P9-ASJ-577

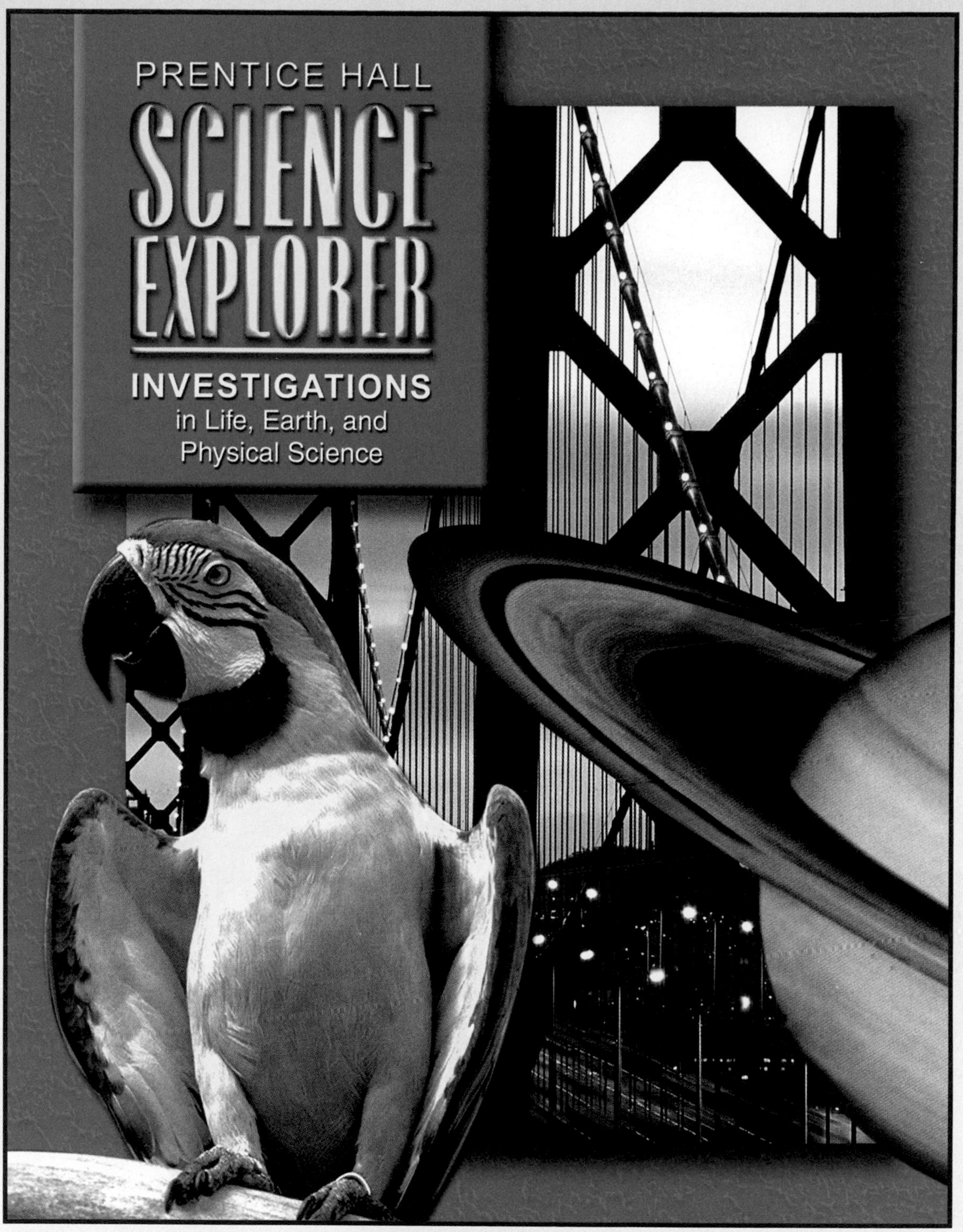

PRENTICE HALL

SCIENCE EXPLORER

INVESTIGATIONS
in Life, Earth, and Physical Science

Needham, Massachusetts
Upper Saddle River, New Jersey

Investigations in Life, Earth, and Physical Science

Print Resources

Student Edition
Annotated Teacher's Edition
Unit Resource Books, including:

- Chapter Project Support
- Lesson Plans
- Section Summaries
- Review and Reinforce Worksheets
- Enrich Workshops
- Student Edition Lab Worksheets
- Answer Keys

Color Transparencies
Chapter Tests
Performance Assessments
Standardized Test Preparation Workbook
Test-Taking Tips With Transparencies
Laboratory Manual, Student Edition
Laboratory Manual, Teacher's Edition
Guided Reading and Study Workbook
Guided Reading and Study Workbook, Teacher's Edition
Inquiry Skills Activity Book
Student-Centered Science Activity Books
Reading in the Content Area With Literature Connections
How to Assess Student Work
How to Manage Instruction in the Block
Teacher's ELL Handbook

Media/Technology

Resource Pro® CD-ROM
Exam View®Computer Test Bank Book with CD-ROM
Probeware Laboratory Manual with CD-ROM
Section Summaries on Audio CD
Presentation Pro CD-ROM
Order Assistant Plus CD-ROM
Computer Microscope and Lab Manual
Lab Activity Video Library
Concept Video Library
Companion Web site at PHSchool.com

Materials Kits

Consumable Materials Kit
Nonconsumable Materials Kit

Acknowledgments

Excerpt on page 88 from *The Amateur Naturalist* by Gerald Durrell. Copyright © 1982 by Gerald Durrell. Published by Alfred A. Knopf, a division of Random House, Inc.

Excerpt on page 603 from *Dust Storm Disaster* by Woody Guthrie. Copyright © 1960 (Renewed) by Ludlow Music, Inc. c/o The Richmond Organization. All rights reserved.

Excerpt on page 649 from *The Hymn to Hapy* from Volume 1 of Ancient Egyptian Literature, by Miriam Lichtheim. Copyright © 1973-1980 Regents of the University of California.

Activity on page 681 is from *Exploring Planets in the Classroom,* Copyright Hawaii Space Grant Consortium, based on a concept developed by Dale Olive.

Note: Every effort has been made to locate the copyright owner of material used in this textbook. Omission brought to our attention will be corrected in subsequent editions.

ISBN 0-13-115414-1 3 4 5 6 7 8 9 10 07 06 05 04

Program Authors

Michael J. Padilla, Ph.D.
Professor
Department of Science Education
University of Georgia
Athens, Georgia

Michael Padilla is a leader in middle school science education. He has served as an editor and elected officer for the National Science Teachers Association. He has been principal investigator of several National Science Foundation and Eisenhower grants and served as a writer of the National Science Education Standards.

As lead author of *Science Explorer,* Mike has inspired the team in developing a program that meets the needs of middle grades students, promotes science inquiry, and is aligned with the National Science Education Standards.

Ioannis Miaoulis, Ph.D.
Dean of Engineering
College of Engineering
Tufts University
Medford, Massachusetts

Martha Cyr, Ph.D.
Director, Engineering Educational Outreach
College of Engineering
Tufts University
Medford, Massachusetts

Science Explorer was created in collaboration with the College of Engineering at Tufts University. Tufts has an extensive engineering outreach program that uses engineering design and construction to excite and motivate students and teachers in science and technology education.

Faculty from Tufts University participated in the development of *Science Explorer* chapter projects, reviewed the student books for content accuracy, and helped coordinate field testing.

Series Authors

Elizabeth Coolidge-Stolz, M.D.
Medical Writer
North Reading, Massachusetts

Linda Cronin-Jones, Ph.D.
Professor, College of Education
University of Florida
Gainesville, Florida

Donald Cronkite, Ph.D.
Professor of Biology
Hope College
Holland, Michigan

Joseph D. Exline, M.A., Ed.D.
President
Exline Consulting Services, Inc.
Beaverdam, Virginia

David V, Frank, Ph.D.
Head, Department of Physical Sciences
Ferris State University
Big Rapids, Michigan

Dawn Graff-Haight, Ph.D., CHES
Associate Professor, Health Education
Linfield College
McMinnville, Oregon

Fred Holtzclaw
Science Instructor
Oak Ridge High School
Oak Ridge, Tennessee

Jan Jenner, Ph.D.
Science Writer
Talladega, Alabama

John G. Little
Science Teacher
St. Mary's High School
Stockton, California

Steve Miller
Science Writer
State College, Pennsylvania

Jay M. Pasachoff, Ph.D.
Professor of Astronomy
Williams College
Williamstown, Massachusetts

Barbara Brooks Simons
Science Writer
Boston, Massachusetts

Carole Garbuny Vogel, M.A.T.
Science Writer
Lexington, Massachusetts

Camille L. Wainwright, Ph.D.
Professor of Science Education
Pacific University
Forest Grove, Oregon

Thomas R. Wellnitz
Science Teacher
The Paideia School
Atlanta, Georgia

Contributing Writers

W. Russell Blake, Ph.D.
Planetarium Director
Plymouth Community Intermediate School
Plymouth, Massachusetts

Alfred B. Bortz, Ph.D.
School of Education
Duquesne University
Pittsburgh, Pennsylvania

Rose-Marie Botting
Science Teacher
Broward County School District
Fort Lauderdale, Florida

Doug E. Bowman
Health/Physical Education Teacher
Welches Middle School
Welches, Oregon

Mary Sue Burns
Science Teacher
Pocahontas County High School
Dunmore, West Virginia

Jeffrey C. Callister
Science Instructor
Newburgh Free Academy
Newburgh, New York

Colleen Campos
Science Teacher
Laredo Middle School
Aurora, Colorado

John Coffey
Science/Mathmatics Teacher
Venice Area Middle School
Venice, Florida

Patricia M. Doran
Science Teacher
Rondout Valley Junior High School
Stone Ridge, New York

Holly Estes
Science Instructor
Hale Middle School
Stow, Massachusetts

Edward Evans
Former Science Teacher
Hilton Central School
Hilton, New York

Theresa K. Holtzclaw
Former Science Instructor
Clinton, Tennesse

Jorie Hunken
Science Consultant
Woodstock, Connecticut

Greg Hutton
Science and Health Curriculum Coordinator
School Board of Sarasota County
Sarasota, Florida

Mark Illingworth
Teacher
Hollis Public Schools
Hollis, New Hampshire

James Robert Kaczynski, Jr.
Science Teacher
Barrington Middle School
Barrington, Rhode Island

Lauren Magruder
Science Instructor
St. Michael's Country Day School
Newport, Rhode Island

Thomas L. Messer
Science Teacher
Cape Cod Academy
Osterville, Massachusetts

Susan Offner
Biology Teacher
Milton High School
Milton, Massachusetts

Warren Phillips
Science Teacher
Plymouth Community Intermediate School
Plymouth, Massachusetts

Emery Pineo
Science Teacher
Barrington Middle School
Barrington Rhode Island

Linda Shoulberg
Science Teacher
Millbrook High School
Raleigh, North Carolina

Karen Riley Sievers
Science Teacher
Callanan Middle School
Des Moines, Iowa

Evan P. Silberstein
Science Teacher
Spring Valley High School
Spring Valley, New York

Sharon M. Stroud
Science Teacher
Widefield High School
Colorado Springs, Colorado

Joseph Stukey, Ph.D.
Department of Biology
Hope College
Holland, Michigan

Reading Consultant

Bonnie B. Armbruster, Ph.D.
Department of Curriculum and Instruction
University of Illinois
Champaign, Illinois

Interdisciplinary Consultant

Heidi Hayes Jacobs, Ed.D.
Teachers College
Columbia University
New York, New York

Safety Consultants

W. H. Breazeale, Ph.D.
Department of Chemistry
College of Charleston
Charleston, South Carolina

Ruth Hathaway, Ph.D.
Hathaway Consulting
Cape Girardeau, Missouri

Content Reviewers

Jack W. Beal, Ph.D.
Department of Physics
Fairfield University
Fairfield, Connecticut

W. Russell Blake, Ph.D.
Planetarium Director
Plymouth Community Intermediate School
Plymouth, Massachusetts

Howard E. Buhse, Jr., Ph.D.
Department of Biological Sciences
University of Illinois
Chicago, Illinois

Dawn Smith Burgess, Ph.D.
Department of Geophysics
Stanford University
Palo Alto, California

A. Malcolm Campbell, Ph.D.
Assistant Professor
Davidson College
Davidson, North Carolina

Elizabeth A. De Stasio, Ph.D.
Associate Professor of Biology
Lawrence University
Appleton, Wisconsin

John M. Fowler, Ph.D.
Former Director of Special Projects
National Science Teachers Association
Arlington, Virginia

Jonathan Gitlin, M.D.
School of Medicine
Washington University
St. Louis, Missouri

Dawn Graff-Haight, Ph.D., CHES
Department of Health, Human Performance, and Athletics
Linfield College
McMinnville, Oregon

Deborah L. Gumucio, Ph.D.
Associate Professor
Department of Anatomy and Cell Biology
University of Michigan
Ann Arbor, Michigan

William S. Harwood, Ph.D.
Dean of University Division and Associate Professor of Education
Indiana University
Bloomington, Indiana

Cyndy Henzel, Ph.D.
Department of Geography and Regional Development
University of Arizona
Tucson, Arizona

Greg Hutton
Science and Health Curriculum Coordinator
School Board of Sarasota County
Sarasota, Florida

Susan K. Jacobson, Ph.D.
Department of Wildlife Ecology and Conservation
University of Florida
Gainesville, Florida

Judy Jernstedt, Ph.D.
Department of Agronomy and Range Science
University of California, Davis
Davis, California

John L. Kermond, Ph.D.
Office of Global Programs
National Oceanographic and Atmospheric Administration
Silver Spring, Maryland

David E. LaHart, Ph.D.
Institute of Science and Public Affairs
Florida State University
Tallahassee, Florida

Joe Leverich, Ph.D.
Department of Biology
St. Louis University
St. Louis, Missouri

Dennis K. Lieu, Ph.D.
Department of Mechanical Engineering
University of California
Berkeley, California

Cynthia J. Moore, Ph.D.
Science Outreach Coordinator
Washington University
St. Louis, Missouri

Joseph M. Moran, Ph.D.
Department of Earth Science
University of Wisconsin–Green Bay
Green Bay, Wisconsin

Joseph Stukey, Ph.D.
Department of Biology
Hope College
Holland, Michigan

Seetha Subramanian
Lexington Community College
University of Kentucky
Lexington, Kentucky

Carl L. Thurman, Ph.D.
Department of Biology
University of Northern Iowa
Cedar Falls, Iowa

Edward D. Walton, Ph.D.
Department of Chemistry
California State Polytechnic University
Pomona, California

Robert S. Young, Ph.D.
Department of Geosciences and Natural Resource Management
Western Carolina University
Cullowhee, North Carolina

Edward J. Zalisko, Ph.D.
Department of Biology
Blackburn College
Carlinville, Illinois

Tufts University Program Reviewers

Behrouz Abedian, Ph.D.
Department of Mechanical Engineering

Wayne Chudyk, Ph.D.
Department of Civil and Environmental Engineering

Eliana De Bernardez-Clark, Ph.D.
Department of Chemical Engineering

Anne Marie Desmarais, Ph.D.
Department of Civil and Environmental Engineering

David L. Kaplan, Ph.D.
Department of Chemical Engineering

Paul Kelley, Ph.D.
Department of Electro-Optics

George S. Mumford, Ph.D.
Professor of Astronomy, Emeritus

Jan A. Pechenik, Ph.D.
Department of Biology

Livia Racz, Ph.D.
Department of Mechanical Engineering

Robert Rifkin, M.D.
School of Medicine

Jack Ridge, Ph.D.
Department of Geology

Chris Swan, Ph.D.
Department of Civil and Environmental Engineering

Peter Y. Wong, Ph.D.
Department of Mechanical Engineering

Teacher Reviewers

Stephanie Anderson
Sierra Vista Junior High School
Canyon Country, California

John W. Anson
Mesa Intermediate School
Palmdale, California

Pamela Arline
Lake Taylor Middle School
Norfolk, Virginia

Lynn Beason
College Station Jr. High School
College Station, Texas

Richard Bothmer
Hollis School District
Hollis, New Hampshire

Jeffrey C. Callister
Newburgh Free Academy
Newburgh, New York

Judy D'Albert
Harvard Day School
Corona Del Mar, California

Betty Scott Dean
Guilford County Schools
McLeansville, North Carolina

Sarah C. Duff
Baltimore City Public Schools
Baltimore, Maryland

Melody Law Ewey
Holmes Junior High School
Davis, California

Sherry L. Fisher
Lake Zurich Middle School North
Lake Zurich, Illinois

Melissa Gibbons
Fort Worth ISD
Fort Worth, Texas

Debra J. Goodding
Kraemer Middle School
Placentia, California

Jack Grande
Weber Middle School
Port Washington, New York

Steve Hills
Riverside Middle School
Grand Rapids, Michigan

Sandra M. Justin
Swift Junior High School
Oakville, Connecticut

Carol Ann Lionello
Kraemer Middle School
Placentia, California

Jaime A. Morales
Henry T. Gage Middle School
Huntington Park, California

Patsy Partin
Cameron Middle School
Nashville, Tennessee

Deedra H. Robinson
Newport News Public Schools
Newport News, Virginia

Bonnie Scott
Clack Middle School
Abilene, Texas

Charles M. Sears
Belzer Middle School
Indianapolis, Indiana

Barbara M. Strange
Ferndale Middle School
High Point, North Carolina

Jackie Louise Ulfig
Ford Middle School
Allen, Texas

Kathy Usina
Belzer Middle School
Indianapolis, Indiana

Heidi M. von Oetinger
L'Anse Creuse Public School
Harrison Township, Michigan

Pam Watson
Hill Country Middle School
Austin, Texas

Activity Field Testers

Nicki Bibbo
Russell Street School
Littleton, Massachusetts

Connie Boone
Fletcher Middle School
Jacksonville Beach, Florida

Rose-Marie Botting
Broward County School District
Fort Lauderdale, Florida

Colleen Campos
Laredo Middle School
Aurora, Colorado

Elizabeth Chait
W. L. Chenery Middle School
Belmont, Massachusetts

Holly Estes
Hale Middle School
Stow, Massachusetts

Laura Hapgood
Plymouth Community Intermediate School
Plymouth, Massachusetts

Sandra M. Harris
Winman Junior High School
Warwick, Rhode Island

Jason Ho
Walter Reed Middle School
Los Angeles, California

Joanne Jackson
Winman Junior High School
Warwick, Rhode Island

Mary F. Lavin
Plymouth Community Intermediate School
Plymouth, Massachusetts

James MacNeil, Ph.D.
Concord Public Schools
Concord, Massachusetts

Lauren Magruder
St. Michael's Country Day School
Newport, Rhode Island

Jeanne Maurand
Glen Urquhart School
Beverly Farms, Massachusetts

Warren Phillips
Plymouth Community Intermediate School
Plymouth, Massachusetts

Carol Pirtle
Hale Middle School
Stow, Massachusetts

Kathleen M. Poe
Kirby-Smith Middle School
Jacksonville, Florida

Cynthia B. Pope
Ruffner Middle School
Norfolk, Virginia

Anne Scammell
Geneva Middle School
Geneva, New York

Karen Riley Sievers
Callanan Middle School
Des Moines, Iowa

David M. Smith
Howard A. Eyer Middle School
Macungie, Pennsylvania

Derek Strohschneider
Plymouth Community Intermediate School
Plymouth, Massachusetts

Sallie Teames
Rosemont Middle School
Fort Worth, Texas

Gene Vitale
Parkland Middle School
McHenry, Illinois

Zenovia Young
Meyer Levin Junior High School (IS 285)
Brooklyn, New York

Contents

Investigations in Life, Earth, and Physical Science

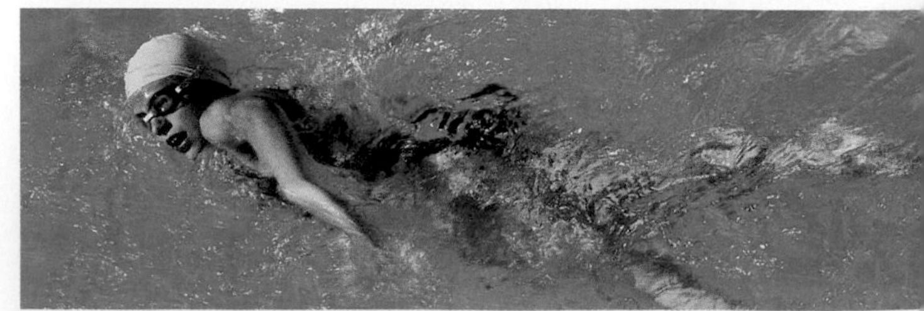

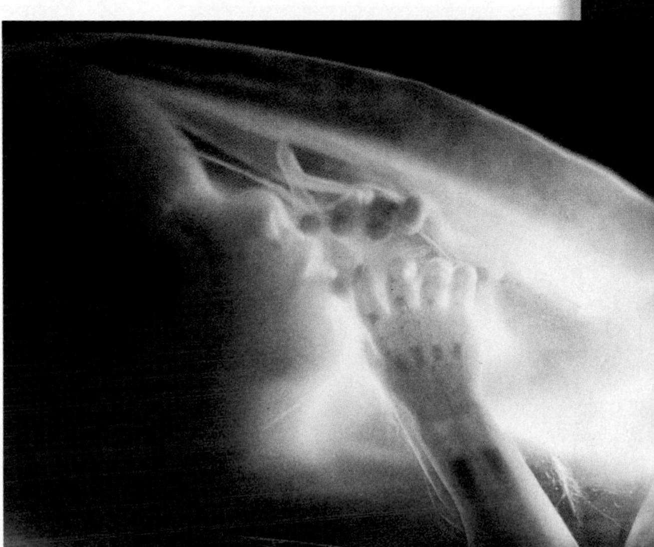

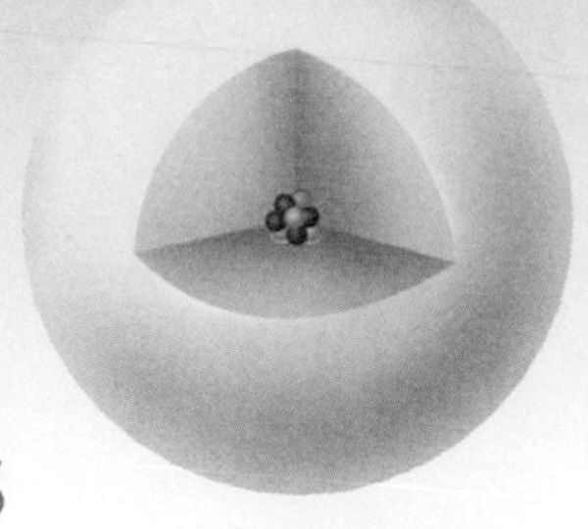

Unit 3 Chemical Interactions

Unit 4 Sound and Light

Unit 5 Earth's Changing Surface

Unit 6 Astronomy

Reference Section

Activities

Inquiry Activities

CHAPTER PROJECT

Opportunities for long-term inquiry

DISCOVER

Exploration and inquiry before reading

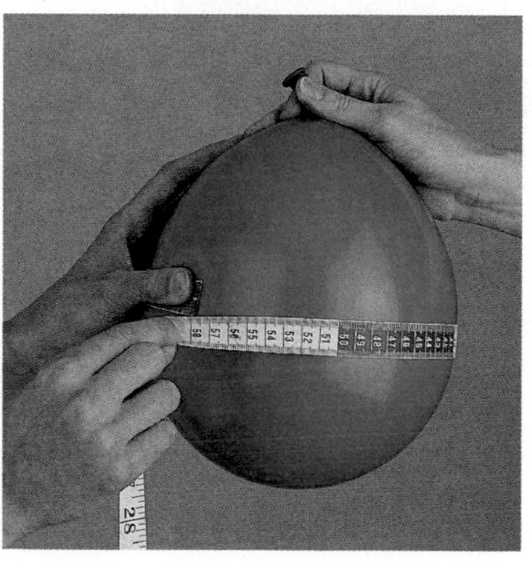

PRENTICE HALL
SCIENCE EXPLORER
INVESTIGATIONS
in Life, Earth, and Physical Science

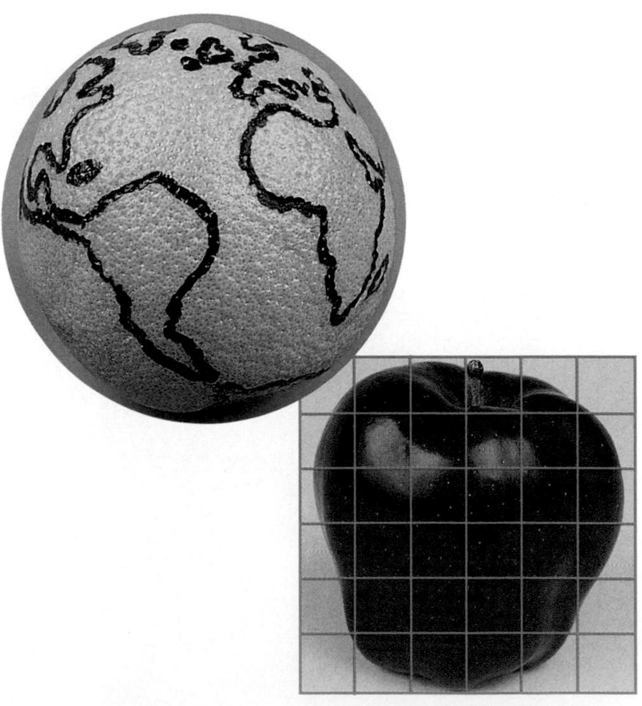

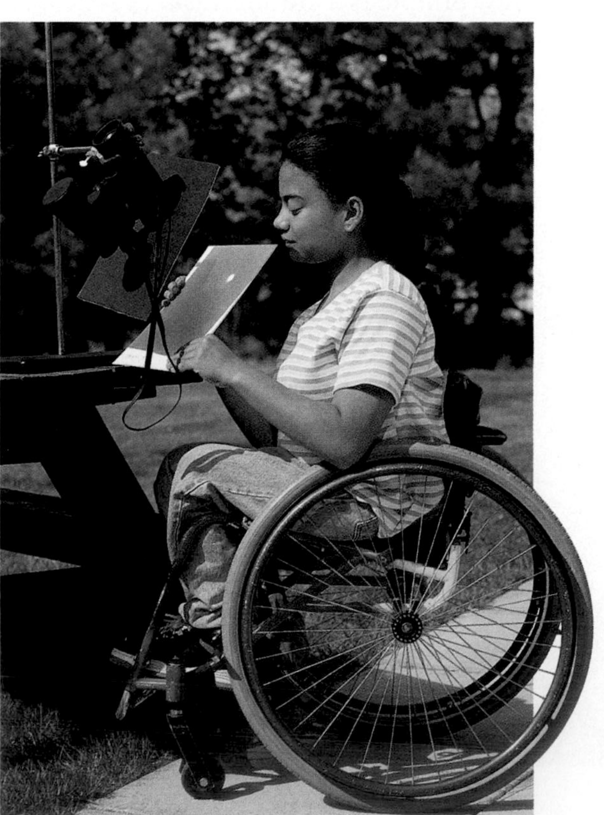

Sharpen your Skills

Practice of specific science inquiry skills

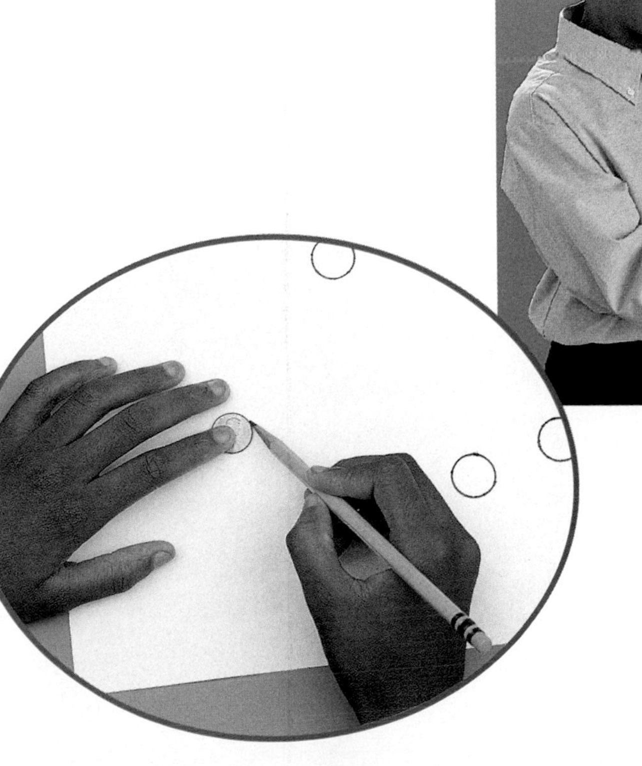

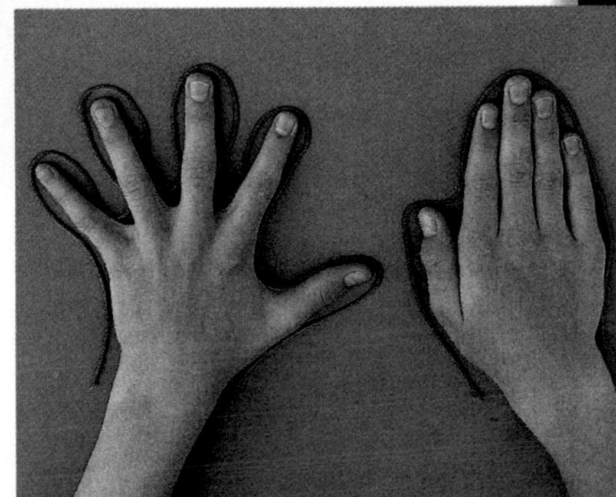

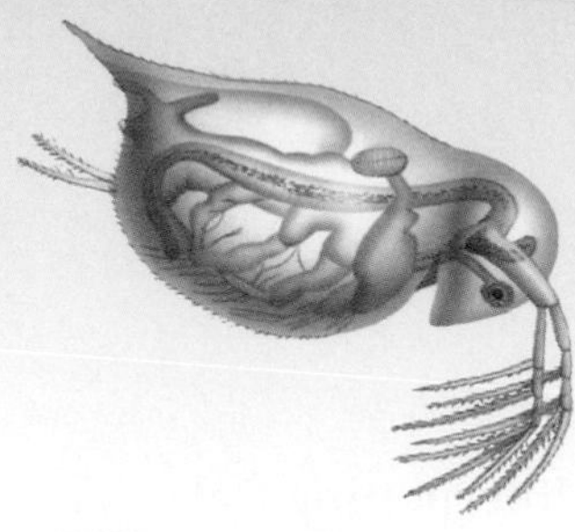

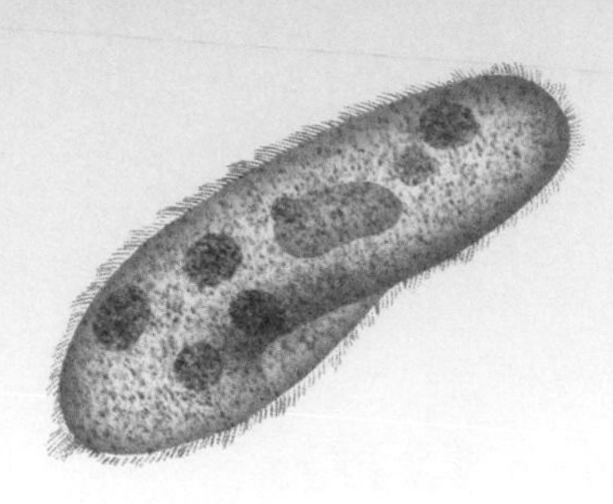

TRY THIS

Reinforcement of key concepts

Skills Lab

In-depth practice of inquiry skills

Real-World Lab

Everyday application of science concepts

Interdisciplinary Activities

EXPLORING

Visual exploration of concepts

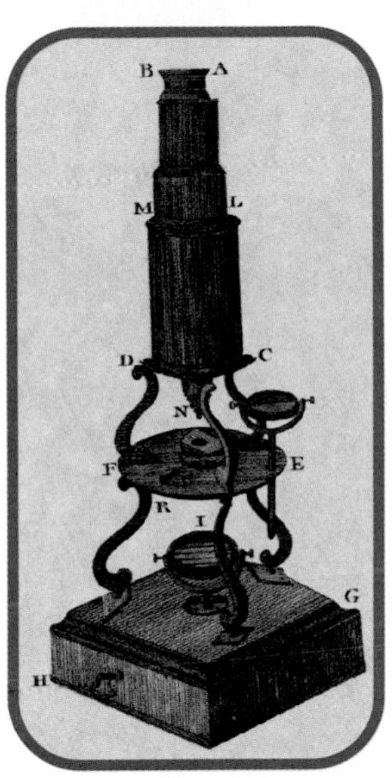

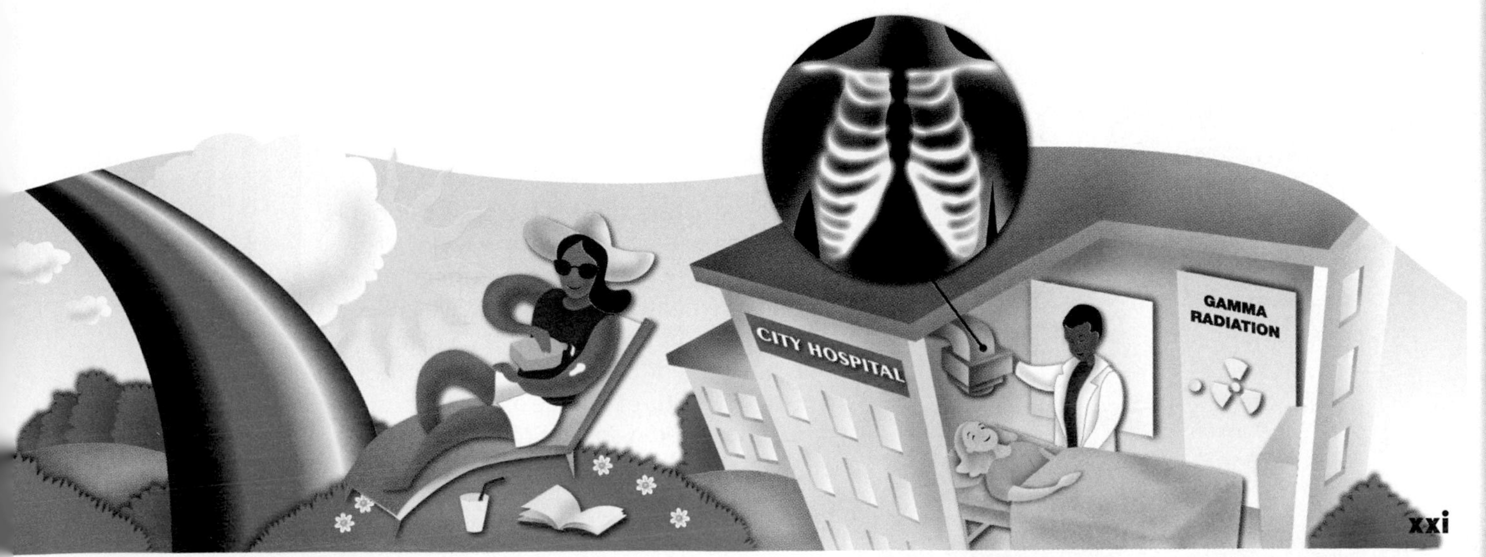

Protecting Desert Wildlife

Elroy Masters likes working outdoors. One day he hikes a mountain trail, looking for desert tortoises. The next morning he may be in a boat on the Colorado River, counting birds along the riverbank. Another day he may be in the Arizona hills, building a water container for thirsty bighorn sheep. Elroy is a biologist working for the federal government's Bureau of Land Management (BLM). His job is to protect wildlife habitat in the desert along the Colorado River between California and Arizona.

"People may come in wanting to run a pipeline across public land or needing to build a road," he explains. "Part of my job is to check out the biological effect of that action on different species of animals and plants. If people are going to build a road where there are a lot of tortoises, we might try to have them work from November to March. Since tortoises hibernate during those months, we reduce the chance of a tortoise getting run over."

Growing up in Arizona, Elroy lived in a farming community. "I was always outdoors. I was able to have animals that a lot of people don't have—chickens, pigeons, ducks, and a horse. I always loved animals. I always hoped for some type of career with them."

Elroy Masters studied biology at Phoenix College and Northern Arizona University. He started working for the Bureau of Land Management when he was still a college student. He now works as a Wildlife Management Biologist. In this photograph, Elroy is about to release a razorback sucker, an endangered species of fish, into the Colorado River.

Today, Elroy and his co-workers make surveys of desert animals. They count the animals in different areas and make maps of their habitats. They locate where the animals live, what they eat, and where they build their nests and raise their young. Elroy uses that information to protect the animals when natural events or human activities threaten them.

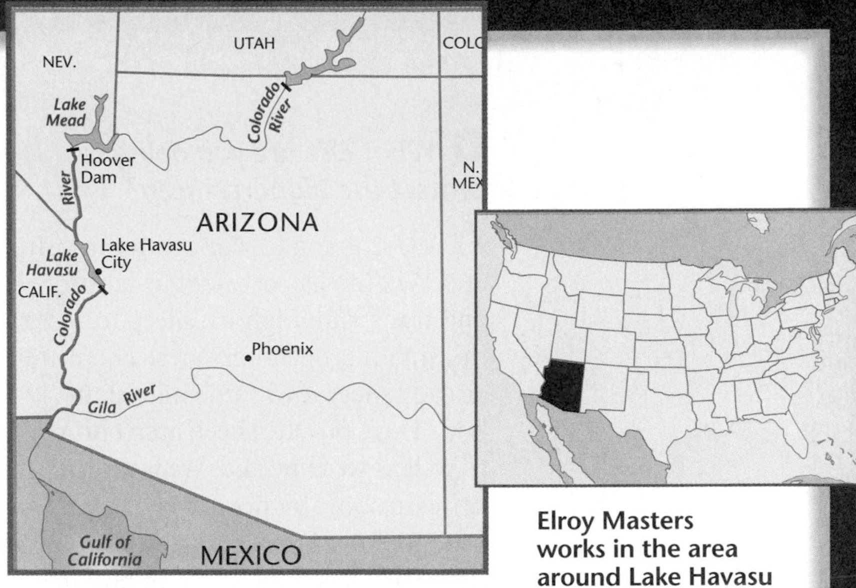

Elroy Masters works in the area around Lake Havasu in western Arizona.

Talking with Elroy Masters

Q ***What wildlife do you protect?***

A One of the neatest animals we deal with is the desert bighorn sheep. In an average summer, it can get as hot as 120 degrees here. Sometimes the heat lasts for weeks. But with the number of people living around the river, the animals are no longer able to travel to water. So we go up into the mountains to construct catchments (containers) to collect water and store it. That way the sheep can stay in the mountains without trying to cross freeways to get to water.

We fly in big storage tanks that hold about 10,000 gallons of water. We bury them in the ground or put them on a platform. We use paint to mask them into the color of the scenery. We sometimes build a dam or put out a metal sheet to catch drizzle rain.

A catchment can hold 10,000 gallons of water (right). It is buried in the ground. The drinking container provides water for desert bighorn sheep (below), mule deer, and other wildlife.

Q ***What else are you doing to protect the bighorn sheep?***

A We're going to work with the Fish and Wildlife Department to capture and transplant bighorn sheep to a mountain range in my area. There are already sheep and some mountain lions here. But the sheep aren't doing as well as we expected. We want to bring in some bighorn sheep that are used to lions. We hope these lion-savvy sheep will teach the sheep in our area how to avoid lions. To catch the sheep, we'll use a helicopter. We'll shoot a net over the sheep and a couple of guys will jump out to secure the animals and then bring them to our herd.

Q ***What other animals are you responsible for protecting?***

A I work a lot with desert tortoises. I'm responsible for two different populations, one on either side of the river. The tortoises live in the drier, hilly areas away from the river. Any time we go out into the field, we try to collect data. We keep track of where they've been and where they feed.

Q ***How do you find the tortoises?***

A We have maps that indicate their habitat. Based on the habitat, we'll go out, walk around, and look under rocks and boulders to see if we can find a burrow. The tortoises are good diggers. They find a good boulder and go underground 10 or 12 feet. That's where they'll spend the winter.

The Colorado River valley is home to the Southwestern willow flycatcher and the desert tortoise.

Southwestern willow flycatcher

Desert tortoise

Q ***Do you also work with birds?***

A Right now we're working with the Southwestern willow flycatcher. It's a small bird that depends on thick riparian (riverbank) vegetation to build nests and breed. The flycatcher is a migratory bird. Each spring, the birds fly to Arizona from Central America and Mexico. In the early summer months, we go out to find how many are breeding. We're trying to learn what's needed to prevent flycatchers from becoming extinct. We need to survey and protect the remaining stands of habitat. The flycatchers like to nest in thick stands of willow. But they will also build nests in another tree, salt cedar. The birds don't prefer it, but sometimes salt cedar is the only vegetation remaining, so they use it.

Q ***What's threatening the riverbank plants?***

A The low water level in the river—due to human use—is a big threat. So is fire. During summer months, there are large numbers of recreational boats. Careless boaters can cause fires. Some fires get pretty big along the river and destroy a lot of the habitat where the birds nest and raise their young.

Q ***Can you see the benefits of your work?***

A Yes, I see it especially in riverbank zones where areas are protected so that vegetation and trees can grow back. This year we did a new bird count in one area. Species that hadn't been seen in a while, like tanagers, showed up. Some of the migratory birds are already stopping in young cottonwood trees. That's the best gauge I've had—seeing birds returning to these new trees.

There are also quick results with the water catchments in the hills. We put the water in a year ago. They're aimed at bighorn sheep and mule deer. But now we've also got a lot of different birds—doves and quails—that come into the area.

Elroy Masters also works with populations of the California leaf-nosed bat. This bat has large ears and a leaf-shaped, turned-up nose. The bats are threatened by the loss of their habitat.

In Your Journal

Elroy Masters and his co-workers "survey" the wildlife in their area in order to learn how to protect them. Think of a wild animal that lives in a park or open area near you—squirrels, frogs, birds, even insects. Work out a step-by-step plan to draw a simple map marking the places where the animal is found.

What Is SCIENCE?

GUIDE FOR READING

- What skills do scientists use in their work?
- Why are safe laboratory practices important?

Reading Tip Before you read, make a list of the boldfaced terms. As you read, write a definition in your own words for each term.

Elroy Masters's work as a biologist for the Bureau of Land Management requires him to collect information on the organisms and habitats he is studying. When he analyzes this information to draw conclusions, he is applying the principles of science.

Science is both a way of learning about the natural world and the knowledge gained in that process. This body of knowledge is always growing and changing as scientists explore new ideas.

Another term for the many ways in which scientists study the world around them is **scientific inquiry.** Scientific inquiry is used every day by the engineers and scientists at NASA. You don't have to be an engineer or a scientist to use the methods of scientific inquiry. In fact, you have already used some kinds of scientific thinking. If you have ever tried to figure out why a radio has stopped working or decided on the best location for a garden, you have used scientific inquiry.

Thinking Like a Scientist

Elroy Masters and his co-workers use scientific inquiry as they study the effects of habitat changes on desert animals. In their work, they use a variety of skills.

Some of the skills that scientists use are posing questions, making observations and inferences, developing hypotheses, designing experiments, collecting data and making measurements, interpreting data, and drawing conclusions. Sometimes scientists make models of scientific events to help them solve problems. Scientists also must communicate their findings to others. Scientists may use only some or all of these skills in any single investigation.

You can use the skills of scientific inquiry as you make discoveries yourself. For example, look at the picture of the hang glider in Figure 1. How does the hang glider stay in the air? Where was his starting point? What will happen when he lands?

Figure 1 How does this hang glider defy gravity and stay up in the air? Unusual sights or events often lead to questions.

If you ask questions about things and events around you, you are thinking like a scientist. You have begun the process of scientific inquiry.

Posing Questions Are you curious? Curiosity drives scientific inquiry by leading people to think about a question or a problem. You may have questions about the natural world. Have you ever had a roll of film developed and seen shadows in your photos like the ones in Figure 2? Did you become curious about shadows? Perhaps it made you wonder, "What causes shadows to occur?" or "What makes shadows longer or shorter?"

Making Observations and Inferences In order to learn more about shadows, you use the skill of observation. **Observation** involves using one or more of the five senses—sight, hearing, touch, smell, and taste—to gather information. Using your sight, for example, you may observe that shadows can change in length.

An observation is important, but it's only one part of a larger process. Observations usually lead to inferences. An **inference** is a logical interpretation based on observations or prior knowledge. You may infer, for example, that the length of an object's shadow depends on how near the object is to the light source.

It is important to remember that an inference is just one possible interpretation. Scientists must keep an open mind and consider many possible interpretations of their observations.

☑ ***Checkpoint*** *What senses can the skill of observation involve?*

Figure 2 Photographers make use of shadows to create interesting photos. ***Posing Questions*** *Think of some questions about light and shadows that a photographer might investigate in order to take photographs like these?*

Developing Hypotheses

Scientific inquiry moves forward when ideas are tested. In doing so, scientists often work from one or more hypotheses. A **hypothesis** is a possible explanation for a set of observations or an answer to a scientific question. In science, a hypothesis must be testable by observation or experimentation. In this way, information can be collected that may or may not support the hypothesis.

In your study of shadows, you might develop the following hypothesis: *The distance between an object and a light source affects the length of the object's shadow.* You could then design an experiment to test this idea. You might even predict the outcome of the experiment based on previous observations you have made. Perhaps you would predict that an object's shadow gets smaller as the light source is moved farther from it.

☑ *Checkpoint* *What is a hypothesis?*

Figure 3 The position of a light source can affect the size of an object's shadow. ***Inferring*** *How would you explain the length of the shadows in this photograph?*

Designing Controlled Experiments To test a hypothesis, scientists examine all the factors that can change during an experiment. Such factors are called **variables.** The variable that a scientist changes is called the **manipulated variable,** or independent variable. The variable that is expected to change in response to the manipulated variable is the **responding variable,** or dependent variable.

The manipulated variable for the hypothesis being tested in Figure 4 is the distance between the light source and the object. The responding variable is the length of the shadow. To be sure that changes in the manipulated variable are causing the changes in the responding variable, scientists test, or change, only one variable at a time. All other variables must be controlled—that is, kept constant. In this example, some of the variables that must be controlled are the type of light source, the angle at which the light hits the object, and the distance between the object and the wall. An investigation in which all variables except one remain constant is called a **controlled experiment.**

Collecting Data and Making Measurements The facts, figures, and other information that are collected during an experiment are called **data.** Scientists carefully record their data in order to have a permanent account of the results of their experiments.

Scientific data may include both qualitative and quantitative descriptions. Qualitative data are descriptions, such as color, odor, or sound, that don't involve measurements or numbers. Quantitative data are

Figure 4 In this experiment, the distance between the flashlight and the ruler is the manipulated variable. ***Applying Concepts*** *Why is the length of the ruler's shadow the responding variable?*

measurements made using standard units, such as degrees Celsius (°C) for temperature or meters per second (m/s) for speed.

To make it easier to share data, scientists express measurements in a standard way. They use a system of measurement called the International System of Units. This measurement system is abbreviated as SI (for the French, *Système International d'Unités*). SI is based on the metric system used in many countries around the world. By using SI, scientists from all over the world can understand one another's data.

Notice that the data for the shadow experiment are measured in the metric unit known as centimeters. Before you conduct any experiments, learn more about making scientific measurements on pages 778–779 of the Skills Handbook.

Interpreting Data Scientists interpret data, or find out what the data mean, by identifying trends or patterns. Data are often organized in tables or graphs. Figure 5 shows a data table and graph for the shadow experiment. To learn more about data tables and graphs, see pages 786–788 in the Skills Handbook.

Distance Between Object and Light (cm)	Length of Shadow (cm)
10	32
15	27
20	25
25	23
30	22
35	21
40	20

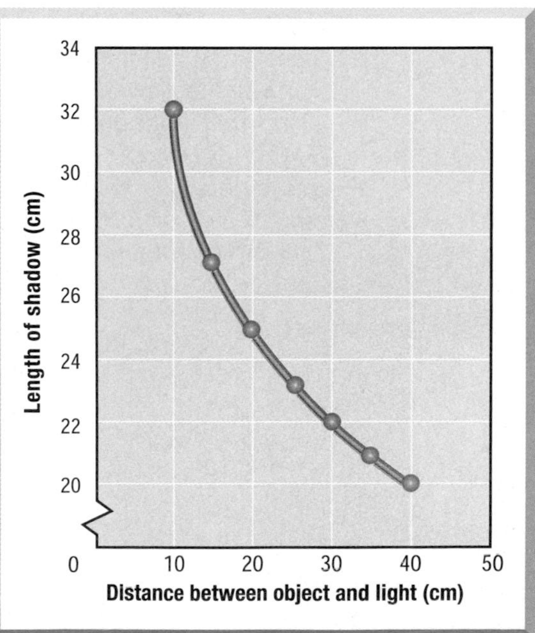

Figure 5 The distances and lengths recorded in this data table are examples of quantitative data. Notice that the heading for each column indicates the units used to make the measurements. When these data are graphed, the result is a curved line.

Drawing Conclusions After interpreting the data from an experiment, you are ready to draw a conclusion. A conclusion states whether or not the data support the hypothesis. For example, based on the data in Figure 5, you would conclude that the length of a shadow *does* decrease as the light source is moved farther away.

In this example, the data support the hypothesis. However, experimental data often do not support a hypothesis. Does this mean that the investigation was a failure? Quite the contrary. What may be most surprising to you is that failure is often an important step in the scientific process! What seems like a dead end can lead to new questions that need to be investigated further. Then the process of inquiry begins all over again. When answers come, they may increase scientific knowledge in small steps. Or, they may lead to a giant leap of understanding.

Making Models and Simulations Sometimes scientists cannot test a hypothesis by doing a controlled experiment. Another way to test a hypothesis is to use a model or simulation.

A scientific model can be a three-dimensional representation, or it can be a diagram such as a map. Many scientists today use computers to make models of complex objects or events.

A simulation is a model that imitates a real-world situation. For example, scientists who study weather may use computer simulations to predict the path that hurricanes will take. The computer uses data from past hurricanes as well as current conditions in its simulations.

Scientific models and simulations are important tools that help scientists understand complex events and make predictions about the future.

Figure 6 An understanding of light and shadows helps artists and performers create visual effects that delight and surprise the viewer. ***Predicting*** *If the photographer wanted to make the shadow of the musician look larger, how would the light source have to change?*

Figure 7 This scientist is standing behind a three-dimensional model of a disease-fighting molecule found in the human body.

But even the most sophisticated models have limitations because they are still only simplified versions of the real world. Scientists always work to improve the accuracy of the models and simulations they use. They do this by gathering new data and revising their models to reflect all of the latest information available to them.

Communicating Information

Sixteen nations are working together to build the parts of the International Space Station. It's the largest space-based research center in history. The engineers designing these parts must communicate with each other frequently. Communication is the sharing of ideas and experimental findings with others through writing and speaking.

Scientists communicate directly with one another when they are working on the same project. They also communicate with the whole scientific community by writing articles in scientific journals, speaking at scientific meetings, and by using the Internet. In addition, scientists may communicate their findings to the public using nontechnical terms that most people can understand easily.

☑ ***Checkpoint** List three ways in which scientists communicate with one another.*

Developing Scientific Laws and Theories

As a body of knowledge, science is built up cautiously. Scientists do not accept a new hypothesis with just a few successful experiments. Instead, it is tested repeatedly by different scientists. Some hypotheses have become so well established that they are called laws. A **scientific law** is a statement that describes what scientists expect to happen every time under a particular set of conditions. One law in science describes how objects fall toward Earth in a certain way.

Sometimes a large body of related information can be explained by a single major idea. If that idea is supported by many tests, it may develop into a scientific theory. A **scientific theory** is a well-tested idea that explains and connects a wide range of observations. For example, the theory that matter is made of atoms helps explain a huge number of observations related to changes in matter. It is possible, however, that a scientific theory will be contradicted by new evidence. If that happens, scientists will change the theory or abandon it.

Figure 8 Following laboratory safety rules keeps scientists safe and makes experiments run smoothly. ***Observing*** *What steps has this student taken to protect himself while carrying out this experiment?*

Laboratory Safety

You will carry out experiments and other activities as you learn about science. During these investigations, be sure to observe safe laboratory practices. Always follow your teacher's instructions, and show respect and courtesy to your teacher and classmates. Before you begin an activity, make sure you understand every step of the procedure and the accompanying safety information. Handle all laboratory materials carefully.

Before conducting any experiment or activity, read and learn the rules for laboratory safety and the meaning of each safety symbol in Appendix A: Laboratory Safety on pages 789–791. The safety symbols alert you to necessary precautions, such as wearing a lab apron or heat-resistant gloves. **Remember, safe laboratory practices will not only protect you and your classmates from injury but will also make your investigations run more smoothly.**

☑ *Checkpoint* *What are three important safety rules to follow when performing a scientific investigation?*

SWING TIME

You can study the movement of a pendulum by hanging an object—the bob—on a string.

Problem

Does the swing of a pendulum take longer for an object of greater mass?

Materials

stand with clamp
large paper clip
ruler
string, 50 cm in length
5 metal washers
stopwatch

Procedure

1. Read the whole procedure. Write a hypothesis describing how the mass of the bob will affect the time of its swing. Then create a data table like the one shown.
2. Tie one end of a string to a clamp on a stand. Tie the other end to a large paper clip. Pull out one side of the paper clip to serve as a hook.
3. Place a metal washer on the hook, and let it hang down. If necessary, raise the clamp so that the bob swings freely.
4. Pull the bob back so that the string makes an angle of about 45° with the stand. Have your partner measure the height of the bob above the table top. Record this height as the starting position of the bob.

DATA TABLE

Number of washers	Time for 10 swings (s)	Average time per swing (s)
1		
2		

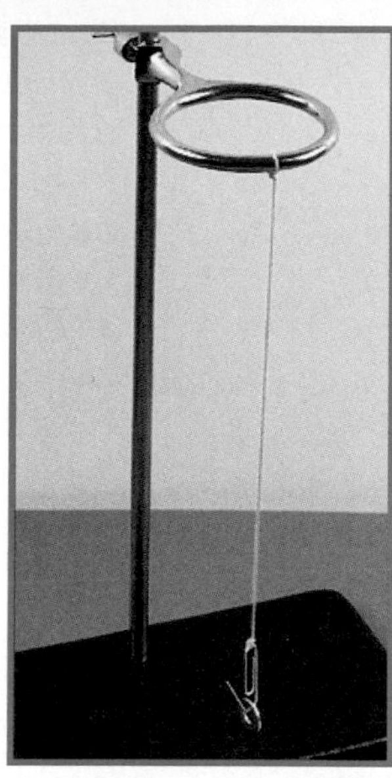

5. Release the bob gently, without pushing it. During a complete swing, the bob will move from its starting position and back again. Your partner should time 10 complete swings.
6. Record the time for 10 swings to the nearest tenth of a second. Then divide that time by 10 to find the average time for one swing.
7. Repeat Steps 5 and 6, increasing the mass of the bob each time by adding a washer. Make sure you always start the bob at the same height.

Analyze and Conclude

1. Graph your results. (*Hint:* Place the number of washers on the horizontal axis and the average time per swing on the vertical axis.)
2. Use the graph to decide if your data support your hypothesis.
3. What conclusion can you draw from this experiment?
4. **Think About It** How did this experiment enable you to test your hypothesis?

Design an Experiment

Design an experiment to test how the average time for a pendulum swing changes when the mass is constant but the length of the string changes. Obtain your teacher's approval before carrying out this experiment.

Branches of Science

There are four main branches of science—physical science, Earth science, life science, and environmental science. Physical science includes the study of motion and forces, sound and light, and electricity and magnetism. It also includes the study of the matter that makes up everything around you.

Earth science is the study of Earth and its place in the universe. Earth science includes the study of rivers, oceans, landforms, weather, climate, and the bodies that make up the solar system.

Life science is the study of living things, including plants, animals, and microscopic life forms. The study of the human body is a part of life science, too. Life scientists also study how living things interact with each other and with their surroundings.

Environmental science deals with the effects of human activities on Earth's land, air, water, and living things. Environmental scientists study problems, such as pollution, that result from human activities and the use of Earth's natural resources.

The branches of science are not really separate from one another. For example, in working with desert wildlife, Elroy Masters uses his knowledge of physical science as he builds water containers for bighorn sheep. He uses his knowledge of environmental science as he studies the changes in the riverbanks where Southwestern willow flycatchers nest. And he uses his knowledge of life science as he collects data on the habits of desert tortoises.

In Figure 9 you can see some of the diverse jobs that scientists perform. You can find scientists at work almost anywhere—from the depths of the oceans, to laboratories, mountains, and jungles on Earth, to space stations out in space. Wherever people are asking scientific questions and searching for answers, they are using the methods of science.

☑ ***Checkpoint*** *Name the four main branches of science.*

Technology and the Internet

Today, many scientists use the latest technology in their research. For example, life scientists today use powerful microscopes, some of which can magnify images up to one million times their size. Space scientists use telescopes that can detect objects in space more clearly than ever before. Most modern scientific equipment is connected to computers, which allow scientists to quickly record, store, and analyze the data they collect. You have already read how important computers are for creating models and running simulations of scientific events.

Technology also helps scientists communicate information to one another and to the public. You can find large amounts of information about discoveries and current research in science on the Internet. Many government agencies maintain Web sites. Hospitals and universities that have research centers often have Web sites, too. The publisher of this textbook maintains a Web site, **www.PHSchool.com**. This site includes links to other Web sites that may help you as you study science.

Figure 9 This is just a small sampling of the types of work that scientists do.
(A) Environmental chemists study the chemicals found in air, soil, and water.
(B) Botanists study plants. Some botanists investigate interactions between plants and other living things. Others help identify ways to increase crop yields.
(C) Audiologists test hearing ability through the use of specialized equipment.
(D) Structural engineers assess the safety of building designs, using their knowledge of building materials, loads, and the effects of weather and earthquakes.

Study Guide

Key Ideas

- Science is an organized way of learning about the natural world. Through observations and logical reasoning, scientists investigate problems and look for answers.
- Scientists use many specific skills, including posing questions, making observations and inferences, developing hypotheses, designing experiments, collecting data and making measurements, interpreting data, drawing conclusions, making models, and communicating information.
- A scientific hypothesis states a possible explanation for observations in a way that can be tested.
- In a controlled experiment, the manipulated variable is changed in order to determine its effect on the responding variable. All other variables are kept constant.
- Data from an experiment are analyzed to determine whether or not they support the hypothesis being tested.
- Safe laboratory practices prevent injuries and make lab investigations run more smoothly.

Key Terms

science	manipulated variable
scientific inquiry	responding variable
observation	controlled experiment
inference	data
hypothesis	scientific law
variable	scientific theory

Reviewing Content

Multiple Choice

Choose the letter of the best answer.

1. A logical interpretation based on observations or prior knowledge is called
   a. scientific inquiry. **b.** an inference.
   c. communication. **d.** an observation.
2. The scientific skill in which the senses are used to gather information is
   a. posing questions.
   b. drawing conclusions.
   c. observing.
   d. developing hypotheses.
3. A statement that is tested through scientific experiments is called a
   a. conclusion. **b.** variable.
   c. law. **d.** hypothesis.
4. In an experiment in which you change only the temperature, temperature is the
   a. responding variable.
   b. manipulated variable.
   c. hypothesis.
   d. controlled variable.
5. A well-tested idea that explains and connects a wide range of observations is a
   a. scientific law.
   b. scientific theory.
   c. hypothesis.
   d. conclusion.

True or False

If the statement is true, write true. If it is false, change the underlined word or words to make the statement true.

6. A <u>hypothesis</u> sums up what was learned from an experiment.
7. The facts and figures collected during an experiment are called <u>data</u>.
8. A factor that can change during an experiment is called a <u>variable</u>.
9. A <u>scientific theory</u> describes what is always expected to happen under a given set of conditions.
10. <u>Scientific inquiry</u> is the process of sharing information with other scientists.

Checking Concepts

11. Explain the difference between an observation and an inference.

12. Why is controlling variables an essential part of a scientific experiment?

13. How does a hypothesis guide a scientist in setting up an experiment?

14. Why is it an advantage for scientists to use one system of measurement when collecting data?

15. Explain how scientists use models and simulations.

16. Why is communication an important skill in science?

17. Writing to Learn The process of science usually begins with one or more questions. Write a question that you have about the natural world. Then write a plan describing how you might find an answer to your question.

Thinking Critically

18. Making Generalizations A friend tells you that science is all the information found in this textbook. Do you agree with that statement? Why or why not?

19. Applying Concepts You are about to conduct an experiment in which you drop a ball from different heights to find out how high the ball bounces at each height. Create a table to show your data. (You can refer to the Skills Handbook, pages 786–788.)

20. Problem Solving Suppose a company advertises a piece of sports equipment that's "guaranteed to improve your game." How could you use the idea of a controlled experiment to safely test that claim?

21. Making Judgments Why does everyone involved in science activities have to take responsibility for the class's safety?

Test Preparation

Use these questions to prepare for standardized tests.

Read the information below. Then answer Questions 22–25.

Three students wanted to find out whether the mass of an object affects how fast it falls. They designed an experiment in which different stacks of washers would be released from the same height. They tied the washers together and determined how long each stack took to reach the ground. Here is their data.

Number of Washers	Time (s)			
	Trial 1	Trial 2	Trial 3	Average
2	2.9	2.8	3.3	3.0
10	3.0	2.9	3.1	3.0
20	2.9	2.9	3.2	3.0

22. What is the manipulated variable?
- **a.** number of trials
- **b.** starting height
- **c.** number of washers
- **d.** time of the drop

23. What is the responding variable?
- **a.** number of trials
- **b.** starting height
- **c.** number of washers
- **d.** time of the drop

24. Which of the following could be the hypothesis for this experiment?
- **a.** The height from which an object is dropped affects how fast it falls.
- **b.** The mass of an object affects how fast it falls.
- **c.** The mass of an object affects the force with which it hits the ground.
- **d.** The height from which an object is dropped affects the force with which it hits the ground.

25. Based on the results of this experiment, what can you conclude about objects dropped from the same height?
- **a.** Objects having greater mass will drop faster than objects with less mass.
- **b.** Objects having less mass will drop faster than objects with greater mass.
- **c.** All objects take 3 seconds to drop.
- **d.** The mass of an object has no effect on the rate at which it falls.

CHAPTER 1

Populations and Communities

WEB ACTIVITY www.phschool.com

SECTION 1 Living Things and the Environment

Discover What's in the Scene?
Try This With or Without Salt?
Skills Lab A World in a Jar

Integrating Mathematics

SECTION 2 Studying Populations

Discover What's the Population of Beans in a Jar?
Sharpen Your Skills Calculating
Try This Elbow Room
Real-World Lab Counting Turtles

SECTION 3 Interactions Among Living Things

Discover How Well Can You Hide a Butterfly?
Sharpen Your Skills Classifying

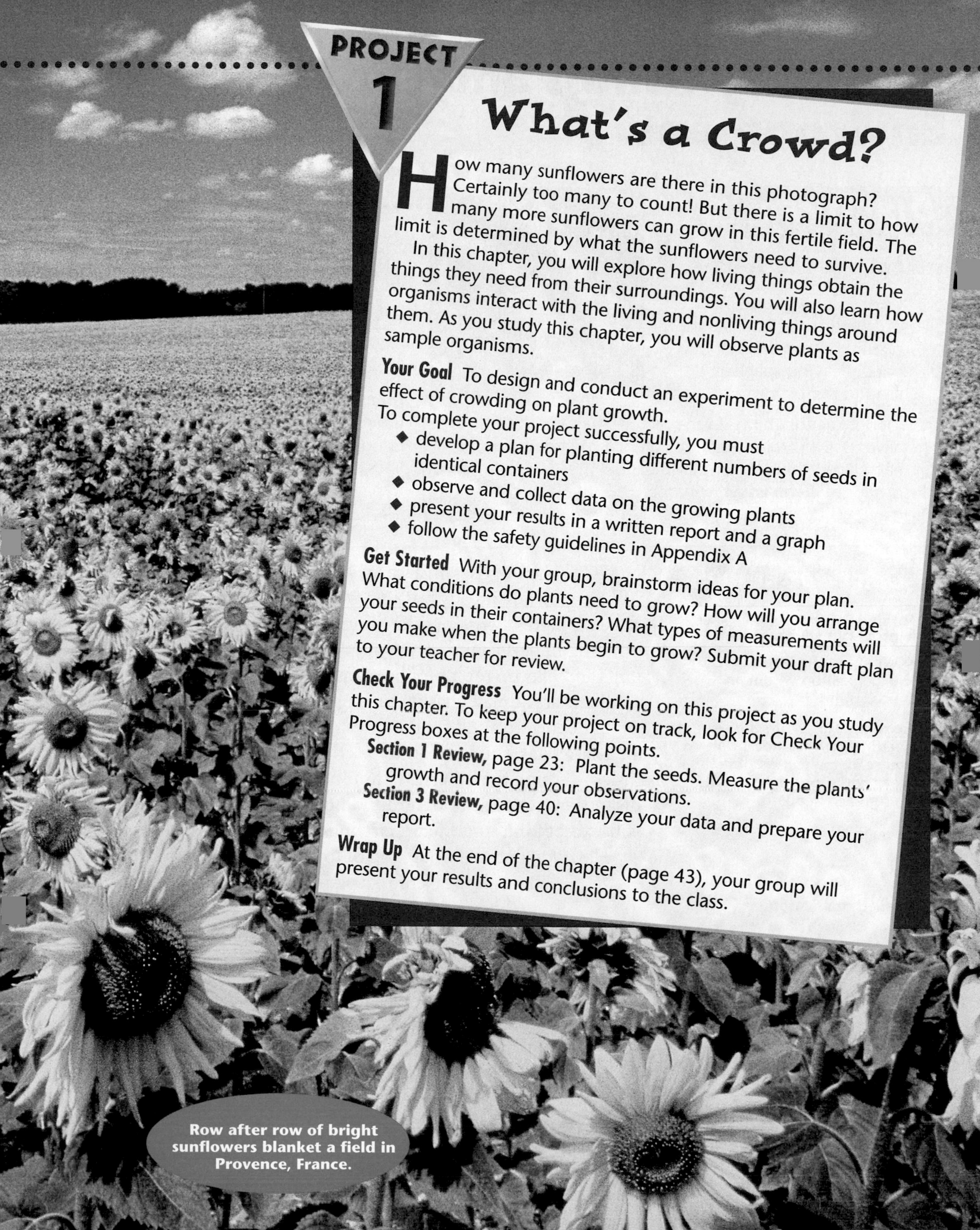

PROJECT 1

What's a Crowd?

How many sunflowers are there in this photograph? Certainly too many to count! But there is a limit to how many more sunflowers can grow in this fertile field. The limit is determined by what the sunflowers need to survive.

In this chapter, you will explore how living things obtain the things they need from their surroundings. You will also learn how organisms interact with the living and nonliving things around them. As you study this chapter, you will observe plants as sample organisms.

Your Goal To design and conduct an experiment to determine the effect of crowding on plant growth.

To complete your project successfully, you must

- develop a plan for planting different numbers of seeds in identical containers
- observe and collect data on the growing plants
- present your results in a written report and a graph
- follow the safety guidelines in Appendix A

Get Started With your group, brainstorm ideas for your plan. What conditions do plants need to grow? How will you arrange your seeds in their containers? What types of measurements will you make when the plants begin to grow? Submit your draft plan to your teacher for review.

Check Your Progress You'll be working on this project as you study this chapter. To keep your project on track, look for Check Your Progress boxes at the following points.

Section 1 Review, page 23: Plant the seeds. Measure the plants' growth and record your observations.

Section 3 Review, page 40: Analyze your data and prepare your report.

Wrap Up At the end of the chapter (page 43), your group will present your results and conclusions to the class.

Row after row of bright sunflowers blanket a field in Provence, France.

Section 1 Living Things and the Environment

Discover — Activity

What's in the Scene?

1. Choose a magazine picture of a nature scene. Paste the picture onto a sheet of paper, leaving space all around the picture.
2. Identify all the things in the picture that are alive. Use a colored pencil to draw a line from each living thing, or organism. Label the organism if you know its name.
3. Use a different colored pencil to draw a line from each nonliving thing and label it.

Think It Over

Inferring How do the organisms in the picture depend on the nonliving things? Using a third color, draw lines connecting organisms to the nonliving things they need.

Guide for Reading

- What needs are met by an organism's surroundings?
- What are the levels of organization within an ecosystem?

Reading Tip Write the section headings in your notebook. As you read, make a list of main ideas and supporting details under each heading.

As the sun rises on a warm summer morning, the Nebraska town is already bustling with activity. Some residents are hard at work building homes for their families. They are building underground, where it is dark and cool. Other inhabitants are collecting seeds for breakfast. Some of the town's younger residents are at play, chasing each other through the grass.

Suddenly, an adult spots a threatening shadow approaching—an enemy has appeared in the sky! The adult cries out several times, warning the others. Within moments, the town's residents disappear into their underground homes. The town is silent and still, except for a single hawk circling overhead.

Have you guessed what kind of town this is? It is a prairie dog town on the Nebraska plains. As these prairie dogs dug their burrows, searched for food, and hid from the hawk, they interacted with their environment, or surroundings. The prairie dogs interacted with living things, such as the grass and the hawk, and with nonliving things, such as the soil. All the living and nonliving things that interact in a particular area make up an **ecosystem.**

Black-tailed prairie dogs ▼

A prairie is just one of the many different ecosystems found on Earth. Other ecosystems in which living things make their homes include mountain streams, deep oceans, and dense forests.

Habitats

A prairie dog is one type of organism, or living thing. Organisms live in a specific place within an ecosystem. **An organism obtains food, water, shelter, and other things it needs to live, grow, and reproduce from its surroundings.** The place where an organism lives and that provides the things the organism needs is called its **habitat.**

A single ecosystem may contain many habitats. For example, in a forest ecosystem, mushrooms grow in the damp soil, bears live on the forest floor, termites live in fallen tree trunks, and flickers build nests in the trunks.

Organisms live in different habitats because they have different requirements for survival. A prairie dog obtains the food and shelter it needs from its habitat. It could not survive in a tropical rain forest or on the rocky ocean shore. Likewise, the prairie would not meet the needs of a gorilla, a penguin, or a hermit crab.

Figure 1 A stream tumbles over mossy rocks in a lush Tennessee forest. This ecosystem contains many different habitats. ***Comparing and Contrasting*** *How is the mushrooms' habitat in the forest different from the flicker's habitat?*

Biotic Factors

An organism interacts with both the living and nonliving things in its environment. The living parts of an ecosystem are called **biotic factors** (by AHT ik factors). Biotic factors in the prairie dogs' ecosystem include the grass and plants that provide seeds and berries. The hawks, ferrets, badgers, and eagles that hunt the prairie dogs are also biotic factors. In addition, worms, fungi, and bacteria are biotic factors that live in the soil underneath the prairie grass. These organisms keep the soil rich in nutrients as they break down the remains of other living things.

☑ ***Checkpoint*** *Name a biotic factor in your environment.*

Figure 2 This eastern banjo frog is burrowing in the sand to stay cool in the hot Australian desert. ***Interpreting Photographs*** *With which abiotic factors is the frog interacting in this scene?*

With or Without Salt?

ACTIVITY

In this activity you will explore salt as an abiotic factor.

1. Label four 600-mL beakers A, B, C, and D. Fill each with 500 mL of room-temperature spring water.
2. Set beaker A aside. It will contain fresh water. To beaker B, add 2.5 grams of noniodized salt. Add 7.5 grams of salt to beaker C and 15 grams of salt to beaker D. Stir beakers B, C, and D.
3. Add $\frac{1}{8}$ teaspoon of brine shrimp eggs to each beaker.
4. Cover each beaker with a square of paper. Keep them away from direct light or heat. Wash your hands.
5. Observe the beakers daily for three days.

Drawing Conclusions In which beakers did the eggs hatch? What can you conclude about the amount of salt in the shrimps' natural habitat?

Abiotic Factors

The nonliving parts of an ecosystem are called **abiotic factors** (ay by AHT ik factors). Abiotic factors that affect living things in the prairie are similar to those found in most ecosystems. They include water, sunlight, oxygen, temperature, and soil.

Water All living things require water to carry out their life processes. Water also makes up a large part of the bodies of most organisms. Your body, for example, is about 65 percent water. A watermelon consists of more than 95 percent water! Water is particularly important to plants and algae. These organisms use water, along with sunlight and carbon dioxide, to make food in a process called **photosynthesis** (foh toh SIN thuh sis). Other living things eat the plants and algae to obtain energy.

Sunlight Because sunlight is necessary for photosynthesis, it is an important abiotic factor for plants, algae, and other living things. In places that do not receive sunlight, such as dark caves, plants cannot grow. Without plants or algae to provide a source of food, few other organisms can live.

Oxygen Most living things require oxygen to carry out their life processes. Oxygen is so important to the functioning of the human body that you can live only a few minutes without it. Organisms that live on land obtain oxygen from the air, which is about 20 percent oxygen. Fish and other water organisms obtain dissolved oxygen from the water around them.

Temperature The temperatures that are typical of an area determine the types of organisms that can live there. For example, if you took a trip to a warm tropical island, you would see palm trees, bright hibiscus flowers, and tiny lizards. These organisms could not survive on the frozen plains of Siberia. But the thick, warm fur of wolves and short, strong branches of dwarf willows are suited to the blustery winters there.

Some animals alter their environments to overcome very hot or very cold temperatures. For example, prairie dogs dig underground dens to find shelter from the blazing summer sun. They line the dens with grass. The grass keeps the prairie dogs warm during the cold and windy winters.

Soil Soil is a mixture of rock fragments, nutrients, air, water, and the decaying remains of living things. Soil in different areas consists of varying amounts of these materials. The type of soil in an area influences the kinds of plants that can grow there. Many animals, such as the prairie dogs, use the soil itself as a home. Billions of microscopic organisms such as bacteria also live in the soil. These tiny organisms play an important role in the ecosystem by breaking down the remains of other living things.

☑ *Checkpoint* *How do biotic factors differ from abiotic factors?*

Populations

In 1900, travelers saw a prairie dog town in Texas covering an area twice the size of the city of Dallas. The sprawling town contained more than 400 million prairie dogs! These prairie dogs were all members of one species, or single kind, of organism. A **species** (SPEE sheez) is a group of organisms that are physically similar and can reproduce with each other to produce fertile offspring.

All the members of one species in a particular area are referred to as a **population.** The 400 million prairie dogs in the Texas town are one example of a population. All the pigeons in New York City make up a population, as do all the daisies in a field. In contrast, all the trees in a forest do not make up a population, because they do not all belong to the same species. There may be pines, maples, birches, and many other tree species in the forest.

The area in which a population lives can be as small as a single blade of grass or as large as the whole planet. Scientists studying a type of organism usually limit their study to a population in a defined area. For example, they might study the population of bluegill fish in a pond, or the population of alligators in the Florida Everglades.

Some populations, however, do not stay in a contained area. For example, to study the population of finback whales, a scientist might need to use the entire ocean.

Figure 3 This milkweed plant is home to a small population of ladybug beetles.

Organism

Population

Communities

Of course, most ecosystems contain more than one type of organism. The prairie, for instance, includes prairie dogs, hawks, grasses, badgers, and snakes, along with many other organisms. All the different populations that live together in an area make up a **community.**

Figure 4 shows the levels of organization in the prairie ecosystem. **The smallest unit of organization is a single organism, which belongs to a population of other members of its species. The population belongs to a community of different species. The community and abiotic factors together form an ecosystem.**

To be considered a community, the different populations must live close enough together to interact. One way the populations in a community may interact is by using the same resources, such as food and shelter. For example, the tunnels dug by the prairie dogs also serve as homes for burrowing owls and black-footed ferrets. The prairie dogs share the grass with other animals. Meanwhile, prairie dogs themselves serve as food for many species.

What Is Ecology?

Because the populations in the prairie ecosystem interact with one another, any changes in a community affect all the different populations that live there. The study of how living things interact with each other and with their environment is called **ecology.** Ecologists, scientists who study ecology, look at how all the biotic and abiotic factors in an ecosystem are related.

Language Arts CONNECTION

The word *ecology* comes from two Greek root words: *oikos,* which means house or place to live, and *logos,* which means *study.* Put together, these root words create a term for studying organisms in the place where they live. Many science terms are derived from Greek and Latin root words.

In Your Journal

Use a dictionary to find root words for the following terms from this section: *habitat, biotic, community,* and *population.* For each root word, list its meaning, original language, and other English words containing the root.

Community

Ecosystem

Figure 4 The smallest level of ecological organization is an individual organism. The largest is the entire ecosystem.

As part of their work, ecologists study how organisms react to changes in their environment. Living things constantly interact with their surroundings, responding to changes in the conditions around them. Some responses are very quick. When a prairie dog sees a hawk overhead, it gives a warning bark. The other prairie dogs hear the bark and respond by returning to their burrows to hide. Other responses to change in the environment occur more slowly. For example, after a fire on the prairie, it takes some time for the grass to reach its former height and for all the animals to return to the area.

Section 1 Review

1. What basic needs are provided by an organism's habitat?
2. List these terms in order from the smallest unit to the largest: population, organism, ecosystem, community.
3. Explain how water and sunlight are two abiotic factors that are important to all organisms.
4. Why do ecologists study both biotic and abiotic factors in an ecosystem?
5. **Thinking Critically Applying Concepts** Would all the insects in a forest be considered a population? Why or why not?

CHAPTER PROJECT 1

Check Your Progress

After your teacher has reviewed your plan, prepare the containers and plant the seeds. Design a data table to record the information you will use to compare the growth in the different containers. When the plants begin to grow, examine them daily and record your observations. Be sure to continue caring for your plants according to your plan. *(Hint:* Use a metric ruler to measure your growing plants. Besides size, look for differences in leaf color and the number of buds among the plants.)

Skills Lab

Making Models

A World in a Jar

In this lab, you will study the interactions that take place between biotic and abiotic factors in a model ecosystem.

Problem

How can organisms live in a closed ecosystem?

Materials

aquarium gravel
plastic stirring rod
2-day-old tap water
2 guppies
metric ruler
dip net
2 aquatic plants
2 small pond snails
large jar with cover (about 2 liters)
UL-listed lamp with a 60-watt bulb

Procedure   

1. In this lab, you will put guppies, snails, and plants together in a sealed jar of water. Record your prediction about whether this habitat will meet the needs of these organisms.
2. Find a safe location for the jar away from windows and other areas where light and temperature are likely to change often. There should be an electrical outlet nearby for the lamp.
3. Add aquarium gravel to the jar to a depth of 5 cm. Add water to about 6 cm from the top.
4. Place the plants in the jar one at a time. Use a stirring rod to gently brush aside a little gravel. Position the roots of each plant against the bottom of the jar. Move gravel back over the roots to hold the plant in place.
5. Using a dip net, carefully place the guppies in the water. Gently place the snails in the jar. Put the lid on the jar, and close it tightly.
6. Position the lamp so that the light shines into the jar. The light bulb should be 15 to 20 cm from the jar. **CAUTION:** *Lighted bulbs get very hot. Do not allow the bulb to touch any objects.*
7. Observe the jar every day. Record your observations in your notebook.
8. Within 5 days, the water in the jar should turn slightly green. The green color indicates the presence of algae. If the water is bright green, move the light away from the jar. If the water is not green after 5 days, move the light closer to the jar. Record in your notebook any changes to the setup.
9. Observe the jar for at least one more week.

Analyze and Conclude

1. What biotic and abiotic factors are part of the ecosystem in the jar?
2. Are any biotic or abiotic factors able to enter the sealed jar? If so, which one(s)?
3. Where did the green algae come from?
4. Draw a diagram of the interactions between the biotic and abiotic factors in the jar.
5. Would the guppies, snails, and plants be able to live alone in separate jars? Why or why not?
6. **Think About It** Explain how your jar and its contents model an ecosystem. How is your model different from an ecosystem on Earth?

More to Explore

Make a plan to model a saltwater or land ecosystem. How would this model be different from the freshwater ecosystem? Obtain your teacher's approval before carrying out your plan.

SECTION 2

Studying Populations

DISCOVER

ACTIVITY

What's the Population of Beans in a Jar?

1. Fill a plastic jar with dried beans. This is your model population.
2. Your goal is to determine the number of beans in the jar, but you will not have time to count every bean. You may use any of the following to help you determine the size of the bean population: a ruler, a small beaker, another large jar. Set a timer for two minutes when you are ready to begin.

3. After two minutes, record your answer. Then count the actual number of beans. How close was your answer?

Think It Over

Forming Operational Definitions In this activity, you came up with an estimate of the size of the bean population. Write a definition of the term *estimate* based on what you did.

GUIDE FOR READING

- **How do ecologists determine the size of a population?**
- **What causes populations to change in size?**
- **What factors limit population growth?**

Reading Tip **Before you read, predict some factors that might cause a population to increase or decrease.**

How would you like to change jobs for the day? Instead of being a student, today you are an ecologist. You are working on a project to study the bald eagle population in your area. One question you might ask is how the population has changed over time. Is the number of bald eagles more, less, or the same as it was 50 years ago? To answer these questions, you must first determine the present size of the bald eagle population.

Population Density

One way to state the size of a population is in terms of **population density**— the number of individuals in a specific area. Population density can be written as an equation:

$$\textit{Population density} = \frac{\textit{Number of individuals}}{\textit{Unit area}}$$

For instance, suppose you counted 50 monarch butterflies in a garden measuring 10 square meters. The population density would be 50 butterflies per 10 square meters, or 5 butterflies per square meter.

Bald eagles in Alaska ▶

Figure 5 These cone-shaped structures are nests built by cliff swallows in Dinosaur National Monument, Utah. Counting the nests is one way to estimate the cliff swallow population.

Determining Population Size

In your work as an ecologist, how can you determine the size of the population you are studying? **Some methods of determining the size of a population are direct and indirect observations, sampling, and mark-and-recapture studies.**

Direct Observation The most obvious way to determine the size of a population is to count, one by one, all of its members. You could count all the bald eagles that live along a river, all the red maple trees in a forest, or all the elephants in a valley in Kenya.

Indirect Observation The members of a population may be small or hard to find. It may then be easier to observe their tracks or other signs rather than the organisms themselves. Look at the mud nests built by cliff swallows in Figure 5. Each nest has one entrance hole. By counting the entrance holes, you can determine the number of swallow families nesting in this area. Suppose that the average number of swallows per nest is four: two parents and two offspring. If there are 120 nests in an area, you can find the number of swallows by multiplying 120 by 4, or 480 swallows.

Sampling In most cases, it is not possible to count every member of a population. The population may be very large, or it may be spread over a wide area. It may be hard to find every individual or to remember which ones have already been counted. Instead, ecologists usually make an estimate. An **estimate** is an approximation of a number, based on reasonable assumptions.

One type of estimating involves counting the number of organisms in a small area (a sample), and then multiplying to find the number in a larger area. To get an accurate estimate, the sample should have the same population density as the larger area. For example, suppose you count 8 red maples in a 10-meter-by-10-meter area of the forest. If the entire forest were 100 times that size, you would multiply your count by 100 to estimate the total population, or 800 red maples.

Sharpen your Skills

Calculating ACTIVITY

A bed of oysters measures 100 meters long and 50 meters wide. In a one-square-meter area you count 20 oysters. Estimate the population of oysters in the bed. (*Hint:* Drawing a diagram may help you set up your calculation.)

Mark-and-Recapture Studies Another estimating method is a technique called "mark and recapture." This technique gets its name because some animals are first captured, marked, and released into the environment. Then another group of animals is captured. The number of marked animals in this second group indicates the population size. For example, if half the animals in the second group are marked, it means that the first sample represented about half the total population.

Here's an example showing how mark and recapture works. First, deer mice in a field are caught in a trap that does not harm the mice. Ecologists count the mice and mark each mouse's belly with a dot of hair dye before releasing it again. Two weeks later, the researchers return and capture mice again. They count how many mice have marks, showing that they were captured the first time, and how many are unmarked. Using a mathematical formula, the scientists can estimate the total population of mice in the field. You can try this technique for yourself in the Real-World Lab at the end of this section.

Figure 6 This young hawk is part of a mark-and-recapture study in a Virginia marsh. *Inferring What is the purpose of the silver band on the hawk's leg?*

☑ *Checkpoint* *When is sampling used to estimate a population?*

Changes in Population Size

By returning to a location often and using one of the methods described above, ecologists can monitor the size of a population over time. **Populations can change in size when new members enter the population or when members leave the population.**

Births and Deaths The major way in which new individuals are added to a population is through the birth of offspring. The **birth rate** of a population is the number of births in a population in a certain amount of time. For example, suppose a population of 1,000 snow geese produces 1,400 goslings in a year. The birth rate in this population would be 1,400 goslings per year.

Similarly, the major way that individuals leave a population is by dying. The **death rate** is the number of deaths in a population in a certain amount of time. Suppose that in the same population, 100 geese die in a year. The death rate would be 100 geese per year.

Figure 7 The birth of new individuals can increase the size of a population. This cheetah mother added five offspring to the population in her area.

The Population Equation When the birth rate in a population is greater than the death rate, the population will generally increase in size. This statement can be written as a mathematical statement using the "is greater than" sign:

If birth rate > death rate, population size increases.

For example, in the snow goose population, the birth rate of 1,400 goslings per year was greater than the death rate of 100 geese per year, and the population would increase in size.

However, if the death rate in a population is greater than the birth rate, the population size will generally decrease. This can also be written as a mathematical statement:

If death rate > birth rate, population size decreases.

Immigration and Emigration The size of a population also can change when individuals move into or out of the population, just as the population of your town changes when families move into town or move away. **Immigration** (im ih GRAY shun) means moving into a population. **Emigration** (em ih GRAY shun) means leaving a population. Emigration can occur when part of a population gets cut off from the rest of the population. For instance, if food is scarce, some members of an antelope herd may wander off in search of better grassland. If they become permanently separated from the original herd, they will no longer be part of that population.

Graphing Changes in Population You can see an example of changes in a population of rabbits in Figure 8. The vertical axis shows the numbers of rabbits in the population, while the horizontal axis shows time. The graph shows the size of the population over a 10-year period.

☑ ***Checkpoint*** *Name two ways individuals can join a population.*

Math TOOLBOX

Inequalities

The population statement is an example of an inequality. An inequality is a mathematical statement that compares two expressions. Two signs that represent inequalities are:

$<$ (is less than)

$>$ (is greater than)

For example, an inequality comparing the fraction $\frac{1}{2}$ to the decimal 0.75 would be written:

$$\frac{1}{2} < 0.75$$

Write an inequality comparing each pair of expressions below.

1. 5 **?** −6
2. 0.4 **?** $\frac{3}{5}$
3. −2 − (−8) **?** 7 − 1.5

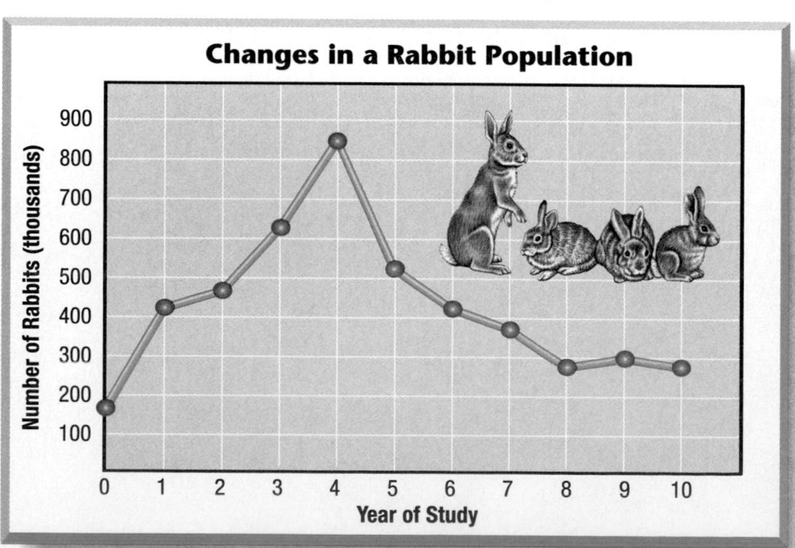

Figure 8 From Year 0 to Year 4, more rabbits joined the population than left it, so the population increased. From Year 4 to Year 8, more rabbits left the population than joined it, so the population decreased. From Year 8 to Year 10, the rates of rabbits leaving and joining the population were about equal, so the population remained steady. ***Interpreting Graphs*** *In what year did the rabbit population reach its highest point? What was the size of the population in that year?*

Figure 9 These gannets seem to have heard the saying "Birds of a feather flock together." When there are more birds than the space can support, the population will have exceeded the carrying capacity of the shore.

Limiting Factors

When conditions are good, a population will generally increase. But a population does not keep growing forever. Eventually, some factor in its environment causes the population to stop growing. A **limiting factor** is an environmental factor that prevents a population from increasing. **Some limiting factors for populations are food, space, and weather conditions.**

Food Organisms require food to survive. In an area where food is scarce, this becomes a limiting factor. Suppose a giraffe needs to eat 10 kilograms of leaves each day to survive. The trees in an area can provide 100 kilograms of leaves a day while remaining healthy. Five giraffes could live easily in this area, since they would only require a total of 50 kilograms of food. But 15 giraffes could not all survive—there would not be enough food for all of them. No matter how much shelter, water, and other resources there might be, the population will not grow much higher than 10 giraffes. The largest population that an environment can support is called its **carrying capacity.** The carrying capacity of this environment is 10 giraffes.

Space The birds in Figure 9 are rarely seen on land. These birds, called gannets, spend most of their lives flying over the ocean. They only land on this rocky shore to nest. But as you can see, the shore is very crowded. If a pair of gannets does not have room to build a nest, that pair will not be able to produce any offspring.

Elbow Room

ACTIVITY

Using masking tape, mark off several one-meter squares on the floor of your classroom. Your teacher will form groups of 2, 4, and 6 students. Each group's task is to put together a small jigsaw puzzle in one of the squares. All the group members must keep their feet within the square. Time how long it takes your group to finish the puzzle.

Making Models How long did it take each group to complete the task? How does this activity show that space can be a limiting factor? What is the carrying capacity of puzzle-solvers in a square meter?

Figure 10 A snowstorm can limit the size of the orange crop.

Those gannets will not contribute to an increase in the gannet population. This means that space for nesting is a limiting factor for these gannets. If the shore were bigger, more gannets would be able to nest there, and the population would increase.

Space is often a limiting factor for plants. The amount of space in which a plant grows can determine how much sunlight, water, and other necessities the plant can obtain. For example, many pine seedlings sprout each year in a forest. But as the trees get bigger, those that are too close together do not have room to spread their roots underground. Other tree branches block out the sunlight they need to live. Some of the seedlings die, limiting the size of the pine population.

Weather Weather conditions such as temperature and amount of rainfall can also limit population growth. Many insect species breed in the warm spring weather. As winter begins, the first frost kills many of the insects. This sudden rise in the death rate causes the insect population to decrease.

A single severe weather event can dramatically change the size of a population by killing many organisms. For instance, a flood or hurricane can wash away nests and burrows just as it damages the homes of humans. If you live in a northern state, you may have seen an early frost limit the population of tomato plants in a vegetable garden.

Section 2 Review

1. List four ways of determining population size.
2. How is birth rate related to population size?
3. List three limiting factors for populations. Choose one and explain how this factor can limit population growth.
4. Explain why it is often necessary for ecologists to estimate the size of a population.
5. **Thinking Critically Problem Solving** A field measures 50 meters by 90 meters. In one square meter, you count 3 mice. Estimate the total population of mice in the field. What method did you use to make your estimate?

Science at Home

Choose a page of a dictionary or other book that has a lot of type on it. Challenge your family members to estimate the number of words on the page. After everyone has come up with an estimate, have each person explain the method he or she used. Now count the actual number of words on the page. Whose estimate was closest?

Careers in Science

Counting Turtles

Real-World Lab

For three years, ecologists have been using the mark-and-recapture method to monitor the population of turtles in a pond. In this lab, you will model recapturing the turtles to complete the study. Then you will analyze the results.

Problem

How can the mark-and-recapture method help ecologists monitor the size of a population?

Skills Focus

calculating, graphing, predicting

Materials

model paper turtle population
calculator
graph paper

Procedure

1. The data table shows the results from the first three years of the study. Copy it into your notebook, leaving spaces for your data as shown.
2. Your teacher will give you a box representing the pond. Fifteen of the turtles have been marked, as shown in the data table for Year 4.
3. Capture a member of the population by randomly selecting one turtle. Set it aside.
4. Repeat Step 3 nine times. Record the total number of turtles you captured.
5. Examine each turtle to see whether it has a mark. Count the number of recaptured (marked) turtles. Record this number in your data table.

Analyze and Conclude

1. Use the equation below to estimate the turtle population for each year. The first year is done for you as a sample. If your answer is a decimal, round it to the nearest whole number so that your estimate is in "whole turtles." Record the population for each year in the last column of the data table.

$$\text{Total population} = \frac{\text{Number marked} \times \text{Total number captured}}{\text{Number recaptured (with marks)}}$$

Sample (Year 1):

$$\frac{32 \times 28}{15} = 59.7 \text{ or } 60 \text{ turtles}$$

2. Graph the estimated total populations for the four years. Mark years on the horizontal axis. Mark population size on the vertical axis.
3. Describe how the turtle population has changed over the four years of the study. Suggest three possible causes for the changes.
4. **Apply** Use your graph to predict the turtle population in Year 5. Explain your prediction.

DATA TABLE

Year	Number Marked	Total Number Captured	Number Recaptured (with Marks)	Estimated Total Population
1	32	28	15	
2	25	21	11	
3	23	19	11	
4	15			

Getting Involved

Find out whether any wildlife populations in your area are being monitored by national, state, or local agencies. Make a poster or write an article for the school paper about the population and the method being used to study it.

Animal Overpopulation: How Can People Help?

Populations of white-tailed deer are growing rapidly in many parts of the United States. As populations soar, food becomes a limiting factor. Many deer die of starvation. Others grow up small and unhealthy. In search of food, hungry deer move closer to where humans live. There they eat farm crops, garden vegetables, shrubs, and even trees. This affects birds and small animals that depend on the plants for shelter or food. In addition, increased numbers of deer near roads can cause more automobile accidents.

People admire the grace, beauty, and swiftness of deer. Most people don't want these animals to suffer from starvation or illness. Should people take action to limit growing deer populations?

The Issues

Should People Take Direct Action? Many people argue that hunting is the simplest way to reduce animal populations. Wildlife managers look at the supply of resources in an area and determine its carrying capacity. Then hunters are issued licenses to help reduce the number of deer to the level that can be supported.

Other people favor nonhunting approaches to control deer populations. One plan is to trap the deer and relocate them. But this method is expensive and requires finding another location that can accept the deer without unbalancing its own system. Few such locations are available.

Scientists are also working to develop chemicals to reduce the birth rate in deer populations. This plan will help control overpopulation, but it is effective for only one year at a time.

Should People Take Indirect Action? Some suggest bringing in natural enemies of deer, such as wolves, mountain lions, and bears, to areas with too many deer. But these animals could also attack cattle, dogs, cats, and even humans. Other communities have built tall fences around areas they don't want deer to invade. Although this solution can work for people with small yards, it is impractical for farmers or ranchers.

Should People Do Nothing? Some people oppose any kind of action. They support leaving the deer alone and allowing nature to take its course. Animal populations in an area naturally cycle up and down over time. Doing nothing means that some deer will die of starvation or disease. But eventually, the population will be reduced to a size within the carrying capacity of the environment.

You Decide

1. Identify the Problem
In your own words, explain the problem created by the overpopulation of white-tailed deer.

2. Analyze the Options
List the ways that people can deal with overpopulation of white-tailed deer. State the negative and positive points of each method.

3. Find a Solution
Suppose you are an ecologist in an area that has twice as many deer as it can support. Propose a way for the community to deal with the problem.

Section 3 Interactions Among Living Things

Discover Activity

How Well Can You Hide a Butterfly?

1. Using the outline at the right, trace a butterfly on a piece of paper.
2. Look around the classroom and pick a spot where you will place your butterfly. The butterfly must be placed completely in the open. Color your butterfly so it will blend in with the spot you choose.
3. Tape your butterfly to its spot. Someone will now enter the room to look for the butterflies. This person will have one minute to find all the butterflies he or she can. Will your butterfly be found?

Think It Over

Predicting Over time, how do you think the population size would change for butterflies that blend in with their surroundings?

Guide for Reading

- **How do an organism's adaptations help it to survive?**
- **What are the major types of interactions among organisms?**
- **What are the three forms of symbiotic relationships?**

Reading Tip **As you read, use the section headings to make an outline. Fill in details under each heading.**

Imagine giving a big hug to the plant in the photo. Ouch! The sharp spines on its trunk would make you think twice before hugging—or even touching—the saguaro (suh GWAHR oh) cactus. But if you could spend a day hidden inside a saguaro, you would see that many species do interact with this spiky plant.

As the day breaks, you hear a twittering noise coming from a nest tucked in one of the sagauro's arms. Two young red-tailed hawks are preparing to fly for the first time. Farther down the trunk, a tiny elf owl peeks out of its nest in a small hole. The elf owl is so small it could fit in your palm! A rattlesnake slithers around the base of the saguaro, looking for lunch. Spying a nearby shrew, the snake moves in for the kill. With a sudden movement, it strikes the shrew with its sharp fangs.

The activity around the saguaro doesn't stop after the sun goes down. At night, long-nosed bats feed on the nectar from the saguaro's blossoms. They stick their faces into the flowers to feed, covering their long snouts with a dusting of white pollen in the process. As the bats move from plant to plant, they carry the pollen along. This enables the cactuses to reproduce.

Saguaro cactus in the Arizona desert

Adapting to the Environment

Each organism in this desert ecosystem has some unique characteristics. In response to their environments, species evolve, or change over time. The changes that make organisms better suited to their environments develop through a process called **natural selection.**

Natural selection works like this: Individuals in a population have different characteristics. Those individuals whose characteristics are best suited for their environment tend to survive and produce offspring. Offspring that inherit the characteristics that made their parents successful also live to reproduce. Over many generations individuals with those characteristics continue to reproduce. Individuals that are poorly suited to the environment are less likely to survive and reproduce. Over time, these poorly suited characteristics may disappear from the population. This process results in **adaptations,** the behaviors and physical characteristics of species that allow them to live successfully in their environment.

Every organism has a variety of adaptations that are suited to its specific living conditions. The adaptations of the organisms in the desert ecosystem create unique roles for each organism. An organism's particular role, or how it makes its living, is called its **niche.** A niche includes the type of food the organism eats, how it obtains this food, and which other species use the organism as food. The niche also includes when and how the organism reproduces and the physical conditions it requires to survive.

An organism's niche may include how it interacts with other organisms. During your day in the saguaro community, you observed a range of such interactions. **There are three major types of interactions among organisms: competition, predation, and symbiosis.**

Figure 11 The organisms in the saguaro community are well adapted to their desert environment. ***Observing*** *Identify two interactions between organisms that are taking place in this scene.*

Figure 12 Each of these warblers occupies a different niche in its spruce tree habitat. By feeding in different areas of the tree, the birds avoid competing with each other for food.

Competition

Different species can share the same habitat, such as the many animals that live in and around the saguaro. Different species can also share similar food requirements. For example, the red-tailed hawk and the elf owl both live on the saguaro and eat similar food. However, these two species do not occupy exactly the same niche. The hawk is active during the day, while the owl is active mostly at night. If two species occupy the same niche, one of the species will eventually die off. The reason for this is **competition,** the struggle between organisms to survive in a habitat with limited resources.

An ecosystem cannot satisfy the needs of all the living things in a particular habitat. There is a limited amount of food, water, and shelter. Organisms that survive have adaptations that enable them to reduce competition. For example, the three species of warblers in Figure 12 live in the same spruce forest habitat. They all eat insects that live in the spruce trees. How do these birds avoid competing for the limited insect supply? Each warbler "specializes" in feeding in a certain part of a spruce tree. By finding their own places to feed, the three species can coexist.

INTEGRATING CHEMISTRY Many plants use chemicals to ward off their competition. Plants often compete with one another for growing space and water. Some shrubs release toxic, or poisonous, chemicals into the ground around them. These chemicals keep grass and weeds from growing around the shrubs, sometimes forming a ring of bare ground a meter or two wide.

☑ ***Checkpoint*** *Why can't two species occupy the same niche?*

Predation

A tiger shark lurks beneath the surface of the clear blue water, looking for shadows of young albatross floating above it. The shark sees a chick and silently swims closer. Suddenly, the shark bursts through the water and seizes the albatross with one snap of its powerful jaw. This interaction between two organisms has an unfortunate ending for the albatross.

An interaction in which one organism kills and eats another is called **predation.** The organism that does the killing, in this case the tiger shark, is the **predator.** The organism that is killed, the albatross, is the **prey.**

Predator Adaptations Predators have adaptations that help them catch and kill their prey. For example, a cheetah can run very fast for a short time, enabling it to catch its prey. A jellyfish's tentacles contain a poisonous substance that paralyzes tiny water

EXPLORING *Defense Strategies*

Organisms display a wide array of adaptations that help them avoid becoming prey.

Camouflage ▲
These delicate spiny bugs are a perfect match for their branch habitat. The more an organism resembles its surroundings, the less likely it is that a predator will notice it. Some animals, such as flounder, can even change their colors to match a variety of settings.

Protective Coverings
This sea urchin sends a clear message to predators: "Don't touch!" Porcupines, hedgehogs, and cactuses all use the same spiny strategy. After a few painful encounters, a predator will look for less prickly prey. ▼

animals. You can probably think of many predators that have claws, sharp teeth, or stingers. Some plants, too, have adaptations for catching prey. The sundew is covered with sticky bulbs on stalks—when a fly lands on the plant, it remains snared in the sticky goo while the plant digests it.

Some predators have adaptations that enable them to hunt at night. For example, the big eyes of an owl let in as much light as possible to help it see in the dark. Bats can hunt without seeing at all. Instead, they locate their prey by producing pulses of sound and listening for the echoes. This precise method enables a bat to catch a flying moth in complete darkness.

Prey Adaptations How do prey organisms manage to avoid being killed by such effective predators? In *Exploring Defense Strategies*, below, you can see some examples of how an organism's physical characteristics can help protect it.

Warning Coloring ▲
A frog this bright certainly can't hide. How could such a color be an advantage? The bright red and blue of this poison arrow frog warn predators not to eat it—glands on the frog's back that release toxic chemicals make it a bad choice for a meal.

Mimicry
If you've ever been stung by a bee, you'd probably keep your distance from this insect. But actually this "bee" is a harmless fly. The fly's resemblance to a stinging bee protects it from birds and other predators, who are fooled into staying away. ▼

◀ **False Coloring**
Which way is this butterfly fish swimming? The black dot on its tail is a false eye. A predator may bite this end of the fish, allowing it to escape with only part of its tail missing.

Figure 13 The populations of wolves and moose on Isle Royale are related. The predator wolf population depends on the size of the prey moose population, and vice versa.
Predicting *How might a disease in the wolf population one year affect the moose population the next year?*

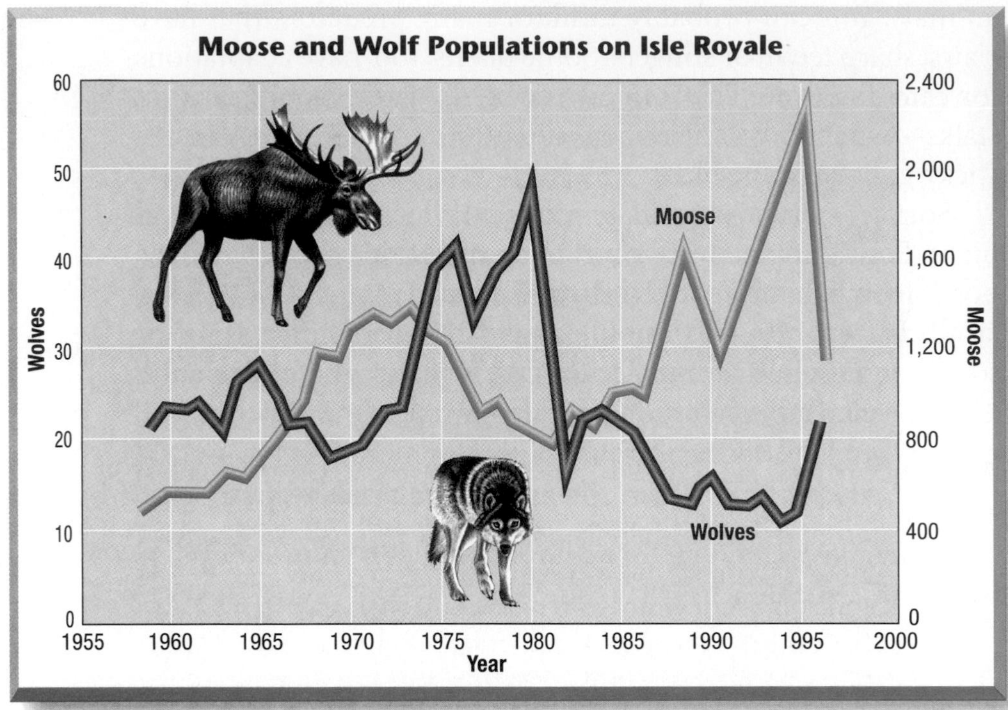

The Effect of Predation on Population Size Predation can have a major effect on the size of a population. As you learned in Section 2, when the death rate exceeds the birth rate in a population, the size of the population usually decreases. If predators are very effective at hunting their prey, the result is often a decrease in the size of the prey population. But a decrease in the prey population in turn affects the predator population.

To see how predator and prey populations can affect each other, look at the graph above. The graph shows the number of moose and wolves living on Isle Royale, an island in Lake Superior. From 1965 to 1975, the number of prey moose increased. The wolves now had enough to eat, so more of them survived. Within a few years, the wolf population began to increase. The growing number of wolves killed more and more moose. The moose population decreased. By 1980, the lack of moose had greatly affected the wolves. Some wolves starved, and others could not raise as many young. Soon the moose population began to climb again. This cycle for the two species has continued.

Of course, other factors also affect the populations on Isle Royale. For instance, cold winters and disease can also reduce the size of one or both of the populations.

☑ *Checkpoint* ***If predation removes more members of a population than are born, how will the population change?***

Symbiosis

Many of the interactions in the saguaro community you read about earlier are examples of symbiosis. **Symbiosis** (sim bee OH sis) is a close relationship between two species that benefits at least one of the species. **The three types of symbiotic relationships are mutualism, commensalism, and parasitism.**

Mutualism A relationship in which both species benefit is called **mutualism** (MYOO choo uh liz um). The relationship between the saguaro and the long-eared bats is an example of mutualism. The bat benefits because the cactus flowers provide it with food. The saguaro benefits as its pollen is carried to another plant on the bat's nose.

INTEGRATING HEALTH At this very moment, you are participating in a mutualistic relationship with a population of bacteria in your large intestine. These bacteria, called *Escherichia coli*, live in the intestines of most mammals. The bacteria break down some foods that the mammal cannot digest. The bacteria benefit by receiving food and a place to live. You also benefit from the relationship because the bacteria provide you with vitamin K, a nutrient that is needed to make your blood clot.

Commensalism A relationship in which one species benefits and the other species is neither helped nor harmed is called **commensalism** (kuh MEN suh liz um). The red-tailed hawks' interaction with the saguaro is an example of commensalism. The hawks are helped by having a place to build their nest, while the cactus is not affected by the birds.

Commensalism is not very common in nature because two species are usually either helped or harmed a little by any interaction. For example, by creating a small hole for its nest in the cactus trunk, the elf owl slightly damages the cactus.

Classifying

ACTIVITY

Classify each interaction as an example of mutualism, commensalism, or parasitism. Explain your answers.

- A remora fish attaches itself to the underside of a shark without harming the shark, and eats leftover bits of food from the shark's meals.
- A vampire bat drinks the blood of horses.
- Bacteria living in cows' stomachs help them break down the cellulose in grass.

Figure 14 Three yellow-billed oxpeckers get a cruise and a snack aboard an obliging hippopotamus. The oxpeckers eat ticks living on the hippo's skin. Since both the birds and the hippo benefit from this interaction, it is an example of mutualism.

Figure 15 The white objects on this sphinx moth larva are wasp cocoons. When the wasps emerge, they will feed on the larva. ***Applying Concepts*** *Which organism in this interaction is the parasite? Which organism is the host?*

Parasitism The third type of symbiosis is called parasitism. **Parasitism** (PA ruh sit iz um) involves one organism living on or inside another organism and harming it. The organism that benefits is called a **parasite,** and the organism it lives on or in is called a **host.** The parasite is usually smaller than the host. In a parasitic relationship, the parasite benefits from the interaction while the host is harmed.

Some common parasites you may be familiar with are fleas, ticks, and leeches. These parasites have adaptations that enable them to attach to their host and feed on its blood. Other parasites live inside the host's body, such as tapeworms that live inside the digestive systems of many mammals, such as dogs and wolves.

Unlike a predator, a parasite does not usually kill the organism it feeds on. If the host dies, the parasite loses its source of food. An interesting example of this rule is shown by a species of mite that lives in the ears of moths. The mites almost always live in just one of the moth's ears. If they live in both ears, the moth's hearing is so badly affected that it is likely to be quickly caught and eaten by its predator, a bat.

Section 3 Review

1. How do an organism's adaptations help it to survive?
2. Name and define the three major types of interactions among organisms.
3. List the three types of symbiosis. For each one, explain how the two organisms are affected.
4. A walking stick is an insect that resembles a small twig. How do you think this insect avoids predators?
5. **Thinking Critically Comparing and Contrasting** How are parasitism and predation similar? How are they different?

CHAPTER PROJECT 1

Check Your Progress

By now you should be making your final observations of your plants and planning your report. How can you present your data in a graph? Think about what you should put on each axis of your graph. (*Hint:* Draft the written portion of your report early enough to look it over and make any necessary changes.)

CHAPTER 1 STUDY GUIDE

Living Things and the Environment

Key Ideas

- An organism's habitat provides food, water, shelter, and other things the organism needs to live, grow, and reproduce.
- An ecosystem includes both biotic and abiotic factors. Abiotic factors found in many environments include water, sunlight, oxygen, temperature, and soil.
- A population consists of a single species. The different populations living together in one area make up a community. The community plus abiotic factors form an ecosystem.
- Ecologists study how the biotic and abiotic factors interact within an ecosystem.

Key Terms

ecosystem
habitat
biotic factor
abiotic factor
photosynthesis
species
population
community
ecology

Studying Populations

INTEGRATING MATHEMATICS

Key Ideas

- Ecologists can estimate population size by direct and indirect observations, sampling, and mark-and-recapture studies.
- A population changes in size as a result of changes in the birth rate or death rate, or when organisms move into or out of the population.
- Population size is controlled by limiting factors such as food, space, and weather conditions.

Key Terms

population density
estimate
birth rate
death rate
immigration
emigration
limiting factor
carrying capacity

SECTION 3 Interactions Among Living Things

Key Ideas

- Over time, species of organisms develop specialized adaptations and behaviors that help them succeed in their environments.
- The major types of interactions among organisms are competition, predation, and symbiosis.
- Symbiosis is a close relationship between two species. The three types of symbiotic relationships are mutualism, commensalism, and parasitism.

Key Terms

natural selection
adaptation
niche
competition
predation
predator
prey
symbiosis
mutualism
commensalism
parasitism
parasite
host

Organizing Information

Concept Map Copy the concept map about interactions among organisms onto a sheet of paper. Complete it and add a title. (For more on concept maps, see the Skills Handbook.)

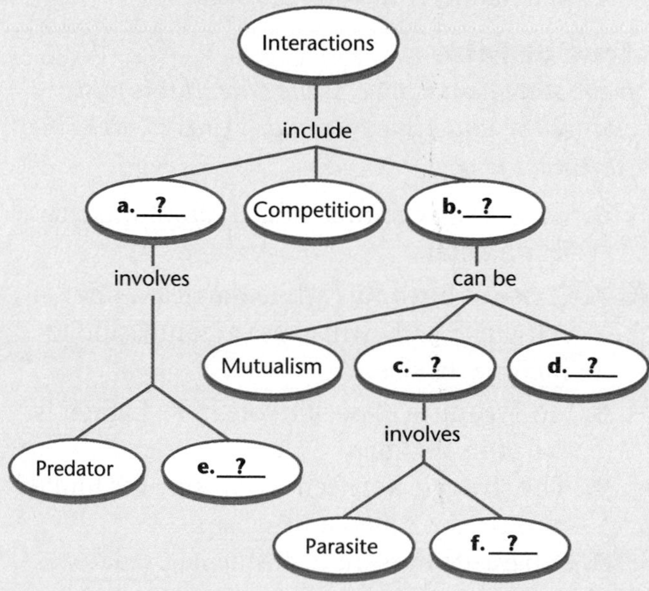

CHAPTER 1 ASSESSMENT

Reviewing Content

Multiple Choice

Choose the letter of the best answer.

1. Which of the following is *not* an example of a population?
   a. the pets in your neighborhood
   b. the people in a city
   c. the rainbow trout in a stream
   d. the ants in an anthill
2. A prairie dog, a hawk, and a badger all are members of the same
   a. habitat. b. community.
   c. species. d. population.
3. All of the following are examples of limiting factors for populations *except*
   a. space b. food
   c. time d. weather
4. In which type of interaction do both species benefit?
   a. predation b. mutualism
   c. commensalism d. parasitism
5. Which of these relationships is an example of parasitism?
   a. a bird building a nest on a tree branch
   b. a bat pollinating a saguaro cactus
   c. a flea living on a cat's blood
   d. *Escherichia coli* bacteria making vitamin K in your intestine

True or False

If the statement is true, write true. If it is false, change the underlined word or words to make the statement true.

6. Grass is an example of a(n) abiotic factor in a habitat.
7. A rise in birth rate while the death rate remains steady will cause a population to increase in size.
8. An organism's specific role in its habitat is called its niche.
9. The struggle between organisms for limited resources is called mutualism.
10. A parasite lives on or inside its predator.

Checking Concepts

11. Name two biotic and two abiotic factors you might find in a forest ecosystem.
12. Explain how sunlight is used by plants and algae. How is this process important to other living things in an ecosystem?
13. Describe how ecologists use the technique of sampling to estimate population size.
14. Give an example showing how space can be a limiting factor for a population.
15. What are two adaptations that prey organisms have developed to protect themselves? Describe how each adaptation protects the organism.
16. **Writing to Learn** Write a description of your niche in the environment. Include details about your habitat, including both biotic and abiotic factors around you. Be sure to describe your feeding habits as well as any interactions you have with members of other species.

Thinking Critically

17. **Making Generalizations** Explain why ecologists usually study a specific population of organisms rather than studying the entire species.
18. **Problem Solving** In a summer job working for an ecologist, you have been assigned to estimate the population of grasshoppers in a field. Propose a method to get an estimate and explain how you would carry it out.
19. **Relating Cause and Effect** Competition for resources in an area is usually more intense within a single species than between two different species. Can you suggest an explanation for this observation? (*Hint:* Consider how niches help organisms avoid competition.)
20. **Comparing and Contrasting** Explain how parasitism and mutualism are similar and how they are different.

Applying Skills

Ecologists monitoring a deer population collected data during a 30-year study. Use the data to answer Questions 21–24.

Year	0	5	10	15	20	25	30
Population (thousands)	15	30	65	100	40	25	10

21. Graphing Make a line graph using the data in the table. Plot years on the horizontal axis and population on the vertical axis.

22. Interpreting Data In which year did the deer population reach its highest point? Its lowest point?

23. Communicating Write a few sentences describing how the deer population changed during the study.

24. Developing Hypotheses In Year 16 of the study, this region experienced a very severe winter. How might this have affected the deer population?

Performance Assessment
CHAPTER PROJECT 1

Project Wrap Up Review your report and graph to be sure that they clearly state your conclusion about the effects of crowding on plant growth. With your group, decide how you will present your results. Do a practice run-through to make sure all group members feel comfortable with their part.

Reflect and Record Compare your group's results with those of your classmates. Suggest possible explanations for any differences. How could you have improved your plan for your experiment?

Test Preparation

Use these questions to prepare for standardized tests.

Study the graph. Then answer Questions 25–28.

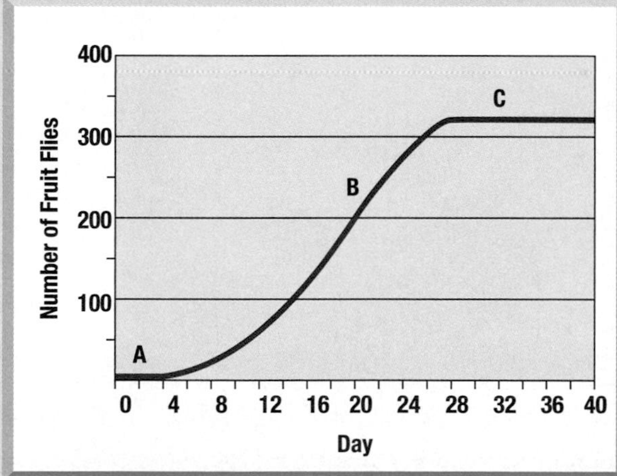

25. What is the best title for this graph?
a. Fruit Fly Population Density
b. Abiotic Factors and Fruit Flies
c. Fruit Fly Population Growth
d. Fruit Fly Death Rate

26. At what point on the graph is the population of fruit flies increasing?
a. Point A **b.** Point B
c. Point C **d.** none of the above

27. Which of the following statements may be true of the fruit fly population at Point C?
a. The death rate is approximately equal to the birth rate.
b. A limiting factor in the environment is preventing the population from increasing.
c. There may not be enough food or space to support a larger population.
d. All of the above statements may be true.

28. Based on the graph, what is the carrying capacity of the environment in which the fruit flies live?
a. approximately 320 fruit flies
b. approximately 220 fruit flies
c. approximately 410 fruit flies
d. approximately 160 fruit flies

Chapter 2 Ecosystems and Biomes

WEB ACTIVITY www.phschool.com

Section 1 Energy Flow in Ecosystems

Discover Where Did Your Dinner Come From?
Sharpen Your Skills Observing
Try This Weaving a Food Web

Section 2 Cycles of Matter

Integrating Chemistry

Discover Are You Part of a Cycle?
Sharpen Your Skills Developing Hypotheses

Section 3 Biogeography

Discover How Can You Move a Seed?

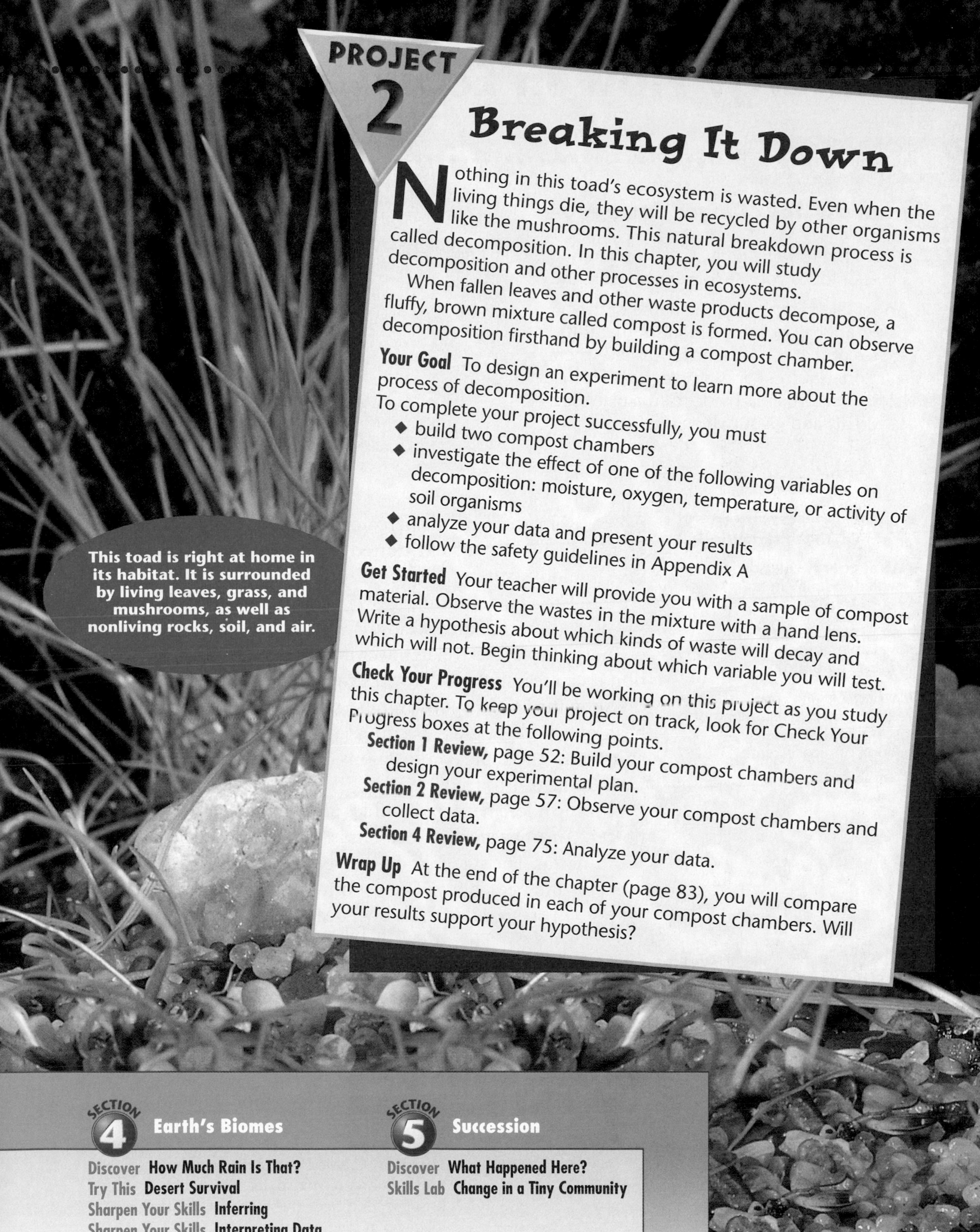

PROJECT 2

Breaking It Down

Nothing in this toad's ecosystem is wasted. Even when the living things die, they will be recycled by other organisms like the mushrooms. This natural breakdown process is called decomposition. In this chapter, you will study decomposition and other processes in ecosystems.

When fallen leaves and other waste products decompose, a fluffy, brown mixture called compost is formed. You can observe decomposition firsthand by building a compost chamber.

Your Goal To design an experiment to learn more about the process of decomposition.

To complete your project successfully, you must

- build two compost chambers
- investigate the effect of one of the following variables on decomposition: moisture, oxygen, temperature, or activity of soil organisms
- analyze your data and present your results
- follow the safety guidelines in Appendix A

Get Started Your teacher will provide you with a sample of compost material. Observe the wastes in the mixture with a hand lens. Write a hypothesis about which kinds of waste will decay and which will not. Begin thinking about which variable you will test.

Check Your Progress You'll be working on this project as you study this chapter. To keep your project on track, look for Check Your Progress boxes at the following points.

Section 1 Review, page 52: Build your compost chambers and design your experimental plan.

Section 2 Review, page 57: Observe your compost chambers and collect data.

Section 4 Review, page 75: Analyze your data.

Wrap Up At the end of the chapter (page 83), you will compare the compost produced in each of your compost chambers. Will your results support your hypothesis?

This toad is right at home in its habitat. It is surrounded by living leaves, grass, and mushrooms, as well as nonliving rocks, soil, and air.

Section 1 Energy Flow in Ecosystems

Discover Activity

Where Did Your Dinner Come From?

1. Across the top of a page, list the different types of foods you ate for dinner last night.
2. Under each item, write the name of the plant, animal, or other organism that is the source of that food. Some foods have more than one source. For example, bread is made from flour (which is made from a plant such as wheat) and yeast (which is a fungus).

Think It Over

Classifying Count the different organisms that contributed to your dinner. How many of your food sources were plants? How many were animals?

Guide for Reading

- ◆ What energy roles do organisms play in an ecosystem?
- ◆ How much energy is available at each level of an energy pyramid?

Reading Tip As you read, create a flowchart showing one possible path of energy through an ecosystem.

Pushing off from its perch on an oak tree limb, the kestrel glides over a field dotted with yellow flowers. In the middle of the field, the bird pauses. It hovers above the ground like a giant hummingbird. Despite strong gusts of wind, the bird's head remains steady as it looks for prey. It takes a lot of energy for the kestrel to hover in this way, but from this position it can search the field below for food.

Soon the kestrel spots a mouse munching the ripening seedhead of a blade of grass. Seconds later the kestrel swoops down and grasps the mouse in its talons. The bird carries the mouse back to the tree to feed.

Meanwhile, a lynx spider hides among the petals of a nearby flower. An unsuspecting bee lands on the flower for a sip of nectar. The spider grabs the bee and injects its venom into the bee's body. The venom kills the bee before it can respond with its own deadly sting.

This sunny field is an ecosystem, made up of living and nonliving things that interact with one another. You can see that many interactions in this ecosystem involve eating. The spider eats a bee that eats nectar, while the kestrel eats a mouse that eats grass. Ecologists study such feeding patterns to learn how energy flows within an ecosystem.

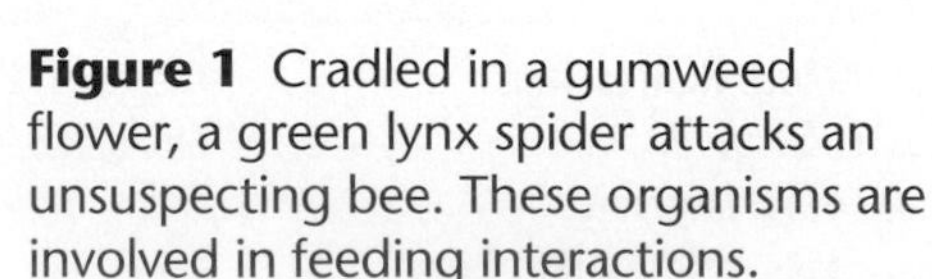

Figure 1 Cradled in a gumweed flower, a green lynx spider attacks an unsuspecting bee. These organisms are involved in feeding interactions.

Energy Roles

Do you play an instrument in your school band? If so, you know that each instrument has a role in a piece of music. For instance, the flute may provide the melody, while the drum provides the beat. Although the two instruments are quite different, they both play important roles in creating the band's music. In the same way, each organism has a role in the movement of energy through its ecosystem. This role is part of the organism's niche in the ecosystem. The kestrel's role is different from that of the giant oak tree where it was perched. But all parts of the ecosystem, like all parts of the band, are necessary for the ecosystem to work.

An organism's energy role is determined by how it obtains energy and how it interacts with the other living things in its ecosystem. **An organism's energy role in an ecosystem may be that of a producer, consumer, or decomposer.**

Producers Energy first enters most ecosystems as sunlight. Some organisms, such as plants, algae, and some bacteria, are able to capture the energy of sunlight and store it as food energy. As Figure 2 shows, these organisms use the sun's energy to turn water and carbon dioxide into molecules such as sugars and starches. As you recall from Chapter 1, this process is called photosynthesis.

An organism that can make its own food is a **producer.** Producers are the source of all the food in an ecosystem. For example, the grass and oak tree are the producers for the field ecosystem you read about at the beginning of the section.

In a few ecosystems the producers obtain energy from a source other than sunlight. One such ecosystem is found in rocks deep beneath the ground. Since the rocks are never exposed to sunlight, how is energy brought into this ecosystem? Certain bacteria in this ecosystem produce their own food using the energy in a gas, hydrogen sulfide, that is found in their environment.

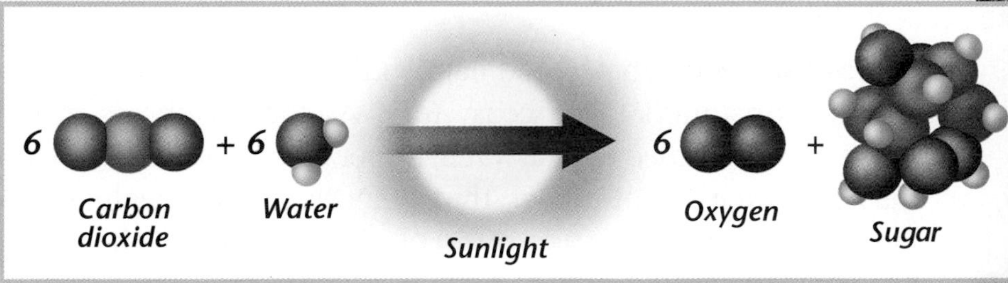

Figure 2 The sunlight streaming through this redwood forest is the source of energy for the ecosystem. Plants convert the sun's energy to stored food energy through the process of photosynthesis.
Interpreting Diagrams *What substances are needed for photosynthesis? What substances are produced?*

Figure 3 Consumers are classified by what they eat. **A.** An agile gerenuk stands on its hind legs to reach these leaves. Consumers that eat plants are called herbivores. **B.** Carnivores like this collared lizard eat only animals. **C.** A black vulture is a scavenger, a carnivore that feeds on the remains of dead organisms.

Consumers Other members of the ecosystem cannot make their own food. These organisms depend on the producers for food and energy. An organism that obtains energy by feeding on other organisms is a **consumer.**

Consumers are classified by what they eat. Consumers that eat only plants are called **herbivores.** This term comes from the Latin words *herba,* which means grass or herb, and *vorare,* which means to eat. Some familiar herbivores are caterpillars, cattle, and deer. Consumers that eat only animals are called **carnivores.** This term comes from the same root word *vorare,* plus the Latin word for flesh, *carnis.* Lions, spiders, and snakes are some examples of carnivores. A consumer that eats both plants and animals is called an **omnivore.** The Latin word *omni* means all. Crows, goats, and most humans are examples of omnivores.

Some carnivores are scavengers. A **scavenger** is a carnivore that feeds on the bodies of dead organisms. Scavengers include catfish and vultures.

Decomposers What would happen if there were only producers and consumers in an ecosystem? As the organisms in the ecosystem continued to take water, minerals, and other raw materials from their surroundings, these materials would begin to run low. If these materials were not replaced, new organisms would not be able to grow.

All the organisms in an ecosystem produce waste and eventually die. If these wastes and dead organisms were not somehow removed from the ecosystem, they would pile up until they overwhelmed the living things. Organisms that break down wastes and

Observing ACTIVITY

Sprinkle a few drops of water on a slice of bread. Enclose the bread in a sealable plastic bag. Seal the bag tightly with tape and put it in a warm, dark place. Observe the bread daily for about two weeks. **CAUTION:** *Do not open the bag.* Write a few sentences describing the changes you observe. What is responsible for the change?

dead organisms and return the raw materials to the environment are called **decomposers.** Two major groups of decomposers are bacteria and fungi, such as molds and mushrooms. While obtaining energy for their own needs, decomposers return simple molecules to the environment. These molecules can be used again by other organisms.

Figure 4 A cluster of honey mushrooms grows among dead leaves. Mushrooms are familiar decomposers.

☑ *Checkpoint* *What do herbivores and carnivores have in common?*

Food Chains and Food Webs

As you have read, energy enters most ecosystems as sunlight, and is converted into sugar and starch molecules by producers. This energy is transferred to each organism that eats a producer, and then to other organisms that feed on these consumers. The movement of energy through an ecosystem can be shown in diagrams called food chains and food webs.

A **food chain** is a series of events in which one organism eats another and obtains energy. You can follow one food chain from the field ecosystem below. The first organism in a food chain is always a producer, such as the grass in the field. The second organism is a consumer that eats the producer, and is called a first-level consumer. The mouse is a first-level consumer. Next, a second-level consumer eats the first-level consumer. The second-level consumer in this example is the kestrel.

A food chain shows one possible path along which energy can move through an ecosystem. But just as you do not eat the same thing every day, neither do most other organisms. Most producers and consumers are part of many food chains. A more realistic way to show the flow of energy through an ecosystem is a food web. A **food web** consists of the many overlapping food chains in an ecosystem.

Figure 5 These organisms make up one food chain in a field ecosystem. ***Classifying*** *Which organism shown is acting as an herbivore? Which is a carnivore?*

EXPLORING a Food Web

A food web consists of many interconnected food chains. Trace the path of energy through the producers, consumers, and decomposers.

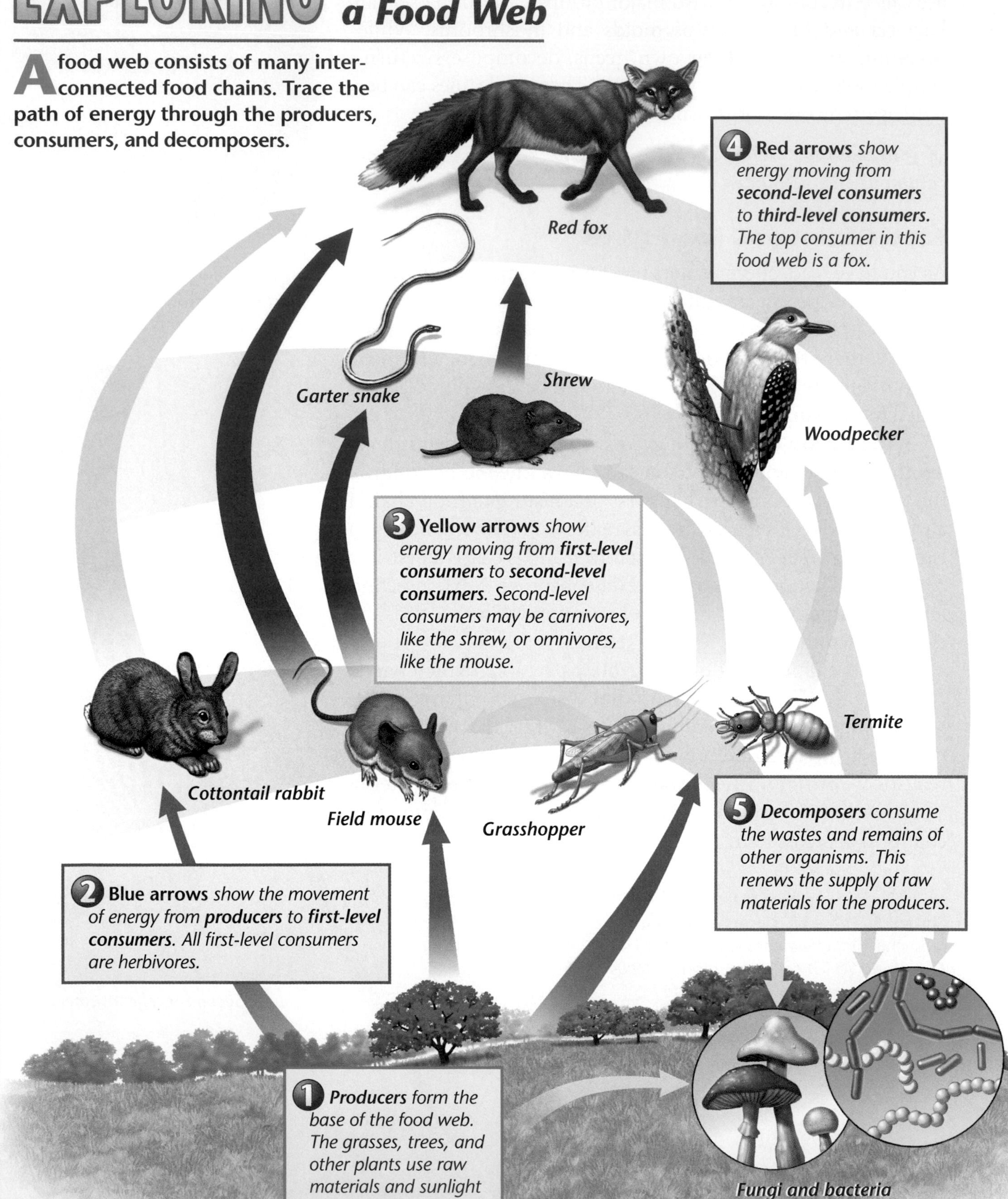

1 Producers *form the base of the food web. The grasses, trees, and other plants use raw materials and sunlight to make sugars and starches.*

2 Blue arrows *show the movement of energy from* **producers** *to* **first-level consumers***. All first-level consumers are herbivores.*

3 Yellow arrows *show energy moving from* **first-level consumers** *to* **second-level consumers***. Second-level consumers may be carnivores, like the shrew, or omnivores, like the mouse.*

4 Red arrows *show energy moving from* **second-level consumers** *to* **third-level consumers***. The top consumer in this food web is a fox.*

5 Decomposers *consume the wastes and remains of other organisms. This renews the supply of raw materials for the producers.*

In *Exploring a Food Web* on the facing page, you can trace the many food chains in a woodland ecosystem. Note that an organism may play more than one role in an ecosystem. For example, an omnivore such as the mouse is a first-level consumer when it eats grass. But when the mouse eats a grasshopper, it is a second-level consumer.

☑ *Checkpoint What are the organisms in one food chain shown in the food web on the facing page?*

Energy Pyramids

When an organism in an ecosystem eats, it obtains energy. The organism uses some of this energy to move, grow, reproduce, and carry out other life activities. This means that only some of the energy will be available to the next organism in the food web.

A diagram called an **energy pyramid** shows the amount of energy that moves from one feeding level to another in a food web. The organisms at each level use some of the energy to carry out their life processes. **The most energy is available at the producer level. At each level in the pyramid, there is less available energy than at the level below.** An energy pyramid gets its name from the shape of the diagram—wider at the base and narrower at the top, resembling a pyramid.

In general, only about 10 percent of the energy at one level of a food web is transferred to the next, higher, level. The other

Weaving a Food Web

ACTIVITY

This activity shows how the organisms in a food web are interconnected.

1. Your teacher will assign you a role in the food web.
2. Hold one end of each of several pieces of yarn in your hand. Give the other ends of your yarn to the other organisms to which your organism is linked.
3. Your teacher will now eliminate one of the organisms. Everyone who is connected to that organism should drop the yarn connecting them to it.

Making Models How many organisms were affected by the removal of one organism? What does this activity show about the importance of each organism in a food web?

Figure 6 Organisms use energy to carry out their life activities. A lioness uses energy to chase her zebra prey. The zebras use energy to flee.

Figure 7 This energy pyramid diagram shows the energy available at each level of a food web. Energy is measured in kilocalories, or kcal. ***Calculating*** *How many times more energy is available at the producer level than at the second-level consumer level?*

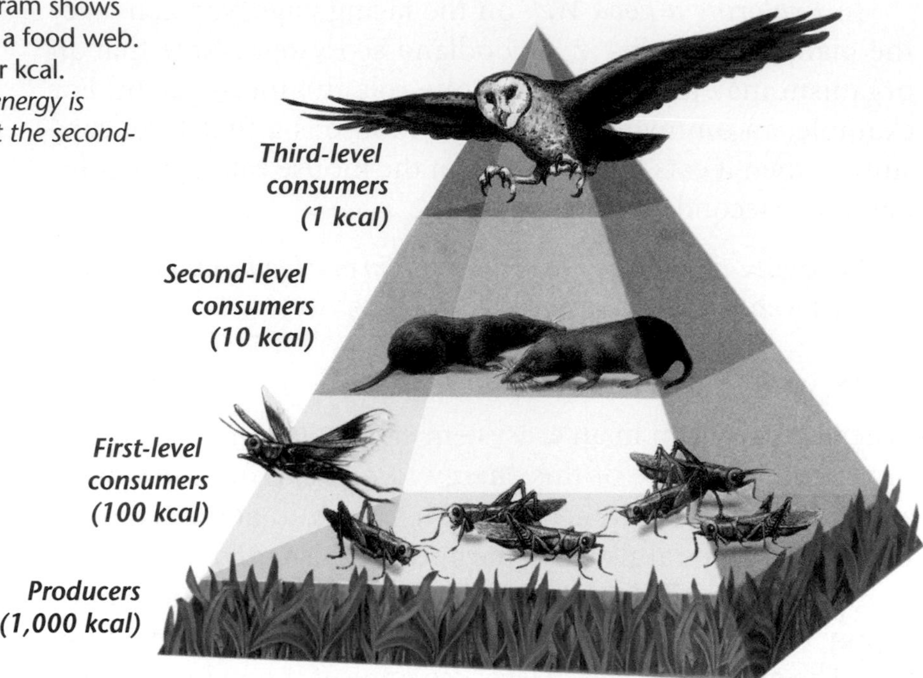

90 percent of the energy is used for the organism's life processes or is lost as heat to the environment. Because of this, most food webs only have three or four feeding levels. Since 90 percent of the energy is lost at each step, there is not enough energy to support many feeding levels.

But the organisms at higher feeding levels of an energy pyramid do not necessarily require less energy to live than organisms at lower levels. Since so much energy is lost at each level, the amount of energy in the producer level limits the number of consumers the ecosystem can support. As a result, there usually are few organisms at the highest level in a food web.

Section 1 Review

1. Name the three energy roles of organisms in an ecosystem. How does each type of organism obtain energy?
2. How does the amount of available energy change from one level of an energy pyramid to the next level up?
3. Name and define the four types of consumers.
4. What is the source of energy for most ecosystems?
5. **Thinking Critically Making Generalizations** Why are food webs a more realistic way of portraying ecosystems than food chains?

Check Your Progress

CHAPTER PROJECT 2

By now you should have constructed your compost chambers and chosen a variable to investigate. Design your plan for observing the effect of this variable on the decomposition process. Submit your plan to your teacher for approval. (*Hint:* As part of your plan, include how you will collect data to measure decomposition in your compost chambers.)

Cycles of Matter

DISCOVER — ACTIVITY

Are You Part of a Cycle?

1. Hold a small mirror a few centimeters from your mouth.
2. Exhale onto the mirror.
3. Observe the surface of the mirror.

Think It Over

Inferring What is the substance that forms on the mirror? Where did this substance come from?

GUIDE FOR READING

- **What three major processes make up the water cycle?**
- **How is carbon dioxide used by producers?**

Reading Tip **As you read, use the section headings to make an outline of the section.**

A pile of crumpled cars is ready for loading into a giant compactor. Junkyard workers have already removed many of the cars' parts. The aluminum and copper pieces were removed so that they could be recycled, or used again. Now a recycling plant will reclaim the steel in the bodies of the cars. Earth has a limited supply of aluminum, copper, and the iron needed to make steel. Recycling old cars is one way to provide a new supply of these materials.

Recycling Matter

The way matter is recycled in ecosystems is similar to the way the metal in old cars is recycled. Like the supply of metal for building cars, the supply of matter in an ecosystem is limited. If matter could not be recycled, ecosystems would quickly run out of the raw materials necessary for life.

Energy, on the other hand, is not recycled. You must constantly supply a car with energy in the form of gasoline. Ecosystems must also be constantly supplied with energy, usually in the form of sunlight. Gasoline and the sun's energy cannot be recycled—they must be constantly supplied.

As you read in Section 1, energy enters an ecosystem and moves from the producers to the consumers to the decomposers. In contrast, matter cycles through an ecosystem over and over. Matter in an ecosystem includes water, oxygen, carbon, nitrogen, and many other substances. To understand how these substances cycle through an ecosystem, you need to know a few basic terms that describe the structure of matter. Matter is made

Cars awaiting recycling at a Utah plant ▼

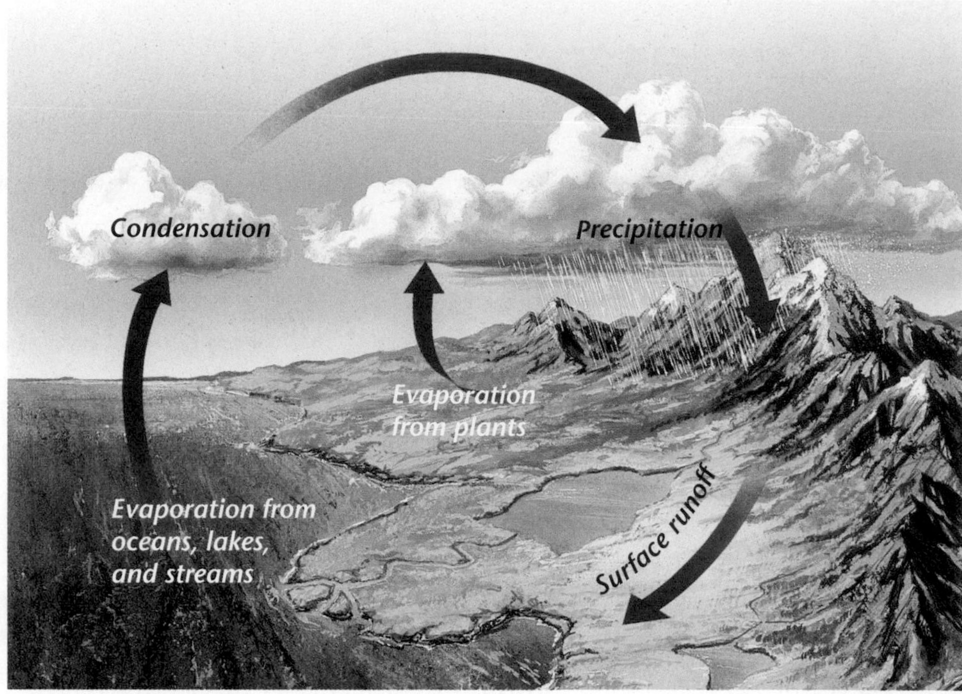

Figure 8 In the water cycle, water moves continuously from Earth's surface to the atmosphere and back. ***Interpreting Diagrams*** *In which step of the water cycle does water return to Earth's surface?*

up of tiny particles called atoms. Combinations of two or more atoms chemically bonded together are called molecules. For example, a molecule of water consists of two hydrogen atoms bonded to one oxygen atom. In this section, you will learn about some of the most important cycles of matter: the water cycle, the carbon and oxygen cycles, and the nitrogen cycle.

The Water Cycle

How could you determine whether life has ever existed on another planet in the solar system? One piece of evidence scientists look for is the presence of water. This is because water is the most common compound in all living cells on Earth. Water is necessary for life as we know it.

Water is recycled through the water cycle. The **water cycle** is the continuous process by which water moves from Earth's surface to the atmosphere and back. **The processes of evaporation, condensation, and precipitation make up the water cycle.** As you read about these processes, follow the cycle in Figure 8.

Evaporation The process by which molecules of liquid water absorb energy and change to the gas state is called **evaporation.** In the water cycle liquid water evaporates from Earth's surface and forms water vapor, a gas, in the atmosphere. Most water evaporates from the surfaces of oceans and lakes. The energy for evaporation comes from the sun.

Developing Hypotheses

ACTIVITY

You're having cocoa at a friend's house on a cold, rainy day. As your friend boils some water, you notice that a window next to the stove is covered with water droplets. Your friend thinks the window is leaking. Using what you know about the water cycle, can you propose another explanation for the water droplets on the window?

Some water is also given off by living things. For example, plants take in water through their roots and release water vapor from their leaves. You take in water when you drink and eat. You release liquid water in your wastes and water vapor when you exhale.

Condensation What happens next to the water vapor in the atmosphere? As the water vapor rises higher in the atmosphere, it cools down. When it cools to a certain temperature the vapor turns back into tiny drops of liquid water. The process by which a gas changes to a liquid is called **condensation.** The water droplets collect around particles of dust in the air, eventually forming clouds like those in Figure 8.

Precipitation As more water vapor condenses, the drops of water in the cloud grow larger and heavier. Eventually the heavy drops fall back to Earth as a form of **precipitation**—rain, snow, sleet, or hail. Most precipitation falls back into oceans or lakes. The precipitation that falls on land may soak into the soil and become groundwater. Or the precipitation may run off the land, ultimately flowing into a river or ocean once again.

☑ *Checkpoint* *What change of state occurs when water from the surface of the ocean enters the atmosphere as water vapor?*

The Carbon and Oxygen Cycles

Two other chemicals necessary for life are carbon and oxygen. The processes by which they are recycled are linked together, as shown in Figure 9. Carbon is the building block for the matter that makes up the bodies of living things. It is present in the atmosphere in the gas carbon dioxide. Producers take in carbon dioxide from

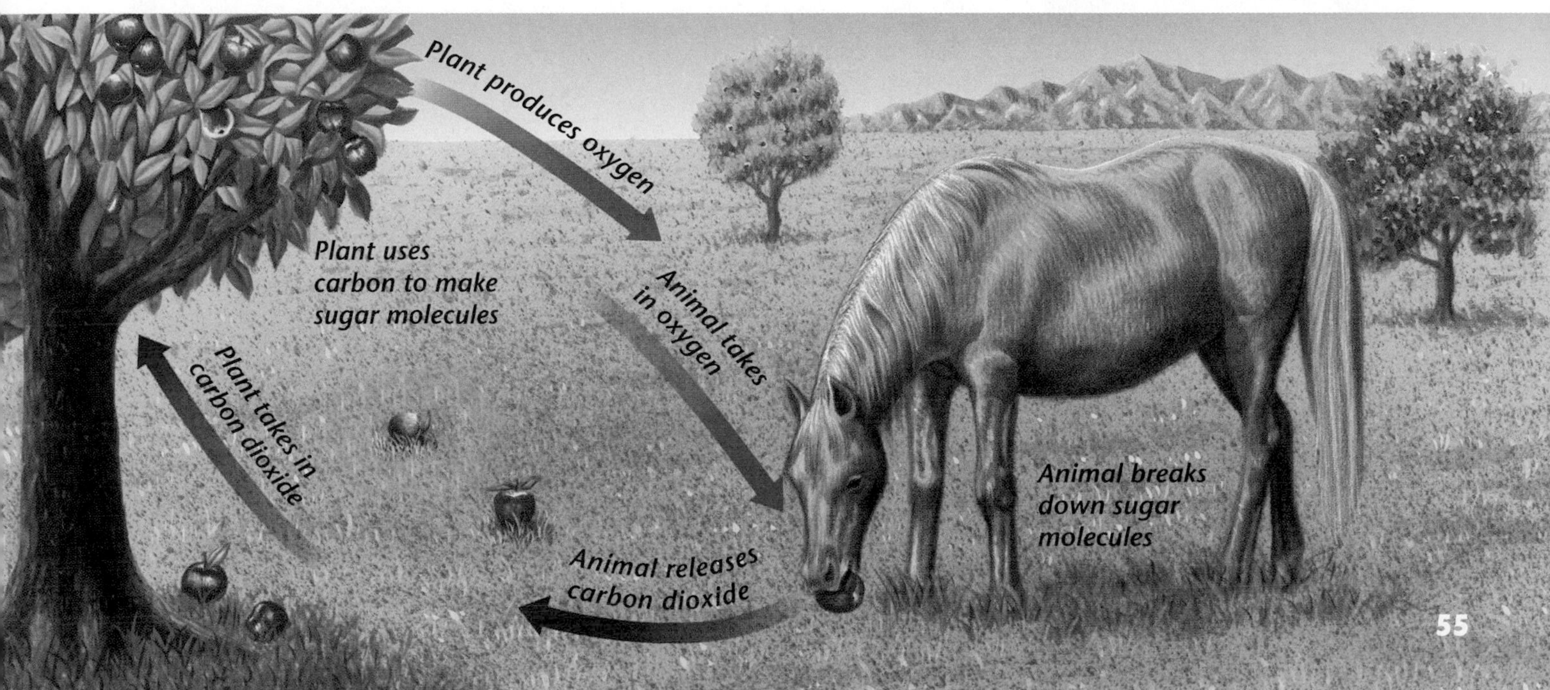

Figure 9 This scene shows how the carbon and oxygen cycles are linked together. Producers use carbon dioxide to carry out photosynthesis. In this process, carbon is used to create sugar molecules such as those found in apples. The producers release oxygen, which is then used by other organisms. These organisms take in carbon in food and release it in the form of carbon dioxide again.

the atmosphere during photosynthesis. **In this process, the producers use carbon from the carbon dioxide to produce other carbon-containing molecules.** These molecules include sugars and starches. To obtain energy from these molecules, consumers break them down into simpler molecules. Consumers release water and carbon dioxide as waste products.

At the same time, oxygen is also cycling through the ecosystem. Producers release oxygen as a result of photosynthesis. Other organisms take in oxygen from the atmosphere and use it in their life processes.

☑ *Checkpoint* *How is oxygen returned to the environment?*

The Nitrogen Cycle

Like carbon, nitrogen is a necessary building block in the matter that makes up living things. Since the air around you is about 78 percent nitrogen gas, you might think that it would be easy for living things to obtain nitrogen. However, most organisms cannot use the nitrogen gas in the air. Nitrogen gas is called "free" nitrogen, meaning it is not combined with other kinds of atoms. Most organisms can use nitrogen only once it has been "fixed," or combined with other elements to form nitrogen-containing compounds. You can follow this process in Figure 10 below.

Figure 10 In the nitrogen cycle, nitrogen moves from the air to the soil, into living things, and back into the air.
Interpreting Diagrams *How do consumers obtain nitrogen?*

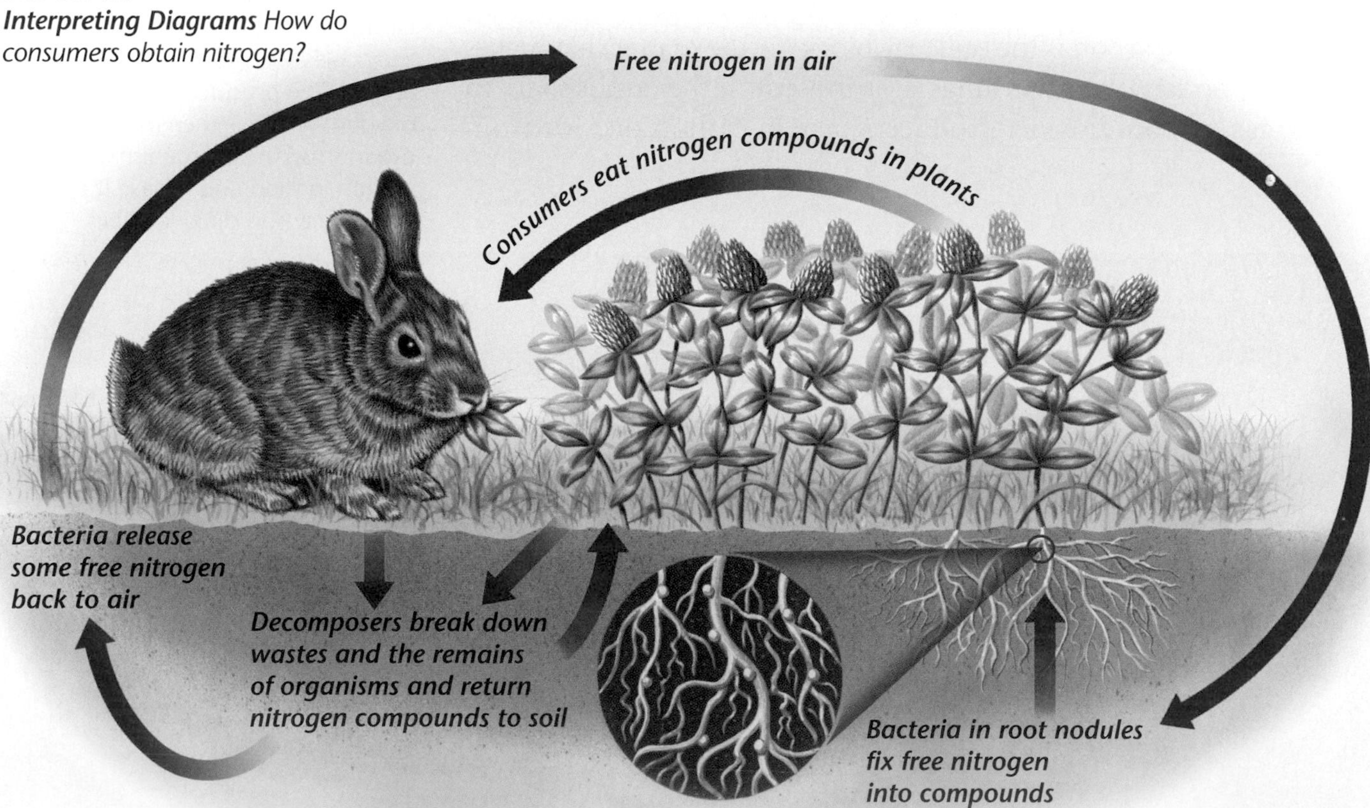

Nitrogen Fixation The process of changing free nitrogen gas into a usable form of nitrogen is called **nitrogen fixation.** Most nitrogen fixation is performed by certain kinds of bacteria. Some of these bacteria live in bumps called **nodules** (NAHJ oolz) on the roots of certain plants. These plants, known as legumes, include clover, beans, peas, alfalfa, and peanuts.

The relationship between the bacteria and the legumes is an example of mutualism. As you recall from Chapter 1, a symbiotic relationship in which both species benefit is called mutualism. Both the bacteria and the plant benefit from this relationship: The bacteria feed on the plant's sugars, and the plant is supplied with nitrogen in a usable form.

INTEGRATING TECHNOLOGY Many farmers make use of the nitrogen-fixing bacteria in legumes to enrich their fields. Every few years, a farmer may plant a legume such as alfalfa in a field. The bacteria in the alfalfa roots build up a new supply of nitrogen compounds in the soil. The following year, the new crops planted in the field benefit from the improved soil.

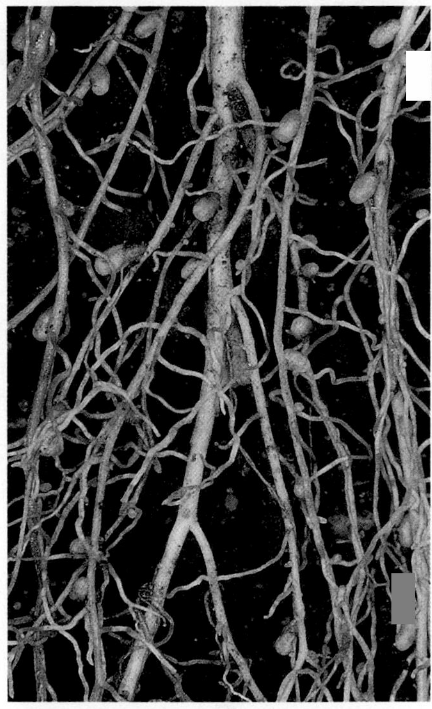

Figure 11 Lumpy nodules are clearly visible on the roots of this clover plant. Bacteria inside the nodules carry out nitrogen fixation.

Return of Nitrogen to the Environment Once the nitrogen has been fixed into chemical compounds, it can be used by organisms to build proteins and other complex substances. Decomposers break down these complex compounds in animal wastes and in the bodies of dead organisms. This returns simple nitrogen compounds to the soil. Nitrogen can cycle from the soil to producers and consumers many times. At some point, however, bacteria break down the nitrogen compounds completely. These bacteria release free nitrogen back into the air. Then the cycle starts again.

Section 2 Review

1. Name and define the three major processes that occur during the water cycle.
2. Explain the role of plants in the carbon cycle.
3. How is nitrogen fixation a necessary part of the nitrogen cycle?
4. Where do nitrogen-fixing bacteria live?
5. **Thinking Critically Comparing and Contrasting** Explain how the movement of matter through an ecosystem is different than the movement of energy through an ecosystem.

Check Your Progress

CHAPTER PROJECT 2

Once your teacher has approved your plan, place the waste into your compost chambers. Record your hypothesis about the effect of the variable you are investigating. Observe the two containers daily. (*Hint:* If there are no signs of decomposition after several days, you may wish to stir the contents of each chamber. Stirring allows more oxygen to enter the mixture.)

SECTION 3 Biogeography

DISCOVER ACTIVITY

How Can You Move a Seed?

1. Place a few corn kernels at one end of a shallow pan.
2. Make a list of ways you could move the kernels to the other side of the pan. You may use any of the simple materials your teacher has provided.
3. Now try each method. Record whether or not each was successful in moving the kernels across the pan.

Think It Over

Predicting How might seeds be moved from place to place on Earth?

GUIDE FOR READING

- **How does dispersal of organisms occur?**
- **What factors can limit the distribution of a species?**

Reading Tip **As you read, look for reasons why organisms live in certain places in the world. Make a list of these reasons.**

◀ **Australian wallaby**

Imagine how European explorers must have felt when they saw the continent of Australia for the first time. Instead of familiar grazing animals such as horses and deer, they saw what looked like giant rabbits with long tails. Peering into the branches of eucalyptus trees, these explorers saw bearlike koalas. And who could have dreamed up an egg-laying animal with a beaver's tail, a duck's bill, and a thick coat of fur? You can see why people who heard the first descriptions of the platypus accused the explorers of lying!

Ecologists had many questions about the plants and animals of Australia. Why had no one ever seen a kangaroo, a eucalyptus tree, or a koala in Europe? Why were there no reindeer, camels, or gorillas in Australia?

Different species live in different parts of the world. The study of where organisms live is called **biogeography.** The word *biogeography* is made up of three Greek word roots: *bio,* meaning "life"; *geo,* meaning "Earth"; and *graph*, meaning "description." Together, these root words tell what biogeographers do—they describe where living things are found on Earth.

Continental Drift

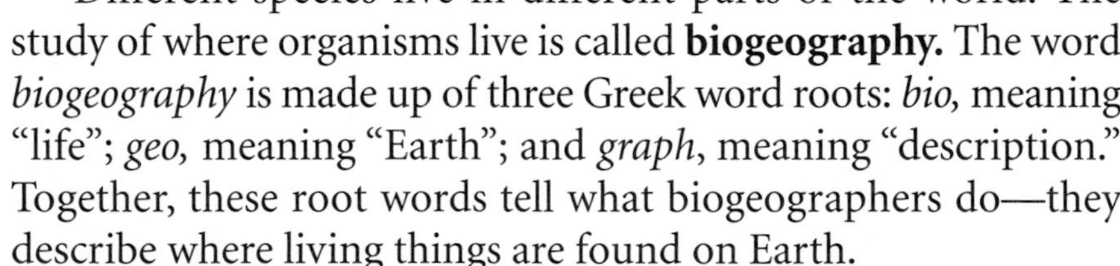

INTEGRATING EARTH SCIENCE

In addition to studying where species live today, biogeographers also study how these species spread into different parts of the world. One factor that has affected how species are distributed is the motion of Earth's continents.The continents are huge blocks of solid rock floating on a layer of hot, dense liquid. The very slow motion of the continents is called **continental drift.**

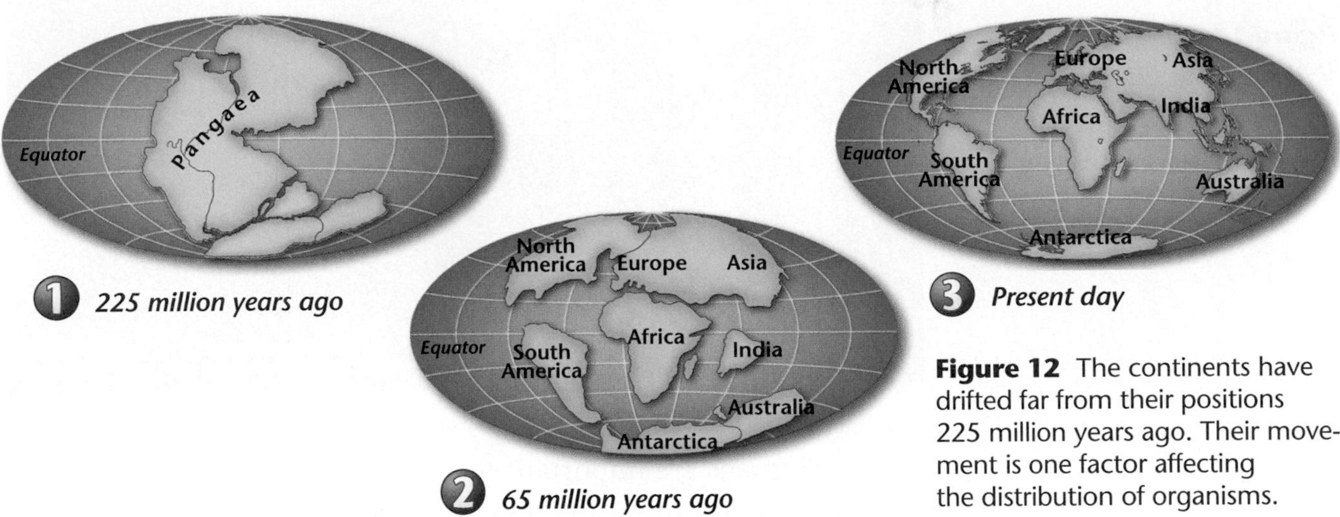

Figure 12 The continents have drifted far from their positions 225 million years ago. Their movement is one factor affecting the distribution of organisms.

Figure 12 shows how much the continents have moved. About 225 million years ago, all of today's continents were part of one large land mass called Pangaea. But after millions of years of slow drifting, they have moved to their present locations. Looking at the globe today, it is hard to believe that at one time India was next to Antarctica, or that Europe and North America once were connected.

The movement of the continents has had a great impact on the distribution of species. Consider Australia, for example. Millions of years ago Australia drifted apart from the other land masses. Organisms from other parts of the world could not reach the isolated island. Kangaroos, koalas, and other unique species developed in this isolation.

Means of Dispersal

The movement of organisms from one place to another is called **dispersal.** Organisms may be dispersed in several different ways. **Dispersal can be caused by wind, water, or living things, including humans.**

Wind and Water Many animals move into new areas by simply walking, swimming, or flying. But plants and small organisms need assistance to move from place to place. Wind provides a means of dispersal for seeds, the spores of fungi, tiny spiders, and many other small, light organisms. Similarly, water transports objects that float, such as coconuts and leaves. Insects and other small animals may get a free ride to a new home on top of these floating rafts.

Other Living Things Organisms may also be dispersed by other living things. For example, a goldfinch may eat seeds in one area and deposit them elsewhere in its wastes. A duck may carry algae or fish eggs on its feet from pond to pond. And if your dog or cat has ever come home covered with sticky plant burs, you know another way seeds can get around.

Figure 13 The stiff brown pods of the milkweed plant contain seeds fringed with silky threads. ***Inferring*** *By what means of dispersal are milkweed seeds spread?*

Figure 14 Clumps of purple loosestrife line the banks of a Massachusetts river. Loosestrife is an exotic species that has thrived in its new home, often crowding out native species.

Humans are important to the dispersal of other species. As people move around the globe, they take plants, animals, and other organisms with them. Sometimes this is intentional, such as when people bring horses to a new settlement. Sometimes it is unintentional, such as when someone carries a parasite into a country.

Species that have naturally evolved in an area are referred to as **native species.** When an organism is carried into a new location by people, it is referred to as an **exotic species.** Some exotic species are so common in their new environment that people think of them as native. For example, you probably know the dandelion, one of the most common flowering plants in North America. But the dandelion is not a native species. It was brought by colonists who valued its leaves for eating and for tea for the sick.

☑ *Checkpoint How can humans disperse a species?*

Social Studies CONNECTION

Many important crops are actually exotic species. When settlers in new lands brought crops with them from their old homes, they caused the dispersal of these species. Some examples of crops dispersed by people are peanuts, potatoes, cotton, corn, and rice.

In Your Journal

Choose a crop to investigate. Research your crop to learn where it is a native species and how it spread to different parts of the world. In what conditions does it grow well? (*Hint:* Almanacs and encyclopedias are good sources of this information.)

Limits to Dispersal

With all these means of dispersal, you might expect to find the same organisms everywhere in the world. Of course, that's not so. Why not? What determines the limits of a species' distribution? **Three factors that limit dispersal of a species are physical barriers, competition, and climate.**

Physical Barriers Barriers such as water, mountains, and deserts are hard to cross. These features can limit the movement of organisms. For example, once Australia became separated from the other continents, the ocean acted as a barrier to dispersal. Organisms could not easily move to or from Australia.

Competition When an organism enters a new area, it must compete for resources with the species already there. To survive, the organism must find a unique niche. If the existing species are thriving, they may outcompete the new species. In this case competition is a barrier to dispersal. Sometimes, however, the new species is more successful than the existing species. The native species may be displaced.

Climate The typical weather pattern in an

INTEGRATING EARTH SCIENCE area over a long period of time is the area's **climate.** Climate is different from weather, which is the day-to-day conditions in an area. Climate is largely determined by temperature and precipitation.

Differences in climate can be a barrier to dispersal. For example, conditions at the top of the mountain shown in Figure 15 are very different from those at the base. The base is warm and dry. Low shrubs and cactuses grow there. Just up the mountain, mostly grasses grow. Higher up the mountain, the climate becomes cooler and wetter. Larger trees such as pines, oaks, and firs can grow. The squirrel in the closeup lives in this region. Climate differences act as a barrier that keeps the squirrel species from dispersing down or up the mountain. Near the top of the mountain, it is very cold and windy. Small alpine wildflowers and mosses grow best in this region.

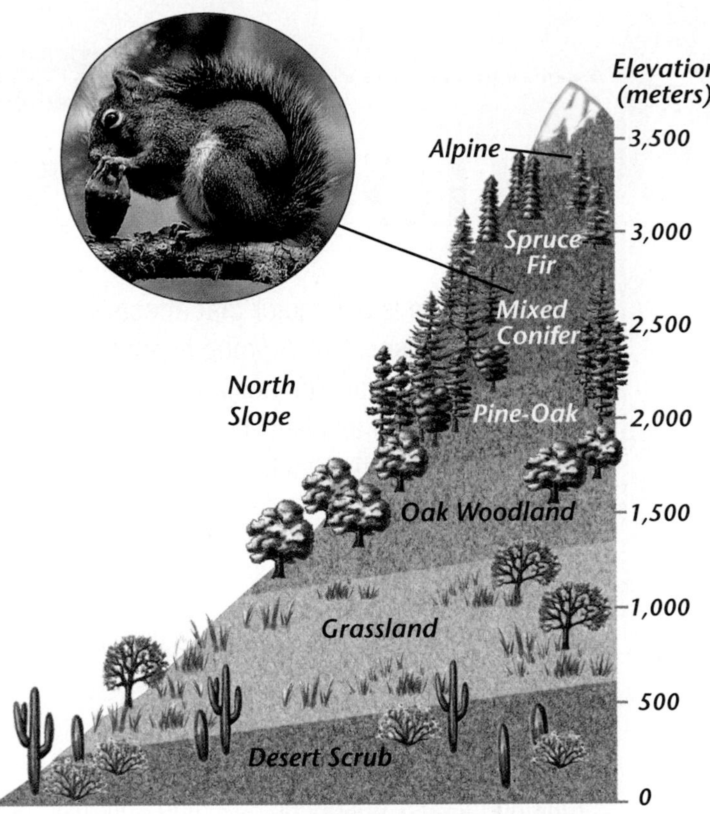

Figure 15 Climate conditions change at different elevations on this mountainside. These conditions determine the distribution of species on the mountain. Each zone begins at a lower elevation on the north slope of the mountain, which is cooler than the south slope.

Places with similar climates tend to have species that occupy similar niches. For example, most continents have a large area of flat, grassy plains. The organisms that occupy the niche of "large, grazing mammal" on each continent have some similarities. In North America, the large, grazing mammals of the grasslands are bison; in Africa, they are wildebeests and antelopes; in Australia, they are kangaroos.

Section 3 Review

1. List three ways that species can disperse.
2. Explain how mountain ranges and climate can each limit a species' distribution.
3. What is biogeography?
4. Give an example of a physical barrier. How might it affect where species are found?
5. **Thinking Critically Predicting** If an exotic insect species were introduced to your area, do you think it would be easy or difficult to eliminate the species? Give reasons to support your answer.

Science at Home

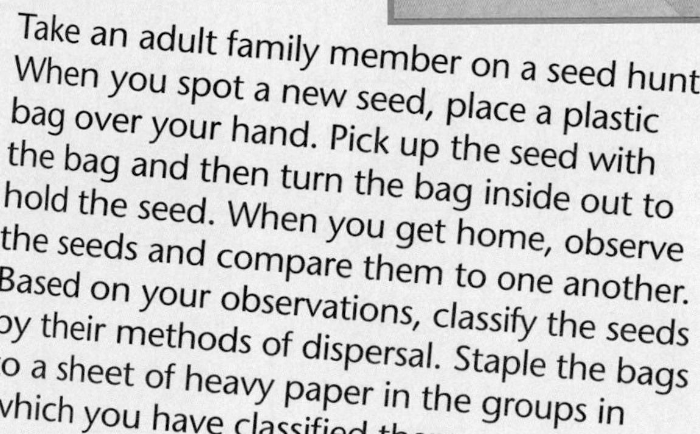

Take an adult family member on a seed hunt. When you spot a new seed, place a plastic bag over your hand. Pick up the seed with the bag and then turn the bag inside out to hold the seed. When you get home, observe the seeds and compare them to one another. Based on your observations, classify the seeds by their methods of dispersal. Staple the bags to a sheet of heavy paper in the groups in which you have classified them.

Real-World Lab

How It Works

BIOMES IN MINIATURE

Climate is one factor that affects where organisms live. A group of ecosystems with similar climates and organisms is called a biome. In this lab, you will investigate some key factors that make biomes different from each other.

Problem

What biotic and abiotic factors create different biomes around the world?

Skills Focus

making models, observing, drawing conclusions

Materials

scissors
index card
10 impatiens seeds
5 lima bean seeds
about 30 rye grass seeds
empty, clean cardboard milk carton
sandy soil or potting soil
clear plastic wrap
lamp
tape
stapler

Procedure

1. Your teacher will assign your group a biome. You will also observe the other groups' biomes. Based on the chart below, predict how well you think each of the three kinds of seeds will grow in each set of conditions. Record these predictions in your notebook. Then copy the data table on the facing page four times, once for each biome.
2. Staple the spout of the milk carton closed. Completely cut away one of the four sides of the carton. Poke a few holes in the opposite side for drainage, then place that side down.
3. Fill the carton to 3 centimeters from the top with the type of soil given in the table. Divide the surface of the soil into three sections by making two lines in it with a pencil.
4. In the section near the spout, plant the impatiens seeds. In the middle section, plant the lima bean seeds. In the third section, scatter the rye grass seeds on the surface.

GROWING CONDITIONS

Biome	Soil Type	Hours of Light Per Day	Watering Instructions
Forest	Potting soil	1–2 hours direct light	Let the surface dry, then add water.
Desert	Sandy soil	5–6 hours direct light	Let the soil dry to a depth of 2.5 cm below the surface.
Grassland	Potting soil	5–6 hours direct light	Let the surface dry, then add water.
Rain forest	Potting soil	No direct light; indirect light for 5–6 hours	Keep the surface of the soil moist.

DATA TABLE

Name of biome: ______________

Day	Impatiens	Lima Beans	Rye Grass
1			
2			
3			

5. Water all the seeds well. Then cover the open part of the carton with plastic wrap.
6. On an index card, write the name of your biome, the names of the three types of seeds in the order you planted them, and the names of your group members. Tape the card to the carton. Put it in a warm place where it will not be disturbed.
7. Once the seeds sprout, provide your biome with light and water as specified in the chart. Keep the carton covered with plastic wrap except when you add water.
8. Observe all the biomes daily for at least one week. Record your observations.

Analyze and Conclude

1. In which biome did each type of seed grow best? In which biome did each type of seed grow least well?
2. How was each type of seed affected by the soil type, amount of light, and availability of water? How do your results relate to biomes in nature?
3. Ecologists studying land biomes often begin a description of the biome by describing key abiotic factors and the typical plants. Why do you think they do this?
4. **Apply** Describe the rainfall pattern and other abiotic factors that make up the climate where you live. How do those factors affect the kinds of plants and animals that live there?

Design an Experiment

After reading Section 4, write a plan for setting up a model rain forest or desert terrarium. Include typical plants found in that biome. Obtain your teacher's approval before trying this activity.

SECTION 4

Earth's Biomes

DISCOVER — ACTIVITY

How Much Rain Is That?

The table shows the average amount of precipitation that falls each year in four different regions. With your classmates, you will create a full-size bar graph on a wall to help you visualize these amounts of rain.

Biome	Rainfall (cm)
Mojave Desert	15
Illinois prairie	70
Smoky Mountains	180
Costa Rican rain forest	350

1. Using a meter stick, measure a strip of adding-machine paper 15 centimeters long. Label this piece of paper "Mojave Desert."
2. Repeat Step 1 for the other three locations. If necessary, tape strips of paper together to make the correct length. Label each strip.
3. Now find a place where you can display the four strips vertically. If the wall of your classroom is not tall enough, you may need to use another wall in your school building. Follow your teacher's instructions to hang your precipitation strips.

Think It Over

Developing Hypotheses Which ecosystem receives the most precipitation? Which receives the least? What effect do you think the amount of rainfall might have on the types of species that live in these ecosystems?

GUIDE FOR READING

- **What determines the type of biome found in an area?**
- **Where can photosynthesis occur in water biomes?**

Reading Tip **As you read, make a list of the biomes described in this section. Under each biome name, take notes on the characteristics of that biome.**

Congratulations! You and your classmates have been selected as the student members of an around-the-world scientific expedition. Your mission is to study the major types of ecosystems on Earth. You will be collecting data on the climate conditions and typical organisms found in each of these ecosystems. The result of this expedition will be a database of information on the biomes you visit. A **biome** is a group of ecosystems with similar climates and organisms.

Classifying ecosystems into biomes helps ecologists describe the world. As you might expect, not all ecologists agree on the exact number and kinds of biomes. The scientists guiding your expedition have chosen to focus on six major land biomes and two major water biomes.

Be sure to pack a variety of clothing for your journey. During your trip, you will visit places ranging from frozen, windy Arctic plains to steamy tropical jungles. **In fact, it is mostly the climate conditions—temperature and rainfall—in an area that determine its biome.** This is because climate limits the distribution of plants in the area. In turn, the types of plants determine the kinds of animals that live there.

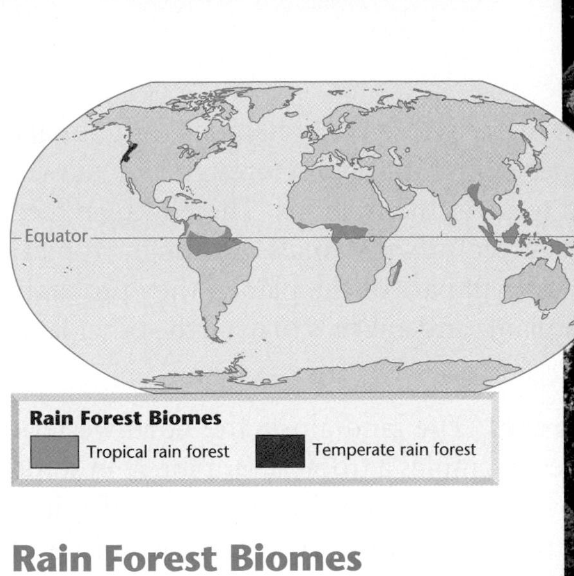

Rain Forest Biomes

The first stop on your expedition is a tropical rain forest close to the equator. The rain forest is warm and humid—in fact, it's pouring rain! Fortunately, you remembered to pack a poncho. After just a short shower, the sun reappears. But even though the sun is shining, very little light penetrates the thick vegetation.

Plants are everywhere in the rain forest. Some, such as the ferns, orchids, and vines you observe hanging from tree limbs, even grow on other plants. Among the plants are many species of birds as bright as the numerous flowers all around you.

Tropical Rain Forests Tropical rain forests are found in warm regions close to the equator. Tropical rain forests typically receive a lot of rain. The warm temperatures do not vary much throughout the year, and the sunlight is fairly constant all year.

Tropical rain forests contain an astounding variety of species. For example, scientists studying a 100-square-meter area of one rain forest identified 300 different kinds of trees! These trees form several distinct layers. The tall trees form a leafy roof called the **canopy.** A few giant trees poke out above the canopy. Below the canopy, a second layer of shorter trees and vines form an **understory.** Understory plants grow well in the shade formed by the canopy. Finally, some plants thrive in the near-darkness of the forest floor.

Figure 16 Tropical rain forests contain an amazing variety of plants and other organisms. In the large photo, a river winds through the lush Indonesian rain forest. The top closeup shows a young orangutan swinging from tree limbs. In the bottom closeup, a tarantula climbs over a brightly colored bracket fungus on the forest floor.

The abundant plant life provides many habitats for animals. The number of insect species in tropical rain forests is not known, but has been estimated to be in the millions. These in turn feed many bird species, which feed other animals. Although tropical rain forests cover only a small part of the planet, they probably contain more species of plants and animals than all the other land biomes combined.

Temperate Rain Forests The land along the northwestern coast of the United States resembles a tropical rain forest in some ways. This region receives more than 300 centimeters of rain a year. Huge trees grow there, including cedars, redwoods, and Douglas firs. However, it is difficult to classify this region. It is too far north and too cool to be a tropical rain forest. Instead many ecologists refer to this ecosystem as a temperate rain forest. The term *temperate* means having moderate temperatures.

Desert Biomes

The next stop on your expedition is a desert. It couldn't be more different from the tropical rain forest you just left. You step off the bus into the searing summer heat. At midday, you cannot even walk into the desert—the sand feels as hot as the hot water that comes from your bathroom faucet at home.

A **desert** is an area that receives less than 25 centimeters of rain per year. The amount of evaporation in a desert is greater than the amount of precipitation. Some of the driest deserts may not receive any rain at all in a year! Deserts often also undergo large shifts in temperature during the course of a day. A scorching hot desert like the

Figure 17 Desert organisms have adaptations that enable them to live in the harsh conditions of their biome. For example, this shovel-snouted lizard "dances" to avoid burning its feet on the hot sand dunes of the Namib Desert in Africa. ***Making Generalizations*** *Describe the climate conditions of a typical desert.*

Namib Desert cools rapidly each night when the sun goes down. Other deserts, such as the Gobi in central Asia, are cooler, even experiencing freezing temperatures in the winter.

The organisms that live in the desert are adapted to the lack of rain and to the extreme temperatures. For example, the trunk of a saguaro cactus has folds that work like the pleats in an accordion. The trunk of the cactus expands to hold more water when it is raining. Many desert animals are most active at night when the temperatures are cooler. A gila monster, for instance, spends much of its time in a cool underground burrow. It may go for weeks without coming up to the surface of the desert.

Checkpoint *What are some adaptations that help an organism to live in the desert?*

Grassland Biomes

The next stop on the expedition is a grassland called a prairie. The temperature here is much more comfortable than that in the desert. The breeze carries the scent of soil warmed by the sun. This rich soil supports grass as tall as you and your classmates. Sparrows flit among the grass stems, looking for their next meal. Startled by your approach, a rabbit quickly bounds away.

Like other grasslands located in the middle latitudes, this prairie receives more rain than deserts, but not enough for many trees to grow. A **grassland** receives between 25 and 75 centimeters of rain each year, and is typically populated by grasses and other non-woody plants. Grasslands that are located closer to the equator than prairies, called **savannas,** receive as much as 120 centimeters of

Desert Survival

ACTIVITY

Use a hand lens to carefully observe a small potted cactus. Be careful of the spines! With a pair of scissors, carefully snip a small piece from the tip of the cactus. Observe the inside of the plant. Note any characteristics that seem different from those of other plants.

Observing How is the inside of the cactus different from the outside? Suggest how the features you observe might be related to its desert habitat.

Figure 18 Migrating wildebeest make their way across a vast Kenyan savanna.

Figure 19 This Michigan forest in autumn is a beautiful example of a deciduous forest. The closeup shows a red fox, a common resident of North American deciduous forests. ***Comparing and Contrasting*** *How do deciduous forests differ from rain forests?*

rain each year. Scattered shrubs and small trees grow on savannas along with the grass.

Grasslands are home to many of the largest animals on Earth—herbivores such as bison, antelopes, zebras, rhinoceros, giraffes, and kangaroos. Grazing by these large herbivores helps to maintain the grasslands. They keep young trees and bushes from sprouting and competing with the grass for water and sunlight.

Deciduous Forest Biomes

Your trip to the next biome takes you to another forest. It is now late summer. Cool mornings here give way to warm days. Several members of the expedition are busy recording the numerous plant species. Others are looking through their binoculars, trying to identify the songbirds in the trees. You step carefully to avoid a small salamander on the forest floor. Chipmunks chatter at all the disturbance.

You are now visiting the deciduous forest biome. The trees found in this forest, called **deciduous trees** (dee SIJ oo us), shed their leaves and grow new ones each year. Oaks and maples are examples of deciduous trees. Deciduous forests receive enough rain to support the growth of trees and other plants, at least 50 centimeters per year. Temperatures vary during the year. The growing season usually lasts five to six months. As in the rain forest, different plants grow to different heights, ranging from a canopy of tall trees to small ferns and mosses on the forest floor.

The variety of plants in the forest creates many different habitats. You and your classmates note that different species of birds live at each level, eating the insects and fruits that live and grow there. You observe opossums, mice, and a skunk looking for food in the thick layer of damp leaves on the ground. Other common North American deciduous forest species include wood thrushes, white-tailed deer, and black bears.

If you were to return to this biome in the winter, you would not see much of the wildlife you are now observing. One reason is that many of the bird species migrate to warmer areas. Some of the mammals enter a low-energy state similar to sleep called **hibernation.** During hibernation an animal relies on fat it has stored in its body.

☑ *Checkpoint* *What are deciduous trees?*

Inferring ACTIVITY

Observe the map on the facing page showing the locations of deciduous and boreal forests. How do they compare? Can you suggest a reason why no boreal forests are shown in the Southern Hemisphere?

Boreal Forest Biomes

Now the expedition heads north into a colder climate. The expedition leaders claim they can identify the next biome, a boreal forest, by its smell. When you arrive, you catch a whiff of the spruce and fir trees that blanket the hillsides. Feeling the chilly early fall air, you pull a jacket and hat out of your bag.

This forest contains **coniferous trees** (koh NIF ur us), that produce their seeds in cones and have leaves shaped like needles. The boreal forest is sometimes referred to by its Russian name, the *taiga* (TY guh). Winters in these forests are very cold. The yearly

Figure 20 Common organisms of the boreal forest include moose like this one in Alaska's Denali National Park, and porcupines.

snowfall can reach heights well over your head—or even two or three times your height! Even so, the summers are rainy and warm enough to melt all the snow.

A limited number of trees have adapted to the cold climate of boreal forests. Fir, spruce, and hemlock are the most common species because their thick, waxy needles keep water from evaporating. Since water is frozen for much of the year in these areas, prevention of water loss is a necessary adaptation for trees in the boreal forest.

Many of the animals of the boreal forest eat the seeds produced by the conifers. These animals include red squirrels, insects, and birds such as finches and chickadees. Some of the larger herbivores, such as porcupines, deer, elk, moose, and beavers, eat tree bark and new shoots. This variety of herbivores in the boreal forest supports a variety of large predators, including wolves, bears, wolverines, and lynxes.

Tundra Biomes

The driving wind brings tears to the eyes of the members of the expedition as you arrive at your next stop. It is now fall. The slicing wind gives everyone an immediate feel for this biome, the tundra. The **tundra** is an extremely cold, dry, land biome. Expecting deep snow, many are surprised that the tundra may receive no more precipitation than a desert. Most of the soil in the tundra is frozen all year. This frozen soil is called **permafrost**.

Figure 21 Far from being a barren terrain, the tundra explodes with color in summer. Mosses, wildflowers, and shrubs flourish despite the short growing season. ***Relating Cause and Effect*** *Why are there no tall trees on the tundra?*

During the short summer the top layer of soil on the tundra thaws, but the underlying soil remains frozen.

Plants on the tundra include mosses, grasses, shrubs, and dwarf forms of a few trees, such as willows. Looking across the tundra, you observe that the landscape is already brown and gold. The short growing season is over. Most of the plant growth takes place during the long summer days when many hours of sunshine combine with the warmest temperatures of the year. North of the Arctic Circle the sun does not set during midsummer.

Figure 22 Many waterfowl spend summers on the tundra. This black brant is tending her nest.

If you had visited the tundra during the summer, the animals you might remember most are insects. Swarms of black flies and mosquitos provide food for many birds. The birds take advantage of the plentiful food and long days by eating as much as they can. Then, when winter approaches again, many birds migrate south to warmer climates.

Mammals of the tundra include caribou, foxes, wolves, and hares. The animals that remain in the tundra during the winter grow thick fur coats. What can these animals find to eat on the tundra in winter? The caribou scrape snow away to find lichens, which are fungi and algae that grow together on rocks. Wolves follow the caribou and look for weak members of the herd to prey upon.

☑ *Checkpoint* *What is the climate of the tundra?*

Mountains and Ice

Some areas of land on Earth do not fall into one of the major land biomes. These areas include mountain ranges and land that is covered with thick sheets of ice.

You read in Section 3 that the climate conditions of a mountain change from its base to its summit. As a result, different species of plants and other organisms inhabit different parts of the mountain. If you hiked to the top of a tall mountain, you would pass through a series of biomes. At the base of the mountain, you might find a grassland. As you climbed, you might pass through a deciduous forest, and then a boreal forest. Finally, as you neared the top, the trees would disappear. Your surroundings would resemble the rugged tundra.

Some land on Earth is covered year-round with thick ice sheets. Most of the island of Greenland and the continent of Antarctica fall into this category. Some organisms are adapted to life on the ice, including penguins, polar bears, and seals.

Interpreting Data

ACTIVITY

An ecologist has collected climate data from two locations. The total yearly precipitation is 250 cm in Location A and 14 cm in Location B. The graph below shows the average monthly temperature in the two locations. Based on this information, of which biome is each location a part? Explain.

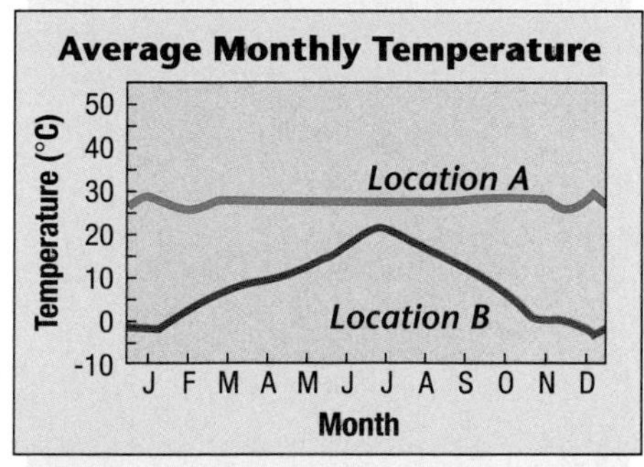

Figure 23 Ponds and rivers are two types of freshwater habitats. **A.** At the edge of a pond, two western pond turtles sun themselves on a log. **B.** A brown bear fishes for salmon in the rushing waters of a river. ***Comparing and Contrasting*** *How are these habitats similar? How are they different?*

Freshwater Biomes

The next stops for the expedition are located in water biomes. Since almost three quarters of Earth's surface is covered with water, it is not surprising that many living things make their homes in the water. Water biomes include both freshwater and saltwater (also called marine) biomes. All of these are affected by the same abiotic factors: temperature, sunlight, oxygen, and salt content.

An especially important factor in water biomes is sunlight. Sunlight is necessary for photosynthesis in the water just as it is on land. **However, because water absorbs sunlight, there is only enough light for photosynthesis near the surface or in shallow water.** The most common producers in most water biomes are algae rather than plants.

Ponds and Lakes First stop among the freshwater biomes is a calm pond. Ponds and lakes are bodies of standing, or still, fresh water. Lakes are generally larger and deeper than ponds. Ponds are often shallow enough that sunlight can reach the bottom even in the center of the pond, allowing plants to grow there. Plants that grow along the shore have their roots in the soil, while their leaves stretch to the sunlit water at the surface. In the center of a lake, algae floating at the surface are the major producers.

Many animals are adapted for life in the still water. Along the shore of the pond you observe insects, snails, frogs, and salamanders. Sunfish live in the open water, feeding on insects and algae from the surface. Scavengers such as catfish live near the pond bottom. Bacteria and other decomposers also feed on the remains of other organisms.

Streams and Rivers When you arrive at a mountain stream, you immediately notice how different it is from the still waters of a lake. Where the stream begins, called the headwaters, the cold, clear water flows rapidly. Animals that live in this part must be adapted to the strong current. Trout, for instance, have streamlined bodies that allow them to swim despite the pull of the rushing water. Insects and other small animals may have hooks or suckers to help them cling to rocks. Few plants or algae can grow in this fast-moving water. Instead, first-level consumers rely on leaves and seeds that fall into the stream.

As the river flows along, it is joined by other streams. The current slows. The water becomes cloudy with soil. With fewer rapids, the slower-moving, warmer water contains less oxygen. Different organisms are adapted to live in this lower part of the river. More plants take root among the pebbles on the river bottom, providing homes for insects and frogs. As is true in every biome, organisms are adapted to live in this specific habitat.

☑ *Checkpoint* ***What are two abiotic factors that affect organisms in a river?***

Marine Biomes

Next the members of the expedition head down the coast to explore some marine biomes. The oceans contain many different habitats. These habitats differ in sunlight amount, water temperature, wave action, and water pressure. Different organisms are adapted to life in each type of habitat. The first habitat, called an **estuary** (ES choo ehr ee), is found where the fresh water of a river meets the salt water of the ocean.

Estuaries The shallow, sunlit water, plus a large supply of nutrients carried in by the river, makes an estuary a very rich habitat for living things. The major producers in estuaries are plants, such as marsh grasses, as well as algae.

Figure 24 Fresh river water and salty ocean water meet in an estuary. Estuaries such as this Georgia salt marsh provide a rich habitat for many organisms, including a wading tricolored heron.

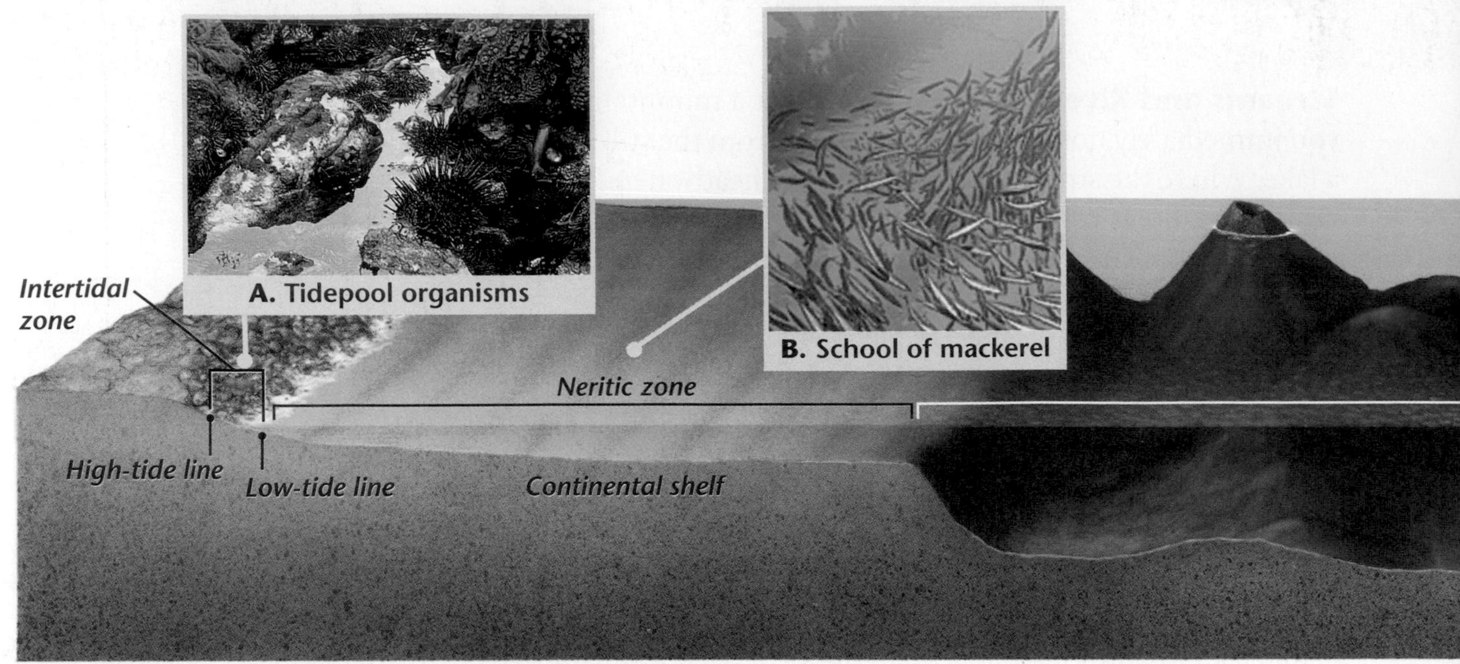

Figure 25 The marine biome is divided into several zones. **A.** Tidepools are common in the intertidal zone. This zone lies between the highest high-tide line and lowest low-tide line. **B.** Many fish, such as these silvery mackerel, inhabit the shallow waters over the continental shelf, called the neritic zone. **C.** A humpback whale feeds on algae at the surface of the open-ocean zone. **D.** This eerie deep-sea gulper is a predator in the deepest part of the ocean.

These organisms provide food and shelter for a variety of animals, including crabs, worms, clams, oysters, and fish. Many of these organisms use the calm waters of estuaries for breeding grounds.

Intertidal Zone Next, you take a walk along the rocky shoreline. The part of the shore between the highest high-tide line and the lowest low-tide line is called the **intertidal zone.** Organisms here must be able to withstand the pounding action of waves, sudden changes in temperature, and being both covered with water and then exposed to the air. It is a difficult place to live! You observe many animals, such as barnacles and sea stars, clinging to the rocks. Others, such as clams and crabs, burrow in the sand.

Neritic Zone Now it's time to set out to sea to explore the waters near shore. From your research vessel, your group will explore the next type of marine habitat. The edge of a continent extends into the ocean for a short distance, like a shelf. Below the low-tide line is a region of shallow water, called the **neritic zone** (nuh RIT ik), that extends over the continental shelf. Just as in freshwater biomes, the shallow water in this zone allows photosynthesis to occur. As a result, this zone is particularly rich in living things. Many large schools of fish such as sardines and anchovies feed on the algae in the neritic zone. In the warm ocean waters of the tropics, coral reefs may form in the neritic zone. Though a coral reef may look like stone, it is actually a living home to a wide variety of other organisms.

Surface Zone Out in the open ocean, light penetrates through the water only to a depth of a few hundred meters. Algae floating in these surface waters carry out photosynthesis. These algae

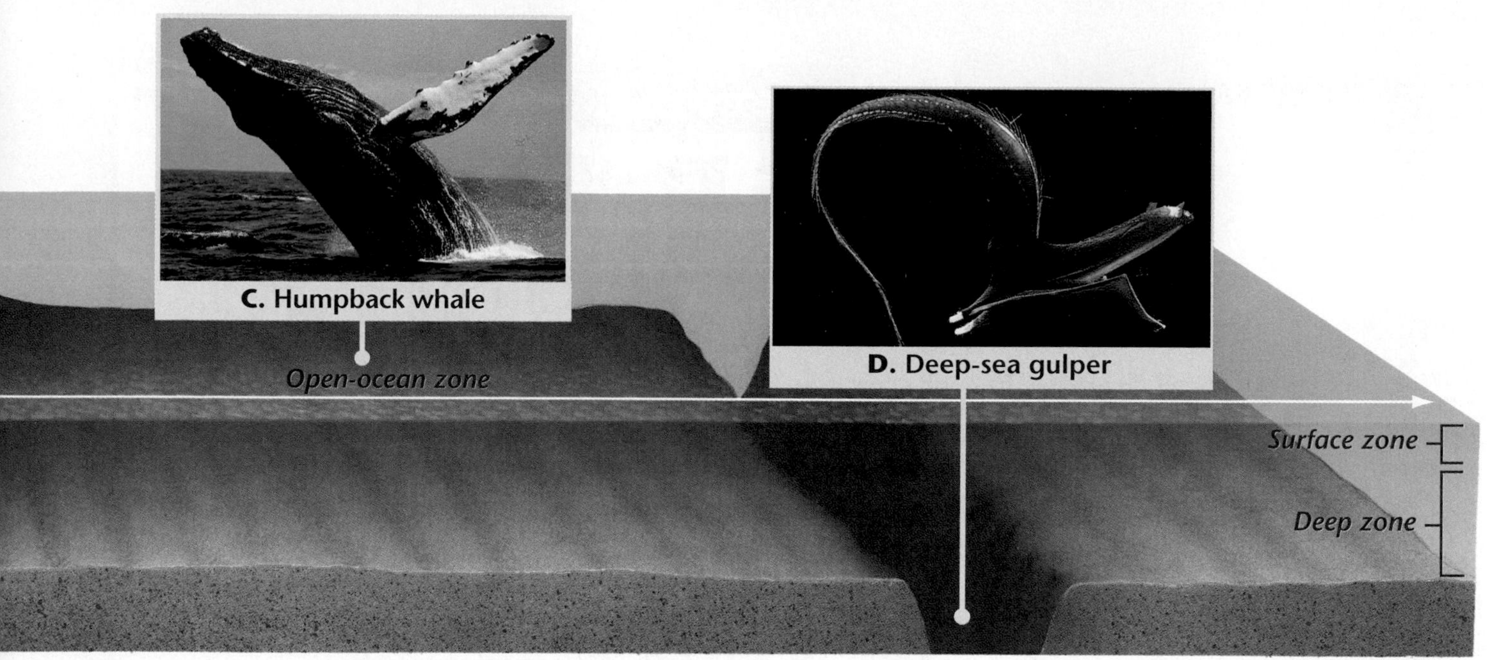

C. Humpback whale

D. Deep-sea gulper

are the producers that form the base of almost all open-ocean food webs. Other marine animals, such as tuna, swordfish, and whales, depend directly or indirectly on the algae for food.

Deep Zone The deep zone is located in the open ocean below the surface zone. Throughout most of the deep ocean, the water is completely dark. Your expedition will need to use a submarine with bright headlights to explore this region. How can anything live in a place with no sunlight? Most animals in this zone feed on remains of organisms that sink down from the surface zone. The deepest parts of the deep zone are home to bizarre-looking animals, such as giant squid that glow in the dark and fish with rows and rows of sharp teeth.

After you have recorded your deep-zone observations, your long expedition is over at last. You can finally return home.

Section 4 Review

1. How does climate determine a biome's characteristics?
2. Where in water biomes can photosynthesis occur?
3. Which land biome receives the most precipitation? Which two receive the least?
4. In which biome would you find large herbivores such as antelope and elephants? Explain your answer.
5. **Thinking Critically Comparing and Contrasting** How are the three forest biomes (rain forests, deciduous forests, and boreal forests) alike? How are they different?

CHAPTER PROJECT 2

Check Your Progress

By now you should be ready to start analyzing the data you have collected about your compost chambers. Do your observations of the two chambers support your hypothesis? Begin to prepare your report.

Skills Lab

Observing

CHANGE IN A TINY COMMUNITY

The types of organisms in an ecosystem may change gradually over time. You will learn more about this process, called succession, in the next section. In this lab you will observe succession in a pond community.

Problem

How does a pond community change over time?

Materials

hay solution	pond water
small baby-food jar	wax pencil
plastic dropper	microscope slide
coverslip	microscope

Procedure 

1. Use a wax pencil to label a small jar with your name.
2. Fill the jar about three-fourths full with hay solution. Add pond water until the jar is nearly full. Examine the mixture, and record your observations in your notebook.
3. Place the jar in a safe location out of direct sunlight where it will remain undisturbed. Always wash your hands thoroughly with soap after handling the jar or its contents.
4. After two days, examine the contents of the jar, and record your observations.
5. Use a plastic dropper to collect a few drops from the surface of the solution in the jar. Make a slide following the procedures in the box at the right. **CAUTION:** *Slides and coverslips are fragile, and their edges are sharp. Handle them carefully.*
6. Examine the slide under a microscope using both low and high power following the procedures in the box at the right. Draw each type of organism you observe. Estimate the number of each type in your sample. The illustration below shows some of the organisms you might see.
7. Repeat Steps 5 and 6 with a drop of solution taken from the side of the jar beneath the surface.
8. Repeat Steps 5 and 6 with a drop of solution taken from the bottom of the jar. When you are finished, follow your teacher's directions about cleaning up.
9. After 3 days, repeat Steps 5 through 8.
10. After 3 more days, repeat Steps 5 through 8 again. Then follow your teacher's directions for returning the solution.

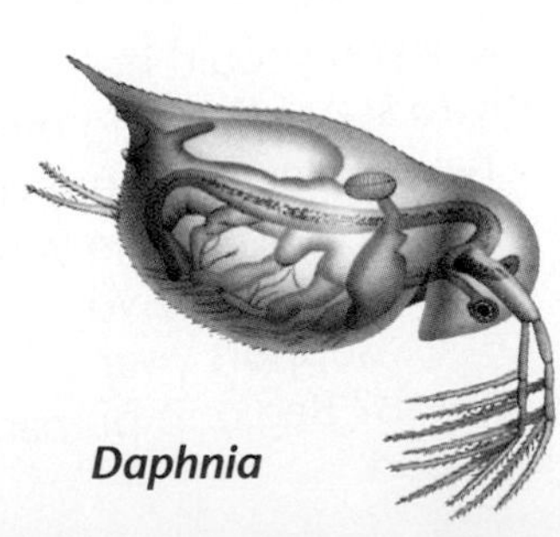

Daphnia

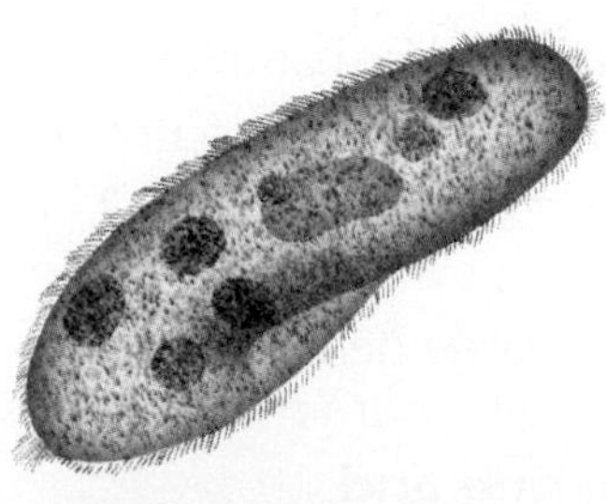

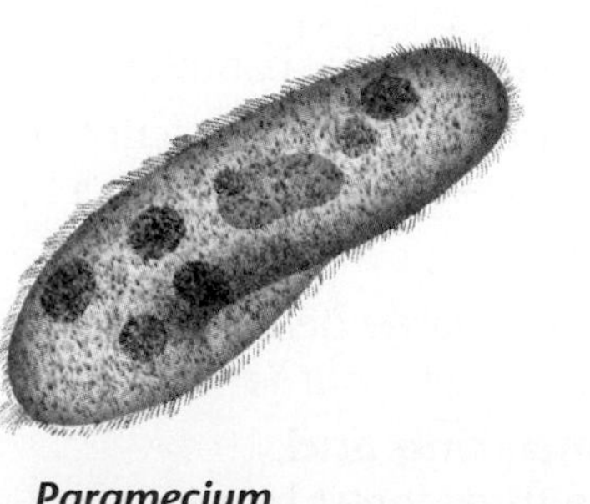

Paramecium

Spirogyra

Making and Viewing a Slide

A. Place one drop of the solution to be examined in the middle of a microscope slide. Place one edge of a coverslip at the edge of the drop, as shown above. Gently lower the coverslip over the drop. Try not to trap any air bubbles.

B. Place the slide on the stage of a microscope so the drop is over the opening in the stage. Adjust the stage clips to hold the slide.

C. Look from the side of the microscope, and use the coarse adjustment knob to move the low-power objective close to, but not touching, the coverslip.

D. Look through the eyepiece, and use the coarse adjustment knob to raise the body tube and bring the slide into view. Use the fine adjustment knob to bring the slide into focus.

E. To view the slide under high power, look from the side of the microscope, and revolve the nosepiece until the high-power objective clicks into place just over, but not touching, the slide.

F. While you are looking through the eyepiece, use the fine adjustment knob to bring the slide into focus.

Analyze and Conclude

1. Identify as many of the organisms you observed as possible. Use the diagrams on the facing page and any other resources your teacher provides.
2. How did the community change over the time that you made your observations?
3. What factors may have influenced the changes in this community?
4. Where did the organisms you observed in the jar come from?
5. **Think About It** Do you think your observations gave you a complete picture of the changes in this community? Explain your answer.

Design an Experiment

Write a hypothesis about what would happen if you changed one biotic or abiotic factor in this activity. Design a plan to test your hypothesis. Obtain your teacher's permission before carrying out your experiment.

SECTION 5 Succession

DISCOVER ACTIVITY

What Happened Here?

1. The two photographs at the right show the same area in Yellowstone National Park in Wyoming. Photograph A was taken soon after a major fire. Photograph B was taken a few years later. Observe the photographs carefully.
2. Make a list of all the differences you notice between the two scenes.

Think It Over

Posing Questions How would you describe what happened during the time between the two photographs? What questions do you have about this process?

GUIDE FOR READING

◆ **How are primary and secondary succession different?**

Reading Tip **Before you read, write a definition of what you think the term *succession* might mean. As you read, revise your definition.**

In 1988, a huge fire raged through Yellowstone National Park. The fire was so hot that it jumped from tree to tree without burning along the ground between them. In an instant, huge trees burst into flame from the intense heat. It took weeks for the fires to burn themselves out. All that remained of that part of the forest were thousands of blackened tree trunks sticking out of the ground like charred toothpicks.

You might think it unlikely that Yellowstone could recover from such a disastrous fire. But within just a few months, signs of life had returned. First tiny green shoots of new grass appeared in the black ground. Then small tree seedlings began to grow again. The forest was coming back!

Fires, floods, volcanoes, hurricanes, and other natural disasters can change communities in a very short period of time. But even without a disaster, communities change. The series of predictable changes that occur in a community over time is called **succession.** This section describes two types of succession: primary succession and secondary succession.

Primary Succession

Primary succession is the series of changes that occur in an area where no ecosystem previously existed. Such an area might be a new island formed by the eruption of an undersea volcano, or an area of rock uncovered by a melting sheet of ice.

You can follow the series of changes an area might undergo in Figure 26 below. These scenes show an area after a violent volcanic eruption. At first there is no soil, just ash and rock. The first species to populate the area are called **pioneer species.** Pioneer species are often lichens and mosses carried to the area by wind or water. These species can grow on bare rocks with little or no soil. As these organisms grow, they help break up the rocks. When they die, they provide nutrients that enrich the thin layer of soil that is forming on the rocks.

Over time, plant seeds land in the new soil and begin to grow. The specific plants that grow depend on the biome of the area. For example, in a cool, northern area, early seedlings might include alder and cottonwood trees. As the soil grows older and richer, these trees might be replaced by spruce and hemlock. Eventually, succession may lead to a community of organisms that does not change unless the ecosystem is disturbed. Reaching this stable community can take centuries.

☑ ***Checkpoint*** *What are some pioneer species?*

Figure 26 Primary succession occurs in an area where no ecosystem previously existed. **A.** After a volcanic eruption, the ground surface consists of ash and rock. **B.** The first organisms to appear are lichens and moss. **C.** Weeds and grasses take root in the thin layer of soil. **D.** Eventually, tree seedlings and shrubs sprout. ***Applying Concepts*** *What determines the particular species that appear during succession?*

Figure 27 Secondary succession occurs following a disturbance to an ecosystem, such as clearing a forest for farmland. When the farm is abandoned, the forest gradually returns. **A.** After two years, weeds and wildflowers fill the field. **B.** After five years, pine seedlings and other plants populate the field. **C.** After 30 years, a pine forest has grown up. **D.** After 100 years, a mixed forest of pine, oak, and hickory is developing in the field.

Secondary Succession

The changes following the Yellowstone fire were an example of secondary succession. **Secondary succession** is the series of changes that occur after a disturbance in an existing ecosystem. Natural disturbances that have this effect include fires, hurricanes, and tornadoes. Human activities, such as farming, logging, or mining, may also disturb an ecosystem. **Unlike primary succession, secondary succession occurs in a place where an ecosystem has previously existed.**

Secondary succession occurs somewhat more rapidly than primary succession. Consider, for example, an abandoned field in the southeastern United States. Follow the process of succession in such a field in Figure 27. After a century, a hardwood forest is developing. This forest is very stable and will remain for a long time. Of course, the particular species that come and go in the process of succession depend on the biome.

Section 5 Review

1. How are primary and secondary succession different?
2. What is a pioneer species?
3. Give two examples of natural disturbances and two examples of human disturbances that can result in secondary succession.
4. **Thinking Critically Classifying** Grass poking through the cracks in a sidewalk is an example of succession. Is this primary or secondary succession? Explain.

Science at Home

Interview an older family member or neighbor who has lived in your neighborhood for a long time. Ask the person to describe how the neighborhood has changed over time. Have areas that were formerly grassy been paved or developed? Have any farms, parks, or lots returned to a wild state? Write a summary of your interview. Can you classify any of the changes as examples of succession?

CHAPTER 2 STUDY GUIDE

Energy Flow in Ecosystems

Key Ideas

- The energy role of an organism is that of a producer, consumer, or decomposer.
- Producers are the source of all the food in an ecosystem.
- Consumers include herbivores, carnivores, omnivores, and scavengers.
- Decomposers return nutrients to the environment where they can be used again.
- A food web shows feeding relationships.
- At each level in an energy pyramid, there is less available energy than at the level below.

Key Terms

producer
consumer
herbivore
carnivore
omnivore
scavenger
decomposer
food chain
food web
energy pyramid

Cycles of Matter

INTEGRATING CHEMISTRY

Key Ideas

- Matter cycles through an ecosystem. Energy must be supplied constantly.
- The processes of evaporation, condensation, and precipitation form the water cycle.

Key Terms

water cycle
evaporation
condensation
precipitation
nitrogen fixation
nodule

Biogeography

Key Ideas

- Means of dispersal of organisms include continental drift, wind, water, and living things.
- Three factors that limit dispersal are physical barriers, competition, and climate.

Key Terms

biogeography
continental drift
dispersal
native species
exotic species
climate

Earth's Biomes

Key Ideas

- Temperature and rainfall mostly determine the biome in an area. Land biomes include rain forests, deserts, grasslands, deciduous forests, boreal forests, and tundras.
- Photosynthesis occurs only near the surface or in shallow areas of water biomes.

Key Terms

biome
canopy
understory
desert
grassland
savanna
deciduous tree
hibernation
coniferous tree
tundra
permafrost
estuary
intertidal zone
neritic zone

Succession

Key Idea

- Primary succession occurs where no previous ecosystem exists. Secondary succession occurs after a disturbance.

Key Terms

succession
primary succession
pioneer species
secondary succession

Organizing Information

Cycle Diagram Complete the cycle diagram to show how carbon cycles through an ecosystem.

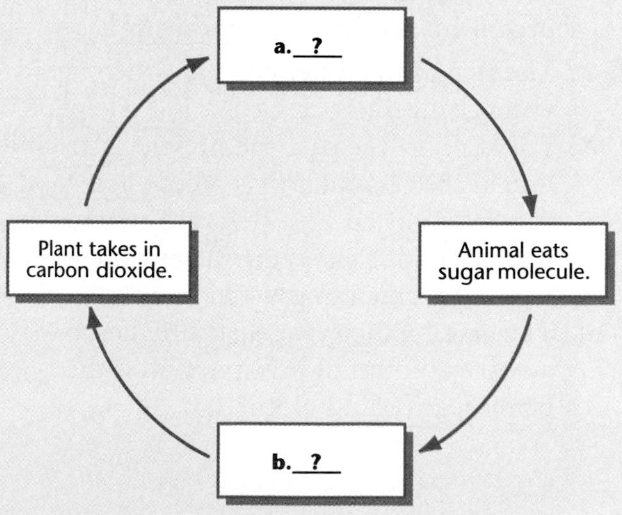

CHAPTER 2 ASSESSMENT

Reviewing Content

Multiple Choice

Choose the letter of the best answer.

1. Which of the following organisms are typical decomposers?
   a. grasses and ferns
   b. bacteria and mushrooms
   c. mice and deer
   d. lions and snakes
2. A diagram that shows how much energy is available at each feeding level in an ecosystem is a(n)
   a. food chain. b. food web.
   c. succession. d. energy pyramid.
3. Which of the following is *not* recycled in an ecosystem?
   a. carbon b. nitrogen
   c. water d. energy
4. Organisms may be dispersed in all the following ways *except* by
   a. wind. b. water.
   c. temperature. d. other organisms.
5. Much of Canada is covered in pine and spruce forests. The winter is cold and long. What is this biome?
   a. tundra b. boreal forest
   c. deciduous forest d. grassland

True or False

If the statement is true, write true. If it is false, change the underlined word or words to make the statement true.

6. An organism that eats the remains of dead organisms is called a(n) <u>herbivore</u>.
7. The step of the water cycle in which liquid water changes to water vapor is <u>evaporation</u>.
8. The study of the past and present distribution of species on Earth is called <u>succession</u>.
9. <u>Precipitation</u> and temperature are the two major abiotic factors that determine what types of plants can grow in an area.
10. The land biome that gets the highest average amount of precipitation is the tropical <u>grassland</u> biome.

Checking Concepts

11. Name and briefly define each of the three energy roles organisms can play in an ecosystem.
12. How are food chains and food webs different?
13. What is the source of energy for most ecosystems?
14. Describe the role of nitrogen-fixing bacteria in the nitrogen cycle.
15. How has continental drift affected the distribution of species on Earth?
16. Explain the difference between a native species and an exotic species.
17. What organisms are the producers in most marine ecosystems?
18. **Writing to Learn** Choose any of the biomes described in this chapter. Imagine that you are a typical animal found in that biome. Write a paragraph describing the conditions and other organisms in your animal's biome.

Thinking Critically

19. **Relating Cause and Effect** Every few years, a farmer plants clover in a wheat field. Explain how this practice might benefit the farmer.
20. **Inferring** Polar bears are very well adapted to life around the Arctic Ocean. Their white fur camouflages them in the snow. They can withstand freezing temperatures for a long time. They swim and hunt in very cold water. Is the distribution of polar bears limited by physical barriers, competition, or climate? Explain your answer.
21. **Comparing and Contrasting** How are the desert biome and the tundra biome similar? How are they different?
22. **Predicting** A volcano has just erupted in the ocean near Hawaii, forming a new island. How might succession change this island over time?

Applying Skills

Use the diagram of a food web below to answer Questions 23–25.

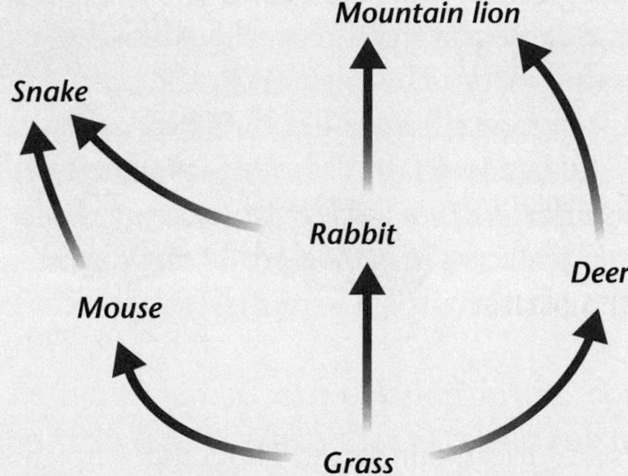

23. **Classifying** Identify the energy role of each organism in this food web. For consumers, specify whether they are first-level, second-level, or third-level.

24. **Inferring** Which level of the food web contains the greatest amount of available energy?

25. **Predicting** If a disease were to kill most of the rabbits in this area, predict how the snakes, deer, and mountain lions would be affected.

Performance Assessment (Chapter Project 2)

Project Wrap Up Check over your report, poster, or other product. It should clearly present your data and conclusions about the effect of your variable on the decomposition process.

Reflect and Record In your notebook, compare your results to your predictions about the different waste materials in the compost mixture. Were you surprised by any of your results? Based on what you have learned from your project and those of your classmates, make a list of the ideal conditions for decomposition.

Test Preparation

Use these questions to prepare for standardized tests.

Study the diagram. Then answer Questions 26–29.

26. Which of the following is a producer in the jar ecosystem?
    a. fresh water
    b. fish
    c. snails
    d. water plants

27. Which of the following is a consumer in the jar ecosystem?
    a. gravel
    b. snails
    c. water plants
    d. fresh water

28. Which gas do the snails and fish release into the water?
    a. hydrogen
    b. oxygen
    c. carbon dioxide
    d. nitrogen

29. A gas released by the water plants as a result of photosynthesis is
    a. hydrogen
    b. oxygen
    c. carbon dioxide
    d. nitrogen

African Rain Forests

Preserving Diversity

What forest—

is home to a beetle with wings larger than a sparrow's?

contains a frog that's 30 cm long?

is home to gorillas, chimpanzees, and pygmy hippos?

▲ Ball python

▲ Comet moth

It's an African rain forest. Thousands of plants and animals live here, from colorful orchids to fruit bats, tree frogs, and elephants.

The rain forests of Africa grow in a band near the equator. About 80 percent of the rain-forested area is in central Africa, in the vast basin of the great Congo River. Some parts of the central African rain forest are so dense and hard to reach that explorers have never visited them. East Africa, which is drier and more heavily populated, has only scattered areas of rain forest.

The rain forest regions of the world have similar life forms and niches. But the rain forests of different continents have very different species.

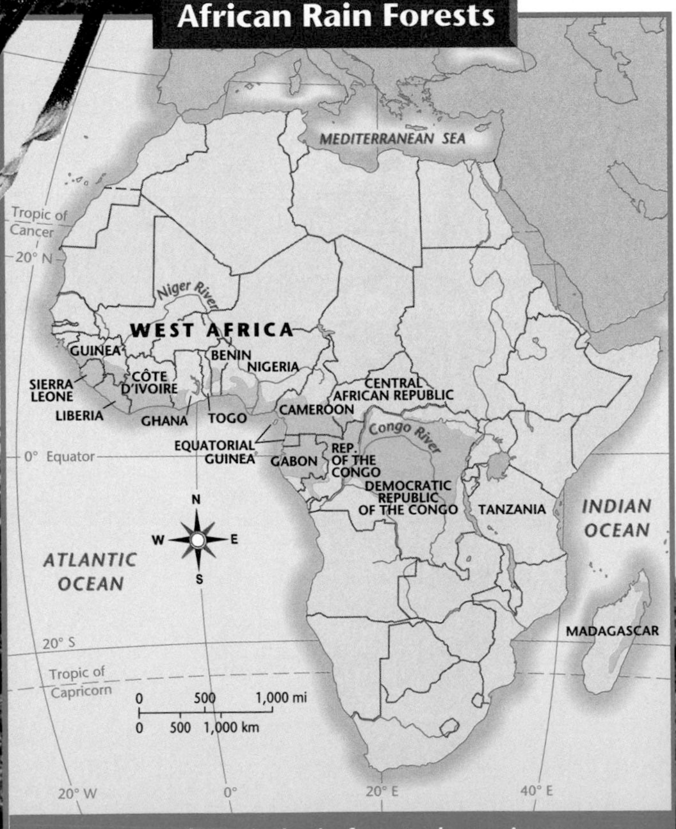

Major areas of tropical rain forest, shown in green on the map, cover only 7 percent of Africa.

Bonobo chimpanzee ▶

Layers of the Rain Forest

From above, the rain forest may look like a mass of broccoli. But it's really many forests in one—like different levels in an apartment building.

Each layer from the forest floor to the emergent, or top, layer varies in climate and is home to different plants and animals. The emergent layer captures the most rain, sunlight, heat, and wind. Colobus monkeys swing from vines and branches. Vast numbers of birds live in the trees.

Over time, African rain forest plants and animals have developed unusual adaptations to life at different layers of the forest. Some monkeys living in the canopy have long, muscular legs. They can run and leap through the branches. Guenons and baboons have strong teeth and jaws that allow them to crunch fruits, nuts, and seeds. Other monkeys have shorter tails but longer front legs. They live mainly on the forest floor.

In the understory, small animals such as frogs and squirrels "fly." They have tough membranes that stretch between their front and hind legs and allow them to glide from branch to branch.

The forest floor is dark, humid, and still. Termites feed on dead leaves and brush. Many plants have large leaves that allow them to catch the dim light. Some animals, such as frogs and insects, grow to gigantic sizes. Others are little, like the pygmy hippo that runs through the forest.

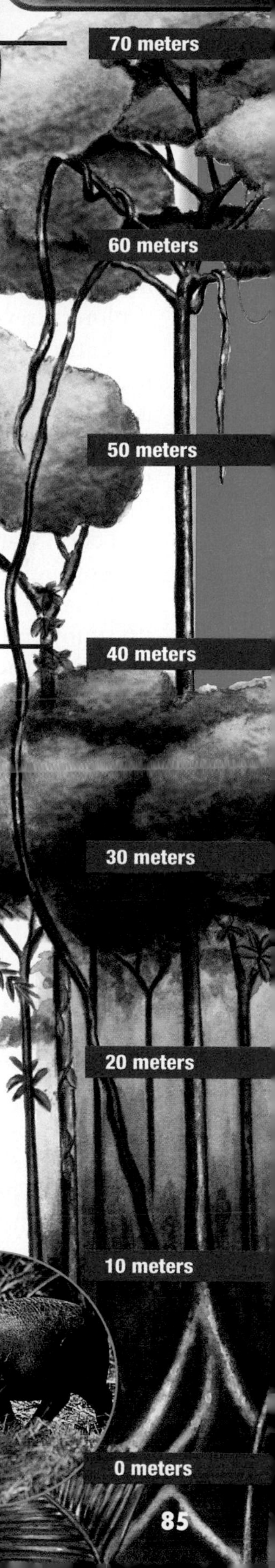

__The emergent layer__ is formed by a few taller trees that poke through the canopy. Some of these trees are as much as 70 meters high—about as tall as a 17-story building. __Colobus monkeys__ (above) live at this level.

__The canopy,__ from 10 to 40 meters high, is the dense "roof" of the rain forest. The crowns of trees capture sunlight to use in photosynthesis. Rainwater and sunlight filter through thick vegetation. __Epiphytic orchids__ grow to the top of the canopy (below).

__The understory__ has trees and plants that need little light. Pythons lurk in the vegetation. On the forest floor live other animals like the __pygmy hippo__ and the gorilla.

70 meters
60 meters
50 meters
40 meters
30 meters
20 meters
10 meters
0 meters

Science Activity

Design a rain forest animal that is adapted to life at a certain level of the rain forest. Consider how your animal lives, how it travels, and what food it eats. Outline its characteristics and explain how each adaptation helps the animal survive. Draw a sketch.

Mathematics

Reaching for Sunlight

Most rain forest trees are evergreens with broad leathery leaves. Some, like the African yellowwood, are conifers. Because the forest is so dense, trees must grow tall and straight to reach sunlight at the top of the canopy.

Along rivers, the floor and understory of the rain forest are a tangle of plants. Early explorers traveling the rivers assumed that the entire rain forest had similar thick vegetation, or jungle. In fact, the rain forest floor is surprisingly bare.

The canopy trees block the sunlight from plants below. Shaded by the dense canopy, the understory and forest floor are humid and dark. Water drips from the leaves of the canopy high overhead. Young trees have the best chance to grow when trees fall, opening up sunny clearings.

West Africa's tropical forests contain many valuable trees. African mahogany and teak are used to make furniture, tools, and boats. Oil from the oil palm is used in soaps, candles, and some foods. Trees such as ebony that can tolerate shade, grow slowly and develop dark, hard, long-lasting wood.

Math Activity

The table on this page gives the height of some of the trees in the rain forest. Use the information in the table to make a bar graph. On the horizontal axis, label the trees. Use the vertical axis to show the height of the trees.

- Which tree has the greatest maximum height? The least maximum height?
- What is the height difference between the tallest and the shortest trees?
- What is the average height of all the trees shown in the graph?

Trees of the Rain Forest

Tree	Maximum Height
African oil palm	18 m
African yellowwood	20 m
Cape fig	7 m
Ebony	30 m
Kapok	70 m
Raffia palm	12 m
Teak	46 m

African oil palms ▲ grow in Nigeria.

◀ This African sculpture is made of wood from the African rain forest.

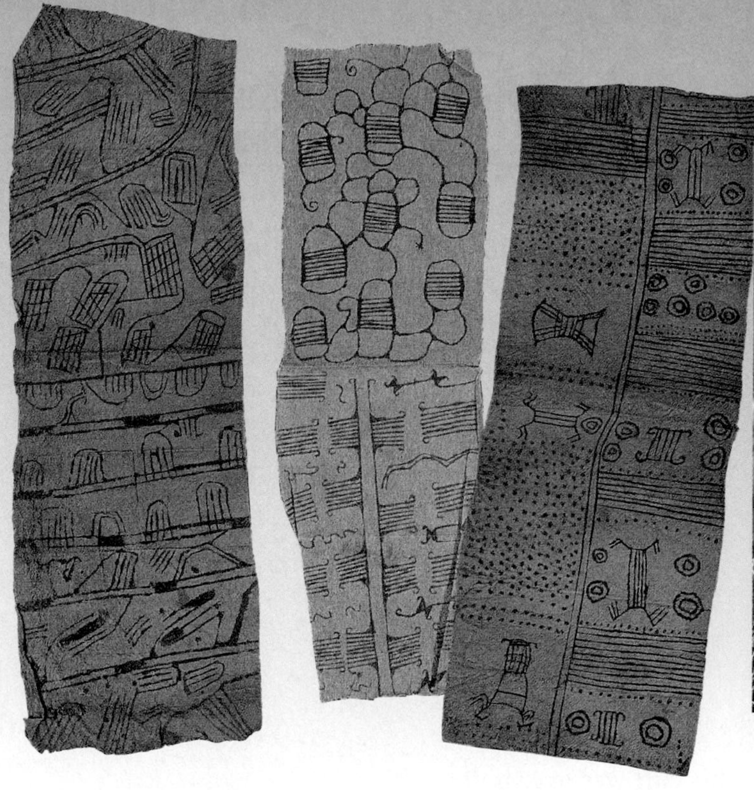

The Mbuti (above) hunt and fish along the Congo River. Their clothing is made of bark cloth (left).

Ituri Forest People

The native peoples of the African rain forest live as they have for thousands of years—by hunting and gathering. The forest supplies them with everything they need—food, water, firewood, building materials, and medicines.

One group of rain forest dwellers is the Mbuti people. The Mbuti live in the Ituri forest of the Democratic Republic of the Congo. Many of the Mbuti are quite small. The men hunt game, such as gazelle and antelope. The women gather wild fruits, nuts, and greens. Their traditional Mbuti clothing is made of tree bark and is wrapped around the waist. The bark is beaten to make it soft. Then it's decorated with geometric designs.

Most Mbuti live as nomads, with no single settled home. Every few months they set up new hunting grounds. They build temporary dome-shaped huts of branches and leaves. Hunting groups of about 10 to 25 families live together. They divide the hunting area among the family groups. On occasion, larger groups gather for ceremonies with dances and ritual music.

Modern Africa has brought changes to the forest people, especially for those who live near the edges of the rain forest. For a few months of the year, some Mbuti work as laborers for farmers who live in villages at the edge of the forest. When their work is finished, the Mbuti return to the Ituri forest. Most forest people prefer not to cultivate their own land. Since the farmers don't hunt, they trade their goods for meat. In exchange for meat, the Mbuti receive goods such as iron tools, cooking pots, clothes, bananas, and other farm produce.

Social Studies Activity

List the goods that forest people and farmers might have to trade. Assume that no modern conveniences, such as tractors and stoves, are available. Write a paragraph or two explaining how goods might be exchanged. Assign a value to the farmers' goods and the Mbuti goods, depending upon each group's needs. For example, decide how much meat a farmer should pay for medicines from the rain forest. How would the trading process change if money were exchanged?

Climbing the Canopy

Much of the rain forest is still a mystery because it's so difficult for scientists to study the canopy. Native forest people sometimes climb these tall trees using strong, thick vines called lianas as support. But rain forest scientists have had to find different methods. Naturalist Gerald Durrell, working in the African rain forest, was lucky enough to find another way to observe the canopy. He describes it here:

While the canopy is one of the most richly inhabited regions of the forest it is also the one that causes the naturalist the greatest frustration. There he is, down in the gloom among the giant tree trunks, hearing the noises of animal life high above him and having half-eaten fruit, flowers, or seeds rained on him by legions of animals high in their sunlit domain—all of which he cannot see. Under these circumstances the naturalist develops a very bad temper and a permanent crick in the neck.

However, there was one occasion when I managed to transport myself into the forest canopy, and it was a magical experience. It happened in West Africa when I was camped on the thickly forested lower slopes of a mountain called N'da Ali. Walking through the forest one day I found I was walking along the edge of a great step cut out of the mountain. The cliff face, covered with creepers, dropped away for about 50 yards, so that although I was walking through forest, just next to me and slightly below was the canopy of the forest growing up from the base of the cliff. This cliff was over half a mile in length and provided me with a natural balcony from which I could observe the treetop life simply by lying on the cliff edge, concealed in the low undergrowth.

Over a period of about a week I spent hours up there and a whole pageant of wildlife passed by. The numbers of birds were incredible, ranging from minute glittering sunbirds in rainbow coloring, zooming like helicopters from blossom to blossom as they fed on the nectar, to the flocks of huge black hornbills with their monstrous yellow beaks who flew in such an ungainly manner and made such a noise over their choice of forest fruits.

From early morning to evening when it grew too dark to see, I watched this parade of creatures. Troops of monkeys swept past, followed by attendant flocks of birds who fed eagerly on the insects that the monkeys disturbed during their noisy crashing through the trees. Squirrels chased each other, or hotly pursued lizards, or simply lay spread-eagled on branches high up in the trees, enjoying the sun.

Language Arts Activity

- Besides being an experienced naturalist and writer, Gerald Durrell is also a careful observer. In this selection, he describes in detail the "magical experience" of being in the canopy. Reread Durrell's description. Now work with a partner to write and design a pamphlet that will persuade visitors to come to an African rain forest. For your pamphlet, write strong, lively descriptions of what you might see, hear, and experience. Be persuasive.

Tie It Together

Celebrate Diversity

Rain forests have the greatest biodiversity—variety of plant and animal life—of any ecosystem on Earth. Many species have yet to be discovered! Plan a display for your school to celebrate biodiversity in the rain forests. Include drawings, photos, and detailed captions.

- On a large map, locate and label Earth's tropical rain forests. Divide into groups to choose one rain forest region to research, such as Africa, Brazil, Costa Rica, Hawaii, or Borneo.
- Have your group study several animal and plant species in its chosen rain forest. You might choose monkeys, butterflies, birds, orchids, or medicinal plants.
- For each species, describe its appearance, where it occurs in the rain forest, its role in the ecosystem, and how it is useful to humans.

British conservationist Gerald Durrell wrote about his adventures with wildlife around the world. He established a zoo on the British island of Jersey and worked to preserve threatened species. In the photo, Durrell holds an anteater.

CHAPTER 3

Bones, Muscles, and Skin

www.phschool.com

Integrating Health

Section 1 Body Organization and Homeostasis

Discover How Do You Lift Books?
Try This How Is a Book Organized?

Section 2 The Skeletal System

Discover Hard as a Rock?
Try This Soft Bones?
Sharpen Your Skills Classifying
Science at Home Exercising Safely

Section 3 The Muscular System

Discover How Do Muscles Work?
Try This Get a Grip
Skills Lab A Look Beneath the Skin

PROJECT 3

On the Move

People are able to perform an amazing variety of movements. For example, a baseball player can swing a bat, a chef can twirl pizza dough, and an artist can mold clay into a sculpture. Behind every human movement, there's a complex interaction of bones, muscles, and other parts of the body.

In this chapter, you'll find out how bones and muscles work. And in this project, you'll take a close look at a simple movement, such as stretching a leg, bending an arm at the elbow, or another movement you choose.

Your Goal To make a working model that shows how bones and muscles interact to move the body in a specific way.

To complete this project you will

- select a specific movement, and identify all of the major bones, joints, and muscles that are involved
- design an accurate physical model of the movement
- explain how the bones and muscles make the movement possible
- follow the safety guidelines in Appendix A

Get Started Let all group members name a motion from a sport or other familiar activity that they'd like to investigate. If the motion is long or complicated, discuss how to simplify it for the project. Also consider what kind of model you'll make, such as a wood or cardboard cutout, clay structure, or computer animation. Then write up a plan for your teacher's approval.

Check Your Progress You'll be working on this project as you study this chapter. To keep your project on track, look for Check Your Progress boxes at the following points.

Section 1 Review, page 99: Choose a simple motion to analyze and sketch.

Section 3 Review, page 112: Create your working model.

Wrap Up At the end of the chapter (page 123), you'll demonstrate your working model.

For this baseball player to hit the ball, his bones and muscles must work together in a coordinated manner.

SECTION 4 **The Skin**

Discover **What Can You Observe About Skin?**
Try This **Sweaty Skin**
Real-World Lab **Sun Safety**
Science at Home **Protection From the Sun**

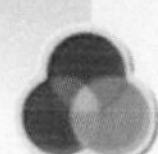

SECTION 1

Body Organization and Homeostasis

DISCOVER ACTIVITY

How Do You Lift Books?

1. Stack one book on top of another one.
2. Lift the two stacked books in front of you so the lowest book is about level with your shoulders. Hold the books in this position for 30 seconds. While you are performing this activity, note how your body responds. For example, how do your arms feel at the beginning and toward the end of the 30 seconds?
3. Balance one book on the top of your head. Walk a few steps with the book on your head.

Think It Over

Inferring List all the parts of your body that worked together as you performed the activities in Steps 1 through 3.

GUIDE FOR READING

- What are the levels of organization in the body?
- What are the four basic types of tissue in the human body?
- What is homeostasis?

Reading Tip Before you read, preview information about levels of organization in the body. Write down any unfamiliar words. Then, as you read, write their definitions.

The bell rings—lunchtime at last! You hurry down the noisy halls toward the cafeteria. The unmistakable aroma of hot pizza makes your mouth water. At last, after waiting in line, you pick up a plate with a slice of pizza and some salad. When you get to the cashier, you dig in your pocket for lunch money. Then, carefully balancing your tray, you scan the crowded cafeteria for your friends. You spot them, walk to their table, sit down, and begin to eat.

Think for a minute about how many parts of your body were involved in the simple act of getting and eating your lunch. You heard the bell with your ears and smelled the pizza with your nose. Bones and muscles worked together as you walked to the cafeteria, picked up your food, and sat down at the table. Without your brain, you couldn't have remembered where you put your lunch money. Once you began to eat, your teeth chewed the food and your throat muscles swallowed it. Then other parts of your digestive system, such as your stomach, began to process the food for your body to use.

Levels of Organization

Every minute of the day, whether you are eating, studying, playing basketball, or even sleeping, your body is busily at work. Each part of the body has a specific job to do, and all the different parts work together. This smooth functioning is due partly to the way in which the human body is organized. **The levels of organization in the human body consist of cells, tissues, organs, and organ systems.** The smallest unit is the cell, and the largest is the organ system.

Cells

A **cell** is the basic unit of structure and function in a living thing. Complex organisms are composed of many cells in the same way a building is composed of many bricks. The human body contains about 100 trillion cells. Cells are quite tiny, and most cannot be seen without a microscope.

Most animal cells, including those in the human body, have a structure similar to the cell in Figure 1. The **cell membrane** forms the outside boundary of the cell. Inside the cell membrane is a large structure called the **nucleus.** The nucleus is the control center that directs the cell's activities and contains information that determines the cell's characteristics. When the cell divides, or reproduces, this information is passed on to the newly formed cells. The area between the cell membrane and the nucleus is called the **cytoplasm.** The cytoplasm contains a clear, jellylike substance in which many important cell structures, called organelles, are found.

Cells carry on the processes that keep organisms alive. Inside cells, for example, molecules from digested food undergo chemical reactions that provide energy for the body's activities. Cells also get rid of waste products, grow, and reproduce.

☑ ***Checkpoint*** *What is the function of the nucleus?*

How Is a Book Organized?

ACTIVITY

In this activity, you will analyze the levels of organization in a book.

1. Examine this textbook to see how it is subdivided—into chapters, sections, and so on.
2. Make a concept map that shows this pattern of organization. Place the largest subdivision at the top of the map and the smallest at the bottom.
3. Compare the levels of organization in this book to those in the human body.

Making Models Which level of organization in the book represents cells? Which represent tissues, organs, and organ systems?

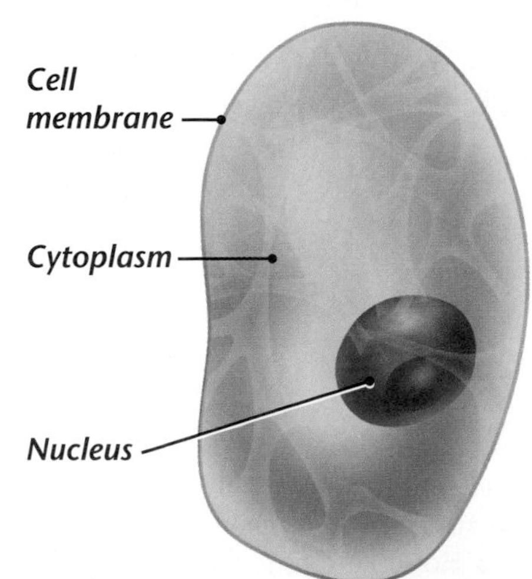

Figure 1 The cells in your body are surrounded by a cell membrane, and most have a nucleus. The cytoplasm is the area between the cell membrane and the nucleus.

Tissues

Tissue is the next largest unit of organization in your body. A **tissue** is a group of similar cells that perform the same function. **The human body contains four basic types of tissue: muscle tissue, nerve tissue, connective tissue, and epithelial tissue.** To see examples of each of these tissues, look at Figure 2.

Like the muscle cells that form it, **muscle tissue** can contract, or shorten. By doing this, muscle tissue makes parts of your body move.

While muscle tissue carries out movement, nerve tissue directs and controls it. **Nerve tissue** carries messages back and forth between the brain and every other part of the body. Your brain is made up mostly of nerve tissue.

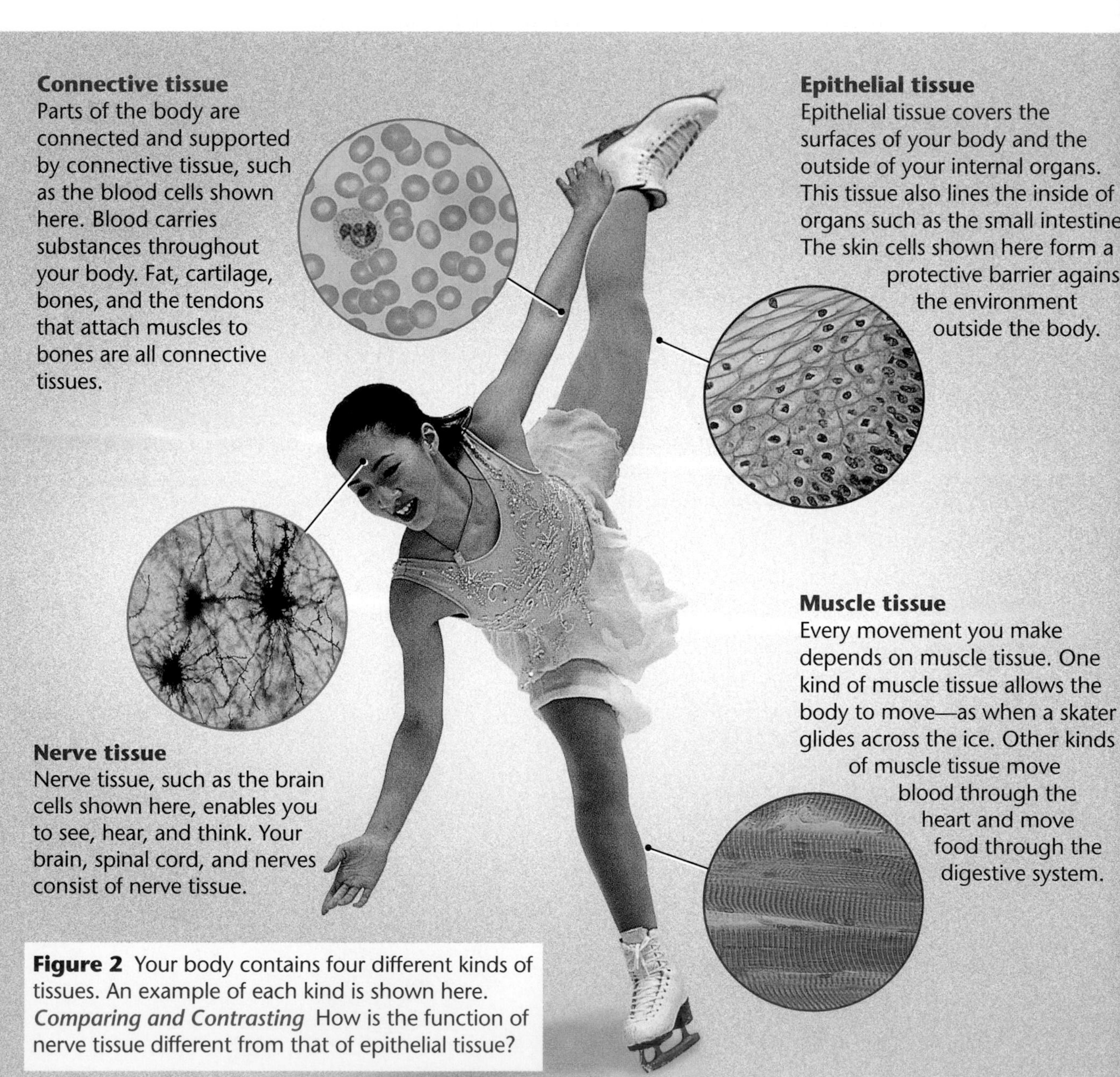

Figure 2 Your body contains four different kinds of tissues. An example of each kind is shown here. *Comparing and Contrasting* How is the function of nerve tissue different from that of epithelial tissue?

Connective tissue provides support for your body and connects all its parts. Bone is one kind of connective tissue; its strength and hardness support your body and protect its internal structures. Fat is also a connective tissue. It pads parts of your body, provides insulation from cold, and stores energy.

Epithelial tissue (ep uh THEE lee ul) covers the surfaces of your body, inside and out. Some epithelial tissue, such as the outermost layer of your skin, protects the delicate structures that lie beneath it. Other kinds of epithelial tissue absorb or release substances. The lining of your digestive system consists of epithelial tissue that releases chemicals used in digestion.

Organs and Organ Systems

Your stomach, heart, brain, and lungs are all organs. An **organ** is a structure that is composed of different kinds of tissue. Like a tissue, an organ performs a specific job. The job of an organ, however, is generally more complex than that of a tissue. The heart, for example, pumps blood throughout your body, over and over again. The heart contains all four kinds of tissue—muscle, nerve, connective, and epithelial. Each tissue type contributes to the overall job of pumping blood.

Each organ in your body is part of an **organ system,** a group of organs that work together to perform a major function. Your heart is part of your circulatory system, which carries oxygen and other materials throughout the body. Besides the heart, blood vessels are organs in the circulatory system. Figure 3 describes the major organ systems in the human body.

Figure 3 The human body is made up of eleven organ systems. *Interpreting Charts* Which two systems work together to get oxygen to your cells?

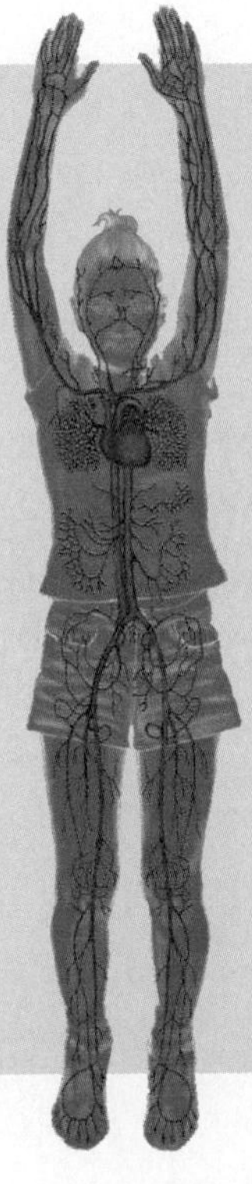

Organ Systems in the Human Body

◀ **Circulatory** Carries needed materials to the body cells; carries wastes away from body cells; helps fight disease.

Digestive Takes food into the body, breaks food down, and absorbs the digested materials.

Endocrine Controls many body processes—such as intake of sugar by cells—by means of chemicals.

Excretory Removes wastes.

Immune Fights disease.

Muscular Enables the body to move; moves food through the digestive system; keeps the heart beating.

Nervous Detects and interprets information from the environment outside the body and from within the body; controls most body functions.

Reproductive Produces sex cells that can unite with other sex cells to create offspring; controls male and female characteristics.

Respiratory Takes oxygen into the body and eliminates carbon dioxide.

Skeletal Supports the body, protects it, and works with muscles to allow movement; makes blood cells and stores some materials.

Skin Protects the body, keeps water inside the body, and helps regulate body temperature.

Homeostasis

The different organ systems work together and depend on one another. You can compare the functioning of the human body to the work it takes to put on a school play. A play needs actors, of course, but it also needs a director, someone to make the costumes, and people to sell tickets. Similarly, when you ride a bike, you use your muscular and skeletal systems to steer and push the pedals. But you also need your nervous system to direct your arms and legs to move. Your respiratory, digestive, and circulatory systems work together to fuel your muscles with the energy they need. And your excretory system removes the wastes produced while your muscles are hard at work.

The systems of the body work together to maintain **homeostasis** (hoh mee oh STAY sis), the body's tendency to keep an internal balance. **Homeostasis is the process by which an organism's internal environment is kept stable in spite of changes in the external environment.**

To see homeostasis in action, all you have to do is take your temperature when the air is cold. Then take it again in an overheated room. No matter what the temperature of the air around you, your internal body temperature will be close to 37 degrees Celsius, as long as you are healthy. If you get sick, your body temperature may rise. But when you get well again, it returns to 37 degrees.

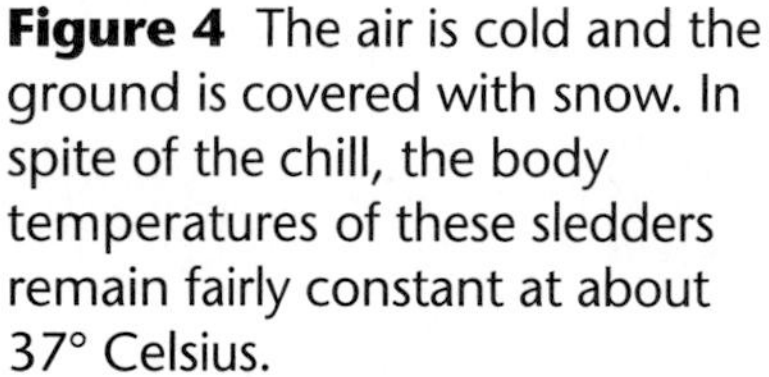

Figure 4 The air is cold and the ground is covered with snow. In spite of the chill, the body temperatures of these sledders remain fairly constant at about 37° Celsius.
Applying Concepts *What is the term for the body's tendency to maintain a stable internal environment?*

Your body has various ways of maintaining homeostasis. For example, you need food and water to stay alive. When your body is low on either of these substances, your brain sends signals that result in your feeling hungry or thirsty. When you eat or drink, you maintain homeostasis by providing your body with substances that it needs.

Stress and Homeostasis

The school play is about to begin. Nervously, you walk out on stage. Your heart is beating rapidly and your breathing quickens. Your body's reactions are signs of stress. **Stress** is the reaction of your body and mind to threatening, challenging, or disturbing events. Many things can act as stressors, or events that cause stress. A snarling dog, an argument with a friend, or an upcoming oral report can all be stressors. Stress upsets homeostasis, and your body reacts in specific ways.

Physical Responses to Stress Figure 5 shows what happens in your body within seconds after you experience stress. During this stage, which is called the alarm stage, your body releases a chemical called adrenaline into your bloodstream. Adrenaline gives you a burst of energy and causes many other changes in your body. These changes prepare you to take quick action.

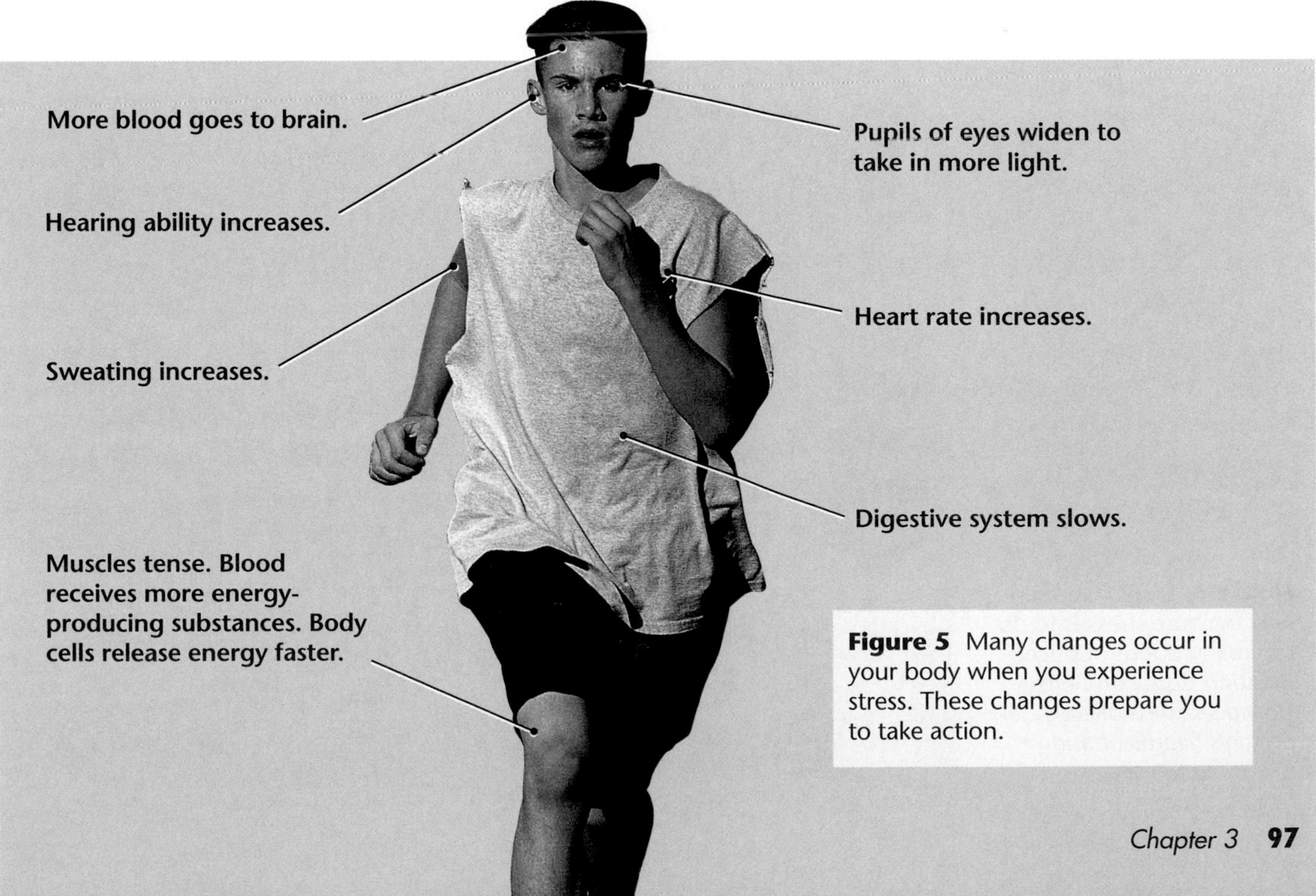

Figure 5 Many changes occur in your body when you experience stress. These changes prepare you to take action.

Language Arts CONNECTION

In Edgar Allan Poe's story, "The Pit and the Pendulum," the author's detailed descriptions paint a vivid picture of a person's physical reactions to a stressor. The character was frightened by a razor-sharp pendulum swinging overhead. "I at once started to my feet, trembling compulsively in every fibre....Perspiration burst from every pore, and stood in cold, big beads upon my forehead."

In Your Journal

Create a situation in which a character faces an extremely stressful situation. Describe the character's physical reactions and feelings. Make sure to use vivid and precise descriptive words that clearly convey the character's reactions.

The effects of adrenaline, which take only a few seconds, are dramatic. Your breathing quickens, sending more oxygen to your body cells to provide energy for your muscles. That extra oxygen gets to your cells rapidly because your heart begins to beat faster. The faster heartbeat increases the flow of blood to your muscles and some other organs. In contrast, less blood flows to your skin and digestive system, so that more is available for your arms and legs. The pupils of your eyes become wider, allowing you to see better.

Fight or Flight The reactions caused by adrenaline are sometimes called the "fight-or-flight" response, because they prepare you either to fight the stressor or to take flight and escape. Scientists think that the fight-or-flight response was important for primitive people who faced wild-animal attacks and similar dangers. Today, the same reactions still occur with any stressor, whether it is a snarling dog or a social studies test.

During the fight-or-flight response, your body systems work together to respond to the stressor. For example, your respiratory system provides you with extra oxygen, which your circulatory system delivers to the parts of your body that need it. Your muscular system, in turn, works with your skeletal system to help you move—fast.

☑ ***Checkpoint*** *During the alarm stage, how do your eyes and ears respond?*

Figure 6 Oops! One sure way to cause stress is to do too many things at once. ***Relating Cause and Effect*** *How does stress affect a person's heartbeat and breathing rates?*

Long-Term Stress

The alarm stage of stress only lasts for a short time. If the stress is over quickly, your body soon returns to its normal state. Some kinds of stressors, however, continue for a long time. Suppose, for example, you are stressed because you are moving to a new community. You cannot fight the stressor, and you cannot run away from it either. When a stressful situation does not go away quickly, your body cannot restore homeostasis. If you do not deal with the stress, you may become tired, irritable, and have trouble getting along with others. In addition, you may be more likely to become ill.

Figure 7 When you are under stress, it is important to find ways to relax.

Dealing With Stress

Stress is a normal part of life. No one can avoid stress entirely. When you are in a stressful situation, it is important that you recognize it and take action to deal with it, rather than pretending that the stressor doesn't exist. For example, suppose you aren't doing well in math class. If you accept the problem and deal with it—perhaps by asking your teacher for help—your stress will probably decrease.

In addition, when you are experiencing long-term stress, physical activity can help you feel better. Riding a bike, skating, or even raking leaves can take your mind off the stress. It is also important to talk about the situation and your feelings with friends and family members.

Section 1 Review

1. List the four levels of organization in the human body. Give an example of each level.
2. Name the four types of tissue in the human body. Give an example of where each is located.
3. What is homeostasis?
4. Describe what happens during the alarm stage of stress.
5. **Thinking Critically Applying Concepts** What systems of the body are involved when you prepare a sandwich and then eat it?

Check Your Progress

CHAPTER PROJECT 3

By now, you should have your teacher's approval for modeling the movement you chose. Ask a classmate or friend to perform the movement. Make drawings to study the motion. Find out what bones are involved, and determine their sizes and shapes. (*Hint:* Notice the direction of bone movement and the kinds of joints that are involved.)

SECTION 2 The Skeletal System

DISCOVER ACTIVITY

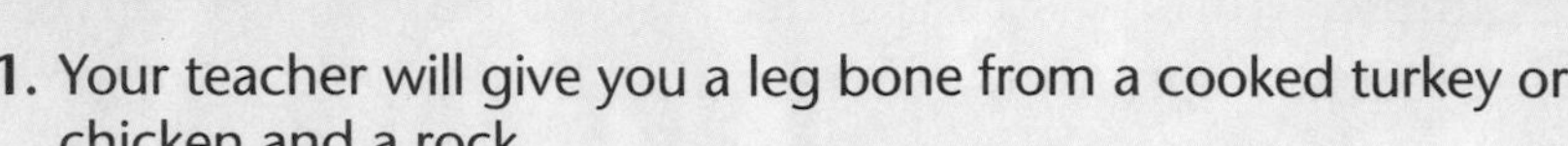

Hard as a Rock?

1. Your teacher will give you a leg bone from a cooked turkey or chicken and a rock.
2. Use a hand lens to examine both the rock and the bone.
3. Gently tap both the rock and the bone on a hard surface.
4. Pick up each object to feel how heavy it is.
5. Wash your hands. Then make notes of your observations.

Think It Over

Observing Based on your observations, why do you think bones are sometimes compared to rocks? List some ways in which bones and rocks are similar and different.

GUIDE FOR READING

- **What are the functions of the skeleton?**
- **What role do movable joints play in the body?**
- **How can you keep your bones strong and healthy?**

Reading Tip **Before you read, rewrite the headings in the section as *how, why,* or *what* questions. As you read, write answers to the questions.**

A construction site is a busy place. After workers have prepared the building's foundation, they begin to assemble thousands of steel pieces into a frame for the building. People watch as the steel pieces are joined to create a rigid frame that climbs toward the sky. By the time the building is finished, however, the building's framework will no longer be visible.

Like a building, you also have an inner framework, but it is made up of bones instead of steel. Your framework, or skeleton, is shown in Figure 9. The number of bones in your skeleton depends on your age. A newborn baby has about 275 bones. An adult, however, has about 206 bones. As a baby grows, some of the bones fuse together. For example, as a baby, you had many more individual bones in your skull than you do now. As you grew, some of your bones grew together to form the larger bones of your skull.

What the Skeletal System Does

Just as a building could not stand without its frame, you would collapse without your skeleton. **Your skeleton has five major functions. It provides shape and support, enables you to move, protects your internal organs, produces blood cells, and stores certain materials until your body needs them.**

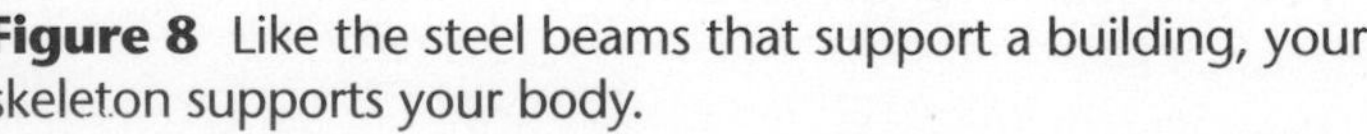

Figure 8 Like the steel beams that support a building, your skeleton supports your body.

Your skeleton determines the shape of your body, much as a steel frame determines the shape of a building. The backbone, or vertebral column, is the center of the skeleton. Locate the backbone in Figure 9. Notice that all the bones in the skeleton are in some way connected to this column. If you move your fingers down the center of your back, you can feel the 26 small bones, or **vertebrae** (VUR tuh bray)(singular *vertebra*), that make up your backbone. Bend forward at the waist and feel the bones adjust as you move. You can think of each individual vertebra as a bead on a string. Just as a beaded necklace is flexible and able to bend, so too is your vertebral column. If your backbone were just one bone, you would not be able to bend or twist.

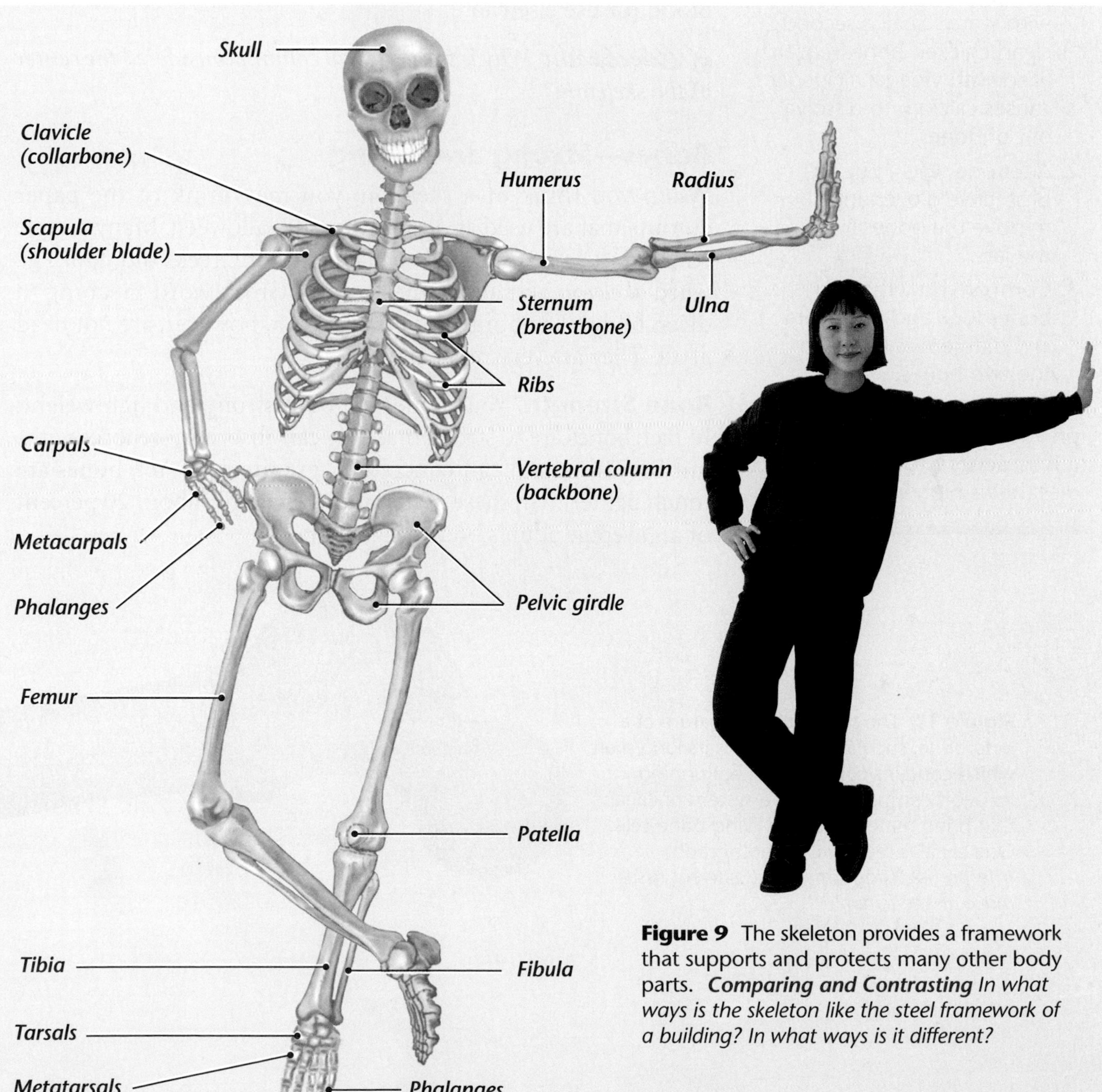

Figure 9 The skeleton provides a framework that supports and protects many other body parts. ***Comparing and Contrasting*** *In what ways is the skeleton like the steel framework of a building? In what ways is it different?*

Soft Bones?

In this activity, you will explore the role that calcium plays in bones.

1. Put on protective gloves. Soak one clean chicken bone in a jar filled with water. Soak a second clean chicken bone in a jar filled with vinegar. (Vinegar causes calcium to dissolve out of bone.)
2. After one week, put on protective gloves and remove the bones from the jars.
3. Compare how the two bones look and feel. Note any differences between the two bones.

Drawing Conclusions Based on your results, explain why it is important to consume a diet that is high in calcium.

Your skeleton also allows you to move. Most of the body's bones are associated with muscles. The muscles pull on the bones to make the body move. Bones also protect many of the organs in your body. For example, your skull protects your brain, and your breastbone and ribs form a protective cage around your heart and lungs.

Some of the bones in your body produce substances that your body needs. You can think of the long bones of your arms and legs as factories that make blood cells. Bones also store minerals such as calcium and phosphorus. Calcium and phosphorus make bones strong and hard. When the body needs these minerals, the bones release small amounts of them into the blood for use elsewhere.

Checkpoint *Why is the vertebral column considered the center of the skeleton?*

Bones—Strong and Living

When you think of a skeleton, you may think of the paper cutouts that are used as decorations at Halloween. Many people connect skeletons with death. The ancient Greeks did, too. The word *skeleton* actually comes from a Greek word meaning "a dried body." The bones of your skeleton, however, are not dead at all. They are very much alive.

Bone Strength Your bones are both strong and lightweight. In fact, bones are so strong that they can absorb more force without breaking than can concrete or granite rock. Yet, bones are much lighter than these materials. In fact, only about 20 percent of an average adult's body weight is bone.

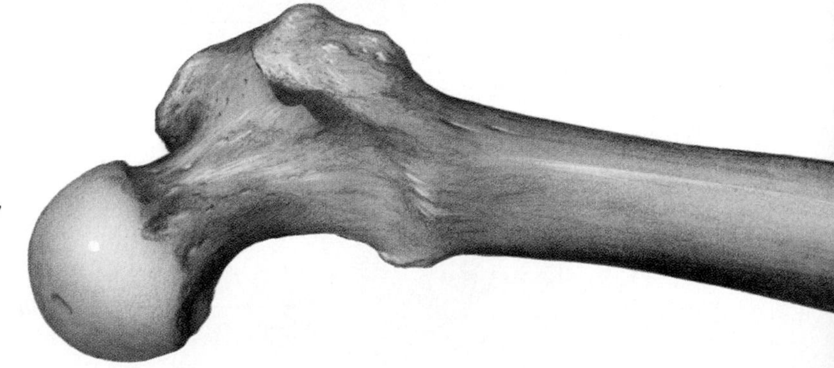

Figure 10 The most obvious feature of a long bone, such as the femur, is its long shaft, which contains compact bone. Running through compact bone is a system of canals that bring materials to the living bone cells. One canal is seen in the photograph. ***Interpreting Diagrams*** *What different tissues make up the femur?*

Have you ever heard the phrase "as hard as a rock"? Most rock is hard because it is made up of minerals that are packed tightly together. In a similar way, bones are hard because they are made up of two minerals—phosphorus and calcium.

Bone Growth Bones also contain cells and tissues, such as blood and nerves. And, because your bone cells are alive, they form new bone tissue as you grow. But even after you are grown, bone tissue continues to form within your bones. For example, every time you play soccer or basketball, your bones absorb the force of your weight. They respond by making new bone tissue.

Sometimes, new bone tissue forms after an accident. If you break a bone, for example, new bone tissue forms to fill the gap between the broken ends of the bone. The healed region of new bone may be stronger than the original bone.

The Structure of Bones

Figure 10 shows the structure of the femur, or thighbone. The femur, which is the body's longest bone, connects the pelvic bones to the lower leg bones. Notice that a thin, tough membrane covers all of the bone except the ends. Blood vessels and nerves enter and leave the bone through the membrane. Beneath the membrane is a layer of compact bone, which is hard and dense, but not solid. As you can see in Figure 10, small canals run through the compact bone. These canals carry blood vessels and nerves from the bone's surface to the living cells within the bone.

Just inside the compact bone is a layer of spongy bone. Spongy bone is also found at the ends of the bone. Like a sponge, spongy bone has many small spaces within it. This structure makes spongy bone lightweight but strong.

CANAL

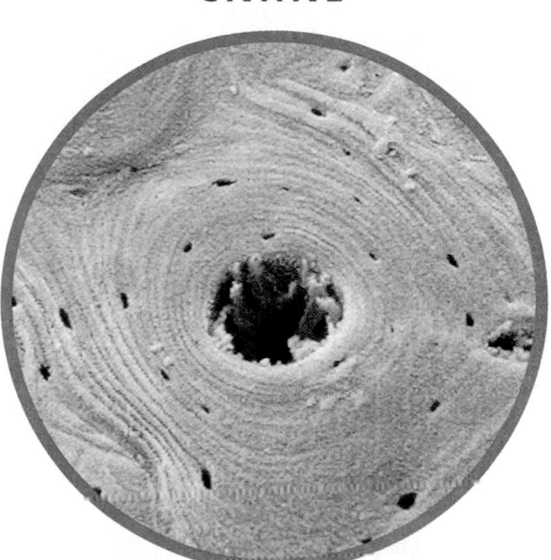

COMPACT BONE

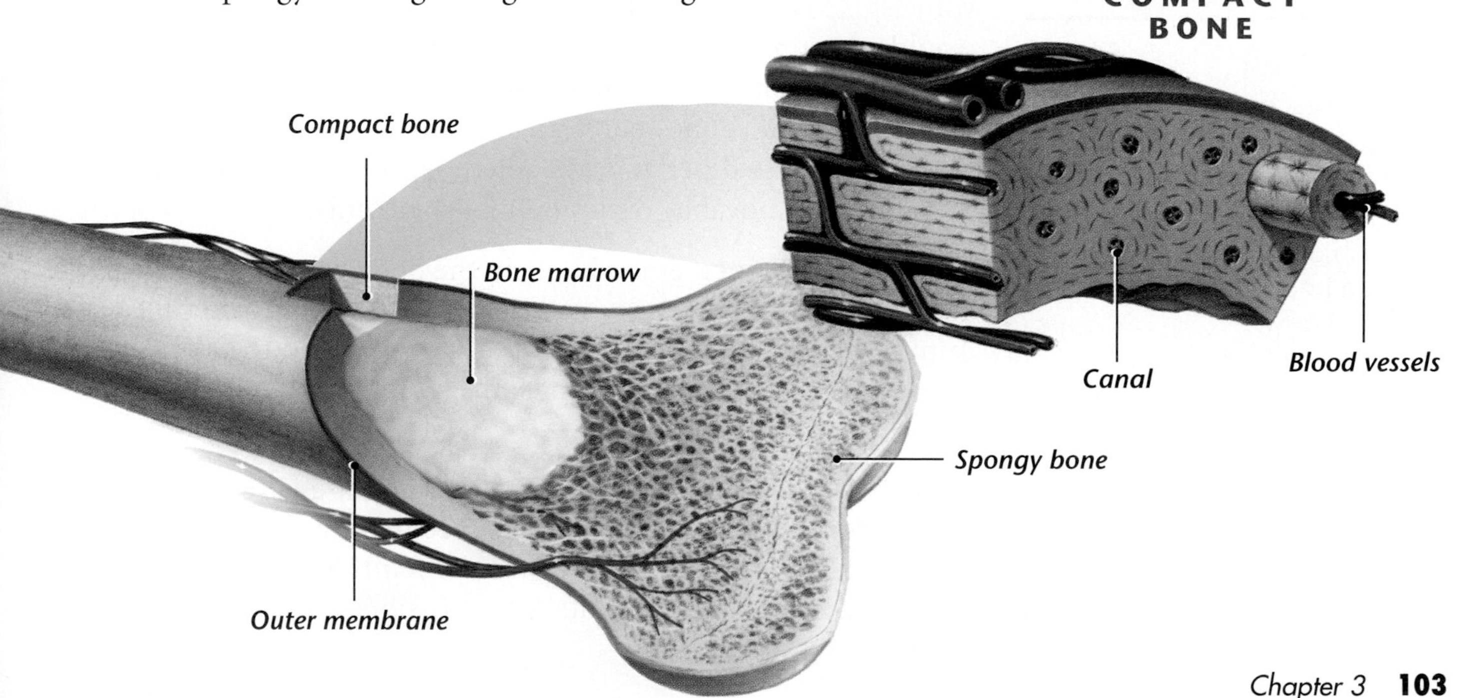

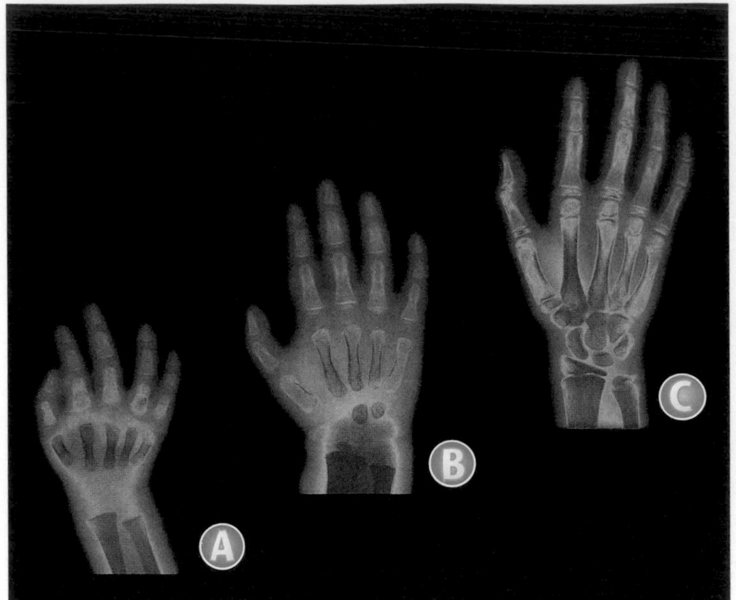

Figure 11 X-rays of the hands of a 1-year-old **(A)** and a 3-year-old **(B)** show that the cartilage in the wrist has not yet been replaced by bone. In the X-ray of the 13-year-old's hand **(C)**, the replacement of cartilage by bone is almost complete.

The spaces in bone contain a soft connective tissue called **marrow.** There are two types of marrow—red and yellow. Red bone marrow produces the body's blood cells. As a child, most of your bones contained red bone marrow. As a teenager, only the ends of your femurs, skull, hip bones, and sternum (breastbone) contain red marrow. Your other bones contain yellow marrow. This marrow stores fat, which serves as an energy reserve.

How Bones Form

Try this activity: Move the tip of your nose from side to side between your fingers. Notice that the tip of your nose is not stiff. That is because it contains cartilage. **Cartilage** (KAHR tuh lij) is a connective tissue that is more flexible than bone. As an infant, much of your skeleton was cartilage. Over time, most of the cartilage has been replaced with hard bone tissue.

The replacement of cartilage by bone tissue usually is complete by the time you stop growing. But not all of your body's cartilage is replaced by bone. Even in adulthood, cartilage covers the ends of many bones. For example, in the knee, cartilage acts like a cushion that keeps your femur from rubbing against the bones of your lower leg.

☑ *Checkpoint* *What happens to cartilage as you grow?*

Joints of the Skeleton

Imagine what life would be like if your femur ran the length of your leg. How would you get out of bed in the morning? How would you run for the school bus? Luckily, your body contains many small bones rather than fewer large ones. A place in the body where two bones come together is a **joint.** Joints allow bones to move in different ways. There are two kinds of joints in the body—immovable joints and movable joints.

Immovable Joints Some joints in the body connect bones in a way that allows little or no movement. These joints are called immovable joints. The bones of the skull are held together by immovable joints. The joints that attach the ribs to the sternum are also immovable.

Movable Joints Most of the joints in the body are movable joints. **Movable joints allow the body to make a wide range of movements.** Look at *Exploring Movable Joints* to see the variety of movements that these joints make possible.

Classifying

Perform each of the activities listed below:

- move your arm in a circle
- push open a door
- lift a book from a desk
- kneel down
- wave your hand
- twist your head from side to side.

Determine which type of joint or joints is involved in performing each activity. Give a reason to support your classifications.

EXPLORING *Movable Joints*

Without movable joints, your body would be as stiff as a board. The four types of movable joints shown here allow your body to move in a variety of ways.

Ball-and-socket joint Ball-and-socket joints allow the greatest range of motion. In your shoulder, the top of the arm bone fits into the deep, bowl-like socket of the scapula (shoulder blade). The joint allows you to swing your arm freely in a circle. Your hips also have ball-and-socket joints.

Pivot joint A pivot joint allows one bone to rotate around another. The pivot joint in the top of your neck gives you limited ability to turn your head from side to side.

Gliding joint A gliding joint allows one bone to slide over another. The gliding joint in your wrist enables you to bend and flex your wrist, as well as make limited side-to-side motions. Your ankles also have gliding joints.

Hinge joint Like the hinge of a door, a hinge joint allows extensive forward or backward motion. Your knee is a hinge joint that allows you to bend and straighten your leg. Your elbow is also a hinge joint.

The bones in movable joints are held together by strong connective tissues called **ligaments.** Cartilage that covers the ends of the bones keeps them from rubbing against each other. In addition, a fluid lubricates the ends of the bones, allowing them to move smoothly over each other.

Taking Care of Your Bones

INTEGRATING HEALTH Because your skeleton performs so many necessary functions, it is important to keep it healthy. This is especially true while you are still growing. **A combination of a balanced diet and regular exercise can start you on the way to a lifetime of healthy bones.**

One way to ensure healthy bones is to eat a well-balanced diet. A well-balanced diet includes enough calcium and phosphorus to keep your bones strong while they are growing. Meats, whole grains, and leafy green vegetables are all excellent sources of both calcium and phosphorus. Dairy products, including milk, are excellent sources of calcium.

Visual Arts CONNECTION

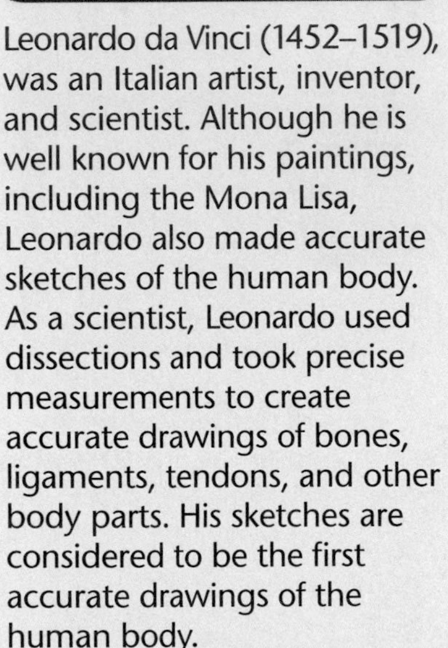

Leonardo da Vinci (1452–1519), was an Italian artist, inventor, and scientist. Although he is well known for his paintings, including the Mona Lisa, Leonardo also made accurate sketches of the human body. As a scientist, Leonardo used dissections and took precise measurements to create accurate drawings of bones, ligaments, tendons, and other body parts. His sketches are considered to be the first accurate drawings of the human body.

In Your Journal

Leonardo da Vinci relied on measurements and visual observations to make his drawings. Use a metric ruler to measure the lengths of the bones in your arm or leg. Then try to make an accurate drawing of your arm or leg.

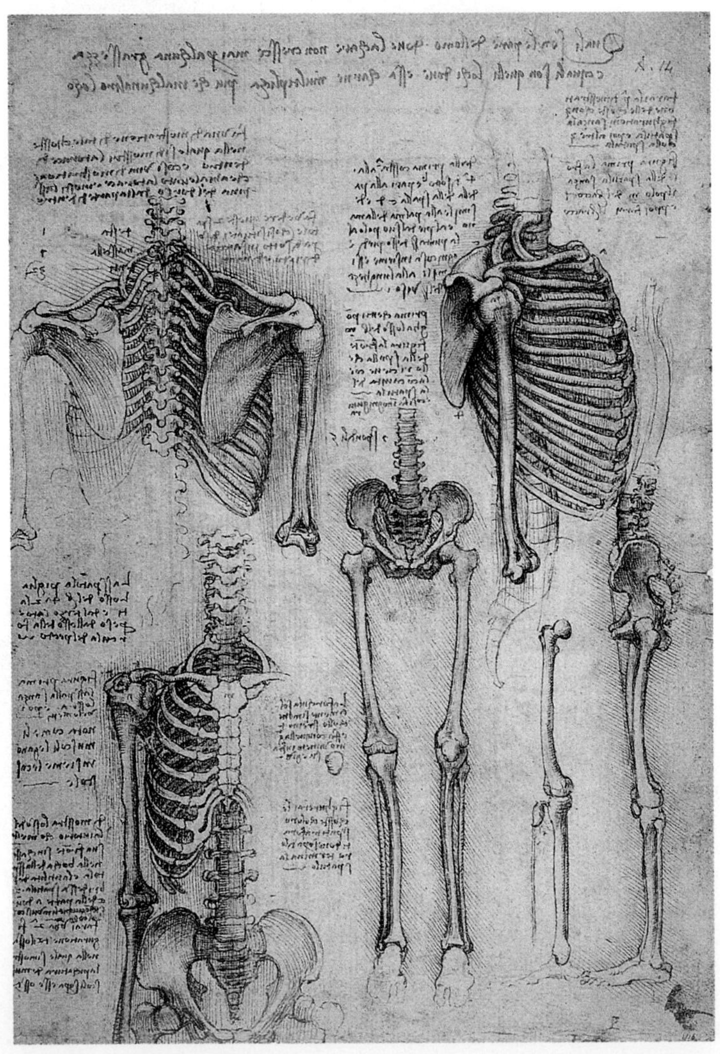

Figure 12 Leonardo da Vinci drew these sketches of the human chest, hip, and leg bones in 1510.

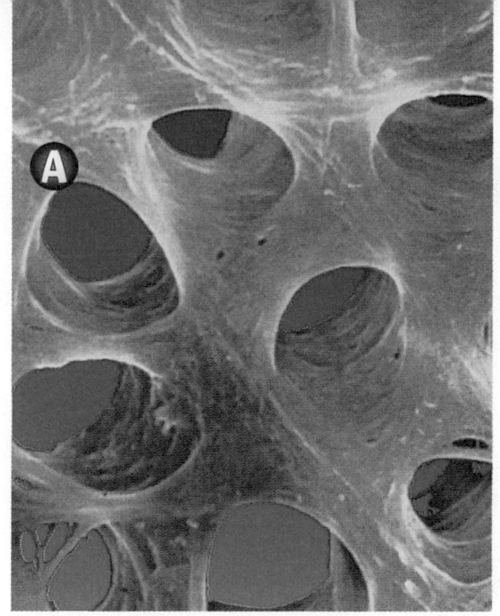

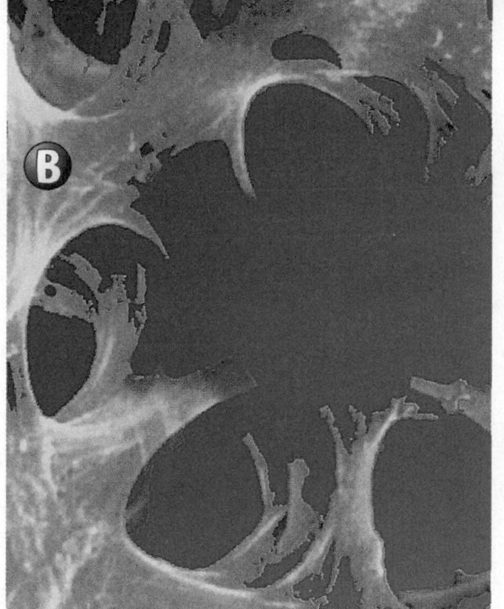

Figure 13 Without enough calcium in the diet, a person's bones weaken. **A.** This magnified view of healthy bone shows a continuous framework. **B.** Notice the large empty space in this bone from a person with osteoporosis. ***Relating Cause and Effect*** *What can you do to prevent osteoporosis?*

Another way to build and maintain strong bones is to get plenty of exercise. During activities such as walking, soccer, or basketball, your bones support the weight of your entire body. This helps your bones grow stronger and denser. Running, skating, and aerobics are other activities that help keep your bones healthy and strong. To prevent injuries while exercising, be sure to wear appropriate safety equipment, such as a helmet, knee pads, or shoulder pads.

As people become older, their bones begin to lose some of the minerals they contain. Mineral loss can lead to **osteoporosis** (ahs tee oh puh ROH sis), a condition in which the body's bones become weak and break easily. You can see the effect of osteoporosis in Figure 13B. Osteoporosis is more common in women than in men. Evidence indicates that regular exercise throughout life can help prevent osteoporosis. A diet with enough calcium can also help prevent osteoporosis. If you eat enough calcium-rich foods now, during your teenage years, you may help prevent osteoporosis later in life.

Section 2 Review

1. List five important functions that the skeleton performs in the body.
2. What is the role of movable joints in the body?
3. What behaviors are important for keeping your bones healthy?
4. Compare the motion of a hinge joint to that of a pivot joint.
5. **Thinking Critically Predicting** How would your life be different if your backbone consisted of just one bone?

Science at Home

List the types of exercise you and your family members do. With your family, brainstorm a list of safety gear and precautions to use for each activity. (For example, for bicycling, you might list wearing a helmet, stretching before riding, and avoiding busy streets and nighttime riding.) How can you put these safety measures into practice?

SECTION 3

The Muscular System

DISCOVER ACTIVITY

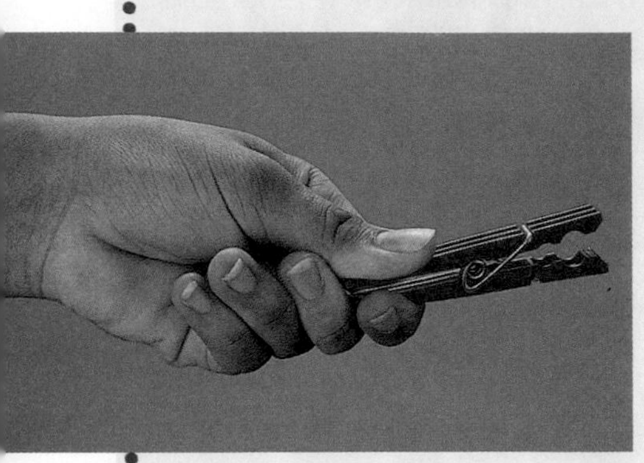

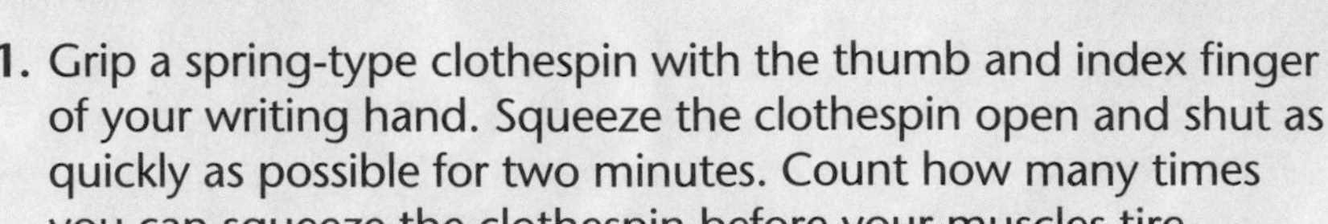

How Do Muscles Work?

1. Grip a spring-type clothespin with the thumb and index finger of your writing hand. Squeeze the clothespin open and shut as quickly as possible for two minutes. Count how many times you can squeeze the clothespin before your muscles tire.
2. Rest for one minute. Then repeat Step 1.

Think It Over

Predicting What do you think would happen if you repeated Steps 1 and 2 with your other hand? Give a reason for your prediction. Then test your prediction.

GUIDE FOR READING

- **What three types of muscles are found in the body?**
- **Why do skeletal muscles work in pairs?**

Reading Tip **Before you read, preview Figure 14. Predict the functions of skeletal, smooth, and cardiac muscle. After you read the section, look back at your predictions to see whether they were correct.**

A rabbit becomes still when it senses danger. The rabbit sits so still that it doesn't seem to move a muscle. Could you sit without moving any muscles? If you tried to, you'd find that it is impossible to sit still for very long. Saliva builds up in your mouth. You swallow. You need to breathe. Your chest expands to let air in. All of these actions involve muscles.

There are about 600 muscles in your body. Muscles have many functions. For example, they keep your heart beating, pull your mouth into a smile, and move the bones of your skeleton.

Muscle Action

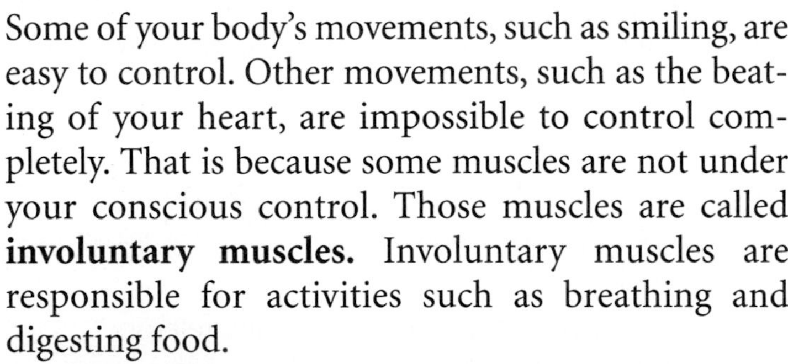

Some of your body's movements, such as smiling, are easy to control. Other movements, such as the beating of your heart, are impossible to control completely. That is because some muscles are not under your conscious control. Those muscles are called **involuntary muscles.** Involuntary muscles are responsible for activities such as breathing and digesting food.

The muscles that are under your control are called **voluntary muscles.** Smiling, turning a page in a book, and getting out of your chair when the bell rings are all actions controlled by voluntary muscles.

◀ **A rabbit "frozen" in place**

Types of Muscles

Your body has three types of muscle tissue—skeletal muscle, smooth muscle, and cardiac muscle. In Figure 14, you see a magnified view of each type of muscle in the body. Both skeletal and smooth muscles are found in many places in the body. Cardiac muscle is found only in the heart. Each muscle type performs specific functions in the body.

Skeletal Muscle Every time you type on a computer keyboard, shoot a basketball, or walk across a room, you are using skeletal muscles. As their name suggests, **skeletal muscles** are attached

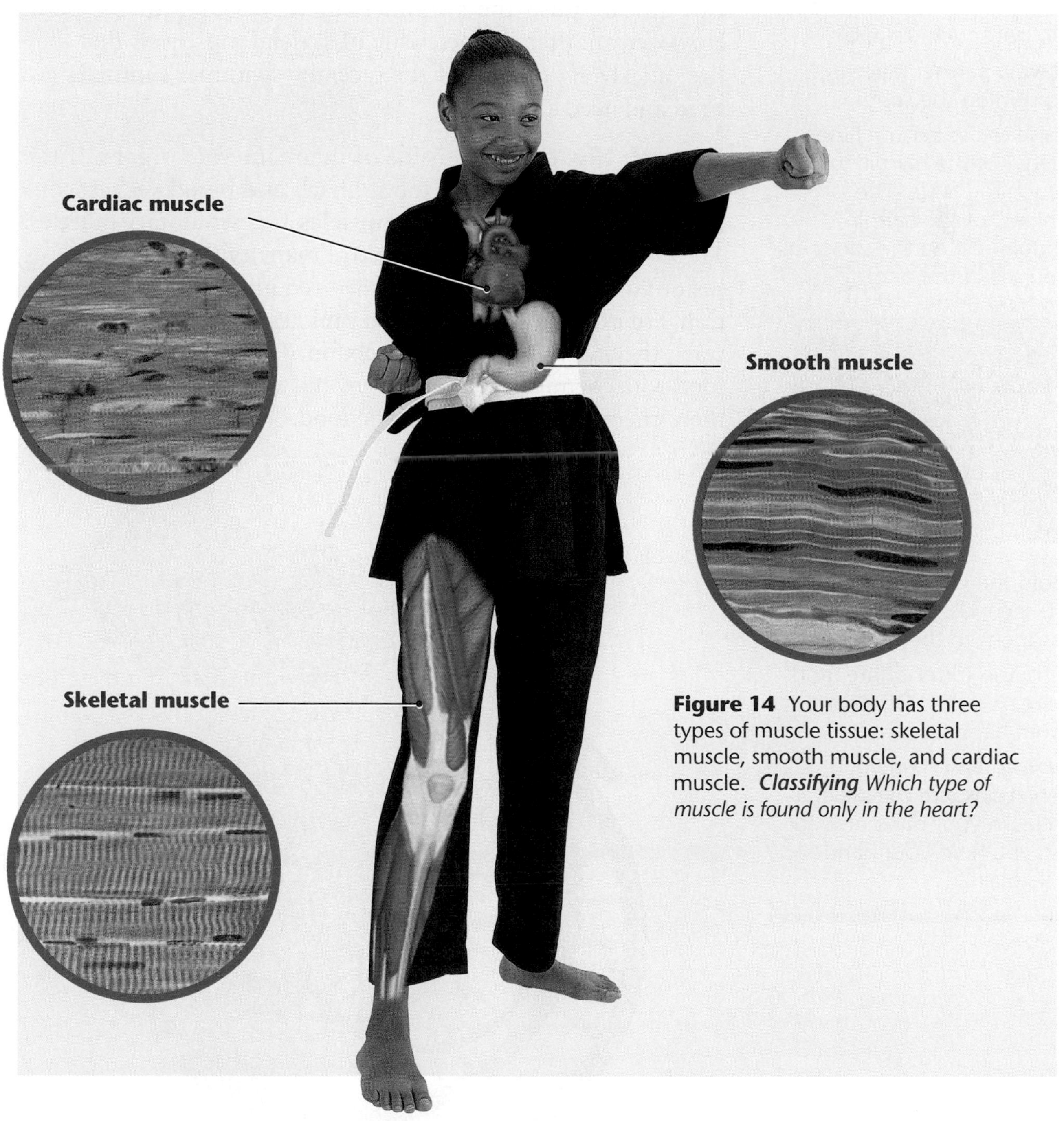

Figure 14 Your body has three types of muscle tissue: skeletal muscle, smooth muscle, and cardiac muscle. ***Classifying*** *Which type of muscle is found only in the heart?*

Get a Grip

ACTIVITY

Are skeletal muscles at work when you're not moving? Try this activity and see.

1. Hold a stirrer in front of you, parallel to a table top. Do not touch the table.
2. Have a partner place a hairpin on the stirrer.
3. Raise the stirrer until the "legs" of the hairpin just touch the table. The "head" of the hairpin should rest on the stirrer, as you see in the photo.

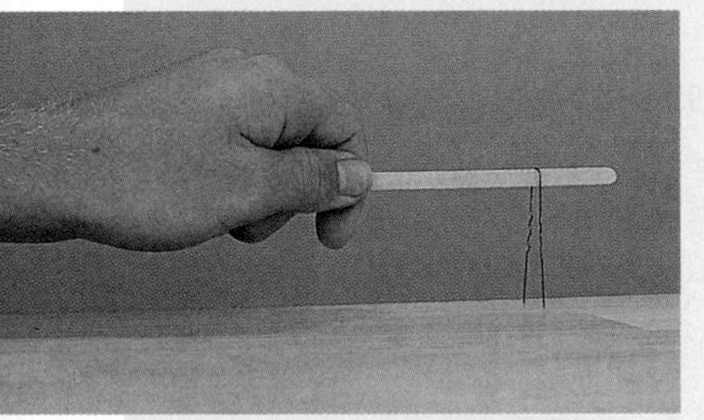

4. Hold the stirrer steady for 20 seconds. Observe what happens to the hairpin.
5. Grip the stirrer tighter and repeat Step 4. Observe what happens.

Inferring Based on your observations, are the skeletal muscles in your hand at work when you hold your hand still? Explain.

to the bones of your skeleton. These muscles provide the force that moves your bones. At each end of a skeletal muscle is a tendon. A **tendon** is a strong connective tissue that attaches muscle to bone. As you can see in Figure 14, skeletal muscle cells appear banded, or striated (STRY ay tid). For this reason, skeletal muscle is sometimes called striated muscle.

Because you have conscious control of skeletal muscles, they are classified as voluntary muscles. One characteristic of skeletal muscles is that they react very quickly. You can see an example of just how quickly skeletal muscle reacts by watching a swim meet. Immediately after the starting gun sounds, a swimmer's leg muscles quickly push the swimmer off the block into the pool. However, another characteristic of skeletal muscles is that they tire quickly. By the end of the race, the swimmer's muscles are tired and need a rest.

Smooth Muscle The inside of many internal organs of the body, such as the walls of the stomach and blood vessels, contain smooth muscles. **Smooth muscles** are involuntary muscles. They work automatically to control many types of movements inside your body, such as those involved in the process of digestion. For example, as the smooth muscles of your stomach contract, they produce a churning action. The churning mixes the food with chemicals produced by your stomach. This action and these chemicals help to digest the food.

Unlike skeletal muscles, smooth muscle cells are not striated. Smooth muscles behave differently than skeletal muscles, too. Smooth muscles react more slowly and tire more slowly.

Cardiac Muscle The tissue called **cardiac muscle** has characteristics in common with both smooth and skeletal muscles. Like smooth muscle, cardiac muscle is involuntary. Like skeletal muscle, cardiac muscle cells are striated. However, unlike skeletal muscle, cardiac muscle does not get tired. It can contract repeatedly. You call those repeated contractions heartbeats.

☑ ***Checkpoint*** *Which type of muscle reacts and tires quickly?*

Muscles at Work

Has anyone ever asked you to "make a muscle"? If so, you probably tightened your fist, bent your arm at the elbow, and made the muscles in your upper arm bulge. Like other skeletal muscles, the muscles in your arm do their work by contracting, or becoming shorter and thicker. Muscle cells contract when they receive messages from the nervous system. **Because muscle cells can only contract, not extend, skeletal muscles must work in pairs. While one muscle contracts, the other muscle in the pair returns to its original length.**

Figure 15 shows the muscle action involved in bending the arm at the elbow. First, the biceps muscle on the front of the upper arm contracts to bend the elbow, lifting the forearm and hand. As the biceps contracts, the triceps on the back of the upper arm returns to its original length. Then to straighten the elbow, the triceps muscle contracts. As the triceps contracts to extend the arm, the biceps returns to its original length. Another example of muscles that work in pairs are those in your thigh that bend and straighten the knee joint.

Figure 15 Because muscles can only contract, or shorten, they must work in pairs. To bend the arm at the elbow, the biceps contracts while the triceps returns to its original length. ***Interpreting Diagrams*** *What happens to each muscle to straighten the arm?*

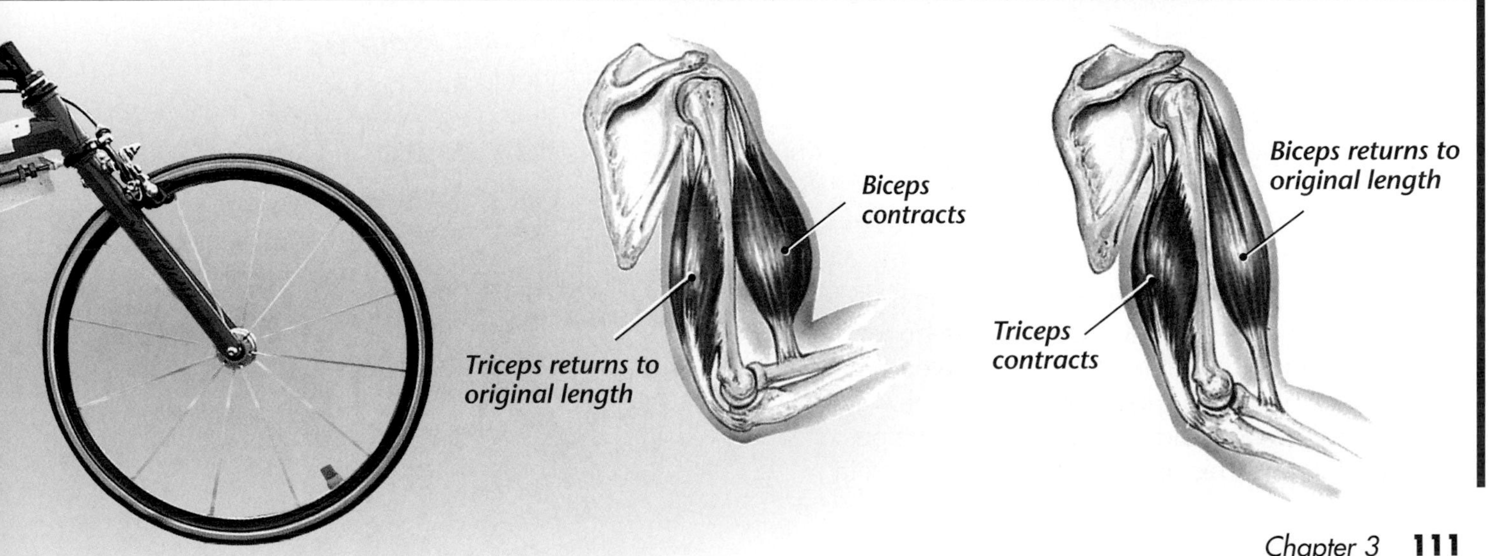

Figure 16 When you warm up before exercising, you increase the flexibility of your muscles.

Taking Care of Your Skeletal Muscles

Exercise is important for maintaining both muscular strength and flexibility. Exercise makes individual muscle cells grow wider. This, in turn, causes the whole muscle to become thicker. The thicker a muscle is, the stronger the muscle is. When you stretch and warm up thoroughly, your muscles become more flexible. This helps prepare your muscles for the work involved in exercising or playing.

Like your bones and joints, your skeletal muscles are subject to injuries. Some of the same precautions that help prevent bone and joint injuries can also help prevent muscle injuries. For example, warming up increases the flexibility of joints as well as muscles. In addition, using proper safety equipment can protect all of your tissues, including muscles and tendons.

Sometimes, despite taking proper precautions, muscles can become injured. A muscle strain, or a pulled muscle, can occur when muscles are overworked or overstretched. Tendons can also be overstretched or partially torn. After a long period of exercise, a skeletal muscle can cramp. When a muscle cramps, the entire muscle contracts strongly and stays contracted. If you injure a muscle or tendon, it is important to follow medical instructions and to rest the injured area until it heals.

Section 3 Review

1. Name the three types of muscle tissue. Where is each type found?
2. Describe how the muscles in your upper arm work together to bend and straighten your arm.
3. How do voluntary and involuntary muscles differ? Give an example of each type of muscle.
4. **Thinking Critically Predicting** The muscles that move your fingers are attached to the bones in your fingers by long tendons. Suppose one of the tendons in a person's index finger were cut all the way through. How would this injury affect the person's ability to move his or her index finger? Explain.

Check Your Progress — CHAPTER PROJECT 3

You should now be assembling your working model. Be sure that you include the muscles involved in the movement you are modeling. Also, remember that your model must show how muscle contractions produce the chosen movement. (*Hint:* After you have assembled your model, do a final check to be sure it functions the way it should.)

Observing

Skills Lab

A Look Beneath the Skin

In this lab, you will learn about your own skeletal muscles by observing the "arm" muscles of a chicken.

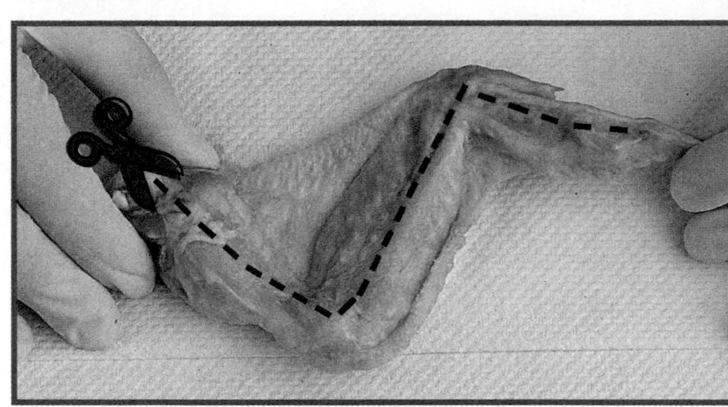

Problem

What are some characteristics of skeletal muscles? How do skeletal muscles work?

Materials

protective gloves
paper towels
scissors
water
dissection tray
uncooked chicken wing, treated with bleach

Procedure   

1. Put on protective gloves. **CAUTION:** *Wear gloves whenever you handle the chicken.*
2. Your teacher will give you a chicken wing. Rinse it well with water, dry it with paper towels, and place it in a dissecting tray.
3. Carefully extend the wing to find out how many major parts it has. Draw a diagram of the external structure. Label the upper arm, elbow, lower arm, and hand (wing tip).
4. Use scissors to remove the skin. Cut along the cut line as shown in the photo. Only cut through the skin. **CAUTION:** *Cut away from your body and your classmates.*
5. Examine the muscles, the bundles of pink tissue around the bones. Find the two groups of muscles in the upper arm. Hold the arm down at the shoulder, and alternately pull on each muscle group. Observe what happens.
6. Find the two groups of muscles in the lower arm. Hold down the arm at the elbow, and alternately pull on each muscle group. Then make a diagram of the wing's muscles.
7. Find the tendons—shiny white tissue at the ends of the muscles. Notice what parts the tendons connect. Add the tendons to your diagram.
8. Remove the muscles and tendons. Find the ligaments, the whitish ribbonlike structures between bones. Add them to your diagram.
9. Dispose of the chicken parts according to your teacher's instructions. Wash your hands.

Analyze and Conclude

1. How does a chicken wing move at the elbow? How does the motion compare to how your elbow moves? What type of joint is involved?
2. What happened when you pulled on one of the arm muscles? What muscle action does the pulling represent?
3. Classify the muscles you observed as smooth, cardiac, or skeletal.
4. **Think About It** Why is it valuable to record your observations with accurate diagrams?

More to Explore

Use the procedures from this lab to examine an uncooked chicken thigh and leg. Compare how the chicken leg and a human leg move.

Section 4 The Skin

Discover Activity

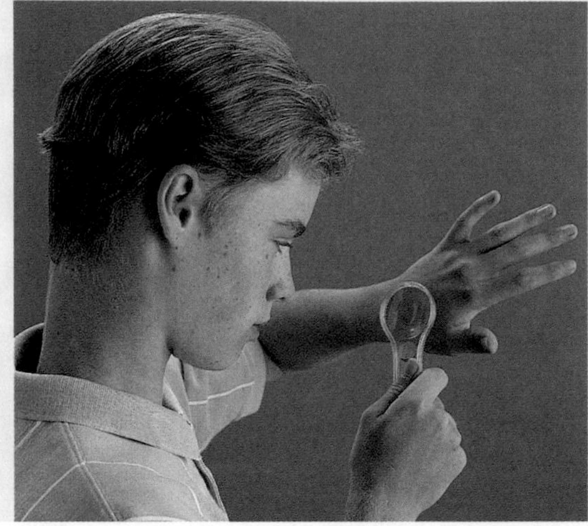

What Can You Observe About Skin?

1. Using a hand lens, examine the skin on your hand. Look for pores and hairs on both the palm and back of your hand.
2. Place a plastic glove on your hand. After five minutes, remove the glove. Then examine the skin on your hand with the hand lens.

Think It Over

Inferring Compare your hand before and after wearing the glove. What happened to the skin when you wore the glove? Why did this happen?

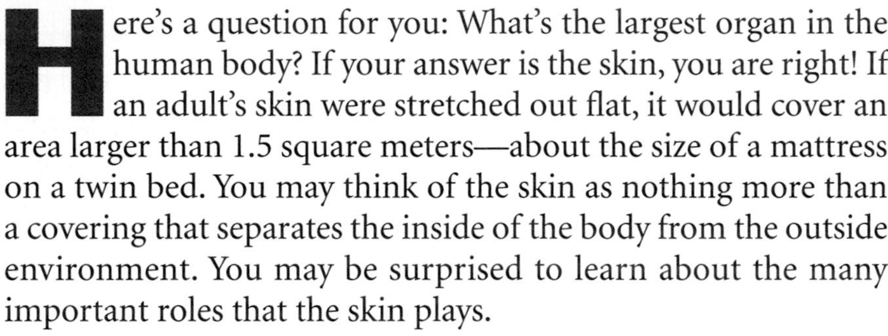

Guide for Reading

- **What are the functions of skin?**
- **What habits can help keep your skin healthy?**

Reading Tip **As you read, create a table that shows the two major layers of skin. Include columns to record the location, structures, and functions of each layer.**

Here's a question for you: What's the largest organ in the human body? If your answer is the skin, you are right! If an adult's skin were stretched out flat, it would cover an area larger than 1.5 square meters—about the size of a mattress on a twin bed. You may think of the skin as nothing more than a covering that separates the inside of the body from the outside environment. You may be surprised to learn about the many important roles that the skin plays.

The Body's Tough Covering

The skin performs several major functions in the body. **The skin covers the body and prevents the loss of water. It protects the body from injury and infection. The skin also helps to regulate body temperature, eliminate wastes, gather information about the environment, and produce vitamin D.**

Figure 17 The skin forms a barrier that protects the inside of the body from substances such as the chlorine in pool water.

The skin protects the body by forming a barrier that keeps disease-causing microorganisms and harmful substances outside the body. In addition, the skin helps keep important substances inside the body. Like plastic wrap that keeps food from drying out, the skin prevents the loss of important fluids such as water.

Figure 18 When you exercise, your body becomes warmer. Sweat glands in the skin produce perspiration, which leaves the body through pores like the one you see here. ***Relating Cause and Effect*** *How does perspiration help cool your body?*

Another function of the skin is to help the body maintain a steady temperature. Many blood vessels run through skin. When you become too warm, these blood vessels enlarge to increase the amount of blood that flows through them. This allows heat to move from your body into the outside environment. In addition, sweat glands in the skin respond to excess heat by producing perspiration. As perspiration evaporates from your skin, heat moves into the air. Because perspiration contains some dissolved waste materials, your skin also helps to eliminate wastes.

The skin also gathers information about the environment. To understand how the skin does this, place your fingertips on the skin of your arm and press down firmly. Then lightly pinch yourself. You have just tested some of the nerves in your skin. The nerves in skin provide information about such things as pressure, pain, and temperature. Pain messages are important because they warn you that something in your surroundings may have injured you.

Lastly, some skin cells produce vitamin D in the presence of sunlight. Vitamin D is important for healthy bones. This is because Vitamin D helps the cells in your digestive system to absorb the calcium in your food. Your skin cells need only a few minutes of sunlight to produce all the vitamin D you need in a day.

☑ ***Checkpoint*** *How does your skin help eliminate waste materials from your body?*

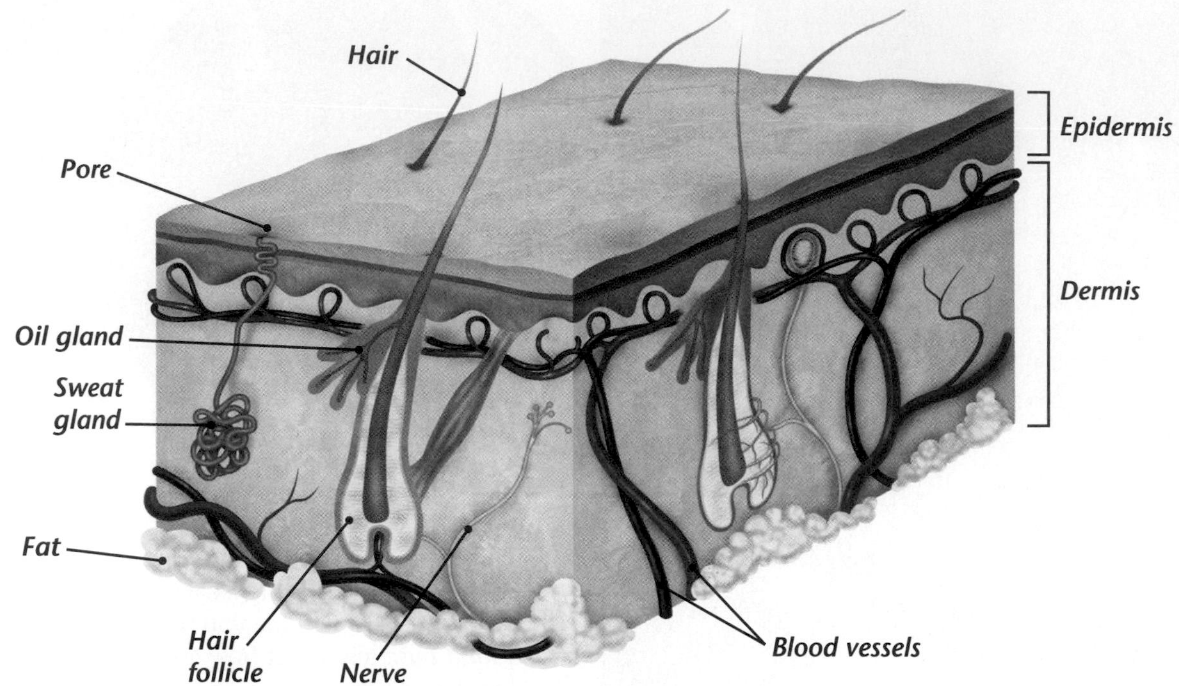

Figure 19 The skin is made of two main layers. The top layer is called the epidermis. The bottom layer is called the dermis. ***Interpreting Diagrams*** *In which layer of the skin do you find blood vessels?*

The Epidermis

The skin is organized into two main layers, the epidermis and the dermis. You can see these layers in Figure 19. The **epidermis** is the outermost layer of the skin. In most places, the epidermis is thinner than the dermis. The epidermis does not have nerves or blood vessels. This is why you usually don't feel pain from very shallow scratches and why shallow scratches do not bleed.

Dead or Alive? The cells in the epidermis have a definite life cycle. Each epidermal cell begins life deep in the epidermis, where cells divide to form new cells. The new cells gradually mature and move upward in the epidermis as new cells form beneath them. After about two weeks, the cells die and become part of the surface layer of the epidermis. Under a microscope, this surface layer of dead cells resembles flat bags laid on top of each other. Cells remain in this layer for about two weeks. Then they are shed and replaced by the dead cells below.

Protecting the Body In some ways, the cells of the epidermis are more valuable to the body dead than alive. Most of the protection provided by the skin is due to the layer of dead cells on the surface. The thick layer of dead cells on your fingertips, for example, protects and cushions your fingertips. The shedding of dead cells also helps to protect the body. As the cells fall away, they carry with them bacteria and other substances that settle on the skin. Every time you rub your hands together, you lose hundreds, even thousands, of dead skin cells.

Some cells in the inner layer of the epidermis help to protect the body, too. On your fingers, for example, some cells produce hard fingernails, which protect the fingertips from injury and help you scratch and pick up objects.

Other cells deep in the epidermis produce **melanin,** a pigment, or colored substance, that gives skin its color. The more melanin in your skin, the darker it is. Exposure to sunlight stimulates the skin to make more melanin. Melanin production helps to protect the skin from burning.

☑ *Checkpoint* *How do dead skin cells help to protect the body?*

The Dermis

The **dermis** is the lower layer of the skin. Find the dermis in Figure 19. Notice that it is located below the epidermis and above a layer of fat. This fat layer pads the internal organs and helps keep heat in the body.

The dermis contains nerves and blood vessels. The dermis also contains other structures as well—sweat glands, hairs, and oil glands. Sweat glands produce perspiration, which reaches the surface through openings called **pores.** Strands of hair grow within the dermis in structures called **follicles** (FAHL ih kulz). The hair that you see above the skin's surface is made up of dead cells. Oil produced in glands around the hair follicles waterproofs the hair. In addition, oil that reaches the surface helps to keep the skin moist.

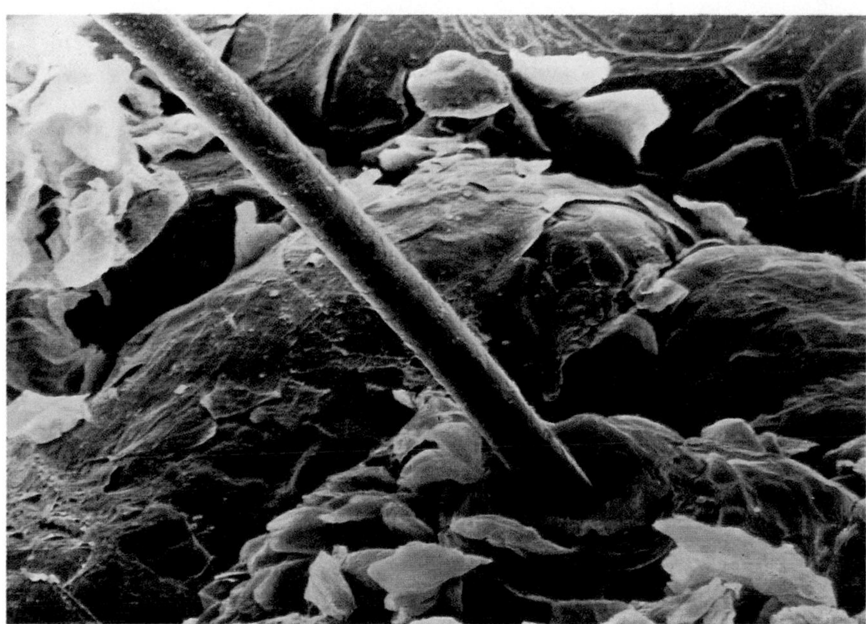

Figure 20 Hairs grow from follicles in the dermis of the skin. Hair is made of dead cells.

Sweaty Skin

ACTIVITY

This activity illustrates one of the skin's important functions.

1. Put on your safety goggles. Wrap a wet cotton ball around the bulb of one thermometer. Place a second thermometer next to the first one.

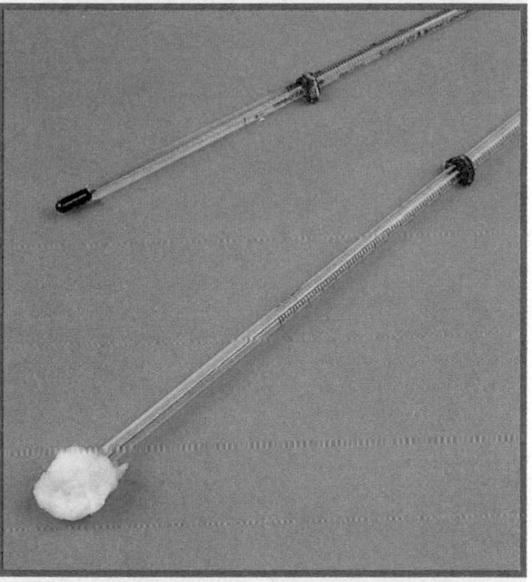

2. After two minutes, record the temperature reading on each thermometer.
3. Using a piece of cardboard, fan both thermometers for several minutes. The cardboard should be at least 10 cm from the thermometers. Then record the temperatures.

Measuring Which of the two thermometers had a lower temperature after Step 3? How does this activity relate to the role of skin in regulating body temperature?

Caring for Your Skin

Because your skin has so many important functions, it is important to take care of it. **Four simple habits can help you keep your skin healthy. Eat properly. Drink enough water. Limit your exposure to the sun. Keep your skin clean and dry.**

Eating Properly Your skin is always active. The cells in the epidermis are replaced, hair strands and nails grow, and oil is produced. These activities require energy—and a well-balanced diet provides the energy needed for these processes. You will learn more about healthy diets in Chapter 4.

Real-World Lab

You and Your Environment

In this lab, you'll investigate how sunscreen products and various fabrics protect your skin from the sun.

Problem

How well do different materials protect the skin from the sun?

Skills Focus

predicting, observing, drawing conclusions

Materials

scissors
3 different fabrics
photosensitive paper
white construction paper
resealable plastic bag
pencil
plastic knife
metric ruler
stapler
staple remover
2 sunscreens with SPF ratings of 4 and 30

Procedure

1. Read over the procedure. Then write a prediction about how well each of the sunscreens and fabrics will protect against the sun.

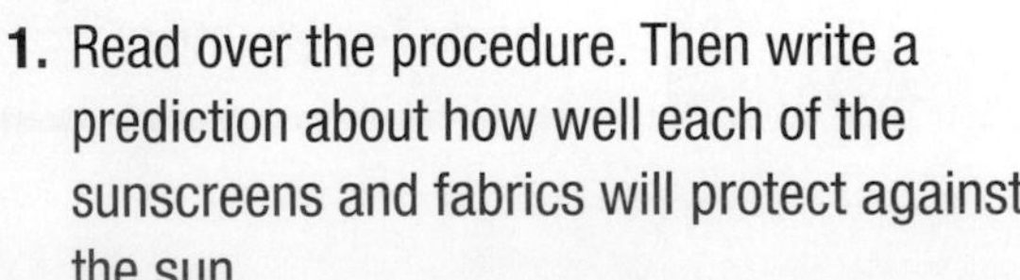

2. Use scissors to cut five strips of photosensitive paper that measure 5 cm by 15 cm.
3. Divide each strip into thirds by drawing lines across the strips as shown in the photo.
4. Cover one third of each strip with a square of white construction paper. Staple each square down.
5. Use a pencil to write the lower SPF (sun protection factor) rating on the back of the first strip. Write the other SPF rating on the back of a second strip. Set the other three strips aside.
6. Place the two strips side by side in a plastic bag. Seal the bag, then staple through the white squares to hold the strips in place.

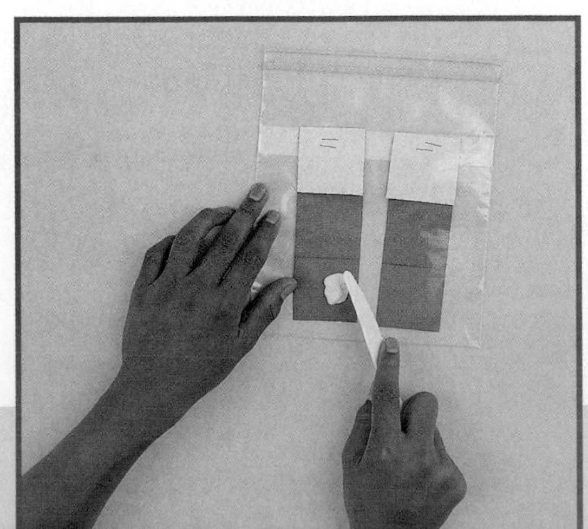

Drinking Water To keep your skin healthy, it is also important to drink plenty of water. When you participate in strenuous activities, such as playing soccer, you can perspire up to 10 liters of liquid a day. You need to replace the water lost in perspiration by drinking water or other beverages and by eating foods, such as fruits, that contain water.

Limiting Sun Exposure You can also take actions to protect your skin from cancer and early aging. **Cancer** is a disease in which some body cells divide uncontrollably. Repeated exposure to sunlight can damage skin cells and cause them to become

7. With a plastic knife, spread a thin layer of each sunscreen on the bag over the bottom square of its labeled strip. Make certain each layer has the same depth. Be sure not to spread sunscreen over the middle squares. Place the bag in a drawer or cabinet.
8. Obtain three fabric pieces of different thicknesses. Using the other three photo-sensitive strips, staple a square of each fabric over the bottom square of one of the strips. Write a description of the fabric on the back of the strip.
9. Remove the bag from the drawer or cabinet. Make sure the bag is sunscreen-side up and the fabric strips are fabric-side up. Place the strips in sunlight until the color of the middle squares stops changing.
10. Remove the strips from the bag. Take off the construction paper and fabrics. Rinse the strips for one minute in cold water, then dry them flat.
11. Observe all the squares. Record your observations.

Analyze and Conclude

1. Did the sunscreens protect against sun exposure? How do you know?
2. Which sunscreen provided more protection? Was your prediction correct?
3. Did the fabrics protect against sun exposure? How do you know?
4. Which fabric provided the most protection? The least protection? How did your results compare with your predictions?
5. **Apply** What advice would you give people about protecting their skin from the sun?

Design an Experiment

Design an experiment to find out whether ordinary window glass protects skin against sun exposure. Obtain your teacher's approval before carrying out this experiment.

Figure 21 This person is taking precautions to protect her skin from the sun. ***Applying Concepts*** *What other behaviors can provide protection from the sun?*

cancerous. In addition, exposure to the sun can cause the skin to become leathery and wrinkled.

There are many things you can do to protect your skin from damage by the sun. When you are outdoors, wear a hat and sunglasses and use a sunscreen on exposed skin. The clothing you wear can also protect you. Choose clothing made of tightly woven fabrics for the greatest protection. In addition, avoid exposure to the sun between the hours of 10 A.M. and 2 P.M. That is the time when sunlight is the strongest.

Keeping Skin Clean When you wash your skin with mild soap, you get rid of dirt and harmful bacteria. Good washing habits are particularly important during the teenage years when oil glands are more active. When oil glands become clogged with oil, bacterial infections can occur.

One bacterial infection of the skin that can be difficult to control is known as **acne.** If you develop acne, your doctor may prescribe an antibiotic to help control the infection. When you wash, you help to control oiliness and keep your skin from becoming infected with more bacteria.

Other organisms, called fungi, can also live on and infect the skin. Fungi grow best in warm, moist surroundings. Athlete's foot is a very common fungal infection that occurs on the feet, especially between the toes. You can prevent athlete's foot by keeping your feet, especially the spaces between your toes, clean and dry.

Section 4 Review

1. Describe the functions of the skin.
2. List three things you can do to keep your skin healthy.
3. Describe the structure of the two layers of skin.
4. **Thinking Critically Making Judgments** Do you think it is possible to wash your skin too much and damage it as a result? Why or why not?

Science at Home

With a family member, look for products in your home that provide protection from the sun. You may also want to visit a store that sells these products. Make a list of the products and place them in categories such as sunblocks, clothing, eye protectors, and other products. Explain to your family member why it is important to use such products.

CHAPTER 3 STUDY GUIDE

Body Organization and Homeostasis

INTEGRATING HEALTH

Key Ideas

- The levels of organization in the body consist of cells, tissues, organs, and organ systems.
- Homeostasis is the process by which an organism's internal environment is kept stable in spite of changes in the external environment.

Key Terms

cell	muscle tissue	organ
cell membrane	nerve tissue	organ system
nucleus	connective tissue	homeostasis
cytoplasm	epithelial tissue	stress
tissue		

The Skeletal System

Key Ideas

- The skeleton provides shape and support, enables movement, protects internal organs, produces blood cells, and stores materials.
- Movable joints allow the body to make a wide range of motions.
- A combination of a balanced diet and regular exercise helps keep bones healthy.

Key Terms

vertebra	cartilage	ligament
marrow	joint	osteoporosis

The Muscular System

Key Ideas

- Skeletal muscles are voluntary muscles that are attached to the bones of the skeleton.
- Smooth muscles, which are involuntary muscles, line the walls of many internal organs and blood vessels. Cardiac muscles are involuntary muscles found only in the heart.

Key Terms

involuntary muscle	tendon
voluntary muscle	smooth muscle
skeletal muscle	cardiac muscle

The Skin

Key Ideas

- Skin covers and protects the body from injury and infection. It also helps to regulate body temperature, get rid of wastes, gather information about the environment, and produce vitamin D.
- The epidermis is the top layer of the skin. The dermis is the lower layer of the skin.
- For healthy skin, eat a well-balanced diet and drink enough water. Also limit your exposure to the sun and keep your skin clean.

Key Terms

epidermis	follicle
melanin	cancer
dermis	acne
pore	

Organizing Information

Concept Map Copy the concept map about muscles onto a separate sheet of paper. Then complete it and add a title. (For more information on concept maps, see the Skills Handbook.)

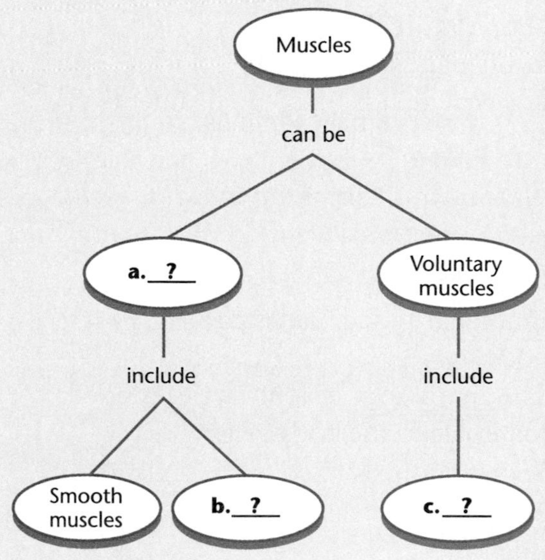

Reviewing Content

Multiple Choice

Choose the letter of the best answer.

1. A group of similar cells that perform a similar function is called a(n)
   a. cell.
   b. organ.
   c. tissue.
   d. organ system.
2. The term most closely associated with homeostasis is
   a. growth.
   b. stability.
   c. temperature.
   d. energy.
3. Blood cells are produced in
   a. compact bone.
   b. red bone marrow.
   c. cartilage.
   d. ligaments.
4. Muscles that help the skeleton move are
   a. cardiac muscles.
   b. smooth muscles.
   c. skeletal muscles.
   d. involuntary muscles.
5. Which structures help to maintain body temperature?
   a. oil glands **b.** follicles
   c. sweat glands **d.** ligaments

True or False

If the statement is true, write true. If it is false, change the underlined word or words to make the statement true.

6. <u>Epithelial</u> tissue makes parts of your body move.
7. The <u>circulatory</u> system carries needed materials to the body cells.
8. Spongy bone is filled with <u>cartilage</u>.
9. <u>Skeletal</u> muscle is sometimes called striated muscle.
10. The <u>epidermis</u> contains nerve endings and blood vessels.

Checking Concepts

11. Explain the relationship among cells, tissues, organs, and organ systems.
12. How does hunger help your body maintain homeostasis?
13. Think of a situation that might cause long-term stress. Identify some ways in which a person might deal with that stress.
14. Describe the structure of a bone.
15. List the four kinds of movable joints. Describe how each kind of joint functions.
16. How does the appearance of smooth muscle differ from that of skeletal muscle when viewed with a microscope?
17. Explain how skeletal muscles work in pairs to move a body part.
18. Why is it important to limit your exposure to the sun?
19. **Writing to Learn** Write an article for your school newspaper about preventing skeletal and muscular injuries. The article should focus on ways in which athletes can strengthen their muscles and bones and decrease the risk of injuries during sports.

Thinking Critically

20. **Inferring** Why do you think scientists classify blood as a connective tissue?
21. **Making Generalizations** How is homeostasis important to survival?
22. **Applying Concepts** At birth, the joints in an infant's skull are flexible and not yet fixed. As the child develops, the bones become more rigid and grow together. Why is it important that the bones of an infant's skull not grow together too rapidly?
23. **Predicting** If smooth muscle had to be consciously controlled, what problems could you foresee in day-to-day living?
24. **Relating Cause and Effect** A person who is exposed to excessive heat may suffer from a condition known as heat stroke. The first sign of heat stroke is that the person stops sweating. Why is this condition a life-threatening emergency?

Applying Skills

The graph below shows the effects of the temperature of the environment on a girl's skin temperature and on the temperature inside her body. Use the graph to answer Questions 25–27.

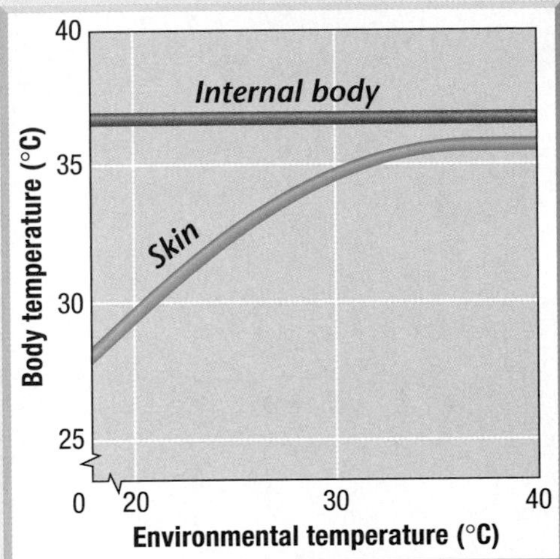

25. **Interpreting Data** As the temperature of the environment rises, what happens to the girl's internal temperature? How does this demonstrate homeostasis?

26. **Inferring** What happens to the temperature of the girl's skin? Why is this pattern different from the pattern shown by the girl's internal temperature?

27. **Developing Hypotheses** Suppose the girl went outdoors on a chilly fall morning. Write a hypothesis that predicts what would happen to her internal body temperature and skin temperature.

Performance Assessment (Chapter Project 3)

Project Wrap Up Demonstrate your model for the class. Explain how your model shows your chosen motion. Describe how the contraction of muscle is involved.

Reflect and Record Why did you select the motion that you modeled? What new information did you discover about the human body? If you could do the project again, what would you change? Write your thoughts in your journal.

Test Preparation

Use these questions to prepare for standardized tests.

Read the passage. Then answer Questions 28–30.

Magnetic resonance imaging, or MRI, is a method used to take clear images of both the bones and soft tissues of the body. An MRI scanner is a large cylinder that contains electromagnets. The person is placed on a platform that slides into the center of the cylinder. The person is then exposed to short bursts of magnetic energy. This magnetic energy causes atoms within the body to vibrate, or resonate. A computer then analyzes the vibration patterns and produces an image of the area.

MRI can produce images of body tissues at any angle. The images clearly show muscles and other soft tissues that an X-ray image cannot show. Another advantage of MRI is that it does not damage cells. Because MRI machines are very expensive to buy and use, this technique is not used to examine broken bones.

28. Which of the following is the best title for this passage?
- **a.** Using X-Rays to Diagnose Bone Injuries
- **b.** Using MRI to Diagnose Injuries
- **c.** The Dangers of MRI
- **d.** Two Methods for Diagnosing Injuries

29. Why is MRI often used to diagnose muscle and other soft tissue injuries?
- **a.** MRI creates clear images of soft tissues.
- **b.** MRI can produce images from many angles.
- **c.** MRI does not damage body cells.
- **d.** all of the above

30. According to the passage, why are X-rays used instead of MRI to examine broken bones?
- **a.** X-ray images are less expensive to produce.
- **b.** MRI involves placing a person inside a cylinder.
- **c.** Vibration of atoms is uncomfortable.
- **d.** MRI causes damage to cells.

CHAPTER 4

Food and Digestion

WEB ACTIVITY www.phschool.com

SECTION 1 Food and Energy

Discover Food Claims—Fact or Fiction?
Sharpen Your Skills Predicting
Real-World Lab Iron for Breakfast

Integrating Health

SECTION 2 Healthy Eating

Discover Do Snack Foods Contain Fat?

SECTION 3 The Digestive Process Begins

Discover How Can You Speed up Digestion?
Try This Modeling Peristalsis
Skills Lab As the Stomach Churns

PROJECT 4

What's for Lunch?

When you see fresh vegetables in a market, which kinds appeal to you? In the school cafeteria at lunch time, which foods do you select? When you're hungry and grab a snack, what do you choose? This chapter looks at foods and the process of digestion that goes on in your body. It also explains how your food choices affect your health. In this project, you'll take a close look at the foods you select each day.

Your Goal To compare your eating pattern to the recommendations in the Food Guide Pyramid.

To complete this project successfully, you must

- keep an accurate record of everything you eat and drink for three days
- create graphs to compare your eating pattern with the recommendations in the Food Guide Pyramid
- make changes, if needed, during another three-day period to bring your diet closer to the recommendations in the Food Guide Pyramid

Get Started Begin by deciding how to best keep an accurate, complete food log. How will you make sure you record everything you eat, including snacks and drinks? How will you decide which category each food falls into? How will you determine serving sizes? Prepare a plan for keeping a food log, and give it to your teacher for approval.

Check Your Progress You'll be working on this project as you study this chapter. To keep your project on track, look for Check Your Progress boxes at the following points.

Section 1 Review, page 133: Keep a food log for three days.

Section 2 Review, page 139: Create graphs to compare your food choices to the recommended number of servings.

Section 4 Review, page 151: Make changes to improve your diet.

Wrap Up At the end of the chapter (page 155), you'll prepare a written summary of what you've learned.

Take your pick! Local markets offer a wide choice of tasty fruits and vegetables.

SECTION 4 **Final Digestion and Absorption**

Discover **Which Surface Is Larger?**
Try This **Break Up!**

SECTION 1 Food and Energy

DISCOVER ACTIVITY

Food Claims—Fact or Fiction?

1. Examine the list of statements at the right. Copy the list onto a separate sheet of paper.
2. Next to each statement, write *agree* or *disagree.* Give a reason for your response.
3. Discuss your responses with a small group of classmates. Compare the reasons you gave for agreeing or disagreeing with each statement.

Fact or Fiction?

a. Athletes need more protein in their diets than other people do.
b. The only salt that a food contains is the salt that you have added to it.
c. As part of a healthy diet, everyone should take vitamin supplements.
d. You can go without water for longer than you can go without food.

Think It Over

Posing Questions List some other statements about nutrition that you have heard. How could you find out whether the statements are true?

GUIDE FOR READING

- **What are the six nutrients needed by the body?**
- **What is the function of water in the body?**

Reading Tip **As you read, create a table that includes the function and sources of each nutrient group.**

Imagine a Thanksgiving dinner—roast turkey on a platter, delicious stuffing, and lots of vegetables—an abundance of colors and aromas. Food is an important part of many happy occasions, of times shared with friends and family. Food is also essential. Every living thing needs food to stay alive.

Why You Need Food

Foods provide your body with materials for growing and for repairing tissues. Food also provides energy for everything you do—running, playing a musical instrument, reading, and even sleeping. By filling those needs, food enables your body to maintain homeostasis. Recall that homeostasis is the body's ability to keep a steady internal state in spite of changing external conditions. Suppose, for example, that you cut your finger. Food provides both the raw materials necessary to grow new skin and the energy that powers this growth.

Your body converts the foods you eat into nutrients. **Nutrients** (NOO tre unts) are the substances in food that provide the raw materials and energy the body needs to carry out all the essential processes. **There are six kinds of nutrients necessary for human health—carbohydrates, fats, proteins, vitamins, minerals, and water.**

INTEGRATING PHYSICS Carbohydrates, fats, and proteins all provide the body with energy. When nutrients are used by the body for energy, the amount of energy they release can be measured in units called calories. One **calorie** is the amount of energy needed to raise the temperature of one gram of water by one Celsius degree. Most foods contain many thousands of calories of energy. Scientists usually use the term *Calorie,* with a capital *C,* to measure the energy in foods. One Calorie is the same as 1,000 calories. For example, one serving of popcorn may contain 60 Calories, or 60,000 calories, of energy. The more Calories a food has, the more energy it contains.

You need to eat a certain number of Calories each day to meet your body's energy needs. This daily energy requirement depends on a person's level of physical activity. It also changes as a person grows and ages. Infants and small children grow very rapidly, so they generally have the highest energy needs. Your current growth and level of physical activity affect the number of Calories you need. The more active you are, the higher your energy needs are.

Carbohydrates

The nutrients called **carbohydrates** (kar boh HY drayts), which are composed of carbon, oxygen, and hydrogen, are a major source of energy. One gram of carbohydrate provides your body with four Calories of energy. Carbohydrates also provide the raw materials to make parts of cells. Based on their chemical structure, carbohydrates are divided into two groups, simple carbohydrates and complex carbohydrates.

Figure 1 Your body obtains energy from carbohydrates. The sugars in fruits are simple carbohydrates. Starch is a complex carbohydrate found in grains and other plant products.

Sharpen your Skills

Predicting

ACTIVITY

Obtain food samples from your teacher. Write a prediction stating whether each food contains starch. Then test your predictions. First, put on your apron. Then use a plastic dropper to add three drops of iodine to each food sample. **CAUTION:** *Iodine can stain skin and clothing. Handle it carefully.* If the iodine turns blue-black, starch is present. Which foods contain starch?

Simple Carbohydrates Simple carbohydrates are also known as sugars. There are many types of sugars. They are found naturally in fruits, milk, and some vegetables. Sugars are also added to foods such as cookies, candies, and soft drinks. One sugar, **glucose** (GLOO kohs), is the major source of energy for your body's cells. However, most foods do not contain large amounts of glucose. The body converts other types of sugars into glucose, the form of sugar the body can use.

Complex Carbohydrates Complex carbohydrates are made up of many sugar molecules linked together in a chain. Starch is a complex carbohydrate found in plant foods such as potatoes, rice, corn, and grain products, such as pasta, cereals, and bread. To use starch as an energy source, your body first breaks it down into smaller, individual sugar molecules. Only then can your body release the molecules' energy.

Like starch, **fiber** is a complex carbohydrate found in plant foods. However, unlike starch, fiber cannot be broken down into sugar molecules by your body. Instead, the fiber passes through the body and is eliminated. Because your body cannot digest it, fiber is not considered a nutrient. Fiber is an important part of the diet, however, because it helps keep the digestive system functioning properly. Fruits, vegetables, and nuts contain fiber. So do products made with whole grains, such as some breads and cereals.

Nutritionists recommend that 50 to 60 percent of the Calories in a diet come from carbohydrates. When choosing foods containing carbohydrates, it is better to eat more complex carbohydrates than simple carbohydrates. Sugars can give a quick burst of energy, but starches provide a more even, long-term energy source. In addition, foods that are high in starch usually contain a variety of other nutrients. Foods made with a lot of sugar, such as candy, cookies, and soft drinks, usually have few valuable nutrients.

☑ ***Checkpoint*** *What are the two types of carbohydrates? Give an example of each.*

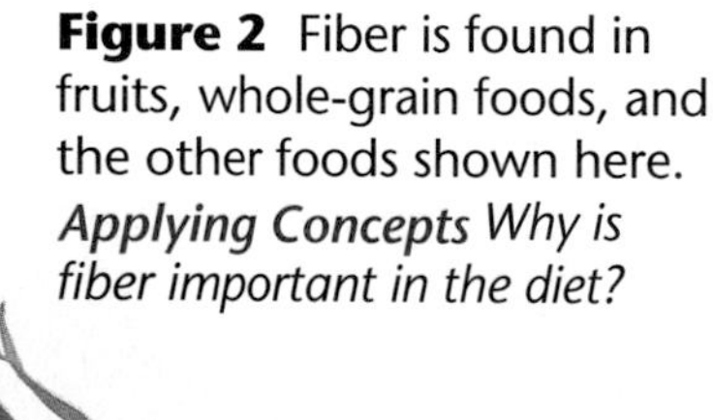

Figure 2 Fiber is found in fruits, whole-grain foods, and the other foods shown here. ***Applying Concepts*** *Why is fiber important in the diet?*

Figure 3 You obtain fats from foods such as steak, ice cream, and cooking oils.
Classifying *Which of these foods contain saturated fats?*

Fats

Like carbohydrates, **fats** are high-energy nutrients that are composed of carbon, oxygen, and hydrogen. However, fats contain more than twice as much energy as an equal amount of carbohydrates. In addition, fats perform other important functions. For example, they form part of the structure of cells. Fatty tissue also protects and supports your internal organs and acts as insulation to keep heat inside your body.

Fats are classified as either unsaturated fats or saturated fats, based on their chemical structure. **Unsaturated fats** are usually liquid at room temperature. Most oils, such as olive oil and canola oil, are unsaturated fats. Unsaturated fat is also found in some types of seafood, such as salmon. **Saturated fats** are usually solid at room temperature. Animal products, such as meat, dairy products, and egg yolks, contain relatively large amounts of saturated fat. Some oils, such as palm oil and coconut oil, are also high in saturated fat.

Foods that contain saturated fat often contain cholesterol as well. **Cholesterol** (kuh LES tur awl) is a waxy, fatlike substance found only in animal products. Like fats, cholesterol is an important part of your body's cells. But your liver makes all of the cholesterol your body needs. Therefore, cholesterol is not a necessary part of the diet.

Although people need some fats in their diet, they only need a small amount. Nutritionists recommend that no more than 30 percent of the Calories eaten each day come from fats. In particular, people should limit their intake of saturated fats and cholesterol. Extra fats and cholesterol in the diet can lead to a buildup of a fatty material in the blood vessels. This fatty buildup can cause heart disease. You will learn about the connections among fats, cholesterol, and heart disease in Chapter 5.

Math TOOLBOX

Calculating Percent

A percent (%) is a number compared to 100. For example, 30% means 30 out of 100.

Here is how to calculate the percent of Calories from fat in a person's diet. Suppose that a person eats a total of 2,000 Calories in one day. Of those Calories, 500 come from fats.

1. Write the comparison as a fraction:

$$\frac{500}{2{,}000}$$

2. Multiply the fraction by 100% to express it as a percent:

$$\frac{500}{2{,}000} \times \frac{100\%}{1} = 25\%$$

Calories from fat made up 25% of the person's diet that day.

Figure 4 Meats and these other foods are sources of protein.

Proteins

Proteins are nutrients that contain nitrogen as well as carbon, hydrogen, and oxygen. Proteins are needed for tissue growth and repair. They also play a part in chemical reactions within cells. Proteins can serve as a source of energy, but they are a less important source of energy than carbohydrates or fats. Foods that contain high amounts of protein include meat, poultry, fish, dairy products, nuts, beans, and lentils. About 12 percent of your daily Calorie intake should come from proteins.

Amino Acids Proteins are made up of small units called *INTEGRATING CHEMISTRY* **amino acids** (uh MEE noh), which are linked together chemically to form large protein molecules. Thousands of different proteins are built from only about 20 different amino acids. Your body can make about half of the amino acids it needs. The others, called essential amino acids, must come from the foods you eat.

Complete and Incomplete Proteins Proteins from animal sources, such as meat and eggs, are called complete proteins because they contain all the essential amino acids. Proteins from plant sources, such as beans, grains, and nuts, are called incomplete proteins because they are missing one or more essential amino acids. Different plant foods lack different amino acids. Therefore, to obtain all the essential amino acids from plant sources alone, people need to eat a variety of plant foods.

☑ *Checkpoint What is meant by the term* incomplete protein?

Vitamins

The life of a sailor in the 1700s could be difficult indeed. For one thing, sailors on long voyages ate hard, dry biscuits, salted meat, and not much else. In addition, many sailors developed a serious disease called scurvy. People with scurvy suffer from bleeding gums, stiff joints, and sores that do not heal.

Social Studies CONNECTION

Industry grew rapidly in the 1800s. During that time, many children of factory workers developed rickets, a condition in which the bones become soft. Rickets is caused by a lack of vitamin D. The main source of vitamin D is sunlight, which acts on skin cells to produce the vitamin.

Factory workers in the 1800s often lived in cities with dark, narrow streets. Air pollution from factories also blocked some sunlight. One researcher, Theobald A. Palm, wrote this statement in 1890: "It is in the narrow alleys, the haunts and playgrounds of the children of the poor, that this exclusion of sunlight is at its worst, and it is there that the victims of rickets are to be found in abundance."

In Your Journal

Write several questions that a newspaper reporter might have asked Dr. Palm about rickets among poor city residents. Then write the answers he might have given.

A Scottish doctor, James Lind, hypothesized that scurvy was the result of the sailors' poor diet. Lind divided sailors with scurvy into groups and fed different foods to each group. The sailors who were fed citrus fruits—oranges and lemons—quickly recovered from the disease. In 1754, Lind recommended that all sailors eat citrus fruits. When Lind's recommendations were finally carried out by the British Navy in 1795, scurvy disappeared from the navy.

Scurvy is caused by the lack of a nutrient called vitamin C. **Vitamins** act as helper molecules in a variety of chemical reactions within the body. The body needs only small amounts of vitamins. Figure 5 lists the vitamins necessary for health. The body can make a few of these vitamins. For example, bacteria that live in your intestines make small amounts of vitamin K.

Figure 5 Both fat-soluble vitamins and water-soluble vitamins are necessary to maintain health. ***Interpreting Charts*** *What foods provide a supply of both vitamins A and B_6?*

Essential Vitamins

Vitamin	Sources	Function
Fat-soluble		
A	Dairy products; eggs; liver; yellow, orange, and dark green vegetables; fruits	Maintains healthy skin, bones, teeth, and hair; aids vision in dim light
D	Fortified dairy products; fish; eggs; liver; made by skin cells in presence of sunlight	Maintains bones and teeth; helps in the use of calcium and phosphorus
E	Vegetable oils; margarine; green, leafy vegetables; whole-grain foods; seeds; nuts	Aids in maintenance of red blood cells
K	Green, leafy vegetables; milk; liver; made by bacteria in the intestines	Aids in blood clotting
Water-soluble		
B_1 (thiamin)	Pork; liver; whole-grain foods; legumes; nuts	Needed for breakdown of carbohydrates
B_2 (riboflavin)	Dairy products; eggs; leafy, green vegetables; whole-grain breads and cereals	Needed for normal growth
B_3 (niacin)	Many protein-rich foods; milk; eggs; meat; fish; whole-grain foods; nuts; peanut butter	Needed for release of energy
B_6 (pyridoxine)	Green and leafy vegetables; meats; fish; legumes; fruits; whole-grain foods	Helps in the breakdown of proteins, fats, and carbohydrates
B_{12}	Meats; fish; poultry; dairy products; eggs	Maintains healthy nervous system; needed for red blood cell formation
Biotin	Liver; meat; fish; eggs; legumes; bananas; melons	Aids in the release of energy
Folic acid	Leafy, green vegetables; legumes; seeds; liver	Needed for red blood cell formation
Pantothenic acid	Liver; meats; fish; eggs; whole-grain foods	Needed for the release of energy
C	Citrus fruits; tomatoes; potatoes; dark green vegetables; mangoes	Needed to form connective tissue and fight infection

However, people must obtain most vitamins from foods. If people eat a wide variety of foods, they will probably get enough of each vitamin. Most people do not need to take vitamin supplements.

Vitamins are classified as either fat-soluble or water-soluble. Fat-soluble vitamins dissolve in fat, and they are stored in fatty tissues in the body. Vitamins A, D, E, and K are all fat-soluble vitamins. Water-soluble vitamins dissolve in water and are not stored in the body. This fact makes it especially important to include sources of water-soluble vitamins—vitamin C and all the B vitamins—in your diet every day.

☑ **Checkpoint** *List the fat-soluble vitamins.*

Figure 6 Eating a variety of foods each day provides your body with the minerals it needs. ***Interpreting Charts*** *Which minerals play a role in regulating water levels in the body?*

Minerals

Like vitamins, minerals are needed by your body in small amounts. **Minerals** are nutrients that are not made by living things. They are present in soil and are absorbed by plants through their roots. You obtain minerals by eating plant foods or animals that have eaten plants. Figure 6 lists some minerals you

◀ Source of calcium

▼ Source of potassium

Source of sodium ▶

Essential Minerals

Mineral	Sources	Function
Calcium	Milk; cheese; dark green, leafy vegetables; tofu; legumes	Helps build bones and teeth; important for blood-clotting, nerve and muscle function
Chlorine	Table salt; soy sauce; processed foods	Helps maintain water balance; aids in digestion
Fluorine	Fluoridated drinking water; fish	Helps form bones and teeth
Iodine	Seafood; iodized salt	Makes up part of hormones that regulate the release of energy
Iron	Red meats; seafood; green, leafy vegetables; legumes; dried fruits	Forms an important part of red blood cells
Magnesium	Green, leafy vegetables; legumes; nuts; whole-grain foods	Needed for normal muscle and nerve function; helps in the release of energy
Phosphorus	Meat; poultry; eggs; fish; dairy products	Needed for healthy bones and teeth; helps in the release of energy
Potassium	Grains; fruits; vegetables; meat; fish	Helps maintain water balance; needed for normal muscle and nerve function
Sodium	Table salt; soy sauce; processed foods	Helps maintain water balance; needed for normal nerve function

need. As you know from Chapter 3, calcium is needed for strong bones and teeth. Iron is needed for the proper function of red blood cells.

Figure 7 Like all living things, you need water. Without regular water intake, your body cannot carry out the processes that keep you alive.

Water

Imagine that a boat is sinking. The people are getting into a lifeboat. They have room for one of the following: a bag of fruit, a can of meat, a loaf of bread, or a jug of water. Which item should they choose?

You might be surprised to learn that the lifeboat passengers should choose the water. Although people can probably survive for weeks without food, they will die within days without fresh water. Water is the most abundant substance in the body. It accounts for about 65 percent of the average person's body weight.

Water is the most important nutrient because the body's vital processes—including chemical reactions such as the breakdown of nutrients—take place in water. Water makes up most of the body's fluids, including blood. Nutrients and other important substances are carried throughout the body dissolved in the watery part of the blood. Your body also needs water to produce perspiration.

Under normal conditions, you need to take in about 2 liters of water every day. You can do this by drinking water and other beverages, and by eating foods with lots of water, such as fruits and vegetables. If the weather is hot or you are exercising, you need to drink even more to replace the water that you lose in sweat.

Section 1 Review

1. List the six nutrients that are needed by the body.
2. Give three reasons why water is necessary for the body to function.
3. Why should you eat more complex carbohydrates than simple carbohydrates?
4. What is the difference between fat-soluble vitamins and water-soluble vitamins?
5. **Thinking Critically Applying Concepts** Why is it especially important that vegetarians eat a varied diet?

Check Your Progress

CHAPTER PROJECT 4

By now, you should have given your teacher your plan for keeping your food log. Adjust the plan as your teacher suggests. Then start your three days of record-keeping. If possible, your record-keeping should span two weekdays and one weekend day. Be sure to keep an accurate record of all the foods and beverages you consume. (*Hint:* Either make your log portable, or plan a method for recording your food intake when you're away from home.)

Real-World Lab

You, the Consumer

Iron for Breakfast

Have you ever looked at the nutrition facts on a cereal box? Some of the listed nutrients occur naturally in the cereal. Others are added as the cereal is processed. In this lab, you will look for evidence that extra iron has been added to some cereals.

Problem

How can you test whether iron has been added to cereals?

Skills Focus

observing, predicting, interpreting data

Materials

long bar magnet
white paper towels
instant oatmeal
watch or clock
wooden dowel
2 dry breakfast cereals
3 sealable plastic freezer bags
plastic jar with sealable cover
balance
plastic spoon
warm water

Procedure

1. Read the nutrition facts listed on the packages of the cereals that you'll be testing. Record the percentage of iron listed for each of the cereals.
2. Put a paper towel on the pan of a balance. Use a spoon to measure out 50 grams of instant oatmeal. **CAUTION:** *Do not eat any of the cereals in this lab.*
3. Place the oatmeal in a plastic bag. Push down gently on the bag to remove most of the air, then seal the bag. Roll a dowel over the oatmeal repeatedly to crush it into a fine powder.

4. Pour the powdered oatmeal into a plastic jar. Add water to the jar so that the water line is about five centimeters above the oatmeal.
5. Stir the mixture with a bar magnet for about five minutes.
6. Rinse the bar magnet gently in clear water. Wipe the magnet with a white paper towel. Observe the particles on the paper towel. Record your observations.
7. Repeat Steps 2 through 6 with your other cereal samples.

Analyze and Conclude

1. Describe the material you saw on the paper towel. What evidence do you have that this material is iron?
2. Which sample appeared to have the most added iron? The least? Were those results consistent with the listed amounts?
3. Why is it likely that any iron metal present in the cereal was added during the processing?
4. What roles does iron play in the body?
5. **Apply** Why might adding iron to breakfast cereal be a good way to ensure that children receive an adequate amount of that mineral?

More to Explore

Read the labels on five snack foods. Make a bar graph showing their iron content.

Section 2 Healthy Eating

DISCOVER — ACTIVITY

Do Snack Foods Contain Fat?

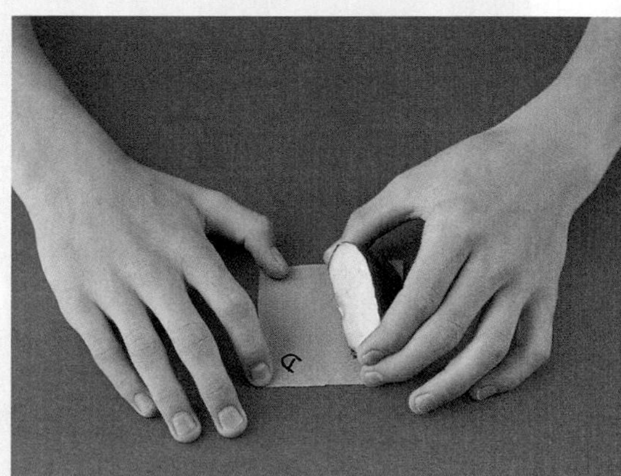

1. Cut four small squares from a brown paper bag. Label them *A, B, C,* and *D.*
2. Rub some crushed potato chips on square A. **CAUTION:** *Do not eat any of the foods in this activity.*
3. Repeat Step 2 using crushed pretzels (on square B), a piece of chocolate (on square C), and an apple slice (on square D).
4. Remove any food. Allow the paper squares to dry.
5. Note which squares have spots of oil on them.

Think It Over

Classifying If a food contains fat, it will leave oily spots on the brown paper. What does this tell you about the foods you tested?

GUIDE FOR READING

- **How can the Food Guide Pyramid help you plan a healthy diet?**
- **What kind of information is included on food labels?**

Reading Tip **Before you read, preview *Exploring the Food Guide Pyramid* on page 137. Write a list of questions about the pyramid. As you read, try to answer your questions.**

What does healthy eating mean to you? Eating more fresh fruits and vegetables? Not skipping breakfast? Cutting down on soft drinks and chips? You have just learned about the six types of nutrients—carbohydrates, fats, proteins, vitamins, minerals, and water—that are part of a healthy diet. You may now be wondering how you can use this information to make healthful changes in your diet.

With so many foods available, it may seem more difficult, not easier, to establish a healthful diet. Luckily, nutritionists have developed some aids—the Food Guide Pyramid and food labels.

Figure 8 Fruits and vegetables are essential parts of a healthy diet. Some people enjoy picking these foods right off the plant.

The Food Guide Pyramid

The **Food Guide Pyramid** was developed by nutritionists to help people plan a healthy diet. **The Food Guide Pyramid classifies foods into six groups. It also indicates how many servings from each group should be eaten every day to maintain a healthy diet.** You can combine the advice within the pyramid with knowledge of your own food preferences. By doing this, you can have a healthy diet containing foods you like.

You can see the six food groups in *Exploring the Food Guide Pyramid.* Notice that the food group at the base of the pyramid includes foods made from grains, such as bread, cereal, rice, and pasta. This bottom level is the widest part of the pyramid. The large size indicates that these foods should make up the largest part of the diet.

Figure 9 If you are very active, you need to eat more servings within the ranges specified for each food group in the Food Guide Pyramid.

The second level in the pyramid is made of two food groups, the Fruit group and the Vegetable group. Notice that this level is not as wide as the bottom level. This size difference indicates that people need fewer servings of these foods than of foods from the bottom level. The third level of the pyramid contains the Milk, Yogurt, and Cheese group, and the Meat, Poultry, Fish, Dry Beans, Eggs, and Nuts group. People need still smaller amounts of food from the third level.

At the top of the pyramid are foods containing large amounts of fat, sugar, or both. Notice that this is the smallest part of the pyramid. The small size indicates that intake of these foods should be limited. There is a good reason for this advice. Foods in the other groups already contain fats and sugars. Limiting intake of *additional* fats and sugars can help you prevent heart disease and other problems.

☑ ***Checkpoint*** *What types of foods should make up the largest portion of a person's diet?*

Food Labels

After a long day, you and your friends stop into a store on your way home from school. What snack should you buy? How can you make a wise choice? One thing you can do is to read the information provided on food labels. The United States Food and Drug Administration (FDA) requires that all food items except meat, poultry, fresh vegetables, and fresh fruit must be labeled with specific nutritional information.

EXPLORING *the Food Guide Pyramid*

The Food Guide Pyramid recommends the number of servings that a person should eat each day from six food groups. Note that each number of servings is listed as a range. Active, growing teenagers may need to eat the larger number of servings for each group.

Fats, Oils, and Sweets (Use sparingly.) Soft drinks, candy, ice cream, mayonnaise, and other foods in this group have few valuable nutrients. In addition, these foods are high in Calories. They should be eaten only in small quantities.

Milk, Yogurt, and Cheese Group (2–3 servings) Milk and other dairy products are rich in proteins, carbohydrates, vitamins, and minerals. Try to select low-fat dairy foods, such as low-fat milk.

Meat, Poultry, Fish, Dry Beans, Eggs, and Nuts Group (2–3 servings) These foods are high in protein. They also supply vitamins and minerals. Since eggs, nuts, and some meats are high in fat, they should be eaten sparingly.

Vegetable Group (3–5 servings) Vegetables are low-fat sources of carbohydrates, fiber, vitamins, and minerals.

Fruit Group (2–4 servings) Fruits are good sources of carbohydrates, fiber, vitamins, and water.

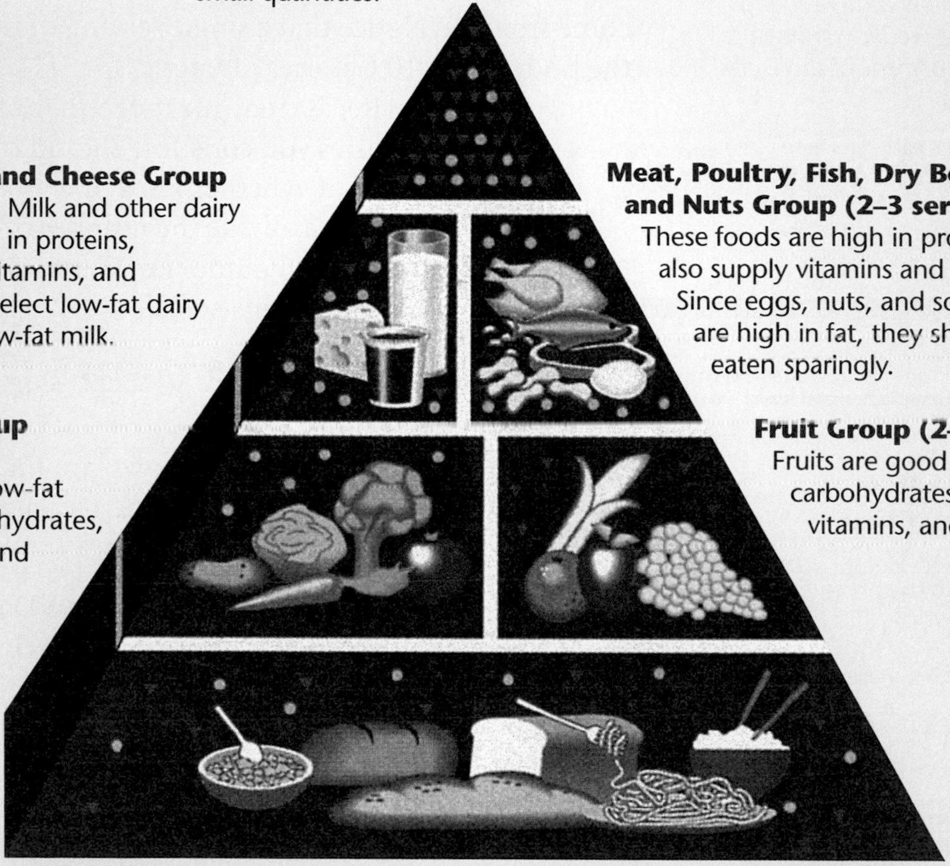

Bread, Cereal, Rice, and Pasta Group (6–11 servings) The foods at the base of the pyramid are rich in complex carbohydrates and also provide proteins, fiber, vitamins, and some minerals.

● *Fat (naturally occurring and added)*

▲ *Sugars (naturally occurring and added)*

Figure 10 shows a food label that might appear on a box of cereal. Refer to that label as you read about some of the important nutritional information it contains.

Serving Size Notice that the serving size and the number of servings in the container are listed at the top of the label. The FDA has established standard serving sizes for all types of foods. This means that all containers of ice cream, for example, use the same serving size on their labels. The information on the rest of the label, including Calorie counts and nutrient content, is based on the serving size. Therefore, if you eat a portion that's twice as large as the serving size, you'll consume twice the number of Calories and nutrients listed on the label.

Figure 10 By law, specific nutritional information must be listed on food labels. ***Calculating*** *How many servings of this product would you have to eat to get 90 percent of the Daily Value for iron?*

Nutrition Facts

Serving Size	1 cup (30g)
Servings Per Container	About 10
Amount Per Serving	
Calories 110	Calories from Fat 15
	% Daily Value*
Total Fat 2g	**3%**
Saturated Fat 0g	**0%**
Cholesterol 0mg	**0%**
Sodium 280mg	**12%**
Total Carbohydrate 22g	**7%**
Dietary Fiber 3g	**12%**
Sugars 1g	
Protein 3g	

Vitamin A	10%	Vitamin C	20%
Calcium	4%	Iron	45%

* Percent Daily Values are based on a 2,000 Calorie diet. Your daily values may be higher or lower depending on your caloric needs:

	Calories	2,000	2,500
Total Fat	Less than	65g	80g
Sat. Fat	Less than	20g	25g
Cholesterol	Less than	300mg	300mg
Sodium	Less than	2,400mg	2,400mg
Total Carbohydrate		300g	375g
Fiber		25g	30g

Calories per gram:
Fat 9 • Carbohydrate 4 • Protein 4

Ingredients: Whole grain oats, sugar, salt, milled corn, oat fiber, dried whey, hone[illegible] almonds[illegible]

Calories from Fat The next item on the food label is the number of Calories in a serving and the number of Calories that come from fat. Notice that a single serving of this cereal supplies the body with 110 Calories of energy.

Recall that no more than 30 percent of the Calories you consume should come from fats. To calculate whether a specific food falls within this guideline, divide the number of Calories from fat by the total number of Calories, then multiply by 100%. For this cereal,

$$\frac{15}{110} \times \frac{100\%}{1} = 13.6\%.$$

That number shows you that a serving of this cereal is well within the recommended limits for fat intake.

Daily Values Locate the % Daily Value column on the label. The **Percent Daily Value** indicates how the nutritional content of one serving fits into the diet of a person who consumes a total of 2,000 Calories a day. One serving of this cereal contains 280 milligrams of sodium. That's 12 percent of the total amount of sodium a person should consume in one day.

As you have learned, the number of Calories you need daily depends on your age, size, and level of activity. An active teenager may require 2,500 Calories or more each day. If your needs exceed 2,000 Calories, you should take in more of each nutrient in your daily diet. Some food labels include a list of the nutrient needs for both a 2,000-Calorie and a 2,500-Calorie diet.

Ingredients Packaged foods, such as crackers and soup mixes, usually contain a mixture of ingredients. The food label lists those ingredients in order by weight, starting with the main ingredient. In a breakfast cereal, for example, that may be corn, oats, rice, or wheat. Often, sugar and salt are added for flavor. The list can alert you to substances that have been added to a food to improve its flavor or color, or to keep it from spoiling. In addition, some people can become sick or break out in a rash if they eat certain substances. By reading ingredients lists, people can avoid foods that contain those substances.

Using Food Labels You can use food labels to help you make healthful food choices. **Food labels allow you to evaluate a single food as well as to compare the nutritional value of two foods.** Suppose you are shopping for breakfast cereals. By reading the labels, you might find that one cereal contains little fat and a high percentage of the Daily Value for valuable nutrients such as complex carbohydrates and several vitamins. Another cereal might have fewer complex carbohydrates and vitamins and contain significant amounts of fat. You can see that the first cereal would be a better choice as a regular breakfast food. If you really enjoy the other cereal, however, you might make it an occasional treat rather than an everyday choice.

Figure 11 Food labels allow you to compare the nutritional content of similar kinds of foods.

Section 2 Review

1. What information does the Food Guide Pyramid provide? Into how many groups are foods classified?
2. Explain how food labels can help a person make healthy food choices.
3. Why are foods in the Bread, Cereal, Rice, and Pasta group placed at the bottom of the Food Guide Pyramid?
4. **Thinking Critically Applying Concepts** Why might a runner need more servings from the Bread, Cereal, Rice, and Pasta group than a less active person?

CHAPTER PROJECT 4

Check Your Progress

By this point, you should have completed three full days of record keeping. Now create bar graphs to compare your food intake to the recommended numbers of servings in the Food Guide Pyramid. Analyze your graphs to identify changes you could make in your diet.

SECTION 3 The Digestive Process Begins

DISCOVER ACTIVITY

How Can You Speed up Digestion?

1. Obtain two plastic jars with lids. Fill the jars with equal amounts of water.
2. At the same time, place a whole sugar cube into one jar. Place a crushed sugar cube into the other jar.
3. Fasten the lids on the jars. Holding one jar in each hand, shake the two jars gently and equally.
4. Place the jars on a flat surface. Observe whether the whole cube or the crushed cube dissolves faster.

Think It Over

Predicting Use the results of this activity to predict which would take longer to digest: a large piece of food or one that has been cut up into many small pieces. Explain your answer.

GUIDE FOR READING

- **What general functions are carried out in the digestive system?**

Reading Tip **Before you read, preview the headings in this section. Predict the functions of the mouth, the esophagus, and the stomach.**

In June of 1822, nineteen-year-old Alexis St. Martin was wounded in the stomach while hunting. William Beaumont, a doctor with the United States Army, saved St. Martin's life. However, the wound left an opening in St. Martin's stomach that never closed completely. Beaumont realized that by looking through the opening, he could observe what was happening inside St. Martin's stomach.

Beaumont observed that milk changed chemically inside the stomach. He hypothesized that chemical reactions inside the stomach broke down foods into smaller particles. To test his hypothesis, Beaumont removed liquid from St. Martin's stomach. He had the liquid analyzed to determine what materials it contained. The stomach liquid contained an acid that could break down foods into simpler substances.

Dr. William Beaumont ▼

Functions of the Digestive System

Beaumont's observations helped scientists understand the role of the stomach in the digestive system. The digestive system has three main functions. **First, it breaks down food into molecules the body can use. Then, the molecules are absorbed into the blood and carried throughout the body. Finally, wastes are eliminated from the body.**

The process by which your body breaks down food into small nutrient molecules is called **digestion.** There are two kinds of digestion—mechanical and chemical. In mechanical digestion, foods are physically broken down into smaller pieces. Mechanical digestion occurs when you bite into a sandwich and chew it into small pieces. In chemical digestion, chemicals produced by the body break foods into their smaller chemical building blocks. For example, the starch in bread is broken down into individual sugar molecules.

After your food is digested, the molecules are ready to be transported throughout your body. **Absorption** (ab SAWRP shun) is the process by which nutrient molecules pass through the wall of your digestive system into your blood. Materials that are not absorbed, such as fiber, are eliminated from the body as wastes.

Figure 12 shows the organs of the digestive system, which is about nine meters long from beginning to end. As food moves through the digestive system, the processes of digestion, absorption, and elimination occur one after the other in an efficient, continuous process.

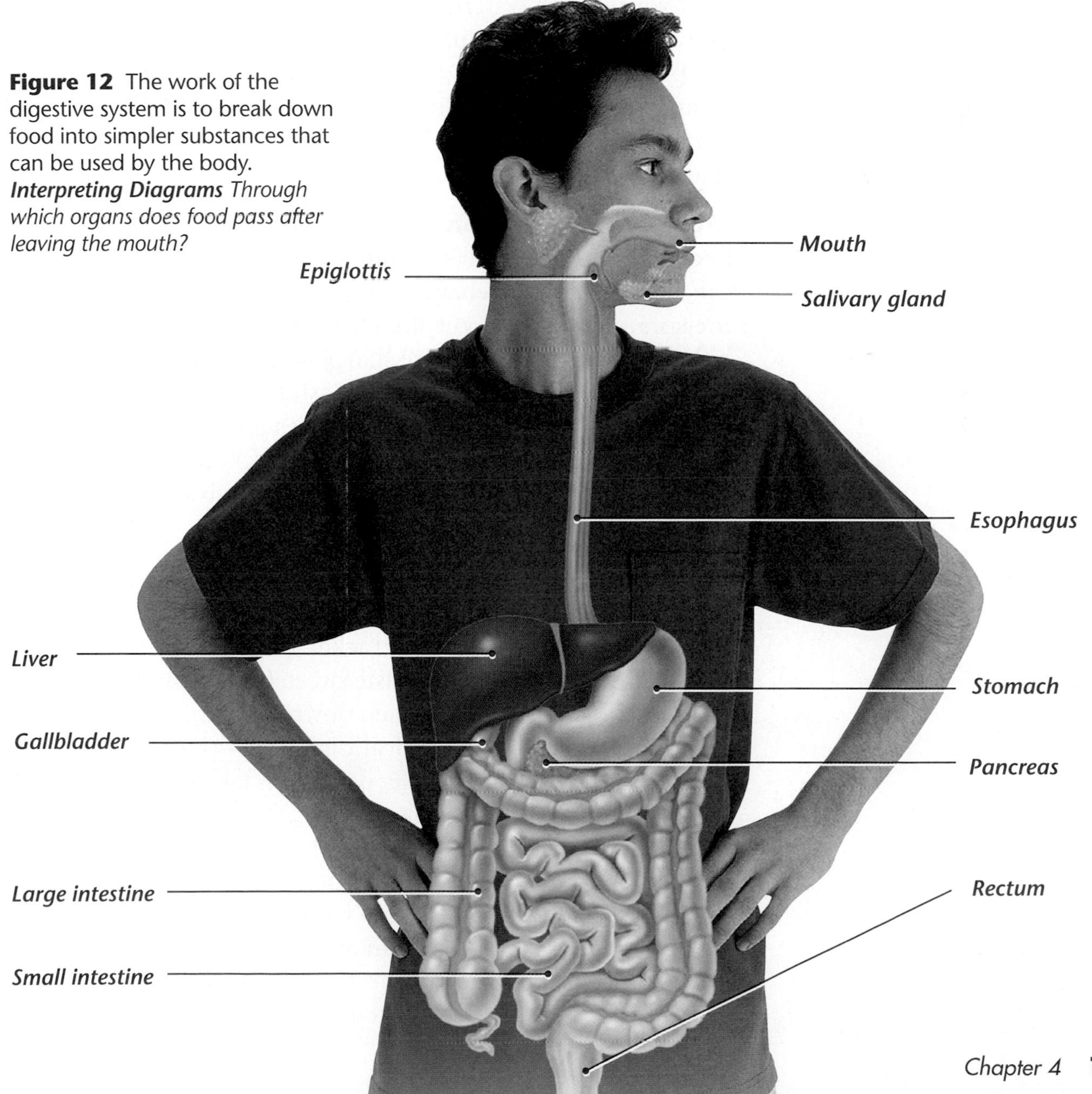

Figure 12 The work of the digestive system is to break down food into simpler substances that can be used by the body. ***Interpreting Diagrams*** *Through which organs does food pass after leaving the mouth?*

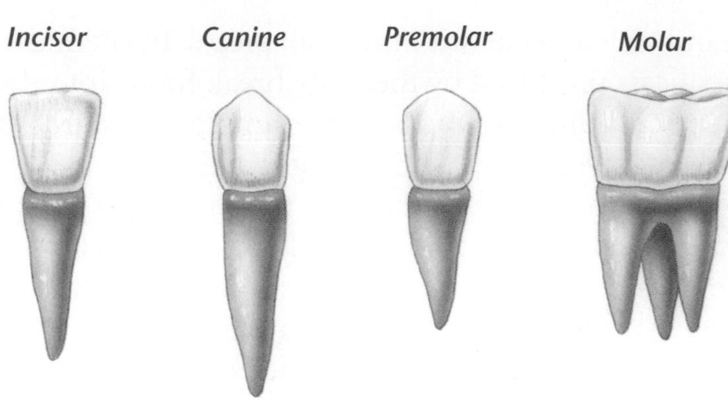

Figure 13 Mechanical digestion begins in the mouth, where the teeth cut and tear food into smaller pieces. ***Observing*** *Which teeth are specialized for biting into a juicy apple?*

The Mouth

Have you ever walked past a bakery or restaurant and noticed your mouth watering? Smelling or even just thinking about food when you're hungry is enough to start your mouth watering. This response isn't accidental. Your body is responding to hunger and thoughts of food by preparing for the delicious meal it expects. The fluid released when your mouth waters is called **saliva** (suh LY vuh). Saliva plays an important role in both the mechanical and chemical digestive processes that take place in the mouth.

Mechanical Digestion The process of mechanical digestion begins as you take your first bite of food. Your teeth carry out the first stage of mechanical digestion. Your center teeth, or incisors (in SY zurz), cut the food into bite-sized pieces. On either side of the incisors are sharp, pointy teeth called canines (KAY nynz). These teeth tear and slash the food in your mouth into smaller pieces. Behind the canines are the premolars and molars, which crush and grind the food. As the teeth do their work, saliva mixes with the pieces of food, moistening them into one slippery mass.

Chemical Digestion Like mechanical digestion, chemical *INTEGRATING CHEMISTRY* digestion begins in the mouth. If you take a bite of a cracker and roll it around your mouth, the cracker begins to taste sweet. It tastes sweet because a chemical in the saliva has broken down the starch in the cracker into sugar molecules. Chemical digestion—the breakdown of complex molecules into simpler ones—has taken place. Chemical digestion is accomplished by enzymes. An **enzyme** is a protein that speeds up chemical reactions in the body. The chemical in saliva that digests starch is an enzyme. Your body produces many different enzymes. Each enzyme has a specific chemical shape. Its shape enables it to take part in only one kind of chemical reaction. For example, the enzyme that breaks down starch into sugars cannot break down proteins into amino acids.

The Esophagus

If you've ever choked on food, someone may have said that your food "went down the wrong way." That's because there are two openings at the back of your mouth. One opening leads to your windpipe, which carries air into your lungs. Usually, your body keeps food out of your windpipe. As you swallow, muscles in your throat move the food downward. While this happens, a flap of tissue called the **epiglottis** (ep uh GLAHT is) seals off your windpipe, preventing the food from entering. As you swallow, food goes into the **esophagus** (ih SAHF uh gus), a muscular tube that connects the mouth to the stomach. The esophagus is lined with mucus. **Mucus** is a thick, slippery substance produced by the body. In the digestive system, mucus makes food easier to swallow and to be moved along.

Food remains in the esophagus for only about 10 seconds. After food enters the esophagus, contractions of smooth muscles push the food toward the stomach. These involuntary waves of muscle contraction are called **peristalsis** (pehr ih STAWL sis). The action of peristalsis is shown in Figure 14. Peristalsis also occurs in the stomach and farther down the digestive system. These muscular waves keep food moving in one direction.

☑ ***Checkpoint*** *How is food prevented from entering the windpipe?*

Modeling Peristalsis

ACTIVITY

1. Obtain a clear, flexible plastic straw.
2. Put on your goggles. Hold the straw vertically and insert a small bead into the top of the straw. The bead should fit snugly into the straw. Do not blow into the straw.
3. Pinch the straw above the bead so that the bead begins to move down the length of the tubing.
4. Repeat Step 3 until the bead exits the straw.

Making Models How does this action compare with peristalsis? What do the bead and the straw represent in this model?

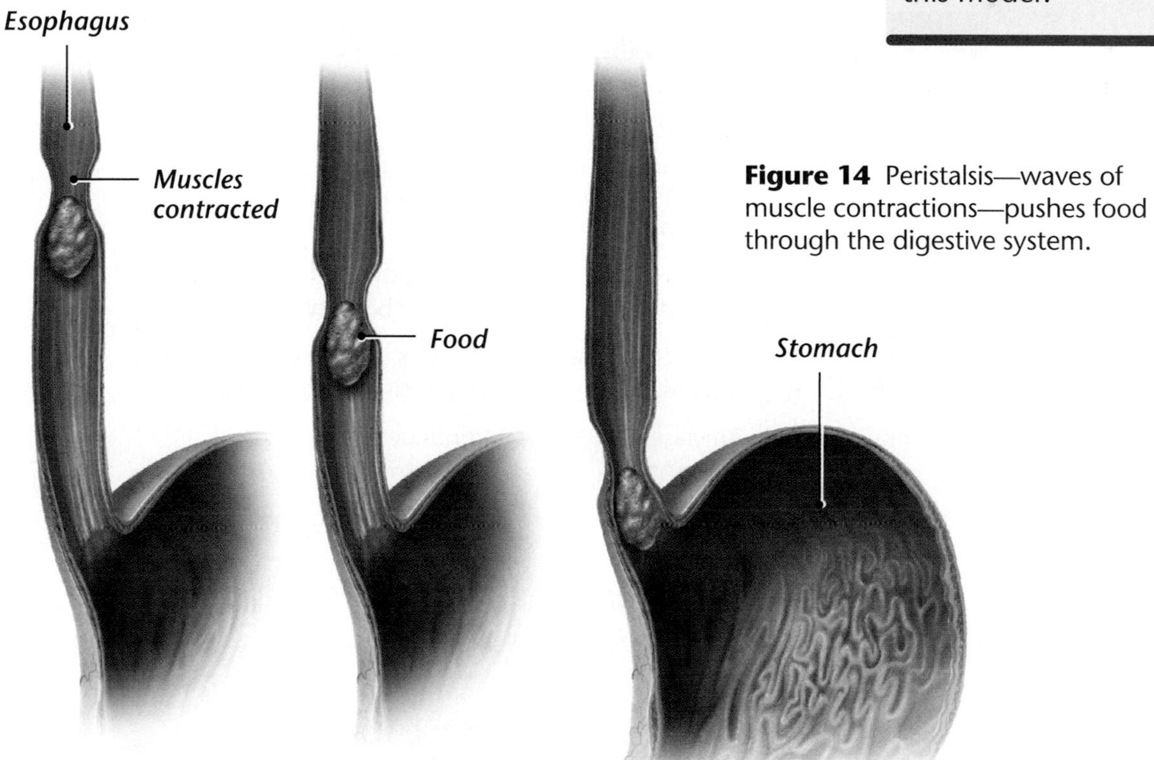

Figure 14 Peristalsis—waves of muscle contractions—pushes food through the digestive system.

The Stomach

When food leaves the esophagus, it enters the **stomach,** a J-shaped, muscular pouch located in the abdomen. As you eat, your stomach expands to hold all of the food that you swallow. An average adult's stomach holds about 2 liters of food.

Most mechanical digestion occurs in the stomach. Three strong layers of muscle contract to produce a churning motion. This action squeezes the food, mixing it with fluids in somewhat the same way that clothes and soapy water are mixed in a washing machine.

INTEGRATING CHEMISTRY While mechanical digestion is taking place, so too is chemical digestion. The churning of the stomach mixes food with digestive juice, a fluid produced by cells in the lining of the stomach.

Digestive juice contains the enzyme pepsin. Pepsin chemically digests the proteins in your food, breaking them down into amino acids. Digestive juice also contains hydrochloric acid, a very strong acid. This acid would burn a hole in clothes if it were spilled on them. Without this strong acid, however, your stomach could not function properly. First, pepsin works best in an acid environment. Second, the acid kills many bacteria that you swallow along with your food.

Since the acid is so strong, you may wonder why it doesn't burn a hole in your stomach. The reason is that digestive juice

Figure 15 As food passes through the digestive system, the digestive juices gradually break down large food molecules into smaller molecules. ***Interpreting Charts*** *Which enzymes aid in protein digestion?*

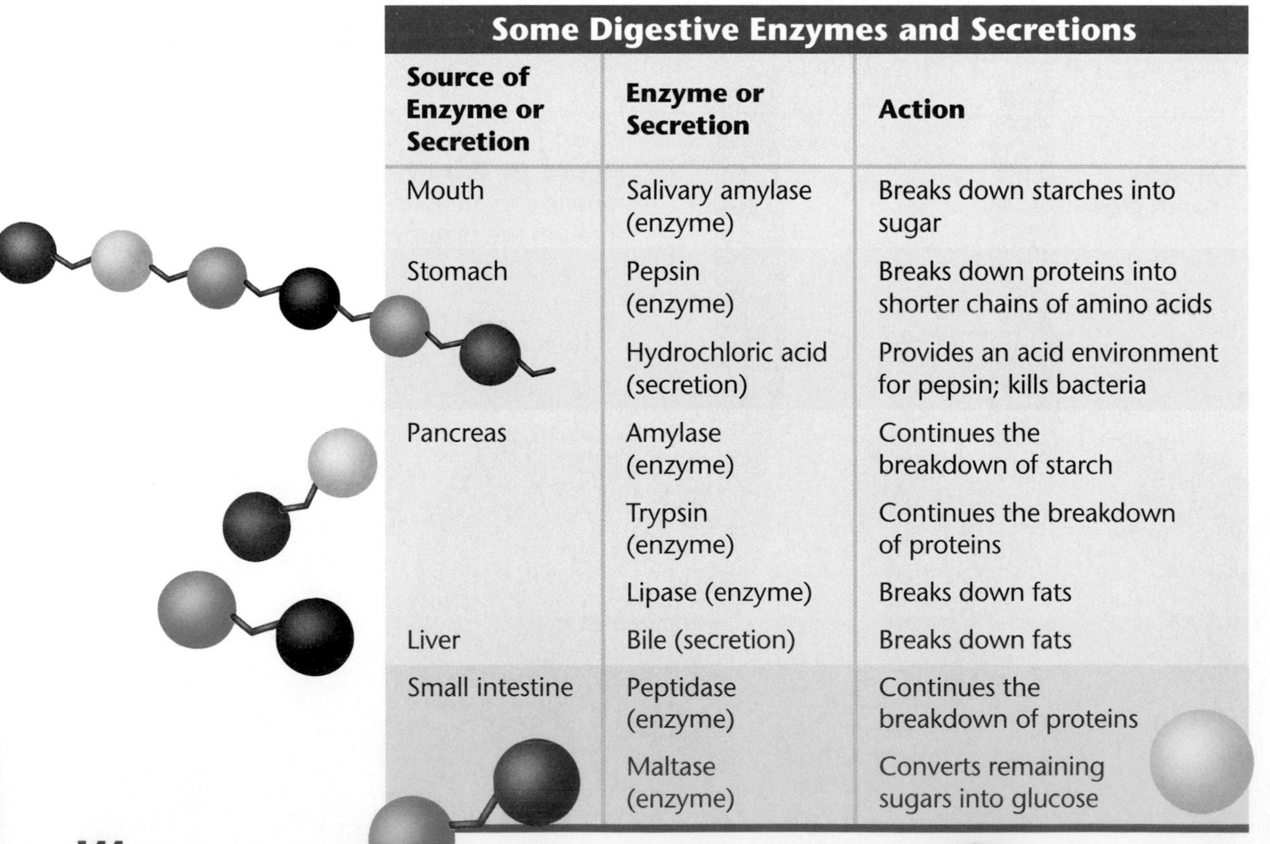

Some Digestive Enzymes and Secretions

Source of Enzyme or Secretion	Enzyme or Secretion	Action
Mouth	Salivary amylase (enzyme)	Breaks down starches into sugar
Stomach	Pepsin (enzyme)	Breaks down proteins into shorter chains of amino acids
	Hydrochloric acid (secretion)	Provides an acid environment for pepsin; kills bacteria
Pancreas	Amylase (enzyme)	Continues the breakdown of starch
	Trypsin (enzyme)	Continues the breakdown of proteins
	Lipase (enzyme)	Breaks down fats
Liver	Bile (secretion)	Breaks down fats
Small intestine	Peptidase (enzyme)	Continues the breakdown of proteins
	Maltase (enzyme)	Converts remaining sugars into glucose

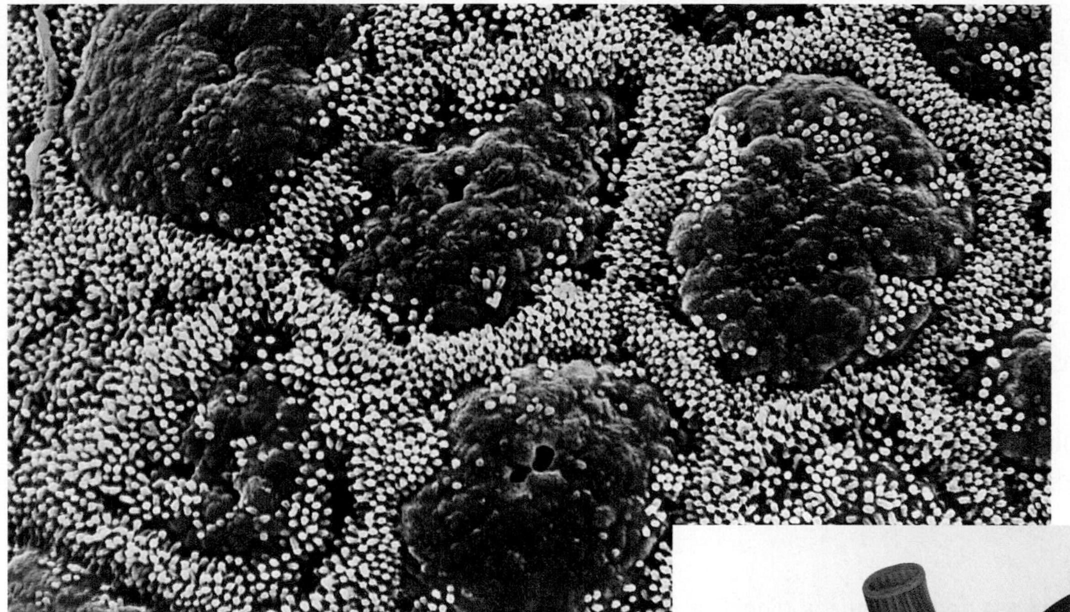

Figure 16 The stomach walls (left) produce mucus, shown here in yellow. Mucus protects the stomach from its own acid and enzymes. The stomach has powerful muscles (below) that help grind up food.

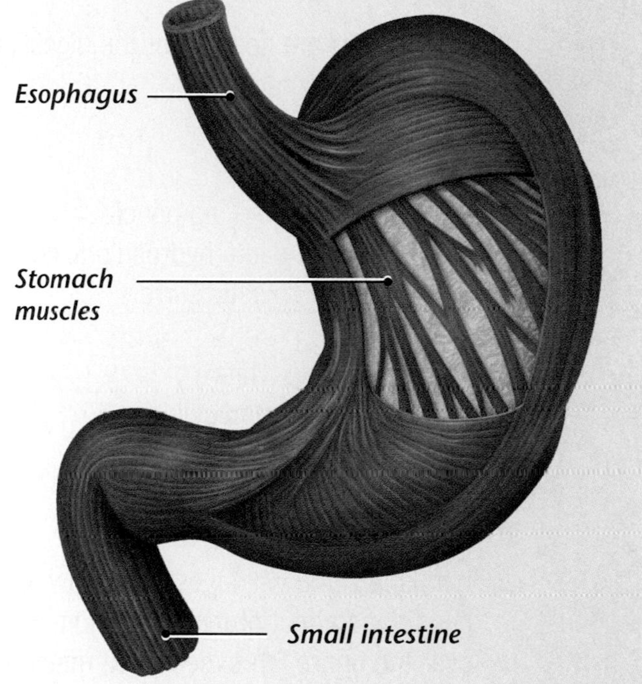

also contains mucus, which coats and protects the lining of your stomach. In addition, the cells that line the stomach are quickly replaced when they are damaged or worn out.

Food remains in the stomach until all of the solid material has been broken down into liquid form. A few hours after you finish eating, the stomach completes mechanical digestion of the food. By that time, most of the proteins have been chemically digested into shorter chains of amino acids. The food, now a thick liquid, is released into the next part of the digestive system. That is where final chemical digestion and absorption will take place.

Section 3 Review

1. List the functions of the digestive system.
2. What role does saliva play in digestion?
3. Describe peristalsis and explain its function in the digestive system.
4. What is the function of pepsin?
5. **Thinking Critically Predicting** If your stomach could no longer produce acid, how do you think that would affect digestion?

Science at Home

Explain to your family what happens when people choke on food. With your family, find out how to recognize when a person is choking and what to do to help the person. Learn about the Heimlich maneuver and how it is used to help someone who is choking.

Skills Lab

Drawing Conclusions

AS THE STOMACH CHURNS

The proteins you eat are constructed of large, complex molecules. Your body begins to break down those complex molecules in the stomach. In this lab, you will draw conclusions about the process by which proteins are digested.

Problem

What conditions are needed for the digestion of proteins in the stomach?

Materials

test tube rack
pepsin
water
litmus paper
cubes of boiled egg white
10-mL plastic graduated cylinder
4 test tubes with stoppers
marking pencil
dilute hydrochloric acid
plastic stirrers

Procedure   

1. In this lab, you will investigate how acidic conditions affect protein digestion. Read over the entire lab to see what materials you will be testing. Write a prediction stating which conditions you think will speed up protein digestion. Then copy the data table into your notebook.
2. Label four test tubes *A, B, C,* and *D* and place them in a test tube rack.
3. In this lab, the protein you will test is boiled egg white, which has been cut into cubes about 1 cm on each side. Add 3 cubes to each test tube. Note and record the size and overall appearance of the cubes in each test tube. **CAUTION:** *Do not put any egg white into your mouth.*
4. Use a graduated cylinder to add 10 mL of the enzyme pepsin to test tube A. Observe the egg white cubes to determine whether an immediate reaction takes place. Record your observations under *Day 1* in your data table. If no changes occur, write "no immediate reaction."
5. Use a clean graduated cylinder to add 5 mL of pepsin to test tube B. Then rinse the graduated cylinder and add 5 mL of water to test tube B. Observe whether or not an immediate reaction takes place.
6. Use a clean graduated cylinder to add 10 mL of hydrochloric acid to test tube C. Observe whether or not an immediate reaction takes place. **CAUTION:** *Hydrochloric acid can burn skin and clothing. Avoid direct contact with it. Wash any splashes or spills with plenty of water, and notify your teacher.*

DATA TABLE

Test Tube	Egg White Appearance		Litmus Color	
	Day 1	Day 2	Day 1	Day 2
A				
B				
C				
D				

7. Use a clean graduated cylinder to add 5 mL of pepsin to test tube D. Then rinse the graduated cylinder and add 5 mL of hydrochloric acid to test tube D. Observe whether or not an immediate reaction takes place. Record your observations.
8. Obtain four strips of blue litmus paper. (Blue litmus paper turns pink in the presence of an acid.) Dip a clean plastic stirrer into the solution in each test tube, and then touch the stirrer to a piece of litmus paper. Observe what happens to the litmus paper. Record your observations.
9. Insert stoppers in the four test tubes and store the test tube rack as directed by your teacher.
10. The next day, examine the contents of each test tube. Note any changes in the size and overall appearance of the egg white cubes. Then test each solution with litmus paper. Record your observations in your data table.

Analyze and Conclude

1. Which material(s) were the best at digesting the egg white? What observations enabled you to determine this?
2. Do you think that the chemical digestion of protein in food is a fast reaction or a slow one? Explain.
3. What did this lab demonstrate about the ability of pepsin to digest protein?
4. Why was it important that the cubes of egg white all be about the same size?
5. **Think About It** How did test tubes A and C help you draw conclusions about protein digestion in this investigation?

Design an Experiment

Design a way to test whether protein digestion is affected by the size of the food pieces. Write down the hypothesis that you will test. Then create a data table for recording your observations. Obtain your teacher's permission before carrying out your plan.

Final Digestion and Absorption

Discover — Activity

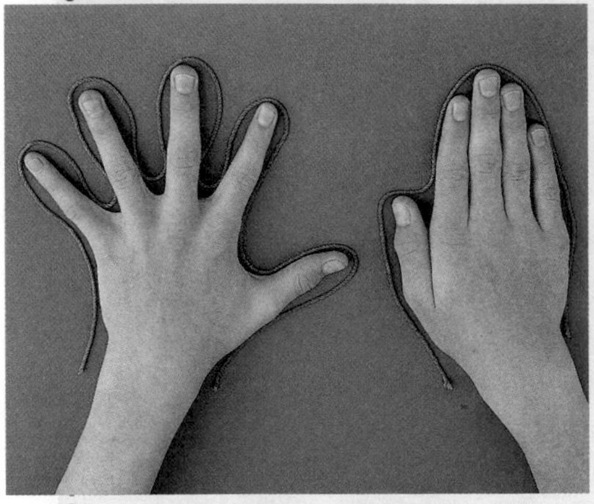

Which Surface Is Larger?

1. Work with a partner to carry out this investigation.
2. Begin by placing your hand palm-side down on a table. Keep your thumb and fingers tightly together. Lay string along the outline of your hand. Have your partner help you determine how long a string you need to outline your hand.
3. Use a metric ruler to measure the length of that string.

Think It Over

Predicting How long would you expect your hand outline to be if you spread out your thumb and fingers? Use string to test your prediction. Compare the two string lengths.

GUIDE FOR READING

- **What roles do the small intestine and large intestine play in digestion?**

Reading Tip **As you read, create a table with the headings *Small Intestine, Liver, Pancreas,* and *Large Intestine.* Under each heading, list that organ's digestive function.**

Have you ever been part of a huge crowd attending a concert or sports event? Barriers and passageways often guide people in the right direction.Ticket takers make sure that only those with tickets get in, and that they enter in an orderly fashion.

In some ways, the stomach can be thought of as the "ticket taker" of the digestive system. Once the food has been changed into a thick liquid, the stomach releases a little liquid at a time into the next part of the digestive system. This slow, smooth passage of food through the digestive system ensures that digestion and absorption take place smoothly.

The Small Intestine

After the thick liquid leaves the stomach, it enters the small intestine. The **small intestine** is the part of the digestive system where most of the chemical digestion takes place. If you look back at Figure 12, you may wonder how the small intestine got its name. After all, at about 6 meters—longer than some full-sized cars—it makes up two thirds of the digestive system. The small intestine was named for its small diameter. It is about two to three centimeters wide, about half the diameter of the large intestine.

When food reaches the small intestine, it has already been mechanically digested into a thick liquid. But chemical digestion has just begun. Although starches and proteins have been partially broken down, fats haven't been digested at all. **Almost all chemical digestion and absorption of nutrients takes place in the small intestine.**

The small intestine is bustling with chemical activity. As the liquid moves into the small intestine, it mixes with enzymes and secretions. The enzymes and secretions are produced in three different organs—the small intestine, the liver, and the pancreas. The liver and the pancreas deliver their substances to the small intestine through small tubes.

The Role of the Liver The **liver** is located in the upper portion of the abdomen. It is the largest and heaviest organ inside the body. You can think of the liver as an extremely busy chemical factory that plays a role in many body processes. For example, the liver breaks down medicines and other substances, and it helps eliminate nitrogen from the body. As part of the digestive system, the liver produces **bile,** a substance that breaks up fat particles. Bile flows from the liver into the **gallbladder,** the organ that stores bile. After you eat, bile passes through a tube from the gallbladder into the small intestine.

Bile is not an enzyme. It does not chemically digest foods. It does, however, break up large fat particles into smaller fat droplets. You can compare the action of bile on fats with the action of soap on a greasy frying pan. Soap physically breaks up the grease into small droplets that can mix with the soapy water and be washed away. Bile mixes with the fats in food to form small fat droplets. The droplets can then be chemically broken down by enzymes produced in the pancreas.

Break Up!

In this activity, you will model the breakup of fat particles in the small intestine. ACTIVITY

1. Fill two plastic jars half full of water. Add a few drops of oil to each jar.
2. Add $\frac{1}{4}$ teaspoon baking soda to one of the jars.
3. Stir the contents of both jars. Record your observations.

Observing In which jar did the oil begin to break up? What substance does the baking soda represent?

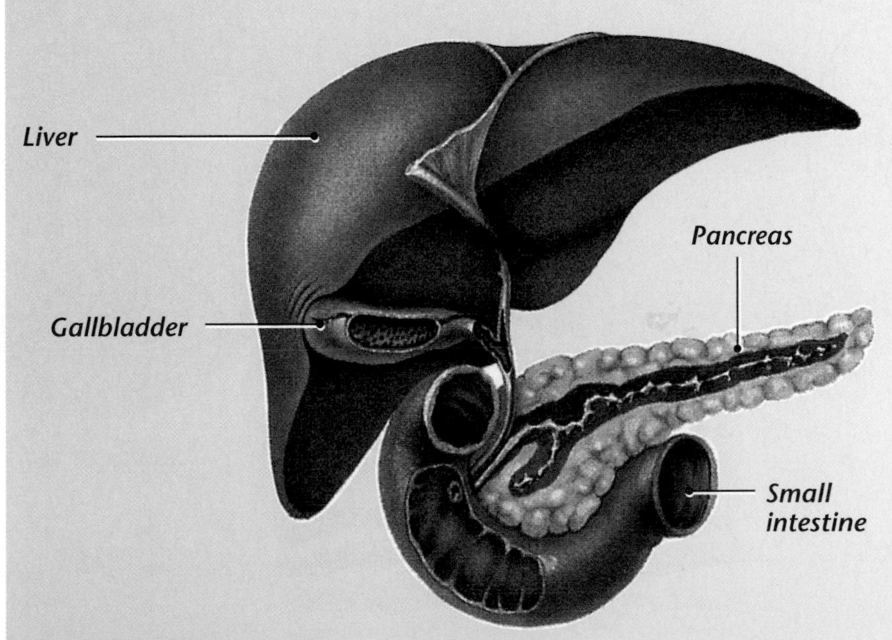

Figure 17 Substances produced by the liver and pancreas aid in the digestion of food.
Applying Concepts *Where is bile produced? Where is it stored before it is released into the small intestine?*

Help From the Pancreas The **pancreas** is a triangular organ that lies between the stomach and the first part of the small intestine. Like the liver, the pancreas plays a role in many body processes. As part of the digestive system, the pancreas produces enzymes that flow into the small intestine. These enzymes help break down starches, proteins, and fats.

The digestive enzymes produced by the pancreas and other organs do not break down all food substances, however. Recall that the fiber in food isn't broken down. Instead, fiber thickens the liquid material in the intestine. This makes it easier for peristalsis to push the material forward.

☑ *Checkpoint How does the pancreas aid in digestion?*

Absorption in the Small Intestine After chemical digestion takes place, the small nutrient molecules are ready to be absorbed by the body. The structure of the small intestine makes it well suited for absorption. The inner surface, or lining, of the small intestine looks bumpy. Millions of tiny finger-shaped structures called **villi** (VIL eye) (singular *villus*) cover the surface. The villi absorb nutrient molecules. Notice that tiny blood vessels run through the center of each villus. Nutrient molecules pass from cells on the surface of a villus into blood vessels. The blood carries the nutrients throughout the body for use by body cells.

The presence of villi increases the surface area of the small intestine. If all of the villi were laid out flat, the total surface area of the small intestine would be about as large as a tennis court.

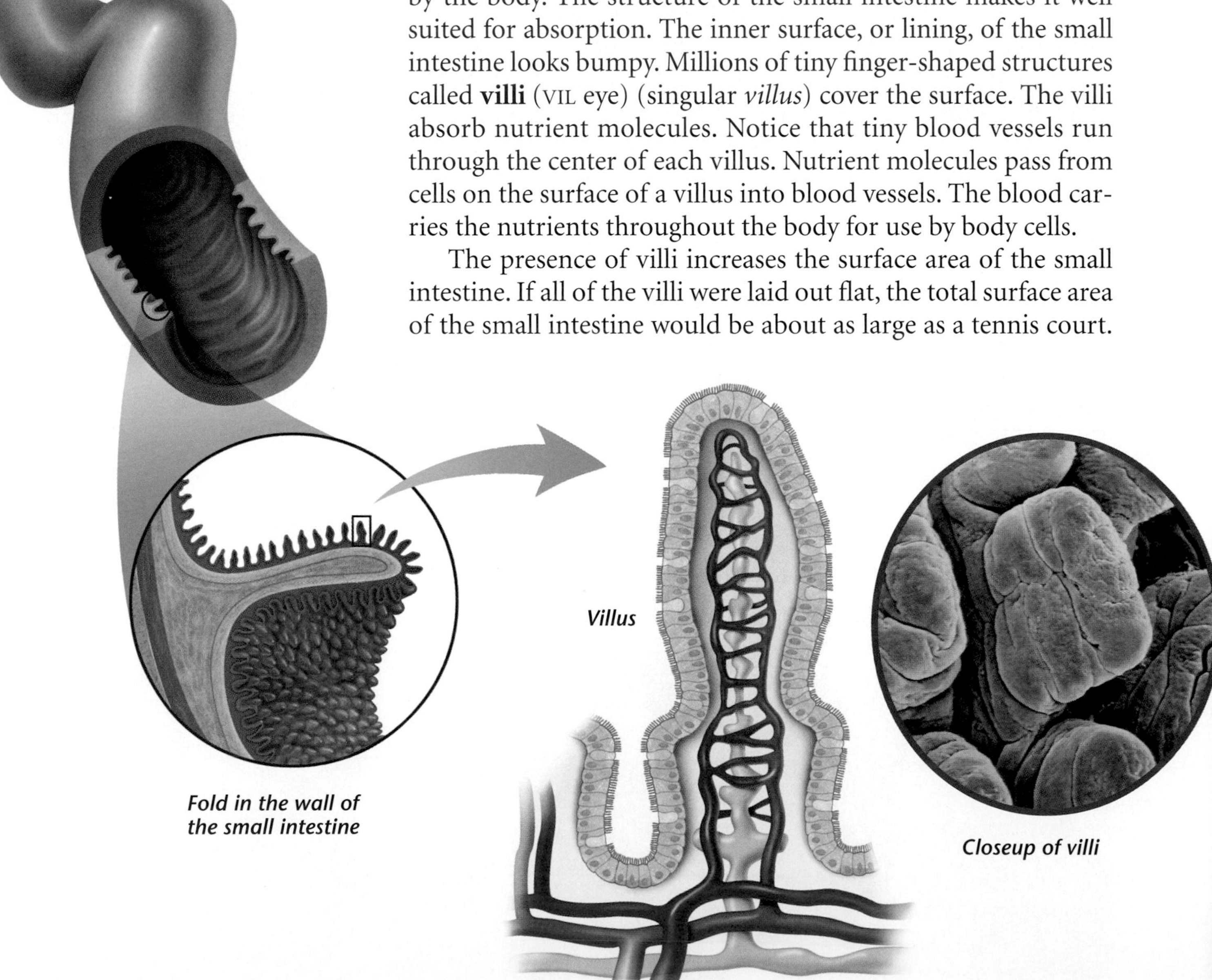

Figure 18 Tiny finger-shaped projections called villi line the inside of the small intestine. In the diagram, you can see that the blood vessels in the villi are covered by a single layer of cells. The photograph shows a closeup view of villi. ***Interpreting Diagrams*** *How does the structure of the villi help them carry out their function?*

This greatly increased surface enables digested food to be absorbed faster than if the walls of the small intestine were smooth.

The Large Intestine

By the time material reaches the end of the small intestine, most nutrients have been absorbed. The remaining material moves from the small intestine into the large intestine. The **large intestine** is the last section of the digestive system. It is about one and a half meters long—about as long as the average bathtub. As you can see in Figure 19, the large intestine is shaped somewhat like a horseshoe. It runs up the right-hand side of the abdomen, across the upper abdomen, and then down the left-hand side. The large intestine contains bacteria that feed on the material passing through. These bacteria normally do not cause disease. In fact, they are helpful because they make certain vitamins, including vitamin K.

The material entering the large intestine contains water and undigested food such as fiber. **As the material moves through the large intestine, water is absorbed into the bloodstream. The remaining material is readied for elimination from the body.**

The large intestine ends in a short tube called the **rectum.** Here waste material is compressed into a solid form. This waste material is eliminated from the body through the **anus,** a muscular opening at the end of the rectum.

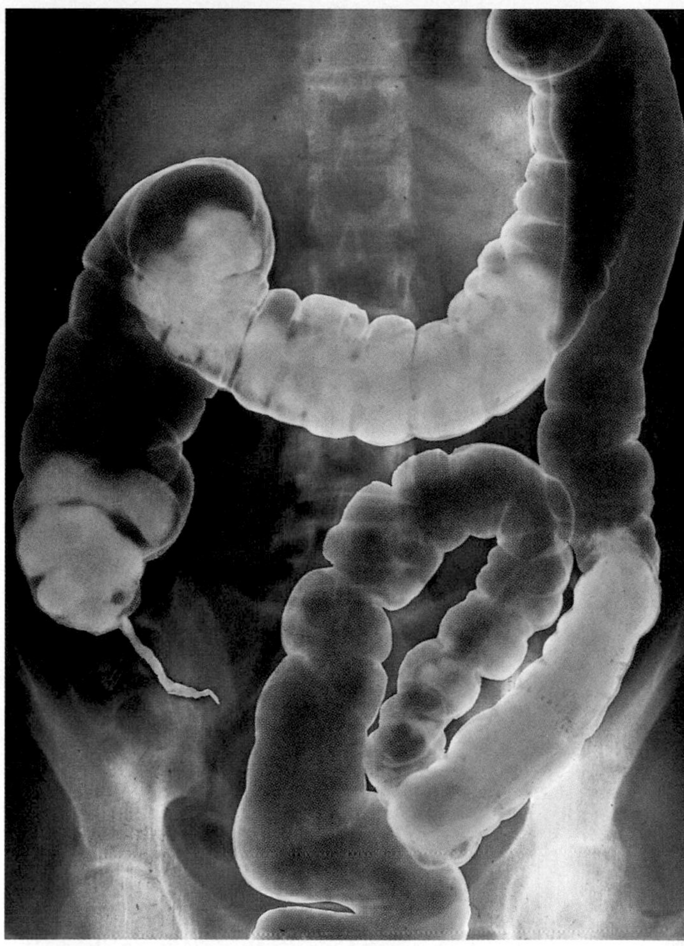

Figure 19 Notice the shape of the large intestine. As material passes through this structure, most of the water is absorbed by the body.

Section 4 Review

1. What two digestive processes occur in the small intestine? Briefly describe each process.
2. Which nutrient is absorbed in the large intestine?
3. How do the liver and pancreas function in the digestive process?
4. **Thinking Critically Relating Cause and Effect** Some people are allergic to a protein in wheat. When these people eat foods made with wheat, a reaction destroys the villi in the small intestine. What problems would you expect these people to experience?

CHAPTER PROJECT 4

Check Your Progress

You should now be trying to eat a more healthful diet. Be sure you keep an accurate log of your food intake during this three-day period. Then graph the results. (*Hint:* You might find it helpful to focus on one food category when trying to improve your eating habits.)

Advertising and Nutrition

Millions of children enjoy Saturday morning television programs. As they watch, they see advertisements for high-sugar cereals, candy, soft drinks, and fat-filled foods. Such foods are not healthy choices. For example, in some cereals marketed to children, added sugar makes up almost half the cereal's weight. How greatly are children's eating habits influenced by food ads? Should these ads be allowed on children's television programs?

The Issues

Does Advertising Influence Children?
Advertising products to children between the ages of four and twelve works. Overall, companies spend more than $300 million a year advertising to that age group. In turn, children influence adults to spend more than 500 times that amount—at least $165 billion a year.

Should Food Companies Advertise on Children's Television? Some people want to regulate food ads on children's shows. Evidence indicates that children choose particular foods based on ads. The foods children eat can affect their health not just during childhood but for the rest of their lives.

Other people point out that children don't try to buy every food they see advertised. It is usually parents, not children, who decide what foods to buy. In addition, companies pay for advertisements. Without this money, television producers might not be able to afford to make good programs.

What Responsibilities Do Families and Schools Have? Many people believe that parents and teachers should teach children about nutrition. These people argue that adults should teach children to read food labels and to recognize misleading advertisements. For the rest of children's lives, they will be surrounded by advertising. If they learn to analyze ads critically, children will become wise consumers as adults.

You Decide

1. Describe the Issue
Summarize the debate about food advertisements on children's television.

2. Analyze the Options
List some possible solutions to the problem of food advertisements on children's television. How would each solution affect children and advertisers?

3. Find a Solution
Prepare a leaflet proposing one solution to the problem. Use persuasive arguments to support your proposal.

Food and Energy

Key Ideas

- ◆ The six nutrients necessary for human health are carbohydrates, fats, proteins, vitamins, minerals, and water.
- ◆ Water is the most important nutrient because it is necessary for all body processes.

Key Terms

nutrient
calorie
carbohydrate
glucose
fiber
fat
unsaturated fat
saturated fat
cholesterol
protein
amino acid
vitamin
mineral

Healthy Eating

INTEGRATING HEALTH

Key Ideas

- ◆ The Food Guide Pyramid classifies foods into six major groups and tells how many servings from each group to eat.
- ◆ Food labels list the nutrients in foods and show how the foods fit into your daily diet.

Key Terms

Food Guide Pyramid
Percent Daily Value

The Digestive Process Begins

Key Ideas

- ◆ The functions of the digestive system are to break down food, absorb food molecules into the blood, and eliminate wastes.
- ◆ During mechanical digestion, food is ground into small pieces. During chemical digestion, large food molecules are broken into small molecules by enzymes.
- ◆ Food first passes from the mouth into the esophagus, and then into the stomach. Waves of muscle contractions, known as peristalsis, keep the food moving in one direction.

Key Terms

digestion
absorption
saliva
enzyme
epiglottis
esophagus
mucus
peristalsis
stomach

Final Digestion and Absorption

Key Ideas

- ◆ Almost all chemical digestion and absorption of nutrients takes place in the small intestine.
- ◆ Nutrients are absorbed into the bloodstream through the villi of the small intestine.
- ◆ As material moves through the large intestine, water is absorbed. The remaining material is readied for elimination.

Key Terms

small intestine
liver
bile
gallbladder
pancreas
villus
large intestine
rectum
anus

Organizing Information

Flowchart Copy the flowchart below onto a sheet of paper. Complete the flowchart with the names and functions of the missing organs. (For more on flowcharts, see the Skills Handbook.)

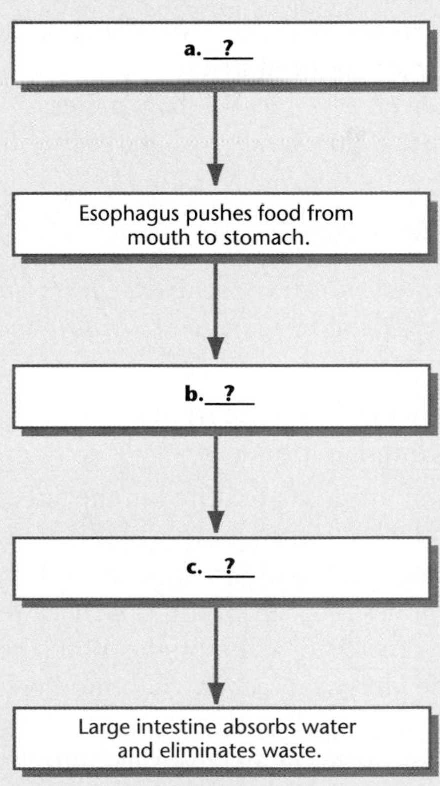

Reviewing Content

Multiple Choice

Choose the letter of the best answer.

1. Which nutrient makes up about 65 percent of the body's weight?
   - **a.** carbohydrate
   - **b.** protein
   - **c.** water
   - **d.** fat
2. According to the Food Guide Pyramid, from which group should you eat the most servings?
   - **a.** Milk, Yogurt, and Cheese
   - **b.** Meat, Poultry, Fish, Beans, Eggs, and Nuts
   - **c.** Vegetables
   - **d.** Bread, Cereal, Rice, and Pasta
3. Most mechanical digestion takes place in the
   - **a.** mouth.
   - **b.** esophagus.
   - **c.** stomach.
   - **d.** small intestine.
4. The enzyme in saliva chemically breaks down
   - **a.** fats.
   - **b.** proteins.
   - **c.** sugars.
   - **d.** starches.
5. Bile is produced by the
   - **a.** liver.
   - **b.** pancreas.
   - **c.** small intestine.
   - **d.** large intestine.

True or False

If the statement is true, write true. If it is false, change the underlined word or words to make the statement true.

6. Proteins that come from animal sources are <u>incomplete</u> proteins.
7. Vitamins that are stored in the fatty tissue of the body are <u>water-soluble</u>.
8. To determine which of two cereals supplies more iron, you can check the <u>Percent Daily Value</u> on the food label.
9. The physical breakdown of food is called <u>mechanical</u> digestion.
10. Most materials are absorbed into the bloodstream in the <u>large</u> intestine.

Checking Concepts

11. How does a person's level of physical activity affect his or her daily energy needs?
12. Why is fiber necessary in a person's diet even though it is not considered a nutrient?
13. Why does the Food Guide Pyramid give the recommended daily servings as a range instead of a single number?
14. Describe the location and function of the epiglottis.
15. Explain the role of peristalsis in the digestive system.
16. What is the function of villi? Where are villi located?
17. **Writing to Learn** Imagine that you are a bacon, lettuce, and tomato sandwich. Describe your journey through a person's digestive system, starting in the mouth and ending with absorption.

Thinking Critically

18. **Applying Concepts** Before winter arrives, animals that hibernate often prepare by eating foods that contain a lot of fat. How is this behavior helpful?
19. **Comparing and Contrasting** The digestive system is sometimes said to be "an assembly line in reverse." Identify some similarities and some differences between your digestive system and an assembly line.
20. **Relating Cause and Effect** "Heartburn" occurs when stomach acid enters the esophagus. Use your knowledge of the digestive system to explain how this condition affects the esophagus and how "heartburn" got its name.
21. **Inferring** Why is it important for people to chew their food thoroughly before swallowing?
22. **Relating Cause and Effect** Suppose a medicine killed all the bacteria in your body. How might this affect vitamin production in your body? Explain.

Applying Skills

Use the chart below to answer Questions 23–25.

Food (1 cup)	Calcium (% Daily Value)	Calories	Calories from Fat
Chocolate Milk	30	230	80
Low-fat Milk	35	110	20
Plain Yogurt	35	110	35

23. Classifying To which group in the Food Guide Pyramid do the foods in the chart belong? What is the recommended range of daily servings for that group?

24. Interpreting Data How many cups of low-fat milk provide the daily recommended percentage of calcium?

25. Calculating Which of the foods meet the recommendation that no more than 30 percent of a food's calories come from fat? Explain.

Performance Assessment

CHAPTER PROJECT 4

Project Wrap Up Write a summary of what you've learned from keeping a food log. Address these questions in your summary: How close were your eating patterns to those recommended in the Food Guide Pyramid? How did you attempt to change your diet during the second three days? How successful were you at making those changes in your diet?

Reflect and Record Did your eating patterns surprise you? What additional changes could help you improve your diet? How might others help you make those changes? If your eating patterns match those that are recommended in the Food Guide Pyramid, how can you be sure to continue those patterns?

Test Preparation

Use these questions to prepare for standardized tests.

Use the information to answer Questions 26–29.

A scientist performed an experiment to determine the amount of time needed to digest protein. She placed small pieces of hard-boiled egg white (a protein) in a test tube containing hydrochloric acid, water, and the enzyme pepsin. She measured the rate at which the egg white was digested over a 24-hour period. Her data are recorded in the table below.

Time (hours)	Percentage of Egg White Digested
0	0%
4	15%
8	25%
12	40%
16	70%
20	85%
24	90%

26. During which 4-hour period did the most digestion take place?
a. 0–4 hours **b.** 4–8 hours
c. 8–12 hours **d.** 12–16 hours

27. After about how many hours would you estimate that half of the protein was digested?
a. 8 hours **b.** 12 hours
c. 14 hours **d.** 16 hours

28. How much digestion occurred in 16 hours?
a. 25% **b.** 40%
c. 70% **d.** 90%

29. What would have happened if no hydrochloric acid were added to the test tube?
a. The protein would have been digested faster.
b. The protein would have been digested slower.
c. There would have been no change in the rate of protein digestion.
d. Pepsin alone would have digested the protein.

CHAPTER 5

Circulation

www.phschool.com

The Body's Transportation System

Discover How Hard Does Your Heart Work?

A Closer Look at Blood Vessels

Discover How Does Pressure Affect the Flow of Blood?
Sharpen Your Skills Creating Data Tables
Skills Lab Heart Beat, Health Beat

Blood and Lymph

Discover What Kinds of Cells Are in Blood?
Try This Caught in the Web
Real-World Lab Do You Know Your A-B-O's?

PROJECT 5

Travels of a Red Blood Cell

Every day, you travel from home to school and then back home again. Your path makes a loop, or circuit, ending where it began. In this chapter, you'll learn how your blood also travels in circuits. You'll find out how your heart pumps your blood throughout your body, bringing that essential fluid to all your living cells. As you learn more about the heart and circulatory system, you'll create a display to show how blood circulates throughout the body.

Your Goal To design and construct a display showing a complete journey of a red blood cell through the human body.

To complete the project successfully, your display must

- show a red blood cell that leaves from the heart and returns to the same place
- show where the red blood cell picks up and delivers oxygen and carbon dioxide
- provide written descriptions of the circuits made by the red blood cell, either with captions or in a continuous story
- be designed following the safety guidelines in Appendix A

Get Started Look ahead at the diagrams in the chapter. Then discuss the kinds of displays you could use, including a three-dimensional model, posters, a series of drawings, a flip-book, or a video animation. Write down any content questions you'll need to answer.

Check Your Progress You'll be working on this project as you study this chapter. To keep your project on track, look for Check Your Progress boxes at the following points.

Section 1 Review, page 164: Make a sketch of your display.
Section 2 Review, page 169: Begin to construct your display.
Section 3 Review, page 176: Add a written description to your display.

Wrap Up At the end of the chapter (page 185), you will use your display to show how blood travels through the body.

Blood cells travel in blood vessels to all parts of the body.

Integrating Health

SECTION 4 **Cardiovascular Health**

Discover **Which Foods Are "Heart Healthy"?**
Try This **Blocking the Flow**

The Body's Transportation System

DISCOVER ACTIVITY

How Hard Does Your Heart Work?

1. Every minute, your heart beats about 75 to 85 times. With each beat, it pumps about 60 milliliters of blood. Can you work as hard and fast as your heart does?
2. Cover a table or desk with newspapers. Place two large plastic containers side by side on the newspapers. Fill one with 2.5 liters of water, which is about the volume of blood that your heart pumps in 30 seconds. Leave the other container empty.
3. With a plastic cup that holds about 60 milliliters, transfer water as quickly as possible into the empty container without spilling any. Have a partner time you for 30 seconds. As you work, count how many transfers you make in 30 seconds.
4. Multiply your results by 2 to find the number of transfers for one minute.

Think It Over

Inferring Compare your performance with the number of times your heart beats every minute. What do your results tell you about the strength and speed of a heartbeat?

GUIDE FOR READING

- **What is the function of the cardiovascular system?**
- **What role does the heart play in the cardiovascular system?**
- **What path does blood take through the circulatory system?**

Reading Tip **As you read, create a flowchart that shows the path that blood follows as it circulates through the body.**

In the middle of the night, a truck rolls rapidly through the darkness. Loaded with fresh fruits and vegetables, the truck is headed for a city supermarket. The driver steers off the interstate and onto a smaller highway. Finally, after driving through narrow city streets, the truck reaches its destination. As dawn begins to break, store workers unload the cargo. They work quickly, because other trucks—carrying meats, canned goods, and freshly baked breads—are waiting to be unloaded. And while workers fill the store with products to be sold, a garbage truck removes yesterday's trash. All these trucks have traveled long distances over roads. Without a huge network of roads, big and small, the supermarket couldn't stay in business.

Movement of Materials

Like the roads that link all parts of the country, your body has a "highway" network, called the cardiovascular system, that links all parts of your body. The **cardiovascular system,** or circulatory system, consists of the heart, blood vessels, and blood. **The cardiovascular system carries needed substances to cells and carries waste products away from cells.** In addition, blood contains cells that fight disease.

Needed Materials Most substances that need to get from one part of the body to another are carried by blood. For example, blood carries oxygen from your lungs to your body cells. Blood also transports the glucose your cells use to produce energy.

Waste Products The cardiovascular system also picks up wastes from cells. For example, when cells use glucose, they produce carbon dioxide as a waste product. The carbon dioxide passes from the cells into the blood. The cardiovascular system then carries carbon dioxide to the lungs, where it is exhaled.

Disease Fighters The cardiovascular system also transports cells that attack disease-causing microorganisms. This process can keep you from becoming sick. If you do get sick, these disease-fighting blood cells will kill the microorganisms to help you get well.

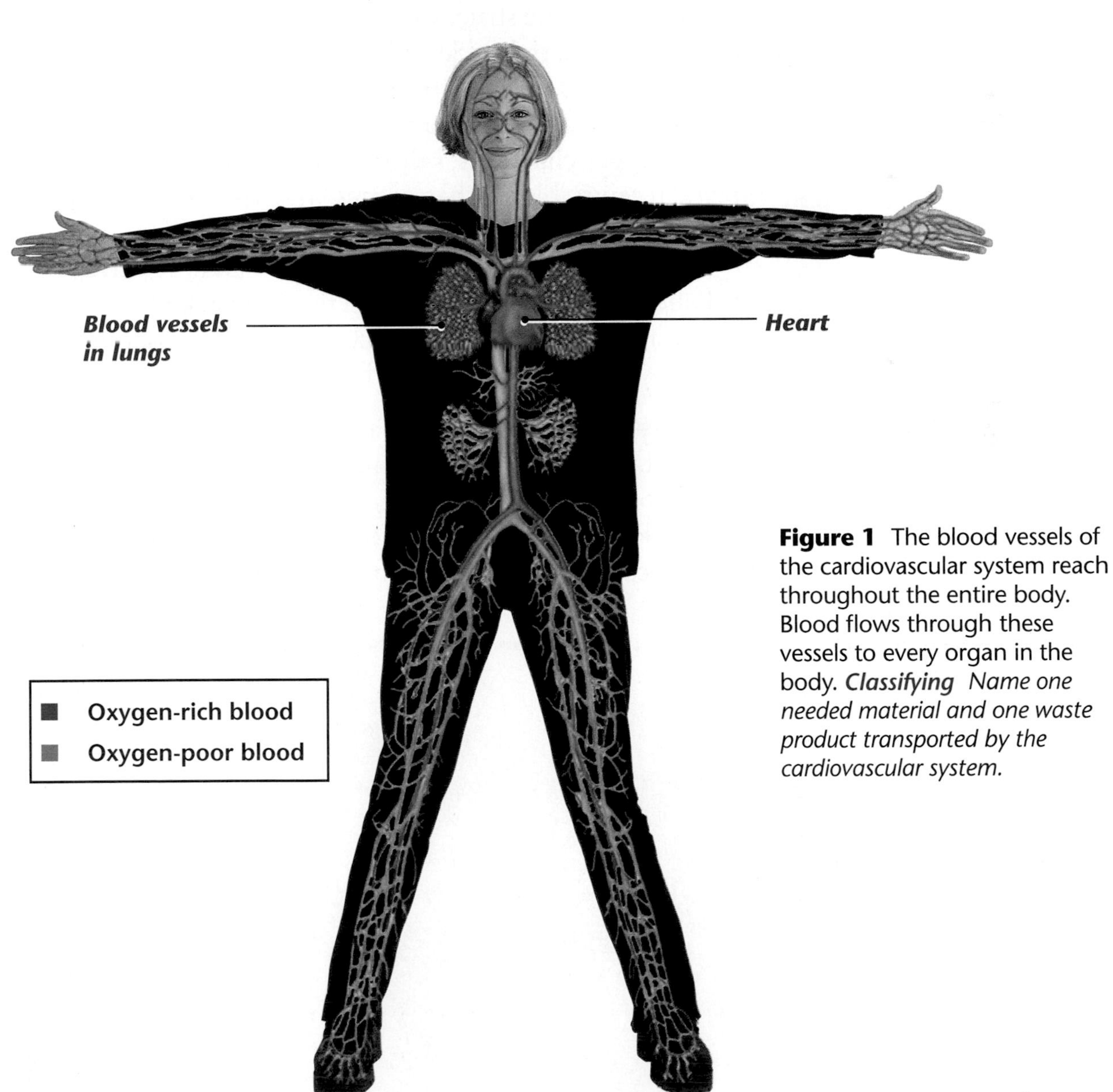

Figure 1 The blood vessels of the cardiovascular system reach throughout the entire body. Blood flows through these vessels to every organ in the body. ***Classifying*** *Name one needed material and one waste product transported by the cardiovascular system.*

Figure 2 This small stone sculpture, created by ancient Egyptians, represents the heart. Ancient Egyptians believed that feelings, thoughts, and memories were created by the heart.

The Heart

Without the heart, blood wouldn't go anywhere. The **heart** is a hollow, muscular organ that pumps blood throughout the body. Your heart, which is about the size of your fist, is located in the center of your chest. The heart lies behind the breastbone and inside the ribs. These bones protect the heart from injury.

Each time the heart beats, it pushes blood through the blood vessels of the cardiovascular system. As you learned in Chapter 3, the heart is made of cardiac muscle, which can contract over and over without getting tired. The heart beats continually throughout a person's life, resting only between beats. During your lifetime, your heart may beat over 3 billion times. In a year, it pumps enough blood to fill over 30 competition-size swimming pools.

The Heart's Structure Look closely at *Exploring the Heart* as you read about the structure of the heart. Notice that the heart has two sides—a right side and a left side—completely separated from each other by a wall of tissue. Each side has two compartments, or chambers—an upper and a lower chamber. Each of the two upper chambers, called an **atrium** (AY tree um) (plural *atria*), receives blood that comes into the heart. Each lower chamber, called a **ventricle,** pumps blood out of the heart. The atria are separated from the ventricles by valves. A **valve** is a flap of tissue that prevents blood from flowing backward. Valves are also located between the ventricles and the large blood vessels that carry blood away from the heart.

How the Heart Works The action of the heart has two main phases. In one phase, the heart muscle relaxes and the heart fills with blood. In the other phase, the heart muscle contracts and pumps blood forward. A heartbeat, which sounds something like *lub-dup,* can be heard during the pumping phase.

Figure 3 As blood flows out of the heart and toward the lungs, it passes through the valve shown in the photograph. The illustration shows how blood flows through the open valve.
Applying Concepts *What is the function of the valves in the heart?*

When the heart muscle relaxes, blood flows into the chambers. Then the atria contract. This muscle contraction squeezes blood out of the atria, through the valves, and then into the ventricles. Next the ventricles contract. This contraction closes the valves between the atria and ventricles, making the *lub* sound and squeezing blood into large blood vessels. As the valves between the ventricles and the blood vessels snap shut, they make the *dup* sound. All of this happens in less than a second.

☑ ***Checkpoint*** *Contrast the functions of atria and ventricles.*

EXPLORING the Heart

Every second of your life, your heart pumps blood through your body. The right side of the heart pumps blood to the lungs, while the left side pumps blood to the rest of the body.

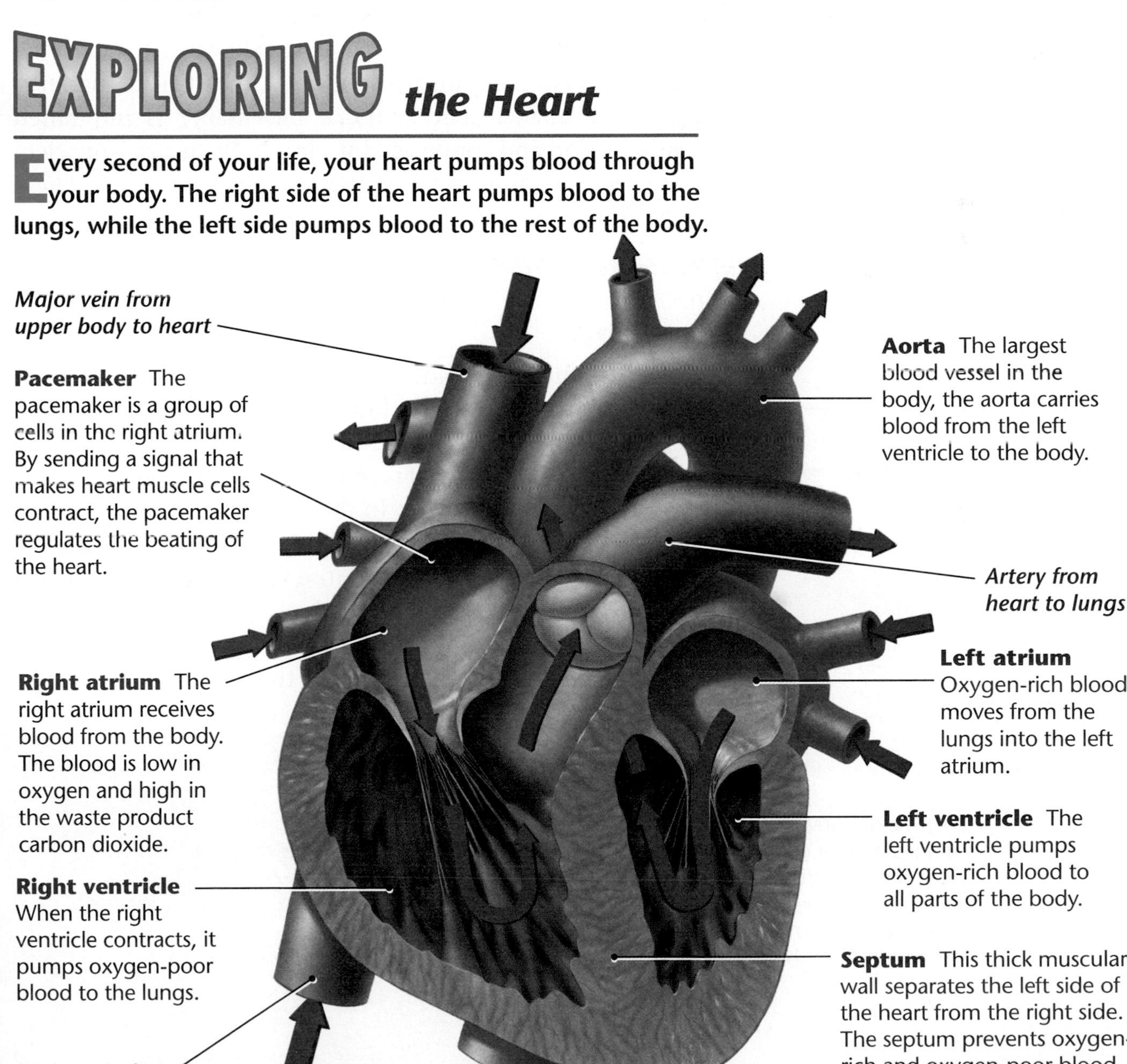

Language Arts CONNECTION

When you say that a person has a "heart of gold," you mean that the person is kind and generous—not that the person's heart is actually made of gold metal. "Heart of gold" is an idiom—an expression with a meaning that cannot be understood from the ordinary meanings of the words in it. The words *heart* and *blood* are found in many idioms. For example, a "blood-chilling scream" frightens you, but it doesn't lower the temperature of your blood.

In Your Journal

Learn what each of the following idioms means:

- a change of heart
- a heart-to-heart talk
- make the blood boil

Then write a sentence using each of these idioms.

Regulation of Heartbeat

A group of cells called the **pacemaker,** which is located in the right atrium, sends out signals that make the heart muscle contract. The pacemaker constantly receives messages about the body's oxygen needs. It then adjusts the heart rate to match. Your heart beats much faster when you are exercising than when you are sitting quietly. When you are exercising, the entire process from the beginning of one heartbeat to the beginning of the next can take less than half a second. Your muscles need more oxygen during exercise. Your rapid heartbeat supplies blood that carries the oxygen.

In some people, the pacemaker becomes damaged as a result of disease or an accident. This often results in an irregular or slow heartbeat. In the 1950s, doctors and engineers developed an artificial, battery-operated pacemaker. The artificial pacemaker is implanted beneath the skin and connected by wires to the heart. Tiny electric impulses travel from the battery through the wires. These impulses make the heart contract at a normal rate.

☑ ***Checkpoint*** *What is the function of the pacemaker?*

Two Loops

After leaving the heart, blood travels in blood vessels through the body. Your body has three kinds of blood vessels—arteries, capillaries, and veins. **Arteries** are blood vessels that carry blood away from the heart. From the arteries, blood flows into tiny vessels called **capillaries.** In the capillaries, substances are exchanged between the blood and body cells. From capillaries, blood flows into **veins,** which are the vessels that carry blood back to the heart.

The overall pattern of blood flow through the body is something like a figure eight. The heart is at the center where the two

Figure 4 Activities such as swimming require a lot of energy. A person's heart beats fast in order to supply the muscles with the blood they need. The heart's pacemaker regulates the speed at which the heart beats.

loops cross. **In the first loop, blood travels from the heart to the lungs and then back to the heart. In the second loop, blood is pumped from the heart throughout the body and then returns again to the heart.** The heart is really two pumps, one on the right and one on the left. The right side pumps blood to the lungs, and the left side pumps blood to the rest of the body.

Blood travels in only one direction. If you were a drop of blood, you could start at any point in the figure eight and eventually return to the same point. The entire trip would take less than a minute. As you read about the path that blood takes through the cardiovascular system, trace the path in Figure 5.

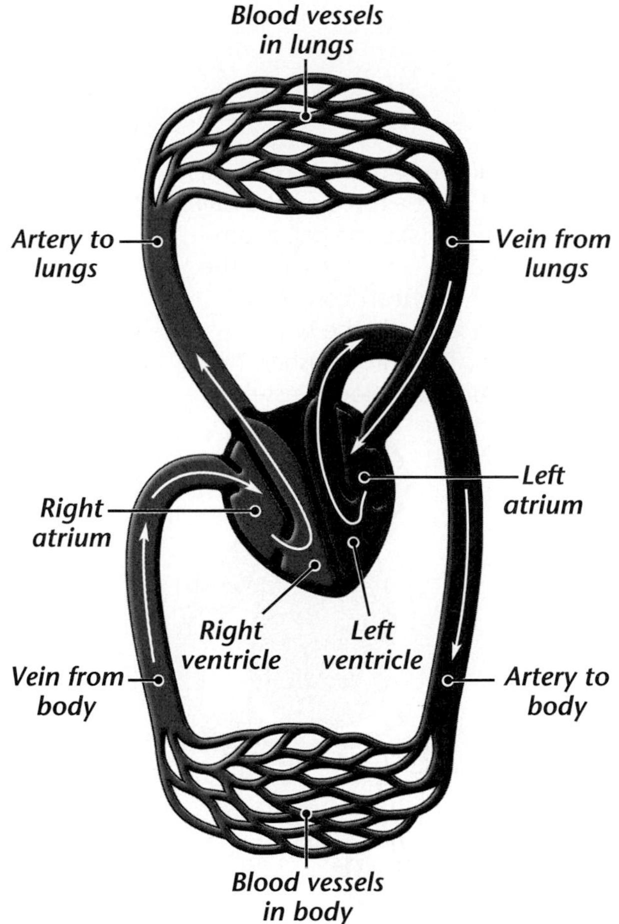

Figure 5 Blood circulates through the body in two loops with the heart at the center. Use the arrows to trace the path of blood, beginning at the right atrium. ***Interpreting Diagrams*** *Where does the blood that enters the left atrium come from?*

Loop One: to the Lungs and Back When blood from the body flows into the right atrium, it contains little oxygen but a lot of carbon dioxide. This oxygen-poor blood is dark red. The blood then flows from the right atrium into the right ventricle. Then the ventricle pumps the oxygen-poor blood into the arteries that lead to the lungs.

As blood flows through the lungs, large blood vessels branch into smaller ones. Eventually, blood flows through tiny capillaries that are in close contact with the air that comes into the lungs. The air in the lungs has more oxygen than the blood in the capillaries, so oxygen moves from the lungs into the blood. In contrast, carbon dioxide moves in the opposite direction—from the blood into the lungs. As the blood leaves the lungs, it is now rich in oxygen and poor in carbon dioxide. This blood, which is bright red, flows to the left side of the heart to be pumped through the second loop.

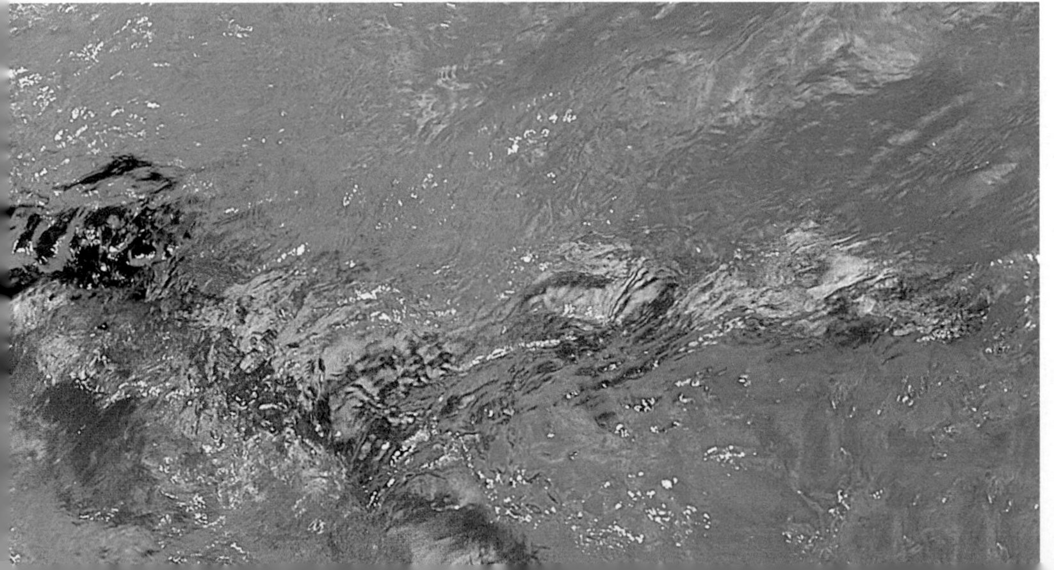

Loop Two: to the Body and Back The second loop begins as the left atrium fills with oxygen-rich blood coming from the lungs. The blood then moves into the left ventricle. From the left ventricle, the blood is pumped into the **aorta** (ay AWR tuh), the largest artery in the body.

Eventually, after passing through branching arteries, blood flows through tiny capillaries in different parts of your body, such as your brain, liver, and legs. These vessels are in close contact with body cells. Oxygen moves out of the blood and into the body cells. At the same time, carbon dioxide passes from the body cells and into the blood. The blood then flows back to the right atrium of the heart through veins, completing the second loop.

Figure 6 If the batter hits the ball, the bat will exert a force on the ball. This force will make the ball zoom through the air. Similarly, when the ventricles of the heart contract, they exert a force on the blood inside them. This force pushes blood through the blood vessels.

The Force of the Ventricles

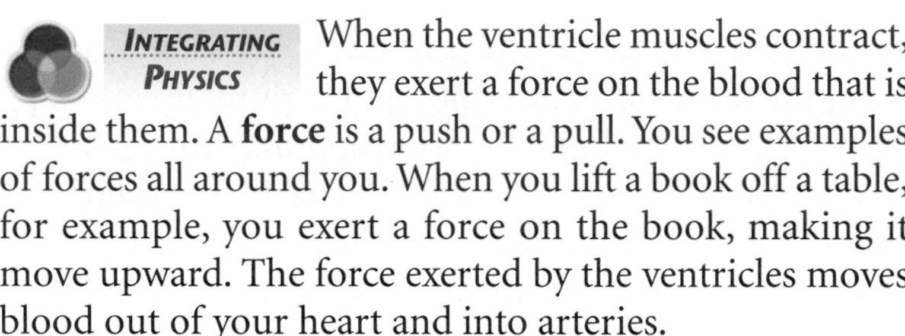

INTEGRATING PHYSICS When the ventricle muscles contract, they exert a force on the blood that is inside them. A **force** is a push or a pull. You see examples of forces all around you. When you lift a book off a table, for example, you exert a force on the book, making it move upward. The force exerted by the ventricles moves blood out of your heart and into arteries.

The contraction of the left ventricle exerts much more force than the contraction of the right ventricle. The right ventricle only pumps blood to the lungs. In contrast, the left ventricle pumps blood throughout the body. As a way of understanding this, think of the force it would take to bunt a baseball. Then think about how hard you would need to hit the ball if you wanted to hit a home run.

Section 1 Review

1. What is the function of the cardiovascular system?
2. What function does the heart perform?
3. Describe the route that blood takes through the cardiovascular system. Begin with blood leaving the left ventricle.
4. What is the heart's pacemaker? What causes the pacemaker to change the rate at which the heart beats?
5. **Thinking Critically Comparing and Contrasting** Most of the arteries in the body carry oxygen-rich blood away from the heart. One artery, however, carries blood that has little oxygen away from the heart. From which ventricle does that artery carry blood? To where does that artery carry blood?

CHAPTER PROJECT 5

Check Your Progress

At this point, you should have sketched out the two loops your red blood cell will travel. Make sure each pathway forms a complete circuit back to the heart. Begin to plan how you will construct your display. Keep a running list of the materials or equipment you'll need. (*Hint:* Think about how you will show the movement of the blood cell in your display.)

A Closer Look at Blood Vessels

DISCOVER ACTIVITY

How Does Pressure Affect the Flow of Blood?

1. Spread newspapers over a table or desktop. Then fill a plastic squeeze bottle with water.
2. Hold the bottle over a dishpan. Squeeze the bottle with one hand. Observe how far the water travels.
3. Now grasp the bottle with both hands and squeeze again. Observe how far the water travels this time.

Think It Over

Inferring Blood is pushed through arteries with much more force than it is pushed through veins. Which part of the activity models an artery? Which part models a vein? Which organ in the body provides the pushing force?

GUIDE FOR READING

- **What are the functions of arteries, capillaries, and veins?**
- **What causes blood pressure?**

Reading Tip **As you read, use the text headings to make an outline of the information in this section.**

Like corridors in a large building, blood vessels run through all of the tissues of your body. While some blood vessels are as wide as your thumb, most of them are much finer than a human hair. If all the arteries, capillaries, and veins in your body were hooked together, end to end, they would stretch a distance of almost 100,000 kilometers. That's long enough to wrap around Earth twice—with a lot left over!

Arteries

When blood leaves the heart, it travels through arteries. The right ventricle pumps blood into the arteries that go to the lungs. The left ventricle pumps blood into the aorta, the largest artery in your body. Every organ receives blood from arteries that branch off the aorta. The first branches, called the **coronary arteries,** carry blood to the heart itself. Other branches carry blood to the brain, intestines, and other organs. Each artery branches into smaller and smaller arteries.

Artery Structure The walls of arteries are generally very thick. In fact, artery walls consist of three layers. The innermost layer, which is made up of epithelial

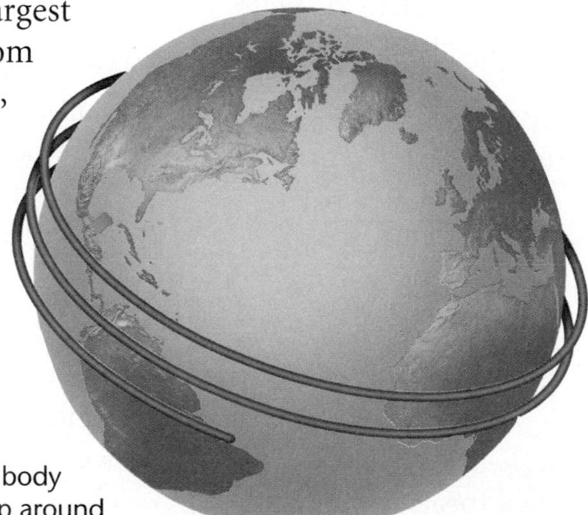

Figure 7 If all the blood vessels in your body were joined end to end, they would wrap around the world almost two and a half times.

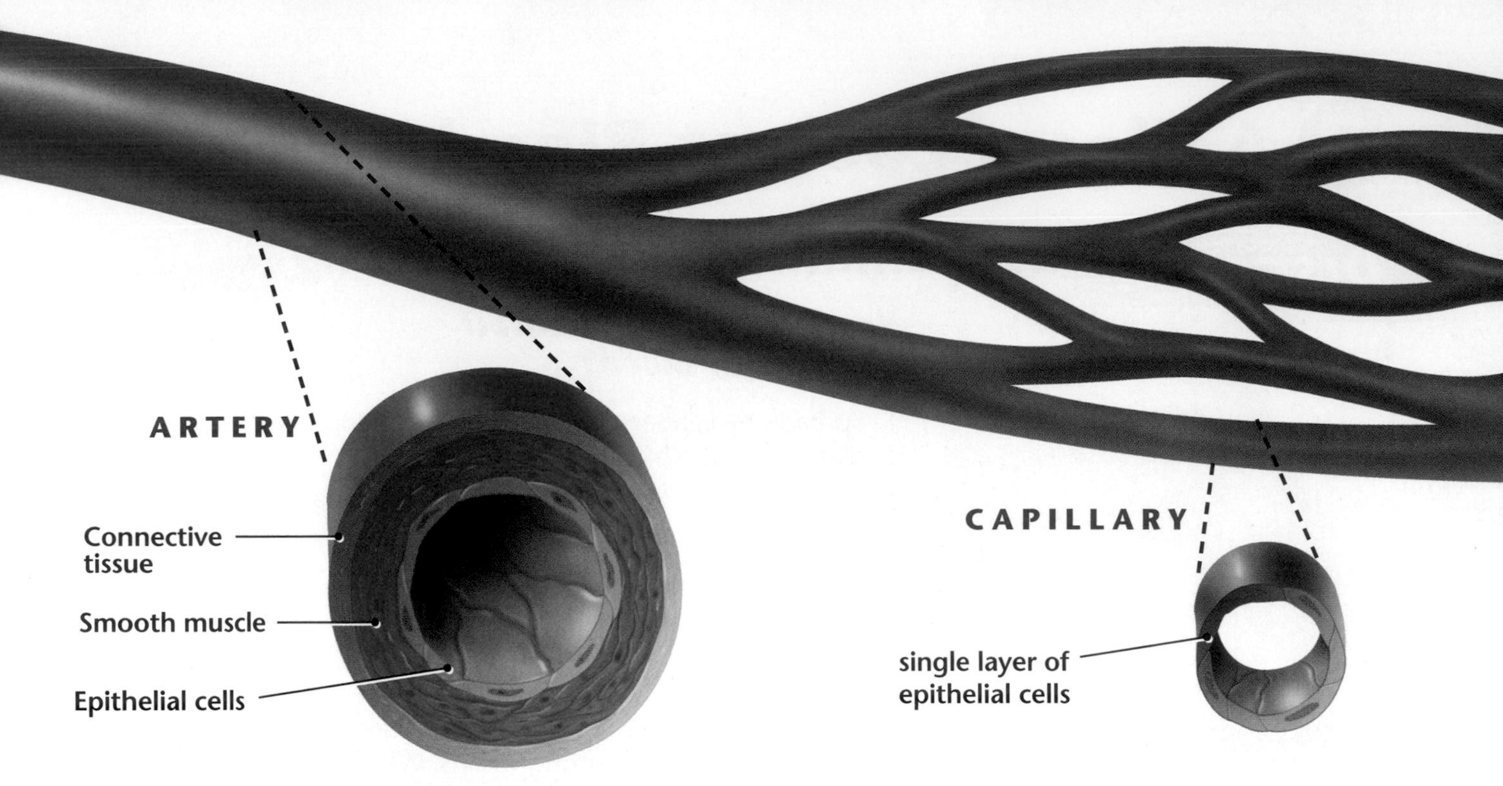

Math Toolbox

Pulse Rate

A rate is the speed at which something happens. When you calculate a rate, you compare the number of events with the time period in which they occur. Here is how you can calculate the pulse rate of a person whose heart beats 142 times in 2 minutes.

1. Write the comparison as a fraction.

$$\frac{142 \text{ heartbeats}}{2 \text{ minutes}}$$

2. Divide the numerator and the denominator by the denominator.

$$\frac{142 \div 2}{2 \div 2} = \frac{71}{1}$$

The person's pulse rate is 71 heartbeats per minute.

tissue, is smooth. This smooth surface enables blood to flow freely. The middle layer consists mostly of muscle tissue. The outer wall is made up of flexible connective tissue. Because of this layered structure, arteries have both strength and flexibility. Arteries are able to withstand the enormous pressure of blood pumped by the heart, and to expand and relax in response to that pumping.

Pulse If you lightly touch the inside of your wrist, you can feel the artery in your wrist rise and fall repeatedly. The pulse that you feel is caused by the alternating expansion and relaxation of the artery wall. Every time the heart's ventricles contract, they send a spurt of blood out through all the arteries in your body. As this spurt travels through the arteries, it pushes the artery walls and makes them expand. After the spurt passes, the artery walls become narrower again. When you count the number of times an artery pulses beneath your fingers, you are counting heartbeats. By taking your pulse rate, you can determine how fast your heart is beating.

Regulating Blood Flow The muscles in the middle wall of an artery are involuntary muscles, which contract without your thinking about it. When they contract, the opening in the artery becomes smaller. When they relax, the opening becomes larger. These muscles act as control gates, adjusting the amount of blood sent to different organs. For example, after you eat, your stomach

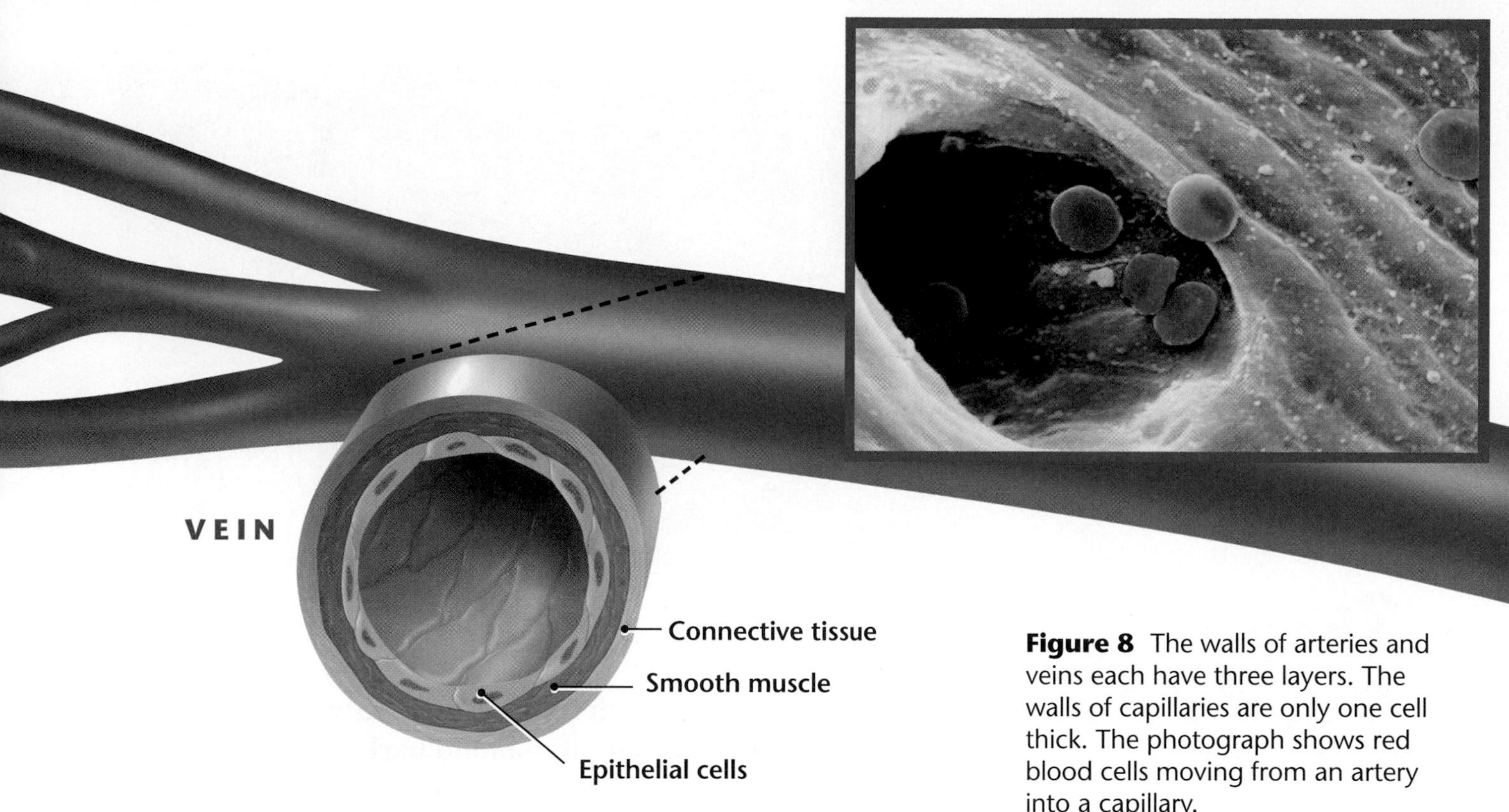

Figure 8 The walls of arteries and veins each have three layers. The walls of capillaries are only one cell thick. The photograph shows red blood cells moving from an artery into a capillary.

and intestines need a greater blood supply to help power digestion. The arteries leading to those organs open wider, so that more blood flows through them. In contrast, when you are running, your stomach and intestines need less blood than the muscles in your legs. The arteries leading to the stomach and intestines become narrower, decreasing the blood flow to those organs.

☑ *Checkpoint* *What causes the pulse that you feel in your wrist?*

Capillaries

Eventually, blood flows from small arteries into the tiny capillaries. **In the capillaries, materials are exchanged between the blood and the body's cells.** Capillary walls are only one cell thick. Because capillaries have thin walls, materials can pass easily through them. Materials such as oxygen and glucose pass from blood, through the thin capillary walls, to the cells. Cellular waste products travel in the opposite direction—from cells, through the capillary walls, and into blood.

Integrating Chemistry One way in which materials are exchanged between the blood and the body cells is by diffusion. **Diffusion** is the process by which molecules move from an area in which they are highly concentrated to an area in which they are less concentrated. For example, glucose is more highly concentrated in blood than it is in the body cells. Therefore, glucose diffuses from the blood, through the capillary wall, and into the body cells.

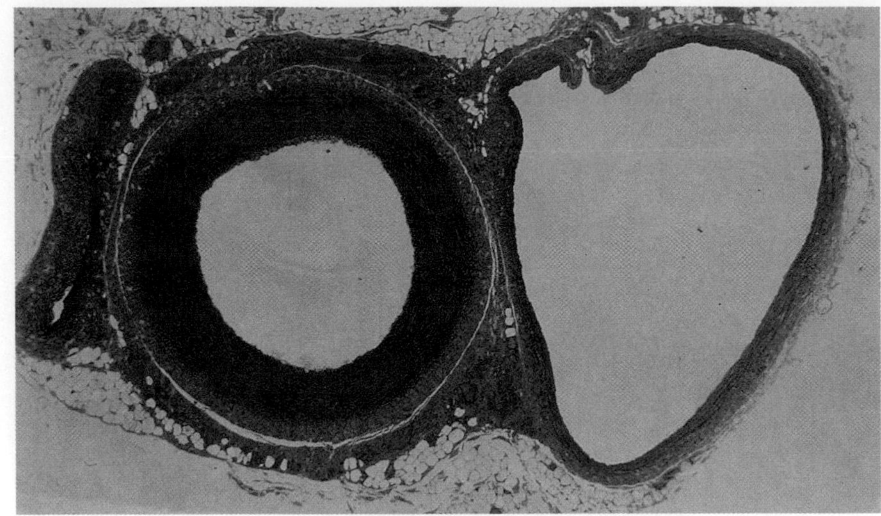

Figure 9 The wall of the artery (left) is much thicker than that of the vein (right).
Making Generalizations *Why is it important for artery walls to be both strong and flexible?*

Creating Data Tables

ACTIVITY

Scientists measured the volume of blood that different organs receive, first when a person was resting and then when the person was engaged in vigorous exercise.

- At rest, the organs of the abdomen received approximately 1,400 mL of blood per minute (mL/min). During vigorous exercise, they received 600 mL/min.
- At rest, skeletal muscles received about 1,200 mL/min. During vigorous exercise, the same muscles received about 12,500 mL/min.
- At rest, the kidneys received about 1,100 mL/min. During vigorous exercise, they received 600 mL/min.

Create a table to record these data. Then use the data to explain why some organs receive more blood during exercise, while some receive less.

Veins

After blood moves through capillaries, it enters larger blood vessels called veins, which carry blood back to the heart. The walls of veins, like those of arteries, have three layers, with muscle in the middle layer. However, the walls of veins are generally thinner than those of arteries.

By the time blood flows into veins, the pushing force of the heart has less effect than it did in the arteries. Several factors help move blood through veins. First, because many veins are located near skeletal muscles, the contraction of the muscles helps push the blood along. For example, as you run or walk, the skeletal muscles in your legs contract and squeeze the veins in your legs. Second, larger veins in your body have valves in them that prevent blood from flowing backward. Third, breathing movements, which exert a squeezing pressure against veins in the chest, also force blood toward the heart.

Checkpoint *How do skeletal muscles help move blood in veins?*

Blood Pressure

INTEGRATING PHYSICS

Suppose that you are washing a car. You attach the hose to the faucet and turn on the faucet. The water flows out in a slow, steady stream. Then, while your back is turned, your little brother turns the faucet on all the way. Suddenly, the water spurts out rapidly, and the hose almost jumps out of your hand.

As water flows through a hose, it pushes against the walls of the hose, creating pressure on the walls. **Pressure** is the force that something exerts over a given area. When your brother turned on the faucet all the way, the additional water flow increased the pressure exerted on the inside of the hose. The extra pressure made the water spurt out of the nozzle faster.

What Causes Blood Pressure? Blood traveling through blood vessels behaves in a manner similar to that of water moving through a hose. Blood exerts a pressure, called **blood pressure,** against the walls of blood vessels. **Blood pressure is caused by the force with which the ventricles contract.** In general, as blood moves away from the heart, its pressure decreases. This happens because the farther away from the heart the blood moves, the lower the force of the ventricles. Blood flowing through arteries exerts the highest pressure. Blood pressure in capillaries and veins is much lower than in the arteries.

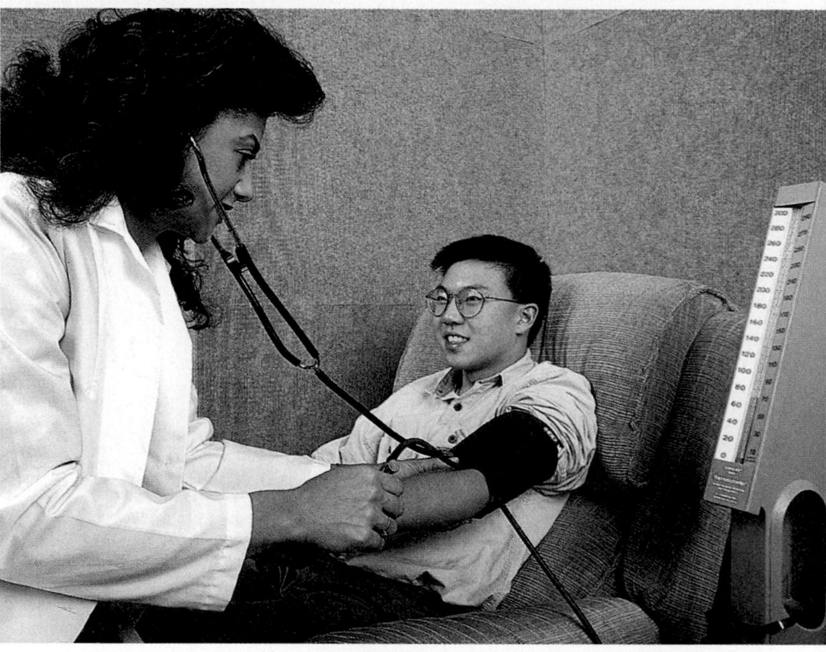

Figure 10 Blood pressure is measured with a sphygmomanometer. The cuff is wrapped around the patient's arm. His blood pressure is recorded by the height of the mercury column in the instrument on the right.

Measuring Blood Pressure Blood pressure can be measured with an instrument called a **sphygmomanometer** (sfig moh muh NAHM uh tur). Many sphygmomanometers contain a tube of mercury. Blood pressure is expressed in millimeters of mercury and is recorded as two numbers. The first number is a measure of the blood pressure while the ventricles contract and pump blood into the arteries. The second number, which is lower, measures the blood pressure while the ventricles relax between heartbeats. The two numbers are expressed as a fraction: the contraction pressure over the relaxation pressure. A typical blood pressure reading for a young adult is 120/80. You will learn about the effects of high blood pressure in Section 4.

Section 2 Review

1. Contrast the functions of arteries, capillaries, and veins.
2. What causes blood pressure?
3. Explain the factors that enable blood in your leg veins to return to the heart in spite of the downward pull of gravity.
4. **Thinking Critically Applying Concepts** Arteries adjust the amount of blood flowing to different parts of the body, depending on where blood is needed. Use this fact to explain why it may not be a good idea to exercise vigorously shortly after you eat.

CHAPTER PROJECT 5

Check Your Progress

By now you should have begun constructing your display. Make sure that the blood vessels are depicted accurately. Also check that your display correctly shows the path of a red blood cell and the place where the red blood cell picks up oxygen. *(Hint:* Start to prepare a rough draft of your written description.)

Skills Lab

Measuring

Heart Beat, Health Beat

Problem

How does physical activity affect your pulse rate?

Materials

watch with second hand or heart rate monitor
graph paper

Procedure

1. Predict how your pulse rate will change as you go from resting to being active, then back to resting again. Then copy the data table into your notebook.
2. Locate your pulse by placing the index and middle finger of one hand on your other wrist at the base of your thumb. Move the two fingers slightly until you feel your pulse. If you are using a heart rate monitor, see your teacher for instructions.
3. Work with a partner for the rest of this lab. Begin by determining your resting pulse rate. Count the number of beats in your pulse for exactly one minute while your partner times you. Record your resting pulse rate in your data table.

CAUTION: *Do not complete the rest of these procedures if there is any medical reason why you should avoid physical activities.*

4. Walk in place for one minute while your partner times you. Stop and immediately take your pulse for one minute. Record the number in your data table.
5. Run in place for one minute. Take your pulse again, and record the result.
6. Sit down right away, and have your partner time you as you rest for one minute. Then take your pulse rate again.
7. Have your partner time you as you rest for 3 more minutes. Then take your pulse rate again and record it.

DATA TABLE

Activity	Pulse Rate
Resting	
Walking	
Running	
Resting after Exercise (1 min)	
Resting after Exercise (3+ min)	

Analyze and Conclude

1. Use the data you obtained to create a bar graph of your pulse rate under the different conditions you tested.
2. What conclusion can you draw about the relationship between physical activity and a person's pulse rate?
3. What happens to the pulse rate when the physical activity has stopped?
4. What can you infer about the heartbeat when the pulse rate increases?
5. **Think About It** Do you think the pulse measurements you made are completely accurate? Why or why not? How could you improve the accuracy of your measurements?

Design an Experiment

Do the resting pulse rates of adults, teens, and young children differ? Write a plan to answer this question. Obtain your teacher's permission before carrying out your plan.

SECTION 3 Blood and Lymph

DISCOVER ACTIVITY

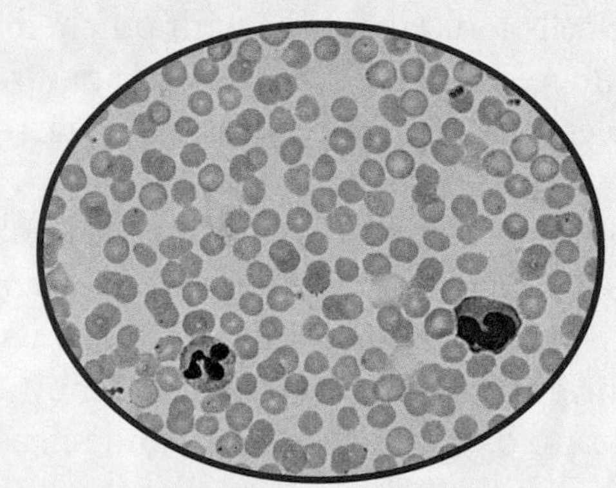

What Kinds of Cells Are in Blood?

1. Obtain a microscope slide of human blood. Look at the slide under the microscope, first under low power and then under high power.
2. Look carefully at the different kinds of cells that you see.
3. Make several drawings of each kind of cell. Use red pencil for the red blood cells.

Think It Over

Observing How many kinds of cells did you see? How do they differ from each other?

GUIDE FOR READING

- **What are the four components of blood?**
- **What determines the type of blood that a person can receive in transfusion?**

Reading Tip **As you read, write definitions for each boldfaced term in your own words.**

If someone fills a test tube with blood and lets it sit for a while, the blood separates into layers. The top layer is a clear, yellowish liquid. A dark red material rests on the bottom. The top layer is **plasma,** which is the liquid part of blood. The red material at the bottom is a mixture of blood cells. **Blood is made up of four components: plasma, red blood cells, white blood cells, and platelets.** About 45 percent of the volume of blood is made up of cells. The rest consists of plasma.

Plasma

Blood, as you have learned, transports materials from one part of the body to another. Most of those materials travel in plasma. In fact, 10 percent of plasma is made up of these dissolved materials. The other 90 percent of plasma is water.

Plasma carries molecules that come from the breakdown of digested food, such as glucose and fats. The vitamins and minerals your body needs also travel in plasma. Plasma also carries chemical messengers that direct body activities such as the uptake of glucose by your cells. In addition, many wastes produced by cell processes are carried away by plasma.

Protein molecules give plasma its yellow color. There are three groups of plasma proteins. One group helps to regulate the amount of water in blood. The second group, which is produced by white blood cells, helps fight disease. The third group of proteins interacts with platelets to form blood clots.

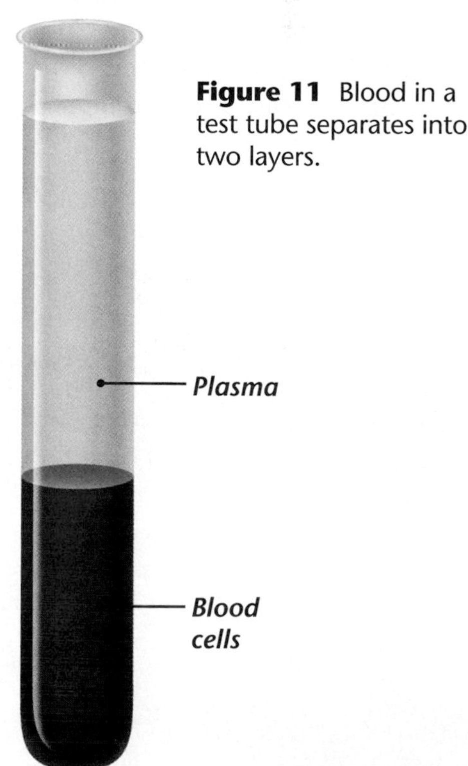

Figure 11 Blood in a test tube separates into two layers.

Red Blood Cells

Without red blood cells, your body could not use the oxygen that you breathe in. **Red blood cells** take up oxygen in the lungs and deliver it to cells elsewhere in the body. Red blood cells, like most blood cells, are produced in bone marrow.

Exploring Blood Cells shows what red blood cells look like. Under a microscope, these cells look like disks with pinched-in centers. Because they are thin, red blood cells can bend and twist easily. This flexibility enables them to squeeze through narrow capillaries.

A red blood cell is made mostly of **hemoglobin** (HEE muh gloh bin), which is an iron-containing protein that binds chemically to oxygen molecules. When hemoglobin combines with oxygen, the cells become bright red. Without oxygen, they are dark red. Hemoglobin picks up oxygen in the lungs and releases it as blood travels through capillaries in the rest of the body. Hemoglobin also picks up some of the carbon dioxide produced by cells. However, most of the carbon dioxide is carried by plasma. The blood carries the carbon dioxide to the lungs, where it is released from the body.

EXPLORING *Blood Cells*

Blood consists of liquid plasma and three kinds of cells—red blood cells, white blood cells, and platelets.

Red Blood Cells
Oxygen is carried throughout your body by red blood cells. Your blood contains more red blood cells than any other kind of cell.

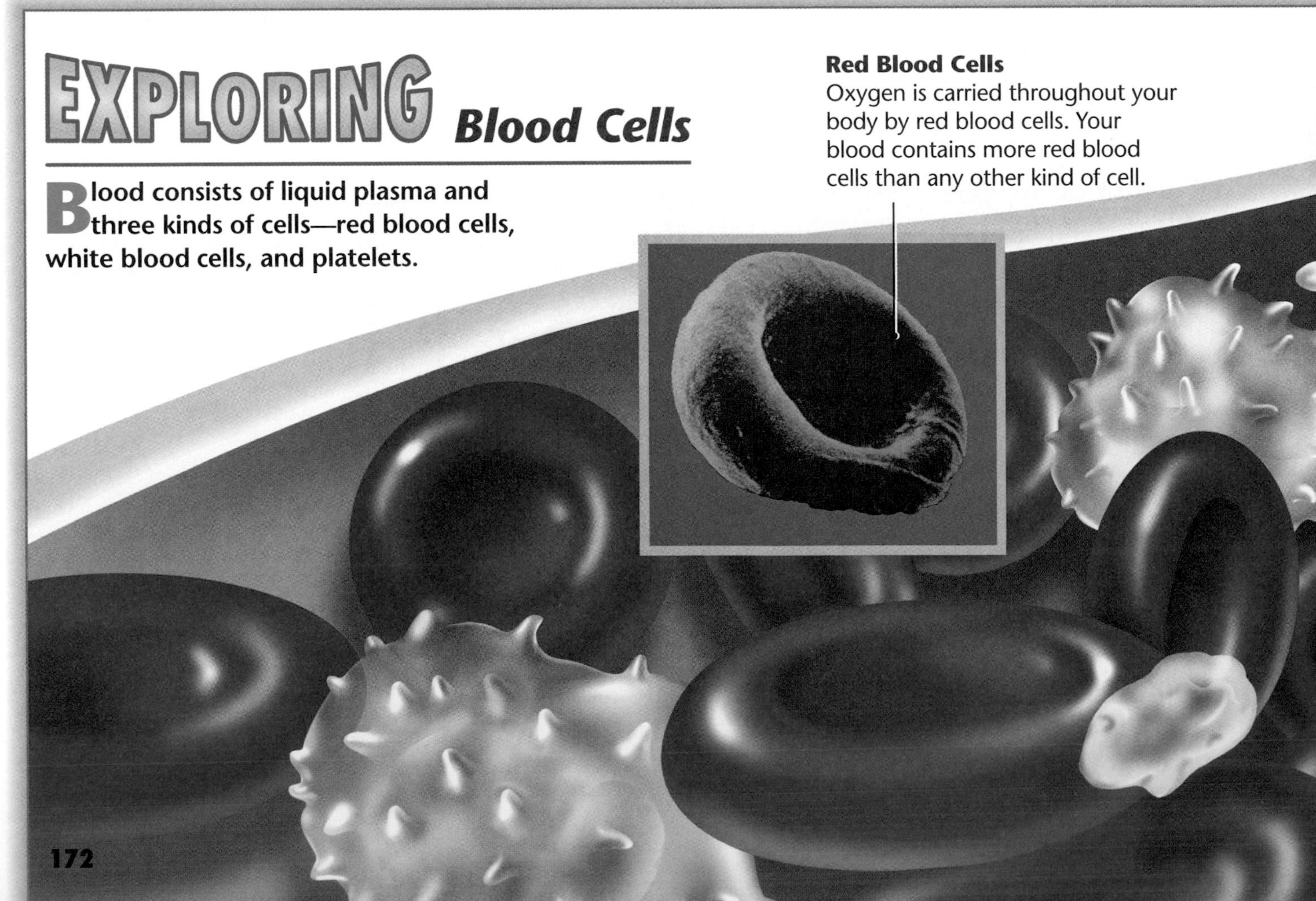

Mature red blood cells have no nuclei. Without a nucleus, a red blood cell cannot reproduce or repair itself. Red blood cells live only about 120 days. Every second, about 2 million red blood cells in your body die. Fortunately, your bone marrow produces new red blood cells at the same rate.

☑ *Checkpoint* *What is the shape of a red blood cell?*

White Blood Cells

Like red blood cells, white blood cells begin their existence in bone marrow. **White blood cells** are the body's disease fighters. Some white blood cells recognize disease-causing organisms such as bacteria, and alert the body that it has been invaded. Other white blood cells produce chemicals to fight the invaders. Still others surround and kill the organisms. You will learn more about the functions of white blood cells in Chapter 7.

White blood cells are different from red blood cells in several important ways. There are fewer of them—only about one white blood cell for every 500 to 1,000 red blood cells. White blood cells are also bigger than red blood cells, and they have nuclei. And most white blood cells live for months or even years.

White Blood Cells
By finding and destroying disease-causing organisms, white blood cells fight disease. Most white blood cells are larger than red blood cells.

Platelets
When you cut yourself, platelets help form the blood clot that stops the bleeding. Platelets aren't really whole cells—instead, they are small pieces of cells that don't have nuclei.

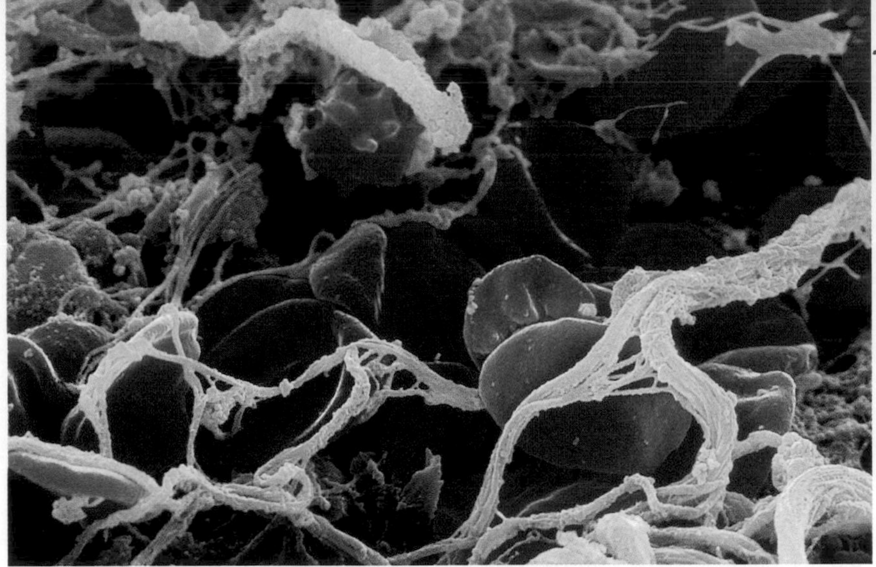

Figure 12 When you cut your skin, a blood clot forms. The blood clot consists of blood cells trapped in a fiber net. Platelets produce the material of which the fibers are made.

Platelets

When you cut your finger, blood flows out of the cut. After a short time, however, a blood clot forms, stopping the blood flow. **Platelets** (PLAYT lits) are cell fragments that play an important part in forming blood clots.

When a blood vessel is cut, platelets collect and stick to the vessel at the site of the wound. The platelets release chemicals that start a chain reaction. This series of reactions eventually produces a chemical called **fibrin** (FY brin). Fibrin gets its name from the fact that it weaves a net of tiny fibers across the cut in the blood vessel. The fiber net traps blood cells. As more and more platelets and blood cells become trapped in the net, a blood clot forms. A scab is a dried blood clot on the skin surface.

☑ *Checkpoint* *What role do platelets play in forming blood clots?*

Caught in the Web

ACTIVITY

In this activity, you will model part of the process by which a blood clot forms.

1. Cover the opening of a sturdy plastic cup with a piece of cheesecloth. Use a rubber band to hold the cheesecloth in place.
2. Put some water, paper clips, and coins in another cup.
3. Carefully pour the water, coins, and paper clips into the middle of the cheesecloth.

Making Models The paper clips and coins represent blood cells. What does the cheesecloth represent? What starts the production of the substance that the cheesecloth represents?

Blood Types

If a person loses a lot of blood—from a wound or during surgery—he or she may be given a **blood transfusion.** A blood transfusion is the transference of blood from one person to another. Most early attempts at blood transfusion failed, but no one knew why until the early 1900s. At that time Karl Landsteiner, an Austrian American physician, tried mixing blood samples from pairs of people. Sometimes the two blood samples blended smoothly. In other cases, however, the red blood cells clumped together. This clumping accounted for the failure of many blood transfusions. If clumping occurs within the body, it clogs the capillaries and may kill the person.

Marker Molecules Landsteiner went on to discover that there are four types of blood—A, B, AB, and O. Blood types are determined by marker molecules on red blood cells. If your blood type is A, you have the A marker. If your blood type is B, you have the B marker. People with type AB blood have both A and B markers. The red blood cells of people with type O blood contain neither A nor B markers.

Your plasma contains clumping proteins that recognize red blood cells with "foreign" markers and make those cells clump together. For example, if you have blood type A, your blood contains clumping proteins that act against cells with B markers. So if you receive a transfusion of type B blood, your clumping proteins will make the "foreign" type B cells clump together.

Safe Transfusions Landsteiner's work led to a better understanding of transfusions. **The marker molecules on your red blood cells determine your blood type and the type of blood that you can safely receive in transfusions.** A person with type A blood can receive transfusions of either type A or type O blood. Neither of these two blood types has B markers. Thus they would not be recognized as foreign by the clumping proteins in type A blood. A person with type AB blood can receive all blood types in transfusion, because type AB blood has no clumping proteins. Figure 13 shows which transfusions are safe for each blood type.

If you ever receive a transfusion, your blood type will be checked. Then donated blood that you can safely receive will be found. This process is called cross matching. You may have heard a doctor on a television show give the order to "type and cross." The doctor wants to find out what blood type the patient has and then cross match it against donated blood.

Blood Types

Blood Type	Marker Molecules on Red Blood Cells	Clumping Proteins	Blood Types That Can Be Safely Received in a Transfusion
A	A A A A A A	anti-B	A and O
B	B B B B B B	anti-A	B and O
AB	A B B A A B	no clumping proteins	A, B, AB, and O
O		anti-A and anti-B	O

Figure 13 The chemical markers on a person's red blood cells determine the types of blood he or she can safely receive in a transfusion. ***Interpreting Charts*** *What types of blood can be given safely to a person with blood type AB? Who can safely receive blood type O?*

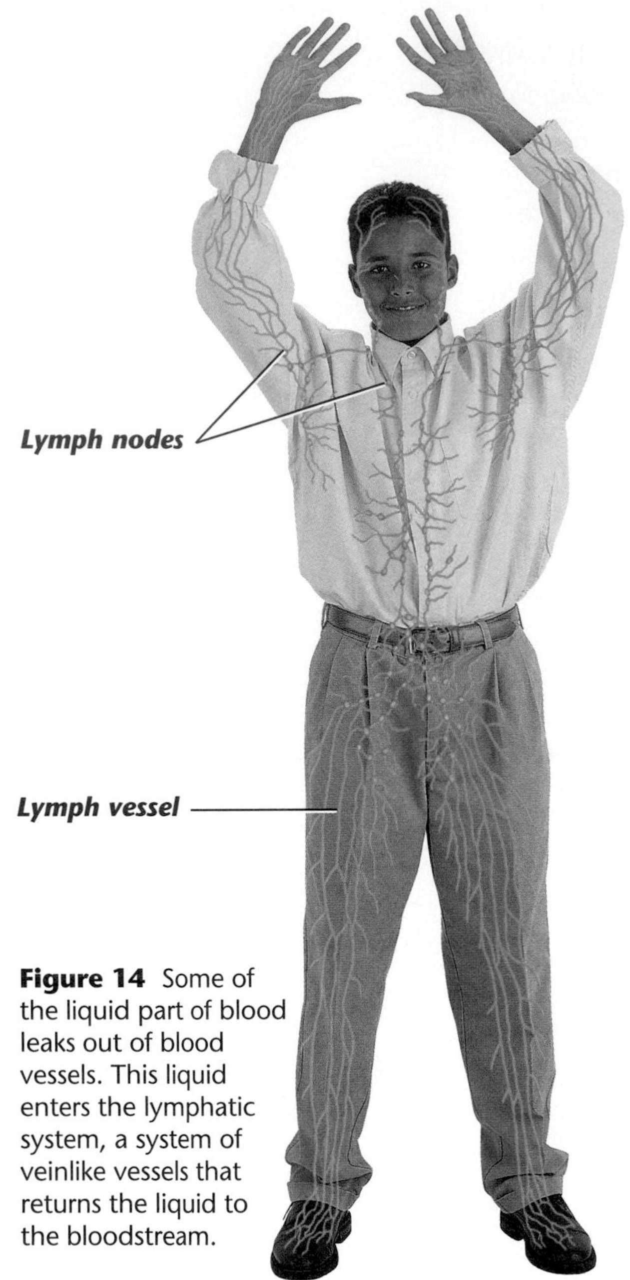

Figure 14 Some of the liquid part of blood leaks out of blood vessels. This liquid enters the lymphatic system, a system of veinlike vessels that returns the liquid to the bloodstream.

The Lymphatic System

As blood travels through the capillaries in the cardiovascular system, some of the fluid leaks out. It moves through the walls of capillaries and into surrounding tissues. This fluid carries materials that the cells in the tissues need.

After bathing the cells, this fluid moves into the lymphatic system. The **lymphatic system** (lim FAT ik) is a network of veinlike vessels that returns the fluid to the bloodstream. The lymphatic system acts something like rain gutters after a rainstorm, carrying the fluid away.

Lymph Once the fluid is inside the lymphatic system, it is called **lymph.** Lymph consists of water and dissolved materials such as glucose. It also contains some white blood cells that have left the capillaries.

The lymphatic system has no pump, so lymph moves slowly. Lymphatic vessels, which are part of the cardiovascular system, connect to large veins in the chest. Lymph empties into these veins and once again becomes part of blood plasma.

Lymph Nodes As lymph flows through the lymphatic system, it passes through small knobs of tissue called **lymph nodes.** Lymph nodes filter the lymph, trapping bacteria and other microorganisms that cause disease. When the body is fighting an infection, the lymph nodes enlarge. If you've ever had "swollen glands" when you've been sick, you've actually had swollen lymph nodes.

Section 3 Review

1. List the four components of blood. Identify whether each is a cell, a part of a cell, or a liquid.
2. Explain why a person with type O blood cannot receive a transfusion of type A blood.
3. Where does lymph come from? What happens to lymph after it travels through the lymphatic system?
4. **Thinking Critically Relating Cause and Effect** People with the disease hemophilia do not produce the chemical fibrin. Explain why hemophilia is a serious disease.

CHAPTER PROJECT 5

Check Your Progress

By now, you should be completing your display. Write out your description using the correct names of blood vessels and other terms that you've learned in this chapter. *(Hint:* If your display has moving parts, test it to make sure that it works the way you expect it to.)

You and Your Community

Real-World Lab

Do You Know Your A-B-O's?

Donated blood is used for blood transfusions. But not every type of blood can be safely donated to every individual. In this lab, you'll investigate why type O blood is especially useful in blood transfusions.

Problem

Which blood types can safely receive transfusions of type A blood? Which can receive type O blood?

Materials

4 paper cups
marking pen
4 plastic droppers
8 plastic petri dishes
white paper
toothpicks
four model "blood" types

Procedure

1. Write down your ideas about why type O blood might be in higher demand than other blood types. Then make two copies of the data table in your notebook.
2. Label 4 paper cups A, B, AB, and O. Fill each cup about one-third full with the model "blood" supplied by your teacher. Insert one clean plastic dropper into each cup. Use each dropper to transfer only that one type of blood.
3. Label the side of each of 4 petri dishes with a blood type: A, B, AB, or O. Place the petri dishes on a sheet of white paper.
4. Use the plastic droppers to place 10 drops of each type of blood in its labeled petri dish. Each sample represents the blood of a potential receiver of a blood transfusion. Record the original color of each sample in your data table as yellow, blue, green, or colorless.

DATA TABLE

Donor: Type ______

Potential Receiver	Original Color	Final Color of Mixture	Safe or Unsafe?
A			
B			
AB			
O			

5. Label your first data table Donor: Type A. To test whether each potential receiver can safely receive type A blood, add 10 drops of type A blood to each sample. Stir each mixture with a separate, clean toothpick.
6. Record the final color of each mixture in the data table. If the color stayed the same, write "safe" in the last column. If the color of the mixture changed, write "unsafe."
7. Label your second data table Donor: Type O. Obtain four clean petri dishes, and repeat Steps 3 through 6 to determine who could safely receive type O blood.

Analyze and Conclude

1. Which blood types can safely receive a transfusion of type A blood? Type O blood?
2. If some blood types are not available, how might type O blood be useful?
3. **Apply** Why should hospitals have an adequate supply of different types of blood?

More to Explore

Repeat this activity to find out which blood types can safely receive donations of type B and type AB blood.

 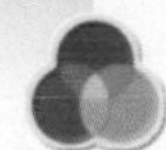

SECTION 4 Cardiovascular Health

DISCOVER — ACTIVITY

Which Foods Are "Heart Healthy"?

1. Your teacher will give you an assortment of foods. If they have nutrition labels, read the information.
2. Sort the foods into three groups. In one group, put those foods that you think are good for your cardiovascular system. In the second group, put foods that you think might damage your cardiovascular system if eaten often. Place foods you aren't sure about in the third group.

Think It Over

Forming Operational Definitions How did you define a "heart-healthy" food?

GUIDE FOR READING

- **What behaviors can help maintain cardiovascular health?**

Reading Tip **Before you read, rewrite the headings in the section as questions that begin with *how, why,* or *what.* Write short answers to these questions as you read.**

Shortly after sunrise, when most people are just waking up, the rowers are already out on the river. Rhythmically, with perfectly coordinated movement, the rowers pull on the oars, making the boat glide swiftly through the water. Despite the chilly morning air, sweat glistens on the rowers' faces and arms. And inside their chests, their hearts are pounding, delivering blood to the arm and chest muscles that power the oars.

Rowers cannot perform at their peaks unless their cardiovascular systems are in excellent condition. But cardiovascular health is important to all people, not just athletes. Cardiovascular

disease is the leading cause of death in the United States. However, people can practice behaviors that decrease their risks of developing cardiovascular problems.

Cardiovascular Disease

Compare the two arteries shown in Figure 15. The one on the left is a healthy artery. It has a large space in the center through which blood can flow easily. The artery on the right, in contrast, has a thick wall and only a small space in the middle. This artery exhibits **atherosclerosis** (ath uh roh skluh ROH sis), a condition in which an artery wall thickens as a result of the buildup of fatty materials. One of these fatty materials is cholesterol, a waxy, fat-like substance. Atherosclerosis restricts the flow of blood in the arteries.

Atherosclerosis can develop in the coronary arteries that supply the heart. When that happens, the heart muscle receives less blood and therefore less oxygen. This condition may lead to a heart attack. A **heart attack** occurs when blood flow to part of the heart muscle is blocked. Cells die in the part of the heart that does not receive blood. This permanently damages the heart.

Treatment for mild atherosclerosis usually includes a low-fat diet and a moderate exercise program. In addition, medications that lower the levels of cholesterol and fats in the blood may be prescribed. People with severe atherosclerosis may need to undergo surgery or other procedures to unclog blocked arteries.

☑ ***Checkpoint*** *Why is atherosclerosis especially serious when it affects the coronary arteries?*

Hypertension

High blood pressure, or **hypertension** (hy pur TEN shun), is a disorder in which a person's blood pressure is consistently higher than normal—greater than 140/90. Hypertension makes the heart work harder. It also may damage the walls of the blood

Blocking the Flow

ACTIVITY

Use this activity to find out how fatty deposits affect the flow of blood through an artery.

1. Put a funnel in the mouth of a plastic jar. The funnel will represent an artery.
2. To model blood flowing through the artery, slowly pour 100 mL of water into the funnel. Have your partner time how many seconds it takes for all the water to flow through the funnel. Then discard the water.
3. Use a plastic knife to spread a small amount of peanut butter along the bottom of the funnel's neck. Then, with a toothpick, carve out a hole in the peanut butter so that the funnel is partly, but not completely, clogged.
4. Repeat Steps 1 and 2.

Predicting If the funnels were arteries, which one—blocked or unblocked—would do a better job of supplying blood to tissues? Explain.

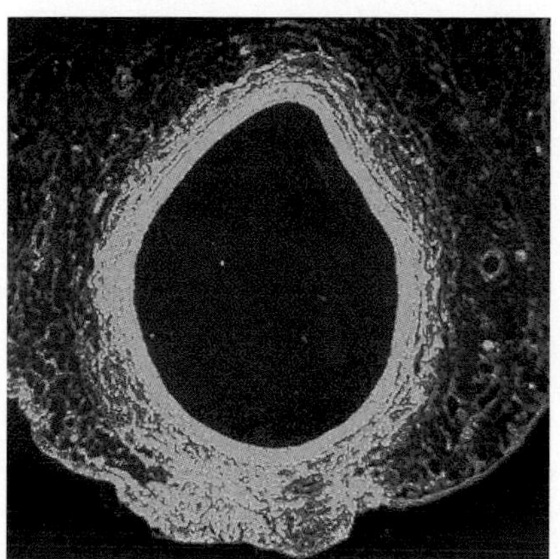

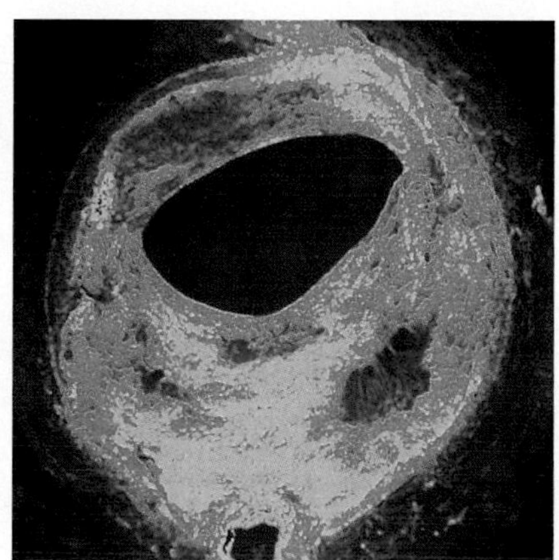

Figure 15 The healthy artery on the left is unblocked. In contrast, notice the narrow opening in the artery on the right. This person has atherosclerosis, which is caused by fatty deposits on the artery walls. ***Relating Cause and Effect*** *What kind of diet can lead to atherosclerosis?*

vessels. Over time, both the heart and arteries can be severely harmed by hypertension. Because people with hypertension often have no obvious symptoms to warn them, hypertension is sometimes called the "silent killer."

Hypertension and atherosclerosis are closely related. As the arteries narrow, blood pressure increases. Being overweight and failing to get enough exercise can also increase a person's risk of developing hypertension.

Cardiovascular Advances in the Twentieth Century

Scientists today have an in-depth understanding of how the cardiovascular system works and how to treat cardiovascular problems. This time line describes some advances of the twentieth century.

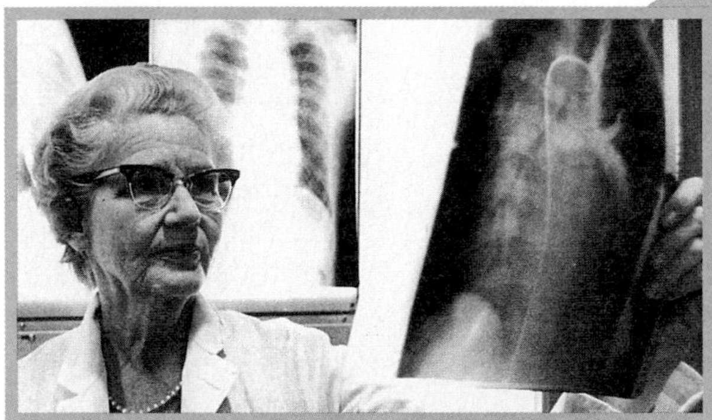

1944
Treatment for "Blue Babies"

Helen Taussig identified the heart defect that causes the skin of some newborn babies to be bluish in color. The blood of these "blue babies" does not receive an adequate amount of oxygen. Taussig and another surgeon, Alfred Blalock, developed an operation to correct the defect and save these babies' lives.

1900 **1920** **1940**

1901
Discovery of Blood Types

Karl Landsteiner demonstrated that people have different blood types, which are determined by marker molecules on their red blood cells. Landsteiner's discovery enabled blood transfusions to be done safely.

1930s–1940s
Blood Banks

Charles Drew demonstrated that emergency transfusions could successfully be done with plasma if whole blood was not available. During World War II, Drew established blood banks for storing donated blood. His work helped save millions of lives on and off the battlefield.

For mild hypertension, regular exercise and careful food choices may be enough to lower blood pressure. People with hypertension need to limit their intake of sodium, which can increase their blood pressure. Sodium is found in salt and in processed foods such as soups and packaged snack foods. For some people who have hypertension, however, medications are needed to reduce their blood pressure.

☑ ***Checkpoint*** *Why is hypertension called the "silent killer"?*

In Your Journal

Choose one of the scientists whose work is described here. Imagine that you are on a committee that has chosen him or her to receive an award. Write the speech you would give at the award ceremony. The speech should explain the importance of the scientist's contributions.

1967

First Heart Transplant

Christiaan Barnard, a South African surgeon, performed the first transplant of a human heart. Louis Washkansky, the man who received the heart, lived for only 18 days after the transplant. But Barnard's work paved the way for future successes in transplanting hearts and other organs.

1992

Laser Beam Unclogs Arteries

The United States government approved a device that uses a laser beam to burn away the material causing blockage in some arteries. This device can help some people with atherosclerosis.

1960 | 1980 | 2000

1982

Artificial Heart

An artificial heart, developed by Robert Jarvik, was implanted into a patient by surgeon William DeVries at the University of Utah. Barney Clark, the man who received the artificial heart, lived for 112 days. Today artificial hearts are sometimes used temporarily in people waiting for heart transplants.

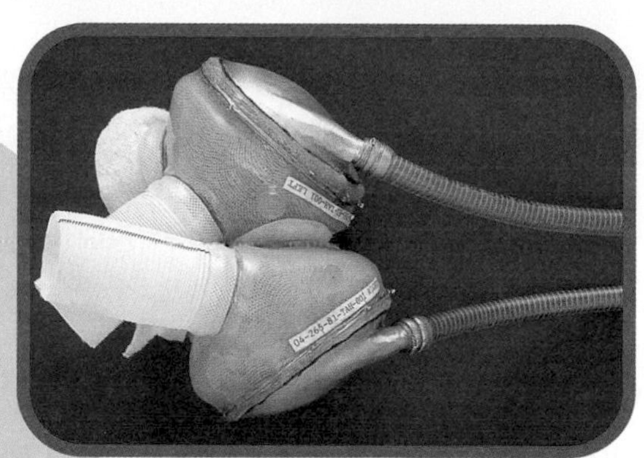

Keeping Your Cardiovascular System Healthy

Few young people have heart attacks, but atherosclerosis can begin to develop in people as young as 20 years old. You can establish habits now that will lessen your risk of developing atherosclerosis and hypertension. **To help maintain cardiovascular health, people should exercise regularly; eat a balanced diet that is low in fat, cholesterol, and sodium; and avoid smoking.**

Figure 16 Eating foods that are low in fat can help keep your cardiovascular system healthy.

Exercise Do you participate in sports, ride a bike, swim, dance, or climb stairs instead of taking the elevator? Every time you do one of those activities, you are helping to maintain your cardiovascular health. Exercise strengthens your heart muscle and also helps prevent atherosclerosis.

A Balanced Diet Foods that are high in cholesterol and fats can lead to a buildup of fatty deposits on artery walls. In addition, eating too many high-fat foods can lead to excessive weight gain. Foods such as red meats, eggs, and cheese are high in cholesterol. These foods also contain substances that your body needs. Therefore, a smart approach might be to eat them, but only in small quantities. Some foods that are especially high in fat include butter and margarine, potato chips, doughnuts, and fried foods such as French fries. Eat high-fat foods only occasionally, if at all.

Avoid Smoking Smokers are more than twice as likely to have a heart attack than are nonsmokers. Every year, almost 180,000 people in the United States die from cardiovascular disease caused by smoking. If smokers quit, however, their risk of death from cardiovascular disease decreases.

Section 4 Review

1. List three things you can do to help your cardiovascular system stay healthy.
2. What is atherosclerosis?
3. How does hypertension affect blood vessels?
4. **Thinking Critically Relating Cause and Effect** Coronary heart disease is much less common in some countries than it is in the United States. What factors might account for this difference?

Science at Home

With your family, discuss some things that you all can do to maintain healthy cardiovascular systems. Make a list of exercise activities, such as bicycling and swimming, that family members can enjoy together. You might also work with your family to cook and serve a "heart-healthy," low-fat meal.

CHAPTER 5 STUDY GUIDE

The Body's Transportation System

Key Ideas

- The heart pumps blood through the blood vessels. The heart has four chambers. The two atria receive blood, and the two ventricles pump blood out of the heart.
- Blood travels from the heart to the lungs and back to the heart. It is then pumped to the body and returns again to the heart.

Key Terms

cardiovascular system	valve	vein
heart	pacemaker	aorta
atrium	artery	force
ventricle	capillary	

A Closer Look at Blood Vessels

Key Ideas

- Arteries carry blood from the heart to the capillaries. In the capillaries, materials are exchanged between the blood and the body's cells. From the capillaries, blood flows into veins that carry it back to the heart.

Key Terms

coronary artery	blood pressure
diffusion	sphygmomanometer
pressure	

Blood and Lymph

Key Idea

- Red blood cells, which contain hemoglobin, carry oxygen and deliver it to body cells. White blood cells fight disease. Platelets are important in forming blood clots.

Key Terms

plasma	fibrin
red blood cell	blood transfusion
hemoglobin	lymphatic system
white blood cell	lymph
platelet	lymph node

Cardiovascular Health

INTEGRATING HEALTH

Key Ideas

- Atherosclerosis is a condition in which an artery wall thickens due to the buildup of cholesterol and other fatty materials.
- Hypertension is a disorder in which the blood pressure is higher than normal.
- To help prevent atherosclerosis and hypertension, people need to exercise regularly; eat a diet low in fat, cholesterol, and salt; and avoid smoking.

Key Terms

atherosclerosis	hypertension
heart attack	

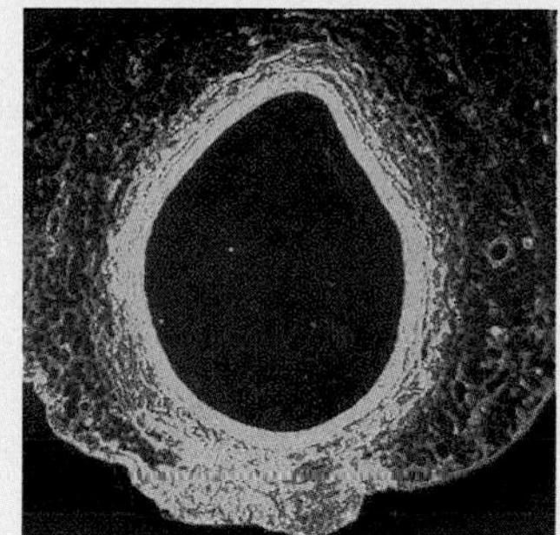

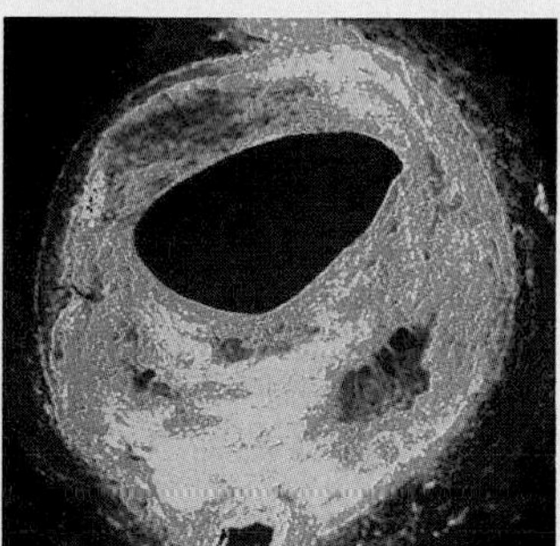

Organizing Information

Compare/Contrast Table Compare the three types of blood vessels by copying and completing the table below. (For more on compare/contrast tables, see the Skills Handbook.)

Blood Vessel	Function	Structure of Wall
Artery	**a.** ?	3 layers: inner—epithelial tissue middle—muscle outer—connective tissue
b. ?	exchange of materials between cells and blood	**c.** ?
Vein	**d.** ?	**e.** ?

Reviewing Content

Multiple Choice

Choose the letter of the best answer.

1. The heart's upper chambers are called
   a. ventricles. b. atria.
   c. valves. d. hemoglobins.
2. Oxygen-rich blood enters the heart through the
   a. left atrium.
   b. right atrium.
   c. left ventricle.
   d. right ventricle.
3. Which of the following is *not* important in moving blood through veins?
   a. the force with which the atria contract
   b. valves
   c. breathing movements of the chest
   d. the contraction of skeletal muscles
4. Platelets help the body to
   a. control bleeding.
   b. carry oxygen.
   c. fight infection.
   d. regulate the amount of water in plasma.
5. Cholesterol is a fatlike substance associated with
   a. lymph nodes.
   b. fibrin.
   c. atherosclerosis.
   d. salt.

True or False

If the statement is true, write true. If it is false, change the underlined word or words to make the statement true.

6. The two lower heart chambers are called <u>ventricles</u>.
7. <u>White blood cells</u> contain hemoglobin.
8. The <u>capillaries</u> are the narrowest blood vessels in the body.
9. A person with blood type B can receive a transfusion of blood types B and <u>AB</u>.
10. Elevated blood pressure is called <u>hypertension</u>.

Checking Concepts

11. A red blood cell is moving through an artery in your leg. Describe the path that blood cell will follow back to your heart. Identify the chamber of the heart to which it will return.
12. Contrast the forces with which the right and left ventricles contract. How does this relate to each ventricle's function?
13. How is a capillary's structure adapted to its function?
14. What is the function of hemoglobin in the body?
15. Give two reasons why the food choices that people make are important to their cardiovascular health.
16. **Writing to Learn** Write an ad that encourages teenagers to exercise. Your ad will appear in a teen magazine. The ad should point out the health benefits of exercise and identify some ways that teenagers can exercise.

Thinking Critically

17. **Predicting** Some babies are born with an opening between the left and right ventricles of the heart. How would this heart defect affect the ability of the cardiovascular system to deliver oxygen to body cells?
18. **Comparing and Contrasting** Contrast the direction of movement of oxygen in lung capillaries and other capillaries in the body.
19. **Relating Cause and Effect** People who do not have enough iron in their diets sometimes develop a condition in which their blood cannot carry a normal amount of oxygen. Explain why this is so.
20. **Making Generalizations** Why are atherosclerosis and hypertension sometimes called "lifestyle diseases"?

Applying Skills

The graph below shows how average blood pressure, measured when the ventricles contract, changes as men and women grow older. Use the graph to answer Questions 21–23.

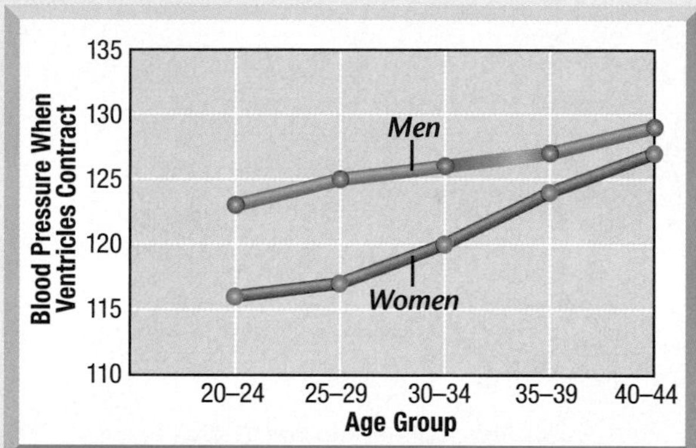

21. **Interpreting Data** At age 20, who is likely to have the higher blood pressure—a man or a woman?
22. **Drawing Conclusions** In general, what happens to people's blood pressure as they age?
23. **Predicting** Do you think that there is some age at which both men and women have about the same blood pressure? Use the graph lines to explain your prediction.

Performance Assessment — Chapter Project 5

Project Wrap Up You should now be ready to present your display. First show it to a small group of classmates to make sure it is clear and accurate. When you present your display, be ready to answer questions.

Reflect and Record As you look at all the different projects, decide which display did the best job of teaching you. Use your journal to write about how the display looked and worked. Did you learn more from that display or from working on your own? As you write, try to decide which way of learning works best for you.

Test Preparation

Use these questions to prepare for standardized tests.

Study the table. Then answer Questions 24–27.

Blood Types

Name	Blood Type	Marker Molecules	Clumping Proteins
Juan	A	A	anti-B
Wanda	B	B	anti-A
Kyoko	AB	A and B	none
Eddie	O	none	anti-A and anti-B

24. What clumping proteins does Kyoko have in her blood?
   a. anti-A
   b. anti-B
   c. anti-A and anti-B
   d. none
25. What marker molecules does Wanda have on her red blood cells?
   a. A
   b. B
   c. A and B
   d. none
26. If you have Type B blood, from whom could you receive a blood transfusion?
   a. Wanda and Kyoko
   b. Wanda and Eddie
   c. only Wanda
   d. only Eddie
27. If you have Type AB blood, from whom could you receive a blood transfusion?
   a. only Juan
   b. only Juan and Wanda
   c. only Eddie
   d. Juan, Wanda, Kyoko, and Eddie

CHAPTER 6

Respiration and Excretion

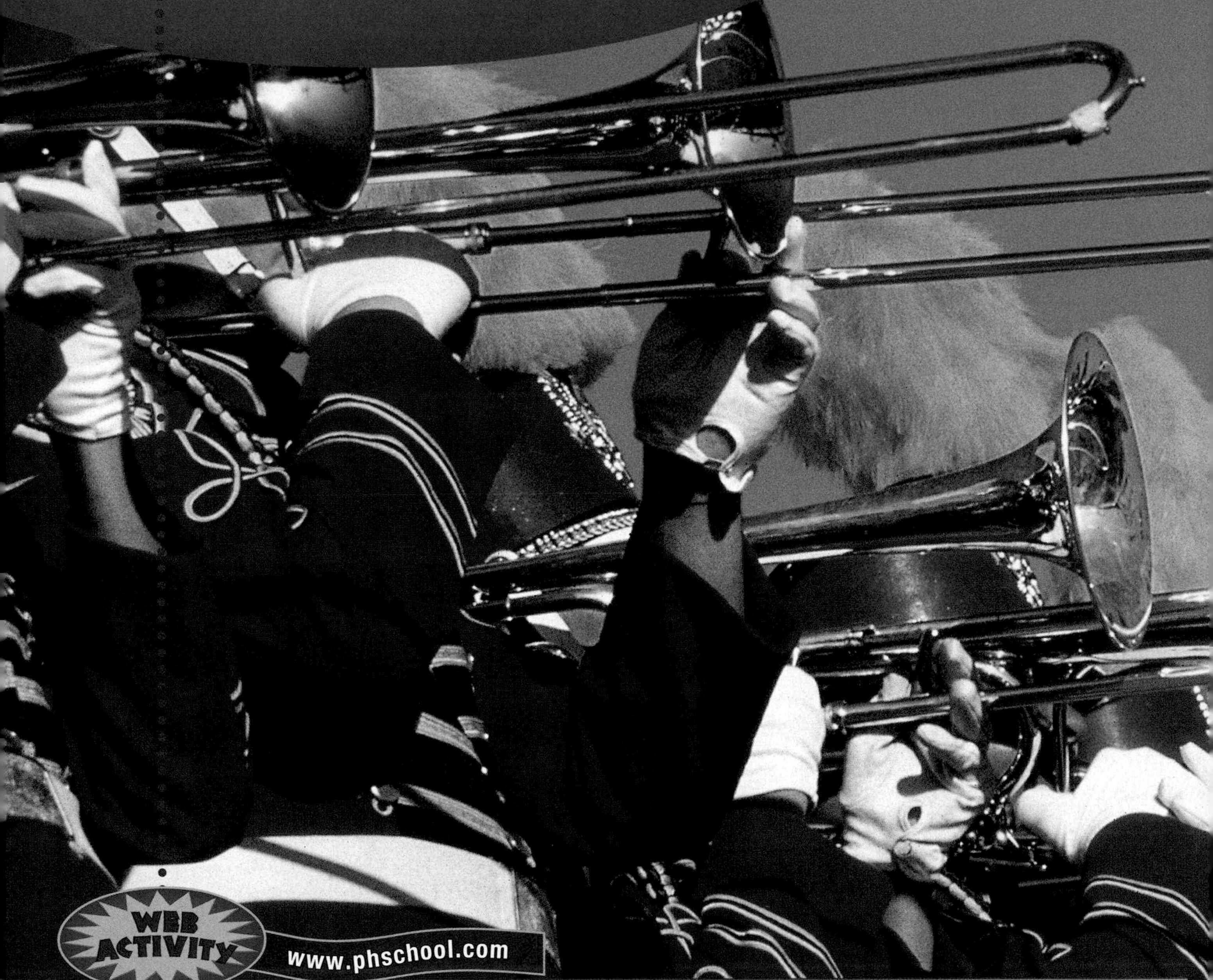

WEB ACTIVITY www.phschool.com

SECTION 1 The Respiratory System

Discover How Big Can You Blow Up a Balloon?
Try This Do You Exhale Carbon Dioxide?
Skills Lab A Breath of Fresh Air

Integrating Health

SECTION 2 Smoking and Your Health

Discover What Are the Dangers of Smoking?
Sharpen Your Skills Calculating

SECTION 3 The Excretory System

Discover How Does Filtering a Liquid Change What Is in It?
Real-World Lab Clues About Health

PROJECT 6

Get the Message Out

Lively music fills the air as the band marches along the parade route. To play many musical instruments, you need powerful, healthy lungs, which are part of the respiratory system. In this chapter, you will learn about the respiratory and excretory systems.

One way that people can keep their respiratory systems healthy is by choosing not to smoke. You've probably seen antismoking advertisements on television and in magazines. Imagine that you're part of a team of writers and designers who create advertisements. You've just been given the job of creating antismoking ads for different age groups. As you learn about the respiratory system, you can use your knowledge in your ad campaign.

Your Goal To create three different antismoking ads: one telling young children about the dangers of smoking; the second one discouraging teenagers from trying cigarettes; and the third encouraging adult smokers to quit.

To complete the project successfully, each ad must

- accurately communicate at least three health risks associated with smoking
- address at least two pressures that influence people to start or continue smoking
- use images and words in convincing, creative ways that gear your message to each audience

Get Started Brainstorm a list of reasons why people smoke. Consider the possible influence of family and friends as well as that of ads, movies, videos, and television. Also decide which types of ads you will produce, such as magazine ads or billboards. Begin to plan your ads.

Check Your Progress You'll be working on this project as you study this chapter. To keep your project on track, look for Check Your Progress boxes at the following points.

Section 2 Review, page 202: Plan your ads.

Section 3 Review, page 208: Design and produce your ads.

Wrap Up At the end of the chapter (page 211), you will display your completed ads. Be prepared to discuss your reasons for choosing the images and persuasive messages that you used.

Trombone players in a marching band need strong, healthy lungs.

The Respiratory System

Discover

How Big Can You Blow Up a Balloon?

1. Take a normal breath, then blow as much air as possible into a balloon. Twist the end and hold it closed. Have your partner measure around the balloon at its widest point.
2. Let the air out of the balloon. Repeat Step 1 and calculate the average of the two measurements.
3. Compare your results with those of your classmates. The bigger the circumference, the greater the volume of air exhaled.

Think It Over

Inferring What factors might affect the volume of air a person can exhale?

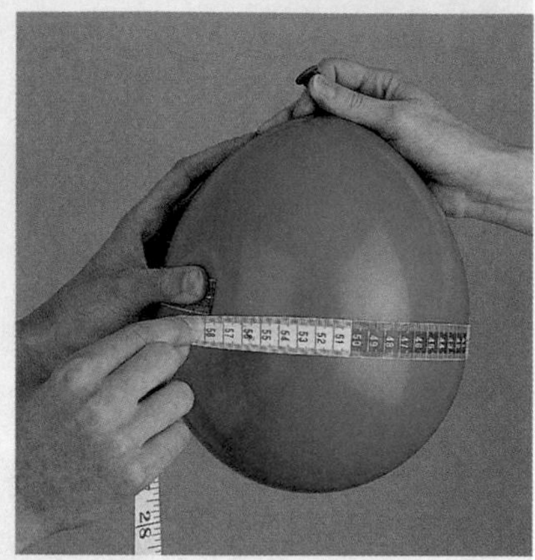

Guide for Reading

- What are the functions of the respiratory system?
- What structures does air pass through as it travels to the lungs?
- How do oxygen, carbon dioxide, and water move in the lungs?

Reading Tip Before you read, preview *Exploring the Respiratory System* on page 191. Write down any unfamiliar terms.

Jerry, the main character in Doris Lessing's story "Through the Tunnel," is on vacation at the seaside. Day after day, he watches some older boys dive into deep water on one side of a huge rock. The boys mysteriously reappear on the other side. Jerry figures out that there must be an underwater tunnel in the rock. He finds the tunnel beneath the water and decides to swim through it. Once inside, though, he is terrified. The walls are slimy, and rocks scrape his body. He can barely see where he is going. But worst of all, Jerry has to hold his breath for far longer than ever before. The author describes Jerry this way: "His head was swelling, his lungs were cracking."

Jerry's behavior could have killed him. No one can go for very long without breathing. Your body cells need oxygen, and they get that oxygen from the air you breathe. **The respiratory system moves oxygen from the outside environment into the body. It also removes carbon dioxide and water from the body.**

Why the Body Needs Oxygen

The energy-releasing chemical reactions that take place inside your cells require oxygen. As a result of these reactions, your cells are able to perform all the tasks that keep you alive. Like a fire, which cannot burn without oxygen, your cells cannot "burn" enough substances to keep you alive without oxygen.

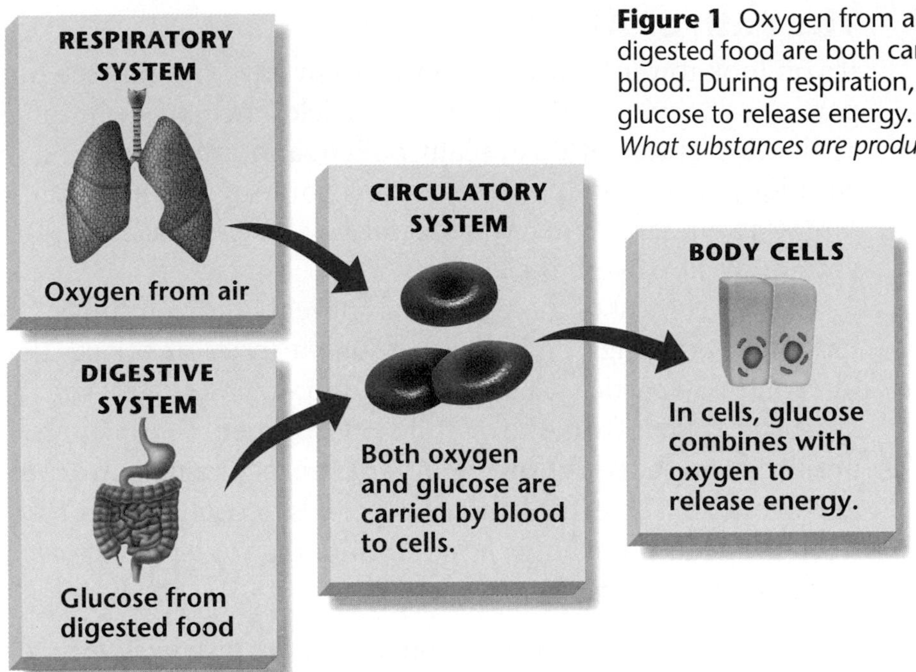

Figure 1 Oxygen from air and glucose from digested food are both carried to cells by the blood. During respiration, oxygen reacts with glucose to release energy. ***Applying Concepts*** *What substances are produced during respiration?*

Respiration is the process in which oxygen and glucose undergo a complex series of chemical reactions inside cells. These chemical reactions release the energy that fuels growth and other cell processes. Besides releasing energy, respiration produces carbon dioxide and water. Your body eliminates the carbon dioxide and some of the water through your lungs. To a scientist, *breathing* and *respiration* mean different things. Respiration, which is also called cellular respiration, refers to the chemical reactions inside cells. Breathing refers to the movement of air into and out of the lungs.

Your respiratory system gets oxygen into your lungs. However, respiration could not take place without your circulatory and digestive systems. The digestive system absorbs glucose from food. The circulatory system carries both oxygen from your lungs and glucose from food to your cells.

☑ *Checkpoint* *Why does your body need oxygen?*

The Air You Breathe

INTEGRATING EARTH SCIENCE The oxygen your body needs comes from the atmosphere, which is the blanket of gases that surrounds Earth. The atmosphere is made up of a mixture of gases. Only about 21 percent of air is oxygen. Nitrogen makes up about 78 percent, and the remaining 1 percent includes carbon dioxide, helium, and other gases. Your body doesn't use most of the air that you breathe into your lungs. When you exhale, most of the air goes back into the atmosphere.

The Path of Air

If you look toward a window on a bright day, you may see tiny particles dancing in the air. These particles include such things as floating grains of dust, plant pollen, and ash from fires. In addition, air contains microorganisms, some of which can cause disease in humans. When you breathe in, all these materials enter your body along with the air.

However, most of these materials never enter your lungs. On its way to the lungs, air passes through a series of organs that filter and trap particles. These organs also warm and moisten the air. **As air travels from the outside environment to the lungs, it passes through the following organs: nose, pharynx, trachea, and bronchi.** It takes air only a few seconds to complete the route from the nose to the lungs. You can trace that route in *Exploring the Respiratory System.*

The Nose Your nose has two openings, or nostrils, which are separated by a thin wall. Air enters the body through the nostrils and then moves into the nose cavities, or nasal cavities. The lining of the nasal cavities contains many blood vessels. Warm blood flowing through these vessels heats the air. Some of the cells lining the cavities produce mucus. This sticky material moistens the air and keeps the delicate tissue from drying out. Mucus also traps particles, such as dust and bacteria. The cells that line the nasal cavities have **cilia** (SIL ee uh), tiny hairlike extensions that can move together like whips. The whiplike motion of these cilia sweeps the mucus into the throat, where you swallow it. In the stomach, the mucus, along with the particles and bacteria trapped in it, is destroyed by stomach acid.

Figure 2 The cilia that line the nasal passages help remove trapped particles. The brown particles in the photograph are dust; the orange particles are pollen grains. When a person sneezes, many of the trapped particles are shot out into the air.

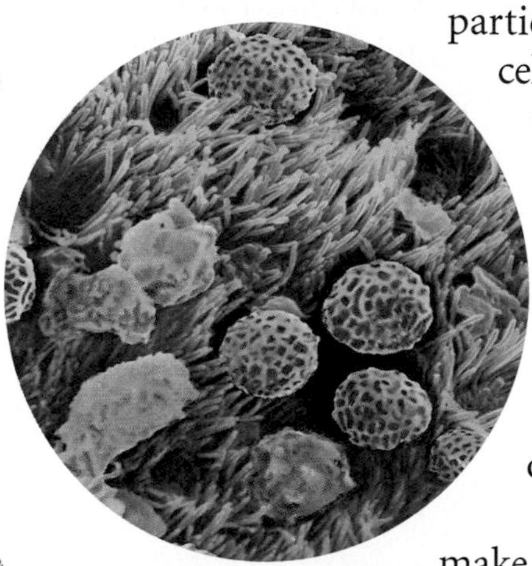

Some particles and bacteria never make it to your stomach. They irritate the lining of your nose or throat, and you sneeze. The powerful force of a sneeze shoots the particles and bacteria out of your nose and into the air.

The Pharynx After flowing through the nasal cavities, air enters the **pharynx** (FAR ingks), or throat. The pharynx is the only part of the respiratory system that is shared with another system—the digestive system. If you look at *Exploring the Respiratory System,* you can see that both the nose and the mouth connect to the pharynx.

☑ ***Checkpoint*** *To what two body systems does the pharynx belong?*

The Trachea From the pharynx, air moves into the **trachea** (TRAY kee uh), or windpipe. You can feel your trachea if you gently run your fingers down the center of your neck. The trachea feels like a tube with a series of ridges. The firm ridges are rings of cartilage that strengthen the trachea and keep it open.

The trachea, like the nose, is lined with cilia and mucus. The cilia in the trachea sweep upward, moving mucus toward the pharynx, where it is swallowed. The trachea's cilia and mucus

EXPLORING the Respiratory System

On its path from outside the body into the lungs, air passes through several structures that clean, warm, and moisten it. Once in the lungs, the oxygen in the air can enter your bloodstream.

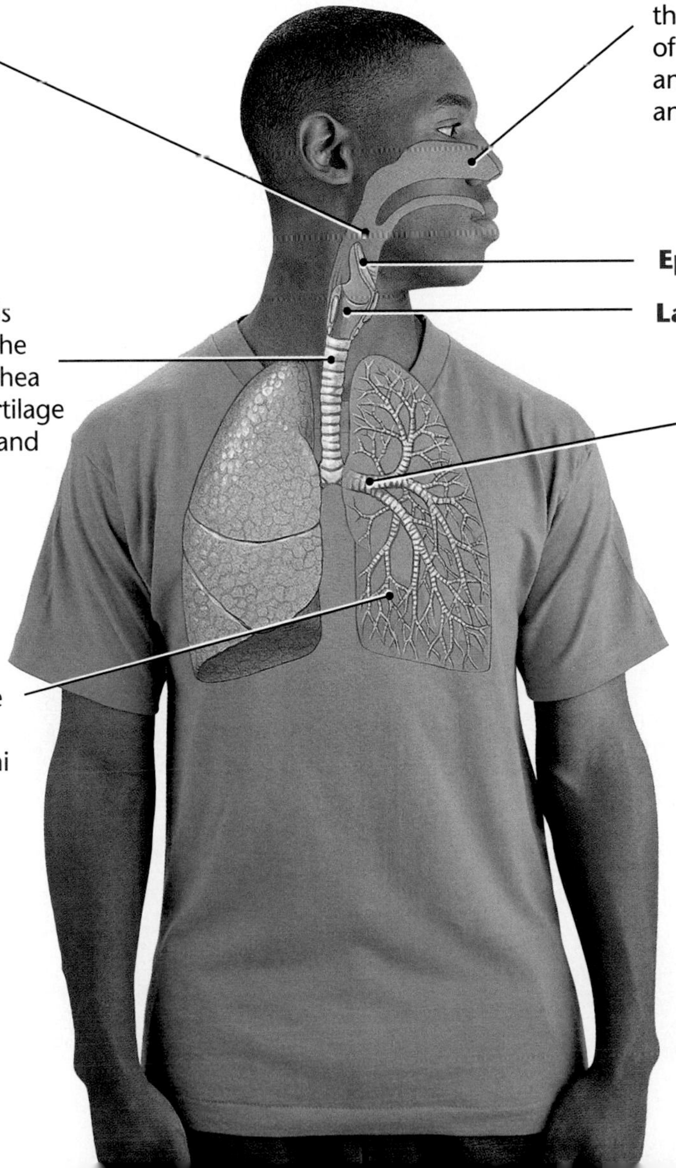

Pharynx Air moves from the nose downward into the throat, or pharynx. Part of the pharynx is also a passageway for food.

Nose Air enters the body through two nostrils. The lining of the nose is coated with cilia and mucus, which trap particles and warm and moisten the air.

Epiglottis

Larynx

Trachea The trachea leads from the pharynx toward the lungs. The walls of the trachea are made up of rings of cartilage which protect the trachea and keep it from collapsing.

Bronchi Air moves from the trachea into the right and left bronchi. One bronchus leads to each lung. Part of each bronchus is outside the lung and part is inside.

Lungs After it reaches the lungs, air moves through smaller and smaller bronchi until it reaches the alveoli. In the alveoli, oxygen passes into the blood and carbon dioxide passes out of the blood.

continue the cleaning and moistening of air that began in the nose. If particles irritate the lining of the trachea, you cough. A cough, like a sneeze, sends harmful materials flying out of your body and into the air.

Normally, only air—not food—enters the trachea. If food does enter the trachea, the food can block the opening and prevent air from getting to the lungs. When that happens, a person chokes. Fortunately, food rarely gets into the trachea. Remember from Chapter 4 that the epiglottis is a small flap of tissue that folds over the trachea. The epiglottis seals the trachea off while you swallow.

The Bronchi and Lungs Air moves from the trachea to the **bronchi** (BRAHNG ky)(singular *bronchus*), the passages that direct air into the lungs. The **lungs** are the main organs of the respiratory system. The left bronchus leads into the left lung, and the right bronchus leads into the right lung. Inside the lungs, each bronchus divides into smaller and smaller tubes in a pattern that resembles the branches of a tree.

At the end of the smallest tubes are small structures that look like bunches of grapes. The "grapes" are **alveoli** (al VEE uh ly) (singular *alveolus*), tiny sacs of lung tissue specialized for the movement of gases between air and blood. Notice in Figure 3 that each alveolus is surrounded by a network of capillaries. It is here that the blood picks up its cargo of oxygen from the air.

☑ *Checkpoint* *Describe the structure of the bronchi.*

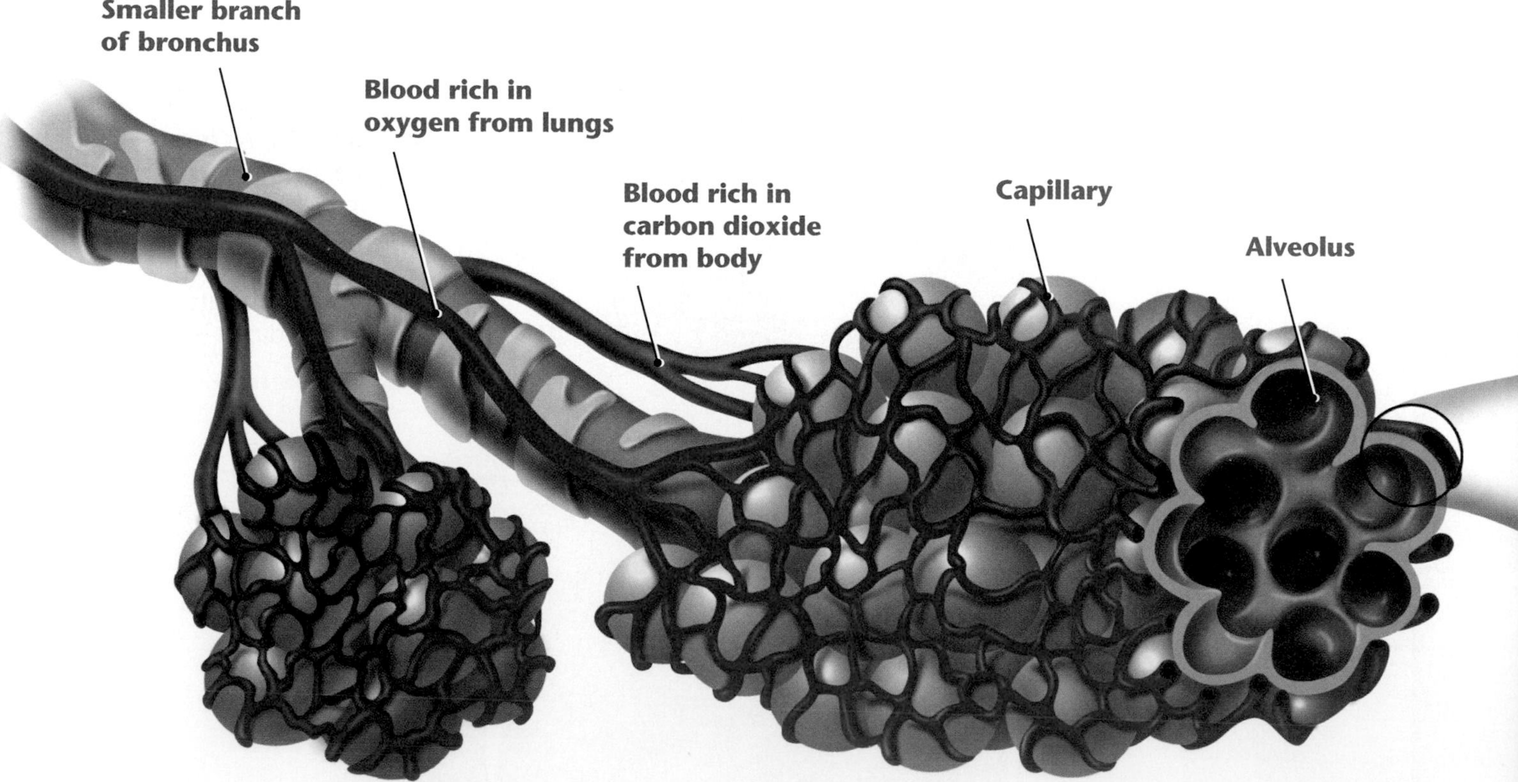

Gas Exchange

Because the walls of both the alveoli and the capillaries are very thin, materials can pass through them easily. **After air enters an alveolus, oxygen passes through the wall of the alveolus and then through the capillary wall into the blood. Carbon dioxide and water pass from the blood into the alveoli.** This whole process is known as gas exchange.

How Gas Exchange Occurs Imagine that you are a drop of blood beginning your journey through a capillary that wraps around an alveolus. When you begin that journey, you are carrying a lot of carbon dioxide and little oxygen. As you move through the capillary, oxygen gradually attaches to the hemoglobin in your red blood cells. At the same time, you are getting rid of carbon dioxide. At the end of your journey around the alveolus, you are rich in oxygen and poor in carbon dioxide.

A Large Surface Area Your lungs can absorb a large amount of oxygen because of the large surface area of the alveoli. An adult's lungs contain about 300 million alveoli. If you removed the alveoli, opened them, and spread them out on a flat surface, you would have a surface area of about 70 square meters. That's about the area of three lanes in a bowling alley!

INTEGRATING MATHEMATICS

The huge surface area of the alveoli enables the lungs to absorb a large amount of oxygen. The lungs can therefore supply the oxygen that people need—even when they are performing strenuous activities. When you play a musical instrument or a fast-paced game of basketball, you have your alveoli to thank.

Your lungs are not the only organs that provide a large surface area in a relatively small space. Remember that the small intestine contains numerous, tiny villi that increase the surface available to absorb food molecules.

Do You Exhale Carbon Dioxide?

ACTIVITY

Learn whether carbon dioxide is present in exhaled air.

1. Put on your goggles. Label two test tubes A and B.
2. Fill each test tube with 10 mL of water and a few drops of bromthymol blue solution. Bromthymol blue solution turns green or yellow in the presence of carbon dioxide.
3. Using a straw, blow air into the liquid in test tube A for a few seconds. Blow gently—if you blow hard, the liquid will bubble out of the test tube. **CAUTION:** *Use the straw to exhale only. Do not suck the solution back through the straw.*
4. Compare the solutions in the test tubes. Wash your hands when you have finished.

Predicting Suppose you had exercised immediately before you blew into the straw. Predict how this would have affected the results.

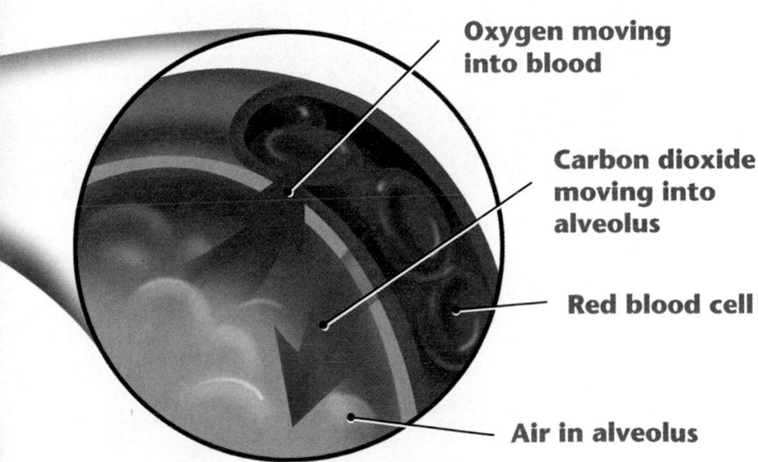

Figure 3 Alveoli are hollow air sacs surrounded by capillaries. As blood flows through the capillaries, oxygen moves from the alveoli into the blood. At the same time, carbon dioxide moves from the blood into the alveoli. ***Interpreting Diagrams*** *How is the structure of the alveoli important for gas exchange?*

Social Studies CONNECTION

Have you ever seen movies or read about climbers scaling mountains in the Andes or Himalayas? Some of the peaks in the Andes rise to almost 7,000 meters. Mount Everest in the Himalayas, which rises to 8,848 meters, is the world's tallest mountain. People who climb these mountains usually experience mountain sickness—dizziness, headaches, and shortness of breath. Their symptoms are due to a shortage of oxygen in their blood. The amount of oxygen in air decreases the farther one goes above sea level.

In contrast to visitors, people who live high in these mountain ranges do not experience these symptoms. Their respiratory and circulatory systems have adjusted to compensate for the low levels of oxygen. For example, they inhale a greater volume of air with each breath than do people at lower levels. In addition, their blood contains a greater number of red blood cells for transporting oxygen.

In Your Journal

Locate the Andes Mountains and Himalaya Mountains on a globe or map. Then imagine that you are climbing a mountain in one of these ranges. Write a diary entry describing your physical reactions and what you might see.

How You Breathe

In an average day, you may breathe more than 20,000 times. The rate at which you breathe depends on your body's need for oxygen. When you exercise, your body needs a lot of oxygen to supply energy. The more oxygen you need, the faster you breathe.

Muscles for Breathing Pay attention to your breathing as you read this paragraph. Can you feel the air flowing in and out through your nose? Do you notice the gentle lift and fall of your chest?

Breathing, like other body movements, is controlled by muscles. Figure 5 shows the structure of the chest, including the muscles that enable you to breathe. Notice that the lungs are surrounded by the ribs, which have muscles attached to them. At the base of the lungs is the **diaphragm** (DY uh fram), a large, dome-shaped muscle that plays an important role in breathing.

The Process of Breathing Here is what happens when you

INTEGRATING PHYSICS

inhale, or breathe in. The rib muscles contract, lifting the chest wall upward and outward. At the same time, the diaphragm contracts and moves downward. The combined action of these muscles makes the chest cavity larger, providing extra space for the lungs to expand.

When the chest cavity has expanded, there is more room for air. For a brief moment, however, there is no extra air to fill the space. Because the same amount of air now occupies a larger

Figure 4 These people live high in the Andes Mountains in Ecuador. Despite the low oxygen levels, these people experience no symptoms of mountain sickness. Their respiratory systems have adjusted in order to get enough oxygen into their bodies.

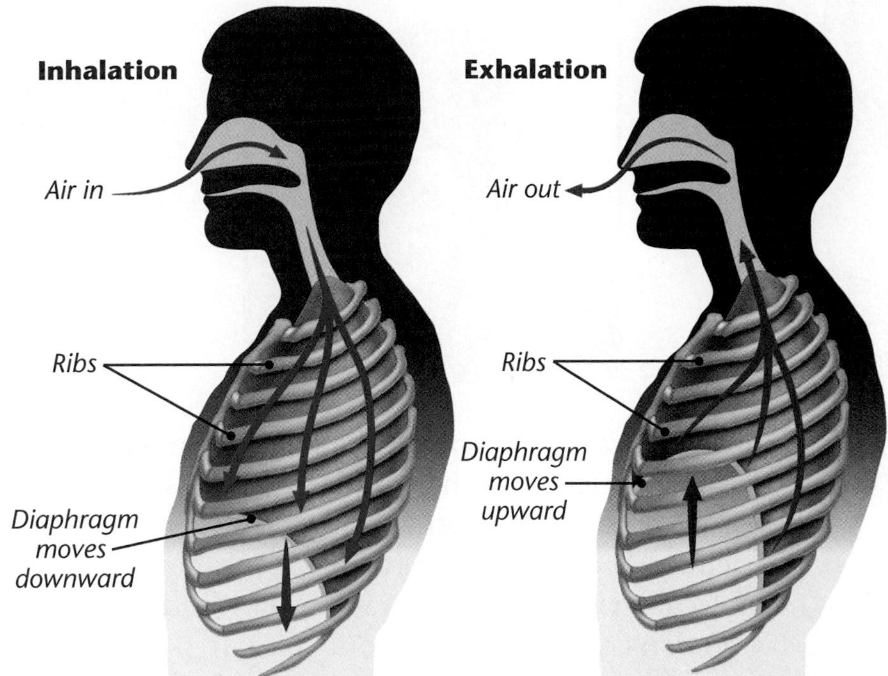

Figure 5 When you inhale, the diaphragm moves downward, allowing more room in the lungs for air. In contrast, when you exhale, the diaphragm moves upward. This upward movement increases the pressure in the lungs and pushes the air out. ***Interpreting Diagrams*** *How does the downward movement of the diaphragm affect the pressure of air inside the chest cavity?*

space, the pressure of the air inside your lungs decreases. This means that the pressure of air inside the chest cavity is lower than the pressure of the atmosphere pushing on the body. Because of this difference in air pressure, air rushes into your chest, in the same way that air is sucked into a vacuum cleaner. You have inhaled.

In contrast, when you exhale, or breathe out, the rib muscles and diaphragm relax, and the chest cavity becomes smaller. This decrease in size squeezes air out of the lungs, the way squeezing a container of ketchup pushes ketchup out of the opening.

☑ ***Checkpoint*** ***What muscles cause the chest to expand during breathing?***

How You Speak

The **larynx** (LAR ingks), or voice box, is located in the top part of the trachea, underneath the epiglottis. You can see the larynx if you look back at *Exploring the Respiratory System* on page 191. Place your fingers on your Adam's apple, which sticks out from the front of your neck. You can feel some of the cartilage that makes up the larynx. Two **vocal cords,** which are folds of connective tissue that produce your voice, stretch across the opening of the larynx.

How the Vocal Cords Work If you've ever let air out of a balloon while stretching its neck, you've heard the squeaking sound that the air makes. The neck of the balloon is something like your vocal cords. The vocal

INTEGRATING PHYSICS

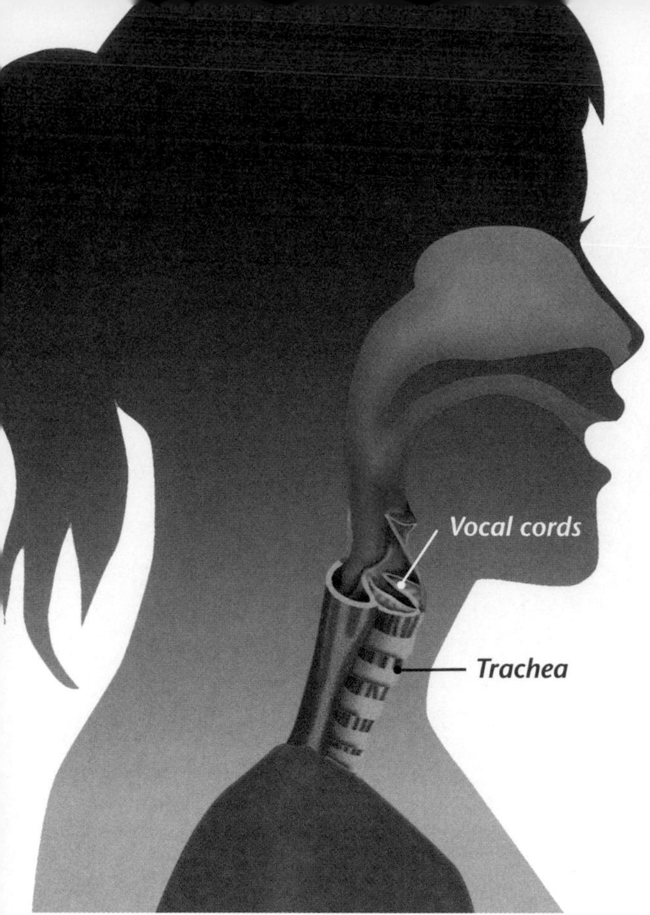

Figure 6 Air moving over this singer's vocal cords causes them to vibrate and produce sound. When her vocal cords contract, or shorten, she sings higher notes. When her vocal cords lengthen, she sings lower notes.

cords have a slitlike opening between them. When you speak, muscles make the vocal cords contract, narrowing the opening. Air from the lungs rushes through this opening. The movement of the vocal cords makes the air molecules vibrate, or move rapidly back and forth. This vibration creates a sound—your voice.

High and Low Tones The length of the vocal cords affects whether you produce low or high tones. When the vocal cords contract and shorten, you speak in a higher voice. When they are longer and in a relaxed position, you speak in a lower voice.

The length of vocal cords changes during a person's lifetime. Small children have high-pitched voices because their larynxes are small and their vocal cords are short. The vocal cords of both boys and girls are about the same length. During the teenage years, however, the vocal cords of boys grow longer than those of girls. This is why men have deeper voices than women.

Section 1 Review

1. List the functions of the respiratory system.
2. Describe the path that a molecule of oxygen takes as it moves from the air into the alveoli.
3. Explain what happens to carbon dioxide in the blood that flows through capillaries in the alveoli.
4. Why does air rush into your body when you inhale?
5. **Thinking Critically Relating Cause and Effect** When there is a lot of dust in the air, people often cough and sneeze. Explain why this happens.

Science at Home

Use a shoe box and a set of blocks to show your family how the alveoli increase the surface area of the lungs. The shoe box represents a lung, and each block represents an alveolus. Fill the box with as many blocks as will fit inside. Then have your family imagine how much surface would be covered if all of the blocks were opened up and put together to form a large sheet. How would the surface area of the blocks compare with that of the shoe box?

Making Models

Skills Lab

A Breath of Fresh Air

How does air get into your lungs? In this lab, you will make a model of the lungs to demonstrate how breathing takes place.

Problem

What causes your body to inhale and exhale air?

Materials

small balloon large balloon
scissors
transparent plastic bottle with narrow neck

Procedure 

1. In your notebook, explain how you think air gets into the lungs during the breathing process.
2. Cut off and discard the bottom of a small plastic bottle. Trim the cut edge so there are no rough spots.
3. Stretch a small balloon, then blow it up a few times to stretch it further. Insert the round end of the balloon through the mouth of the bottle. Then, with a partner holding the bottle, stretch the neck of the balloon and pull it over the mouth of the bottle.
4. Stretch a large balloon, then blow it up a few times to stretch it further. Cut off the balloon's neck, and discard it.
5. Have a partner hold the bottle while you stretch the remaining part of the balloon over the bottom opening of the bottle, as shown in the photo.
6. Use one hand to hold the bottle firmly. With the knuckles of your other hand, push upward on the large balloon, causing it to form a dome. Remove your knuckles from the balloon, letting the balloon flatten. Repeat this procedure a few times. Observe what happens to the small balloon. Record your observations in your notebook.

Analyze and Conclude

1. Make a diagram of the completed model in your notebook. Add labels to show which parts of your model represent the chest cavity, diaphragm, lungs, and trachea.
2. In this model, what is the position of the diaphragm just after you have exhaled? What do the lungs look like just after you have exhaled?
3. In this model, how does the diaphragm move? How do these movements of the diaphragm affect the lungs?
4. **Think About It** How does this model show that pressure changes are responsible for breathing?

More to Explore

How could you improve on this model to more closely show what happens in the chest cavity during the process of breathing? Obtain your teacher's permission before making a new model.

Section 2 Smoking and Your Health

DISCOVER

What Are the Dangers of Smoking?

Pair up with a partner. Read each question below and decide on a reasonable answer based on your current knowledge.

1. In the United States, about how many people die each year from smoking-related illnesses?
2. What percentage of lung cancer deaths are related to smoking?
3. On the average, how much longer do nonsmokers live than smokers?
4. What percentage of smokers say they want to quit smoking?
5. What percentage of smokers actually succeed in quitting?

Think It Over

Inferring Why do you think people start smoking when they know that smoking can cause serious health problems?

GUIDE FOR READING

- **What harmful chemicals are contained in tobacco smoke?**
- **How does tobacco smoke harm the respiratory and circulatory systems?**

Reading Tip **Before you read, make a list of smoking-related health problems that you already know about. Add to your list as you read.**

Whoosh! Millions of tiny but dangerous aliens are invading the respiratory system. The aliens are pulled into the nose with an inhaled breath. The cilia in the nasal cavities trap some aliens, and others get stuck in mucus. But many aliens get past these defenses. After tumbling in air currents, thousands of the invaders enter the lungs. The aliens implant themselves in the alveoli!

The "aliens" are not tiny creatures from space. They are the substances found in cigarette smoke. In this section you will learn how tobacco smoke damages the respiratory system.

Chemicals in Tobacco Smoke

With each puff, a smoker inhales over 4,000 different chemicals. **Some of the most deadly chemicals in tobacco smoke are tar, carbon monoxide, and nicotine.**

Tar The dark, sticky substance that forms when tobacco burns is called **tar.** When someone inhales tobacco smoke, some tar settles on cilia that line the trachea and other respiratory organs. Tar makes cilia clump together so they can't function to prevent harmful materials from getting into the lungs. Tar also contains chemicals that have been shown to cause cancer.

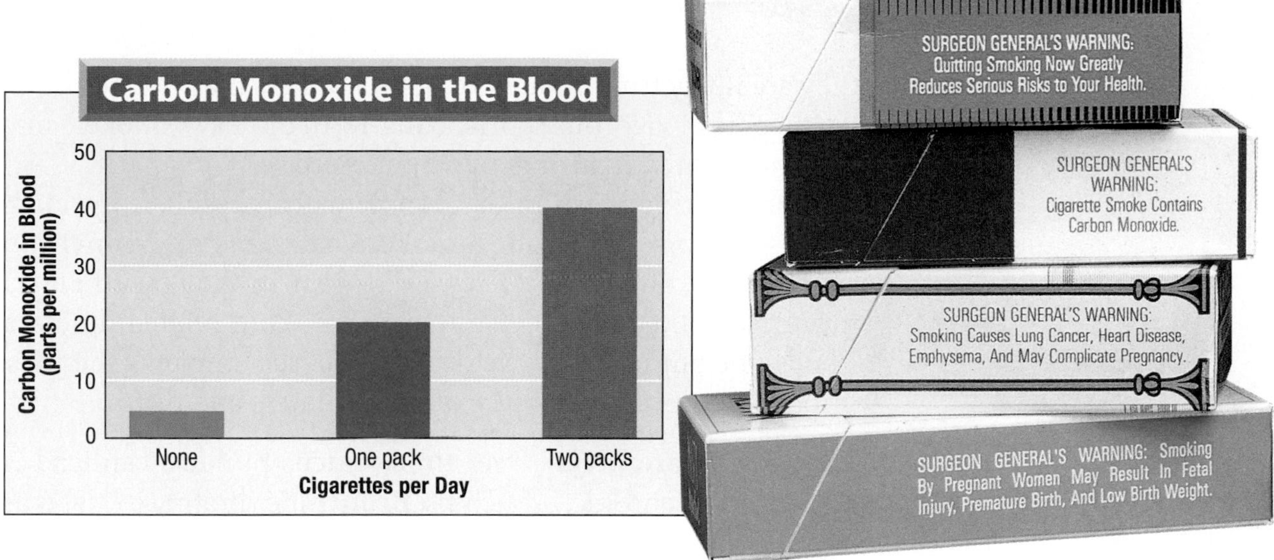

Figure 7 The more cigarettes a person smokes, the more carbon monoxide he or she inhales. ***Relating Cause and Effect*** *How does carbon monoxide deprive the body of oxygen?*

Carbon Monoxide When substances—including tobacco—are burned, a colorless, odorless gas called **carbon monoxide** is produced. Carbon monoxide is dangerous to inhale because its molecules bind to hemoglobin in red blood cells. When carbon monoxide binds to hemoglobin, it takes the place of some of the oxygen that the red blood cells normally carry. The carbon monoxide molecules are something like cars that have taken parking spaces reserved for other cars.

When carbon monoxide binds to hemoglobin, red blood cells carry less than their normal load of oxygen throughout the body. To make up for the decrease in oxygen, the breathing rate increases and the heart beats faster. Smokers' blood may contain too little oxygen to meet their bodies' needs.

Nicotine Another dangerous chemical found in tobacco smoke is **nicotine.** Nicotine is a drug that speeds up the activities of the nervous system, heart, and other organs. It makes the heart beat faster and blood pressure rise. Nicotine produces an **addiction,** or physical dependence. Smokers feel an intense need, or craving, for a cigarette if they go without one. Addiction to nicotine is one reason why smokers have difficulty quitting.

☑ ***Checkpoint*** *How does the tar in cigarette smoke affect the body?*

Respiratory System Problems

Tobacco smoke harms the respiratory system in several ways. For example, because their cilia can't sweep away mucus, many smokers have a frequent cough. The mucus buildup also limits the space for air flow, and this decreases oxygen intake. Because they are not getting enough oxygen, smokers may not be able to participate in vigorous sports. Long-term or heavy smokers may be short of breath during even light exercise.

Some serious respiratory problems can result from long-term smoking. **Over time, smokers can develop bronchitis, emphysema, and lung cancer.** Every year in the United States, more than 400,000 people die from smoking-related illnesses. That's one out of every five deaths. Tobacco smoke is the most important preventable cause of major illness and death.

Chronic Bronchitis Over time, mucus buildup can lead to long-term, or chronic, bronchitis. **Bronchitis** (brahng KY tis) is an irritation of the breathing passages in which the small passages become narrower than normal and may be clogged with mucus. People with bronchitis have a hard time breathing. If bronchitis lasts a long time, it can cause permanent damage to the breathing passages. Chronic bronchitis is often accompanied by infection with disease-causing microorganisms. Chronic bronchitis is five to ten times more common in heavy smokers than in nonsmokers.

Figure 8 These people stay healthy by exercising and by choosing not to smoke.

Emphysema The chemicals in tobacco smoke damage lung tissue as well as breathing passages. **Emphysema** (em fuh SEE muh) is a serious disease that destroys lung tissue and causes difficulty in breathing. People with emphysema do not get enough oxygen and cannot adequately eliminate carbon dioxide. Therefore, they are always short of breath. Some people with emphysema even have trouble blowing out a match. Unfortunately, the damage caused by emphysema is permanent, even if a person stops smoking.

Lung Cancer About 140,000 Americans die each year from lung cancer caused by smoking. Cigarette smoke contains over 40 different chemicals that cause cancer, including chemicals in tar. Cancerous growths, or tumors, take away space in the lungs that should be used for gas exchange. Unfortunately, lung cancer is difficult to detect early, when treatment would be most effective.

☑ *Checkpoint* *How does emphysema affect a person's lungs?*

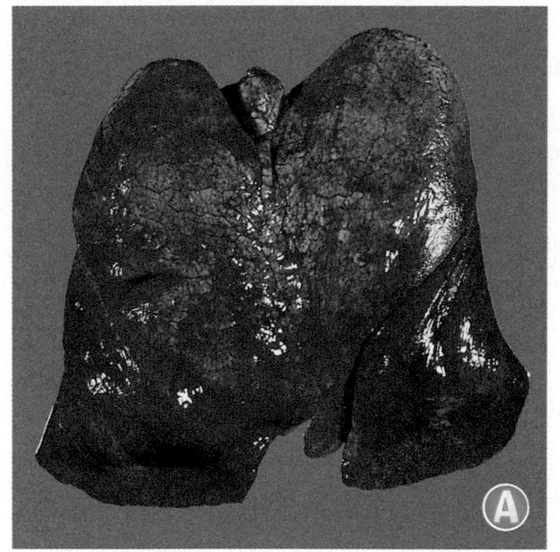

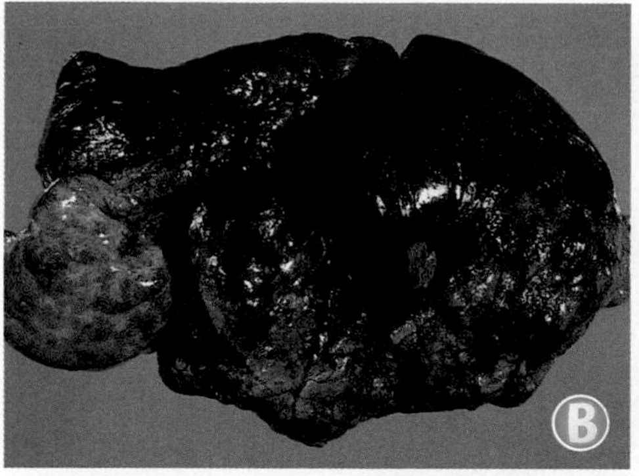

Figure 9 Over time, smoking damages the lungs and leads to serious health problems. Compare the lungs of a nonsmoker **(A)** to those of a person with emphysema **(B)** and a person with lung cancer **(C)**.

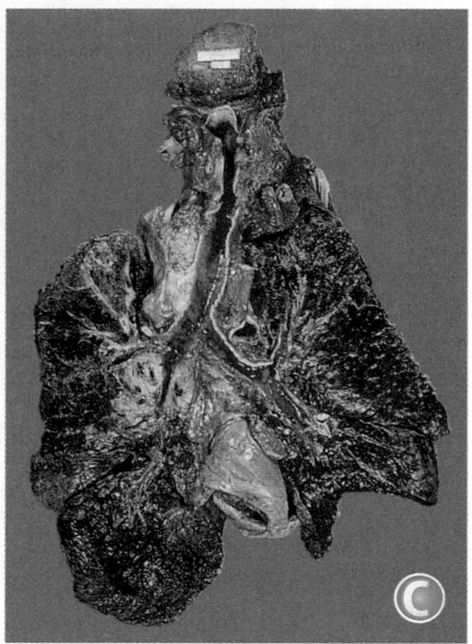

Circulatory System Problems

The chemicals in tobacco smoke that damage the lungs also harm the circulatory system. Some of the chemicals get into the blood and are absorbed by the blood vessels. The chemicals then irritate the walls of the blood vessels. This irritation contributes to the buildup of the fatty material that causes atherosclerosis. Atherosclerosis can lead to heart attacks. **Compared to nonsmokers, smokers are more than twice as likely to have heart attacks.**

Conditions that harm the lungs, such as bronchitis and emphysema, also strain the circulatory system. The respiratory and circulatory systems work together to get oxygen to the cells and to remove carbon dioxide from the body. If either system is damaged, the other one must work harder.

Passive Smoking

Smokers are not the only people to suffer from the effects of tobacco smoke. In **passive smoking,** people involuntarily inhale the smoke from other people's cigarettes, cigars, or pipes. Since this smoke contains the same harmful chemicals that smokers inhale, it can cause health problems. Each year, passive smoking causes about 300,000 young children in the United States to develop respiratory problems such as bronchitis. In addition, long-term exposure to cigarette smoke increases people's risks of heart disease and cancer.

Calculating

ACTIVITY

Heavy smokers may smoke two packs of cigarettes every day. Find out what one pack of cigarettes costs. Then use that price to calculate how much a person would spend on cigarettes if he or she smoked two packs a day for 30 years.

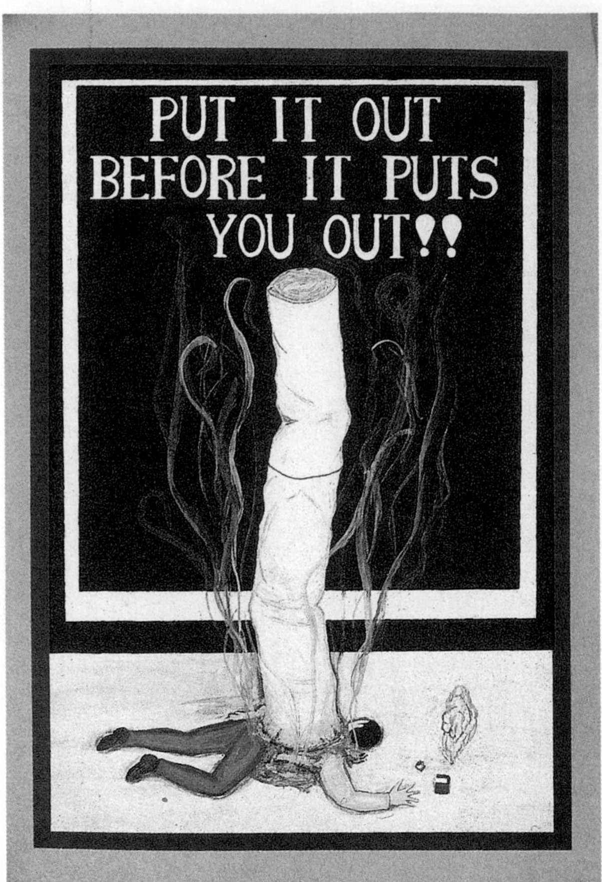

Figure 10 This antismoking advertisement was created by a teenager to encourage smokers to quit.

Choosing Not to Smoke

Today about 50 million Americans are smokers. Of those people, more than 90 percent began smoking when they were teenagers. Studies show that if people do not start smoking when they are teenagers, they probably will not start smoking later in life.

You may be tempted to try smoking. Friends may pressure you, or advertisements may appeal to you. Tobacco advertisements show smokers as young, attractive, popular people. The ads try to make you think that you will be like these people if you use tobacco products.

It is important to remember that it's very hard to quit smoking once you start. Many teenage smokers think that they will quit when they are older—but because nicotine is addictive, they have trouble doing so. And smoking hurts people right away, not just later in life. The lungs of teenagers who smoke develop more slowly than those of nonsmokers and may never reach the same peak level of functioning. In addition, teenage smokers may develop coughs and bronchitis. If someone asks you to try a cigarette, think of your health and politely refuse.

Section 2 Review

1. Name three harmful substances in tobacco smoke. Describe the effects of each substance.
2. Identify three respiratory problems caused by smoking.
3. Describe the effect of smoking on the circulatory system.
4. Identify two factors that may pressure teenagers to try smoking.
5. **Thinking Critically Relating Cause and Effect** Scientists estimate that about 3,000 nonsmoking Americans die every year from smoking-related lung cancer. Explain why.

CHAPTER PROJECT 6

Check Your Progress

By now you should have sketched what your ads might look like and written what they might say. In planning your ads, be sure to consider all the effects of smoking, not just those related to health—for example, the expense of smoking. Plan to use ideas and images that are appropriate for each age group. (*Hint:* Look through a variety of magazines to find ads aimed at different age groups. Which techniques seem to work best? How can you use those techniques in your ads?)

Section 3 The Excretory System

DISCOVER 

How Does Filtering a Liquid Change What Is in It?

1. Your teacher will give you 50 milliliters of a liquid in a small container. Pour a small amount of sand into the liquid.
2. Use a glucose-test strip to determine whether glucose is present in the liquid.
3. Put filter paper in a funnel. Then put the funnel into the mouth of a second container. Slowly pour the liquid through the funnel into the second container.

4. Look for any solid material on the filter paper. Remove the funnel and carefully examine the liquid that passed through the filter.
5. Test the liquid again to see whether it contains glucose.

Think It Over

Observing Which substances passed through the filter, and which did not? How might a filtering device be useful in the body?

The human body faces a challenge that is a bit like trying to keep a home clean. You learned in Chapter 4 that the body takes in foods through the digestive system and breaks them down into nutrients. As cells use those nutrients in respiration and other processes, wastes are created. **The excretory system is the system in the body that collects wastes produced by cells and removes the wastes from the body.** The removal process is known as **excretion.**

If wastes were not taken away, they would pile up and make you sick. Excretion helps maintain homeostasis by keeping the body's internal environment stable and free of harmful materials.

GUIDE FOR READING

- What is the function of the excretory system?
- How is urine produced in the kidneys' nephrons?
- In addition to the kidneys, what other organs play a role in excretion?

Reading Tip As you read, write a brief summary of the information under each heading.

The Kidneys

As you already know, some wastes that your body must eliminate are carbon dioxide and excess water. Another waste product is urea. **Urea** (yoo REE uh) is a chemical that comes from the breakdown of proteins. Your two **kidneys,** which are the major organs of the excretory system, eliminate urea, excess water, and some other waste materials. These wastes are eliminated in **urine,** a watery fluid produced by your kidneys.

The kidneys act something like filters. As blood flows through the kidneys, they remove wastes from the blood. After the process is complete, urine flows from the kidneys through two narrow tubes called **ureters** (yoo REE turz). The ureters carry the urine to the **urinary bladder,** a sacklike muscular organ that stores urine. When the bladder is full enough that its walls are stretched, you feel a need to urinate. Urine flows from the body through a small tube called the **urethra** (yoo REE thruh), which you can see in *Exploring a Kidney.*

☑ ***Checkpoint*** *What is the role of the ureters?*

The Filtering Process

The kidneys are champion filters. Every drop of blood in your body passes through your kidneys and is filtered more than 300 times a day. Contrast this to a typical swimming-pool filter, which only cleans the pool water about 5 times a day.

Each of your kidneys contains about a million tiny filtering factories called **nephrons.** The nephrons are the tiny structures that remove wastes from blood and produce urine. **Urine formation takes place in a number of stages. First, both wastes and needed materials, such as glucose, are removed from the blood. Then, much of the needed material is returned to the blood.**

Filtering Out Wastes After entering the kidneys, blood flows through smaller and smaller arteries. Eventually it reaches a cluster of capillaries in a nephron. These capillaries are surrounded

EXPLORING *a Kidney*

Each kidney contains about a million tiny filtering units called nephrons. Urine is produced in the nephrons.

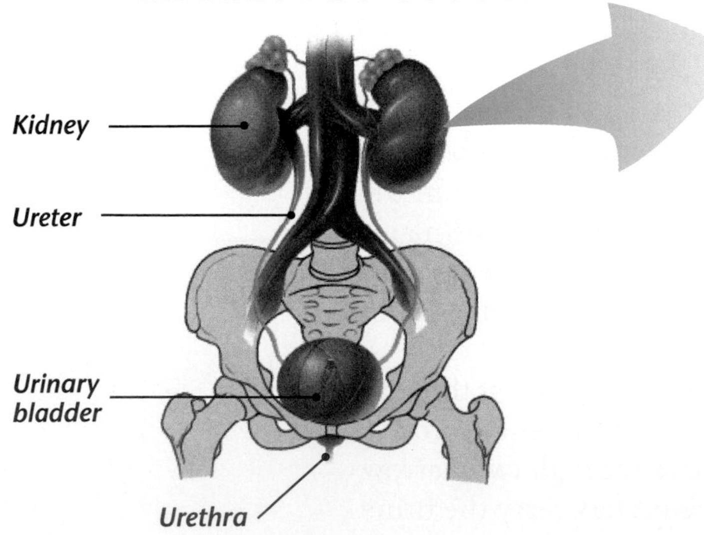

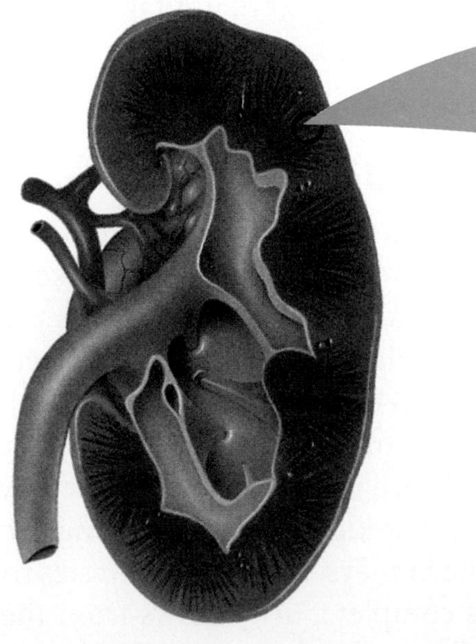

by a thin-walled, hollow capsule that is connected to a long tube. Find the capillary cluster, the capsule, and the tube in *Exploring a Kidney*. In the capillary cluster, urea, glucose, other chemicals, and some water move out of the blood and into the capsule. In contrast, blood cells and most protein molecules do not move into the capsule. Instead, they remain in the capillaries.

Formation of Urine Urine forms from the filtered material that passes into the capsule. This filtered material flows through the long, twisting tube. Some of the substances that collect in the capsule are needed by the body. As the liquid moves through the tube, many of these substances are reabsorbed, or returned to the blood. Normally all the glucose, most of the water, and small amounts of other materials pass back into the blood in the capillaries that surround the tube. In contrast, urea and other wastes remain in the tube.

The filtering process is something like cleaning your locker by throwing everything in your locker into a wastebasket, and then putting back the things that you want to keep. You can think of the locker as your blood and the wastebasket as the capsule. After the entire filtering and reabsorbing process is complete, the fluid that remains in the tube is urine.

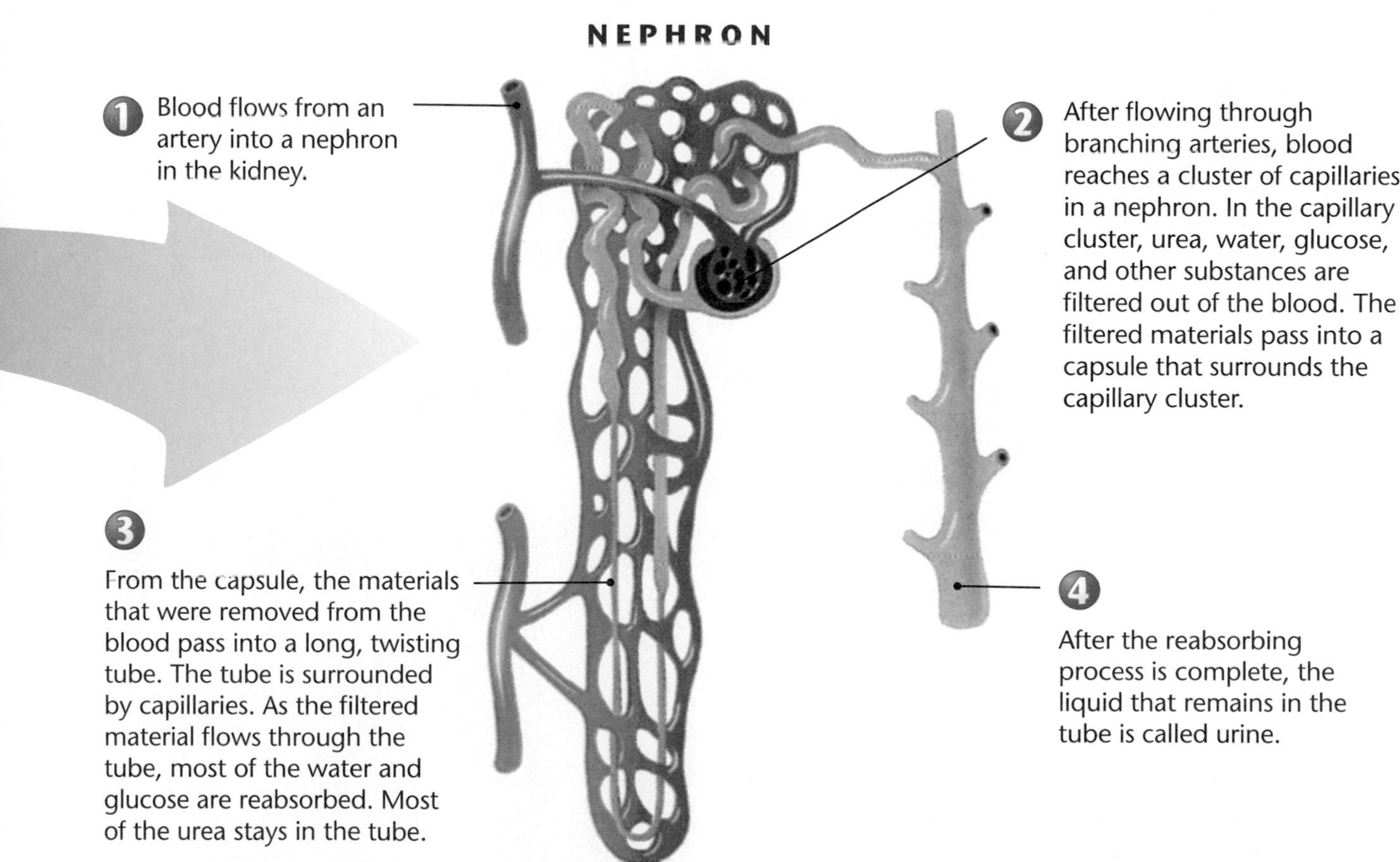

Analyzing Urine for Signs of Disease INTEGRATING HEALTH When people go to a doctor for a medical checkup, they usually have their urine analyzed. A chemical analysis of urine can be useful in detecting some medical problems. Normally, urine contains almost no glucose or protein. If glucose is present in urine, it may indicate that a person has diabetes, a condition in which body cells cannot absorb enough glucose from the blood. Protein in urine can be a sign that the kidneys are not functioning properly.

Real-World Lab

You Solve the Mystery

CLUES ABOUT HEALTH

In this lab, you'll become a medical detective as you carry out urine tests to uncover evidence of disease.

Problem

How can you test urine for the presence of glucose and protein?

Skills Focus

observing, interpreting data, drawing conclusions

Materials

test tubes, 6
plastic droppers, 6
glucose solution
marking pencil
glucose test strips
simulated urine samples, 3
test tube rack
water
protein solution
white paper towels
Biuret solution

Procedure

Part 1 Testing for Glucose

1. Label six test tubes as follows: "W" for water, "G" for glucose, "P" for protein, and "A," "B," and "C" for three patients' "urine samples." Place the test tubes in a test tube rack.
2. Label six glucose test strips with the same letters.
3. Copy the data table into your notebook.
4. Fill each test tube about 3/4 full with the solution that corresponds to its label.
5. Place the W glucose test strip on a clean, dry section of a paper towel. Then use a clean plastic dropper to place 2 drops of the water from test tube W on the test strip. Record the resulting color of the test strip in your data table. If no color change occurs, write "no reaction."

Water Balance in the Body

The kidneys also help maintain homeostasis by regulating the amount of water in your body. Remember that as urine is being formed, water passes from the tube back into the bloodstream. The exact amount of water that is reabsorbed depends on conditions both outside and within the body. Suppose that it's a hot day. You've been sweating a lot, and you haven't had much to drink. In that situation, almost all of the water in the tube will be reabsorbed, and you will excrete only a small amount of urine. If,

DATA TABLE

	Test Tube					
Test for	W (water)	G (glucose)	P (protein)	A (Patient A)	B (Patient B)	C (Patient C)
Glucose						
Protein						

6. Use the procedure in Step 5 to test each of the other five solutions with the correctly labeled glucose test strip. Record the color of each test strip in the data table.

Part 2 Testing for Protein

7. Obtain a dropper bottle containing Biuret solution. Record the original color of the solution in your notebook.
8. Carefully add 30 drops of Biuret solution to test tube W. **CAUTION:** *Biuret solution can harm skin and damage clothing. Handle it with care.* Gently swirl the test tube to mix the two solutions together. Hold the test tube against a white paper towel to help you detect any color change. Observe the color of the final mixture, and record that color in your data table.
9. Repeat Step 8 for each of the other test tubes.

Analyze and Conclude

1. Which of the three patients' urine samples tested normal? How do you know?
2. Which urine sample(s) indicated that diabetes might be present? How do you know?
3. Which urine sample(s) indicated that kidney disease might be present? How do you know?
4. When a person's health is normal, how are the kidneys involved in keeping glucose and protein out of urine?
5. **Apply** Do you think a doctor should draw conclusions about the presence of a disease based on a single urine sample? Explain.

More to Explore

Propose a way to determine whether a patient with glucose in the urine could reduce the level through changes in diet.

Figure 11 Your skin and lungs also function as excretory organs. Water and some chemical wastes are excreted in perspiration. And when you exhale on a cold morning, you can see the water in your breath. *Applying Concepts What other waste product does your exhaled breath contain?*

however, the day is cool and you've drunk a lot of water, less water will be reabsorbed. Your body will produce a larger volume of urine.

Every day, you need to take at least 2 liters of water into your body. You can do this either by drinking or by eating foods such as apples that contain a lot of water. This helps your kidneys maintain the proper water balance in your body.

Other Organs of Excretion

Most of the wastes produced by the body are removed through the kidneys, but not all. **The other organs of excretion are the lungs, skin, and liver.** You've already learned how the lungs and skin remove wastes. When you breathe out, carbon dioxide and some water are removed from the body. Sweat glands also function in excretion, because water and some chemical wastes are excreted in perspiration.

Have you ever torn apart a large pizza box so that it could fit in a wastebasket? If so, then you can understand that some wastes need to be broken down before they can be excreted. The liver performs this function. For example, urea, which comes from the breakdown of proteins, is produced by the liver. The liver also converts part of the hemoglobin molecule from old red blood cells into substances such as bile. Recall from Chapter 4 that bile helps break down fats during digestion. Because the liver produces a usable material from old red blood cells, you can think of the liver as a recycling factory.

Section 3 Review

1. What is the function of the excretory system?
2. Describe the two stages of urine formation.
3. What roles do the lungs, skin, and liver play in excretion?
4. How do the kidneys help regulate the amount of water in the body?
5. **Thinking Critically Predicting** On a long bus trip, Laura does not drink any water for several hours. How will the volume of urine she produces that day compare to the volume on a day when she drinks several glasses of water? Explain.

CHAPTER PROJECT 6

Check Your Progress

By now you should be creating your ads. If you are producing ads for a newspaper or magazine, you need to create original drawings or use images from other sources. If you are preparing television or radio ads, you need to arrange for actors and any necessary props. Write and edit the text or script of your ads. Arrange for a place to display your ads or for a time to present the ads.

CHAPTER 6 STUDY GUIDE

The Respiratory System

Key Ideas

- The respiratory system moves oxygen into the body and removes carbon dioxide from the body.
- In the process of respiration in cells, glucose is broken down using oxygen to produce energy.
- As air travels from the outside environment to the lungs, it passes through the nose, pharynx, trachea, and bronchi.
- In the alveoli, oxygen moves from the air into the blood, while carbon dioxide and water pass from the blood into the air.
- During inhalation, the diaphragm and rib muscles make the chest cavity expand. The air pressure inside the lungs decreases, and air rushes into the lungs. During exhalation, the chest cavity becomes smaller, pushing air out of the body.
- When air passes over the vocal cords, which are folds of tissue in the larynx, they vibrate to produce sound.

Key Terms

respiration
cilia
pharynx
trachea
bronchi
lungs
alveoli
diaphragm
larynx
vocal cords

Smoking and Your Health

INTEGRATING HEALTH

Key Ideas

- The most harmful substances in tobacco smoke are tar, carbon monoxide, and nicotine.
- When people inhale tobacco smoke, they increase their chances of developing respiratory diseases such as chronic bronchitis, emphysema, and lung cancer.
- Smokers are more likely to have heart attacks than are nonsmokers.

Key Terms

tar
carbon monoxide
nicotine
addiction
bronchitis
emphysema
passive smoking

The Excretory System

Key Ideas

- The excretory system removes carbon dioxide, urea, water, and other wastes from the body.
- The kidneys are the major organs of excretion. By filtering the blood, the kidneys produce urine.
- Urine travels from the kidneys through the ureters to the urinary bladder.
- In the kidney's nephrons, wastes and other materials are filtered from the blood. Some useful substances, such as glucose and water, are then reabsorbed into the blood.
- The lungs, skin, and liver are also organs of excretion.

Key Terms

excretion
urea
kidney
urine
ureters
urinary bladder
urethra
nephron

Organizing Information

Flowchart The kidneys eliminate wastes from the body in a series of steps. Copy the flowchart below and complete it by filling in the missing steps.

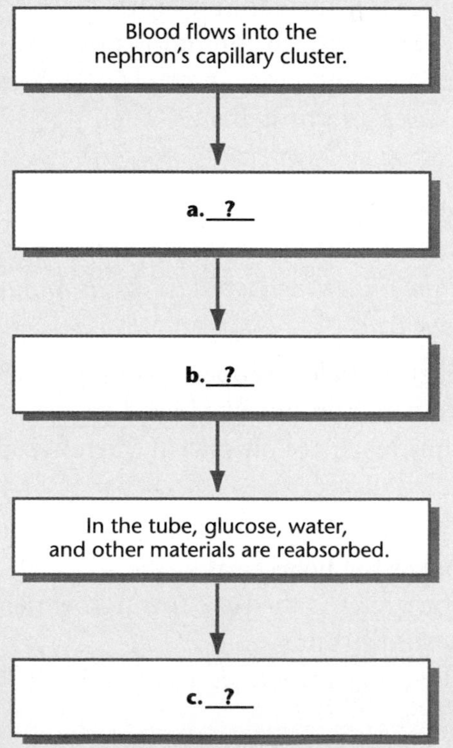

CHAPTER 6 ASSESSMENT

Reviewing Content

Multiple Choice

Choose the letter of the best answer.

1. The process in which glucose and oxygen react in cells to release energy is called
  a. digestion.
  b. respiration.
  c. breathing.
  d. gas exchange.

2. The trachea divides into two tubes called
  a. bronchi.
  b. alveoli.
  c. windpipes.
  d. diaphragms.

3. Your voice is produced by the
  a. pharynx.
  b. larynx.
  c. trachea.
  d. alveoli.

4. The disease in which the respiratory passages become narrower than normal is called
  a. bronchitis.
  b. lung cancer.
  c. diabetes.
  d. emphysema.

5. Normal urine contains both
  a. water and carbon monoxide.
  b. water and large amounts of glucose.
  c. urea and proteins.
  d. urea and water.

True or False

If the statement is true, write true. If it is false, change the underlined word or words to make the statement true.

6. Dust particles trapped in mucus are swept away by tiny, hairlike blood vessels.

7. The clusters of air sacs in the lungs are called alveoli.

8. Tar is a chemical in tobacco smoke that makes the heart beat faster.

9. The ureter is the tube through which urine leaves the body.

10. The lungs are excretory organs.

Checking Concepts

11. Explain the difference between breathing and respiration.

12. Explain how the alveoli provide a large surface area for gas exchange in the lungs.

13. Describe how the diaphragm and rib muscles work together to control inhaling and exhaling.

14. Why do men have deeper voices than women?

15. Describe what happens when carbon monoxide enters the body. How does this affect the body?

16. Explain two ways in which the kidneys help to maintain homeostasis in the body.

17. Writing to Learn Imagine that you are a molecule of oxygen. Write an adventure story that describes what happens to you between the time you are inhaled through someone's nose and the time you are used in respiration in a body cell.

Thinking Critically

18. Comparing and Contrasting How is respiration similar to the burning of fuel? How is it different?

19. Inferring If you exhale onto a mirror, the mirror will become clouded with a thin film of moisture. Explain why this happens.

20. Applying Concepts Explain how babies can develop smoking-related respiratory problems.

21. Making Judgments Do you think that drugstores, which sell medicines, should also sell cigarettes and other tobacco products? Why or why not?

22. Predicting If the walls of the capillary cluster in a nephron were damaged or broken, what substance might you expect to find in urine that is not normally present? Explain.

Applying Skills

Use your knowledge of the respiratory system and the information in the graphs to answer Questions 23–25.

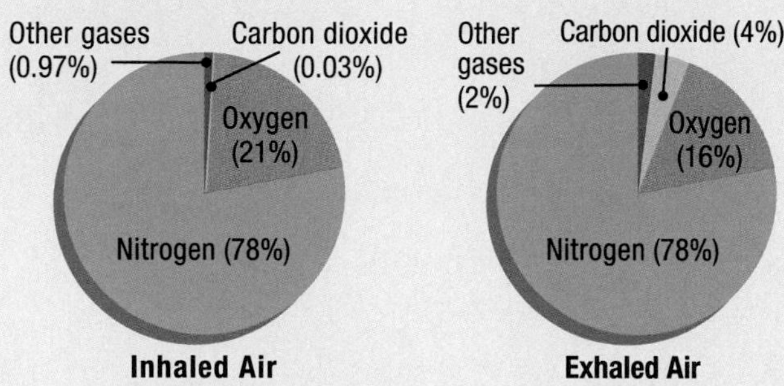

23. **Interpreting Data** Compare the percentage of carbon dioxide in inhaled air and in exhaled air. How can you account for the difference?
24. **Drawing Conclusions** Based on the data, which gas is used by the body? How is this gas used?
25. **Inferring** Explain why the percentage of nitrogen is the same in both inhaled air and exhaled air.

Performance Assessment (Chapter Project 6)

Project Wrap Up Your three ads should be ready for display. Be prepared to explain why you chose the message you did for each group of viewers. Why do you think your ads would be effective?

Reflect and Record Of all the ads produced by your classmates, which seemed the most effective? Why? Did any ads change your own ideas about smoking? How can you protect yourself from pressures that might tempt you to smoke? Record your ideas in your journal.

Test Preparation

Use these questions to prepare for standardized tests.

Study the table. Then answer Questions 26–29.

Average Daily Loss of Water in Humans (mL)

Source	Normal Weather	Hot Weather	Extended Heavy Exercise
Lungs	350	250	650
Urine	1,400	1,200	500
Sweat	450	1,750	5,350
Digestive Waste	200	200	200

26. During normal weather, what is the major source of water loss?
    a. lungs **b.** urine
    c. sweat **d.** digestive waste
27. During hot weather, what is the major source of water loss?
    a. lungs **b.** urine
    c. sweat **d.** digestive waste
28. What is the total amount of water lost on a hot weather day?
    a. 2,400 mL **b.** 3,200 mL
    c. 3,400 mL **d.** 6,700 mL
29. In cool weather, which of the following is most likely to happen?
    a. The body would lose 600 mL of water in digestive wastes.
    b. The body would lose no water.
    c. The body would lose less water in sweat than urine.
    d. The body would lose more water than on a hot day.

Fighting Disease

A white blood cell (shown in purple) attacks a cancer cell (yellow).

www.phschool.com

Infectious Disease

Discover How Does a Disease Spread?
Sharpen Your Skills Posing Questions

The Body's Defenses

Discover Which Pieces Fit Together?
Try This Stuck Together
Real-World Lab The Skin as a Barrier

Preventing Infectious Disease

Discover What Substances Can Kill Pathogens?

PROJECT 7

Stop the Invasion!

When you catch a cold, your body is being attacked. The attackers are cold viruses. If they're not stopped, they'll multiply in great numbers and cause infection. Many other diseases are also caused in this way—by viruses or bacteria that invade your body. In this chapter, you'll learn how your body defends itself against such invasions. And you'll put that knowledge to use as you develop a series of informative news reports in this chapter project.

Your Goal To create a series of imaginary news broadcasts from "battlefield sites" where the body is fighting an infectious disease.

To complete the project successfully you must

- choose a specific disease and represent the sequence of events that occur when that disease strikes the body
- describe the stages of the disease as if they were battles between two armies
- present your story creatively in at least three reports using newspaper, radio, or television news-reporting techniques

Get Started With some classmates, list your ideas about delivering a good newspaper, radio, or television news report. Think about what techniques reporters use to make stories interesting or to explain complicated information. Also, recall the times you've had a cold, flu, or other infectious disease. Write down how your body responded, how long you were sick, and any other useful information you can remember.

Check Your Progress You'll be working on this project as you study this chapter. To keep your project on track, look for Check Your Progress boxes at the following points.

Section 1 Review, page 218: Select a specific disease to research. Learn how it affects the body and how the body responds.
Section 2 Review, page 225: Write scripts for your news reports.
Section 5 Review, page 242: Make any necessary revisions, and practice your presentation.

Wrap Up At the end of the chapter (page 245), you will "broadcast" your news reports for the rest of the class.

Noninfectious Disease

Discover What Happens When Airflow Is Restricted?
Sharpen Your Skills Drawing Conclusions
Skills Lab Causes of Death, Then and Now

Integrating Environmental Science

Cancer and the Environment

Discover What Does Sunlight Do to the Beads?

Section 1 Infectious Disease

Discover Activity

How Does a Disease Spread?

1. On a sheet of paper, write three headings: *Round 1, Round 2,* and *Round 3.*
2. Everyone in the class should shake hands with two people. Under *Round 1,* record the names of the people whose hand you shook.
3. Now shake hands with two different people. Record the name of each person whose hand you shook under *Round 2.*
4. Once again, shake hands with two additional people. Under *Round 3,* record the names of the people whose hand you shook.

Think It Over

Calculating Suppose you had a disease that was spread by shaking hands. Everyone whose hand you shook has caught the disease. So has anyone who later shook those people's hands. Calculate how many people you "infected."

Guide for Reading

- **What kinds of organisms cause disease?**
- **Where do pathogens come from?**

Reading Tip **As you read, use the headings in the section to make an outline. Write the important concepts under each heading.**

Before the twentieth century, surgery was a very risky business. Even if people lived through an operation, they were not out of danger. After the operation, many patients' wounds became infected, and the patients often died. No one knew what caused these infections.

In the 1860s, a British surgeon named Joseph Lister hypothesized that microorganisms caused the infections. To protect his patients, Lister used carbolic acid, a chemical that kills microorganisms. Before performing an operation, Lister washed his hands and surgical instruments with carbolic acid. After the surgery, he covered the patient's wounds with bandages dipped in carbolic acid.

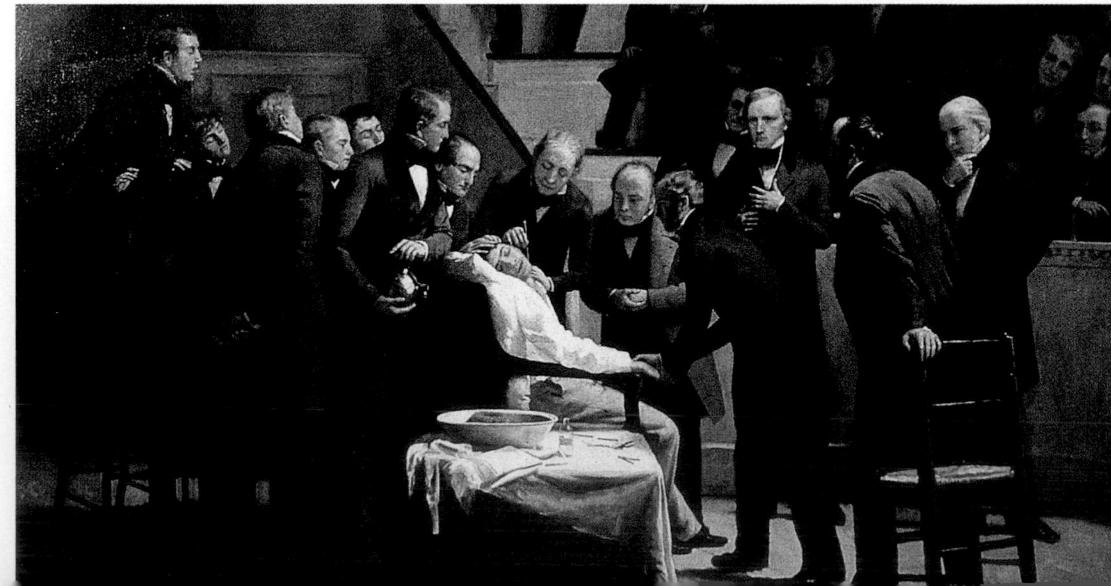

Figure 1 Doctors at Massachusetts General Hospital perform surgery on a patient in 1846. In the 1800s, surgery was performed under conditions that were very different from those used today.

Lister's results were dramatic. Before he used his new method, about 45 percent of his surgical patients died from infection. With Lister's new techniques, only 15 percent died.

Disease and Pathogens

Like the infections that Lister observed after surgery, many illnesses, such as ear infections and food poisoning, are caused by living things that are too small to see. Organisms that cause disease are called **pathogens.** Diseases caused by pathogens are infectious. An **infectious disease** is a disease that can pass from one organism to another.

When you have an infectious disease, pathogens have gotten inside your body and harmed it. Pathogens make you sick by damaging individual cells, even though you may feel pain in a whole organ or throughout your body. For example, when you have strep throat, pathogens have damaged cells in your throat.

☑ ***Checkpoint*** *What causes infectious disease?*

Understanding Infectious Disease

Until Lister's time, few people thought that living organisms could cause disease. Before that, people believed that things like evil spirits or swamp air made people sick.

Several scientists in the late 1800s contributed to the understanding of infectious diseases. Joseph Lister was influenced by the work of Louis Pasteur, a French scientist. In the 1860s, Pasteur showed that microorganisms cause certain kinds of diseases. In addition, Pasteur showed that killing the microorganisms could prevent the spread of those diseases. In the 1870s and 1880s, a German physician named Robert Koch demonstrated that each infectious disease is caused by a specific kind of pathogen. In other words, one kind of pathogen causes pneumonia, another kind causes chicken pox, and still another kind causes rabies.

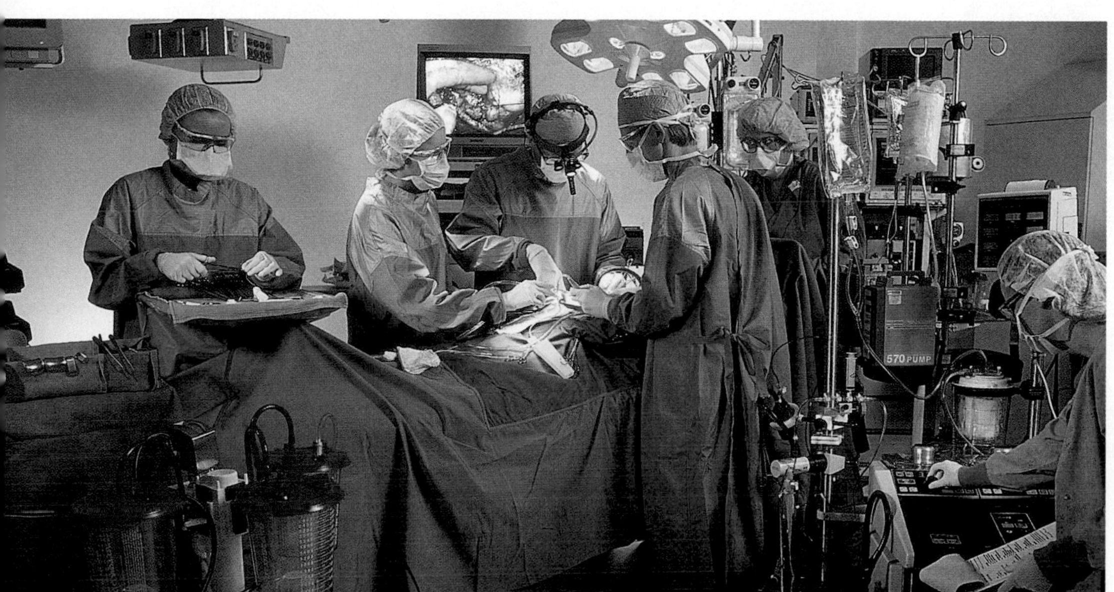

Figure 2 Surgery today is performed in operating rooms that have been cleaned thoroughly to eliminate disease-causing organisms.
Comparing and Contrasting *Contrast Figures 1 and 2. How does surgery today differ from surgery in 1846?*

Kinds of Pathogens

You share Earth with many kinds of organisms. Most are harmless, but some can make you sick. Some diseases are caused by many-celled animals, such as worms. However, most pathogens are too small to be seen without a microscope. **The four major groups of human pathogens are bacteria, viruses, fungi, and protists.** Look at Figure 3 to see examples of pathogens.

Bacteria Bacteria are one-celled microorganisms. They cause a wide variety of diseases, including ear infections, food poisoning, and tuberculosis, which is a disease of the lungs. Some bacterial pathogens damage body cells directly. Strep throat, for example, is caused by streptococcus bacteria that invade cells in your throat. Other bacterial pathogens do not enter cells, but instead produce a poison, or **toxin,** that damages cells. For example, when the bacteria that cause tetanus get into a wound, they can produce a toxin that damages the nervous system. Tetanus is also called lockjaw because the nerve damage can lock the muscles that control the jaws.

Figure 3 Most infectious diseases are caused by microscopic organisms. **A.** Bacteria like this rod-shaped one cause tetanus, a disease that harms the nervous system. **B.** When you have a cough and a sore throat, this round virus, called an adenovirus may be to blame. **C.** This fungus causes ringworm, a skin disease.

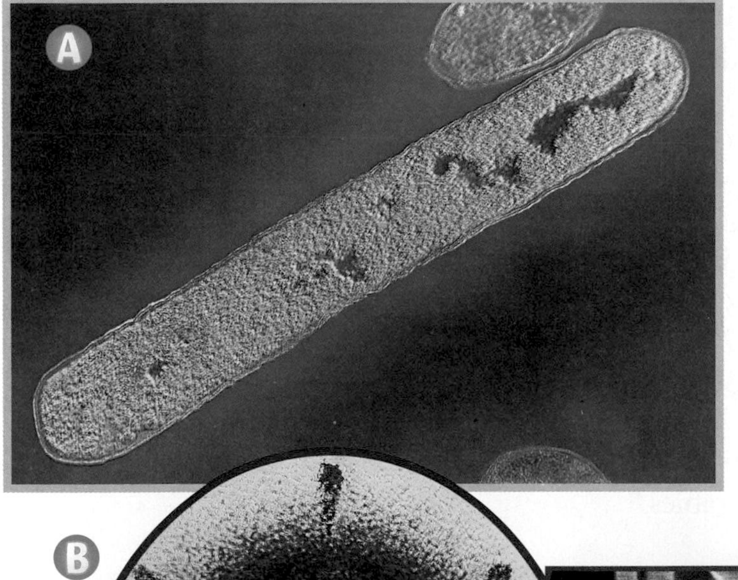

Viruses Viruses are tiny particles, much smaller than bacteria and other pathogens. Viruses cannot reproduce unless they are inside living cells. The cells are damaged or destroyed in the process, releasing new viruses to infect other cells. Both colds and influenza—or flu—are caused by viruses that invade cells in the respiratory system. In fact, there are over 200 different kinds of cold viruses, and each of them can give you a sore throat and a runny nose! Chicken pox and AIDS are also caused by viruses. You will learn more about AIDS later in the chapter.

Fungi and Protists Fungi, which include molds, yeasts, and other organisms, cause some infectious diseases, including athlete's foot. Malaria, an infection of the blood that is common in tropical areas, is one disease caused by protists.

☑ *Checkpoint* *What are two ways in which bacteria cause disease?*

How Diseases Are Spread

Pathogens are something like ants at a picnic. They aren't trying to harm you. However, like the ants, pathogens need food. They also need a place to live and reproduce. Unfortunately, your body may be just the right place for a pathogen to meet those needs.

You can become infected by a pathogen in one of several ways. **Sources of pathogens include another person, a contaminated object, an animal bite, and the environment.**

Person-to-Person Transfer Many pathogens are transferred from one person to another person. Pathogens often pass from one person to another through direct physical contact, such as kissing, hugging, and shaking hands. For example, if you kiss someone who has a cold sore, cold-sore viruses can then get into your body.

Diseases are also spread through indirect contact with an infected person. For example, if a person with pneumonia sneezes, pathogens shoot into the air. Pathogens from a sneeze can travel most of the way across a small room! Other people may catch pneumonia if they inhale these pathogens. Colds, flu, and tuberculosis can be spread through coughing and sneezing.

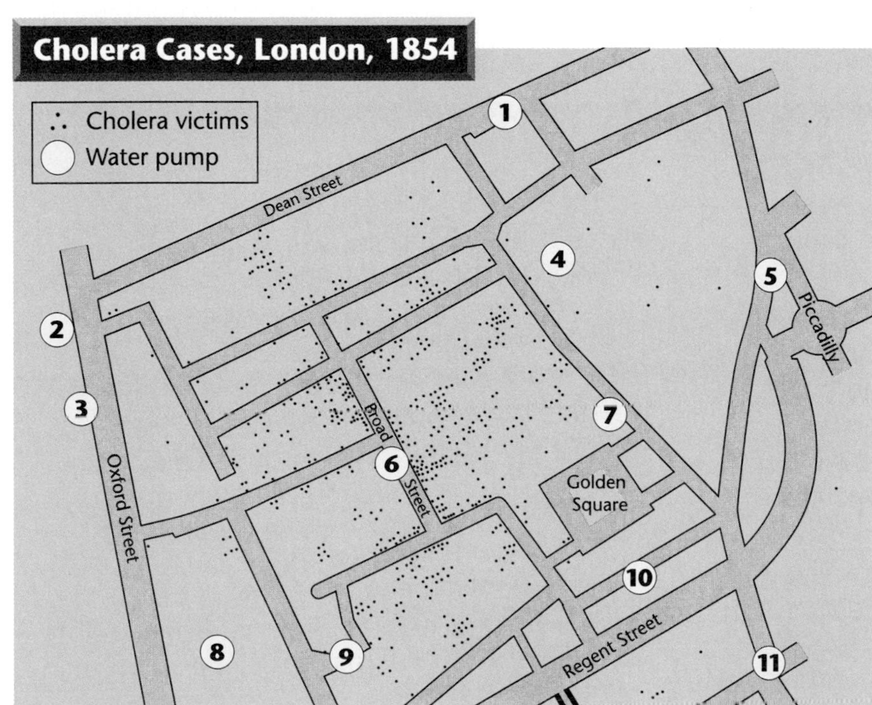

Figure 4 The map shows the location of cholera cases in the 1854 epidemic in London, England.

Posing Questions

ACTIVITY

Cholera is a deadly disease that is spread through food or water contaminated with cholera bacteria. In 1854, cholera spread through London, England. Dr. John Snow analyzed where most of the cholera victims lived, as well as the locations of the water pumps in the area. The map in Figure 4 shows Dr. Snow's findings. Dr. Snow hypothesized that the disease was spread by water that came from one of the pumps. Which pump was probably the source of the contaminated water?

Suppose that Dr. Snow just learned that two additional people had died of cholera. What questions would Dr. Snow most likely ask about the additional cholera cases?

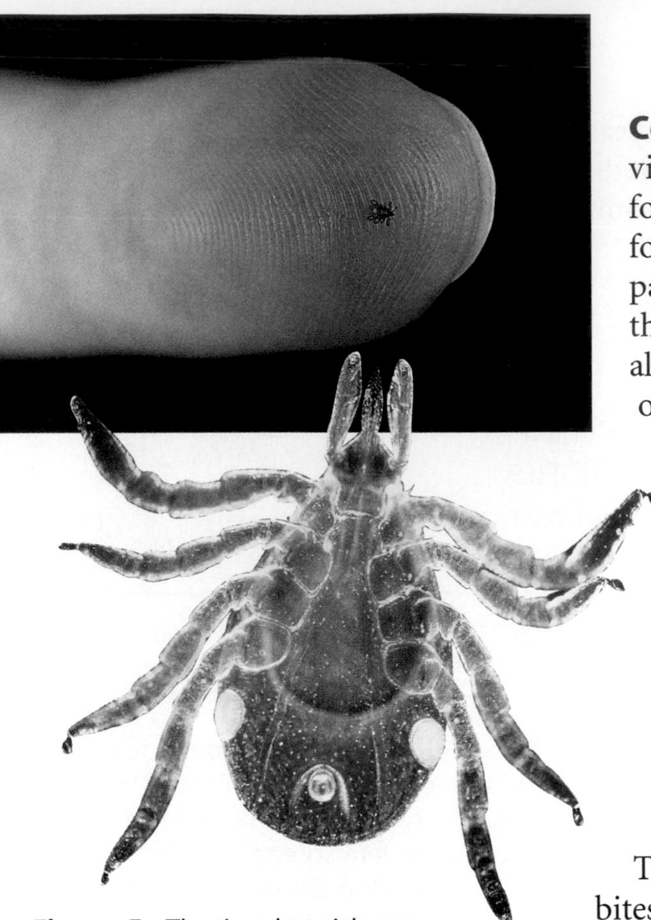

Figure 5 The tiny deer tick may carry the bacteria that cause Lyme disease, a serious condition that can damage the joints. If a deer tick that is carrying Lyme disease bacteria bites a person, the person may get Lyme disease. ***Problem Solving*** *How might people reduce their risk of catching Lyme disease?*

Contaminated Objects Some pathogens can survive for a time outside a person's body. Water and food can become contaminated. If people then eat the food or drink the water, they may become sick. Some pathogens that cause severe diarrhea are spread through contaminated food and water. People can also pick up pathogens by using objects, such as towels or silverware, that have been handled by an infected person. Colds and flu can be spread in this way. Tetanus bacteria can enter the body if a person steps on a contaminated nail.

Animal Bites If an animal is infected with certain pathogens and then bites a person, it can pass the pathogens to the person. People can get rabies, a serious disease that affects the nervous system, from the bite of an infected animal, such as a dog or a raccoon. Lyme disease and Rocky Mountain spotted fever are both spread by tick bites. The protist that causes malaria is transferred by the bites of mosquitoes that live in tropical regions.

Pathogens from the Environment Some pathogens occur naturally in the environment. The bacteria that cause tetanus live in soil or water. The bacteria that cause botulism, an especially severe form of food poisoning, also live in soil. Botulism bacteria can produce a toxin in foods that have been improperly canned. The toxin is extremely powerful.

Section 1 Review

1. Name four kinds of pathogens that cause disease in humans.
2. Describe four ways that pathogens can infect humans.
3. Explain how Pasteur and Koch contributed to the understanding of infectious disease.
4. **Thinking Critically Applying Concepts** If you have a cold, what steps can you take to keep from spreading it to other people? Explain.

CHAPTER PROJECT 7

Check Your Progress

At this stage, you should have chosen a specific infectious disease to research. You should also decide whether to do newspaper articles, radio programs, or a television series. Begin to plan how you will explain the way in which the body is invaded by pathogens. Also begin thinking about how you will make your show appropriate for your audience. (*Hint:* To get ideas on how to present news stories, read newspapers or watch or listen to real news programs about international conflicts.)

SECTION 2

The Body's Defenses

DISCOVER ACTIVITY

Which Pieces Fit Together?

1. Your teacher will give you a piece of paper with one jagged edge.
2. One student in the class has a piece of paper whose edges match your paper edge, like two pieces of a jigsaw puzzle.
3. Find the student whose paper matches yours and fit the two edges together.

Think It Over

Inferring Imagine that one of each pair of matching pieces is a pathogen. The other is a cell in your body that defends your body against the invading pathogen. How many kinds of invaders can each defender cell recognize?

GUIDE FOR READING

- **What is the body's first line of defense against pathogens?**
- **What happens during the inflammatory response?**
- **How does the immune system respond to pathogens?**

Reading Tip **Before you read, preview *Exploring the Immune Response* on page 223. List any unfamiliar terms. As you read, write definitions of those terms in your own words.**

Your eyes are glued to the screen. The situation in the video game is desperate. Enemy troops have gotten through an opening in the wall. Your soldiers have managed to hold back most of the invaders. However, some enemy soldiers are breaking through the defense lines. You need your backup defenders. They can zap the invaders with their powerful weapons. If your soldiers can fight off the enemy until the backup team arrives, you can save your fortress.

Video games create fantasy wars, but in your body, real battles happen all the time. In your body, the "enemies" are invading pathogens. You are hardly ever aware of these battles. The body's disease-fighting system is so effective that most people get sick only occasionally. By eliminating pathogens that can destroy your cells, your body maintains homeostasis.

Figure 6 The pathogens that invade your body are something like the enemy soldiers in a video game. Your body has to defend itself against the pathogens.

Barriers That Keep Pathogens Out

Your body has three lines of defense against pathogens. The first line consists of barriers that keep pathogens from getting into the body. You do not wear a sign that says "Pathogens Keep Out," but that doesn't matter. **Barriers such as the skin, breathing passages, mouth, and stomach trap and kill most pathogens with which you come into contact.**

Figure 7 Skin is covered with bacteria. The dots in the photo are colonies of bacteria living on a person's hand.
Relating Cause and Effect *How can a cut in the skin lead to an infection?*

The Skin When pathogens land on the skin, they are exposed to destructive chemicals in oil and sweat. Even if these chemicals don't kill them, the pathogens may fall off with dead skin cells. If the pathogens manage to stay on the skin, they must get through the tightly packed dead cells that form a barrier on top of living skin cells. Most pathogens get through the skin only when it is cut. Scabs form over cuts so rapidly that the period in which pathogens can enter the body in this way is very short.

The Breathing Passages As you know, you can inhale pathogens when you breathe in. The nose, pharynx, trachea, and bronchi, however, contain mucus and cilia. Together, the mucus and cilia trap and remove most of the pathogens that enter the respiratory system. In addition, irritation by pathogens may make you sneeze or cough. Both actions force the pathogens out of your body.

The Mouth and Stomach Some pathogens are found in foods, even if the foods are handled safely. The saliva in your mouth contains destructive chemicals and your stomach produces acid. Most pathogens that you swallow are destroyed by saliva or stomach acid.

General Defenses

In spite of barriers, pathogens sometimes get into your body and begin to damage cells. When body cells are damaged, they release chemicals that trigger the **inflammatory response,** which is the second line of defense. **In the inflammatory response, fluid and certain types of white blood cells leak from blood vessels into nearby tissues. The white blood cells then fight the pathogens.** Because the inflammatory response is the same no matter what the pathogen, it is sometimes called the body's general defense.

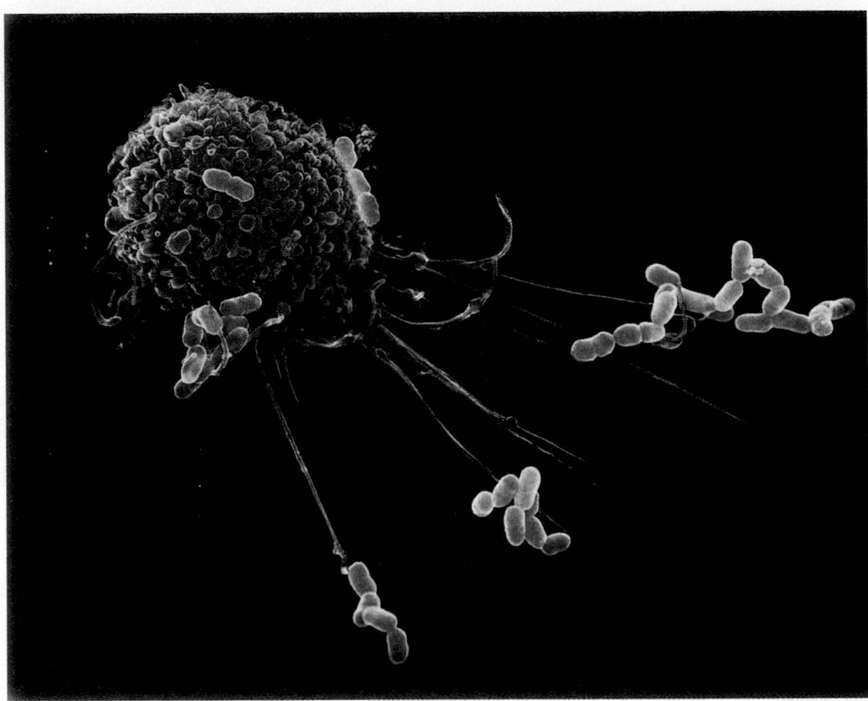

Figure 8 Caught! The bacteria, shown in green, don't stand a chance against the phagocyte, shown in red. Phagocytes are white blood cells that engulf and destroy bacteria.

All white blood cells are disease fighters, but there are different types, each with its own particular function. The kinds involved in the inflammatory response are called phagocytes. A **phagocyte** (FAG uh syt) is a white blood cell that engulfs pathogens and destroys them by breaking them down.

During the inflammatory response, blood vessels widen in the area affected by the pathogens. This enlargement increases the flow of blood to the area. The enlarged blood vessels—and the fluid that leaks out of them—make the affected area red and swollen. If you touch the swollen area, it will feel slightly warmer than normal. In fact, the term *inflammation* comes from a Latin word meaning "to set on fire."

In some cases, chemicals produced during the inflammatory response cause a fever, raising your body temperature above its normal temperature of 37° Celsius. Although fever makes you feel bad, it actually may help your body fight the infection. Some pathogens may not grow and reproduce well at higher temperatures.

Checkpoint *What role do white blood cells play in the inflammatory response?*

Social Studies CONNECTION

Today the Panama Canal is an important shipping route that links the Atlantic and Pacific oceans. But because of two diseases that cause high fever—malaria and yellow fever—the Panama Canal almost didn't get built. Much of the canal, which links the Atlantic and Pacific oceans, passes through the mosquito-filled rain forests of Panama. Mosquitoes carry the pathogens that cause malaria and yellow fever.

In 1889 an attempt at digging a canal was abandoned, partly because so many workers became sick. In 1904, an American physician, Colonel William C. Gorgas, began a project in which swamps in the work area were drained. In addition, brush and grass were cut down. Gorgas's project destroyed the places where mosquitoes lived and reproduced. This action greatly reduced the mosquito population. The Panama Canal was completed in 1914.

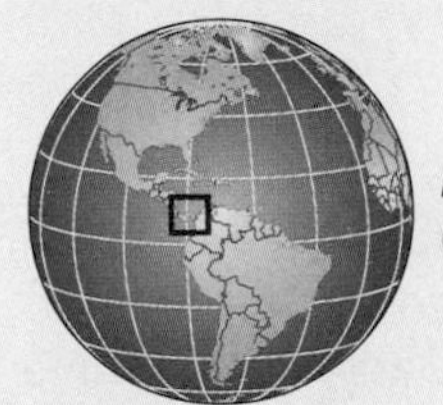

In Your Journal

Write a newspaper article about the construction of the Panama Canal. The article should focus on the problem of disease and the contribution of Colonel Gorgas.

The Immune System

If a pathogen infection is severe enough to cause a fever, it also triggers the third line of defense—the **immune response.** The immune response is controlled by the immune system, your body's disease fighting system. **The cells of the immune system can distinguish between different kinds of pathogens. The immune-system cells react to each kind of pathogen with a defense targeted specifically at that pathogen.** The white blood cells that do this are called **lymphocytes** (LIM fuh syts). There are two major kinds of lymphocytes—T lymphocytes and B lymphocytes, which are also called T cells and B cells. In *Exploring the Immune Response*, you can see how T cells and B cells work together to destroy flu viruses.

T Cells A major function of **T cells** is to identify pathogens and *INTEGRATING CHEMISTRY* distinguish one kind of pathogen from another. You have tens of millions of T cells circulating in your blood. Each kind of T cell recognizes a different kind of pathogen. What T cells actually recognize are marker molecules, called antigens, found on each pathogen. **Antigens** are molecules on cells that the immune system recognizes either as part of your body or as coming from outside your body. All cells have antigens, and each person's antigens are different from those of all other people.

You can think of antigens as something like the uniforms that athletes wear. When you watch a track meet, you can look at the runners' uniforms to tell which school each runner comes from. Like athletes from different schools, each different pathogen has its own kind of antigen. Antigens differ from one another because each kind of antigen has a different chemical structure.

Figure 9 By looking at the runners' uniforms, you can tell that they come from different schools. Similarly, the immune system recognizes a pathogen by its antigens—marker molecules on the pathogen. ***Applying Concepts*** *What is the name of the cell that distinguishes one pathogen from another?*

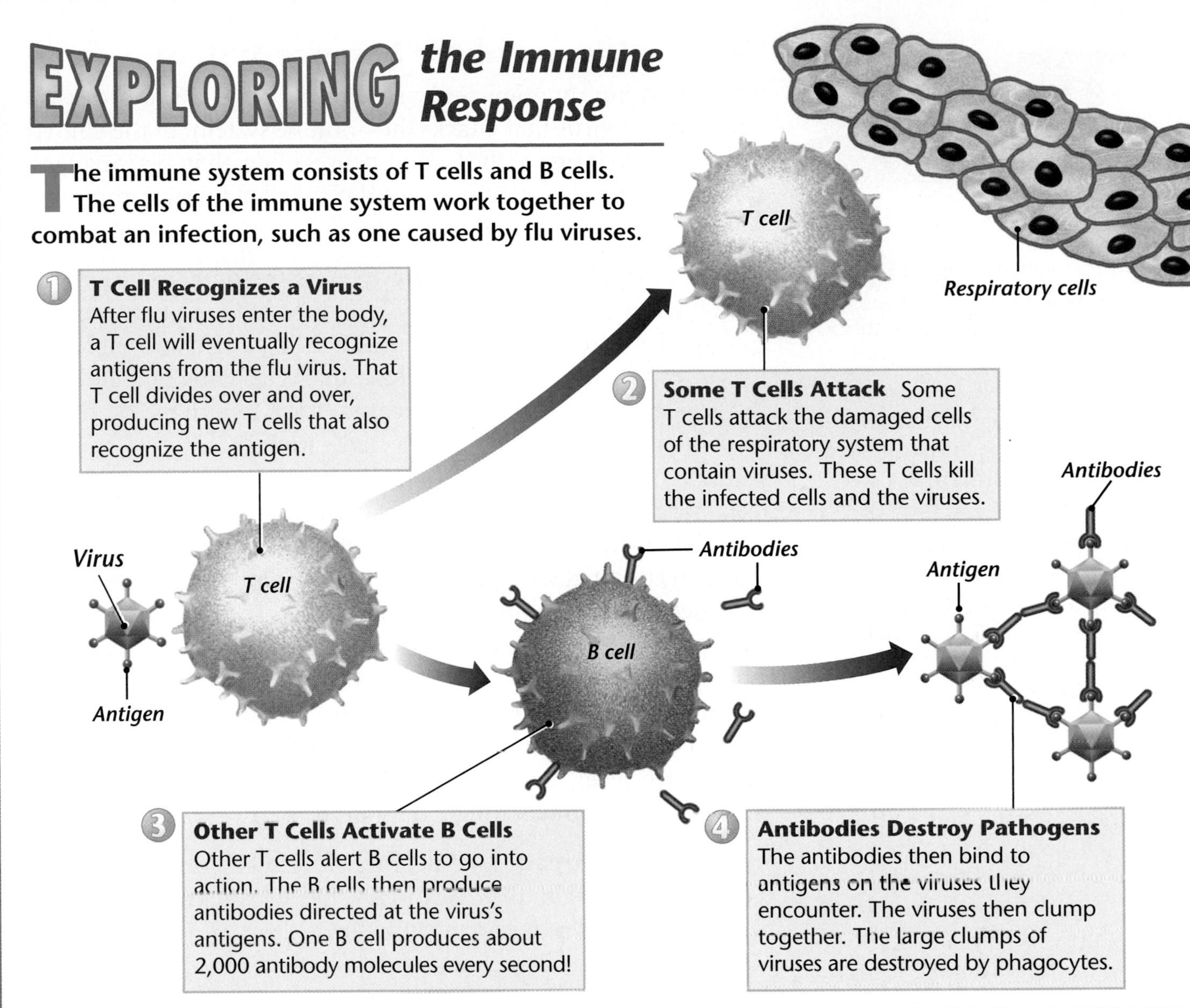

B Cells The lymphocytes called **B cells** produce chemicals that help destroy each kind of pathogen. These chemicals are called **antibodies.** Antibodies lock onto antigens. Each kind of B cell produces only one kind of antibody. Each kind of antibody has a different structure. Antigen and antibody molecules fit together, like pieces of a puzzle. An antigen on a flu virus will only bind to one kind of antibody—the antibody that acts against that flu virus.

INTEGRATING CHEMISTRY

When antibodies bind to the antigens on a pathogen, they mark the pathogen for destruction. Some antibodies make pathogens clump together. Others keep pathogens from attaching to the body cells that they might damage. Still other antibodies make it easier for phagocytes to destroy the pathogens.

☑ *Checkpoint* *What is the function of an antibody?*

Stuck Together

In this activity, you will model one way in which an antibody prevents a pathogen from infecting a body cell.

1. Use a large ball to represent a body cell, and a smaller ball to represent a pathogen.
2. Press a lump of modeling clay onto the small ball. Then use the clay to stick the two balls together. This models how a pathogen attaches itself to a body cell.
3. Pull the two balls apart, keeping the clay on the small ball (the pathogen).
4. Put strips of tape over the clay, so that the clay is completely covered. The tape represents an antibody.
5. Now try to reattach the small ball to the larger one.

Making Models Use the model to explain how antibodies prevent pathogens from attaching to body cells.

AIDS, a Disease of the Immune System

Acquired immunodeficiency syndrome, or **AIDS,** is a disease caused by a virus that attacks the immune system. In the United States, AIDS is one of the leading causes of death in persons aged 25 to 44. The virus that causes AIDS is called human immunodeficiency virus, or HIV.

How HIV Affects the Body HIV is the only kind of virus known to attack the immune system directly. Once it invades the body, HIV enters T cells and reproduces inside them. People can be infected with HIV—that is, have the virus living in their body cells—for years before they become sick. More than 30 million people in the world may be infected with HIV.

Eventually HIV begins to destroy the T cells it has infected. Damage to the immune system is usually slow. But as the viruses destroy T cells, the body loses its ability to fight disease. Most persons infected with HIV eventually develop the disease AIDS.

Because their immune systems no longer function properly, people with AIDS become sick with diseases not normally found in people with healthy immune systems. Many people survive attack after attack of such diseases. But eventually their immune systems fail, ending in death. At this time, there is no cure for AIDS. However, new drug treatments allow people with the disease to survive much longer than in the past.

How HIV Is Spread Like all other viruses, HIV can only reproduce inside cells. In the case of HIV, the virus reproduces inside T cells. However, it can survive for a short time outside the human body in body fluids, such as blood and the fluids produced by the male and female reproductive systems.

HIV can spread from one person to another only if body fluids from an infected person come in contact with those of an uninfected person. Sexual contact is one way in which this can happen. HIV may also pass from an infected woman to her baby

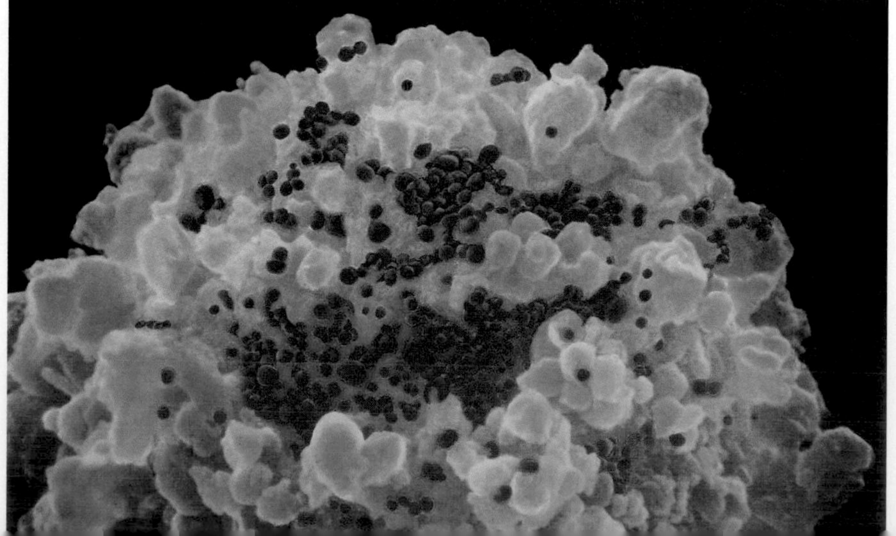

Figure 10 The tiny red particles are HIV viruses emerging from a T cell. The viruses multiply inside the T cell and eventually cause the cell to die.
Relating Cause and Effect *Why does the death of T cells interfere with the body's ability to fight disease?*

Figure 11 You cannot get HIV, the virus that causes AIDS, by hugging someone infected with the virus.

during pregnancy or childbirth or through breast milk. In addition, when drug users share needles, some infected blood may get into the needle and then infect the next person who uses it. A person can also get HIV through a transfusion of blood that contains the virus. But since 1985, all donated blood in the United States has been tested for signs of HIV, and infected blood is not used in transfusions.

It is important to know the many ways in which HIV is *not* spread. HIV does not live on skin, so you cannot be infected by hugging or shaking hands with an infected person. You can't get infected by using a toilet seat after it has been used by someone with HIV. And HIV is not spread when you bump into someone while playing sports.

Section 2 Review

1. Name four barriers that prevent pathogens from getting into the body. Explain how each barrier prevents infection.
2. Describe the inflammatory response.
3. What is the function of the immune system?
4. How is HIV different from other virus pathogens?
5. **Thinking Critically Applying Concepts** Explain why you can't contract HIV by touching a doorknob that someone infected with the virus has touched.

CHAPTER PROJECT 7

Check Your Progress

At this point you should begin writing the newspaper articles or scripts for each of your broadcasts. Before you begin writing, outline the main ideas that you want to communicate. Work to make your descriptions sound like real news. (*Hint:* Make sure that your articles or scripts include information about each of the body's three lines of defense).

Real-World Lab

How It Works

The Skin as a Barrier

Bacteria are all around you. Many of those bacteria can cause disease, yet you usually remain free of disease. In this lab, you will investigate how the skin protects you from infectious disease.

Problem

How does skin act as a barrier to pathogens?

Skills Focus

making models, controlling variables, drawing conclusions

Materials

sealable plastic bags, 4	marking pen
fresh apples, 4	paper towels
rotting apple	toothpick
cotton swabs	rubbing alcohol

Procedure 

1. Read over the entire procedure to see how you will treat each of four fresh apples. Write a prediction in your notebook about the change(s) you expect to see in each apple. Then copy the data table into your notebook.
2. Label four plastic bags *1, 2, 3,* and *4.*
3. Gently wash four fresh apples with water, then dry them carefully with paper towels. Place one apple in plastic bag 1, and seal the bag.
4. Insert a toothpick tip into a rotting apple and withdraw it. Lightly draw the tip of the toothpick down the side of the second apple without breaking the skin. Repeat these actions three more times, touching the toothpick to different parts of the apple without breaking the skin. Insert the apple in plastic bag 2, and seal the bag.

5. Insert the toothpick tip into the rotting apple and withdraw it. Use the tip to make a long, thin scratch down the side of the third apple. Be sure to pierce the apple's skin. Repeat these actions three more times, making additional scratches on different parts of the apple. Insert the apple into plastic bag 3, and seal the bag.
6. Repeat Step 5 to make four scratches in the fourth apple. However, before you place the apple in the bag, dip a cotton swab in rubbing alcohol, and swab the scratches. Then place the apple in plastic bag 4, and seal the bag. **CAUTION:** *Alcohol and its vapors are flammable. Work where there are no sparks, exposed flames, or other heat sources.*
7. Store the four bags in a warm, dark place. Wash your hands thoroughly with soap and water.
8. Every day for one week, remove the apples from their storage place, and observe them without opening the bags. Record your observations, then return the bags to their storage location. At the end of the activity, dispose of the unopened bags as directed by your teacher.

Analyze and Conclude

1. How did the appearance of the four apples compare? Explain your results.
2. In this activity, what condition in the human body is each of the four fresh apples supposed to model?
3. What is the control in this experiment?
4. What is the role of the rotting apple in this activity?
5. **Apply** How does this investigation show why routine cuts and scrapes should be cleaned and bandaged?

Design an Experiment

Using apples as you did in this activity, design an experiment to model how washing hands can prevent the spread of disease. Obtain your teacher's permission before carrying out your investigation.

DATA TABLE

Date	Apple 1 (no contact with decay)	Apple 2 (contact with decay, unbroken skin)	Apple 3 (contact with decay, scratched, untreated)	Apple 4 (contact with decay, scratched, treated with alcohol)

SECTION 3 Preventing Infectious Disease

DISCOVER ACTIVITY

What Substances Can Kill Pathogens?

1. Your teacher will give you a variety of products, such as disinfectant soaps and mouthwashes, that claim to kill pathogens. Read the labels to learn the pathogens that each product is supposed to destroy.
2. Also note the ingredients in each product that act against pathogens. These are labeled "active ingredients."

Think It Over

Designing Experiments How could you determine which of two different soaps is more effective at killing bacteria? Design an experiment to find out. Do not perform the experiment without obtaining your teacher's approval.

GUIDE FOR READING

- What is active immunity?
- What is passive immunity?

Reading Tip **Before you read, rewrite the headings in the section as questions that begin with *how, why,* or *what.* As you read, write short answers to those questions.**

Itch, itch, itch. That's probably what you remember about chicken pox, if you ever had it. But once you got better, you could be pretty sure that you would never get that disease again. As people recover from some diseases, they develop immunity to the diseases. **Immunity** is the body's ability to destroy pathogens before they can cause disease. There are two basic types of immunity—active and passive.

Active Immunity

If you've been sick with chicken pox, your body was invaded by chicken pox viruses. Your immune system responded to the virus antigens by producing antibodies against them. The next time that chicken pox viruses invade your body, your immune system will probably produce antibodies so quickly that you won't become sick. You now have **active immunity** to chicken pox, because your own body has produced the antibodies that fight the chicken pox pathogens. **Active immunity occurs when a person's own immune system produces antibodies in response to the presence of a pathogen.**

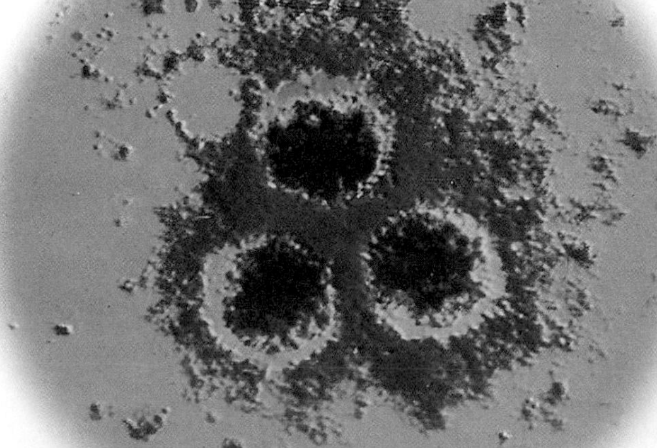

Figure 12 These virus particles cause chicken pox. Once you have had chicken pox you will probably never get that disease again.

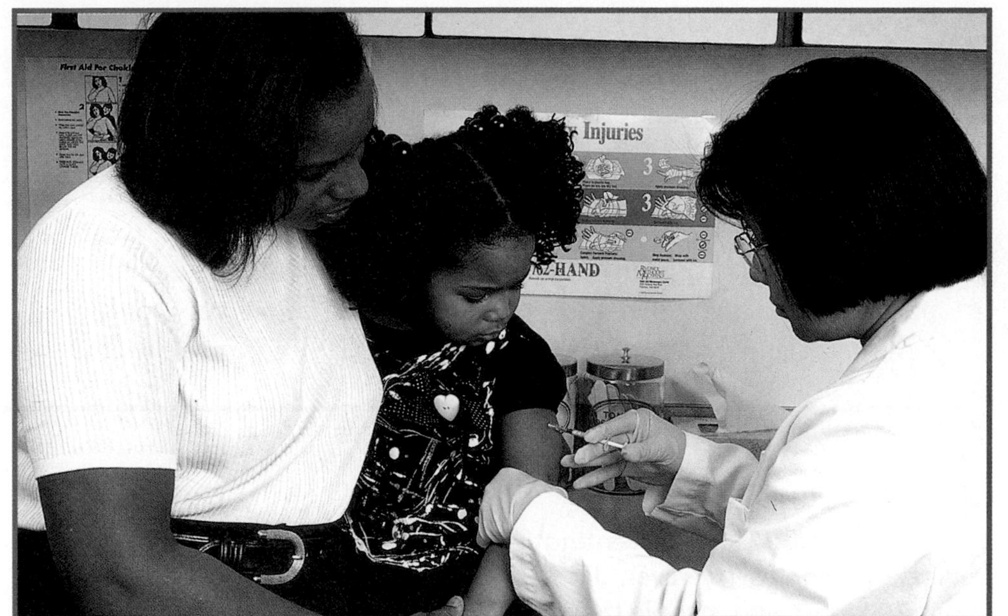

Figure 13 Ouch! The injection may sting a bit, but it is a vaccination that will protect the little girl against disease. Vaccinations consist of dead or weakened pathogens that do not make you sick. ***Classifying*** *Why does a vaccination produce active immunity to a disease?*

How Active Immunity Is Produced Active immunity is produced by the cells of a person's immune system as part of the immune response. Remember that during the immune response, T cells and B cells help destroy the disease-causing pathogens. After the person recovers, some of the T cells and B cells keep the "memory" of the pathogen's antigen. If that kind of pathogen enters the body again, these memory cells recognize the pathogen's antigen. The memory cells start the immune response so quickly that the person usually doesn't get sick. Active immunity usually lasts for many years, and sometimes it lasts for life.

Vaccination One way in which you can gain active immunity is by coming down with the disease. Another way is by being vaccinated against the disease. **Vaccination** (vac suh NAY shun), or immunization, is the process by which harmless antigens are deliberately introduced into a person's body to produce active immunity. Vaccinations are given by injection or by mouth. Vaccinations can prevent polio, chicken pox, and other diseases.

The substance that is used in a vaccination is called a vaccine. A **vaccine** (vak SEEN) usually consists of pathogens that have been weakened or killed but can still trigger the immune system to go into action. The T cells and B cells still recognize and respond to the antigens of the weakened or dead pathogen. When you receive a vaccination, the weakened pathogens usually do not make you sick. However, your immune system responds by producing memory cells and active immunity to the disease.

☑ ***Checkpoint*** *What are two ways in which a person can gain active immunity?*

Passive Immunity

Some diseases, such as rabies, are so uncommon that people rarely receive vaccinations against them. If a person is bitten by an animal that might have rabies, however, the person is usually given injections that contain antibodies to the rabies antigen. The protection that the person acquires this way is an example of passive immunity. This type of immunity is called **passive immunity** because the antibodies are given to the person—the person's own immune system did not make them.

Fighting Infectious Disease

From ancient times, people have practiced methods for preventing disease and caring for sick people. Ancient peoples, however, did not know what caused disease. About 200 years ago, people began to learn much more about the causes of infectious diseases and how to protect against them.

1854

Florence Nightingale

As an English nurse caring for British soldiers during the Crimean War, Florence Nightingale insisted that army hospitals be kept clean. By doing this, she saved many soldiers' lives. She is considered to be the founder of the modern nursing profession.

1800 **1825** **1850**

1796

Edward Jenner

Edward Jenner, a country doctor in England, successfully vaccinated a child against smallpox, a deadly viral disease. Jenner used material from a sore of a person with cowpox, a mild but similar disorder. Although Jenner's procedure was successful, he did not understand why it worked.

1860s

Joseph Lister

Joseph Lister, an English surgeon, used carbolic acid to prevent infections in surgical patients. Because of Lister's techniques, far more people recovered from surgery than before.

Passive immunity occurs when the antibodies that fight the pathogen come from another source rather than from the person's own body. Unlike active immunity, which is long-lasting, passive immunity usually lasts no more than a few months.

A baby acquires passive immunity to some diseases before birth. This happens because antibodies from the mother's body pass into the baby's body. After birth, these antibodies protect the baby for a few months. After that time, the baby's own immune system has begun to function.

In Your Journal

Learn more about the work of one of these people. Then imagine that a new hospital is going to be dedicated to that person, and that you have been chosen to deliver the dedication speech. Write a speech that praises the person's contributions to fighting disease.

1882

Robert Koch

In Germany, Robert Koch identified one kind of microorganism in many samples of tissue taken from people with tuberculosis. Because he always found the same microorganism, Koch hypothesized that each infectious disease is caused by one specific pathogen.

1875 1900 1925

1868

Louis Pasteur

In France, Louis Pasteur showed that microorganisms were the cause of a disease in silkworms. Pasteur reasoned that he could control the spread of disease by killing microorganisms. He also proposed that infectious diseases in humans are caused by microorganisms.

1928

Alexander Fleming

In Britain, Alexander Fleming observed that bacteria growing on laboratory plates were killed when some kinds of fungi grew on the same plate. He discovered that one fungus produced a substance—penicillin—that killed bacteria. Penicillin became the first antibiotic.

Staying Healthy

You almost certainly have immunity to some diseases, either because you have had the diseases or because you have been vaccinated against them. However, no one is immune to all diseases. But there are several steps you can take to decrease your risk of getting and spreading infectious diseases. Figure 14 summarizes these steps.

Unfortunately, you will probably become sick from time to time. When that happens, there are ways in which you can help yourself recover. Get plenty of rest. In addition, unless your stomach is upset, you should eat well-balanced meals. Drink plenty of fluids. These actions are all that you need to recover from most mild illnesses.

Preventing Infectious Diseases

- Don't share items that might carry pathogens, such as toothbrushes, drinking straws, or silverware.
- Keep clean. Wash your hands before eating and after using the bathroom.
- Cover your mouth when sneezing or coughing.
- Get eight hours of sleep every night.
- Eat a well-balanced diet.
- Get regular exercise.

Figure 14 Your actions can help prevent the spread of infectious diseases. ***Applying Concepts*** *How does keeping clean prevent the spread of disease?*

Sometimes when you are sick, medications can help you get better. If you have a disease that is caused by bacteria, you may be given an antibiotic. An **antibiotic** (an tih by AHT ik) is a chemical that kills bacteria or slows their growth without harming body cells. Unfortunately, there are no medications that cure viral illnesses, including the common cold. The best way to deal with most viral diseases is to get plenty of rest.

Some medicines don't kill pathogens but may help you feel more comfortable while you get better. Many of these are over-the-counter medications—drugs that can be purchased without a doctor's prescription. Such medications may reduce fever, clear your nose so you can breathe more easily, or stop a cough. Be sure you understand and follow the instructions for all types of medications. And if you don't start to feel better in a short time, you should see a doctor.

Section 3 Review

1. What is active immunity? How is it produced?
2. How is passive immunity produced? How does passive immunity differ from active immunity?
3. Identify four things that you can do that will help you avoid catching an infectious disease.
4. **Thinking Critically Applying Concepts** After receiving a vaccination, you may develop mild symptoms of the disease. Explain why.

Science at Home

With a family member, make a list of the vaccinations you have received. For each, note when you received the vaccination. Then, with your family member, learn about one of the diseases for which you were vaccinated. What kind of pathogen causes the disease? What are the symptoms of the disease? Is the disease still common in the United States?

Noninfectious Disease

Discover

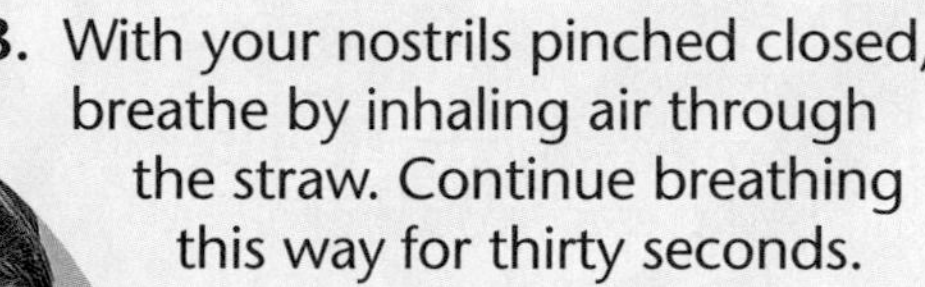

What Happens When Airflow Is Restricted?

1. Asthma is a disorder in which breathing passages become narrower than normal. This activity will help you understand how this condition affects breathing. Begin by breathing normally, first through your nose and then through your mouth. Observe how deeply you breathe.
2. Put one end of a drinking straw in your mouth. Then gently pinch your nostrils shut so that you cannot breathe through your nose.
3. With your nostrils pinched closed, breathe by inhaling air through the straw. Continue breathing this way for thirty seconds.

Think It Over

Observing Compare your normal breathing pattern to that when breathing through the straw. Which way were you able to take deeper breaths? Did you ever feel short of breath?

GUIDE FOR READING

- What is an allergy?
- How does diabetes affect the body?
- What is cancer?

Reading Tip As you read, create a table in which you record the characteristics of each noninfectious disease.

Americans are living longer today than ever before. A person who was born in 1990 can expect to live about 75 years. In contrast, a person born in 1950 could expect to live only about 68 years.

Progress against infectious disease is one reason why life spans have increased. However, as infectious diseases have become less common, noninfectious diseases have grown more prevalent. **Noninfectious diseases** are diseases that are not spread from person to person. Unlike infectious diseases, noninfectious diseases are not caused by microorganisms. A noninfectious disease, cardiovascular disease, is the leading cause of death in America. Allergies, diabetes, and cancer are other noninfectious diseases.

Allergies

Spring has arrived. Flowers are in bloom, and the songs of birds fill the air. Unfortunately for some people, sneezing is another sound that fills the air. People who sneeze and cough in the spring may not have colds. Instead, they may be suffering from an **allergy** to plant pollen in the air. **An allergy is a disorder in which the immune system is overly sensitive to a foreign substance—something not normally found in the body.**

▼ Plant pollen

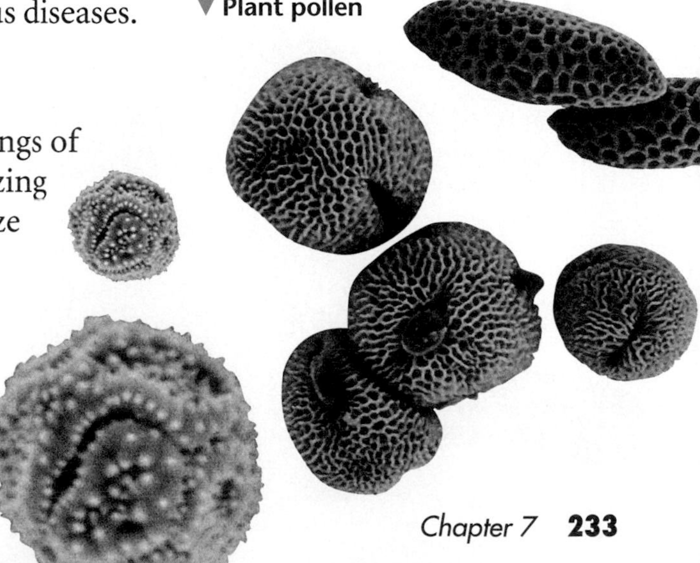

Sharpen your Skills

Drawing Conclusions

ACTIVITY

Two weeks ago, after you ate strawberry shortcake with whipped cream, you broke out in an itchy rash. Besides strawberries, the ingredients in the dessert were sugar, flour, butter, eggs, vanilla, baking powder, salt, and cream. Then last night, you ate a strawberry custard tart with whipped cream and again broke out in a rash. The tart's ingredients were strawberries, sugar, cornstarch, milk, eggs, flour, shortening, salt, and vanilla.

You think that you may be allergic to strawberries. Do you have enough evidence to support this conclusion? If so, why? If not, what additional evidence do you need?

Allergens An **allergen** is any substance that causes an allergy. In addition to different kinds of pollen, people may be allergic to dust, molds, some foods, and even some medicines. If you are lucky, you have no allergies at all. However, many people are allergic to one or more substances.

Reaction to Allergens Allergens may get into your body when you inhale them, eat them in food, or touch them with your skin. When lymphocytes encounter the allergen, they produce antibodies. These antibodies, unlike the ones made during the immune response, signal cells in the body to release a chemical called histamine. **Histamine** (HIS tuh meen) is a chemical that is responsible for the symptoms of an allergy, such as sneezing and watery eyes. Drugs that interfere with the action of histamine, called antihistamines, may lessen this reaction. However, if you have an allergy, the best strategy is to try to avoid the substance to which you are allergic.

Asthma If some people inhale a substance to which they are allergic, they may develop a condition called asthma. **Asthma** (AZ muh) is a disorder in which the respiratory passages narrow significantly. This narrowing causes the person to wheeze and become short of breath. Asthma attacks may be brought on by factors other than allergies, such as stress and exercise. People who have severe asthma attacks may require emergency care. If you have asthma, avoid the substances or activities that trigger asthma attacks and learn how to treat an attack.

☑ *Checkpoint* *What is the effect of histamine on the body?*

Figure 15 Some people have allergic reactions to cats (left) or dust mites, tiny animals found in dust (below).

Diabetes

The pancreas produces a chemical called insulin. **Insulin** (IN suh lin) enables body cells to take in glucose from the blood and use it for energy. In the condition known as **diabetes** (dy uh BEE tis), either the pancreas fails to produce enough insulin or the body's cells can't use it properly. **As a result, a person with diabetes has high levels of glucose in the blood and excretes glucose in the urine. The person's body cells, however, do not have enough glucose.**

Effects of Diabetes People with diabetes may lose weight, feel weak, and be hungry all the time. These symptoms occur because the cells are unable to take in the glucose they need to function efficiently. In addition, these people may urinate frequently and feel thirsty as the kidneys work to eliminate the excess glucose from the body.

Diabetes is a serious condition that, if not treated properly, can result in death. Even with proper treatment, diabetes can have serious long-term effects. These effects can include blindness, kidney failure, and heart disease.

Figure 16 Many people with diabetes must test their blood frequently to determine the level of glucose in their blood. ***Relating Cause and Effect*** *What accounts for the high level of glucose in the blood of people with diabetes?*

Forms of Diabetes There are two main forms of diabetes. Type I diabetes, the more serious form, usually begins in childhood or early adulthood. In Type I diabetes, the pancreas produces little or no insulin. People with this condition must get insulin injections.

Type II diabetes usually develops during adulthood. In this condition, either the pancreas doesn't make enough insulin or body cells do not respond normally to insulin. People with Type II diabetes may not need to take insulin. Instead, they may be able to control the symptoms of diabetes through proper diet, weight control, and exercise.

☑ ***Checkpoint*** *What are some symptoms of diabetes?*

Cancer

Under normal conditions, the body produces new cells at about the same rate that other cells die. In a condition known as **cancer,** however, the situation is quite different. **Cancer is a disease in which cells multiply uncontrollably, over and over, destroying healthy tissue in the process.** The word *cancer* is the Latin word for crab. Cancerous growths act something like a crab, pinching healthy tissues as they grow.

Tumor Formation As cancerous cells divide over and over, they often form abnormal tissue masses called **tumors.** Cancerous tumors invade the healthy tissue around them and destroy the tissue. Cancer cells can break away from a tumor and invade blood or lymph vessels. The blood or lymph then carries the cancer cells to other parts of the body, where they may begin to divide and form new tumors. Unless stopped by treatment, cancer progresses through the body.

Causes of Cancer Different factors may work together to determine what makes cells become cancerous. One such factor is the characteristics that people inherit from their parents. Because of their inherited characteristics, some people are more likely than others to develop certain kinds of cancer. For example, women whose mothers had breast cancer have a higher risk of developing breast cancer than do women with no family history of the disease.

Some substances or factors in the environment, called **carcinogens** (kahr SIN uh junz), can cause cancer. The tar in cigarette smoke is a carcinogen. Ultraviolet light, which is part of sunlight, can also be a carcinogen.

Cancer Treatment Surgery, drugs, and radiation are all used to treat cancer. If cancer is detected before it has spread, doctors remove the cancerous tumors through surgery. Sometimes, however, a surgeon can't remove all of the cancer. In some cases, drugs or radiation may be used to kill the cancer cells or slow their spread.

INTEGRATING PHYSICS Radiation treatment uses high-energy waves to kill cancer cells. X-rays and gamma rays are two types of radiation used in cancer treatment. These waves are similar to sunlight and the

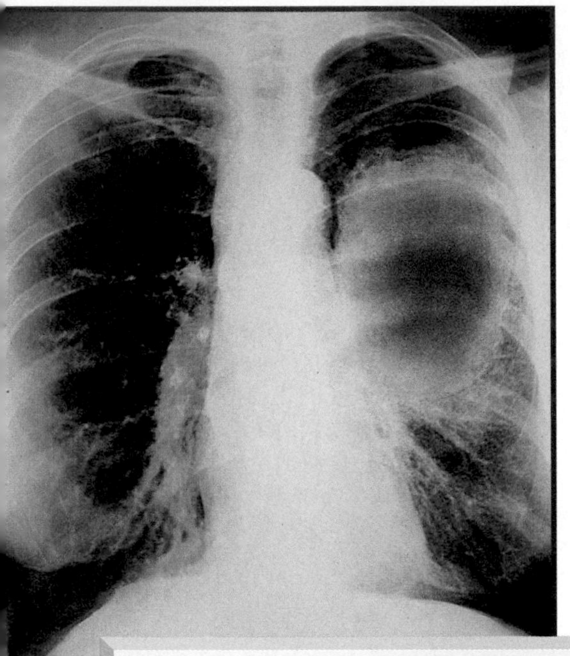

Figure 17 The large orange mass in the X-ray is a cancerous tumor in the lung. The graph shows leading types of cancer that affect men and women in the United States. *Interpreting Graphs Do more women or men develop lung cancer each year?*

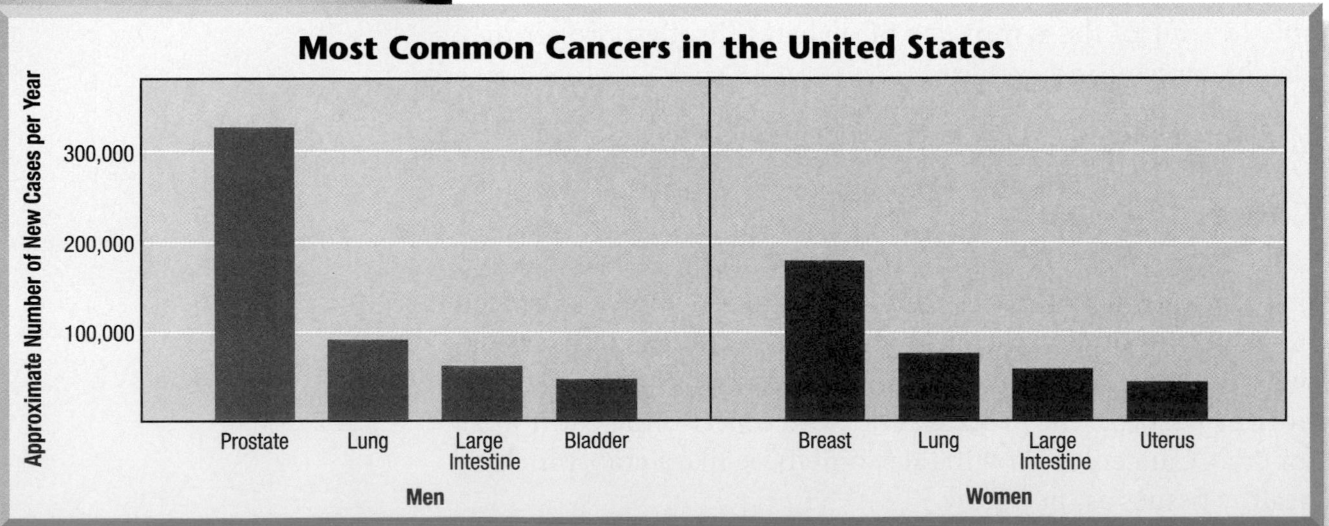

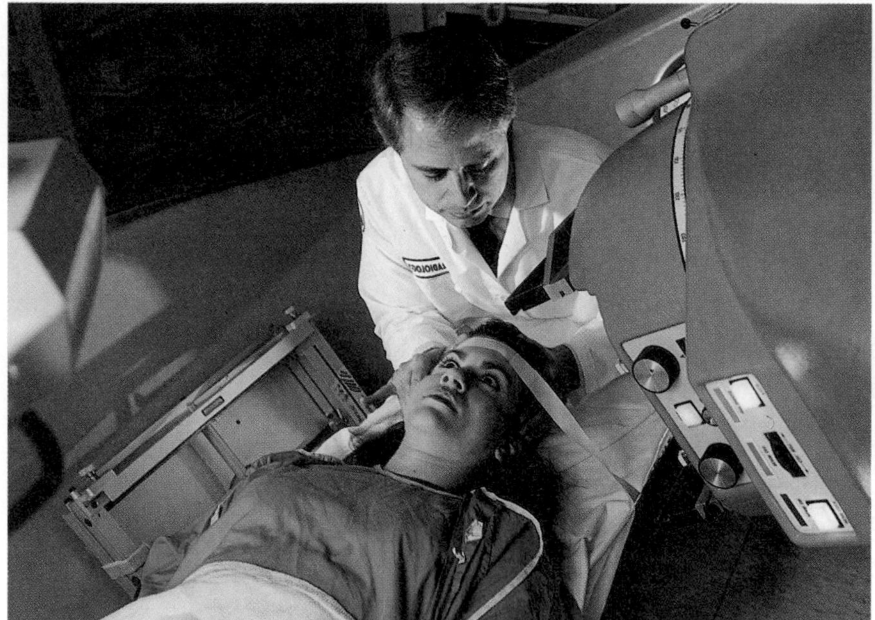

Figure 18 Radiation is one method that is used to treat cancer. The machine beams high-energy radiation at the tumor. This radiation kills cancer cells.

waves that make radios and microwave ovens work. However, X-rays and gamma rays have far more energy than sunlight, radio waves, or microwaves. When X-rays and gamma rays are aimed at tumors, they blast the cancer cells and kill them.

Cancer Prevention People can take steps to reduce their risk of developing cancer. For instance, they can avoid any form of tobacco, since tobacco and tobacco smoke contain carcinogens. Chewing tobacco and snuff contain carcinogens as well—they can cause cancers in the mouth. To prevent skin cancer, people can protect their skin from exposure to too much sunlight. A diet that is low in fat and includes plenty of fruits and vegetables can help people avoid some kinds of cancer, such as certain cancers of the digestive system.

Regular medical checkups are also important. Physicians or nurses may notice signs of cancer during a checkup. The earlier cancer is detected, the more likely it can be treated successfully.

Section 4 Review

1. What is an allergy? Describe how the body reacts to the presence of an allergen.
2. How does diabetes affect the level of glucose in the blood?
3. Describe how cancer cells harm the body.
4. **Thinking Critically Inferring** Doctors sometimes recommend that people with diabetes eat several small meals rather than three large ones. Why do you think doctors give this advice?

Science at Home

Explain to your family what allergies are and how allergens affect the body. Make a list of any substances your family members are allergic to. Use this list to determine whether certain allergies occur frequently in your family.

Skills Lab

Interpreting Data

Causes of DEATH, Then and Now

In this lab you'll compare data on the leading causes of death in 1900 and today.

Problem

How do the leading causes of death today compare with those of a hundred years ago?

Materials

colored pencils
calculator (optional)
compass
ruler
protractor

Procedure 

1. The data table on the next page shows the leading causes of death in the United States during two different years. Examine the data and note that two causes of death—accidents and suicides—are not diseases. The other causes are labeled either "I," indicating an infectious disease, or "NI," indicating a noninfectious disease.

Part 1 Comparing Specific Causes of Death

2. Look at the following causes of death in the data table: **(a)** pneumonia and influenza, **(b)** heart disease, **(c)** accidents, and **(d)** cancer. Construct a bar graph that compares the numbers of deaths from each of those causes in 1900 and today. Label the horizontal axis "Causes of Death." Label the vertical axis "Deaths per 100,000 People." Draw two bars side by side for each cause of death. Use a key to show which bars refer to 1900 and which refer to today.

Part 2 Comparing Infectious and Noninfectious Causes of Death

3. In this part of the lab, you will make two circle graphs showing three categories: infectious diseases, noninfectious diseases, and "other." You may want to review the information on creating circle graphs on page 272 of the Skills Handbook.

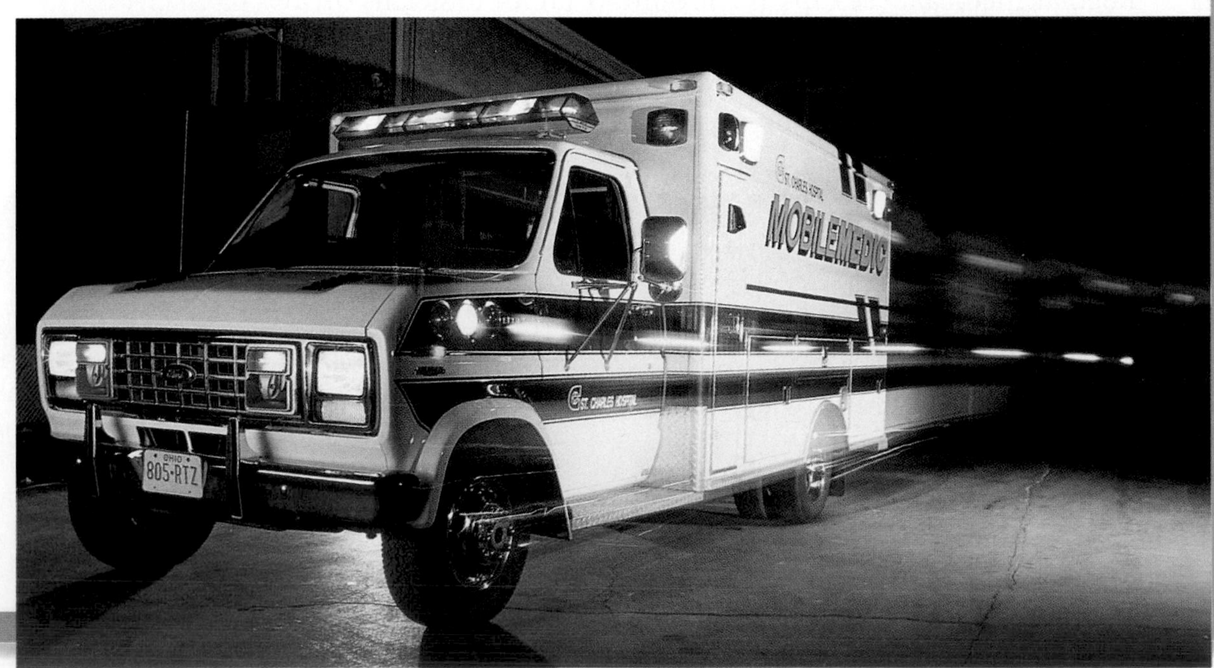

Ten Leading Causes of Death in the United States, 1900 and Today			
1900		Today	
Cause of Death	**Deaths per 100,000**	**Cause of Death**	**Deaths per 100,000**
Pneumonia, influenza (I)*	215	Heart disease (NI)	281
Tuberculosis (I)	185	Cancer (NI)	205
Diarrhea (I)	140	Stroke (NI)	59
Heart disease (NI)	130	Lung disease (NI)	39
Stroke (NI)	110	Accidents	35
Kidney disease (NI)	85	Pneumonia (I)	31
Accidents	75	Diabetes (NI)	22
Cancer (NI)	65	HIV Infection (I)	16
Senility (NI)	55	Suicide	12
Diphtheria (I)	40	Liver disease (NI)	10
Total	**1,100**	**Total**	**710**

*"I" indicates an infectious disease. "NI" indicates a noninfectious disease.

4. Start by grouping the data from 1900 into the three categories—infectious diseases, noninfectious diseases, and other causes. Find the total number of deaths for each category. Then find the size of the "pie slice" (the number of degrees) for each category, and construct your circle graph. To find the size of the infectious disease slice for 1900, for example, use the following formula:

$$\frac{\text{number of deaths from infectious diseases}}{\text{1,100 deaths total}} = \frac{x}{360°}$$

5. Calculate the percentage represented by each category using this formula:

$$\frac{\text{number of degrees in a slice}}{360°} \times 100 = \underline{\ ?\ }\,\%$$

6. Repeat Steps 4 and 5 using the data from today to make the second circle graph. What part of the formula in Step 4 do you need to change?

Analyze and Conclude

1. What kind of information did you learn just from examining the data table in Step 1?
2. According to your bar graph, which cause of death showed the greatest increase between 1900 and today? The greatest decrease?
3. In your circle graphs, which category decreased the most from 1900 to today? Which increased the most?
4. Suggest an explanation for the change in the number of deaths due to infectious diseases from 1900 to today.
5. **Think About It** How do graphs help you identify patterns and other information in data that you might otherwise overlook?

More to Explore

Write a question related to the data table that you have not yet answered. Then create a graph or work with the data in other ways to answer your question.

 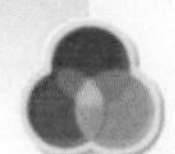

SECTION 5 Cancer and the Environment

DISCOVER ACTIVITY

What Does Sunlight Do to the Beads?

1. Your teacher will give you beads that change color under certain conditions. Thread five beads on a pipe cleaner. Observe what the beads look like. Record your observations.
2. Wrap the pipe cleaner around your wrist. Go outdoors for one minute. Observe what happens to the beads.

Think It Over

Developing Hypotheses The ultraviolet light in sunlight causes the reaction you observed. Form a hypothesis about how you might prevent the beads from reacting as they did. How can you test your hypothesis?

GUIDE FOR READING

- **How can people's environments affect their chances of developing cancer?**

Reading Tip **As you read, write short summaries of the information under each heading.**

You are trapped in a place that is dark, tight, and so warm that it is hard to breathe. You climb upwards, carefully feeling for footholds as you inch along. The surfaces are so warm that your knees begin to feel hot as they scrape against the walls. Grimy dirt falls on your face, and you blink to keep it out of your eyes. This story sounds like a nightmare. But it was real life for the boys who worked as chimney sweeps.

Chimney Sweeps and Skin Cancer

In 1775, about one million people lived in London, England. Their homes were heated by coal fires. Because burning coal produces lots of grimy black soot, the soot had to be cleaned out of the chimneys regularly. Chimney sweeps did this job by crawling into the chimneys and scraping the soot off the walls.

Because chimney sweeps had to be small and thin enough to fit inside a chimney, most were boys rather than men. Since the work was dangerous, only boys who badly needed a job were willing to do it. Therefore, chimney sweeps were usually poor. Their homes did not have a water supply, and bathing was difficult. At the end of a hard day, chimney sweeps were covered with soot, but few washed it off.

A Link Between Soot and Cancer Percivall Pott, a London doctor, saw many chimney sweeps at his medical clinic. Pott noticed that the chimney sweeps often had soot ground deeply into their skin. He also observed that an alarmingly high number of chimney sweeps developed skin cancer. Pott hypothesized that something in soot caused the cancer. He recommended frequent bathing to reduce the risk of skin cancer. Many years later, scientists identified the carcinogens in soot. They are the same substances that make up the tar in cigarette smoke.

Carcinogens in the Environment Percivall Pott was one of the first scientists to understand that the environment can affect people's health. Cancer is one disease that can be caused by harmful environmental factors. **People's environments may contain carcinogens. To reduce the risk of cancer, the carcinogens need to be removed or people need to be protected from them.**

Pott's work led to present-day efforts to control environmental carcinogens. In the United States, the Environmental Protection Agency (EPA) is in charge of enforcing environmental laws. The EPA identifies environmental carcinogens and develops strategies for protecting people from them.

☑ *Checkpoint* *What did Pott recommend that chimney sweeps do in order to reduce their risk of skin cancer?*

Figure 19 Percivall Pott followed scientific procedure as he figured out the cause of skin cancer in chimney sweeps.

1770s — Observations
Percivall Pott notices that chimney sweeps have a high rate of cancer.

1775 — Formation of hypothesis
Pott hypothesizes that something in soot causes skin cancer.

1775 — Testing of hypothesis
Pott recommends that chimney sweeps bathe frequently, thus removing the cancer-causing soot.

1892 — Result of testing
Evidence shows that chimney sweeps who bathe regularly develop skin cancer at a lower rate than sweeps who rarely bathe.

Early 1900s — Confirmation of hypothesis
Certain substances in soot are found to cause skin cancer in laboratory animals.

Figure 20 These asbestos ceiling panels were installed before people knew that asbestos can cause cancer. To protect the people who use the building, a worker is removing the panels.

Environmental Carcinogens Today

Scientists have identified many carcinogens found in the environment. Two important environmental carcinogens are asbestos and ultraviolet light.

Asbestos The mineral asbestos, which occurs in the form of fibers, is strong and does not burn. Because of these characteristics, asbestos was once widely used in materials such as roof shingles, brake linings, and insulation. However, scientists have since discovered that asbestos fibers can sometimes cause lung cancer when people inhale them repeatedly. Because of the dangers of asbestos, in 1989 the United States banned the manufacture and use of most asbestos products.

Ultraviolet Light As you learned in Chapter 3, skin cancer can result from overexposure to sunlight. Ultraviolet light is the part of sunlight that causes cancer. Fortunately, as sunlight travels from the sun to Earth, much of its ultraviolet light is absorbed high in the atmosphere, before it can reach Earth's surface. The gas ozone is the substance that absorbs most of the ultraviolet light.

In the 1970s and 1980s, scientists noticed that ozone levels in the upper atmosphere were decreasing. This decrease in ozone means that more ultraviolet light is reaching Earth's surface. At the same time, cases of skin cancer have been increasing. While the causes of the increase in skin cancer are complicated, some scientists believe that it is linked to the loss of ozone in the atmosphere.

Section 5 Review

1. How can the environment increase a person's risk for getting cancer?
2. What did Percivall Pott observe about the relationship between skin cancer and soot?
3. Why is asbestos dangerous?
4. **Thinking Critically Predicting** If ozone levels in the atmosphere decrease, what will probably happen to the number of skin cancers that develop each year? Explain.

Check Your Progress

CHAPTER PROJECT 7

Before your presentation, make your final revisions. If you are doing broadcasts, practice reading your scripts aloud. Experiment with different ways of bringing your series to a dramatic ending. Try to include answers to questions that might occur to your audience. For instance, are people around the patient at risk of invasion? If so, how can they defend themselves?

CHAPTER 7 STUDY GUIDE

Infectious Disease

Key Ideas

- ◆ Infectious diseases are caused by pathogens: bacteria, viruses, fungi, and protists.
- ◆ Pathogens that infect humans can come from another person, a contaminated object, an animal bite, or the environment.

Key Terms

pathogen   infectious disease   toxin

The Body's Defenses

Key Ideas

- ◆ The body has three lines of defense against pathogens.
- ◆ The immune system targets specific pathogens. T cells identify pathogens and distinguish one kind from another. B cells produce antibodies that destroy pathogens.
- ◆ HIV, the virus that causes AIDS, infects and destroys T cells.

Key Terms

inflammatory response	antigen
phagocyte	B cell
immune response	antibody
lymphocyte	AIDS
T cell	

Preventing Infectious Disease

INTEGRATING HEALTH

Key Ideas

- ◆ In active immunity, a person's own immune system produces antibodies. A person can acquire active immunity by having the disease or by being vaccinated.
- ◆ In passive immunity, the antibodies come from a source other than the person's body.

Key Terms

immunity	vaccination	passive immunity
active immunity	vaccine	antibiotic

Noninfectious Disease

Key Ideas

- ◆ Noninfectious diseases are diseases that are not spread from person to person.
- ◆ An allergy is a disorder in which the immune system is overly sensitive to a foreign substance, called an allergen.
- ◆ In diabetes, the body does not produce enough insulin or can't use it properly.
- ◆ In cancer, cells multiply uncontrollably, destroying healthy tissues.

Key Terms

noninfectious disease	cancer
allergy	insulin
allergen	diabetes
histamine	tumor
asthma	carcinogen

Organizing Information

Flowchart Complete the flowchart, which shows what happens after tuberculosis bacteria begin to multiply in the lungs. (For more information on flowcharts, see the Skills Handbook.)

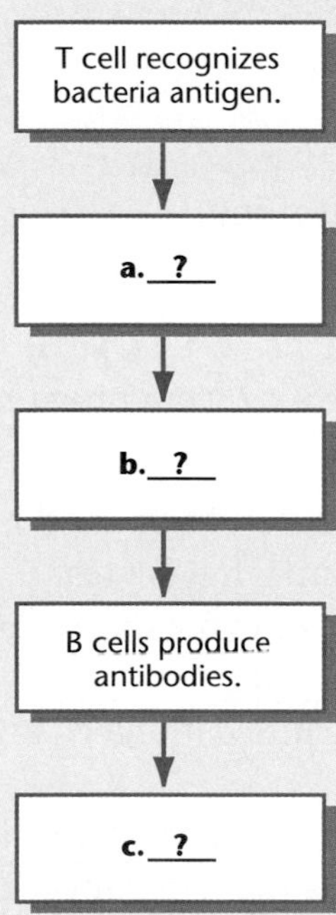

CHAPTER 7 ASSESSMENT

Reviewing Content

Multiple Choice

Choose the letter of the best answer.

1. Some pathogenic bacteria produce poisons called
a. histamines.
b. toxins.
c. phagocytes.
d. pathogens.

2. Antibodies are produced by
a. phagocytes.
b. B cells.
c. T cells.
d. pathogens.

3. Which disease is caused by HIV?
a. diabetes
b. flu
c. AIDS
d. tetanus

4. A chemical that kills bacteria or slows their growth without harming body cells is called a(n)
a. pathogen
b. antibiotic
c. allergen
d. histamine

5. A carcinogen causes
a. cancer.
b. colds.
c. allergies.
d. food poisoning.

True or False

If a statement is true, write true. If it is false, change the underlined word or words to make the statement true.

6. Bacteria, viruses, fungi, and protists are the major human phagocytes.

7. People can get Lyme disease and rabies from animal bites.

8. A T cell engulfs pathogens and destroys them.

9. Vaccination produces active immunity.

10. A tumor is a mass of cancer cells.

Checking Concepts

11. Why is it important not to share a drinking straw with someone else?

12. Explain why it is difficult for pathogens to get to a part of the body in which they can cause disease.

13. What is the relationship between antigens and antibodies?

14. Explain the differences between active immunity and passive immunity. Then describe one way in which a person can acquire each type of immunity.

15. How does diabetes harm the body?

16. Identify two factors that can make a person likely to develop cancer.

17. Writing to Learn A patient of Joseph Lister is angry because Lister has covered her surgery wound with a bandage dipped in carbolic acid. The acid stings and the bandage is uncomfortable. Write a conversation between Lister and the patient in which Lister explains why she shouldn't take the bandage off.

Thinking Critically

18. Inferring Given all the sources of pathogens detailed in this chapter, name as many things as you can that must be sterilized in a hospital operating room.

19. Applying Concepts Can you catch a cold by sitting in a chilly draft? Explain.

20. Comparing and Contrasting Compare the functions of T cells and B cells.

21. Relating Cause and Effect Why can the immune system successfully fight most pathogens, but not HIV?

22. Making Generalizations If diabetes is not treated, the body cells of the diabetic person do not get enough glucose to function properly. List four symptoms of diabetes. Then explain how the lack of glucose can lead to each of the symptoms you listed.

Applying Skills

A person had an illness caused by bacteria. The table shows how the person's temperature and antibody level changed over the course of the disease. Use the table to answer Questions 23–25.

Week	Body Temperature (°C)	Antibody Level
0	37	low
1	39.8	low
2	39	medium
3	37	high
4	37	medium
5	37	low

23. **Graphing** Make a line graph of the temperature data. Label the horizontal axis "Week Number" and the vertical axis "Body Temperature."

24. **Interpreting Data** During what week did the person's temperature return to normal?

25. **Drawing Conclusions** When do antibody levels start to rise? What effect do antibodies have on the illness? Explain.

Performance Assessment (Chapter Project 7)

Project Wrap Up Now you can share your news series with your classmates. Before your presentation, make sure any sound effects and props support the story.

Reflect and Record In your notebook, reflect on what you learned by using your imagination to explore a science topic. Did it help you to better understand how the body fights disease? What new information did you learn from presentations made by other groups? If you had your project to do over, what would you do differently?

Test Preparation

Use these questions to prepare for standardized tests.

Use the information to answer Questions 26–28.

A Glucose Tolerance Test is used to determine whether a person may have diabetes. A doctor gives a patient a sugar drink (at time 0) and measures the blood glucose level every 30 minutes for two hours. The graph below reveals that Person A is normal, while Person B has diabetes.

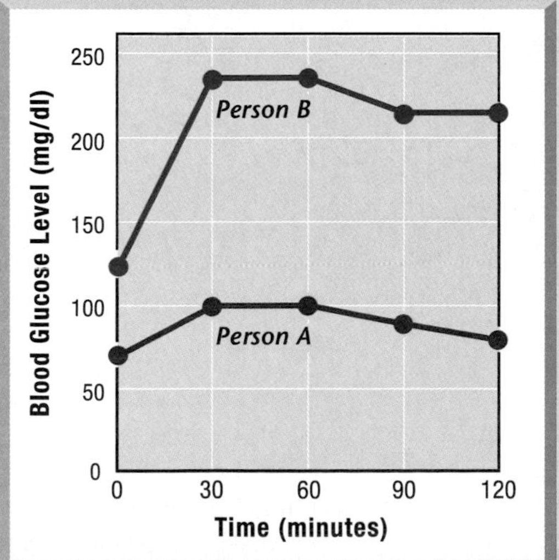

26. What would be the best title for this graph?
    a. How Blood Glucose Levels Rise Over Time
    b. Blood Glucose Levels in a Diabetic and a Non-Diabetic
    c. Normal Blood Glucose Levels
    d. How to Measure Blood Glucose Levels

27. According to the graph, which of the following statements is true?
    a. Person A's starting glucose level is higher than Person B's.
    b. Person A's glucose level rose quickly and then fell to near the starting level.
    c. Person B's glucose level rose quickly and then fell to near the starting level.
    d. Person A's blood glucose level was highest after 90 minutes.

28. What is the name of the hormone that normally controls blood glucose levels?
    a. estrogen
    b. testosterone
    c. insulin
    d. collagen

CHAPTER

8 The Nervous System

WEB ACTIVITY www.phschool.com

SECTION 1 How the Nervous System Works

Discover **How Simple Is a Simple Task?**
Skills Lab **Ready or Not!**

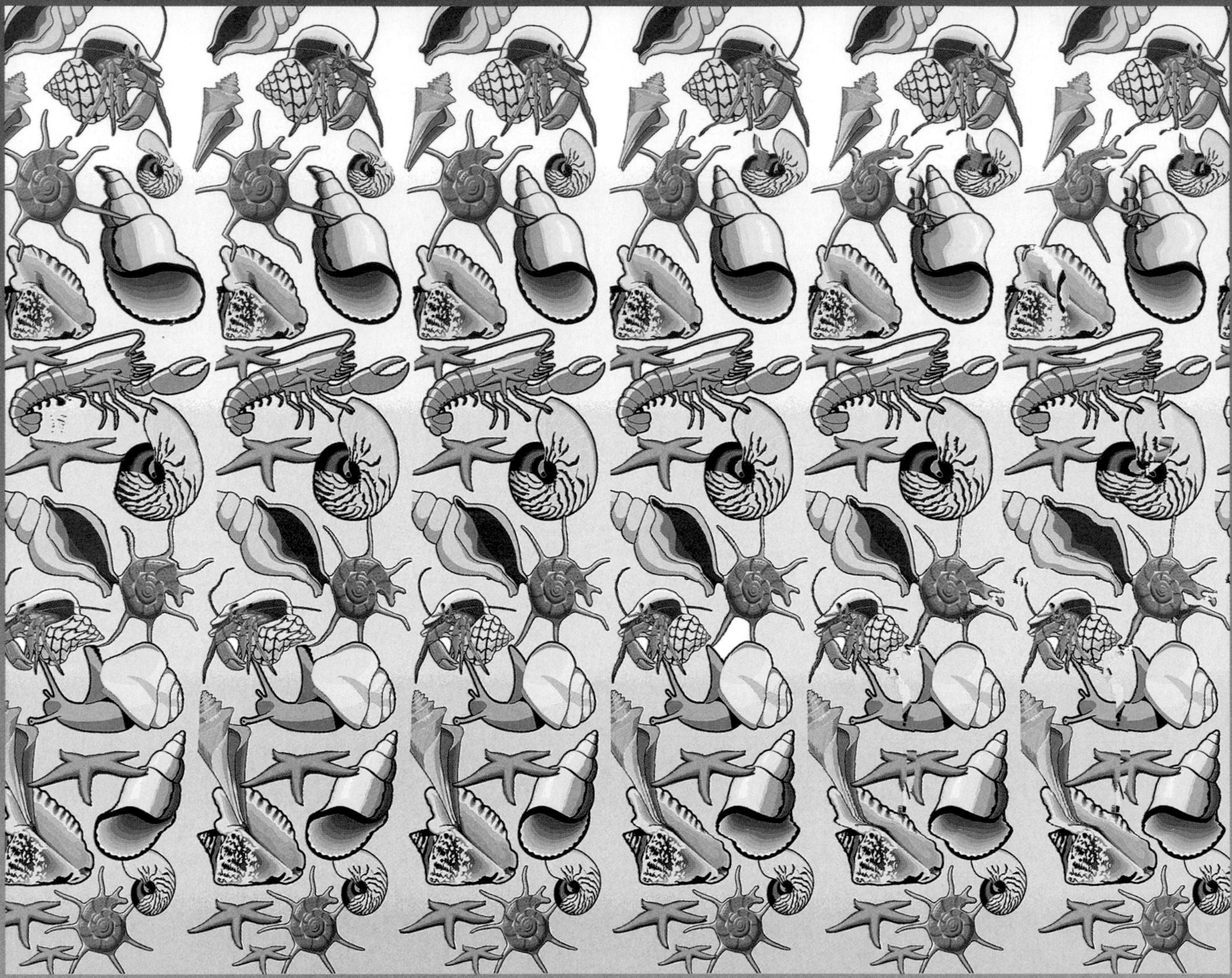

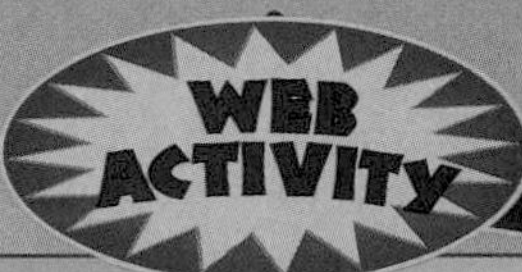

SECTION 2 Divisions of the Nervous System

Discover **How Does Your Knee React?**
Sharpen Your Skills **Controlling Variables**

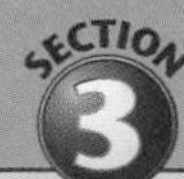

SECTION 3 The Senses

Discover **What's in the Bag?**
Try This **Why Do You Need Two Eyes?**
Try This **Tick, Tick, Tick**
Sharpen Your Skills **Designing Experiments**

Now you see it. Now you don't. Sometimes your eyes can play tricks on you. The picture shows rows of seashells and sea animals. Or does it?

Stare at the picture for several seconds, as if it were far away. The picture should look slightly out of focus. After a while, does anything seem to pop out from the picture?

PROJECT 8

Tricks and Illusions

Can you be sure of what you see, hear, smell, taste, or touch? In this chapter, you'll learn how you experience your environment through your senses. You'll see how the senses send information to your nervous system and how your brain interprets the messages.

But things aren't always what they seem. For example, an optical illusion is a picture or other visual effect that tricks you into seeing something incorrectly. In this project, you'll investigate how your senses can sometimes be fooled by illusions.

Your Goal To set up a science fair booth to demonstrate how different people respond to one or more illusions.

To complete this project, you must

- try out a variety of illusions, including some that involve the senses of hearing or touch as well as sight
- select one or more illusions, and set up an experiment to monitor people's responses to the illusions
- learn why the illusions fool the senses
- follow the safety guidelines in Appendix A

Get Started In a small group, discuss optical illusions or other illusions that you know about. Look in books to learn about others. Try them out. Which illusions would make an interesting experiment? How could you set up such an experiment at a science fair?

Check Your Progress You'll be working on this project as you study this chapter. To keep your project on track, look for Check Your Progress boxes at the following points.

Section 2 Review, page 260: Plan the experiment you will perform.
Section 3 Review, page 269: Carry out your experiment.
Section 4 Review, page 278: Explain why the illusions trick the senses.

Wrap Up At the end of the chapter (page 281), be prepared to share your findings with your classmates. Then explain how your illusions work.

Integrating Health

Alcohol and Other Drugs

Discover **How Can You Best Say No?**
Sharpen Your Skills **Communicating**
Real-World Lab **With Caffeine or Without?**

How the Nervous System Works

DISCOVER — ACTIVITY

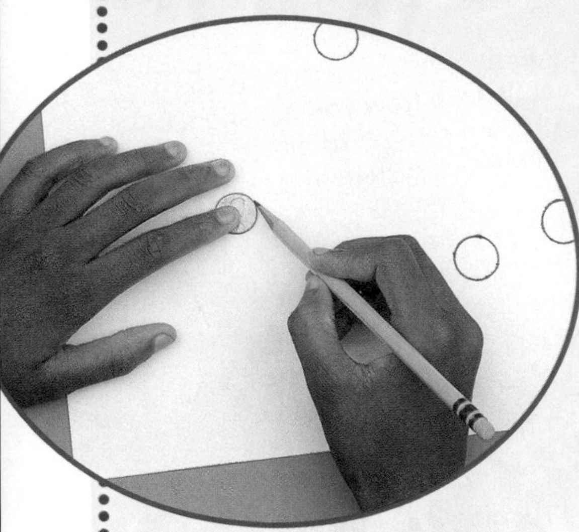

How Simple Is a Simple Task?

1. Trace the outline of a penny in twelve different places on a piece of paper.
2. Number the circles from 1 through 12. Write the numbers randomly, in no particular order.
3. Now pick up the penny again. Put it in each circle, one after another, in numerical order, beginning with 1 and ending with 12.

Think it Over

Inferring Make a list of all the sense organs, muscle movements, and thought processes in this activity. Compare your list with your classmates' lists. What organ system coordinated all the different processes involved in this task?

GUIDE FOR READING

- What are the functions of the nervous system?
- What are the three types of neurons and how do they interact?

Reading Tip Before you read, preview *Exploring the Path of a Nerve Impulse* on page 251. List any unfamiliar terms. Then, as you read, write a definition for each term.

The drums roll, and the crowd suddenly becomes silent. The people in the audience hold their breaths as the tightrope walker begins his long and dangerous journey across the wire. High above the circus floor, he inches along, slowly but steadily. One wrong movement could mean disaster.

To keep from slipping, tightrope performers need excellent coordination and a keen sense of balance. In addition, they must remember what they have learned from years of practice.

Even though you aren't a tightrope walker, you too need coordination, a sense of balance, memory, and the ability to learn. Your nervous system carries out all those functions. The nervous system consists of the brain, spinal cord, and nerves that run throughout the body. It also includes sense organs such as the eyes and ears.

Jobs of the Nervous System

The Internet lets people gather information from anywhere in the world with the click of a button. Like the Internet, your nervous system is a communications network. Your nervous system is much more efficient, however.

The nervous system receives information about what is happening both inside and outside your body. It also directs the way in which your body responds to this information. In addition, your nervous system helps maintain homeostasis. Without your nervous system, you could not move, think, feel pain, or taste a spicy taco.

Receiving Information Because of your nervous system, you are aware of what is happening in the environment around you. For example, you know that a soccer ball is zooming toward you, that the wind is blowing, or that a friend is telling a funny joke. Your nervous system also checks conditions inside your body, such as the level of glucose in your blood.

Figure 1 The sparkling water is a stimulus. This toddler responds by thrusting her hands into the water and splashing.

Responding to Information Any change or signal in the environment that can make an organism react is a **stimulus** (STIM yoo lus)(plural *stimuli*). A zooming soccer ball is a stimulus. After your nervous system analyzes the stimulus, it causes a response. A **response** is what your body does in reaction to a stimulus—you kick the ball toward the goal.

Some nervous system responses, such as kicking a ball, are voluntary, or under your control. However, many processes necessary for life, such as heartbeat rate, are controlled by involuntary actions of the nervous system.

Maintaining Homeostasis The nervous system helps maintain homeostasis by directing the body to respond appropriately to the information it receives. For example, when you are hungry, your nervous system directs you to eat. This action maintains homeostasis by supplying your body with nutrients and energy it needs.

☑ *Checkpoint* *What is a stimulus?*

The Neuron—A Message-Carrying Cell

The cells that carry information through your nervous system are called **neurons** (NOO rahnz), or nerve cells. The message that a neuron carries is called a **nerve impulse.** The structure of a neuron enables it to carry nerve impulses.

The Structure of a Neuron A neuron has a large cell body that contains the nucleus. The cell body has threadlike extensions. One kind of extension, a **dendrite,** carries impulses toward the cell body. An **axon** carries impulses away from the cell body. Nerve impulses begin in a dendrite, move toward the cell body, and then move down the axon. A neuron can have many dendrites, but it has only one axon. An axon, however, can have more than one tip, so the impulse can go to more than one other cell.

Axons and dendrites are sometimes called nerve fibers. Nerve fibers are often arranged in parallel bundles covered with connective tissue, something like a package of uncooked spaghetti wrapped in cellophane. A bundle of nerve fibers is called a **nerve.**

Kinds of Neurons Different kinds of neurons perform different functions. **Three kinds of neurons are found in the body—sensory neurons, interneurons, and motor neurons. Together they make up a chain of nerve cells that carry an impulse through the nervous system.** *Exploring the Path of a Nerve Impulse* shows how these three kinds of neurons work together.

A **sensory neuron** picks up stimuli from the internal or external environment and converts each stimulus into a nerve impulse. The impulse travels along the sensory neuron until it reaches an interneuron, usually in the brain or spinal cord. An **interneuron** is a neuron that carries nerve impulses from one neuron to another. Some interneurons pass impulses from sensory neurons to motor neurons. A **motor neuron** sends an impulse to a muscle, and the muscle contracts in response.

☑ *Checkpoint* *What is the function of an axon?*

Figure 2 A neuron, or nerve cell, has one axon and many dendrites that extend from the cell body. The dendrites carry a nerve message toward the cell body, and the axon carries the message away from the cell body. ***Applying Concepts*** *How many axons can a neuron have?*

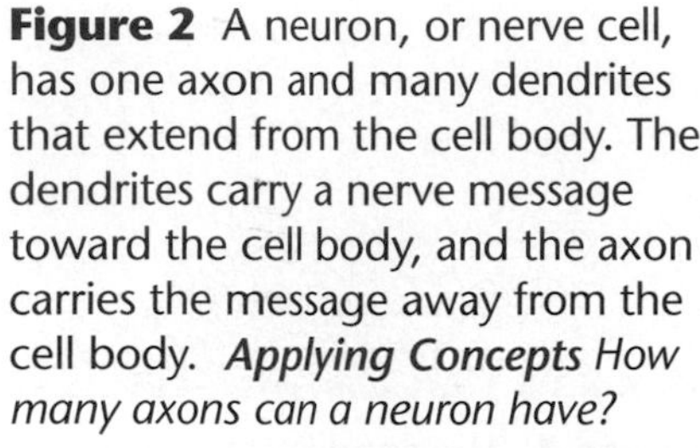

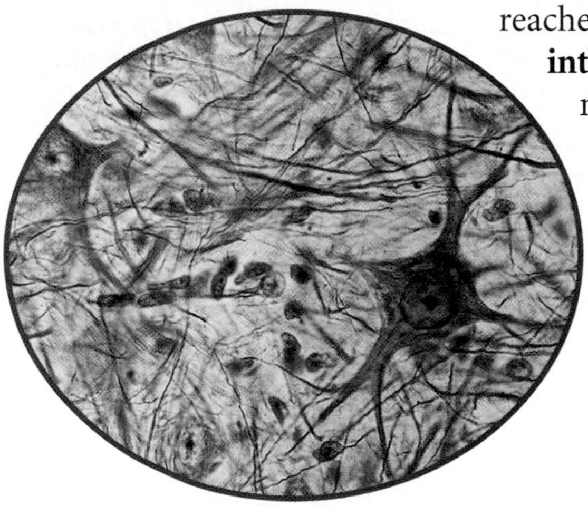

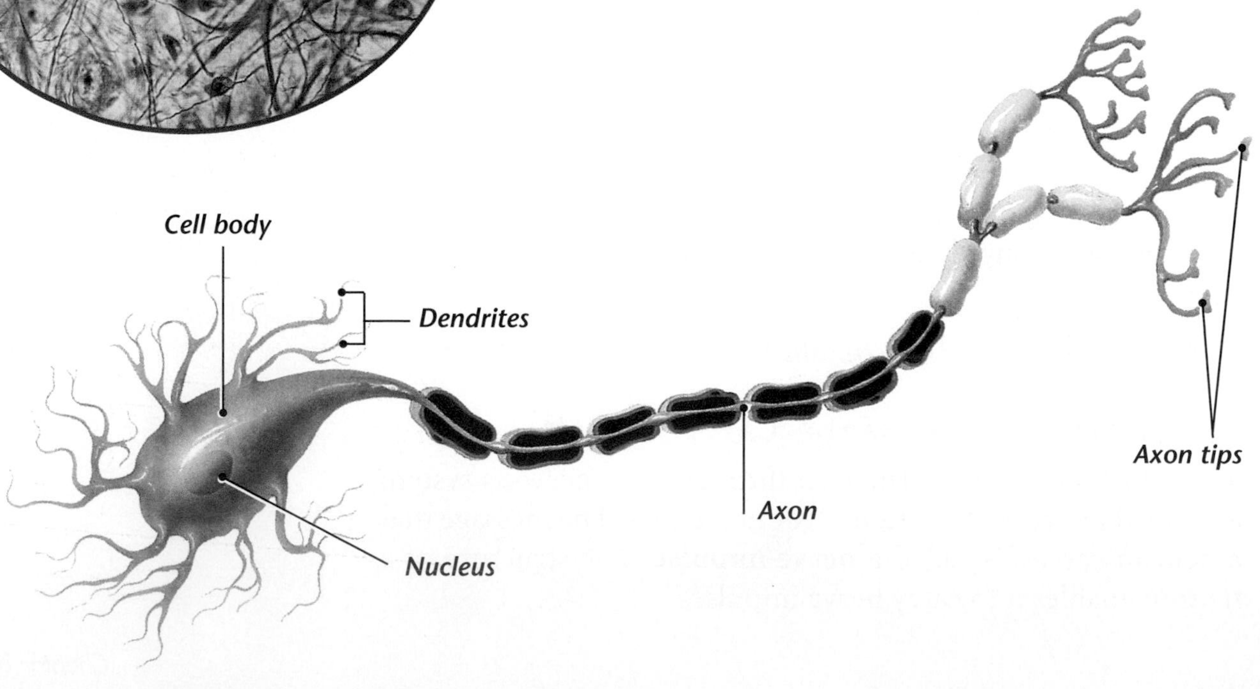

Cell body
Dendrites
Axon tips
Axon
Nucleus

EXPLORING the Path of a Nerve Impulse

When you hear the phone ring, you pick it up to answer it. Many sensory neurons, interneurons, and motor neurons are involved in this action.

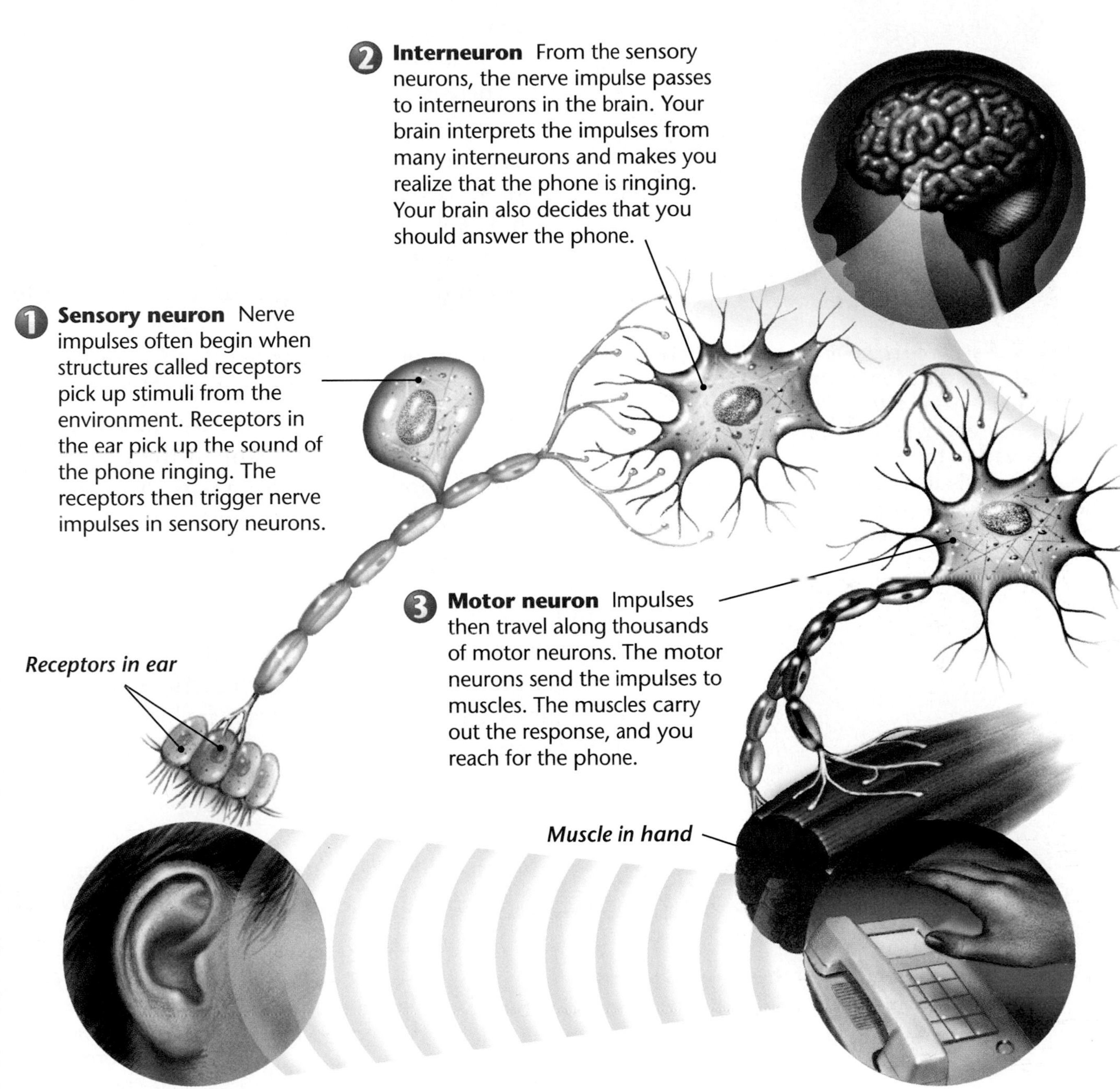

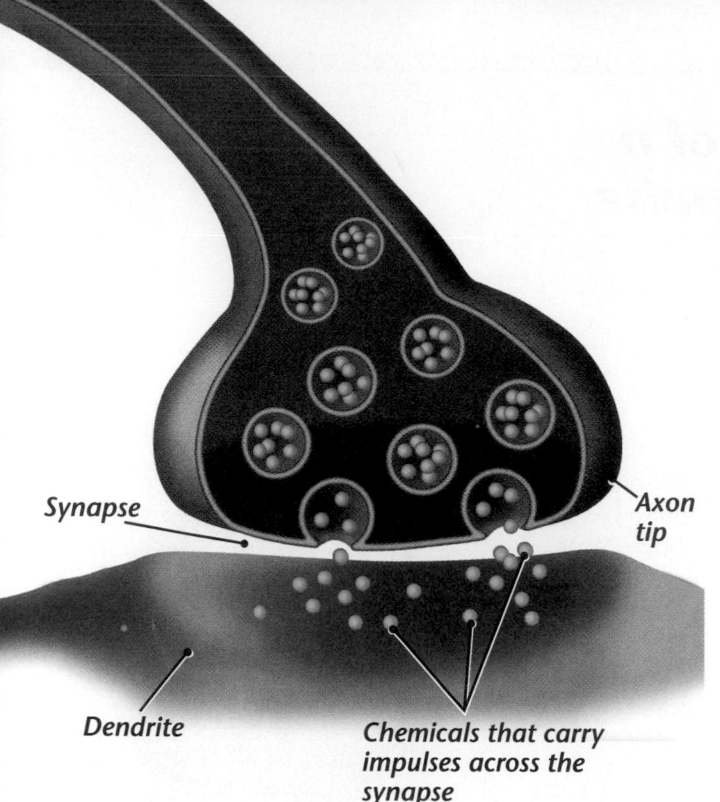

Figure 3 A synapse is the tiny space between the axon of one neuron and the dendrite of another neuron. When a nerve impulse reaches the end of an axon, chemicals are released into the synapse. These chemicals enable the nerve impulse to cross the synapse.

How a Nerve Impulse Travels

Every day of your life, millions of nerve impulses travel through your nervous system. Each of those nerve impulses begins in the dendrites of a neuron. The impulse moves rapidly toward the neuron's cell body and then down the axon until it reaches the axon tip. A nerve impulse travels along the neuron in the form of electrical and chemical signals. Nerve impulses can travel as fast as 120 meters per second!

There is a tiny space called a **synapse** (SIN aps) between each axon tip and the next structure. Sometimes this next structure is a dendrite of another neuron. Other times the next structure can be a muscle or a cell in another organ, such as a sweat gland. Figure 3 illustrates a synapse between the axon of one neuron and a dendrite of another neuron.

In order for a nerve impulse to be carried along, it must cross the gap between the axon and the next structure. The axon tips release chemicals that enable the impulse to cross the synapse. If that didn't happen, the impulse would stop at the end of the axon. The impulse would not be passed from sensory neuron, to interneuron, to motor neuron. Nerve impulses would never reach your brain or make your muscles contract.

You can think of a synapse as a river, and an axon as a road that leads up to the riverbank. The nerve impulse is like a car traveling on the road. To get to the other side, the car has to cross the river. The car gets on a ferry boat, which carries it across the river. The chemicals that the axon tips release are like a ferry that carries the nerve impulse across the synapse.

Section 1 Review

1. Describe three functions of the nervous system.
2. Identify the three kinds of neurons that are found in the nervous system. Describe how they interact to carry nerve impulses.
3. How does a nerve impulse cross a synapse?
4. **Thinking Critically Predicting** What would happen to a nerve impulse carried by an interneuron if the tips of the interneuron's axon were damaged? Explain.

Science at Home

During dinner, ask a family member to pass the salt and pepper to you. Observe what your family member then does. Explain that the words you spoke were a stimulus and that the family member's reaction was a response. Discuss other examples of stimuli and responses with your family.

Designing Experiments

Skills Lab

Ready or Not

Do people carry out tasks better at certain times of day? In this lab, you will design an experiment to answer this question.

Problem

Do people's reaction times vary at different times of day?

Materials

meter stick

Design a Plan

Part 1 Observing a Response to a Stimulus

1. Have your partner hold a meter stick with the zero end about 50 cm above a table.
2. Get ready to catch the meter stick by positioning the top of your thumb and forefinger just at the zero position as shown in the photograph.
3. Your partner should drop the meter stick without any warning. Using your thumb and forefinger only (no other part of your hand), catch the meter stick as soon as you can. Record the distance in centimeters that the meter stick fell. This distance is a measure of your reaction time.

Part 2 Design Your Experiment

4. With your partner, discuss how you can use the activity from Part 1 to find out whether people's reaction times vary at different times of day. Be sure to consider the questions below. Then write up your experimental plan.
   - What hypothesis will you test?
   - What variables do you need to control?
   - How many people will you test? How many times will you test each person?

5. Submit your plan for your teacher's review. Make any changes your teacher recommends. Create a data table to record your results. Then perform your experiment.

Analyze and Conclude

1. In this lab, what is the stimulus? What is the response? Is this response voluntary or involuntary? Explain.
2. Why can you use the distance on the meter stick as a measure of reaction time?
3. Based on your results, do people's reaction times vary at different times of day? Explain.
4. **Think About It** In Part 2, why is it important to control all variables except the time of day?

More to Explore

Do you think people can do arithmetic problems more quickly and accurately at certain times of the day? Design an experiment to investigate this question. Obtain your teacher's permission before trying your experiment.

Divisions of the Nervous System

Discover Activity

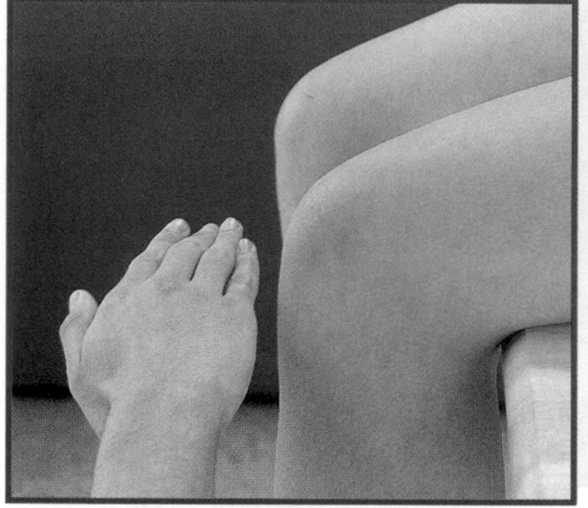

How Does Your Knee React?

1. Sit on a table or counter so that your legs dangle freely. Your feet should not touch the floor.
2. Have your partner use the side of his or her hand to *gently* tap one of your knees just below the kneecap. Observe what happens to your leg. Note whether you have any control over your reaction.
3. Change places with your partner. Repeat Steps 1 and 2.

Think It Over

Inferring When might it be an advantage for your body to react very quickly and without your conscious control?

Guide for Reading

- **What is the function of the central nervous system?**
- **What functions does the peripheral nervous system perform?**
- **What is a reflex?**

Reading Tip **As you read, make a list of main ideas and supporting details about the central and peripheral nervous systems.**

A concert is about to begin. The conductor gives the signal, and the musicians begin to play. The sound of music, beautiful and stirring, fills the air.

To play music in harmony, an orchestra needs both musicians and a conductor. The musicians play the music, and the conductor directs the musicians and coordinates their playing.

Similarly, your nervous system has two divisions that work together—the central nervous system and the peripheral nervous system. The **central nervous system** consists of the brain and spinal cord. The **peripheral nervous system** consists of all the nerves located outside of the central nervous system. The central nervous system is like a conductor. The nerves of the peripheral nervous system are like the musicians.

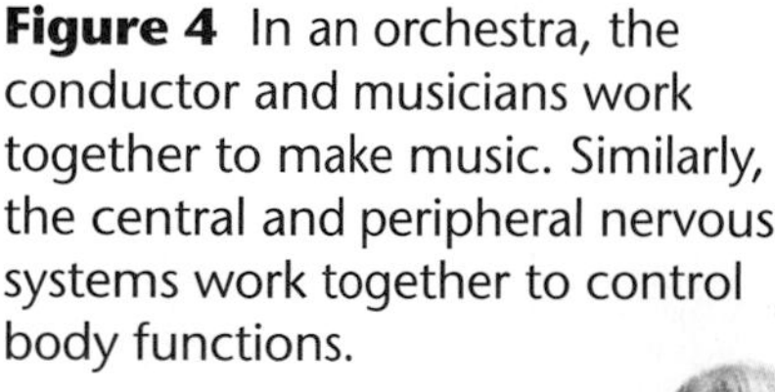

Figure 4 In an orchestra, the conductor and musicians work together to make music. Similarly, the central and peripheral nervous systems work together to control body functions.

The Central Nervous System

You can see the central and peripheral nervous systems in Figure 5. **The central nervous system is the control center of the body.** All information about what is happening in the world inside or outside your body is brought to the central nervous system. The **brain,** located in the skull, is the part of the central nervous system that controls most functions in the body. The **spinal cord** is the thick column of nerve tissue that links the brain to most of the nerves in the peripheral nervous system.

Most impulses from the peripheral nervous system travel through the spinal cord to get to the brain. Your brain then directs a response. The response usually travels from the brain, through the spinal cord, and then to the peripheral nervous system.

For example, here is what happens when you reach under the sofa to find a lost quarter. Your fingers move over the floor, searching for the quarter. When your fingers finally touch the quarter, the stimulus of the touch triggers nerve impulses in sensory neurons in your fingers. These impulses travel through nerves of the peripheral nervous system to your spinal cord. Then the impulses race up to your brain. Your brain interprets the impulses, telling you that you've found the quarter. Your brain starts nerve impulses that move down the spinal cord. From the spinal cord, the impulses travel through motor nerves in your arm and hand. The impulses in the motor neurons cause your fingers to grasp the quarter.

☑ ***Checkpoint*** *What does the spinal cord do?*

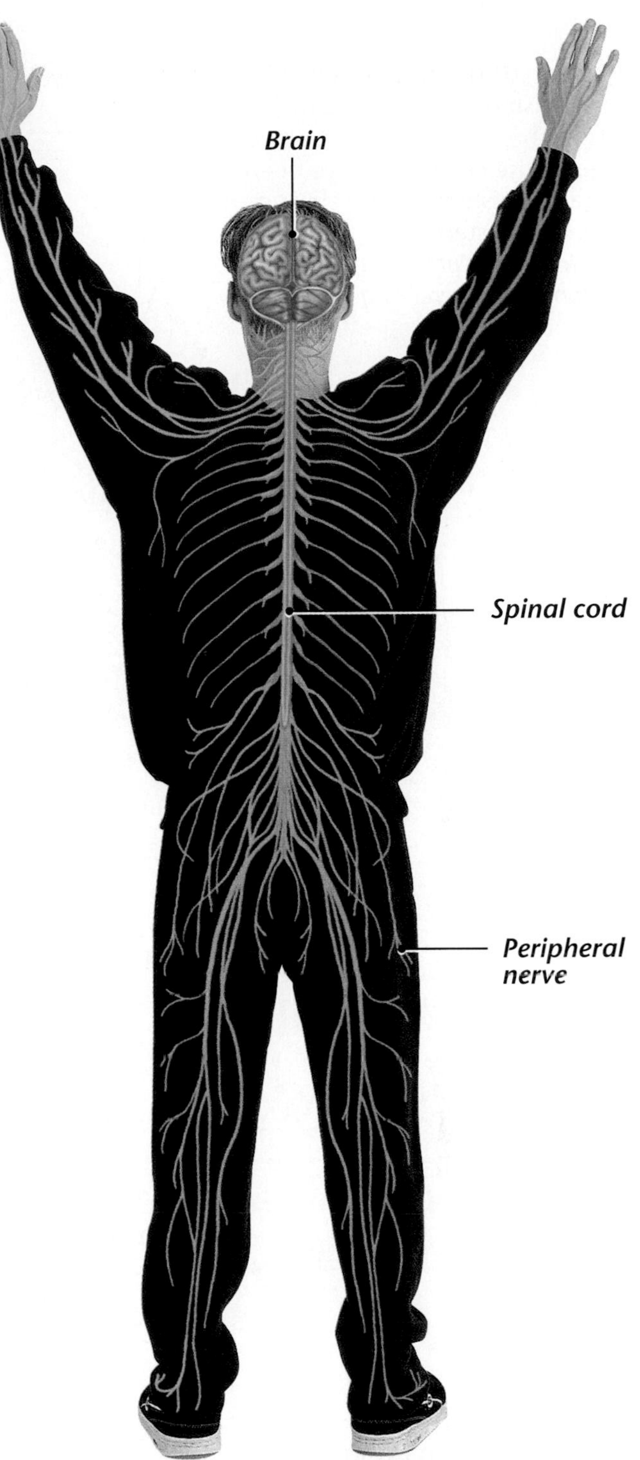

Figure 5 The central nervous system consists of the brain and spinal cord. The peripheral nervous system contains all the nerves that branch out from the brain and spinal cord.

The Brain

Your brain contains about 100 billion neurons, all of which are interneurons. Each of those neurons may receive messages from up to 10,000 other neurons and may send messages to about 1,000 more! Three layers of connective tissue cover the brain. The space between the outermost layer and the middle layer is filled with a watery fluid. The skull, layers of connective tissue, and fluid all help protect the brain from injury.

Figure 6 The cerebrum, cerebellum, and brainstem are the three main parts of the human brain. The two halves of the cerebrum have been separated to show the cerebellum and the brainstem.
Applying Concepts What are three functions of the cerebrum?

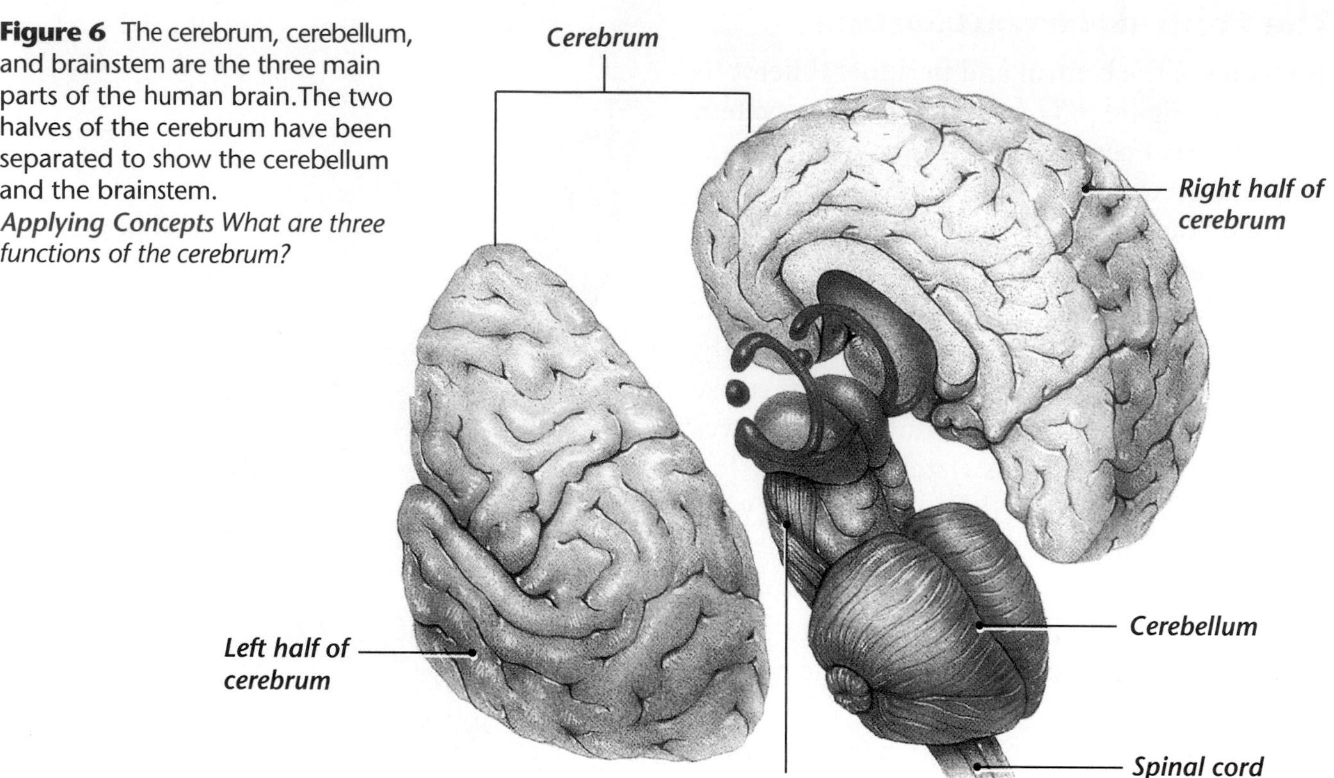

Controlling Variables

ACTIVITY

Are people better able to memorize a list of words in a quiet room or in a room where soft music is playing? First write a hypothesis. Then design an experiment to test your hypothesis. Make sure that all variables are controlled except the one you are testing—music versus quiet. Check your procedure with your teacher. Then perform your experiment. Analyze your results to see whether they support your hypothesis.

Cerebrum There are three main regions of the brain. These are the cerebrum, the cerebellum, and the brainstem. Find each in Figure 6. The largest part of the brain is called the cerebrum. The **cerebrum** (suh REE brum) interprets input from the senses, controls the movement of skeletal muscles, and carries out complex mental processes such as learning, remembering, and making judgments. Because of your cerebrum, you can find the comics in a newspaper and locate your favorite comic strip on the page. Your cerebrum also enables you to read the comic strip and laugh at its funny characters.

Notice in Figure 6 that the cerebrum is divided into a right and a left half. The two halves have somewhat different functions. The right half of the cerebrum contains the neurons that send impulses to the skeletal muscles on the left side of the body. In contrast, the left half of the cerebrum controls the right side of the body. When you reach with your right hand for a pencil, the messages that tell you to do so come from the left half of your cerebrum.

In addition, each half of the cerebrum controls slightly different kinds of mental activity. The right half of the cerebrum is usually associated with creativity and artistic ability. The left half, in contrast, is associated with mathematical skills, speech, writing, and logical thinking.

Cerebellum and Brainstem The second largest part of your brain is called the cerebellum. The **cerebellum** (sehr uh BEL um) coordinates the actions of your muscles and helps you keep your balance. When you put one foot in front of the other as you walk, the motor neuron impulses that tell your feet to move start in your cerebrum. However, your cerebellum gives you the muscular coordination and sense of balance that keep you from falling down.

The **brainstem,** which lies between the cerebellum and spinal cord, controls your body's involuntary actions—those that occur automatically. For example, the brainstem regulates your breathing and helps control your heartbeat.

☑ ***Checkpoint*** *What part of your brain coordinates the contractions of your muscles?*

The Spinal Cord

Run your fingers down the center of your back to feel the bones of the vertebral column. The vertebral column surrounds and protects the spinal cord. The spinal cord is the link between your brain and the peripheral nervous system. The layers of connective tissue that surround and protect the brain also cover the spinal cord. In addition, like the brain, the spinal cord is further protected by a watery fluid.

Visual Arts CONNECTION

Some artists deliberately create works of art that can be interpreted by the brain in more than one way. The Dutch artist M. C. Escher (1898–1972) delighted in creating illustrations that played visual tricks on his viewers. Glance quickly at Escher's illustration in Figure 7. Then look at it again. Do you see the two different scenes in this single picture?

In Your Journal

Which scene did you see when you first looked at Figure 7? Did your brain interpret the picture differently the second time? Write a description of the visual trick that Escher has played in this illustration.

Figure 7 This illustration, by the Dutch artist M. C. Escher, is called "Day and Night." Escher created this picture in 1938.

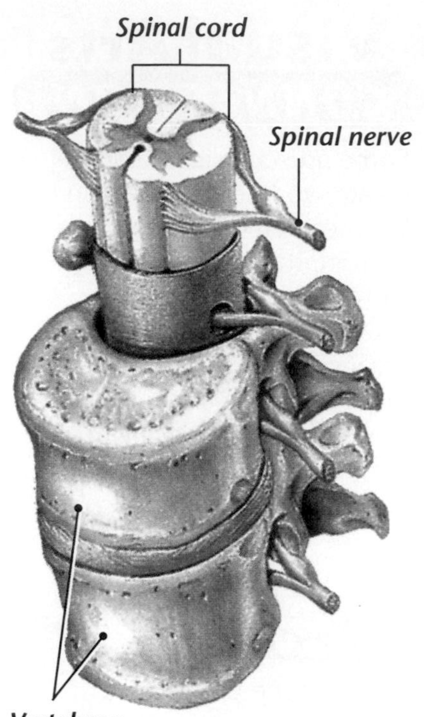

Figure 8 The spinal nerves, which connect to the spinal cord, emerge from spaces between the vertebrae. Each spinal nerve consists of both sensory and motor neurons.

The Peripheral Nervous System

The second division of the nervous system is the peripheral nervous system. **The peripheral nervous system consists of a network of nerves that branch out from the central nervous system and connect it to the rest of your body.** A total of 43 pairs of nerves make up the peripheral nervous system. Twelve pairs originate in the brain. The other 31 pairs—the spinal nerves—begin in the spinal cord. One nerve in each pair goes to the left side of the body, and the other goes to the right. As you can see in Figure 8, spinal nerves leave the spinal cord through spaces between the vertebrae.

Two-Way Traffic A spinal nerve is a little bit like a two-lane highway. Impulses travel on a spinal nerve in two directions—both to and from the central nervous system. Each spinal nerve contains axons of both sensory and motor neurons. The sensory neurons carry impulses from the body to the central nervous system. The motor neurons carry impulses in the opposite direction—from the central nervous system to the body.

Somatic and Autonomic Systems The nerves of the peripheral nervous system can be divided into two groups, called the somatic (soh MAT ik) and autonomic (awt uh NAHM ik) nervous systems. The nerves of the **somatic nervous system** control voluntary actions such as using a fork or tying your shoelaces. In contrast, nerves of the **autonomic nervous system** control involuntary actions. For example, the autonomic nervous system regulates the contractions of the smooth muscles that adjust the diameter of blood vessels.

Figure 9 The somatic nervous system controls voluntary actions. The girl's somatic nervous system is at work as she shapes the pot with her hands. ***Classifying*** *What part of the peripheral nervous system helps regulate the girl's heartbeat?*

Reflexes

Imagine that you are watching an adventure movie. The movie is so thrilling that you don't notice a fly circling above your head. When the fly zooms right in front of your eyes, however, your eyelids immediately blink shut. You didn't decide to close your eyes. The blink, which is an example of a **reflex,** happened automatically. **A reflex is an automatic response that occurs very rapidly and without conscious control.** If you did the Discover activity, you saw another example of a reflex.

As you have learned, the contraction of skeletal muscles is usually controlled by the brain. However, in some reflex actions, skeletal muscles contract with the involvement of the spinal cord only—not the brain. Figure 10 shows the reflex action that occurs when you touch a sharp object, such as a cactus thorn. When your finger touches the object, sensory neurons send impulses to the spinal cord. The impulses then pass to interneurons in the spinal cord. From there the impulses pass directly to motor neurons in your arm and hand. The muscles then contract, and your hand jerks up and away from the sharp object. By removing your hand quickly, this reflex protects you from getting badly cut.

At the same time that some nerve impulses make your arm muscles contract, other nerve impulses travel up your spinal cord and to your brain. When these impulses reach your brain, your brain interprets them. You then feel a sharp pain in your finger.

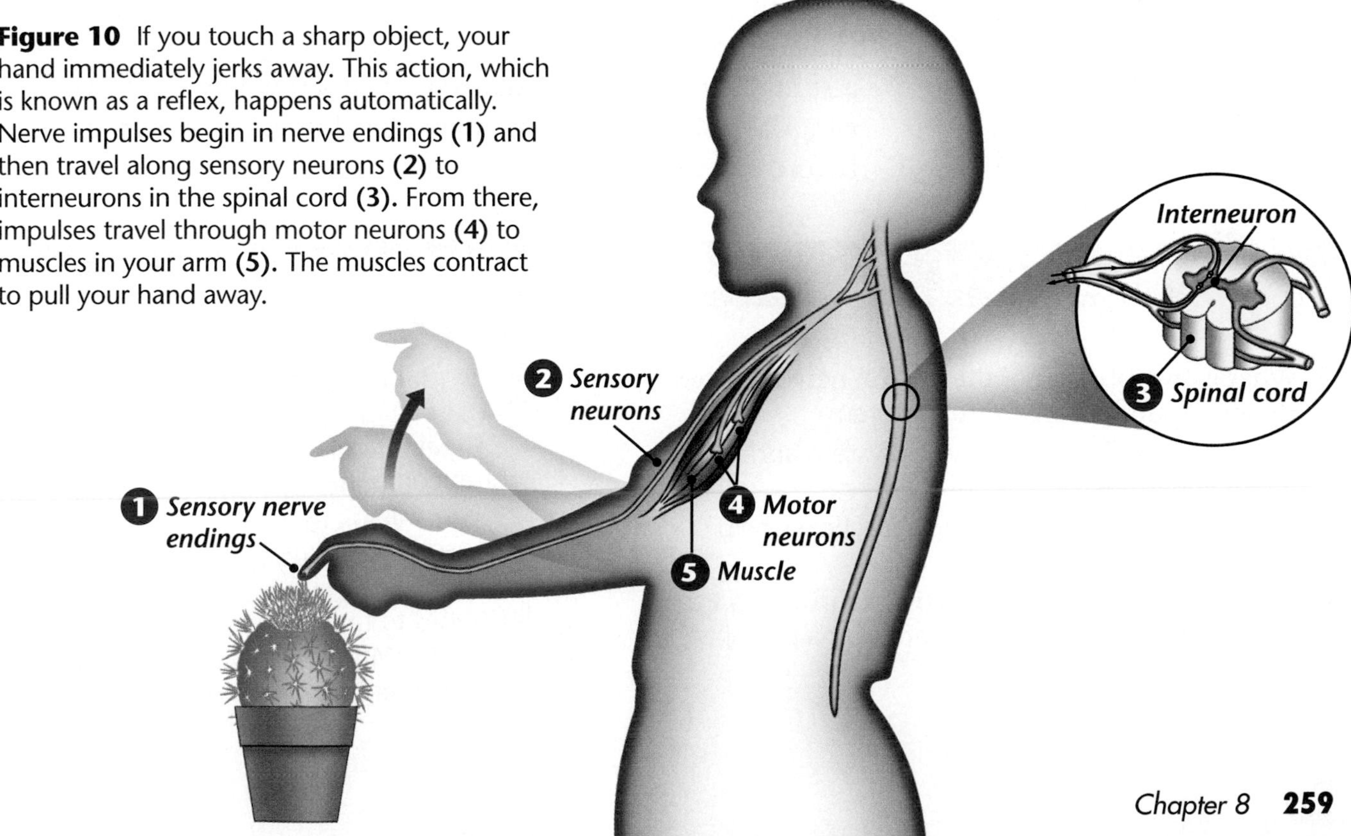

Figure 10 If you touch a sharp object, your hand immediately jerks away. This action, which is known as a reflex, happens automatically. Nerve impulses begin in nerve endings **(1)** and then travel along sensory neurons **(2)** to interneurons in the spinal cord **(3).** From there, impulses travel through motor neurons **(4)** to muscles in your arm **(5).** The muscles contract to pull your hand away.

Figure 11 By wearing a helmet, this skateboarder is helping to prevent injury to his brain.

It takes longer for the pain impulses to get to the brain and be interpreted than it does for the reflex action to occur. By the time you feel the pain, you have already moved your hand away from the sharp object.

Safety and the Nervous System

INTEGRATING HEALTH Like other parts of the body, the nervous system can suffer injuries that interfere with its functioning. Concussions and spinal cord injuries are two ways in which the nervous system can be damaged.

A **concussion** is a bruiselike injury of the brain. A concussion occurs when soft tissue of the cerebrum bumps against the skull. Concussions can happen during a hard fall, an automobile accident, or contact sports such as football. With most concussions, you may have a headache for a short time, but the injured tissue heals by itself. However, if you black out, experience confusion, or feel drowsy after the injury, you should be checked by a doctor. To decrease your chances of getting a brain injury, wear a helmet when bicycling, skating, or performing other activities in which you risk bumping your head.

Spinal cord injuries occur when the spinal cord is cut or crushed. When the spinal cord is cut, all the nerve axons in that region are split, so impulses cannot pass through them. This type of injury results in paralysis, which is the loss of movement in some part of the body. Car crashes are the most common cause of spinal cord injuries. You can help protect yourself from a spinal cord injury by wearing a seatbelt when you travel in a car. Also, when you swim, make sure the water is deep enough before you dive in.

Section 2 Review

1. What is the function of the central nervous system? Which organs are part of this system?
2. What is the peripheral nervous system and what are its functions?
3. Explain what a reflex is. How do reflexes help protect the body from injury?
4. **Thinking Critically Relating Cause and Effect** What symptoms might indicate that a person's cerebellum has been injured?

Check Your Progress

CHAPTER PROJECT 8

At this point, you should have chosen one or more illusions to investigate. Now write up the plan for your experiment. List some questions that you will ask to monitor people's responses to the illusions. (*Hint:* Try out your illusions and your questions on classmates to find out what responses to expect.) With your classmates, make plans for setting up the science fair.

Should People Be Required to Wear Bicycle Helmets?

Bicycle riding is an enjoyable activity. But unfortunately, many bicycle riders become injured while riding. Each year about 150,000 children alone are treated in hospitals for head injuries that occur while bicycling. Head injuries can affect everything your brain does—thinking, remembering, seeing, and being able to move. Experts estimate that as many as 85 percent of bicycle-related head injuries could be prevented if all bicyclists wore helmets. But only about 18 percent of bicyclists wear helmets. What is the best way to get bicycle riders to protect themselves from head injury?

The Issues

Should Laws Require the Use of Bicycle Helmets? About 15 states have passed laws requiring bicycle riders to wear helmets. Nearly all of these laws, however, apply only to children. Some supporters of bicycle laws want to see the laws extended to all bicycle riders. Supporters point out that laws increase helmet use by 47 percent. In contrast, educational programs without laws to back them up increase bicycle helmet use by only 18 percent.

What Are the Drawbacks of Helmet Laws? Opponents of helmet laws believe it is up to the individual, not the government, to decide whether or not to wear a helmet. They say it is not the role of the government to stop people from taking risks. Rather than making people who don't wear helmets pay fines, governments should educate people about the benefits of helmets. Car drivers should also be educated about safe driving procedures near bicycles.

Are There Alternatives to Helmet Laws? Instead of laws requiring people to wear helmets, some communities and organizations have set up educational programs that teach about the advantages of helmets. Effective programs teach about the dangers of head injuries and how helmets protect riders. In addition, they point out that safe helmets can be lightweight and comfortable. Effective education programs, though, can be expensive. They also need to reach a wide audience, including children, teens, and adults.

You Decide

1. **Identify the Problem**
   In your own words, explain the issues concerning laws requiring people to wear bicycle helmets.
2. **Analyze the Options**
   List two different plans for increasing helmet use by bicycle riders. List at least one advantage and one drawback of each plan.
3. **Find a Solution**
   You are a member of the city government hoping to increase helmet use. Write a speech outlining your position for either a helmet law or an alternative plan. Support your position.

Section 3 The Senses

Discover

What's in the Bag?

1. Your teacher will give you a paper bag that contains several objects. Your challenge is to use only your sense of touch to identify each object. You will not look inside the bag.
2. Put your hand in the bag and carefully touch each object. Observe the shape of each object. Note whether its surface is rough or smooth. Also note other characteristics, such as its size, what it seems to be made of, and whether it can be bent.
3. After you have finished touching each object, write your observations on a sheet of paper. Then write your inference about what each object is.

Think It Over

Observing What could you determine about each object without looking at it? What could you not determine?

GUIDE FOR READING

- **What overall function do the senses perform?**
- **How do your eyes enable you to see?**
- **How do you hear?**

Reading Tip **As you read, write an outline of this section. Use the headings in the section as the main topics in the outline.**

You waited in line to get on the ride, and now it's about to begin. You grip the bars as the ride suddenly starts to move. Before you know it, you are lifted high above the ground and you feel the air whipping by. All you see is a dizzy blur.

You can thrill to the speed of amusement park rides because of your senses. **Each of your major senses—vision, hearing, balance, smell, taste, and touch—picks up a specific type of information about your environment. The sense organs change that information into nerve impulses and send the impulses to your brain.** Your brain then interprets the information. Because of the way in which your senses and brain work together, you learn a great deal about your environment.

Figure 12 Riders and bright lights whizzing by—that's what you see when you watch this amusement park ride.

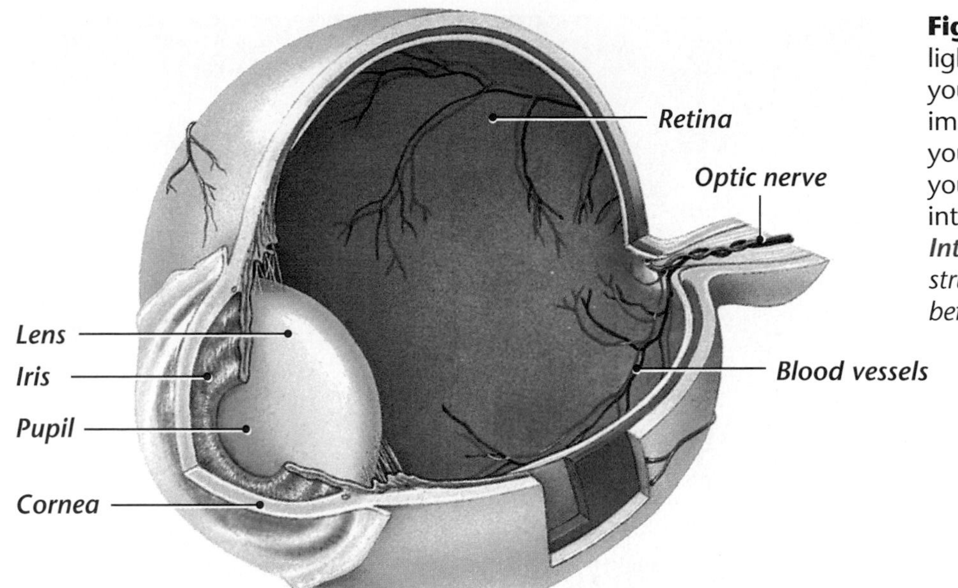

Figure 13 You see an object when light coming from the object enters your eye. The light produces an image on your retina. Receptors in your retina then send impulses to your cerebrum, and your cerebrum interprets these impulses. ***Interpreting Diagrams*** *What structures must light pass through before it reaches your retina?*

Vision

Your eyes are the sense organs that enable you to see the objects in your environment. They let you see this book in front of you, the window across the room, and the world outside the window. **Your eyes respond to the stimulus of light. They convert that stimulus into impulses that your brain interprets, enabling you to see.**

How Light Enters Your Eye When rays of light strike the eye, they pass through the structures shown in Figure 13. First, the light strikes the **cornea** (KAWR nee uh), the clear tissue that covers the front of the eye. The light then passes through a fluid-filled chamber behind the cornea and reaches the pupil. The **pupil** is the opening through which light enters the eye.

You may have noticed that people's pupils change size when they go from a dark room into bright sunshine. In bright light, the pupil becomes smaller. In dim light, the pupil becomes larger. The size of the pupil is adjusted by muscles in the iris. The **iris** is a circular structure that surrounds the pupil and regulates the amount of light entering the eye. The iris also gives the eye its color. If you have brown eyes, your irises are brown.

How Light Is Focused Light that passes through the pupil strikes the lens. The **lens** is a flexible structure that focuses light. The lens of your eye functions something like the lens of a camera, which focuses light on photographic film. Because of the way in which the lens of the eye bends the light rays, the image it produces is upside down and reversed. Muscles that attach to the lens adjust its shape. This adjustment produces an image that is clear and in focus.

Why Do You Need Two Eyes?

ACTIVITY

In this activity, you will investigate how your two eyes work together to allow you to see.

1. With your arms fully extended, hold a plastic drinking straw in one hand and a pipe cleaner in the other.
2. With both eyes open, try to insert the pipe cleaner into the straw.
3. Now close your right eye. Try to insert the pipe cleaner into the straw.
4. Repeat Step 3, but this time close your left eye instead of your right eye.

Inferring How does closing one eye affect your ability to judge distances?

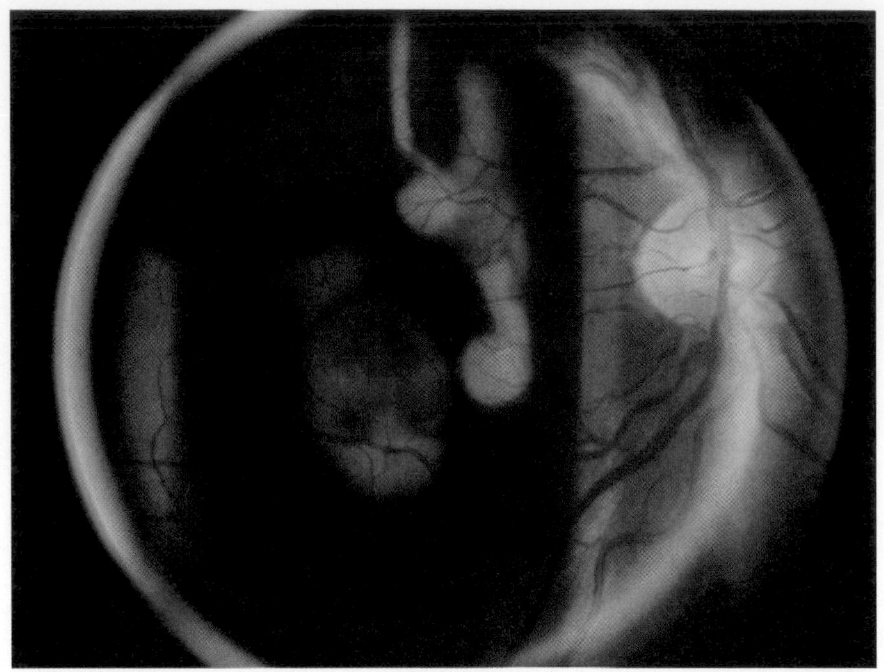

Figure 14 An upside-down image is focused on the retina. ***Applying Concepts*** *When you see an object, why does it appear right-side up?*

How You See an Image After passing through the lens, the focused light rays pass through a transparent, jellylike fluid. Then the light rays strike the **retina** (RET 'n uh), the layer of receptor cells that lines the back of the eye. The retina contains about 130 million receptor cells that respond to light. There are two types of receptors, rods and cones. Rod cells work best in dim light and enable you to see black, white, and shades of gray. In contrast, cone cells only work well in bright light and enable you to see colors. This difference between rods and cones explains why you see colors best in bright light, but you see only shadowy gray images in dim light.

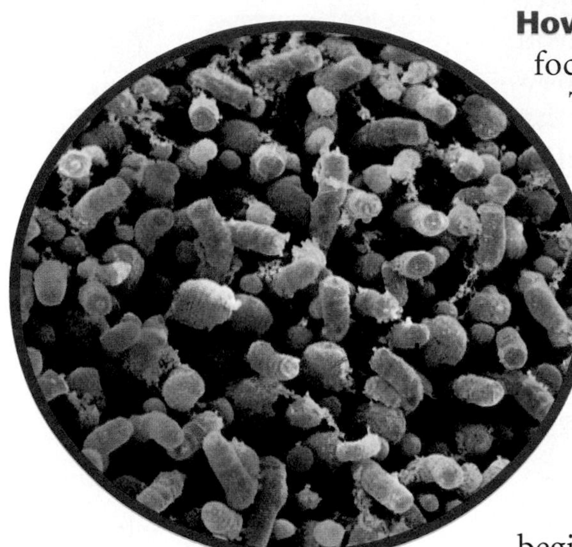

Figure 15 The retina of the eye contains light-sensitive cells. In this photograph, the rods have been colored pink, and the cones have been colored blue.

When light strikes the rods and cones, nerve impulses begin. These nerve impulses travel to the cerebrum through the optic nerves. One optic nerve comes from the left eye and the other one comes from the right. In the cerebrum, two things happen. The brain turns the reversed image right-side up. In addition, the brain combines the images from each eye to produce a single image.

Correcting Vision Problems

INTEGRATING PHYSICS A lens—whether it is in your eye, in a camera, or in eyeglasses—is a curved, transparent object that bends light rays as they pass through it. If the lens of the eye does not focus light properly on the retina, vision problems result. The glass or plastic lenses in eyeglasses can help correct such vision problems.

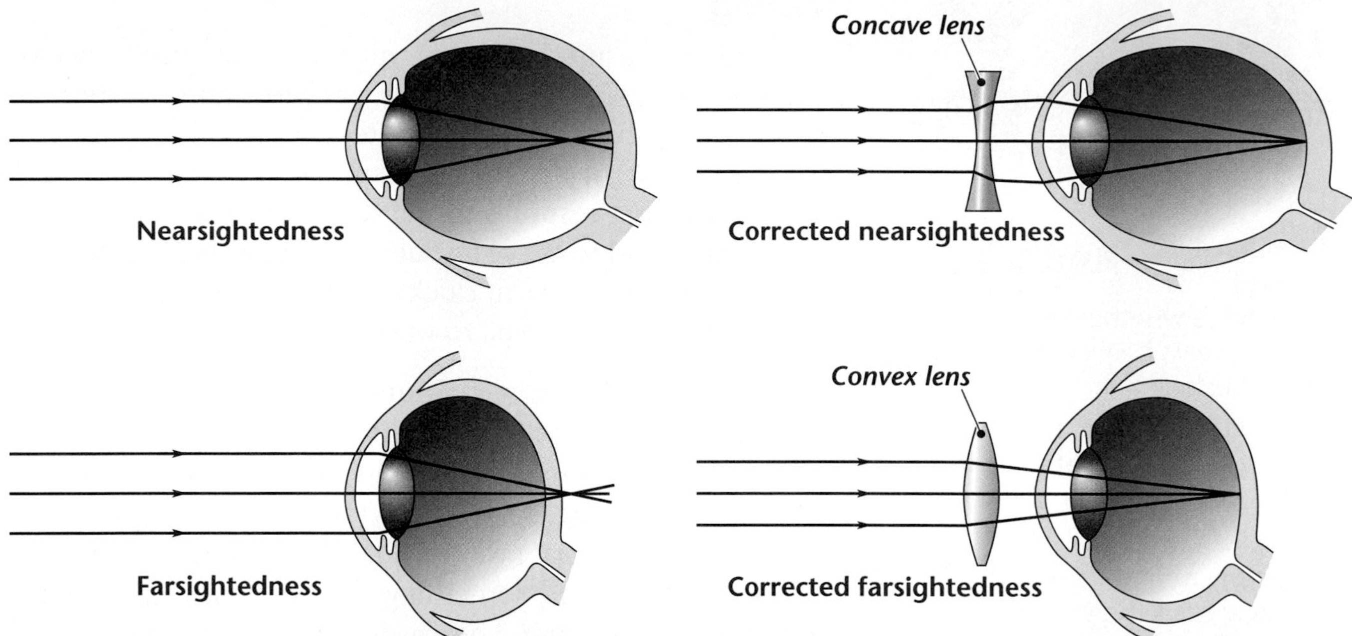

Figure 16 Nearsightedness and farsightedness are conditions in which images do not focus properly on the retina. The diagrams on the left show where the images are focused in both of these conditions. The diagrams on the right show how lenses in eyeglasses can help correct these conditions.

Nearsightedness People with **nearsightedness** can see nearby objects clearly. However, they have trouble seeing objects that are far away. Nearsightedness is caused by an eyeball that is too long. Because of the extra length that light must travel to reach the retina, distant objects do not focus sharply on the retina. Instead, the lens of the eye makes the image come into focus at a point in front of the retina, as shown in Figure 16.

To correct nearsightedness, a person needs to wear eyeglasses with concave lenses. A concave lens is a lens that is thicker at the edges than it is in the center. When light rays pass through a concave lens, they are bent away from the center of the lens. The concave lenses in glasses make light rays spread out before they reach the lens of the eye. Then, when these rays pass through the lens of the eye, they focus on the retina rather than in front of it.

Farsightedness People with **farsightedness** can see distant objects clearly. Nearby objects, however, look blurry. The eyeballs of people with farsightedness are too short. Because of this, the lens of the eye bends light from nearby objects so that the image does not focus properly on the retina. If light could pass through the retina, the image would come into sharp focus at a point behind the retina, as shown in Figure 16.

Convex lenses are used to help correct farsightedness. A convex lens is thicker in the middle than the edges. The convex lens makes the light rays bend toward each other before they reach the eye. Then the lens of the eye bends the rays even more. This bending makes the image focus exactly on the retina.

☑ ***Checkpoint*** *What type of lens is used to correct nearsightedness?*

Tick! Tick! Tick!

In this activity, you will determine whether one of a person's ears hears better than the other one.

1. Work in teams of three. Hold a ticking watch next to the right ear of one team member.
2. Slowly move the watch away from the ear. Stop moving it at the point where the student can no longer hear the ticking.
3. At that point, have the third team member measure the distance between the watch and the student's right ear.
4. Repeat Steps 1 through 3 to test the student's left ear.

Measuring How did the two distances compare? Do you think this is an accurate way to evaluate someone's hearing? Why or why not?

Hearing

What wakes you up in the morning? Maybe an alarm clock buzzes, or perhaps your parent calls you. On a summer morning, you might hear birds singing. Whatever wakes you up, there's a good chance that it's a sound of some sort. **Your ears are the sense organs that respond to the stimulus of sound. The ears convert the sound to nerve impulses that your brain interprets.** So when you hear an alarm clock or other morning sound, your brain tells you that it's time to wake up.

How Sound Is Produced Sound is produced by vibrations.

INTEGRATING PHYSICS

The material that is vibrating, or moving rapidly back and forth, may be almost anything—a guitar string, an insect's wings, or splashing water.

The vibrations create waves. The waves move outward from the source of the sound, something like ripples moving out from a stone dropped in water. The waves consist of moving particles, such as the molecules that make up air. When you hear a friend's voice, for example, sound waves have traveled from your friend's larynx to your ears. In addition to being able to travel through gases such as air, sound waves can also travel through liquids such as water and solids such as wood.

Sound Vibrations and the Ear The ear is structured to receive sound vibrations. As you can see in Figure 18, the ear consists of three parts—the outer ear, middle ear, and inner ear. The outer ear includes the part of the ear that you see. The visible part of the outer ear is shaped like a funnel.

Figure 17 When a wolf howls, its vocal cords vibrate. The vibrating vocal cords produce sound waves. When the sound waves reach a person's ear, the person hears the wolf.

This funnel-like shape enables the outer ear to gather sound waves. The sound waves then travel down the ear canal, which is also part of the outer ear.

At the end of the ear canal, sound waves reach the eardrum. The **eardrum,** which separates the outer ear from the middle ear, is a membrane that vibrates when sound waves strike it. Your eardrum vibrates in much the same way that the surface of a drum vibrates when it is struck. Vibrations from the eardrum pass to the middle ear, which contains the three smallest bones in the body—the hammer, anvil, and stirrup. The names of these bones are based on their shapes. The vibrating eardrum makes the hammer vibrate. The hammer passes the vibrations to the anvil, and the anvil passes them to the stirrup.

How You Hear The stirrup vibrates against a thin membrane that covers the opening of the inner ear. The membrane channels the vibrations into the fluid in the cochlea. The **cochlea** (KAHK le uh) is a snail-shaped tube that is lined with receptors that respond to sound. When the fluid in the cochlea vibrates, it stimulates these receptors. Sensory neurons then send nerve impulses to the cerebrum through the auditory nerve. These impulses are interpreted as sounds that you hear.

☑ ***Checkpoint*** *Where in the ear is the cochlea located?*

Your Sense of Balance

Your ear also controls your sense of balance. Above the cochlea in your inner ear are the **semicircular canals,** which are the structures in the ear that are responsible for your sense of balance.

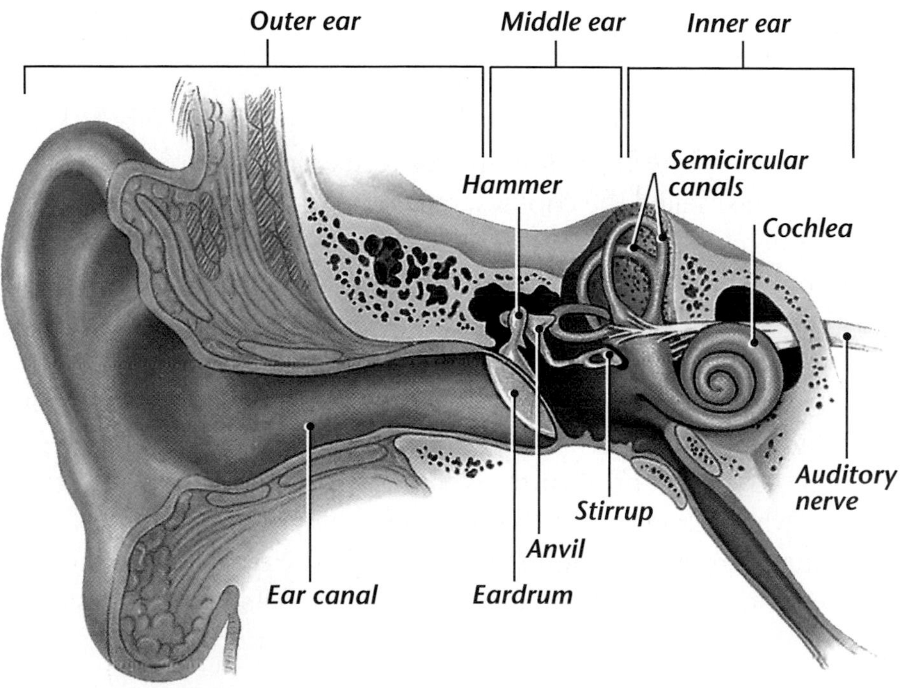

Figure 18 The ear has three regions—the outer ear, the middle ear, and the inner ear. Sound waves enter the outer ear and make structures in the middle ear vibrate. When the vibrations reach the inner ear, nerve impulses travel to the cerebrum through the auditory nerve. ***Predicting*** *What would happen if the bones of the middle ear were stuck together and could not move?*

Figure 19 The semicircular canals of the inner ear enable people to keep their balance—even in very tricky situations!

You can see how these structures got their name if you look at Figure 19. These canals, as well as two tiny sacs located behind them, are full of fluid. The canals and sacs are also lined with tiny cells that have hairlike extensions.

When your head moves, the fluid in the semicircular canals is set in motion. The moving fluid makes the cells' hairlike extensions bend. This bending produces nerve impulses in sensory neurons. The impulses travel to the cerebellum. The cerebellum then analyzes the impulses to determine the way your head is moving and the position of your body. If the cerebellum senses that you are losing your balance, it sends impulses to muscles that help you restore your balance.

Designing Experiments

ACTIVITY

Can people tell one food from another if they can taste the foods but not smell them? Design an experiment to find out. Use these foods: a peeled pear, a peeled apple, and a peeled raw potato. Be sure to control all variables except the one you are testing. Write your hypothesis and a description of your procedure. Show these to your teacher. Do not perform your experiment until your teacher approves your procedure.

Smell and Taste

You walk into the house and smell the aroma of freshly baked cookies. You bite into one and taste its rich chocolate flavor. When you smelled the cookies, receptors in your nose reacted to chemicals carried by the air from the cookies to your nose. When you took a bite of a cookie, taste buds on your tongue responded to chemicals in the food. These food chemicals were dissolved in saliva, which came in contact with your taste buds.

The senses of smell and taste work closely together, and both depend on chemicals. The chemicals trigger responses in receptors in the nose and mouth. Nerve impulses then travel to the brain, where they are interpreted as smells or tastes.

The nose can distinguish at least 50 basic odors. In contrast, there are only four main kinds of taste buds—sweet, sour, salty, and bitter. When you eat, however, you experience a much wider variety of tastes. The flavor of food is determined by both the the senses of smell and taste. When you have a cold, your favorite foods may not taste as good as they usually do. That is because a stuffy nose can decrease your ability to smell food.

Figure 20 Blind people use their sense of touch to read. To do this, they run their fingers over words written in Braille. Braille uses raised dots to represent letters and numbers. Here a teacher shows a blind child how to read Braille.

Touch

Unlike vision, hearing, balance, smell, and taste, the sense of touch is not found in one specific place. Instead, the sense of touch is found in all areas of your skin. Your skin is your largest sense organ!

Your skin contains different kinds of touch receptors. Some of these receptors respond to light touch and others to heavy pressure. Still other receptors pick up sensations of pain and temperature change.

The receptors that respond to light touch are in the upper part of the dermis. They tell you when something brushes against your skin. These receptors also let you feel the textures of objects, such as smooth glass and rough sandpaper. Receptors deeper in the dermis pick up the feeling of pressure. Press down hard on the top of your desk, for example, and you will feel pressure in your fingers.

The dermis also contains receptors that respond to temperature and pain. Pain is unpleasant, but it can be one of the body's most important feelings, because it alerts the body to possible danger. Have you ever stepped into a bathtub of very hot water and then immediately pulled your foot out? If so, you can appreciate how pain can trigger an important response in your body.

Section 3 Review

1. What overall role do the senses perform in the body?
2. Describe the process by which your eyes produce an image of your surroundings. Begin at the point at which light is focused by the lens.
3. How do sound vibrations affect structures in the ear to produce the sensation of hearing?
4. How are the senses of taste and smell similar? How are they different?
5. **Thinking Critically Relating Cause and Effect** Infections of the inner ear sometimes make people more likely to lose their balance and fall. Explain why this is so.

Check Your Progress

CHAPTER PROJECT 8

By now, you should have submitted your plans for your experiment to your teacher. Make any necessary changes in the plan. Prepare all the materials for the fair, including the illusions and questionnaire. Have a data table ready so you can record all responses. (*Hint:* Be sure the people you test cannot see or hear each other's responses. Also, test a large enough number of individuals.)

Section 4 Alcohol and Other Drugs

DISCOVER — ACTIVITY

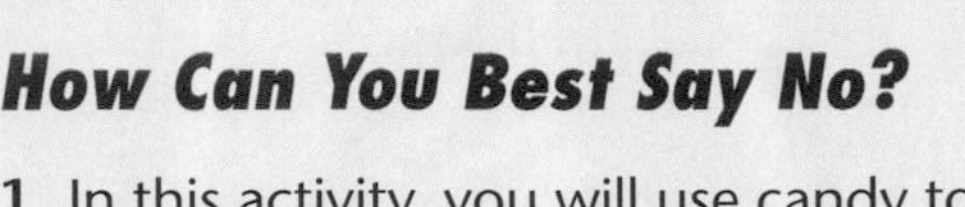

How Can You Best Say No?

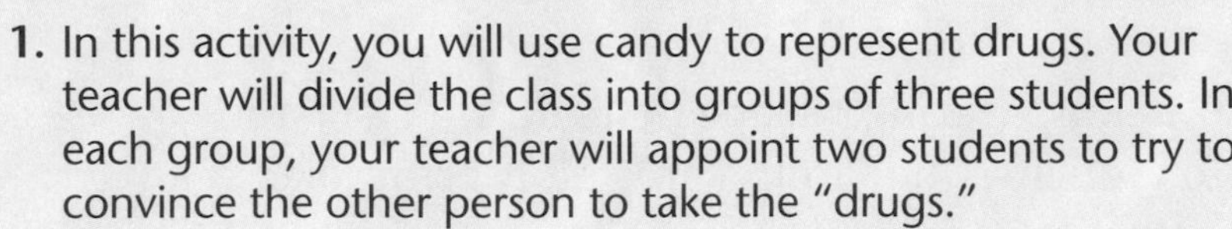

1. In this activity, you will use candy to represent drugs. Your teacher will divide the class into groups of three students. In each group, your teacher will appoint two students to try to convince the other person to take the "drugs."

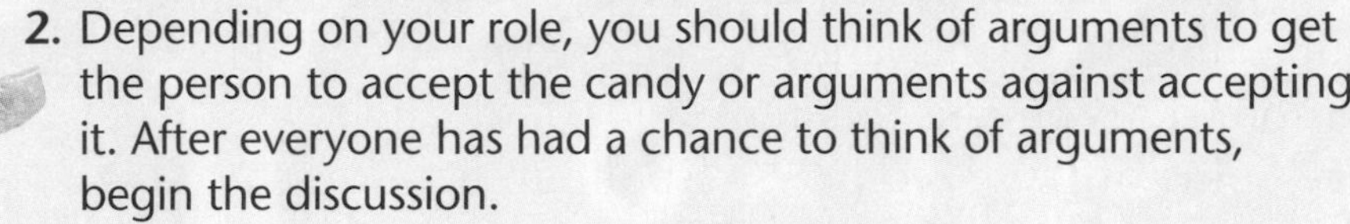

2. Depending on your role, you should think of arguments to get the person to accept the candy or arguments against accepting it. After everyone has had a chance to think of arguments, begin the discussion.
3. After a while, students in each group should exchange roles.

Think It Over

Inferring What role does peer pressure play in whether or not a person decides to abuse drugs?

GUIDE FOR READING

- **How do commonly abused drugs affect the body?**
- **How does alcohol abuse harm the body?**

Reading Tip **Before you read, preview the table on page 273. List some ways in which drugs affect the central nervous system.**

Drugs! You probably hear and see that word in a lot of places. Drugstores sell drugs to relieve headaches, soothe upset stomachs, and stop coughs. Radio and television programs and magazine articles explore drug-related problems. Your school probably has a program to educate students about drugs. When people talk about drugs, what do they mean? To a scientist, a **drug** is any chemical that causes changes in a person's body or behavior. Many drugs affect the functioning of the nervous system.

Medicines

Medicines are legal drugs that help the body fight disease and injury. Aspirin, for example, is a medicine that can relieve pain. To purchase some medicines, you need a doctor's prescription. Other medicines, however, can be bought in drugstores or supermarkets without a prescription. If medicines are used properly, they can help you stay healthy or speed your recovery from sickness. Whenever you take medicines of any kind, it is important to follow the directions for their proper use.

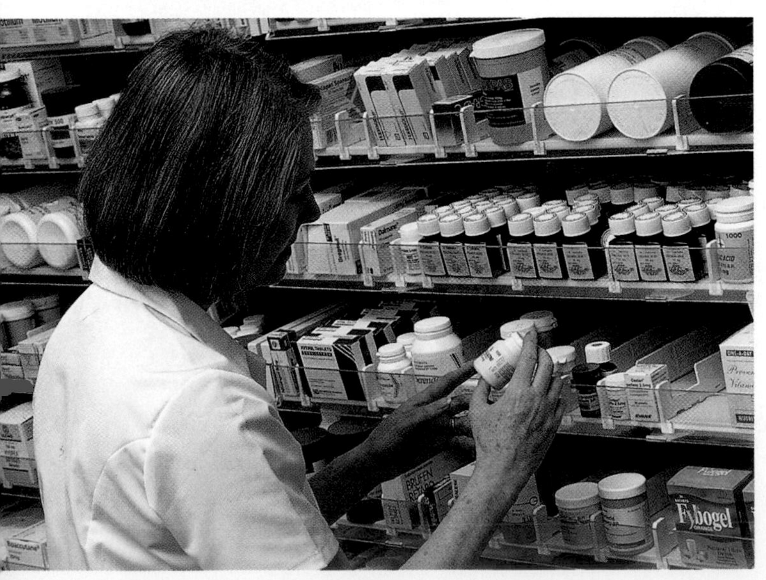

◀ Medicines in a drugstore

Drug Abuse

The deliberate misuse of drugs for purposes other than medical ones is called **drug abuse.** Medicines can be abused drugs if they are used in a way for which they were not intended. Many abused drugs, however, such as cocaine and heroin, are illegal under any circumstances. The use of these drugs is against the law because their effects on the body are almost always very dangerous.

Immediate Effects of Abused Drugs Abused drugs start to affect the body very shortly after they are taken. Different drugs have different effects. Some drugs cause nausea and a fast, irregular heartbeat. Others can cause sleepiness. Drug abusers may also experience headaches, dizziness, and trembling.

Most commonly abused drugs, such as marijuana, alcohol, and cocaine, are especially dangerous because they act on the brain and other parts of the nervous system. For example, alcohol can cause confusion, poor muscle coordination, and blurred vision. These effects are especially dangerous in situations in which an alert mind is essential, such as driving a car.

Most abused drugs can alter, or change, a person's mood and feelings. Because of this effect, these drugs are often called mood-altering drugs. For example, the mood of a person under the influence of marijuana may change from calm to anxious. Alcohol can sometimes make a person angry and even violent. Mood-altering drugs also affect patterns of thinking and the way in which the brain interprets information from the senses.

Tolerance If a person takes a drug regularly, the body may develop a tolerance to the drug. **Tolerance** is a state in which a drug user needs larger and larger amounts of the drug to produce the same effect on the body. Tolerance can cause people to take a very large amount of a drug, or an overdose. People who take an overdose may become unconscious or even die.

Figure 21 Abused drugs such as these can cause serious physical and emotional problems.
Applying Concepts *List three ways in which drugs can affect the body.*

Communicating

Plan a 30-second television commercial aimed at teenagers to help them avoid the pressure to try drugs. Your commercial should reveal some harmful effects of drugs and give strategies for avoiding drugs. Create several storyboards to show what the commercial will look like. Then write a script for your commercial.

Addiction For many commonly abused drugs, repeated use can result in addiction. The body becomes physically dependent on the drug. If a drug addict misses a few doses of the drug, the body reacts to the lack of the drug. The person may experience headaches, fever, vomiting, body aches, and muscle cramps. The person is experiencing **withdrawal,** a period of adjustment that occurs when a person stops taking a drug.

Some drugs may also cause a person to become emotionally dependent on them. The person becomes accustomed to the feelings and moods produced by the drug. Therefore, the person has a strong desire to continue using the drug.

☑ *Checkpoint* *What is meant by a tolerance to a drug?*

Other Effects of Drug Abuse

Drugs can also affect a person's health indirectly. Drug users sometimes share needles. When a person uses a needle to inject a drug, some of the person's blood remains in the needle after it is withdrawn. If the person has HIV or another pathogen in the blood, the next person to use the needle may become infected with the pathogen.

The abuse of drugs also has serious legal and social effects. A person who is caught using or selling an illegal drug may have to pay a fine or go to jail. Drug abuse can also make a person unable to get along with others. Drug abusers often have a hard time doing well in school or holding a job.

Kinds of Drugs

Figure 22 lists and describes the characteristics of some commonly abused drugs. Notice in the chart that some drugs are classified as depressants. **Depressants** are drugs that slow down the activity of the central nervous system. When people take depressants, their muscles relax and they may become sleepy. They may take longer than normal to respond to stimuli. For example, depressants may prevent people from reacting quickly to the danger of a car rushing toward them. Alcohol and narcotics, such as heroin, are depressants.

Stimulants, in contrast, speed up body processes. They make the heart beat faster and make the breathing rate increase. Cocaine and nicotine are stimulants, as are amphetamines. Amphetamines (am FET uh meenz) are prescription drugs that are sometimes sold illegally.

Some Effects of Commonly Abused Drugs

Drug Type	Short-Term Effects	Long-Term Effects	Addiction?	Emotional Dependence?
marijuana (including hashish)	anxiety, panic, excitement, sleepiness	difficulty with concentration and memory, respiratory disease and lung cancer	probably not	yes
nicotine (in cigarettes, cigars, chewing tobacco)	stimulant; nausea, loss of appetite, headache	heart and lung disease, difficulty breathing, heavy coughing	yes, strongly so	yes
alcohol	depressant; decreased alertness, poor reflexes, nausea, emotional depression	liver and brain damage, inadequate nutrition	yes	yes
inhalants (glue, nail polish remover, paint thinner)	sleepiness, nausea, headaches, emotional depression	damage to liver, kidneys, and brain; hallucinations	no	yes
cocaine (including crack)	stimulant; nervousness, disturbed sleep, loss of appetite	mental illness, damage to lining of nose, irregular heartbeat, heart or breathing failure, liver damage	yes	yes, strongly so
amphetamines	stimulant; restlessness, rapid speech, dizziness	restlessness, irritability, irregular heartbeat, liver damage	possible	yes
hallucinogens (LSD, mescaline, PCP)	hallucinations, anxiety, panic; thoughts and actions not connected to reality	mental illness; fearfulness; behavioral changes, including violence	no	yes
barbiturates (Phenobarbital, Nembutal, Seconal)	depressant; decreased alertness, slowed thought processes, poor muscle coordination	sleepiness, irritability, confusion	yes	yes
tranquilizers (Valium, Xanax)	depressant; blurred vision, sleepiness, unclear speech, headache, skin rash	blood and liver disease	yes	yes
narcotics (opium, codeine, morphine, heroin)	depressant; sleepiness, nausea, hallucinations	convulsion, coma, death	yes, very rapid development	yes, strongly so
anabolic steroids	mood swings	heart, liver, and kidney damage; hypertension; overgrowth of skull and facial bones	no	yes

Figure 22 Abused drugs can have many serious effects on the body. ***Interpreting Charts*** *What are the long-term effects of using inhalants?*

Some substances, called inhalants, produce mood-altering effects when they are inhaled, or breathed in. Inhalants include paint thinner, nail polish remover, and some kinds of cleaning fluids. Hallucinogens, such as LSD and mescaline, can make people see or hear things that do not really exist.

Some athletes try to improve their performance by taking drugs known as steroids. **Anabolic steroids** (an uh BAH lik steer oydz) are synthetic chemicals that are similar to hormones produced in the body. You will learn more about hormones in Chapter 9.

Anabolic steroids may increase muscle size and strength. However, steroids can cause mood changes that lead to violence.

Real-World Lab

You, the Consumer

With Caffeine or Without?

Caffeine is a stimulant found in some beverages and foods, such as coffee and cola drinks. In this lab, you'll observe the effect that caffeine has on a nonhuman organism to help understand how caffeine may affect your own body.

Problem

What body changes does caffeine produce in blackworms *(Lumbriculus)*?

Skills Focus

developing hypotheses, designing experiments

Materials

blackworms
plastic dropper
paraffin specimen trough
noncarbonated spring water
adrenaline solution
beverages with and without caffeine
stereomicroscope
stopwatch or clock with second hand

Procedure

Part 1 Observing Effects of a Known Stimulant

1. Use a dropper to remove one worm and a drop or two of water from the blackworm population provided by your teacher.
2. Place the worm and the water in the trough of the paraffin block. Use the dropper or the corner of a paper towel to remove any excess water that does not fit in the trough. Let the blackworm adjust to the block for a few minutes.
3. Place the paraffin block under the stereomicroscope. Select the smallest amount of light and the lowest possible power to view the blackworm.
4. Look through the stereomicroscope and locate a segment near the middle of the worm. Count the number of times blood pulses through this segment for 30 seconds. Multiply this number by two to get the pulse in beats per minute. Record the pulse.

In addition, steroid abuse can cause serious health problems, such as heart damage, liver damage, and increased blood pressure. Steroid use is especially dangerous for teenagers, whose growing bodies can be permanently damaged.

Alcohol

Alcohol is a drug found in many beverages, including beer, wine, cocktails, and hard liquor. Alcohol is a powerful depressant. In the United States, it is illegal for people under the age of 21 to buy or possess alcohol. In spite of this fact, alcohol is the most commonly abused drug in people aged 12 to 17.

5. Remove the block from the stereomicroscope. Use the dropper to add 1 drop of adrenaline solution to the trough. (Adrenaline is a substance that is produced by the human body and that acts in a manner similar to a stimulant.) Let the worm sit in the adrenaline solution for 5 minutes.
6. Place the paraffin block under the stereomicroscope. Again locate a segment near the middle of the worm. Count the number of pulses through this segment for 30 seconds. Multiply this number by two to get the pulse in beats per minute. Record the blackworm's pulse with adrenaline.

Part 2 Testing the Effects of Caffeine

7. Using the procedures you followed in Part 1, design an experiment that tests the effect of caffeine on the blackworm's pulse. You can use beverages with and without caffeine in your investigation. Be sure to write a hypothesis and control all necessary variables.
8. Submit your experimental plan to your teacher for review. After making any necessary changes, carry out your experiment.

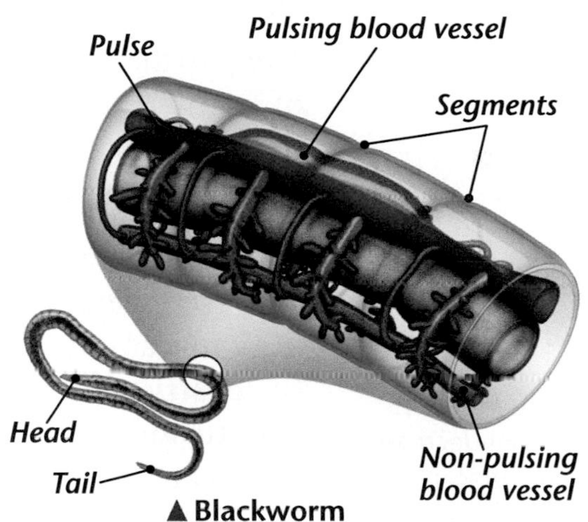

▲ Blackworm

Analyze and Conclude

1. What effect does a stimulant have?
2. In Part 1, how did you know that adrenaline acted as a stimulant?
3. In Part 2, did caffeine act as a stimulant?
4. **Apply** Based on your work in Part 2, how do you think your body would react to drinks with caffeine? To drinks without caffeine?

Design an Experiment

Do you think that "decaffeinated" products will act as a stimulant in blackworms? Design a controlled experiment to find out. Obtain your teacher's approval before performing this experiment.

How Alcohol Affects the Body Alcohol is absorbed by the digestive system quickly. If a person drinks alcohol on an empty stomach, the alcohol enters the blood and gets to the brain and other organs almost immediately. If alcohol is drunk with a meal, it takes longer to get into the blood.

To understand what alcohol does to the body, look at *Exploring the Effects of Alcohol.* The more alcohol in the blood, the more serious the effects. The amount of alcohol in the blood is usually expressed as blood alcohol concentration, or BAC. A BAC value of 0.1 percent means that one tenth of one percent of the fluid in the blood is alcohol. In some states, if car drivers have a BAC of 0.08 percent or more, they are legally drunk. In other states, drivers with a BAC of 0.1 are considered drunk.

Alcohol produces serious effects, including loss of normal judgment, at a BAC of less than 0.08 percent. This loss of judgment can have serious consequences. For example, people who have been drinking may not realize that they cannot drive a car safely. In the United States, alcohol is involved in about 40 percent of traffic-related deaths. About every two minutes, a person in the United States is injured in a car crash related to alcohol.

Long-Term Alcohol Abuse Many adults drink occasionally, and in moderation, without serious safety or health problems. However, heavy drinking, especially over a long period, can result in significant health problems. **The abuse of alcohol can cause the destruction of cells in the brain and liver, and it can also lead to addiction and emotional dependence.** Damage to the brain can cause mental disturbances, such as hallucinations and

Figure 23 Alcohol is involved in many car crashes. Alcohol decreases a driver's ability to react quickly to traffic and road conditions.

loss of consciousness. The liver, which breaks down alcohol for elimination from the body, can become so scarred that it does not function properly. In addition, long-term alcohol abuse can increase the risk of getting certain kinds of cancer.

Abuse of alcohol can result in **alcoholism,** a disease in which a person is both physically addicted to and emotionally dependent on alcohol. To give up alcohol, alcoholics must go through withdrawal, as with any addictive drug. To give up drinking,

EXPLORING *the Effects of Alcohol*

Alcohol is a drug that affects every system of the body. It also impacts a person's thought processes and judgment.

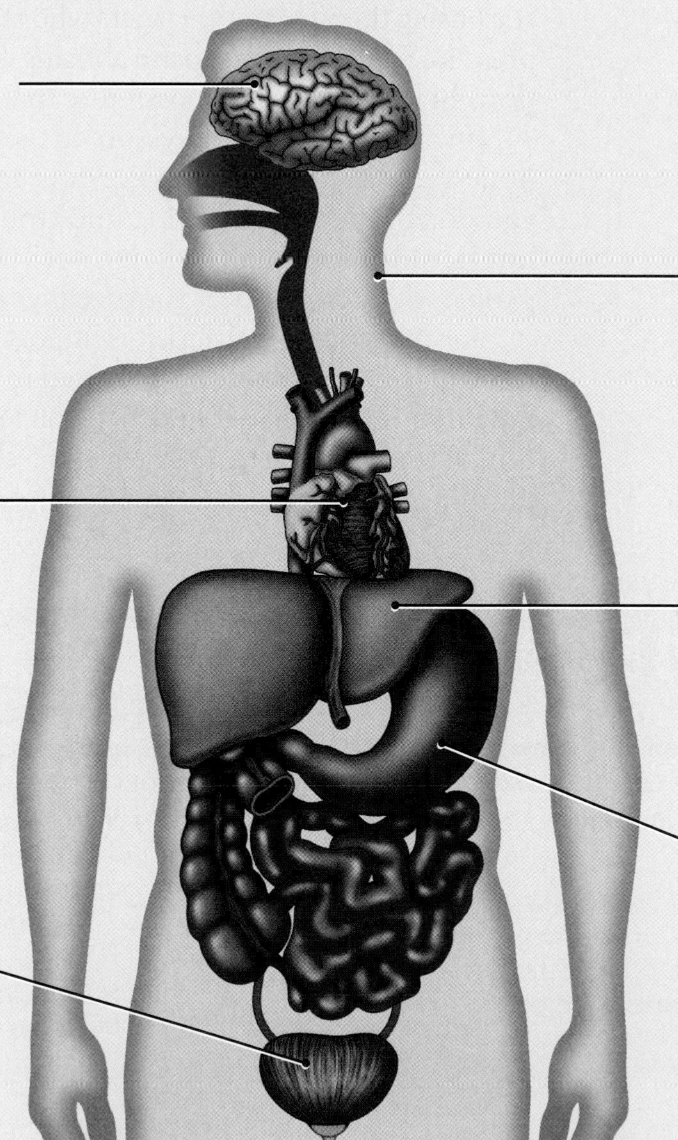

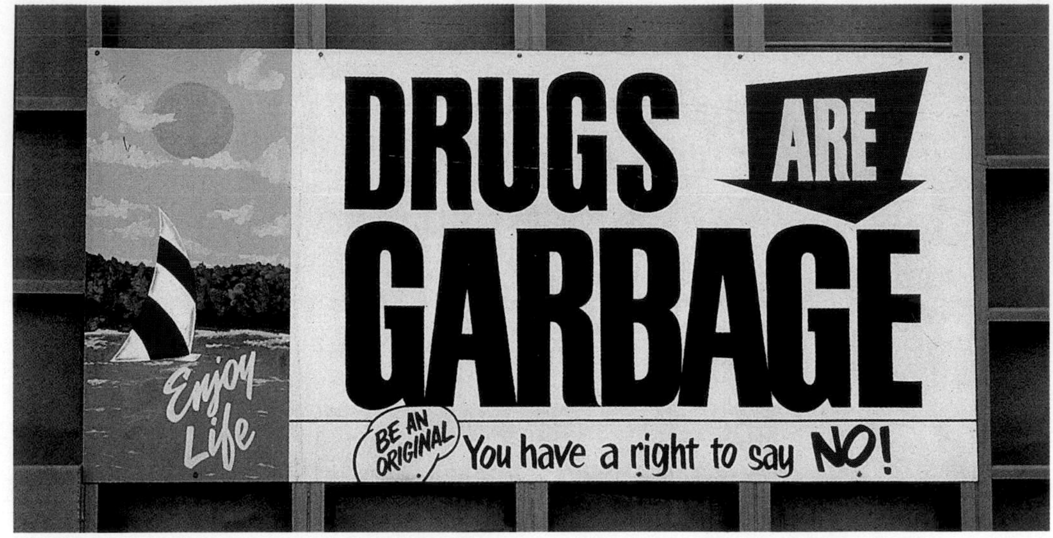

Figure 24 The message is clear: drugs are dangerous, and you have the right to refuse to take them.

alcoholics need both medical and emotional help. Medical professionals and organizations such as Alcoholics Anonymous can help a person stop drinking.

Avoiding Drugs and Alcohol

The best way to avoid depending on drugs and alcohol is not to start using them. Many teenagers who start do so because of peer pressure from people who are abusing drugs. Try to avoid situations in which there is a possibility that drugs may be used.

If you are faced with pressure to use drugs, give a simple but honest reason for your refusal. For example, you might say that you don't want to risk getting into trouble with the law. You do not need to apologize for your decision. And remember that people who don't respect your feelings aren't very good friends.

To stay away from drugs, it is important to find healthy things to do with friends. Become involved in sports and other school or community activities in which you and your friends can have fun together. Such activities help you feel good about yourself. By deciding not to use drugs, you are protecting your health.

Section 4 Review

1. How do abused drugs affect the nervous system? Why can these effects be dangerous?
2. What are the effects of long-term alcohol abuse?
3. What is alcoholism?
4. **Thinking Critically Comparing and Contrasting** Contrast the effects that stimulants and depressants have on the body.

CHAPTER PROJECT 8

Check Your Progress

By now you should have finished collecting your data and recording your observations. Now begin preparing a report about your findings. Think about the best way to communicate the procedures you followed and the results you obtained. Your report should explain how you think the illusions you chose trick the senses. Decide how to use graphs and other visuals in your report.

CHAPTER 8 STUDY GUIDE

How the Nervous System Works

Key Idea

- The nervous system receives information about the external and internal environment and helps maintain homeostasis.

Key Terms

stimulus, response, neuron, nerve impulse, dendrite, axon, nerve, sensory neuron, interneuron, motor neuron, synapse

Divisions of the Nervous System

Key Ideas

- The central nervous system consists of the brain and spinal cord.
- The peripheral nervous system links the central nervous system to the rest of the body.

Key Terms

central nervous system, peripheral nervous system, brain, spinal cord, cerebrum, cerebellum, brainstem, somatic nervous system, autonomic nervous system, reflex, concussion

The Senses

Key Ideas

- The senses change information about the environment to nerve impulses.
- After light enters the eye, it passes through the lens, which focuses it on the retina. Impulses then travel to the brain.
- Sound waves start vibrations in structures in the ear. When the vibrations reach the cochlea, impulses are sent to the brain.

Key Terms

cornea, pupil, iris, lens, retina, nearsightedness, farsightedness, eardrum, cochlea, semicircular canal

Alcohol and Other Drugs

Integrating Health

Key Ideas

- Abused drugs act on the nervous system. Depressants slow down the central nervous system. Stimulants speed up body processes. Marijuana, alcohol, amphetamines, and anabolic steroids are commonly abused drugs.
- The long-term abuse of alcohol can damage the liver and brain and lead to alcoholism.

Key Terms

drug, drug abuse, tolerance, withdrawal, depressant, stimulant, anabolic steroid, alcoholism

Organizing Information

Concept Map Complete the following concept map about nerve cells and their functions. (For more on concept maps, see the Skills Handbook.)

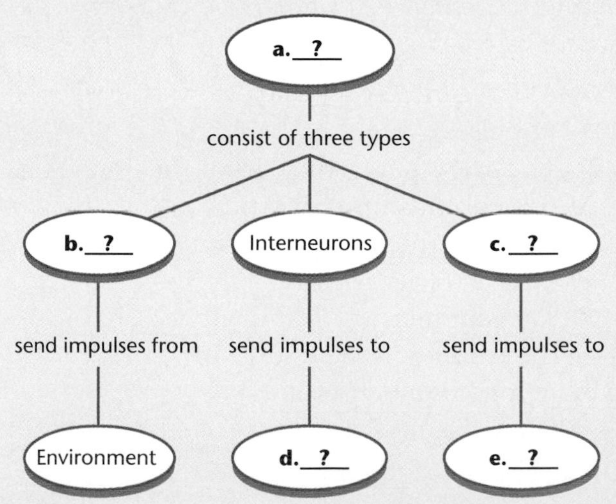

Reviewing Content

Multiple Choice

Choose the letter of the best answer.

1. A change or signal in the environment that makes the nervous system react is called a
   a. stimulus. b. response.
   c. receptor. d. synapse.
2. The structures that carry messages toward a neuron's cell body are
   a. axons.
   b. dendrites.
   c. nerves.
   d. impulses.
3. Which structure links the brain and the peripheral nervous system?
   a. the cerebrum
   b. the cerebellum
   c. the cochlea
   d. the spinal cord
4. Which structure adjusts the size of the pupil?
   a. the cornea
   b. the retina
   c. the lens
   d. the iris
5. Physical dependence on a drug is called
   a. withdrawal.
   b. response.
   c. addiction.
   d. tolerance.

True or False

If the statement is true, write true. If it is false, change the underlined word or words to make the statement true.

6. A nerve message is also called a <u>nerve impulse</u>.
7. The <u>brainstem</u> is the part of the brain that controls involuntary actions.
8. In <u>nearsightedness</u>, a person cannot see nearby objects clearly.
9. The hammer, anvil, and <u>wrench</u> are the three bones in the middle ear.
10. Alcohol is a <u>depressant</u>.

Checking Concepts

11. Compare the functions of axons and dendrites.
12. What is the function of the autonomic nervous system?
13. How do the cerebrum and cerebellum work together when you ride a bicycle?
14. What are some steps you can take to protect your central nervous system from injury?
15. Describe how lenses in eyeglasses correct nearsightedness and farsightedness.
16. List all the structures in your ear that must vibrate before you hear a sound. List them in the order in which they vibrate.
17. What are the effects of anabolic steroids on the body?
18. **Writing to Learn** Imagine that Earth has been invaded by space aliens who are exactly like humans except for the fact that they have no sense of touch. These aliens plan to take over Earth. Write a plan for fighting the aliens that makes use of the fact that they lack a sense of touch.

Thinking Critically

19. **Relating Cause and Effect** When a person has a stroke, blood flow to part of the brain is reduced, and severe brain damage can result. Suppose that after a stroke, a woman is unable to move her right arm and right leg. In which side of her brain did the stroke occur? Explain.
20. **Applying Concepts** As a man walks barefoot along a beach, he steps on a sharp shell. His foot automatically jerks upward, even before he feels pain. What process is this an example of? How does it help protect the man?
21. **Making Judgments** If someone tried to persuade you to take drugs, what arguments would you use as a way of refusing? Why do you think these arguments would be effective?

Applying Skills

A person with normal vision stood at different distances from an eye chart and tried to identify the letters on the chart. The table gives the results. Use the table to answer Questions 22–24.

Distance from Eye Chart	Percent of Letters Identified Correctly
2 meters	100
4 meters	92
6 meters	80
8 meters	71
10 meters	60

22. Graphing Make a line graph of the data. Plot the distance from the chart on the horizontal axis. On the vertical axis, plot the percent of letters identified correctly.

23. Controlling Variables What was the manipulated variable in this experiment? What was the responding variable?

24. Predicting How would you expect the results to differ for a farsighted person? Explain.

Performance Assessment

Project Wrap Up Your report should include an explanation of how you did your research, what you were trying to find out, and how your actual results compared with your expected results. Also, include information on how the nervous system was involved in your illusions. If you can, try to explain why the illusions work.

Reflect and Record In your journal, summarize what you learned from doing this project. Did the project go as you expected, or were you surprised by some results? If you had a chance to continue your investigations, what would you do next? Why?

Test Preparation

Use these questions to prepare for standardized tests.

Study the diagram. Then answer Questions 25–28.

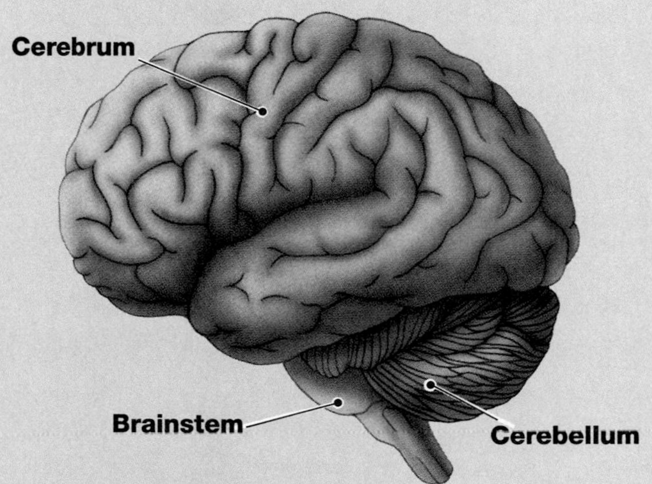

25. Which part of the brain controls muscle coordination and balance?
a. right half of cerebrum
b. left half of cerebrum
c. cerebellum
d. brainstem

26. Which part of the brain controls involuntary actions such as breathing and the heartbeat?
a. right half of cerebrum
b. left half of cerebrum
c. cerebellum
d. brainstem

27. Which part of the brain controls your ability to raise your right hand high over your head?
a. right half of cerebrum
b. left half of cerebrum
c. spinal cord
d. brainstem

28. Which body system consists of the brain and spinal cord?
a. central nervous system
b. peripheral nervous system
c. somatic nervous system
d. autonomic nervous system

CHAPTER 9

The Endocrine System and Reproduction

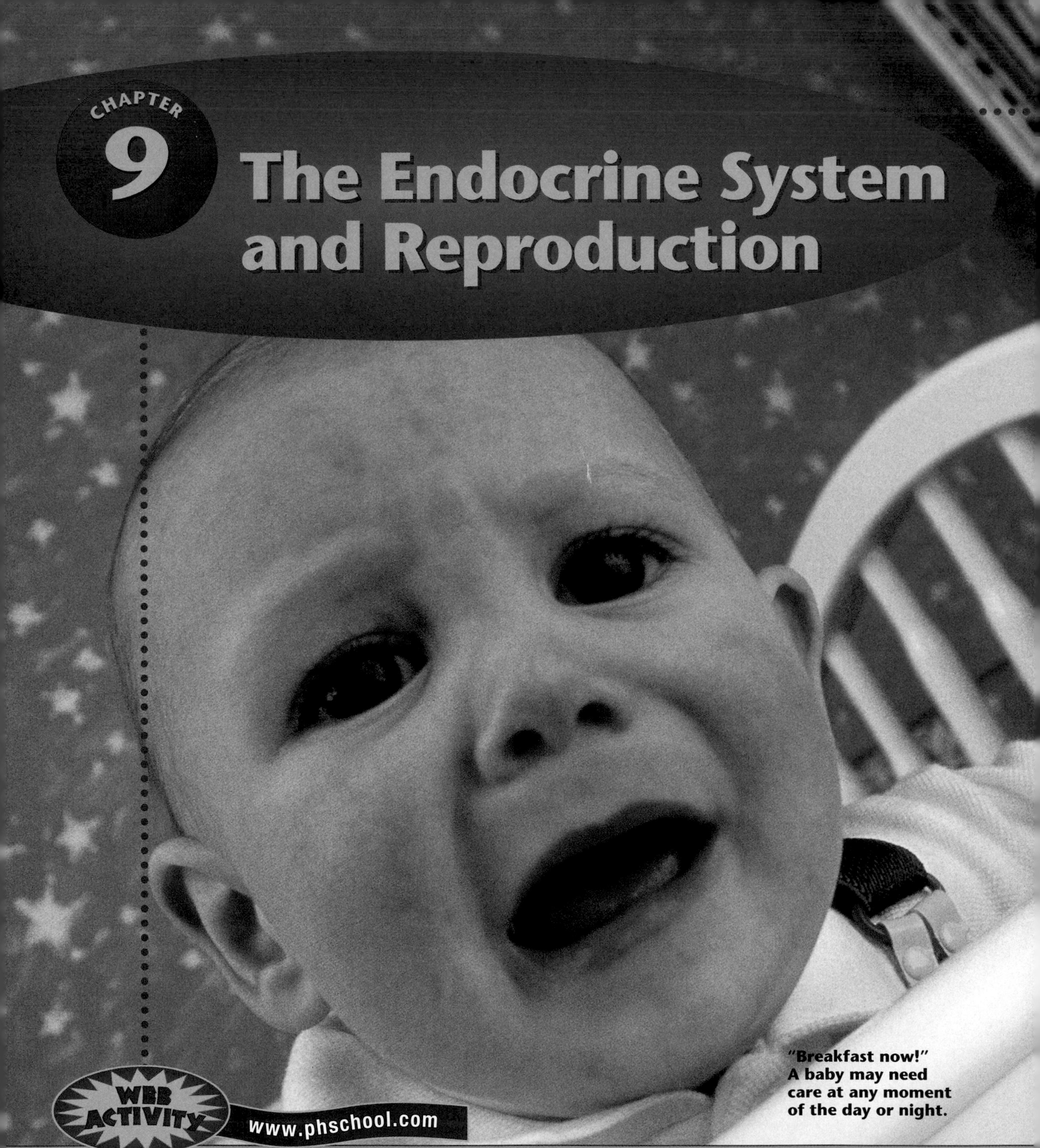

"Breakfast now!" A baby may need care at any moment of the day or night.

www.phschool.com

The Endocrine System

Discover **What's the Signal?**

The Male and Female Reproductive Systems

Discover **What's the Big Difference?**
Sharpen Your Skills **Graphing**

Pregnancy, Birth, and Childhood

Discover **How Many Ways Does a Child Grow?**
Try This **Way to Grow!**
Sharpen Your Skills **Designing Experiments**

PROJECT 9

A Precious Bundle

With the arrival of their first baby, most new parents discover that their lives are totally changed. Their usual schedules are disrupted, and they suddenly need a new set of skills. Parents must begin to learn how to keep the infant comfortable and happy.

As you learn about reproduction and development, you'll experience what it's like to care for a "baby." Although your baby will be only a physical model, you'll have a chance to learn about the responsibilities of parenthood.

Your Goal To develop and follow a plan to care for a "baby" for three days and nights.

To complete this project, you must

- list all the essential tasks involved in caring for a young infant, and prepare a 24-hour schedule of those tasks
- make a model "baby" from a bag of flour, and care for the baby according to your schedule
- keep a journal of your thoughts and feelings as you care for your "baby," making entries at least twice a day

Get Started With classmates write down all the things that parents must do when caring for infants. Prepare a plan describing how to carry out those activities with your "baby." List the materials you'll need. If you require more information, write down your questions, then consult adult caregivers, day care facilities, or other resources.

Check Your Progress You'll be working on this project as you study this chapter. To keep your project on track, look for Check Your Progress boxes at the following points.

Section 1 Review, page 288: Present your child-care plan to your teacher for review.

Section 2 Review, page 294: Care for your "baby," and record your experiences in your journal.

Section 4 Review, page 307: Summarize your experiences.

Wrap Up At the end of the chapter (page 311), you'll share what you learned about parenthood.

Integrating Health

SECTION 4

Adolescence—A Time of Change

Discover **How Do Ads Portray Teenagers?**

Skills Lab **Growing Up**

SECTION 1 The Endocrine System

DISCOVER

What's the Signal?

1. Stand up and move around the room until your teacher says "Freeze!" Then stop moving immediately. Stay perfectly still until your teacher says "Start!" Then begin moving again.
2. Anyone who moves between the "Freeze!" command and the "Start!" command has to leave the game.
3. Play until only one person is left in the game. That person is the winner.

Think It Over

Inferring Why is it important for players in this game to respond to signals? What types of signals does the human body use?

GUIDE FOR READING

- **What is the function of the endocrine system?**
- **How does negative feedback control hormone levels?**

Reading Tip **Before you read, preview *Exploring the Endocrine System* on pages 286–287. List the terms in the diagram that are new to you. Look for their meanings as you read.**

You're playing softball on a hot afternoon. Without warning, thick, dark clouds form. Suddenly, there's a flash of lightning. Thunder cracks overhead. Someone screams, you jump, and everyone runs for cover. Your heart is pounding, your palms are sweaty, and your muscles are tight.

Your body's reaction to the sudden storm was caused mainly by your body's endocrine system. In this section, you will learn about the role of the endocrine system in many body processes—from the quick response to a thunder clap, to the slower body changes that turn a child into an adult.

The Role of the Endocrine System

The human body has two systems that regulate its activities. You learned about one, the nervous system, in Chapter 8. The endocrine system is the other regulating system. **The endocrine system controls many of the body's daily activities as well as long-term changes such as development.**

The endocrine system is made up of glands. Glands are organs that produce chemicals. You already know about some glands, such as those that produce saliva or sweat. Those glands release their chemicals into tiny tubes. The tubes deliver the chemicals to a specific location within the body or to the skin's surface.

The endocrine system does not have delivery tubes. **Endocrine glands** (EN duh krin) produce and release their chemical products directly into the bloodstream. The blood then carries those chemicals throughout the body.

Figure 1 The endocrine system controls the body's response to an exciting situation (left) as well as the changes that occur as a child grows (right).
Applying Concepts *What substances produced by endocrine glands control these body processes?*

Hormones

The chemical product of an endocrine gland is called a **hormone.** Hormones turn on, turn off, speed up, or slow down the activities of different organs and tissues. You can think of a hormone as a chemical messenger. Because hormones are carried by blood, they can regulate activities in tissues and organs far from the glands that produced them.

Hormone Production What causes the release of hormones? In situations such as a sudden storm, nerve impulses from the senses travel to the brain. There, information, such as the sound of thunder, is interpreted. The brain then sends a nerve impulse to a specific endocrine gland. That gland, in turn, releases the hormone adrenaline into the bloodstream. As you read in Chapter 3, adrenaline causes your heart rate to increase, makes you breathe faster and deeper, and releases sugars that power your muscles.

In contrast to the body's response to a nerve impulse, hormones cause a slower, but longer-lasting, response. For example, the brain sends a quick signal to an endocrine gland to release adrenaline into the bloodstream. When the adrenaline reaches the heart, it makes the heart beat more rapidly. The heart continues to race until the amount of adrenaline in the blood drops to a normal level.

Target Cells When a hormone enters the bloodstream, why does it affect some organs but not others? **INTEGRATING CHEMISTRY** The answer lies in its chemical structure. A hormone interacts only with certain **target cells,** cells that recognize the hormone's chemical structure. A hormone and its target cell fit together the way a key fits into a lock. Hormones not meant for a particular organ will travel through the bloodstream until they find the "lock" that they fit.

Each endocrine gland releases different hormones and thus controls different processes. *Exploring the Endocrine System* shows the locations of the endocrine glands and describes some activities they control.

The Hypothalamus

The nervous system and the endocrine system work together. The **hypothalamus** (hy poh THAL uh mus), a tiny part of the brain near the middle of your head, is the link between the two systems. Nerve messages controlling sleep, hunger, and other conditions come from the hypothalamus. The hypothalamus also produces hormones that control other endocrine glands and organs. Through its nerve impulses and hormones, the hypothalamus plays a major role in maintaining homeostasis.

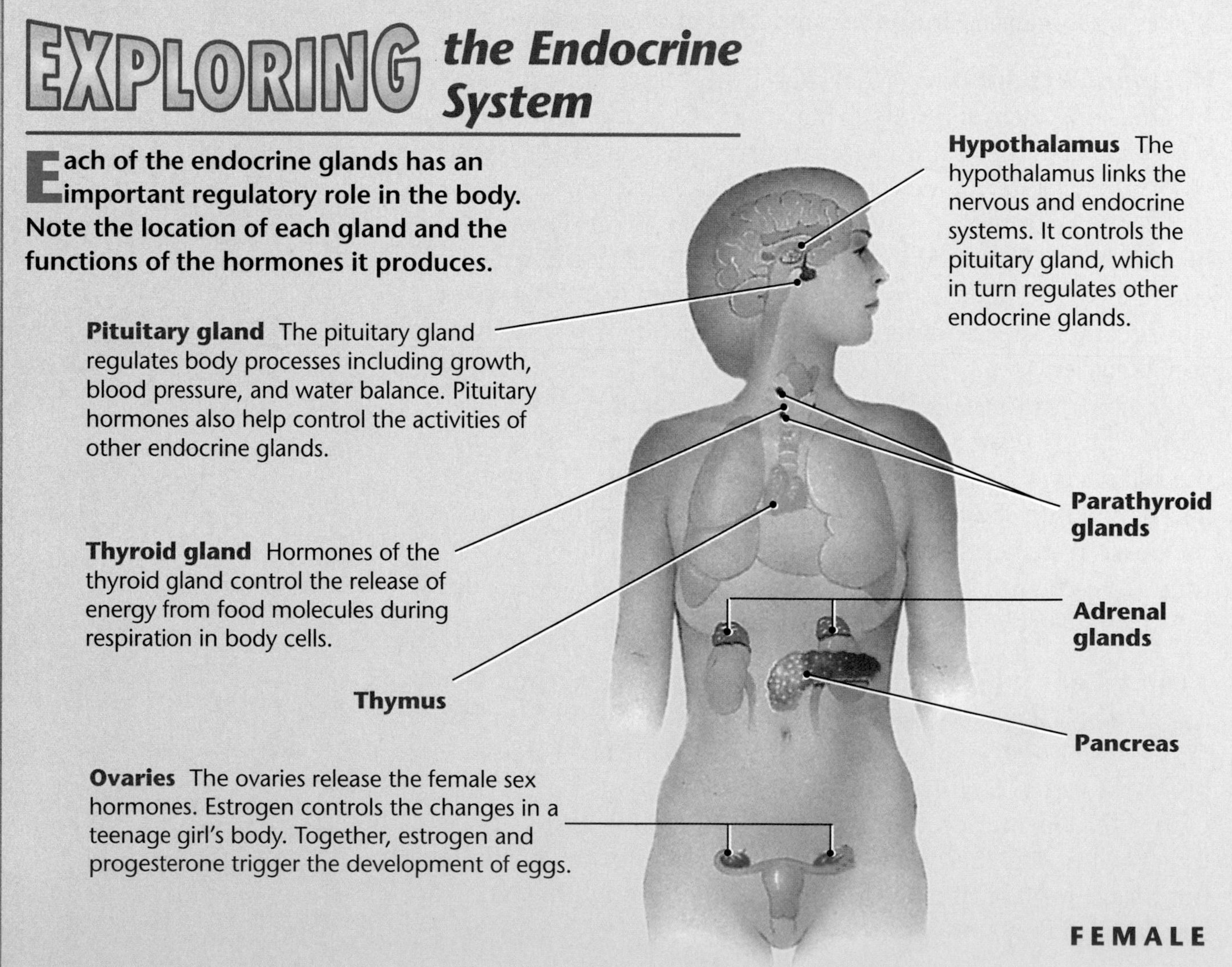

The Pituitary Gland

Just below the hypothalamus is an endocrine gland about the size of a pea. The **pituitary gland** (pih TOO ih tehr ee) communicates with the hypothalamus to control many body activities. In response to nerve impulses or hormone signals from the hypothalamus, the pituitary gland releases its hormones. Some of those hormones act as an "on" switch for other endocrine glands. For example, one pituitary hormone signals the thyroid gland to produce hormones. Other pituitary hormones control body activities directly. Growth hormone regulates growth from infancy to adulthood. Another pituitary hormone directs the kidneys to regulate the amount of water in the blood.

☑ *Checkpoint* *What causes the pituitary gland to release hormones?*

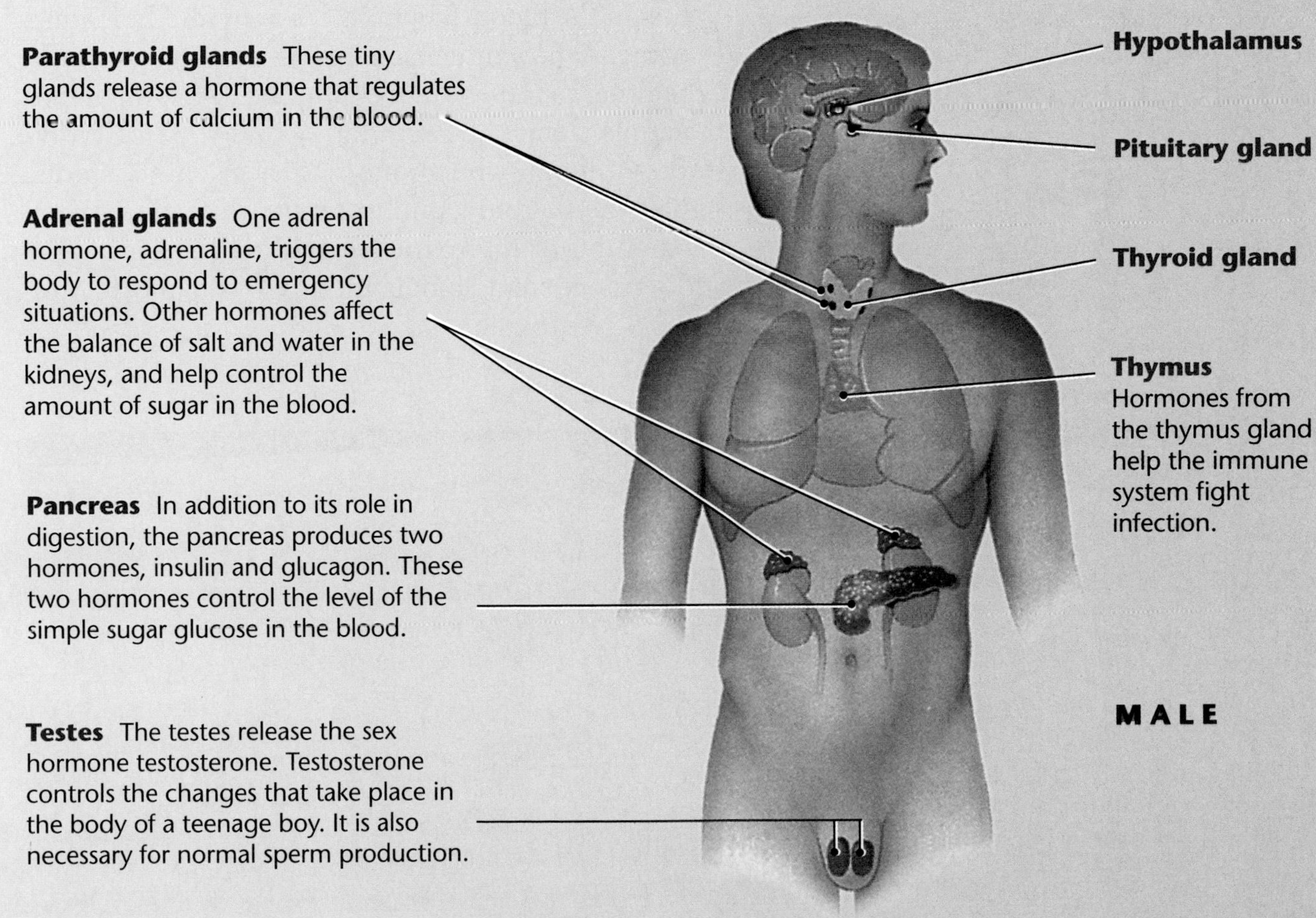

Hypothalamus senses cells need more energy

Pituitary releases TSH

Thyroid produces thyroxine

Hypothalamus senses cells have enough energy

Pituitary stops producing TSH

Thyroid stops producing thyroxine

Figure 2 The release of the hormone thyroxine is controlled through negative feedback. When enough thyroxine is present, the system signals the thyroid gland to stop releasing the hormone. ***Predicting*** *What happens when the amount of thyroxine becomes too low?*

Negative Feedback

One way that the endocrine system maintains homeostasis may remind you of the way a heating system works. Suppose you set a thermostat at 20°C. If the temperature falls below 20°, the thermostat signals the furnace to turn on. When the furnace heats the area to the proper temperature, information about the warm conditions "feeds back" to the thermostat. The thermostat then gives the furnace a negative signal that means "no more heat." That signal turns the furnace off.

The type of signal used in a heating system is called **negative feedback** because the system is turned off by the condition it produces. The endocrine system often works in this way. Through negative feedback, when the amount of a particular hormone in the blood reaches a certain level, the endocrine system sends signals that stop the release of that hormone. **Negative feedback is an important way that the body maintains homeostasis.**

You can see an example of negative feedback in Figure 2. Like a thermostat in a cool room, the endocrine system senses when there's not enough thyroxine in the blood. Thyroxine is a thyroid hormone. It controls how much energy is available to cells. When there's not enough energy available, the hypothalamus signals the pituitary gland to release thyroid-stimulating hormone (TSH). That hormone signals the thyroid gland to release thyroxine. When the amount of thyroxine reaches the right level, the endocrine system signals the thyroid gland to stop releasing thyroxine.

Section 1 Review

1. What role does the endocrine system play in the body? What are the organs of the endocrine system called?
2. Explain how negative feedback helps to maintain homeostasis in the body.
3. How do the hypothalamus and the pituitary gland interact?
4. **Thinking Critically Making Judgments** Years ago, one of the endocrine glands was called the "master gland." Which part of the endocrine system would you consider the master gland? Explain.

CHAPTER PROJECT 9

Check Your Progress

You should now be ready to turn in your plan for your teacher's review. Your plan should include your daily schedule and a list of the materials you'll need. Be sure to describe the kind of journal you plan to keep. (*Hint:* Discuss with your teacher any problems you foresee in caring for the "baby" for three full days and nights.)

SECTION 2 The Male and Female Reproductive Systems

DISCOVER

What's the Big Difference?

1. Your teacher will provide prepared slides of eggs and sperm.
2. Examine each slide under the microscope, first under low power, then under high power. Be sure you view at least one sample of egg and sperm from the same species.
3. Sketch and label each sample.

Think It Over

Observing What differences did you observe between sperm cells and egg cells? What general statement can you make about eggs and sperm?

GUIDE FOR READING

- **What are the organs of the male and female reproductive systems?**
- **What events occur during the menstrual cycle?**

Reading Tip **As you read, create a table comparing the male and female reproductive systems. Include the type of sex cells and primary reproductive organs of each.**

Many differences between an adult animal and its young are controlled by the endocrine system. In humans, two endocrine glands—the ovaries in girls and the testes in boys—control many of the changes that occur as a child matures. These glands release hormones that cause the body to develop as a person grows older.

Sex Cells

You may find it hard to believe that you began life as a single cell. That single cell was produced by the joining of two other cells, an egg and a sperm. An **egg** is the female sex cell. A **sperm** is the male sex cell.

The joining of a sperm and an egg is called **fertilization.** Fertilization is an important part of **reproduction,** the process by which living things produce new individuals of the same type. When fertilization occurs, a fertilized egg, or **zygote,** is produced. Every one of the trillions of cells in your body is descended from the single cell that formed during fertilization.

Figure 3 This gosling began its life as a single cell. When it is fully grown, it will be made up of millions of cells.

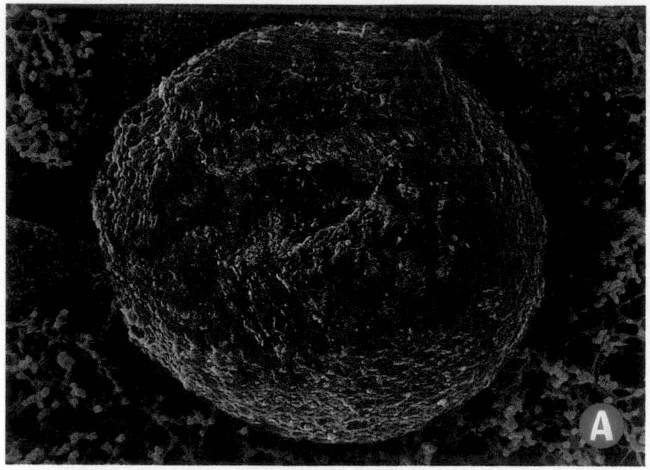

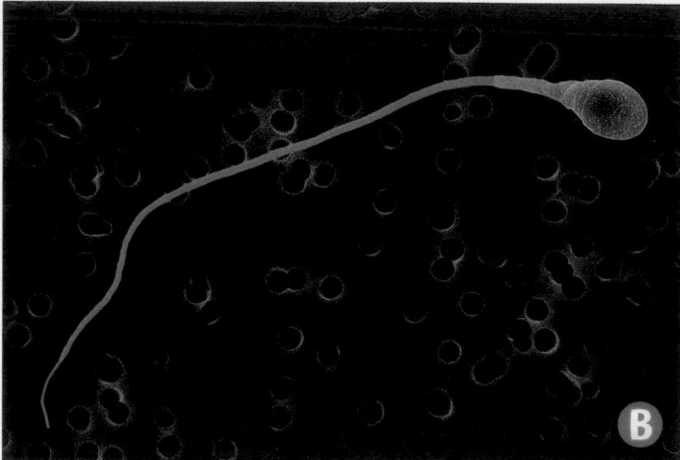

Figure 4 The human reproductive system produces either eggs or sperm. **A.** An egg is one of the largest cells in the body. **B.** A sperm, which is much smaller than an egg, has a tail that allows it to move.

Like other cells in the body, sex cells contain rod-shaped structures called chromosomes. **Chromosomes** (KROH muh sohmz) carry the information that controls inherited characteristics, such as eye color and blood type. Every cell in the human body, except the sex cells, contains 46 chromosomes. Each sex cell contains half that number, or 23 chromosomes. During fertilization, the 23 chromosomes in a sperm join the 23 chromosomes in an egg. The result is a zygote with 46 chromosomes. The zygote contains all of the information needed to produce a new human being.

☑ *Checkpoint* *What happens to the number of chromosomes when a male sex cell and a female sex cell join?*

The Male Reproductive System

The male reproductive system is shown in Figure 5. **The male reproductive system is specialized to produce sperm and the hormone testosterone.**

The Testes The oval-shaped **testes** (tes teez) (singular *testis*) are the organs of the male reproductive system in which sperm are produced. The testes are actually clusters of hundreds of tiny coiled tubes. Sperm are formed inside the tubes.

The testes also produce the hormone **testosterone** (tes TAHS tuh rohn). Testosterone controls the development of physical characteristics in men. Some of those characteristics include facial hair, a deep voice, broad shoulders, and the ability to produce sperm.

Notice in Figure 5 that the testes are located in an external pouch of skin called the **scrotum** (SKROH tum). That external location keeps the testes about 2° to 3°C below the usual body temperature of 37°C. That temperature difference is important. Sperm need the slightly cooler conditions to develop normally.

Sperm Production The production of sperm cells begins in males at some point during the teenage years. Each sperm is composed of a head that contains chromosomes and a long, whiplike tail. Basically, a sperm cell is a tiny package of chromosomes that can swim.

The Path of Sperm Cells Once sperm cells form in the testes, they travel through other structures in the male reproductive system. During this passage, sperm mix with fluids produced by nearby glands. This mix of sperm cells and fluids is called **semen** (SEE mun). Semen contains a huge number of sperm—about 5 to 10 million per drop! The fluids in semen provide an environment in which sperm can swim. Semen also contains nutrients that the moving sperm use as a source of energy.

Semen leaves the body through an organ called the **penis.** The male urethra runs through the penis. The urethra is the tube through which the semen travels as it leaves the body.

Urine also leaves the body through the urethra, as you learned in Chapter 6. When semen passes through the urethra, however, muscles near the bladder contract. Those muscles prevent urine and semen from mixing.

☑ *Checkpoint* *What is a sperm composed of?*

Figure 5 In the male reproductive system, the testes produce sperm and the hormone testosterone. ***Interpreting Diagrams*** *What pathway do sperm follow to reach the urethra?*

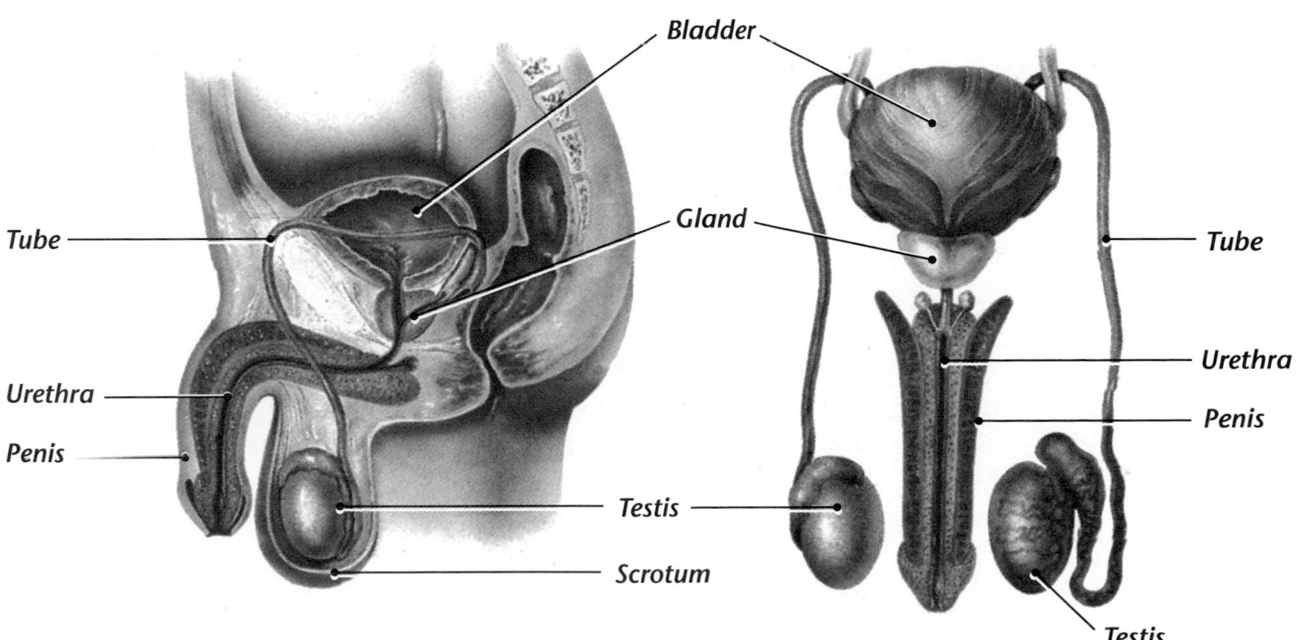

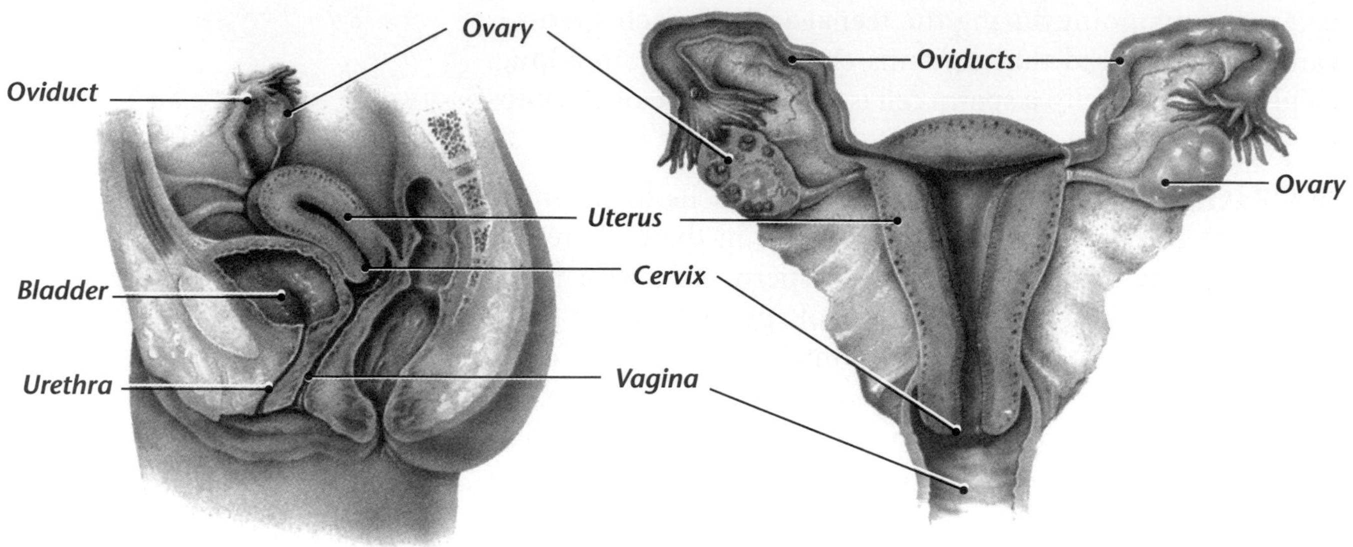

Figure 6 In the female reproductive system, the two ovaries produce eggs and hormones such as estrogen. From an ovary, an egg travels through an oviduct to the uterus. ***Interpreting Diagrams*** *Through what opening does an unfertilized egg pass when leaving the uterus?*

The Female Reproductive System

Unlike the male reproductive system, almost all of the female reproductive system is inside the body. **The role of the female reproductive system is to produce eggs and, if an egg is fertilized, to nourish a developing baby until birth.** The organs of the female reproductive system are shown in Figure 6.

The Ovaries Find the two ovaries in Figure 6. The **ovaries** (OH vuh reez) are located slightly below the waist, one on each side of the body. The name for these organs comes from the word *ova,* meaning "eggs." One major role of the ovaries is to produce egg cells.

Like the testes in males, the ovaries also are endocrine glands that produce hormones. One hormone, **estrogen** (ES truh jun), triggers the development of some adult female characteristics. For example, estrogen causes the hips to widen and the breasts to develop. Estrogen also plays a role in the process by which egg cells develop.

The Path of the Egg Cell As you can see in Figure 6, each ovary is located near an **oviduct** (OH vih duct). The two oviducts are passageways for eggs. They are also the places where fertilization usually occurs. Each month, one of the ovaries releases a mature egg, which enters the nearest oviduct. The egg moves through the oviduct, which leads to the uterus, or womb. The **uterus** (YOO tur us) is a hollow muscular organ about the size of a pear. If the egg has been fertilized, it remains in the uterus and begins to develop.

An egg that has not been fertilized starts to break down as it enters the uterus. It leaves the uterus through an opening at its base called the cervix. The egg then enters the vagina. The **vagina** (vuh JY nuh) is a muscular passageway leading to the outside of the body. The vagina is also called the birth canal. It is the passageway through which a baby leaves the mother's body during the birth process.

☑ *Checkpoint* *What is one of the roles of the ovaries?*

The Menstrual Cycle

When the female reproductive system becomes mature during the teenage years, there are about 400,000 undeveloped eggs in a woman's ovaries. However, only about 500 of those eggs will actually leave the ovaries and reach the uterus. An egg is released about once a month in a mature female's body. The monthly cycle of changes that occurs in the female reproductive system is called the **menstrual cycle** (MEN stroo ul).

During the menstrual cycle, an egg develops in an ovary. At the same time, the uterus prepares for the arrival of a fertilized egg. In this way, the menstrual cycle prepares the female's body for pregnancy, the condition that begins after fertilization has taken place.

Stages of the Cycle The menstrual cycle begins when an egg starts to mature in one of the ovaries. At the same time, the lining of the uterus begins to thicken. About halfway through a typical cycle, the mature egg is released from the ovary into an oviduct. This process is called **ovulation** (OH vyuh lay shun).

Graphing ACTIVITY

A woman's hormone levels change throughout the menstrual cycle. The table below shows the levels of one female hormone, known as LH, during the menstrual cycle.

Day	Level of LH
1	12
5	14
9	14
13	70
17	12
21	12
25	8

Construct a line graph using the information in the table. Label the horizontal axis *Day*. Label the vertical axis *Hormone Level*. What event takes place about the same time that LH reaches its highest level?

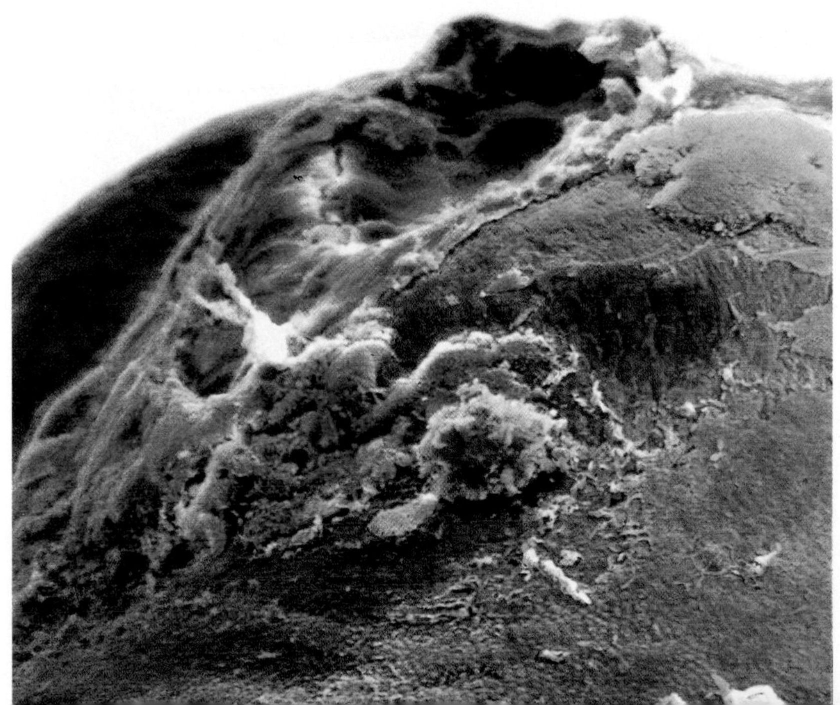

Figure 7 During ovulation an egg bursts from the side of an ovary. In this photograph, the egg is the round red structure on the right.

Once the egg is released, it can be fertilized for the next few days if sperm are present in the oviduct. If the egg is not fertilized, it begins to break down. The lining of the uterus also breaks down. The extra blood and tissue of the thickened lining pass out of the body through the vagina. This process is called **menstruation** (men stroo AY shun). On average, menstruation lasts about 4 to 6 days. At the same time that menstruation occurs, a new egg begins to mature in the ovary, and the cycle continues. You can follow the main steps in the cycle in Figure 8.

Endocrine Control The menstrual cycle is controlled by hormones of the endocrine system. Hormones also trigger a girl's first menstruation. Many girls begin menstruation between the ages of 10 and 14 years. Some girls start earlier, while others start later. Women continue to menstruate until about age 50. At around that age, production of sex hormones drops. As a result, the ovaries stop releasing mature egg cells.

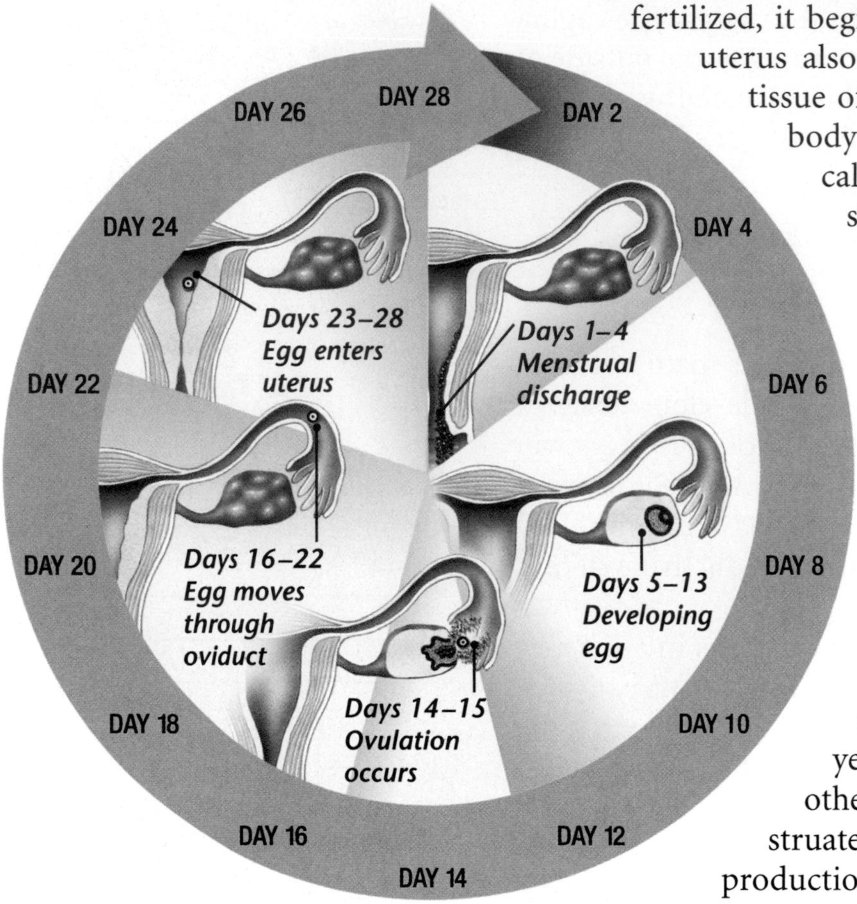

Figure 8 During the menstrual cycle, the lining of the uterus builds up with extra blood and tissue. About halfway through a typical cycle, ovulation takes place. If the egg is not fertilized, menstruation occurs.

Section 2 Review

1. What specialized cells are produced in the male and female reproductive systems?
2. How does the uterus change during the menstrual cycle?
3. How does a sperm's structure help it function?
4. What is ovulation? How often does it occur?
5. **Thinking Critically Comparing and Contrasting** In what ways are the functions of the ovaries and the testes similar? How do their functions differ?

Check Your Progress

CHAPTER PROJECT 9

You should now be caring for your "baby," taking it with you everywhere or arranging for a responsible person to care for it. You or your substitute must continue to perform all the child-care tasks, such as feeding the baby, changing diapers, and playing with the baby. Whenever you travel, you must have a safe method for transporting the baby. Don't forget to make at least two journal entries each day.

Section 3 Pregnancy, Birth, and Childhood

Discover Activity

How Many Ways Does a Child Grow?

1. Compare the two photographs at the left. One shows a baby girl. The other shows the same girl at the age of five.
2. Make two lists—one of the similarities and the other of the differences you see.
3. Compare your lists with those of your classmates.

Think It Over

Observing Based on your observations, list three physical changes that occur in early childhood.

Guide for Reading

- **What are the stages of human development that occur before birth?**
- **What happens during childbirth?**

Reading Tip **As you read, use the headings to outline the events that occur during pregnancy, birth, and childhood.**

An egg can be fertilized during the first few days after ovulation. When sperm are deposited into the vagina, the sperm move through the uterus into the oviducts. If a sperm fertilizes an egg, pregnancy can occur. Then the amazing process of human development begins.

A fertilized egg, or zygote, is no larger than the period at the end of this sentence. Yet after fertilization, the zygote undergoes changes that result in the formation of a new human. **The zygote develops first into an embryo and then into a fetus.** About nine months after fertilization, a baby is born.

The Zygote

After an egg cell and sperm cell join, the zygote moves down the oviduct toward the uterus. During this trip, which takes about four days, the zygote begins to divide. The original cell divides to make two cells, these two cells divide to make four, and so on. Eventually, the growing mass of hundreds of cells forms a hollow ball. The ball attaches to the lining of the uterus. For the next eight weeks or so, the developing human is called an **embryo** (EM bree oh).

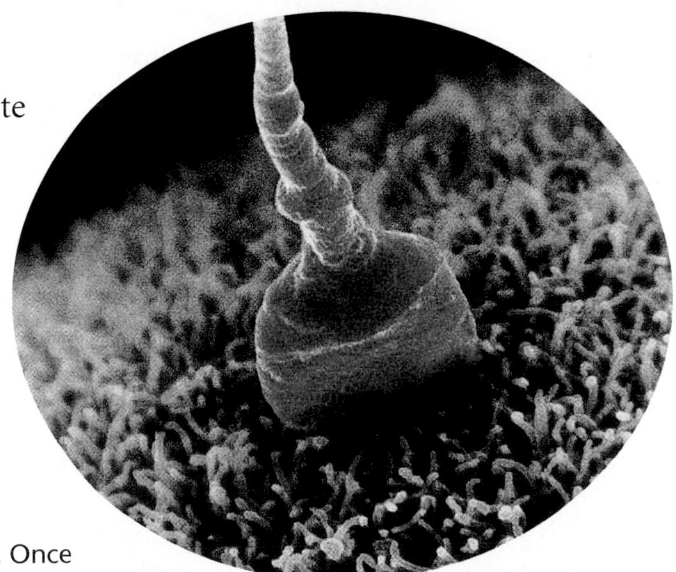

Figure 9 Only one sperm can fertilize an egg. Once fertilization occurs, the process of human development begins.

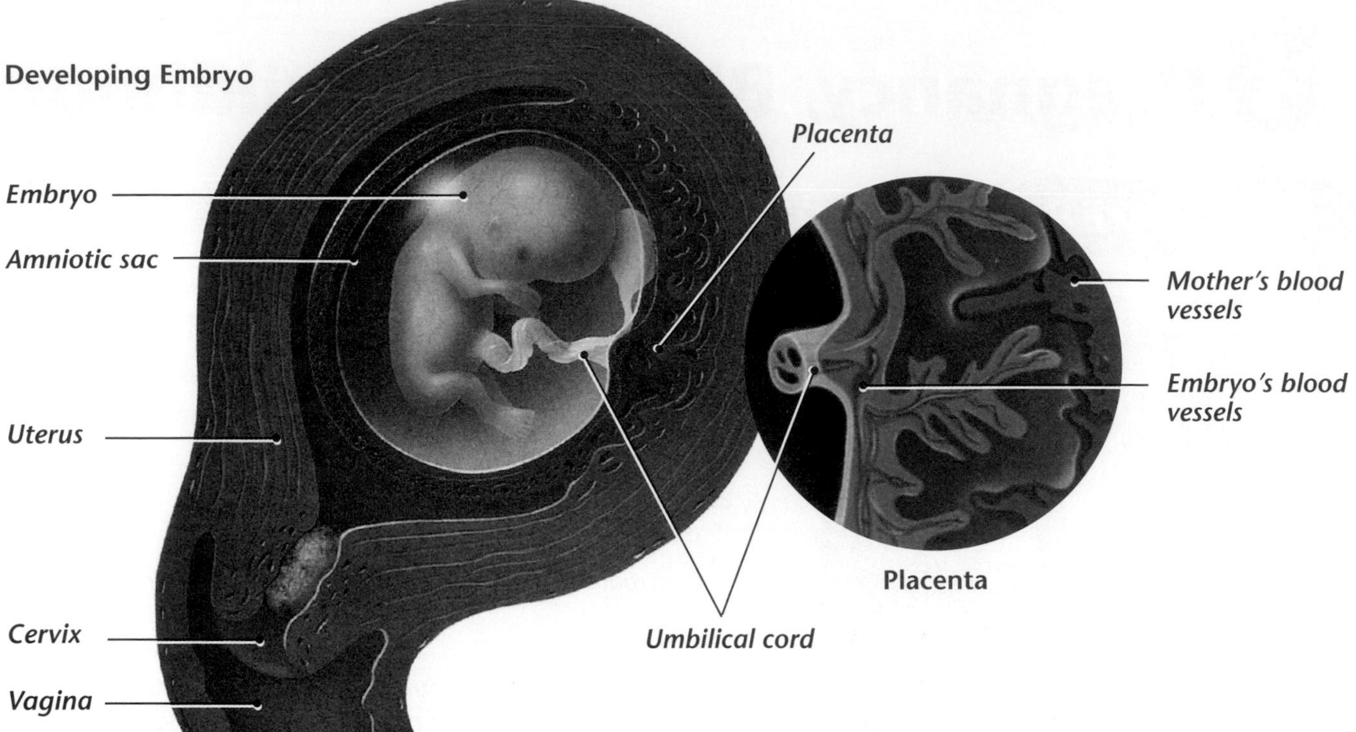

Figure 10 The placenta connects the mother and the developing embryo. But the mother's and the embryo's blood vessels remain separate, as you can see in the closeup of the placenta. ***Interpreting Diagrams*** *What structure carries nutrients and oxygen from the placenta to the embryo?*

The Development of the Embryo

Soon after the embryo attaches to the uterus, many changes take place. The hollow ball of cells grows inward. New membranes form.

One membrane surrounds the embryo and develops into a fluid-filled sac called the **amniotic sac** (am nee AHT ik). Locate the amniotic sac surrounding the embryo in Figure 10. The fluid in the amniotic sac cushions and protects the developing baby.

Another membrane that forms is the **placenta** (pluh SEN tuh). The placenta becomes the link between the embryo and the mother. In the placenta, the embryo's blood vessels are located next to the mother's blood vessels. Blood from the two systems does not mix, but many substances are exchanged. The embryo receives nutrients, oxygen, and other substances from the mother. It gives off carbon dioxide and other wastes.

The embryo soon moves a short distance from the placenta. A ropelike structure called the **umbilical cord** forms between the embryo and the placenta. It contains blood vessels that link the embryo to the mother, but the two circulatory systems remain separated by a thin barrier.

INTEGRATING HEALTH The barrier that separates the embryo's and the mother's blood prevents some diseases from spreading from the mother to the embryo. However, substances such as chemicals in tobacco smoke, alcohol, and some other drugs can pass through the barrier to the embryo. For this reason, pregnant women should not smoke tobacco, drink alcohol, or take any drug without a doctor's approval.

☑ ***Checkpoint*** *How does an embryo obtain oxygen?*

The Development of the Fetus

From the ninth week of development until birth, the embryo is called a **fetus** (FEE tus). Although the fetus starts out about as small as a walnut shell, it now looks more like a baby. Many internal organs have developed. The head is about half the body's total size. The fetus's brain is developing rapidly. It also has dark eye patches, fingers, and toes. By the end of the third month, the fetus is about 9 centimeters long and has a mass of about 26 grams.

Between the fourth and sixth months, the tissues of the fetus continue to develop into more recognizable shapes. Bones become distinct. A heartbeat can be heard with a stethoscope. A layer of soft hair grows over the skin. The arms and legs develop more completely. The fetus begins to move and kick, a sign that its muscles are growing. At the end of the sixth month, the mass of the fetus is approaching 700 grams. Its body is about 20 centimeters long.

The final 3 months prepare the fetus to survive outside the mother's body. The brain surface develops grooves and ridges. The lungs become developed enough to carry out the exchange of oxygen and carbon dioxide. The eyelids can open. Eyelashes and eyebrows grow. The fetus doubles in length. Its mass may reach 3 kilograms or more.

Figure 11 At the beginning of the fourth month of development, a fetus has developed internal organs, portions of the eyes, fingers, and toes. Later, its eyes will open, and fingernails and toenails will form.

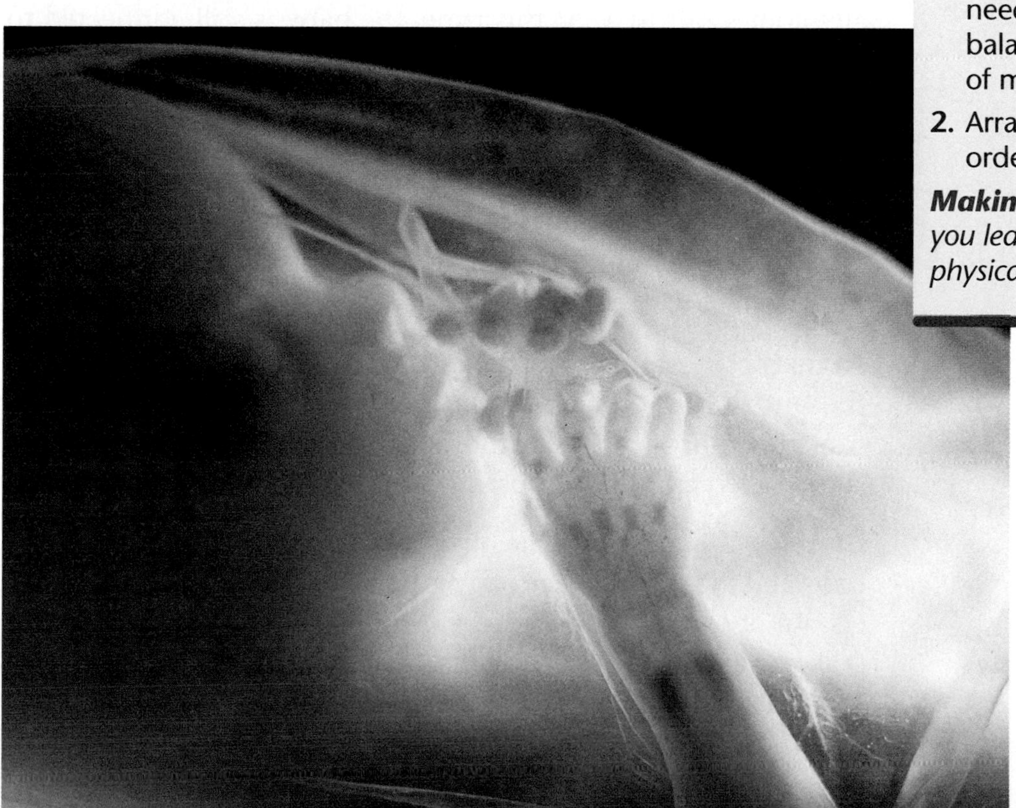

Way to Grow!

ACTIVITY

The table lists the average mass of a developing baby at different months of pregnancy.

Month of Pregnancy	Mass (grams)
1	0.02
2	2.0
3	26
4	150
5	460
6	640
7	1,500
8	2,300
9	3,200

1. Use a balance to identify an everyday object with a mass equal to each mass listed in the table. You may need to use different balances to cover the range of masses listed.
2. Arrange the objects in order by month.

Making Models *What did you learn by gathering these physical models?*

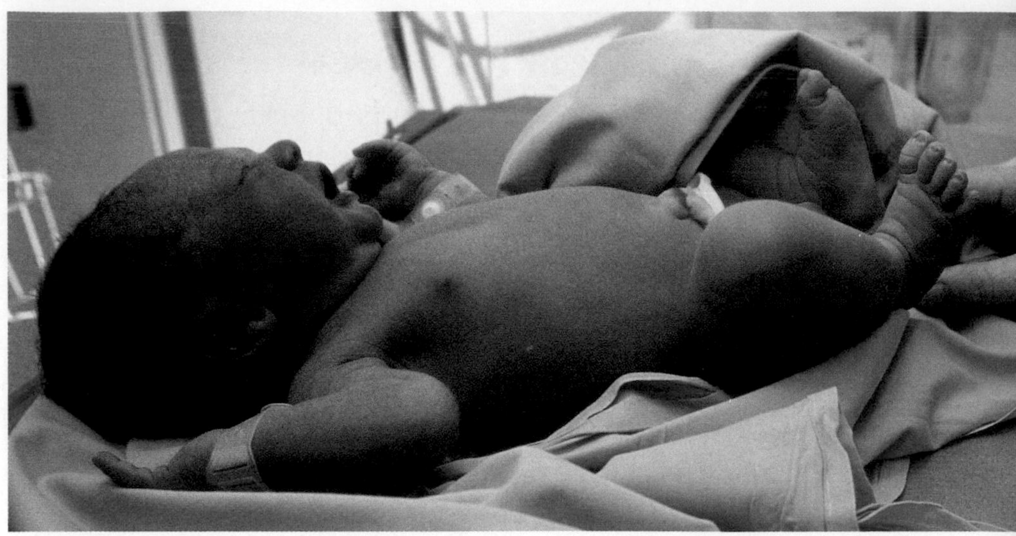

Figure 12 After about 9 months of growth and development inside the uterus, a baby is born. You can see where the umbilical cord of this newborn was clamped and cut.

Birth

After about 9 months of development inside the uterus, the baby is ready to be born. **The birth of a baby takes place in three stages—labor, delivery, and afterbirth.**

Labor During the first stage of birth, strong muscular contractions of the uterus begin. These contractions are called labor. The contractions cause the cervix to enlarge, eventually allowing the baby to fit through the opening. As labor progresses, the contractions become stronger and more frequent. Labor may last from about 2 hours to more than 20 hours.

Delivery The second stage of birth is called delivery. During delivery, the baby is pushed completely out of the uterus, through the vagina, and out of the mother's body. The head usually comes out first. At this time, the baby is still connected to the placenta by the umbilical cord. Delivery usually takes less time than labor does—from several minutes to a few hours.

Shortly after delivery, the umbilical cord is clamped, then cut about five centimeters from the baby's abdomen. Cutting the umbilical cord does not cause the baby any pain. Within 7 to 10 days, the remainder of the umbilical cord dries up and falls off, leaving a scar called the navel, or belly button.

Afterbirth About 15 minutes after delivery, the third stage of the birth process begins. Contractions push the placenta and other membranes out of the uterus through the vagina. This stage, called afterbirth, is usually completed in less than an hour.

Birth and the Baby The birth process is stressful for both the baby and the mother. The baby is pushed and squeezed as it travels out of the mother's body. Contractions put pressure on the placenta and umbilical cord, briefly cutting off the baby's supply of oxygen.

In response to the changes, the baby's endocrine system releases adrenaline. The baby's heart rate increases. Within a few seconds of delivery, a baby may cry or cough. This action helps rid the lungs of fluid and fills them with air. The newborn's heart rate then slows to a steady pace. Blood travels to the lungs and picks up oxygen from the air that the baby breathes in. The newborn's cry helps it adjust to the changes in its surroundings.

☑ *Checkpoint* *What events occur during labor?*

Multiple Births

The delivery of more than one baby from a single pregnancy is called a multiple birth. In the United States, a set of twins is born in about one out of every 90 births. Triplets are born in about one out of every 7,000 births.

There are two types of twins: identical twins and fraternal twins. Identical twins develop from a single fertilized egg, or zygote: Early in development, the embryo splits into two identical embryos. The two embryos have identical inherited traits and are the same sex. Fraternal twins develop when two eggs are released from the ovary and are fertilized by two different sperm. Fraternal twins are no more alike than any other brothers or sisters. Fraternal twins may or may not be the same sex.

Triplets and other multiple births can occur when three or more eggs are produced and fertilized by different sperm. Such births can also occur when an embryo splits into three or more identical embryos.

Sharpen your Skills

Designing Experiments

ACTIVITY

How does the frequency of twins in your school compare to the frequency given in the text? Develop a plan to find out. With your teacher's permission, carry out your plan. Then collect and analyze your data. Of the total number of students, how many are twins? Are your results close to 1 out of 90?

Figure 13 Identical twins (left) develop from the same zygote; they share identical characteristics. Fraternal twins (right) develop from two different fertilized eggs. ***Applying Concepts*** *Why can fraternal twins be different sexes while identical twins cannot?*

Figure 14 During infancy, many physical and mental skills develop. Babies can usually crawl by about seven months of age (left). By the age of two (right), most babies are coordinated enough to feed themselves. ***Making Generalizations*** *What other skills develop during infancy?*

Infancy

What can a newborn baby do? You might say "Not much!" A newborn can perform only simple actions, such as crying, sucking, yawning, and blinking. But during infancy—the first two years of life—babies undergo many changes and learn to do many things.

Physical Changes A baby's shape and size change greatly during infancy. When a baby is born, its head makes up about one fourth of its body length. As the infant develops, its head grows more slowly, and its body, legs, and arms begin to catch up. Its nervous and muscular systems become better coordinated. The baby then starts to develop new physical skills.

The exact ages at which physical skills develop vary from baby to baby. A newborn cannot lift its head. But after about 3 months, it can hold its head up and reach for objects. Within the next 2 months or so, the infant can grasp objects. At about 7 months, most infants can move around by crawling. Somewhere between 10 and 16 months, most infants begin to walk by themselves.

Other Changes How does an infant communicate? You may think that babies display feelings mostly by crying. But young infants can show pleasure by smiling and laughing. They can turn their heads or spit out food they don't like. Babies also begin to make babbling sounds. Sometime between the ages of one and three years, many children speak their first word. By the end of infancy, children can do many things for themselves, such as understand simple directions, feed themselves, and play with toys. However, infants are too young to know when something can hurt them. They must be watched carefully at all times.

Childhood

Infancy ends and childhood begins at about two years of age. Childhood continues until about the age of 13 years. Children gradually become more active and independent, and experience many physical and mental changes.

Physical Changes Throughout childhood, children continue to grow. They become taller and heavier as their bones and muscles increase in size. They become more coordinated as they practice skills such as walking, holding a fork, using a pencil, and playing games. Over a period of several years, baby teeth fall out and are replaced by permanent teeth. Toward the end of childhood, the bones, especially the legs, begin to grow faster. An increased appetite signals that the body needs more nutrients for its next stage of growth and development.

Other Changes As they develop, children show a growing curiosity and increasing mental abilities. Their curiosity helps them learn about their surroundings. With the help of family members and teachers, children learn to read and to solve problems. Language skills improve rapidly. For example, most four-year-olds can express themselves clearly and can carry on conversations.

Over time, children learn to make friends, care about others, and behave responsibly. Between the ages of 3 and 6, they learn to share and play with others. As children think about and care more for others, friends become more important. About the age of 10, children develop a strong wish to fit in with others of their age group. As their independence increases, children take on more responsibilities at home and school.

Figure 15 During childhood, children learn to get along with others. Their physical activities and games help them become stronger and more coordinated.

Section 3 Review

1. What three stages of development does a fertilized egg go through before birth?
2. Briefly describe what happens during each of the three stages of birth.
3. What is the function of the amniotic sac? What is the function of the placenta?
4. List two physical changes that occur during infancy.
5. **Thinking Critically Relating Cause and Effect** Why is it dangerous for a pregnant woman to drink alcohol or to smoke?

Science at Home

Discuss with a family member some of the physical and other changes that take place during infancy and childhood. If possible, find out about some of your own milestones—when you first smiled, walked, or talked, for example. Discuss how these milestones relate to the physical changes that occur at each stage.

INTEGRATING HEALTH 

Section 4 Adolescence—A Time of Change

DISCOVER ACTIVITY

How Do Ads Portray Teenagers?

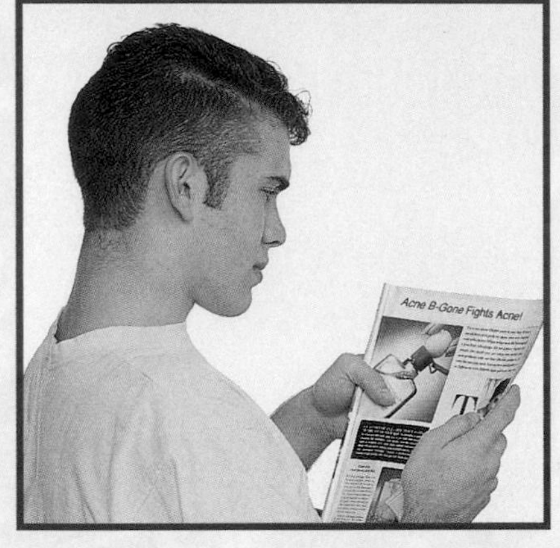

1. Carefully examine an advertisement taken from a teen magazine. The ad should show one or more teenagers. Be sure to read the text and examine the picture.
2. Think about how the ad portrays the teenagers. How do they look and act? Do you think they are typical teens? How accurate is this "picture" of teenagers? Write down your thoughts.

Think It Over

Drawing Conclusions How does the ad use teenagers to try to influence people your age? Explain your opinion. Do you think the ad is effective?

GUIDE FOR READING

- **What is the difference between adolescence and puberty?**
- **What mental and social changes are associated with adolescence?**

Reading Tip **As you read, make a list of the changes that take place during adolescence.**

If you compared a current photo of yourself with one taken three years ago, you would notice many changes. Starting at about the age of 12, you gradually begin to change from a child to an adult. Although many changes happen during infancy and childhood, some of the most significant changes occur during adolescence. **Adolescence** (ad ul ES uns) is the stage of development when children become adults physically and mentally.

By the end of adolescence, you will be able to do things you could not do during childhood. You will become eligible for privileges such as a driver's license and the right to vote. Along

Figure 16 During adolescence, teens mature both physically and mentally. It's a time when many teens try new experiences and take on more responsibilities. Working in the community is one way that teens can explore their interests while helping others.

with these privileges, you will be expected to take on adult responsibilities, such as driving safely. Adolescence is the time to work to become the healthy adult you want to be.

Physical Changes

Adolescence is a time of rapid physical growth. A person grows taller and heavier, and begins to look like an adult. However, some of the most important physical changes take place inside the body. These physical changes are controlled by the hormones of the endocrine system.

Puberty Sometime between the ages of about 9 and 14 years, a child enters puberty. **Puberty** (PYOO bur tee) is the period of sexual development in which the body becomes able to reproduce. Some people think that the term *puberty* is another word for adolescence, but that is not correct. **Adolescence includes more than just the physical changes of puberty. Many important mental and social changes take place as well.**

In girls, hormones produced by the pituitary gland and the ovaries control the physical changes of puberty. The sex organs develop. Ovulation and menstruation begin. The breasts begin to enlarge, and the hips start to widen. The skin begins to produce more oils, and body odor increases.

In boys, hormones from the testes and the pituitary gland govern the changes. The sex organs develop, and sperm production begins. The voice deepens. Hair appears on the face and sometimes on the chest. As with girls, more skin oils are produced, and body odor increases.

Figure 17 Despite their different sizes, each of these teens is developing normally. ***Relating Cause and Effect*** *What body system controls the rate at which changes occur during puberty?*

Bone and Muscle Growth Just as infants and children experience growth spurts, or periods of rapid growth, so do adolescents. Girls tend to experience their growth spurt slightly younger than boys do. Thus, during early adolescence girls tend to be taller than boys. Later in adolescence boys display rapid growth. Overall, boys tend to reach taller adult heights than girls.

Have you ever heard the phrase "growing pains"? Some adolescents grow so rapidly that they experience aches in their arms and legs. A sudden change in height or weight can cause a teen to feel clumsy or awkward at times. It takes time to adjust to a new body size and shape. Regular exercise can help a teen adjust more quickly. Teens should not over-exercise, however, as growing bones and muscles can be injured if overworked.

Another effect rapid growth can produce is hunger. It's normal for teens to go through periods when they eat huge amounts of food. The extra food provides the raw materials and energy required by the growing body. Nutritious meals and snacks can supply the body with the nutrients it needs.

When Puberty Begins As adolescents mature, they may compare their physical development with that of their peers. Teens of the same age can be at different stages of growth. This is because the age at which puberty begins varies from person to person.

These different rates of physical development may lead to misunderstandings. Adolescents whose bodies mature at a younger age may be expected to have adult judgment and take on more responsibilities than other teens. Those whose bodies develop later may face different challenges. They may be treated like children because of their young appearance.

☑ *Checkpoint* *What is a growth spurt?*

Mental and Social Changes

Adolescents may notice changes in the way they think, feel, and get along with others. Many teenagers have mixed feelings about the changes they are experiencing. They may feel excited and happy about them one day, and shy and confused the next day. **Adolescents undergo many mental and social changes as they become more mature.**

Mental Changes Between about the ages of 13 and 15, a teenager gradually becomes able to think and reason like an adult. Teens can think in ways that they could not as children. For example, young children think of hunger only when their stomachs are empty, or of pain only when they are hurt. They don't think beyond what's happening at the moment. Teenagers' thoughts are no longer limited to their immediate experiences. They begin to consider the consequences of their actions and make thoughtful judgments. Memory and problem-solving skills also improve. These and other mental abilities are often developed at school or through interests such as music or theater.

Adolescence is a time when individuals begin to question things that they accepted as children. Adolescents may wonder about the opinions and actions of friends and family members. They may also begin to ask themselves questions such as "Who am I?" and "What will I do with my life?" Often teens find answers by talking with parents, religious leaders, and other adults. Other times teens try out new experiences—from new hairstyles and clothes to volunteering their time to help others.

Social Studies CONNECTION

In many cultures, adolescence is seen as a passage from childhood to adulthood. In the Apache culture, girls who have entered puberty and begun their menstrual cycles undergo the Changing Woman ceremony. Often the whole community enjoys the feasting, dancing, and performances that are part of the ceremony. The girl dresses in a decorated buckskin dress and is sprinkled with cattail pollen. Other parts of the ceremony include fasting followed by special meals and prayer. After the ceremony, the girl is considered a woman by tribal members.

In Your Journal

Imagine you have just witnessed the Changing Woman ceremony. Write a short letter to a friend describing the event. Include information about the significance of the ceremony. Relate the experience to events with which you are familiar.

Figure 18 In the ceremony being celebrated here, tribal members help this 14-year-old Apache girl mark her passage to adulthood.

Figure 19 During the adolescent years, teens place a high value on friendships. ***Making Judgments*** *How can friends help each other develop skills that will be important throughout life?*

Social Changes It is common for adolescents to experience changes in their relationships with others. As they become more independent, teens spend more time with their friends. Because friends' opinions are very important, teens may worry whether friends approve of their clothing, looks, personality, and interests. Some teens may also become interested in members of the opposite sex.

Peer pressure may influence the decisions and actions of teenagers. Peer pressure can produce both negative and positive results. Negative peer pressure can lead teens to do things that go against their values. The support of friends, on the other hand, can encourage teens to work toward their goals or develop new interests and skills.

☑ *Checkpoint* *What social changes occur during adolescence?*

Life as an Adult

At what point does adolescence end and adulthood begin? On a certain birthday? When people are physically mature? When people start to live on their own? If you look up the word *adult* in the dictionary, it is defined as being grown up, or mature. Legally, Americans are considered to be adults at the age of 16 or 18 for some activities and at the age of 21 for others. From a physical and mental standpoint, however, it is difficult to say when adulthood begins.

Physical changes continue to occur throughout adulthood. After about the age of 30, a process known as aging begins. Aging becomes more noticeable between the ages of 40 and 65. The skin starts to become wrinkled, the eyes lose their ability to focus on close objects, the hair may lose its coloring, and muscle strength decreases. During this period, females stop menstruating and ovulating. Males usually continue to produce sperm throughout their lives, although the number of sperm they produce decreases with age.

After age 65, aging intensifies, often leading to less efficient heart and lung action. But the effects of aging can be slowed if people follow sensible diets and good exercise plans. With the help of such healthy behaviors, more and more adults remain active throughout their lives.

Figure 20 Adulthood is a time when opportunities and choices expand. Adults can also share their knowledge and experience with younger people.

Responsibilities—as well as opportunities, rights, and privileges—arrive with adulthood. During adolescence you learn to take care of yourself. Eventually, no one will tell you how to spend your money or what to eat. As an adult, you may need to make decisions that affect not just yourself, but your spouse and your children as well. You will need know what values are important to you, and make decisions that match those values.

Section 4 Review

1. What is the difference between puberty and adolescence? Describe three physical changes that occur in boys and girls during puberty.
2. Name two mental changes and one social change that adolescents experience.
3. Why do adolescents sometimes feel clumsy or awkward?
4. What behaviors can adults practice to slow down the effects of aging?
5. **Thinking Critically Making Judgments** "Developing a sense of who you are is the most important part of adolescence." What does this statement mean? Do you agree with it? Explain.

CHAPTER PROJECT 9

Check Your Progress

By now, you should be preparing a summary of what you learned about being a parent. What skills do parents need? What are some of the rewards of parenthood? What are some of the challenges? How would you feel if you had to continue caring for the "baby" past the project deadline? Write answers to these questions as your final journal entry.

Skills Lab

Interpreting Data

Growing Up

Problem

How do the proportions of the human body change during development?

Procedure

1. Examine the diagram below. Notice that the figures are drawn against a graph showing percents. You can use this diagram to determine how the lengths of major body parts compare to each figure's height. Make a data table in which to record information about each figure's head size and leg length.
2. Look at Figure D. You can use the graph to estimate that the head is about 15% of the figure's full height. Record that number in your data table.
3. Examine Figures A through C. Determine the percent of the total height that the head makes up. Record your results. (*Hint:* Figure A shows the legs folded. You will need to estimate the data for that figure.)
4. Now compare the length of the legs to the total body height for Figures A through D. Record your results.

Analyze and Conclude

1. How do the percents for head size and leg length change from infancy to adulthood?
2. What can you infer about the rate at which different parts of the body grow? Explain.
3. **Think About It** If you made a line graph using the data in the diagram, what would be on the horizontal axis? On the vertical axis? What additional information could you gain from this line graph?

Design an Experiment

Make a prediction about the relationship between the circumference of the head compared to body height. Then design an experiment to test your prediction, using people for test subjects. Obtain your teacher's permission before carrying out the experiment.

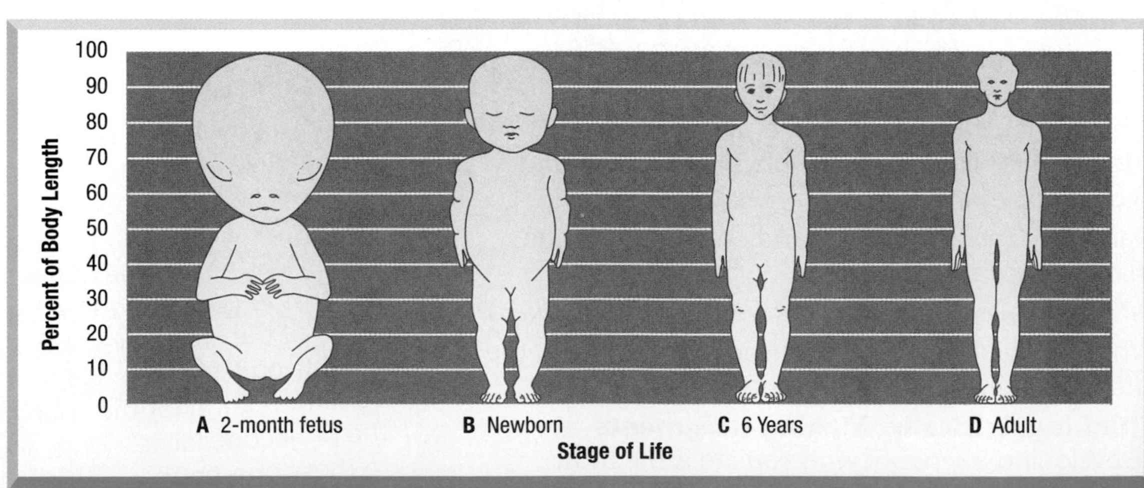

The Endocrine System

Key Ideas

- ◆ The endocrine system controls many of the body's daily activities, as well as the body's overall development.
- ◆ The endocrine system releases chemical messages called hormones. Hormones travel through the bloodstream to their target organs.
- ◆ Homeostasis in the body is maintained partly through negative feedback: the right amount of a particular hormone signals the body to stop producing that hormone.

Key Terms

endocrine gland
hormone
target cell
hypothalamus
pituitary gland
negative feedback

The Male and Female Reproductive Systems

Key Ideas

- ◆ The male reproductive system is specialized to produce sperm and the hormone testosterone.
- ◆ The role of the female reproductive system is to produce eggs and to nourish a developing baby until birth.
- ◆ Eggs are produced in the ovaries of the female. During the menstrual cycle, an egg develops, and the uterus prepares for the arrival of a fertilized egg.

Key Terms

egg
sperm
fertilization
reproduction
zygote
chromosome
testis
testosterone
scrotum
semen
penis
ovary
estrogen
oviduct
uterus
vagina
menstrual cycle
ovulation
menstruation

The Human Life Cycle

INTEGRATING HEALTH

Key Ideas

- ◆ If an egg is fertilized, pregnancy begins. The zygote develops into an embryo and then a fetus.
- ◆ A fetus develops inside the mother's uterus for about 9 months before it is born. Birth takes place in three stages—labor, delivery, and afterbirth.
- ◆ Infancy is a time of rapid physical growth and mastery of basic skills. During childhood, children become more independent.
- ◆ Adolescence includes the physical changes of puberty as well as mental and social changes.
- ◆ Puberty is the period of sexual development in which the body becomes able to reproduce.

Key Terms

embryo
amniotic sac
placenta
umbilical cord
fetus
adolescence
puberty
peer pressure

Organizing Information

Flowchart Copy this flowchart and fill in the main stages that occur between fertilization and birth. (For more on flowcharts, see the Skills Handbook.)

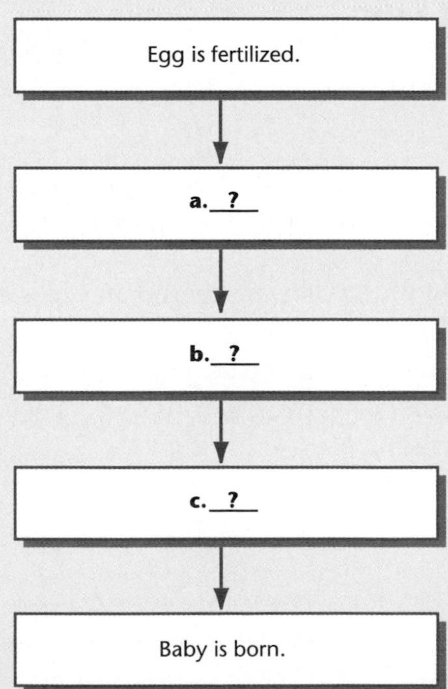

CHAPTER 9 ASSESSMENT

Reviewing Content

Multiple Choice

Choose the letter of the best answer.

1. Which structure links the nervous system and the endocrine system?
a. pituitary gland
b. adrenal gland
c. parathyroid gland
d. hypothalamus

2. What is the male sex cell called?
a. testis **b.** sperm
c. egg **d.** ovary

3. The release of an egg from an ovary is known as
a. ovulation.
b. fertilization
c. menstruation.
d. afterbirth.

4. Two individuals that develop from the same zygote are called
a. embryos.
b. fraternal twins.
c. identical twins.
d. triplets.

5. Sex organs develop rapidly during
a. infancy. **b.** childhood.
c. puberty. **d.** adulthood.

True or False

If the statement is true, write true. If it is false, change the underlined word or words to make the statement true.

6. The <u>pituitary</u> gland produces adrenaline.

7. The female reproductive glands are the <u>ovaries</u>.

8. The joining of a sperm and an egg is called <u>fertilization</u>.

9. An <u>oviduct</u> is the passageway through which an egg travels from the ovary to the uterus.

10. The physical changes of adolescence are controlled by the <u>nervous</u> system.

Checking Concepts

11. What is the function of the hypothalamus in the body?

12. When enough thyroxine has been released into the blood, what signal is sent to the thyroid gland? How is that signal sent?

13. What changes occur in the uterus during the menstrual cycle?

14. What is a zygote and how does it form? What happens to the zygote about four days after it forms?

15. Describe how a fetus receives food and oxygen and gets rid of wastes.

16. Summarize the physical changes that take place during infancy.

17. List six changes a ten-year-old boy should expect to occur in the next five years. Include physical, mental, and social changes.

18. Writing to Learn Imagine you're a skeleton in the body of a sixteen-year-old person. Write about the changes you've experienced since infancy.

Thinking Critically

19. Inferring The pancreas produces insulin, a hormone that lowers the level of sugar in the blood. Glucagon, another hormone of the pancreas, increases the level of sugar in the blood. Suggest how these two hormones might work together to maintain homeostasis in the body.

20. Applying Concepts In what ways is the functioning of the endocrine system similar to the way in which a heating system works? What part of the endocrine system functions like the heating system's thermostat? Explain.

21. Relating Cause and Effect How can playing games help children develop important skills?

22. Comparing and Contrasting In what way is development during adolescence similar to development before birth? How are the two stages different?

Applying Skills

The data table below shows how the length of a developing baby changes during pregnancy. Use the table to answer Questions 23–25.

Week of Pregnancy	Average Length (mm)	Week of Pregnancy	Average Length (mm)
4	7	24	300
8	30	28	350
12	75	32	410
16	180	36	450
20	250	38	500

23. **Measuring** Use a metric ruler to mark each length on a piece of paper. During which four-week period did the greatest increase in length occur?
24. **Graphing** Graph the data by plotting time on the horizontal axis and length on the vertical axis.
25. **Interpreting Data** At the twelfth week, a developing baby measures about 75 mm. By which week has the fetus grown to four times that length? Six times that length?

Performance Assessment — Chapter Project 9

Project Wrap Up You now have the chance to discuss what you learned as you cared for your "baby." What do you now know about parenting that you didn't know before? Consider reading passages from your journal to the class, including the summary you wrote.

Reflect and Record In your journal, describe how well you carried out this project. Did you care for the baby for three complete days? Did you do each task as carefully as you would have for a real infant? How do you think this project was similar to caring for a real baby? How was it different?

Test Preparation

Use these questions to prepare for standardized tests.

Study the graph. Then answer Questions 26–29.

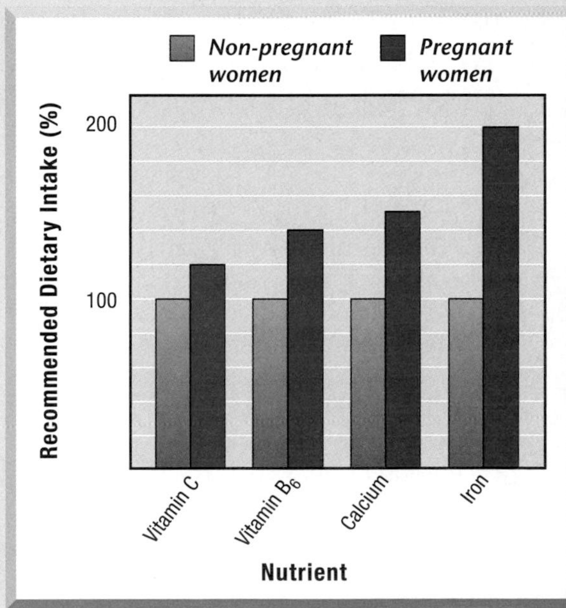

26. What would be the best title for this graph?
    a. Nutrient Needs of Pregnant Women
    b. Recommended Dietary Intake
    c. Vitamin Needs of Pregnant Women
    d. Mineral Needs of Non-pregnant Women
27. How much more iron does a pregnant woman need than a non-pregnant woman?
    a. 20% **b.** 100%
    c. 120% **d.** 150%
28. If non-pregnant adult women normally need 800 mg of calcium a day, how much calcium do pregnant women need?
    a. 800 mg **b.** 1,000 mg
    c. 1,200 mg **d.** 1,600 mg
29. Which nutrient do pregnant women need in the greatest amount?
    a. vitamin C
    b. vitamin B_6
    c. iron
    d. can't tell from the information in this graph

NATURE OF SCIENCE

Finding a Balance in NUTRITION

Nutritionist Alex Martinez's first experiment in science was on himself. Alex says that when he was growing up, he was quite chubby. Then as a high school freshman he began to play football and run track.

"My weight really hindered my athletic performance," he says. "It was very hard to turn down good cooking. But I knew if I wanted to get in shape, my eating habits would have to change." So Alex decided to change his diet by cutting back on fried foods and eating more fruits and vegetables. He also tried eating rice and chicken instead of beef, and he exercised.

"I became the subject of my own lab test, experimenting with different foods," Alex says. "And I could see the results. I lost weight and had more energy and endurance. I could run longer distances, and sometimes even passed my friends down the home stretch in the 100-yard dash. I felt a lot better about myself."

Alex Martinez, a Mexican American, grew up in New Mexico. He has a degree in nutrition and food science from New Mexico State University. He works as a roving health instructor, traveling to different cities in New Mexico to teach people about nutrition. An outdoor enthusiast, Alex spends his free time in the mountains—hiking, bicycling, and rock climbing.

That experience inspired Alex to pursue a career in nutrition, studying how the body uses food to grow and produce energy. Today, Alex is a nutritionist and health educator in New Mexico.

"For me, food is a science," Alex says. "Most people don't think of it that way. But food causes chemical reactions in the body. And those reactions all have specific effects."

Alex plans nutritious diets for people. At a camp for diabetic children, he helped young people plan diets to keep their blood sugar levels balanced. Currently he speaks to parent and student groups about healthy eating habits. He believes that eating right is not hard.

"There's no such thing as good food and bad food," Alex says. "All foods are good. We just have to balance them in our lives."

Talking With Alex Martinez

Q ***How did you become interested in nutrition?***

A When I was training for track and football as a teen, I did a lot of reading about the right things to eat. My coaches were always talking about proper nutrition for athletes. When I found out there were college programs in nutrition, I knew that's what I wanted to study.

Q ***How much science is involved in nutrition?***

A Quite a lot. I studied chemistry, biology, and human physiology. I learned how the body works—what allows me to run down the street, and how my body converts food into energy. Good nutrition is the starting point for this energy.

Q ***Why should young people be concerned about nutrition?***

A Two reasons: Around the age of 11 or 12, teens start to go through growth spurts. A good, balanced diet is critically important to meet the demands of a changing body. Also, the habits young people develop at an early age stay with them for the rest of their life. If they want to be healthy when they grow up, they should be developing healthy eating habits right now.

Exercising (top) and eating a variety of nutritious foods (left) are keys to good health.

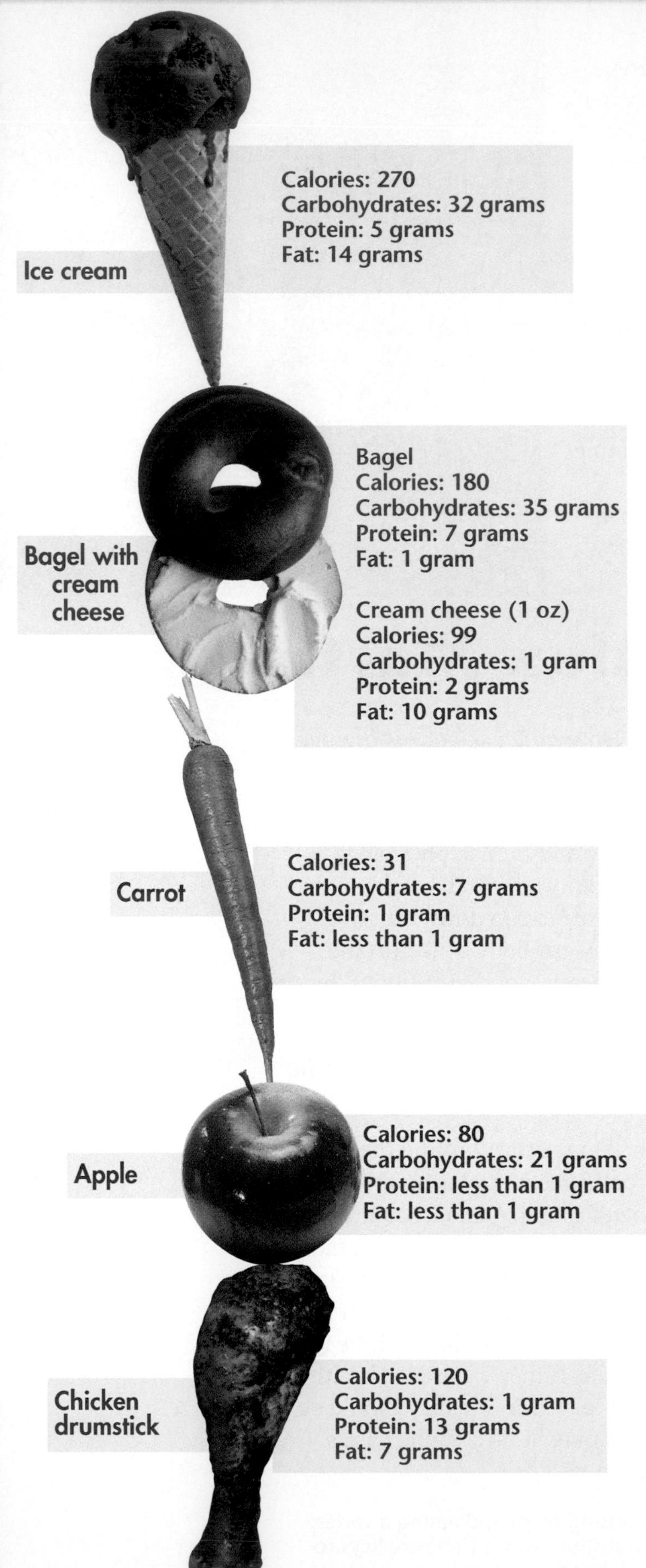

Q ***What ingredients in foods are important to teens?***

A Iron is very important for developing muscles and for helping to carry oxygen through the bloodstream. Without enough iron, people may feel overly tired. Calcium is also important. It plays a critical role in strong bone development. It's especially important for teenage girls to build strong bones. Later in life, women's bones tend to break more easily.

Q ***What about fat?***

A Fat is very important. It helps regulate hormones and vitamin absorption. But there are good fats and bad fats. Too many saturated fats, like those found in steak or hamburger, aren't good for people. Monounsaturated fats, found in foods such as nuts, are much healthier.

Q ***Is sugar important?***

A Yes, although like fat, people tend to eat too much of it. Sugar is a kind of carbohydrate. It's a person's primary energy source. But people shouldn't get sugar from candy bars and soda. Those are simple carbohydrates, low in nutrition. It's better to get sugar from foods such as fruits. They contain vitamins and minerals in addition to sugars.

Q ***Are there specific foods that young people should avoid?***

A My philosophy is that people can eat almost anything they want, as long as they balance it out. If they're dying for a hamburger and french fries one day, there's nothing wrong with that. They just have to balance it the next day by eating fruits and vegetables, and by getting more exercise.

Fresh fruits are good sources of carbohydrates, vitamins, and minerals.

Q ***What kinds of problems can an unbalanced diet create?***

A I'll give you an example. A patient of mine loves ice cream—she eats it all the time. Her diet was really high in fat and lacking in a lot of vitamins and minerals. She wasn't overweight. But she was always feeling tired.

Q ***What did you recommend?***

A I suggested that she eat less ice cream and instead add more natural sources of carbohydrates, such as grains, cereal, and fruit. She could still eat the same number of Calories, but from different, healthier sources.

Q ***How do you determine the proper diet for a person?***

A I use a formula based on age, weight, and a person's activity level to calculate the caloric intake—how much the person should eat every day. Then I try to get an idea about what he or she is already eating. Gradually I help the person convert to a healthy balance of about 60 percent carbohydrates and 30 percent fat.

Q ***Why is exercise important?***

A Every Calorie we take in, we have to burn off—otherwise, it stays around our hips and waist, especially when we get older. Also, exercising releases endorphins, a substance in our body that makes us feel good. Exercise keeps us healthy and feeling good about ourselves.

Q ***What goal should people set?***

A The goal is to be healthy. We can't all be professional athletes. But we can try to eat right and stay fit. And as long as we're trying, that makes a world of difference.

In Your Journal

Alex describes how his personal experiences influenced his career choice. Think about how experiences growing up can help a person choose a career many years later. Describe an experience in your life that might influence your career choice in the future.

CHAPTER 10

Chemical Reactions

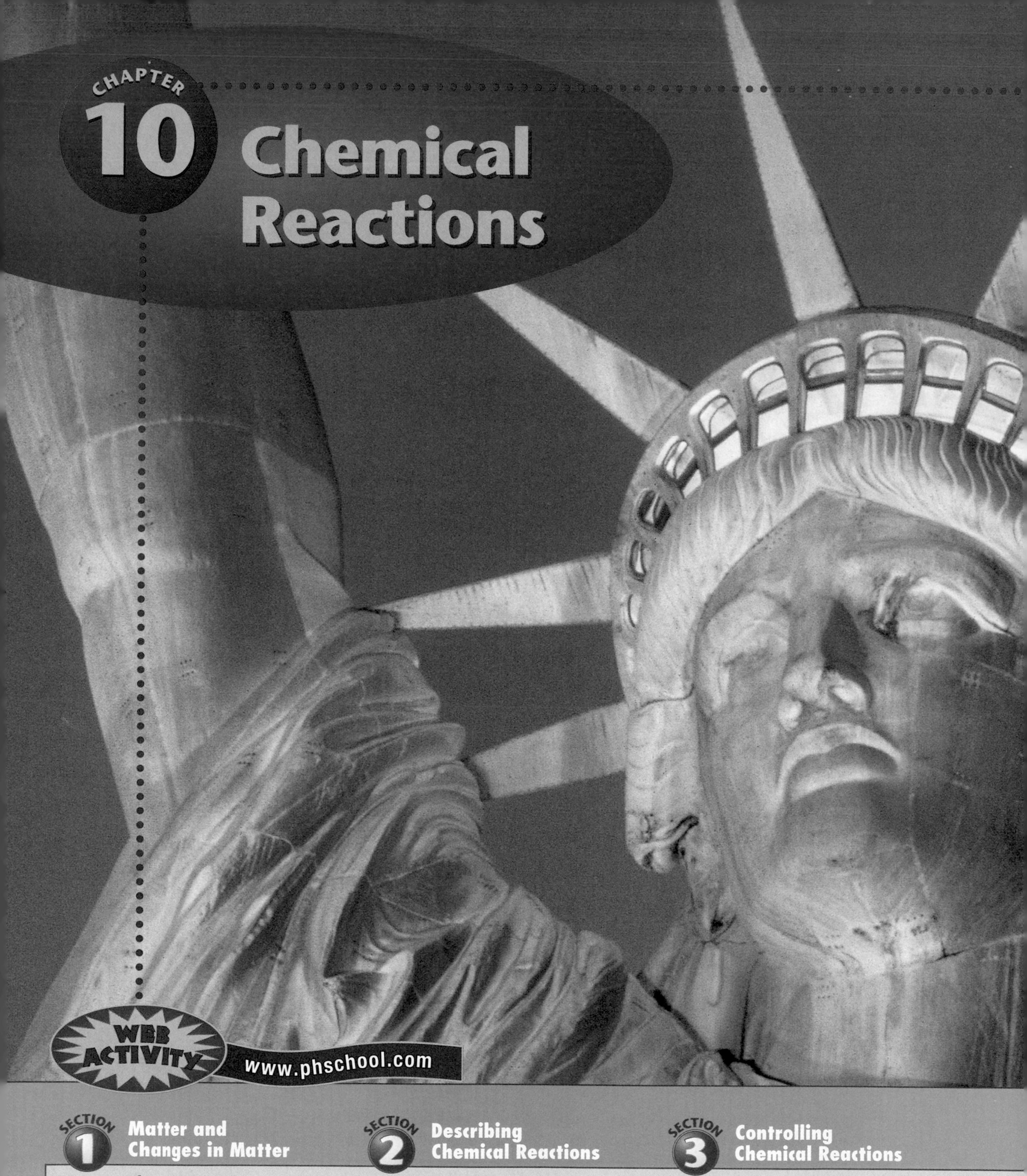

WEB ACTIVITY www.phschool.com

SECTION 1 Matter and Changes in Matter

Discover **What Happens When Chemicals React?**
Try This **Mostly Cloudy**
Skills Lab **Where's the Evidence?**

SECTION 2 Describing Chemical Reactions

Discover **Do You Lose Anything?**
Try This **Still There**
Sharpen Your Skills **Calculating**

SECTION 3 Controlling Chemical Reactions

Discover **Can You Speed Up or Slow Down a Reaction?**
Sharpen Your Skills **Interpreting Data**
Real-World Lab **Peroxide, Catalase, and You!**

PROJECT 10

Keep a Chemical Change Log

Look around. All sorts of changes are taking place. Some changes involve growth. For example, you and your classmates are growing. Other changes produce something that wasn't there before. A factory turns raw materials into desirable products, for instance. Rust coats the surface of a once-silvery fence. Even the green color of the Statue of Liberty comes from a change to the statue's copper metal covering. All of these changes are the result of chemical reactions, or changes in which substances react to form new substances.

In this chapter, you will learn more about the changes in matter that result from chemical reactions. Your project involves keeping a log of chemical changes occurring around you.

Your Goal To identify and observe chemical changes in your daily life and to record evidence for those changes.

To complete the project you must

- determine what evidence indicates that a chemical change has taken place
- record observations of the different chemical changes you notice in your life during one week
- classify the types of chemical changes you observe
- follow the safety guidelines in Appendix A

Get Started Begin by previewing the chapter to learn what a chemical change is. With a group, discuss some changes you observe regularly. Try to decide if each change is a chemical change.

Check Your Progress You'll be working on this project as you study this chapter. To keep your project on track, look for Check Your Progress boxes at the following points.

Section Review 1, page 325: List evidence of chemical changes.

Section Review 2, page 335: Construct a table for observations.

Wrap Up At the end of the chapter (page 351), you will compare your table of chemical changes with those of your classmates and classify the changes.

Integrating Health

SECTION 4 **Fire and Fire Safety**

Discover **How Does Baking Soda Affect a Fire?**

The copper-covered Statue of Liberty has stood in Upper New York Bay for more than 100 years.

Matter and Changes in Matter

DISCOVER — ACTIVITY

What Happens When Chemicals React?

1. Put on your safety goggles.
2. Put 2 teaspoons of baking soda into a clear plastic cup.
3. Holding the cup over a large bowl or sink, add about 125 mL of vinegar. Swirl the cup gently.
4. Observe any changes to the material in the cup. Feel the outside of the cup. What do you notice about the temperature?
5. Carefully fan some air over the liquid toward you. What does the mixture smell like?

Think It Over

Observing Looking at an experiment is not the only way to get information. Your other senses can be equally useful in making observations. What changes did you detect using your senses of smell and touch?

GUIDE FOR READING

- **What simple substances make up matter?**
- **How can you tell a chemical reaction has occurred?**
- **What happens to chemical bonds in chemical reactions?**

Reading Tip **As you read, use the headings of the section to make an outline describing matter and its changes.**

A jet sits on the runway, waiting to fly across the ocean. On a signal from the control tower, the pilot eases the plane forward. Suddenly there is a rumbling sound. The plane starts to shake and picks up speed. Passengers looking out the window watch the runway zip by as the jet moves faster and faster. Suddenly the jet is off the ground. As the thrust of the engines shoots the plane into the air, the passengers feel as though they are being pushed back into their seats.

The jet's giant engines move matter from one city to another. **Matter** is anything that has mass and takes up space. The jet, and the people and the baggage on it, are forms of matter. In fact, everything you can see, taste, touch, or smell is matter.

Inside the jet's powerful engines, the energy needed for the flight comes from changes in the matter that makes up the fuel supply. When the fuel reacts with oxygen from the air, new materials are made and tremendous amounts of energy are released. The release of this energy moves the huge jet fast enough to keep it in the air and speeding on its way.

Chemistry is the study of the properties of matter and how matter changes. Some changes are spectacular, like those in the engines that power a jet. Others are as quiet as a cake baking in an oven. But however dramatic or calm a change is, it always involves matter.

◀ **The engines of this jet get their energy from chemical changes.**

Figure 1 A geodesic dome, a bridge, and a skyscraper are all made from steel, but their appearances and uses are very different.

Building Blocks of Matter

Take an imaginary walk through your city or town and notice all the buildings. Their shapes, sizes, and uses are very different. You would never confuse a doghouse with an airport terminal or a gas station with a 50-story office tower. But they are all constructed of a few kinds of materials. Bricks, wood, glass, stone, concrete, and steel are some of the most common building materials. Using these materials, people have built many different structures. No two are exactly alike.

Elements Just as many different buildings are made from just a few kinds of materials, all the different kinds of matter in the universe are made from about 100 different substances, called elements. An **element** is a substance that cannot be broken down into any other substances by chemical or physical means.

You have seen some elements in their pure form in the world around you. Examples include aluminum in foil, carbon in the form of graphite pencil lead, copper that coats pennies, and tungsten that composes the wire that glows in a light bulb. **All the matter around you is composed of one element or a combination of two or more elements.**

Math TOOLBOX

Ratios

A ratio compares two numbers. It tells you how much you have of one item in comparison to how much you have of another. For example, a recipe for cookies calls for 2 cups of flour for every 1 cup of sugar. You can write the ratio of flour to sugar as:

2 to 1 or 2 : 1

The elements in a compound are present in a specific ratio. If two compounds contain the same elements in different ratios, they are different compounds.

Compounds Most elements are not found in their pure form in nature. They are more likely found as parts of compounds. A **compound** is a substance made of two or more elements chemically combined in a specific ratio, or proportion. For example, the carbon dioxide gas (CO_2) you breathe out of your lungs is made of carbon atoms and oxygen atoms in a 1 to 2 ratio (one part carbon to two parts oxygen).

You use many compounds every day. The sugar that makes juice taste sweet, the water you drink when you're thirsty, and the cavity-fighting ingredient in your toothpaste are all compounds made from different combinations of elements.

Sugar, for example, is made of the elements carbon, hydrogen, and oxygen. Think about the white crystals in a sugar bowl. Do they seem much like the black powdery carbon of pencil lead, and colorless hydrogen and oxygen gases? When elements combine to make a compound, the resulting compound has properties that are different from the elements.

Mixtures Most matter you find in your environment occurs as parts of mixtures. A **mixture** consists of two or more pure substances—elements, compounds, or both—that are in the same place but are not chemically combined. Unlike in a compound, the parts of a mixture may be present in varying ratios. Soil, for example, can be any combination of sand, clay, water, and other materials. Yet it is still soil. Also, the different parts of a mixture keep their individual properties. You can easily distinguish the many parts of a handful of soil just by looking closely at it.

In some mixtures the individual substances are not easily seen. A **solution** is a well-mixed mixture. If you have ever tasted sea water, you know the salt is present even though you can't see it in the water. But if you let a glass of salt water sit on a sunny windowsill for a few days, the water evaporates and only the salt remains. When the salt and water mix, they are still salt and water. No new materials form.

☑ ***Checkpoint*** *Why can you call elements the building blocks of matter?*

Figure 2 Some items in this picture are made of compounds, while others are mixtures. ***Applying Concepts*** *What do the compositions of all these items have in common?*

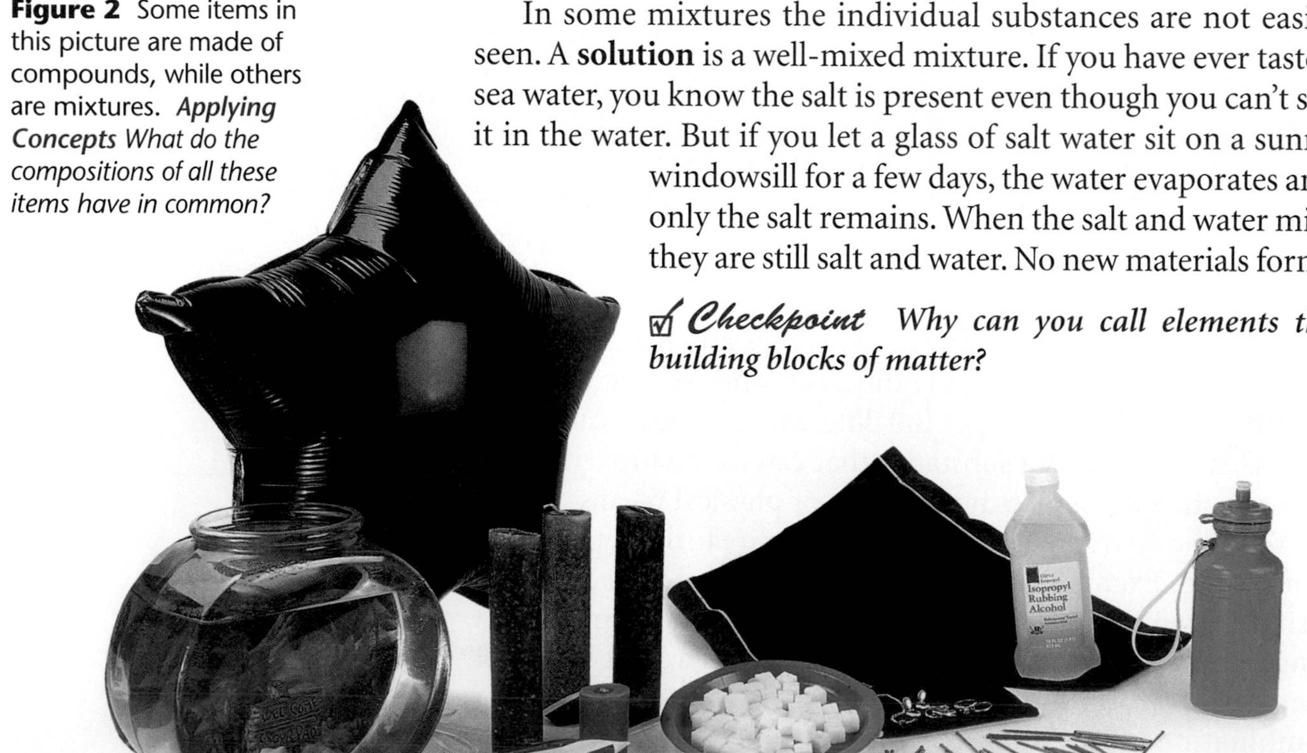

Changes in Matter

Chemistry is not just the study of kinds of matter but also of the changes in matter. Clouds, a plant seed, gasoline in a lawn mower engine, a book of matches—all of these are examples of matter. All of them are useful. They are useful as a result of the changes they undergo.

Figure 3 Matter commonly exists in three different forms, or states. ***Interpreting Photographs*** *Name two states of water shown in this photograph. Which state of water is invisible?*

Physical Change Not all changes produce different material. A change that alters the form or appearance of a material but does not convert the material into new substances is called a **physical change.**

When you think about water in its different forms, you are thinking about physical changes. When it is cooled in a freezer or at the cold regions of Earth, liquid water becomes solid ice. You can change ice to liquid water by leaving an ice cube on your kitchen counter. If it is heated on your stove or by the energy of the sun, liquid water becomes an invisible gas called water vapor. When water vapor becomes liquid again, it returns to the ground as rain. These are all physical changes. Water is still the same substance in all three forms. It is still made of two parts hydrogen and one part oxygen (H_2O).

Chemical Change A change in matter that forms one or more new substances is called a **chemical change.** The new substances are made of the same elements as the original substance, but are now in different combinations. Elements and compounds rearrange to make new materials. Elements may combine to make compounds, compounds may be broken down into elements, or compounds may change into other compounds.

Think about elements and compounds as if they were letters and words. Every word is made of specific letters in a certain combination. Likewise, every compound is made of specific elements in a certain combination. A physical change is like printing the same word in a different style of type:

stampedes → *stampedes*

A chemical change, or **chemical reaction,** is like scrambling the letters of a word to make new words:

stampedes → **made** + **steps**

Figure 4 Over time, the surface of a polished bronze statue darkens as it reacts with oxygen in air.

Examples of chemical reactions are commonplace in your life. Rusting turns the strong iron metal of a car body into iron oxide, a compound you can easily knock a hole through. When wood burns, the compounds that make up the wood combine with oxygen in the air to make carbon dioxide and water.

☑ ***Checkpoint*** *How is a physical change different from a chemical change?*

Observing Chemical Reactions

Imagine you are toasting marshmallows over a campfire. You use your senses to detect chemical changes. You see the burning logs change from a hard solid to a pile of soft ash. You hear popping and hissing sounds as gases produced by the reaction cause the wood to expand. You smell the smoke. You feel the heat. You even taste the results of one chemical change. The brown surface and gooey interior of the toasted marshmallow is a big change from the soft, white marshmallow just out of its bag.

You can detect many chemical reactions by observing changes in the properties of the materials, or matter, involved. Such changes result when new substances form. But how can you tell when a new substance is present? Sometimes a gas is produced, which you might see as bubbles in a liquid. Other times, a solid may appear when two solutions are mixed. A solid that forms from solution during a chemical reaction is called a **precipitate** (pree SIP uh tayt). Still other times, a color change or a change in other properties may tell you that a new substance has formed.

All of these kinds of evidence are good indicators of a chemical reaction. But they do not necessarily mean that a chemical reaction has taken place. Sometimes physical changes give similar results. Take, for example, the changes to water described earlier. When water boils, gas bubbles form. When water freezes, solid ice crystals appear. The properties of solid, liquid, and gaseous water differ also. Ice is a hard, sometimes milky white, brittle solid. Liquid water is clear and colorless. Some of the properties differ, but water vapor, ice, and liquid water all are made of hydrogen and oxygen in a 2 to 1 ratio. **The key characteristic of a chemical reaction is the production of new materials that are chemically different from the starting materials.**

Mostly Cloudy

How can you tell if a chemical reaction is taking place?

1. Put on your safety goggles and apron.
2. Pour about 5 mL of limewater into a plastic cup.
3. Pour an equal amount of plain water into another plastic cup.
4. Add about 5 mL of carbonated water to each of the cups.

Inferring In which cup do you think a chemical reaction occurred? What evidence supports your inference?

EXPLORING Evidence for Chemical Reactions

Chemical reactions produce new substances. The signs of a reaction vary, but many reactions include one or more of the following types of evidence.

Precipitation Two clear solutions react when mixed, forming a red precipitate. The presence of the precipitate tells you a new substance has formed. So you know a chemical change has taken place.

Color Change A color change often is a sign that a chemical reaction has occurred. The brilliant colors of fall foliage result when green chlorophyll in leaves breaks down. Then colors of other substances in the leaves become visible.

Gas Production Oxygen bubbles formed during photosynthesis collect on the leaves of this underwater plant. Oxygen is a product of the reaction between carbon dioxide and water inside the cells of the plant.

Changes in Temperature The burning of natural gas (a chemical reaction) supplies heat to boil water (a physical change). An increase or decrease in temperature can result from the changes in energy during a chemical reaction.

Changes in Properties Baking turns flour, water, and other ingredients into light, flaky bread. The loaf of bread with its crunchy crust has very different properties from the soft dough that went into the oven.

Chemical Reactions on a Small Scale

If you walk along a beach, you leave footprints in the sand. Over time, the incoming tide erases them. A beach is constantly changing, as each wave carries new sand in from the ocean and takes some of the shore sand back with it. Sometimes a violent storm can change the outline of a shore in just a few hours, but mostly the beach is changed by wind and water moving sand a little at a time.

Chemical reactions also occur one small step at a time. When you observe evidence of a chemical change, you are detecting the combined effect of countless small, invisible changes. These changes involve tiny particles of matter.

Atoms and Molecules The matter you see is made of particles you can't see. The smallest particle of an element is an **atom.** All the atoms of an element have the same chemical properties, and these are different from the properties of atoms of other elements. Atoms are unbelievably small. One grain of sand on a beach contains more atoms than there are sand grains on the entire beach!

A **molecule** is a particle made of two or more atoms bonded together. Some molecules are made of atoms that are all alike, as in the oxygen gas (O_2) that you breathe. Most molecules, though, are made of more than one type of atom. Water molecules have 2 hydrogen atoms combined with 1 oxygen atom (H_2O).

Figure 5 The sandy cliffs protecting this lighthouse from the ocean have been worn away as wind and water shifted sand one tiny grain at a time. Moving one piece of sand on a large beach doesn't make a change you can see, but moving billions of pieces changes the shoreline forever.

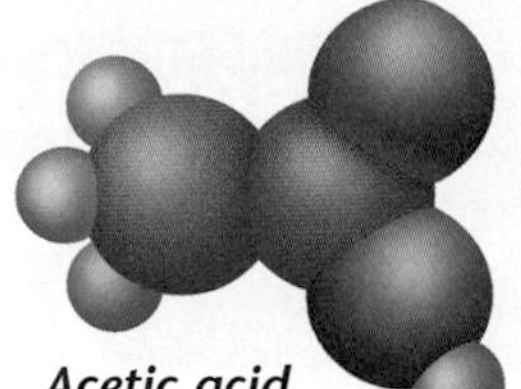

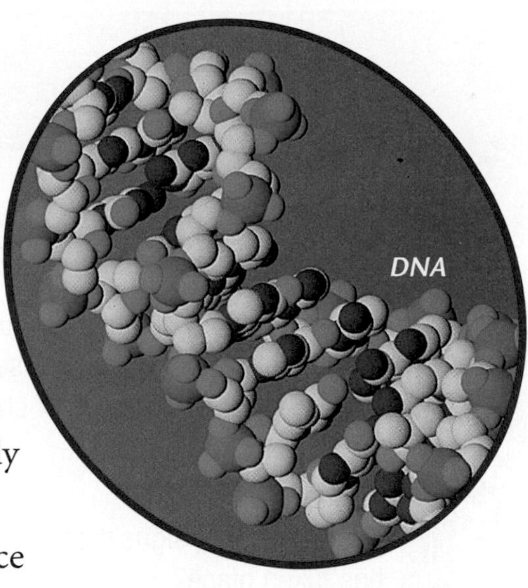

Figure 6 Molecules may be as simple as oxygen. Or, they may be as complex as the DNA in living cells. However, all molecules are made of atoms. (The computer image of DNA was made using a color code for atoms different from the code used in this book.) ***Classifying*** *Which one of these is a molecule of an element? How do you know?*

Acetic acid, the compound that gives vinegar its sharp odor and sour taste, has 2 carbon atoms, 4 hydrogen atoms, and 2 oxygen atoms ($C_2H_4O_2$). Some of the molecules in your body are made of millions of atoms.

Chemical Bonds and Chemical Reactions The force that holds atoms together is called a **chemical bond.** You can think of chemical bonds as the "glue" that makes atoms "stick" to each other. The types of atoms and how they are joined by chemical bonds determine the properties of a substance. **Chemical reactions occur when chemical bonds break or when new bonds form.** When bonds are broken and new ones are formed, atoms are shuffled, making new substances with different properties.

Some chemical bonds are strong and hard to change. Others break apart easily. Glass is unreactive because the chemical bonds that hold it together are strong. Windows in buildings hundreds of years old show no damage from weather, while wood frames around the glass have rotted away. The wood is made of compounds that react easily with other substances in the environment. It can be softened by water and rotted by fungi. Or it can burn in a fire.

Section 1 Review

1. Tell how an element, a compound, and a mixture differ.
2. What forms of evidence show that a chemical reaction has taken place?
3. What is the difference between an atom and a molecule?
4. What happens to the chemical bonds in a molecule during a chemical reaction?
5. **Thinking Critically Classifying** Classify each of the following as a chemical or a physical change: ice cream melting; sugar dissolving in water; a candle burning; a bathroom mirror fogging as someone showers; milk turning sour.

CHAPTER PROJECT 10

Check Your Progress

Use the information from the section to make a list of signs or evidence that a chemical reaction is taking place. Discuss your list with another classmate. (*Hint:* Look outside your home, think about reactions inside your body, and look for reactions that may occur either very slowly or very quickly.)

Skills Lab

Observing

Where's the Evidence?

Chemical reactions occur all around you. In this lab you will observe different types of evidence of chemical reactions.

Problem

What are some signs that a chemical reaction has taken place?

Materials

4 small plastic cups
2 plastic spoons
tongs
matches
sodium carbonate (powder)
graduated cylinder, 10 mL
aluminum foil, about 10-cm square
dilute hydrochloric acid in a dropper bottle
copper sulfate solution
sodium carbonate solution
birthday candles
sugar
clay

Procedure    

Preview the steps for each reaction and copy the data table into your notebook.

Part 1

1. Put a pea-sized pile of sodium carbonate into a clean plastic cup. Record the appearance of the sodium carbonate in the data table.
2. Observe a dropper containing hydrochloric acid. Record the appearance of the acid. **CAUTION:** *Hydrochloric acid can burn you or anything else it touches. Wash spills with water.*
3. Make a prediction about how you think the acid and the sodium carbonate will react when mixed. Record your prediction.
4. Add about 10 drops of hydrochloric acid to the sodium carbonate. Swirl to mix the contents of the cup. Record your observations.

Part 2

5. Fold up the sides of the aluminum foil square to make a small tray.
6. Use a plastic spoon to place a pea-sized pile of sugar into the tray.
7. Carefully describe the appearance of the sugar in your data table.

DATA TABLE

Reaction	Observations Before Reaction	Predictions	Observations During Reaction	Observations After Reaction
1. Sodium carbonate (powder) + hydrochloric acid				
2. Sugar + heat				
3. Copper sulfate + sodium carbonate solutions				

8. Secure a small candle on your desktop in a lump of clay. Carefully light the candle with a match only after being instructed to do so by your teacher. **CAUTION:** *Tie back long hair and loose clothing.*
9. Predict what you think will happen if you heat the sugar. Record your prediction.
10. Use tongs to hold the aluminum tray. Heat the sugar slowly by moving the tray gently back and forth over the flame. Make observations while the sugar is heating.
11. When you think there is no longer a chemical reaction occurring, blow out the candle.
12. Allow the tray to cool for a few seconds and set it down on your desk. Record your observations of the material left in the tray.

Part 3

13. Put about 2 mL of copper sulfate solution in one cup. **CAUTION:** *Copper sulfate is poisonous and can stain your skin and clothes. Do not touch it or get it in your mouth.* Put an equal amount of sodium carbonate solution in another cup. Record the appearance of both liquids.
14. Predict what you think will happen when the two solutions are mixed. Record your prediction.
15. Combine the two solutions and record your observations. **CAUTION:** *Dispose of the solutions as directed by your teacher.*
16. Wash your hands when you have finished working.

Analyze and Conclude

1. How do the results of each reaction compare with your predictions for that reaction?
2. How did you know when Reaction 1 was over?
3. Was the product of the reaction in Part 1 a solid, a liquid, or a gas? How do you know?
4. How are the properties of the material remaining after the reaction in Part 2 different from those of the sugar?
5. Was the product of the reaction in Part 3 a solid, a liquid, or a gas? How do you know?
6. How do you know if new substances were formed in each reaction?
7. **Think About It** What senses did you use to make observations during this lab? How might you use scientific instruments to extend your senses in order to make more observations?

More to Explore

Use your observation skills to find evidence of chemical reactions involving foods in your kitchen. Look for production of gases, color changes, and formation of precipitates. Share your findings with your classmates.

Describing Chemical Reactions

DISCOVER — ACTIVITY

Do You Lose Anything?

1. Place about two dozen coins on a table. Sort them into stacks of pennies, nickels, dimes, and quarters.
2. Count and record the number of coins in each stack. Calculate and record the value of each stack and the total value of all stacks combined.
3. Mix all the coins together and then divide them randomly into four unsorted stacks.
4. Again calculate the value of each stack and the total amount of money. Count the total number of each type of coin.
5. Repeat Steps 3 and 4.

Think It Over

Making Models What happened to the total value and types of coins in this activity? Did rearranging the coins change any individual coin? If you think of the coins as representing different types of atoms, what does this model tell you about chemical reactions?

GUIDE FOR READING

- **What does a chemical equation tell you?**
- **How does mass change during a chemical reaction?**
- **What are three categories of chemical reactions?**

Reading Tip **As you read, describe how each boldfaced word relates to a chemical reaction.**

Suppose you were to take a walk in a foreign country where the language is unfamiliar to you. Think of the signs you might see—two doors with drawings of a man and a woman, the receiver of a telephone, a drawing of a bicycle, and a picture of a trash can with something dropping into it. You would have no trouble figuring out what these signs mean.

Symbols express a concept in a shorter form. "Hydrogen molecules react with oxygen molecules to form water molecules" is a sentence that describes the reaction between hydrogen and oxygen. But writing it is slow and awkward. A **chemical equation** is a shorter, easier way to show chemical reactions, using symbols instead of words.

Figure 7 Symbols are used as short and easy-to-recognize ways of saying something. ***Inferring*** *What information does each of these symbols tell you?*

Symbols of Common Elements			
Element	**Symbol**	**Element**	**Symbol**
Oxygen	O	Gold	Au
Hydrogen	H	Silver	Ag
Carbon	C	Sulfur	S
Helium	He	Calcium	Ca
Nitrogen	N	Neon	Ne
Chlorine	Cl	Phosphorus	P
Aluminum	Al	Potassium	K
Iron	Fe	Iodine	I
Sodium	Na	Silicon	Si

Figure 8 The symbols for most elements are the first one or two letters of their names. Some elements have symbols that come from their Latin, Greek, or Arabic names.

Writing Chemical Equations

To write a chemical equation, you have to know what chemicals you are starting with and what new chemicals you get during the reaction. Then you can use symbols to stand for the elements and compounds involved. A **symbol** in chemistry is a one-letter or two-letter set of characters used to identify an element.

Chemical Formulas Most elements are represented by a one- or two-letter symbol. So, how do you represent a compound? If you've looked at Figure 9, you may already know the answer: with a formula. A **chemical formula** is a combination of symbols that represent the elements in a compound. For example, NaCl is the formula for table salt. If you think of symbols of the elements as being like letters of the alphabet, a formula is like a "word" that represents a compound.

Look at the formula for propane in Figure 9. The formula tells you that the compound propane is made of the elements carbon and hydrogen. But a formula does more than just identify the elements in a compound. Notice that there are numbers in the formula that are written smaller and lower than the letter symbols. These numbers are subscripts. **Subscripts** show the number of atoms of an element in a molecule or the ratio of elements in a compound. The formula for propane shows that it has three atoms of carbon and eight atoms of hydrogen.

If a letter symbol in a chemical formula doesn't have a subscript, the number 1 is understood to be there. Carbon dioxide (CO_2), for example, has one carbon atom and two oxygen atoms. Its ratio of carbon atoms to oxygen atoms is 1 to 2. How many atoms in total does a water molecule (H_2O) have? Since the absence of a subscript means that there is one oxygen atom, there are three atoms altogether in a water molecule.

Figure 9 Formulas for compounds tell you what elements as well as how many atoms of each element are present. ***Observing*** *How many oxygen atoms are present in water, carbon dioxide, and sugar?*

Formulas of Familiar Compounds	
Compound	**Formula**
Water	H_2O
Carbon dioxide	CO_2
Carbon monoxide	CO
Methane	CH_4
Propane	C_3H_8
Sugar (sucrose)	$C_{12}H_{22}O_{11}$
Rubbing alcohol	C_3H_8O
Ammonia	NH_3
Sodium chloride	$NaCl$
Washing soda	Na_2CO_3
Baking soda	$NaHCO_3$

Structure of an Equation A chemical equation summarizes a reaction. It tells you the substances you start with and the substances you get at the end. The materials you have at the beginning are called the **reactants.** When the reaction is complete, you have different materials, called the **products** of the reaction. **A chemical equation uses symbols and formulas to show the reactants and the products of a chemical reaction.**

Chemical equations have a definite structure. The formulas for all the reactants are written on the left side of the equation, followed by an arrow. You read the arrow as "yields." The formulas for all the products are on the right:

$$\text{Reactant} + \text{Reactant} \rightarrow \text{Product} + \text{Product}$$

The number of reactants and products can vary. Some reactions have only one reactant or product. Other reactions have two, three, or more reactants or products. Look at the equation for a reaction that forms hydrogen peroxide and count the number of reactants:

$$\underset{\text{Reactant}}{H_2} + \underset{\text{Reactant}}{O_2} \rightarrow \underset{\text{Product}}{H_2O_2}$$

Conservation of Mass

No matter how many reactants and products are involved, all the atoms present at the start of a reaction are present at the end. Think about what happens when classes change at your school. A class is made up of a group of students and a teacher together in one room. When the bell rings, people from each class move from room to room, ending up in different classes. The number of students and teachers in the school has not changed. But their arrangement is different and the new groups interact differently.

Figure 10 When iron filings and sulfur are mixed and heated, the product is the compound iron sulfide. ***Interpreting Diagrams*** *How do you know that mass has been conserved in the reaction?*

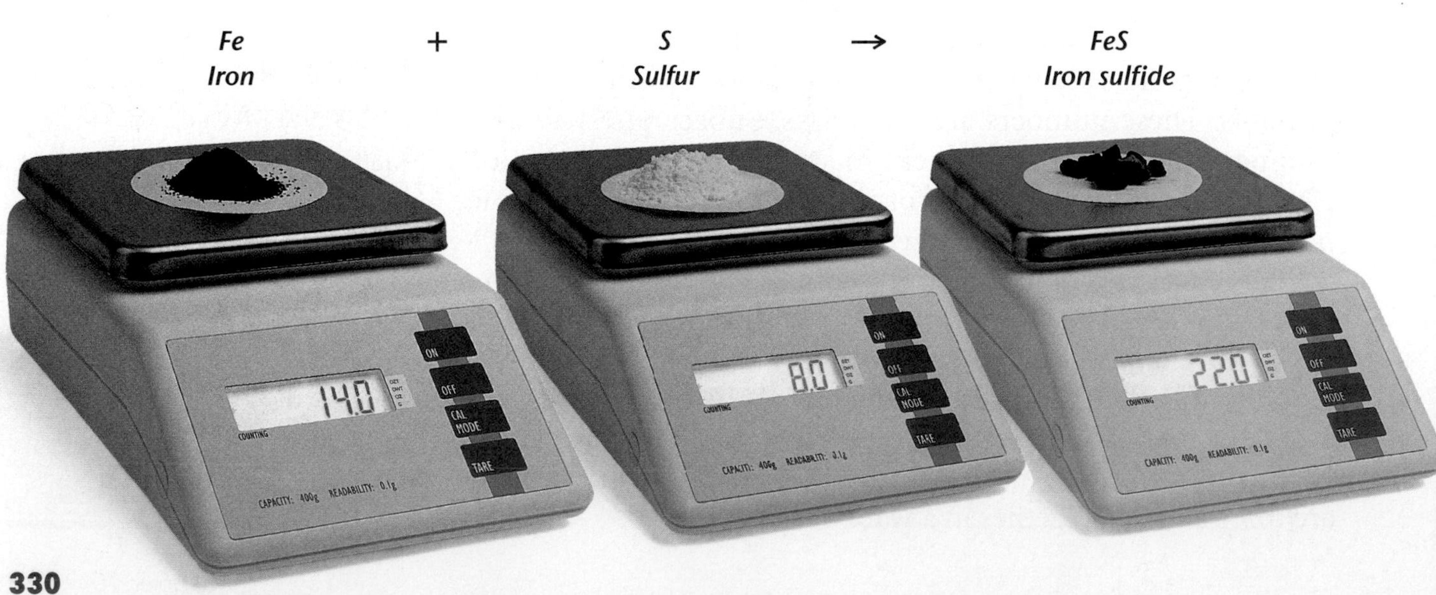

Figure 11 Burnt wood and gray ash are all that remain from a roaring fire.
Problem Solving *When wood burns, it reacts with oxygen in the air. What masses would you need to measure before and after the fire to show conservation of mass?*

Now imagine that all the students and teachers are atoms, and each class is a molecule. At the end of a reaction (similar to a class change), the same atoms are present, but they are grouped together in different molecules. **The amount of matter in a chemical reaction does not change. Therefore, the total mass of the reactants must equal the total mass of the products.** This principle, called the **conservation of mass,** means that during a chemical reaction, matter is not created or destroyed.

At first glance, some reactions seem to violate the principle of conservation of mass. If you measured the cooled ash left from a wood fire, for example, it wouldn't have the same mass as the wood that had been burned. What happened to the missing mass? Much of it escaped into the air as carbon dioxide gas and water vapor. If you could trap and measure these gases, you'd be able to prove that the mass didn't change.

☑ ***Checkpoint*** *How do the numbers and masses of the atoms in the reactants of a chemical reaction compare with the atoms in the products?*

Balancing Chemical Equations

What does the principle of conservation of mass mean for a chemical equation? Matter is not created or destroyed in a reaction. This means that the same number of atoms exists in the products as in the reactants. To accurately describe a reaction, a chemical equation must show the same number of each type of atom on both sides of the equation. When it does, chemists say the equation is balanced. To balance an equation, first look at the formulas.

$$H_2 \quad + \quad O_2 \quad \rightarrow \quad H_2O$$

How many atoms does an oxygen molecule have? How about hydrogen? How many of each kind of atom are present in one water molecule?

Still There

ACTIVITY

Use nuts and bolts to model the principle of conservation of mass.

1. Measure the mass of a collection of bolts, each with a nut attached to it.
2. Remove all the nuts from the bolts. Measure the total mass of the nuts. Then do the same with the bolts. Add these values.
3. Rearrange your collection, putting two or three nuts on one bolt, one nut on another bolt, and so on. You can even leave a few pieces unattached.
4. Measure the total mass again. Compare this figure with the totals from Steps 1 and 2.

Making Models How are the nuts and bolts similar to atoms and molecules in a chemical reaction? How do your observations model conservation of mass?

Calculating ACTIVITY

Each chemical formula below is written just as it might be in a balanced chemical equation. For each formula, calculate the number of each kind of atom.

$3\ H_2O$
$2\ H_2SO_4$
$4\ Fe_2O_3$
$6\ NaCl$
NO_2

When a coefficient is in front of a formula, how do you find the total number of atoms of one kind? What do you do if there is no coefficient?

Look at the chemical equation and models for the reaction:

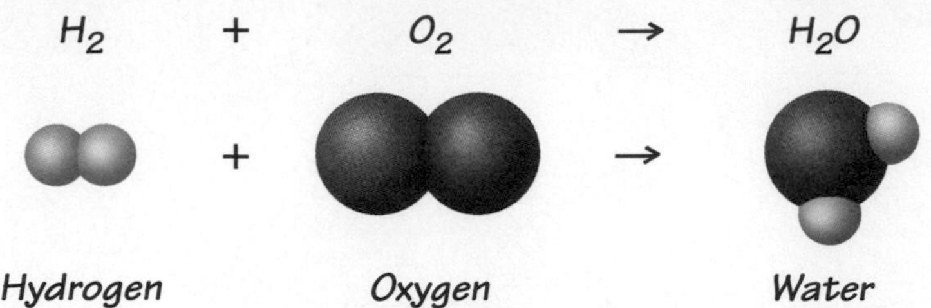

Count the number of atoms of each element on each side of the equation. You find 2 atoms of oxygen in the reactants but only 1 atom of oxygen in the products.

How can you get the number of oxygen molecules on both sides to be the same? You might be tempted to balance the oxygen by changing the formula for water to H_2O_2. Don't even think about it! Remember that H_2O_2 is the formula for hydrogen peroxide, a completely different compound.

To balance the equation, use a coefficient. A **coefficient** (koh uh FISH unt) is a number placed *in front of* a chemical formula in the equation. It tells you how many atoms or molecules of each reactant and product take part in the reaction. If the coefficient is 1, you don't need to write it. Balance the number of oxygen atoms by writing the coefficient 2 for water. It's like saying "$2 \times H_2O$." Now there are 2 oxygen atoms in the product.

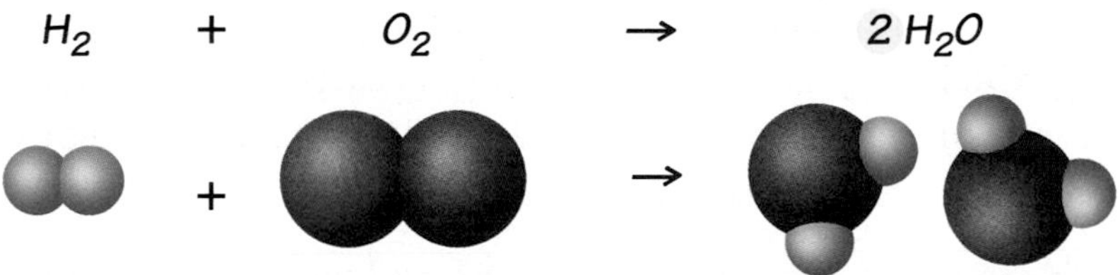

Okay, you've balanced the oxygen atoms. But now there are 2 hydrogen atoms in the reactants and 4 in the product. How can you balance the hydrogen? Try doubling the number of hydrogen atoms on the left side of the equation by changing the coefficient for hydrogen to 2. You've got it! Here is the balanced equation:

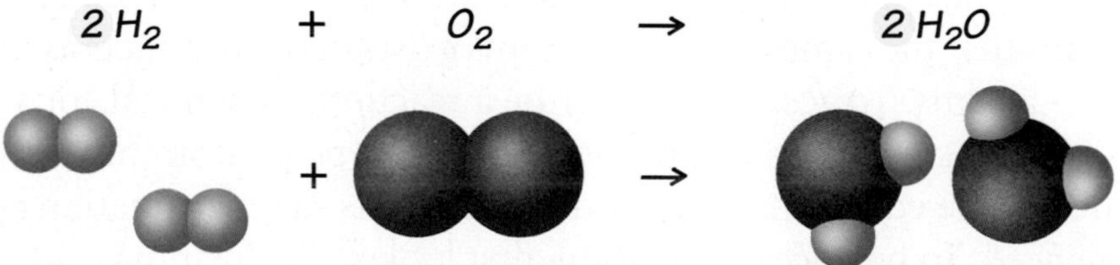

Now there are 4 hydrogen atoms and 2 oxygen atoms on each side. The equation is balanced. It tells you that 2 molecules of hydrogen react with 1 molecule of oxygen to yield 2 molecules of water. Count the atoms in the last diagram. Prove to yourself that the balanced equation is correct.

Sample Problem

When magnesium metal, Mg, reacts with oxygen, O_2, the product of the reaction is magnesium oxide, MgO. Write a balanced equation for this reaction.

Write the word equation.	Magnesium + Oxygen → Magnesium oxide
Write the chemical equation.	$Mg + O_2 \rightarrow MgO$
Count the number of atoms of each element on each side of the equation.	Mg one; O two → Mg one, O one
Choose coefficients to balance the equation.	$2\,Mg + O_2 \rightarrow 2\,MgO$
Think about it.	The answer shows 2 magnesium atoms and 2 oxygen atoms on each side, so the equation is balanced.

Practice Problems

1. Balance the equation: $C + Cl_2 \rightarrow CCl_4$
2. Balance the equation: $Al_2O_3 \rightarrow Al + O_2$

Classifying Chemical Reactions

Chemical reactions can be classified by what happens to the reactants and products. Substances may add together to make a more complex substance. They may break apart to make simpler substances. Or substances may even exchange parts. In each case, new materials form. **Many chemical reactions can be classified in one of three categories: synthesis, decomposition, or replacement.** As you read about each of these kinds of reactions, look at the examples. Compare the reactants and the products to see how they change.

Synthesis Have you ever listened to music from a synthesizer? You can hear many different notes and types of musical sounds. The synthesizer combines these sounds to make a complicated piece of music. When two or more substances (elements or compounds) combine to make a more complex substance, the process is called **synthesis** (SIN thuh sis). To synthesize is to put things together. Look back at the reaction of hydrogen and oxygen to make water. You should see now that this is a synthesis reaction—two elements come together, making a compound.

Figure 12 When a ribbon of magnesium metal burns in air (left), it combines with oxygen to form magnesium oxide (right). The shiny metal and colorless gas become a white powdery solid. ***Classifying*** *Why is this a synthesis reaction?*

Integrating Environmental Science

Acid rain is a product of synthesis reactions. In one case, sulfur dioxide, oxygen, and water combine to make sulfuric acid. Look at the equation for the reaction. Can you find the 8 oxygen atoms on each side of the equation?

$2\,SO_2$	+	O_2	+	$2\,H_2O$	→	$2\,H_2SO_4$
Sulfur dioxide		Oxygen		Water		Sulfuric acid

Sulfur dioxide comes from car engines or from power plants that burn coal. Oxygen and water vapor are in the air. Together they produce sulfuric acid, which causes rainwater to become corrosive. This acid water then eats away at stone and metal, and can damage living organisms.

Decomposition While a synthesis reaction builds compounds from simpler reactants, a process called **decomposition** breaks down compounds into simpler products. Remember the bottle of hydrogen peroxide used to clean cuts? If you keep such a bottle for a very long time, you'll have water instead. The hydrogen peroxide decomposes into water and oxygen gas.

$$2\,H_2O_2 \rightarrow 2\,H_2O + O_2$$

The oxygen that is produced escapes into the air.

☑ *Checkpoint* *How do synthesis and decomposition differ?*

Figure 13 Safety airbags in cars inflate as a result of a decomposition reaction. On impact, a detonator cap inside the air bag explodes. The explosion causes a compound made of sodium and nitrogen to decompose. One product is a large quantity of nitrogen gas.
Applying Concepts *Why would quick inflation of airbags be important?*

Replacement When one element replaces another in a compound, or when two elements in different compounds trade places, the process is called **replacement.** Copper metal, for example, can be obtained by heating rock containing copper oxide in the presence of charcoal. The carbon of the charcoal takes the place of copper in the copper oxide. You can write the reaction as:

$$2\ CuO + C \rightarrow 2\ Cu + CO_2$$

Obtaining copper metal from rock is a simple replacement reaction. However, not all chemical reactions can be classified clearly as synthesis, decomposition, or replacement. Look carefully at the formulas of the reactants and products for clues to what type of reaction the equation shows.

Figure 14 Copper metal can be chemically obtained from copper ore. Copper oxide (in the ore) reacts with carbon in a replacement reaction.

Section 2 Review

1. What information do you need in order to write a chemical equation?
2. What is the principle of conservation of mass?
3. List and define three categories of chemical reactions.
4. **Thinking Critically Applying Concepts** Balance the following chemical equations by adding coefficients:
   a. $HCl + NaOH \rightarrow H_2O + NaCl$
   b. $Fe_2O_3 + C \rightarrow Fe + CO_2$
   c. $SO_2 + O_2 \rightarrow SO_3$
5. **Thinking Critically Classifying** Classify each of the following reactions as synthesis, decomposition, or replacement:
   a. $2\ NH_4NO_3 \rightarrow 2\ N_2 + O_2 + 4\ H_2O$
   b. $2\ Al + Fe_2O_3 \rightarrow Al_2O_3 + 2\ Fe$
   c. $MgCl_2 + K_2S \rightarrow MgS + 2\ KCl$
   d. $P_4O_{10} + 6\ H_2O \rightarrow 4\ H_3PO_4$

Check Your Progress

CHAPTER PROJECT 10

Prepare a table to keep track of the chemical changes you observe. Have your teacher check your table to be sure it contains the proper headings. Record the different chemical changes you observe for a week. Make sure you can describe the evidence for each chemical change. If possible, classify each reaction as a synthesis, decomposition, or replacement reaction. Also classify it as occurring in a living or nonliving setting.

Section 3 Controlling Chemical Reactions

Discover Activity

Can You Speed Up or Slow Down a Reaction?

1. Put on your safety goggles and lab apron.
2. Obtain about 125 mL each of three solutions of vitamin C and water—one at room temperature, one at about 75°C, and one chilled to between 5° and 10°C.
3. Add three drops of iodine solution to each container and stir each with a clean spoon. Compare changes you observe in the solutions.
4. Clean up your work area and wash your hands.

Think It Over

Inferring What conclusion can you make about the effect of temperature on the reaction of iodine and vitamin C?

Guide for Reading

- **How is energy related to chemical reactions?**
- **How can you control the rate of a chemical reaction?**

Reading Tip **As you read, make a list of factors affecting reaction rate.**

You are working on an engineering team that tears down buildings. "3, 2, 1 . . . Let it go!" You push a button and suddenly a loud rumbling sound starts. The ground shakes, and clouds of dust pour into the street. In 15 seconds, a tall building is reduced to a pile of rubble. Careful control of energy in the explosion is critical to collapse the building without even breaking a window next door. If the demolition expert on your team doesn't understand the chemical reactions used, people could be injured or property damaged.

Although you may never demolish a building, you do use energy from controlled chemical reactions every day. Every time your body converts your lunch into the energy to play sports or you go for a ride in a car, you are using controlled reactions.

Figure 15 Building demolition requires a good understanding of chemical reactions.

Energy in Chemical Reactions

Light is a type of energy. Other forms of energy include electricity and the energy of a moving object. **Every chemical reaction involves a change of energy. Some reactions release energy and others absorb energy.**

The reaction between gasoline and oxygen in a car engine yields carbon dioxide, water, and other products. It also releases a lot of energy. You can detect one form of this energy as heat. The engine of a car gets hot enough to burn you if you touch it. A reaction that releases energy in the form of heat is called an **exothermic reaction** (ek soh THUR mik).

If you did the Discover activity in Section 1, you observed that the mixture became colder. When baking soda (sodium bicarbonate) reacts with vinegar, the reaction takes heat from the solution, making it feel cooler. This kind of reaction, which absorbs energy, is called an **endothermic reaction** (en doh THUR mik).

Figure 17 compares the changes in energy of exothermic and endothermic reactions. Notice that the energy of the products in an exothermic reaction is lower than the energy of the reactants. In an exothermic reaction, energy is released. This is the case when gasoline burns. Now see how an endothermic reaction is different. In an endothermic reaction, the energy of the products is greater than the energy of the reactants. This means energy is absorbed. That's what happened with the baking soda and vinegar.

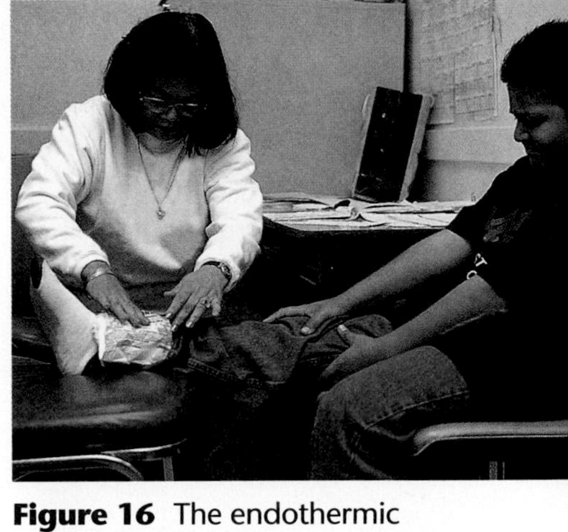

Figure 16 The endothermic reaction inside a cold pack helps cool this boy's injured ankle. Such rapid treatment after an injury reduces pain and speeds up healing.

Getting Reactions Started

Trace each diagram in Figure 17 from left to right with your finger. As your finger moves, do you notice how the curve goes up and over a rise? Then your finger moves down toward the products. All chemical reactions need energy to get started. The **activation energy** is the minimum amount of energy needed to start a chemical reaction.

Figure 17 Every chemical reaction needs a certain amount of energy to get started. ***Interpreting Diagrams*** *Where are increases and decreases in energy shown in each diagram?*

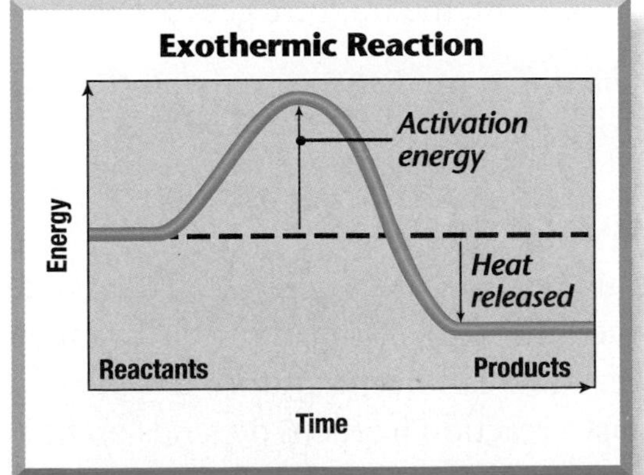

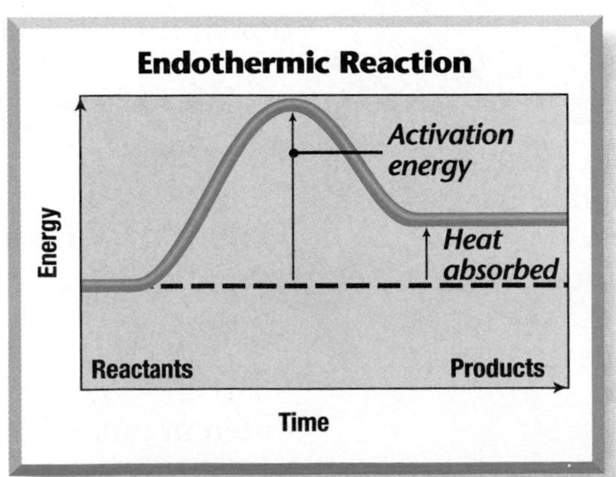

Figure 18 The rock at the top of this hill cannot roll down the hill until a small push gets it going.

The reaction that makes water from hydrogen and oxygen is very exothermic. It gives off tremendous amounts of energy. But if you make a mixture of hydrogen and oxygen, it could remain unchanged for years. For the reaction to start, a tiny amount of activation energy—just a spark—is needed. Once a few molecules of hydrogen and oxygen react, the rest will follow, because the large amount of energy released provides the activation energy for more molecules to react.

Think of a chemical reaction as being like a rock resting behind a ridge at the top of a hill. The rock stays put until someone or something adds energy by giving it a push. With enough energy, the rock can move over the hump and roll down the hill. The same idea applies to a chemical reaction. With enough energy, reactants can get "over the hump" and form products.

It's not always clear where the energy to start a reaction comes from. In the case of vinegar and baking soda, heat already in the solution provides the energy to get the reaction started. This reaction is endothermic. To keep it going, more energy is continually drawn from the solution. As a result, the mixture gets cooler.

☑ **Checkpoint** ***What is the difference between an endothermic reaction and an exothermic reaction?***

Social Studies CONNECTION

In the early part of the 1900s, people sometimes traveled in airships called dirigibles. Unlike modern airships, which are filled with unreactive helium, some dirigibles contained flammable hydrogen. On May 6, 1937, the airship *Hindenburg* came in for a landing over Lakehurst, New Jersey. Somehow the ship caught fire. Seconds later, its 200,000 cubic meters of hydrogen gas burst into flame, killing 36 people. The *Hindenburg* was a tragic example of how much energy can be released during a chemical reaction.

In Your Journal

Pretend you are a reporter covering the *Hindenburg* disaster. Write a brief news article explaining how the reaction between hydrogen and oxygen affected the disaster.

Rates of Chemical Reactions

Chemical reactions don't all occur at the same rate. Some, like explosions, are very fast. Others, like the rusting of metal, are much slower. Also, a particular reaction can occur at different rates in different conditions. How fast a reaction happens depends on how easily the particles of the reactants can get together.

If you want to make a reaction happen faster, you need to get more particles of the reactants together more often. To slow down a reaction, you need to do the opposite—get fewer particles together less often. Chemists do this by controlling the conditions of a reaction. **The rate of a chemical reaction is affected by such factors as concentration, surface area, and temperature, and by using substances called catalysts and inhibitors.**

Figure 19 Bubbles of hydrogen form when magnesium reacts with an acid. The test tube on the left has a lower concentration of acid than the test tube on the right. ***Relating Cause and Effect*** *How does the concentration of acid affect the rate of the reaction?*

Concentration One way to increase the rate of a reaction is to increase the concentration of the reactants. **Concentration** is the amount of one material in a given volume of another material. For example, adding a small spoonful of sugar to a glass of lemonade will make it sweet. But adding a large spoonful of sugar makes the lemonade a lot sweeter! The glass with more sugar has a greater concentration of sugar molecules.

Increasing the concentrations of the reactants makes more particles available to react. Compare the test tubes in Figure 19. In the test tube on the right, the greater concentration of acid means more acid particles are present to react with the magnesium metal. You can see evidence for the increased rate of reaction in the greater number of bubbles that are produced.

Surface Area When a chunk of solid material reacts with a liquid or a gas, only the particles on the surface of the solid come in contact with the other reactant. Now suppose you break the solid into smaller pieces. What happens? You've increased the

Figure 20 The concrete walls of this grain elevator in Kansas were blown apart by an explosion when grain particles and oxygen above the stored wheat exploded. Grain dust has a much greater surface area exposed to air than the top surface of a pile of grain does.

Interpreting Data

1. Measure the length and width of a face of a gelatin cube.
2. Calculate the area of that face of the cube.
   Area = length × width
   Repeat for each of the other five faces. Then add the six values together to get the total surface area.
3. Using a plastic knife, cut the cube in half and repeat Steps 1 and 2 for each piece of gelatin. Add the surface areas of the two pieces to get the new total surface area.

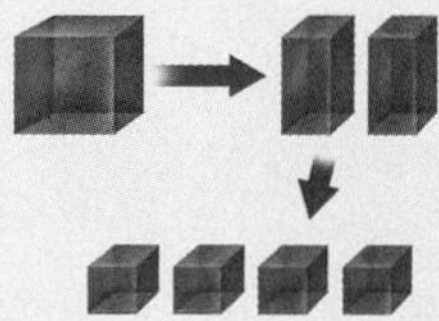

4. How did the total surface area of the cube before it was cut compare with the total surface area after it was cut?
5. Predict what would happen to the total surface area if you cut each cube in two again. If you have time, test your prediction.

surface area of the solid. More particles of the material are exposed, so the reaction happens faster. That's also what happens when you chew your food. Chewing breaks the food into smaller pieces. Your digestive juices can then work more quickly to change the food into nutrients your body can use.

Temperature A third way to increase the rate of a reaction is to increase its temperature. When you heat a substance, its particles move faster. Faster-moving particles increase the reaction rate in two ways. First, they come in contact more often, which means there are more chances for a reaction to happen. Second, faster-moving particles have more energy. This energy helps the reactants get over the activation energy "hump."

Did you ever leave a glass of milk out on the kitchen counter when you left for school? When you picked it up again later, the milk may have had a sour smell. When foods are left unrefrigerated, bacteria in them reproduce quickly. As they live and reproduce, the bacteria carry out thousands of chemical reactions. Some reactions can cause food to spoil. Keeping foods cold slows these reactions and the growth of the organisms that cause them. Your food stays fresh longer.

Catalysts Another way to control the rate of a reaction is to change the activation energy. If you decrease the activation energy, the reaction happens faster. A **catalyst** (KAT uh list) is a material that increases the rate of a reaction by lowering the activation energy. Catalysts help with the reaction, but they are not permanently changed in the reaction. Therefore, they are not considered reactants.

Figure 21 Unrefrigerated foods quickly spoil from the chemical reactions carried out by microorganisms. Keeping foods cold slows these changes.

INTEGRATING LIFE SCIENCE Many chemical reactions happen at temperatures that would be deadly to living things. Yet, some of these reactions are necessary for life. The cells in your body (as in all living things) contain biological catalysts called **enzymes** (EN zymz). Enzymes provide a surface on which reactions take place. This helps reactions happen at lower temperatures because it lowers activation energy. In this way, enzymes safely increase the reaction rates of chemical reactions necessary for life. An enzyme breaks away unchanged at the end of a reaction.

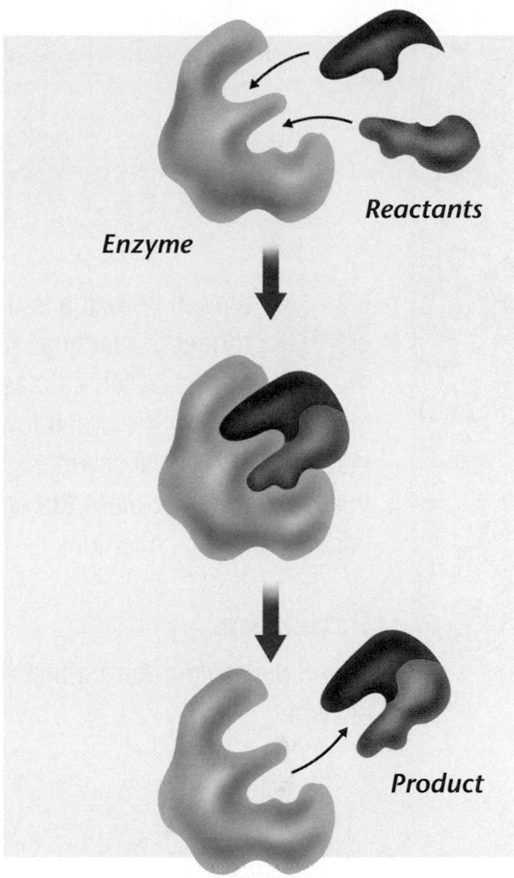

Figure 22 Enzyme molecules are shaped in ways that help reactant molecules come together.

Inhibitors Sometimes a reaction is more useful when it can be slowed down rather than speeded up. A material used to decrease the rate of a reaction is called an **inhibitor.**

The discovery of one inhibitor had an important effect on the construction industry. Nitroglycerin is a powerful liquid explosive that decomposes quickly, releasing tremendous energy. An explosion can be caused just by shaking the bottle! In the 1860s, Alfred Nobel tried adding certain solid materials, such as wood pulp, to the nitroglycerin. The solids absorbed the liquid and kept it from reacting until it was detonated. This mixture could be handled more safely and still be used for blasting. Nobel's discovery is the more easily controlled material known as dynamite.

Section 3 Review

1. Compare the change of energy in an exothermic reaction to that in an endothermic reaction.
2. Which has greater surface area: a sugar cube or an equal mass of sugar crystals? Explain.
3. Compare and contrast catalysts and inhibitors.
4. **Thinking Critically Relating Cause and Effect** Copy and complete the table below to show how some factors increase, decrease, or have no effect on rate of a reaction.

Changes	Effect on Reaction Rate
Decreased concentration	
Increased surface area	
Heat added	
Catalyst	

Science at Home

Place an iron nail in a plastic cup. Add enough water to almost cover the nail. Place a small piece of fine steel wool in another cup and add the same amount of water. Ask family members to predict what will happen overnight. The next day, examine the nail and steel wool. Compare the amount of rust on each. Were your family's predictions correct? Explain how reaction rates are affected by surface areas.

Real-World Lab

How It Works

Peroxide, Catalase, & You!

Hydrogen peroxide is a poisonous waste product of reactions in living cells. An enzyme called catalase, found in the blood, speeds up the breakdown of hydrogen peroxide into harmless water and oxygen gas. In this lab, you will explore the action of catalase under changing conditions.

Problem

How does temperature affect the action of an enzyme?

Skills Focus

measuring, controlling variables, drawing conclusions

Materials

forceps
stopwatch
test tube with a one-hole stopper
0.1% hydrogen peroxide solution
filter paper disks soaked in liver preparation (catalase enzyme) and kept at four different temperatures (room temperature, 0–4°C, 37°C, and 100°C)
container to hold water (beaker or bowl)

Procedure

1. Form a hypothesis that predicts how the action of the catalase enzyme will differ at the different temperatures to be tested.
2. Fill a container with water. Then fill a test tube with 0.1% hydrogen peroxide solution until the test tube is overflowing. Do this over a sink or the container of water.
3. Make a data table similar to the one shown.

DATA TABLE

Temperature (°C)	Time (sec)	Average Time for Class (sec)

4. Moisten the small end of a one-hole stopper with water.
5. Using forceps, remove a filter paper disk soaked in liver preparation (catalase enzyme) that has been kept at room temperature. Stick it to the moistened end of the one-hole stopper.
6. Your partner should be ready with the stopwatch for the next step.
7. Place the stopper firmly into the test tube, hold your thumb over the hole, and quickly invert the test tube. Start the stopwatch. Put the inverted end of the test tube into the container of water, as shown in the photograph, and remove your thumb.
8. Observe what happens to the filter paper inside the test tube. Record the time it takes for the disk to rise to the top. If the disk does not rise within 2 minutes, record "no reaction" and go on to Step 9.
9. Rinse the test tube and repeat the procedure with catalase enzyme disks kept at 0°C, 37°C, and 100°C. **CAUTION:** *When you remove the disk kept in the hot water bath, do not use your bare hands. Avoid spilling the hot water.*

Analyze and Conclude

1. What makes the disk float to the top of the test tube?
2. Calculate the average time for each temperature based on the results of the entire class. Enter the results in your data table.
3. Make a line graph of the data you collected. Label the horizontal axis (*x*-axis) "Temperature" with a scale from 0°C to 100°C. Label the vertical axis (*y*-axis) "Time" with a scale from 0 to 30 seconds. Plot the class average time for each temperature.
4. What evidence do you have that your hypothesis from Step 1 is either supported or not supported?
5. How is the time it takes the disk to rise to the top of the tube related to the rate of the reaction?
6. What can you conclude about the activity of the enzyme at the various temperatures you tested? (*Hint:* Enzyme activity is greater when the rate of reaction is faster.)
7. Make a prediction about how active the enzyme would be at 10°C, 60°C, and 75°C. Give reasons to support your prediction.
8. **Apply** Oxygen kills many kinds of bacteria that can cause infection. Explain why hydrogen peroxide is often used as a treatment on cuts and scrapes.

Design an Experiment

The activity of an enzyme also depends upon the concentration of the enzyme. Design an experiment that explores the relationship between enzyme activity and enzyme concentration. (Your teacher can give you disks soaked with different enzyme concentrations.)

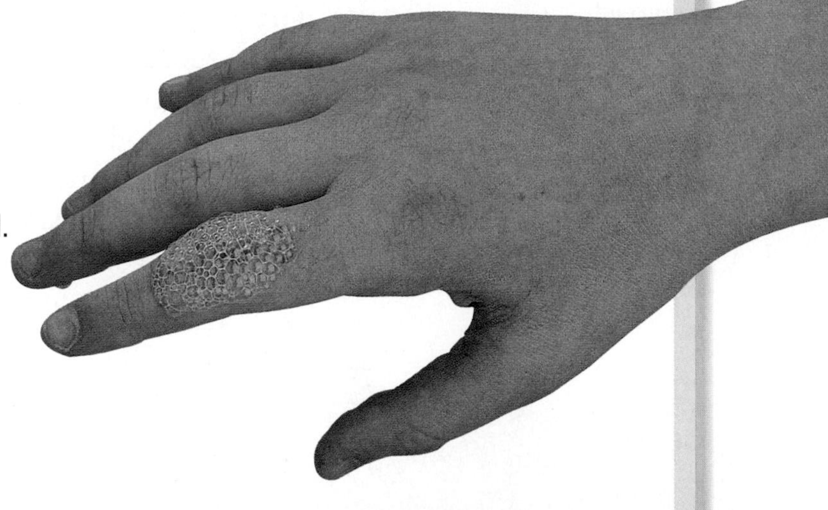

Fire and Fire Safety

DISCOVER

ACTIVITY

How Does Baking Soda Affect a Fire?

1. Put on your safety goggles.
2. Secure a small candle in a holder or some clay. After instructions from your teacher, use a match to light the candle.
3. Place a beaker next to the candle. Measure 1 large spoonful of baking soda into the beaker. Add about 112 mL of water and stir. Add about 112 mL of vinegar.
4. As soon as the mixture stops foaming, tip the beaker as if you are pouring something out of it onto the flame. **CAUTION:** *Do not pour any liquid on the candle.*
5. Observe what happens to the flame.

Think It Over

Developing Hypotheses The gas produced in the beaker was carbon dioxide. Based on the results of this experiment, develop a hypothesis to explain what you observed in Step 5.

GUIDE FOR READING

- **What are the three things necessary to maintain a fire?**
- **How does water stop combustion?**

Reading Tip **Before you read, predict what conditions contribute to the start of a fire. Revise your predictions as you read.**

What picture comes to mind when you hear the word *fire?* Do you think of a warm campfire on a cold night or a house reduced to a pile of ashes? All fires are chemically similar, but a fire can be useful or disastrous depending on whether or not it is controlled. You can keep fires under control, but only if you understand fire as a chemical reaction.

Understanding Fire

Fire is the result of **combustion,** a rapid reaction between oxygen and a substance called a fuel. A **fuel** is a material that releases energy when it burns. Some fuels you probably know about are oil, coal, wood, gasoline, and paper. Combustion of these types of fuel always produces carbon dioxide and water. Sometimes products such as smoke and poisonous gases may form from incomplete combustion or the presence of other materials.

The Fire Triangle Although a combustion reaction is very exothermic and fast, a fire cannot start unless conditions are right. **Three things are necessary to start and maintain a fire—fuel, oxygen, and heat.**

You just read about some different fuels. The second part of the fire triangle is oxygen. Where does oxygen come from? About 20 percent of the air around you is composed of oxygen gas. If air can reach the fuel, so can oxygen. A large fire can actually draw oxygen toward it. As other gases in the air around the flame are heated, they move rapidly away from the fire. Cooler air flows toward the fire, bringing a fresh supply of oxygen. If you stand in front of a fire in a fireplace, you can often feel the flow of air to the fire.

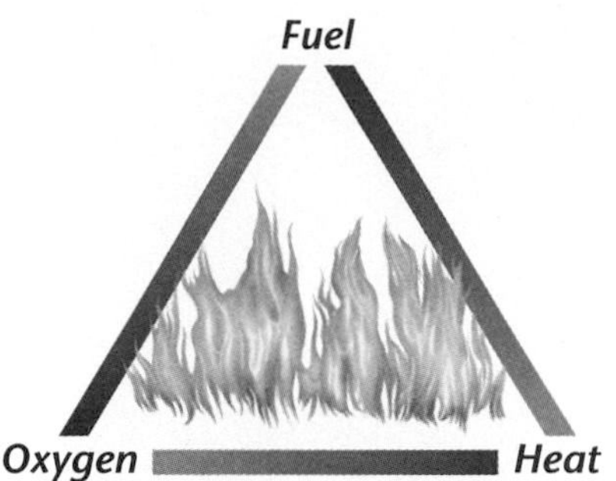

Figure 23 If any point of the fire triangle is missing, a fire will not continue. ***Applying Concepts*** *How does putting a lid over a burning pot of food affect the fire triangle?*

The third part of the fire triangle is heat. Fuel and oxygen can be together, but they won't react until something provides enough activation energy to start the combustion reaction. This energy can come from a lighted match, an electric spark, lightning, or the heat from a stove. Once the reaction starts, the heat released by the combustion can keep the reaction going.

Once a fire has started, it can continue as long as all three components of the fire triangle are available. Coal in abandoned mines underneath the town of Centralia, Pennsylvania, started burning in 1962 and still burns. Many old ventilation shafts lead into the tunnels, but they have never been mapped. Since not all the shafts can be located and sealed, air (containing oxygen) continues to flow into the mines, supporting the fire. Heat and poisonous gases coming up from the fire through cracks in the ground made living in Centralia difficult. Everyone eventually moved away. No one knows how long this fire will burn.

☑ ***Checkpoint*** *What is necesssary to start a fire?*

Controlling Fire Use your knowledge of chemical reactions to think of ways to control a fire. What if you removed one part of the fire triangle? For example, you could get the fuel away from the flames. You could keep oxygen from getting to the fuel, or cool the combustion reaction below its activation energy. Any of these actions may help bring a fire under control.

Think about how firefighters put out a fire in a building. They use large hoses to spray huge amounts of water on the flaming part of the building.

Figure 24 Firefighters use water to cool a fire and prevent oxygen from reaching the fuel.

Water removes two parts of the fire triangle. First, water covers the fuel, which keeps it from coming into contact with oxygen. Second, evaporation of the water uses a large amount of heat, causing the fire to cool. Without heat, there isn't enough energy to reach the activation energy of combustion, so the reaction stops.

Home Fire Safety

Every year, fire claims thousands of lives in the United States. If you know how to prevent fires in your home and what to do if a fire starts, you are better prepared to take action. You may save your home or even your life!

Common Sources of Fires The two most common sources of home fires are small heaters and fires that start in the kitchen during cooking. Another common cause is faulty electrical wiring. The fires that cause the most deaths start from carelessness with cigarettes.

Fighting Fires You can fight a small fire by using what you know about the fire triangle. For example, carbon dioxide gas can be used to smother a fire by preventing contact between the fuel and oxygen in the air. If a small fire should start on the stove,

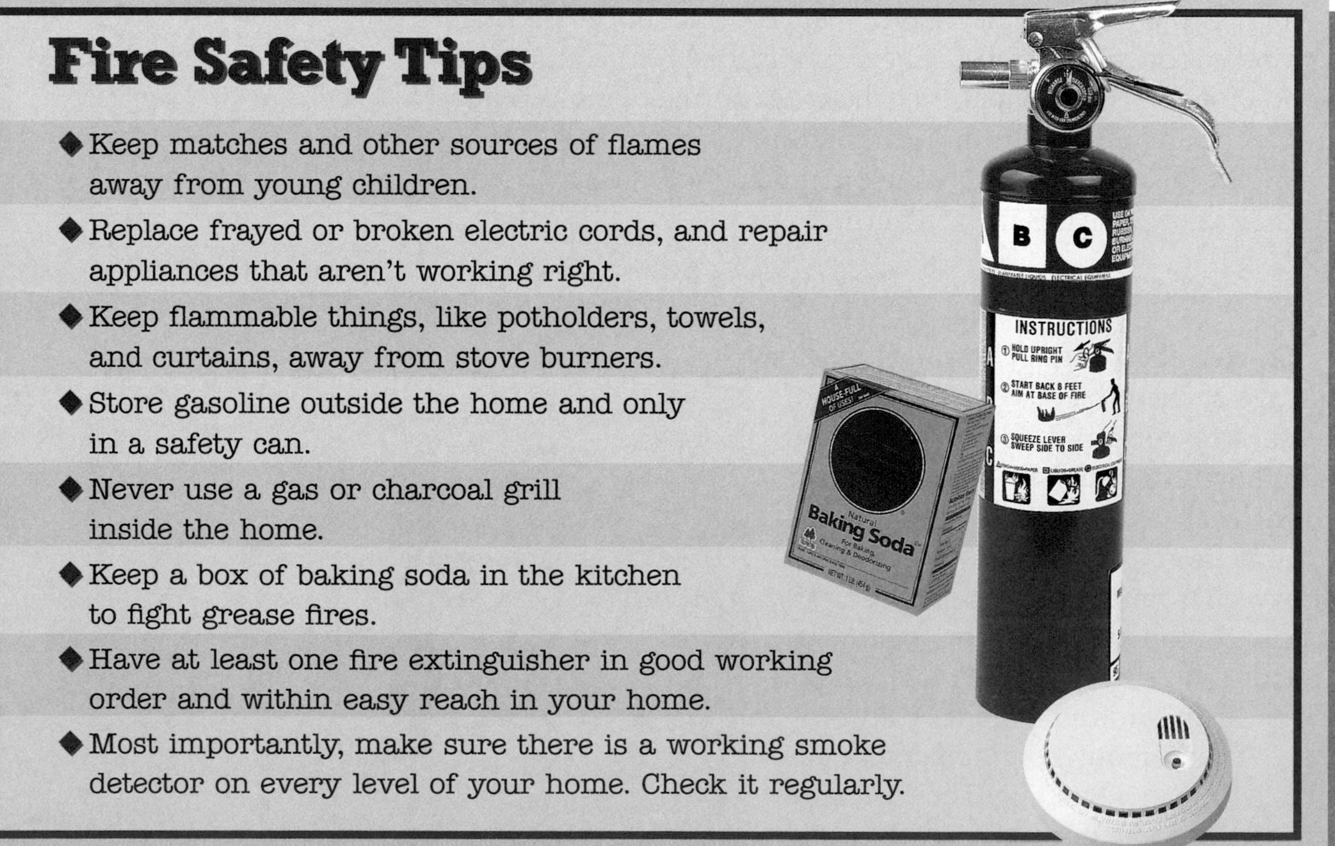

Figure 25 Families can take several steps to prevent fire and to be ready for action if one should start. ***Making Judgments*** *Which of these fire safety aids do you think a home should have?*

covering it with baking soda may put the fire out. Liquids in food will react with baking soda to produce carbon dioxide. The baking soda itself will help smother the fire, too.

The smaller a fire is, the easier it is to control. You can cool a match enough to stop combustion just by blowing on it. A small fire in a trash can may be doused with a pan of water. If the fire spreads to the curtains, however, even a garden hose might not deliver enough water to put it out.

One of the most effective ways to fight a small fire is with a fire extinguisher. Extinguishers designed for home use are effective when used properly. But a fire that is growing as you fight it is out of control. If this happens, there is only one safe thing to do—get away from the fire and let the fire department handle it.

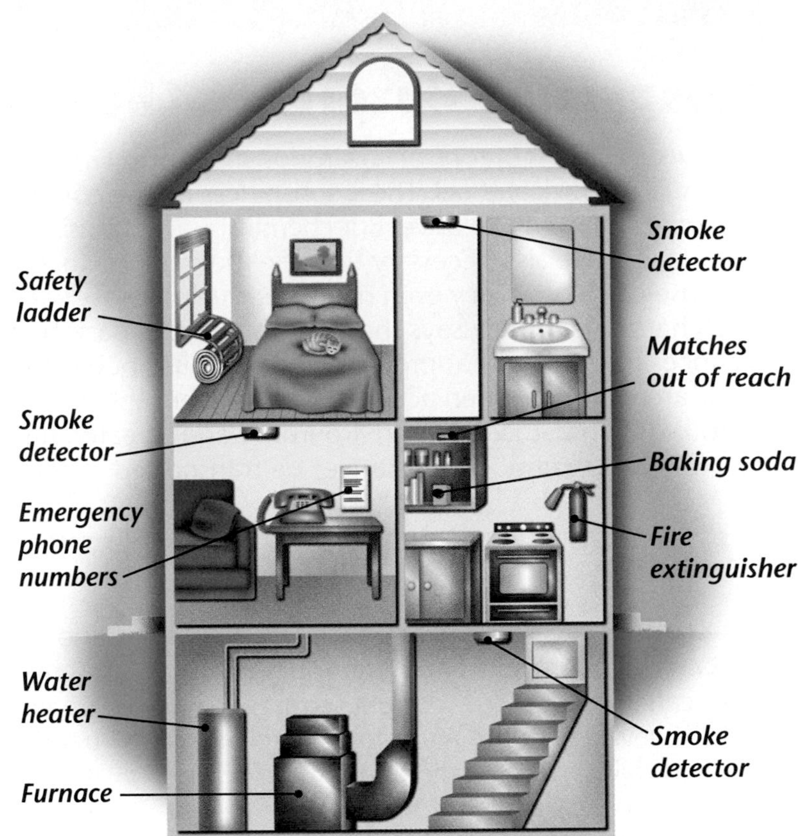

Figure 26 This fire-safe house has many of the fire-prevention features listed in Figure 25. ***Interpreting Illustrations*** *Which of those safety features can you find in the picture?*

Preventing Trouble The best form of fire safety is fire prevention. With your family, check your home for fire hazards and fire-fighting aids. Look at the list on the opposite page for some things you and your family can do.

Fires can be dangerous and deadly, but many fires can be prevented if you are careful. Understanding the chemistry of fire gives you a way to reduce risk and increase your family's safety.

Section 4 Review

1. What are the three points of the fire triangle?
2. Why is water a good tool for fighting most fires?
3. List some of the products of combustion.
4. How does adding carbon dioxide gas to cover a fire control or stop it? Use the fire triangle in your answer.
5. **Thinking Critically Making Judgments** Why is fire prevention one of the best ways to fight fires?

Science at Home

Work with your family to formulate a fire safety plan. How can fires be prevented in your home? How can fires be put out if they occur? Is there a functioning smoke detector on each floor of the home, especially near the bedrooms? How can the fire department be contacted in an emergency? Design a fire escape route. Make sure all family members know the route as well as a meeting place outside.

SCIENCE AND SOCIETY

Transporting Hazardous Chemicals

Each year, millions of tons of hazardous substances criss-cross the country by truck and rail. These substances can be poisonous, flammable, and even explosive. But chemical reactions using these materials are also necessary to make the products that people use every day. They even make the trucks themselves run.

The chemical industry says that the transport of hazardous substances is safe and that problems are rare. But public health officials are worried. When accidents do happen, these compounds can damage the environment and threaten human lives. How can hazardous substances be transported safely?

The Issues

Why Do People Transport Hazardous Substances? Transporting hazardous substances can be dangerous. Useful products are made, however, from the hazardous materials that trucks and trains carry. Would people give up cars, computers, and CDs?

For example, CDs are made from plastics. To produce these plastics, manufacturers use compounds such as benzene and styrene. Benzene fumes are poisonous and flammable. Styrene can explode when exposed to air. Public health experts say it is important to find safe substitutes for dangerous substances. But finding alternatives will be difficult and expensive.

What Are the Risks? Serious accidents are rare. But in the United States in a recent year, there were over 300 accidents involving hazardous chemical releases. Public health experts say that some substances are too hazardous to transport on roads and railroads. An accidental release of these substances near a city could harm many people.

Some people say that vehicles carrying chemically reactive or hazardous substances should be restricted to isolated roads. However, many factories that use the chemical compounds are located in cities. Chemicals often must be transported from where they are made to where they are used. In the case of gasoline, cars are everywhere. Trucks and trains must transport the fuel to every neighborhood and region of the country.

How Should Transportation Be Regulated? Manufacturers that use hazardous chemicals say that there already are adequate laws. The Hazardous Materials Transportation Act (1975, revised 1994) requires carriers of hazardous substances to follow strict labeling and packaging rules. They must keep records of what they carry and where they travel. Local emergency officials in communities near transportation routes must also be trained to handle accidents involving these substances.

On the other hand, public health experts say there are not enough inspectors to check all trucks and trains and make sure rules are followed. But hiring more inspectors would cost additional tax money.

You Decide

1. Identify the Problem
In your own words, explain the problem of safely transporting hazardous substances.

2. Analyze the Options
Examine the pros and cons of greater regulation of the transport of hazardous substances. In each position, consider the effects on chemical industries and on the general public.

3. Find a Solution
Suppose there is a chemical factory in your city. You are the emergency planning director. Create regulations for transporting hazardous substances through your community.

CHAPTER 10 STUDY GUIDE

Matter and Changes in Matter

Key Ideas

- Matter may be in the form of elements, compounds, or mixtures.
- Chemical changes result in the formation of new substances. Physical changes do not.
- Chemical reactions occur when chemical bonds are formed or broken.

Key Terms

chemistry	chemical change
element	chemical reaction
compound	precipitate
mixture	atom
solution	molecule
physical change	chemical bond

Describing Chemical Reactions

Key Ideas

- A chemical equation uses symbols for the reactants and products of a chemical reaction.
- Chemical reactions may be classified by the types of changes in reactants and products.

Key Terms

chemical equation	conservation of mass
symbol	coefficient
chemical formula	synthesis
subscript	decomposition
reactants	replacement
products	

Controlling Chemical Reactions

Key Ideas

- A chemical reaction involves a change in energy.
- The rate of a chemical reaction can be controlled by such factors as concentration, surface area, temperature, and use of a catalyst or inhibitor.

Key Terms

exothermic reaction	catalyst
endothermic reaction	enzyme
activation energy	inhibitor
concentration	

Fire and Fire Safety

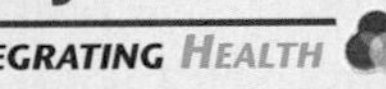

Key Ideas

- The fire triangle shows the three things necessary to start a fire and keep it burning: fuel, oxygen, and heat.
- Water stops combustion by keeping the fuel from coming in contact with oxygen. Also, evaporation of water uses a great deal of heat and cools the fire.

Key Terms

combustion	fuel

Organizing Information

Concept Map Copy the concept map, then complete it and add a title.

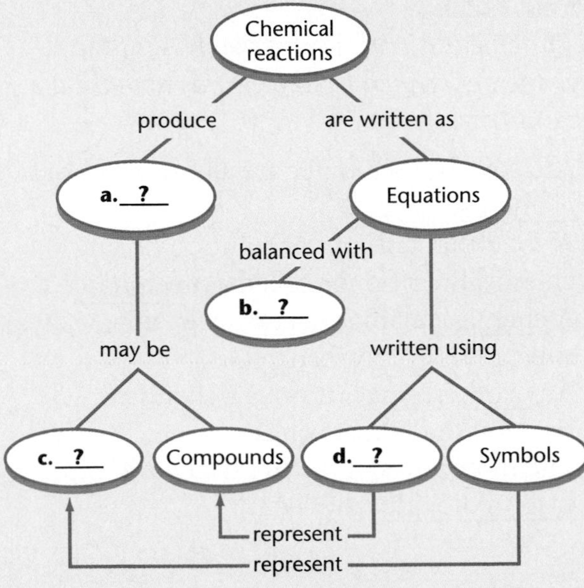

Reviewing Content

Multiple Choice

Choose the letter of the best answer.

1. A chemical equation shows
   a. elements and mixtures.
   b. hydrogen and oxygen.
   c. reactants and products.
   d. chemical bonds.
2. You can balance a chemical equation by changing the
   a. coefficients. b. products.
   c. reactants. d. formulas.
3. The reaction between sulfur trioxide and water ($SO_3 + H_2O \rightarrow H_2SO_4$) is a
   a. replacement reaction.
   b. synthesis reaction.
   c. decomposition reaction.
   d. physical change.
4. The rate of a chemical reaction can be increased by all the following, except:
   a. increasing temperature.
   b. increasing concentration.
   c. decreasing concentration.
   d. increasing surface area.
5. To extinguish a fire, do *not*
   a. remove fuel.
   b. add oxygen.
   c. reduce heat.
   d. add baking soda.

True or False

If the statement is true, write true. If it is false, change the underlined word or words to make the statement true.

6. Air, soil, and sea water are all examples of <u>elements</u>.
7. A solid that falls out of solution during a chemical reaction is called a <u>precipitate</u>.
8. A <u>chemical</u> change occurs when new substances are formed.
9. An <u>exothermic</u> reaction is a chemical reaction that absorbs heat.
10. The three parts of the fire triangle are fuel, <u>carbon dioxide</u>, and heat.

Checking Concepts

11. How can millions of compounds exist if there are only about 100 elements?
12. Why can't you balance a chemical equation by changing the subscripts?
13. You find the mass of a piece of iron metal, let it rust, and measure the mass again. The mass has increased. Does this violate the law of conservation of mass? Explain.
14. A fire starts in a frying pan in your kitchen. You grab a box of baking soda and throw its contents into the pan. Bubbling and foaming occur, and the fire goes out. What is the evidence that a chemical reaction has occurred?
15. **Writing to Learn** Imagine you are teaching a group of younger students about the difference between chemical and physical changes. One of the students claims the change from liquid water to water vapor is chemical. Write a brief paragraph of what you would say to convince the student otherwise.

Thinking Critically

16. **Applying Concepts** Balance the following equations and tell whether they are synthesis, decomposition, or replacement reactions.
    a. $Fe + HCl \rightarrow FeCl_2 + H_2$
    b. $N_2 + O_2 \rightarrow N_2O_5$
    c. $H_2CO_3 \rightarrow H_2O + CO_2$
    d. $CuO + H_2SO_4 \rightarrow CuSO_4 + H_2O$
17. **Problem Solving** Steel that is exposed to water and salt rusts quickly. If you were a shipbuilder, how would you protect a new ship? Explain why your solution works.
18. **Relating Cause and Effect** Firefighters open doors very carefully, because sometimes a room will explode into flames when the door is opened. Based on your knowledge of reaction rates and the fire triangle, why does this happen?

Applying Skills

Use the energy diagram to answer Questions 19–21.

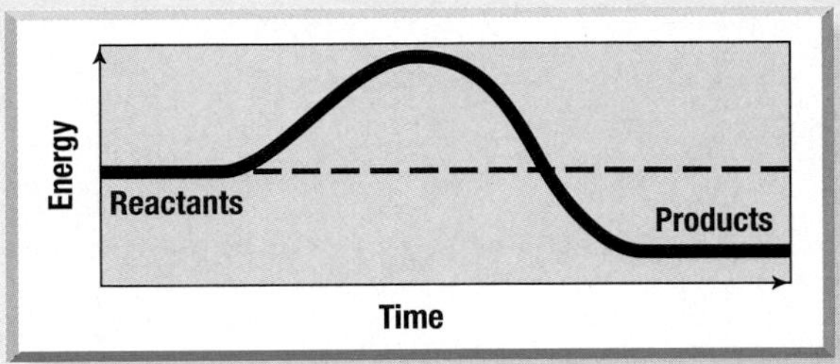

19. **Interpreting Data** How does the energy of the products compare with the energy of the reactants?
20. **Classifying** Tell whether this reaction is exothermic or endothermic.
21. **Predicting** What would happen to the graph if a catalyst were added to the reaction? Would adding heat to the reaction change the height of the curve? Explain.

Performance Assessment (Chapter Project 10)

Project Wrap Up Compare the reactions in your chemical change log with those of your classmates. How many of the same processes did you observe? Defend your opinions as to whether or not your observations were chemical changes. Together make a list of the types of evidence you observed, and classify the reactions as endothermic or exothermic.

Reflect and Record In your journal, answer these questions. What evidence of chemical change is easiest to detect? What types of chemical reactions did you observe most frequently? Give an example of a chemical reaction you suspect was taking place, but for which you could not find direct evidence.

Test Preparation

Use these questions to prepare for standardized tests.

Read the information below. Then answer Questions 22–26.

A laboratory assistant was experimenting with chemical reactions when she combined a small amount of zinc (Zn) with hydrochloric acid (HCl). She discovered that zinc chloride ($ZnCl_2$) and hydrogen (H_2) were produced.

22. Which of the following substances are the reactants?
    a. Zn + HCl
    b. $ZnCl_2 + H_2$
    c. $Zn + H_2$
    d. $ZnCl_2$ + HCl
23. Which of the following substances are the products?
    a. Zn + HCl
    b. $ZnCl_2 + H_2$
    c. $Zn + H_2$
    d. $ZnCl_2$ + HCl
24. Which equation correctly describes this reaction?
    a. $Zn + HCl \rightarrow ZnCl_2 + H_2$
    b. $ZnCl_2 + H_2 \rightarrow Zn + 2\ HCl$
    c. $Zn + 2HCl \rightarrow ZnCl_2 + H_2$
    d. $2\ Zn + 2\ HCl \rightarrow 2\ (ZnCl_2 + H_2)$
25. How should the assistant classify this reaction?
    a. synthesis
    b. decomposition
    c. replacement
    d. combustion
26. Which of the following actions would probably speed up the reaction between zinc and hydrochloric acid?
    a. making sure the masses of the reactants and the products are the same
    b. cooling down the reactants before combining them
    c. adding an inhibitor
    d. breaking up the zinc into smaller pieces

CHAPTER 11

Atoms and Bonding

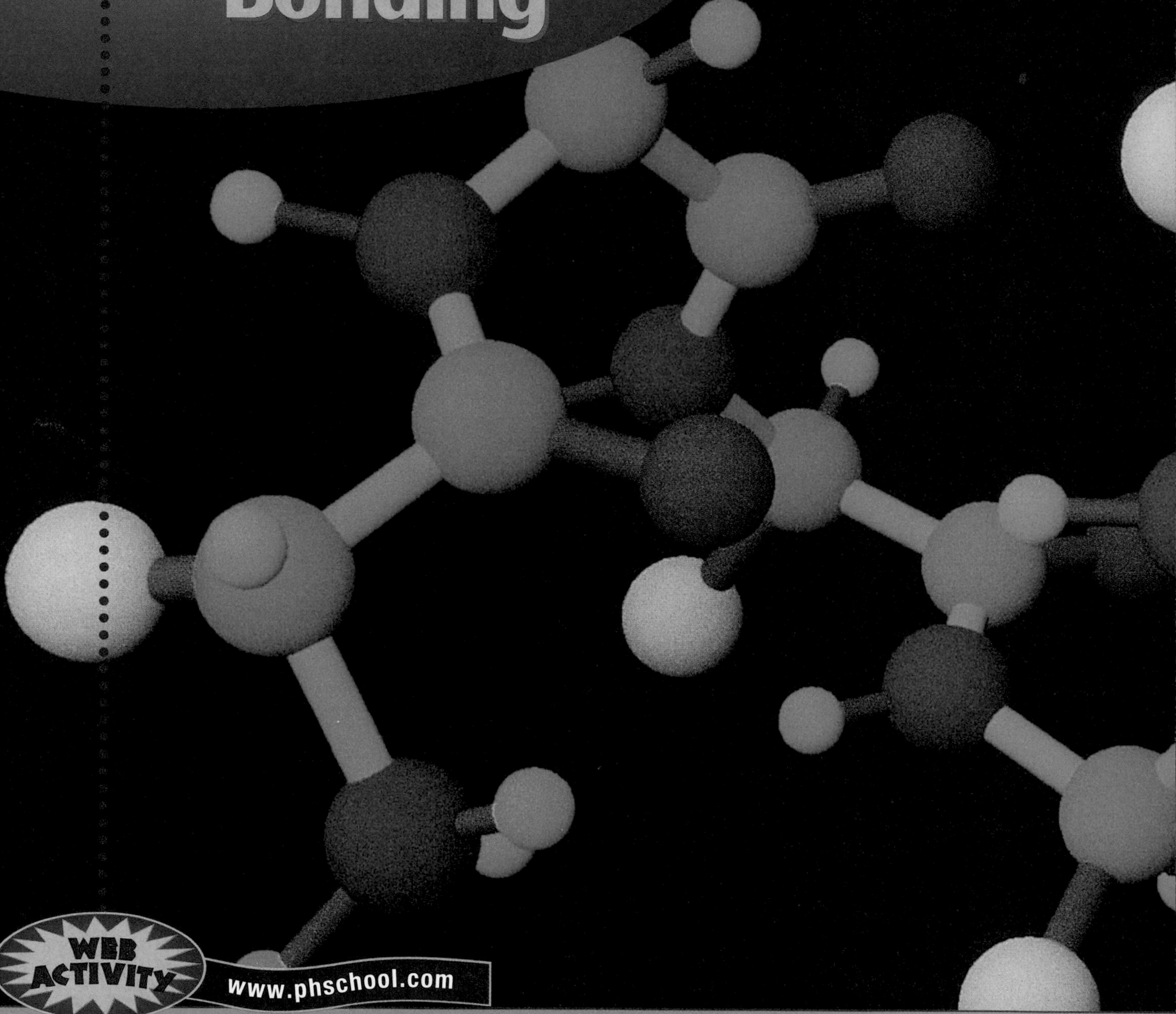

www.phschool.com

Section 1 Inside an Atom

Discover How Far Away Is the Electron?

Section 2 Atoms in the Periodic Table

Discover What Are the Trends in the Periodic Table?

Sharpen Your Skills Classifying

Skills Lab Comparing Atom Sizes

Section 3 Ionic Bonds

Discover How Do Ions Form?

Sharpen Your Skills Interpreting Data

Try This Crystal Clear

PROJECT 11

Molecule Models

With computer-made models like these, you can see molecules up close and personal. Many compounds are made of molecules—much tinier, of course, than these models.

In this chapter, you will learn why atoms react with one another. You will also learn about the different types of chemical bonds that can hold atoms together. In your project you can use fruits, vegetables, or other materials to make models of atoms and show the way they bond in compounds.

Your Goal To make models demonstrating how atoms bond in compounds that contain ionic and covalent bonds.

To complete the project you must
- select appropriate materials to make models of atoms
- design a way to tell the difference between the atoms of various elements
- indicate the correct number of bonds each atom forms
- use your model atoms to compare compounds that contain ionic and covalent bonds

Get Started Brainstorm with some your classmates about materials you can use to represent atoms and chemical bonds. You may want to look ahead in the chapter to preview covalent and ionic bonding.

Check Your Progress You'll be working on this project as you study this chapter. To keep your project on track, look for Check Your Progress boxes at the following points.

Section 1 Review, page 358: Make models of atoms.
Section 3 Review, page 368: Build models of ionic compounds.
Section 4 Review, page 373: Build models of compounds that contain covalent bonds.

Wrap Up At the end of the chapter (page 381), you will present and explain your models to the class.

A computer-made model of a protein shows the many atoms that are bonded together in the molecule.

Section 4 Covalent Bonds

Discover **Why Don't Water and Oil Mix?**
Sharpen Your Skills **Designing Experiments**
Skills Lab **Shedding Light on Chemical Bonds**

Integrating Earth Science
Section 5 Crystal Chemistry

Discover **How Small Do They Get?**

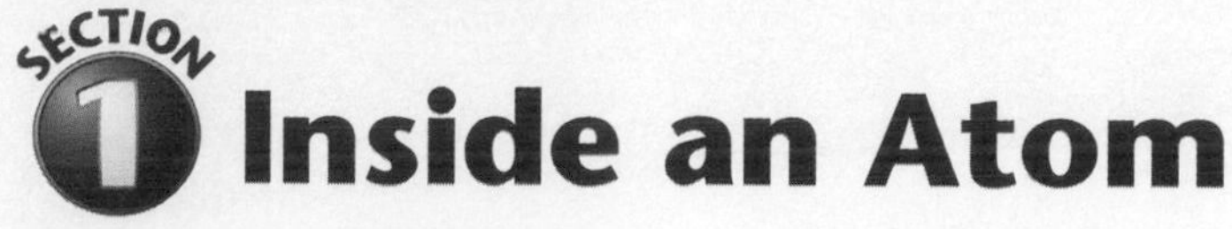

SECTION 1 Inside an Atom

DISCOVER

How Far Away Is the Electron?

1. On a piece of paper, make a small circle no bigger than a dime. The circle represents the nucleus, or center, of a model atom.
2. Measure the diameter of the circle in centimeters.
3. Now predict where you think the outer edge of this model atom will be. For example, will the outer edge be within the edges of the paper? Your desk? The classroom? The school building?

Think It Over

Making Models The diameter of an actual atom can be 100,000 times the diameter of its nucleus. Calculate the diameter of your model atom. How close was your prediction in Step 3 to your calculation? (*Hint:* To compare your result to the real world, change the units of your prediction from centimeters to meters.)

GUIDE FOR READING

- **What is the structure of an atom?**
- **What role do valence electrons play in forming chemical bonds?**

Reading Tip **As you read, make a table listing the particles found in an atom. Include the name of each particle, its charge, and where in an atom the particle is located.**

Picture this: It's –5°C, five degrees below the freezing temperature of water. Two white solids—ice and salt—are side by side. You begin to heat the materials to see how each one will change. As the temperature rises, the ice melts at 0°C, making liquid water. It then boils into a gas at 100°C. The water is long gone before you notice a change in the salt. Finally, at 801°C the salt begins to melt. It boils away when the temperature reaches 1,413°C.

Although these materials were both solids when you started heating them, they showed very different properties as conditions changed. These differences are caused in part by the kinds of chemical bonds that hold their atoms together. To understand how atoms bond, you first need to know more about atoms themselves.

Structure of an Atom

Ice, salt, and all other materials in your world are made of atoms. Atoms are so small it would take about two million to make a line across the period at the end of this sentence. It's amazing that things so tiny are the building blocks of all substances in the universe.

If you could look into a single atom, what might you see? Figuring out what atoms are made of hasn't been simple. Theories about their shape and structure have changed many times over the past 200 years and continue to change even now. But some properties of atoms are well understood. For one thing, scientists know atoms are made of even smaller particles.

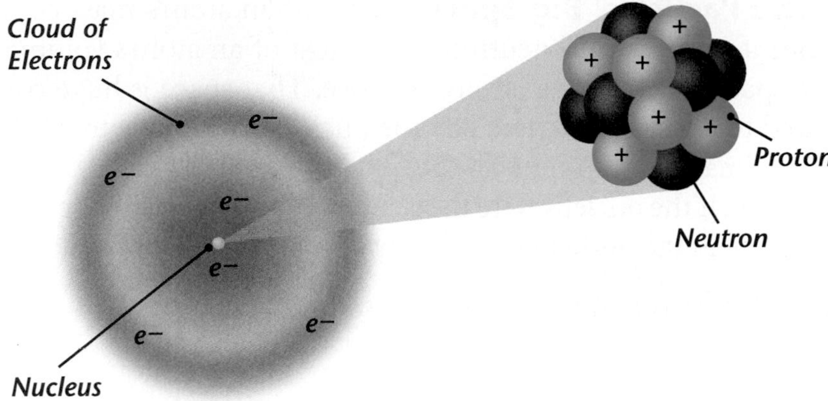

Figure 1 An atom's tiny nucleus contains protons and neutrons. The electrons move in the space around the nucleus.
Applying Concepts *Is this carbon atom negatively charged, positively charged, or neutral overall?*

An atom consists of a nucleus surrounded by one or more electrons. The **nucleus** (NOO klee us) is the tiny, central core of an atom. It contains particles called protons and neutrons. **Protons** have a positive electric charge (indicated by a plus symbol, +). **Neutrons** have no charge. They are neutral. (Could you guess that from their name?) A third type of particle moves in the space around the outside of the nucleus. These very energetic particles, called **electrons,** move rapidly in all directions. Electrons carry a negative charge (indicated by a negative symbol, –).

Look at the carbon atom illustrated in Figure 1. If you count the number of protons and electrons, you'll see there are six of each. In an atom, the number of protons equals the number of electrons. As a result, the total positive charge and total negative charge balance each other, making the atom neutral. The number of neutrons in an atom may be the same as the number of protons, but not always.

Although the charges of a proton and an electron cancel each other out, the particles differ greatly in mass. A proton is almost 2,000 times as massive as an electron! Neutrons, however, have about the same mass as protons.

☑ ***Checkpoint*** *Which particles in an atom are in the nucleus?*

Electrons in Atoms

Electrons move around the nucleus so fast that it is impossible to know exactly where any electron is at a particular time. Think about the blades of a fan that is turned on. They go too fast to be seen. As electrons move around the nucleus, the effect is like the fan blades, but in three dimensions. You can think of the space around the nucleus as a spherical cloud of negatively charged electrons.

Figure 2 When a fan is turned on, you see a blur instead of separate blades. A fan is a model for the way electrons fill the space around the nucleus of an atom.

Little Particles, Big Spaces Most of an atom's mass comes from its protons and neutrons. But most of an atom's volume is the space in which the electrons move. That space is huge compared to the space occupied by the nucleus. To picture the difference, imagine standing at the pitcher's mound in a baseball stadium. If the nucleus were the size of a pencil eraser, the electrons could be in the outfield or as far away as the top row of seats!

☑ ***Checkpoint*** *Where are the electrons in an atom?*

Models of Atoms

For over two centuries, scientists have worked on models of atoms in an effort to understand why matter behaves as it does. As scientists have learned more, the model of the atom has changed.

1808

Dalton Model

British chemist John Dalton published his *New System of Chemical Philosophy*, explaining that each element is made of small atoms and that different elements have atoms of different mass. Dalton imagined atoms as tiny, solid balls.

1897

Thomson Model

British scientist J. J. Thomson proposed a new model. He suggested that an atom is a positively charged sphere with electrons embedded in it. His model could be described as looking like a muffin with berries scattered through it.

1800 — **1900**

For almost 100 years, not much new information was learned about atoms.

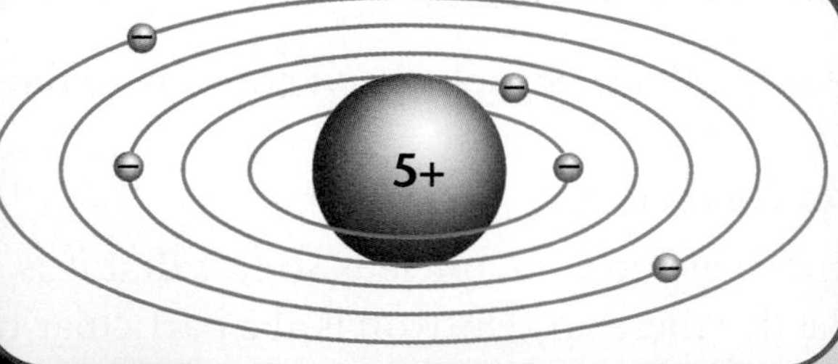

1904 Nagaoka Model

Japanese physicist Hantaro Nagaoka proposed a model of the atom that had a large sphere in the center with a positive charge. His model showed the electrons revolving around this sphere like the planets around the sun.

Valence Electrons An atom's electrons are not all the same distance from the nucleus. Nor are they held to the atom with equal strength. Those farthest away or most loosely held are called **valence electrons** (VAY luns). The number of valence electrons in an atom determines many properties of the atom, and therefore, of an element. For example, only valence electrons are involved in chemical bonding.

In Your Journal

Find out more about one of the scientists who worked on models of the atom. Write an imaginary interview with this person in which you discuss his work with him.

1911

Rutherford Model

British physicist Ernest Rutherford concluded that the atom is mostly empty space. Electrons orbit randomly around a small, positively charged nucleus.

1932

Chadwick Model

British physicist James Chadwick discovered the neutron, a particle having about the same mass as the proton but with no electrical charge. The existence of the neutron explained why atoms were heavier than the total mass of their protons and electrons.

1910 | 1920 | 1930 | 1940 | 1950

1913

Bohr Model

Danish physicist Niels Bohr determined that electrons aren't randomly located around the nucleus. His model showed electrons moving in specific layers, or shells. He said that atoms absorb or give off energy when the electrons move from one shell to another.

1920s to Present

Modern Model

The current model of the atom came from the work of many scientists from the 1920s to the present. It shows the electrons as forming a negatively charged cloud around the nucleus. It is impossible to determine exactly where an electron is at any given time.

Figure 3 In electron dot diagrams, each dot represents one outer, or valence, electron of an atom. ***Interpreting Diagrams*** *Each hydrogen atom has only one electron, but an argon atom has 18 electrons. How many of argon's electrons are valence electrons?*

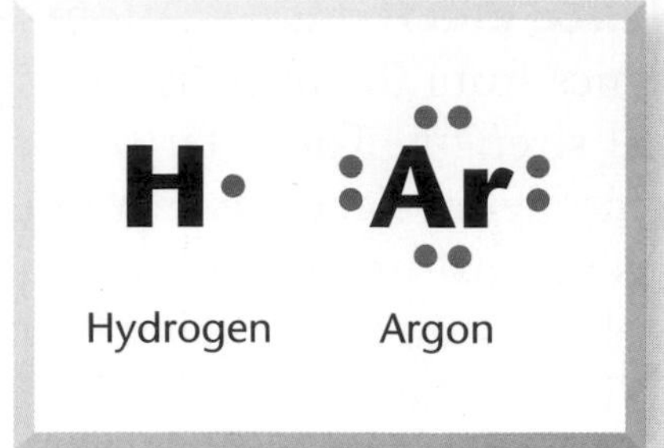

One way to show the number of valence electrons that an atom has is with an **electron dot diagram.** It includes the symbol for an element surrounded by dots. Each dot stands for one valence electron.

Why Atoms Form Bonds

A neutral atom never has more than eight valence electrons. Most kinds of atoms have fewer. When atoms form bonds with each other, one of two things usually happens. Either the number of valence electrons increases to a total of eight, or all the valence electrons are given up. When atoms end up with eight or zero valence electrons, they become less reactive than they were before. Chemists say that such atoms are more chemically stable.

A chemical bond forms between two atoms when valence electrons move between them. Electrons may be transferred from one atom to another, or they may be shared between the atoms. In either case, the change causes the atoms to become connected, or bonded. Chemical reactions occur when bonds between atoms form. Reactions also occur when bonds are broken. Each time, electrons are moved around. The result is the formation of new substances.

Section 1 Review

1. Describe the parts of an atom and tell where each is found.
2. Explain why the electrical charge on an atom is zero, or neutral.
3. What happens to valence electrons during the formation of chemical bonds?
4. Explain why electrons make up much of an atom's volume but not much of its mass.
5. **Thinking Critically Applying Concepts** What information can you get from an electron dot diagram?

Check Your Progress

CHAPTER PROJECT 11

Select materials to use to build your models. Start by making models of several common elements such as hydrogen, oxygen, nitrogen, carbon, chlorine, sodium, potassium, and sulfur. (*Hint:* You will need to represent the valence electrons on each atom.) Make several atoms of each element and save them. Select materials to represent the chemical bonds.

Atoms in the Periodic Table

DISCOVER — ACTIVITY

What Are the Trends in the Periodic Table?

1. Examine closely the periodic table of the elements your teacher provides. Each square shows the chemical symbol for an element plus information about the element.
2. Look in each square for the whole number located above the symbol of the element. As you read across a row from left to right, what trend do you see?
3. Now look at a column from top to bottom. What pattern do you see in these numbers?

Think It Over

Interpreting Data Are the elements organized in alphabetical order? Can you explain why one row ends and a new row starts? Why do you think certain elements are in the same column? What questions would you need to ask in order to understand how the elements are organized?

GUIDE FOR READING

- **How is the periodic table organized?**
- **What do elements in a family have in common?**

Reading Tip **As you read, use the periodic table in Appendix D for reference. Look for repeating patterns.**

Mix some elements together and nothing happens. Mix other elements together and they react as explosively as the sodium and bromine in Figure 4. Other combinations of elements react either slowly or only when heated. Recall that atoms react with each other as a result of how many valence electrons each has. Therefore, knowing the number of valence electrons in atoms is a clue to which elements combine, and how. But where do you look for this information? You can look in the periodic table of the elements.

Organizing the Elements

The periodic table is a system used worldwide for organizing elements into categories based on how they react. The way the elements are organized in the periodic table also tells you something about their protons and electrons.

All the atoms of one kind of element have the same number of protons. For example, all carbon atoms have six protons, and all hydrogen atoms have only one. The **atomic number** is the number of protons in the nucleus of an atom. **Look at any periodic table and you will see that elements are arranged from left to right and top to bottom in order of increasing atomic number.** Remember that if you know the number of protons in an atom, you also know the number of electrons.

Figure 4 The elements sodium and bromine react with an explosion.

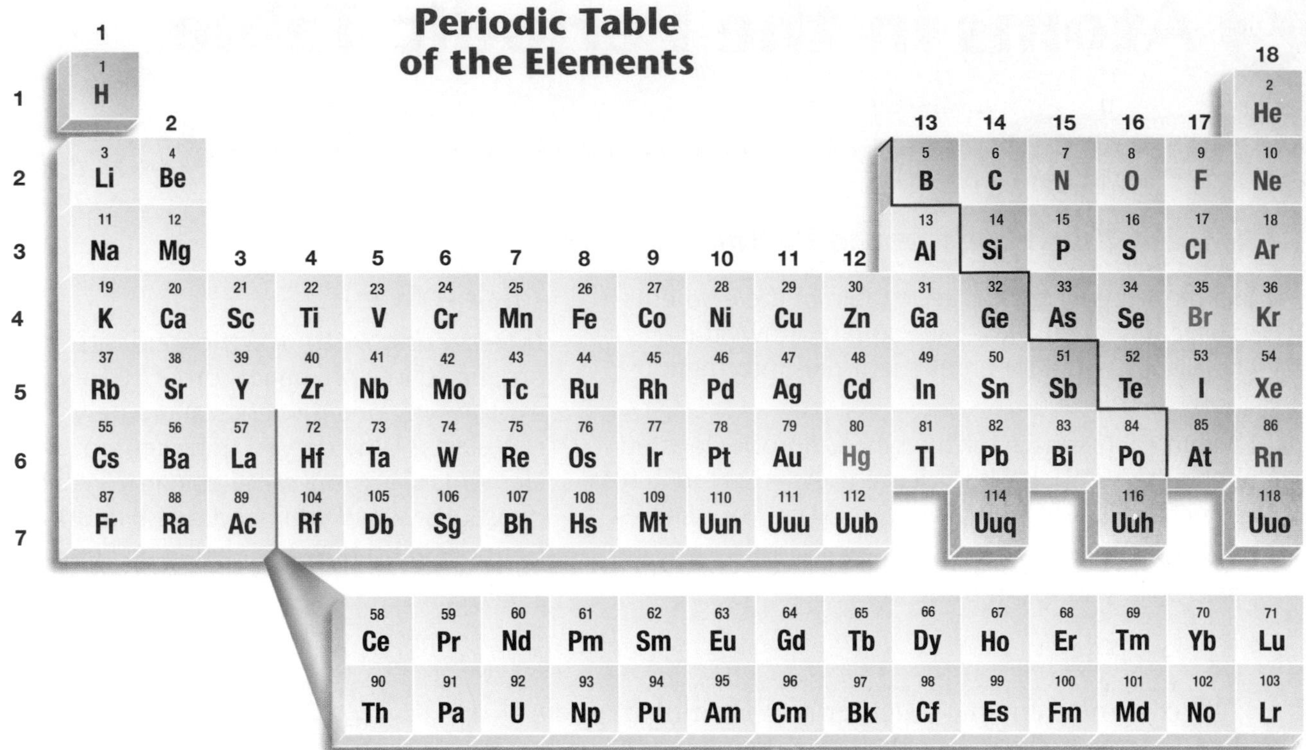

Figure 5 The periodic table organizes the elements into rows and columns.

Classifying

ACTIVITY

Match each element on the left with the element on the right that has the most similar chemical properties. Use the periodic table to help you.

Krypton (Kr)	Sodium (Na)
Phosphorus (P)	Neon (Ne)
Potassium (K)	Calcium (Ca)
Magnesium (Mg)	Sulfur (S)
Silicon (Si)	Nitrogen (N)
Oxygen (O)	Carbon (C)

Why did you match the pairs as you did?

Elements in the same column, up and down, are called a **group,** or **family.** Notice the numbers 1 through 18 across the tops of the columns in Figure 5. These numbers identify the group to which an element belongs. For example, carbon (C) is in Group 14 and oxygen (O) is in Group 16.

A row across the table is called a **period.** Hydrogen and helium make up the first period. The second period starts with lithium (Li) and continues across to neon (Ne). Notice that the atomic number increases one at a time from left to right across the periodic table. The number of valence electrons increases from left to right, too. Figure 6 shows the electron dot diagrams for the elements in the second period of the table.

☑ ***Checkpoint*** *What is the difference between a group and a period in the periodic table?*

Comparing Families of Elements

If you saw a flock of ducks on a pond, would you notice any similarities among the birds? Would they share characteristics that would set them apart from crows or robins on the nearby shore? **Each family in the periodic table has its own characteristic properties based on its number of valence electrons.**

Noble Gases Group 18 at the far right side of the table is a good place to start learning about the characteristics of the families. Except for helium, atoms of these elements have eight valence electrons. (Look at the electron dot diagram for neon at right, as an example.) The Group 18 elements are known as the noble gases or inert gases. *Inert* means "inactive." Since they already have the maximum number of valence electrons, noble gas atoms don't react very easily with other atoms. Helium, which is as unreactive as the other noble gases, is stable with only two valence electrons.

Reactive Nonmetals Now look at the column to the left of the noble gases. The elements in Group 17, also called the **halogen** family, are very reactive. Atoms of these elements have seven valence electrons, as illustrated by fluorine in Figure 6. A gain of just one electron leads to the more stable number of eight. As a result, elements in the halogen family react easily with other elements whose atoms can give up electrons.

Reactive Metals At the far left side of the periodic table is Group 1, the elements of the alkali metal family. If alkali metals lose one electron, the atoms are left with zero valence electrons. They become more chemically stable. This property makes the alkali metals very reactive elements. If the alkali metals lose electrons easily and the halogens gain electrons easily, what happens when they come in contact with each other? They react violently! This explains the explosive reaction between sodium and bromine shown at the beginning of this section. These two elements form the compound sodium bromide.

Hydrogen is located above Group 1 on the periodic table because it has only one valence electron. Like the alkali metal elements, hydrogen is extremely reactive.

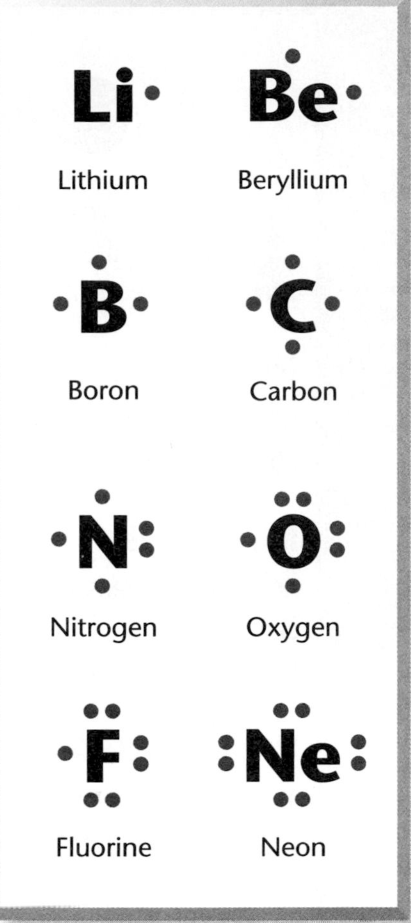

Figure 6 These eight elements make up the second period. ***Calculating*** *What is the trend in number of valence electrons from lithium to neon?*

Section 2 Review

1. What is the basis for arranging the elements in the periodic table?
2. Why are the elements in each group in the periodic table considered a family?
3. What properties are shared by the noble gases?
4. **Thinking Critically Applying Concepts** How can you use the arrangement of elements in the periodic table to predict how they will react with other elements to form compounds?

Science at Home

People use many organization systems. Think of tools in a workshop or baseball cards in a collection. Look around your home for as many different systems of organization you can find. Check out drawers and cabinets. Look for things lined up in rows. Then discuss with your family how these systems of organization compare with the periodic table of the elements.

Skills Lab

Making Models

Comparing Atom Sizes

In this lab, you will be using models to compare the sizes of atoms in one family of elements in the periodic table.

Problem

How is the radius of an atom related to its atomic number?

Materials

drawing compass
calculator
periodic table of the elements (Appendix D)

Procedure 

1. Using the periodic table as a reference, predict whether the size (radius) of atoms will increase, remain the same, or decrease as you go from the top to the bottom of a chemical family.
2. Look at the table on this page that lists each element in Group 2 and its atomic radius. Copy the table into your notebook.
3. Calculate the relative radius of each atom compared to beryllium, the smallest atom listed. Do this by dividing each radius in the table by the value for beryllium. (*Hint:* The relative radius of magnesium would be 160 divided by 112, or 1.4.) Record these values, rounded to the nearest tenth, in your data table.
4. Using a compass, draw a circle for each element with a radius that corresponds to the relative radius you calculated in Step 3. Use centimeters as your unit for the radius of each of these circles. **CAUTION:** *Do not push the sharp point of the compass against your skin.*
5. Label each model with the symbol of the element it represents.

DATA TABLE

Atomic Number	Element	Radius (pm)*	Relative Radius
4	Be	112	1
12	Mg	160	
20	Ca	197	
38	Sr	215	
56	Ba	222	

*A picometer (pm) is one billionth of a millimeter.

Analyze and Conclude

1. Based on your models, was your prediction in Step 1 correct? Explain your answer.
2. Make a graph of the data given in the first and third columns of your table. Label the horizontal axis Atomic Number. Mark the divisions from 0 to 60. Then label the vertical axis Radius and mark its divisions from 0 to 300 picometers.
3. Do your points fall on a straight line or on a curve? What pattern does your graph show?
4. Predict where you would find the largest atom in any chemical family. What evidence would you need to tell if your prediction is correct?
5. **Think About It** If an atom has an actual radius of 100 to 200 picometers, why would drawing a model with a radius of about one to two centimeters be useful?

More to Explore

Look up the atomic masses for the Group 2 elements. Devise a plan to model their relative atomic masses using real-world objects.

SECTION 3 Ionic Bonds

DISCOVER ACTIVITY

How Do Ions Form?

1. Place three pairs of checkers (three red and three black) on your desk. The red represent electrons and the black represent protons.
2. Place nine pairs of checkers (nine red and nine black) in a separate group on your desk.
3. Move a red checker from the smaller group to the larger group.
4. Count the number of positive charges (protons) and negative charges (electrons) in each group.
5. Now sort the checkers into a group of four pairs and a group of eight pairs. Repeat Steps 3 and 4, this time moving two red checkers from the smaller group to the larger group.

Think It Over

Modeling What is the total charge on each group before you moved the red checkers (electrons)? What is the charge on each group after you moved the checkers? Based on this activity, what do you think happens to the charge of an atom when it loses electrons? When it gains electrons?

Imagine you are walking down the street with your best friend. A market has a bin of apples for sale. A sign says that they cost 40 cents each. You both want an apple, but your friend has only 35 cents while you have 45 cents. What can you do? It doesn't take you long to figure out that if you give your friend a nickel, you can each buy an apple. Transferring the nickel to your friend gets both of you what you want. Your actions model, in a simple way, what can happen between atoms.

GUIDE FOR READING

- **How does an atom become an ion?**
- **What are the characteristic properties of ionic compounds?**
- **How are the ions in an ionic compound held together?**

Reading Tip **As you read, make an outline describing the characteristics of compounds containing ionic bonds.**

Electron Transfer

Like your friend with not quite enough money to buy an apple, an atom with five, six, or seven valence electrons has not quite enough to total the more stable number of eight. On the other hand, an atom with one, two, or three valence electrons can lose a few and become stable. When atoms have fewer than four valence electrons, they can transfer these to other atoms that have more than four. In this way, atoms either gain electrons or lose electrons, becoming more stable.

Figure 7 When an atom loses one of its negatively charged electrons, it becomes a positively charged ion.

An **ion** (EYE ahn) is an atom or group of atoms that has become electrically charged. **When an atom loses an electron, it loses a negative charge and becomes a positive ion. When an atom gains an electron, it gains a negative charge and becomes a negative ion.**

Figure 8 Positively charged ions have lost one or more electrons. Negatively charged ions have gained one or more electrons. ***Classifying*** *Which ions in the table are positively charged and which are negatively charged?*

Ions and Their Charges		
Name	**Charge**	**Symbol or Formula**
Lithium	1+	Li^+
Sodium	1+	Na^+
Potassium	1+	K^+
Ammonium	1+	NH_4^+
Calcium	2+	Ca^{2+}
Magnesium	2+	Mg^{2+}
Aluminum	3+	Al^{3+}
Fluoride	1–	F^-
Chloride	1–	Cl^-
Iodide	1–	I^-
Bicarbonate	1–	HCO_3^-
Nitrate	1–	NO_3^-
Oxide	2–	O^{2-}
Sulfide	2–	S^{2-}
Carbonate	2–	CO_3^{2-}
Sulfate	2–	SO_4^{2-}
Phosphate	3–	PO_4^{3-}

Forming an Ionic Bond

Consider what can happen if sodium and chlorine atoms combine. Sodium has one valence electron and chlorine has seven. Suppose sodium's valence electron is transferred to chlorine. Then both atoms become ions. The sodium atom becomes a positive ion (Na^+). The chlorine atom becomes a negative ion (Cl^-). Negative and positive electric charges attract each other, so the oppositely charged Na^+ and Cl^- ions come together. They form sodium chloride, which you know as table salt.

An **ionic bond** is the attraction between two oppositely charged ions. This attraction is similar to the attraction between the opposite poles of two magnets. When the two ions come together, the opposite charges cancel out. Every sodium ion (with a charge written as 1+) is balanced by a chloride ion (with a charge written as 1–). The formula for sodium chloride, NaCl, shows you this 1 : 1 ratio.

Compounds are electrically neutral. When ions come together, they do so in a way that balances out the charges on the ions. Figure 8 lists some common ions. Look at the charge of the magnesium ion. How many chloride ions would be needed to cancel out the 2+ charge of magnesium in the compound magnesium chloride? The formula for magnesium chloride, $MgCl_2$, tells you the answer is two.

☑ ***Checkpoint*** *What effect does gaining an electron have on the charge of an atom?*

EXPLORING *Ionic Bonds*

Reactions between metals and nonmetals often form ionic compounds. These reactions occur easily between the metals in Group 1 and the halogens in Group 17. Here you can see what happens when an ionic bond forms between a sodium atom and a chlorine atom.

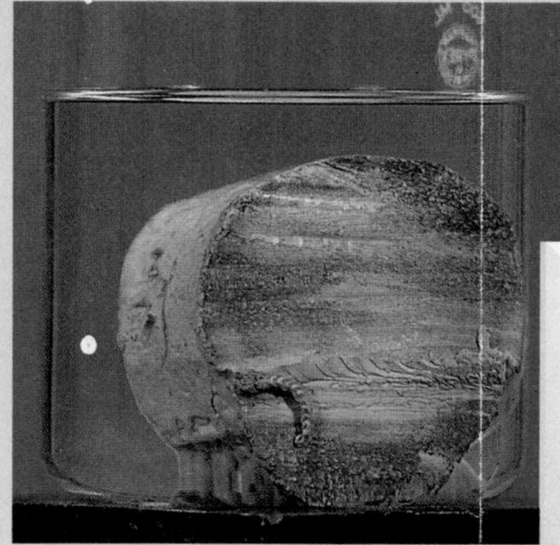

Sodium metal

Sodium atoms have one valence electron. When the electron is lost, the atoms become more stable.

Na·

1 valence electron

Chlorine gas

Chlorine atoms become more stable when they gain just one electron.

·Cl: (with dot pairs above and below)

7 valence electrons

One electron is transferred from the sodium atom to the chlorine atom.

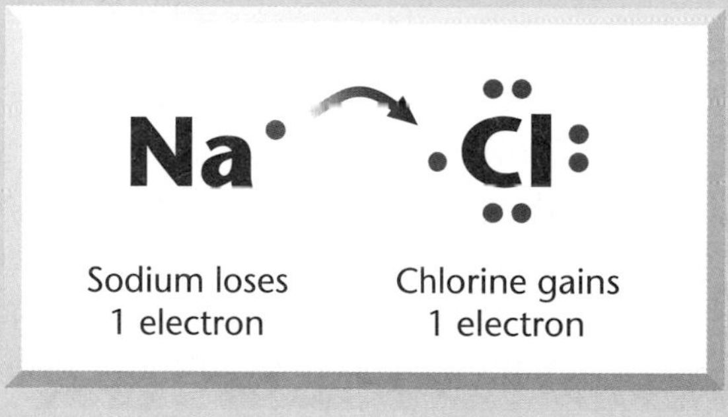

Na· → ·Cl:

Sodium loses 1 electron

Chlorine gains 1 electron

After losing an electron, the sodium atom becomes a sodium ion with a 1+ charge.

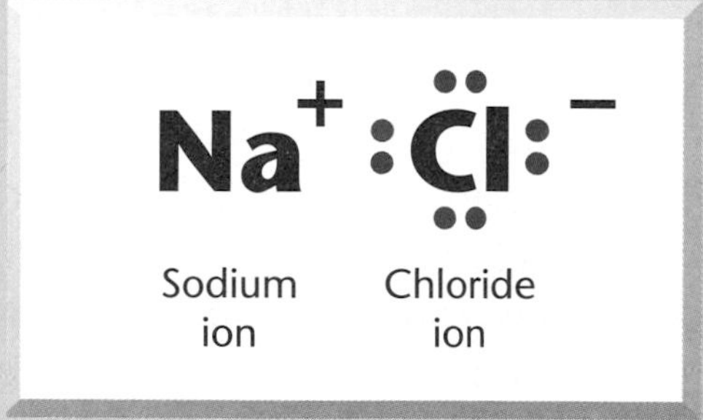

Na^{+} :Cl:$^{-}$

Sodium ion

Chloride ion

After gaining an electron, the chlorine atom becomes a chloride ion with a 1– charge.

Oppositely charged ions attract each other. This attractive force is an ionic bond. In sodium chloride, each sodium ion balances the charge of one chloride ion. Overall, the compound sodium chloride is electrically neutral.

Sodium chloride

Figure 9 What do seashells, chalk, limestone, and eggshells have in common? They all contain calcium carbonate, which is an ionic compound made of Ca^{2+} and CO_3^{2-} ions.

Polyatomic Ions

Some ions are made of more than one atom. Ions that are made of more than one atom are examples of **polyatomic ions** (pahl ee uh TAHM ik). The prefix *poly* means "many," so the word *polyatomic* means "many atoms." You can think of a polyatomic ion as a group of atoms that react as one. Each polyatomic ion has an overall positive or negative charge. If a polyatomic ion combines with another ion of opposite charge, an ionic compound forms. Think, for example, about the carbonate ion (CO_3^{2-}). It is made of one carbon atom and three oxygen atoms and has an overall charge of 2–. This ion can combine with a calcium ion (Ca^{2+}), forming calcium carbonate ($CaCO_3$). Calcium carbonate is the main compound in limestone.

Naming Ionic Compounds

Magnesium chloride, sodium bicarbonate, sodium oxide—where do these names come from? For an ionic compound, the name of the positive ion comes first, followed by the name of the negative ion. The name of the positive ion is usually the name of a metal. It may also be the name of a positive polyatomic ion, such as ammonium. If the negative ion is an element, the end of its name changes to *-ide*. For example, MgO is magnesium oxide. If the negative ion is polyatomic, its name remains unchanged. For example, the chemical name for washing soda (Na_2CO_3) is sodium carbonate.

Checkpoint *What kind of atom has a name change when it becomes an ion?*

Sharpen your Skills

Interpreting Data

ACTIVITY

Look at the list of compounds below. Use the periodic table and Figure 8 to identify the charges of the ions in each compound. Then write the formula for each compound.

- sodium fluoride
- lithium oxide
- magnesium sulfide
- boron chloride
- aluminum sulfide

How did you know how many of each atom to write in the formula?

Properties of Ionic Compounds

Do you think table salt, iron rust, baking soda, and limestone are very much alike? If you answer no, you're right. If you answer yes, you're right, too! You wouldn't want to season your food with rust, or construct a building out of baking soda. But despite their differences, these compounds share some similarities because they all contain ionic bonds. **The characteristic properties of ionic compounds include crystal shape, high melting points, and electrical conductivity.**

Crystal Shape The object in Figure 10 that looks like a glass sculpture is really a chunk of halite, or table salt. Halite is an ionic compound. All samples of halite have sharp edges, corners, and flat surfaces. The shapes result from how the ions are arranged. In solid sodium chloride, the Na^+ and Cl^- ions come together in an alternating pattern, as shown in the diagram. The ions form an orderly, three-dimensional arrangement called a **crystal.**

In an ionic compound, every ion is attracted to ions near it that have an opposite charge. Positive ions tend to be near negative ions and farther from other positive ions. As a result, a positive sodium ion isn't attracted to just one negative chloride ion. It is attracted to ions above, below, and to all sides. Because chloride ions are attracted to sodium ions in the same way, a crystal forms. This pattern holds true no matter what the size of the crystal. In a single grain of salt, the crystal can extend for millions of ions in every direction. The number of sodium ions and chloride ions in the crystal is equal. The formula for sodium chloride, NaCl, represents this 1 : 1 ratio.

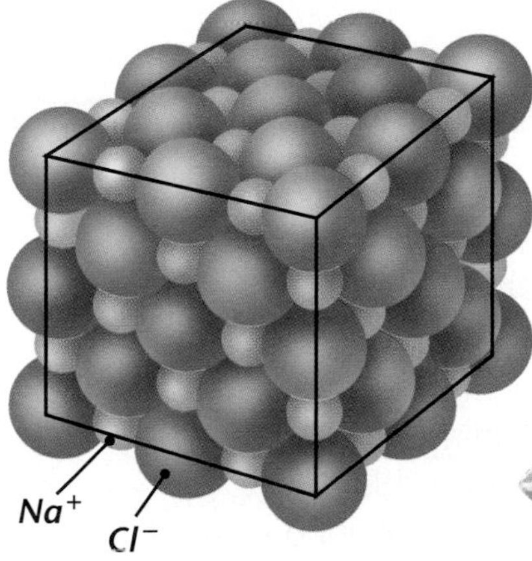

Figure 10 A halite crystal contains sodium and chloride ions in an alternating pattern.
Making Generalizations *What general characteristics of crystals can you observe in the photograph of halite?*

Crystal Clear

Can you grow a salt crystal?

1. Add salt to a jar containing about 200 mL of hot tap water, and stir. Keep adding salt until no more dissolves and it settles out when you stop stirring.
2. Tie a large crystal of coarse salt into the middle of a piece of thread.
3. Tie one end of the thread to the middle of a pencil.
4. Suspend the other end of the thread in the solution by laying the pencil across the mouth of the jar. Do not allow the crystal to touch the solution.
5. Place the jar in a quiet, undisturbed area. Check the size of the crystal over the next few days.

Observing Does the salt crystal change size over time? What is its shape? What do you think is happening to the salt in the solution?

Figure 11 A conductivity tester shows that a solution of salt in water conducts electricity. The bulb lights up because the ions in the salt solution complete the circuit for the flow of electricity.

High Melting Points What happens when you heat an ionic compound such as table salt? Remember, the ions are held together in a crystal by attractions between oppositely charged particles. When the particles have enough energy to overcome the attractive forces between them, they break away from each other. It takes a temperature of 801°C to reach this energy for table salt. Ionic bonds are strong enough to cause all ionic compounds to be solids at room temperature.

Electrical Conductivity When ionic compounds dissolve in water, the solution conducts electricity. Electricity is the flow of electric charge, and ions have electric charges. However, if you connect wires from a salt crystal to a battery and a light bulb, don't expect anything to happen. A solid ionic compound does not conduct electricity very well. The ions in the crystal are tightly bound to each other. If the charged particles do not move, electricity does not flow. But what if the ions are broken apart? When ionic compounds dissolve in water, the ions separate. These ions then move freely, and the solution conducts electricity.

INTEGRATING PHYSICS

Melting ionic compounds also allows them to conduct electricity. Can you figure out why? Think about the difference between the particles in a solid and a liquid. In a solid, the particles do not move from place to place. But in a liquid, the particles slip and slide past each other. As long as the ions can move around, electricity can flow.

Section 3 Review

1. How does an ion form from an atom?
2. What properties may be used to identify ionic compounds?
3. Why are ions in an ionic compound attracted to each other?
4. Name these compounds: NaF, BeI_2, K_2SO_4, CaO, H_2S, $MgCO_3$.
5. Solid salt does not conduct electricity. How does dissolving salt in water allow electricity to flow?
6. **Thinking Critically Problem Solving** The metal scandium (Sc) has three valence electrons. What is the formula of the ionic compound formed when scandium reacts with iodine?

CHAPTER PROJECT 11

Check Your Progress

Use your materials to make models of compounds containing ionic bonds, such as sodium chloride (NaCl), magnesium chloride ($MgCl_2$), or potassium oxide (K_2O). (*Hint:* Figure out whether each atom forms a positive or negative ion. Then use combinations that result in a neutral compound.)

Covalent Bonds

DISCOVER ACTIVITY

Why Don't Water and Oil Mix?

1. Pour water into a small jar that has a tight-fitting top until the jar is about a third full.
2. Add an equal amount of vegetable oil to the water and cover the jar tightly.
3. Shake the jar vigorously for approximately 15–20 seconds. Observe the contents.
4. Allow the jar to sit undisturbed for about 1 minute. Observe the contents again.
5. Remove the top and add 2–3 drops of liquid soap. Repeat Steps 3 and 4.

Think It Over

Inferring Describe how adding soap affected the mixing of the oil and water. How might your observations depend on chemical bonds in the soap, oil, and water molecules?

GUIDE FOR READING

- **How do electrons allow covalent bonds to form?**
- **Why do some atoms in covalent bonds have slight negative or positive charges?**
- **How are polar and nonpolar compounds different?**

Reading Tip **Before you read, preview the illustrations in the section. Predict how covalent bonds differ from ionic bonds.**

Remember the market with apples selling for 40 cents each? On another day, the apples are also on sale at two for 70 cents. You and your friend check your pockets and find 35 cents each. What can you do? You could give your friend a nickel to make enough money for one apple. Then you would have only 30 cents, not enough to get one for yourself. But if you share your money, together you can buy two apples.

Electron Sharing

Just as you and your friend can buy apples by sharing money, atoms can become more stable by sharing valence electrons. A chemical bond formed when two atoms share electrons is called a **covalent bond.**

Unlike ionic bonds, which form between metals and nonmetals, covalent bonds often form between two or more nonmetals. Oxygen, carbon, nitrogen, and the halogens are examples of atoms that frequently bond to other nonmetals by sharing electrons.

The element fluorine forms molecules made of two fluorine atoms. Each fluorine atom shares one of its seven valence electrons with the other atom. When you count the number of electrons on one atom, you count the shared pair each time. By sharing, both atoms have eight valence electrons. **In a covalent bond, both atoms attract the two shared electrons at the same time.**

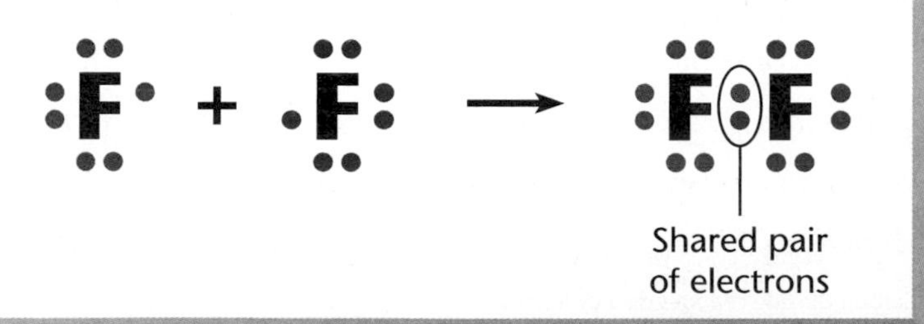

Figure 12 The shared pair of electrons in a molecule of fluorine is a single covalent bond.

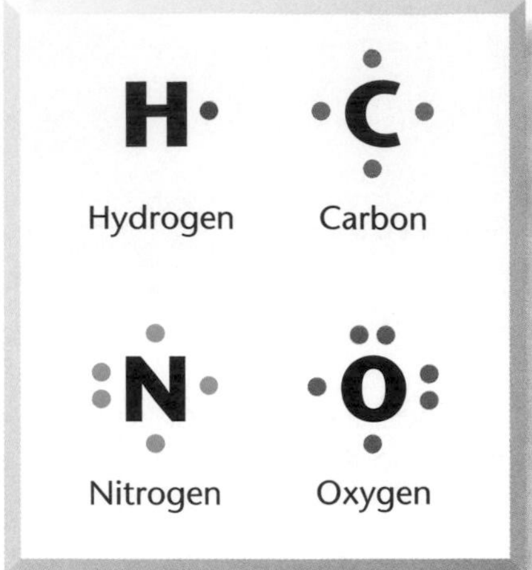

H:O:
H
Water

H:N:H
H
Ammonia

O::O
Oxygen

O::C::O
Carbon dioxide

:N:::N:
Nitrogen

Figure 13 The electron dot diagrams for hydrogen, carbon, nitrogen, and oxygen (left) show the number of valence electrons for each. The diagrams of molecules (right) show how the electrons are shared in covalent bonds. ***Interpreting Diagrams*** *How many bonds does each nitrogen atom form?*

How Many Bonds?

Look at the electron dot diagrams for oxygen, nitrogen, and carbon atoms in Figure 13. Count the dots around each atom. The number of bonds these atoms can form equals the number of valence electrons needed to make a total of eight.

For example, oxygen has six valence electrons, so it can form two covalent bonds. In a water molecule, oxygen forms one covalent bond with each hydrogen atom. Since nitrogen has five valence electrons, it can form three bonds. In ammonia (NH_3), a nitrogen atom bonds with three hydrogen atoms.

Next, look at the diagram of a molecule of oxygen. Do you see something different? This time *two* pairs of electrons are shared between the oxygen atoms, forming a **double bond.** In a carbon dioxide molecule, carbon forms a double bond with each oxygen atom. Elements such as nitrogen and carbon can even form triple bonds in which three pairs of electrons are shared.

Count the electrons around any atom in the molecules in Figure 13. Remember that shared pairs count for both atoms forming a bond. You'll find that each atom has eight valence electrons. The exception is hydrogen, which can have no more than two electrons and forms one bond.

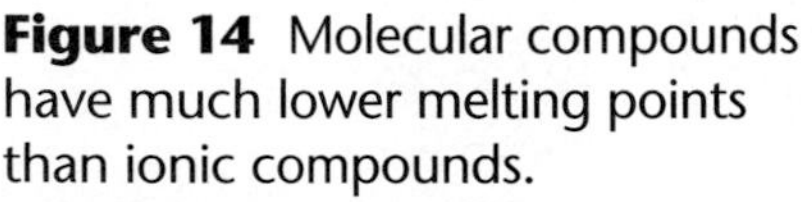

Figure 14 Molecular compounds have much lower melting points than ionic compounds.

Melting and Boiling Points of Some Molecular Compounds

Compound	Formula	Melting Point (°C)	Boiling Point (°C)
Water	H_2O	0	100
Methane	CH_4	–182	–164
Carbon dioxide	CO_2	—	–78.6*
Ammonia	NH_3	–77.7	–33.6
Rubbing alcohol	C_3H_8O	–89.5	82.4
Table sugar	$C_{12}H_{22}O_{11}$	185–186	(decomposes)

*Carbon dioxide changes directly from a solid to a gas.

Properties of Molecular Compounds

Molecular compounds consist of molecules having covalently bonded atoms. Such compounds have very different properties from ionic compounds.

Look at Figure 14, which lists the melting and boiling points for some molecular compounds. There's quite a difference between these melting points and the 801°C described earlier for table salt! In molecular solids, the molecules are held close to each other. But the forces holding them are much weaker than those holding ions together in an ionic solid. Less heat is needed to separate molecules than is needed to separate ions. Some molecular compounds, such as table sugar and water, do form crystals. But these compounds, like other molecular solids, melt and boil at much lower temperatures than ionic compounds do.

Most molecular compounds are poor conductors of electricity. No charged particles are available to move, and electricity does not flow. That's why molecular compounds, such as plastic and rubber, are used to insulate electric wires. Even as liquids, molecular compounds are poor conductors. Pure water, for example, does not conduct electricity. Neither does water with table sugar dissolved in it.

☑ *Checkpoint* *Why are molecular compounds poor conductors?*

Unequal Sharing of Electrons

Have you ever played tug of war? If you have, you know that if both teams have equal strength, the contest is a tie. But what if the teams pull on the rope with unequal force? Then the rope moves closer to one side or the other. The same is true of electrons in a covalent bond. **Some atoms pull more strongly on the shared electrons than other atoms do. As a result, the electrons move closer to one atom, causing the atoms to have slight electrical charges.** These charges are not as strong as the charges on ions. But the unequal sharing is enough to make one atom slightly negative and the other atom slightly positive. A covalent bond in which electrons are shared unequally is **polar.**

Designing Experiments

ACTIVITY

Suppose you have samples of two colorless, odorless gases. You are told that one gas is methane (CH_4) and the other is carbon dioxide (CO_2). How could you use the information in Figure 14 to find out which gas is which? Describe the experiment you would set up. Tell what conditions you would control and what you would change. What result would you look for to get an answer?

Figure 15 The unequal sharing of the electrons in a polar covalent bond is like a tug of war in which one atom is slightly stronger than the other atom.

Figure 16 In the nonpolar bond in F_2, the two flourine atoms pull equally on the shared electrons. In the polar bond in HF, fluorine pulls more strongly on the shared electrons than hydrogen does.

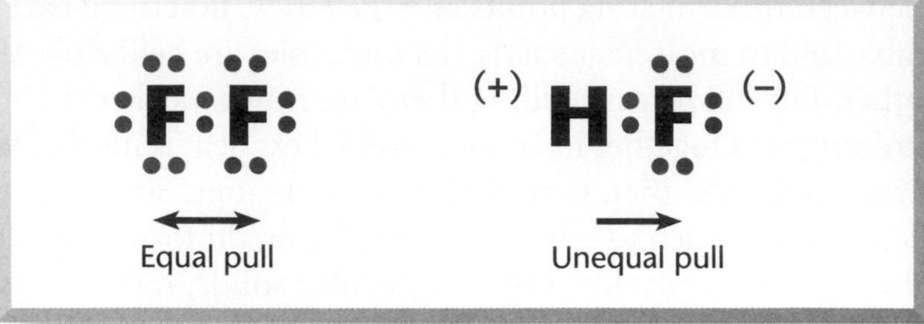

If two atoms pull equally on the electrons, neither atom becomes charged. This is the case when the two atoms are identical, as in fluorine gas (F_2). The valence electrons are shared equally and the bond is **nonpolar.** Compare the bond in F_2 with the polar bond in hydrogen fluoride (HF) in Figure 16.

Nonpolar Molecules Keep tug of war in mind as you look at the carbon dioxide (CO_2) molecule in Figure 17. Oxygen attracts electrons much more strongly than carbon, so bonds between oxygen and carbon are polar. But the two oxygen atoms are pulling with equal strength in opposite directions. In a sense, they cancel each other out. Overall, a carbon dioxide molecule is nonpolar even though it has polar bonds. A molecule is nonpolar if it contains polar bonds that cancel each other. As you might guess, molecules that contain only nonpolar bonds are also nonpolar.

Polar Molecules Water molecules are polar. As you can see in Figure 17, the shape of the molecule leaves the two hydrogen atoms more to one end and the oxygen atom toward the other. The oxygen atom pulls electrons closer to it from both hydrogen atoms. Overall, the molecule is polar. It has a slightly negative charge at the oxygen end and a slightly positive charge near the hydrogen atoms.

☑ ***Checkpoint*** *What makes a covalent bond polar?*

Attractions Between Molecules

If you could shrink small enough to move among a bunch of water molecules, what would you find? The negatively charged oxygen ends and positively charged hydrogen ends behave like poles of a bar magnet. They attract the opposite ends of other water molecules. These attractions between positive and negative ends pull water molecules toward each other.

What about carbon dioxide? There is no pulling between these molecules. Remember, carbon dioxide molecules are nonpolar. No oppositely charged ends means there are no strong attractions between the molecules.

Language Arts CONNECTION

Breaking a word into its parts can help you understand its meaning. Take *covalent,* for example. The prefix *co-* means "together." The *-valent* part comes from "valence electrons." So "valence electrons together" can remind you that in a covalent bond, valence electrons are shared.

In Your Journal

The prefix *co-* is used in many other words—*coauthor, coexist,* and *cooperate* are just a few. Add five more *co-* words to this list and try to define them all without looking them up. Then check their meanings in a dictionary and write sentences that use each one.

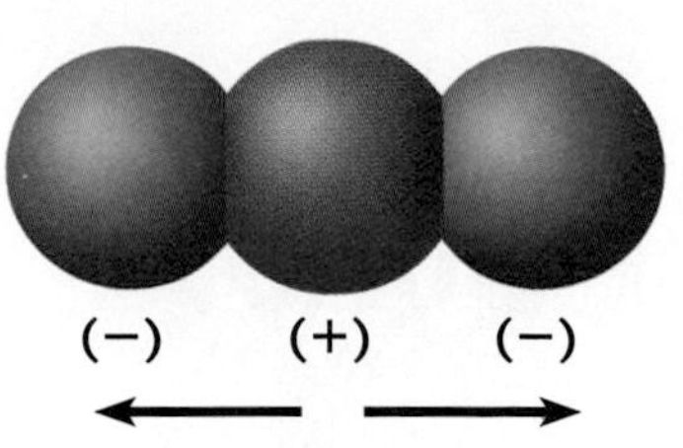

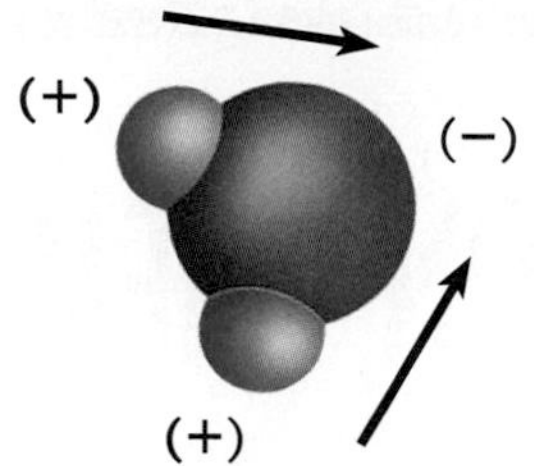

Figure 17 CO_2 molecules are nonpolar, and H_2O molecules are polar. Attractions between the slightly positive and slightly negative ends of water molecules pull the molecules toward each other (below).

Differences in the attractions between molecules lead to different properties in polar and nonpolar compounds. For example, water and vegetable oil don't mix. Oil is nonpolar, and nonpolar compounds do not dissolve well in water. The polar water molecules are attracted more strongly to each other than to the molecules of oil. Water stays with water and oil stays with oil.

INTEGRATING TECHNOLOGY These differences in attractions come in handy when you wash laundry. Many kinds of dirt—for example, grease—are nonpolar compounds. Their molecules won't mix well with plain water. So how can you wash dirt out of your clothes?

If you did the Discover activity, you found that adding soap helped the oil and water to mix. When you do laundry, detergent causes the nonpolar dirt to mix with the polar water. Soaps and detergents have long molecules. One end of a soap molecule is polar, and the other end is nonpolar. Soaps and detergents dissolve in water because the polar ends of their molecules are attracted to water molecules. Meanwhile, their nonpolar ends mix easily with the dirt. When the water washes down the drain, the soap and the dirt go with it.

Section 4 Review

1. How are valence electrons involved in the formation of a covalent bond?
2. How do atoms in covalent bonds become slightly negative or slightly positive?
3. Explain how attractions between molecules could cause polar water to have a higher boiling point than nonpolar carbon dioxide.
4. **Thinking Critically Comparing and Contrasting** In terms of electrons, how is a covalent bond different from an ionic bond?

CHAPTER PROJECT 11

Check Your Progress

Use your materials to build molecules with single covalent bonds. Also make models of molecules containing double or triple bonds. (*Hint:* After you make bonds, each atom should have a total of eight valence electrons or, in the case of hydrogen, two valence electrons.)

Skills Lab

Interpreting Data

Shedding Light on Chemical Bonds

Electricity is the flow of electric charges. In this lab, you will interpret data about which compounds conduct electricity in order to determine the nature of their bonds.

Problem

How can you use a conductivity tester to determine whether a compound contains ionic or covalent bonds?

Materials

- 2 dry cells, 1.5-V
- small light bulb and socket
- 4 lengths of wire with insulation scraped off the ends

(or conductivity probe)

- small beaker
- small plastic spoon
- sodium chloride
- 100-mL graduated cylinder
- additional substances supplied by your teacher

DATA TABLE

Sample	Observations
Water	
Sodium chloride in water	

Procedure

1. Make a conductivity tester as described below or, if you are using a conductivity probe, see your teacher for instructions. Then make a data table in your notebook similar to the one above.
2. Pour about 50 mL of water into a small beaker. Place the free ends of the two wires of the conductivity tester into the water. Be sure the ends are close but not touching each other. Record your observations.

Making a Conductivity Tester

A. Use wire to connect the positive terminal of a dry cell to a lamp socket. **CAUTION:** *The bulb is fragile and can break.*

B. Use another wire to connect the negative terminal to the positive terminal of a second dry cell.

C. Connect a third wire to the negative terminal of the second dry cell.

D. Connect a fourth wire to the other terminal of the lamp socket.

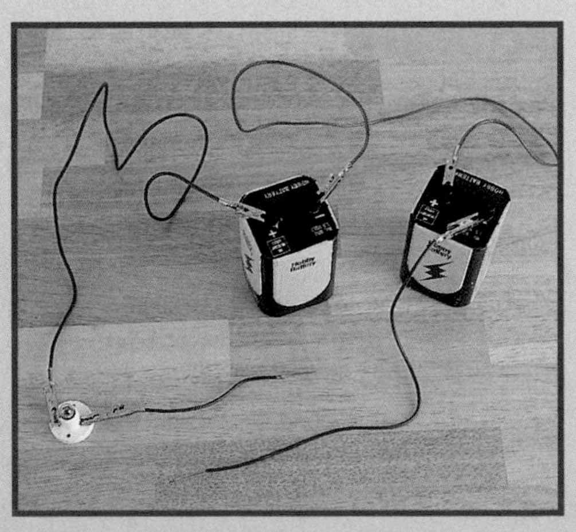

3. Remove the conductivity tester and add a small sample (about 3 spoonfuls) of sodium chloride to the water in the small beaker. Stir with the spoon until mixed.
4. Repeat the conductivity test and record your observations in your data table.
5. Rinse the beaker, spoon, and wire ends with clear water. Then repeat Steps 3 and 4 for each substance provided by your teacher.
   - If the substance is a solid, mix 1 to 3 spoonfuls of it with about 50 mL of fresh water. Test the resulting mixture.
   - If the substance is a liquid, simply pour about 50 mL into the beaker. Test it as you did the solutions.

Analyze and Conclude

1. Why did you test plain water first?
2. Based on your observations, add a column to your chart indicating whether each substance tested contained ionic or covalent bonds.
3. Explain why one substance is a better conductor of electricity than another.
4. Did all the substances that conducted electricity show the same amount of conductivity? How do you know?
5. **Think About It** How might varying the amount of each substance added to the water have affected your results? How could you better control the amount of each substance?

Design an Experiment

Design another experiment to compare a different property of compounds containing ionic and covalent bonds. You might want to examine properties such as the ability to dissolve in water or in some other liquid. Present your experimental plan to your teacher before proceeding.

SECTION 5 Crystal Chemistry

DISCOVER ACTIVITY

How Small Do They Get?

1. Place a piece of rock salt on a hard surface. Make a rough sketch of the shape of your sample.
2. Put on your goggles. Cover the salt with a paper towel. Use the back of a metal spoon or a rock hammer to break the salt into smaller pieces.
3. Look at these smaller pieces with a hand lens. Then draw a picture of the shapes you see.
4. Crush a few of these smaller pieces with the spoon. Repeat Step 3.

Think It Over

Predicting What do you think the crystals would look like if you crushed them into such small pieces that you needed a microscope to see them?

GUIDE FOR READING

- **How are the properties of a mineral related to chemical bonds?**

Reading Tip **As you read, make a list of the ways in which a mineral can be described or identified.**

A class of earth science students gathers rock samples on a field trip. They want to know whether the rocks contain any of the minerals they have been studying. The teacher takes a hammer and strikes one rock. It cracks open to reveal a few small crystals peeking out of the new surface. The crystals are mostly the same shape and have a metallic shine. The teacher tries to scratch one crystal, first with her fingernail and then with a copper penny. Only the penny leaves a mark. By now, the students have enough information to make an inference about the identity of the crystals. They'll do more tests back in their classroom to be sure the mineral is what they think it is.

Properties of Minerals

A **mineral** is a naturally occurring solid that has a crystal structure and a definite chemical composition. A few minerals, such as sulfur and gold, are pure elements. But most minerals are compounds.

Mineralogists, scientists who study minerals, identify minerals by looking at certain properties. These properties include color, shininess, density, crystal shape, hardness, and magnetism. Color and shininess can be judged just by looking at a mineral. Other properties, however, require measurements or testing. For example, scientists rate a mineral's hardness by comparing it with something harder or softer. You can scratch the softest mineral, talc, with your fingernail. Diamond is the hardest mineral. Other minerals are somewhere in between.

Figure 18 The mineral sulfur (above) is a pure element. The mineral galena (right) is a compound of sulfur and lead.

Figure 19 Mica's flakes **(A)** are a result of how the mineral splits when it breaks. The crystals of fluorite **(B)** and tourmaline **(C)** grew in the shapes you see. ***Observing*** *How do the shapes of fluorite crystals and tourmaline crystals differ?*

Another key property is the way a mineral breaks apart. Some minerals break into regular shapes. Mica, for example, splits easily along flat surfaces and at sharp angles. Crystals also grow in characteristic shapes. All the properties of a mineral depend on its chemical composition. Since each mineral has a different composition, its properties will not be exactly like those of any other mineral.

☑ *Checkpoint* *What is a mineral?*

Bonding in Mineral Crystals

Every mineral has a crystal structure. The repeating pattern of particles creates a shape that may be visible to your eye. Or, you may have to look under a microscope to see it. Either way, the structure of the crystal is a characteristic property of the mineral.

Mineral crystals may be made of ions, or they may contain atoms that are covalently bonded together. **The arrangement of particles in a mineral and the kind of bonds holding them together determine properties such as crystal shape, hardness, and the way the crystal breaks apart.**

An Ionic Crystal In Section 3, you read about halite, a mineral made of sodium chloride (NaCl). You can easily scratch halite with a steel knife. If you put a crystal of halite into water, it would dissolve. The oppositely charged sodium and chloride ions in a halite crystal alternate in every direction, making a pattern something like a three-dimensional checkerboard. This arrangement affects the shape in which halite crystals grow.

If you break a piece of halite, the smaller pieces of halite have the same shape as the bigger piece. When bonds in an ionic crystal break, they break along a face of ions. A blow or crushing action shifts the ions slightly so that positive ions are next to other positive ions and negative ions are next to other negative ions. The effect is the same as bringing the

Figure 20 The particles in an ionic crystal such as halite can shift because of a blow or pressure.

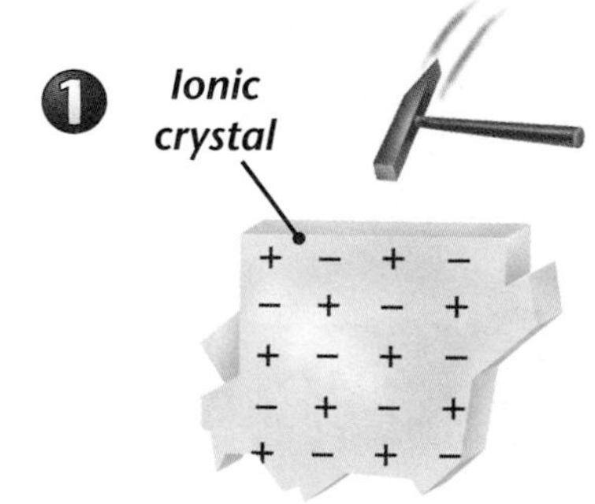

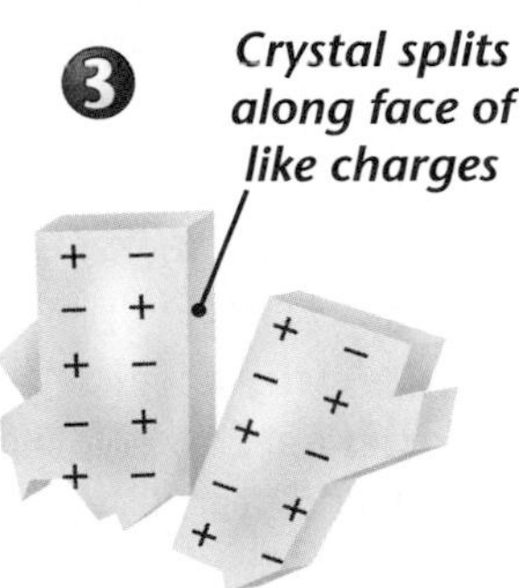

Figure 21 The uneven surfaces on this crystal are typical of broken quartz.
Comparing and Contrasting *How does the way quartz breaks compare to the way mica breaks?*

north ends of two magnets together. It creates a weakness in the crystal. The ions push each other away, breaking bonds along a flat surface or face. The result is that the smaller crystals retain the cube shape that is characteristic of halite.

A Covalent Crystal If you picked up a handful of sand, most likely you would be holding some quartz. Quartz is a compound made of silicon and oxygen atoms covalently bonded together to form the compound silicon dioxide (SiO_2). The covalent bonds in quartz are much stronger than the ionic bonds in halite. Quartz won't dissolve in water. You can't scratch it with a knife. In fact, you could use quartz to scratch steel! Because of its strong bonds, a quartz crystal doesn't have clear lines of weakness. You can't crush it into predictable shapes with a hammer. Instead, it breaks into smaller pieces with irregular shapes. The broken surfaces have shell-like ridges similar to chipped glass. These features help identify the mineral as quartz.

Comparing Crystals

Not all mineral crystals made of ions have the same properties as halite. Similarly, not all minerals made of covalently bonded atoms are like quartz. Properties such as hardness, for example, depend on the strength of the bonds in a crystal. The stronger bonds of quartz make it harder than halite. But other crystals with covalently bonded atoms are stronger than quartz. Still others have weaknesses in their bonds that cause the minerals to break apart the same way every time.

Experienced mineralogists can usually identify a mineral just by looking at it. But when there is a question, they test the sample for characteristics such as hardness and the way the crystals break. The results give the answer.

Section 5 Review

1. Name two properties of minerals that depend on chemical bonds.
2. What property of a mineral can be determined by scratching it?
3. How does the way in which a mineral crystal breaks apart help to identify it?
4. **Thinking Critically Comparing and Contrasting** Name three ways in which a halite crystal differs from a quartz crystal.

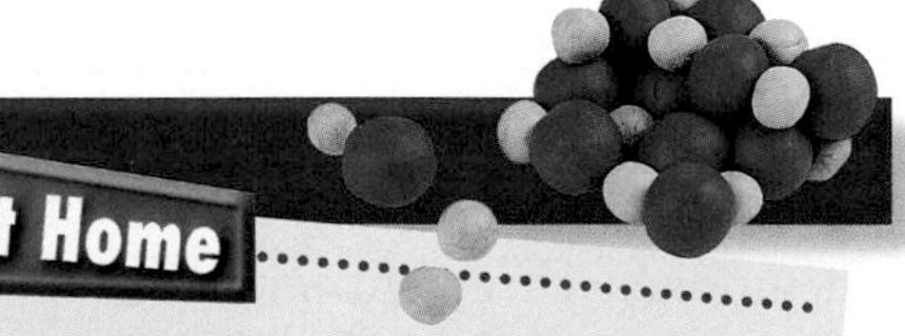

Science at Home

Construct a model of an ionic crystal. Place round objects of two different sizes (such as balls of clay) in a checkerboard pattern to make the first layer. Now place one smaller object on top of each larger one and vice versa to make the second layer. Continue until the first layer is completely covered. Construct a third layer in a similar way. Explain to your family how your model represents an ionic crystal.

CHAPTER 11 STUDY GUIDE

Inside an Atom

Key Ideas

- An atom consists of a nucleus of protons and neutrons, surrounded by rapidly moving electrons.
- Chemical reactions involve the valence electrons of atoms. Chemical bonds form when electrons are transferred or shared between atoms.

Key Terms

nucleus
proton
neutron
electron
valence electron
electron dot diagram

Atoms in the Periodic Table

Key Ideas

- The periodic table organizes the elements according to atomic number.
- Families of elements have similar chemical properties.
- The noble gases (Group 18) are the least reactive elements. Elements in groups 1 and 17 are highly reactive.

Key Terms

atomic number
group
family
period
halogen

Ionic Bonds

Key Ideas

- Ions form when atoms become charged after gaining or losing electrons.
- Ionic compounds exist in the form of crystals made of many ions, each attracted to all the surrounding ions of opposite charge.
- Ionic compounds have high melting and boiling points. They conduct electricity when dissolved in water.

Key Terms

ion
ionic bond
polyatomic ion
crystal

Covalent Bonds

Key Ideas

- In covalent bonds, pairs of electrons are shared between atoms.
- In polar covalent bonds, the shared electrons are attracted more to one atom than the other.
- Attractions between polar molecules are stronger than attractions between nonpolar molecules, leading to differences in properties.

Key Terms

covalent bond
double bond
molecular compound
polar
nonpolar

Crystal Chemistry

INTEGRATING EARTH SCIENCE 

Key Ideas

- Minerals have characteristic properties, such as hardness, density, color, crystal shape, and the way the crystal breaks and grows.
- The properties of a mineral depend on its chemical composition and its bonding.
- The stronger the chemical bonds in a mineral crystal, the harder the crystal is.

Key Term

mineral

Organizing Information

Venn Diagram Copy and complete the diagram, and add a title.

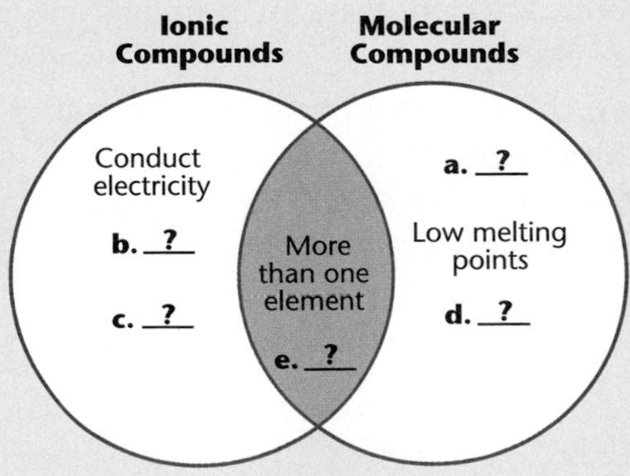

Reviewing Content

Multiple Choice

Choose the letter of the best answer.

1. The atomic number of an atom is determined by the number of
   a. protons. b. electrons.
   c. neutrons. d. valence electrons.
2. The vertical columns on the periodic table organize elements by
   a. periods. b. metals.
   c. families. d. nonmetals.
3. When an atom loses an electron, it
   a. becomes a negative ion.
   b. becomes a positive ion.
   c. forms a covalent bond.
   d. gains protons.
4. Which of these is a property of an ionic compound?
   a. low melting point
   b. poor conductor of electricity
   c. crystal shape
   d. shared electrons
5. A chemical bond in which a pair of electrons is shared between two atoms is called
   a. ionic. b. covalent.
   c. polyatomic. d. triple.

True or False

If the statement is true, write true. If it is false, change the underlined word or words to make the statement true.

6. Using the periodic table, you can determine that a potassium atom has <u>one</u> valence electron.
7. When a chlorine atom gains an electron, it becomes a <u>positive ion</u>.
8. When atoms share electrons unequally, a <u>polar</u> bond forms.
9. Two polar molecules have <u>weaker</u> attractions between them than two nonpolar molecules do.
10. <u>Hardness</u> is determined by how easily a mineral can be scratched.

Checking Concepts

11. Strontium is classified as an alkaline earth metal. Look at the periodic table and name the other elements that are alkaline earth metals.
12. Use the periodic table to identify what type of chemical bond is involved in each of these compounds: NaF, NO_2, CBr_4, MgS. Explain your reasoning.
13. How is a covalent bond between two atoms affected when each atom attracts electrons equally?
14. Of all the elements, fluorine atoms attract electrons most strongly. When fluorine atoms form covalent bonds with other kinds of atoms, are the bonds polar or nonpolar?
15. **Writing to Learn** Imagine you are a chlorine atom. Write a first-person description of the changes you undergo when forming an ionic bond with sodium. Compare these with what happens when you form a covalent bond with another chlorine atom.

Thinking Critically

16. **Making Generalizations** How does the location of an element on the periodic table help you determine how reactive that element might be?
17. **Applying Concepts** Use the periodic table to find the number of valence electrons for calcium (Ca), aluminum (Al), rubidium (Rb), oxygen (O), sulfur (S), and iodine (I).Then use that information to predict the formula for each of the following compounds: calcium oxide, aluminum iodide, rubidium sulfide, and aluminum oxide.
18. **Inferring** Element Z is a yellow solid that melts at about 100°C and does not conduct electricity. What type of bond holds the element's atoms together? Explain the reasoning for your answer.
19. **Problem Solving** Suppose you were given two mineral crystals that looked alike. How would you determine the identity of each?

Applying Skills

Element X exists as a nonpolar molecule made of two identical atoms. When individual atoms of element X react with sodium, they form ions with a 2– charge. Use the periodic table in Appendix D to answer Questions 20–24.

20. **Classifying** To what group of elements does element *X* belong?
21. **Inferring** How many valence electrons does an atom of element *X* have?
22. **Predicting** Sodium can react with element *X* to form a compound. How many atoms of sodium are needed for each atom of element *X*? Write the formula for the compound.
23. **Calculating** How many covalent bonds can element *X* form?
24. **Posing Questions** In order to identify element *X*, what additional questions would you need to ask?

Performance  **Assessment**

Project Wrap Up Before you present your models to the class, use an index card for each model to make a key telling what each part of the model represents. Explain why you chose particular items to model the atoms and the chemical bonds. How are your models alike or different from models of the same compounds made by other students?

Reflect and Record In your journal, compare your models containing ionic bonds with those containing covalent bonds. Which were easier to show? Why? What more would you like to know about bonding that could help improve your models?

Test Preparation

Use these questions to prepare for standardized tests.

Use the diagram to answer Questions 25–28.

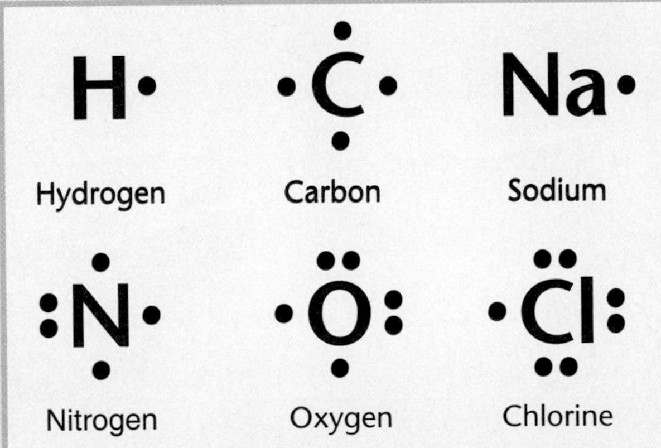

25. When one nitrogen atom joins with another nitrogen atom forming a molecule of nitrogen gas, the atoms are held together by a(n)
    a. single bond
    b. double bond
    c. triple bond
    d. ionic bond

26. When nitrogen and hydrogen combine, the ratio of hydrogen atoms to nitrogen atoms in a molecule of the resulting compound is
    a. 2 to 1
    b. 3 to 1
    c. 1 to 3
    d. 1 to 1

27. Atoms of which pair of elements are most likely to form a polar covalent bond?
    a. H and O
    b. C and O
    c. Na and Cl
    d. Cl and Cl

28. The correct symbol for an ion of oxygen is
    a. O^+
    b. O^{2+}
    c. O^-
    d. O^{2-}

CHAPTER 12

Acids, Bases, and Solutions

WEB ACTIVITY www.phschool.com

Section 1 Working With Solutions

Discover **What Makes a Mixture a Solution?**
Try This **Does It Dissolve?**
Sharpen Your Skills **Graphing**
Sharpen Your Skills **Controlling Variables**
Skills Lab **Speedy Solutions**

Section 2 Describing Acids and Bases

Discover **What Colors Does Litmus Paper Turn?**

Section 3 Acids and Bases in Solution

Discover **What Can Cabbage Juice Tell You?**
Try This **pHone Home**
Real-World Lab **The Antacid Test**

PROJECT 12

Make Your Own Indicator

These delicious-looking fruits are more than just nutritious, juicy treats. Most fruits are acidic. And some fruits contain chemicals that change color in an acid or a base. Such chemicals are called acid-base indicators. These natural indicators can be found in different parts of many plants. You can find them in flowers, leaves, and the skins of some fruits.

As you learn about acids and bases in this chapter, you can make your own solutions that will tell you if something is an acid or a base. Then you can use your solutions to test for acids and bases among substances found in your home.

Your Goal To make acid-base indicators from flowers, fruits, vegetables, or other common plant materials.

To complete the project you must

- make one or more indicators that will turn colors in acids and bases
- use your indicators to test a number of substances
- compare your indicators to a standard pH scale
- rank the tested substances according to their pH
- follow the safety guidelines in Appendix A

Get Started Brainstorm with your classmates about foods, spices, flowers, or other plant materials that have definite, deep colors. Think about fruits and vegetables you may find in a supermarket. These materials are good candidates for your indicators.

Check Your Progress You'll be working on this project as you study this chapter. To keep your project on track, look for Check Your Progress boxes at the following points.

Section 2 Review, page 399: Prepare the indicators.
Section 3 Review, page 405: Perform the tests.
Section 4 Review, page 410: Compare with pH paper results.

Wrap Up At the end of the chapter (page 413), you will demonstrate your indicators and rank the tested substances by acidity.

Fruits and fruit juices often contain weak acids.

Integrating Life Science

Digestion and pH

Discover **Where Does Digestion Begin?**

Working With Solutions

DISCOVER

What Makes a Mixture a Solution?

1. Put about 50 mL of water into a plastic cup. Add a spoonful of pepper and stir well.
2. To a second cup of water, add a spoonful of salt. Stir well.
3. Compare the appearance of the two mixtures.

Think It Over

Observing What is the difference between the two mixtures? What other mixtures have you seen that are similar to pepper and water? That are similar to salt and water?

GUIDE FOR READING

- **What happens to the particles of a solute when a solution forms?**
- **What factors affect the solubility of a substance?**
- **How do solutes affect the freezing point and boiling point of a solvent?**

Reading Tip **As you read, make a list of main ideas about solutions.**

Imagine a hot summer day. You've been outdoors and now you're really thirsty. A tall, cool glass of just plain water would taste great. Or would it? Have you ever tasted distilled water from the supermarket? It tastes flat. Distilled water is "just plain water." To make it, you boil tap water so it becomes a gas. Then you recollect it as a liquid. This process separates the water from dissolved materials that give it flavor.

Tap water is a mixture of pure water (H_2O) and a variety of other substances, such as chlorine, fluoride, and metallic ions. Gases, such as oxygen and carbon dioxide, are also dissolved in water. Like all mixtures, the composition of tap water can vary. Tap water can differ from one home to the next, across a town, or from state to state. Tap water is an example of a kind of mixture called a solution.

Solutions and Suspensions

What happens if you make a mixture of water and pepper? Not much. No matter how much you stir pepper and water, the two never really seem to "mix." When you stop stirring, you can still see pepper flakes floating on the water's surface and collecting at the bottom of the cup. You could scoop them out if you wanted to. Pepper and water make a suspension. A **suspension** (suh SPEN shun) is a mixture in which particles can be seen and easily separated by settling or filtration. If you tasted the pepper suspension, you might find that one mouthful of it tastes peppery, but another mouthful does not. Such a mixture is not evenly mixed.

On the other hand, if you stir table salt into water, the salt disappears. Water and table salt form a **solution,** a well-mixed mixture. If you taste a salt solution, any sip tastes just as salty as the next. A solution has the same properties throughout. Solutions and suspensions differ in other ways, too. The particles of a solution—too small to see—are much smaller than those of a suspension. Solutions and suspensions differ in the way the parts of the mixture can be separated. You cannot separate table salt from water by filtering it or by letting it settle. Boiling the water away, however, will work. Letting the water evaporate will also separate the salt.

Figure 1 Glitter mixes with the water when you shake the paperweight, but settles out later. ***Classifying*** *Are the glitter particles in solution or in suspension?*

Solvents and Solutes

All solutions have at least two parts: the solvent and the solute. The **solvent** is the part of a solution present in the largest amount. It dissolves the other substances. A substance that is present in a solution in a smaller amount and dissolved by the solvent is the **solute.** In salt water, the solvent is water and the solute is salt.

Water as a Solvent In many common solutions, the solvent is water. Sugar in water, for example, is the starting solution for flavored soft drinks. Adding food coloring gives the drink color. Dissolving carbon dioxide gas in the mixture produces a soda. Water dissolves so many substances that it is often called the "universal solvent."

INTEGRATING LIFE SCIENCE Life depends on water solutions. Nutrients used by plants are dissolved in water in the soil. Sap is a solution that carries sugar to tree cells. Water is the solvent in blood, saliva, and tears. Reactions in cells take place in solution. To keep cells working, you must replace the water you lose in sweat and urine—two other water solutions.

Figure 2 When air bubbles are blown through a fish tank, oxygen gas dissolves in the water. Fish take in this oxygen through their gills. Without oxygen, the fish would die.

Figure 3 Solutions can be made from any combination of the three states of matter. ***Interpreting Tables*** *In which of these solutions is the solvent a substance other than water?*

Examples of Common Solutions		
Solute	**Solvent**	**Solution**
Gas	Gas	Air (oxygen and other gases in nitrogen)
Gas	Liquid	Soda water (carbon dioxide in water)
Liquid	Liquid	Antifreeze (ethylene glycol in water)
Solid	Liquid	Dental filling (silver in mercury)
Solid	Liquid	Ocean water (sodium chloride and other compounds in water)
Solid	Solid	Brass (zinc and copper)

Solutions Without Water Many solutions are made with solvents other than water. For example, gasoline is a solution of several different liquid fuels. You don't even need a liquid solvent to make solutions. Solutions can be made of various combinations of gases, liquids, and solids.

Particles in a Solution

Why do solutes seem to disappear when you mix them with water? If you had a microscope powerful enough to look at the particles in the mixture, what would you see? **Whenever a solution forms, particles of the solute leave each other and become surrounded by particles of the solvent.**

Ionic Solids in Water Figure 4 shows what happens when an ionic solid mixes with water. The positive and negative ions are attracted to polar water molecules. Water molecules surround each ion as it leaves the surface of the crystal. As each layer of the solid is exposed, more ions can dissolve.

Figure 4 Water molecules surround and separate positive and negative ions as an ionic solid dissolves. Notice that sodium ions attract the oxygen ends of the water molecules.

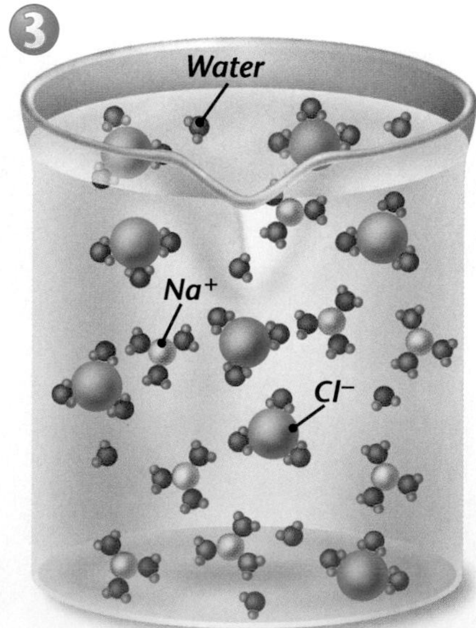

Molecular Solids in Water Not every substance breaks into ions when it dissolves in water. A molecular solid, such as sugar, breaks up into individual neutral molecules. The polar water molecules attract the slightly polar sugar molecules. This causes the sugar molecules to move away from each other. But covalent bonds within the molecules are undisturbed. Like ions, the sugar molecules become surrounded by water.

Solutions and Conductivity You have a solution, but you don't know if it was made with salt or sugar in water. How could you use what you know about particles to find out? (Remember, a smart scientist never tastes chemicals!) Think about what you learned about the electrical conductivity of compounds. Ionic compounds dissolved in water conduct electricity, but molecular compounds do not. You could test the conductivity of the solution. If no ions were present (as in a sugar solution), electricity would not flow.

☑ ***Checkpoint*** *How do ionic and molecular solids differ from each other in solution?*

Concentration

Suppose you make two cups of hot herbal tea. You leave a tea bag in the first cup for fifteen seconds. You put another tea bag in the second cup for a few minutes. When you're done, the tea in the second cup is darker than the tea in the first cup.

The two cups of tea differ in their concentrations. That is, they differ in the amount of solute (tea) dissolved in a certain amount of solvent (water). Chemists describe the first mixture as a **dilute solution** because only a little solute is dissolved in the water. By comparison, the darker tea is a **concentrated solution** because it has more solute dissolved in the water.

Does It Dissolve?

ACTIVITY

Compare how well a few common substances dissolve in water.

1. Put on your safety goggles.
2. Put half a spoonful of soap flakes into a small plastic cup. Add about 50 mL of water and stir. Did the soap flakes mix with water?
3. Clean out the cup and repeat the test for each of several other solids and liquids, such as baking soda, chalk dust, hand cream, and fruit juice. Decide which materials are soluble in water and which are not.

Creating Data Tables Make a table and record your results. Which dissolve more easily, solids or liquids?

Figure 5 Tea is made of several solutes dissolved in water. "Weak" tea is a dilute solution of these solutes. "Strong" tea is a more concentrated solution.

Solubility in 100 g Water at 0°C	
Compound	**Solubility (g)**
Salt (NaCl)	35.7
Baking soda ($NaHCO_3$)	6.9
Carbon dioxide (CO_2)	0.348
Sugar ($C_{12}H_{22}O_{11}$)	180

Figure 6 Each compound listed in the table dissolves in water, but they have different solubilities. ***Comparing and Contrasting*** *Which compound is the most soluble? Which is the least soluble?*

Solubility

If a substance dissolves in water, a question you might ask is, "How well does it dissolve?" Suppose you add sugar to a glass of iced tea. You could add half a spoonful to make it taste slightly sweet. Or, you could add two spoonfuls to make it sweeter. Is there a limit to how "sweet" you can make the tea? Yes. At the temperature of iced tea, several spoonfuls of sugar are about all you can add. No matter how much you stir the tea, no more sugar will dissolve. **Solubility** is a measure of how well a solute can dissolve in a solvent at a given temperature.

When you've added so much solute that no more dissolves, you have a **saturated solution.** Any more sugar would just fall to the bottom of the glass and not make the tea any sweeter. On the other hand, if you can continue to dissolve more solute, you still have an **unsaturated solution.**

The solubility of a substance tells you the limit on how much you can add before you make a saturated solution. Because solubility is a characteristic property of matter, you can use it to help identify a compound. The solubility of a substance is usually described for a specific solvent (such as water) and under certain conditions (such as temperature). Figure 6 compares the solubilities of some familiar compounds when they dissolve in water.

From the table you can see that 35.7 g of salt will dissolve in 100 g of water at 0°C. But the same quantity (mass) of water at the same temperature will dissolve 180 g of sugar! If you had two white solids, you could use solubility to tell the difference without tasting them.

☑ *Checkpoint* ***Why doesn't solute added to a saturated solution dissolve?***

Changing Solubility

Which holds more sugar, iced tea or hot tea? You have already read that there is a limit on solubility. An iced tea and sugar solution quickly becomes saturated. Yet a hot, steaming cup of the same tea can hold several more spoonfuls of sugar before the limit is reached. Later, if the solution is cooled, the solubility of sugar decreases. Sugar crystals will form. The solubilities of sugar and other substances change when conditions change. **Among the factors that affect the solubility of a substance are temperature and type of solvent.**

Figure 7 Rock candy is made by dissolving sugar in hot water. As the sugar water cools, sugar crystals collect on a string.

Figure 8 Has this ever happened to you? Opening a bottle of soda water can sometimes produce quite a spray as dissolved gas comes out of solution. ***Relating Cause and Effect*** *Why does more gas escape from a warm bottle of soda water than from a cold bottle?*

Temperature Sugar is one of many solids that dissolve better when the temperature of the solvent increases. Cooks apply this principle to prepare certain foods. A cook cannot dissolve enough sugar at room temperature to make candy or fudge. The cook must heat the liquid mixture to dissolve the sugar. Later, when the food cools, it will taste sweeter than if it were made at room temperature.

Unlike most solids, gases become less soluble when the temperature goes up. For example, more carbon dioxide will dissolve in cold water than in hot water. Carbon dioxide makes soda water fizzy when you pour it into a glass. If you open a warm bottle of soda water, carbon dioxide escapes the liquid in greater amounts than if the soda water had been chilled. Why does warm soda taste "flat"? It contains less gas. If you like soda water that's very fizzy, open it when it's cold!

Solvents If you've ever shaken a bottle of salad dressing, you've seen how quickly water and oil separate. This is because water is polar and oil is nonpolar. Polar compounds and nonpolar compounds do not mix very well. For liquid solutions, the solvent affects how well a solute dissolves. The expression "like dissolves like" gives you a clue to which solutes are soluble in which solvents. Ionic and polar compounds dissolve in polar solvents. Nonpolar compounds do not dissolve in polar solvents. If you work with paints, you know that water-based (latex) paints can be cleaned up with just soap and water. But oil-based paints may require cleanup with a nonpolar solvent, such as turpentine.

Graphing ACTIVITY

The table below shows how many grams of potassium nitrate (KNO_3) can dissolve in 100 g of water at different temperatures. Use the data to make a graph. Label the horizontal axis *Temperature* and the vertical axis *Solubility.*

Temperature (°C)	Solubility (g/100g H_2O)
0	13
20	31
40	65
60	108
80	164
100	247

What does the graph show?

Sharpen your Skills

Controlling Variables

ACTIVITY

How does the quantity (mass) of a solute affect the boiling temperature of water? Design an experiment using a solute, water, a balance, a hot plate, and a thermometer.

What variables should remain constant in your experiment? What is the manipulated variable? What will be the responding variable?

With approval from your teacher, do the experiment. Report on your results.

Effects of Solutes on Solutions

Have you ever made ice cream? First you mix cream, sugar, and other ingredients. Then you freeze the mixture by packing it in ice and water. But ice water by itself is not cold enough to do the job. Cream freezes at a temperature lower than the freezing point of water (0°C). Adding salt to the ice water creates a mixture that is several degrees cooler. This salty ice water is cold enough to freeze the cream. Mmm!

You can use salt to affect boiling, too. When cooking spaghetti, people often add table salt to the water. As a result, the water boils at a temperature higher than 100°C, the boiling point of water. One small spoonful of salt in about a liter of water will raise the boiling point about 0.25 degrees. A few large spoonfuls of salt in a pot of water could increase the boiling temperature by about 0.5 degrees. This change is enough to cook the spaghetti faster.

Why does salt make cold water colder when it freezes and hot water hotter when it boils? The answer to both parts of this question depends on solute particles.

Lower Freezing Points **Solutes lower the freezing point of a solvent.** When liquid water freezes, the movement of molecules slows considerably. Instead, they form crystals of solid ice. Look at Figure 9 to compare the particles in pure water with those in a saltwater solution. Notice that pure water is made only of water molecules. In the salt solution, solute particles are present, too. In fact, they're in the way. The solute particles make it harder for the water molecules to form crystals. The temperature must drop lower than 0°C for a solid to form.

Figure 9 The freezing point and boiling point of water are affected by the presence of solute particles. Solute particles interfere with the change of state.

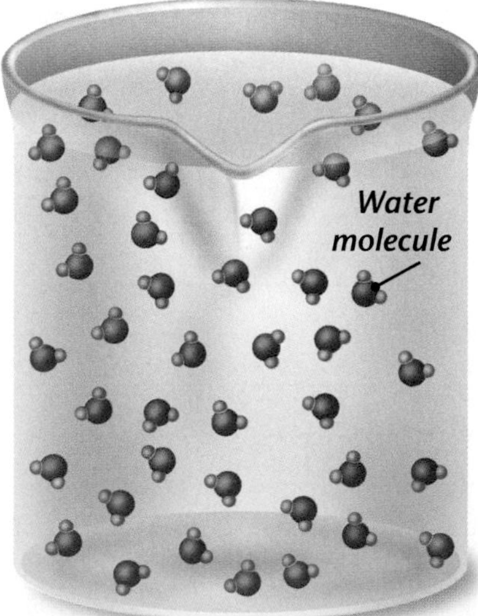

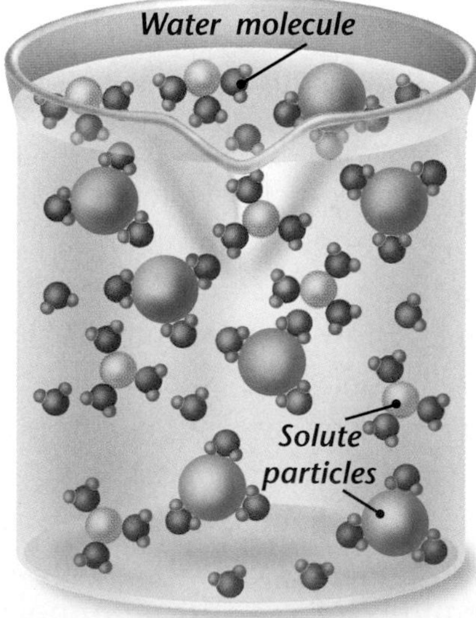

Higher Boiling Points **Solutes raise the boiling point of a solvent.** To see why, think about the difference between the molecules of a liquid and those of a gas. In a liquid, molecules are moving close to each other. In a gas, they are far apart and moving much more rapidly. As the temperature of a liquid rises, the molecules gain energy and escape into the air. Now compare the left and right beakers in Figure 9 again. In pure water, all the molecules are water. In the solution, however, some of the particles are water molecules and others are particles of solute. The presence of the solute makes it harder for the water molecules to escape, so more energy is needed. The temperature must go higher than 100°C for the water to boil.

Figure 10 The coolant in a car radiator is a solution.
Predicting *On a very cold day, what might happen to a car that had only water in the radiator?*

INTEGRATING TECHNOLOGY Car manufacturers make use of the effects of solutes to protect engines from heat and cold. The coolant in a car radiator is a solution of water and another liquid called antifreeze. Often the antifreeze is ethylene glycol, which freezes at –13°C and boils at 197°C. The mixture of the two liquids has a lower freezing point and higher boiling point than water alone. This solution safely absorbs heat given off by the running engine. Risk of damage to the car from overheating is greatly reduced. So is the risk of damage from freezing in very cold weather.

Section 1 Review

1. Describe what happens to the molecules of a solid, such as a sugar cube, when it dissolves in water. How does the process differ for an ionic compound, such as table salt?
2. Why would an ionic compound be more likely to dissolve in water than in oil?
3. Would you expect a concentrated solution of sugar in water to boil at 100°C? Explain.
4. **Thinking Critically Relating Cause and Effect** Why is the temperature needed to freeze ocean water lower than the temperature needed to freeze the surface of a freshwater lake?

Science at Home

With your family, make a saturated solution of baking soda in water. Add one small spoonful of baking soda to about 250 mL of cool water. Stir until the baking soda dissolves. Continue adding baking soda in this manner until no more dissolves. Keep track of how much baking soda you use. Then ask your family to predict what would happen if you used warm water instead. Test their predictions and compare the results with those of the first test.

Skills Lab

Designing Experiments

Speedy Solutions

In this lab, you will design an experiment to find out how a chosen variable affects the speed at which salt dissolves in water.

Problem

How can you control the rate at which salt dissolves in water?

Materials

spoon
thermometers
balance
ice
test tube rack
solid stoppers, #4
hot plate
stirring rods
timer or watch
test tubes, 25×150 mm
coarse, rock, and table salt
graduated cylinders and beakers, various sizes

Design a Plan 

1. Make a list of all the variables you can think of that could affect the speed with which salt dissolves in water.
2. Compare your list with your classmates' lists, and add other variables.
3. Choose one variable from your list to test.
4. Write a hypothesis predicting the effect of your chosen variable on the speed of dissolving.
5. Decide how to work with your choice.
   - ◆ If you choose temperature, you might perform tests at 10°C, 20°C, 30°C, 40°C, and 50°C.
   - ◆ If you choose stirring, you might stir for various amounts of time.
6. Plan at least three tests for whichever variable you choose. Remember to control all other variables.
7. Write down a series of steps for your procedure and safety guidelines for your experiment. Be quite detailed in your plan.
8. As part of your procedure, prepare a data table in which to record your results. Fill in the headings on your table that identify your manipulated variable and the responding variable. (*Hint:* Remember to include units.)
9. Have your teacher approve your procedure, safety guidelines, and data table.
10. Perform the experiment.

DATA TABLE

Manipulated Variable	Dissolving Time		
	Test 1	Test 2	Test 3

Analyze and Conclude

1. Which is the manipulated variable in your experiment? Which is the responding variable? How do you know which is which?
2. List three variables you held constant in your procedure. Explain why controlling these variables makes your data more reliable.
3. Make a line graph of your data. Label the horizontal axis with the manipulated variable. Label the vertical axis with the responding variable. Use an appropriate scale for each axis and label the units.
4. Study the shape of your graph. Write a conclusion about the effect of the variable you tested on the speed of salt dissolving in water.
5. Does your conclusion support the hypothesis you wrote in Step 4? Explain.
6. How do your results relate to what you have learned about particles and solubility?
7. What advantage would there be in running your tests a second or third time?
8. **Think About It** If you switched procedures with another student who tested the same variable as you, do you think you would get the same results? Explain why or why not.

More to Explore

Choose another variable from the list you made in Steps 1 and 2. Repeat the process with that variable. Of the two variables you chose, which was easier to work with? Explain.

SECTION 2 Describing Acids and Bases

DISCOVER ACTIVITY

What Colors Does Litmus Paper Turn?

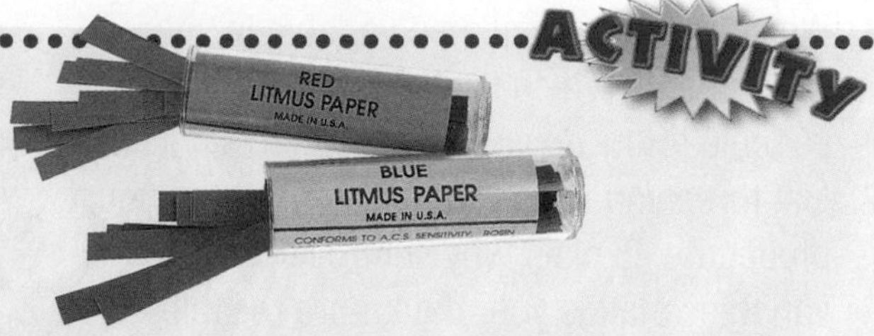

1. Use a plastic dropper to put a drop of lemon juice on a clean piece of red litmus paper. Put another drop on a clean piece of blue litmus paper. Observe.
2. Rinse your dropper with water. Then test other substances the same way. You might test orange juice, ammonia cleaner, tap water, vinegar, and solutions of soap, baking soda, and table salt. Record all your observations.
3. Wash your hands when you are finished.

Think It Over

Classifying Group the substances based on how they make the litmus paper change color. Do you notice any other characteristics that the members of each group have in common?

GUIDE FOR READING

- What properties can you use to identify acids?
- What properties can you use to identify bases?

Reading Tip Before you read, preview *Exploring Uses of Acids* and *Exploring Uses of Bases.* List examples of acids and bases you are already familiar with.

Did you eat any fruit for breakfast today—perhaps an orange, an apple, or fruit juice? If so, an acid was part of your meal. The last time you washed your hair, did you use shampoo? If your answer is yes, then you may have used a base.

You use many products that contain acids and bases. Manufacturers, farmers, and builders depend on acids and bases in their work. The chemical reactions of acids and bases even keep you alive! What are acids and bases? How do they react, and what are their uses? In this section you will start to find out.

Properties of Acids

What is an acid and how do you know when you have one? Test its properties. **Acids** are compounds that share some characteristic properties. **An acid is a substance that tastes sour, reacts with metals and carbonates, and turns blue litmus paper red.**

Sour Taste If you've ever tasted a lemon, you've had firsthand experience with the sour taste of acids. Can you think of other foods that sometimes taste sour, or tart? Citrus fruits—lemons, grapefruits, oranges, and limes—are acidic. They all contain citric acid. Other fruits (cherries, tomatoes, apples) contain acids also. The vinegar used in salad dressing is made from a solution of water and acetic acid. Tea is acidic, too. So is spoiled milk, but you might not want to drink it!

Although sour taste is a property of many acids, it is not one you would use to identify a compound as

Figure 11 A sour taste often means that food is acidic.

an acid. Scientists never taste chemicals in order to identify them. Though acids in sour foods may be safe to eat, many other acids are not.

Reactions With Metals Do you notice bubbles in Figure 13? Acids react with certain metals to produce hydrogen gas. Not all metals react this way, but magnesium, zinc, and iron do. When they react, the metals seem to disappear in the solution. This observation is one reason acids are described as **corrosive,** meaning they "eat away" at other materials.

INTEGRATING TECHNOLOGY The metal plate in Figure 13 is being etched with acid. Etching is one method of making printing plates that are then used to print works of art on paper. To make an etching, an artist first coats a metal plate with an acid-resistant material—often beeswax. Then the design is cut into the beeswax with a sharp tool, exposing some of the metal. When the plate is treated with acid, the acid eats away the design in the exposed metal. Later, ink applied to the plate collects in the grooves made by the acid. The ink is transferred to the paper when the etching is printed.

Some Important Acids

Acid	Formula
Hydrochloric acid	HCl
Nitric acid	HNO_3
Sulfuric acid	H_2SO_4
Carbonic acid	H_2CO_3
Acetic acid	$HC_2H_3O_2$
Phosphoric acid	H_3PO_4

Figure 12 The table lists the names and formulas of some common acids.

Figure 13 Metal etching takes advantage of the reaction of an acid with a metal. Lines are cut in a wax coating on a plate. Here, hydrochloric acid eats away at the exposed zinc metal, forming bubbles you can see in the close-up. ***Applying Concepts*** *What gas forms in this reaction?*

Language Arts CONNECTION

Putting someone to the "acid test" has nothing to do with litmus. The phrase is a figure of speech. It refers to a situation that tests someone's character, ability, courage, or other personal qualities. It comes from an old use of nitric acid to test the purity of gold. Many metals react with acid, but gold does not. Fake gold corrodes, while the value and quality of real gold are revealed.

In Your Journal

Write about a time you or someone you know went through an "acid test." What was hard about the situation? What did you learn from it about yourself or the other person?

Reactions With Carbonates Acids also react with carbonate ions in a characteristic way. Recall that an ion is an atom or a group of atoms that has an electric charge. Carbonate ions contain carbon and oxygen atoms bonded together. They carry an overall negative charge (CO_3^{2-}). When acids react with carbonate compounds, a gas forms. In this case, the gas is carbon dioxide.

INTEGRATING EARTH SCIENCE Geologists, scientists who study Earth, use the reaction of acids with carbonates to identify limestone. Limestone is made of calcium carbonate ($CaCO_3$). If a dilute solution of hydrochloric acid (HCl) is poured on a limestone rock, bubbles of carbon dioxide appear. Look at the equation for this reaction.

$$2\,HCl + CaCO_3 \rightarrow CaCl_2 + CO_2 + H_2O$$

Many forms of limestone come from organisms that live in the ocean. Coral rock, for example, comes from coral reefs. Reefs are large structures made of the skeletons of millions of tiny sea animals that produce an outer covering of calcium carbonate. Chalk is another form of limestone. It forms from the hard parts of microscopic sea animals, deposited in thick layers. Over time, these layers are pressed together and harden into chalk.

Reactions With Indicators If you did the Discover activity, you used litmus paper to test several substances. Litmus is an example of an **indicator,** a compound that changes color when in contact with an acid or a base. Vinegar and lemon juice turn blue litmus paper red. In fact, acids always turn litmus paper red. Sometimes chemists use other indicators to test for acids, but litmus is one of the easiest to use.

☑ *Checkpoint* *What is the purpose of using an indicator?*

Figure 14 Hydrangea flowers are natural indicators. They may range in color from bright pink to blue, depending on the acidity of the soil in which the bush grows.

EXPLORING Uses of Acids

Acids play important roles in the chemistry of living things. Acids also are used to make valuable products for homes, farms, and industries.

Acids and food
Many of the vitamins in the foods you eat are acids.

Oranges and tomatoes contain ascorbic acid, or vitamin C.

Folic acid, needed for healthy cell growth, is found in green leafy vegetables.

Acids in the body
Acids are useful in the body and are also waste products of cell processes.

Acid in the stomach helps to digest protein.

During exercise, lactic acid builds up in hard-working muscles.

In solution, acids often look just like water, but they react very differently. A concentrated acid can burn a hole in metal, cloth, skin, wood, and other materials.

Acids in the home
People often use dilute solutions of acids to clean brick and other surfaces. Hardware stores sell muriatic (hydrochloric) acid, which is used to clean bricks and metals.

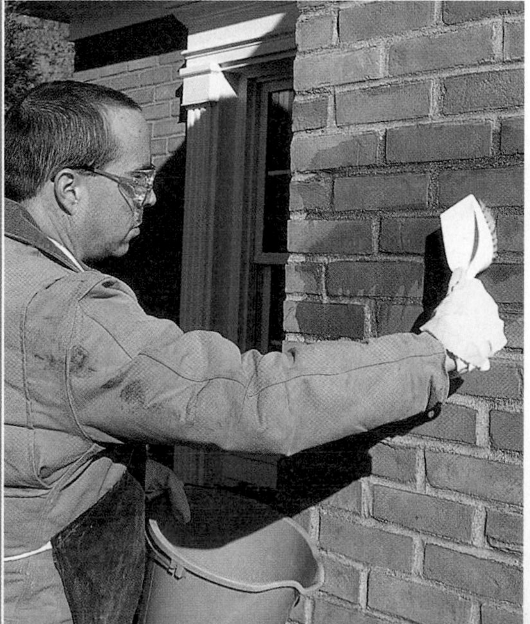

Acids and industry
Farmers and manufacturers depend on acids for many uses.

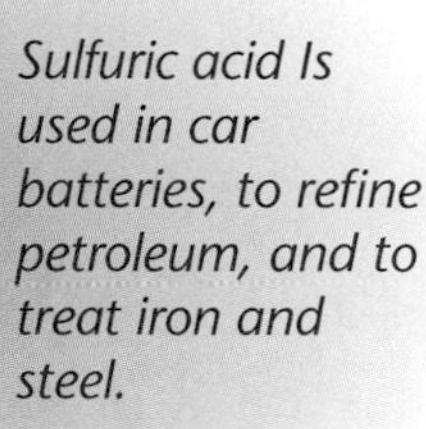

Sulfuric acid Is used in car batteries, to refine petroleum, and to treat iron and steel.

Nitric acid and phosphoric acid are used to make fertilizers for crops, lawns, and gardens.

EXPLORING Uses of Bases

The reactions of bases make them valuable raw materials for a range of products.

Bases and food

Baking soda reacts with acids to produce carbon dioxide gas in baked goods. Without these gas bubbles, this delicious variety of breads, biscuits, cakes, and cookies would not be light and fluffy.

Bases in the home

Ammonia solutions are safe to spray with bare hands, but gloves must be worn when working with drain cleaners.

Drain cleaners contain sodium hydroxide (lye).

You can't mistake the odor of household cleaning products made with ammonia.

In solution, bases sometimes look like water, or they may be cloudy white. Strong bases can burn your skin.

Base

Bases and health

Bases such as milk of magnesia (magnesium hydroxide) and calcium carbonate help ease effects of too much stomach acid.

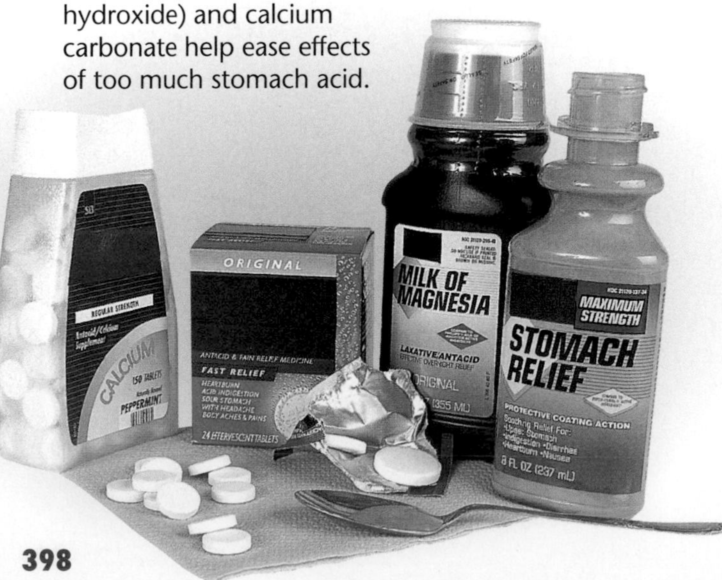

Bases and industry

Mortar and cement are manufactured using the bases calcium oxide and calcium hydroxide. Gardeners sometimes add calcium oxide to soil to make the soil less acidic for plants.

Properties of Bases

Bases are another group of compounds that can be identified by their common properties. **A base is a substance that tastes bitter, feels slippery, and turns red litmus paper blue.** Bases often are described as the "opposites" of acids.

Bitter Taste Have you ever tasted tonic water? The slightly bitter taste is caused by the base quinine. Bases taste bitter. Soaps, some shampoos, and detergents are bases. But you wouldn't want to identify them as bases by a taste test.

Slippery Feel Picture yourself washing your hands. You reach for a bar of soap and rub it between your hands underwater. Think about how slippery your hands feel. This slippery feeling is another property of bases. But just as you avoid tasting a substance to identify it, you wouldn't want to touch it. Strong bases can irritate or burn your skin. A safer way to identify bases is by their other properties.

Reactions With Indicators As you might guess, if litmus paper can be used to test acids, it can be used to test bases too. Bases turn red litmus blue. Like acids, bases react with other indicators. But litmus paper gives a reliable, safe test. An easy way to remember which color litmus turns for acids or bases is to remember the letter *b*. **B**ases turn litmus paper **b**lue.

Reactions of Bases Unlike acids, bases don't react with metals or carbonates. At first, you may think it is useless to know that a base doesn't react with certain chemicals. But if you know what a compound *doesn't* do, you know something about it. For example, you know it's not an acid. Another important property of bases is how they react with acids. You will learn more about these reactions in Section 3.

Some Important Bases

Base	Formula
Sodium hydroxide	$NaOH$
Potassium hydroxide	KOH
Calcium hydroxide	$Ca(OH)_2$
Magnesium hydroxide	$Mg(OH)_2$
Aluminum hydroxide	$Al(OH)_3$
Ammonia	NH_3
Calcium oxide	CaO

Figure 15 The table lists the names and formulas of some common bases.
Predicting *What color would any of these compounds turn litmus paper?*

Section 2 Review

1. How can you use litmus paper to distinguish an acid from a base?
2. How can you tell if a food may contain an acid or a base as one of its ingredients?
3. Name at least two ways that acids and bases are useful around your home.
4. **Thinking Critically Comparing and Contrasting** Make a table that compares at least three properties of acids and bases.

Check Your Progress

CHAPTER PROJECT 12

Select sources for your indicators. Explore ways to crush each material and squeeze out its juice. You may have to add some water and remove any solid. (*Hint:* Refrigerate any samples you are not going to use immediately.) Write down your procedure and get your teacher's approval before preparing your indicators.

Section 3 Acids and Bases in Solution

Discover Activity

What Can Cabbage Juice Tell You?

1. Using a dropper, put five drops of red cabbage juice into each of three separate plastic cups.
2. Add 10 drops of lemon juice (an acid) to one cup. Add 10 drops of ammonia cleaner (a base) to another. Keep the third cup for comparison. Record the colors you see.
3. Now add ammonia, one drop at a time, to the cup containing lemon juice. Keep adding ammonia until the color no longer changes. Record all color changes you see.
4. Add lemon juice a drop at a time to the ammonia until the color no longer changes. Record the changes you see.

Think It Over

Forming Operational Definitions Based on your observations, how could you expand your definitions of acids and bases?

Guide for Reading

- **What kind of ions do acids and bases form in water?**
- **What does pH tell you about a solution?**
- **What happens in a neutralization reaction?**

Reading Tip **As you read, write one sentence to summarize the main idea discussed under each heading.**

A chemist pours hydrochloric acid into a beaker. Then she adds sodium hydroxide to the acid. The mixture looks the same, but the beaker becomes warm. If she tested the solution with litmus paper, what color would the paper turn? Would you be surprised if it did not turn color at all? If *exactly* the right amounts and concentrations of the acid and the base were mixed, the beaker would hold nothing but salt water! How could those two corrosive chemicals produce something harmless to the touch? In this section, you will find the answer.

Acids in Solution

What do acids have in common? Notice that each formula in Figure 16 begins with hydrogen. The acids you will learn about are made of one or more hydrogen ions and a negative ion. A **hydrogen ion** (H^+) is an atom of hydrogen that has lost its electron. The negative ion may be a nonmetal or a polyatomic ion. But hydrogen ions are the key to the reactions of acids.

Figure 16 You can find at least one hydrogen atom in the formula of each of these acids.

Acid Formulas	
Name	**Formula**
Hydrochloric acid	HCl
Nitric acid	HNO_3
Sulfuric acid	H_2SO_4
Acetic acid	$HC_2H_3O_2$

Acids in water solution separate into hydrogen ions (H^+) and negative ions. In the case of hydrochloric acid, hydrogen ions and chloride ions (Cl^-) form.

$$HCl \xrightarrow{\text{water}} H^+ + Cl^-$$

If another acid were substituted for HCl, the negative ions would be different. But hydrogen ions would be produced in each case.

Figure 17 Acids share certain chemical and physical properties when dissolved in water. Most acids are very soluble.

Now you can add to the definition of acids you learned in Section 2. **An acid is any substance that produces hydrogen ions (H^+) in water.** These hydrogen ions cause the properties of acids. For instance, when you add certain metals to an acid, hydrogen ions interact with the metal atoms. One product of the reaction is hydrogen gas (H_2). Hydrogen ions also react with blue litmus paper, turning it red. That's why every acid gives the same litmus test result.

Bases in Solution

The formulas of bases give you clues to what ions they have in common. Look at Figure 18. Many bases are made of metals combined with hydroxide ions. The **hydroxide ion (OH^-)** is a negative ion made of oxygen and hydrogen.

When bases dissolve in water, positive metal ions and hydroxide ions separate. Look, for example, at what happens to sodium hydroxide.

$$NaOH \xrightarrow{water} Na^+ + OH^-$$

Not every base contains hydroxide ions. For example, the gas ammonia (NH_3) does not. But in the solvent water, ammonia is a base that reacts with water to form hydroxide ions.

$$NH_3 + H_2O \rightarrow NH_4^+ + OH^-$$

Notice that in both reactions, there are negative hydroxide ions. These examples give you another way to define a base. **A base is any substance that produces hydroxide ions (OH^-) in water.** Hydroxide ions are responsible for the bitter taste and slippery feel of bases. Hydroxide ions also turn red litmus paper blue.

Checkpoint *What is a hydroxide ion made of?*

Figure 18 Many, but not all, bases dissolve well in water. ***Making Generalizations*** *What do all of the base formulas in the table have in common?*

Base Formulas

Name	Formula
Sodium hydroxide	NaOH
Potassium hydroxide	KOH
Calcium hydroxide	$Ca(OH)_2$
Magnesium hydroxide	$Mg(OH)_2$

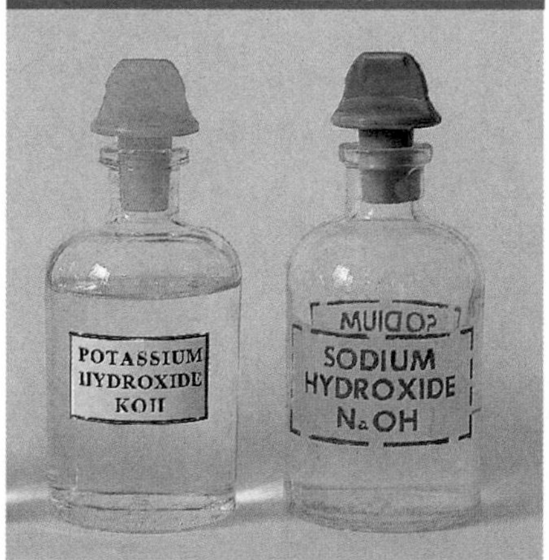

Figure 19 In a solution of a strong acid, all the acid molecules break up into ions. In a solution of a weak acid, however, fewer molecules do so.

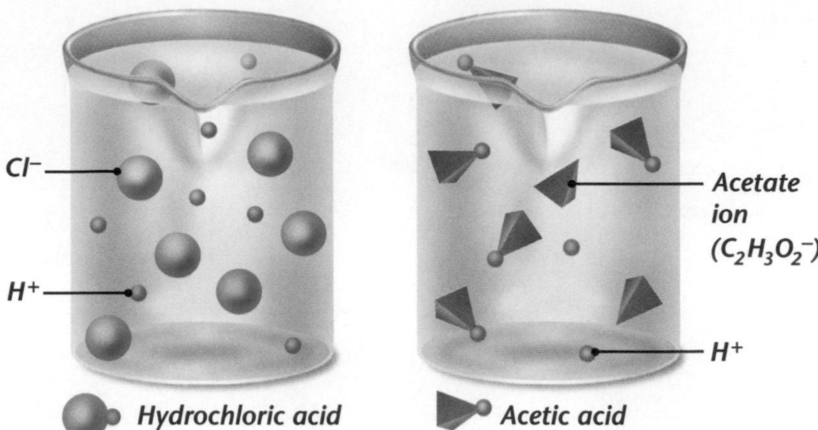

pHone Home

ACTIVITY

Find out the pH of familiar substances in your home.

1. Put on your safety goggles and apron.
2. Select substances such as fruit juices, soda water, coffee, tea, or antacids.
3. Predict which substances are most acidic or most basic.
4. If the sample is solid, dissolve some in a cup of water. Use a liquid as is.
5. Using a plastic dropper, transfer a drop of each sample onto a fresh strip of paper for testing pH.
6. Compare the color of the strip to the pH values on the package.
7. Repeat for all your samples. Remember to rinse the dropper between tests.

Interpreting Data List the samples from lowest to highest pH. Which results, if any, surprised you?

Strengths of Acids and Bases

Acids and bases may be strong or weak. Strength refers to how well an acid or base produces ions in water. With a strong acid, most of the molecules react to form hydrogen ions in solution. With a weak acid, fewer molecules do. At the same concentration, a strong acid produces more hydrogen ions (H^+) than a weak acid does. Examples of strong acids include hydrochloric acid, sulfuric acid, and nitric acid. Most other acids, such as acetic acid, are weak acids.

Strong bases react in a water solution in a similar way to strong acids. A strong base produces more hydroxide ions (OH^-) than does an equal concentration of a weak base. Ammonia is a weak base. Lye, or sodium hydroxide, is a strong base.

Strength determines, in part, how safe acids and bases are to use. For example, all the acids that are safe to eat, such as acetic acid and citric acid, are weak. Ammonia cleaner may irritate your hands slightly if you use it. But the same concentration of drain cleaner, which contains sodium hydroxide, would burn your skin.

People often say that a solution is weak when they mean it is dilute. This could be a dangerous mistake! Even a dilute solution of hydrochloric acid can eat a hole in your clothing or sting your skin. An equal concentration of acetic acid would not.

☑ ***Checkpoint*** *How would a weak base differ from an equal concentration of a strong base in solution?*

Measuring pH

Knowing the concentration of hydrogen ions is the key to knowing how acidic or basic a solution is. To find out the concentration of ions, chemists use a numeric scale called pH. The **pH scale** is a range of values from 0 to 14. It expresses the concentration of hydrogen ions in a solution.

Figure 20 shows where some familiar substances fit on the pH scale. Notice that the most acidic substances are at the low end of the scale. At the same time, the most basic substances are at the high end of the scale. You need to remember two important points about pH. **A low pH tells you that the concentration of hydrogen ions is high. By comparison, a high pH tells you that the concentration of hydrogen ions is low.** If you keep these ideas in mind, you can make sense of how the scale works.

You can find the pH of a solution by using indicators. The student in Figure 20 is using indicator paper that turns a different color for each pH value. Matching the color of the paper with the colors on the test scale tells how acidic or basic the solution is. A pH lower than 7 is acidic. A pH higher than 7 is basic. If the pH is 7, the solution is neutral. That means it's neither an acid nor a base. Pure water has a pH of 7.

A concentrated solution of acetic acid can have a lower pH than a dilute solution of hydrochloric acid. In order to handle acids and bases safely, you need to know both their pH and their concentration. Hydrochloric acid is more acidic (has a lower pH) than acetic acid. But a concentrated (strong) solution of acetic acid can have a lower pH than a dilute (weak) solution of hydrochloric acid. To safely handle acids and bases, you need to know the pH of the *solutions* you are using.

Figure 20 The pH scale classifies solutions as acidic or basic. Indicator paper turns a different color for each pH value. ***Interpreting Diagrams*** *If a solution has a pH of 9, is it acidic or basic? What can you say about a solution with a pH of 3?*

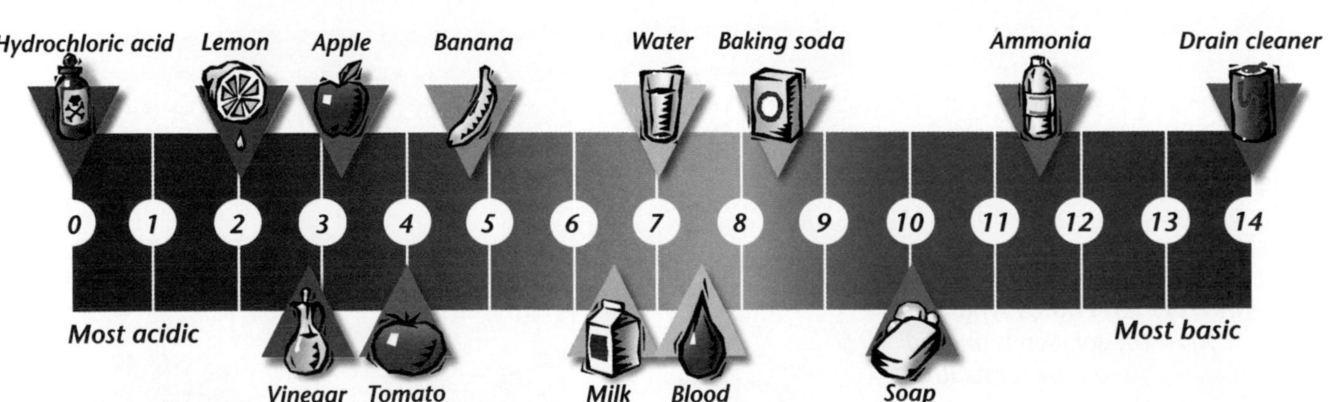

Figure 21 Acid rain weakens trees by damaging their leaves and removing nutrients from the soil. Portions of forests can die off when weakened trees become diseased or are further damaged by severe cold or drought.

Acid Rain

Normal rainfall is slightly acidic, with a pH of approximately 5.5. *INTEGRATING ENVIRONMENTAL SCIENCE* This acidity comes from carbon dioxide in the air. Carbon dioxide dissolves in rainwater, producing carbonic acid, a weak acid.

$$H_2O + CO_2 \rightarrow H_2CO_3$$

Acid rain is more acidic than normal rainwater. The pH of acid rain in the United States today can be as low as about 4.3. The extra acidity comes from nitrogen oxides and sulfur oxides. These gases are released into the air as pollutants from industry and motor vehicles. These oxides react with water in the air to produce acids, including nitric acid and sulfuric acid. Rainwater containing these acids has more hydrogen ions. It has a lower pH and is more corrosive. Acid rain can damage statues and buildings, destroy forests, and kill fishes in lakes.

Acid-Base Reactions

The story at the start of this section describes a chemist who mixed hydrochloric acid with sodium hydroxide. She got a solution of table salt (sodium chloride) and water.

$$HCl + NaOH \rightarrow H_2O + Na^+ + Cl^-$$

If you tested the pH of the mixture, it would be close to 7, or neutral. In fact, a reaction between an acid and a base is called a **neutralization** (noo truh lih ZAY shun). As a result of neutralization, an acid-base mixture is not as acidic or basic as the individual starting solutions were.

Sometimes an acid-base reaction results in a neutral solution, with a pH of 7. But not always. The final pH depends on which acid and base react, how much of each is used, and what their concentrations are. If a small amount of a strong acid is added to a larger amount of strong base, what would be the pH of the mixture? Common sense tells you it would be higher than 7, still somewhat basic.

Figure 22 The solution on the left is acidic. The solution on the right is basic. When mixed, these solutions produced the neutral solution in the center. *Interpreting Photos What tells you if the solution is an acid, a base, or neutral?*

Some Salts and Their Uses		
Salt	**Formula**	**Uses**
Sodium chloride	$NaCl$	Food flavoring; preservative
Potassium iodide	KI	Additive in "iodized" salt that prevents iodine deficiency (goiter)
Calcium chloride	$CaCl_2$	De-icer for roads and walkways
Potassium chloride	KCl	Salt substitute in foods
Calcium carbonate	$CaCO_3$	Found in limestone and seashells
Ammonium nitrate	NH_4NO_3	Fertilizer; active ingredient in some cold packs

Figure 23 Each salt listed in this table can be formed by the reaction between an acid and a base.

Products of Acid-Base Reactions

"Salt" may be the familiar name of the stuff you sprinkle on food. But to a chemist, the word refers to a specific group of compounds. A **salt** is any ionic compound made from the neutralization of an acid with a base. A salt is made from the positive ion of a base and the negative ion of an acid. Look at the equation for the reaction of nitric acid with potassium hydroxide.

$$HNO_3 + KOH \rightarrow H_2O + K^+ + NO_3^-$$

One product of the reaction is water. The other product is potassium nitrate (KNO_3), a salt. Potassium nitrate is written in the equation as separate K^+ and NO_3^- ions because it is soluble in water. **A neutralization reaction produces water and a salt.** Some salts, such as potassium nitrate, are soluble. Others form precipitates because they are insoluble.

Figure 24 These salt flats were left behind in Death Valley, California, when the water in which the salts were dissolved evaporated.

Section 3 Review

1. What ions would you expect to find when an acid dissolves in water? What ions would you expect to find when a base dissolves in water?
2. If the pH of a solution is 6, would you expect to find more or fewer hydrogen ions (H^+) than in a solution with a pH of 3? Explain why.
3. What does the term *salt* mean to a chemist, and how may a salt form?
4. **Thinking Critically Predicting** What salt would form from a reaction between hydrochloric acid, or HCl, and calcium hydroxide, or $Ca(OH)_2$? Explain your answer.

CHAPTER PROJECT 12

Check Your Progress

Use each indicator to test for acids and bases in familiar substances. For example, try vinegar, household ammonia, lemon juice, milk, and soapy water. (*Hint:* Use small amounts of indicator and test samples. Watch for a color change, especially where the sample comes in contact with the indicator. If you do not see any change, add a few more drops of the sample.) Summarize your results in a table.

Real-World Lab

You, the Consumer

The Antacid Test

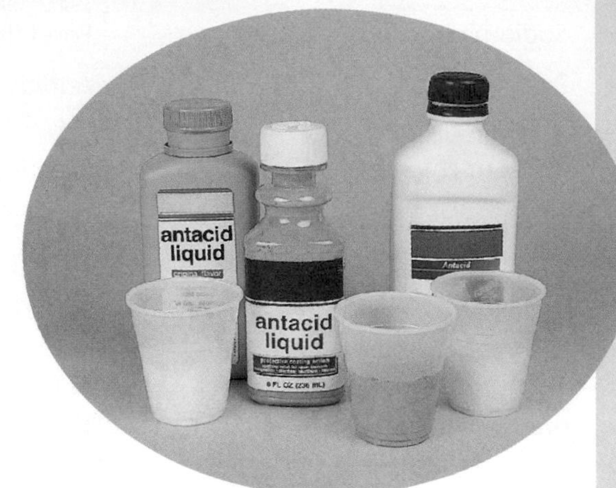

Consumers see or hear ads for antacids on television, radio, and in magazines. Each product claims to "neutralize excess stomach acid" best. You can experiment to see if some antacids really do work better than others.

Problem

Which antacid neutralizes stomach acid with the smallest number of drops?

Skills Focus

designing experiments, measuring, interpreting data

Materials

3 plastic droppers   small plastic cups
dilute hydrochloric acid (HCl), 50 mL
methyl orange solution, 1 mL
liquid antacid, 30 mL of each brand tested

Procedure    

Part 1

1. Using a plastic dropper, put 10 drops of hydrochloric acid (HCl) into one cup. **CAUTION:** *HCl is corrosive. Rinse spills and splashes immediately with water.*
2. Use another plastic dropper to put 10 drops of liquid antacid into another cup.
3. In your notebook, make a data table like the one below. Record the colors of the HCl and the antacid.
4. Add two drops of methyl orange solution to each cup. Record the colors you see.
5. Test each of the other antacids. Discard all the solutions and cups as directed by your teacher.

Part 2

6. Methyl orange changes color at a pH of about 4. Predict the color of the solution you expect to see when an antacid is added to a mixture of methyl orange and HCl.
7. Design a procedure for testing the reactions of each antacid with HCl. Decide how many drops of acid and methyl orange you need to use each time.

DATA TABLE

Substance	Original Color	Color With Indicator
HCl		
Antacid Brand A		
Antacid Brand B		

8. Devise a plan for adding the antacid so that you can detect when a change occurs. Decide how much antacid to add each time and how to mix the solutions in order to be sure the indicator is giving accurate results.
9. Make a second data table to record your observations.
10. Carry out your procedure and record your results.
11. Discard the solutions and cups as directed by your teacher. Rinse the plastic droppers thoroughly.
12. Wash your hands thoroughly when done.

Analyze and Conclude

1. What is the function of the methyl orange solution?
2. Do your observations support your predictions from Step 6? Explain why or why not.
3. Why do you think antacids reduce stomach acid? Explain your answer, using the observations you made.
4. Why is it important to use the same number of drops of HCl in each trial?
5. Which antacid neutralized the HCl with the smallest number of drops? Give a possible explanation for the difference.
6. If you have the same volume (number of drops) of each antacid, which one can neutralize the most acid?
7. Did your procedure give results from which you could draw conclusions about which brand of antacid was most effective? Explain why or why not.
8. **Apply** If you want to buy an antacid, what information do you need in order to decide which brand is the best buy?

Getting Involved

Compare the advertised strength of several brands of antacids. Look for antacids in a local grocery store or drug store. Check the ingredient lists of several brands. What are some of the different bases used in commercial antacids? (*Hints:* Look for compounds containing "hydroxide." Also check any compound identified as the "active ingredient.")

SECTION 4 Digestion and pH

DISCOVER ACTIVITY

Where Does Digestion Begin?

1. Obtain a bite-sized piece of crusty bread.
2. Chew the bread for about one minute. Do not swallow until after you notice a change in taste as you chew.

Think It Over

Inferring How did the bread taste before and after you chewed it? How can you explain the change in taste?

GUIDE FOR READING

- **Why is it necessary for your body to digest food?**
- **How does pH affect digestion?**

Reading Tip **Before you read, preview Figure 27. List the organs of the digestive system in the order in which food passes through them.**

You may have seen the following commercial: A man has a stomachache after eating spicy food. A voice announces that the problem is excess stomach acid. The remedy is an antacid tablet.

Ads like this one highlight the role of chemistry in digestion. You need to have acid in your stomach. But too much acid is a problem. Other parts of your digestive system need to be basic. What roles do acids and bases play in the digestion of food?

What Is Digestion?

Foods are made mostly of water and three groups of compounds: carbohydrates, proteins, and fats. But your body can't use foods in the forms you eat. **Foods must be broken down into simpler substances that your body can use for raw materials and energy.** The process of **digestion** breaks down the complex molecules of foods into smaller molecules.

Digestion involves two processes—mechanical and chemical digestion. **Mechanical digestion** tears, grinds, and mashes large food particles into smaller ones. The result is similar to what happens when a sugar cube is hit with a hammer. The size of the food is reduced, but the foods aren't changed into other compounds. **Chemical digestion** breaks large molecules into smaller molecules. Some molecules provide your body with energy. Others serve as building blocks for the compounds in muscle, bone, blood, skin, and other organs.

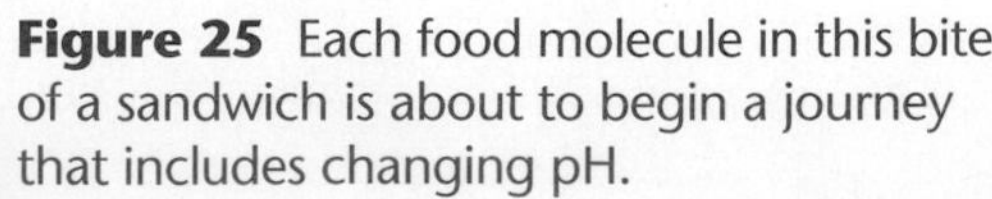

Figure 25 Each food molecule in this bite of a sandwich is about to begin a journey that includes changing pH.

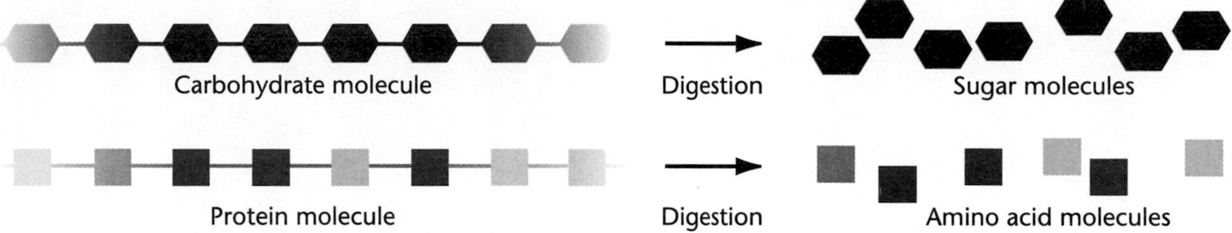

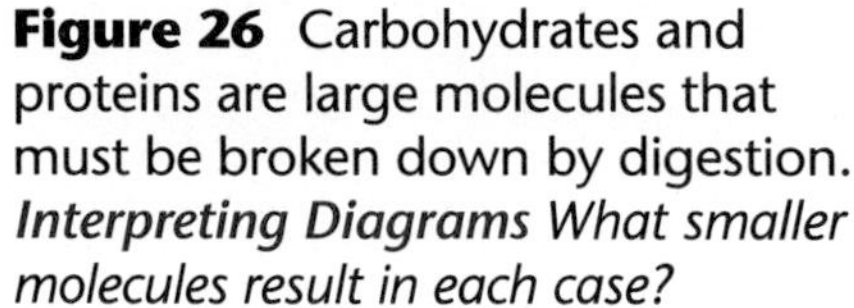
Figure 26 Carbohydrates and proteins are large molecules that must be broken down by digestion. ***Interpreting Diagrams*** *What smaller molecules result in each case?*

Chemical digestion takes place with the help of enzymes. Enzymes are substances that speed up reactions in living things. Enzymes require just the right conditions to work, including temperature and pH. **For some digestive enzymes, the pH must be low. For others, the pH must be high or neutral.**

☑ *Checkpoint* *What happens to foods in your body?*

pH in the Digestive System

A bite of sandwich is about to take a journey through your digestive system. What pH changes will affect the food molecules along the way? Figure 27 shows the main parts of the human digestive system. As you read, trace the food's pathway through the body.

Your Mouth The first stop in the journey is your mouth. Immediately, your teeth chew and mash the food. Also, the food is mixed with a fluid called saliva. Have you ever felt your mouth water at the smell of something delicious? The odor of food can trigger production of saliva.

What would you expect the usual pH inside your mouth to be? Remember that saliva tastes neither sour nor bitter. So you're correct if you think your mouth has a pH near 7, the neutral point.

Saliva contains amylase (AM uh lays), an enzyme that helps break down the carbohydrate starch into smaller sugar molecules. Amylase works best when the pH is near 7. You can sense the action of this enzyme if you chew a piece of bread. After about two minutes in your mouth, the carbohydrates are broken down into sugars. This makes the bread taste sweet.

Your Stomach Next, the food is swallowed and arrives in your stomach. This muscular organ starts digestion of foods that contain protein, such as meat, fish, and beans. Cells in the lining of your stomach release enzymes and hydrochloric acid. Rather than the near-neutral pH of your mouth, the pH drops to a very acidic level of about 2. This pH is even more acidic than the juice of a lemon.

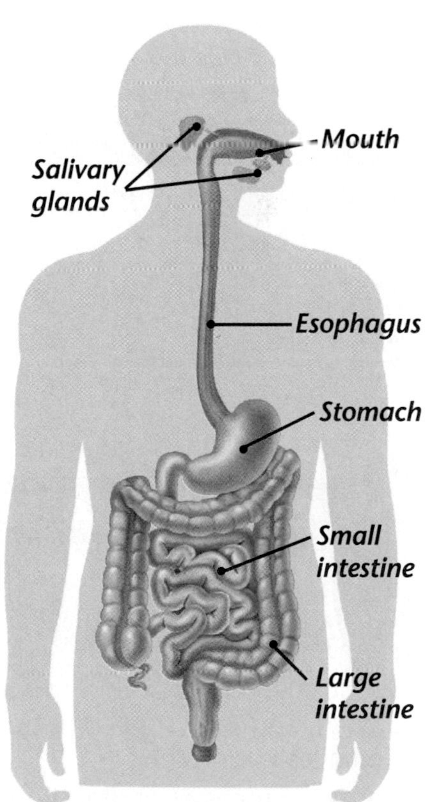

Figure 27 Foods undergo changes in pH as they move through the digestive system.

Figure 28 Shrimp contains protein. Rice and pea pods contain carbohydrates.

The low pH in your stomach helps digestion take place. The main enzyme that works in your stomach is pepsin. It helps break down proteins into small molecules called amino acids. Most enzymes work best in a solution that is nearly neutral. But pepsin is different. It works most effectively in acids.

Your Small Intestine Your stomach empties its contents into the small intestine. Here, other digestive fluids surround the food. One fluid contains the bicarbonate ion (HCO_3^-). This ion creates a slightly basic solution, with a pH of about 8. In the small intestine, other enzymes complete the breakdown of carbohydrates, fats, and proteins. All of these enzymes work best in a slightly basic solution. Most chemical digestion ends in the small intestine.

The food molecules from the bite of sandwich have been split up into smaller ones by now. These smaller molecules pass through the walls of your small intestine into your bloodstream and are carried to the cells that will use them.

Figure 29 The pH varies greatly through the digestive system. ***Relating Cause and Effect*** *Why do certain digestive enzymes work only in certain parts of the digestive system?*

pH Changes During Digestion

Organ	pH
Mouth	7
Stomach	2
Small intestine	8

Section 4 Review

1. How are foods changed by your digestive system?
2. How does pH differ in your mouth, your stomach, and your small intestine? Why are the differences important?
3. What two processes of digestion begin in the mouth? How do they differ?
4. **Thinking Critically Predicting** How would the digestion of food be affected if your stomach did not produce hydrochloric acid?

CHAPTER PROJECT 12

Check Your Progress

Use indicator paper to find the pH of each substance you tested earlier with homemade indicators. Add these pH values to your data table. Compare the data you collected using your indicators with the data you obtained with the indicator paper.

CHAPTER 12 STUDY GUIDE

Working With Solutions

Key Ideas

- A solution is a well-mixed mixture. Particles dissolved in a liquid solution cannot be seen or separated by settling or filtration.
- In a solution, solute particles separate from each other and become surrounded by particles of the solvent.
- Every solute has a specific solubility in a particular solvent. Solubility changes with temperature, pressure, and type of solvent.
- Solutes affect the freezing points and boiling points of solvents.

Key Terms

suspension
solution
solvent
solute
dilute solution
concentrated solution
solubility
saturated solution
unsaturated solution

Describing Acids and Bases

Key Ideas

- An acid tastes sour, reacts with metals and carbonates, and turns litmus paper red.
- A base tastes bitter, feels slippery, and turns litmus paper blue.
- An indicator is a substance that turns different colors in an acid or a base.

Key Terms

acid
corrosive
indicator
base

Acids and Bases in Solution

Key Ideas

- An acid produces hydrogen ions (H^+) when it dissolves in water. A base produces hydroxide ions (OH^-) when it dissolves in water.
- pH describes the acidity of a solution.

Key Terms

hydrogen ion (H^+)
hydroxide ion (OH^-)
pH scale
acid rain
neutralization
salt

Digestion and pH

INTEGRATING LIFE SCIENCE 

Key Ideas

- Digestion breaks foods into smaller molecules.
- Each digestive enzyme works best at a specific pH.

Key Terms

digestion
mechanical digestion
chemical digestion

Organizing Information

Concept Map Copy and complete the concept map, and add a title. (For more on concept maps, see the Skills Handbook.)

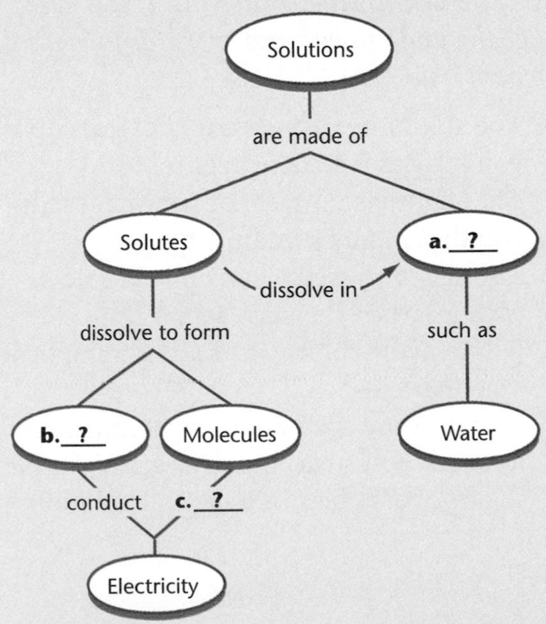

Reviewing Content

Multiple Choice

Choose the letter of the best answer.

1. Sugar water is an example of a
a. suspension. **b.** solution.
c. solute. **d.** solvent.

2. A solution in which as much solute as possible is dissolved in a solvent is a(n)
a. dilute solution.
b. filtered solution.
c. saturated solution.
d. unsaturated solution.

3. Washing soda (sodium carbonate, Na_2CO_3) will make bubbles if you add
a. tap water. **b.** salt water.
c. ammonia cleaner. **d.** lemon juice.

4. Litmus and cabbage juice are examples of
a. indicators.
b. strong acids.
c. strong bases.
d. concentrated solutions.

5. If a base separates completely into ions when dissolved in water, it is a
a. weak acid.
b. weak base.
c. strong acid.
d. strong base.

True or False

If the statement is true, write true. If it is false, change the underlined word or words to make the statement true.

6. The solubility of a gas in water goes up if you <u>increase</u> the temperature.

7. The slightly sour taste of lemonade tells you that it may contain a <u>base</u>.

8. The gas produced when an acid reacts with a carbonate is <u>oxygen</u>.

9. Dilute hydrochloric acid is an example of a <u>strong</u> acid.

10. Amylase, the enzyme in saliva that helps to break down carbohydrates into simple sugars, works best in a <u>neutral</u> solution.

Checking Concepts

11. Describe at least two differences between a dilute solution and a concentrated solution of sugar water.

12. You have three different unknown compounds that are all white solids. How can you use solubility to identify each compound?

13. Tomatoes are acidic. Predict two properties of tomato juice that you would be able to observe.

14. Explain how an indicator helps you distinguish between an acid and a base.

15. What combination of acid and base can be used to make the salt potassium chloride, KCl?

16. Writing to Learn Some of the limestone on the outside of buildings in an area looks as if it is being gradually eaten away. As an investigator for the local air pollution agency, write a brief memo explaining what may be causing the problem.

Thinking Critically

17. Developing Hypotheses Some power plants release hot wastewater into nearby rivers or streams. Fish living in these waters sometimes die from lack of oxygen. Write a hypothesis to explain what has happened to the oxygen in the water.

18. Comparing and Contrasting Compare the types of particles formed in a water solution of an acid with those formed in a water solution of a base.

19. Applying Concepts When calcium oxide (CaO) dissolves in water, it reacts as shown below. Is calcium oxide an acid or a base? Explain.

$$CaO + H_2O \rightarrow Ca^{2+} + 2OH^-$$

20. Predicting Suppose a person took a dose of antacid greater than what is recommended. Predict how this action might affect the digestion of certain foods. Explain.

Applying Skills

The diagram below shows the particles of an unknown acid in a water solution. Use the diagram to answer Questions 21–23.

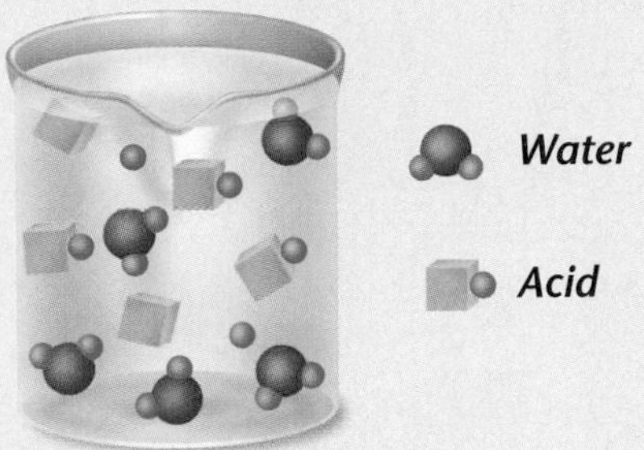

21. **Interpreting Data** How can you tell from the diagram that the solution contains a weak acid?
22. **Making Models** Suppose another unknown acid is a strong acid. Make a diagram to show the particles of this acid dissolved in water.
23. **Drawing Conclusions** Explain how the pH of a strong acid compares with the pH of a weak acid of the same concentration.

Performance CHAPTER PROJECT 12 Assessment

Project Wrap Up Demonstrate the indicators you prepared. Make a list of the substances you tested in order from most acidic to least acidic.

Reflect and Record In your journal, discuss whether or not you would use the same materials as indicators if you did this project again. Explain why. Describe how acid-base indicators could be useful for farmers and gardeners. Would you recommend that they use any of the indicators you made? Why or why not?

Test Preparation

Use these questions to prepare for standardized tests.

Study the graph showing solubilities of four compounds. Then answer Questions 24–27.

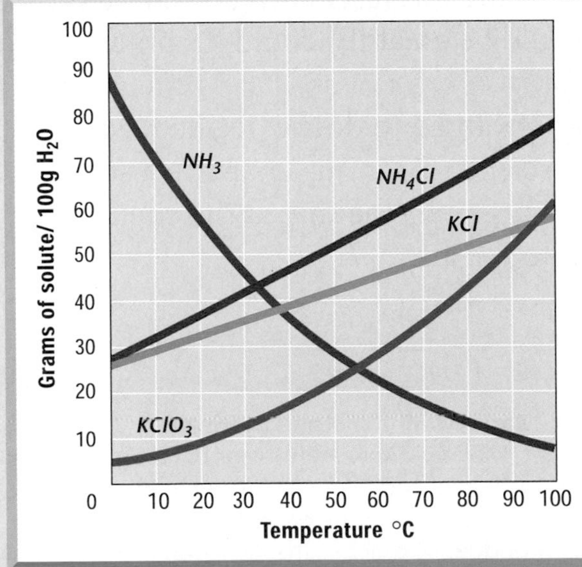

24. At 70°C, about how many grams of ammonium chloride (NH_4Cl) can dissolve in 100 grams of water?
    a. 40 g b. 50 g
    c. 60 g d. 70 g
25. If 30 grams of potassium chloride (KCl) are dissolved in 100 grams of water at 50°C, the solution can be best described as
    a. saturated b. supersaturated
    c. unsaturated d. soluble
26. Which one of the compounds becomes less soluble with increasing temperature?
    a. NH_4Cl b. NH_3
    c. KCl d. $KClO_3$
27. At about what temperature is the solubility of ammonia (NH_3) the same as the solubility of potassium chlorate ($KClO_3$)?
    a. 0°C b. 55°C
    c. 85°C d. 100°C

NATURE OF SCIENCE

SAVING THE OZONE LAYER

As a child growing up in Mexico, long before he won a Nobel Prize in chemistry, Mario Molina enjoyed playing with science. "I was always interested in chemistry sets or toy microscopes. With the microscope in front of me, I'd take a piece of lettuce, put it in water, and let it rot and really stink. To see the life teeming in a drop of water—that for me was fascinating. Even then I realized it would be great if I could become a research scientist."

What Mario wanted to do, he decided, was "actually use science for things that affect society." Mario Molina began by looking at the chemicals people put into the air.

Dr. Mario Molina Born in Mexico City, chemist Mario Molina is now a Professor of Earth, Atmospheric, and Planetary Sciences at the Massachusetts Institute of Technology in Cambridge, Massachusetts. In 1995, Professor Molina, Sherwood Rowland, and Paul Crutzen won the Nobel Prize in Chemistry for their work on CFCs and the ozone layer.

Cycle of Ozone Destruction

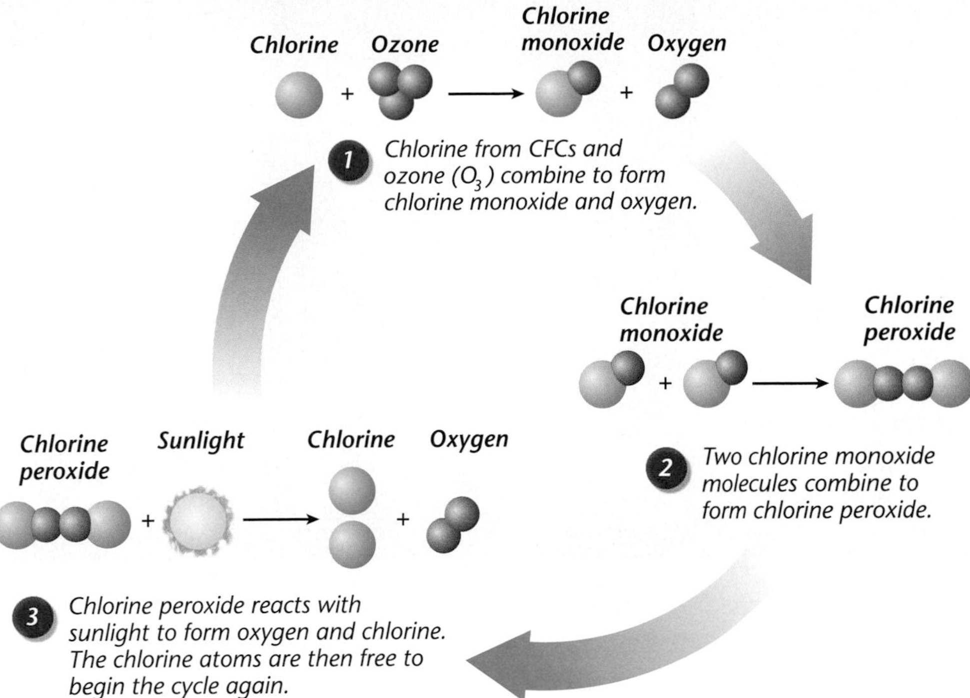

Asking Simple Questions

In the early 1970s, one of Dr. Molina's co-workers, Sherwood Rowland, heard about a group of compounds called chlorofluorocarbons, or CFCs. CFCs were used in air conditioners, refrigerators, and aerosol spray cans, but leaked into the air. "It is something that is not natural, but is now in the atmosphere all over the planet." What happens to these compounds in the air, Rowland and Molina wondered, and what do they do to the air?

"We didn't know ahead of time if CFCs were doing damage or not," Dr. Molina explains. "So what we did was study what was going on. We learned that CFCs aren't changed much down near Earth. But we expected that if they got high enough in the atmosphere, solar radiation would destroy them."

Radiation is how energy from the sun reaches Earth. Ultraviolet (UV) rays, a form of radiation, break compounds apart and change them. "Above a certain altitude, everything falls apart. We had to learn how high CFCs went and how long it took them to get there. Then we asked: What does it mean that CFCs are up there?"

A Protective Shield in the Sky

In his laboratory, Dr. Molina studied how ultraviolet light changes CFCs. "It became clear that these molecules would be destroyed by UV rays in the stratosphere—the upper atmosphere, where the ozone layer is. At the time, I didn't even know what the ozone layer was."

But Mario Molina learned fast. The ozone layer is a thin layer of the atmosphere that contains ozone, a form of oxygen. The ozone blocks out UV rays from the sun. UV rays would be dangerous to living things if they reached Earth's surface.

In a 1987 international treaty, the United States and other industrial nations agreed to reduce the use of CFCs in spray cans and other products.

Changes in the ozone layer over Antarctica, 1979 to 1993

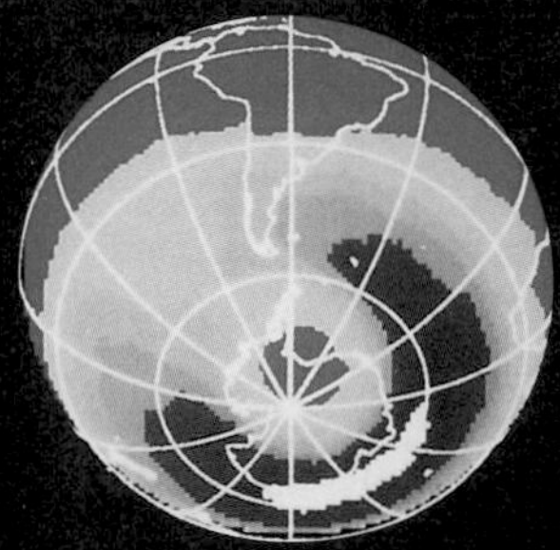

In 1979, thinning of the ozone layer was visible in satellite images.

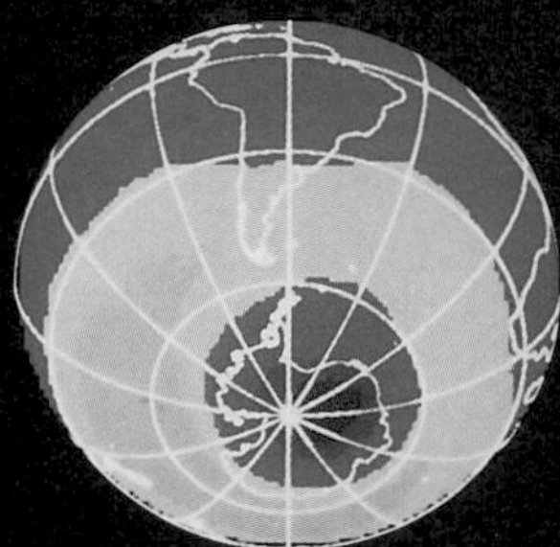

In 1985, a hole in the ozone layer was clearly visible.

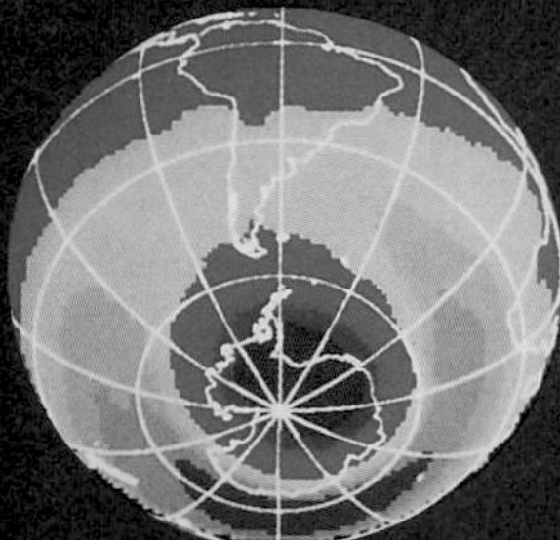

In 1989, the hole in the ozone layer was expanding.

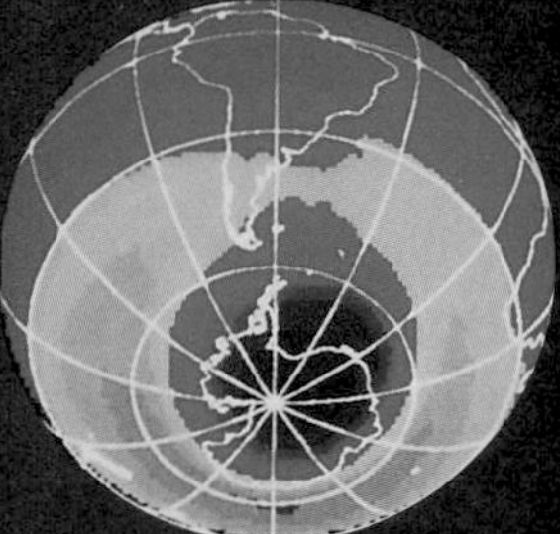

In 1993, the damage to the ozone layer was even worse.

← Less ozone More ozone →

These images of the South Pole, taken by satellite between 1979 and 1993, show a hole developing in the ozone layer of the atmosphere. The changing size and color of the image over the pole represent how quickly the hole increased.

Dr. Molina learned something very disturbing. When the sun's rays break CFCs apart, chlorine forms. A chain of chemical changes that destroys ozone then begins. "Very small amounts of CFCs can have very big effects on ozone."

A Scary Prediction Comes True

Mario Molina and his co-workers made a frightening prediction. If CFCs can reach the stratosphere, they will eventually damage the protective ozone layer. Other scientists thought Mario Molina was wrong or exaggerating. But more and more evidence came in. Researchers sent balloons up into the stratosphere with scientific instruments to measure chlorine formed by CFCs. They found that CFCs were in the stratosphere and that the sun's rays were breaking them down.

Was the ozone layer being hurt? Yes. Over Antarctica, there was an "ozone hole," an opening in the ozone layer. The hole lets in harmful radiation from the sun. "That was a surprise to us and to everybody. It was a very large effect that we hadn't predicted. Some scientists thought the ozone hole was natural, but we thought it was caused by CFCs. We checked it out by doing experiments from Antarctica. In a couple of years it became very clear that this hole was a result of the CFCs."

Scientist and Speaker

Dr. Molina now had to convince people to stop making and using CFCs. "We were lucky that the effect

Shown here is the ER-2 aircraft, which was used to measure gases in the ozone hole over Antarctica. ▶

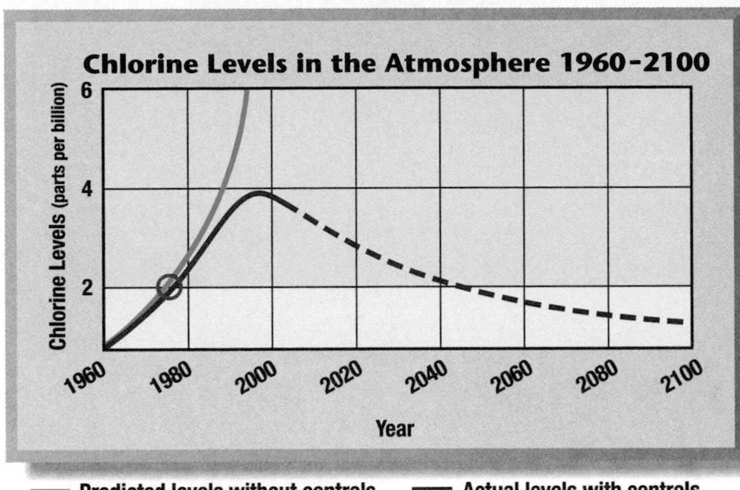

Predicted levels without controls — Actual levels with controls
Antarctica ozone hole found — Predicted levels with controls

The graph shows that the level of chlorine in the atmosphere would have increased rapidly if controls on CFCs had not been passed. With controls in place, the amount of chlorine in the atmosphere should gradually decrease to levels in the light blue region of the graph. The ozone hole should then close.

over Antarctica was so large. That made it easy to measure and test. But similar effects exist everywhere. As scientists we had to inform the public and the government. If you're convinced that you're right and that something dangerous is going to happen, you need to risk speaking out."

Mario Molina went to the U.S. Senate and to other governments. He was able to show how UV radiation was causing damage. "There was damage to some crops, damage to growing fish, damage that we can already see and measure today."

Finally, the world listened. Through the United Nations, an agreement was signed by most industrial nations to stop using CFCs by the year 2000.

Work Still to Do

"Everybody has to work together," chemist Molina says. He has done more than his share. He gave $200,000 of his Nobel Prize money to help train scientists from Latin America and other developing countries. "There is a need to understand our planet, and we need very good minds to work on these problems. There are big challenges out there," he says with a confident smile, "but fortunately science is fascinating."

In Your Journal

Mario Molina particularly wants to know how chemicals made by people get into the atmosphere and change it. Take a walk in your neighborhood. Make a list of ways you can observe—or think of—that people put chemicals into the air. Remember that smoke is a mixture of chemicals.

CHAPTER 13

Characteristics of Waves

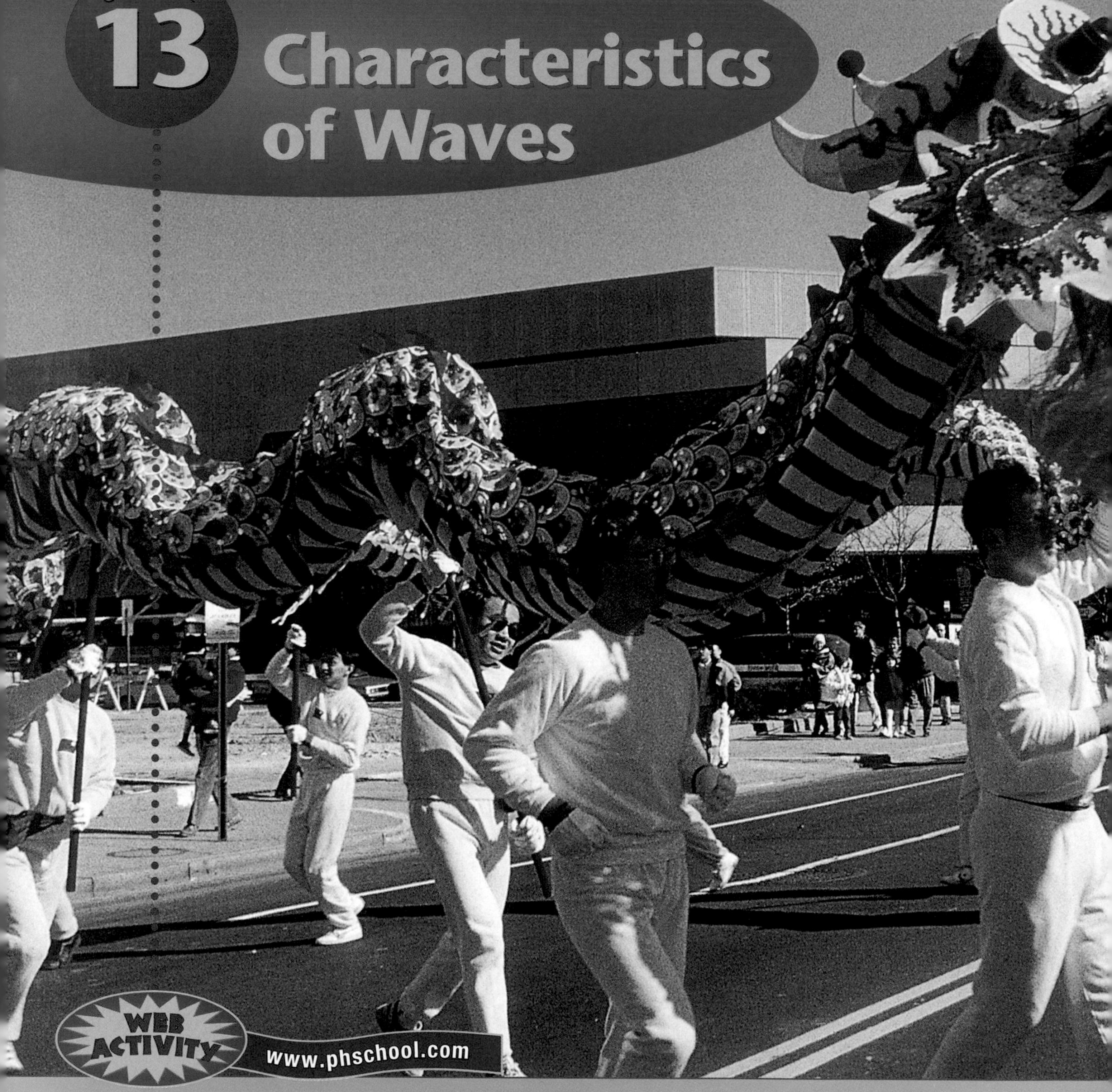

WEB ACTIVITY www.phschool.com

What Are Waves?

Discover How Do Waves Travel?

Properties of Waves

Discover How Can You Change a Wave?
Skills Lab Wavy Motions

Interactions of Waves

Discover How Does a Ball Bounce?
Sharpen Your Skills Observing
Try This Standing Waves
Skills Lab Making Waves

PROJECT 13

Over and Over and Over Again

It's time to celebrate the Chinese New Year! The parade passes through the streets to the delight of the people watching. The dragon dancers use poles to move the dragon up and down. The dragon moves just like a wave.

In this chapter, you will discover how waves travel. Some waves involve repeating patterns, or cycles. Any motion that repeats itself at regular intervals is called periodic motion. The hands moving on a clock, a child swinging on a swing, and a Ferris wheel going round and round are just a few examples. As you work through the project, you will investigate the properties of periodic motion.

Your Goal To find and describe examples of periodic motion.

To complete this project you will
- identify several examples of periodic motion or other events that have periodic characteristics
- collect and organize data on the frequency and duration of each event
- present your findings as a poster, display, or demonstration

Get Started Brainstorm examples of repeating patterns you have observed. Think about objects or events that go back and forth or alternate from high to low, dark to light, loud to quiet, or crowded to uncrowded.

Check Your Progress You'll be working on this project as you study this chapter. To keep your project on track, look for Check Your Progress boxes at the following points.

Section 1 Review, page 423: List examples of periodic motion you'd like to study.

Section 2 Review, page 429: Record your observations of the frequency, length, and amplitude of the periodic events.

Wrap Up At the end of the project (page 443), you will present your findings to your class.

Passers-by watch as the Chinese dragon moves to the music.

Integrating Earth Science 

SECTION 4 **Seismic Waves**

Discover **Can You Find the Sand?**

SECTION 1 What Are Waves?

DISCOVER ACTIVITY

How Do Waves Travel?

1. Fill a shallow pan with about 3 centimeters of water.
2. With a pencil, touch the surface of the water at one end of the pan twice each second for about a minute.
3. Describe the pattern the waves make. Sketch a rough diagram of what you see.
4. Float a cork on the water. How do you think the cork will move if there are waves? Repeat Step 2 to find out.

Think It Over

Observing What happened to the cork in Step 4? How is the cork's movement similar to the wave's movement? How is it different? Draw a diagram of what you see. Use arrows to show the movement of the cork.

GUIDE FOR READING

- What causes waves?
- What are the three main types of waves?

Reading Tip Before you read, think of what comes to mind when you hear the word *wave*. As you read, write a definition of wave.

Far out to sea, the wind disturbs the calm surface of the water. A ripple forms. As the wind continues to blow, the ripple grows into a powerful wave that can travel a great distance. Near the beach, surfers wait eagerly. They quickly paddle into deeper water to catch the monstrous wave. Surfers enjoy the power of nature as they ride the wave to the shore.

What are waves? How can they travel so far? Why are some waves more powerful than others? In this section, you will explore how waves begin and how they move.

Waves and Energy

Waves crashing on a beach show the tremendous energy waves can carry. A **wave** is a disturbance that transfers energy from place to place. In science, **energy** is defined as the ability to do work. To understand waves, think of a boat out on the ocean. If a wave disturbs the surface of the water, it will cause anything floating on the water to be disturbed, too. The energy carried by a wave can lift even a large ship as it passes.

The disturbance caused by a wave is temporary. After the wave has passed, the water is calm again.

◀ A surfer riding a wave

What Carries Waves? Many waves require something to travel through. Water waves travel along the surface of the water, and sound waves travel through air. You can even make a wave travel along a rope. The material through which a wave travels is called a **medium.** Gases (such as air), liquids (such as water), and solids (such as ropes) all act as mediums. Waves that require a medium through which to travel are called **mechanical waves**.

Although waves travel through a medium, they do not carry the medium itself with them. Look at the duck in Figure 1. When a wave moves under the duck, the duck moves up and down. It does not move along the surface of the water. After the wave passes, the water and the duck return to where they started.

Breaking waves at a beach behave a little differently. When waves hit a beach, the water does move along with the wave. This happens because the ocean floor near the beach slopes upward. As the water at the bottom of the wave hits the slope, it moves up toward the top of the wave. The top of the wave gets bigger and continues to move forward. Eventually it topples over, turning white and frothy.

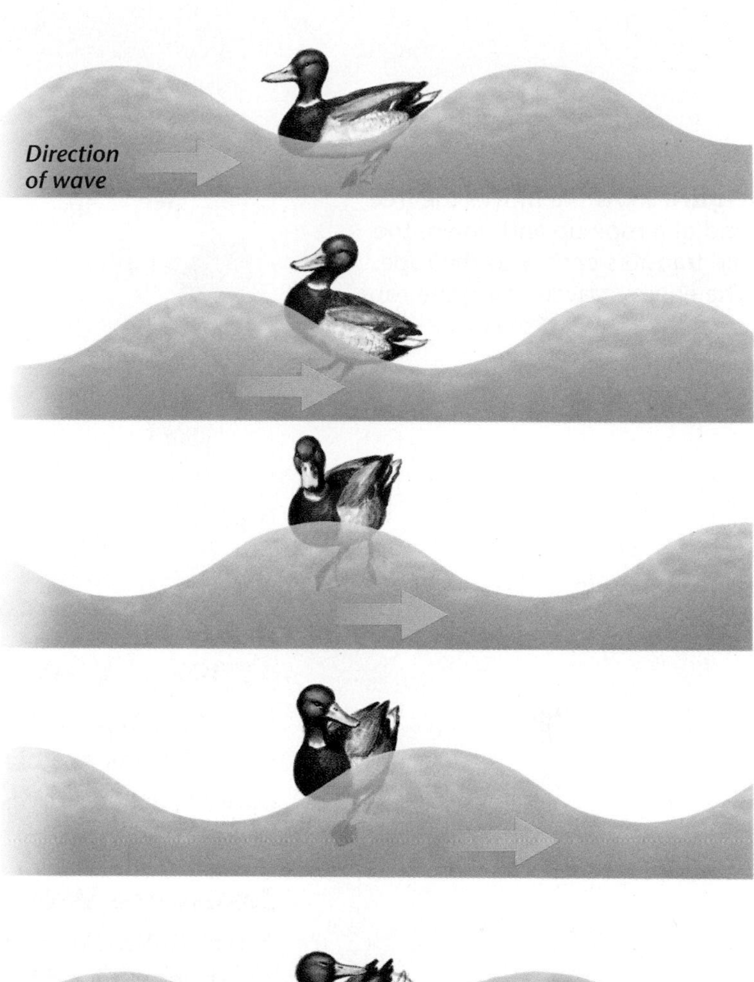

Figure 1 Waves travel through water, but they do not carry the water with them. The duck moves up and down as a wave passes under it. The duck does not travel along with the wave.
Interpreting Diagrams *If you add a sixth sketch to the diagram, which stage should it most resemble?*

Not all waves require a medium to carry them along. Light from the sun, for example, can travel through empty space. Light is an example of an electromagnetic wave. You will learn more about electromagnetic waves in Chapter 15.

What Causes Waves? You can create waves by dipping your finger in water. **Waves are created when a source of energy causes a medium to vibrate.** A **vibration** is a repeated back-and-forth or up-and-down motion. This motion is the wave.

A moving object has energy. The moving object can transfer energy to a nearby medium, creating a wave. For example, as the propellers of a motorboat turn, they disturb the calm water surface. The boat's propeller transfers energy to the water. The propeller produces a wave that travels through the water. As the boat moves through the water, it also causes waves.

☑ ***Checkpoint*** *What are mechanical waves?*

Figure 2 As she moves the free end of a rope up and down, the girl transfers energy to the rope. The energy travels along the rope, creating a transverse wave.

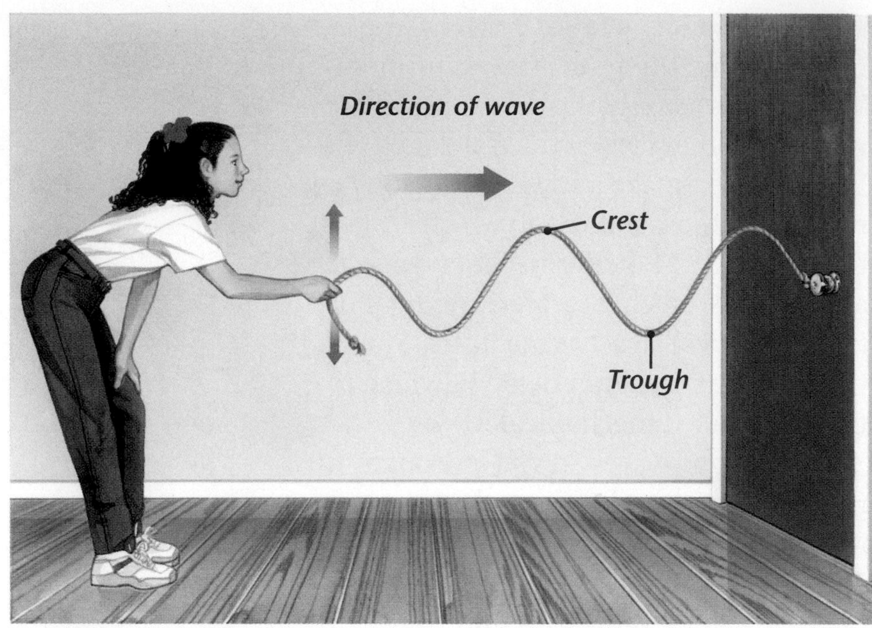

Types of Waves

Different types of waves travel through mediums in different ways. **Waves are classified according to how they move. The three types of waves are transverse waves, longitudinal waves, and surface waves.**

Transverse Waves When you make a wave on a rope, the wave moves from one end of the rope to the other. The rope itself, however, moves up and down or from side to side. Waves that move the medium at right angles to the direction in which the waves are traveling are called **transverse waves.** Transverse means "across." As a transverse wave moves in one direction, the particles of the medium move across the direction of the wave. Figure 2 shows that some parts of the rope are very high while some are very low. The highest parts of the wave are called **crests,** and the lowest parts are called **troughs** (trawfs).

Figure 3 The coils in the spring toy move back and forth parallel to the motion of the wave. This is a longitudinal wave. ***Comparing and Contrasting*** *How does this wave compare with waves on a rope?*

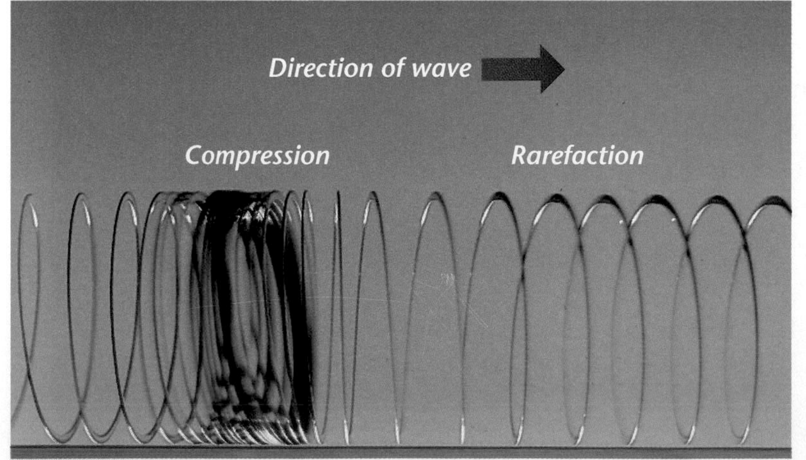

Longitudinal Waves Figure 3 shows a different kind of wave. If you stretch out a spring toy and push and pull one end, you can produce a longitudinal wave. **Longitudinal waves** (lawn juh TOO duh nul) move the particles of the medium parallel to the direction in which the waves are traveling. The coils in the spring move back and forth parallel to the wave motion.

Notice in Figure 3 that in some parts of the spring the coils are close together.

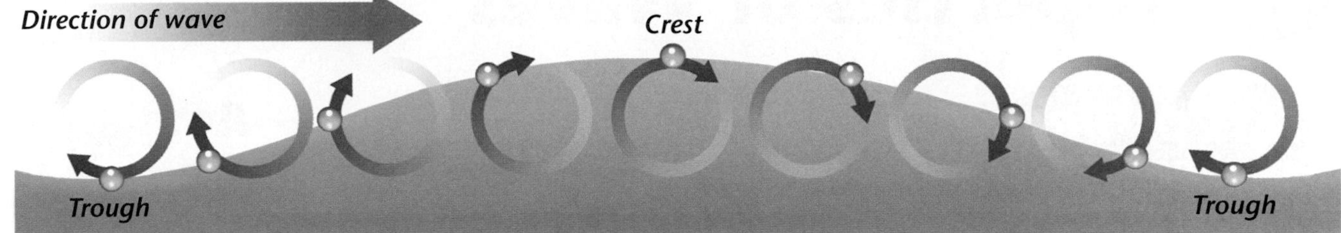

Figure 4 In a surface wave, up-and-down motion combines with back-and-forth motion. The combination produces circular motion.

In other parts, the coils are more spread out. The parts where the coils are close together are called **compressions** (kum PRESH uns). The parts where the coils are spread out, or rarefied, are called **rarefactions** (rair uh FAK shunz).

As compressions and rarefactions travel along the spring toy, each coil moves slightly forward and then back. The energy travels from one end of the spring to the other, creating a wave. After the wave passes, each part of the spring returns to the position where it started.

Combinations of Waves **Surface waves** are combinations of transverse and longitudinal waves. These waves occur at the surface between two mediums, such as water and air. When a wave passes through water, the water (and anything on it) moves up and down, like a transverse wave on a rope. The water also moves back and forth slightly in the direction that the wave is traveling, like the coils of the spring. But unlike the coils of a spring, water does not compress. The up-and-down and back-and-forth movements combine to make each particle of water move in a circle. Figure 4 shows the circular motion of surface waves.

Section 1 Review

1. Where do waves get their energy?
2. Name the three types of waves. Give an example of each type.
3. When a wave passes a ship at sea, how does the wave affect the ship?
4. **Thinking Critically Applying Concepts** The vibrations produced by a jackhammer are used to break up pavement. What type of waves do you think the jackhammer produces in the ground? Explain.

CHAPTER PROJECT 13

Check Your Progress

Find and list as many examples of periodic motion as you can. Look for cycles and patterns that repeat in only a few seconds and others that take hours or days to repeat. Try to find examples that continue day after day, such as the rising and setting of the sun. Don't limit your search to your home or school. Look at the world around you and at the solar system for ideas. Describe and sketch each example you find.

Section 2 Properties of Waves

Discover Activity

How Can You Change a Wave?

1. Lay a rope about 3 meters long on a smooth floor. Securely hold one end. Have a partner hold the other end.
2. Flick the end of the rope left and right about once per second to make a series of waves travel down the rope. Observe the waves as they travel toward your partner.
3. Now flick the end of the rope more often—about two times per second. Again, observe the waves.
4. Switch roles with your partner and repeat Steps 2 and 3.

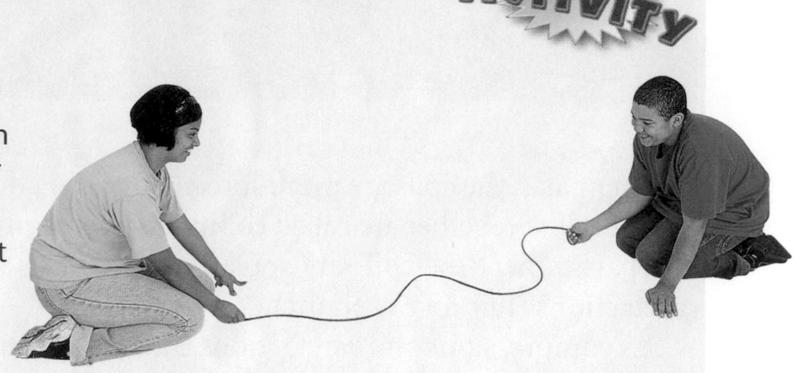

Think It Over

Predicting What happened to the waves when you flicked the rope more often? How will the wave change if you flick the rope less often than once per second? Try it.

GUIDE FOR READING

- **What are the basic properties of waves?**
- **How is a wave's speed related to its wavelength and frequency?**

Reading Tip **As you read, make a list of the properties of waves. Write a sentence that describes each property.**

One of the most elegant and graceful Olympic sports is rhythmic gymnastics. A ribbon dancer flicks a stick attached to a ribbon, making waves travel down the ribbon. Some of the waves are long, while others are shorter. The rate at which the gymnast flicks her hands affects the length and shape of the waves in the ribbon.

There are many different kinds of waves. Waves can carry a little energy or a lot. They can be short or long. They can be rare or frequent. They can travel fast or slow. All waves, however, share certain properties. **The basic properties of waves are amplitude, wavelength, frequency, and speed.**

Rhythmic gymnastics ▶

Wave Diagrams

To understand the properties of waves, it helps to represent a wave on a diagram. Transverse waves like those on a rope are easy to draw. You can draw a transverse wave as shown in Figure 5. Think of the horizontal line as the position of the rope before it is disturbed. This is its rest position. As the wave passes, the rope goes above or below the rest position. Remember that the crests and the troughs are the highest and lowest points on the wave.

To draw longitudinal waves, think of the compressions in the spring toy as being similar to the crests of a transverse wave. The rarefactions in the spring toy are like the troughs of a transverse wave. By treating compressions as crests and rarefactions as troughs, you can draw longitudinal waves in the same way as transverse waves.

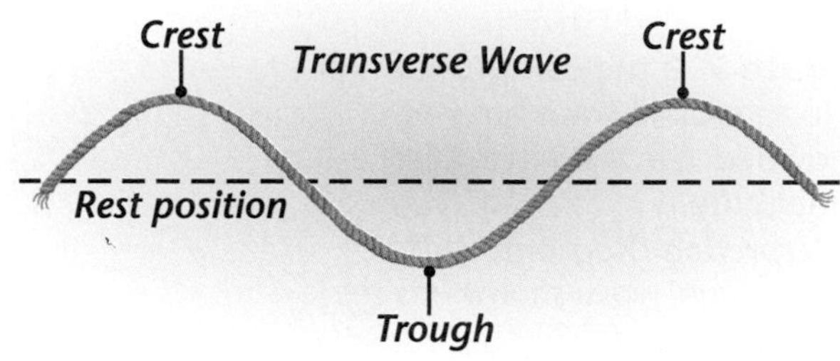

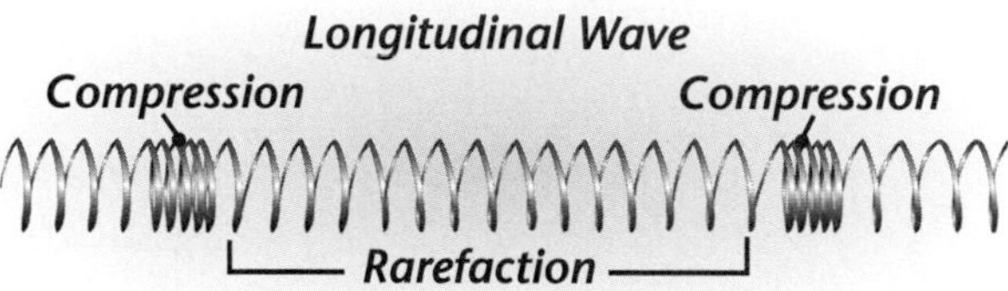

Figure 5 The crests and troughs of a transverse wave are the points at which the medium is farthest from the rest position. The compressions of a longitudinal wave correspond to the crests of a transverse wave.

☑ *Checkpoint Which part of a longitudinal wave is similar to the crest of a transverse wave?*

Amplitude

Some waves are very high, while others are barely noticeable. The distance the medium rises depends on the amplitude of the wave that passes through it. **Amplitude** is the maximum distance the particles of the medium carrying the wave move away from their rest positions. The amplitude is a measure of how much a particle in the medium moves when disturbed by the wave. The amplitude of a water wave is the maximum distance a water particle moves above or below the surface level of calm water.

You know that waves are produced by something vibrating. The farther the medium moves as it vibrates, the larger the amplitude of the resulting waves. You can increase the amplitude of the waves on a rope by moving your hand up and down a greater distance. To do this, you have to use more energy. This greater amount of energy is then transferred to the rope. Thus, the amplitude of a wave is a direct measure of its energy.

Amplitude of Transverse Waves Compare the two transverse waves in Figure 6. You can see that wave A goes up and down a greater distance than wave B. The amplitude of a transverse wave is the maximum distance the medium moves up or down from its rest position. You can find the amplitude of a transverse wave by measuring the distance from the rest position to a crest or to a trough.

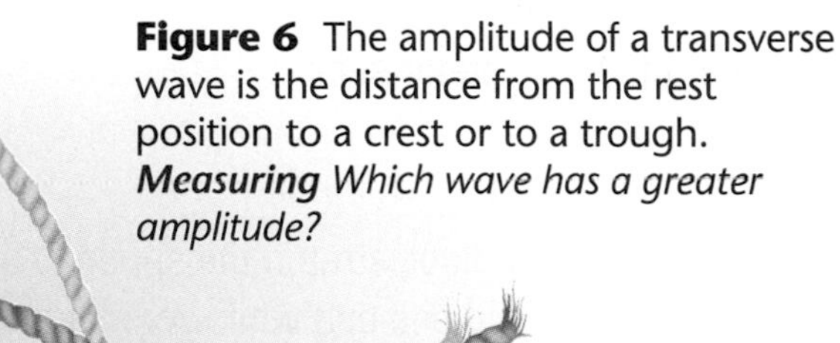

Figure 6 The amplitude of a transverse wave is the distance from the rest position to a crest or to a trough. ***Measuring*** *Which wave has a greater amplitude?*

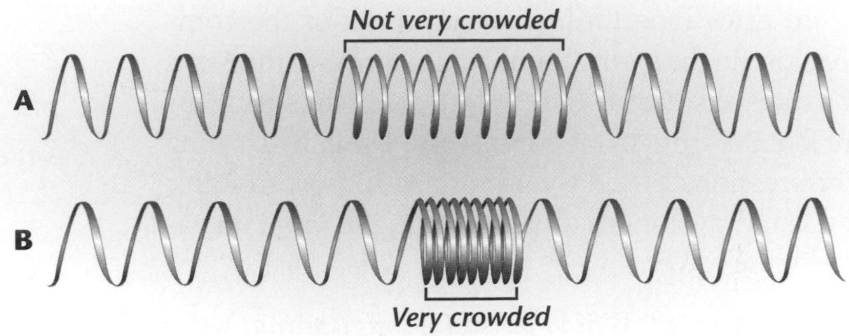

Figure 7 If the compressions of a longitudinal wave are very crowded, the wave has a large amplitude.
Interpreting Diagrams *Which longitudinal wave shown has the larger amplitude?*

Amplitude of Longitudinal Waves The amplitude of a longitudinal wave is a measure of how compressed or rarefied the medium becomes. High-energy vibrations cause the compressions to be very crowded. This makes the rarefactions quite loose. Crowded compressions and uncrowded rarefactions are like high crests and low troughs. They mean that the longitudinal wave has a large amplitude.

Skills Lab

Observing

Wavy Motions

Now it's your turn to make some waves on a spring toy. In this lab, you will observe some properties of waves.

Problem

How do waves travel in a spring toy?

Materials

spring toy meter stick

Procedure

1. On a smooth floor, stretch the spring to about 3 meters. Hold one end while your partner holds the other end. Do not overstretch the spring toy.
2. Pull a few coils of the spring toy to one side near one end of the spring.
3. Release the coils and observe the motion of the spring. What happens when the disturbance reaches your partner? Draw what you observe.
4. Have your partner move one end of the spring toy to the left and then to the right on the floor. Be certain that both ends of the spring are held securely. Draw a diagram of the wave you observe.
5. Repeat Step 4, increasing the rate at which you move the spring toy left and right. Record your observations.
6. Squeeze together several coils of the spring toy, making a compression.
7. Release the compressed section of the spring toy and observe the disturbance as it moves down the spring. Record your observations. Draw and label what you see.

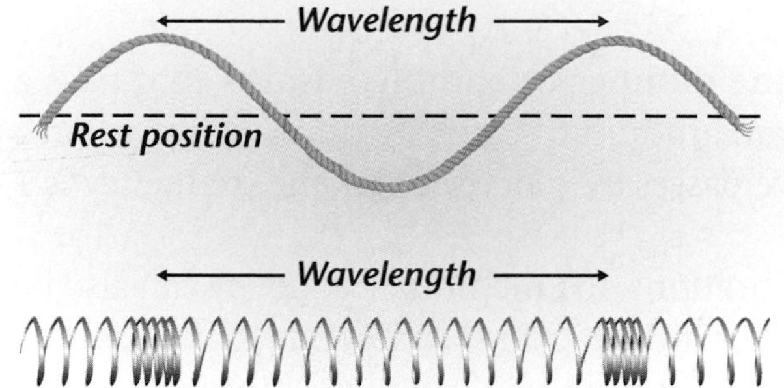

Figure 8 The wavelength of a transverse wave is the distance from crest to crest. The wavelength of a longitudinal wave is the distance from compression to compression.

Wavelength

A wave travels a certain distance before it starts to repeat. The distance between two corresponding parts of a wave is its **wavelength.** You can find the wavelength of a transverse wave by measuring the distance from crest to crest or from trough to trough. You can find the wavelength of a longitudinal wave by measuring the distance from one compression to the next.

Analyze and Conclude

1. Compare the waves generated in Steps 1–5 with the waves generated in Steps 6–7.
2. Were the waves generated in Steps 1–5 transverse or longitudinal? Explain your answer.
3. In Step 3 of the procedure, compare the original wave to the wave that came back.
4. Were the waves generated in Steps 6 and 7 transverse or longitudinal? Explain your answer.
5. What happened to the wavelength and frequency when you increased the rate at which the spring toy moved left and right?
6. How did you change the amplitude of the waves you made?
7. **Think About It** Based on your observations, describe two ways that waves move through a spring toy. Use drawings and written explanations.

More to Explore

Obtain a wide variety of spring toys. Look for different sizes and materials, such as metal and plastic. Explore the differences among the waves you can produce on each spring. What accounts for these differences?

Frequency

Wave **frequency** is the number of complete waves that pass a given point in a certain amount of time. If you make waves on a rope so that one wave passes by every second, the frequency is 1 wave per second.

Since waves are vibrations of a medium, frequency can also be described as the number of vibrations per second. To increase the frequency of the waves on a rope, you can make more vibrations by moving your hand up and down more often, perhaps two or three times per second. To decrease the frequency, you move your hand less often, perhaps once every two or three seconds.

Frequency is measured in units called **hertz (Hz).** A wave or vibration that occurs every second has a frequency of 1 Hz. If two waves pass you every second, then the frequency of the wave is 2 per second, or 2 hertz. The hertz was named after the German scientist Heinrich Hertz, who first produced radio waves in an experimental situation.

☑ *Checkpoint* *How can you increase the frequency of rope waves?*

Speed

Imagine watching a distant thunderstorm on a hot summer day. First you see the flash of lightning. A few seconds later you hear the roll of thunder. Even though the lightning and thunder occurred at the same instant, they reach you seconds apart. This happens because sound and light travel at very different speeds. Light travels much faster than sound. Different waves travel at different speeds. The speed of a wave is how far the wave travels in one unit of time, or distance divided by time.

The speed, wavelength, and frequency of a wave are related to each other by a mathematical formula.

$$\text{Speed} = \text{Wavelength} \times \text{Frequency}$$

If you know any two of the quantities in the speed formula—speed, wavelength, and frequency—you can calculate the third quantity. For example, if you know the speed and the wavelength of a wave, you can calculate the frequency. If you know the speed and the frequency, you can calculate the wavelength.

$$\text{Frequency} = \frac{\text{Speed}}{\text{Wavelength}} \qquad \text{Wavelength} = \frac{\text{Speed}}{\text{Frequency}}$$

Waves in different mediums travel at different speeds. In a given medium and under the same conditions, the speed of a wave is constant. For example, all sound waves traveling through the air at the same pressure and at the same temperature travel

Math TOOLBOX

Calculating With Units

When calculating with quantities that include units, treat the units as you do the numbers.

For example, if an object travels 6 m in 2 s, here is how you find its speed:

$$\text{Speed} = \frac{\text{Distance}}{\text{Time}} = \frac{6\text{ m}}{2\text{ s}} = 3\text{ m/s}$$

A wave on a lake has a wavelength of 0.5 m and a frequency of 2 Hz (2 Hz = 2 per second, or 2/s). To find the speed of the wave, use this formula:

$$\text{Speed} = \text{Wavelength} \times \text{Frequency}$$

Substitute and simplify:

$$\text{Speed} = 0.5\text{ m} \times 2\text{ Hz} = 0.5\text{ m} \times 2/\text{s} = 1\text{ m/s}$$

The speed of the wave is 1 m/s. Note that the answer is in meters per second, which is a correct unit for speed.

at the same speed. If the temperature or pressure changes, the sound waves will travel at a different speed.

If one type of wave travels at a constant speed in one medium, what do you think will happen if the frequency changes? When you multiply the wavelength and frequency after the change, you should get the same speed as before the change. Therefore, if you increase the frequency of a wave, the wavelength must decrease.

Sample Problem

The speed of a wave on a rope is 50 cm/s and its wavelength is 10 cm. What is the frequency?

Analyze. You know speed and wavelength. You want to find frequency.

Write the formula. $\text{Frequency} = \frac{\text{Speed}}{\text{Wavelength}}$

Substitute and solve. $\text{Frequency} = \frac{50 \not{\text{cm}}/\text{s}}{10 \not{\text{cm}}}$

$\text{Frequency} = \frac{5\not{0}\ /\text{s}}{1\not{0}}$

Frequency = 5 /s (5 per second) or 5 Hz.

Think about it. If you move your hand as often as 5 times a second, then fairly short waves, only 10 cm long, will move down the rope.

Practice Problems

1. A wave has a wavelength of 5 mm and a frequency of 2 Hz. At what speed does the wave travel?
2. The speed of a wave on a guitar string is 100 m/s and the frequency is 1,000 Hz. What is the wavelength of the wave?

Section 2 Review

1. List the four basic properties of waves. Describe each property.
2. How are the speed, wavelength, and frequency of a wave related?
3. Can two waves have the same wavelength but different amplitudes? Explain.
4. **Thinking Critically Inferring** When you increase the tension on a piece of wire, the speed of waves on it increases, but the wavelength stays constant. What happens to the frequency of the waves as the tension on the wire is increased?

Check Your Progress

CHAPTER PROJECT 13

Observe the amplitude, wavelength, frequency, and speed of one of the periodic motions on your list. How many complete repetitions of each periodic motion occur in a given amount of time? How long does it take for a periodic event to finish and start again? Compare the highest and lowest position or the nearest and farthest position of the object showing periodic motion. Record your observations in your notebook.

SECTION 3 Interactions of Waves

DISCOVER — ACTIVITY

How Does a Ball Bounce?

1. Choose a spot at the base of a wall. From a distance of 1 m, roll a wet ball along the floor straight at the spot you chose. Watch the angle at which the ball bounces back by looking at the path of moisture on the floor.
2. Wet the ball again. From a different position, roll the ball at the same spot, but at an angle to the wall. Again, observe the angle at which the ball bounces back.

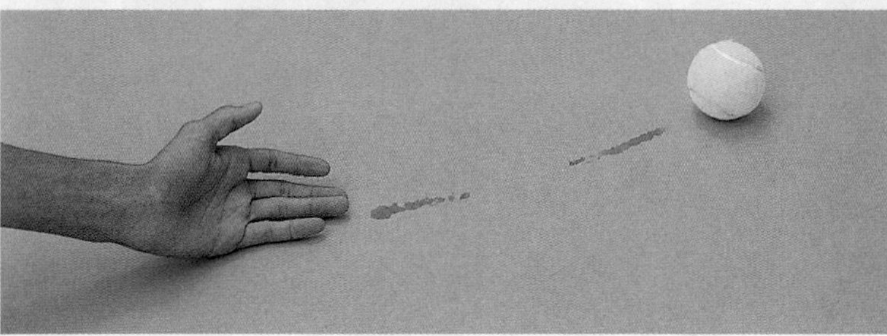

Think It Over

Developing Hypotheses How do you think the angle at which the ball hits the wall is related to the angle at which the ball bounces back? To test your hypothesis, roll the ball from several different positions toward the same spot on the wall.

GUIDE FOR READING

- **What happens when waves hit a surface?**
- **How do waves bend?**
- **How do waves interact with each other?**

Reading Tip **Before you read, preview *Exploring Interactions of Waves* on pages 434–435. Make a list of any unfamiliar words. As you read, write a definition for each word on your list.**

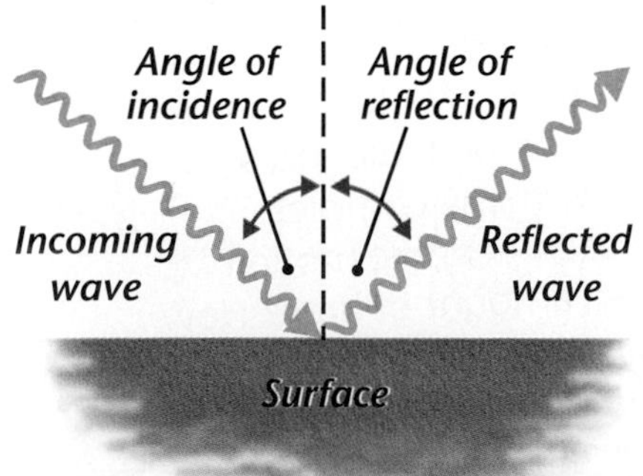

Figure 9 The angle of reflection is equal to the angle of incidence.

It is a hot, sunny day. You are the first person to enter the calm water of the swimming pool. To test the temperature of the water, you dip one foot in first. Your foot causes a series of ripples to travel across the water to the far wall of the pool. As each ripple hits the wall, it bounces off the wall and travels back toward you.

Reflection

When water waves hit the side of a swimming pool, they bounce back. **When an object or wave hits a surface through which it cannot pass, it bounces back.** This is called **reflection.**

To show reflection of a wave, draw a line to represent a surface. Draw another line to show a wave moving toward the surface at an angle. Now imagine a line perpendicular to the surface. The **angle of incidence** is the angle between the incoming wave and the imaginary perpendicular line. The **angle of reflection** is the angle between the reflected wave and the imaginary line. The law of reflection states that the angle of reflection equals the angle of incidence. All waves obey the law of reflection.

There are many examples of reflection in your everyday life. A ball that hits a wall bounces back, or is reflected. When you look in a mirror, you use reflected light to see yourself. An echo is an example of reflected sound.

Refraction

Have you ever pushed a shopping cart that had a stiff wheel? If so, you know how difficult it is to control the direction of the cart. This is because the stiff wheel can't turn as fast as the other wheels. As you push the cart, it tends to veer to the side of the sticky wheel and so changes direction. Waves sometimes change direction when they enter a new medium. If a wave enters the new medium at an angle, one side changes speed before the other side. **When a wave moves from one medium into another medium at an angle, it changes speed as it enters the second medium, which causes it to bend.** The bending of waves due to a change in speed is called **refraction.**

Though all waves change speed when they enter a new medium, they don't always bend. Bending occurs only when one side of the wave enters the new medium before the other side of the wave. The side of the wave that enters the new medium first changes speed first. The other side is still traveling at its original speed. The bending occurs because the two sides of the wave are traveling at different speeds.

☑ *Checkpoint* *What is refraction?*

Diffraction

Somctimes waves can bend around an obstacle in their path. For example, waves can pass through a narrow entrance to a harbor and then spread out inside the harbor. Figure 10 shows water waves diffracting as they enter a harbor.

When a wave passes a barrier or moves through a hole in a barrier, it bends and spreads out. The bending of waves

Sharpen your Skills

Observing ACTIVITY

Here is how you can simulate what happens as waves move from one medium to another.

1. Roll a drinking straw from a smooth tabletop straight onto a thin piece of terry cloth or a paper towel. Describe how the straw's motion changes as it leaves the smooth surface.
2. Repeat Step 1, but roll the straw at an angle to the cloth or paper.

Describe what happens as each side of the straw hits the cloth or paper. How are your results similar to what happens when waves are refracted?

Figure 10 Waves from the ocean enter the harbor and spread out. This is an example of diffraction. ***Predicting*** *How do you think the waves in the harbor would change if the opening were wider?*

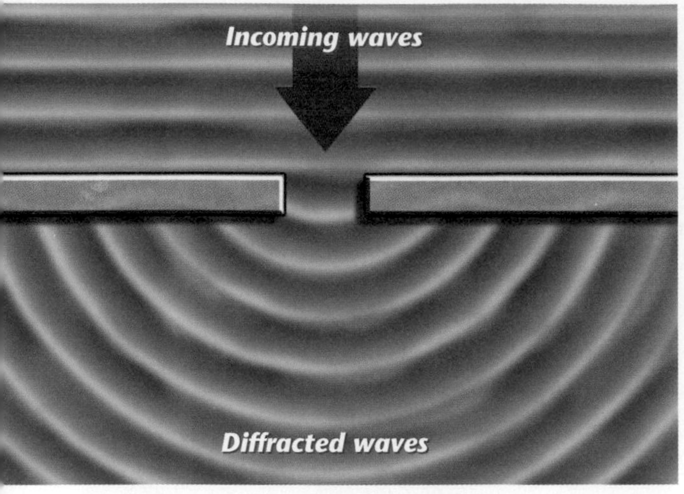

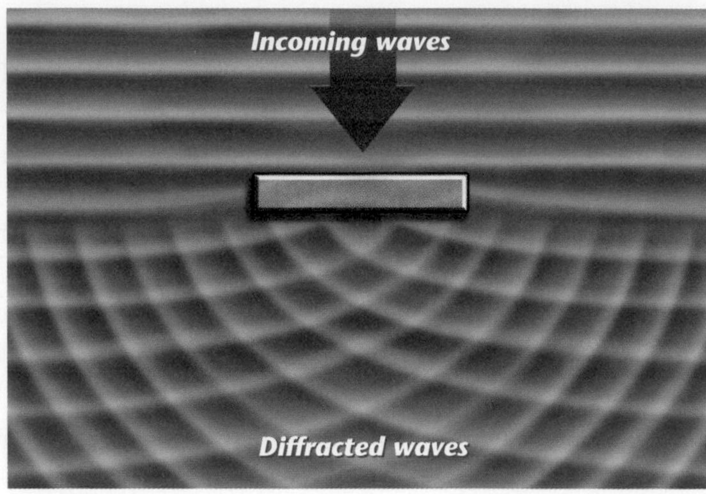

Figure 11 The diagram shows how waves diffract. A wave can go through a hole in a barrier and spread out (left). Or it can bend around a barrier (right).

around the edge of a barrier is known as **diffraction.** Figure 11 shows a water wave passing through a hole in a barrier and another bending around a barrier. In each case, you see the wave diffracting on the other side of the barrier.

☑ *Checkpoint* *What is diffraction?*

Interference

Suppose that you and a friend are each holding one end of a rope. If you both flick the ends at the same time, you send two waves toward each other. What will happen when those two waves meet?

When two or more waves meet, they have an effect on each other. This interaction is called **interference.** There are two types of interference: constructive and destructive.

Constructive Interference **Constructive interference** occurs whenever two waves combine to make a wave with a larger amplitude. You can think of constructive interference as waves "helping each other" to give a stronger result, or combining energy.

Figure 12A shows two identical waves (same amplitude, same wavelength) traveling in the same direction at the same time. If the two waves travel along the same path at the same time, they will behave as one. What will the combined wave look like? The crests of the first wave will occur at the same place as the crests of the second wave. The energy from the two waves will combine. Thus the amplitude of the new wave will be twice the amplitude of either of the original waves.

If the waves have the same wavelength but different amplitudes, the crests will still occur at the same place and add together. The resulting amplitude will be the sum of the two original amplitudes. Similarly, the troughs will occur together, making a deeper trough than either wave alone.

Figure 12 The diagrams show how identical waves can combine.

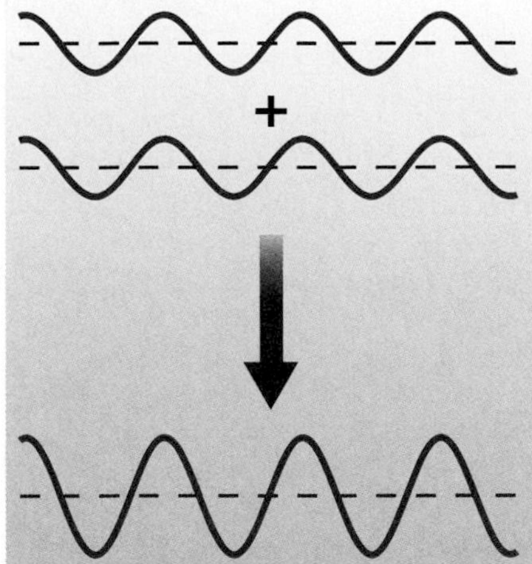
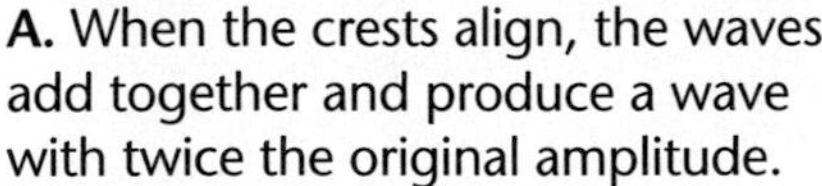

A. When the crests align, the waves add together and produce a wave with twice the original amplitude.

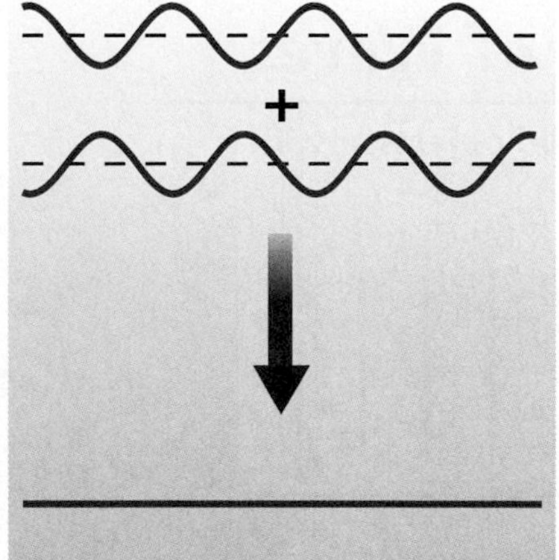

B. When the crests of one wave align with the troughs of another, they cancel each other out.

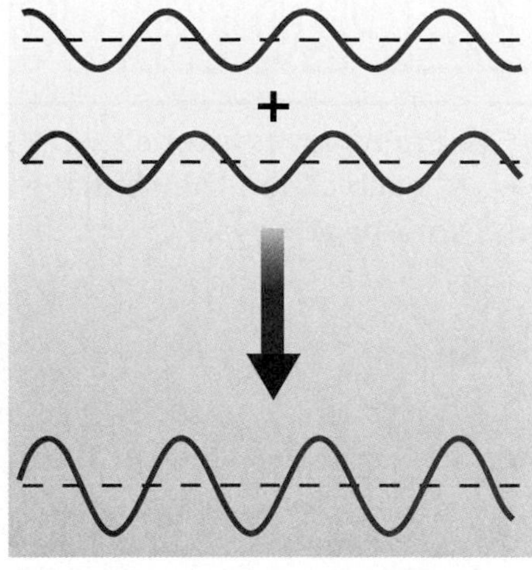

C. If one wave travels a little behind the other, they combine both constructively and destructively at different places.

Destructive Interference When the amplitudes of two waves combine with each other producing a smaller amplitude, the result is called **destructive interference.** What happens if the crests don't meet at the same place? In this case, one wave comes after the other. Figure 12B shows what happens when the crests of the first wave occur at the same place as the troughs of the second wave. The amplitude of the first wave cancels out the amplitude of the second wave. This type of interference produces a wave with an amplitude of zero. The original waves seem to be destroyed. If the two waves have different amplitudes, they will not cancel each other out but will combine to produce a wave with a smaller amplitude.

Two identical waves can travel along the same path, one a little behind the other. When this happens, the waves combine constructively in some places and destructively in others.

Standing Waves

If you tie a rope to a doorknob and continuously shake the free end, waves will travel down the rope, reflect at the end, and come back. The reflected waves will collide with the incoming waves. When the waves meet, interference occurs. After they pass each other, they carry on as if the interference had never occurred.

If the incoming wave and the reflected wave combine at the right places, the combined wave appears to be standing still. A **standing wave** is a wave that appears to stand in one place, even though it is really two waves interfering as they pass through each other. If you make a standing wave on a rope, the wave looks as though it is standing still. But in fact, waves are traveling along the rope in both directions.

Standing Waves

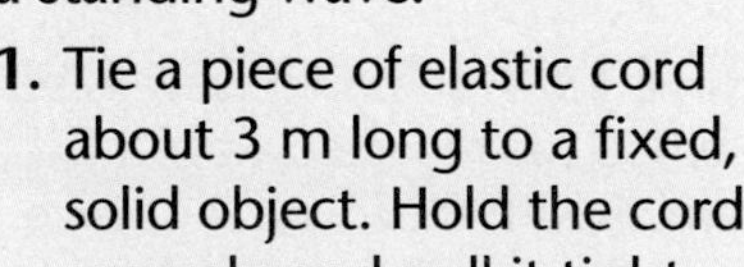

Here's how you can make a standing wave.

1. Tie a piece of elastic cord about 3 m long to a fixed, solid object. Hold the cord securely and pull it tight.
2. Slowly move the end of the cord up and down until you produce a standing wave.
3. Now move the cord up and down twice as fast to double the frequency. What happens?

Predicting What do you think will happen if you triple the original frequency? Try it. Be careful to keep a good grip on the cord.

EXPLORING *Interactions of Waves*

When waves interact with solid objects or with each other, they behave in a variety of ways.

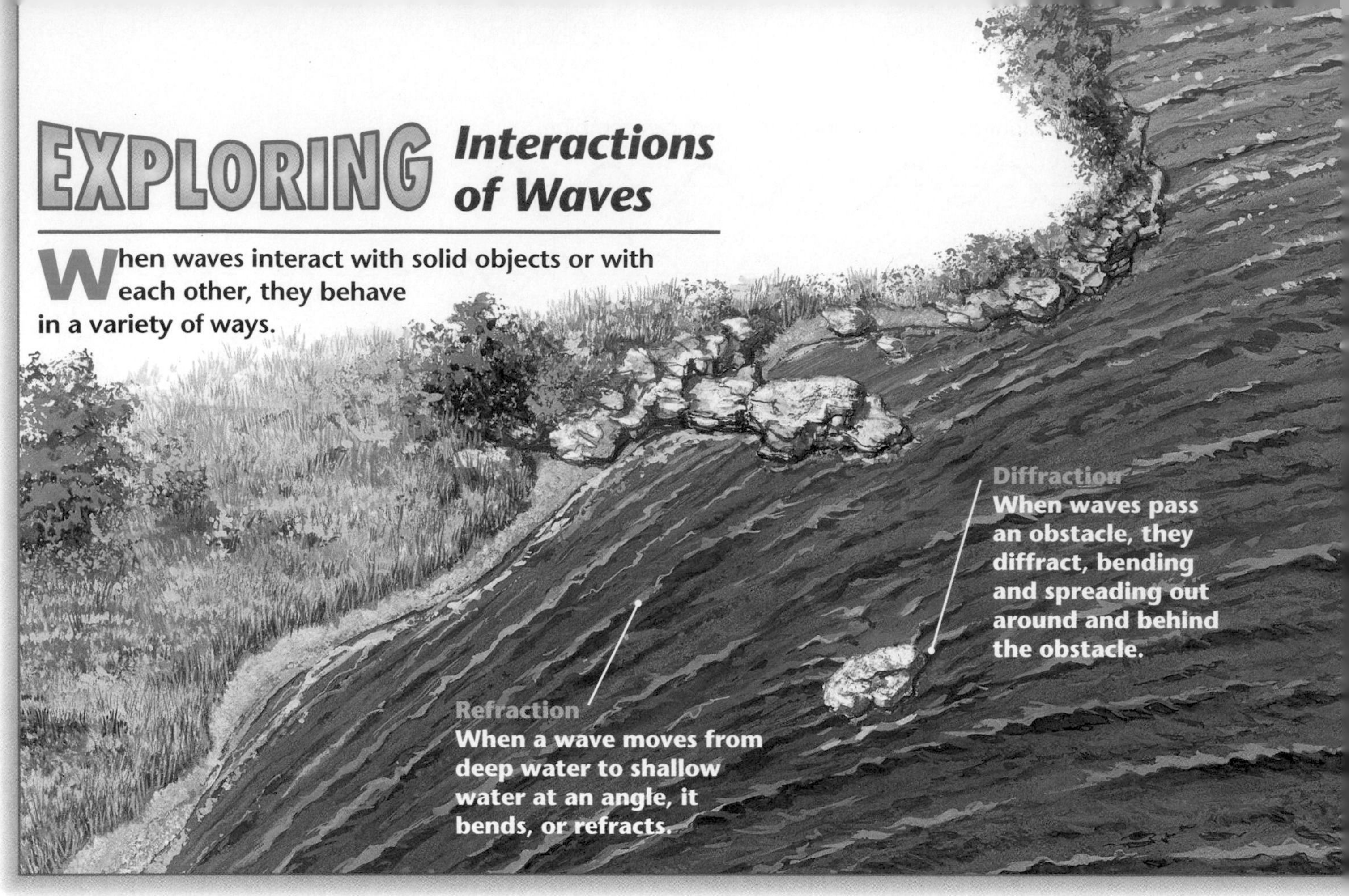

Diffraction
When waves pass an obstacle, they diffract, bending and spreading out around and behind the obstacle.
Refraction
When a wave moves from deep water to shallow water at an angle, it bends, or refracts.

Nodes and Antinodes At certain points, destructive interference causes the two waves to combine to produce an amplitude of zero, as in Figure 13. These points are called **nodes.** The nodes always occur at the same place on the rope. The diagram also shows how the amplitudes of the two waves combine to produce amplitudes greater than zero. The crests and troughs of the standing wave are called **antinodes.** These are the points of maximum energy.

Figure 13 A standing wave is set up when the reflected wave interacts with the incoming wave. The nodes are the points of zero amplitude. The antinodes are the points of maximum amplitude.

Antinode
Incoming wave
Reflected wave
Node

Resonance Have you ever pushed a child on a swing? At first, it is difficult to push the swing. But once you get it going, you need only push gently to keep it going. When an object is vibrating at a certain frequency, it takes very little energy to maintain or increase the amplitude of the wave.

Most objects have a natural frequency of vibration. Their particles vibrate naturally at a certain frequency. **Resonance** occurs when vibrations traveling through an object match the object's natural frequency. If vibrations of the same frequency are added, the amplitude of the object's vibrations increases.

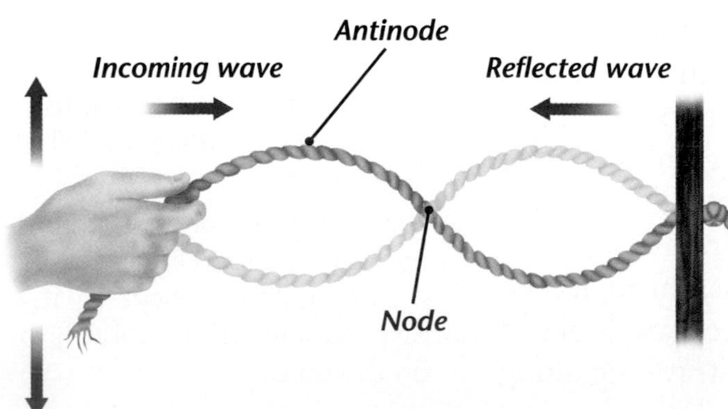

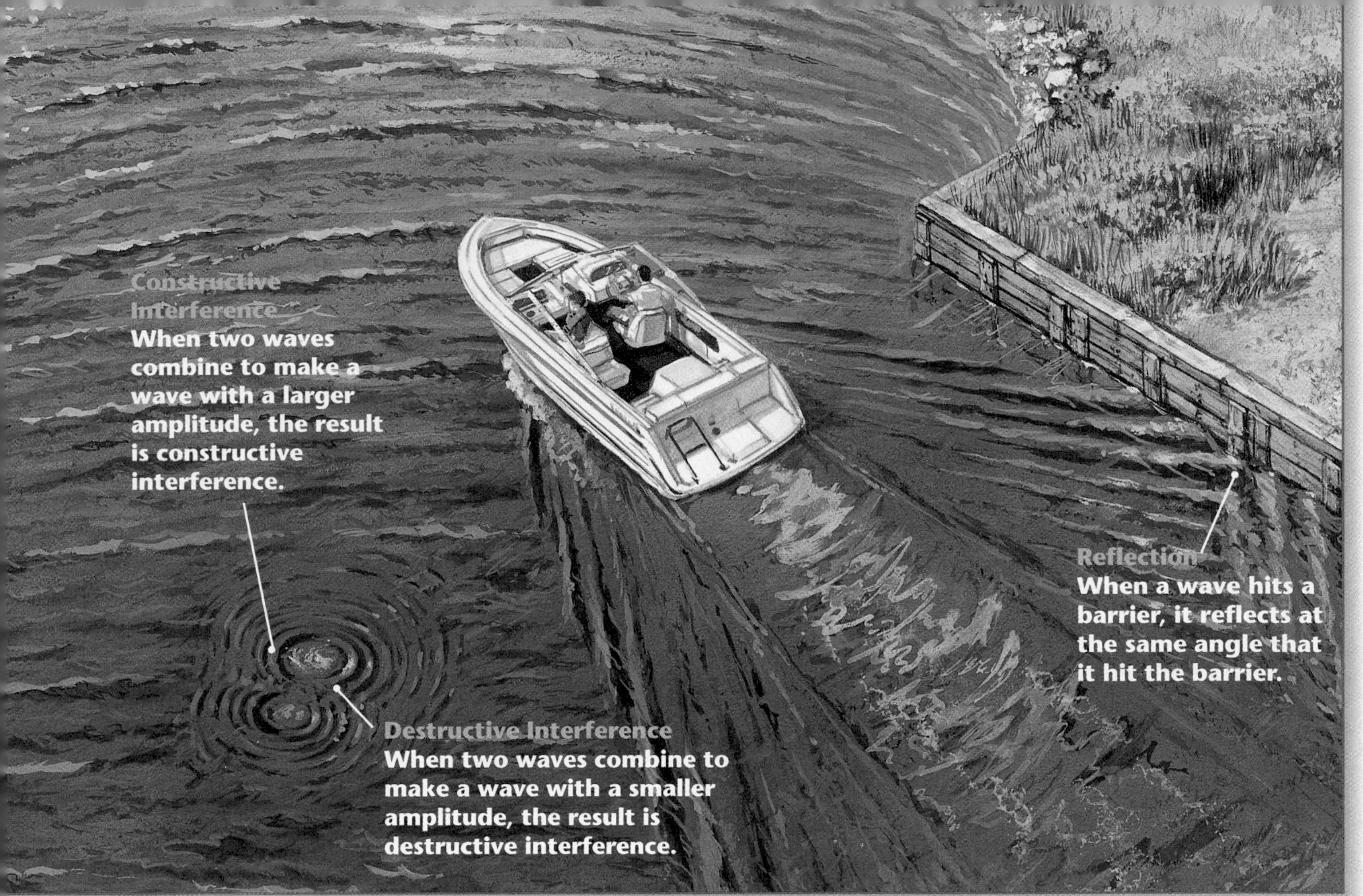

Constructive Interference When two waves combine to make a wave with a larger amplitude, the result is constructive interference.

Reflection When a wave hits a barrier, it reflects at the same angle that it hit the barrier.

Destructive Interference When two waves combine to make a wave with a smaller amplitude, the result is destructive interference.

An object that is vibrating at its natural frequency absorbs energy from objects that vibrate at the same frequency. Resonance occurs in music and adds a distinct quality to the sound.

If an object is not very flexible, resonance can cause it to shatter. For this reason, marching troops are told to break step as they cross a bridge. If they all march across the bridge in perfect step, it is possible that the pounding could match the natural frequency of the bridge. The increased vibration could cause the bridge to collapse.

Section 3 Review

1. What is the law of reflection?
2. What causes refraction?
3. Describe the difference between constructive and destructive interference.
4. What causes a standing wave?
5. **Thinking Critically Predicting** Two water waves have the same wavelength. The crests of one occur at the same place as the crests of the second. If one wave has twice the amplitude of the other, will the waves interfere constructively or destructively? Explain.

Science at Home

With your parent's permission, fill the kitchen sink with water to a depth of about 10 cm. Dip your finger in the water repeatedly to make waves. Demonstrate reflection and interference to your family members. Try to think of ways to demonstrate refraction and diffraction as well.

Skills Lab

Making Models

Making Waves

In this lab, you will use a model to investigate wave behavior.

Problem

How do water waves interact with each other and with solid objects in their paths?

Materials

water
plastic dropper
metric ruler
paper towels
modeling clay
cork or other small floating object
ripple tank (aluminum foil lasagna pan with mirror at the bottom)

Procedure

1. Fill the pan with water to a depth of 1.5 cm. Let the water come to rest. Make a data table like the one shown in your text.
2. Fill a plastic dropper with water. Then release a drop of water from a height of about 10 cm above the center of the ripple tank. Observe the reflection of the waves that form and record your observations.
3. Predict how placing a paper towel across one end of the ripple tank will affect the reflection of the waves. Record your prediction in your notebook.
4. Drape a paper towel across one end of the ripple tank so it hangs in the water. Repeat Step 2, and record your observations of the waves.
5. Remove the paper towel and place a stick of modeling clay in the water near the center of the ripple tank.
6. From a height of about 10 cm, release a drop of water into the ripple tank halfway between the clay and one of the short walls. Record your observations.
7. Place the clay in a different position so that the waves strike it at an angle. Then repeat Step 6.

DATA TABLE

Type of Barrier	Observations Without Cork	Observations With Cork

8. Place two sticks of clay end-to-end across the width of the tank. Adjust the clay so that there is a gap of about 2 cm between the ends of the two pieces. Repeat Step 6. Now change the angle of the barrier in the tank. Again repeat Step 6, and watch to see if the waves interact with the barrier any differently.
9. Cut the two pieces of clay in half. Use the pieces to make a barrier with three 2-cm gaps. Then repeat Step 6.
10. Remove all the clay and add a small floating object, such as a cork, to the water. Then repeat Steps 2–9 with the floating object. Observe and record what happens to the cork in each step.
11. Once you have finished all of the trials, clean and dry your work area.

Analyze and Conclude

1. How are waves affected by the paper towel hanging in the water?
2. What happens when waves strike a barrier head on? When they strike it at an angle?
3. What happens when waves strike a barrier with a gap in it? With three gaps in it?
4. **Think About It** How does the behavior of waves in your model compare to the behavior of waves in a harbor?

Design an Experiment

Predict what would happen if you could send a steady train of uniform waves the length of the tank for an extended time. Use a plastic bottle with a pinhole in the bottom to make a model that will help to test your prediction. Get permission from your teacher to try out your dropper device.

SECTION 4 Seismic Waves

DISCOVER ACTIVITY

Can You Find the Sand?

1. Fill a plastic film canister with sand and replace the lid tightly.
2. Place the canister on a table with four other identical but empty canisters. Mix them around so that a classmate does not know which can is which.
3. With your fist, pound on the table a few times. Have your classmate try to figure out which canister contains the sand.
4. Stick each canister to the table with some modeling clay. Pound on the table again. Now can your classmate figure out which canister contains the sand?

Think It Over

Inferring Pounding on a table makes waves. Why might the canister containing the sand respond differently from the empty canisters?

GUIDE FOR READING

- **What happens when rock beneath Earth's surface moves?**
- **What are the different types of seismic waves?**
- **How does a seismograph work?**

Reading Tip **As you read, make a table comparing primary, secondary, and surface waves.**

Some of the most dramatic waves originate deep inside Earth. On August 27, 1883, the eruption of Krakatau volcano in Indonesia caused a series of earthquakes. Vibrations from the earthquakes formed waves that traveled from the island through the surrounding water. On the open ocean, the waves were only about 1 meter high. As they entered shallower water, near land, the waves traveled more slowly. This caused the waves at the back to catch up to the front and to pile on top. The first wave grew into a wall of water over 35 meters high. People on ships far out at sea could not even tell when the waves went by. But on the islands of Java and Sumatra thousands of people were killed as the enormous waves crashed onto the land.

Figure 14 This illustration shows a giant wave reaching the coast of Java. The wave was caused by earthquakes related to the eruption of Krakatau volcano 40 kilometers away.

Types of Seismic Waves

An earthquake occurs when rock beneath Earth's surface moves. The movement of Earth's plates creates stress in the rock. **When the stress in the rock builds up enough, the rock breaks or changes shape, releasing energy in the form of waves or vibrations.** The waves produced by earthquakes are known as **seismic waves.** (The word *seismic* comes from the Greek word *seismos*, meaning "earthquake.")

Seismic waves ripple out in all directions from the point where the earthquake occurred. As the waves move, they carry the energy through Earth. The waves can travel from one side of Earth to the other. **Seismic waves include primary waves, secondary waves, and surface waves.**

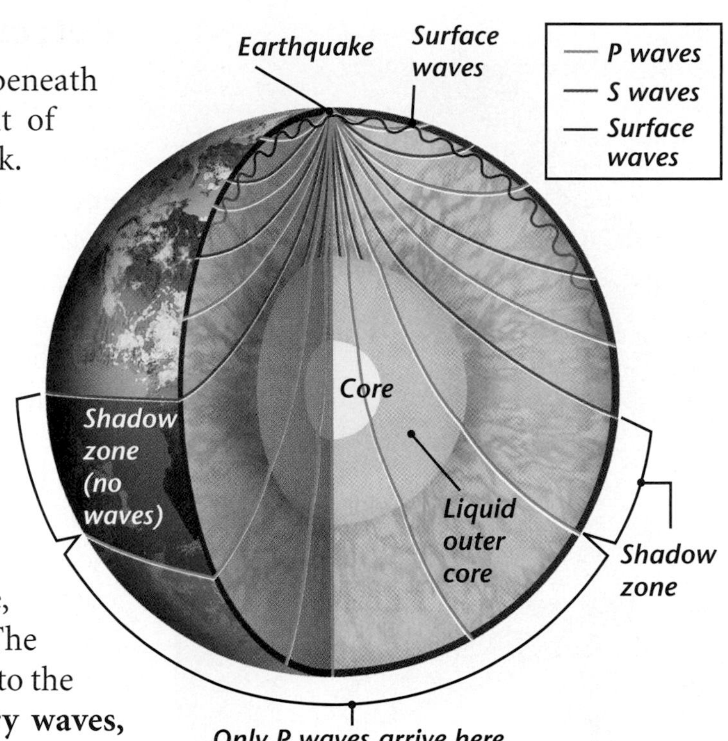

Figure 15 P waves travel through all parts of Earth. S waves do not travel through Earth's core. Surface waves travel only along Earth's surface. The shadow zone is where there are no seismic waves. ***Applying Concepts*** *Why don't S waves travel through Earth's core?*

Primary Waves Some seismic waves are longitudinal waves. Longitudinal seismic waves are known as **primary waves,** or P waves. They are called primary waves because they move faster than other seismic waves and so arrive at distant points before other seismic waves. Primary waves are made up of compressions and rarefactions of rock inside Earth.

Secondary Waves Other seismic waves are transverse waves with crests and troughs. Transverse seismic waves are known as **secondary waves,** or S waves. Secondary waves cannot travel through liquids. Since part of Earth's core is liquid, S waves do not travel directly through Earth and cannot be detected on the side of Earth opposite an earthquake. Because of this, scientists on the side of Earth opposite the earthquake detect mainly P waves.

Surface Waves When P waves and S waves reach Earth's surface, some of them are transformed into surface waves similar to waves on the surface of water. Recall that surface waves are a combination of longitudinal and transverse waves. Even though surface waves travel more slowly than either P or S waves, they produce the most severe ground movements.

Earthquakes that occur underwater can cause huge surface waves on the ocean called **tsunamis** (tsoo NAH meez). Tsunamis can cause great damage when they reach land.

☑ ***Checkpoint*** *How are P waves different from S waves?*

Figure 16 A scientist studies the printout from a seismograph.

Detecting Seismic Waves

If you did the Discover activity, you saw how waves can affect different masses by different amounts. To detect and measure earthquake waves, scientists use instruments called **seismographs** (SYZ muh grafs). **A seismograph records the ground movements caused by seismic waves as they move through Earth.**

The frame of the seismograph is attached to the ground, so the frame shakes when seismic waves arrive at the seismograph's location. Seismographs used to have pens attached to the frame that made wiggly lines on a roll of paper as the ground shook. Now scientists use electronic seismographs that use computers to record data about Earth's motion.

Since P waves travel through Earth faster than S waves, P waves arrive at seismographs before S waves. By measuring the time between the arrival of the P waves and the arrival of the S waves, scientists can tell how far away the earthquake was. By comparing readings from at least three seismographs at different places on Earth, scientists can tell where the earthquake occurred.

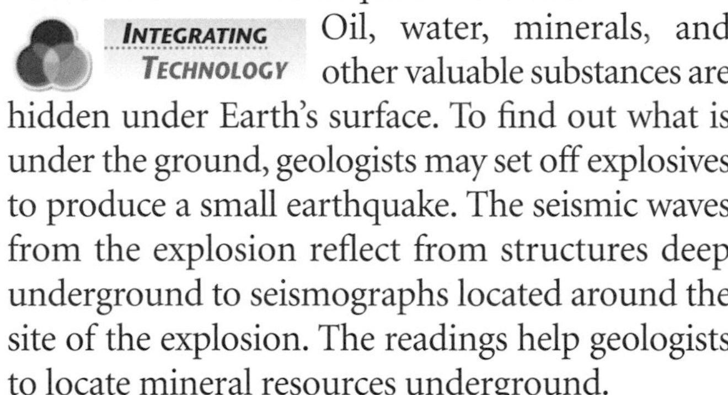

INTEGRATING TECHNOLOGY Oil, water, minerals, and other valuable substances are hidden under Earth's surface. To find out what is under the ground, geologists may set off explosives to produce a small earthquake. The seismic waves from the explosion reflect from structures deep underground to seismographs located around the site of the explosion. The readings help geologists to locate mineral resources underground.

Section 4 Review

1. What causes seismic waves?
2. Describe the different types of seismic waves.
3. How do seismographs help scientists determine where an earthquake occurred?
4. **Thinking Critically Inferring** S waves can travel from one side of the moon, through the core, to the other side. What does this tell you about the center of the moon? Explain.

Science at Home

Find out how disturbances travel through different solids. Have a family member or friend tap one end of the table with a spoon. Now put your ear down on the other side of the table and listen to the tapping again. What difference do you notice? Repeat the tapping on various surfaces around your home. What observations have you made?

CHAPTER 13 STUDY GUIDE

What Are Waves?

Key Ideas

- Waves are created when a source of energy causes a medium to vibrate.
- The three types of waves are transverse waves, longitudinal waves, and surface waves.

Key Terms

wave
energy
medium
mechanical wave
vibration
transverse wave
crest
trough
longitudinal wave
compression
rarefaction
surface wave

Properties of Waves

Key Ideas

- The basic properties of waves are amplitude, wavelength, frequency, and speed.
- The speed, frequency, and wavelength of a wave are related to each other by a mathematical formula.

$$\text{Speed} = \text{Wavelength} \times \text{Frequency}$$

Key Terms

amplitude
wavelength
frequency
hertz (Hz)

Interactions of Waves

Key Ideas

- When an object or wave hits a surface through which it cannot pass, it bounces back.
- When a wave moves from one medium into another medium at an angle, it changes speed as it enters the second medium and bends.
- When a wave passes a barrier or moves through a hole in a barrier, it bends and spreads out.

Key Terms

reflection
angle of incidence
angle of reflection
refraction
diffraction
interference
constructive interference
destructive interference
standing wave
node
antinode
resonance

Seismic Waves

INTEGRATING EARTH SCIENCE

Key Ideas

- When stress in the rock beneath Earth's surface builds up enough, the rock breaks or changes shape, releasing energy in the form of seismic waves.
- Seismic waves include primary waves, secondary waves, and surface waves.
- A seismograph records the ground movements caused by seismic waves as they move through Earth.

Key Terms

seismic wave
primary wave
secondary wave
tsunami
seismograph

Organizing Information

Concept Map Copy the concept map about waves onto a separate sheet of paper. Then complete it and add a title. (For more on concept maps, see the Skills Handbook.)

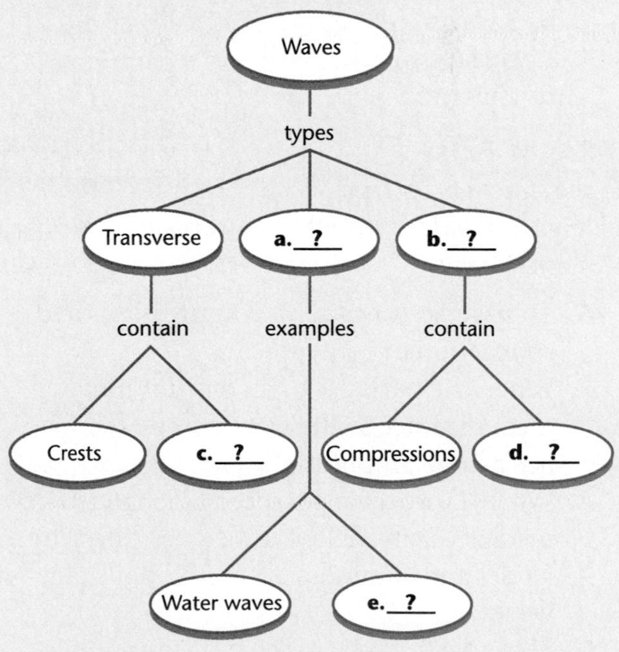

Reviewing Content

Multiple Choice

Choose the letter of the best answer.

1. A wave carries
a. energy. **b.** matter.
c. water. **d.** air.

2. The distance between one crest and the next crest is the wave's
a. amplitude. **b.** wavelength.
c. frequency. **d.** speed.

3. In a given medium, if the frequency of a wave increases, its
a. wavelength increases.
b. speed increases.
c. amplitude decreases.
d. wavelength decreases.

4. The bending of a wave due to a change in its speed is
a. interference.
b. diffraction.
c. reflection.
d. refraction.

5. Seismic waves that do *not* travel through liquids are
a. P waves.
b. S waves.
c. surface waves.
d. tsunamis.

True or False

If the statement is true, write true. If it is false, change the underlined word or words to make the statement true.

6. Transverse waves have compressions and rarefactions.

7. When the particles of a medium move a great distance as the wave passes, the wave has a large amplitude.

8. When a wave changes speed as it enters a new medium at an angle, it undergoes diffraction.

9. Nodes and antinodes occur in longitudinal waves.

10. Secondary waves arrive at distant points before other seismic waves.

Checking Concepts

11. Explain the difference between transverse and longitudinal waves. Use diagrams to illustrate your explanation.

12. How can you find the amplitude of a longitudinal wave?

13. How are a wave's speed, wavelength, and frequency related?

14. Describe the difference between constructive and destructive interference.

15. Explain how seismographs work.

16. Writing to Learn Suppose you are a sportswriter with a background in science. While at a baseball game, you notice that at various times, entire sections of people stand up and sit down again. This "wave" travels around the stadium. Write a short newspaper article that describes what the crowd is doing. Be sure to use terms such as amplitude, frequency, wavelength, and speed in your description. Give your article a title.

Thinking Critically

17. Comparing and Contrasting One wave has half the amplitude of a second wave. The two waves interfere constructively. Draw a diagram and describe the resulting wave. Describe the resulting wave if two waves of equal amplitude interfere destructively.

18. Calculating A wave travels at 10 m/s and has a wavelength of 2 m. What is the frequency of the wave? If the speed of the wave doubles but the wavelength remains the same, what is the new frequency? Show your work.

19. Making Models Describe a way to model refraction of a wave as it enters a new medium.

20. Applying Concepts Suppose a wave moves from one side of a lake to the other. Does the water move across the lake? Explain.

Applying Skills

The wave in the illustration is a giant ocean wave produced by an underwater earthquake. Use the illustration to answer Questions 21–24.

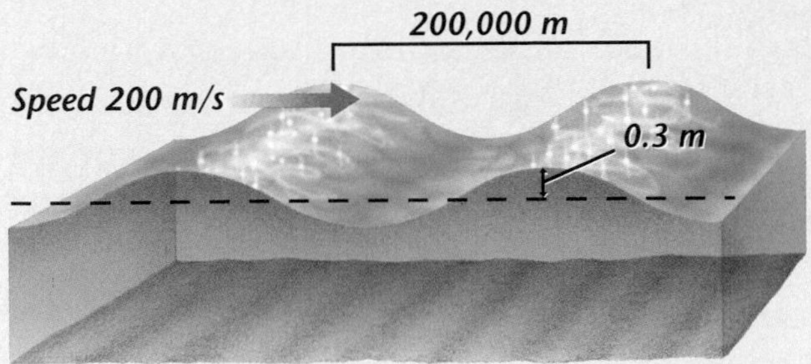

21. Classifying What kind of wave is shown in the above diagram?

22. Interpreting Diagrams What is the amplitude of the wave shown? What is its speed? Find the frequency of the wave. Show your work.

23. Predicting What could happen if this wave hits a coastal city? What property of a wave determines how much damage it could do?

24. Calculating How long would it take this wave to travel 5,000 km?

Performance — Chapter Project 13 — Assessment

Project Wrap Up Share your examples of periodic events and patterns with your classmates. On your display, highlight the repeating patterns and the frequency of each example. Which periodic events involve the transmission of waves through the vibrations of a medium?

Reflect and Record In your journal, describe the common or unusual events in your life that repeat periodically. Did you and your classmates observe the same things, or did your classmates surprise you with the examples they found?

Test Preparation

Use these questions to prepare for standardized tests.

Use the diagram to answer Questions 25–29.

25. What type of waves did you create by throwing the stone?
- **a.** transverse
- **b.** longitudinal
- **c.** surface
- **d.** seismic

26. What is the medium for the waves?
- **a.** stone
- **b.** water
- **c.** leaf
- **d.** air

27. What was transferred by the waves?
- **a.** water
- **b.** energy
- **c.** floating objects
- **d.** air

28. When the leaf was raised to its highest position by the wave, it was at the wave's
- **a.** trough.
- **b.** compression.
- **c.** crest.
- **d.** rarefaction.

29. What two factors do you need to know to determine a wave's speed?
- **a.** amplitude and frequency
- **b.** amplitude and wavelength
- **c.** angle of incidence and angle of reflection
- **d.** wavelength and frequency

CHAPTER 14 Sound

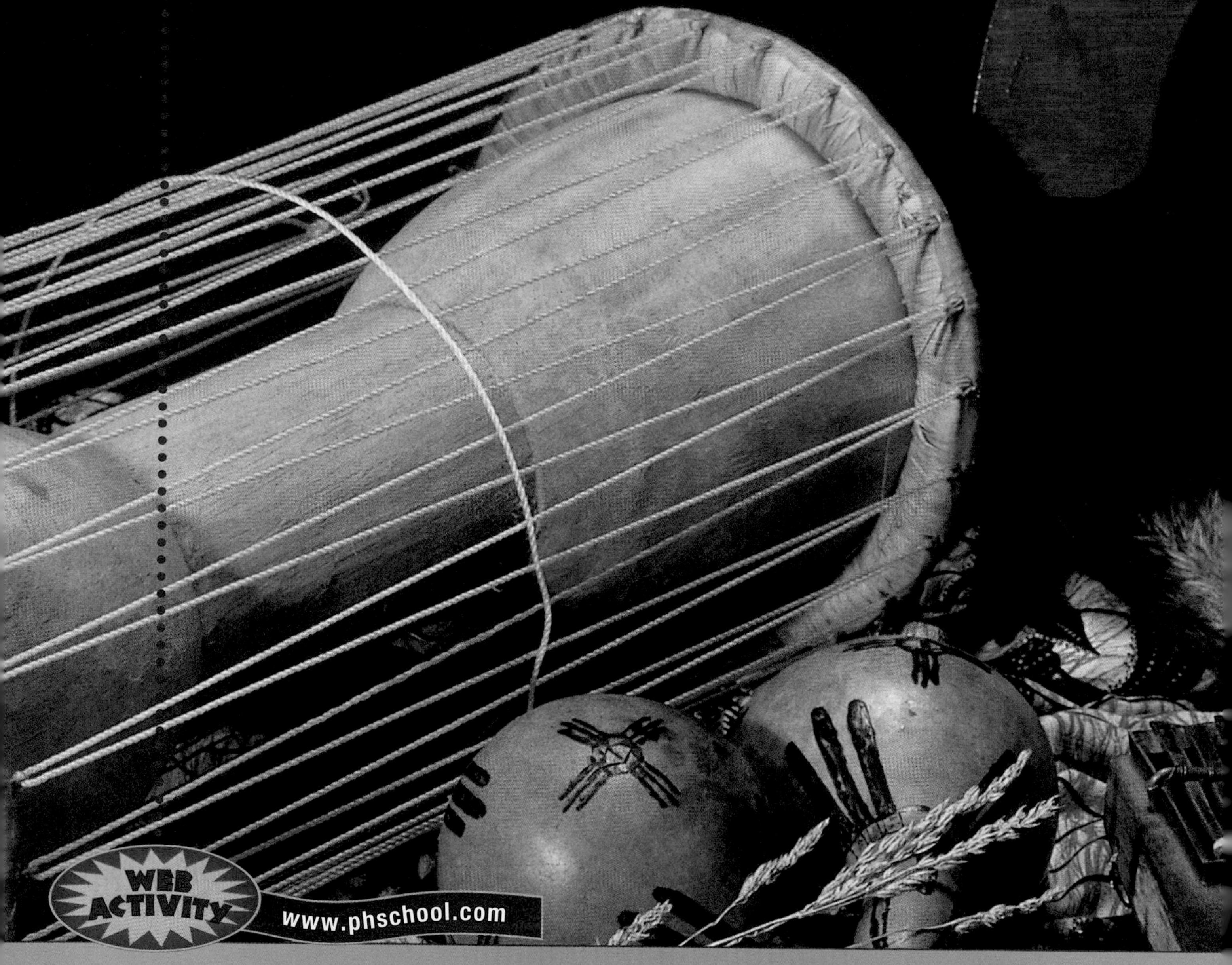

WEB ACTIVITY
www.phschool.com

SECTION 1 The Nature of Sound

Discover **What Is Sound?**
Sharpen Your Skills **Graphing**
Skills Lab **The Speed of Sound**

SECTION 2 Properties of Sound

Discover **How Does Amplitude Affect Loudness?**
Try This **The Short Straw**
Try This **Pipe Sounds**

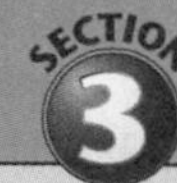

SECTION 3 Combining Sound Waves

Discover **How Can You Produce Patterns of Sound?**
Try This **Plucking Rubber Bands**
Real-World Lab **Musical Notes**

PROJECT 14

Music to Your Ears

Music, one of the oldest arts, forms an important part of many occasions. Early Chinese, Egyptian, and Babylonian people made stringed instruments from animal hair, whistles from bones, and trumpets from animal horns. Today, musical instruments are made of wood, brass, silver, and nylon.

In this chapter you will investigate the properties of sound. You will learn how sound is produced by different objects, including musical instruments. As you work through the chapter, you will gather enough knowledge to help you to complete the project.

Your Goal To design, build, and play a simple musical instrument.

To complete this project you must
- design a simple musical instrument
- construct and modify your instrument
- play a simple tune on your instrument

Get Started Begin now by discussing different kinds of instruments with your classmates. What kind of music do you enjoy? What instruments are common in your favorite type of music? Do you or any of your classmates already play an instrument? Which type of instrument would you like to build?

Check Your Progress You'll be working on this project as you study this chapter. To keep your project on track, look for Check Your Progress boxes at the following points.

Section 2 Review, page 457: Make a list of materials you could use to build your instrument.

Section 3 Review, page 465: Design and construct your instrument.

Section 5 Review, page 476: Test your instrument. Modify and test it again.

Wrap Up At the end of the chapter (page 479), you will demonstrate how you can vary the loudness and pitch of the sound of your instrument and play a simple tune.

These musical instruments play a part in African ceremonial life.

The Nature of Sound

DISCOVER — ACTIVITY

What Is Sound?

1. Fill a bowl with water.
2. Tap a tuning fork against the sole of your shoe. Place the tip of one of the prongs in the water. What do you see?
3. Tap the tuning fork again. Predict what will happen when you hold it near your ear. What do you hear?

Think It Over

Observing How do you think your observations are related to the sound you hear? What might change if you use a tuning fork of a different size? What would change in the sound you hear?

GUIDE FOR READING

- ◆ What is sound?
- ◆ What factors affect the speed of sound?

Reading Tip **Before you read, preview the headings in the section. Record the headings in outline form, leaving room to add notes.**

Here is an old riddle: If a tree falls in a forest and no one is there to hear it, does the tree make a sound? To answer the question, you must decide how to define the word "sound." If sound is something that a person must hear with his or her ears, then you might say that the tree makes no sound.

When a tree crashes down, the energy with which it strikes the forest floor is transmitted through the ground and the surrounding air. This energy causes the ground and the air to vibrate. If sound is a disturbance that travels through the ground or the air, then sound is created even if no one is around. So the tree does make a sound.

Sound and Longitudinal Waves

Just like the waves you studied in Chapter 13, sound begins with a vibration. When a tree crashes to the ground, the surrounding air particles are disturbed. This disturbance causes other vibrations in nearby particles.

How Sound Travels Like all waves, sound waves carry energy through a medium without the particles of the medium traveling along. A common medium for sound is air. Each molecule in the air moves back and forth as the disturbance goes by. **Sound is a disturbance that travels through a medium as a longitudinal wave.** When the disturbance in the air reaches your ears, you hear the sound.

How Sounds Are Made When you beat a drum, the surface of the drum begins to vibrate so quickly that you cannot see it move. Air is made up mostly of tiny particles, or molecules, of gases.

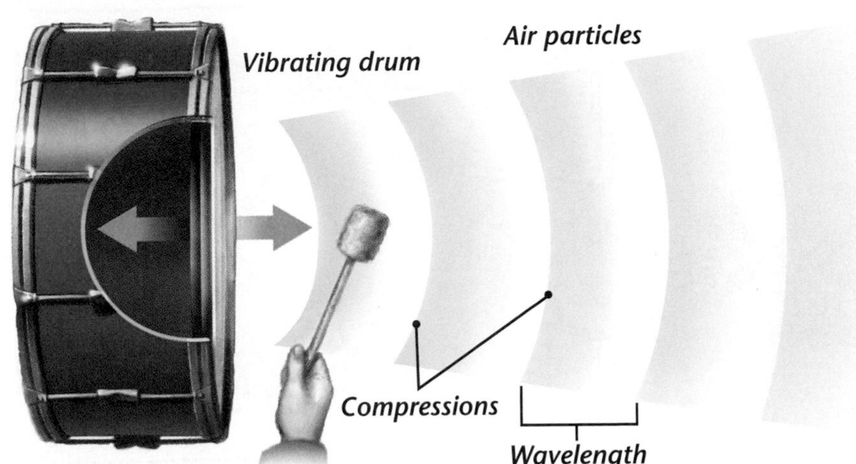

Figure 1 As the drum vibrates back and forth, it creates compressions and rarefactions in the air. ***Classifying*** *What type of wave does a drum make?*

Figure 1 shows how the vibration of a drum creates a disturbance in the molecules in the air near it. When the drumhead moves to the right, it pushes the molecules together, creating a compression. When the drumhead moves to the left, the molecules move farther apart, creating a rarefaction.

When you pluck a guitar string, it vibrates back and forth, creating compressions and rarefactions. These compressions and rarefactions travel through the air as longitudinal waves similar to the longitudinal waves that you saw travel along a spring.

INTEGRATING LIFE SCIENCE Your vocal cords act like vibrating guitar strings. Whenever you speak or sing, you force air from your lungs up through your voice box, or **larynx.** Your larynx consists of two folds of tissue called vocal cords, shown in Figure 2. The forced air rushes by your vocal cords, making them vibrate. As your vocal cords move toward each other, the air between them is compressed. As they move apart, the air spreads out, or is rarefied. Like vibrating guitar strings, your vocal cords produce compressions and rarefactions in the air. The air carries these longitudinal waves to other people's ears as well as to your own.

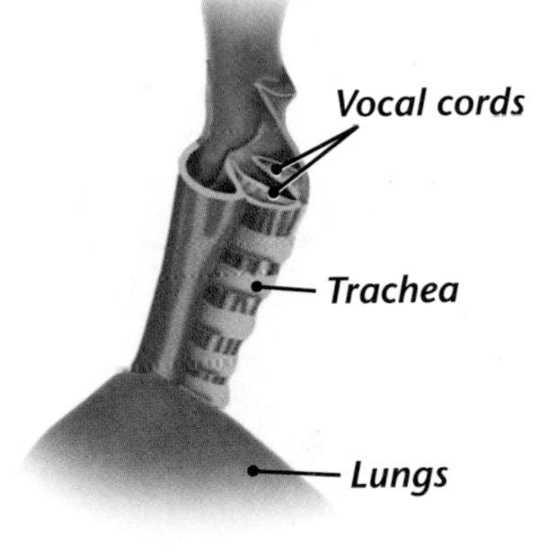

Figure 2 When a person speaks or sings, the vocal cords vibrate. The vibrations produce longitudinal sound waves in the air.

Sound in Solids and Liquids Sound can also travel through solids and liquids. When you knock on a door, the particles of the door vibrate. The vibration creates sound waves that travel through the door. When the sound waves reach the other side of the door, they make sound waves in the air on the far side. In old western movies, you may see someone put an ear to a railway track to tell if a train is on the way.

Figure 3 When sound waves enter a room through an open door, they spread out. This is called diffraction.

The sound of the train travels easily through the steel tracks. If you put your ear to the ground, you might hear distant traffic. Sound waves from the traffic are traveling through the ground as well as through the air.

Sound can travel only if there is a medium to transmit the compressions and rarefactions. In outer space, there are no molecules to compress or rarefy. The energy of the original vibrations has nothing through which to travel. So sound does not travel through outer space.

How Sound Bends When sound waves hit a barrier with a small hole in it, some of the waves pass through the hole. Just as diffraction causes water waves to spread out in a harbor, the sound waves spread out, or diffract, as they go through the hole. When sound waves go through a doorway, they spread out. Even if you are off to the side of the room, you may still hear sound from outside. If you are outside the room and not too far from the doorway, you can hear sound coming from inside the room.

Because of diffraction, you can also hear sounds from around corners. Waves passing a corner spread out as they pass.

The Speed of Sound

If you have ever seen a live band perform, you've noticed that the sounds produced by the different instruments and singers all reach your ears at the same time. If they did not travel at the same speed, the sounds that were played together would reach you at different times and would not sound very pleasant.

The speed of sound depends on the properties of the medium it travels through. At room temperature, about 20°C, sound travels at about 342 m/s. This is much faster than most jet airplanes travel through the air. Figure 4 shows the speed of sound through some common materials.

Figure 4 The speed of sound depends upon the medium through which it is traveling. ***Making Generalizations*** *In general, does sound travel faster in solids, liquids, or gases?*

Speed of Sound

Medium	Speed (m/s)
Gases	
Air (0°C)	330
Air (20°C)	342
Liquids	
Fresh water	1,490
Salt water	1,530
Solids (25°C)	
Lead	1,210
Plastic	1,800
Silver	2,680
Copper	3,100
Gold	3,240
Brick	3,650
Hard wood	4,000
Glass	4,540
Iron	5,100
Steel	5,200

As the properties of a medium change, so too does the speed of the sound that travels through it. **The speed of sound depends on the elasticity, density, and temperature of the medium.**

Figure 5 Some substances are more elastic than others. Sponges and rubber bands are more elastic than modeling clay. ***Predicting*** *Is sound likely to travel faster through a sponge, a rubber band, or a piece of modeling clay?*

Elasticity Since sound is a transfer of energy, its speed depends on how well the particles in the medium bounce back after being disturbed. If you stretch a rubber band and then let it go, it returns to its original shape. However, when you stretch modeling clay and then let it go, it stays stretched. Rubber bands are more elastic than modeling clay. **Elasticity** is the ability of a material to bounce back after being disturbed. If a medium is very elastic, its particles easily go back to their original positions. Sound travels more quickly in mediums that have a high degree of elasticity because when the particles are compressed, they quickly spread out again.

Solid materials are usually more elastic than liquids or gases, so compressions and rarefactions travel very well in solids. The particles of a solid do not move very far, so they bounce back and forth quickly as the compressions and rarefactions of the sound waves go by. Most liquids are not very elastic. Sound is not transmitted as well in liquids as it is in solids. Gases are generally very inelastic and are the poorest transmitters of sound.

Density The speed of sound also depends on how close together the particles of the substance are. The **density** of a medium is how much matter, or mass, there is in a given amount of space, or volume.

In materials in the same state of matter—solid, liquid, or gas—sound travels more slowly in denser mediums. The denser the medium, the more mass it has in a given volume. The particles of a dense material do not move as quickly as those of a less-dense material. Sound travels more slowly in dense metals, such as lead or silver, than in iron or steel.

Temperature In a given medium, sound travels more slowly at lower temperatures and faster at higher temperatures. At a low temperature, the particles of a medium are more sluggish. They are more difficult to move and return to their original positions more slowly.

At 20°C, the speed of sound in air is about 342 m/s. At 0°C, the speed is about 330 m/s. At higher altitudes the air is colder, so sound travels more slowly at higher altitudes.

☑ ***Checkpoint*** *How does elasticity affect the speed of sound?*

Sharpen your Skills

Graphing ACTIVITY

Graph the following data, to show how the speed of sound through air changes with temperature. Show temperature from –20°C to 30°C on the horizontal axis. (*Note:* Negative numbers are less than zero.) Plot speed from 300 m/s to 400 m/s on the vertical axis.

Air Temperature (°C)	Speed (m/s)
–20	318
–10	324
0	330
10	336
20	342
30	348

How does air temperature affect the speed of sound?

Figure 6 On October 14, 1947, Captain Chuck Yeager became the first person to fly a plane faster than the speed of sound (top). On October 15, 1997, Andy Green officially became the first person to drive a land vehicle faster than the speed of sound (bottom).

Moving Faster Than Sound

The supersonic age began with a bang on October 14, 1947. Far above the California desert, Captain Chuck Yeager of the United States Air Force had just "broken the sound barrier." Captain Yeager was at an altitude of 12,000 meters and just about out of fuel. He had used much of his fuel to get to a higher altitude because the speed of sound is slower higher up. Wide open throttles accelerated his plane to over 293 meters per second, the speed of sound at that altitude. Thus, when he hit 294 meters per second, he exceeded the speed of sound at that altitude. At a lower altitude, the speed of sound is much faster and he would not have had the power or speed to exceed it. Yeager's team chose to go high in part because the temperature there is lower and the speed of sound is slower. Each pilot today who "goes supersonic" owes Chuck Yeager a debt of gratitude.

Fifty years later, Andy Green stood poised on Nevada's Black Rock desert. He had traveled all the way from Great Britain to go supersonic—on the ground! He chose the desert because it is flat, wide open, and cold in the morning. All of these factors were important to the attempt. On October 15, 1997, at the coolest time of the day, Green blasted off in his jet-powered car, *Thrust.* A short time later he traveled a measured distance at an average speed of 339 meters per second—7 meters per second faster than the speed of sound at that altitude. Andy Green was the first person to break the sound barrier on the ground.

Section 1 Review

1. How does sound travel through a medium?
2. How do elasticity, density, and temperature affect the speed of sound through a medium?
3. Explain why sound cannot travel through outer space.
4. **Thinking Critically Applying Concepts** Sound travels faster through glass than through gold. Based on this information, which material would you say is more dense? Explain.

Science at Home

Find a long metal railing or water pipe. **CAUTION:** *Beware of sharp edges and rust.* Put one ear to the pipe while a family member taps on the pipe some distance away. Do you hear the sound first with the ear touching the pipe or with your other ear? Compare the sound you hear through the metal with the sound coming through the air. What accounts for the difference?

Measuring

The Speed of Sound

Sound travels at different speeds through different materials. In this lab, you will measure the speed of sound in air.

Problem

How fast does sound travel in air?

Materials

metric tape measure
drum and drumstick (or empty coffee can and metal spoon)
digital stopwatch
thermometer

Procedure

1. With the approval of your teacher, select an outdoor area such as a football field.
2. Record the outdoor air temperature in °C.
3. Measure a distance of 100 meters in a straight line. How long do you think it should take for a sound to travel the 100 m?
4. Stand at one end of this measured distance with the drum. Have two teammates go to the other end with a stopwatch. One teammate, the "watcher," should watch you and the drum. The other, the "listener," should face away from the drum and listen for the sound.
5. Make a short, loud noise by striking the drum.
6. As you strike the drum, the watcher should start the stopwatch. When the listener hears the sound, he or she should immediately say "stop." Then the watcher stops the watch. Record the time to one tenth of a second.
7. Repeat Steps 4–6 five times. How consistent are your times? What might account for any differences?
8. Now switch roles. Repeat Steps 4–6 with different students beating the drum, watching, and listening.

Analyze and Conclude

1. How far did the sound travel? How long did it take? (Calculate the average of the five measured times.)
2. To calculate the speed of sound in air, use this formula:

$$\text{Speed} = \frac{\text{Distance}}{\text{Time}}$$

3. How well does your result compare with the prediction you made in Step 3? Make a list of reasons to account for any differences. What could you do to improve the accuracy of your measurements?
4. **Think About It** Another way to measure the speed of sound would be to stand near a tall building, shout, and wait to hear the echo. To use the echo method, what adjustments would you have to make to the procedure in this lab?

Design an Experiment

How could you find out the effect of changing air temperature on the speed of sound? Write a set of procedures you could use to conduct such an experiment.

2 Properties of Sound

DISCOVER

How Does Amplitude Affect Loudness?

1. Your teacher will give you a wooden board with two nails in it. Fasten a guitar string to the board by wrapping each end tightly around a nail.
2. Hold the string near the middle. Pull it about 1 cm to one side. This distance is the amplitude of vibration. Let it go. How far does the string move to the other side? Describe the sound you hear.
3. Repeat Step 2 four more times. Each time, pull the string back a greater distance. Describe how the sound changes each time.

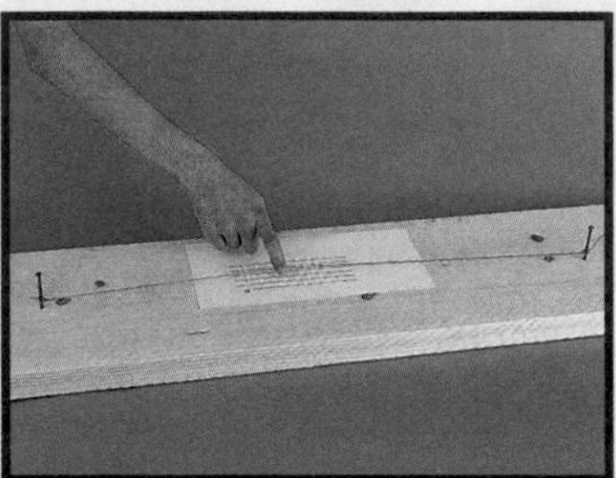

Think It Over

Forming Operational Definitions How would you define the amplitude of the vibration? How did you change the amplitude each time? What effect did changing the amplitude have on the sound?

GUIDE FOR READING

- How are sound intensity and loudness related?
- How are frequency and pitch related?
- What causes the Doppler effect?

Reading Tip As you read, use your own words to write a phrase or sentence describing each boldfaced word.

Suppose you and a friend are standing next to each other. You are talking in your normal speaking voice. After you say good-bye and your friend has walked away, you realize you have forgotten to tell your friend something important. How do you get your friend's attention? You will need to shout to be heard. When you shout, you take a deep breath and exhale very fast, and your voice sounds louder.

Intensity and Loudness

Compare the sound of a whisper to that of a hearty shout. The sounds are different because the amount of energy carried by the sound waves is different. The sound waves caused by a shout carry much more energy than those of a whisper.

Intensity You have seen how you can change the amplitude of a wave along a rope. If you move the rope a greater distance, you give it more energy as you shake it. When a sound wave carries a larger amount of energy, the molecules of the medium move a greater distance as the waves pass by, and the sound wave has a greater amplitude. The **intensity** of a sound wave is the amount of energy the wave carries per second through a unit area. Intensity is measured in watts per square meter (W/m^2).

Loudness If you did the Discover activity with the guitar string, you noticed how pulling the string back different distances affected the loudness of the sound you heard. You changed the amplitude of vibration of the string. Sound waves of higher amplitude have a greater intensity because they carry more energy per second through a given area. The greater the intensity of a sound wave, the louder it is. **Loudness** describes what you actually hear. **A sound wave of greater intensity generally sounds louder.**

Figure 7 A loudspeaker gives out sound by vibrating cones of material. The greater the amplitude of vibration, the greater the volume, or loudness, of the sound.

To increase the loudness of the music coming from a CD player, you adjust the volume control. Loudspeakers or headphones give off sound by vibrating a cone of material. Figure 7 shows how the vibrations make compressions and rarefactions in the air, just like a vibrating drumhead. As you turn up the volume, the cone vibrates with a greater amplitude and the sound you hear is louder.

Loudness, or sound level, is measured in **decibels (dB).** Figure 8 shows the loudness of some familiar sounds. The loudness of a sound you can barely hear is about 0 dB. Each 10 dB increase in sound level represents a tenfold increase in intensity. For example, a sound at 30 dB is ten times more intense than a sound at 20 dB. Sounds louder than 100 dB can cause damage to your ears, especially if you listen to those sounds for long periods of time. Sounds louder than 120 dB can cause pain and sometimes permanent hearing loss.

Checkpoint *How does amplitude affect the loudness of a sound?*

Loudness of Sounds

Sound	Loudness (dB)	Hearing Damage
Threshold of human hearing	0	None
Rustling leaves	10	
Whisper	20	
Very soft music	30	
Classroom	35	
Average home	40–50	
Loud conversation	60–70	
Heavy street traffic	70	
Loud music	90–100	After long exposure
Subway train	100	
Rock concert	115–120	Progressive
Jackhammer	120	Threshold of pain
Jet engine	120–170	
Space shuttle engine	200	Immediate and irreversible

Figure 8 Some sounds are so soft, you can barely hear them. Others are so loud that they can damage your ears. ***Applying Concepts*** *How is the sound of a space shuttle engine different from that of a whisper?*

The Short Straw

Try this activity to see how the length of a straw affects the sound it makes when you blow through it.

1. Flatten one end of a drinking straw and cut the end to form a point.
2. Blow through the straw. Describe what you hear.

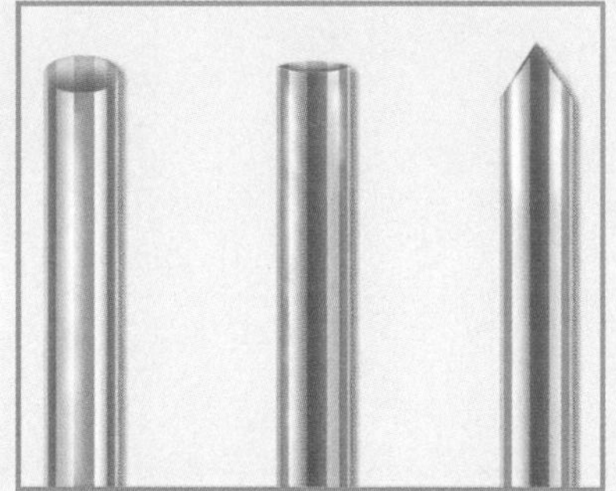

Predicting What changes would you hear if you shortened the straw by cutting off some of the straight end? Test your prediction.

Frequency and Pitch

A barbershop quartet consists of four singers with very different voices. When all four people sing together, the different voices combine to make a pleasing sound.

Frequency When a person sings, muscles in the throat stretch and relax the vocal cords. This changes the frequency of the sound waves. When the vocal cords are stretched, they vibrate more often as the air rushes past them. This creates higher-frequency sound waves. When the vocal cords are relaxed, they vibrate less often and produce lower-frequency sound waves. The frequency of a sound wave is the number of vibrations that occur per second. A frequency of 50 Hz means fifty vibrations per second. A bass singer can produce a range of frequencies from about 80 Hz to about 260 Hz. A trained soprano voice can produce frequencies higher than 1,000 Hz.

Most people can hear sounds with frequencies between 20 Hz and 20,000 Hz. Sound waves with frequencies above the normal human range of hearing are called **ultrasound.** The prefix *ultra-* means "above." Sounds with frequencies below the normal human range of hearing are called **infrasound.** The prefix *infra-* means "below."

Pitch Before a barbershop quartet begins to sing, one member plays a note on a pitch pipe. This gives the lead singer the correct starting note. The **pitch** of a sound is a description of how high or low the sound seems to a person. **The pitch of a sound that you hear depends on the frequency of the sound wave.** Sound waves of high frequency have a high pitch, while sound waves of low frequency have a low pitch.

Figure 9 A barbershop quartet consists of four singers, whose voices sound good together. ***Comparing and Contrasting*** *In what way are the four voices different?*

Figure 10 The key farthest to the left on a piano is attached to the longest string. This key plays the note with the lowest pitch. ***Developing Hypotheses*** *Why do longer strings generally produce lower notes than shorter strings?*

When a string vibrates, the pitch of the sound depends on the length and thickness of the string, the material it is made from, and how tightly it is stretched. You can change the pitch of a sound by changing the properties of the string that produces it. For example, violinists and guitarists tune their instruments by turning knobs that stretch the strings. A tighter string produces a higher frequency. You hear the higher frequency as a sound with higher pitch.

Different lengths of string produce different frequencies, too. In general, a short string produces a higher pitch than a long string under the same tension. Consider the range of notes you can play on a piano. The key farthest to the left on a piano keyboard produces the note with the lowest pitch. It is attached to the longest string, which vibrates at a frequency of about 27 Hz. The key farthest to the right on a piano keyboard produces the note with the highest pitch. It is attached to the shortest string, which vibrates at a frequency of 4,186 Hz.

☑ ***Checkpoint*** *How are frequency and pitch related?*

Figure 11 Some musical instruments can produce notes with vibrations that match the natural frequency of a crystal glass. If the note is sustained, the amplitude of vibration can cause the glass to shatter.

Resonance Have you ever heard of an opera singer who could shatter a glass with a sustained high note? How can that happen? All objects vibrate naturally. The vibrations are so frequent that you usually cannot see them. The frequency of the vibrations depends on the type and shape of the object. If the frequency of sound waves exactly matches the natural frequency of an object, the sound waves can add to the object's vibrations. Resonance occurs when the frequency of the sound waves and the natural frequency of the object are the same.

Suppose a note has the same frequency as the natural vibration of a crystal glass. If the note is played steadily, the sound waves can add to the amplitude of vibration of the glass. If the note is played loudly enough and for long enough, the amplitude of vibration can increase so much that the glass shatters.

Pipe Sounds

Try this activity **ACTIVITY** to see how a single pipe can produce different pitches.

1. Find an open space where there are no objects or people near you.
2. Hold the end of a flexible plastic tube firmly (a vacuum cleaner hose works well) and swing it over your head until it produces a sound. Try to swing the tube by moving only your wrist.
3. Now slowly increase the speed of the tube. Then slow it down. Use varying speeds. Describe what you hear as you change the speed of the whirling tube.

Observing How was the sound produced? How did the pitch change with an increase in speed? What happens if you plug the far end of the tube with a cloth? Explain.

The Doppler Effect

Even though a sound may have a constant frequency, it does not always sound that way to a listener. Have you ever heard a police car speed by with its siren on? If you listen carefully you will notice something surprising. As the car moves toward you, the pitch of the siren is higher. As the car goes by and moves away, the pitch drops. But the frequency of the siren is not really changing. If you were riding in the police car, you would hear the same pitch all the time. The apparent change in frequency as a wave source moves in relation to the listener is called the **Doppler effect.** If the waves are sound waves, the change in frequency is heard as a change in pitch.

The Doppler Demonstration The Doppler effect was named after Christian Doppler, an Austrian scientist who described it about 150 years ago. To demonstrate the effect, Doppler put a musical band on an open flatcar of a train. He stood on the ground nearby. As the train approached him, the notes the musicians played seemed to be a higher pitch. As the train passed, the notes seemed to drop in pitch. Doppler repeated the experiment, but this time he stood on the train and had the musicians play while they were seated on the ground. Doppler heard the same changes in pitch as the train he rode approached and passed the band. The effect was the same regardless of who was moving, the band or Doppler.

Changing Pitch To understand what causes this apparent change in pitch, imagine you are standing still and throwing tennis balls at a wall about 5 meters in front of you. If you throw one ball each second, the balls hit the wall at a rate of one per second. The frequency is 1 per second, or 1 Hz. Now suppose you walk toward the wall, still throwing one ball per second.

Figure 12 As the police car speeds by, the pitch of the siren seems to change. Ahead of the car, the sound waves are piling up, so the pitch is higher. Behind the car the waves spread out, so the pitch is lower.

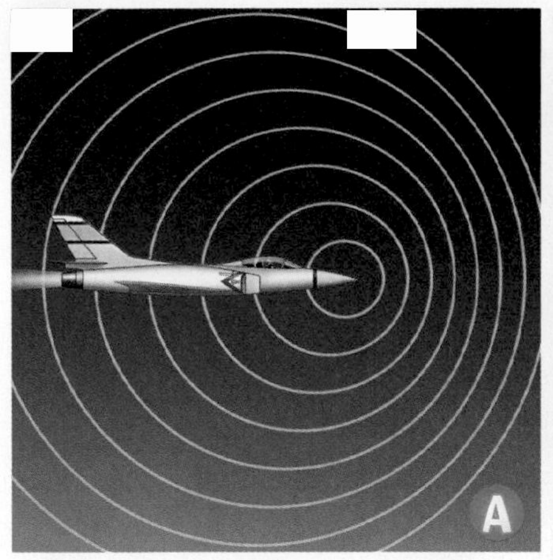

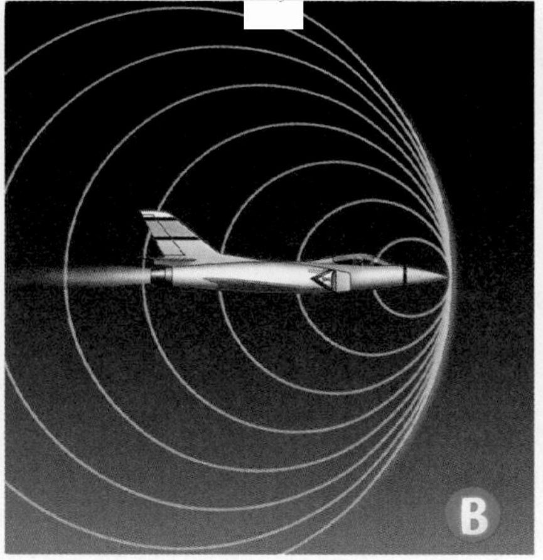

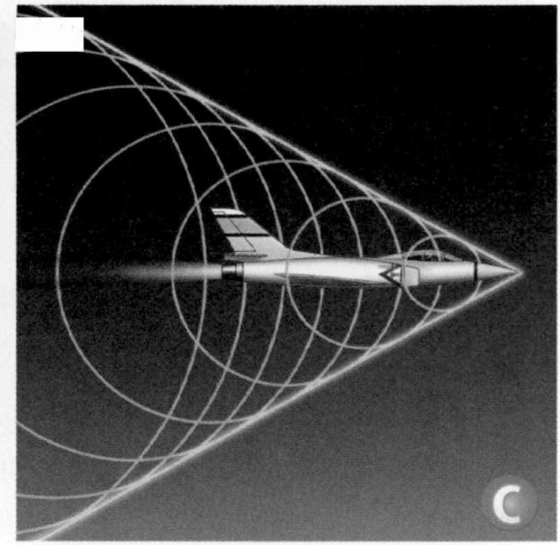

Figure 13 When a plane approaches the speed of sound **(A)**, waves pile up to form the sound barrier **(B)**. When the plane exceeds the speed of sound, it moves through this barrier **(C)**, causing the shock wave that we hear as a sonic boom.

Because each ball has a shorter distance to travel than the one before, it takes less time to get there. The balls hit the wall more often than one per second, or with a higher frequency than before. Similarly, if you throw balls at the wall as you back away, the balls will hit the wall with lower frequency. Each ball has farther to travel before it hits the wall, so it takes longer to get there.

Figure 12 shows how sound waves from a moving source behave. **As a sound source moves toward the listener, the waves reach the listener with a higher frequency. The pitch appears to increase because of the Doppler effect.**

This piling up of sound waves has a spectacular effect in the air. Figures 13A and B show how as a plane travels almost as fast as the speed of sound, the sound waves pile up in front of the plane. This pile-up is the "sound barrier." When the plane flies faster than the speed of sound, it breaks through the barrier. When the sound barrier is broken, as in Figure 13C, a huge amount of energy is released in the form of a shock wave. People on the ground nearby hear a loud noise called a sonic boom.

Section 2 Review

1. What makes some sounds louder than others?
2. Explain the relationship between frequency and pitch.
3. How can you change the pitch produced by a vibrating string?
4. Explain how resonance can cause a crystal glass to shatter.
5. What is the Doppler effect?
6. **Thinking Critically Relating Cause and Effect** If you are riding in a fire truck with the siren blaring, you do not hear the Doppler effect. Explain.

CHAPTER PROJECT 14

Check Your Progress

Think about the design of your instrument and how it will produce sounds. Consider how you will vary the sound produced by your instrument. Make a list of the materials you could use to build your instrument. Begin to collect your materials.

SECTION 3 Combining Sound Waves

DISCOVER ACTIVITY

How Can You Produce Patterns of Sound?

1. Obtain an empty coffee can.
2. Stretch the palm area of a latex glove over the open end. Glue a small mirror tile in the center of the glove.
3. Shine a flashlight so that the light reflects off the mirror and onto a wall.
4. Ask a classmate to continuously tap a spoon on the closed end of the can. Make sure you keep the light shining on the mirror. Observe the light patterns that are reflected on the wall. What do the patterns look like? Draw and label what you observe.
5. Have your classmate change the frequency of the tapping. Draw what you observe.

Think It Over

Inferring What causes the moving patterns on the wall? What happens when you change the frequency of the tapping? Explain.

GUIDE FOR READING

- **What is sound quality?**
- **How are music and noise different?**
- **What happens when two or more sound waves interact?**

Reading Tip **Before you read, list as many musical instruments as you can. Write a short description of how you think each one works. Revise your list as you read.**

Imagine you are waiting for a train at a busy station. In the middle of all the hustle and bustle, you notice lots of different sounds. A baby wails while a teenager listens to a favorite radio station. Then the train rolls in. Why are some sounds pleasing to hear while others make you want to cover your ears? The answer is in the way sound waves combine.

Busy train station ▶

Sound Quality

Think of all the different sounds you hear on a given day. Some sounds are pleasant, such as your favorite kind of music, a babbling brook, or a baby cooing. Other sounds are unpleasant, such as loud power tools, fingernails scratching on a chalkboard, or a constant drip of water from a tap. Your ears hear all kinds of sounds—some that you like and some that you don't.

To understand the quality of sound, consider the example of a violin string. As the string vibrates, waves travel along the string and then reflect back, setting up a standing wave. Figure 14 shows how a string vibrates with different frequencies. The frequency at which a standing wave occurs is the string's resonant frequency. Every object, including musical instruments, has its own resonant frequency.

The resonant frequency produces a pitch called the fundamental tone. However, most of the sounds you hear are not pure tones. Although a tuning fork or pitch pipe produces a single tone, more complex instruments produce several tones at once. For example, a string can vibrate at several frequencies at the same time. The higher frequencies produce sounds heard as having higher pitch. The higher pitches, or overtones, have frequencies of two, three, or four times the frequency of the fundamental tone.

Timbre (TAM bur) describes the quality of the sound you hear. Overtones can be weak, strong, or missing. The timbre of a sound depends on which overtones are present. **The blending of the fundamental tone and the overtones makes up the characteristic sound quality, or timbre, of a particular sound.**

Sounds produced by different instruments have different timbres. The sound of a note played on a trumpet has a different timbre from the same note played on a violin or flute. The trumpet, the violin, and the flute produce different overtones. The size, shape, and materials used also affect the timbre of an instrument.

☑ *Checkpoint What factors affect the quality of a sound?*

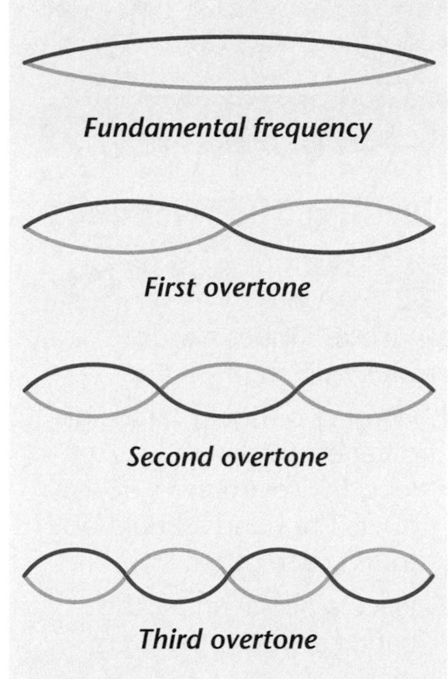

Figure 14 When half a wave takes up the whole string, a fundamental tone is produced (top). Waves half, one third, one fourth, and so on, as long as the fundamental wave produces overtones. ***Inferring*** *How does the pitch of each overtone compare with the pitch of the fundamental tone?*

Plucking Rubber Bands

ACTIVITY

Here's how you can make rubber bands produce different pitches.

1. Wrap two rubber bands of different thickness lengthwise around a 30-cm ruler. The bands should not touch each other.
2. Place a pencil under the bands at about the 5-cm mark.
3. Pluck one band and then the other. What causes the sounds? How are the sounds from the two bands different?
4. With one finger, hold down one of the bands between 5 cm and 30 cm. Pluck the band again.

Drawing Conclusions How is the sound the rubber band made in Step 4 different from the sound it made in Step 3? What caused this difference?

Making Music

If the combination of the fundamental tone and the overtones results in a sound with a pleasing timbre and a clear pitch, the sound is considered **music.** Most music contains only a few fundamental tones and their overtones. **Music is a set of tones combined in ways that are pleasing to the ear.** The design of a musical instrument affects the overtones it produces when a note is played. All musical instruments produce vibrations when played. The material that vibrates varies. The major groups of instruments are strings, brass, woodwinds, and percussion.

Strings Stringed instruments have strings that vibrate when plucked, struck, or rubbed with a bow. A short string vibrates at a higher frequency and so produces a higher-pitched sound than a long string. As they play, musicians place their fingers on different places along the string to vary the pitch. The material, thickness, and tightness of a string also affects the pitch it produces. Instruments such as guitars, violins, and cellos also have a box, or sounding board. The box improves the quality of the sound produced by the strings. Larger stringed instruments, such as the cello and the double bass, produce lower pitches.

Brass and Woodwinds Brass instruments, such as trumpets and trombones, produce sound when the player's lips vibrate against the mouthpiece. This vibration causes the air column inside the instrument to vibrate. The musician adjusts the length of the air column by pressing valves or moving slides.

Figure 15 Violins are stringed instruments, flutes and clarinets are woodwinds, and trumpets are brass instruments.
Making Generalizations *What do all these musical instruments have in common?*

Many woodwind instruments, such as clarinets and oboes, have a thin, flexible strip of material called a reed. When the player blows into the mouthpiece, the reed vibrates along with the column of air. The longer the column of air, the lower the pitch. Larger woodwind and brass instruments, such as the bassoon and the tuba, produce lower pitches.

Percussion Percussion instruments, such as drums, bells, cymbals, and xylophones, vibrate when struck. The sound they produce depends on the material from which they are made. It also depends on the size of the instrument, and the part of the instrument that is played. For example, larger drums produce lower pitches.

Figure 16 Percussion instruments vibrate when struck. ***Predicting*** *Describe the sound produced by a large drum compared with that of a small drum of the same material.*

☑ ***Checkpoint*** *What are the main groups of musical instruments?*

Noise

You are sitting comfortably in your classroom chair, watching a classmate write on the board. Suddenly, you hear the accidental scratch of fingernails as the chalk flies from your friend's grasp. The sound makes you wince.

Why is the squeak of fingernails on a chalkboard so unpleasant? One answer is that the squeak is noise. **Noise** is a mixture of sound waves that do not sound pleasing together. **Noise has no pleasing timbre and no identifiable pitch.** Consider the noise of chalk squeaking on a chalkboard or the noise of a jackhammer working in the street. The vibrations that produce these sounds are random. Even if an engine produces a hum that has a fundamental tone and overtones, the lack of rhythm in the sound makes us call it noise instead of music.

Sounds that are music to some people are noise to others. Some rock bands and orchestras play compositions with tones that seem to have no musical relationship. The sound produced when these notes are played together is called **dissonance.** Dissonance is music to the ears of people who enjoy the sound.

Music CONNECTION

One of the most widely known compositions of Sergei Prokofiev, a Russian composer who lived from 1891 to 1953, is *Peter and the Wolf.* In this work, each instrument, or group of instruments, represents a character in the story.

In Your Journal

Listen to a recording of *Peter and the Wolf.* Write a review of this work. Do you agree with how Prokofiev matched instruments with characters? Which instrument would you have chosen to represent each character?

EXPLORING Making Music

The sound produced by a musical instrument depends on the instrument's size and shape. The material from which the instrument is made and the way it is played also affect the timbre of the sound.

Violin
The violin is a carefully crafted wooden box with strings. The strings are attached to tuning pegs, which can be turned to adjust the tension. When the strings are rubbed with a bow, they vibrate. The violinist controls the pitch by placing the fingers at different positions along the string.

Harp
The harp consists of a row of strings, each one a different length. The harpist gracefully plucks the strings with the fingers to produce music. The short strings produce higher pitches than the long strings do.

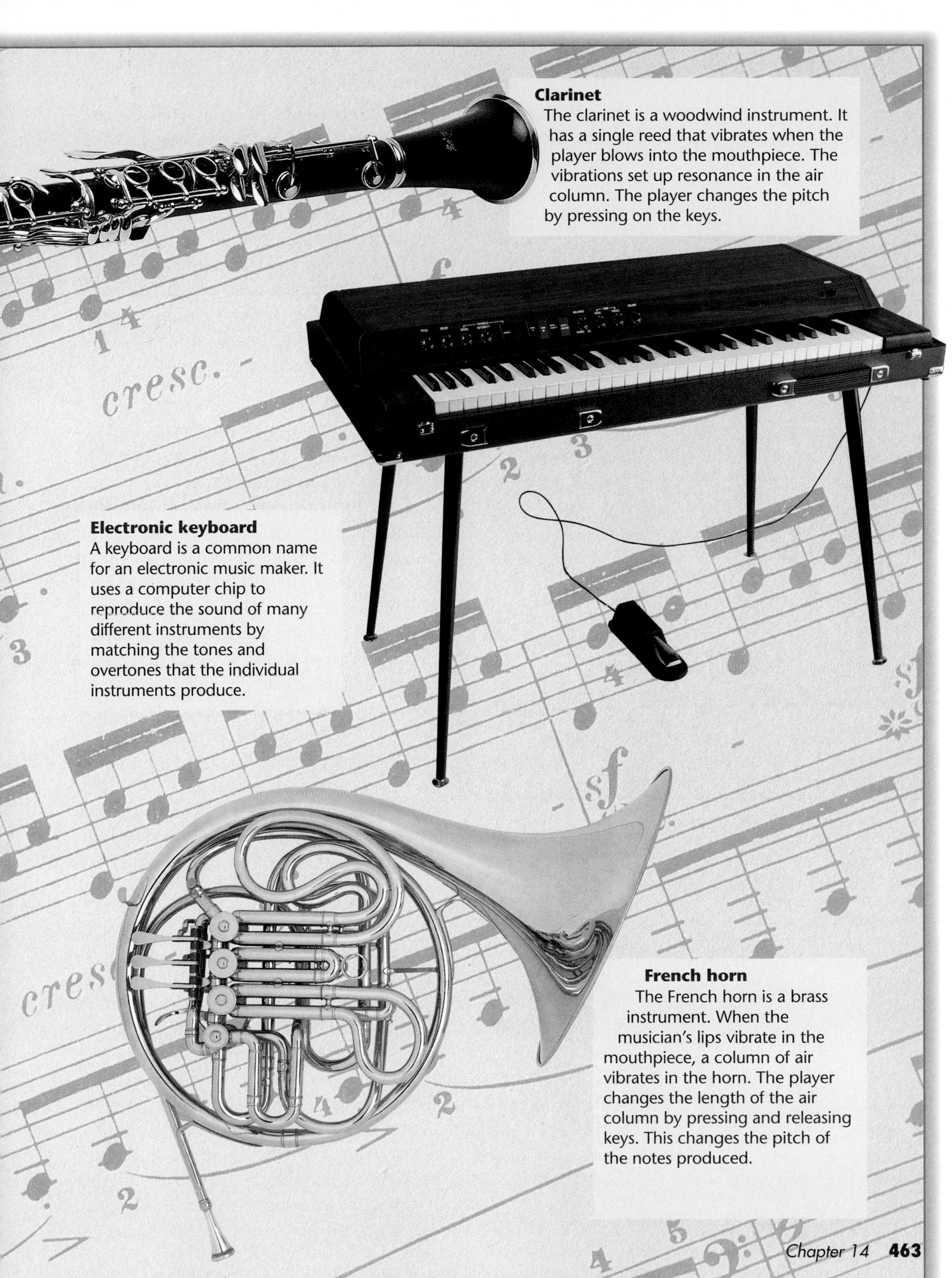

Clarinet
The clarinet is a woodwind instrument. It has a single reed that vibrates when the player blows into the mouthpiece. The vibrations set up resonance in the air column. The player changes the pitch by pressing on the keys.

Electronic keyboard
A keyboard is a common name for an electronic music maker. It uses a computer chip to reproduce the sound of many different instruments by matching the tones and overtones that the individual instruments produce.

French horn
The French horn is a brass instrument. When the musician's lips vibrate in the mouthpiece, a column of air vibrates in the horn. The player changes the length of the air column by pressing and releasing keys. This changes the pitch of the notes produced.

Interference of Sound Waves

You have probably heard sound waves interfering with each other, though you may not have known what you were hearing. **Interference occurs when two or more sound waves interact.** The amplitudes of the two waves combine, causing the loudness of the sound to change. When interference is constructive, compressions of waves occur at the same place and the amplitudes combine. The resulting sound is louder than either of the two original sounds. When the interference is destructive, compressions of one wave occur at the same place as rarefactions of another wave and the amplitudes cancel each other out. The resulting wave is softer or completely concealed.

Figure 17 A concert hall must be designed to provide the highest sound quality possible. The design should eliminate echoes and destructive interference.

Acoustics The way in which sound waves interact is very important in concert halls. In a concert hall, sound waves of different frequencies reach each listener from many directions at the same time. These sound waves may come directly from the orchestra or they may first bounce off the walls or ceiling. People sitting in various seats may hear different sounds because of the particular interactions of sound waves at their locations. In a poorly designed hall, seats may be located where destructive interference occurs. The sound will seem distorted.

Acoustics describe how well sounds can be heard in a particular room or hall. When designing auditoriums, acoustical engineers must carefully consider the shape of the room and the materials used to cover walls, floors, ceilings, and seats. Because they absorb sound instead of reflecting it, some materials can eliminate the reflected waves that cause interference.

Canceling Sounds Sometimes destructive interference is welcome.

INTEGRATING TECHNOLOGY

Airplane passengers use earphones to listen to music, but the throbbing of the plane's engines can drown out much of the sound. Some airline earphones use destructive interference to cancel out the steady engine noise. The earphones produce sound waves that interfere destructively with the engine sound. The passenger's ears receive both the engine sound waves and the sound waves produced by the earphones. These waves cancel each other out, so the passenger hears neither. Only the music is left. This type of technology also allows factories to reduce noise levels to protect the hearing of workers.

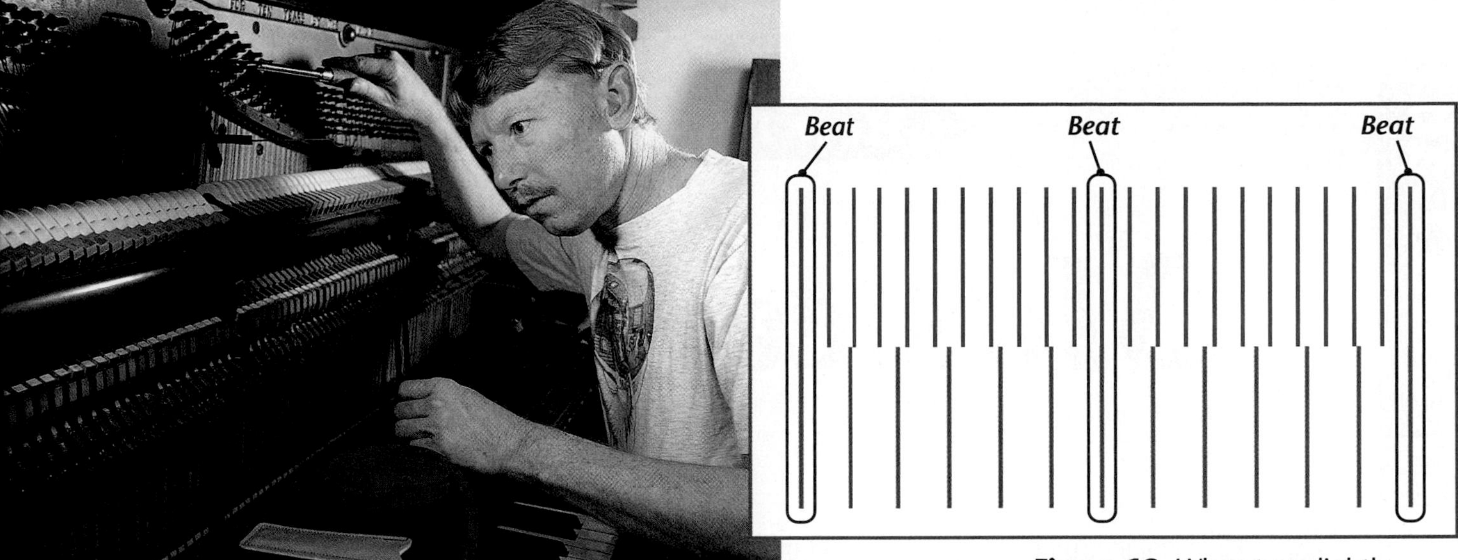

Figure 18 When two slightly different frequencies are combined, they interfere constructively at regular intervals (above right). A piano tuner listens to the sound of a note and a tuning fork together (above left). ***Inferring*** *How does the piano tuner know when a key is perfectly tuned?*

Beats If two sound waves are close in frequency, they can combine so that they interfere both constructively and destructively at regular intervals. Figure 18 shows how two frequencies can combine at certain times. The resulting sound gets louder and softer at regular intervals. The intervals depend on the difference between the two frequencies. The repeated changes in loudness are called **beats.**

Piano tuners use beats to tune pianos. A piano tuner strikes a tuning fork of a particular frequency and hits the corresponding key on a piano at the same time. If the tuner hears beats, that means that the frequency of vibration of the piano string does not exactly match that of the tuning fork. The tuner then adjusts the piano string until no beat can be heard. Then the piano key is perfectly tuned.

Section 3 Review

1. What factors determine the quality of a sound?
2. What is the difference between music and noise?
3. How can sounds cancel each other out?
4. How can the interference of two sound waves produce a louder sound?
5. What are beats?
6. **Thinking Critically Applying Concepts** Explain why a sound in an empty room will sound different from the same sound in a room with a carpet, curtains, and furniture.

Check Your Progress

CHAPTER PROJECT 14

Begin building the instrument you have designed. As you build your instrument, experiment with different materials to find the most appealing sound. How do different kinds of materials affect the sounds? Explore and experiment with the sounds your instrument makes. How does adding or removing certain parts or materials affect the loudness of the sound? How can you vary the pitch of your instrument?

Real-World Lab

How It Works

Musical Notes

Musical instruments produce sound by setting up standing waves. Those waves can be on a string or in a column of air. In this lab, you will see how you can use bottles to produce different musical notes, maybe enough to play a simple tune.

Problem

How can you produce different musical notes with bottles of water?

Skills Focus

predicting, observing, inferring

Materials

3 identical glass bottles
water
masking tape
marking pen
pencil

Procedure

1. Label the bottles A, B, and C.
2. Put water in each bottle so that bottle A is one-fourth full, bottle B is half full, and bottle C is three-fourths full.
3. Copy the data table into your lab notebook. Measure the distance from the top of each bottle to the surface of the water. Then measure the height of the water in each bottle. Record your measurements.
4. Predict the difference in pitch you will hear if you blow across the top of each bottle in turn. Give reasons for your prediction.
5. Test your prediction by blowing over the top of each bottle. Listen to the sound you produce. Describe each sound in terms of its pitch—low, medium, or high. Record the pitch of each sound.

DATA TABLE				
Bottle	Length of Column of Air (cm)	Height of Water (cm)	Pitch Produced by Blowing Across Top of Bottle	Pitch Produced by Tapping Pencil on Side of Bottle
A				
B				
C				

6. When you gently tap the side of a bottle with a pencil, you produce another sound. Do you think the sound will be similar to or different from the sound produced by blowing across the top of the bottle? Explain.
7. Test your prediction by tapping on the side of each bottle with a pencil. Record the pitch of each sound.

Analyze and Conclude

1. Describe how the sound is produced in Step 5. Which bottle produced the highest pitch? Which bottle produced the lowest pitch?
2. What caused the change in pitch from bottle to bottle?
3. Describe how the sound is produced in Step 7. Which bottle produced the highest pitch? Which bottle produced the lowest pitch?
4. What caused the change in pitch from bottle to bottle? What change in pitch can you produce by tapping on a different part of the bottle?
5. Compare the sounds you produced by blowing across the bottles with those produced by tapping on the bottles. What was the difference in pitch for each bottle? Explain your observations.
6. Look at your data table. How does the length of the column of air affect the pitch? How does the height of the water affect the pitch?
7. **Think About It** Based on your observations in this lab, what statements can you make about the relationship between the sounds produced and the medium through which the sound travels?

More to Explore

To play simple tunes, you will need eight notes. Set up a row of eight bottles, each with a different amount of water. Adjust the water level in each bottle until you can play a simple scale. Practice playing a simple tune on your bottles.

How You Hear Sound

DISCOVER — ACTIVITY

Where Is the Sound Coming From?

1. Ask your partner to sit on a chair, with eyes closed.
2. Clap your hands near your partner's left ear. Ask your partner to tell you the direction the sound came from.
3. Now clap near your partner's right ear. Again, ask your partner to tell you the direction the sound came from. Continue clapping above your partner's head, in front of the face, and below the chin in random order. How well can your partner detect the direction the sound is coming from?
4. Switch places with your partner and repeat Steps 1–3.

Think It Over

Observing As you clap, record the answers given by your partner. Which locations are easily identified? Which locations are impossible to identify? Is there a pattern? If so, can you think of a possible explanation for this pattern?

GUIDE FOR READING

- How do you hear sound?
- What causes hearing loss?

Reading Tip **As you read, draw a flowchart to show how you hear sound.**

The house is quiet. You are sound asleep. All of a sudden, your alarm clock goes off. Startled, you jump up out of bed. Your ears detected the sound waves produced by the alarm clock. But how exactly did your brain receive the information?

How You Hear Sound

Once the sound waves enter your ear, how does your brain receive the information? Your ear has three main sections: the outer ear, the middle ear, and the inner ear. Each has a different function. **The outer ear funnels sound waves, the middle ear transmits the waves inward, and the inner ear converts the sound waves into a form that your brain can understand.**

Outer Ear As the alarm clock rings, the sound waves reach your ears. The curved surface of the outermost part of your ear looks and acts like a funnel. It collects sound waves and directs them into a narrower region known as the **ear canal.** Your ear

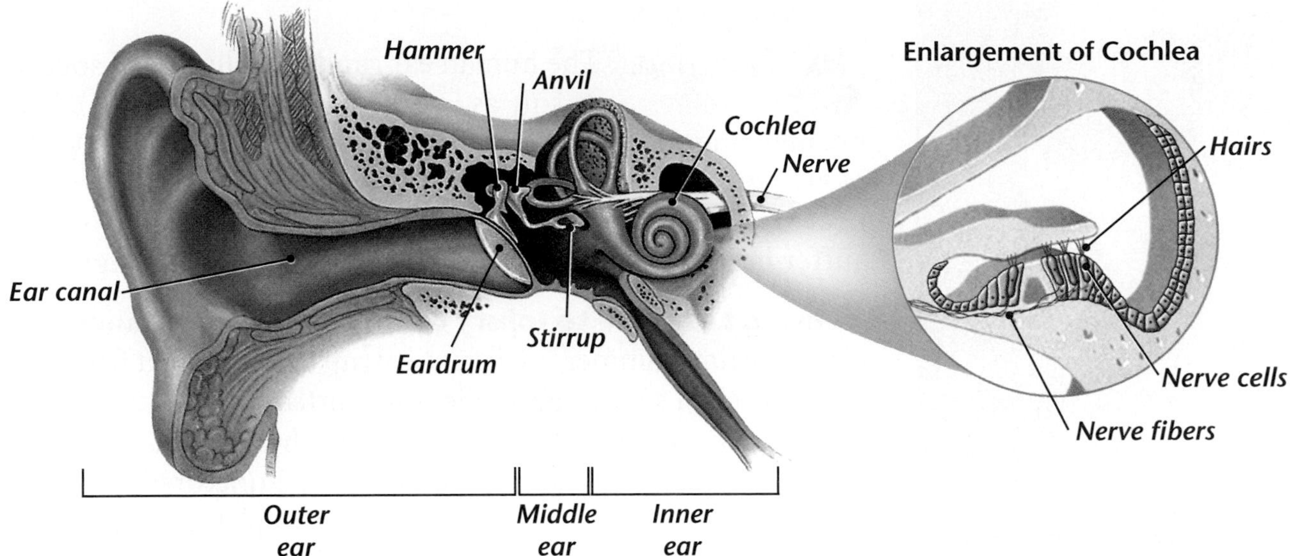

Figure 19 The illustrations show the structure of the human ear and the inside of the cochlea. *Interpreting Diagrams How is sound transmitted through the middle ear?*

canal is a few centimeters long and ends at the eardrum. The **eardrum** is a small, tightly stretched, drumlike membrane. The sound waves make your eardrum vibrate, just as a drum vibrates when you beat it with a drumstick.

Middle Ear Behind the eardrum is an area called the middle ear. The **middle ear** contains the three smallest bones in the human body—the hammer, the anvil, and the stirrup. If you look at them in Figure 19, you'll see how they got their names. The hammer is attached to the eardrum, so when the eardrum vibrates, the hammer does too. The hammer then hits the anvil, which then shakes the stirrup.

Inner Ear The inner ear is separated from the middle ear by another membrane. Behind this membrane is a cavity filled with liquid. This cavity, the **cochlea** (KAHK lee uh), is shaped like a snail shell. Inside, it is lined with more than 10,000 nerve cells. These nerve cells have hairlike structures that float in the liquid in the cochlea. When the stirrup vibrates against the membrane, the vibrations pass into the liquid in the cochlea. As the liquid moves, the hairlike structures sway, sending messages to the brain. The brain processes these messages and tells you that you've heard sound.

Checkpoint *What are the three main areas of the ear?*

Listen to Sounds

How does sound travel to your ears?

1. Tie two strings to the handle of a metal spoon. Each string should be about 40 cm long.
2. Hold one end of each string in each hand. Bump the bowl of the spoon against a desk or other hard solid object. Listen to the sound.
3. Now wrap the ends of the string around your fingers.
4. Put your index fingers up against your ears and bump the spoon against the object again.

Inferring How does the first sound compare with the sound you heard with your fingers up against your ears? What can you conclude about how sound travels to your ears?

Figure 20 Hearing aids can make sounds louder as the sounds enter the ear.

Hearing Loss

INTEGRATING HEALTH The human ear can normally detect sounds as soft as breathing (about 2–10 dB). The normal range of frequencies a person can hear is 20–20,000 Hz. However, when hearing loss occurs, a person may have difficulty hearing soft sounds or high-pitched sounds. **Many people suffer hearing loss as a result of injury, infection, or aging.**

Hearing Loss Due to Injury or Infection A head injury can cause the tiny hammer, anvil, and stirrup to disconnect from one another. Then sound cannot be transmitted through the middle ear. Surgery can usually correct this type of hearing loss.

If your eardrum becomes damaged or punctured, you may experience hearing loss. (Imagine trying to play a torn drum!) For this reason, it is dangerous to put objects into your ear, even to clean it. Viral or bacterial infections can also damage the delicate inner ear, causing permanent hearing loss.

Hearing Loss Due to Aging The most common type of hearing loss occurs gradually. As a person gets older, the tiny hair cells in the cochlea become less effective at detecting the signals. Many older people have difficulty hearing higher-frequency sounds.

Extended exposure to loud sounds can damage the hair cells. If these cells are damaged by loud sounds, they can no longer transmit signals to the brain. You can prevent this type of hearing loss by wearing ear plugs or other hearing protection when you know you are going to be exposed to loud noises.

Some types of hearing loss can be helped with hearing aids. Hearing aids are amplifiers. Some are so tiny that they can fit invisibly in the ear. Others are made specifically for a person's hearing loss and amplify mainly the frequencies that the person has lost the ability to hear.

Section 4 Review

1. How do your ears detect sound waves?
2. How can sound damage your hearing?
3. Describe how the eardrum works.
4. What happens once sound waves enter the ear?
5. **Thinking Critically Classifying** Make a chart that lists some common sounds you might hear in a day. Estimate the loudness of each sound and state whether each one could produce hearing loss. (*Hint:* Refer to Figure 8 on page 453.)

Science at Home

Invite family members to make a survey of the kinds of sounds they hear throughout one day. Have each member rate the sounds as quiet, normal, loud, or painful. Then rate each sound as pleasant, neutral, or annoying. State the source of each sound, the location, the time of day, and the approximate length of time that they are exposed to the sound. How are the ratings alike and different?

SCIENCE AND SOCIETY

Keeping It Quiet...

A construction worker operates a jackhammer; a woman waits in a noisy subway station; a factory worker uses loud machinery. All three are victims of noise pollution. In the United States, 80 million people say they are "continually" bothered by noise, and 40 million face danger to their health.

One burst of sound from a passing truck can be enough to raise blood pressure. People start to feel pain at about 120 decibels. Exposure to even 85 decibels (the noise level of a kitchen blender or a loudly crying baby) can eventually damage the hairlike cells of the cochlea. Noise that "doesn't hurt" can still damage your hearing. As many as 16 million Americans may have permanent hearing loss caused by noise. What can we do to keep it quiet?

The Issues

What Can Individual People Do? Some work conditions are noisier than others. Construction workers, factory employees, and people who drive large vehicles are often at risk. All workers in noisy environments can benefit from ear protectors, such as plugs or headphone-like mufflers. Ear protectors can reduce noise levels by 35 decibels.

A listener at a rock concert, a hunter firing a rifle, or someone using an electric drill can also prevent damage with ear protectors. In addition, people should, if possible, avoid extreme noise. They can buy quieter machines and respect neighbors by not using noisy machines, such as lawn mowers and snow blowers, at quiet times of day or night. Simply turning down the volume on headphones, radios, CD players, and tape players can help prevent permanent hearing loss in young people.

What Can Communities Do? Transportation—planes, trains, trucks, and cars—is the largest source of noise pollution. Fifteen million Americans live near airports or under airport flight paths. Careful planning to locate highways and airports away from homes and buildings can reduce noise. Cities and towns can also prohibit flights late at night.

Many communities have laws against noise of more than a fixed decibel level, but these laws are not always enforced. In some cities "noise police" can fine the owners of noisy equipment.

What Can Government Do? A national Office of Noise Abatement and Control was set up in the 1970s. It required labels on power tools and lawnmowers, telling how much noise they make. In 1982, this office was closed down. Some lawmakers want to bring the office back and have nationwide limits to many types of noise. But critics say that national laws have little effect in controlling noise. The federal government could also encourage—and pay for—research into making quieter vehicles and machines.

You Decide

1. **Identify the Problem**
   In your own words, describe the problem of noise pollution.
2. **Analyze the Options**
   List as many methods as you can for dealing with noise. How would each method work to reduce noise or to protect people from noise? Who would be affected by each method?
3. **Find a Solution**
   Propose one method for reducing noise in your community. Make a poster that encourages people to carry out your proposal.

SECTION 5 Applications of Sound

DISCOVER ACTIVITY

How Can You Use Time to Measure Distance?

1. Measure a distance 3 meters from a wall and mark the spot with a piece of masking tape.
2. Roll a soft ball in a straight line from that spot toward the wall. What happens to the ball?
3. Roll the ball again. Try to roll the ball at the same speed each time. Have a classmate use a stopwatch to record the time it takes for the ball to leave your hand, reflect off the wall, and then return to you.
4. Now move 6 meters away from the wall. Mark the spot with tape. Repeat Steps 2 and 3.
5. Compare the time for both distances.

Think It Over

Inferring What does the difference in time tell you about the distance the ball has traveled?

GUIDE FOR READING

- **How is sonar used to tell distances?**
- **How do animals use sound?**
- **How is ultrasound used in medicine?**

Reading Tip **As you read, write a sentence or two to describe each application of sound waves.**

You and your friend are in a long, dark cave. Every sound you make seems to come right back to you. For fun, both of you shout and scream and then listen as the echoes bounce around the cave.

Reflection of Sound Waves

When a sound wave hits a surface through which it cannot pass, it bounces back, or reflects. A reflected sound wave is called an echo.

Sometimes an echo is much fainter than the original sound. This is usually because some of the energy of the wave is absorbed along the way. Some materials reflect sound very well, while others absorb most of the sound that strikes them. Most of the practical applications of sound are based on the fact that sound reflects off some surfaces.

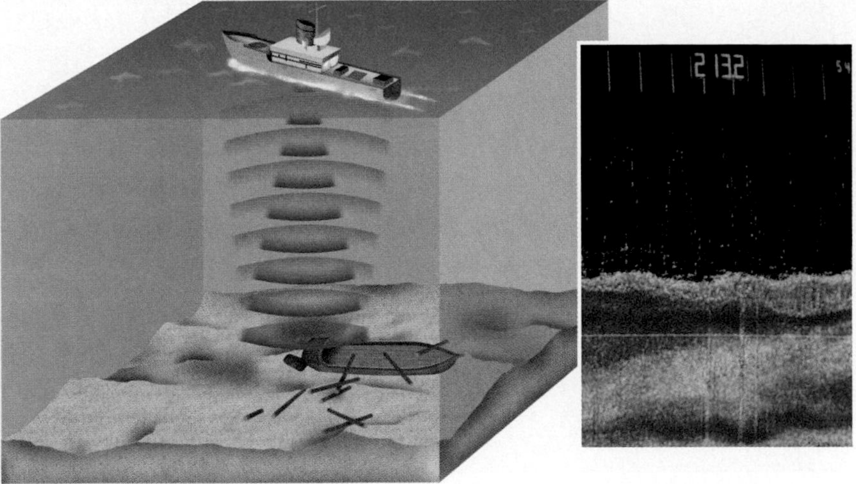

Figure 21 Sonar is used to determine distances and to locate objects under water. ***Applying Concepts*** *What two quantities must be known to calculate how far a sound wave has traveled?*

Sonar

Reflected sound waves have many uses. They can be used to determine the depth of water, to locate a sunken shipwreck or cargo, to find schools of fish, or to locate boats out on the ocean.

Sonar is a system of detecting reflected sound waves. The word *sonar* comes from the initial letters of **so**und **n**avigation **a**nd **r**anging. "Navigation" means finding your way around on the ocean (or in the air), and "ranging" means finding the distance between objects. Submarines and ships use sonar to detect other submarines and ships by sending sound waves through the water close to the surface. When the waves hit another boat near the surface of the water, they reflect back and are picked up by the sonar device.

How Sonar Works A sonar machine, or depth finder, produces a burst of high-frequency ultrasonic sound waves that travels through the water. When the waves hit an object or the ocean floor, they reflect. The reflected waves are detected by the sonar machine. **The sonar device measures the time it takes to detect the reflected sound waves.** It uses the data to calculate the distance that the sound has traveled. The intensity of the reflected waves tells the size and shape of the object that reflected the waves.

Calculating Distances The farther a sound wave travels before bouncing off a barrier, the longer it takes to come back. To calculate the depth of water, the sonar machine must calculate the distance traveled by the sound waves. It measures the time taken for the waves to come back. The sonar device then multiplies the speed of sound in water by the time taken. The total distance traveled by the sound is twice the depth of the water. Because the waves traveled to the bottom and then back, the sonar machine divides the total distance by two to find the actual depth.

☑ *Checkpoint* *What are three uses for sonar?*

Sharpen your Skills

Designing Experiments

ACTIVITY

1. Stand a square piece of cardboard on a table. Prop it up with a book.
2. Put two empty paper towel or aluminum foil tubes on the table. The tubes should be at an angle to each other and almost touching at the end near the cardboard. Leave a gap of about 6 cm between the cardboard and the ends of the tubes.
3. Put your ear near the other end of one of the tubes. Cover one ear with your hand so that the only sounds you hear are coming through the tube.
4. Place a ticking watch in the second tube and cover the open end with your hand. What do you hear?
5. Design an experiment to determine how sound reflects off different materials, such as a variety of fabrics.

Figure 22 Elephants communicate using low-frequency, or infrasonic, sound waves.

Uses of Ultrasound and Infrasound

The dog trainer stands quietly, watching the dog a short distance away. To get the dog's attention, the trainer blows into a small whistle. You don't hear a thing. But the dog stops, cocks an ear, and then comes running toward the trainer. What did the dog hear that you didn't? Dogs can hear ultrasonic frequencies of over 20,000 Hz, well above the upper limit for humans.

Some animals communicate using sounds with frequencies that humans cannot hear. Evidence indicates that elephants communicate with low-frequency, or infrasonic, sound waves—too low for humans to hear. Elephants use infrasound to locate mates and to communicate their location to other members of their group.

Ultrasound in the Ocean Dolphins and whales emit pings of INTEGRATING LIFE SCIENCE sound at frequencies that are high, but not too high for you to hear. **Echolocation** (ek oh loh KAY shun) is the use of sound waves to determine distances or to locate objects. Dolphins and whales use echolocation to find their way in the ocean, and to find their prey.

Figure 23 Dolphins emit high-frequency sounds to communicate with each other, to navigate, and to find food.

It was once thought that fish couldn't hear the high frequencies that dolphins and whales emit. But scientists have discovered that shad, herring, and some other fish can hear sounds as high as 180,000 Hz, nine times as high as the highest frequency you can hear. The fish may use this ability to avoid being eaten by dolphins and whales.

Because sound waves travel so well in water, ultrasound has many uses in the sea. Some fishermen attach ultrasonic beepers to their nets. The ultrasound annoys the dolphins, who then swim away from the nets and do not get caught. Ultrasound technology is also used to measure the thickness of the blubber of Northern right whales as part of a study of their reproductive rate.

Echolocation in Bats Imagine walking around in a totally dark room. You would bump into the walls and furniture quite often. Bats, however, can fly around dark areas and not bump into anything. **Bats use echolocation to navigate and to find food.**

As bats fly, they send out pulses of sound at frequencies of about 100,000 Hz. Then they listen to how long the sound takes to return. By picking up the reflections, or echoes, a bat can tell if it is about to bump into something. Though bats are not blind, they tend to rely more on their hearing than on their vision to "see" where they are going. Echolocation also tells the bat where its prey is. Bats can use echolocation to hunt. Most bats hunt insects, but some hunt small animals such as mice, rats, frogs, or birds.

Figure 24 Bats use echolocation to locate food and to avoid bumping into objects. Their large ears are used for collecting sound waves.

Ultrasound in Medicine Ultrasound allows doctors to get a

INTEGRATING HEALTH

picture, called a **sonogram,** of the inside of the human body. **Doctors use ultrasound to look inside the human body and to diagnose and treat medical conditions.**

To examine a pregnant woman, the doctor holds a small probe on the woman's abdomen. The probe generates very high-frequency sound waves (about 4 million Hz). The ultrasound device detects and measures the ultrasonic waves that bounce back. By analyzing the intensity and frequency of the reflected waves, the device builds up a picture. The sonogram can show the position of the developing baby. Sonograms can also show if more than one baby is to be born. In addition to a still picture, an ultrasound can produce a video of a developing baby in motion.

Because of their high frequency, carefully focused ultrasound waves can also painlessly destroy unwanted tissues. In many cases ultrasound treatment can eliminate the need for surgery.

Figure 25 A doctor examines a pregnant woman with an ultrasound machine. A picture of the developing baby is displayed on a screen.

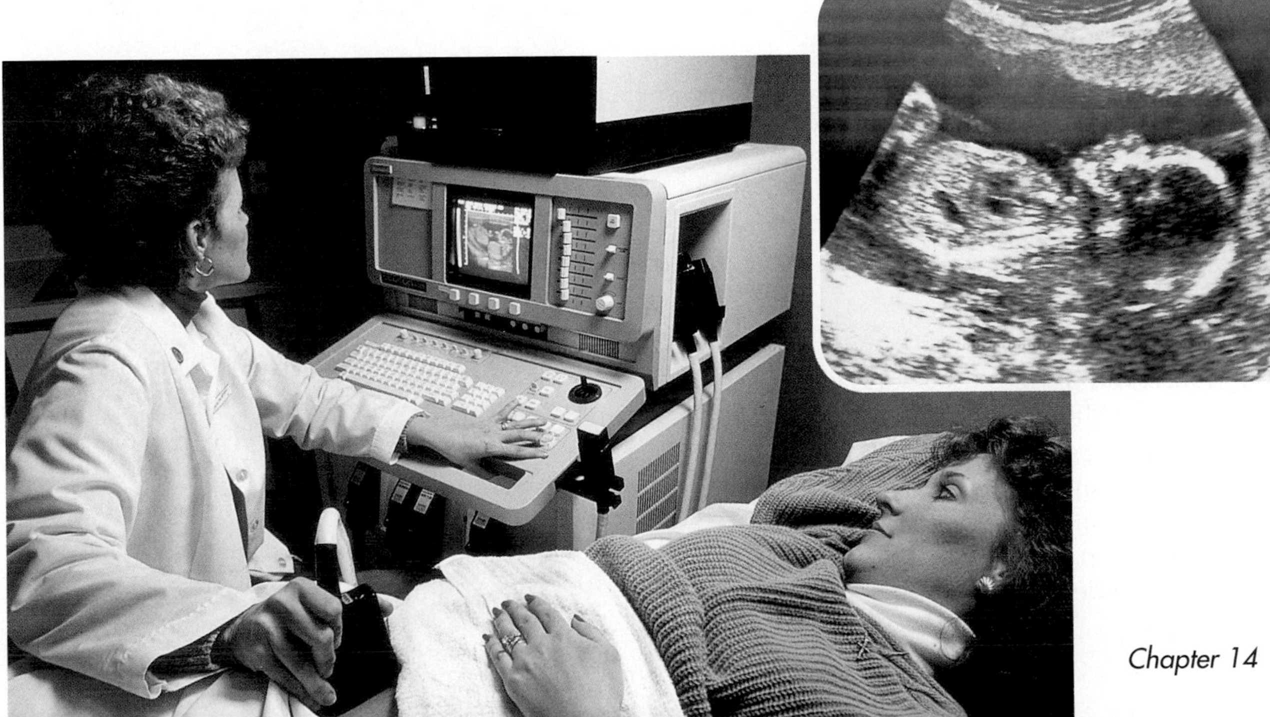

Figure 26 Some examples of common household objects that use ultrasound include an automatic focus camera, an ultrasonic toothbrush, and an ultrasonic jewelry cleaner.

Ultrasound at Home As technology progresses, more and more everyday objects use ultrasonic waves. Imagine cleaning your teeth with sound! If you have used one of the newer electric toothbrushes, you have done just that. The toothbrush sends out high-frequency sound waves that can reach into places that the bristles of the brush cannot.

Ultrasonic jewelry cleaners can clean delicate pieces of jewelry that might be damaged by brushes or harsh detergents. The tub is filled with water and a mild detergent. When the cleaner is switched on, the sound waves move through the water. When they reach the jewelry, the vibrations shake the dirt away, without causing scratches or other damage.

Some cameras use ultrasound to focus automatically. You look through the viewfinder at the object to be photographed. As you push the button to take a picture, the camera sends out ultrasonic waves that reflect off the object and travel back to the camera. The camera measures the time taken for the waves to come back, just like a sonar machine. The camera then calculates the distance to the object and adjusts the lens accordingly.

Section 5 Review

1. What is sonar?
2. How do animals use ultrasound and infrasound?
3. How is ultrasound used in medicine?
4. What household devices use sound waves? What is the function of sound in each device?
5. **Thinking Critically Calculating** The speed of sound in ocean water is about 1,530 m/s. If it takes 3 seconds for a sound to travel from a ship to the bottom of the ocean and back, how deep is the water?

Check Your Progress

CHAPTER PROJECT 14

Test your musical instrument. Is it pleasing to the ear? Can you play a wide range of notes? Can you vary the loudness? Make further adjustments to your instrument. From what you have learned about pitch and frequency, what changes can you make to produce different notes? You may want to try tuning your instrument with a piano or pitch pipe. Try to play a musical scale or a simple song. Or make up your own song.

CHAPTER 14 STUDY GUIDE

The Nature of Sound

Key Ideas

- Sound is a disturbance that travels through a medium as a longitudinal wave.
- The speed of sound depends on the elasticity, density, and temperature of the medium.

Key Terms

larynx elasticity density

Properties of Sound

Key Ideas

- A sound wave of greater intensity sounds louder. Loudness is measured in decibels.
- The pitch of a sound that you hear depends on the frequency of the sound wave.
- As a sound source moves toward the listener, the waves reach the listener with a higher frequency. The pitch appears to increase because of the Doppler effect.

Key Terms

intensity
loudness
decibels (dB)
ultrasound
infrasound
pitch
Doppler effect

Combining Sound Waves

Key Ideas

- The blending of the fundamental tone and the overtones makes up the characteristic sound quality, or timbre, of a particular sound.
- Music is a set of tones that combine in ways that are pleasing to the ear.
- Noise has no pleasing timbre or identifiable pitch.
- Interference occurs when two or more sound waves interact.

Key Terms

timbre
music
noise
dissonance
acoustics
beats

How You Hear Sound

INTEGRATING LIFE SCIENCE

Key Idea

- The outer ear funnels sound waves, the middle ear transmits the sound inward, and the inner ear converts the sound into a form your brain can understand.

Key Terms

ear canal eardrum middle ear cochlea

Applications of Sound

Key Ideas

- A sonar device measures the time it takes to detect reflected sound waves.
- Animals use sound waves to communicate, to navigate, and to find food.

Key Terms

sonar echolocation sonogram

Organizing Information

Concept Map Copy the concept map about sound onto a separate sheet of paper. Then complete it and add a title. (For more on concept maps, see the Skills Handbook.)

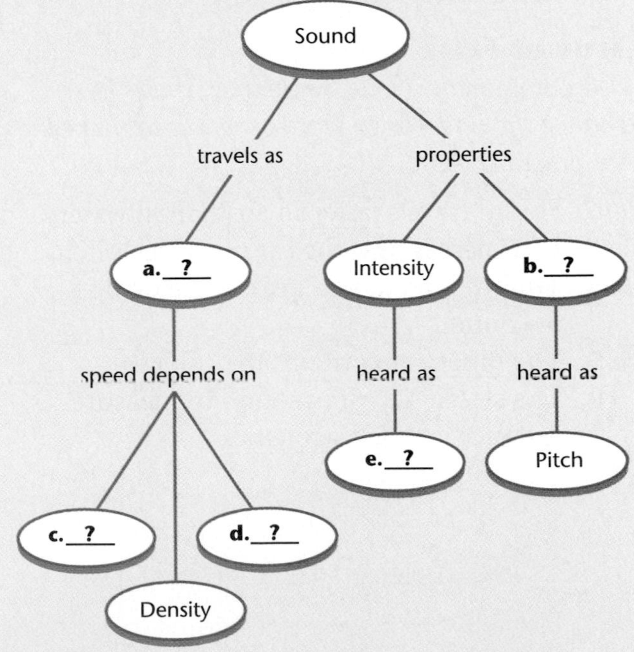

CHAPTER 14 ASSESSMENT

Reviewing Content

Multiple Choice

Choose the letter of the best answer.

1. Sound does *not* travel through
- **a.** water.
- **b.** steel rails.
- **c.** wooden doors.
- **d.** outer space.

2. The Doppler effect causes an apparent change in
- **a.** loudness.
- **b.** intensity.
- **c.** pitch.
- **d.** resonance.

3. Beats result from
- **a.** reflection.
- **b.** refraction.
- **c.** diffraction.
- **d.** interference.

4. The hammer, anvil, and stirrup are in the
- **a.** outer ear.
- **b.** middle ear.
- **c.** inner ear.
- **d.** cochlea.

5. Sonar is used to find
- **a.** time.
- **b.** speed.
- **c.** angle of reflection.
- **d.** distance.

True or False

If the statement is true, write true. If it is false, change the underlined word or words to make the statement true.

6. Sound travels <u>faster</u> in air than in water.

7. Loudness is how the ear perceives <u>pitch</u>.

8. <u>Timbre</u> is what you hear as the quality of sound.

9. The <u>inner</u> ear contains the cochlea.

10. The system of using sound to measure distance is called <u>acoustics</u>.

Checking Concepts

11. When a drum vibrates, the air molecules that begin vibrating next to it do not reach your ear, yet you hear the sound of the drum. Explain.

12. What are the factors that affect the sound of a vibrating guitar string?

13. As a car drives past you, the driver keeps a hand on the horn. Describe what you hear as the car approaches you then passes by.

14. How can loud noises damage your hearing?

15. Why is ultrasound useful in medicine?

16. **Writing to Learn** You have been hired to produce an informational brochure about sound. This brochure will be presented to soon-to-arrive visitors from outer space. They have no concept of sound, and everything they learn will come from your brochure. Write a brief description of sound for the visitors.

Thinking Critically

17. **Comparing and Contrasting** How do sound waves behave like the waves in spring toys? How are they different?

18. **Controlling Variables** If you are measuring the speed of sound, what variable(s) should you try to keep constant?

19. **Calculating** At 0°C, sound travels through air at a speed of 330 m/s. At this speed, how long would it take sound to travel a distance of 1000 m? *(Hint:* Speed = Distance/Time)

20. **Applying Concepts** If one musician plays a note on an instrument and another plays a slightly higher note on a similar instrument, what will you hear?

21. **Inferring** Thunder and lightning happen at the same time. Why do you think you usually see the lightning before you hear the thunder?

Applying Skills

The table below shows the range of frequencies produced and heard by various animals and birds. Use the data to answer Questions 22–23.

Animal	Highest Frequency Heard (Hz)	Highest Frequency Produced (Hz)
Human	20,000	1,100
Dog	50,000	1,800
Cat	65,000	1,500
Bat	120,000	120,000
Porpoise	150,000	120,000
Frog	10,000	8,000

22. Graphing Draw a bar graph to compare the highest frequencies heard by each animal and the highest frequencies produced by each animal.

23. Calculating If the speed of sound in air is 330 m/s, calculate the wavelength of the highest-frequency sound heard by humans. Use the following formula:

$$\text{Wavelength} = \frac{\text{Speed}}{\text{Frequency}}$$

Performance CHAPTER PROJECT 14 Assessment

Project Wrap Up Describe your instrument and explain how it was built. Discuss how you solved any design problems. Using your instrument, demonstrate how you can play different sounds. Show how you change the pitch or loudness of your instrument.

Reflect and Record In your journal write an evaluation of your project. How would you improve on the design of the instrument? How is your instrument like or different from the instruments your classmates built?

Test Preparation

Use these questions to prepare for standardized tests.

Study the chart. Then answer Questions 24–26.

Substance	Speed of Sound (m/s)
Rubber	60
Air at 0°C	330
Air at 25°C	346
Lead	1,210
Water at 25°C	1,498
Silver	2,680
Wood (Oak)	3,850
Glass	4,540
Aluminum	5,000
Iron	5,100
Steel	5,200

24. What information does this table provide?
- **a.** the speed of sound in different states of the same matter
- **b.** the speed of sound over different distances
- **c.** the speed of sound at several different temperatures
- **d.** the speed of sound in different substances

25. In which substance does sound travel most slowly?
- **a.** water
- **b.** air
- **c.** steel
- **d.** rubber

26. Sound travels faster through air at 25°C than it does at 0°C. This shows that sound travels
- **a.** faster at lower temperatures.
- **b.** more slowly at lower temperatures.
- **c.** more slowly at higher temperatures.
- **d.** only at temperatures above 0°C.

CHAPTER 15

The Electromagnetic Spectrum

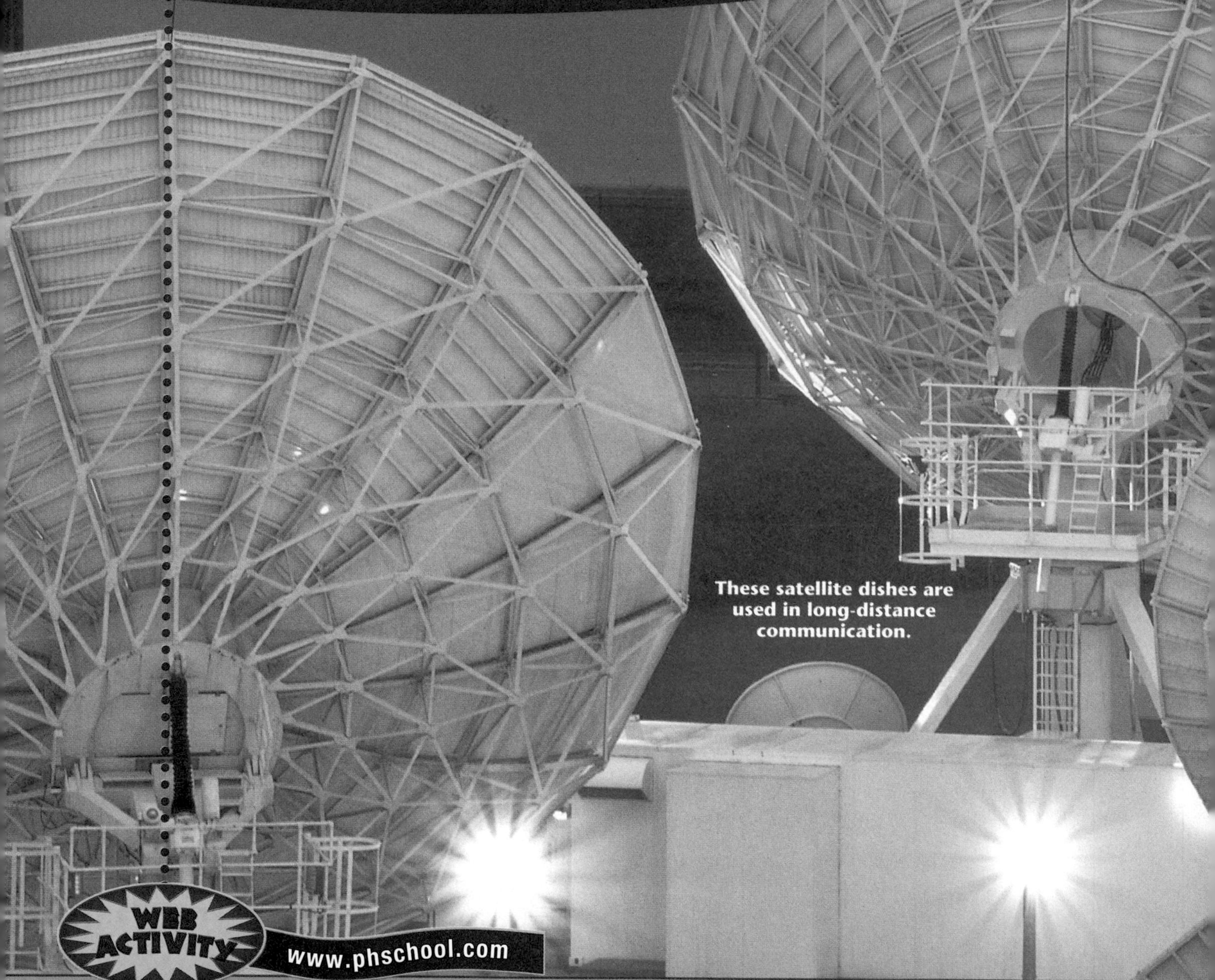

These satellite dishes are used in long-distance communication.

WEB ACTIVITY www.phschool.com

The Nature of Electromagnetic Waves

Discover How Does a Beam of Light Travel?

Try This How Do Light Beams Behave?

Waves of the Electromagnetic Spectrum

Discover What Is White Light?

Try This What Does a Bee See?

Producing Visible Light

Discover How Do Light Bulbs Differ?

Sharpen Your Skills Observing

Real-World Lab Comparing Light Bulbs

PROJECT 15

You're on the Air

Communication technology is developing at a rapid rate. Technology now makes it possible to store and process huge amounts of information. Communication technology will continue to improve as scientific advances are made. Look around you! How do people communicate? Radios, televisions, cellular phones, and electronic pagers are part of everyday life. Wireless communication has made it convenient for people to communicate anytime and anywhere.

In this chapter you will study and research the use of several wireless communication devices.

Your Goal To collect data about when, where, and why people use radios, televisions, cellular telephones, and other kinds of communication devices.

To complete this project you must

- design a survey sheet about the use of communication devices
- distribute your survey sheet to students in your school and to adults in your community
- compile and analyze your data
- create graphs to show your results

Get Started To get started, brainstorm what kinds of questions you will ask. Think about the format and content of your survey sheet. How might you involve students in other classes so you can gather more data?

Check Your Progress You will be working on this project as you study this chapter. To keep your project on track, look for Check Your Progress boxes at the following points.

Section 2 Review, page 494: Design and distribute your survey.

Section 4 Review, page 509: Compile, analyze, and graph your results.

Wrap Up At the end of the chapter (page 515), you will present the results of your survey to the class.

Integrating Technology

SECTION 4 **Wireless Communication**

Discover **How Can Radio Waves Change?**
Try This **Produce Electromagnetic Interference**
Real-World Lab **Build a Crystal Radio**

SECTION 1

The Nature of Electromagnetic Waves

DISCOVER — ACTIVITY

How Does a Beam of Light Travel?

1. Punch a small hole (about 0.5 cm in diameter) in each of four large index cards.
2. Stand each card upright so that the long side of the index card is on the tabletop. Use binder clips or modeling clay to hold the cards upright.
3. Space the cards about 10 cm apart. To make sure the holes in the cards are in a straight line, run a piece of string through the four holes and pull it tight.
4. Place the flashlight in front of the card nearest you. Shut off all the lights, so that the only light you see comes from the flashlight. What do you see on the wall?
5. Move one of the cards sideways about 3 cm and repeat Step 4. Now what do you see on the wall?

Think It Over

Inferring Explain what happened in Step 5. What does this activity tell you about the path of light?

GUIDE FOR READING

- **What is an electromagnetic wave?**
- **What is light?**

Reading Tip **As you read, keep a list of the words that are used to describe the nature of electromagnetic waves.**

Close your eyes for a moment and imagine you are in a shower of rain. Are you getting wet? Do you feel anything? Believe it or not, you are being "showered" all the time. Not by rain but by waves, most of which you cannot feel or hear. As you read this, you are surrounded by radio waves, infrared waves, visible light, ultraviolet waves, and maybe even tiny amounts of X-rays and gamma rays. If you have ever tuned a radio, spoken on a cordless or cellular phone, felt warmth on your skin, turned on a light, or had an X-ray taken, you have experienced electromagnetic waves.

Figure 1 Even though you cannot feel electromagnetic waves, you are being showered by them.

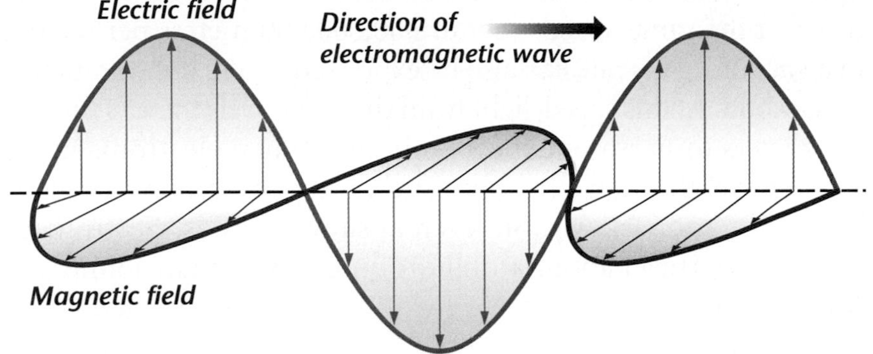

Figure 2 An electromagnetic wave occurs when electric and magnetic fields vibrate at right angles to each other.

Electromagnetic Waves

You have seen waves travel through water and move along ropes and springs. You have also heard sound waves travel through air, metal, and water. All these waves have two things in common—they transfer energy from one place to another, and they require a medium through which to travel.

But a group of waves called electromagnetic waves can transfer energy without a medium. **Electromagnetic waves** are transverse waves that have some electrical properties and some magnetic properties. **An electromagnetic wave consists of changing electric and magnetic fields.**

Electric and Magnetic Fields Electromagnetic waves travel as vibrations in electric and magnetic fields. An electric field is a region in which charged particles can be pushed or pulled. Wherever there is an electric charge, there is an electric field associated with it. A moving electric charge is part of an electric current.

An electric current is surrounded by a magnetic field. A magnetic field is a region in which magnetic forces are present. If you place a paper clip near a magnet, the paper clip moves toward the magnet because of the magnetic field surrounding the magnet.

When the electric field changes, so does the magnetic field. The changing magnetic field causes the electric field to change. When one field vibrates, so does the other. In this way, the two fields constantly cause each other to change. The result is an electromagnetic wave, as shown in Figure 2.

Electromagnetic Radiation The energy that is transferred by electromagnetic waves is called **electromagnetic radiation.** Because electromagnetic radiation does not need a medium, it can travel through the vacuum of outer space. If it could not, light from the sun and stars could not travel through space to Earth. NASA officials could not make contact with space shuttles in orbit.

How Do Light Beams Behave?

ACTIVITY

1. Fill two plastic cups with water. Slowly pour the water from the two cups into a sink. Aim the stream of water from one cup across the path of the water from the other cup.
2. How do the two streams interfere with each other?
3. Now darken a room and project a slide from a slide projector onto the wall. Shine a flashlight beam across the projector beam.
4. How do the two beams of light interfere with each other? What effect does the interference have on the projected picture?

Drawing Conclusions How is the interference between light beams different from that between water streams? Does this activity support a wave model or a particle model of light? Explain.

Speed of Electromagnetic Waves All electromagnetic waves travel at the same speed—about 300,000,000 meters per second in a vacuum. This rate can also be expressed as 300,000 kilometers per second. At this speed, light from the sun travels the 150 million kilometers to Earth in about 8 minutes. When electromagnetic waves travel through a medium such as the atmosphere or glass, they travel more slowly. But even at slower speeds, electromagnetic waves travel about a million times faster than sound can travel in air.

☑ *Checkpoint What is the speed of electromagnetic waves in a vacuum?*

Waves or Particles?

In general, the wave model can explain many of the properties of electromagnetic radiation. However, some properties of electromagnetic radiation do not fit the wave model. **Light has many of the properties of waves. But light can also act as though it is a stream of particles.**

When light passes through a polarizing filter, it has the properties of a wave. An ordinary beam of light has waves that vibrate in all directions. A polarizing filter acts as though it has tiny slits that are either horizontal or vertical. When light enters a polarizing filter, only some waves can pass through. The light that passes through is called **polarized light.**

To help you understand polarization, think of waves of light as being like transverse waves on a rope. They vibrate up and down, left and right, or at any other angle. If you shake a rope through a fence with vertical slats, as shown in Figure 3, only waves that vibrate up and down will pass through. The other waves are blocked. A polarizing filter acts like the slats in a fence. It allows only waves that vibrate in one direction to pass through.

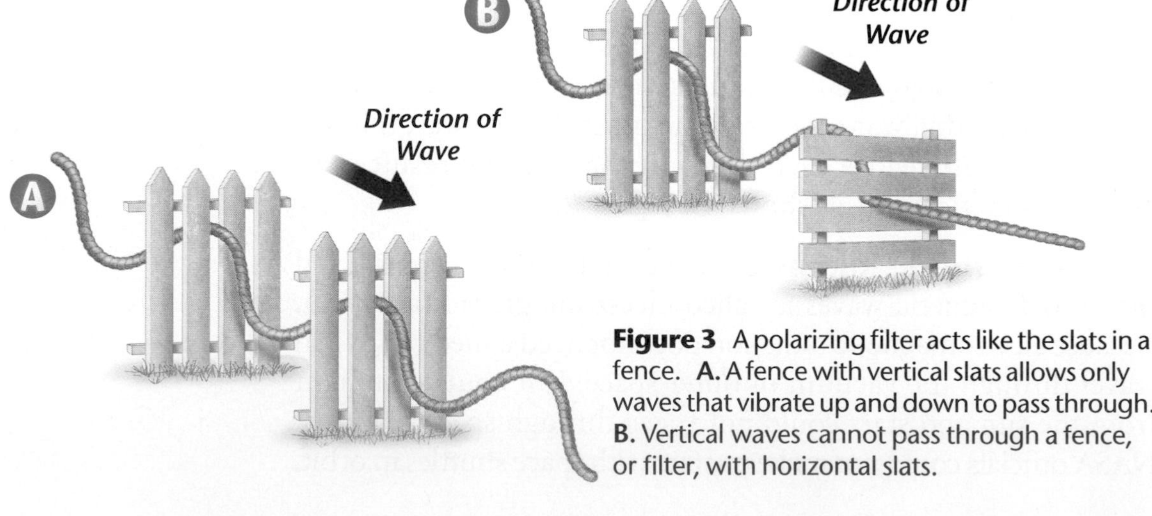

Figure 3 A polarizing filter acts like the slats in a fence. **A.** A fence with vertical slats allows only waves that vibrate up and down to pass through. **B.** Vertical waves cannot pass through a fence, or filter, with horizontal slats.

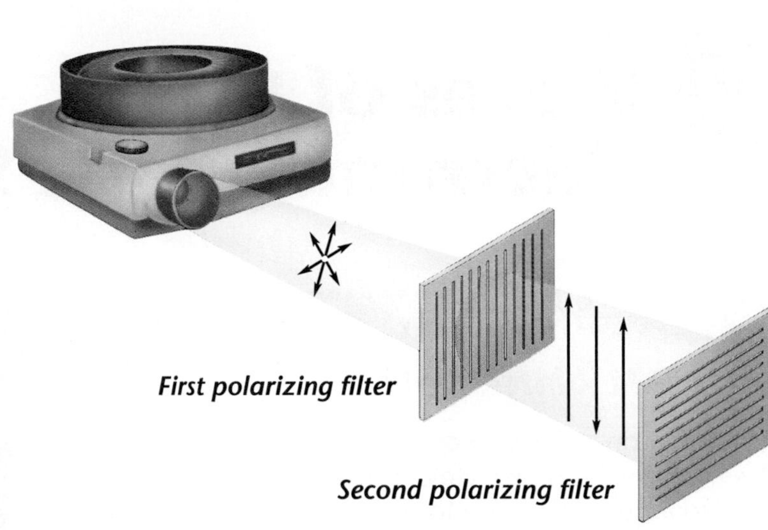

Figure 4 The first polarizing filter allows only waves that vibrate up and down to pass through. When a second polarizing filter is placed in front of the first, and at right angles to it, no light passes through. ***Applying Concepts*** *Does the way that light passes through a polarizing filter support the wave model or the particle model of light?*

If you place one polarizing filter on top of another and rotate one of them, you will see how the amount of light coming through changes. If the two polarizing filters are placed so that one is rotated 90° from the other, no light can come through. All the light is blocked.

Here is an example of how light can act like a stream of particles. When a beam of light shines on some substances, it causes tiny particles called electrons to move. This movement causes an electric current to flow. Sometimes light can even knock electrons out of the substance. This is called the **photoelectric effect.** The photoelectric effect can only be explained by thinking of light as a stream of tiny packets, or particles, of energy. Each packet is called a **photon.** Albert Einstein's explanation of the photoelectric effect in 1905 was important for our understanding of photons as particles of light.

It may be difficult for you to picture light as being particles and waves at the same time. Many scientists find it difficult, too. But both models are necessary to explain all the properties of electromagnetic radiation.

Section 1 Review

1. What do electromagnetic waves consist of?
2. Describe one behavior that shows that light is a set of particles.
3. Describe one behavior that shows that light is a wave.
4. **Thinking Critically Comparing and Contrasting** How are light and sound alike? How are they different?

Science at Home

On the next sunny day, have family members go outside wearing their sunglasses. Compare the sunglasses. Which sunglasses have polarizing lenses? How can you tell? Through the sunglasses, look at surfaces that create glare, such as water or glass. Compare the effects of different pairs of sunglasses. Which kind of sunglasses are best designed to reduce glare on a sunny day? **CAUTION:** *Do not look directly at the sun.*

Waves of the Electromagnetic Spectrum

DISCOVER ACTIVITY

What Is White Light?

1. Line the inside of a cardboard box with white paper. Hold a small triangular prism up to direct sunlight. **CAUTION:** *Do not look directly at the sun.*
2. Rotate the prism until the light coming out of the prism appears on the inside of the box. What colors do you see? What is the order of the colors? Describe how the colors progress from one to the next.

3. Using colored pencils, draw a picture of what you see inside the box.

Think It Over

Forming Operational Definitions The term *spectrum* describes a range. How do you think this term is related to what you just observed?

GUIDE FOR READING

- **How do electromagnetic waves differ from each other?**
- **What are the waves of the electromagnetic spectrum?**

Reading Tip **Before you read, use the headings to make an outline about the different electromagnetic waves. As you read, make notes about each type of wave.**

Can you imagine trying to keep food warm with a flashlight? How about trying to tune in a radio station on your television? Light and radio waves are both electromagnetic. But each has properties that make it useful for some purposes and useless for others. What makes radio waves different from light or ultraviolet rays?

Characteristics of Electromagnetic Waves

All electromagnetic waves travel at the same speed, but they have different wavelengths and different frequencies. Radiation in the wavelengths that your eyes can see is called visible light. Only a small portion of electromagnetic radiation is visible light. The rest of the wavelengths are invisible. Your radio detects wavelengths that are much longer and have a lower frequency than visible light.

Recall how speed, wavelength, and frequency are related:

$$\textit{Speed} = \textit{Wavelength} \times \textit{Frequency}$$

Since the speed of all electromagnetic waves is the same, as the wavelength decreases, the frequency increases. Waves with the longest wavelengths have the lowest frequencies. Waves with the shortest wavelengths have the highest frequencies. The amount of energy carried by an electromagnetic wave increases with frequency. The higher the frequency of a wave, the higher its energy.

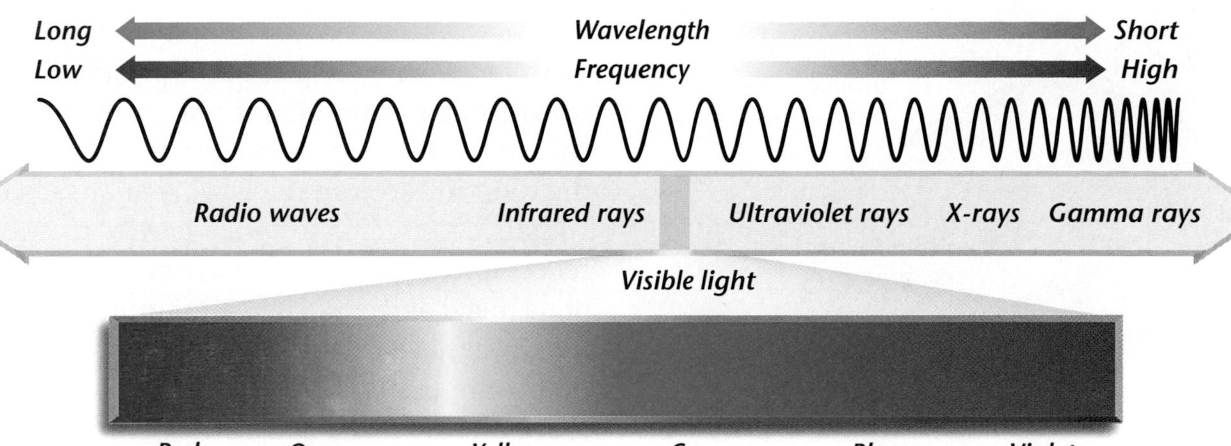

Figure 5 The electromagnetic spectrum shows the different electromagnetic waves in order of increasing frequency and decreasing wavelength. ***Interpreting Diagrams*** *Which electromagnetic waves have the highest frequencies?*

The **electromagnetic spectrum** is the name for the range of electromagnetic waves when they are placed in order of increasing frequency. Figure 5 shows the electromagnetic spectrum. **The electromagnetic spectrum is made up of radio waves, infrared rays, visible light, ultraviolet rays, X-rays, and gamma rays.**

☑ ***Checkpoint*** *How are the frequency and wavelength of electromagnetic waves related?*

Radio Waves

Radio waves are the electromagnetic waves with the longest wavelengths and lowest frequencies. Like all electromagnetic waves, radio waves can travel through a vacuum. Most of the radio waves we receive, though, have traveled through air. Antennas pick up radio waves from the air and send them through wires to your radio. The radio converts the electromagnetic waves into the sound that comes out of the radio speakers.

Each radio station in an area broadcasts at a different frequency. To change the station on your radio, you adjust the tuning dial or press a button. This makes the tuner pick up waves of a different frequency. The numbers on your radio tell you the frequency of the station you are listening to.

Microwaves The radio waves with the shortest wavelengths and the highest frequencies are **microwaves.** One of their most common uses is in microwave ovens. When you switch on a microwave oven, it gives off electromagnetic waves that bounce around inside the oven, penetrating the food. Water molecules in the food absorb the energy from the microwaves, causing the food to get hot.

Social Studies CONNECTION

In 1920, only about 20,000 people using homemade radio sets were receiving radio signals. As an experiment, Frank Conrad of the Westinghouse Company began to broadcast recorded music and sports results. Because public response was so enthusiastic, the company began broadcasting programs on a regular basis. By 1922, there were more than 500 radio stations in the United States.

In Your Journal

Imagine you are the advertising director for an early radio station. Write a letter to a business of your choice telling the owners why they should buy advertising time from your radio station.

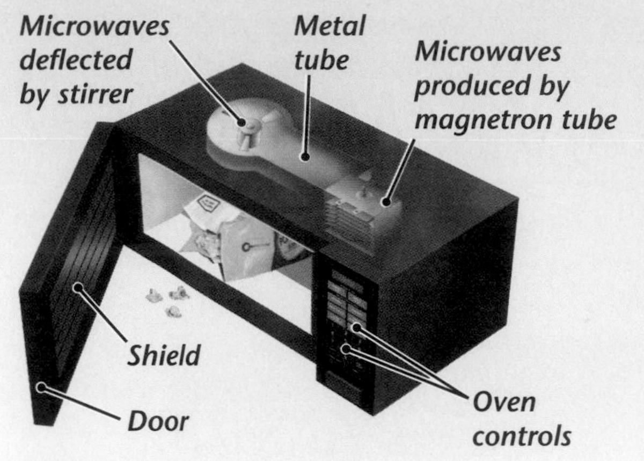

Figure 6 Microwaves produced in a microwave oven are absorbed by water molecules in foods. The energy raises the temperature of the food faster than the heat from an ordinary oven, so the food takes less time to cook.
Applying Concepts *Why are metal containers not suitable for use in a microwave oven?*

Microwaves can pass right through some substances, such as glass and plastic. For this reason, microwaves do not heat glass and plastic containers. If the container gets hot, it is because the food in the container transfers heat to the container. Other substances, such as metals, reflect microwaves. If you have ever accidentally put a metal object, such as aluminum foil, into a microwave oven, you may have seen sparks. The sparks are the result of a buildup of electrical energy in the metal caused by the microwaves. Metal containers and utensils should never be used in microwave ovens.

Microwaves are not easily blocked by structures such as trees, buildings, and mountains. For this reason, microwaves are used to transmit cellular telephone calls. You will read more about cellular phones in Section 4.

Radar Short-wavelength microwaves are used in radar. **Radar,** which stands for **ra**dio **d**etection **a**nd **r**anging, can be used to locate objects. A radar device sends out short pulses of radio waves. These waves are reflected by objects that they strike. A receiver detects the reflected waves and measures the time it takes for them to come back. From the time and the known speed of the waves, the receiver calculates the distance to the object. Radar is used to monitor airplanes landing and taking off at airports, as Figure 7 shows. Radar is also used to locate ships at sea and to track weather systems.

In Chapter 13, you learned how the frequency of a sound wave seems to change when the source of the sound moves toward you or away from you. The Doppler effect occurs with electromagnetic waves too, and has some very useful applications. Police use radio waves and the Doppler effect to find the

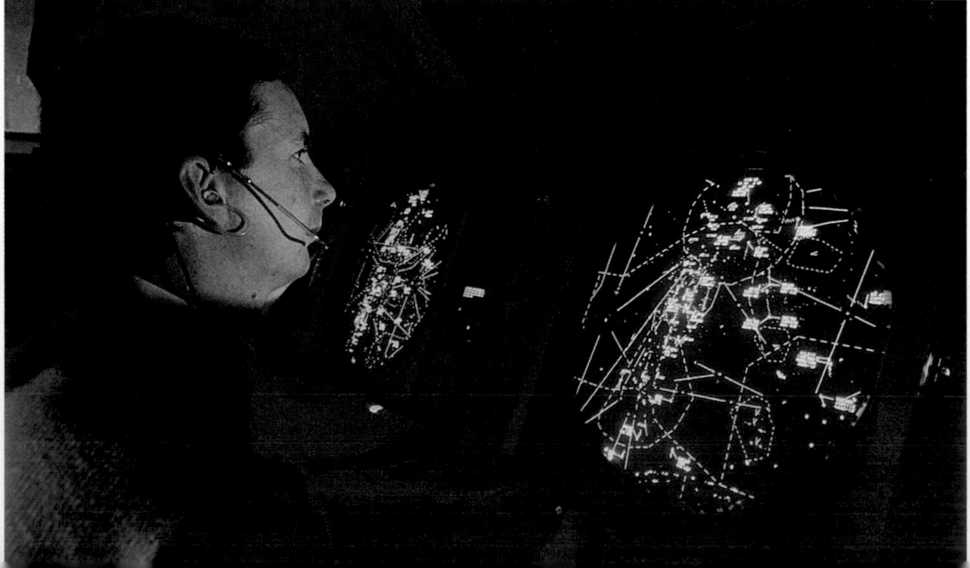

Figure 7 Radar is used to monitor airplanes taking off and landing at airports.

Figure 8 Radio waves and the Doppler effect are used to find the speeds of moving vehicles (left) and of moving balls at sporting events such as tennis matches (right).

speeds of vehicles. A radar gun sends blips of radio waves toward a moving car. The waves are then reflected. Because the car is moving, the frequency at which the reflected blips arrive back at the radar gun is different from the frequency at which the blips were sent out. The radar device uses the difference in frequency to calculate the speed of the car. If the car is going faster than the speed limit, the police often give a speeding ticket.

Radar is also used at some sports events to measure the speed of a moving ball. The radio waves bounce off a moving ball. The speed at which the ball is hit or thrown can then be displayed on a board like the one in Figure 8.

Magnetic Resonance Imaging (MRI) Radio waves are also

INTEGRATING HEALTH

used in medicine to produce pictures of tissues in the human body. This process is called **magnetic resonance imaging,** or MRI. In MRI, a person is placed in a machine that gives out short bursts of radio waves. The radio waves, combined with strong magnetic fields, cause atoms within the body to line up in the same direction. The atoms return to their original directions at different rates. By analyzing the responses, the MRI machine can create pictures of internal organs, including the brain. The pictures show clear images of muscles and other soft tissues that do not show up on X-rays. MRI is particularly useful in detecting brain disorders and disorders of the soft tissue near the spine.

Checkpoint *What are three uses of radio waves?*

Infrared Rays

If you switch on an electric stove, you can feel infrared rays before the element turns red. As the element gets warmer, it gives out energy as heat. This energy is infrared radiation, or infrared rays.

Figure 9 Magnetic resonance imaging (MRI) uses radio waves to create pictures of human tissue. It is used to examine the brain, spinal cord, and other organs.

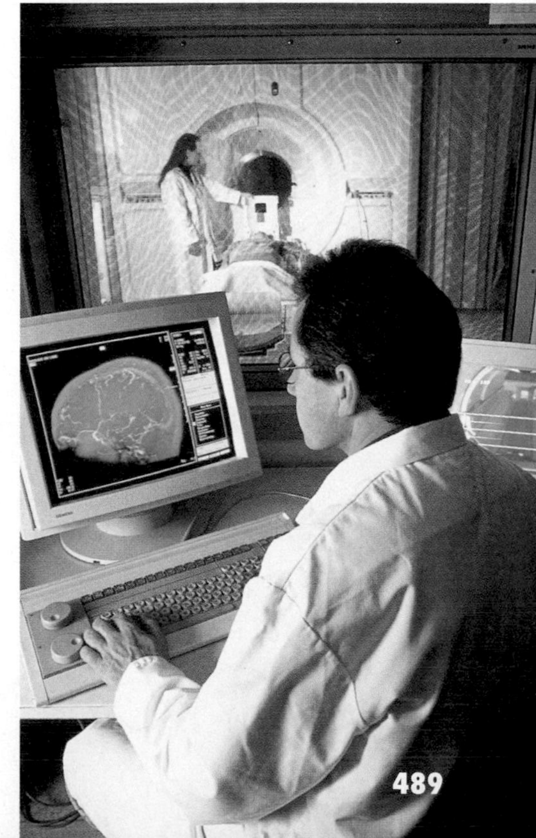

Infrared rays have shorter wavelengths and higher frequencies than radio waves. *Infra-* is a prefix that means "below." So *infrared* means "below red." The next waves in the spectrum are red light.

Infrared rays range in wavelength from a little shorter than radio waves to just longer than visible light. Because you can feel the longest infrared rays as warmth, these rays are often called heat rays. Heat lamps have bulbs that give off more infrared rays and less visible light than regular bulbs. Some people have heat lamps in their bathrooms. You may also have seen heat lamps keeping food warm at cafeteria counters.

Most objects give off some infrared rays. Warmer objects give off infrared waves with more energy and higher frequencies than cooler objects. An infrared camera takes pictures using infrared

the Electromagnetic Spectrum

Electromagnetic waves are all around you—in your home, around your neighborhood and town, at the beach or pool, and in hospitals.

Radio waves, at the long-wavelength, low-frequency end of the electromagnetic spectrum, carry information and entertainment through radio and television.

Microwaves are radio waves with the shortest wavelengths. They are used in microwave ovens and to transmit cellular telephone messages.

Infrared rays provide the energy that makes your morning toast. You can't see the infrared rays, but the toaster element gets hot enough to glow red.

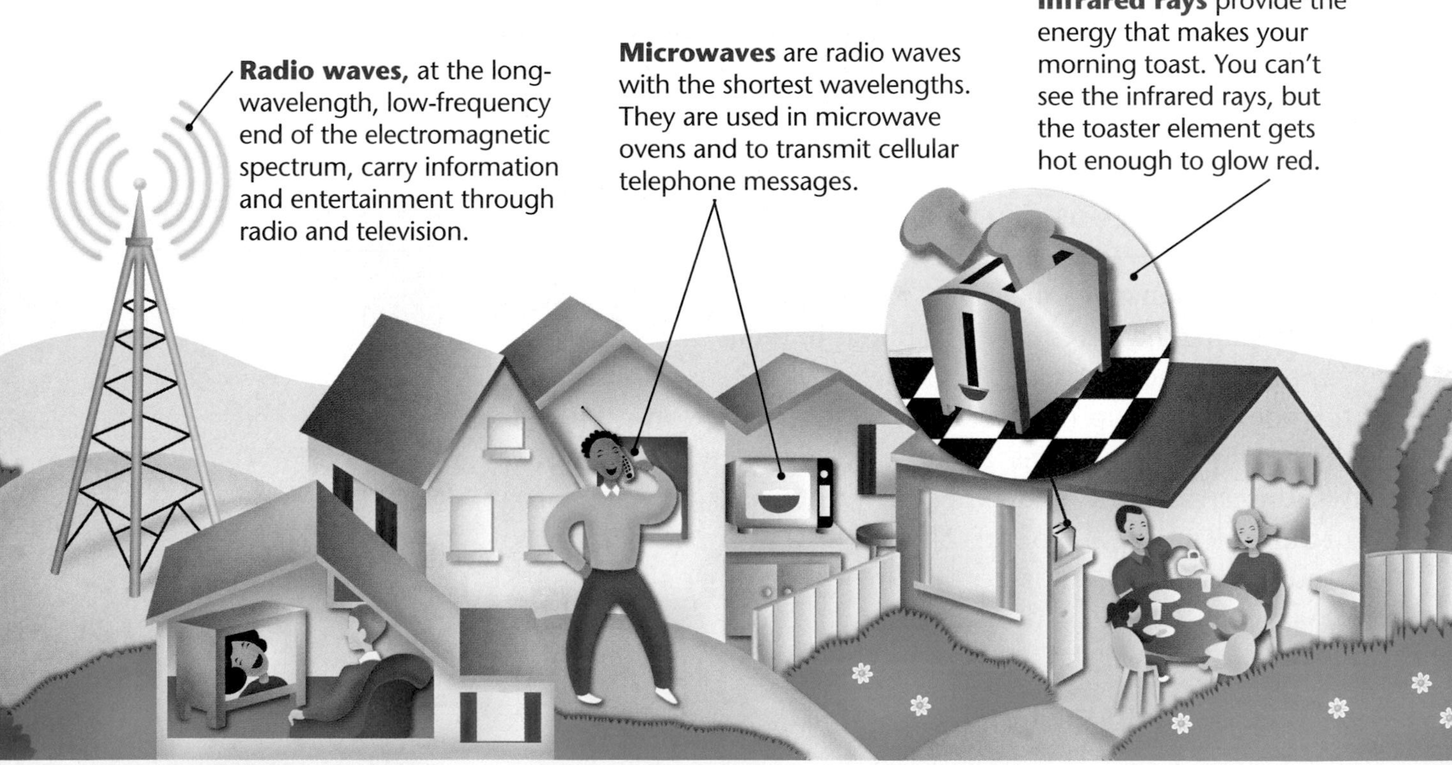

Radio waves
10^3 Hz

Microwaves
10^{10} Hz

Infrared rays
10^{13} Hz

rays instead of light. These pictures are called thermograms. A **thermogram** shows regions of different temperatures in different colors. Figure 10 shows a thermogram of a person. Thermograms identify the warm and cool parts of an object by analyzing infrared rays. Thermograms are especially useful for checking structures, such as houses, for energy leaks.

Even though your eyes cannot see the wavelengths of infrared rays, you can use an infrared camera or binoculars to detect people or animals in the dark. Satellites in space use infrared cameras to study the growth of plants and to observe the motions of clouds to help determine weather patterns.

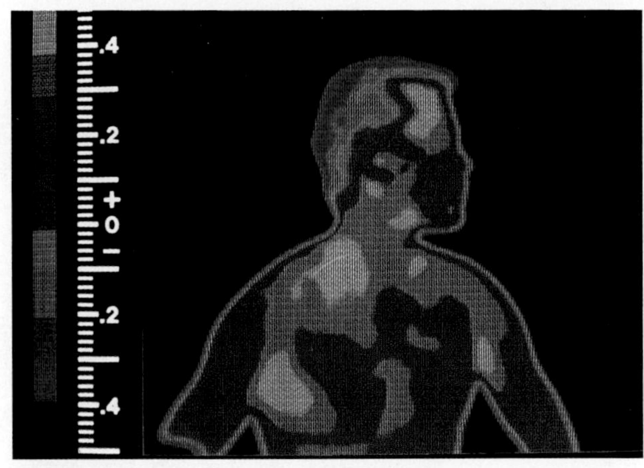

Figure 10 Infrared rays can be used to produce a thermogram. On a thermogram, regions of different temperatures appear in different colors.

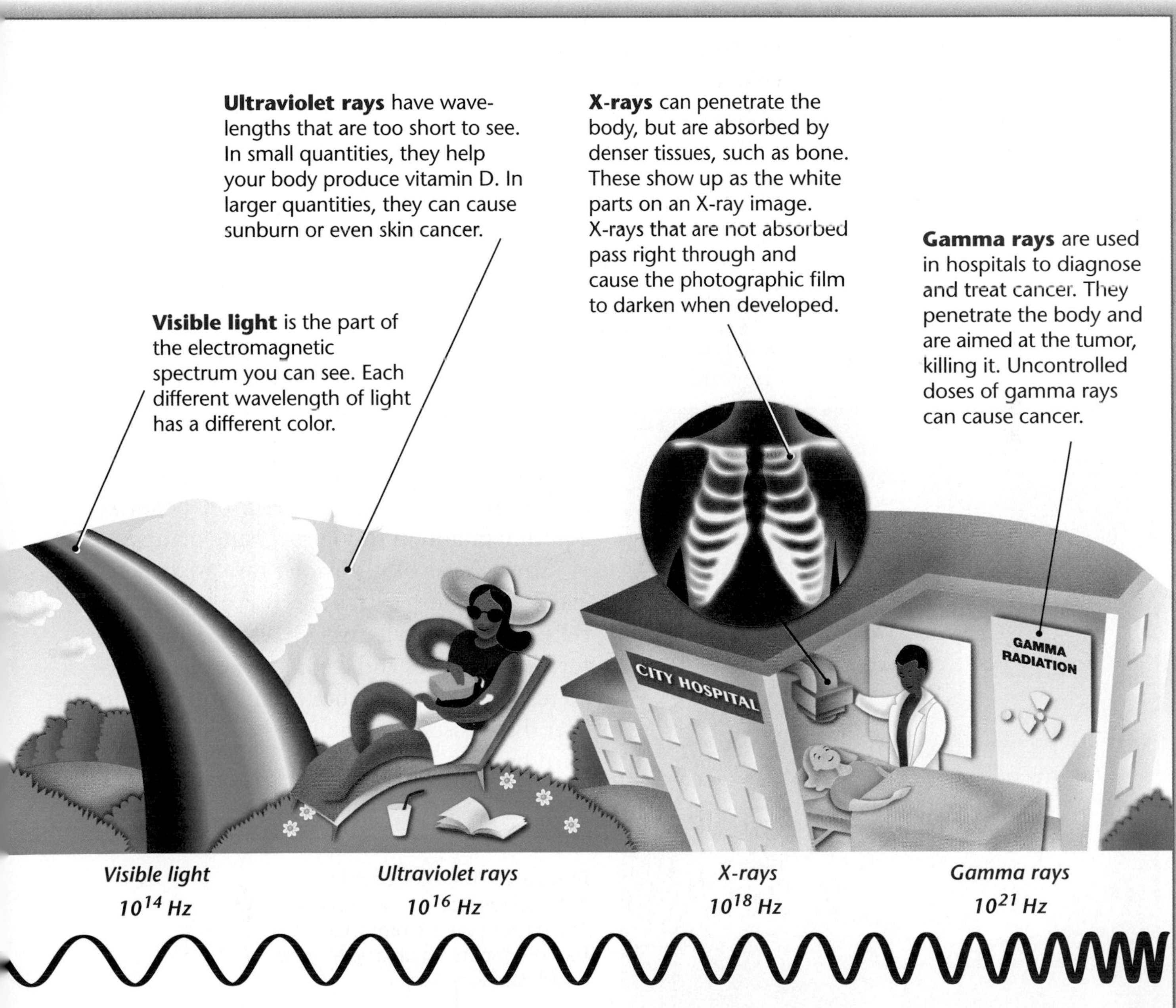

Ultraviolet rays have wavelengths that are too short to see. In small quantities, they help your body produce vitamin D. In larger quantities, they can cause sunburn or even skin cancer.

X-rays can penetrate the body, but are absorbed by denser tissues, such as bone. These show up as the white parts on an X-ray image. X-rays that are not absorbed pass right through and cause the photographic film to darken when developed.

Visible light is the part of the electromagnetic spectrum you can see. Each different wavelength of light has a different color.

Gamma rays are used in hospitals to diagnose and treat cancer. They penetrate the body and are aimed at the tumor, killing it. Uncontrolled doses of gamma rays can cause cancer.

CITY HOSPITAL

GAMMA RADIATION

Visible light	*Ultraviolet rays*	*X-rays*	*Gamma rays*
10^{14} Hz	*10^{16} Hz*	*10^{18} Hz*	*10^{21} Hz*

Visible Light

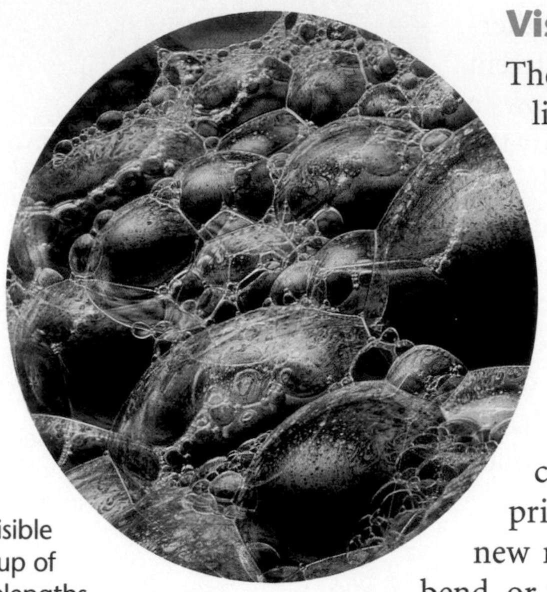

The electromagnetic waves that you can see are light. They make up only a small part of the electromagnetic spectrum. **Visible light** has shorter wavelengths and higher frequencies than infrared waves. The longest wavelengths of visible light are red. As the wavelengths decrease and the frequencies increase, you can see other colors of light. The shortest wavelengths are purple, or violet.

Have you ever seen a rainbow in the sky, colors on a bubble, or light passing through a prism? Recall what happens when waves enter a new medium, such as water or glass. The waves bend, or refract. Different wavelengths of light refract by different amounts, so the waves separate into the various colors. The colors in the visible spectrum are red, orange, yellow, green, blue, and violet, in order of increasing frequencies. Most visible light is made up of a mixture of these colors.

Figure 11 Visible light is made up of different wavelengths. Each wavelength has its own color. When light bounces off a bubble, interference removes some of the colors of visible light and leaves others for us to see.

☑ ***Checkpoint*** *What colors make up the visible spectrum?*

Ultraviolet Rays

Electromagnetic waves with wavelengths just shorter than those of visible light are called **ultraviolet rays,** or UV. *Ultra-* is a Latin prefix that means "beyond." So *ultraviolet* means "beyond violet." UV waves have higher frequencies than visible light, so they carry more energy. Because the energy of ultraviolet rays is great enough to damage or kill living cells, ultraviolet lamps are often used to kill bacteria on hospital equipment and in food processing plants.

Small doses of ultraviolet rays are beneficial to humans. Ultraviolet rays cause skin cells to produce vitamin D, which is needed for healthy bones and teeth. Ultraviolet lamps are used to treat jaundice, a condition of the liver that causes yellowing of the skin, in newborn babies.

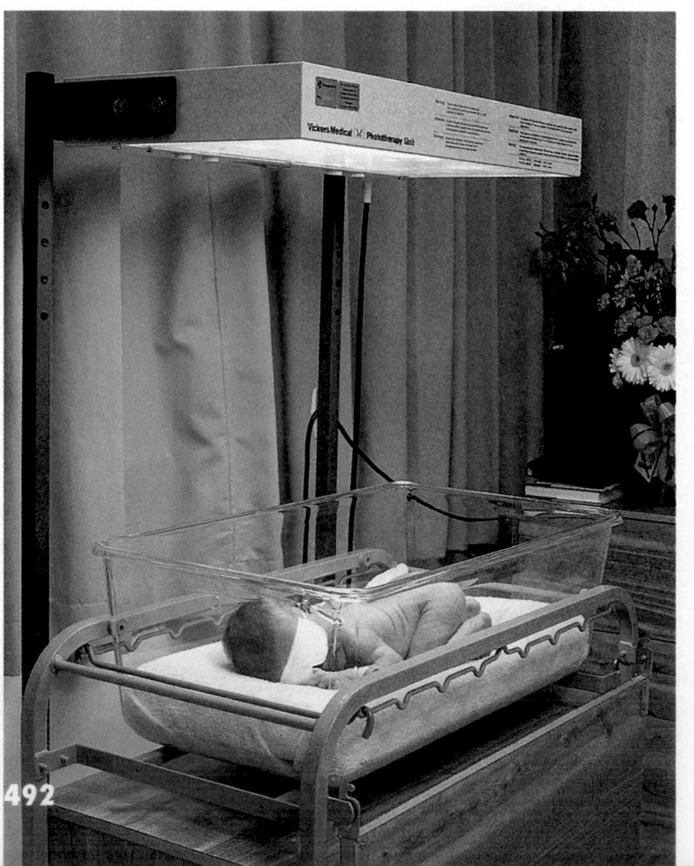

Figure 12 Ultraviolet light is used to treat jaundice in newborn babies. The baby's eyes are protected because too much ultraviolet light could damage them.

The ultraviolet rays present in sunlight can burn your skin. Too much exposure can cause skin cancer and damage your eyes. If you apply sunblock lotion and wear sunglasses, you can limit the damage to your body caused by UV rays.

INTEGRATING LIFE SCIENCE Although ultraviolet light is invisible to humans, many insects can see it. For example, bees have good color vision, but they do not see the same range of wavelengths that humans do. Bees see less of the lower frequency red waves and more of the higher frequency ultraviolet waves. Flowers that appear to be one color to a human appear very different to a honeybee. To the bee, the part of a flower that contains nectar looks different from the rest of the flower. The bee can head straight for the nectar!

What Does a Bee See?

ACTIVITY

Load a roll of UV-sensitive film into a camera. Take photos of a variety of flowers. Include white flowers and flowers that you see bees near. Have the film developed and look at the prints.

Observing What can bees see that you cannot? How is this useful to the bees?

X-Rays

X-rays are electromagnetic waves with very short wavelengths. Their frequencies are just a little higher than ultraviolet rays. Because of their high frequencies, X-rays carry more energy than ultraviolet rays and can penetrate most matter. Dense matter, such as bone or lead, absorbs X-rays and does not allow them to pass through. For this reason, X-rays are used to make images of bones inside the body. X-rays pass right through skin and soft tissues, causing the photographic film in the X-ray machine to darken when it is developed. The bones, which absorb X-rays, appear as the lighter areas on the film, as shown in Figure 13.

Too much exposure to X-rays can cause cancer. If you've ever had a dental X-ray, you'll remember how the dentist gave you a lead apron to wear during the procedure. The lead absorbs X-rays and prevents them from reaching your body.

X-rays are sometimes used in industry and engineering. For example, to find out if a steel or concrete structure has tiny cracks, engineers can take an X-ray image of the structure. X-rays will pass through tiny cracks that are invisible to the human eye. Dark areas on the X-ray film show the cracks. This technology is often used to check the quality of joints in oil and gas pipelines.

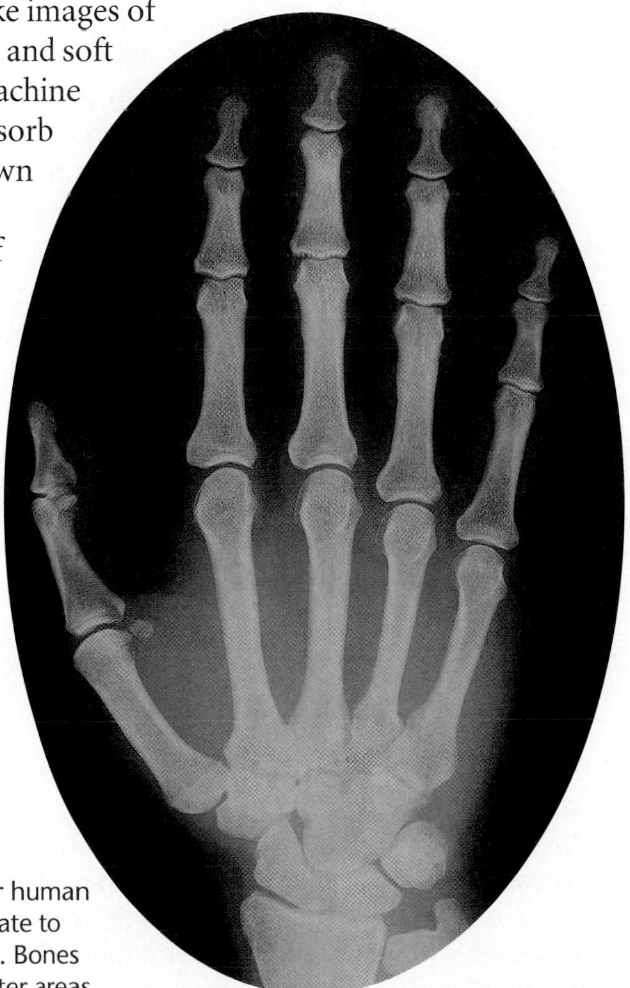

Figure 13 X-rays pass through softer human tissues and cause the photographic plate to darken behind them when developed. Bones absorb X-rays so they show up as lighter areas.

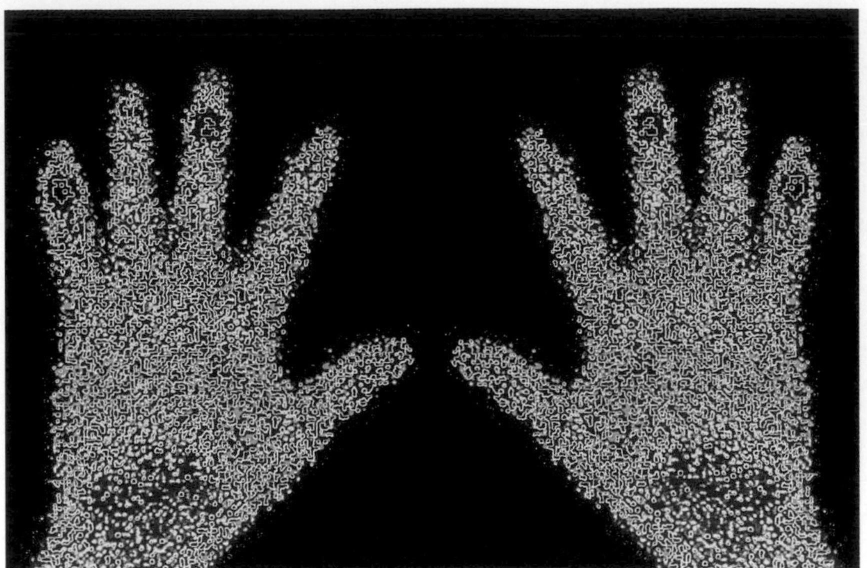

Figure 14 Doctors can inject radioactive liquids into the body and use gamma-ray detectors to trace them. The detectors build images that doctors can use to examine the inside of the body.

Gamma Rays

Gamma rays have the shortest wavelengths and highest frequencies of the electromagnetic spectrum. Because they have the greatest amount of energy, they are the most penetrating of all the electromagnetic waves.

Some radioactive substances and certain nuclear reactions produce gamma rays. Because of their great penetrating ability, gamma rays can cause serious illness. However, when used in controlled conditions, gamma rays have some medical uses. For example, gamma rays can be used to kill cancer cells in radiation therapy. Gamma rays can also be used to examine the body's internal structures. A patient can be injected with a fluid that emits gamma-rays. Then a gamma-ray detector can form an image of the inside of the body.

INTEGRATING SPACE SCIENCE Some objects far out in space give off bursts of gamma rays. The gamma rays travel for billions of years before they reach Earth. Earth's atmosphere blocks these gamma rays, so gamma-ray telescopes that detect them must orbit above Earth's atmosphere. Astronomers think that collisions of dying stars in distant galaxies are one way of producing these gamma rays. Gamma-ray telescopes have also been used to detect the stronger gamma rays given off in the atmosphere as a result of nuclear weapons tests on Earth.

Section 2 Review

1. How are all electromagnetic waves alike? How are they different?
2. List in order of increasing frequency the kinds of waves that make up the electromagnetic spectrum. Name one use for each.
3. Explain how radio waves are used to find the speed of a moving object.
4. How are X-rays useful? How are they dangerous?
5. **Thinking Critically Applying Concepts** As the wavelength of electromagnetic waves decreases, what happens to the frequency? To the energy?

Check Your Progress

CHAPTER PROJECT 15

Write the questions for your survey. Some categories you might want to include are types of communication devices, how often they are used, when and where they are used, and the purposes for which they are used. Do people use these devices for personal reasons or for business? (*Hint:* To make your survey easy to complete, ask questions that require short answers.) Give the survey sheet to your classmates and other students in the school for their families and neighbors to complete.

SCIENCE AND SOCIETY

Food Irradiation

Food sometimes travels a long way to reach your plate. Potatoes from Maine and strawberries from Florida or Mexico must stay fresh until you eat them. But every so often, food makes people ill. Millions of Americans get sick every year from contaminated or spoiled food.

One way to prevent such illness is to treat food by irradiation. In the most common method, gamma rays are sent through fresh or frozen food. The radiation slows decay and kills organisms that could make people sick. It makes food safer to eat and also helps the food stay fresh longer. Five minutes of irradiation will allow strawberries to stay fresh for an extra nine or ten days.

Some people worry about the possible dangers of eating irradiated food. More than 40 countries, including the United States, permit food irradiation. Others forbid it. Is food irradiation safe?

The Issues

Does Irradiation Destroy Nutrients in Food? Radiation kills living cells. But it can also make chemical changes in the food itself. It may destroy useful nutrients, such as vitamins A, B-1, E, and K. Up to ten percent of these vitamins can be lost when food is irradiated. Of course, other methods of protecting and preserving food—such as refrigeration or canning fruits and vegetables—also lead to small losses in nutrition. Even cooking food makes it lose some vitamins.

Does Irradiation Change the Food Itself? Irradiating food doesn't make the food radioactive. But irradiation may change the molecular structure of some foods, creating chemicals such as benzene and formaldehyde. In small doses, these substances have little effect. But large amounts can be harmful to people. Supporters say that these same substances are found naturally in food. Some critics say irradiation should not be used until there is further research. Researchers want to determine whether people who eat irradiated food for a long time are more likely to develop cancer or other diseases. Other experts say that the short-term research already done shows that irradiation is safe. Some alternatives to irradiation, such as spraying with pesticides, are clearly more harmful.

Will Irradiating Food Make People Less Careful About Handling Food? In the United States, all irradiated food must be labeled. But if people are not careful about washing their hands before preparing food, irradiated food can still become contaminated. Also, the amounts of radiation allowed won't kill all harmful organisms. It's still necessary to cook food properly before eating it, especially meat and eggs. Some food experts worry that irradiation will make people feel falsely safe and become careless about preparing food.

You Decide

1. Identify the Problem

In your own words, explain the problem of food irradiation.

2. Analyze the Options

List reasons for and against: (a) requiring all food to be irradiated; (b) permitting, but not requiring, food irradiation; and (c) banning food irradiation.

3. Find a Solution

You see two containers of a food at the supermarket. One is irradiated; one is not. The price is the same. Which would you buy? Explain why.

Producing Visible Light

DISCOVER

How Do Light Bulbs Differ?

1. Your teacher will give you one incandescent and one fluorescent light bulb.
2. Examine each bulb closely. What is the shape and size of each? Describe the differences between the bulbs. Draw each type of bulb and record your observations.
3. How do you think each bulb produces light?

Think It Over

Posing Questions Make a list of five questions you could ask to help you understand how each bulb works.

GUIDE FOR READING

- **What are the different types of light bulbs?**
- **What colors of light are produced by an incandescent bulb?**

Reading Tip **As you read, compare and contrast the different ways in which light can be produced.**

Look around the room. Most of the objects you see are visible because they reflect light. If no light source were present, you could not see the objects. An object that can be seen because it reflects light is an **illuminated** object. Light illuminates the page you are reading and your desk. An object that gives off its own light is a **luminous** object. A light bulb, a burning match, and the sun are examples of luminous objects.

There are many different types of lighting. **Common types of lighting include incandescent, fluorescent, neon, sodium vapor, and tungsten-halogen light bulbs.** Some light bulbs produce a continuous spectrum of wavelengths. Others produce only a few wavelengths of light. You can use an instrument called a **spectroscope** to view the different colors of light produced by each type of bulb.

Incandescent Lights

Have you heard the phrase "red hot"? When some objects get hot enough, they glow, giving off a faint red light. If they get even hotter, the glow turns into white light. The objects are said to be "white hot." **Incandescent lights** (in kun DES unt) glow when a filament inside them gets hot.

Look closely at a clear, unlit incandescent bulb. You'll notice that inside is a thin wire coil called a filament. It is made of a metal called tungsten. When an electric current passes through this filament, it heats up. When the filament gets hot enough, it gives off red light, which has low frequencies. As it gets hotter, the filament begins to give off light waves with higher

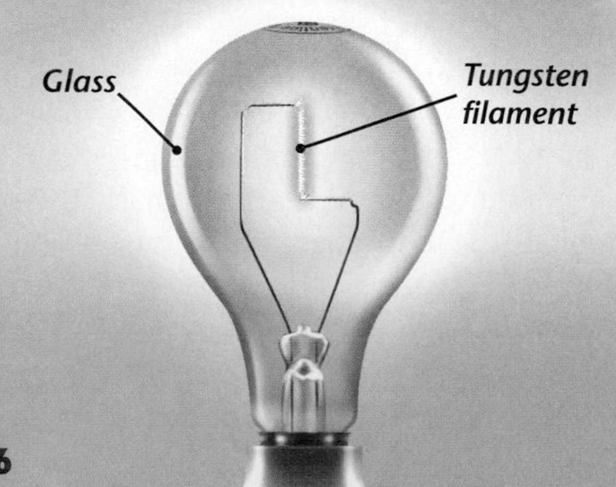

Figure 15 An incandescent light bulb glows when electricity passes through the tungsten filament. ***Inferring*** *Why do incandescent bulbs get so hot?*

frequencies. Once the filament gets hot enough to give off enough violet light, all the frequencies of light combine to produce white light. **Incandescent lights give off all the colors of visible light: red, orange, yellow, green, blue, and violet.**

The American inventor Thomas Edison is credited with developing a long-lasting incandescent light bulb in 1879. Edison knew that if he passed an electric current through a wire, it would get hot and glow. By experimenting with different types of filaments, Edison developed a light bulb that would glow for a long time.

Incandescent bulbs are not very efficient in giving off light. Less than ten percent of the energy is actually given out as light. Most of the energy produced by an incandescent bulb is given off as infrared rays. Incandescent bulbs can get quite hot when they have been left on for a while.

Observing ACTIVITY

Use a spectroscope to observe light from different sources. **CAUTION:** *Do not look at the sun with the spectroscope.*

1. Look through the spectroscope at an incandescent light. Using colored pencils, draw and label the band of colors as they appear in the spectroscope.
2. Now, look at a fluorescent light through the spectroscope. Again, draw and label what you see.

How are the two bands of color the same? How are they different? Can you explain the differences?

Fluorescent Lights

Have you ever noticed the long, narrow light bulbs in stores and offices? They are **fluorescent lights** (floo RES uhnt). Maybe you have some in your school. Each glass tube contains a gas and is coated on the inside with a powder.

When an electric current passes through a fluorescent bulb, it causes the gas to emit ultraviolet waves. When the ultraviolet waves hit the powder coating inside the tube, the coating emits visible light. This process is called fluorescing.

Unlike incandescent lights, fluorescent lights give off most of their energy as light. They usually last longer than incandescent bulbs and use less electricity for the same brightness, which makes them less expensive to run.

☑ *Checkpoint* *Why are fluorescent bulbs more economical than incandescent bulbs?*

Figure 16 Fluorescent lights are commonly used in offices, stores, and schools. They are efficient and inexpensive.

Figure 17 Neon lights are used in advertising signs and decoration. ***Applying Concepts*** *Why are neon lights so colorful?*

Neon Lights

Some gases can be made to produce light by passing an electric current through them. For example, a **neon light** consists of a sealed glass tube filled with neon. When an electric current passes through the neon, particles of the gas absorb energy. However, the gas particles cannot hold the energy for very long. The energy is released in the form of light. This process is called electric discharge through gases.

Pure neon gives out red light. Often, what is called a neon light has a different gas, or a mixture of gases, in the tube. Different gases produce different colors of light. For example, both argon gas and mercury vapor produce greenish blue light. Helium gives a pale pink light. Krypton gives a pale violet light. Sometimes the gases are put into colored glass tubes to produce other colors. Neon lights are commonly used for bright, flashy signs.

Sodium Vapor Lights

Sodium vapor lights contain a small amount of solid sodium as well as some neon and argon gas. When the neon and argon gas are heated, they begin to glow. This glow heats up the sodium, causing it to change from a solid into a gas. The particles of sodium vapor give off energy in the form of yellow light.

Sodium vapor lights are commonly used for street lighting. They require very little electricity to give off a great deal of light, so they are quite economical.

Figure 18 Sodium vapor light bulbs give off a yellow light. They are commonly used to illuminate streets and parking lots.

Tungsten-Halogen Lights

Tungsten-halogen lights work partly like incandescent bulbs. They have tungsten filaments and contain a gas. The gas is one of a group of gases called the halogens. When electricity passes through the filament, the filament gets hot and glows. The halogen makes the filament give off a bright white light.

Tungsten-halogen lights have become very popular because they provide bright light from small bulbs, but use relatively little electricity for the amount of light they give off. They are used in overhead projectors and also in floor lamps. Because halogen bulbs become very hot, they must be kept away from flammable materials, such as paper and curtains.

Figure 19 Tungsten-halogen light bulbs contain a tungsten filament and a halogen gas. Even small bulbs can produce very bright light.

Bioluminescence

INTEGRATING LIFE SCIENCE

Have you ever seen a firefly? On a warm summer evening, they flash their lights in patterns to attract mates. Fireflies are examples of organisms that produce their own light in a process called bioluminescence. **Bioluminescence** (by oh loo muh NES uns) occurs as a result of a chemical reaction among proteins and oxygen in an organism. The reaction produces energy that is given off in the form of light. Unlike a light bulb, which gives off most of its energy as infrared rays, the reaction that produces bioluminescence gives off almost all of its energy as light.

There are also bioluminescent organisms in the oceans. Some types of jellyfish give off light when they are disturbed. Deep in the ocean, where sunlight cannot reach, bioluminescence is the only source of light. Some deep-sea fish use bioluminescence to search for food or to attract mates.

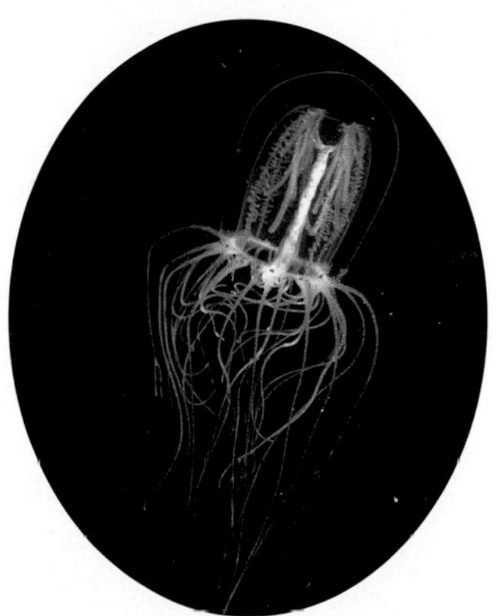

Figure 20 This jellyfish produces its own light by bioluminescence.

Section 3 Review

1. What are five common types of lighting?
2. How does an incandescent light bulb work?
3. Compare luminous objects with illuminated objects. Give two examples of each.
4. Why are fluorescent lights commonly used in businesses and schools?
5. **Thinking Critically Making Judgments** Make a list of the different rooms in your home. Which type of light do you think is best for each room? Give reasons for each choice.

Science at Home

Invite family members to visit a hardware store that sells light bulbs. Ask the salesperson to describe the different kinds of bulbs available. Read the information about each bulb on the side panel of each package. Ask the salesperson to explain any terms you don't understand. Look for the cost and expected life of the bulbs, too. How does this information help you and your family purchase the most economical bulbs?

Real-World Lab

You, the Consumer

Comparing Light Bulbs

In this lab, you will design an experiment to compare the illumination provided by different light bulbs.

Problem

Which light bulb provides the best illumination?

Skills Focus

designing experiments, controlling variables, measuring, drawing conclusions

Materials

a variety of incandescent light bulbs that can fit in the same lamp or socket
medium-sized cardboard box
light socket or lamp (without shade)
meter stick
wax paper
scissors
plain paper

Procedure

1. Following the instructions below, construct your own light box. The box allows you to test the illumination that is provided by each light bulb.
2. Make a data table like the one shown at the right to record your data.
3. With a partner, examine the different bulbs. What is the power (watts), light output (lumens), and life (hours) for each bulb? Predict which light bulb will be the brightest. Explain your choice.
4. How will you test your prediction?
   - What kinds of incandescent light bulbs will you use?
   - What variables will you keep constant? What variables will you change?
5. Review your plan. Will your procedure help you find an answer to the problem?

How to Build and Use a Light Box

A. Use a medium-sized cardboard box, such as the kind of box copy paper comes in. If the box has flaps, cut them off.

B. Carefully cut a viewing hole (about 2 cm × 4 cm) in the bottom of the box. This will be on top when the box is used. This is hole A.

C. Punch another hole (about 1 cm × 1 cm) on one side of the box. This is hole B. It will allow light from the bulb to enter the box.

D. To decrease the amount of light that can enter, cover hole B with two layers of wax paper.

E. Put one of your light bulbs in the lamp and place it to the side of the box, about 1 m from hole B.

F. Have your partner write a secret letter on a piece of plain paper. Put the paper on the table. Place the light box over the paper with the viewing hole facing up.

G. Now look through hole A.

H. Turn the lamp on and move the light toward the box until you can read the secret letter. Measure the distance between the light bulb and hole B.

Bulb #	Brand Name	Power (watts)	Light Output (lumens)	Life (hrs)	Cost ($)	Distance from Bulb to Light Box (cm)

DATA TABLE

6. Ask your teacher to check your procedure.
7. Before you repeat the steps for a second light bulb, look back at your procedure. How could you improve the accuracy of your results?
8. Test the illumination of the rest of your light bulbs.

Analyze and Conclude

1. How does the distance between the bulb and hole B affect how easily you can read the secret letter?
2. Based on your observations, what can you infer about the illumination provided by each bulb? Which bulb gave the most illumination?
3. How did your results compare with your prediction? What did you learn that you did not know when you made your prediction?
4. What factors affect the illumination given by a light bulb?
5. **Apply** Based on your results, do you think that the most expensive bulb is the best?

More to Explore

Modify your light box and repeat the activity. What different materials would you use? Would you make the light box smaller or larger than the original? How do different light boxes compare in testing illumination by light bulbs?

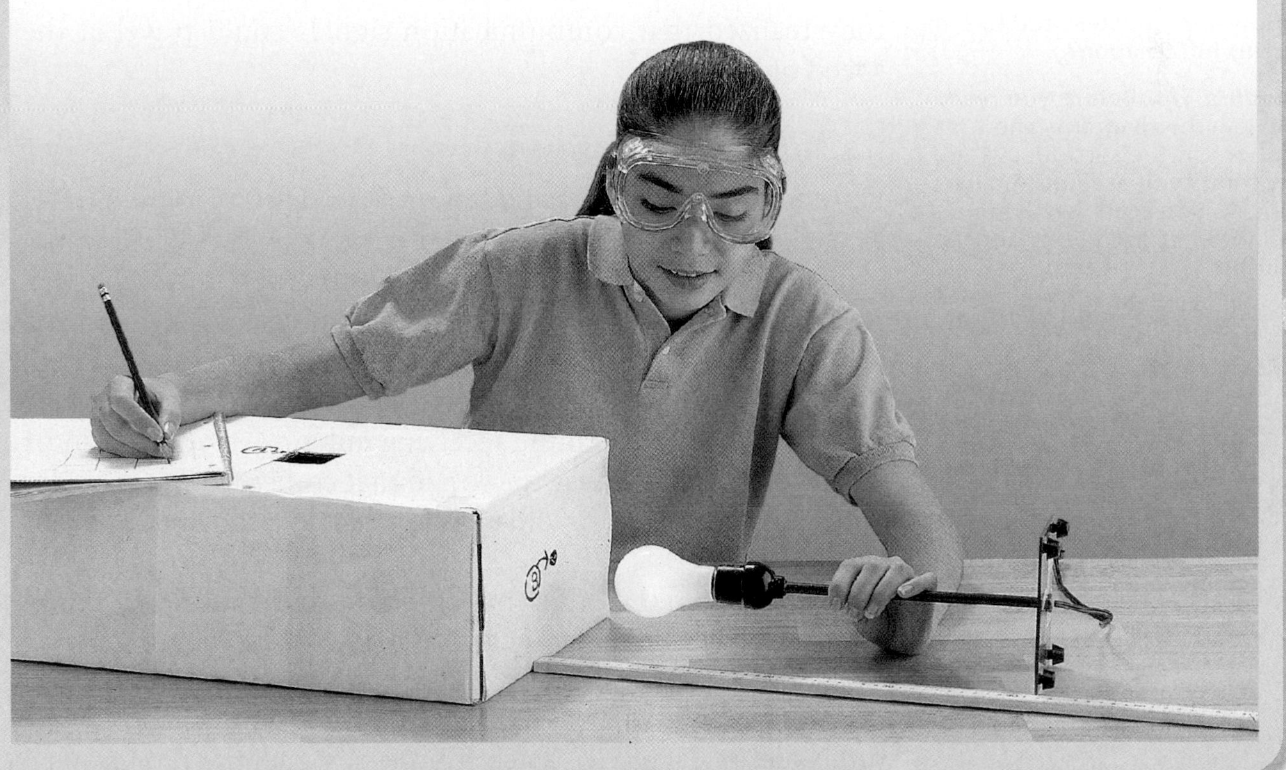

 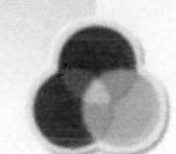

SECTION 4 Wireless Communication

DISCOVER ACTIVITY

How Can Radio Waves Change?

1. Trace the wave diagram onto a piece of tracing paper. Then transfer the wave diagram onto a flat piece of latex from a balloon or latex glove.
2. Stretch the latex horizontally. How is the stretched wave different from the wave on the tracing paper?
3. Now stretch the latex vertically. How is this wave different from the wave on the tracing paper? How is it different from the wave in Step 2?

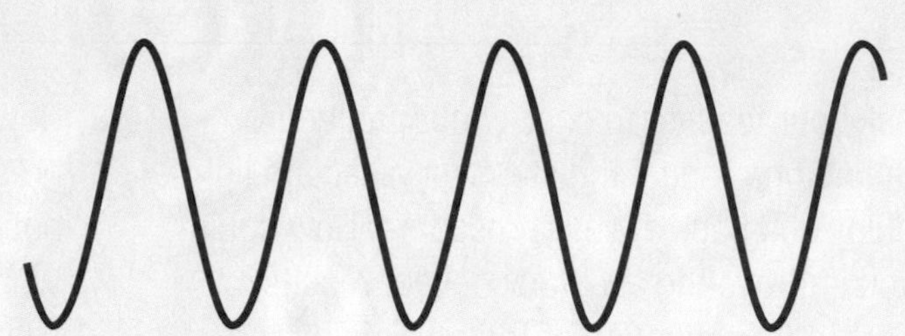

Think It Over

Making Models Which stretch changes the amplitude of the wave? Which stretch changes the frequency of the wave?

GUIDE FOR READING

- **How are radio waves used to transmit information?**
- **How do cellular phones and pagers use electromagnetic waves?**
- **How are satellites used to relay information?**

Reading Tip **Before you read, preview the diagrams and captions in the section. List any terms you are not familiar with. As you read, write the definition of each term on your list.**

Recent advances in technology have turned our world into a global village. Today it is possible to communicate with people on the other side of the world in just seconds. You can watch a television broadcast of a soccer game from Europe or a news report from the Middle East. Once scientists discovered that messages could be carried on electromagnetic waves, they realized that communication signals could travel at the speed of light.

Radio and Television

How does your favorite radio station or television program travel to you? Both radio and television programs are carried, or transmitted, by radio waves. Radio transmissions are produced when charged particles move back and forth in transmission antennas. These transmissions are broadcast, or sent out in all directions. Radio waves carry information from the antenna of a broadcasting station to the receiving antenna of your radio or television. Don't confuse the sound that comes from your radio with radio waves. Your radio converts the radio transmission into sound waves.

There are many different radio and television stations, all sending out signals. So how can each individual program or song come through clearly? As you move your radio tuner up and down the dial, you can hear different radio stations. Look at the radio dial in Figure 21. Each number on the dial represents a

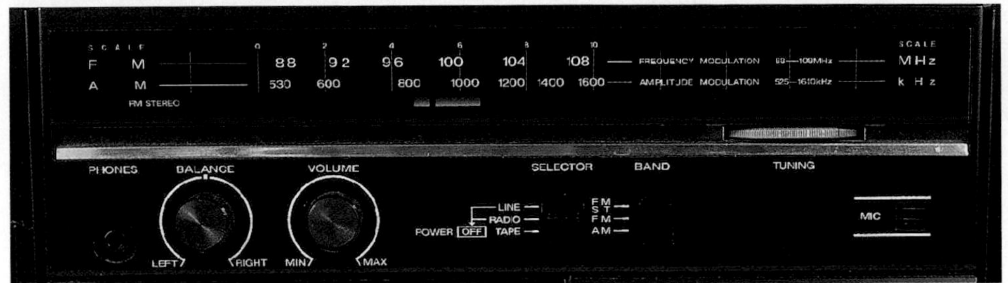

Figure 21 The radio dial shows the FM and AM frequency bands. Each radio station is assigned a different carrier frequency.

different frequency measured in either kilohertz (kHz) or megahertz (MHz).

Recall that a hertz is one cycle per second. If something vibrates 1,000 times a second, it has a frequency of 1,000 Hz, or 1 kilohertz (kHz). (The prefix *kilo-* means "one thousand.") If something vibrates 1,000,000 times a second, it has a frequency of 1,000,000 Hz, or 1 megahertz (MHz). (The prefix *mega-* means "one million" and is represented by a capital M.)

In the United States, the Federal Communications Commission, or FCC, assigns different frequencies of radio waves for different uses. Radio stations are allowed to use one part of the spectrum, and television stations use other parts. Taxi and police radios are also each assigned a set of frequencies. In this way, the entire spectrum of radio waves is divided into bands that are used for different purposes.

Each radio or television station is assigned a basic broadcast frequency, known as a carrier frequency. Each station is identified by the frequency at which it broadcasts. Radio stations broadcast in one of two main frequency bands—AM and FM.

AM Radio AM stands for **amplitude modulation.** On AM broadcasts, the frequency of the wave remains constant. The information that will become sound, such as speech and music, is coded in changes, or modulations, in the amplitude of the wave. **At the broadcasting station, music and speech are converted from sound into electronic signals. The electronic signals for AM broadcasts are then converted into a pattern of changes in the amplitude of a radio wave.**

Figure 22 Sound signals are carried by varying either the amplitude (AM) or the frequency (FM) of radio waves.
Interpreting Diagrams *What remains constant in the AM wave? In the FM wave?*

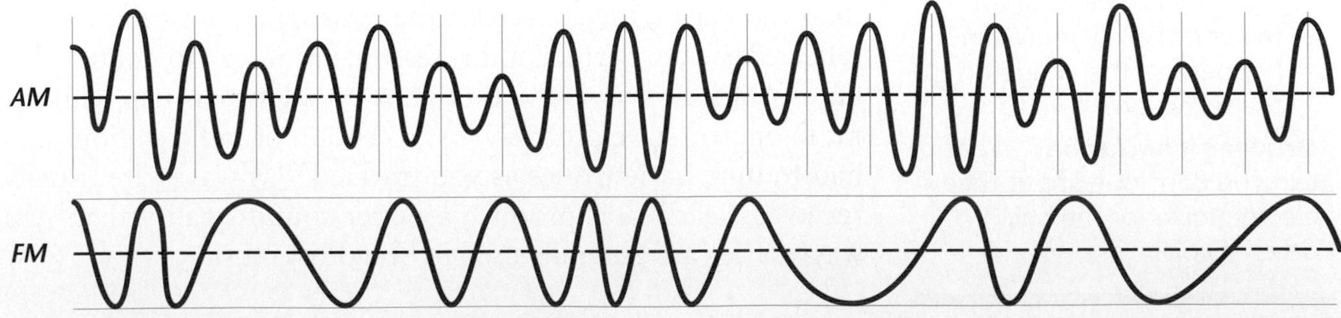

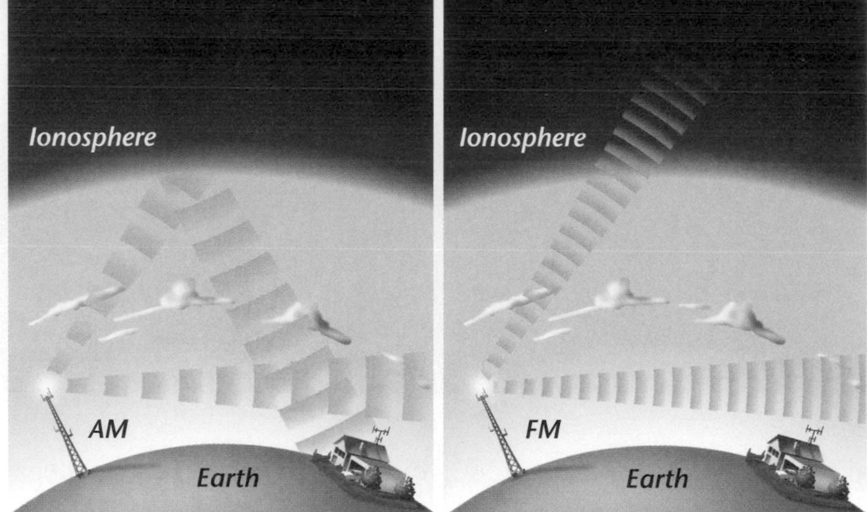

Figure 23 AM radio waves are reflected by the ionosphere. FM radio waves pass through the ionosphere. ***Applying Concepts*** *Which type of broadcast has a longer range on Earth?*

Your radio picks up the wave and converts the coded information back into an electronic signal. This signal travels to your radio's speaker and comes out as sound waves.

The AM frequencies used for radio broadcasts range from 535 kHz to 1,605 kHz. These radio waves vibrate at frequencies from 535 thousand to 1,605 thousand times per second.

AM waves have relatively long wavelengths and are easily reflected by Earth's ionosphere. The ionosphere is an electrically charged layer high in the atmosphere. Figure 23 shows how this reflection allows the AM waves to bounce back to Earth's surface. This is why AM radio stations can broadcast over long distances, especially at night when the absorption of radio waves by the ionosphere is reduced. However, the reception of AM waves is sometimes not very clear. For this reason, AM radio stations usually broadcast more talk shows than music.

FM Radio FM stands for **frequency modulation.** On FM broadcasts, the amplitude of the wave remains constant. **FM signals travel as changes, or modulations, in the frequency of the wave.**

If you look at an FM dial on a radio, you will see that the stations broadcast at frequencies from 88 MHz to 108 MHz. FM radio waves vibrate from 88 million to 108 million times each second. The frequencies of FM stations are much higher than the frequencies of AM radio stations, which vibrate only thousands of times per second.

Because FM waves have higher frequencies and more energy than AM waves, they penetrate the atmosphere instead of being reflected back to Earth. For this reason, FM waves do not travel as far as AM waves. If you've ever gone on a long car trip with the radio on, you have probably lost reception of radio stations and had to tune in new ones as you traveled. FM waves are usually received clearly and produce a better sound quality than AM waves. They are generally used to broadcast music.

Produce Electromagnetic Interference

ACTIVITY

Find out which appliances produce radio waves.

1. Turn on a non-cabled television set. Keep the volume low. Observe the image on the screen.
2. Plug an electric mixer or a hair dryer into a nearby outlet and switch it on. What happens to the image on the television?
3. Change the speed of the mixer or hair dryer. What happens to the image on the television?

Drawing Conclusions What can you conclude about the electric mixer or the hair dryer? Explain.

Television Television broadcasts are similar to radio broadcasts, except that the electromagnetic waves carry picture signals as well as sound. There are two main bands of television wave frequencies: Very High Frequency (VHF) and Ultra High Frequency (UHF). VHF television channels range from frequencies of 54 MHz to 216 MHz, and correspond to Channels 2 through 13 on your television set. This band of frequencies includes some FM radio frequencies, so television stations are restricted from using the frequencies that are reserved for radio stations. UHF channels range from frequencies of 470 MHz to 806 MHz, and correspond to Channels 14 through 69.

Weather can affect the reception of television signals. For better reception, cable companies now pick up the signals, improve them, and send them through cables into homes. Cable television reception is usually clearer than reception with an antenna. The majority of American homes that have television now have cable reception.

☑ *Checkpoint* *What do the terms VHF and UHF mean?*

Cellular Telephones

Cellular phones have become very common. **Cellular telephones transmit and receive signals using high-frequency radio waves, or microwaves.** The cellular system works over regions divided up into many small cells. Each cell has its own transmitter and receiver. Cells that are next to each other are assigned different frequencies, but cells that are not next to each other can be assigned the same frequency. Cellular telephone signals are strong enough to reach only a few nearby cells. They cannot travel great distances. This allows many phones in different areas to use the same frequency at the same time, without interfering with each other.

As cellular phone users travel from one cell to another, the signals are transferred from one cell to another with very little interruption. If you travel outside one cellular phone company's area, another company becomes responsible for transmitting the signals.

Most cellular phones are more expensive to use than wired phones. But they are becoming more and more affordable. Cellular phones allow users to make and receive calls almost anywhere without having to use someone else's phone or look for a pay phone.

Figure 24 Cellular telephones transmit and receive radio waves that travel short distances.

Cordless Telephones

Cellular telephones should not be confused with cordless telephones. The bases of cordless telephones are connected to the telephone system just like ordinary phones. The only difference is that there is no cord between the handset and the base. The information is transmitted from the handset to the base by radio waves, so you can walk away from the base as you talk on the phone.

Pagers

Pagers are small electronic devices that people can carry in their pockets or attach to their clothes. To page someone, you must

Wireless Communication

Since the late 1800s, many developments in communication have turned our world into a global village.

1895
First Wireless Transmission

Italian engineer and inventor Guglielmo Marconi successfully used radio waves to send a coded wireless signal a distance of more than 2 km.

1923
Ship-to-Ship Communication

For the first time, people on one ship could talk to people on another. The signals were sent as electromagnetic waves, received by an antenna, and converted into sound.

1900 **1920**

1888
Electromagnetic Waves

German scientist Heinrich Hertz proved James Clerk Maxwell's prediction that radio waves exist. Hertz demonstrated that the waves could be reflected, refracted, diffracted, and polarized just like light waves.

1901
First Transatlantic Signals

On December 12, the first transatlantic radio signal was sent from Poldhu Cove, Cornwall, England, to Signal Hill, Newfoundland. The coded electromagnetic waves traveled more than 3,000 km through the air.

dial the telephone number of the pager. This can be done from a telephone or another pager. Depending on the pager, you can then enter your telephone number or leave a voice message. Some pagers even allow the user to receive text messages.

When you leave a message for a pager, the information is first sent to a receiving station. There it is coded and sent as electromagnetic waves to the correct pager. The pager then beeps or vibrates, letting the owner know that there is a message. Some pagers are two-way pagers. This means that the pager can return electromagnetic signals to the receiving station, which sends them to the person who sent the original message.

In Your Journal

At your local or school library, find out more about Guglielmo Marconi. Imagine you were hired as his assistant. Write a letter to a friend that describes your new job.

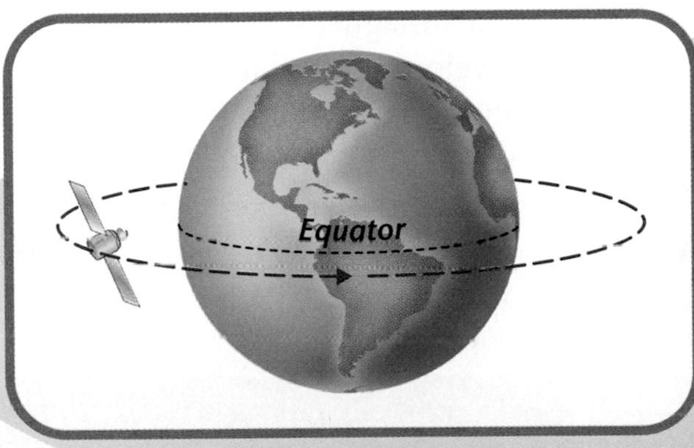

1963

Geosynchronous Orbit

Communications satellites are launched into orbits at altitudes of about 35,000 km. At this altitude, a satellite orbits Earth at the same rate as Earth rotates. A satellite orbiting above the equator remains above the same location as Earth turns.

1940 — 1960 — 1980

1957

Sputnik I

On October 4, the Soviet Union became the first country to successfully launch an artificial satellite into orbit. This development led to a new era in communications. Since then, more than 5,000 artificial satellites have been placed in orbit.

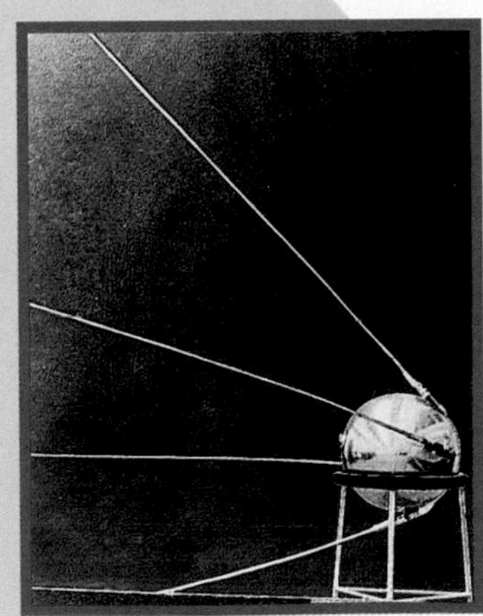

1979

Cellular Phone Network

The world's first cellular phone network was set up in Japan. It allowed people to make and receive telephone calls without wired phones.

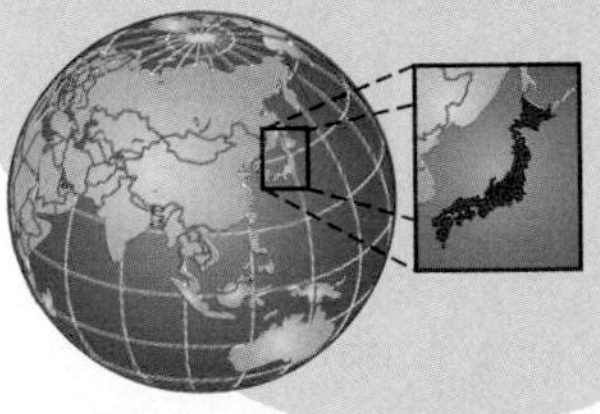

Communications Satellites

Since the development of satellite technology, long-distance communications have become faster and cheaper. Communications satellites work like the receivers and transmitters of a cellular phone system. Satellites orbiting Earth receive radio, television, and telephone signals, and transmit them around the world. **The radio waves are sent from Earth up to the satellite, which then relays the waves to other receivers on Earth.** Most satellites strengthen the signals before sending them back to Earth. Communications satellites can relay several signals at the same time.

Because a satellite can "see" only part of Earth at any given time, it is necessary to have more than one satellite in orbit for any given purpose. In this way, signals can be sent all around the world at any time.

Satellite Telephone Systems The use of telephones has increased so much that telephone companies have had to develop new ways of transmitting electromagnetic waves. Several companies have developed or are developing satellite telephone systems. The radio waves from one phone are sent up through the atmosphere, received by a communications satellite, and transmitted back to Earth to the receiving phone. This system makes calling available anywhere in the world, but it may be more expensive to use than the cellular telephone system.

Figure 25 Communications satellites are remote-controlled spacecraft that orbit Earth. Because electromagnetic waves travel in straight lines, they cannot curve around Earth. Satellites receive signals from Earth and transmit them to parts of the world they could not otherwise reach.

Television Satellites Television networks use communications satellites to send their signals to local stations across the country. The television signals are changed into radio waves using frequency modulation.

Some people have their own antennas to receive signals directly from satellites. Because the antennas are dish-shaped, they are known as satellite dishes. Older satellite dishes were very large. As the signals broadcast from satellites have become more powerful, and as ways to greatly compress the data have been developed, the dishes required to receive the signals have become a lot smaller.

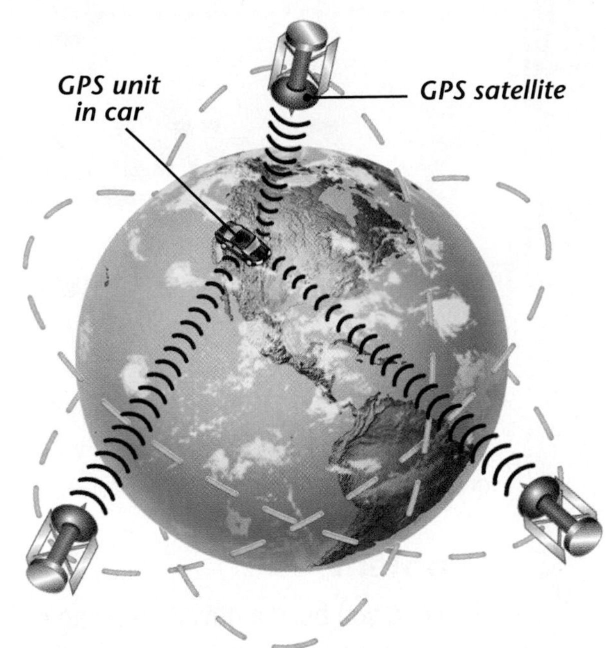

Figure 26 The Global Positioning System (GPS) uses a group of 24 satellites, each traveling in its own orbit. Receivers in cars, boats, and airplanes use signals from at least three satellites at a time to determine their exact location on Earth.

The Global Positioning System The Global Positioning System (GPS) was originally designed for use by the United States military. Now, many thousands of civilians use the system for navigation. The Global Positioning System uses a group of two dozen communications satellites that work together. The GPS satellites broadcast radio signals to Earth. These signals carry information that can tell you your exact location on Earth's surface, or even in the air. Anybody on Earth with a GPS receiver can receive these signals.

GPS systems have grown more sophisticated. Today, receivers are increasingly common in airplanes, boats, and even cars. In some cars you can type your destination into a computer and have the GPS system map out your route. A computerized voice might even tell you when to turn.

Section 4 Review

1. Describe how the sounds from a radio station, such as speech or music, are converted into radio waves.
2. What is the difference between AM and FM radio broadcasts?
3. How does the cellular phone system work?
4. How does a satellite relay radio and television signals?
5. **Thinking Critically Predicting** What do you think might happen if the Federal Communications Commission did not control the use of different frequencies of radio waves?

CHAPTER PROJECT 15

Check Your Progress

Collect your surveys and tally your results. As you analyze your data, look for patterns. You can use bar graphs or circle graphs to display your findings. Include information about cost, time, and any other questions you asked in your survey. Write one or two paragraphs explaining your conclusions.

Real-World Lab

How It Works

Build a Crystal Radio

The first radio, called a crystal set, was invented in the early 1900s. At first, people built their own crystal sets to receive broadcast transmissions from local radio stations. In this lab, you will build your own crystal radio and learn how it works.

Problem

How can you build a device that can collect and convert radio signals?

Skills Focus

measuring, observing, making models, drawing conclusions

Materials

cardboard tube (paper towel roll)
3 pieces of enameled or insulated wire, 1 about 30 m long, and 2 about 30 cm long
wirestrippers or sandpaper
2 alligator clips
scissors
aluminum foil
2 pieces of cardboard (sizes can range from 12.5 cm × 20 cm to 30 cm × 48 cm)
masking tape
crystal diode
earphone
2 pieces of insulated copper antenna wire, 1 about 30 m long, and 1 about 0.5 m long

Procedure

Part 1 Wind the Radio Coil

(*Hint:* All ends of the insulated wires need to be stripped to bare metal. If the wire is enameled, you need to sandpaper the ends.)

1. Carefully punch two holes approximately 2.5 cm apart in each end of a cardboard tube. The holes should be just large enough to thread the insulated wire through.
2. Feed one end of the 30-m piece of insulated wire through one set of holes. Leave a 50-cm lead at that end. Attach alligator clip #1 to this lead. See Figure 1.
3. Wind the wire tightly around the cardboard tube. Make sure the coils are close together but do not overlap one another.
4. Wrap the wire until you come to the end of the tube. Feed the end of the wire through the other set of holes, leaving a 50-cm lead as before. Attach alligator clip #2 to this lead. See Figure 2.

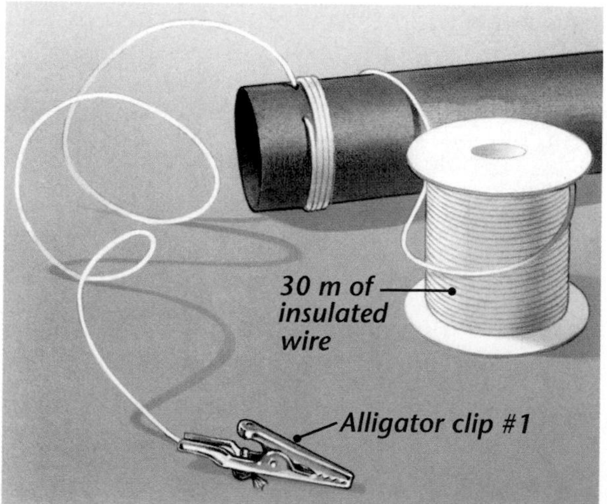

Figure 1 Winding the Coil

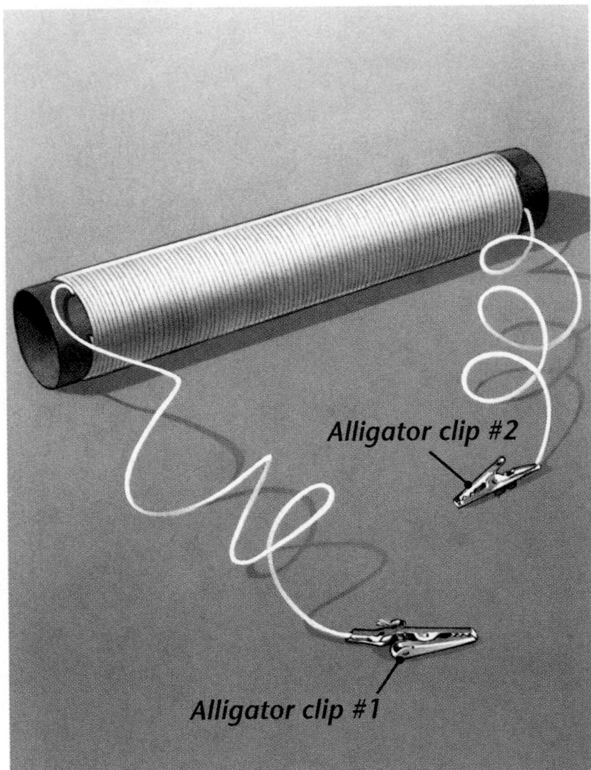

Figure 2 The Finished Coil

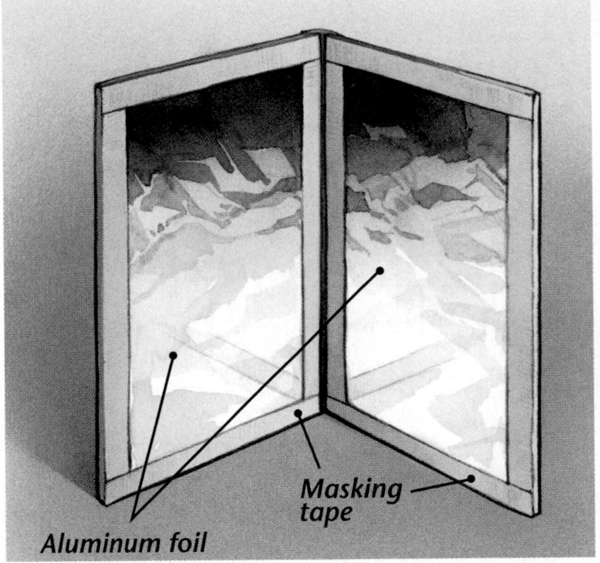

Figure 3 The Tuning Plates

Part 2 Make the Tuning Plates

5. Without wrinkling the aluminum foil, cover one side of each piece of cardboard with the foil. Trim off any excess foil and tape the foil in place.
6. Hold the pieces of cardboard together with the foil facing inward. Tape along one edge to make a hinge. It is important for the foil pieces to be close together but not touching. See Figure 3.
7. Make a small hole through the cardboard and foil near a corner of one side. Feed one of the short pieces of insulated wire through the hole and tape it onto the foil as shown. Tape the other short piece of insulated wire to the corner of the other side. See Figure 4.
8. Connect one end of the wire from the foil to alligator clip #1. Connect the other wire from the foil to alligator clip #2.

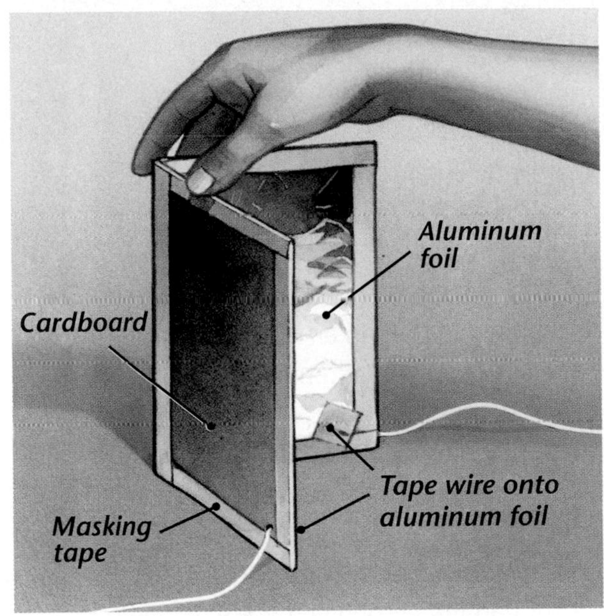

Figure 4 Connecting the Tuning Plates

Part 3 Prepare the Earphone

9. Handle the diode carefully. Connect one wire from the diode to alligator clip #1. The arrow on the diode should point to the earphone. Tape the other end of the diode wire to one of the earphone wires.
10. Connect the other wire from the earphone to alligator clip #2. See Figure 5.

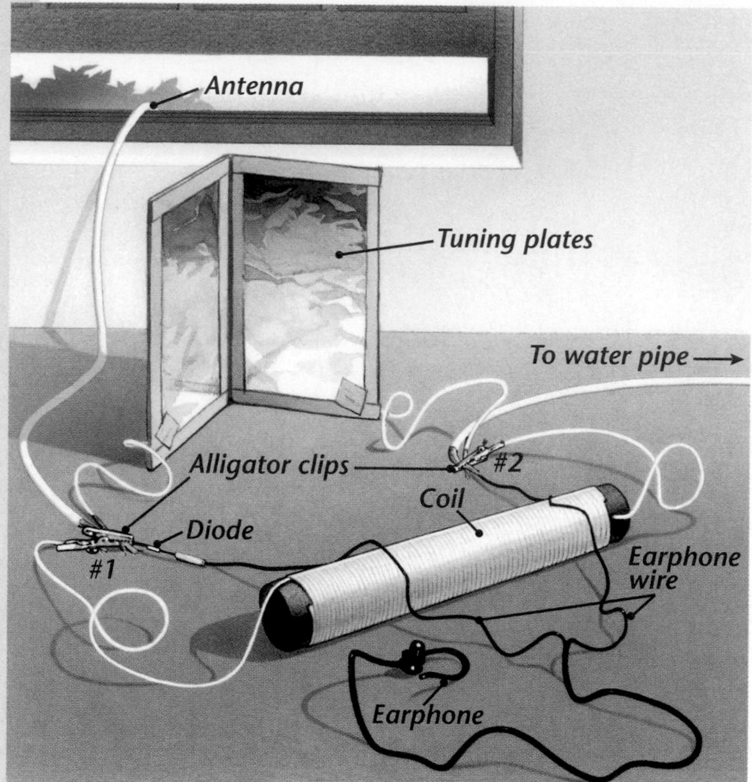

Figure 5 The Completed Radio

Part 4 Hook Up the Antenna

11. String the long piece of antenna wire along the floor to an outside window. Connect the other end of the wire to alligator clip #1.
12. Connect one end of the shorter piece of antenna wire to a cold-water pipe or faucet. Connect the other end to alligator clip #2. See Figure 5.
13. Put on the earphone and try to locate a station by squeezing the tuning plates slowly until you hear a signal. Some stations will come in when the plates are close together. Other stations will come in when the plates are opened far apart.

Analyze and Conclude

1. How many stations can you pick up? Where are the stations located geographically? Which station has the strongest signal? Keep a log of the different stations you receive.
2. How does adjusting the tuning plates affect the radio signals?
3. A crystal radio is not a powerful receiver. You can improve reception by having a good antenna. How can you improve your antenna?
4. **Apply** What are the similarities and differences between a modern radio and a crystal radio? How is one more efficient?

Design an Experiment

Use your crystal radio or any radio to test signal reception at various times of the day. Do you receive more stations at night or in the morning? Why do you think certain times of the day are better for receiving radio waves?

CHAPTER 15 STUDY GUIDE

The Nature of Electromagnetic Waves

Key Ideas

- ◆ An electromagnetic wave transfers energy by means of changing electric and magnetic fields.
- ◆ Sometimes light acts as though it is a set of waves. Sometimes light acts as though it is a stream of particles.

Key Terms

electromagnetic wave
electromagnetic radiation
polarized light
photoelectric effect
photon

Waves of the Electromagnetic Spectrum

Key Ideas

- ◆ All electromagnetic waves travel at the same speed, but they have different wavelengths and different frequencies.
- ◆ The electromagnetic spectrum is made up of radio waves, infrared rays, visible light, ultraviolet rays, X-rays, and gamma rays.
- ◆ Radio waves and the Doppler effect can be used to tell the speeds of moving objects.

Key Terms

electromagnetic spectrum
radio wave
microwave
radar
magnetic resonance imaging
infrared ray
thermogram
visible light
ultraviolet ray
X-ray
gamma ray

Producing Visible Light

Key Idea

- ◆ Light bulbs can be incandescent, fluorescent, neon, sodium vapor, or tungsten-halogen.

Key Terms

illuminated
luminous
spectroscope
incandescent light
fluorescent light
neon light
sodium vapor light
tungsten-halogen light
bioluminescence

Wireless Communication

INTEGRATING TECHNOLOGY

Key Ideas

- ◆ At broadcasting stations, music and speech are converted from sound into an electrical signal and then into a pattern of changes in a radio wave.
- ◆ AM broadcasts transmit information by modifying the amplitude of the signal. FM broadcasts change the frequency of the signal.
- ◆ Cellular telephones transmit and receive signals using high-frequency radio waves.
- ◆ When you leave a message for a pager, the information is first sent to a receiving station. There it is coded and directed to the correct pager.
- ◆ Radio, television, and telephone signals are sent from Earth up to communications satellites, which then relay the signals to receivers around the world.

Key Terms

amplitude modulation (AM)
frequency modulation (FM)

Organizing Information

Concept Map Copy the concept map about electromagnetic waves onto a sheet of paper. Then complete it and add a title. (For more on concept maps, see the Skills Handbook.)

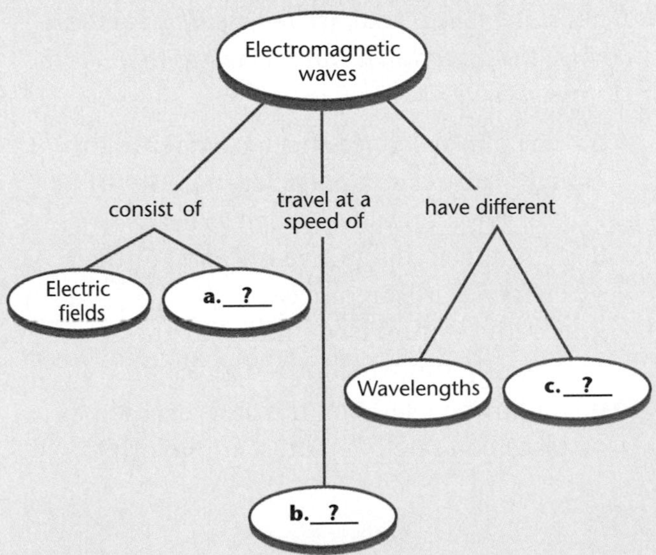

Reviewing Content

Multiple Choice

Choose the letter of the best answer.

1. All electromagnetic waves have the same
   a. frequency.
   b. speed.
   c. wavelength.
   d. energy.
2. The electromagnetic waves with the longest wavelengths are
   a. radio waves.
   b. infrared rays.
   c. X-rays.
   d. gamma rays.
3. Which of the following does *not* belong in the electromagnetic spectrum?
   a. X-ray
   b. sound
   c. infrared ray
   d. radio wave
4. Light bulbs that glow when a filament inside them gets hot are called
   a. bioluminescent lights.
   b. fluorescent lights.
   c. incandescent lights.
   d. neon lights.
5. Television signals are transmitted by
   a. gamma rays. b. infrared rays.
   c. X-rays. d. radio waves.

True or False

If the statement is true, write true. If it is false, change the underlined word or words to make the statement true.

6. The photoelectric effect is evidence that light can act as a <u>particle</u>.
7. <u>Ultraviolet</u> rays can be felt as heat.
8. Fluorescent lights give off most of their energy as <u>infrared rays</u>.
9. A radio station is identified by the <u>amplitude</u> at which it broadcasts.
10. Radio and television transmitters can be placed on <u>satellites</u> and sent into orbit.

Checking Concepts

11. How do you know that electromagnetic waves can travel through a vacuum?
12. How does polarization show that light can act as a wave?
13. How is the Doppler effect used to find the speeds of moving objects?
14. Explain the difference between cellular telephones and cordless telephones.
15. A person lost in the woods at night may signal for help by turning a flashlight on and off according to a code known as Morse code. This is actually a modulated signal. Is it AM or FM? Explain your answer.
16. **Writing to Learn** Develop an advertising campaign to sell fluorescent lights. Your ad should describe two advantages of fluorescent lights over incandescent lights. Be sure to include a catchy slogan.

Thinking Critically

17. **Applying Concepts** What important information can be gathered from a thermogram of a house? How could this information be used to help save energy?
18. **Relating Cause and Effect** The waves of the electromagnetic spectrum that have the greatest frequency are also the most penetrating and can cause the most harm. Explain.
19. **Classifying** List five examples of luminous objects and five examples of illuminated objects.
20. **Problem Solving** Suppose you are building an incubator for young chicks and need a source of heat. What type of light bulbs would you use? Explain.
21. **Comparing and Contrasting** Make a table to compare the different types of wireless communication. Include headings such as: type of information transmitted; distance over which signal can be transmitted; one-way or two-way communication.

Applying Skills

The table below gives information about four radio stations. Use the table to answer Questions 22–24.

Call letters	Frequency
KLIZ	580 kHz
KMOM	103.7 MHz
WDAD	1030 kHz
WJFO	89.7 MHz

22. **Interpreting Data** Which radio station broadcasts at the longest wavelength? The shortest wavelength?
23. **Classifying** Which radio stations are AM? Which are FM?
24. **Predicting** You are going on a car trip across the United States. Which station would you expect to receive for the greater distance: KLIZ or KMOM?

Performance Assessment

Project Wrap Up Now you are ready to present your findings to your classmates. You could mount your graphs on posterboard. Alternatively, you could put your graphs on transparencies and use an overhead projector to show the results of your survey. You could also use a computer to create a slide show.

Reflect and Record What in your results was most surprising? How could you have done a better job of collecting your data? Has this project given you a better understanding of the usage of the various devices? Think about the world 25 years from now. Predict the types of devices that will be used in the future.

Test Preparation

Use these questions to prepare for standardized tests.

Use the diagram to answer Questions 25–29.

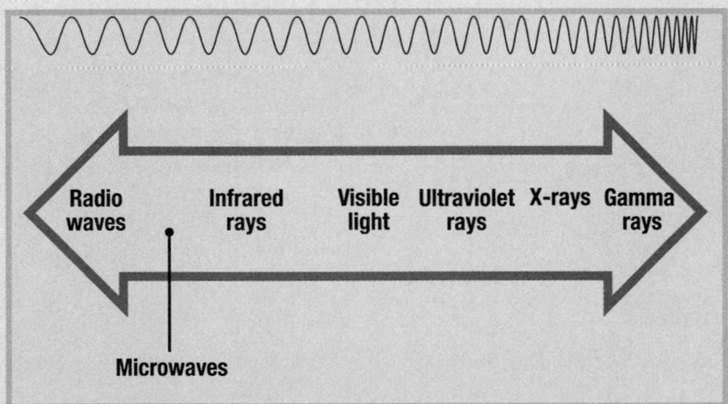

25. Low-frequency waves have
    a. short wavelengths and high energy.
    b. long wavelengths and low energy.
    c. short wavelengths and low energy.
    d. long wavelengths and high energy.

26. Which waves have the lowest frequency?
    a. radio waves
    b. infrared rays
    c. visible light
    d. gamma rays

27. Which waves have the shortest wavelength?
    a. radio waves
    b. infrared rays
    c. visible light
    d. gamma rays

28. Microwaves are a type of
    a. radio waves.
    b. visible light.
    c. X-rays.
    d. ultraviolet rays.

29. Waves with higher frequencies have higher energies. Which rays have the highest energy?
    a. ultraviolet rays
    b. visible light
    c. gamma rays
    d. microwaves

CHAPTER

16 Light

This kaleidoscope image is formed by two mirrors at right angles. Light reflected from colored objects between the mirrors is reflected again to form a repeated pattern.

WEB ACTIVITY www.phschool.com

SECTION 1 Reflection and Mirrors

Discover How Does Your Reflection Wink?
Sharpen Your Skills Classifying

SECTION 2 Refraction and Lenses

Discover How Can You Make an Image Appear on a Sheet of Paper?
Try This Disappearing Glass
Skills Lab Looking at Images

SECTION 3 Color

Discover How Do Colors Mix?
Sharpen Your Skills Developing Hypotheses
Real-World Lab Changing Colors

PROJECT 16

What a Sight!

Look inside a kaleidoscope. Light reflected from small beads or pieces of colored glass is reflected again by mirrors, forming colorful, ever-changing patterns. Kaleidoscopes are optical instruments, devices that use arrangements of mirrors or lenses to produce images.

In this chapter, you will study how mirrors and lenses reflect and refract light. You will learn what causes the colors of objects. You will use these ideas to create your own optical instrument.

Your Goal To construct an optical instrument that serves a specific purpose. It can be a kaleidoscope, a telescope, a periscope, a microscope, or something of your own creation.

To complete this project you must

- design and build an optical instrument that includes at least one mirror or one lens
- demonstrate how your instrument works
- prepare a manual that explains the purpose of each part of your instrument

Get Started Begin to think about what you would like your optical instrument to do. Which would you like to see better—tiny objects or distant objects? Would you like to see around corners? Maybe you would prefer your instrument to produce striking images!

Check Your Progress You'll be working on this project as you study this chapter. To keep your project on track, look for Check Your Progress boxes at the following points.

Section 1 Review, page 522: Draw your optical instrument.
Section 3 Review, page 533: Build your optical instrument.
Section 5 Review, page 548: Test and modify your instrument. Prepare a manual explaining how your instrument works.

Wrap Up At the end of the chapter (page 551), you will demonstrate how your instrument works. You will also present your manual, showing the design and use of the instrument.

Integrating Life Science 

Section 4 Seeing Light

Discover **Can You See Everything With One Eye?**
Try This **True Colors**

Section 5 Using Light

Discover **How Does a Pinhole Viewer Work?**
Try This **What a View!**

Reflection and Mirrors

DISCOVER — ACTIVITY

How Does Your Reflection Wink?

1. Look at your face in a mirror. Wink your right eye. Which eye does your reflection wink?
2. Tape two mirrors together so that they open and close like a book. Open them so they form a 90° angle with each other. **CAUTION:** *Be careful of any sharp edges.*

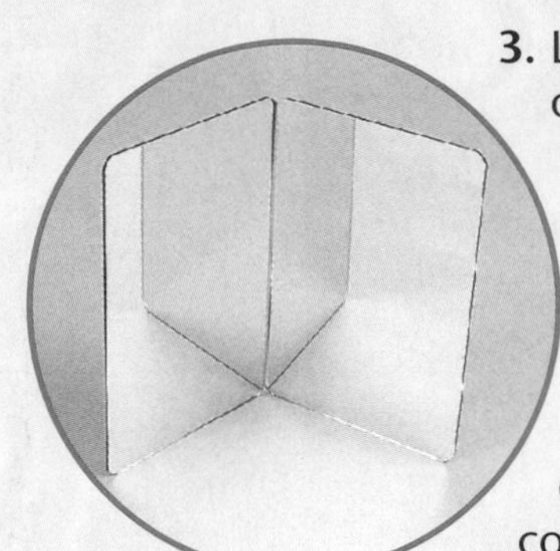

3. Looking into both mirrors at once, wink at your reflection again. Which eye does your reflection wink now?

Think It Over

Observing How does your reflection wink at you? How does the second reflection compare with the first reflection?

GUIDE FOR READING

- **What happens when light strikes an object?**
- **What are the two kinds of reflection?**
- **What types of images are produced by plane, concave, and convex mirrors?**

Reading Tip **Before you read, preview the section and write down any new terms. As you read, find the meaning of each term.**

◄ Glare on a window

Have you ever looked at a store window on a bright, sunny day? In order to see inside, you may have used your hands to block the glare. The glare is actually reflected light. The glare from the store window shows that glass can reflect light. But if you look at a clear glass window with no glare, you can see right through it.

When Light Strikes an Object

When light strikes an object, the light can be reflected, absorbed, or transmitted. Most objects reflect or absorb light. A material that reflects or absorbs all of the light that strikes it is **opaque** (oh PAYK). Most objects are opaque. You cannot see through opaque objects because light cannot pass through them. Examples of opaque materials include wood, metal, and cotton and wool fabrics.

A **transparent** material transmits light. When light strikes a transparent object, it passes right through, allowing you to see what is on the other side. Clear glass, water, and air are examples of transparent materials.

Other materials allow some light to pass through. This type of material is translucent. **Translucent** (trans LOO sunt) materials scatter light as it passes through. You can usually tell that there is something behind a translucent object, but you cannot see details clearly. Frosted glass and wax paper are translucent. Figure 1 shows opaque, transparent, and translucent objects.

Figure 1 The spools of thread are opaque. They reflect light of various colors. The pitcher and glass are transparent. They transmit light, allowing you to see the milk inside. The leaf is translucent. The frog's image can be seen through the leaf but lacks detail.

Kinds of Reflection

When you look at some objects, such as a shiny metal fixture or a mirror, you can see yourself. But when you look at other objects, such as a book, a wooden table, or your pencil, you see only the object itself. **You can see most objects because light reflects, or bounces, off them.** What you see when you look at an object depends on how its surface reflects light.

Regular Reflection To show how light travels and reflects, you can represent light waves as straight lines called **rays.** Light rays reflect from a surface according to the law of reflection: the angle of reflection equals the angle of incidence.

Regular reflection occurs when parallel rays of light hit a smooth surface. All the rays are reflected at the same angle. For example, if you look at a sheet of shiny metal, you can see your own reflection. The light rays coming from you strike the smooth surface and are reflected regularly.

Diffuse Reflection When parallel rays of light hit a bumpy, or uneven, surface, **diffuse reflection** occurs. Each ray obeys the law of reflection. But since each ray hits the surface at a different angle, the rays are reflected at different angles. Because the reflected rays travel in all directions, diffuse reflection allows you to see an object from any position.

Most objects reflect light diffusely. This is because most objects do not have smooth surfaces. Even surfaces that appear to be smooth, such as a freshly painted wall, have small bumps that scatter light. If you look at a wall through a magnifying glass, you will see that the surface is not really smooth.

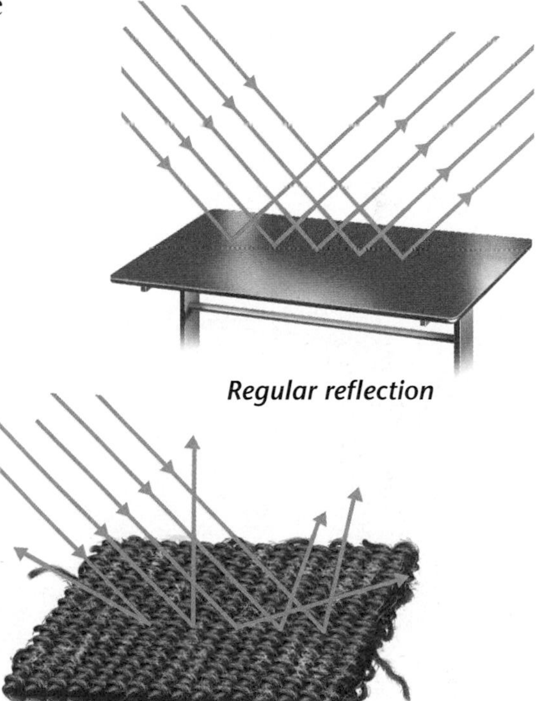

Figure 2 When light strikes a surface at an angle, it is reflected at the same angle. If the surface is smooth, the reflection is regular (top). If the surface is uneven, the reflection is diffuse (bottom).

Sharpen your Skills

Classifying ACTIVITY

Look at the back of a shiny spoon. What kind of image do you see? How does changing the distance between your eyes and the spoon affect what you see? What kind of mirror does the back of the spoon represent? Now look at the front of the spoon. What kind of mirror is the front of the spoon? What kind of image do you see ?

Mirrors

Did you look in a mirror this morning? Maybe you combed your hair or brushed your teeth in front of a mirror. A mirror is a sheet of glass that has a smooth, silver-colored coating on one side. When light passes through the glass, the coating on the back reflects the light regularly, allowing you to see an image. An **image** is a copy of an object formed by reflected or refracted rays of light.

Mirrors can be flat or curved. The shape of the surface determines how the image will look. Depending on the shape of the mirror, the image can be the same size as the object, or it can be larger or smaller.

Plane Mirrors Look into a flat mirror, or **plane mirror.** You will see an image that is the same size as you are. Your image will seem to be the same distance behind the mirror as you are in front of it. **A plane mirror produces an image that is right-side up and the same size as the object being reflected.**

The image you see when you look in a plane mirror is a virtual image. **Virtual images** are right-side up, or upright. "Virtual" describes something that you can see, but does not really exist. You can't reach behind a mirror and touch your image.

Why do you see a virtual image? Figure 3 shows how the image of the dancer is formed by a plane mirror. Light rays reflected from the dancer travel out in all directions. They strike the mirror and are reflected toward the eye. Even though the rays are reflected, the brain treats them as if they had come from behind the mirror. The dashed lines show the points from which the light rays appear to come. Since the light appears to come from behind the mirror, this is where the dancer's image appears to be located.

☑ *Checkpoint* *What is a virtual image?*

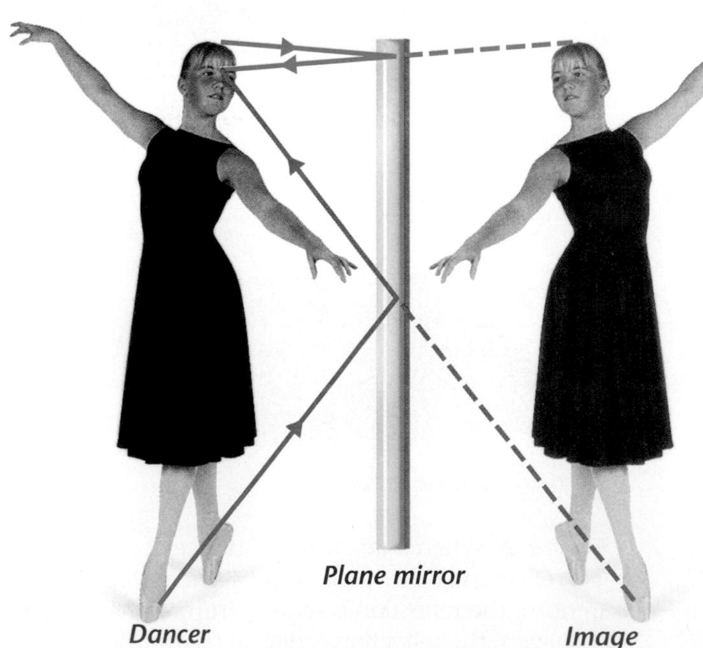

Figure 3 A plane mirror forms a virtual image. When the dancer looks in the mirror, the rays of light reflected from her body are reflected back toward her. The rays appear to come from behind the mirror, where the image is formed.

Concave Mirrors A mirror with a surface that curves inward like the inside of a bowl is a **concave mirror.** Figure 4 shows how a concave mirror can reflect parallel rays of light so that they meet at a point. The point at which the rays meet is called the **focal point.**

Concave mirrors can form either virtual images or real images. The type of image formed by a concave mirror depends on the position of the object in relation to the focal point. Figure 5 shows how concave mirrors form images. If the object is farther away from the mirror than the focal point, the reflected rays form a real image. A **real image** is formed when rays actually meet at a point. Real images are upside down, or inverted. A real image may be larger or smaller than the object. If the object is between the focal point and the mirror, the image appears to be behind the mirror and is right-side up. Then it is a virtual image.

Some concave mirrors are used to project rays of light. For example, a car headlight has a bulb at the focal point of a concave mirror. When the light from the bulb spreads out and hits the mirror, the rays are reflected parallel to each other. This projects the light on the road ahead. Concave mirrors are also used to produce magnified images, as in makeup mirrors.

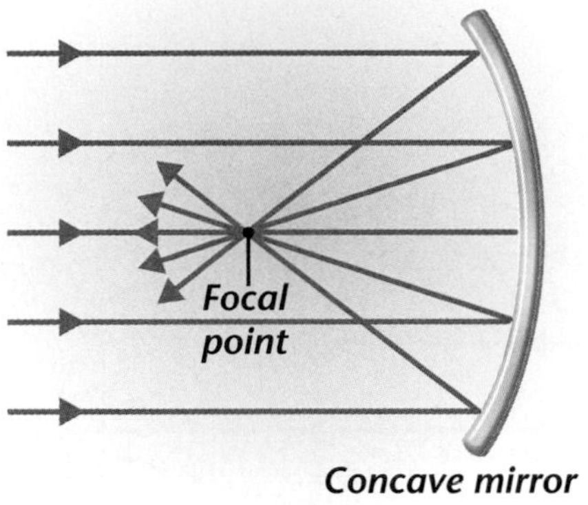

Figure 4 This concave mirror reflects parallel rays of light back through the focal point.

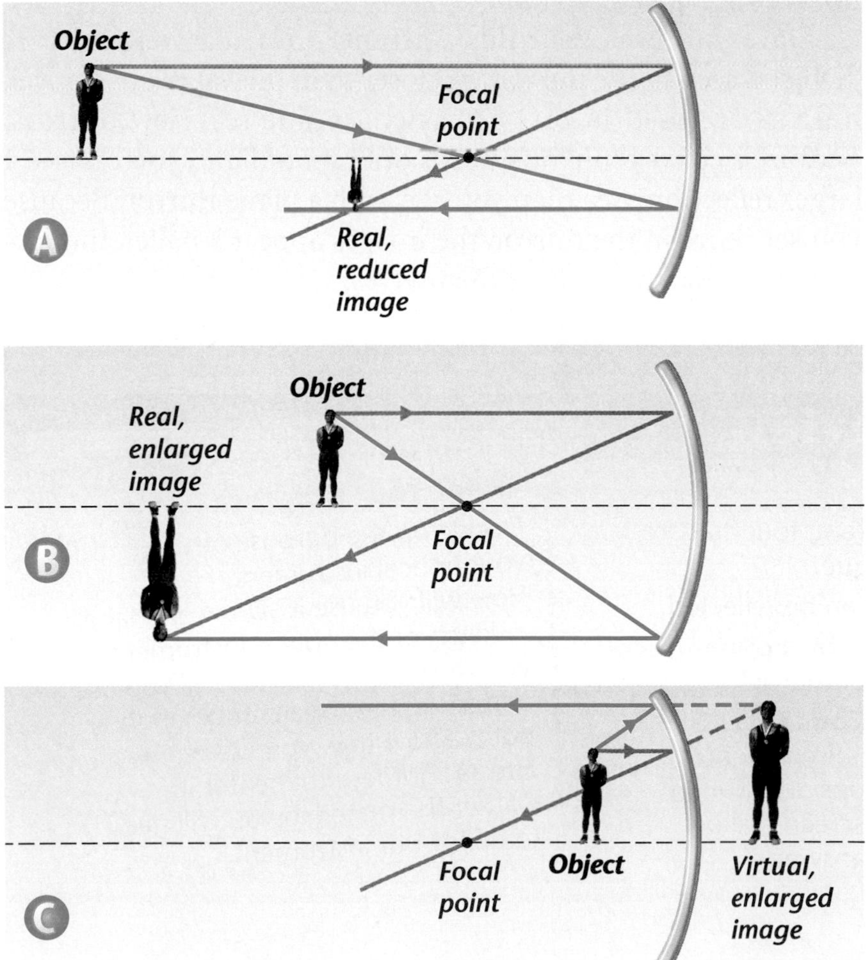

Figure 5 The type of image formed by a concave mirror depends on the position of the object in relation to the focal point. **A,B.** If the object is farther from the mirror than the focal point, the image is real and inverted. **C.** If the object is between the mirror and the focal point, the image is virtual and upright. ***Interpreting Diagrams*** *How can you tell that the images in A and B are real?*

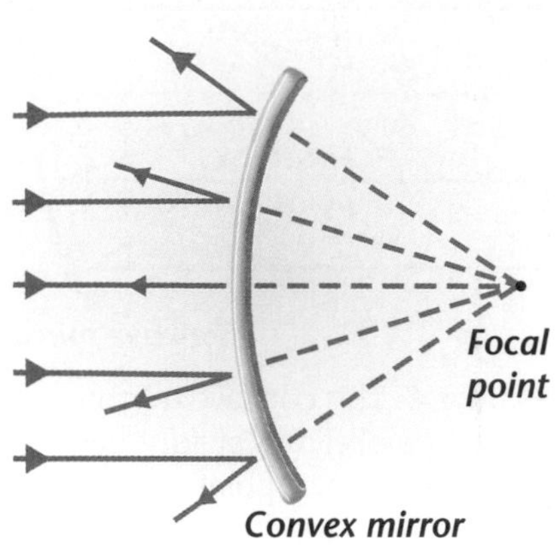

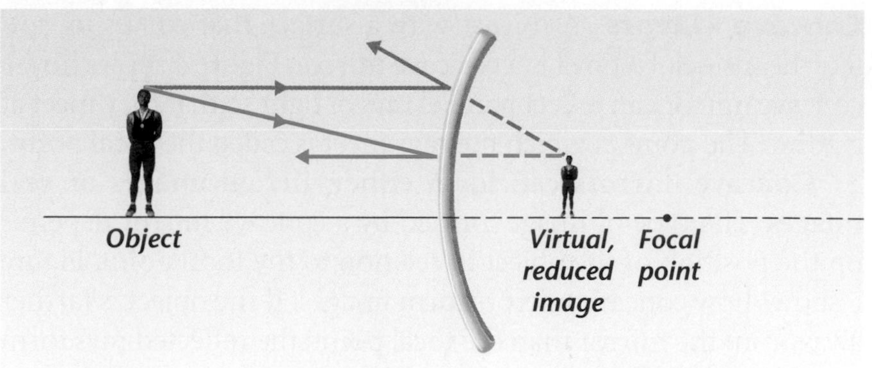

Figure 6 A convex mirror reflects parallel rays of light as though they came from the focal point behind the mirror. The image formed by a convex mirror is always virtual. *Applying Concepts What is a convex mirror?*

Convex Mirrors A mirror with a surface that curves outward is called a **convex mirror.** Figure 6 shows how some convex mirrors reflect parallel rays of light. The rays spread out but appear to come from a focal point behind the mirror. The focal point of a convex mirror is the point from which the rays appear to come. **Since the rays do not actually meet, images formed by convex mirrors are always virtual.**

Have you ever seen this warning on a rearview mirror? "Objects seen in the mirror are closer than they appear." Convex mirrors are used in cars as passenger-side rearview mirrors. Because a convex mirror spreads out rays of light, you can see a larger reflection area than you can with a plane mirror. Because you see more in the mirror, the images appear smaller and farther away than the objects themselves.

Section 1 Review

1. List four materials that are transparent, four that are translucent, and four that are opaque.
2. Describe two ways in which light can be reflected.
3. What types of images are produced by a plane mirror? A concave mirror? A convex mirror?
4. **Thinking Critically Applying Concepts** A slide projector projects an upright image onto a screen. The slides must be placed upside down in the projector. Is the image on the screen real or virtual? Give two reasons for your answer.

Check Your Progress CHAPTER PROJECT 16

Decide on the purpose of your optical instrument. How will you use it? Draw and label a sketch of the optical instrument you would like to build. Will you use mirrors, lenses, or a combination of both? Show how your instrument affects light rays that enter it. Gather the materials you will need to build your instrument.

Section 2 Refraction and Lenses

Discover Activity

How Can You Make an Image Appear on a Sheet of Paper?

1. Hold a hand lens about 2 meters from a window. Look through the lens. What do you see? **CAUTION:** *Do not look at the sun.*
2. Move the lens farther away from your eye. What changes do you notice?
3. Now hold the lens between the window and a sheet of paper, but closer to the paper. Slowly move the lens away from the paper and toward the window. Keep watching the paper. What do you see? What happens as you move the lens?

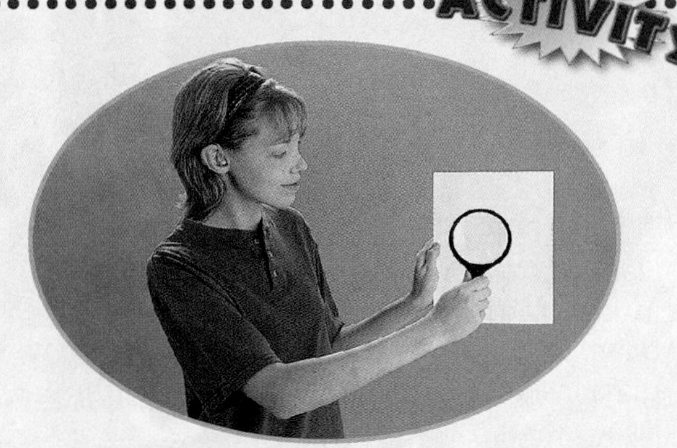

Think It Over

Observing How do you think an image is formed on a sheet of paper? Describe the image. Is it real or virtual? How do you know?

Guide for Reading

- What happens when light rays enter a medium at an angle?
- How do convex and concave lenses form images?

Reading Tip As you read, draw diagrams to show how each type of lens refracts light.

A fish tank can play tricks on your eyes. If you look through the side, the fish seems closer than if you look over the top. If you look through the corner, you may see the same fish twice. You see one image of the fish through the front of the tank and another image through the side of the tank. The two images appear in different places!

Refraction of Light

As you look into a fish tank, you are seeing the light bend as it passes through three different mediums. The mediums are the water, the glass of the tank, and the air. As the light passes from one medium to the next, it refracts. **When light rays enter a new medium at an angle, the change in speed causes them to bend, or change direction.**

Refraction can cause you to see something that may not actually be there. For example, refraction can form a mirage. It can also cause a beautiful sight, a rainbow.

Figure 7 There is only one fish in this tank, but the refraction of light makes it look as though there are two.

Disappearing Glass

Try this activity to see how different liquids refract light.

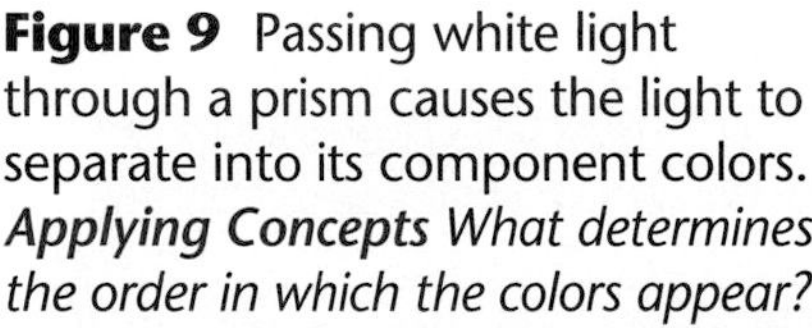

1. Place a small drinking glass inside a larger drinking glass. Can you see the small glass inside the larger one?
2. Fill both glasses with water. Look at the glasses from the side. Can you still see the smaller glass?
3. Empty and dry the glasses and refill them with vegetable oil. Describe what you see.

Inferring Why does the vegetable oil create an effect different from the water?

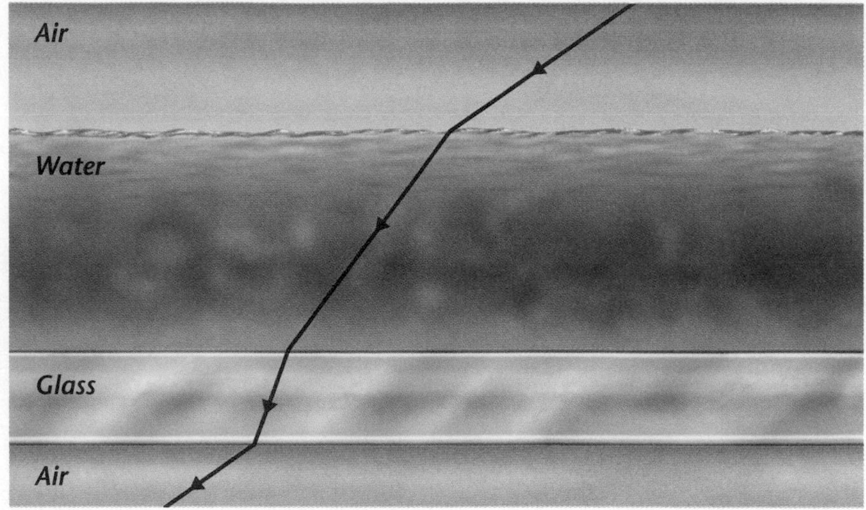

Figure 8 The index of refraction of a medium determines the extent to which light is bent as it passes through the medium. ***Inferring*** *Why does the light leaving the glass and entering the air travel in its original direction?*

Index of Refraction Some mediums cause light to bend more than others. Figure 8 shows how light passes from air into water, from water into glass, and from glass into air again. When light passes from air into water, the light slows down. Light slows down even more when it passes from water into glass. Light travels fastest in air, a little slower in water, and slower still in glass. When light passes from glass back into air, the light speeds up. Notice that the ray that leaves the glass is traveling in the same direction as it was before it entered the water.

Glass causes light to bend more than either air or water because glass refracts light more. Another way to say this is that glass has a higher index of refraction than either air or water. A material's **index of refraction** is a measure of how much a ray of light bends when it enters that material. The higher the index of refraction of a medium, the more it bends light. The index of refraction of a vacuum is 1. The index of refraction of diamond is 2.42.

Figure 9 Passing white light through a prism causes the light to separate into its component colors. ***Applying Concepts*** *What determines the order in which the colors appear?*

Prisms Figure 9 shows that a beam of white light can be separated to show all the colors of the visible spectrum. Remember that white light is actually a mixture of many wavelengths of light, each with its own color. When white light enters a prism, each wavelength is refracted by a different amount. The longer the wavelength, the less the wave will be bent by a prism.

Rainbows When white light from the sun shines through tiny drops of water, a rainbow may appear. **INTEGRATING EARTH SCIENCE** Raindrops act like tiny prisms, refracting and reflecting the light and separating the colors. The colors of the rainbow always appear in the same order because raindrops refract the shorter wavelengths the most. Red, with the longest wavelength, is refracted the least. Violet, with the shortest wavelength, is refracted the most. The result is that white light is separated into the colors of the visible spectrum: red, orange, yellow, green, blue, and violet.

Figure 10 A rainbow forms when sunlight is refracted and reflected by tiny water droplets.

Mirages Imagine that you are in a car moving down a road on a hot, sunny day. The road ahead looks wet. Yet when you get there, the road is perfectly dry. Did the puddles disappear just before you got there? No, they were never there at all! What you saw was a mirage. A **mirage** (mih RAHJ) is an image of a distant object caused by refraction of light.

Figure 11 shows how a mirage forms. The air higher up is cooler than the air near the road. Light travels faster when it reaches the warmer air. As a result, the rays bend as they travel downward. Near the ground, the rays are traveling almost parallel to the ground but continue to bend until they begin to travel upward. As they travel upward they bend in the other direction. Your brain assumes that the rays have traveled in a straight line. They look just like rays reflected off a smooth surface, such as water. The observer sees a mirage.

☑ *Checkpoint* *What causes a mirage?*

Figure 11 Light travels faster through hot air than through cool air. This causes light from the sky to curve as it approaches the ground. You see a mirage when refracted light appears to come from the ground.

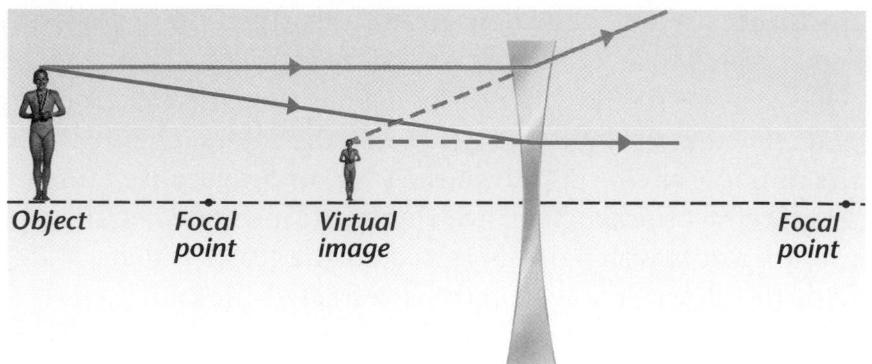

Figure 12 The ray that travels horizontally from the top of the object is refracted as though it is coming from the focal point on the same side of the concave lens as the object. The ray that travels toward the other focal point is refracted so it travels horizontally.
Interpreting Diagrams *Why do the rays from a concave lens never meet?*

Lenses

Have you ever looked through binoculars, used a microscope or a camera, or worn eyeglasses? If so, you have used a lens to bend light. A **lens** is a curved piece of glass or other transparent material that is used to refract light. A lens forms an image by refracting light rays that pass through it. Like mirrors, lenses can have different shapes. The type of image formed by a lens depends on the shape of the lens.

Concave lens

Convex lens

Figure 13 A concave lens refracts parallel rays of light so that they appear to come from one of the focal points. A convex lens refracts parallel rays of light so that they meet at the focal point.

Concave Lenses A **concave lens** is thinner in the center than at the edges. As parallel rays of light pass through a concave lens, they are bent away from the center of the lens. Figure 12 shows how the rays spread out, but appear to come from the focal point on the opposite side of the lens. **Because the light rays never meet, a concave lens can produce only a virtual image.**

Convex Lenses A **convex lens** is thicker in the center than at the edges. As parallel light rays pass through a convex lens, they are bent toward the center of the lens. The rays meet at the focal point of the lens and then continue on. The more curved the lens, the more it refracts light.

A convex lens acts somewhat like a concave mirror, because it focuses rays of light. **The type of image formed by a convex lens depends on the position of the object in relation to the focal point.** Figure 14 shows three examples. If the object is farther away than the focal point, the refracted rays form a real image on the other side of the lens. If the object is between the lens and the focal point, a virtual image forms on the same side of the lens as the object.

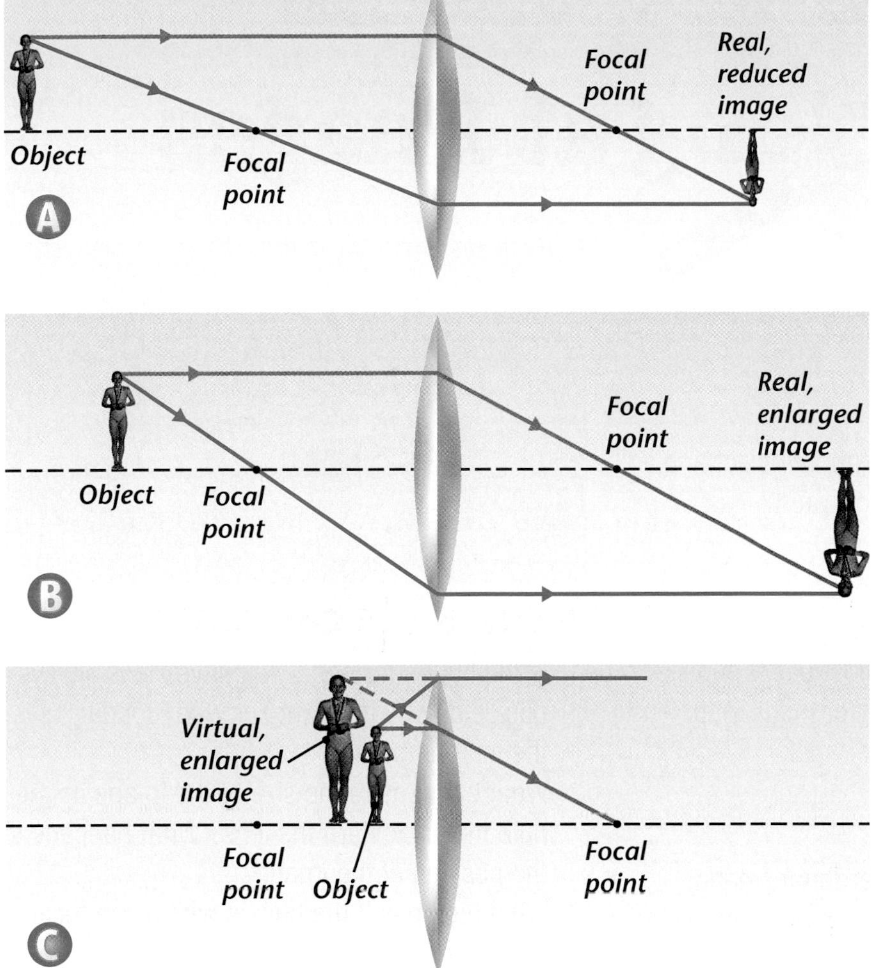

Figure 14 The type and size of image formed by a convex lens depend on the position of the object. **A, B.** If the object is farther from the lens than the focal point is from the lens, the image is real and inverted. **C.** If the object is between the focal point and the lens, the image is virtual.

Section 2 Review

1. What happens to light rays as they pass from one medium into another medium?
2. What determines the type of image that is formed by a convex lens?
3. Why is it impossible for a concave lens to form a real image?
4. Explain why you sometimes see a rainbow during a rain shower or shortly afterward.
5. **Thinking Critically Problem Solving** Suppose you wanted to closely examine the leaf of a plant. Which type of lens would you use? Explain.

Science at Home

Here's how you can bend a pencil without touching it. Put a pencil in a glass of water, as shown in the photograph. Have your family members look at the pencil from the side. Using the idea of refraction, explain to your family why the pencil appears as it does.

Skills Lab

Controlling Variables

Looking at Images

In this lab, you will control variables as you explore how images are formed by a convex lens.

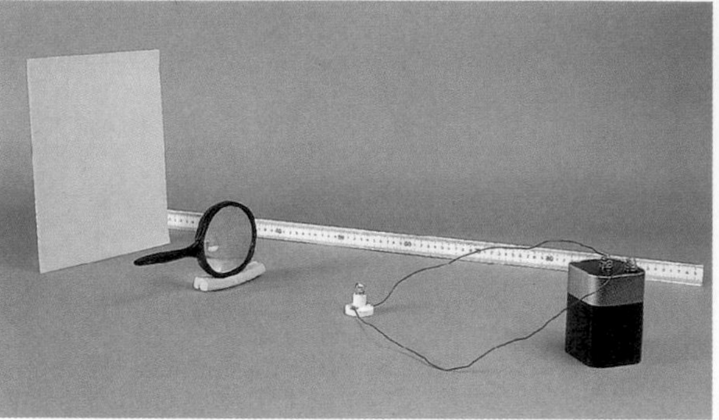

Problem

How does the distance between an object and a convex lens affect the image formed?

Materials

tape
cardboard stand
light bulb and socket
battery and wires
convex lens
blank sheet of paper
clay, for holding the lens
meter stick

Procedure

1. Tape the paper onto the cardboard stand.
2. Place a lit bulb more than 2 m from the paper. Use the lens to focus light from the bulb onto the paper. Measure the distance from the lens to the paper. This is the approximate focal length of the lens you are using.
3. Copy the data table into your notebook.
4. Now place the bulb more than twice the focal length away from the lens. Record the position and size of the focused image on the paper. Measure the height of the bulb image.
5. Now, move the bulb so that it is just over one focal length away from the lens. Record the position and size of the image.

Analyze and Conclude

1. Is the image formed by a convex lens always upside down? If not, under what conditions is the image upright?
2. What happens to the size of the image as the bulb moves toward the lens? What happens to the position of the image?
3. What happens if the bulb is within one focal length of the lens? Explain.
4. **Think About It** Make a list of the variables in this experiment. Which variables did you keep constant? Which was the manipulated variable? Which was the responding variable?

Design an Experiment

With your teacher's approval and supervision, design an experiment to study images formed by convex lenses of various focal lengths. How does the focal length of the lens affect the position and size of the images produced?

DATA TABLE

Focal Length of Lens: ____ cm		Height of Bulb: ____ cm	
Distance From Bulb to Lens (cm)	Distance From Lens to Cardboard (cm)	Image Orientation (upright or upside down)	Image Size (height in cm)

Section 3 Color

Discover Activity

How Do Colors Mix?

1. Carefully cut a disk with a diameter of about 10 cm out of a piece of sturdy white cardboard. Divide the disk into three equal-size segments. Use colored pencils to color one segment red, the next green, and the third blue.
2. Carefully punch two holes, about 2 cm apart, on opposite sides of the center of the disk.

3. Thread a string about 1 m long through the holes. Tie the ends of the string together so that the string forms a loop that passes through both holes.
4. With equal lengths of string on each side of the disk, turn the disk so that you are winding up the string. Predict what color(s) you will see if the disk spins fast.
5. Spin the disk by pulling and relaxing the string.

Think It Over

Observing What color do you see as the wheel spins fast? Was your prediction correct?

Guide for Reading

- What determines the color of an object?
- What are the primary colors of light?
- How is mixing pigments different from mixing light?

Reading Tip Before you read, use the section headings to make an outline about color. Leave space to take notes as you read.

As the morning sun slowly rises over the flower garden, the sunlight begins to reveal bright pink and orange poppies, purple pansies, and a striking display of many other colors. Each flower is beautiful, yet different. The light from the sun allows you to see each color clearly. But sunlight is white light. What makes each flower appear to be a different color?

The Color of Objects

The color of a flower depends on how it reflects light. Each flower absorbs some wavelengths of light and reflects other wavelengths. **The color of an object is the color of the light it reflects.**

Objects in White Light Flowers and other objects reflect different colors of light. For example, when white light strikes the orange petals of a lily, the petals reflect mostly orange wavelengths. The petals absorb the other wavelengths. You see the petals as orange because orange wavelengths of light bounce off them and enter your eyes. On the other hand, the stem and leaves appear green. They reflect mostly green wavelengths and absorb the other colors.

Figure 15 The petals of this lily appear orange because they reflect orange light. The stems and leaves appear green because they reflect green light.

What happens with black and white objects? A skunk looks black and white because some parts of it reflect all wavelengths of light while other parts do not reflect any light. When white light strikes the skunk's stripe, all the colors are reflected. The colors combine, so you see white light. When white light strikes the black parts of the skunk, all the light is absorbed and none is reflected. Your eyes see black.

Even colored and white objects can appear black if there is no light to reflect off them. Imagine being in a dark room. If there is no light present, then no light can reflect off the things in the room. No light enters your eyes, so you see nothing. If there is a small amount of light in the room, you may be able to make out the shapes of objects. However, you will not be able to tell their colors.

Objects in Colored Light Objects can look a different color depending on the color of light in which they are seen. Figure 17 shows two photographs of a desktop, each taken under different light. The first picture was taken under ordinary white light. In it, the keyboard is blue and the folder is red. The second picture was taken under green light. When green light shines on an object,

Figure 16 The white part of this skunk reflects all colors of light. ***Applying Concepts*** *Why do the skunk's legs look black?*

Figure 17 In white light, objects appear in many different colors (left). If viewed under green light, the same objects appear in shades of green or black (right). ***Predicting*** *How would these objects look under blue light?*

the object either reflects or absorbs the green light. Since red and blue objects reflect only red and blue light, they absorb all of the green light. The binder looks black.

Objects Seen Through Filters Some transparent materials allow only certain colors of light to pass through them. They reflect or absorb the other colors. Such materials are called color filters. For example, a red filter is a piece of glass or plastic that allows only red light to pass through. Spotlights on theater stages often use color filters to produce different color effects. Photographic slides are color filters, too. A slide projector shines white light through a combination of color filters. The image you see on the screen shows the colors that each part of the slide allows through.

☑ ***Checkpoint*** *What is a color filter?*

Combining Colors

An understanding of color is very useful in photography, art, theater lighting, and printing. People who work with color must know how to produce a wide range of colors from just a few basic colors. It is possible to produce any color by mixing colors of the spectrum in varying amounts. Three colors that can be used to make any other color are called **primary colors.** Any two primary colors combined in equal amounts produce a **secondary color.**

Mixing Colors of Light **The primary colors of light are red, green, and blue. When combined in equal amounts, the primary colors produce white light.** But if they are combined in varying amounts, they can produce any other color. For example, red and green combine to form yellow light. Yellow is a secondary color of light because it is produced from two primary colors.

Developing Hypotheses

ACTIVITY

1. Carefully make a color wheel with eight segments. Use colored pencils to color alternate blue and yellow segments.
2. Predict what color you will see if you spin the wheel. Write a hypothesis of what you think the outcome will be. Be sure to write your hypothesis as an *"If . . . then . . ."* statement.
3. Spin the wheel. What do you see? Does it confirm your hypothesis?
4. Repeat the activity with color wheels that have different pairs of colors.

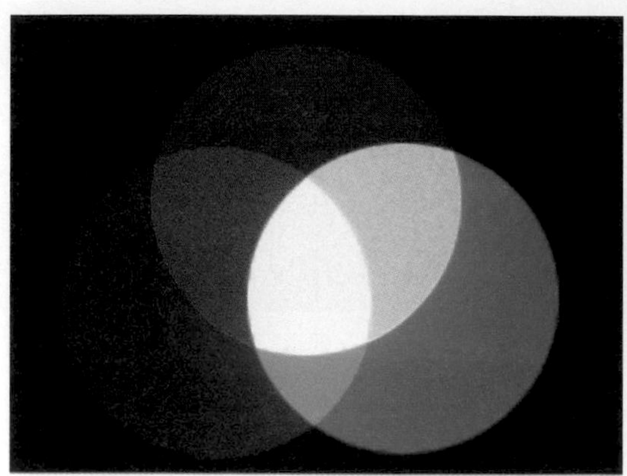

Overlapping primary colors of light

Figure 18 The primary colors of light are red, green, and blue (left). When combined in equal amounts, the primary colors of light form white light. A color television produces all colors of light by combining red, green, and blue light in varying amounts. ***Interpreting Photographs*** *How does a television show black?*

Visual Arts CONNECTION

Ever since the first cave artists painted about 20,000 years ago, pigments made from natural materials have been used to create pictures. In the 1400s, Renaissance painters such as Leonardo da Vinci and Raphael used many more colorful pigments to create their vivid paintings. Pigments were derived from minerals, plants, and animals.

In Your Journal

Look at the color names for markers, paints, or crayons. Do you see vermilion (red), azure (blue) or ochre (brown)? These colors were all originally made from minerals. Now these colors are made from chemicals. Can you find the names of other colors that may have originally come from minerals?

The secondary colors of light are yellow (red + green), cyan (green + blue), and magenta (red + blue). Figure 18 shows the primary and secondary colors of light.

A primary color and a secondary color can combine to make white. Any two colors that combine to form white light are called **complementary colors.** Yellow and blue are complementary colors, as are cyan and red, and magenta and green.

INTEGRATING TECHNOLOGY A color television screen produces only three colors of light. Figure 18 shows a magnified portion of a color television screen. Notice that the picture on the screen is made up of little groups of red, green, and blue lights. By varying the brightness of each colored light, the television produces pictures of many different colors.

Mixing Pigments How do artists produce the many shades of colors you see in paintings? Paints and dyes have different colors because of the pigments they contain. **Pigments** are substances that are used to color other materials. Color pigments are opaque substances that reflect particular colors. The color you see is the color that particular pigment reflects.

Mixing colors of pigments is different from mixing colors of light. **As pigments are added together, fewer colors of light are reflected and more are absorbed.** The more pigments that are combined, the darker the mixture looks.

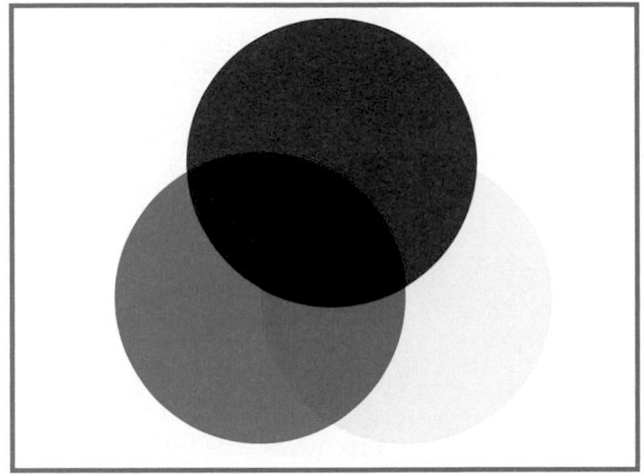

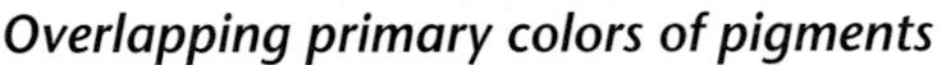

Overlapping primary colors of pigments

Figure 19 The primary colors of pigments are cyan, yellow, and magenta (left). The photograph shows a printed image and the round inset shows an enlargement of part of it. Four-color printing uses the three primary colors of pigments, plus black.

The primary colors of pigments are cyan, yellow, and magenta. If you combine all three primary colors of pigments in equal amounts, you get black. If you combine two primary colors of pigments in equal amounts, you get a secondary color. The secondary colors of pigments are red (magenta + yellow), green (cyan + yellow), and blue (magenta + cyan). By combining pigments in varying amounts, you can produce any other color. Figure 19 shows the primary and secondary colors of pigments.

If you use a magnifying glass to look at color pictures in this book, you will see that the pictures are made up of tiny dots of different colors of ink. The colors used are cyan, yellow, and magenta. Black ink is also used to make pictures darker. Because of the four colors of ink used, the process that produced this book is called four-color printing.

Section 3 Review

1. Why do objects have different colors?
2. What are the primary colors of light? What happens when the primary colors of light are mixed in equal amounts?
3. What happens when the primary colors of pigments are mixed in equal amounts?
4. What colors are used in the four-color printing process?
5. **Thinking Critically Comparing and Contrasting** Make a table that compares and contrasts the primary and secondary colors of light and those of pigments.

CHAPTER PROJECT 16

Check Your Progress

Build your optical instrument according to the sketch you prepared. How does your instrument use reflection or refraction to produce and clarify images? Do you need to be able to change the focus of the image? Does your instrument have moving parts? How will you combine the different parts of the instrument?

Real-World Lab

How It Works

Changing Colors

Stage lighting in theaters uses color filters to control the colors of light on stage. In this lab you will study the effect of color filters on white light.

Problem

How do color filters affect the appearance of white light?

Skills Focus

observing, predicting, inferring

Materials

shoe box
scissors
flashlight
removable tape
red object (such as a ripe tomato)
yellow object (such as a ripe lemon)
blue object (such as blue construction paper)
red, green, and blue cellophane, enough to cover the top of the shoe box

Procedure 

1. Carefully cut a large rectangular hole in the lid of the shoe box.
2. Carefully cut a small, round hole in the center of one of the ends of the shoe box.
3. Tape the red cellophane under the lid of the shoe box, covering the hole in the lid.
4. Place the objects in the box and put the lid on.
5. In a darkened room, shine the flashlight into the shoe box through the side hole. Note the apparent color of each object in the box.
6. Repeat Steps 3–5 using the other colors of cellophane.

Analyze and Conclude

1. What did you see when you looked through the red cellophane? Explain why each object appeared as it did.
2. What did you see when you looked through the blue cellophane? Explain.
3. What color of light does each piece of cellophane allow through?
4. Predict what you would see under each piece of cellophane if you put a white object in the box. Test your prediction.
5. Use diagrams to show how each color of cellophane affects the white light from the flashlight.
6. **Think About It** Do color filters work more like pigments or like colors of light? What would happen if you shined a flashlight through both a red and a green filter? Explain.

Getting Involved

Visit a local theater or talk to a lighting designer to find out how color filters are used to produce different stage effects.

Section 4 Seeing Light

Discover

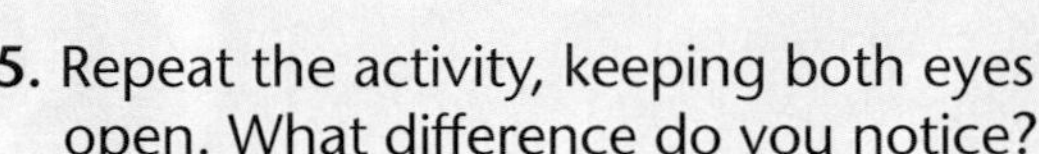

Can You See Everything With One Eye?

1. Write an X and an O on a sheet of paper. They should be about 5 cm apart.
2. Hold the sheet of paper at arm's length.
3. Close or cover your left eye. Stare at the X with your right eye.
4. Slowly move the paper toward your face while staring at the X. What do you notice?
5. Repeat the activity, keeping both eyes open. What difference do you notice?

Think It Over

Posing Questions Write two questions about vision that you could investigate using the X and the O.

The excitement mounts as the pitcher goes into his windup. As he goes through his motion, he keeps his eye on the strike zone. The batter watches the pitcher release the ball, then swings. Crack! The batter hits the ball, drops the bat, and sprints toward first base. From your seat behind home plate, you watch the ball travel toward the outfield. Will it be a base hit? The left fielder watches the ball leave the bat and travel toward him. It goes over his head—a double!

Everyone involved has been following the first rule of baseball: Keep your eye on the ball. As the ball moves, the eyes must adjust continuously to keep it in focus. Fortunately, this change in focus happens automatically.

Guide for Reading

- **How do your eyes allow you to see?**
- **What kinds of lenses are used to correct vision problems?**

Reading Tip **As you read, make a flowchart that shows how light travels through the eye and how the brain interprets the image.**

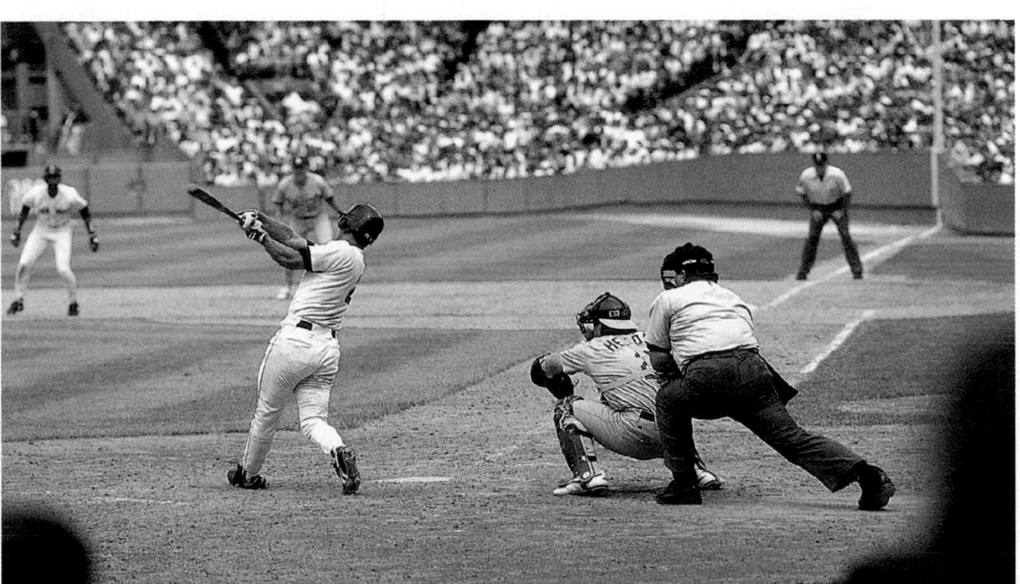

Figure 20 As the ball moves through the air, your eyes must continuously adjust their focus to see the ball.

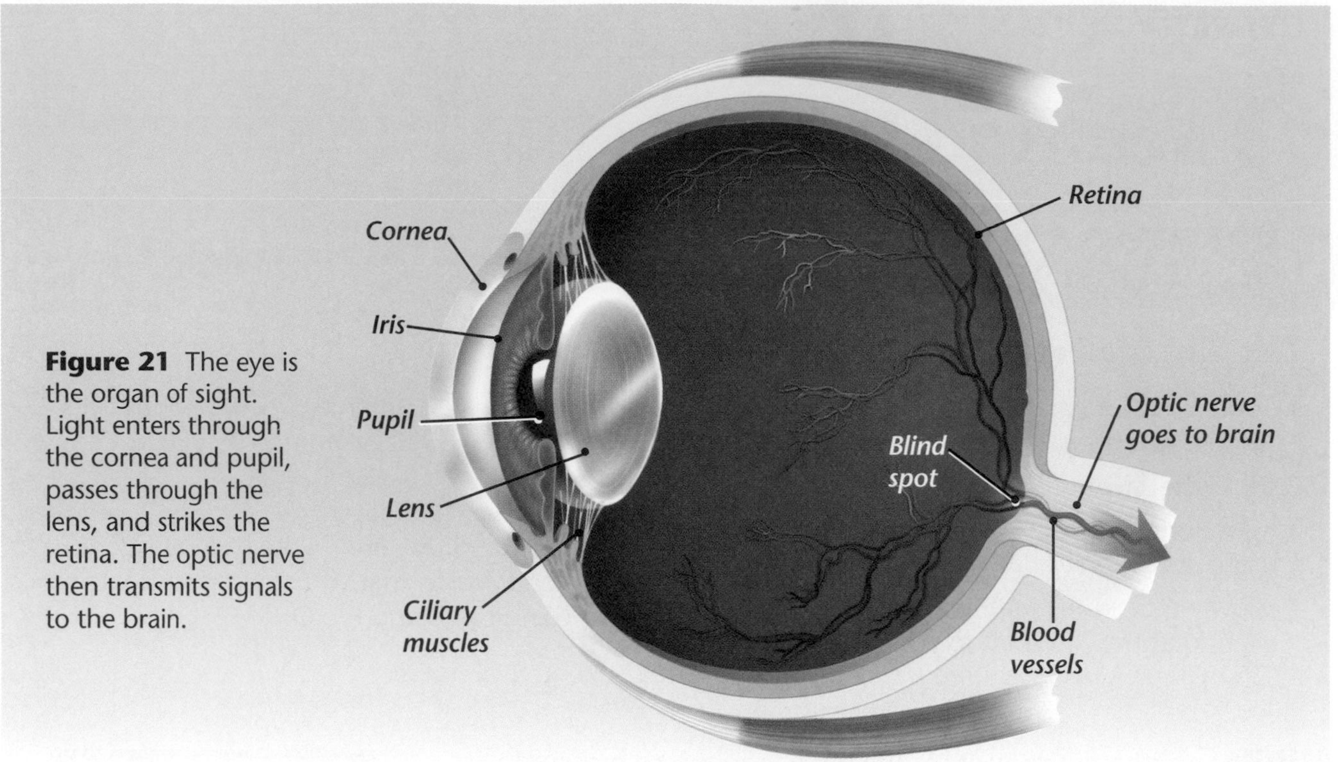

Figure 21 The eye is the organ of sight. Light enters through the cornea and pupil, passes through the lens, and strikes the retina. The optic nerve then transmits signals to the brain.

The Human Eye

Your eyes are complicated organs, with each part playing its own role in helping you see. **You see objects because of a series of steps that involve the structures of the eye and the brain.**

The Cornea Light enters the eye through the transparent front surface called the **cornea.** The cornea protects the eye. It also acts as a lens, bending rays of light as they enter the eye. Each time you blink, your eyelids act like little windshield wipers, cleansing and moistening the cornea.

The Iris The **iris** is a ring of muscle that contracts and expands to change the amount of light that enters the eye. The iris gives the eye its color. In most people the iris is brown; in others it is blue or green.

The Pupil The **pupil** is the part of the eye that looks black. It is actually a hole, covered by the clear cornea. The pupil looks black because it is an opening into the dark inside of the eye. Figure 22 shows how the size of the pupil depends on whether the iris is contracted or expanded. In dim light, the pupil becomes larger, allowing more light in. In very bright light, the pupil becomes smaller, reducing the amount of light that enters the eye.

Figure 22 In dim light, the iris contracts. The pupil gets bigger and allows more light into the eye. ***Relating Cause and Effect*** *What happens in bright light?*

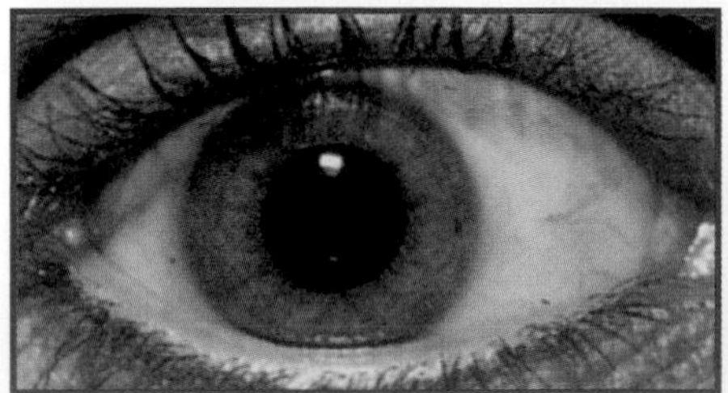

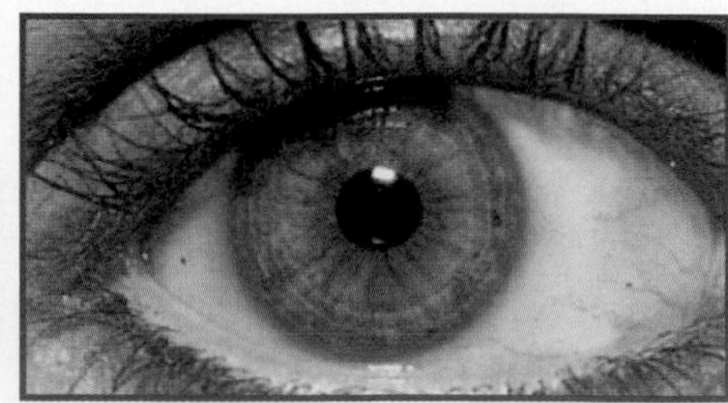

The Lens Just behind the pupil is the lens. The lens of your eye is a convex lens. The lens refracts light, forming an image on the lining of your eyeball. Figure 23 shows how the lens changes its focus. When you focus on a distant object, the ciliary muscles holding the lens relax, making the lens longer and thinner. When you focus on a nearby object, the muscles contract and the lens becomes shorter and fatter.

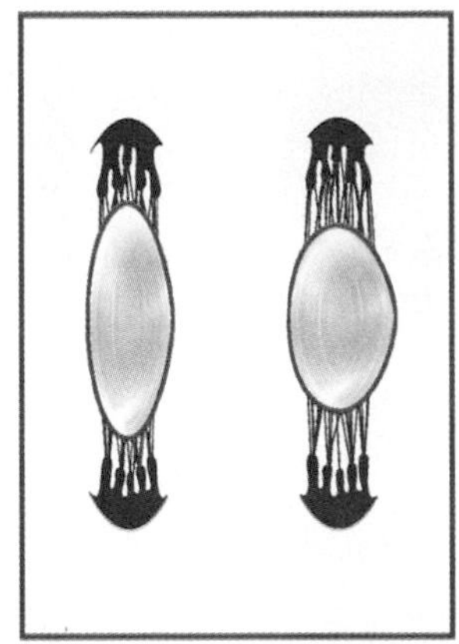

Figure 23 The ciliary muscles holding the lens in place relax (left) or contract (right) to change the shape of the lens.

The Retina The layer of cells lining the inside of the eyeball is the **retina.** As the cornea and the lens refract light, an upside-down image is formed on the retina. The retina is made up of millions of tiny, light-sensitive cells called rods and cones. The rods and cones generate small nerve signals when they are hit by light.

The **rods** contain a pigment that reacts to small amounts of light. The rods distinguish among black, white, and shades of gray. They allow you to see in dim light, so they are important for night vision.

The **cones** respond to colors. There are three types of cones: those that detect red light, those that detect green light, and those that detect blue light. The cone cells function only in bright light. This is why it is difficult to distinguish colors in dim light.

The Optic Nerve and the Brain The signals generated by the rods and cones travel to your brain along a short, thick nerve called the **optic nerve.** When the signals reach your brain, it automatically turns the image right-side up. Your brain also combines the two images, one from each eye, into a single three-dimensional image.

There is one spot on the retina that does not have any rods or cones. This blind spot is the part of the retina where the optic nerve begins. You cannot see light that falls on the blind spot. However, an object whose light falls on the blind spot of one eye can usually be seen with the other eye. If you keep both eyes open, you do not notice the effect of the blind spots.

☑ *Checkpoint* *Where in the eye is the image formed?*

Correcting Vision

In some people, the eyeball is slightly too long or too short, so the image on the retina is slightly out of focus. Fortunately, wearing glasses or contact lenses can usually correct this type of vision problem. **Some lenses in eyeglasses are convex and some are concave. The type of lens used depends on whether the eyeball is too long or too short.**

True Colors ACTIVITY

When you stare too long at a color, the cones in your eyes get tired.

1. Stare at the bottom right star of the flag for at least 60 seconds. Do not move your eyes or blink during that time.
2. Now stare at a sheet of blank white paper.

Observing What do you see when you look at the white paper? How are the colors you see related to the colors in the original art?

Nearsightedness (eyeball too long)

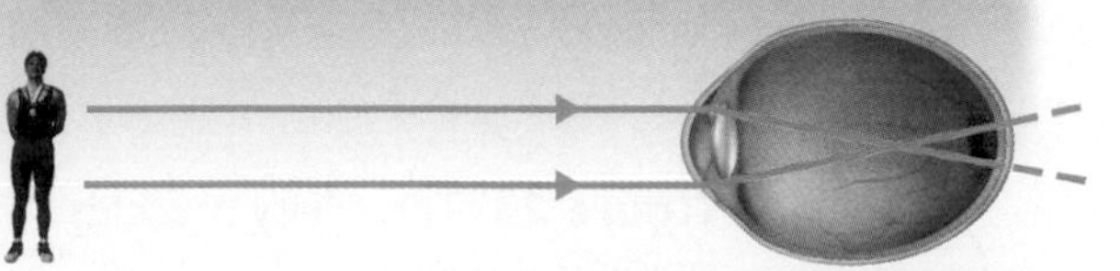

Farsightedness (eyeball too short)

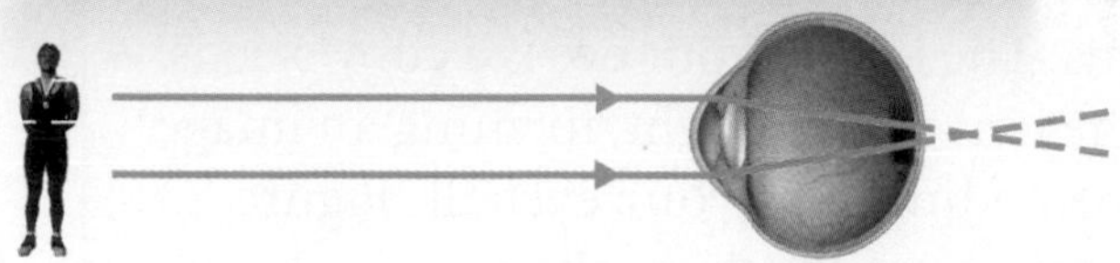

Correction

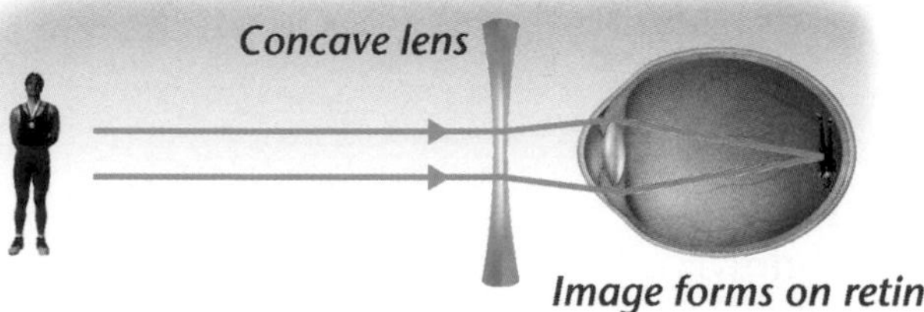

Correction

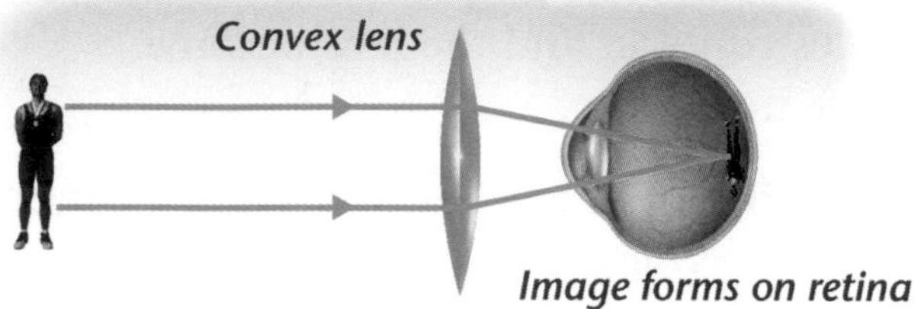

Figure 24 Nearsightedness and farsightedness are caused when the eyeball is a little too long or too short. Both can be corrected by wearing lenses.

Nearsightedness A **nearsighted** person can see nearby things clearly, but objects at a distance appear blurry. This happens because the eyeball is a little too long. The lens focuses the image in front of the retina. A nearsighted person can wear eyeglasses with concave lenses to see more clearly. A concave lens spreads out the rays a little before they enter the lens of the eye. This causes the image to form a little farther back, on the retina.

Farsightedness A **farsighted** person can see distant objects clearly, but nearby objects appear blurry. This happens when the eyeball is a little too short. The lens focuses the rays of light so that they would meet behind the retina. The image that falls on the retina is out of focus. A farsighted person can wear glasses with convex lenses. A convex lens makes the rays bend toward each other a little before they enter the eye. A clear image is then formed on the retina.

Section 4 Review

1. Describe briefly the function of each of these structures in allowing a person to see: cornea, pupil, lens, retina, optic nerve, brain.
2. How and why does the pupil change size?
3. What causes nearsightedness? Farsightedness? How can each be corrected?
4. **Thinking Critically Comparing and Contrasting** Compare and contrast the functions of the rods and the cones.

Science at Home

Roll a sheet of paper into a tube and hold one end up to your right eye. Hold your left hand against the left side of the far end of the tube with your palm facing toward you. Keeping both eyes open, look at a distant object. Draw and label a diagram of what you see. What do you think causes this optical illusion?

SECTION 5 Using Light

DISCOVER

How Does a Pinhole Viewer Work?

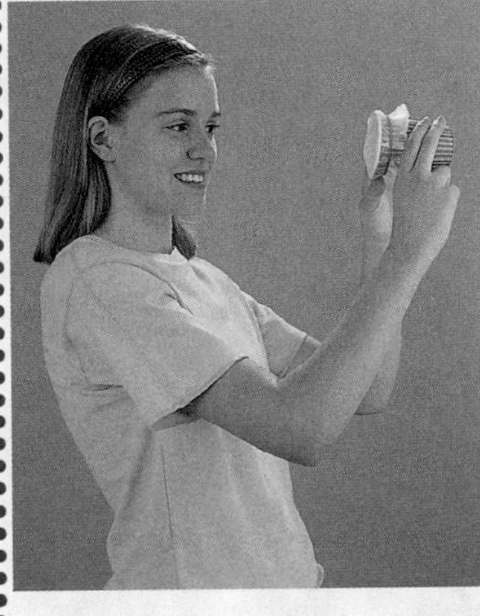

1. Carefully use a pin to make a tiny hole in the center of the bottom of a paper cup.
2. Place a piece of wax paper over the open end of the cup. Hold the paper in place with a rubber band.
3. Turn off the room lights. Point the end of the cup with the hole in it at a bright window. **CAUTION:** *Do not look directly at the sun.*
4. Look at the image formed on the wax paper.

Think It Over

Classifying Describe the image you see. Is it upside down or right-side up? Is it smaller or larger than the actual object? What type of image is it?

Have you ever seen photos of the moons of Jupiter? Have you ever thought it would be exciting to fly close to the rings of Saturn? Of course you know that traveling in space has been done for only a few decades. But you might be surprised to know that the moons of Jupiter and the rings of Saturn had not been seen by anyone before the year 1600. It was only about 1609 that a new invention, the telescope, made those objects visible to people on Earth.

Since the 1600s, astronomers have built more powerful telescopes that allow them to see objects in space that are very far from Earth. The Trifid Nebula, for example, is a cloud of gas and dust in space 28,000 trillion kilometers from Earth. It took about 3,000 years for light from this nebula to travel to Earth.

In this section you will learn how simple a device the telescope is. You may wonder why no one invented it sooner!

GUIDE FOR READING

- **How do telescopes and microscopes work?**
- **How does a camera work?**
- **How is laser light different from ordinary light?**

Reading Tip **Before you read, preview the section to identify devices that use light. As you read, make notes about how each device is commonly used.**

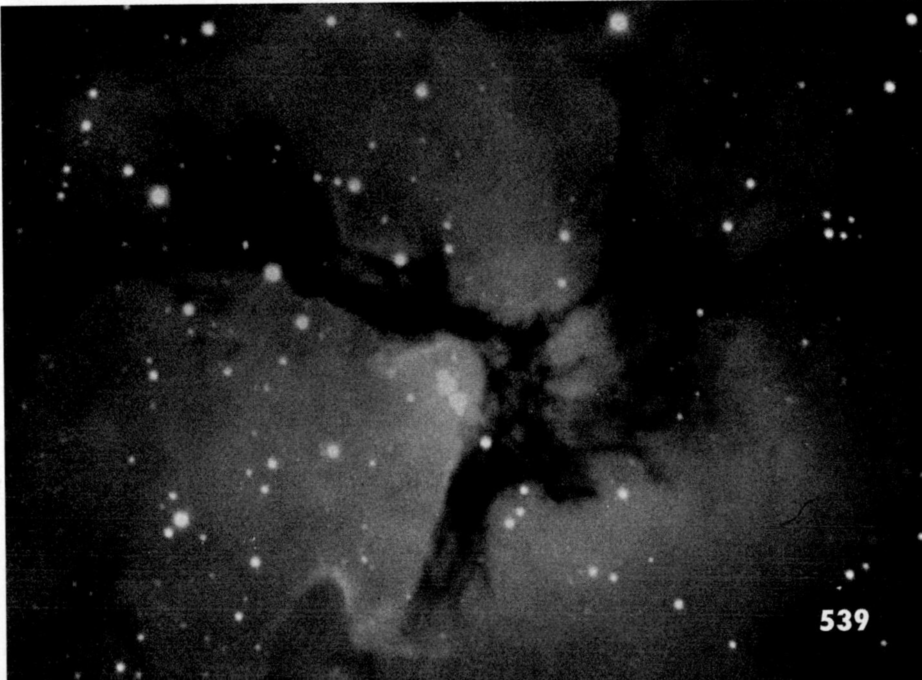

The Trifid Nebula ▶

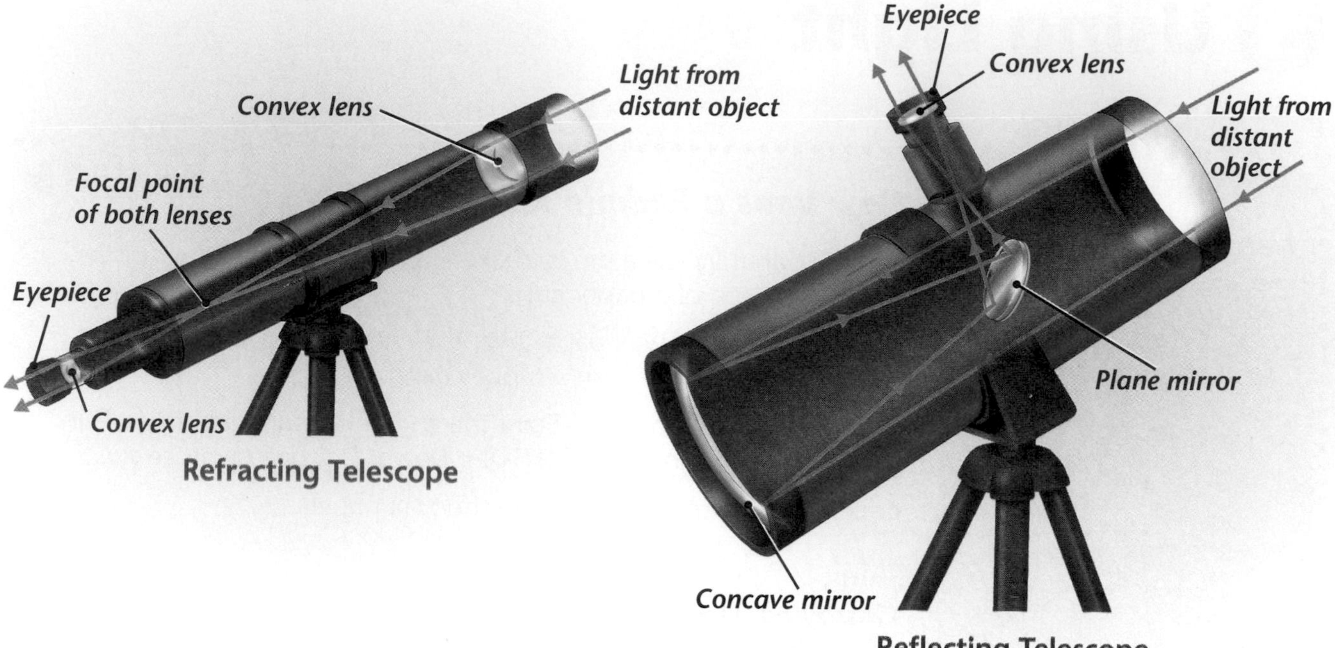

Figure 25 A refracting telescope (left) uses a combination of lenses to form an image. A reflecting telescope (right) uses a combination of lenses and mirrors to form an image.

What a View!

ACTIVITY

You can use two hand lenses of different strengths to form an image.

1. Hold the stronger lens close to your eye.
2. Hold the other lens at arm's length.
3. Use your lens combination to view a distant object. **CAUTION:** *Do not look at the sun.* Adjust the distance of the farther lens until the image is clear.

Classifying What type of image do you see? What type of telescope is similar to this lens combination?

Telescopes

Distant objects are difficult to see because light from them has spread out by the time it reaches your eyes. Your eyes are too small to gather much light. A **telescope** forms enlarged images of distant objects. **Telescopes use lenses or mirrors to collect and focus light from distant objects.** The most common use of telescopes is to collect light from space. This allows astronomers to see objects they could not see with their eyes alone.

There are two main types of telescopes: refracting telescopes and reflecting telescopes. Both types are shown in Figure 25. A **refracting telescope** consists of two convex lenses, one at each end of a long tube. The larger lens is the **objective**. The objective gathers the light coming from an object and focuses the rays to form a real image. The lens close to your eye is in the **eyepiece.** The eyepiece magnifies the image so you can see it clearly. The image you see through the refracting telescope in Figure 25 is upside down.

A **reflecting telescope** uses a large concave mirror to gather light. The mirror collects light from distant objects and focuses the rays to form a real image. A small mirror inside the telescope reflects the image to the eyepiece. The eyepiece can be replaced by a camera to record the image. The image you see through a reflecting telescope is upside down also.

☑ ***Checkpoint*** *What are the two main types of telescopes?*

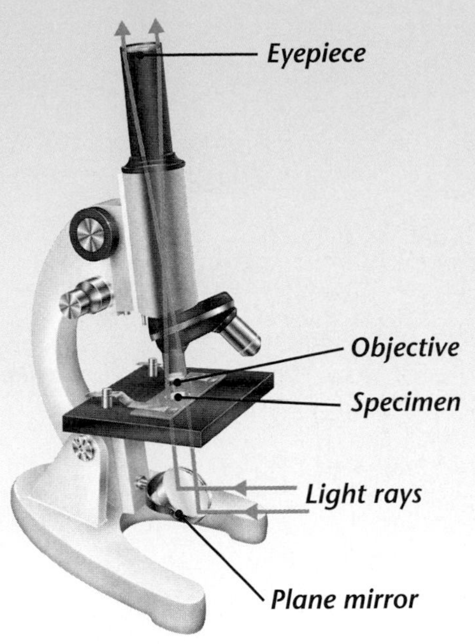

Figure 26 A microscope uses a combination of lenses to form enlarged images of tiny objects. You can use a microscope to look at microorganisms such as these single-celled algae.

Microscopes

What would happen if you used a telescope to look at small objects close up? The principle of a refracting telescope can also be used to enlarge very small objects. A **microscope** forms enlarged images of tiny objects. **A microscope uses a combination of lenses to produce and magnify an image.**

Figure 26 shows how a microscope works. The specimen to be viewed is placed on a glass or plastic slide and covered with a coverslip. The slide is then placed on the platform of the microscope. A light source or a mirror illuminates the slide from below. The objective, placed very close to the slide, forms a real, but enlarged, image of the tiny object. The eyepiece enlarges the image even more. The image can be hundreds of times larger than the object itself. Most microscopes have two or three objectives so you can change the magnifying power.

Cameras

A **camera** uses lenses to focus light and record an image of an object. Cameras range from simple pinhole cameras to high-tech models used by professional photographers. They all work in basically the same way.

In a pinhole camera, rays of light from an object enter a small box through a tiny pinhole. This light forms an upside down, real image on the back of the box. However, most cameras are more complex.

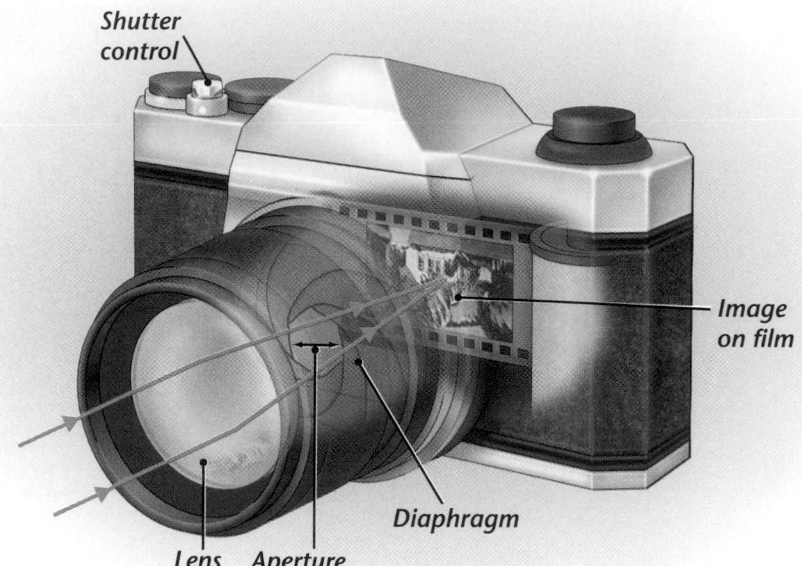

Figure 27 A camera uses a lens to project an image onto film. ***Comparing and Contrasting*** *Compare the lens, diaphragm, aperture, and film of the camera to the corresponding parts of the eye.*

Figure 27 shows the structure of a camera. The shutter is a little door behind an aperture, or hole. **When you press the button of a camera to take a photograph, you briefly open the shutter. This allows light to hit the film.** The shutter speed is the amount of time the shutter is open, or the exposure time. The diaphragm controls the amount of light that enters the camera by changing the size of the aperture. This is similar to the way that the iris of your eye controls the amount of light that enters your eye through the pupil.

Inside the camera, light passes through a convex lens or a combination of lenses. The lens focuses the light to form a real image on the film. To get a clear, properly focused image, the lens must move closer to or away from the film, depending on whether the object is close or far away. Most cameras allow you to move the lens by turning a ring on the front of the camera. An automatic camera moves the lens itself until the image is focused.

Photographic film is a material that undergoes a chemical change when exposed to light. The film is developed into negatives by treating it with chemicals. The negative is used to print the image on paper. The result is a photograph.

☑ *Checkpoint What part of a camera controls the amount of light that enters the camera?*

Lasers

In a laser show, thin beams of light flash across the walls and ceiling. These are not ordinary beams of light. The light can be focused into a narrow beam with very little spread. It can produce a clear, sharp image on a flat surface. The properties of these beams of light allow them to have many different uses.

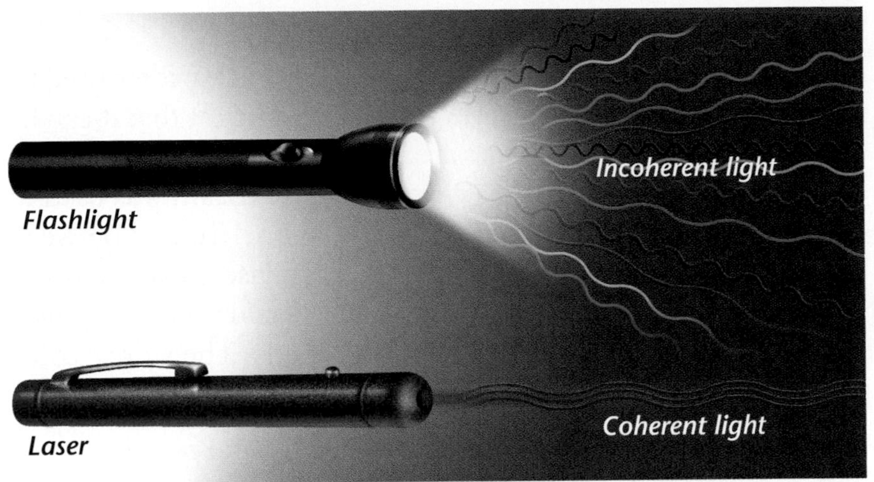

Figure 28 White light is made up of many different wavelengths, or colors. Laser light consists of light of only one wavelength. All the crests of laser light are in step with one another.

When you turn on an ordinary light bulb, the light spreads out and is visible around the room. Ordinary white light is made up of light of many different colors and wavelengths. **A laser beam consists of waves that all have the same wavelength, or color. The waves are coherent, or in step.** All the crests of the waves align with one another, as do all the troughs.

The word **laser** comes from the first letters of the words that describe how it works: **l**ight **a**mplification by **s**timulated **e**mission of **r**adiation. *Light amplification* means that the light is strengthened, or given more energy. *Stimulated emission* means that the atoms emit light when exposed to radiation.

A laser consists of a tube that contains a material such as ruby or a helium-neon mixture. The material used determines the wavelength of the light produced.

Electricity, a light flash, or a chemical reaction causes the material in the tube to emit light. The light travels up and down the tube. One end of the tube is covered with a mirror. This mirror reflects all the photons that hit it. The photons then travel to a partially reflecting mirror at the other end of the tube. As the photons travel in the tube, they bump into other atoms. The atoms then emit more photons with the same amount of energy as the one that caused the collision. The photons then travel together in step with one another. This process continues until there is a stream of in-step photons traveling up and down the tube. Some of the light "leaks" through the partially reflecting mirror. The light that comes out of the tube is the laser beam.

Figure 29 This diagram of a ruby laser shows photons moving up and down the tube. The light that comes out of the tube is the laser beam.

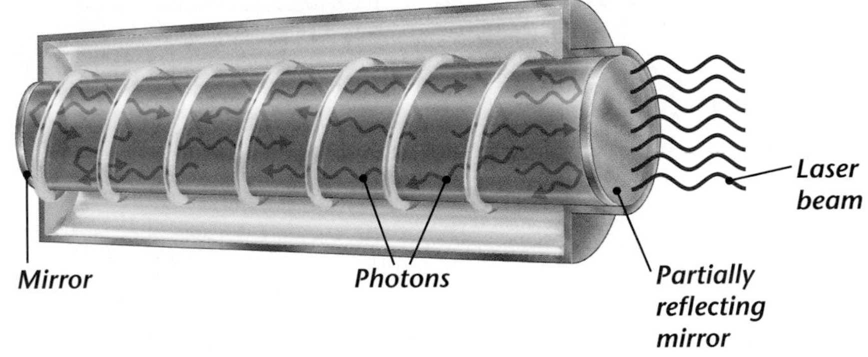

Uses of Lasers

Lasers have many practical applications. Lasers are widely used by surveyors and engineers. A laser beam is so straight that it can be used to make sure that surfaces are level and that bridges and tunnels are properly aligned. For example, a laser beam was used to guide the tunnel diggers who dug the Channel Tunnel between England and France. Some very powerful lasers can even cut through steel. Many stores and supermarkets use lasers. A laser scans the universal product code, or bar code. The store's computer then displays the price of the object.

Compact Discs Lasers can be used to store and read information. A compact disc is produced by converting data into electrical signals. The electrical signals are converted to a laser beam, which cuts a pattern of pits on a blank disc. When you play a compact disc or read one with a computer, a laser beam shines on the surface and is reflected. The reflection patterns vary because

Optical Instruments

The development of optical instruments has changed the way we look at the world and beyond. It has allowed major scientific discoveries.

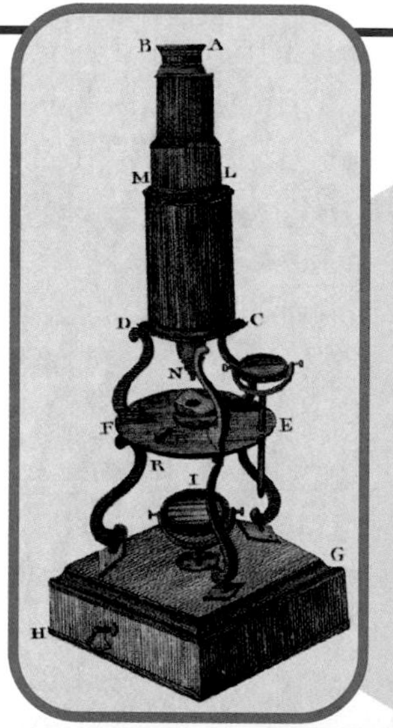

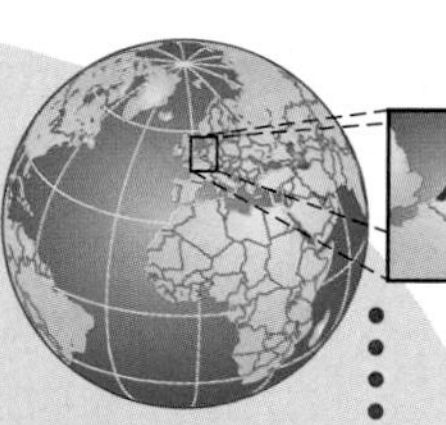

1595 The Netherlands

Microscopes

The first useful microscope is thought to have been constructed by Zacharias Jansen or his father, Hans. The Jansen microscope could magnify images up to nine times the size of the object. By the mid-1600s, microscopes looked like the one shown here.

1300 | 1400 | 1500 | 1600

1350 Italy

Spectacles

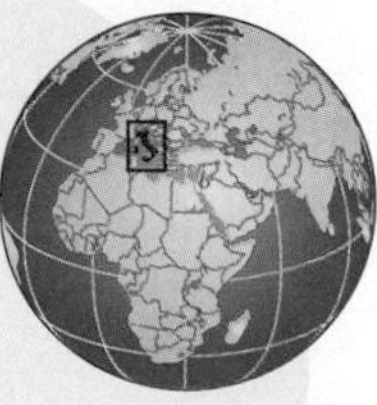

Craftsmen made small disks of glass that could be framed and worn in front of the eyes. Early spectacles consisted of convex lenses. They were used as reading glasses.

1607 The Netherlands

Telescopes

The first telescope was made of two convex lenses. It was from this simple invention that the Italian scientist Galileo developed his more powerful telescopes shown here.

of the pits. The compact disc player or disc drive changes these patterns into electrical signals. The signals are sent to speakers and you hear sound.

Surgery Doctors can use lasers instead of scalpels to make

INTEGRATING HEALTH

incisions. The beam of light can be powerful enough to cut through flesh. As the laser makes the incision, it seals the cut blood vessels. This reduces the amount of blood a patient loses. Laser incisions usually heal faster than scalpel cuts, so the patient's recovery time is reduced.

Eye doctors use lasers to repair detached retinas. If the retina falls away from the inside of the eye, the rods and cones can no longer send signals to the brain. This can lead to total or partial blindness. The doctor can use a laser to "weld" or burn the retina back onto the eyeball. Lasers can also be used to destroy or remove skin blemishes and cancerous growths.

In Your Journal

Find out more about early photography and people's reactions to it. Then imagine you are an early photographer explaining photography to someone who has never seen a photo. Create a two-page dialog in which you answer that person's questions on the process and possible uses of photography.

1990 UNITED STATES

Hubble Space Telescope

This large reflecting telescope was launched by the crew of the space shuttle *Discovery.* It can detect infrared, visible, and ultraviolet rays in space and send pictures back to Earth.

1700 1800 1900 2000

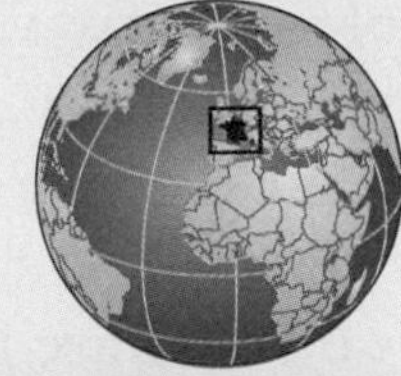

1826 FRANCE

Cameras

The earliest camera, the pinhole camera, was adapted to form and record permanent images by Joseph Nicéphore Niepce and Louis-Jacques-Mandé Daguerre of France. This is one of Nicéphore Niepce's earliest photographic images.

1960 UNITED STATES

Lasers

The first laser, built by American Theodore Maiman, used a rod of ruby to produce light. Since then, lasers have been used in numerous ways, including in engineering, medicine, and communications.

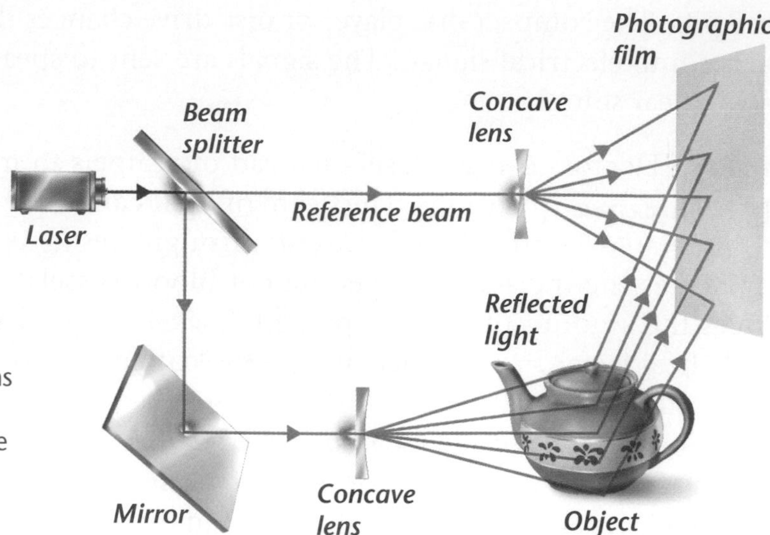

Figure 30 To form a hologram, the light from a laser is split into two beams. When the two beams strike the photographic film, an interference pattern produces the image, or hologram.

Holography Check out your local video store or newsstand. Some videos and magazines have pictures that appear to move as you walk by. A **hologram** is a three-dimensional photograph created by using the light from a laser. The process is called holography.

Figure 30 shows how a hologram is produced. A laser beam is split into two beams. One beam passes through a concave lens, behind which is a piece of photographic film. The concave lens spreads out the rays of light before they hit the film. The second beam is sent to a mirror and reflected toward another concave lens, behind which is the object being photographed. Again, the rays are spread out by the lens before they hit the object. The object then reflects these rays toward the film, where they interfere with rays from the first beam. The interference pattern recorded on the film produces a three-dimensional image when viewed in laser light.

Checkpoint *What are four uses of lasers?*

Figure 31 Optical fibers are thin strands of glass or plastic that carry light.

Optical Fibers

Lasers are also used in communications. A laser beam is electromagnetic radiation of a single wavelength. It is similar to radio waves and so can carry signals by modulation. Unlike radio waves, laser beams are not usually sent through the air. Instead, they are sent through optical fibers. **Optical fibers** are long, thin strands of glass or plastic that can carry light for long distances without allowing the light to fade out. You may have seen optical fibers in lamps or in the small hand-held lights that are sometimes sold at circuses and other shows.

EXPLORING Uses of Lasers

The invention of the laser has led to many developments in technology and communication.

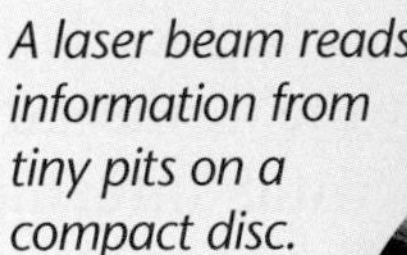

A laser beam reads information from tiny pits on a compact disc. ▲

▲ Civil engineers use laser beams to ensure that buildings are straight.

▼ Optical fibers carry beams of laser light great distances. One tiny fiber can carry thousands more phone conversations than the traditional copper wire cable.

▲ A supermarket scanner reflects a laser off a set of lines known as a universal product code, or UPC. Each product has a unique code. This code represents a number that is programmed into the store's computer. The computer then displays the name of the object and the price on a screen near the cash register.

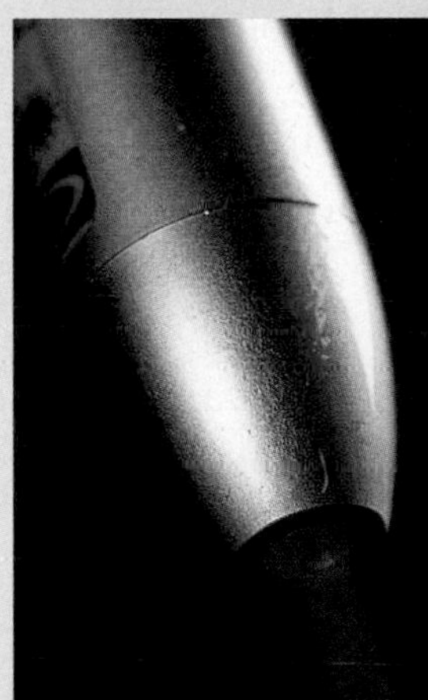

Small, hand-held lasers are commonly used as pointers in lectures and presentations.

◀ Banks now commonly put small holograms on credit cards for security reasons. The hologram makes credit cards difficult to copy.

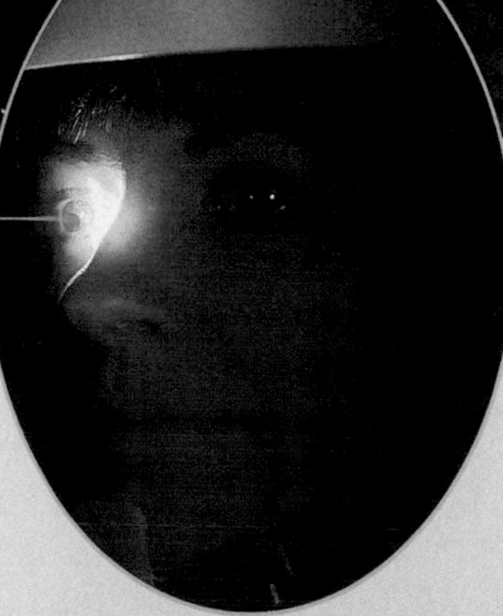

▶ Laser surgery can correct vision by reshaping the cornea of the eye.

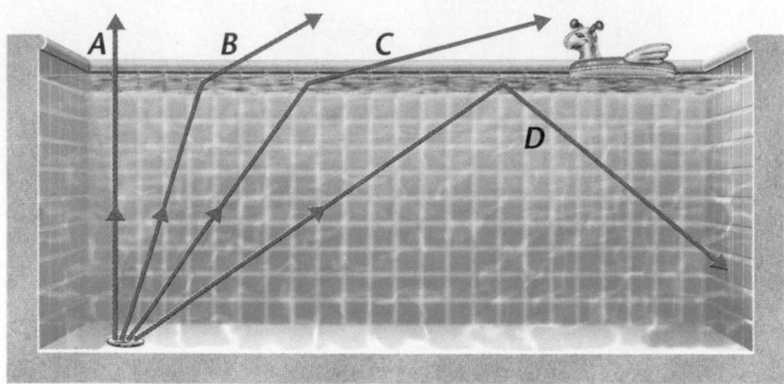

Figure 32 The angle of the light beam determines whether or not the light can leave the medium. If the angle is great enough, the light is reflected back into the water.

Figure 32 shows how light can stay inside a medium and not pass through the surface to the outside. When a light beam hits a surface at a 0° angle of incidence, it goes through the surface without being bent. As the angle of incidence gets larger, the light is bent more and more. When it travels nearly parallel to the surface, all of the light is reflected. This complete reflection of light by the inside surface of a medium is called **total internal reflection.** Figure 33 shows how a laser beam reflects off the inside of an optical fiber and keeps going, even if the optical fiber is curved or curled up.

Communications To send signals through optical fibers, the electrical signals that start out over copper wires are changed into pulses of light by tiny lasers. Then the signals can travel over long ranges in the optical fiber. Optical fibers have led to great improvements in telephone service, computer networks, and cable television systems. Signals sent over optical fibers are usually faster and clearer than those sent over copper wire. One tiny optical fiber can carry thousands of phone conversations at the same time. Optical fibers are so much thinner than copper wire that more fibers can be placed in the same space underground.

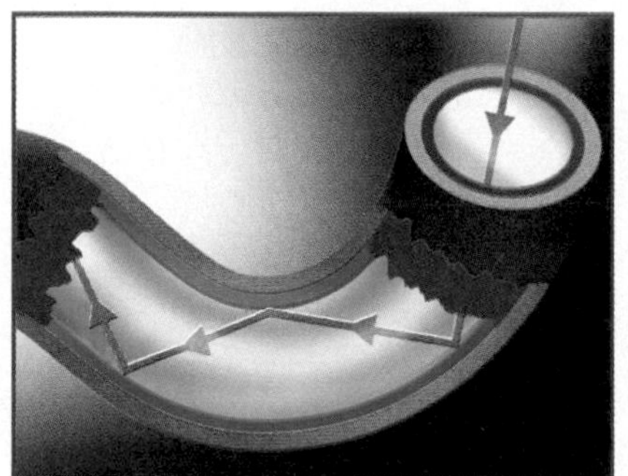

Figure 33 Light travels through an optical fiber by total internal reflection.

Medicine Optical fibers are commonly used in medical instruments. Doctors can insert a thin optical fiber inside various parts of the body, such as the heart or the stomach. The optical fiber can be attached to a microscope or a camera. In this way, doctors can examine internal organs without having to perform surgery.

Section 5 Review

1. Compare and contrast refracting telescopes and reflecting telescopes.
2. How does a microscope work?
3. Why does a camera produce an upside-down image?
4. What is a laser beam composed of?
5. Describe two uses of optical fibers.
6. **Thinking Critically Making Judgments** Laser beams can *severely* damage eyes and skin. Explain why you think this is so.

CHAPTER PROJECT 16

Check Your Progress

Now it is time to test your optical instrument. Does it work as you designed it to? Can you adjust the mirror or lenses to change the focus of the image? Do moving parts move smoothly and easily? Modify any parts of your instrument to help it work better. Prepare a manual that describes and explains each part of the instrument.

CHAPTER 16 STUDY GUIDE

Reflection and Mirrors

Key Ideas

- Light that strikes an object can be reflected, absorbed, or transmitted.
- A plane mirror produces an image that is right-side up and the same size as the object.
- Concave mirrors can form either virtual images or real images. Images formed by convex mirrors are always virtual.

Key Terms

opaque
transparent
translucent
ray
regular reflection
diffuse reflection
image
plane mirror
virtual image
concave mirror
focal point
real image
convex mirror

Refraction and Lenses

Key Ideas

- When light rays hit the surface of a medium at an angle, they bend, or change direction.
- The type of image formed by a convex lens depends on the position of the object in relation to the focal point.
- Concave lenses produce only virtual images.

Key Terms

index of refraction
mirage
lens
concave lens
convex lens

Color

Key Ideas

- You see an object as the color of the light it reflects. The primary colors of light are red, green, and blue.
- As pigments are added together, fewer colors of light are reflected and more are absorbed.

Key Terms

primary color
secondary color
complementary color
pigment

Seeing Light

Integrating Life Science

Key Ideas

- You see objects because of a series of steps that involve the structures of the eye and the brain.
- Lenses can correct some vision problems.

Key Terms

cornea
iris
pupil
retina
rod
cone
optic nerve
nearsighted
farsighted

Using Light

Key Ideas

- A telescope uses lenses or mirrors to gather light.
- A laser beam consists of waves that all have the same wavelength. The waves are coherent.

Key Terms

telescope
refracting telescope
objective
eyepiece
reflecting telescope
microscope
camera
laser
hologram
optical fiber
total internal reflection

Organizing Information

Compare/Contrast Table Copy the tables about mirrors and lenses onto a sheet of paper. Then fill in the empty spaces and add a title to each table. (For more on compare/contrast tables, see the Skills Handbook.)

Type of Mirror	How It Affects Light	Type of Image Formed
Plane	Reflects	**a.** ?
b. ?	**c.** ?	Real or virtual
Convex	Reflects	**d.** ?

Type of Lens	How It Affects Light	Type of Image Formed
Convex	**e.** ?	**f.** ?
g. ?	**h.** ?	Virtual

Reviewing Content

Multiple Choice

Choose the letter of the best answer.

1. A substance that does not transmit light is
   a. translucent.
   b. opaque.
   c. transparent.
   d. polarized.
2. The scattering of light off an uneven surface is called
   a. regular reflection.
   b. refraction.
   c. diffuse reflection.
   d. total internal reflection.
3. A convex lens can form
   a. either a real image or a virtual image.
   b. a virtual image.
   c. a real image.
   d. a reflection.
4. The colored part of the eye is the
   a. retina.
   b. cornea.
   c. iris.
   d. pupil.
5. A laser produces light that
   a. has many colors.
   b. spreads out in many directions.
   c. is incoherent.
   d. is coherent.

True or False

If the statement is true, write true. If it is false, change the underlined word or words to make the statement true.

6. An image that only seems to be where it is seen is a <u>real</u> image.
7. A lens that is thinner in the middle than at the edges is a <u>concave</u> lens.
8. Under green light a red object appears <u>blue</u>.
9. <u>Farsightedness</u> can be corrected by a convex lens.
10. <u>Holograms</u> are long, thin strands of glass or plastic that can carry light for long distances.

Checking Concepts

11. Explain the differences among transparent, translucent, and opaque materials. Give an example of each type of material.
12. Describe the differences and similarities between real and virtual images. How can each type of image be formed?
13. How is the index of refraction of a substance related to the speed of light in the substance?
14. Explain how mirages form.
15. Why do you see the petals of a rose as red and the leaves as green?
16. Explain how the lenses in your eyes adjust to focus on near and distant objects.
17. Explain how a camera works.
18. **Writing to Learn** You have been asked to nominate an optical instrument for an award. Choose the instrument that you think has played the most significant role in society. Write a nomination speech that describes several reasons for your choice.

Thinking Critically

19. **Applying Concepts** Can a plane mirror ever produce a real image? Explain.
20. **Comparing and Contrasting** How is mixing colors of light different from mixing pigments?
21. **Relating Cause and Effect** Explain why you can only see shades of gray in dim light.
22. **Comparing and Contrasting** How is a microscope similar to a refracting telescope? How is it different?
23. **Problem Solving** A telescope produces a real, upside-down image. If you want to see a boat that is far out to sea, how could you modify your telescope so the boat appears right-side up?
24. **Making Generalizations** Explain why laser light can never be white.

Applying Skills

Use the diagram to answer Questions 25–27.

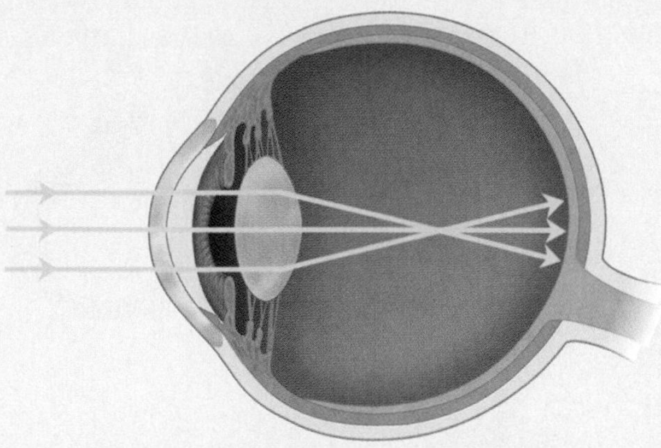

25. Classifying Which type of vision problem does this eye have?

26. Problem Solving What type of lens can correct this vision problem?

27. Communicating Copy the diagram into your notebook. Add a correcting lens to your diagram and show how the lens makes the image focus on the retina.

Performance Assessment (Chapter Project 16)

Project Wrap Up Demonstrate your optical instrument to your class. Explain how your instrument works and how it can be used. Present diagrams that show how the mirrors or lenses in your instrument reflect or refract light.

Reflect and Record Consider the design and performance of your instrument. What parts of the instrument worked as expected? What improvements could you make? What are the similarities and differences between your instrument and other students' instruments?

Test Preparation

Use these questions to prepare for standardized tests.

Read the passage. Then answer Questions 28–31.

As the sun sets, it is still visible for several minutes after it has really sunk below the horizon. This is because light is refracted by Earth's atmosphere. The density of the atmosphere gradually decreases as its altitude above Earth's surface increases. For this reason, the refracted rays bend gradually to produce a curved path.

Refraction can also cause the shape of the sun to appear different just before it rises or sets. When the sun is near the horizon, the rays from the lower edge are bent more than the rays from the upper edge. This makes the sun look oval rather than round.

28. What would be a good title for this passage?
- **a.** The Sun Sets Earlier Each Day
- **b.** Why Light Lingers After the Sunset
- **c.** How the Atmosphere Lights Earth
- **d.** How Sunlight Travels Through the Atmosphere

29. According to this passage, what happens to sunlight as it passes through the atmosphere?
- **a.** It is separated into colors.
- **b.** Its path curves because of reflection.
- **c.** Its path curves because of refraction.
- **d.** It is absorbed and does not reach Earth's surface.

30. How does the fact that the atmosphere is denser in some places than in others affect sunlight?
- **a.** It causes the light to curve.
- **b.** It causes the light to be reflected.
- **c.** It causes the light to stay in the atmosphere.
- **d.** It causes rainbows to form.

31. What is the result of refraction of sunlight?
- **a.** Daytimes are several minutes longer.
- **b.** Daytimes are several minutes shorter.
- **c.** The shape of the sun can be seen even after it has set.
- **d.** The sun appears round when it is really oval in shape.

NATURE OF SCIENCE

Turning Down the Volume on SONIC BOOMS

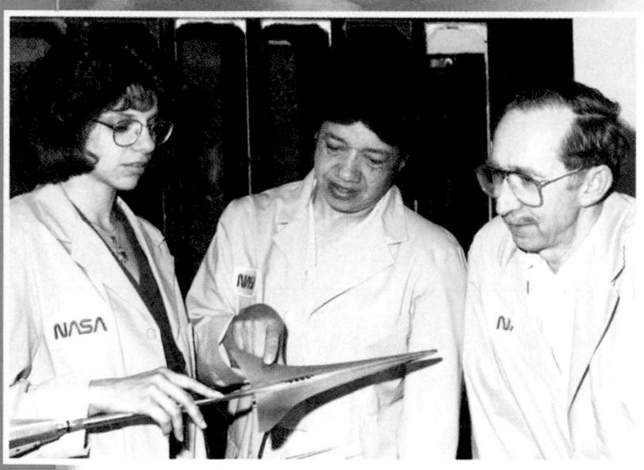

Dr. Christine Mann Darden grew up in Monroe, North Carolina. She received her Ph.D. in Mechanical Engineering at George Washington University in Washington, D.C. A national expert on sonic booms, she now works at NASA's Langley Research Center in Hampton, Virginia. She manages a group of scientists who are developing supersonic airplanes. Dr. Darden (center) is shown here with other members of the Sonic Boom Group, Kathy Needleman (left) and Robert Mack (right).

It happens every time a space shuttle returns to Earth. The spacecraft drops down from orbit and streaks toward its landing site in Florida or California. A few seconds after it passes overhead—BOOM! A window-rattling sound like a giant cannon shot is heard. Most scientists at the space center are monitoring the shuttle itself when it comes down from a mission. But Dr. Christine Darden is more interested in that big boom.

Dr. Darden is a research engineer at the National Aeronautics and Space Administration (NASA). She is in charge of the space agency's Sonic Boom Group. Her team of scientists is investigating the distinctive "sound print" made by aircraft that travel faster than the speed of sound. Dr. Darden and her co-workers are looking for ways to soften sonic booms. They hope to make supersonic travel—travel at speeds faster than the speed of sound—more common in the future.

Talking With Dr. Christine Darden

Both the SR-71 Blackbird (above) and F-16 (opposite page) are military supersonic planes.

Breaking the Sound Barrier

The sound barrier was first broken in 1947. Since then, people have complained about sonic booms so much that the government has passed regulations. It's now against the law to fly most aircraft at supersonic speeds over the United States.

"If it is loud enough, a sonic boom can actually break windows and do damage to buildings," says Dr. Darden. "People find it very disturbing. Right now, the boom is one of the biggest obstacles to commercial supersonic air service."

Today supersonic aircraft fly mainly over the ocean. But what if scientists can find ways to lower the volume of sonic booms? Then someday supersonic commercial jets may be allowed to fly across the country.

What Is a Sonic Boom?

You have probably heard the sound that is made when an airplane breaks the sound barrier. A sonic boom sounds like a clap of thunder or a sharp explosion high in the sky. Just what are you hearing?

"A sonic boom is a compression or pressure wave," Dr. Darden explains. "An airplane pushes a wave of air molecules ahead of it as it travels forward, just as a ship's bow pushes out a wave as it moves through the water. Those compressions travel outward from the plane as a shock wave of high pressure. When that shock wave reaches our ears, we hear it as a boom."

"Think of blowing up a balloon," Dr. Darden says. "With the balloon inflated, the air on the inside is much more compressed than the air on the outside. When the balloon pops, the compression immediately flies outward in the form of a shock wave."

How Do You Research What You Can't See?

"Part of our work is coming up with new ways to observe and measure the phenomenon we're studying," says Dr. Darden. "For example, we know that all waves have similar properties. So we look at how waves behave in water to tell us something about how they behave in the air."

Choosing Engineering

Dr. Darden's study of waves in water and air is a long way from her first career as a math teacher. In the late 1960s, she was teaching in a school in Hampton, Virginia. At that time, the NASA labs nearby were working on a program to send astronauts to the moon. Dr. Darden went to work for NASA as a mathematician.

She quickly became fascinated with the work of the NASA research engineers. "They were the ones who were working with the really tough challenges of the program," she says. "They were doing the interesting, hands-on work." As a result of her experience, she decided to get a graduate degree in engineering.

How Do You Test Supersonic Aircraft?

Working hands-on is one way that Dr. Darden and her team study how airplanes create sonic booms. They

1 **A sonic boom results when an airplane moves at supersonic speed. Air is compressed at the front of the plane, creating shock waves.**

2 **The shock waves move out behind the plane in a cone shape.**

3 **When the shock waves reach the ground, people hear them as a sonic boom.**

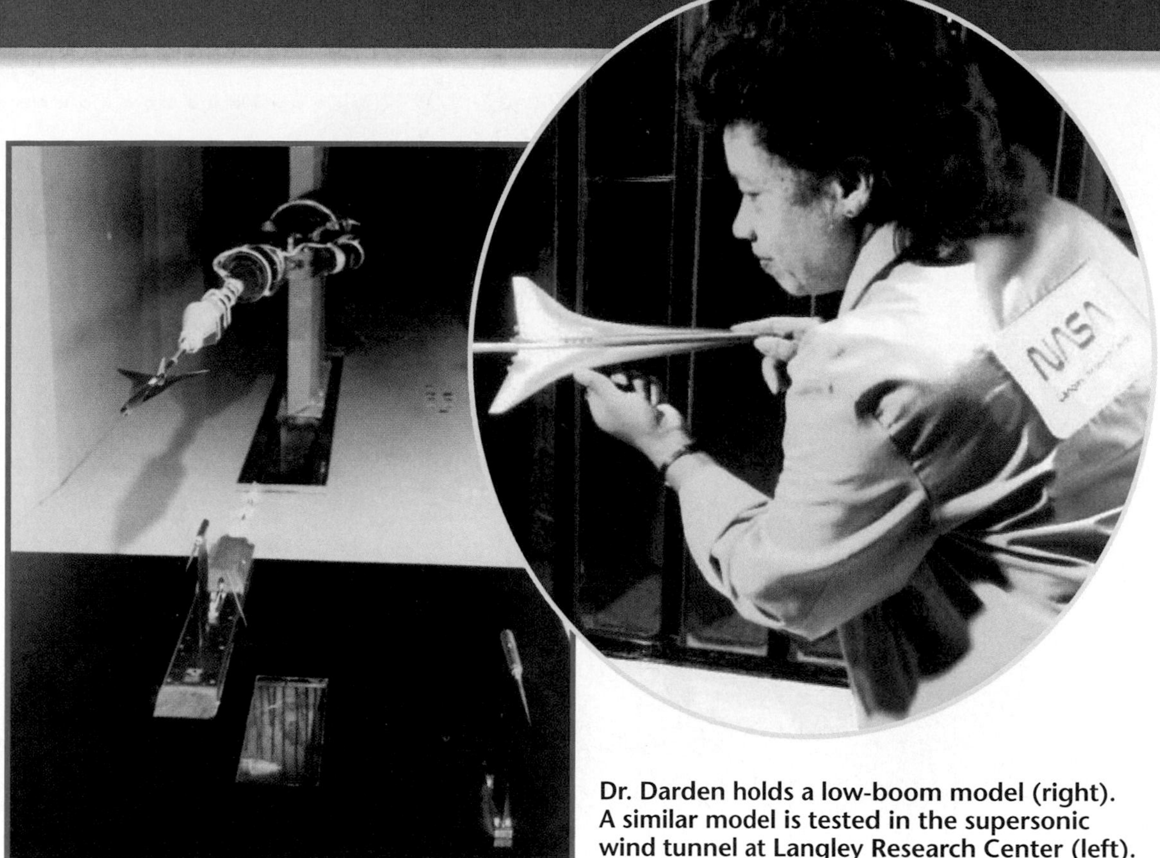

Dr. Darden holds a low-boom model (right). A similar model is tested in the supersonic wind tunnel at Langley Research Center (left).

"fly" model aircraft in a high-speed wind tunnel. The scientists place the steel models in the tunnel and watch how they behave in winds moving at up to three times the speed of sound. (The speed of sound varies with altitude and air pressure. At sea level on a 16°C day, the speed of sound is about 1,207 kilometers per hour.)

Instruments on the sides of the tunnel allow Dr. Darden to "hear" the sonic boom created by the model. By adding very fine smoke, she can even watch how the air moves over the plane. "We can actually see the shock wave," she says.

Can the Sonic Boom Effect Be Reduced?

Dr. Darden and her group at NASA have found that the shape of an aircraft determines the size of the boom it creates. They have performed tests with computer programs, on actual supersonic jets, and in wind tunnels. Their experiments have shown that angling the wings back sharply reduces the size of the shock wave and the loudness of the sonic boom. But the same features that make planes quieter also make them harder to fly.

"You could put a needle up there supersonically and you wouldn't get a sonic boom," explains Dr. Darden. "But you wouldn't have much of an airplane, either."

In Your Journal

In her research, Dr. Darden made predictions about how the angle of an airplane wing might affect a sonic boom. Then her team set up a series of experiments to test these predictions.

Now think of different-shaped boats moving through water: a kayak, a tugboat, and a rowboat. Predict the type of wave that each boat will make. How could you use models to test your predictions?

CHAPTER 17

Mapping Earth's Surface

WEB ACTIVITY www.phschool.com

SECTION 1 **Exploring Earth's Surface**

Discover What Is the Land Like Around Your School?

SECTION 2 **Models of Earth**

Discover How Can You Flatten the Curved Earth?

Try This Where in the World?

Real-World Lab A Borderline Case

Integrating Technology

SECTION 3 **Maps in the Computer Age**

Discover Can You Make a Pixel Picture?

PROJECT 17

Getting on the Map

A shining river winds across a green plain. A plain is one of Earth's landforms. In this chapter, you will learn about plains and other landforms such as mountains and plateaus. You will also learn how to read and use maps that show the shape, height, and slope of Earth's surface. For this chapter project, you will select a small piece of land and draw a map of its physical features.

Your Goal To create a scale map of a small area of your neighborhood.

To complete this project you must
- work with your teacher or an adult family member
- choose and measure a small square or rectangular piece of land
- use a compass to locate north and draw a map to scale
- use symbols and a key to represent natural and human-made features of the land

Get Started Start looking for a suitable site. Your site should be about 300 to 1,000 square meters in area. It could be part of a park, playground, or backyard. Look for an area that includes interesting natural features such as trees, a stream, and changes in elevation or slope. There may be some human-made structures on your site, such as a park bench or sidewalk.

Check Your Progress You'll be working on this project as you study this chapter. To keep your project on track, look for Check Your Progress boxes at the following points.

Section 1 Review, page 562: Choose a site, measure the boundaries, and sketch all the physical features.

Section 2 Review, page 568: Brainstorm ideas for symbols to include on your map.

Section 4 Review, page 577: Complete the final draft of your map, including a key and map scale.

Wrap Up At the end of this chapter (page 581), you will present your map to the class.

The Cheyenne River flows through Buffalo Gap National Grassland near Red Shirt, South Dakota.

SECTION 4 **Topographic Maps**

Section 1 Exploring Earth's Surface

Discover Activity

What Is the Land Like Around Your School?

1. On a piece of paper, draw a small square to represent your school.
2. Choose a word that describes the type of land near your school, such as flat, hilly, or rolling. Write the word next to the square.
3. Use a magnetic compass to determine the direction of north. Assume that north is at the top of your piece of paper.
4. If you travel due north 1 kilometer from your school, what type of land do you find? Choose a word to describe the land in this area. Write that word to the north of the square.
5. Repeat Step 4 for areas located 1 kilometer east, south, and west of your school.

Think It Over

Forming Operational Definitions What phrase could you use to describe the land in your area?

Guide for Reading

- **What determines the topography of Earth's surface?**
- **What are the main types of landforms?**
- **What are the four "spheres" that make up Earth's surface?**

Reading Tip **Before you read, preview *Exploring Landforms* on page 561. Make a list of questions you have about landforms.**

In 1804, an expedition set out from St. Louis to explore the land between the Mississippi River and the Pacific Ocean. The United States had just purchased a part of this vast territory, called Louisiana, from France. Before the Louisiana Purchase, the United States stretched from the Atlantic coast westward to the Mississippi River. Few United States citizens had traveled west of the Mississippi. None had ever traveled over land all the way to the Pacific.

Led by Meriwether Lewis and William Clark, the expedition traveled up the Missouri River, crossed the Rocky Mountains, followed the Columbia River to the Pacific Ocean—and then returned. The purpose of the expedition was to map America's interior and discover resources.

Figure 1 While traveling down the Columbia River, the Lewis and Clark expedition meets the Chinook people.

Topography

On the journey to the Pacific, the Lewis and Clark expedition traveled more than 5,000 kilometers across the continent of North America. As they traveled, Lewis and Clark observed many changes in topography. **Topography** is the shape of the land. An area's topography may be flat, sloping, hilly, or mountainous.

The topography of an area is determined by the area's elevation, relief, and landforms. The desktop where you do homework probably has piles of books, papers, and other objects of different sizes and shapes. Your desktop has both elevation and relief!

Elevation The height above sea level of a point on Earth's surface is its **elevation.** When Lewis and Clark started in St. Louis, they were about 140 meters above sea level. By the time they reached Lemhi Pass in the Rocky Mountains, they were more than 2,200 meters above sea level.

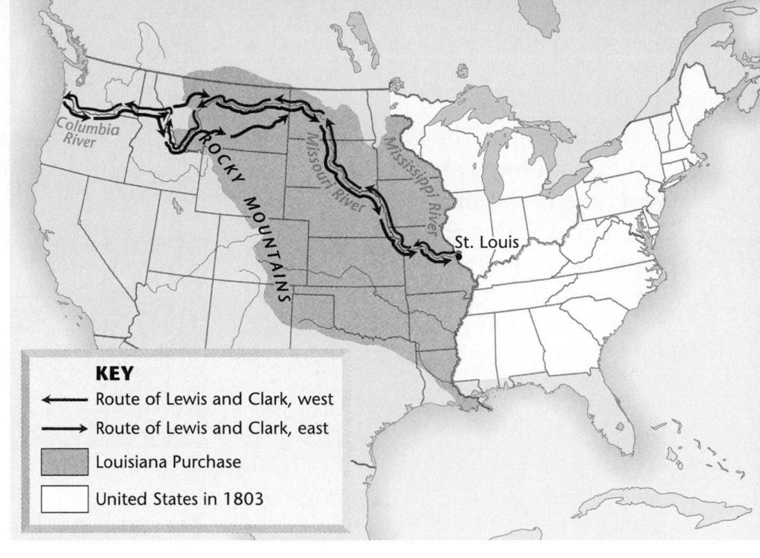

Figure 2 The Lewis and Clark expedition followed major rivers, except when crossing the Rocky Mountains.

Relief The difference in elevation between the highest and lowest parts of an area is its **relief.** As the Lewis and Clark expedition entered the Rocky Mountains, the relief of the land changed from flat or rolling land with low relief to huge mountains with high relief.

Landforms If you followed the route of the Lewis and Clark expedition, you would see many different landforms. A **landform** is a feature of topography formed by the processes that shape Earth's surface. All landforms have elevation and relief. A large area of land where the topography is similar is called a **landform region.** Figure 3 shows the landform regions of the United States not including Alaska or Hawaii.

☑ ***Checkpoint*** *What is the difference between elevation and relief?*

Figure 3 The United States has many different landform regions. ***Interpreting Maps*** *In what regions are Charleston, Topeka, Santa Fe, and Walla Walla located?*

Figure 4 The Great Plains of western North America include a vast area of flat or rolling land. The Great Plains are interior plains. ***Predicting*** *What do you think would be some differences between interior plains and coastal plains?*

Types of Landforms

Landforms can vary greatly in size and shape—from level plains extending as far as the eye can see, to low, rounded hills that you could climb on foot, to jagged mountains that would take you days to walk around. **There are three main types of landforms: plains, mountains, and plateaus.**

Plains A **plain** is a landform made up of flat or gently rolling land with low relief. A plain that lies along a seacoast is called a coastal plain. In North America, a coastal plain wraps like an apron around the continent's eastern and southeastern shores. Coastal plains have both low elevation and low relief.

A plain that lies away from the coast is called an interior plain. Although interior plains have low relief, their elevation can vary. The broad interior plain of North America is called the Great Plains.

The Great Plains extend from Texas north into Canada. From their eastern border in the states of North and South Dakota, Nebraska, Kansas, Oklahoma, and Texas, the Great Plains stretch west to the Rocky Mountains. At the time of the Lewis and Clark expedition, the Great Plains were a vast grassland.

Figure 5 The Bitterroot Mountains in Idaho are part of the Rocky Mountains system.

Mountains A **mountain** is a landform with high elevation and high relief. Mountains usually occur as part of a mountain range. A **mountain range** is a group of mountains that are closely related in shape, structure, and age. After crossing the Great Plains, the Lewis and Clark expedition crossed a rugged mountain range in Idaho called the Bitterroot Mountains.

The different mountain ranges in a region make up a mountain system. The Bitterroot Mountains are one mountain range in the mountain system known as the Rocky Mountains.

Mountain ranges and mountain systems in a long, connected chain form a larger unit called a mountain belt. The Rocky Mountains are part of a great mountain belt that stretches down the western sides of North America and South America.

Plateaus A landform that has high elevation and a more or less level surface is called a **plateau.** A plateau is rarely perfectly smooth on top. Streams and rivers may cut into the plateau's surface. The Columbia Plateau in Washington State is an example. The Columbia River, which the Lewis and Clark expedition followed, slices through this plateau. The many layers of rock that make up the Columbia Plateau are about 1,500 meters thick.

☑ *Checkpoint* *What types of landforms have low relief?*

EXPLORING Landforms

Mountains, plains, and plateaus are just a few of the many landforms that make up the topography of Earth's surface.

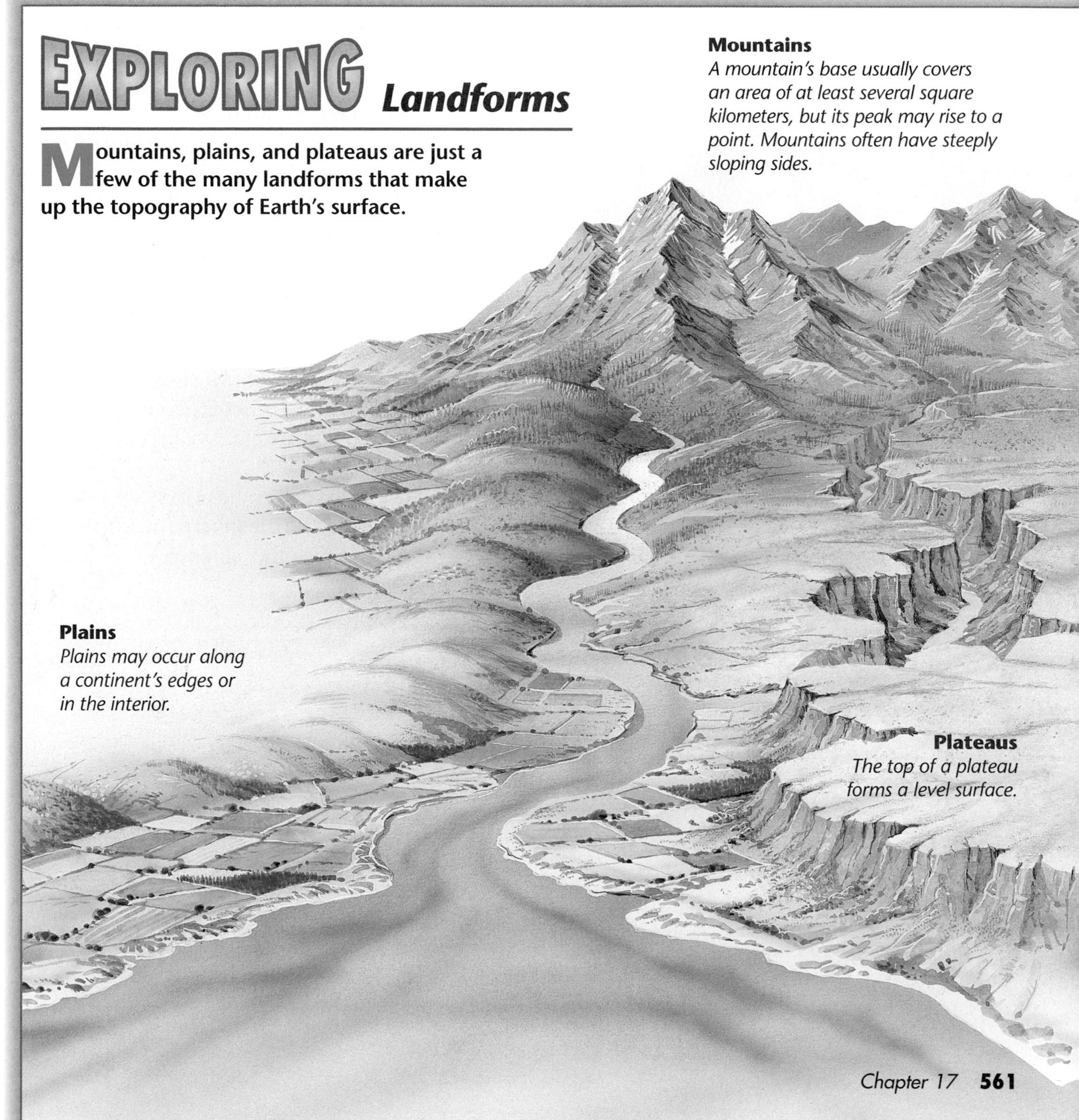

Mountains
A mountain's base usually covers an area of at least several square kilometers, but its peak may rise to a point. Mountains often have steeply sloping sides.

Plains
Plains may occur along a continent's edges or in the interior.

Plateaus
The top of a plateau forms a level surface.

Earth's Four Spheres

Lewis and Clark's two-year journey took them across western North America. Along the way, they observed the land, water, air, and living things. Together, these four things make up everything that is on and around planet Earth. **Scientists divide Earth into four spheres: the lithosphere, hydrosphere, atmosphere, and biosphere.** In this book, you will learn mainly about the lithosphere and how it is affected by each of the other spheres.

Figure 6 A view from space shows all four of Earth's spheres—the atmosphere, hydrosphere, biosphere, and lithosphere. ***Observing*** *What evidence of each of the spheres can you see in the photograph?*

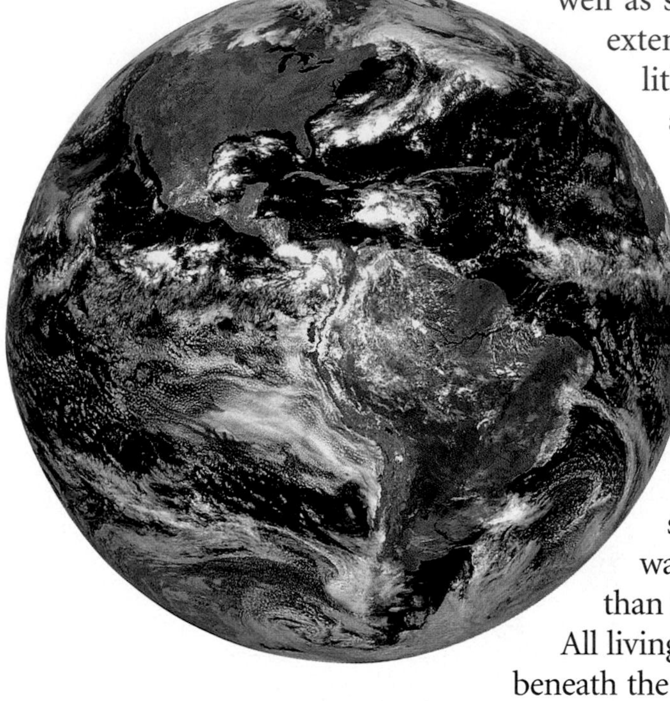

Earth's solid, rocky outer layer is called the **lithosphere** (LITH uh sfeer). The lithosphere is made up of the continents as well as smaller landmasses called islands. The lithosphere extends under the entire ocean floor. The surface of the lithosphere varies from smooth plains to wrinkled hills and valleys to jagged mountain peaks.

The outermost sphere is the **atmosphere** (AT muh sfeer), the mixture of gases that surrounds the planet. By far the most abundant gases are nitrogen and oxygen, but the atmosphere also contains water vapor, carbon dioxide, and other gases. When water vapor condenses, it forms the droplets that make up clouds.

Earth's oceans, lakes, rivers, and ice form the **hydrosphere** (HY druh sfeer). Most of the hydrosphere consists of the salt water in the oceans, but fresh water is also part of the hydrosphere. Oceans cover more than two thirds of Earth.

All living things—whether in the air, in the oceans, or on and beneath the land surface—make up the **biosphere** (BY uh sfeer). The biosphere extends into each of the other spheres.

Section 1 Review

1. What three factors determine the topography of a region?
2. What are the most common types of landforms?
3. Which is larger, a mountain belt or a mountain system?
4. In which of Earth's spheres would you find a cloud? A mountain? A lake? A tree?
5. **Thinking Critically Comparing and Contrasting** How are mountains and plateaus similar? How are they different?

Check Your Progress

CHAPTER PROJECT 17

Choose a site that is as square or rectangular as possible. **CAUTION:** *Make sure to obtain permission from the property owner before you begin.* To start mapping your site, mark the four corners with stakes, stones, or other markers. Measure the boundaries and record the distances on a rough sketch. Your sketch should show your site's topography, plus natural and human-made features. Include a north arrow on your sketch. How can you determine which direction is north?

SECTION 2

Models of Earth

DISCOVER ACTIVITY

How Can You Flatten the Curved Earth?

1. Using a felt-tip pen, make a rough sketch of the outlines of the continents on the surface of an orange or grapefruit.
2. Using a plastic knife, carefully peel the orange. If possible, keep the peel in one large piece so that the continents remain intact.
3. Try to lay the pieces of orange peel flat on a table.

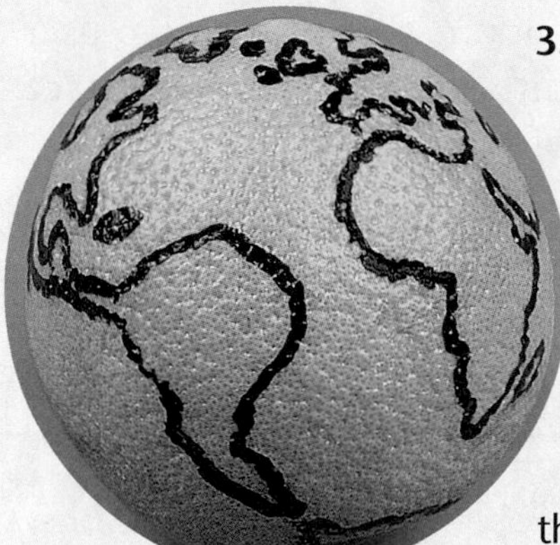

Think It Over

Observing What happens to the continents when you try to flatten the pieces? What adjustments would you need to make to the shapes of the continents to get them to match their shape and position on a sphere?

GUIDE FOR READING

- **How do maps and globes represent Earth's surface?**
- **How are latitude and longitude used to locate points on Earth's surface?**

Reading Tip **Before you read, rewrite the headings in the section as *how, why,* or *what* questions. As you read, look for answers to these questions.**

You want to invite relatives from out of town to a sports event at your school. You could use words to explain how to find the school: Take the third exit off the highway, turn left at the first traffic light, and so on. But verbal directions can be hard to follow. Instead, you might sketch a map of the best route to your school. Maps use a picture instead of words to tell where things are.

Maps and Globes

Maps and globes show the shape, size, and position of Earth's surface features. A **map** is a model on a flat surface of all or part of Earth's surface as seen from above. A **globe** is a sphere that represents Earth's entire surface. A globe correctly shows the relative size and shape of landmasses and bodies of water, much as if you were viewing Earth from space.

Maps and globes are drawn to scale and use symbols to represent topography and other features on Earth's surface. A map's **scale** relates distance on a map to a distance on Earth's surface. Scale is often given as a ratio. For example, one unit on the map equals 25,000 units on the ground. So one centimeter on the map represents 0.25 kilometers. This scale, "one to twenty-five thousand," would be written "1 : 25,000." Figure 7 shows three ways of giving a map's scale.

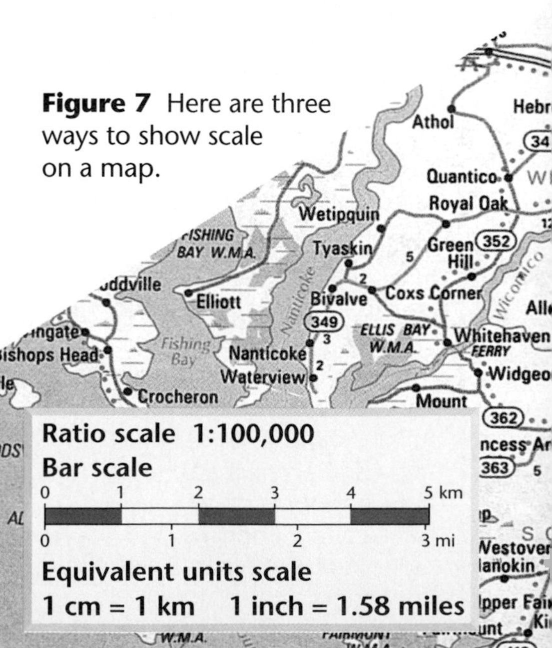

Figure 7 Here are three ways to show scale on a map.

Mapmakers use pictures called **symbols** to stand for features on Earth's surface. A symbol can represent a physical feature, such as a river, lake, mountain, or plain. A symbol also can stand for a human-made feature, such as a highway, a city, or an airport. A map's **key,** or legend, is a list of all the symbols used on the map with an explanation of their meaning.

Maps also include a compass rose or north arrow. The compass rose helps the map user to relate directions on the map to directions on Earth's surface. North usually is located at the top of the map.

☑ *Checkpoint Where can you find the meaning of the symbols on a map?*

Maps and Technology

Centuries ago, people invented instruments for determining compass direction, latitude, and longitude. Mapmakers developed techniques to show Earth's surface accurately.

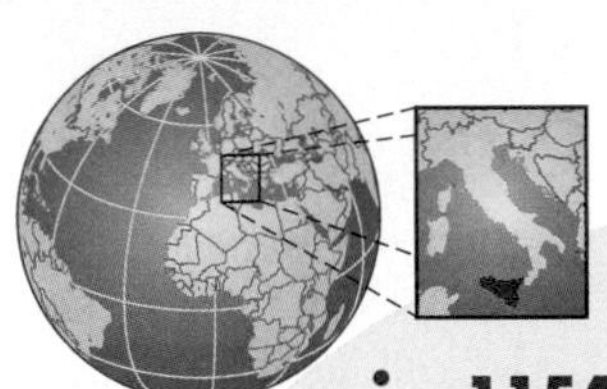

1154 Sicily

The Arab mapmaker Al-Idrisi made several world maps for King Roger of Sicily. Idrisi's maps marked a great advance over other maps of that time. They showed the Arabs' grasp of scientific mapmaking and geography. But unlike modern maps, these maps placed south at the top!

1100 | 1200 | 1300 | 1400

AROUND 1100 China

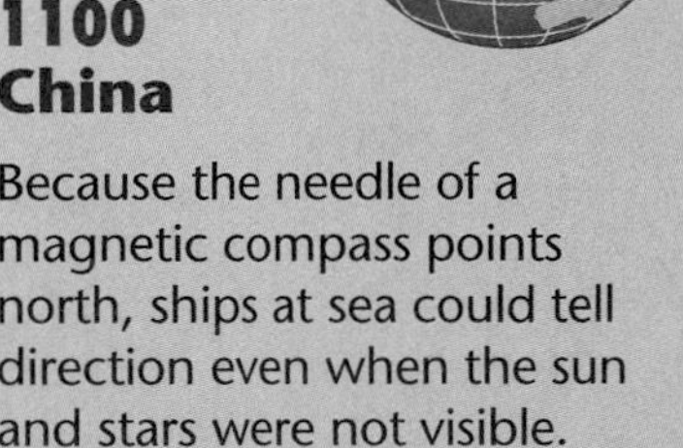

Because the needle of a magnetic compass points north, ships at sea could tell direction even when the sun and stars were not visible. Arabs and Europeans adopted this Chinese invention by the 1200s.

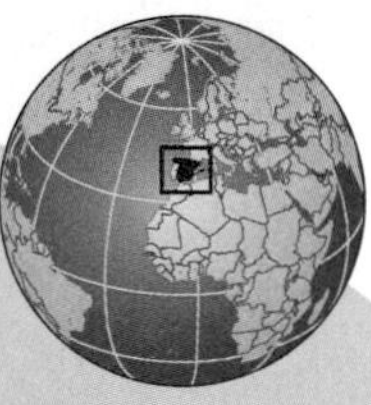

AROUND 1300 Spain

Lines representing wind directions criss-crossed a type of map called a portolan chart. These charts also showed coastlines and harbors. A sea captain would use a portolan chart and a compass when sailing from one harbor to another in the Mediterranean Sea.

An Earth Reference System

When you play chess or checkers, the grid of squares helps you to keep track of where each piece should be. To find a point on Earth's surface, you need a reference system like the grid of squares on a checkerboard. Of course, Earth itself does not have grid lines, but most maps and globes show a grid. The grid is based on two imaginary lines: the equator and the prime meridian.

The Equator Halfway between the North and South poles, the **equator** forms an imaginary line that circles Earth. The equator divides Earth into the Northern and Southern hemispheres. A **hemisphere** (HEH mih sfeer) is one half of the sphere that makes up Earth's surface.

In Your Journal

Choose one period on the time line to learn more about. Use the library to find information about maps in that time. Who used maps? Why were they important? Share what you learn in the form of a letter written by a traveler or explorer who is using a map of that period.

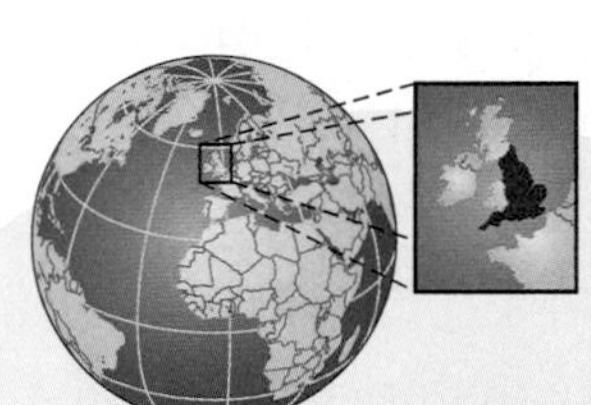

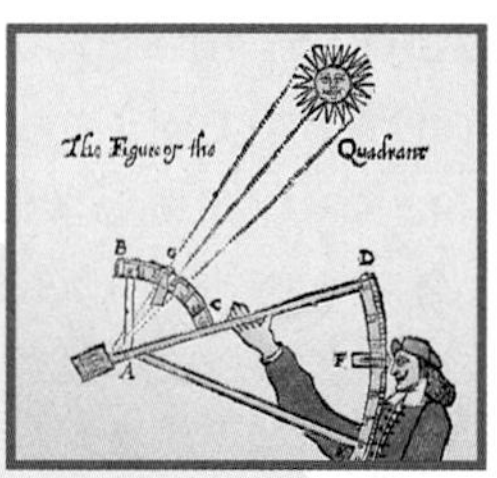

1595 England

To find latitude, sailors used a variety of instruments, including the backstaff. The navigator sighted along the backstaff's straight edge to measure the angle of the sun or North star above the horizon. Later improvements led to modern instruments for navigation.

1684 France

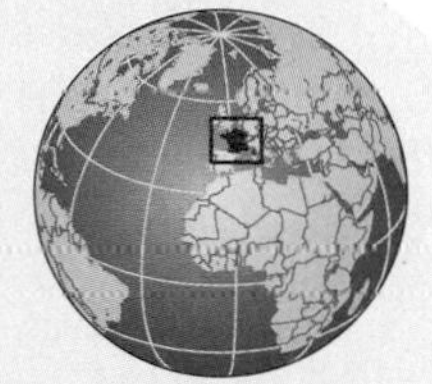

On land, mapmakers developed new ways of measuring land areas accurately. Philippe de La Hire's map of France proved that the country was actually smaller than people had thought. The king of France said that he lost more land because of this map than he would have lost through losing a war.

1500 | 1600 | 1700 | 1800

1569 Belgium

Flemish mapmaker Gerardus Mercator invented the first modern map projection, which bears his name. Mercator and his son, Rumold, also made an atlas and maps of the world such as the one shown below.

1763 England

John Harrison, a carpenter and mechanic, won a prize from the British navy for building a highly accurate clock called a chronometer. Harrison's invention made finding longitudes quicker and easier. With exact longitudes, mapmakers could greatly improve the accuracy of their maps.

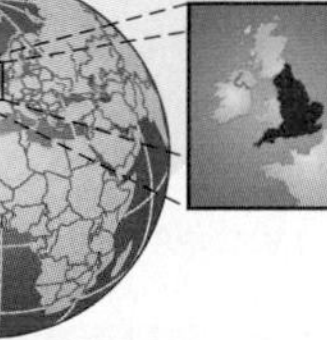

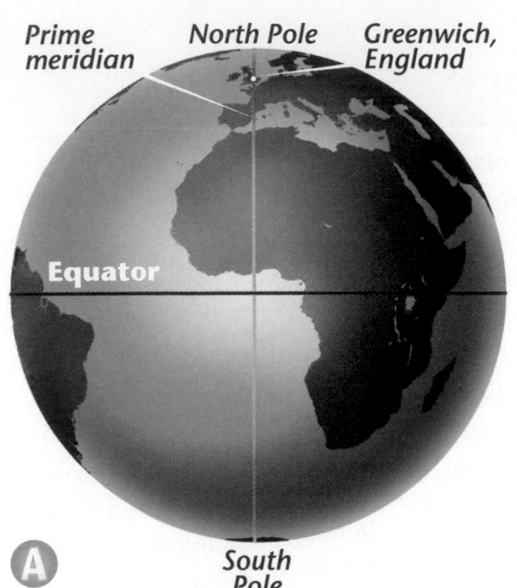

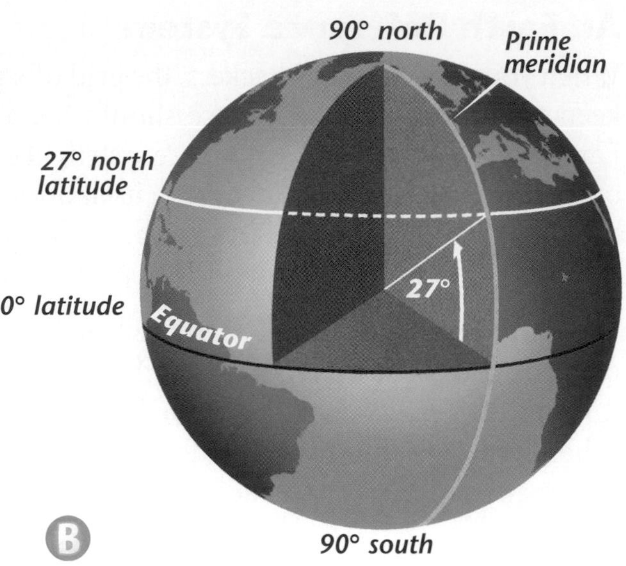

Figure 8 **A.** The equator and the prime meridian divide Earth's surface into hemispheres. **B.** Latitude measures distances north or south of the equator. **C.** Longitude measures distances east or west of the prime meridian. **D.** Cairo, Egypt, is located where the latitude line 30° N crosses the longitude line 31° E.

The Prime Meridian Another imaginary line, called the **prime meridian,** makes a half circle from the North Pole to the South Pole. The prime meridian passes through Greenwich, England. Places east of the prime meridian are in the Eastern Hemisphere. Places west of the prime meridian are in the Western Hemisphere.

Measurements on a Sphere To measure distances around a circle, scientists use units called degrees. A **degree** (°) is $\frac{1}{360}$ of the way around a full circle. As you can see in Figure 8, each degree is a measure of the angle formed by lines drawn from the center of Earth to points on the surface. If you started at the prime meridian and traveled west along the equator, you would travel through 360 degrees before returning to your starting point. If you started at the equator and traveled to one of the poles, you would travel 90 degrees—one quarter of the distance in a full circle.

Where in the World?

ACTIVITY

Using a globe, determine what city is found at each of the following points:

2° S 79° W
38° N 9° W
34° N 135° E
34° S 58° W
55° N 3° W
1° N 103° E

What word is spelled by the first letters of these city names?

☑ ***Checkpoint*** *In what two hemispheres is the United States located?*

Locating Points on Earth's Surface

Using the equator and prime meridian, mapmakers have constructed a grid made up of lines of latitude and longitude. **You can use lines of latitude and longitude to find locations anywhere on Earth.**

Latitude The equator is the starting line for measuring **latitude,** or distance in degrees north or south of the equator. Between the equator and both poles are evenly spaced lines called lines of latitude. All lines of latitude are parallel to the equator. Latitude is measured from the equator, which is at 0°. The latitude of each pole is 90° north or 90° south.

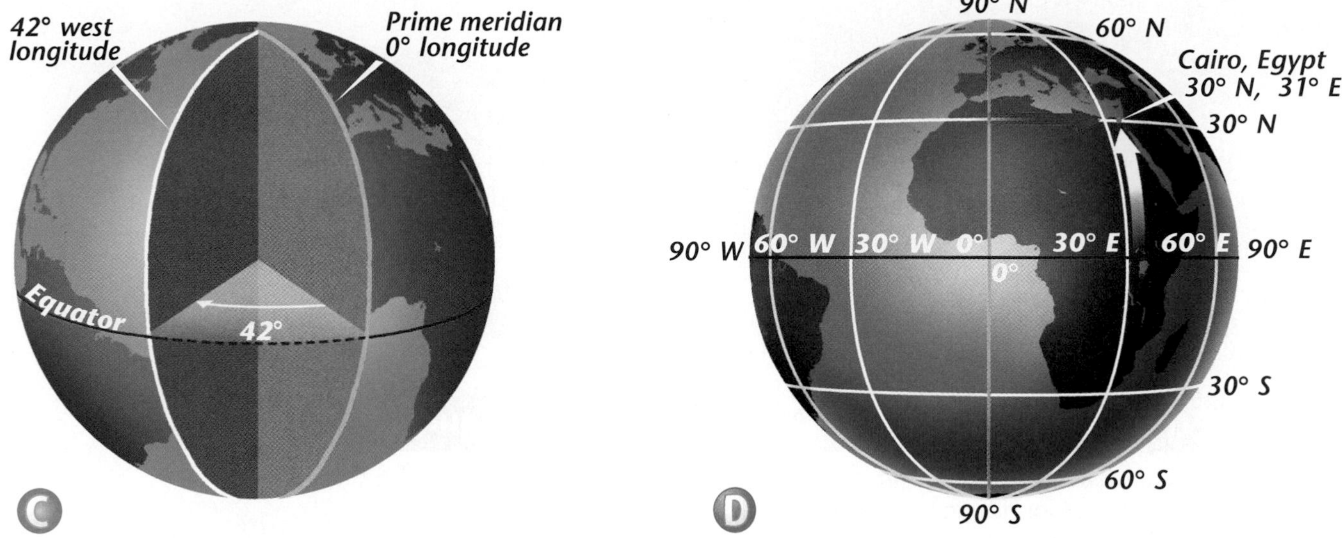

Longitude The distance in degrees east or west of the prime meridian is called **longitude.** There are 360 lines of longitude that run from north to south, meeting at the poles. Each line represents one degree of longitude. The prime meridian, which is the starting line for measuring longitude, is at 0°. Each longitude line crosses the latitude lines, including the equator, at a right angle.

As Figure 9 shows, the longitude lines in each hemisphere are numbered up to 180 degrees. This is one half the total number of degrees in a circle. At 180 degrees east or 180 degrees west lies a single longitude line directly opposite the prime meridian.

Figure 9 Every point on Earth's surface has a particular latitude and longitude. ***Interpreting Maps*** *What are the latitude and longitude of New Orleans? Of Sydney?*

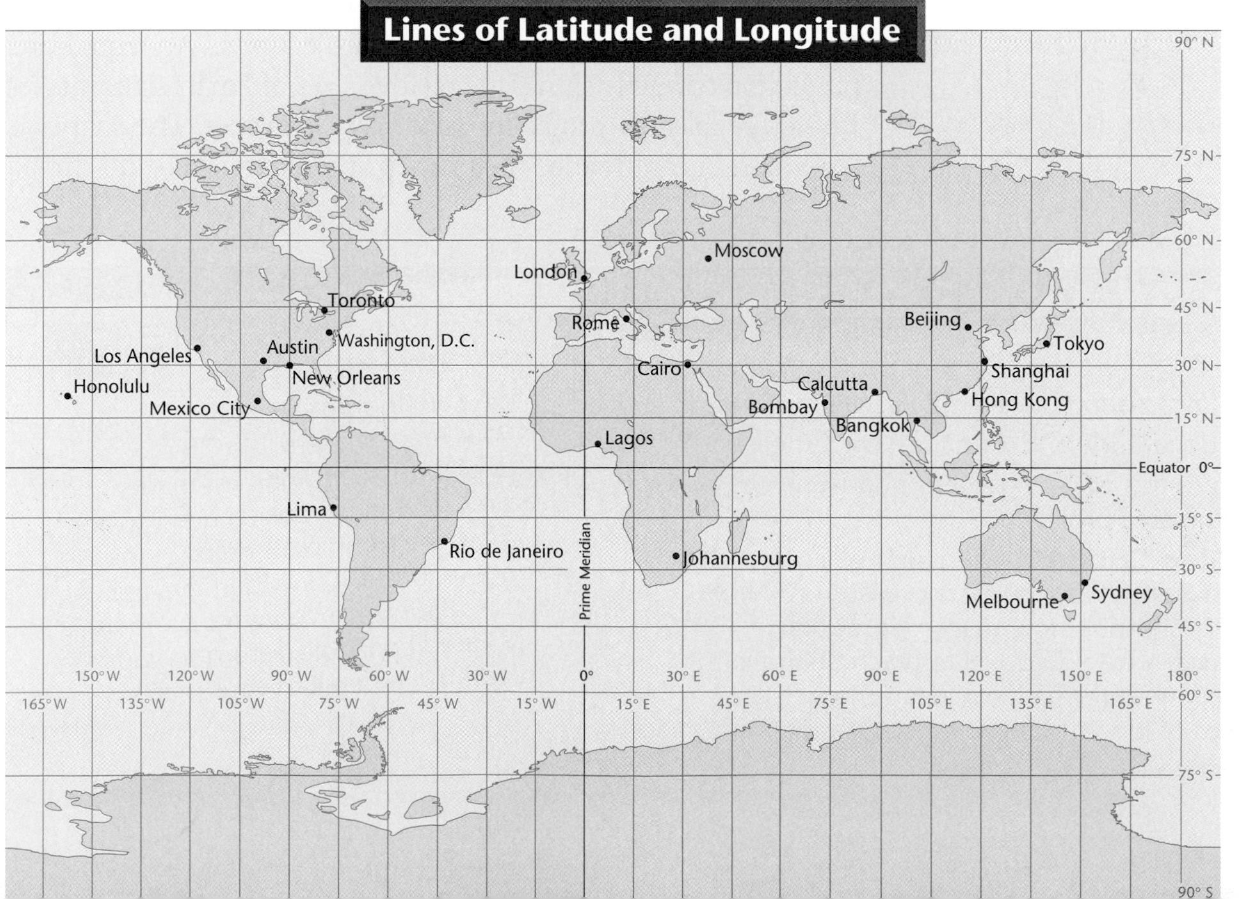

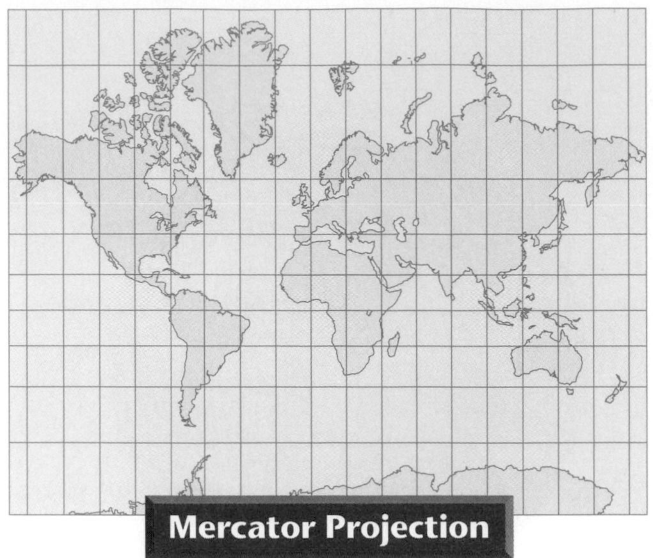

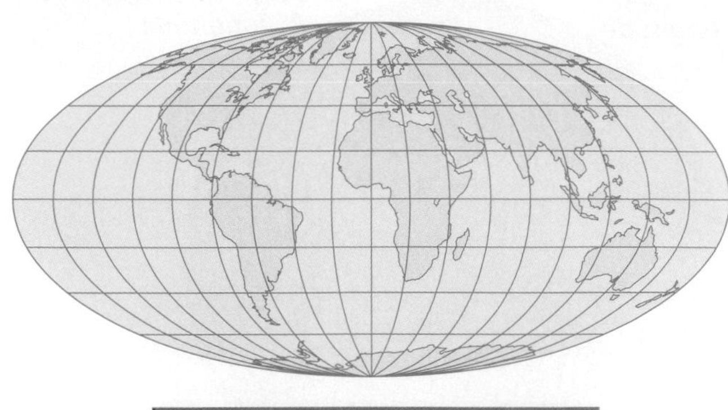

Figure 10 On a Mercator projection (left), lines of longitude are parallel, so shapes near the poles are distorted. An equal-area projection (right) shows areas correctly, but distorts some shapes around its edges.
Comparing and Contrasting *Why does Greenland appear larger on the Mercator projection than on the equal-area projection?*

Map Projections

To show Earth's curved surface on a flat map, mapmakers use map projections. A **map projection** is a framework of lines that helps to show landmasses on a flat surface.

On a Mercator projection, the lines of latitude and longitude all appear as straight, parallel lines that form a rectangle. On a Mercator projection, the size and shape of landmasses near the equator are distorted only a little. But as you go toward the poles, size and shape become more and more distorted. The reason for this distortion is that the lines of longitude do not come together at the poles as they do on a globe. As you can see in Figure 10, this projection also changes the relative sizes of landmasses.

To solve the problem of distortion on Mercator projections, mapmakers developed equal-area projections. An equal-area projection correctly shows the relative sizes of Earth's landmasses. But an equal-area projection also has distortion. The shapes of landmasses near the edges of the map appear stretched and curved.

Section 2 Review

1. What information does a map's scale provide?
2. What do latitude and longitude each measure?
3. What are the advantages and disadvantages of an equal-area projection?
4. **Thinking Critically Measuring** Look at the map in Figure 9. If you fly due east from New Orleans, through how many degrees of longitude must you travel to reach Shanghai? If you flew west from New Orleans, how many degrees of longitude would you pass before reaching Shanghai? Explain.

Check Your Progress

CHAPTER PROJECT 17

Choose an appropriate scale for your map. Make a list of the types of natural and human-made features for which you will need symbols. Examine the samples of maps in the chapter and those provided by your teacher. Brainstorm ideas for symbols to include. If possible, return to your site and add more detail to your map.

You may have wondered how people first decided where to locate the borders between states.

Problem

Which was more important in locating state borders: lines of latitude and longitude or physical features?

Skills Focus

drawing conclusions, observing, inferring

Materials

United States map with latitude, longitude, and state borders
tracing paper   paper clips   colored pencils

Procedure

1. Lay a sheet of tracing paper on top of a map of the United States.
2. Trace over the Pacific and Atlantic coasts of the United States with a blue pencil.
3. Using the blue pencil, trace all Great Lakes shorelines that reach nearby states.
4. Trace all state borders that go exactly north-south with a red pencil. (*Hint:* Some straight-line borders that appear to run north-south, such as the western border of Maine, do not follow lines of longitude.)
5. Use a green pencil to trace all state borders or sections of state borders that go exactly east-west. (*Hint:* Straight-line borders that are slanted, such as the southern border of Nevada, do not follow lines of latitude.)
6. Now use a blue pencil to trace the borders that follow rivers.
7. Use a brown pencil to trace any borders that are not straight lines or rivers.

Analyze and Conclude

1. How many state boundaries are completely defined by longitude and latitude? How many are partially defined by longitude and latitude?
2. What feature is used to define a state border when longitude and latitude are not used? Give examples of specific states.
3. Study the physical map of the United States in Appendix B. What other physical features are used to define borders? Which state borders are defined by these features?
4. Which was used more often in locating state borders: longitude or latitude?
5. How many states do not use longitude and latitude for the location of their borders?
6. **Apply** In which region of the country were lines of latitude and longitude most important in determining state borders? What do you think is the reason for this?

More to Explore

Research the history of your state to find out when and how its borders were established. Are your state's borders based on longitude and latitude, landforms and topography, or both?

Review a map of your county or state. Are any features, other than the state's border, related to longitude and latitude? Which features seem to follow landforms and topography?

INTEGRATING TECHNOLOGY 

SECTION 3 Maps in the Computer Age

DISCOVER ACTIVITY

Can You Make a Pixel Picture?

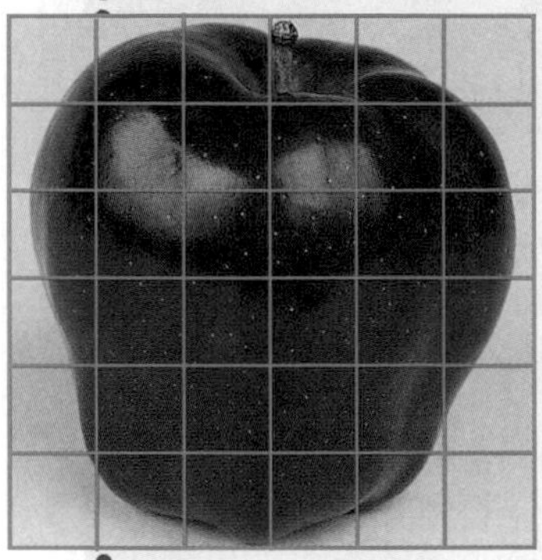

1. With a pencil, draw a square grid of lines spaced 1 centimeter apart. The grid should have 6 squares on each side.
2. On the grid, draw the outline of a simple object, such as an apple.
3. Using a different color pencil, fill in all squares that are completely inside the apple. If a square is mostly inside the apple, fill it in completely. If it is mostly outside, leave it blank.
4. Each square on your grid represents one pixel, or bit of information, about your picture. Looking at your pixel picture, can you recognize the shape you started with?

Think It Over

Predicting How would the pixel picture change if you drew the object smaller? How would the pixel picture look if you used graph paper with squares that are smaller than your grid?

GUIDE FOR READING

- **How are satellites and computers used in mapmaking?**

Reading Tip **Before you read, preview Figures 12 and 13. In your notebook, describe how you think computers may have affected mapmaking.**

For centuries, mapmakers slowly gathered data and then drew maps by hand. Explorers made maps by sketching coastlines as seen from their ships. Mapmakers sometimes drew the land based on reports from people who had traveled there. More accurate maps were made by locating points on the surface in a process called surveying.

During the twentieth century, people learned to make highly accurate maps using photographs taken from airplanes. These photographs are called aerial photographs. Aerial photographs are still important in many types of mapmaking.

Since the 1970s, information gathered by satellites has revolutionized mapmaking. Powerful computers use the satellite data to make maps quickly and accurately.

Figure 11 A satellite image is made up of many pixels. This enlargement of a satellite image shows Tampa Bay and St. Petersburg, Florida.

Satellite Mapping

Beginning in 1972, the United States launched a series of Landsat satellites designed to observe Earth's surface. Landsat uses electronic devices to collect information about the land surface in the form of computer data. **Satellite images** are pictures of the surface based on these data. As Landsat orbits Earth, it collects and stores information about a strip of the surface that is

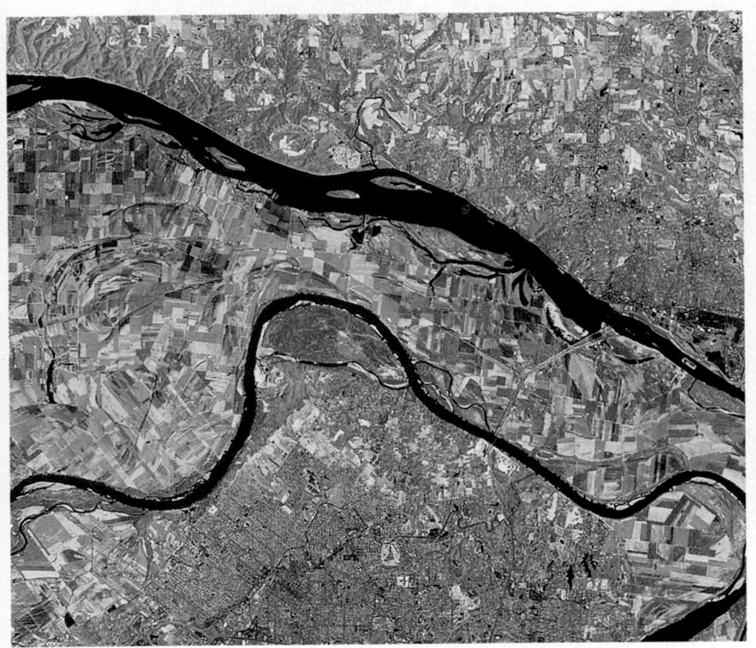

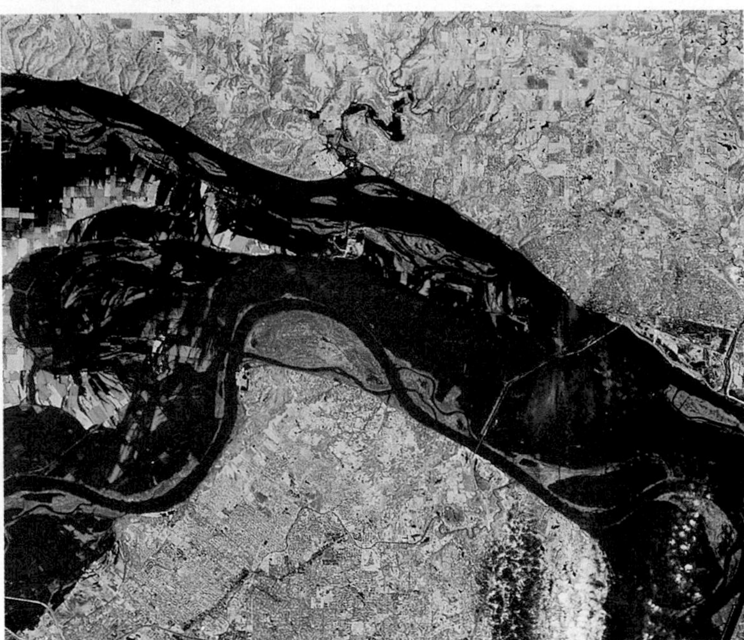

Figure 12 Landsat made these images of part of the Mississippi and Missouri rivers. They show an area just north of St. Louis, before (left) and during (right) a flood in 1993. The Mississippi is the wider river in each image. In both images, north is at the top.
Inferring *What can you infer about the relief of the land between the Mississippi and Missouri rivers?*

185 kilometers wide. The satellite relays the data back to a station on Earth, where computers create images of the surface.

Pictures made by Landsat show what covers the land surface—plants, soil, sand, rock, water, or snow and ice. Large human-made features, such as cities, are also visible.

Printing Satellite Images Unlike a photograph, a satellite image is made up of thousands of tiny dots called **pixels.** A painting made of pixels would have many separate dots of color. Each pixel in a satellite image contains information on the color and brightness of a small part of Earth's surface. This information is stored on a computer as a series of 0's and 1's. When the satellite image is printed, the computer translates these numbers into colors.

Interpreting Satellite Images Scientists learn to identify

INTEGRATING ENVIRONMENTAL SCIENCE

specific features by the "signature," or combination of colors and shapes, that the feature makes on a satellite image. In a satellite image, areas covered by grass, trees, or crops are often shown as red, water as black or blue, and cities as bluish gray. Landsat images may show features such as grasslands, forests, and agricultural crops, as well as desert areas, mountains, or cities. By comparing one image with another made at an earlier time, scientists can see changes due to drought, forest fires, or floods. Figure 12 shows satellite images taken before and during a flood in the Mississippi River valley.

☑ ***Checkpoint*** ***What information does a pixel in a satellite image contain?***

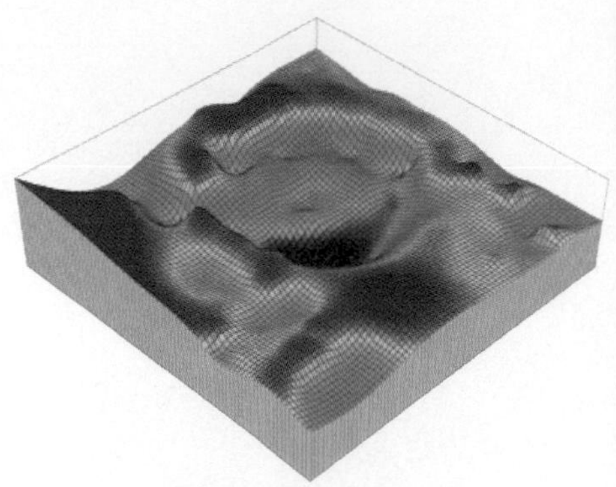

Figure 13 Today computers are an essential tool in making accurate maps. A computer produced the digital model shown above.

Computer Mapping

With computers, mapmakers have new ways of storing and displaying map data. Computer mapmakers use up-to-the-minute data to produce maps quickly and easily.

All of the data used in computer mapping must be in numbers, just like the pixels in a satellite image. The process by which mapmakers convert the location of map points to numbers is called **digitizing.** Once the map data have been digitized, they can be displayed on a computer screen, modified, and printed out in map form.

Computers can automatically create three-dimensional views that might take a person hundreds of hours to draw by hand. The computer image in Figure 13, for example, was made to help geologists search for oil.

Section 3 Review

1. Describe how Landsat collects data about Earth's surface.
2. What are the two ways in which computers are useful in making maps?
3. How are the data for a map put in a form that a computer can use?
4. **Thinking Critically Making Generalizations** In your own words, describe how computers and satellites have improved the accuracy of maps.

Science at Home

Most of the maps that you see today in newspapers and magazines are made using computers. With family members look through newspapers and news magazines. How many different types of maps can you find? Explain to your family the map's scale, symbols, and key. After you have studied the map, try to state the main point of the information shown on the map.

Section 4 Topographic Maps

DISCOVER ACTIVITY

Can a Map Show Relief?

1. Carefully cut the corners off 8 pieces of cardboard so that they look rounded. Each piece should be at least 1 centimeter smaller than the one before.

2. Trim the long sides of the two largest pieces so that the long sides appear wavy. Don't cut any more than one-half centimeter into the cardboard.
3. Trace the largest cardboard piece on a sheet of paper.
4. Trace the next largest piece inside the tracing of the first. Don't let any lines cross.
5. Trace the other cardboard pieces, from largest to smallest, one inside the other, on the same paper.
6. Stack the cardboard pieces in the same order they were traced beside the paper. Compare the stack of cardboard pieces with your drawing. How are they alike? How are they different?

Think It Over

Making Models If the cardboard pieces are a model of a landform, what do the lines on the paper represent?

GUIDE FOR READING

- **What is a topographic map?**
- **How do mapmakers represent elevation, relief, and slope?**
- **What is the Global Positioning System?**

Reading Tip **As you read, make a list of main ideas and supporting details about topographic maps.**

You are an engineer planning a route for a highway over a mountain pass. You need to consider many different factors. To design a safe highway, you need a route that avoids the steepest slopes. To protect the area's water supply, the highway must stay a certain distance from rivers and lakes. You also want to find a route that avoids houses and other buildings. How would you find the best route? You could start by studying a topographic map.

Mapping Earth's Topography

A **topographic map** is a map showing the surface features of an area. Topographic maps use symbols to portray the land as if you were looking down on it from above. **Topographic maps provide highly accurate information on the elevation, relief, and slope of the ground surface.**

Figure 14 Topographic maps provide the data necessary for the planning of highways, bridges, and other large construction projects.

Math TOOLBOX

Scale and Ratios

A ratio compares two numbers by division. For example, the scale of a map given as a ratio is 1 : 250,000. At this scale, the distance between two points on the map measures 23.5 cm. How would you find the actual distance? Begin by writing the scale as a fraction.

$$\frac{1}{250{,}000}$$

Next, write a proportion. Let *d* represent the actual distance between the two points.

$$\frac{1}{250{,}000} = \frac{23.5 \text{ cm}}{d}$$

Then write the cross products.

$$1 \times d = 250{,}000 \times 23.5 \text{ cm}$$

$$d = 5{,}875{,}000 \text{ cm}$$

(*Hint:* To convert cm to km, divide *d* by 100,000.)

Uses of Topographic Maps People find many uses for topographic maps. Businesses use them to help decide where to build new stores, housing, or factories. Cities and towns use them to decide where to build new schools. Topographic maps have recreational uses, too. If you were planning a bicycle trip, you could use a topographic map to see whether your trip would be flat or hilly.

Scale Topographic maps usually are large-scale maps. A large-scale map is one that shows a close-up view of part of Earth's surface. In the United States, most topographic maps are at a scale of 1 : 24,000, or 1 centimeter equals 0.24 kilometers. At this scale, a map can show the details of elevation and features such as rivers and coastlines. Large buildings, airports, and major highways appear as outlines at the correct scale. Symbols are used to show houses and other small features.

Coverage Most nations have a government agency that is responsible for making topographic maps. In the United States, that agency is the U. S. Geological Survey, or USGS. The USGS has produced about 57,000 topographic maps at scales of either 1 : 24,000 or 1 : 25,000. The maps cover all of the United States, except for parts of Alaska. Each map covers an area of roughly 145 square kilometers.

Symbols Mapmakers use a great variety of symbols on topographic maps. If you were drawing a map, what symbols would you use to represent woods, a campground, an orchard, a swamp, or a school? Look at Figure 15 to see the symbols that the USGS uses for these and other features.

☑ ***Checkpoint*** *In the United States, what agency is responsible for producing topographic maps?*

Figure 15 Maps made by the U. S. Geological Survey use more than 150 symbols.

Commonly Used Map Symbols

Contour line: elevation	Primary highway	River
Contour line: depression	Secondary highway	Stream
Building	Divided highway	Waterfall or rapids
School; church	Railroad tracks	Marsh or swamp
Built-up area	Airport	Rock or coral reef (Reef)
Campground; picnic area	Woods	Breakwater; wharf
Cemetery (Cem)	Orchard	Exposed wreck

Figure 16 The contour lines on a topographic map represent elevation and relief. ***Comparing and Contrasting*** *What information does the topographic map provide that the photograph does not?*

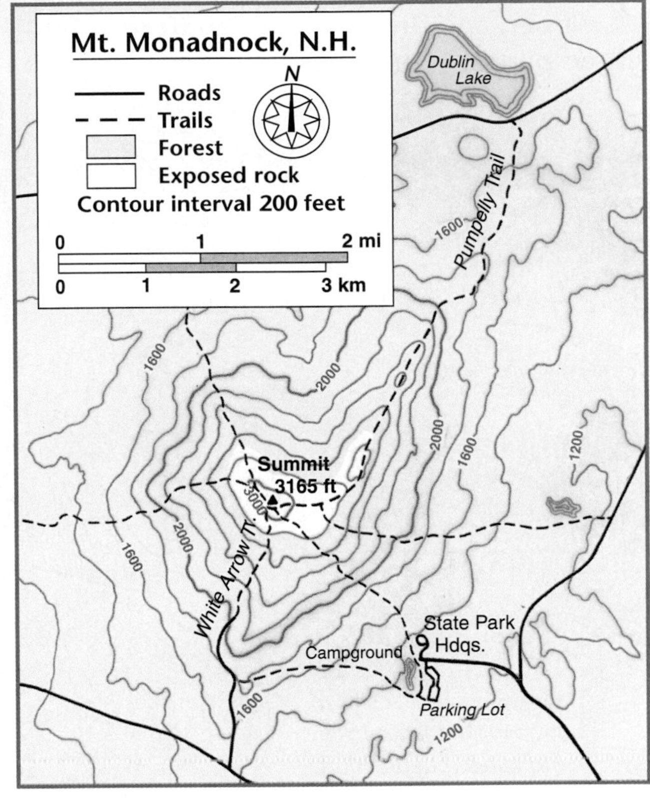

Showing Relief on Topographic Maps

To represent elevation, relief, and slope on topographic maps, mapmakers use contour lines. On a topographic map, a **contour line** connects points of equal elevation.

The change in elevation from contour line to contour line is called the **contour interval.** The contour interval for a given map is always the same. For example, the map in Figure 16 has a contour interval of 200 feet. If you start at one contour line and count up 10 contour lines, you have reached an elevation 2,000 feet above where you started. Usually, every fifth contour line is darker and heavier than the others. These lines are labeled with the elevation in round units, such as 1,600 or 2,000 feet above sea level. Most USGS maps give contour intervals in feet rather than meters.

Looking at a topographic map with many squiggly contour lines, you may feel as if you are gazing into a bowl of spaghetti. But if you follow the rules listed in *Exploring Topographic Maps* on the following page, you can learn to read contour lines. Reading contour lines is the first step toward "seeing" an area's topography by looking at a topographic map.

Interpreting Data

ACTIVITY

You are planning to hike up Mt. Monadnock. Use the topographic map in Figure 16 to determine which route is steeper: the White Arrow Trail or the Pumpelly Trail. What is the difference in elevation between the park headquarters and the summit?

EXPLORING *Topographic Maps*

Topographic maps provide data on elevation, relief, slopes, and the shapes of landforms. This USGS map shows part of Tennessee.

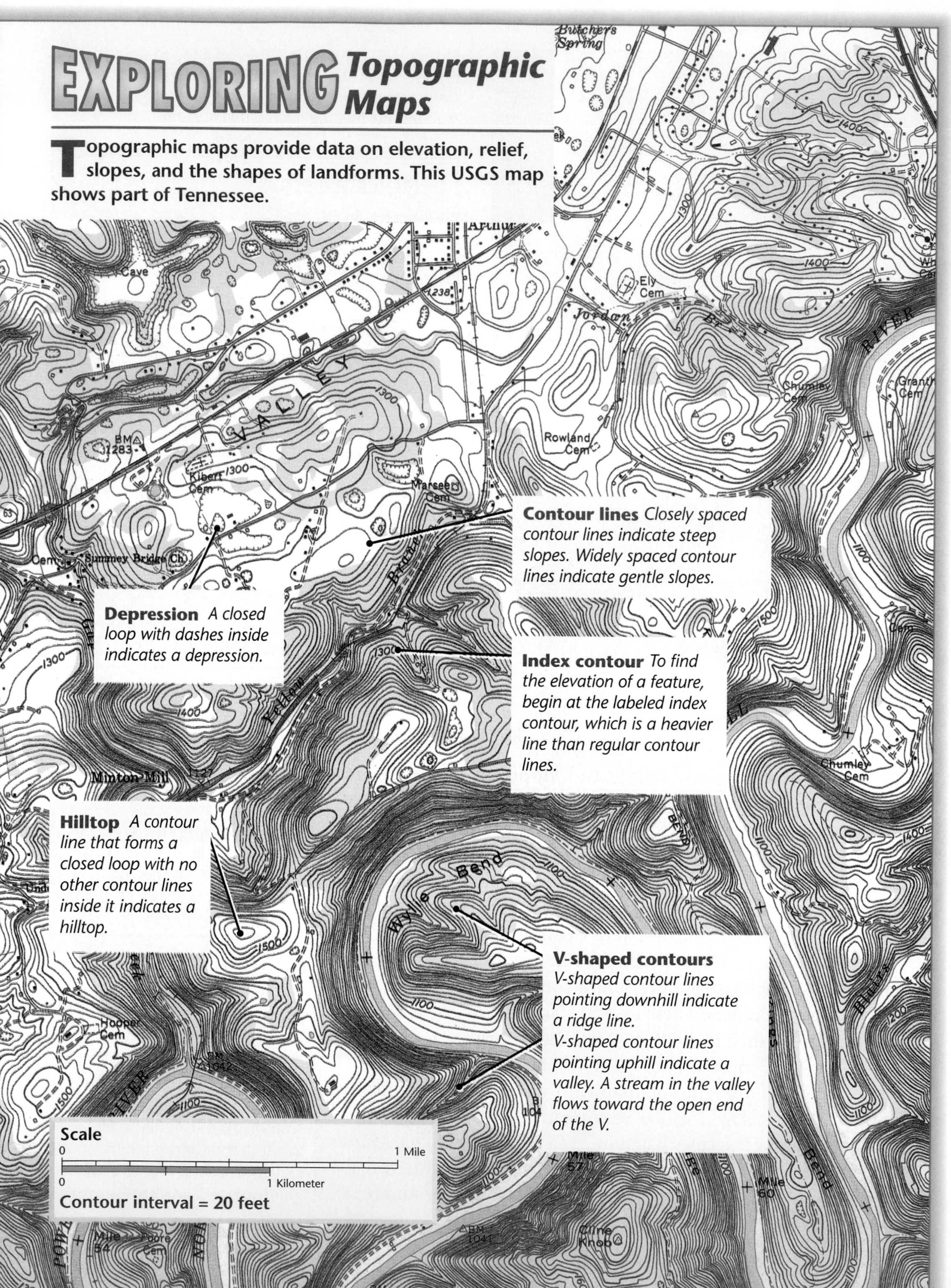

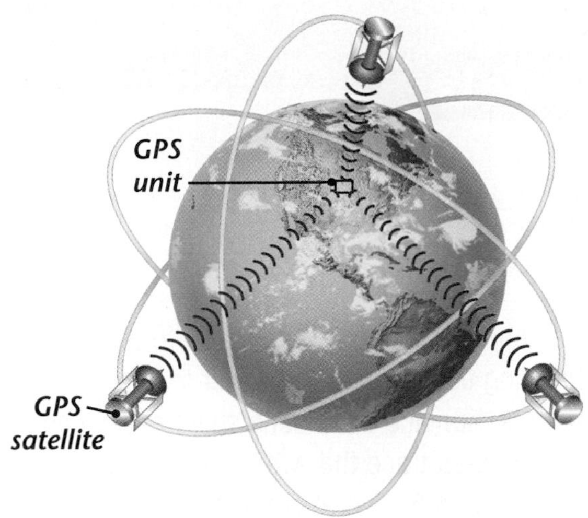

Figure 17 The GPS network includes 24 satellites. Three satellites (left) must be above the horizon to pinpoint the location of the user (right). The user's latitude and longitude appear on the screen of a portable GPS unit like the one in the photograph.

Global Positioning System

Integrating Technology Today, surveyors, pilots, and mapmakers around the world rely on the **Global Positioning System,** or GPS, to determine locations precisely. **The Global Positioning System is a method of finding latitude, longitude, and elevation of points on Earth's surface using a network of satellites.** At any given moment, there are between five and eight GPS satellites above the horizon in a given area. A hand-held unit the size of a cellular phone picks up signals broadcast by these satellites. A computer inside the GPS unit then calculates the user's location and elevation.

Engineers can use GPS to locate points on the ground for a construction project. Airplanes, ships, and hikers can use GPS to navigate. Some cars now contain both a GPS unit and a digital road map stored in a computer. Using GPS, the computer determines the car's location and suggests a route to your destination.

Section 4 Review

1. What kind of information does a topographic map provide about landforms?
2. How do topographic maps represent elevation and relief?
3. What would the highest and lowest points in an area look like on a topographic map?
4. What is the role of satellites in the Global Positioning System?
5. **Thinking Critically Interpreting Maps** Look at the map on page 576. Where is the highest elevation? Where do you find the steepest slopes? The gentlest slopes?

Check Your Progress

CHAPTER PROJECT 17

On a large piece of paper, draw your map to scale. Locate all natural and human-made features on the map using the measurements you recorded on your rough sketch and the symbols you brainstormed earlier. Include a north arrow, a legend, and scale on your map. Show the topography of the land by using contour lines or other symbols that show how the land slopes.

Skills Lab

Making Models

A Map in a Pan

A topographic map is a two-dimensional model of three-dimensional landforms.

Problem

How can you make a topographic map?

Materials

deep-sided pan
marking pencil
clear, hard sheet of plastic
sheet of unlined white paper
water
modeling clay
metric ruler
food coloring

Procedure

1. Place a lump of clay on the bottom of a deep-sided pan. Shape the clay into a model of a hill.
2. Pour colored water into the pan to a depth of 1 centimeter to represent sea level.
3. Place a sheet of hard, clear plastic over the container.
4. Trace the outline of the pan on the plastic sheet with a marking pencil. Then, looking straight down into the pan, trace the outline the water makes around the edges of the clay model. Remove the plastic sheet from the pan.

5. Add another centimeter of water to the pan, bringing the depth of the water to 2 centimeters. Replace the plastic sheet exactly as before, then trace the water level again.
6. Repeat Step 5 several times. Stop when the next addition of water would completely cover your model.
7. Remove the plastic sheet. Trace the outlines that you drew on the plastic sheet onto a sheet of paper.

Analyze and Conclude

1. Looking at your topographic map, how can you tell which parts of your model hill have a steep slope? A gentle slope?
2. How can you tell from the map which point on the hill is the highest?
3. Where on your map would you be likely to find a stream? Explain.
4. Is there any depression on your map where water would collect after it rained? What symbol should you use to identify this depression?
5. **Think About It** Compare your map with the clay landform. How are they alike? How are they different? How could you improve your map as a model of the landform?

More to Explore

Obtain a topographic map that includes an interesting landform such as a mountain, canyon, river valley, or coastline. After studying the contour lines on the map, make a sketch of what you think the landform looks like. Then build a scale model of the landform using clay or layers of cardboard or foamboard. How does your model landform compare with your sketch?

Exploring Earth's Surface

Key Ideas

- Earth's topography is made up of landforms that have elevation and relief, such as plains, mountains, and plateaus.
- The atmosphere, hydrosphere, and biosphere surround Earth's rocky outer layer, the lithosphere.

Key Terms

topography
elevation
relief
landform
landform region
plain
mountain
mountain range
plateau
lithosphere
atmosphere
hydrosphere
biosphere

Mapping Earth's Surface

Key Ideas

- Maps and globes are drawn to scale to show features on Earth's surface as seen from above.
- The grid of latitude and longitude lines can be used to locate points on Earth's surface.

Key Terms

map
globe
scale
symbols
key
equator
hemisphere
prime meridian
degree
latitude
longitude
map projection

Maps in the Computer Age

INTEGRATING TECHNOLOGY

Key Ideas

- Instruments carried aboard satellites in orbit around Earth make pictures of the surface called satellite images.
- Computers are used to store and display the information used in making maps.

Key Terms

satellite image
pixel
digitizing

Topographic Maps

Key Ideas

- Topographic maps portray the elevation, relief, and slope of the landforms in an area.
- Contour lines are used on a topographic map to show elevation and relief.
- The contour interval of a topographic map is the amount that elevation increases or decreases between contour lines.
- In addition to showing elevation and relief, topographic maps include a variety of other natural and human-made features.

Key Terms

topographic map
contour line
contour interval
Global Positioning System

Organizing Information

Concept Map Copy the concept map about landforms onto a separate piece of paper. Then complete it and add a title. (For more on concept maps, see the Skills Handbook.)

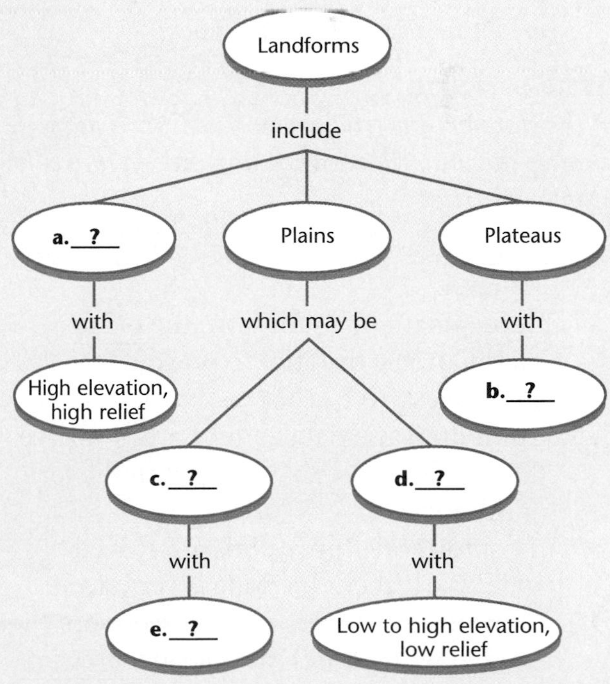

Reviewing Content

Multiple Choice

Choose the letter of the best answer.

1. A landform that has high elevation but a mostly flat surface is a
   a. coastal plain. b. mountain.
   c. mountain belt. d. plateau.
2. Of the Earth's four "spheres," the one that extends into all the others is the
   a. lithosphere. b. hydrosphere.
   c. biosphere. d. atmosphere.
3. Latitude is a measurement of distance north or south of the
   a. hemispheres. b. equator.
   c. axis. d. prime meridian.
4. To show the continents without distorting their relative sizes and shapes, a mapmaker would choose a(n)
   a. Mercator projection.
   b. globe.
   c. equal-area projection.
   d. topographic map.
5. On a topographic map, the contour lines form a V at a
   a. hilltop. b. level area.
   c. depression. d. valley.

True or False

If the statement is true, write true. If it is false, change the underlined word or words to make the statement true.

6. Relief measures a landform's height above sea level.
7. Going north or south from the prime meridian, the distance to one of the poles is 90 degrees.
8. Computers use data about Earth's surface that has been digitized, or put in the form of numbers.
9. If contour lines on a slope are spaced wide apart, then the slope is very steep.
10. Contour lines that form a closed loop marked with dashes indicate a depression.

Checking Concepts

11. What do geologists call an area where there is mostly one kind of topography?
12. What is a mountain range?
13. Compare the elevation of a coastal plain to that of an interior plain.
14. The South Island of New Zealand lies at about 170° E. What hemisphere is it in?
15. Could contour lines on a map ever cross? Explain.
16. Which would be more likely to show a shallow, 1.5-meter-deep depression in the ground: a 1-meter contour interval or a 5-meter contour interval? Explain.
17. **Writing to Learn** With your family, you make a car trip across the United States along the latitude line 35° N. Write a series of postcards to friends describing the landforms that you see on your trip. Use Appendix B to determine what the land is like along your route.

Thinking Critically

18. **Applying Concepts** Earth's diameter is about 13,000 kilometers. If a globe has a diameter of 0.5 meter, write the globe's scale as a ratio. What distance on Earth would 1 centimeter on the globe represent?
19. **Inferring** An airplane flies directly west at 1,000 kilometers per hour. Without changing direction, the plane returns to its starting point in just one hour. What can you infer about the plane's route with regard to lines of latitude and longitude? Explain.
20. **Observing** Using an atlas, find the latitude and longitude of San Francisco, California; Wichita, Kansas; and Richmond, Virginia. What do these three cities have in common?
21. **Comparing and Contrasting** How is mapmaking with computers different from earlier mapmaking techniques?
22. **Problem Solving** Your community has decided to build a zoo for animals from many regions of Earth. How could you use topographic maps of your area to help decide on the best location for the zoo?

Applying Skills

This map shows part of Acadia National Park in Maine. The contour interval is 20 feet. Use the map to answer Questions 23–25.

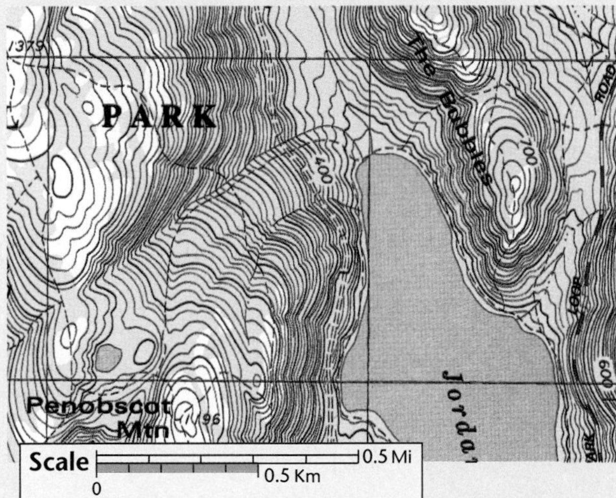

23. Interpreting Maps
- **A.** What is the elevation of the large lake?
- **B.** Which of the two Bubbles is higher?

24. Calculating Use the map scale to calculate the distance from the top of Penobscot Mountain to the large lake.

25. Inferring How can you tell whether the streams flow into or out of the large lake?

Performance Assessment — Chapter Project 17

Project Wrap Up Present your map to the class. Discuss the natural and physical features found on your site. What symbols did you use to represent these features? How did you measure and locate them on your map? How accurate is your map? Ask your classmates how you could improve your map.

Reflect and Record Write an evaluation of your map. What would you change about it? What would you keep the same? Does your map give others a clear idea of what the land looks like?

Test Preparation

Use these questions to prepare for standardized tests.

The map shows part of Earth's surface with a grid of latitude and longitude lines. Study the map. Then answer Questions 26–30.

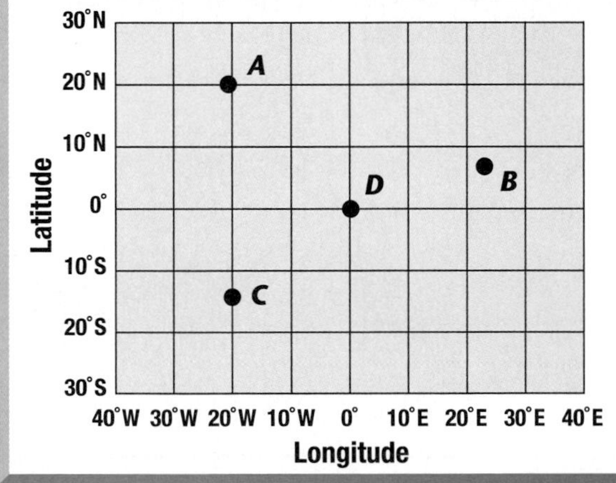

26. The horizontal line labeled 0° is called the
- **a.** horizon line.
- **b.** equator.
- **c.** prime meridian.
- **d.** contour line.

27. The latitude and longitude of point B is best given by
- **a.** 25°S 7°W.
- **b.** 7°N 25°W.
- **c.** 7°E 25°N.
- **d.** 7°N 25°E.

28. In which two hemispheres is point C located?
- **a.** western and southern hemispheres
- **b.** northern and eastern hemispheres
- **c.** eastern and western hemispheres
- **d.** western and northern hemispheres

29. The north-south distance in degrees from point A to Point C is about
- **a.** 15°.
- **b.** 35°.
- **c.** 25°.
- **d.** 0°.

30. Suppose you start at point D and travel southwest to point C. Through how many degrees of longitude have you traveled?
- **a.** 20°
- **b.** 15°
- **c.** 60°
- **d.** 30°

CHAPTER 18

Weathering and Soil Formation

WEB ACTIVITY www.phschool.com

Section 1 Rocks and Weathering

Discover **How Fast Can It Fizz?**
Try This **Rusting Away**
Skills Lab **Rock Shake**

Section 2 Soil Formation and Composition

Discover **What Is Soil?**
Sharpen Your Skills **Predicting**
Try This **A Square Meter of Soil**
Real-World Lab **Getting to Know the Soil**

Integrating Environmental Science

Section 3 Soil Conservation

Discover **How Can You Keep Soil From Washing Away?**

PROJECT 18

Soils for Seeds

High above Paris, weathering attacks limestone statues that are hundreds of years old. The process of weathering affects all rocks exposed on Earth's surface. Weathering breaks rock down into smaller and smaller particles. When other ingredients, such as decayed plant and animal materials, mix with the rock particles, the mixture is called soil. In this chapter, you will test how soil and other growing materials affect the growth of plants.

Your Goal To determine how soil composition affects the growth of bean seeds.

To complete this project successfully, you must

- examine your different growing materials and compare their particle size, shape, and composition
- compare how bean seeds grow in several different growing materials
- determine what type of soil or growing material is best for young bean plants

Get Started With your group, brainstorm what types of soil and other growing materials you will use in your experiment. Also consider these questions: What are the different variables that affect the growth of plants? How will you control these variables in your experiment? How will you measure the growth of your bean plants? Plan your experiment and obtain your teacher's approval.

Check Your Progress You will be working on this project as you study this chapter. To keep your project on track, look for Check Your Progress boxes at the following points.

Section 2 Review, page 599: Describe the different growing materials you have collected, and plant your bean seeds.

Section 3 Review, page 604: Observe and record the results of the growth of bean plants.

Wrap Up At the end of the chapter (page 607), you will present your results to the class. Your presentation will analyze how well bean plants grew in the different types of growing materials.

These stone gargoyles on the Cathedral of Notre Dame in Paris, France, are wearing away because of weathering.

Section 1 Rocks and Weathering

DISCOVER — ACTIVITY

How Fast Can It Fizz?

1. Place a fizzing antacid tablet in a small beaker. Then grind up a second tablet and place it in another beaker. The whole tablet is a model of solid rock. The ground-up tablet is a model of rock fragments.
2. Add 100 mL of warm water to the beaker containing the whole tablet. Then stir with a stirring rod until the tablet dissolves completely. Use a stopwatch to time how long it takes.
3. Add 100 mL of warm water to the beaker containing the ground-up tablet. Then stir until all of the ground-up tablet dissolves. Time how long it takes.

Think It Over

Inferring Which dissolved faster, the whole antacid tablet or the ground-up tablet? What difference between the two affected how long it took them to dissolve?

GUIDE FOR READING

- **What causes mechanical weathering?**
- **What causes chemical weathering?**
- **What determines how fast weathering occurs?**

Reading Tip **As you read, use the headings to make an outline about weathering.**

Imagine a hike that lasts for months and covers hundreds of kilometers. Each year, many hikers go on such treks. They hike trails that run the length of America's great mountain ranges. For example, the John Muir Trail follows the Sierra Nevada mountains. The Sierras extend about 640 kilometers along the eastern side of California. In the east, the Appalachian Trail follows the Appalachian Mountains. The Appalachians stretch more than 2,000 kilometers from Alabama to Maine.

The two trails cross very different landscapes. The Sierras are rocky and steep, with many peaks rising 3,000 meters above sea level. The Appalachians are more rounded and gently sloping, and are covered with soil and plants. The highest peaks in the Appalachians are less than half the elevation of the highest peaks in the Sierras. Which mountain range do you think is older? The Appalachians formed more than 250 million years ago. The Sierras formed only within the last 10 million years. The forces that wear down rock on Earth's surface have had much longer to grind down the Appalachians.

The Effects of Weathering

The process of mountain building thrusts rock up to the Earth's surface. There, the rock becomes exposed to weathering. **Weathering** is the process that breaks down rock and other substances at Earth's surface. Heat, cold, water, and ice all contribute to weathering. So do the oxygen and carbon dioxide in the atmosphere. Repeated freezing

Figure 1 The jagged, rocky peaks of the Sierra Nevadas (left) show that the mountains are young. The more gently sloping Appalachians (right) have been exposed to weathering for 250 million years.

and thawing, for example, can crack rock apart into smaller pieces. Rainwater can dissolve minerals that bind rock together. You don't need to go to the mountains to see examples of weathering. The forces that wear down mountains also cause bicycles to rust, paint to peel, sidewalks to crack, and potholes to form.

The forces of weathering break rocks into smaller and smaller pieces. Then the forces of erosion carry the pieces away. **Erosion** (ee ROH zhun) is the movement of rock particles by wind, water, ice, or gravity. Weathering and erosion work together continuously to wear down and carry away the rocks at Earth's surface.

There are two kinds of weathering: mechanical weathering and chemical weathering. Both types of weathering act slowly, but over time they break down even the biggest, hardest rocks.

☑ *Checkpoint* *What is the difference between weathering and erosion?*

Mechanical Weathering

If you hit a rock hard enough with a hammer, the rock will break into pieces. Some forces of weathering can also break rock into pieces. The type of weathering in which rock is physically broken into smaller pieces is called **mechanical weathering.** These smaller pieces of rock have the same composition as the rock they came from. If you have seen rocks that are cracked or peeling in layers, then you have seen rocks that are undergoing mechanical weathering.

Mechanical weathering breaks rock into pieces by freezing and thawing, release of pressure, growth of plants, actions of animals, and abrasion. The term **abrasion** (uh BRAY zhun) refers to the grinding away of rock by rock particles carried by water, ice, wind, or gravity. Mechanical weathering works slowly. But over very long periods of time, it does more than wear down rocks. Mechanical weathering eventually wears away whole mountains.

INTEGRATING PHYSICS In cool climates, the most important force of mechanical weathering is freezing and thawing of water. Water seeps into cracks in rocks and then freezes when the temperature drops. Water expands when it freezes. Ice therefore acts like a wedge, a simple machine that forces things apart. Wedges of ice in rocks widen and deepen cracks. This process is called **ice wedging.** When the ice melts, the water seeps deeper into the cracks. With repeated freezing and thawing, the cracks slowly expand until pieces of rock break off. *Exploring the Forces of Mechanical Weathering* shows how this process weathers rock.

☑ ***Checkpoint*** *How does ice wedging weather rock?*

EXPLORING the Forces of Mechanical Weathering

Mechanical weathering affects all the rock on Earth's surface. Given enough time, mechanical weathering can break down a massive mountain into tiny particles of sand.

Release of Pressure
As erosion removes material from the surface of a mass of rock, pressure on the rock is reduced. This release of pressure causes the outside of the rock to crack and flake off like the layers of an onion.

Freezing and Thawing
When water freezes in a crack in a rock, it expands and makes the crack bigger. The process of ice wedging also widens cracks in sidewalks and causes potholes in streets.

Chemical Weathering

In addition to mechanical weathering, another type of weathering attacks rock. **Chemical weathering** is the process that breaks down rock through chemical changes. **The agents of chemical weathering include water, oxygen, carbon dioxide, living organisms, and acid rain.**

Chemical weathering produces rock particles that have a different mineral makeup from the rock they came from. Each rock is made up of one or more minerals. For example, granite is made up of several minerals, including feldspar, quartz, and mica. But chemical weathering of granite eventually changes the feldspar minerals to clay minerals.

Plant Growth
Roots of trees and other plants enter cracks in rocks. As the roots grow, they force the cracks farther apart. Over time, the roots of even small plants can pry apart cracked rocks.

Abrasion
Sand and other rock particles that are carried by wind, water, or ice can wear away exposed rock surfaces like sandpaper on wood. Wind-driven sand helped shape the rocks shown here.

Animal Actions
Animals that burrow in the ground—including moles, gophers, prairie dogs, and some insects—loosen and break apart rocks in the soil.

Figure 2 As weathering breaks apart rock, the surface area exposed to further weathering increases.

Chemical weathering creates holes or soft spots in rock, so the rock breaks apart more easily. Chemical and mechanical weathering often work together. As mechanical weathering breaks rock into pieces, more surface area becomes exposed to chemical weathering. The Discover activity in this section shows how increasing the surface area increases the rate of a chemical reaction.

Water Water is the most important agent of chemical weathering. Water weathers rock by dissolving it. When a rock or other substance dissolves in water, it mixes uniformly throughout the water to make a solution. Over time, many rocks will dissolve in water.

Oxygen The oxygen gas in air is an important cause of chemical weathering. If you have ever left a bicycle or metal tool outside in the rain, then you have seen how oxygen can weather iron. Iron combines with oxygen in the presence of water in a process called oxidation. The product of oxidation is rust. Rock that contains iron also oxidizes, or rusts. Rust makes rock soft and crumbly and gives it a red or brown color.

Carbon Dioxide Another gas found in air, carbon dioxide, also causes chemical weathering. Carbon dioxide becomes dissolved in rainwater and in water that sinks through air pockets in the soil. The result is a weak acid called carbonic acid. Carbonic acid easily weathers marble and limestone.

Living Organisms Imagine a seed landing on a rock face. As it sprouts, its roots push into cracks in the rock. As the plant's roots grow, they produce weak acids that slowly dissolve rock around the roots. Lichens—plantlike organisms that grow on rocks—also produce weak acids that chemically weather rock.

Acid Rain Over the past 150 years, people have been burning

INTEGRATING ENVIRONMENTAL SCIENCE

large amounts of coal, oil, and gas for energy. Burning these fuels can pollute the air with sulfur, carbon, and nitrogen compounds. Such compounds react chemically with the water vapor in clouds, forming acids. These acids mix with raindrops and fall as acid rain. Acid rain causes very rapid chemical weathering.

Rusting Away

Here's how you can observe weathering. ACTIVITY

1. Moisten some steel wool and place it in a closed container so it will not dry out.
2. Observe the steel wool after a few days. What has happened to the steel wool?
3. Take a new piece of steel wool and squeeze it between your fingers. Remove the steel wool from the container and squeeze it between your fingers. What happens? Wash your hands when you have finished.

Predicting If you kept the steel wool moist for a longer time, what would eventually happen to it? How is the weathering of steel wool like the weathering of a rock?

Rate of Weathering

Visitors to New England's historic cemeteries may notice a surprising fact. Slate tombstones from the 1700s are less weathered and easier to read than marble gravestones from the 1800s. Why is this so? **The most important factors that determine the rate at which weathering occurs are type of rock and climate.**

Type of Rock Some kinds of rocks weather more rapidly than others. The minerals that make up the rock determine how fast it weathers. Rock made of minerals that do not dissolve easily in water weathers slowly. Rock made of minerals that dissolve easily in water weathers faster.

Some rock weathers easily because it is permeable. **Permeable** (PUR mee uh bul) means that a material is full of tiny, connected air spaces that allow water to seep through it. Permeable rock weathers chemically at a fast rate. Why? As water seeps through the spaces in the rock, it removes dissolved material formed by weathering.

Climate Climate refers to the average weather conditions in an area. Both chemical and mechanical weathering occur faster in wet climates. Rainfall provides the water needed for chemical changes as well as for freezing and thawing.

Chemical reactions occur faster at higher temperatures. That is why chemical weathering occurs more quickly where the climate is both hot and wet. Granite, for example, is a very hard rock that forms when molten material cools inside Earth. Granite weathers so slowly in cool climates that it is often used as a building stone. But in hot and wet climates, granite weathers faster and eventually crumbles apart.

Figure 3 The rate of weathering of these tombstones depends on the type of rock. Slate (top) resists weathering better than marble (bottom). ***Inferring*** *What type of weathering probably wore away the letters on the marble tombstone?*

Section 1 Review

1. What factors cause mechanical weathering?
2. Describe three causes of chemical weathering.
3. What factors affect the rate of weathering?
4. Explain why chemical weathering occurs faster in hot, wet climates than in cool, dry climates.
5. **Thinking Critically Predicting** Suppose you see a large boulder with several cracks in it. What would you expect to see if you could observe the boulder again in several hundred years? Explain.

Science at Home

Here's how to demonstrate one type of weathering for your family. Plug one end of a drinking straw with a small piece of clay. Fill the straw with water. Now plug the top of the straw with clay. Make sure that the clay plugs do not leak. Lay the straw flat in the freezer overnight. Remove the straw the next day. What happened to the clay plugs? What process produced this result? Be sure to dispose of the straw so that no one will use it for drinking.

Skills Lab

Controlling Variables

Rock Shake

Which do you think would weather faster, a rock attacked by plant acids or a rock in the rushing waters of a stream? Many factors affect the rate at which rock weathers. In this lab, you will compare the rates of weathering that take place under different conditions.

Problem

How will shaking and acid conditions affect the rate at which limestone weathers?

Materials

300 mL of water
balance
paper towels
masking tape
2 pieces of thin cloth
marking pen or pencil
300 mL of vinegar, an acid
plastic graduated cylinder, 250 mL
80 small pieces of water-soaked limestone
4 watertight plastic containers with screw-on caps, 500-mL

Procedure

Part 1— Day 1

1. Using masking tape, label the four 500-mL containers A, B, C, and D.
2. Separate the 80 pieces of limestone into four sets of 20.
3. Copy the data table in your notebook. Then place the first 20 pieces of limestone on the balance and record their mass in the data table. Place the rocks in Container A.
4. Repeat Step 3 for the other sets of rocks and place them in containers B, C, and D.
5. Pour 150 mL of water into container A and container B. Put caps on both containers.
6. Pour 150 mL of vinegar into container C and also into container D. Put caps on both containers.
7. Predict the effect of weathering on the mass of the limestone pieces. Which will weather more: the limestone in water or the limestone in vinegar? (*Hint:* Vinegar is an acid.) Also predict the effect of shaking on the limestone in containers B and D. Record your predictions in your notebook.
8. Allow the pieces to soak overnight.

Container	Total Mass Start	Total Mass Next Day	Change in Mass	Percent Change in Mass
A (water, no shaking)				
B (water, shaking)				
C (vinegar, no shaking)				
D (vinegar, shaking)				

Part 2—Day 2

9. Screw the caps tightly on containers B and D. Shake both containers for 10 to 15 minutes. Make sure that each container is shaken for exactly the same amount of time and at the same intensity. After shaking, set the containers aside. Do not shake containers A and C.
10. Open the top of container A. Place one piece of thin cloth over the opening of the container. Carefully pour all of the water out through the cloth into a waste container. Be careful not to let any of the pieces flow out with the water. Dry these pieces carefully and record their mass in your data table.
11. Next, determine how much limestone was lost through weathering in container A. (*Hint:* Subtract the mass of the limestone pieces remaining on Day 2 from the mass of the pieces on Day 1.)
12. Repeat Steps 10 and 11 for containers B, C, and D.

Analyze and Conclude

1. Calculate the percent change in mass of the 20 pieces for each container.

$$\% \text{ change} = \frac{\text{Change in mass} \times 100}{\text{Total mass start}}$$

   Record the results in the data table.
2. Do your data show a change in mass of the 20 pieces in each of the four containers?
3. Is there a greater change in total mass for the pieces in one container than for the pieces in another? Explain.
4. How correct were your predictions of how shaking and acid would affect the weathering of limestone? Explain.
5. If your data showed a greater change in the mass of the pieces in one of the containers, how might this change be explained?
6. **Think About It** Based on your data, which variable do you think was more responsible for breaking down the limestone: the vinegar or the shaking? Explain.

Design an Experiment

Would your results for this experiment change if you changed the variables? For example, you could soak or shake the pieces for a longer time, or test rocks other than limestone. You could also test whether adding more limestone pieces (30 rather than 20 in each set) would make a difference in the outcome. Design an experiment on the rate of weathering to test the effects of changing one of these variables. Have your teacher approve your plan before you begin.

SCIENCE AND SOCIETY

Preserving Stone Monuments

A statue with a human head and a lion's body crouches in the desert beside the pyramids of Egypt. This is the great Sphinx. It was carved out of limestone about 4,500 years ago. Thousands of years of weathering by water, wind, and sand have worn away much of the Sphinx's face. In the 1800s, sand that had protected the Sphinx's body was cleared away. Weathering attacked the newly exposed parts of the Sphinx. Flakes and even chunks of stone fell from the statue. Workers tried to repair the Sphinx with cement. But the repairs weakened the statue and changed its shape.

The Issues

Should Structures Be Restored? Weathering threatens many ancient stone monuments throughout the world. Pollutants in air and rain make stone weather faster. But there are ways to slow the weathering of a monument without changing or damaging it. In 1998, workers in Egypt completed a new restoration of the Sphinx. They removed the added cement. They replaced the damaged stones with new, hand-cut limestone blocks of the same size and weight. The new stone will help protect what remains of the monument. Visitors to the Sphinx will now see only the original statue and repairs made with original materials. The new repairs preserve the statue's original shape.

Most people want the Sphinx and other monuments to be restored. But restoration is time-consuming and very expensive. And in some cases, repair work can damage or change the original structure.

Can New Technology Slow Weathering? Advances in technology may provide some solutions. At the Sphinx, scientists measure wind direction, wind speed, and moisture in the air. This information helps scientists follow the weathering process and provides data that will help prevent more damage. Similar instruments are used at other monuments.

Other scientists are working on a way of coating stone with a chemical compound to strengthen and repair the surface. So far, they have found a compound that sticks well to sandstone, but not to marble or limestone.

What Else Can People Do? Repair and restoration are not the only options. Some say that ancient monuments should be buried again after being uncovered by archaeologists. Some people suggest that the Sphinx itself should be reburied in the sand that protected it for so many centuries. But scholars, archaeologists, and tourists disagree. Meanwhile, as people seek solutions, rain, wind, sun, and polluted air continue to take their toll.

You Decide

1. Identify the Problem
In your own words, explain the difficulties involved in preserving ancient monuments.

2. Analyze the Options
List methods for preserving ancient buildings and monuments. Note the advantages and disadvantages of repair work, technology, and other approaches.

3. Find a Solution
Make a plan to preserve a monument in your city. Write your recommendations in the form of a letter to a city mayor or town council.

Soil Formation and Composition

DISCOVER — ACTIVITY

What Is Soil?

1. Use a toothpick to separate a sample of soil into individual particles. With a hand lens, try to identify the different types of particles in the sample. Wash your hands when you are finished.
2. Write a "recipe" for the sample of soil, naming each of the "ingredients" that you think the soil contains. Include what percentage of each ingredient would be needed to make up the soil.
3. Compare your recipe with those of your classmates.

Think It Over

Forming Operational Definitions Based on your observations, how would you define *soil*?

A bare rock surface does not look like a spot where a plant could grow. But look more closely. In that hard surface is a small crack. Over many years, mechanical and chemical weathering will slowly enlarge the crack. Rain and wind will bring bits of weathered rock, dust, and dry leaves. The wind also may carry tiny seeds. With enough moisture, a seed will sprout and take root. Then, when the plant blossoms a few months later, the rock itself will seem to have burst into flower.

GUIDE FOR READING

- How does soil form?
- What is soil made of?
- What is the role of plants and animals in soil formation?

Reading Tip **Before you read, rewrite the headings as *how, what, where,* and *why* questions. Then look for answers as you read.**

Soil Formation

The crack in the rock seems to have little in common with a flower garden containing thick, rich soil. But soil is what the weathered rock and other materials in the crack have started to become. **Soil** is the loose, weathered material on Earth's surface in which plants can grow. **Soil forms as rock is broken down by weathering and mixes with other materials on the surface.**

Soil is constantly being formed wherever bedrock is exposed. **Bedrock** is the solid layer of rock beneath the soil. Once exposed at the surface, bedrock gradually weathers into smaller and smaller particles that are the basic material of soil.

Figure 4 A crack between rocks holds just enough soil for this plant.

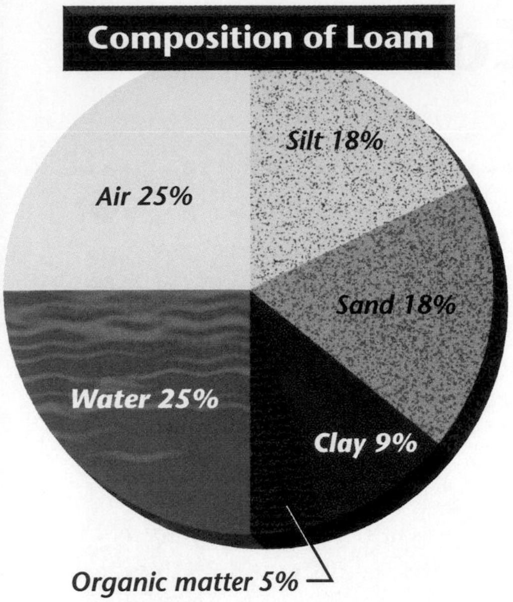

Composition of Loam

Silt 18%
Air 25%
Sand 18%
Water 25%
Clay 9%
Organic matter 5%

Figure 5 Loam, a type of soil, is made up of air, water, and organic matter as well as materials from weathered rock.
Interpreting Graphs *What two materials make up the major portion of this soil?*

Soil Composition

Soil is more than just particles of weathered bedrock. **Soil is a mixture of rock particles, minerals, decayed organic material, air, and water.**

The type of rock particles and minerals in any given soil depends on two factors: the bedrock that was weathered to form the soil and the type of weathering. Together, sand, silt, and clay make up the portion of soil that comes from weathered rock.

The decayed organic material in soil is humus. **Humus** (HYOO mus) is a dark-colored substance that forms as plant and animal remains decay. Humus helps create spaces in soil for the air and water that plants must have. Humus is also rich in the nitrogen, sulfur, phosphorus, and potassium that plants need to grow.

Soil Texture

Sand feels coarse and grainy, but clay feels smooth and silky. These differences are differences in texture. Soil texture depends on the size of individual soil particles.

The particles of rock in soil are classified by size. As you can see in Figure 6, the largest soil particles are gravel. Small pebbles and even large boulders are considered gravel. Next in size are particles of sand, followed by silt particles, which are smaller than sand. The smallest soil particles are clay. Clay particles are smaller than the period at the end of this sentence.

Soil texture is important for plant growth. Soil that is mostly clay has a dense, heavy texture. Some clay soils hold a lot of water, so plants grown in them may "drown" for lack of air. In contrast, sandy soil has a coarse texture. Water quickly drains through it, so plants may die for lack of water.

Soil that is made up of about equal parts of clay, sand, and silt is called **loam.** It has a crumbly texture that holds both air and water. Loam is best for growing most types of plants.

Figure 6 Soil particles range in size from gravel to clay particles too small to be seen by the unaided eye. The sand, silt, and clay shown here have been enlarged.

Soil Horizons

Soil formation continues over a long period of time. Gradually, soil develops layers called horizons. A **soil horizon** is a layer of soil that differs in color and texture from the layers above or below it.

If you dug a hole in the ground about half a meter deep, you would see the different soil horizons. Figure 7 shows how soil scientists classify the soil into three horizons. The A horizon is made up of **topsoil,** a crumbly, dark brown soil that is a mixture of humus, clay, and other minerals. The B horizon, often called **subsoil,** usually consists of clay and other particles washed down from the A horizon, but little humus. The C horizon contains only partly weathered rock.

☑ ***Checkpoint*** *What are soil horizons?*

The Rate of Soil Formation

The rate at which soil forms depends on the climate and type of rock. Remember that weathering occurs most rapidly in areas with a warm, rainy climate. As a result, soil develops more quickly in these areas. In contrast, weathering and soil formation take place slowly in areas where the climate is cold and dry.

Some types of rock weather and form soil faster than others. For example, limestone weathers faster than granite. Thus, soil forms more quickly from limestone than from granite.

Predicting ACTIVITY

Gardeners often improve soil by adding materials to it. These added materials change the soil's composition. They make the soil more fertile or improve its ability to hold water. For example, a gardener might add compost (partly decayed leaves) to sandy soil. How would the compost change the sandy soil?

Figure 7 Soil horizons form in three steps.

1. The C horizon forms as bedrock weathers and rock breaks up into soil particles.

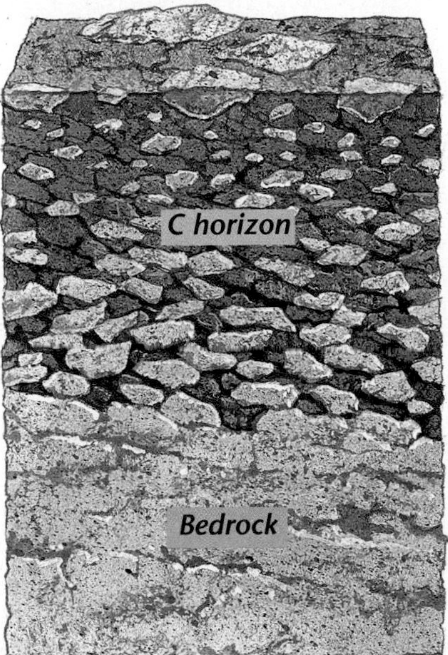

2. The A horizon develops from the C horizon when plant roots weather the rock mechanically and chemically. Plants also add organic material to the soil.

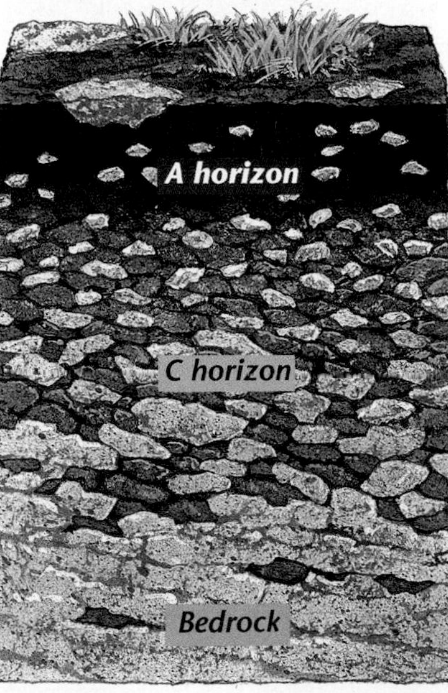

3. The B horizon develops as rainwater washes clay and minerals from the A horizon to the B horizon.

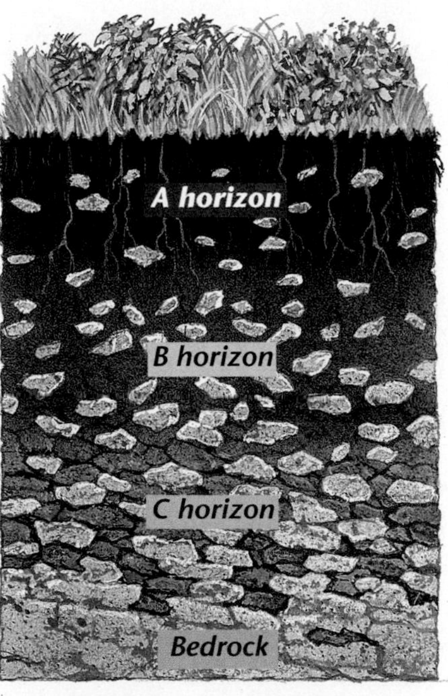

Life in Soil

INTEGRATING LIFE SCIENCE Soil is more than just bits of rock. If you look closely at some soil, you can see that it is teeming with living things. **Some soil organisms mix the soil and make spaces in it for air and water. Other soil organisms make humus, the material that makes soil fertile.** Fertile soil is rich in nutrients that plants need, such as nitrogen and phosphorus.

Plants contribute most of the organic remains that form humus. As plants shed leaves, they form a loose layer called **litter.**

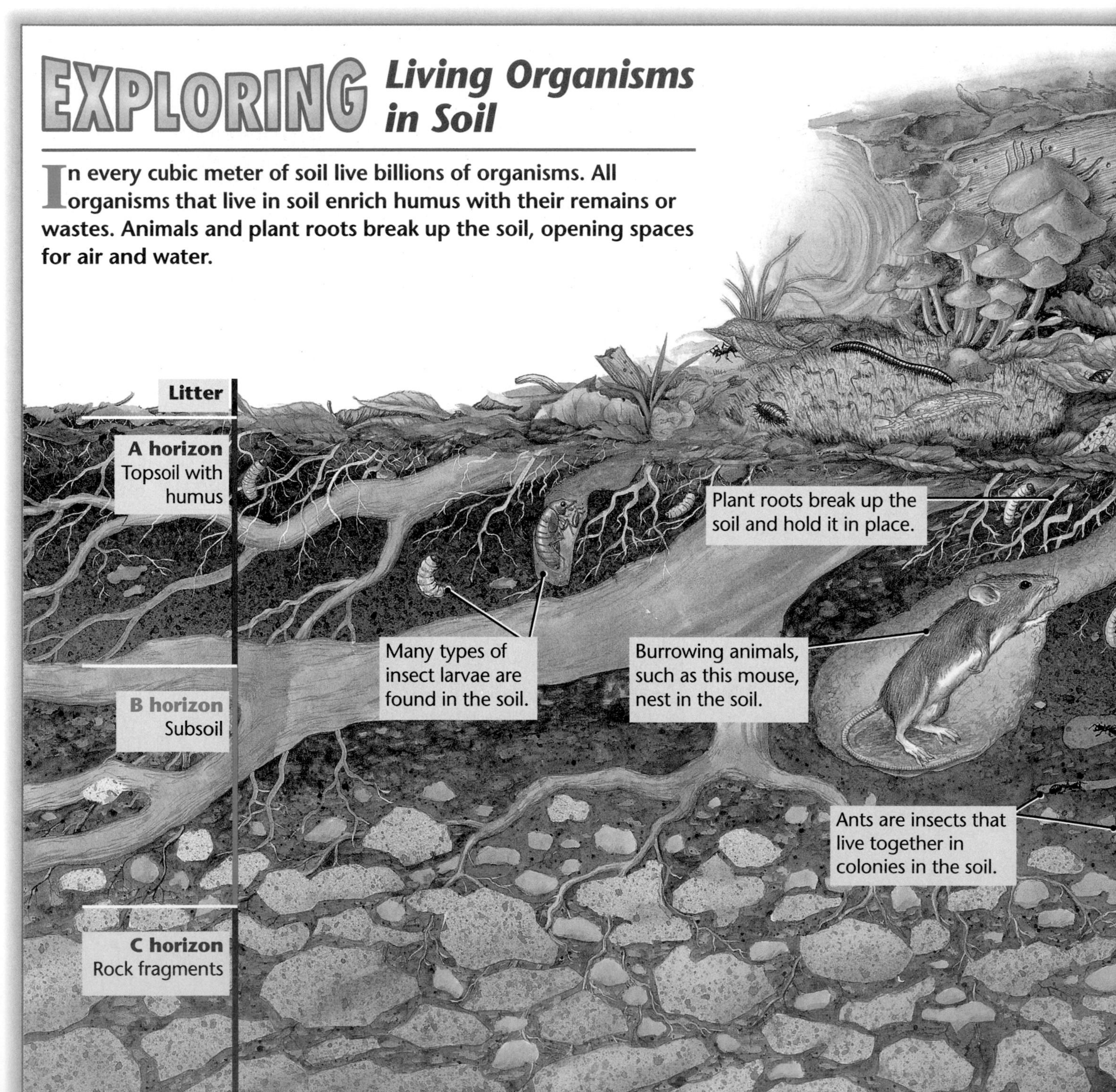

When plants die, their remains fall to the ground and become part of the litter. Plant roots also die and begin to decay underground. Although plant remains are full of stored nutrients, they are not yet humus.

Humus forms in a process called decomposition. As decomposition occurs, organisms that live in soil turn dead organic material into humus. These organisms are called decomposers. **Decomposers** are the organisms that break the remains of dead organisms into smaller pieces and digest them with chemicals.

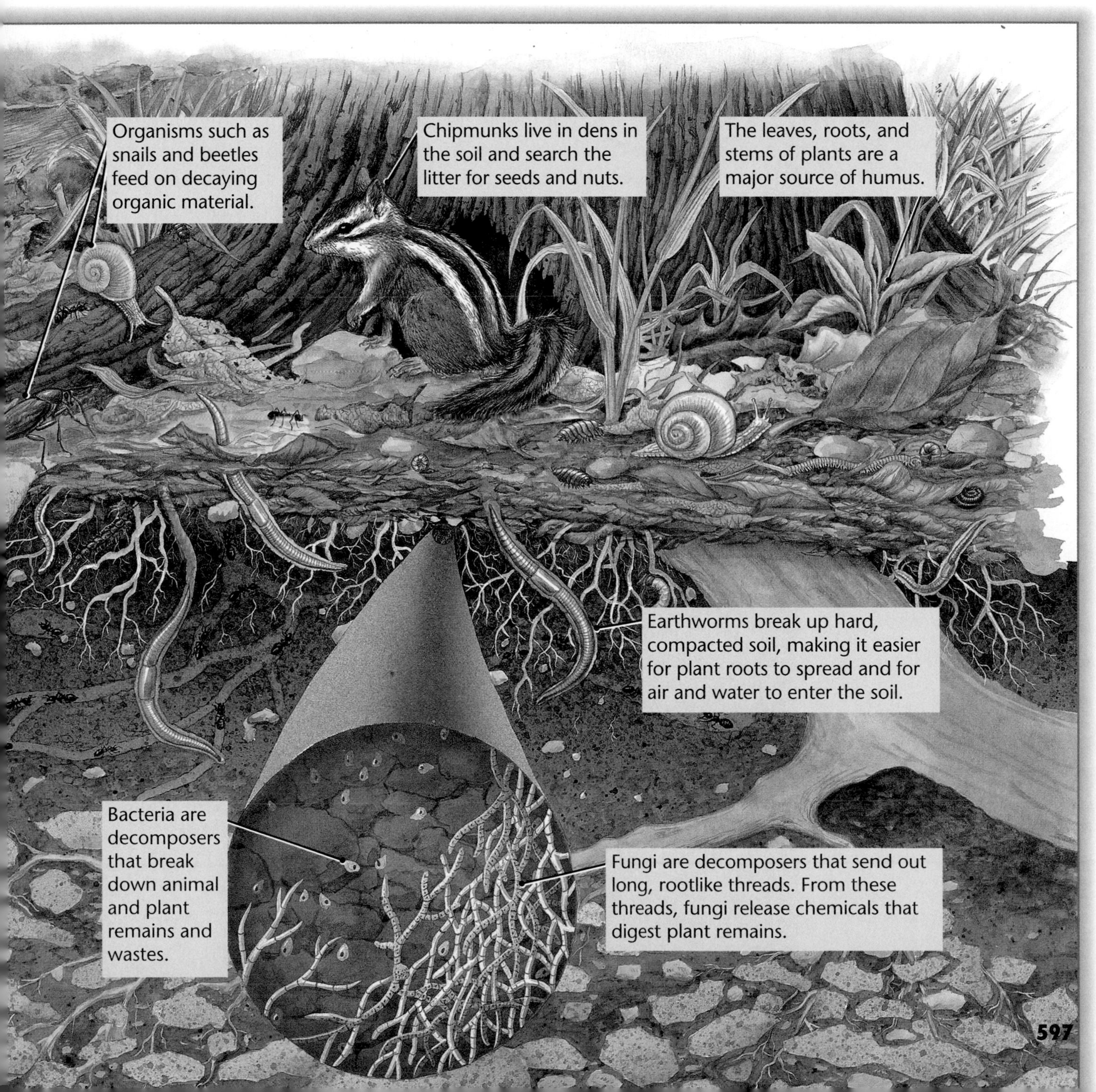

A Square Meter of Soil

ACTIVITY

1. Outdoors, measure an area of one square meter. Mark your square with string.
2. Observe the color and texture of the surface soil. Is it dry or moist? Does it contain sand, clay, or gravel? Are there plants, animals, or humus?
3. Use a trowel to dig down several centimeters into the soil. What is the soil's color and texture there?
4. When you finish, leave the soil as you found it. Wash your hands.

Drawing Conclusions What can you conclude about the soil's fertility? What evidence supports your conclusions?

Fungi, protists, bacteria, and worms are the main soil decomposers. Fungi are organisms such as molds and mushrooms. Fungi grow on, and digest, plant remains. Bacteria are microscopic decomposers that cause decay. Bacteria attack dead organisms and their wastes in soil. Other very small animals, such as mites and worms, also decompose dead organic material and mix it with the soil.

Earthworms do most of the work of mixing humus with other materials in soil. As earthworms eat their way through the soil, they carry humus down to the subsoil and subsoil up to the surface. Earthworms also pass out the soil they eat as waste. The waste soil is enriched with substances that plants need to grow, such as nitrogen.

Many burrowing mammals such as mice, moles, prairie dogs, and gophers break up hard, compacted soil and mix humus through it. These animals also add nitrogen to the soil when they excrete waste. They add organic material when they die and decay.

Earthworms and burrowing animals also help to aerate, or mix air into, the soil. Plant roots need the oxygen that this process adds to the soil.

☑ ***Checkpoint*** *How do decomposers contribute to the formation of soil?*

Soil Types in the United States

If you were traveling across the hills of north-central Georgia, you would see soils that seem to be made of red clay. In other parts of the country, soils can be black, brown, yellow, or gray. In the United States alone, differences in climate and local bedrock have led to the formation of thousands of different types of soil.

Figure 8 Earthworms break up the soil, allowing in air and water. An earthworm eats its own weight in soil every day.

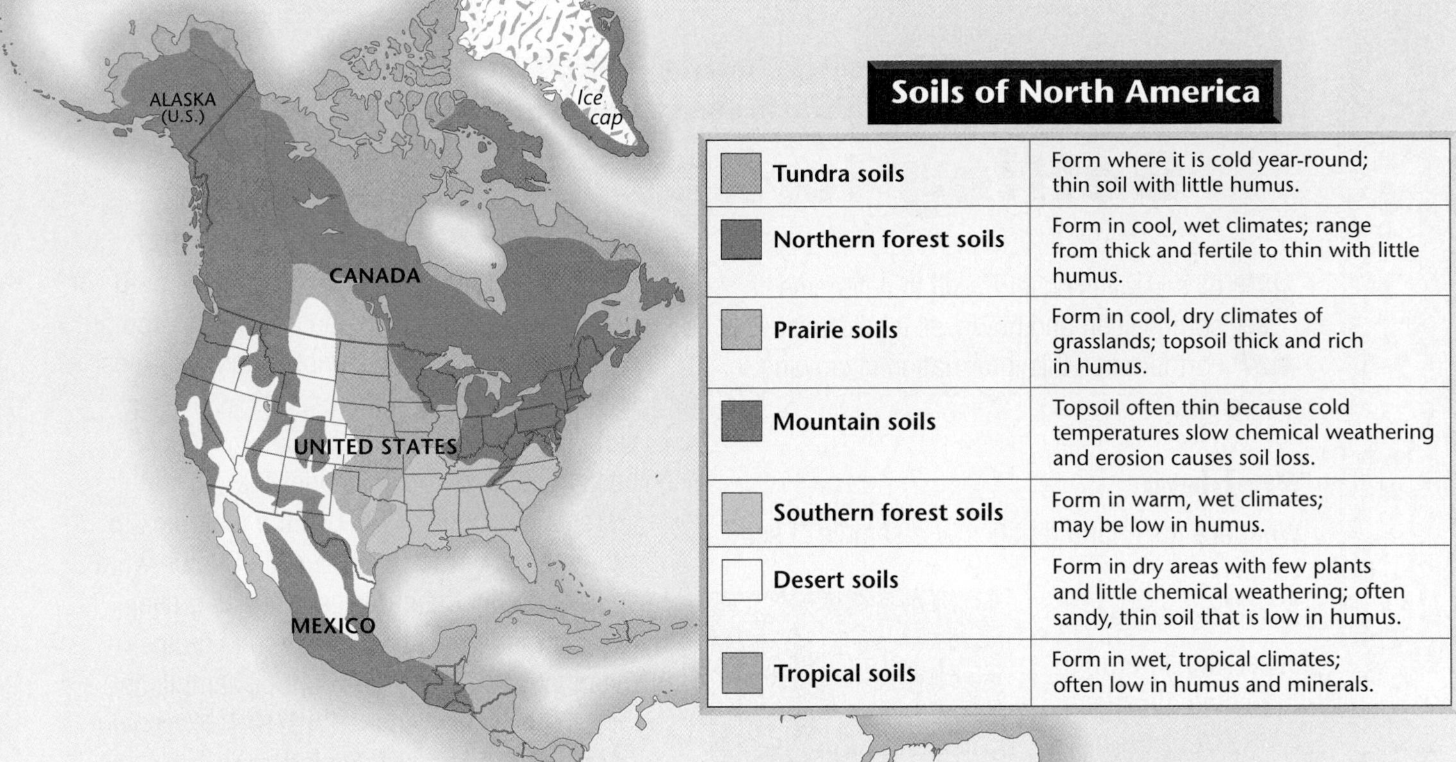

Soils of North America

	Soil type	Description
	Tundra soils	Form where it is cold year-round; thin soil with little humus.
	Northern forest soils	Form in cool, wet climates; range from thick and fertile to thin with little humus.
	Prairie soils	Form in cool, dry climates of grasslands; topsoil thick and rich in humus.
	Mountain soils	Topsoil often thin because cold temperatures slow chemical weathering and erosion causes soil loss.
	Southern forest soils	Form in warm, wet climates; may be low in humus.
	Desert soils	Form in dry areas with few plants and little chemical weathering; often sandy, thin soil that is low in humus.
	Tropical soils	Form in wet, tropical climates; often low in humus and minerals.

Figure 9 An area's climate and plant life help to determine what type of soil forms from bedrock. ***Interpreting Maps*** *Recall that soil forms more rapidly in warm, wet areas than in cold, dry areas. Which types of soil on the map would you expect to form most slowly?*

Scientists classify the different types of soil into groups. These groups are based partly on the climate in a region. The most common plants found in a region are also used to help classify the soil. In addition, scientists classify soil by its composition—whether it is rocky, sandy, or rich in clay. Major soil types found in North America include forest, prairie, desert, mountain, tundra, and tropical soils. Look at Figure 9 to see where each of the major soil types is found. Which soil type is found in your part of the country?

Section 2 Review

1. What role does weathering play in the formation of soil?
2. What are the different materials that make up soil?
3. How do plants and animals affect the formation and composition of soil?
4. How do forest soils differ from prairie soils?
5. **Thinking Critically Relating Cause and Effect** Earthworms breathe by absorbing air in the soil through their skin. Why do you think earthworms crawl to the surface when it rains? Explain.

Check Your Progress

CHAPTER PROJECT 18

Obtain samples of the soil and growing materials you will use to grow your bean seeds. Choices include sand, vermiculite, gravel, potting soil, and local topsoil. **CAUTION:** *Avoid collecting soil near animal droppings. Wash your hands after handling the soil.* Make notes describing each sample. Predict which soil or mixture will be best for the growth of bean seeds. Design a method for recording the growth of your bean plants. Plant the bean seeds in the growing materials.

Careers in Science

Getting to Know the Soil

Soil scientists observe soil to determine its composition and how well it holds water. Farmers use this information in growing their crops.

Problem

What are the characteristics of a sample of soil?

Skills Focus

observing, inferring, posing questions

Materials

20–30 grams of soil
plastic spoon
plastic dropper
toothpick
water
stereomicroscope
graph paper ruled with 1- or 2-mm spacing
plastic petri dish or jar lid

Procedure  

1. Your teacher will give you a dry sample of soil. As you observe the sample, record your observations in your lab notebook.
2. Spread half of the sample on the graph paper. Spread the soil thinly so that you can see the lines on the paper through the soil. Using the graph paper as a background, estimate the sizes of the particles that make up the soil.
3. Place the rest of the sample in the palm of your hand, rub it between your fingers, and squeeze it. Is it soft or gritty? Does it clump together or crumble when you squeeze it?
4. Place about half the sample in a plastic petri dish. Using the dropper, add water one drop at a time. Watch how the sample changes. Does any material in the sample float? As the sample gets wet, do you notice any odor?
5. Look at some of the soil under the stereomicroscope. (*Hint:* Use the toothpick to examine the particles in the soil.) Sketch what you see. Label the particles, such as gravel, organic matter, or strangely shaped grains.
6. Clean up and dispose of your soil sample as directed by your teacher. **CAUTION:** *Wash your hands when you finish handling the soil.*

Analyze and Conclude

1. What did you notice about the appearance of the soil sample when you first obtained it?
2. What can you infer about the composition of the soil from the different sizes of its particles? From your observations of its texture? From how the sample changed when water was added? What surprised you the most about the composition of your sample?
3. Based on the composition of your soil sample, can you determine the type of environment from which it was taken?
4. **Apply** List several questions that a soil scientist would need to answer to determine whether a soil sample was good for growing flowers or vegetables. Did your observations answer these questions for your soil sample?

More to Explore

Repeat the procedure using a soil sample from a different location. How does it compare with the first soil sample you tested?

SECTION 3 Soil Conservation

DISCOVER ACTIVITY

How Can You Keep Soil From Washing Away?

1. Pour about 500 mL of soil into a pie plate, forming a pile.
2. Devise a way to keep the soil from washing away when water is poured over it. To protect the pile of soil, you may use craft sticks, paper clips, pebbles, modeling clay, strips of paper, or other materials approved by your teacher.

3. After arranging your materials to protect the soil, hold a container containing 200 mL of water about 20 cm above the center of the soil. Slowly pour the water in a stream onto the pile of soil.
4. Compare your pan of soil with those of your classmates.

Think It Over

Observing Based on your observations, what do you think is the best way to prevent soil on a slope from washing away?

GUIDE FOR READING

- **Why is soil one of Earth's most valuable resources?**
- **What caused the Dust Bowl?**
- **What are some ways that soil can be conserved?**

Reading Tip **As you read, make a list of human activities that can harm the soil and a list of activities that can help save the soil.**

Suppose you were a settler traveling west in the early 1800s. Much of your journey would have been through vast, open grasslands called prairies. After the forests and mountains of the East, the prairies were an amazing sight. Grass taller than a person rippled and flowed in the wind like a sea of green.

The prairie soil was very fertile. It was rich with humus because of the tall grass. The **sod**—the thick mass of tough roots at the surface of the soil—kept the soil in place and held onto moisture.

The prairies covered a vast area. They included the eastern parts of Kansas, Nebraska, North and South Dakota, as well as Iowa and Illinois. Today, farms growing crops such as corn, soybeans, and wheat have replaced the prairies. But the prairie soils are still among the most fertile in the world.

The Value of Soil

Soil is one of Earth's most valuable resources because everything that lives on land depends directly or indirectly on soil. Plants depend directly on the soil to live and grow. Animals depend on plants—or on other animals that depend on plants—for food. Soil is a renewable resource that can be found wherever weathering occurs. But soil formation takes a long time. It can take hundreds of years for just a few centimeters of soil to form. The thick, fertile soil of the prairies took many thousands of years to develop.

Prairie grasses and wildflowers ►

Figure 10 The world's best soils for farming often are found in river valleys or interior and coastal plains. Areas too dry, too mountainous, or not fertile enough for farming may be used for grazing cattle, sheep, or other livestock.

Fertile soil is valuable because there is a limited supply. Less than one eighth of the land on Earth has soils that are well suited for farming. Figure 10 shows where these regions are located. In many areas, farming is difficult and little food is produced. The reasons for this include low soil fertility, lack of water, steep slopes, or a short growing season.

☑ *Checkpoint* *Why is soil valuable?*

Soil Damage and Loss

Soil is one of Earth's most important resources. But soil can be lost or damaged. For example, soil can become exhausted, or lose its fertility. This occurred in large parts of the South in the late 1800s. Soils in which only cotton had been grown were exhausted. Many farmers abandoned their farms. Early in the 1900s in Alabama, a scientist named George Washington Carver developed new crops and farming methods that helped to restore soil fertility in the South. Peanuts were one crop that helped make the soil fertile again.

Soil can be lost to erosion by water and wind. Water erosion can occur wherever soil is not protected by plant cover. Plants break the force of falling rain, and plant roots hold the soil together. Wind erosion is another cause of soil loss. Wind erosion, combined with farming methods that were not suited to dry conditions, caused the Dust Bowl on the Great Plains.

Figure 11 George Washington Carver (1864–1943) taught new methods of soil conservation to farmers in the South.

The Dust Bowl

Toward the end of the 1800s, farmers had settled most of the prairies. New settlers moved on to the Great Plains farther west. This region sweeps eastward from the base of the Rocky Mountains across the western parts of North and South Dakota, Nebraska, Kansas, Oklahoma, and Texas.

The soil of the Great Plains is fertile. But there is an important difference between the Great Plains and the prairie. Rainfall decreases steadily from east to west across the Great Plains. The tall grass gives way to shorter, thinner grass needing less moisture. **Plowing removed the grass from the Great Plains and exposed the soil. In times of drought, the topsoil quickly dried out, turned to dust, and blew away.**

By 1930, almost all of the Great Plains had been turned into farms or ranches. Then, several very dry years in a row turned the soil on parts of the Great Plains to dust. The wind blew the soil east in great, black clouds. The clouds turned the sky dark as far away as Chicago and even New York City. Eventually the soil blew out over the Atlantic Ocean, where it was lost forever.

The problem was most serious in the southern Plains states. There, the drought and topsoil loss lasted until 1938. This area, shown in Figure 12, was called the **Dust Bowl.** Many people in the Dust Bowl states abandoned their farms and moved away.

Language Arts CONNECTION

Woody Guthrie wrote and sang folk songs. Guthrie lived in Oklahoma and Texas at the time of the Dust Bowl and wrote a series of songs called "Dust Bowl Ballads." (A ballad is a song that tells a story.) One of the ballads describes how

We saw outside our window
Where wheat fields they had grown
Was now a rippling ocean
Of dust the wind had blown.

In Your Journal

Write the words for a ballad that tells the story of a problem in your community and how you think the problem should be solved.

Figure 12 The Dust Bowl included western Oklahoma and parts of the surrounding states. Wind blew dry particles of soil into great clouds of dust that traveled thousands of kilometers.

Figure 13 Contour plowing (above) and conservation plowing (below) help prevent soil erosion. *Predicting How might conservation plowing affect the amount of humus in the soil?*

Soil Conservation

The Dust Bowl helped people appreciate the value of soil. In the 1930s, with government support, farmers in the Great Plains and throughout the country began to take better care of their land. They adopted methods of farming that helped save the soil. Some of the methods were new. Others had been practiced for hundreds of years.

Farmers in the United States adopted modern methods of soil conservation. **Soil conservation** is the management of soil to prevent its destruction. **Two ways that soil can be conserved include contour plowing and conservation plowing.**

Contour plowing is the practice of plowing fields along the curves of a slope. This helps slow the runoff of excess rainfall and prevents it from washing the soil away.

Conservation plowing disturbs the soil and its plant cover as little as possible. Dead weeds and stalks of the previous year's crop are left in the ground to help return soil nutrients, retain moisture, and hold soil in place. This method is also called low-till or no-till plowing.

In grasslands such as the Great Plains, grazing livestock is an important use of the land. But if too many cattle graze on the grass during dry periods, the grass cover protecting the soil may be damaged. This exposes the soil to both wind and water erosion. To prevent damage to the soil, ranchers must limit the size of their herds.

Section 3 Review

1. Explain the importance of soil as one of Earth's resources.
2. How did settlers on the Great Plains help create the Dust Bowl?
3. What are some techniques that farmers use to conserve soil?
4. **Thinking Critically Problem Solving** If you had to plant corn on a steep hillside, how would you do it so that rain would not wash the soil away?

Check Your Progress

CHAPTER PROJECT 18

Check your bean seeds daily and water them as needed. Count and record the number of seeds that sprout. You can also measure the height of each plant, count the number of leaves, and note the leaf color. After about 14 days, you should be able to make comparisons. What differences did you observe in the bean plants grown in the different materials? When did these differences appear? Based on your data, what conclusions can you draw about which material is best for growing bean plants?

CHAPTER 18 STUDY GUIDE

Rocks and Weathering

Key Ideas

- ◆ Rock weathers, or wears down, when it is exposed to air, water, weather, and living things at Earth's surface.
- ◆ Mechanical weathering breaks rock into smaller pieces. The agents of mechanical weathering include freezing and thawing, release of pressure, growth of plants, actions of animals, and abrasion.
- ◆ Chemical weathering changes the mineral content of rock. The agents of chemical weathering are water, oxygen, carbon dioxide, living organisms, and acid rain.
- ◆ Climate and rock type determine how fast weathering occurs.

Key Terms

weathering
erosion
mechanical weathering
abrasion
ice wedging
chemical weathering
permeable

Soil Formation and Composition

Key Ideas

- ◆ Soil is made of small particles of rock mixed with the decaying remains of organisms.
- ◆ Soil forms in layers called horizons as bedrock weathers and organic materials build up.
- ◆ The three soil horizons are the A horizon, the B horizon, and the C horizon. The A horizon is made up of topsoil, which is rich in humus. The B horizon consists of clay and other particles washed down from the A horizon, but little humus. The C horizon is made up of partly weathered rock without clay or humus.
- ◆ Plants and animals break up and mix the soil, and also add the organic materials that form humus.

Key Terms

soil
bedrock
humus
loam
soil horizon
topsoil
subsoil
litter
decomposers

Soil Conservation

INTEGRATING ENVIRONMENTAL SCIENCE

Key Ideas

- ◆ Soil is a valuable resource because life on land depends on it, yet it forms very slowly.
- ◆ Soil can be eroded away and its fertility can be decreased by improper farming practices.
- ◆ Soil can be conserved and its fertility can be maintained by using various methods of soil conservation.

Key Terms

sod
Dust Bowl
soil conservation
contour plowing
conservation plowing

Organizing Information

Concept Map Copy the concept map about soil horizons onto a piece of paper. Then complete it and add a title. (For more on concept maps, see the Skills Handbook.)

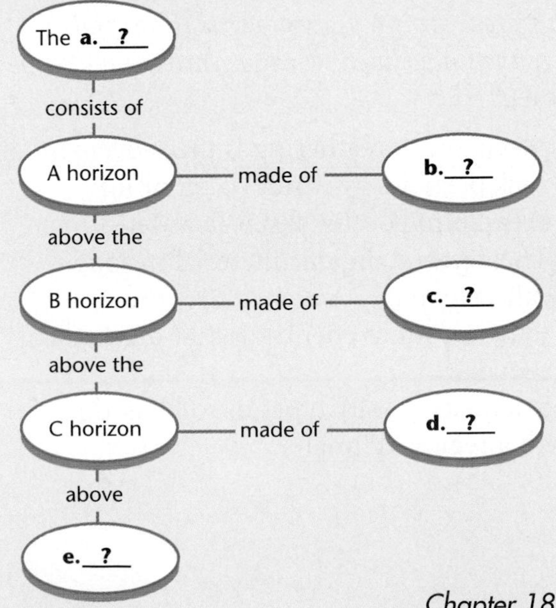

Reviewing Content

Multiple Choice

Choose the letter of the best answer.

1. The most important force of mechanical weathering in cool climates is
  a. oxidation.
  b. freezing and thawing.
  c. animal activity.
  d. abrasion.

2. Most chemical weathering is caused by
  a. acid rain.
  b. water.
  c. oxygen.
  d. carbon dioxide.

3. The B horizon consists of
  a. subsoil.
  b. topsoil.
  c. rock particles.
  d. bedrock.

4. One of the best types of soil for farming is
  a. forest soil.
  b. mountain soil.
  c. tropical soil.
  d. prairie soil.

5. Most of the work of mixing humus into the soil is done by
  a. fungi.
  b. bacteria.
  c. earthworms.
  d. mites.

True or False

If the statement is true, write true. If it is false, change the underlined word or words to make the statement true.

6. <u>Mechanical weathering</u> is the movement of rock particles by wind, water, or ice.

7. Weathering occurs faster in a <u>wet</u> climate.

8. The decayed organic material in soil is called <u>loam</u>.

9. <u>Fungi</u> produce chemicals that digest plant remains.

10. Scientists classify types of soil based partly on a region's <u>climate</u>.

Checking Concepts

11. Where is mechanical weathering likely to occur more quickly: where the winter temperature usually stays below freezing, or where it more often shifts back and forth around the freezing point? Explain.

12. Briefly describe how soil is formed.

13. Which contains more humus, topsoil or subsoil?

14. Explain how plants can act as agents of both mechanical and chemical weathering.

15. What role did grass play in conserving the soil of the prairies?

16. How does conservation plowing contribute to soil conservation?

17. Writing to Learn Write a description of your life as an earthworm. What would it be like to live in the soil? What would you see? What would you eat? How would you move through the soil? How would you change it?

Thinking Critically

18. Predicting Suppose mechanical weathering breaks a rock into pieces. How would this affect the rate at which the rock weathers chemically?

19. Classifying Classify the following examples as either mechanical weathering or chemical weathering:
  A. Cracks appear in a sidewalk next to a large tree.
  B. A piece of limestone develops holes like Swiss cheese.
  C. A rock exposed at the surface slowly turns reddish brown.

20. Developing Hypotheses On the moon there is no air or water. Develop a hypothesis about how fast rocks would weather on the moon compared with their rate of weathering on Earth. Explain.

21. Relating Cause and Effect Two rocks, each in a different location, have been weathering for the same amount of time. Mature soil has formed from one rock but only immature soil from the other. What factors might have caused this difference in rate of soil formation?

Applying Skills

Use the following information to answer Questions 22–24. You have two samples of soil. One is mostly sand and one is mostly clay.

22. **Developing Hypotheses** Which soil sample do you think would lose water more quickly? Why?
23. **Designing Experiments** Design an experiment to test how quickly water passes through each soil sample.
24. **Posing Questions** Suppose you are a farmer who wants to grow soybeans in one of these two soils. What questions would you need to answer before choosing where to plant your soybeans?

Performance  **Assessment**

Project Wrap Up You are ready to present your conclusions about what type of material is best for growing bean plants. Decide how to display the data you collected on the different materials. How did your group's results compare with those of the other groups in your class?

Reflect and Record In your journal, describe how well the results of your experiment matched your predictions. What have you learned from this project about soil characteristics that help plants to grow? What improvements could you make to your experiment?

Test Preparation

Use these questions to prepare for standardized tests.

Use the diagram of soil horizons to answer Questions 25–29.

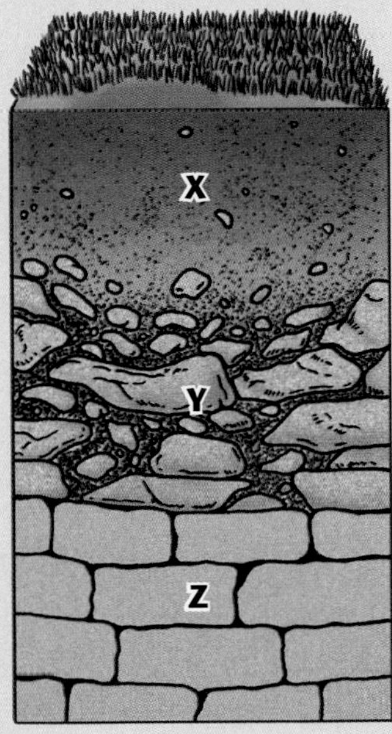

25. Layer X in the diagram consists of a mixture of humus, clay, and other minerals called
    a. litter. **b.** gravel.
    c. subsoil. **d.** topsoil.
26. Layer Y is made up of partly weathered rock called the
    a. C horizon.
    b. B horizon.
    c. A horizon.
    d. humus horizon.
27. One soil horizon, made up of clay and other particles but little humus, has not yet developed in this soil. The missing soil horizon is the
    a. A horizon.
    b. B horizon.
    c. C horizon.
    d. bedrock horizon.
28. The missing soil horizon will develop
    a. above layer X.
    b. below layer Z.
    c. between layers X and Y.
    d. between layers Y and Z.
29. In which layer or layers would you expect to find the most plant roots, insects, and other soil organisms?
    a. layers Y and Z **b.** layer Z
    c. layer Y **d.** layer X

CHAPTER 19

Erosion and Deposition

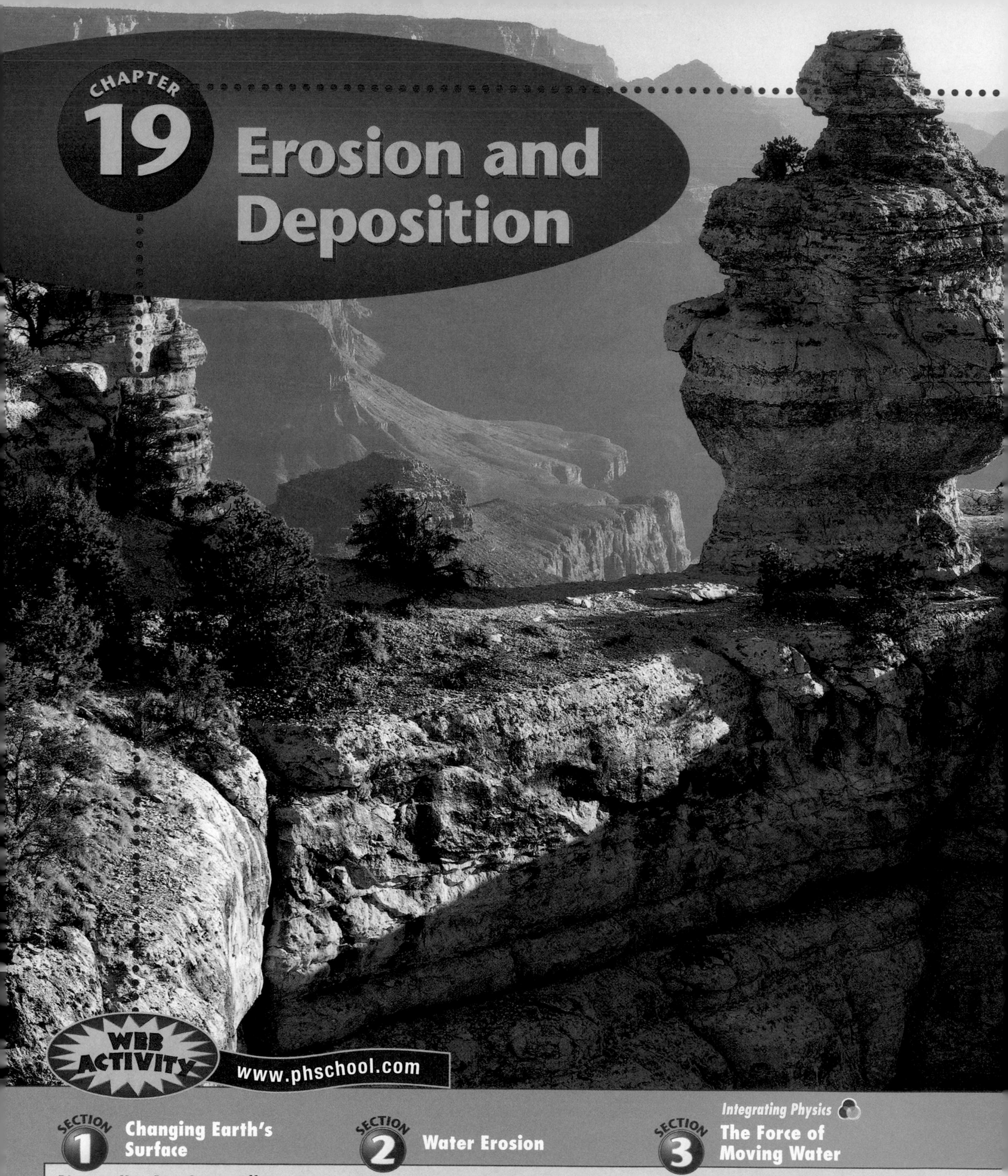

WEB ACTIVITY www.phschool.com

Section 1 Changing Earth's Surface

Discover How Does Gravity Affect Materials on a Slope?
Sharpen Your Skills Observing
Skills Lab Sand Hills

Section 2 Water Erosion

Discover How Does Moving Water Wear Away Rocks?
Try This Raindrops Falling
Real-World Lab Streams in Action

Integrating Physics 

Section 3 The Force of Moving Water

Discover How Are Sediments Deposited?
Sharpen Your Skills Developing Hypotheses

PROJECT 19

Changes In the Land

The walls of the Grand Canyon reveal the colorful rock layers that make up the Colorado Plateau. What force shaped such a vast canyon? For about 6 million years the Colorado River has been cutting and grinding through the plateau. The river also carries away the broken particles of rock.

In this chapter you will explore the forces that change Earth's surface. Flowing water, frozen glaciers, waves, and wind all wear down and build up landforms. Throughout the chapter, you will build models showing how erosion shapes a landscape.

Your Goal To make three-dimensional models that show how the forces of erosion and deposition can change a landscape over millions of years.

To complete this project, you must

- make a three-dimensional model of a landscape
- predict how the model would be affected by erosion
- construct a second model showing how your landscape might look after erosion has continued for millions of years

Get Started Begin now by sketching a mountainous or hilly landscape. Include sharp peaks, deep valleys, a river or stream, and a coastline.

Check Your Progress You will be working on this project as you study this chapter. To keep your project on track, look for Check Your Progress boxes at the following points.

Section 3 Review, page 632: Draw and make your first model.

Section 4 Review, page 637: Begin to make your second model, showing how water and glaciers cause erosion.

Section 5 Review, page 641: Add the effects of wave erosion to the model.

Wrap Up At the end of the chapter (page 647), you will present your models to the class. In your presentation, you will explain how the landscape changed and predict how it might change in the future.

The view from the South Rim of the Grand Canyon in Arizona is one of Earth's most memorable sights.

Glaciers

Discover **How Do Glaciers Change the Land?**

Waves

Discover **What Can Be Learned From Beach Sand?**

Sharpen Your Skills **Calculating**

Wind

Discover **How Does Moving Air Affect Sediment?**

Section 1 Changing Earth's Surface

Discover Activity

How Does Gravity Affect Materials on a Slope?

1. Place a small board flat on your desk. Place a marble on the board and slowly tip the board up slightly at one end. Observe what happens.
2. Place a block of wood on the board. Slowly lift one end of the board and observe the result.
3. Next, cover the board and the wood block with sandpaper and repeat Step 2.

Think It Over

Developing Hypotheses How do the results of each step compare? Develop a hypothesis to explain the differences in your observations.

Guide for Reading

- What processes wear down and build up Earth's surface?
- What force pulls rock and soil down slopes?
- What are the different types of mass movement?

Reading Tip As you read, make a list of main ideas and supporting details about erosion, deposition, and mass movement.

Madison River Canyon is a quiet wilderness area in the Rocky Mountains of Montana. In 1959, something happened to change the canyon forever. When a strong earthquake jolted nearby Yellowstone National Park, a mountainside along the canyon gave way. In a few seconds, nearly 30 million cubic meters of rock, soil, and trees slid into the canyon. If this much material were in the shape of a cube, then each side of the cube would be three times longer than a football field. Rock and soil from the landslide dammed the Madison River, forming a new lake.

Figure 1 During a landslide, loose rock and soil on the side of a mountain suddenly slide away from underlying bedrock. This landslide in Madison River Canyon, Montana, buried a highway and campground.

Wearing Down and Building Up

A landslide like the one in Madison River Canyon is a spectacular example of erosion. **Erosion** is the process by which natural forces move weathered rock and soil from one place to another. A landslide is a very rapid type of erosion. Other types of erosion move soil and rock more slowly. Gravity, running water, glaciers, waves, and wind can all cause erosion. You may have seen water carrying soil and gravel down a driveway after it rains. That's an example of erosion. Erosion also caused the damage to the road in Figure 2.

Figure 2 Heavy winter rains washed out this California highway. ***Relating Cause and Effect*** *What caused the erosion that you can see in the photograph?*

The material moved by erosion is **sediment.** Both weathering and erosion produce sediment. **Deposition** occurs where the agents of erosion lay down sediment. Deposition changes the shape of the land. You may have watched a playing child who picked up several toys and then carried them across a room and put them down. This child was acting something like an agent of erosion and deposition.

Weathering, erosion, and deposition act together in a cycle that wears down and builds up Earth's surface. Erosion and deposition are at work everywhere on Earth. Sometimes they work slowly. At other times, they work more quickly, such as during a thunderstorm. Then, heavy rain soaks into rock and soil. These water-soaked materials may then come loose suddenly and slide down a mountain. But as a mountain wears down in one place, new landforms build up in other places. Erosion and deposition are never-ending.

☑ ***Checkpoint*** *What happens to sediment as a result of erosion and deposition?*

Mass Movement

Imagine that you are sitting on a bicycle at the top of a hill. With only a slight push, you can coast down the hill. If the slope of the hill is very steep, you will reach a high speed before reaching the bottom. The force that pulls you and your bicycle downward is gravity. Gravity pulls everything toward the center of Earth.

Gravity is the force that moves rock and other materials downhill. Gravity causes **mass movement,** any one of several processes that move sediment downhill. Mass movement can be rapid or slow. **The different types of mass movement include landslides, mudslides, slump, and creep.**

Figure 3 A mudflow caused by heavy rains raced through the streets of this town in Italy. *Relating Cause and Effect* *What characteristic of soil can contribute to a mudflow?*

Landslides The most destructive kind of mass movement is a landslide, which occurs when rock and soil slide quickly down a steep slope. Some landslides may contain huge masses of rock. But many landslides contain only a small amount of rock and soil. Such mass movement is common where road builders have cut highways through hills or mountains.

Mudflows A mudflow is the rapid downhill movement of a mixture of water, rock, and soil. The amount of water in a mudflow can be as high as 60 percent. Mudflows often occur after heavy rains in a normally dry area. In clay soils with a high water content, mudflows may occur even on very gentle slopes. Under certain conditions, clay soils suddenly turn to liquid and begin to flow. For example, an earthquake can trigger both mudflows and landslides. Mudflows like the one in Figure 3 can be very dangerous.

Slump If you slump your shoulders, the entire upper part of your body drops down. In the type of mass movement known as slump, a mass of rock and soil suddenly slips down a slope. Unlike a landslide, the material in slump moves down in one large mass. It looks as if someone pulled the bottom out from under part of the slope. Figure 4 shows an example of slump. Slump often occurs when water soaks the base of a mass of soil that is rich in clay.

Figure 4 Slump can look as if a giant spoon has started to scoop a mass of soil out from a hillside.

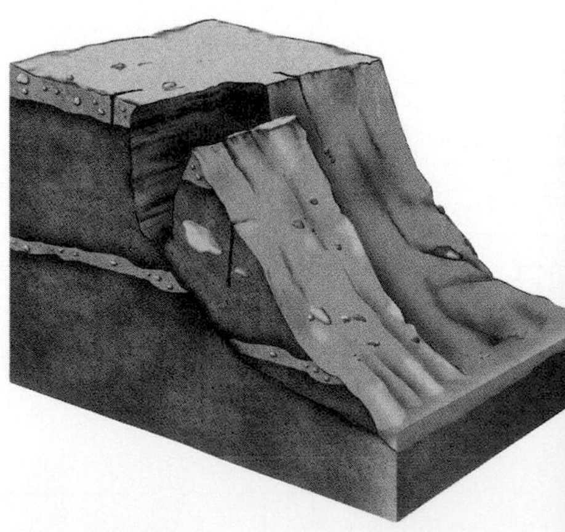

Creep Landscapes affected by creep may have the eerie, out-of-kilter look of a funhouse in an amusement park. Creep is the very slow downhill movement of rock and soil. It can even occur on gentle slopes. Like the movement of an hour hand on a clock, creep is so slow you can barely notice it. But you can see the effects of creep in objects such as telephone poles, gravestones, and fenceposts. Creep may tilt these objects at spooky angles. Creep often results from the freezing and thawing of water in cracked layers of rock beneath the soil. How have the trees in Figure 5 been affected by creep?

Observing ACTIVITY

Compare the examples of mass movement in Figures 4 and 5. Based on your observations, construct a table comparing slump and creep. Include the Earth materials involved, the type of slope, and the speed for each type of mass movement.

Figure 5 Creep has slowly tilted these trees downhill, causing their trunks to grow in a curve. ***Predicting*** *If creep continues, how might it affect the road, the fence, and the electric power lines?*

Section 1 Review

1. Explain the difference between erosion and deposition.
2. What force causes erosion?
3. What are four types of mass movement?
4. **Thinking Critically Relating Cause and Effect** Why would a landslide be more likely on a steep mountain than on a gently sloping hill?

Science at Home

After a rainstorm, take a walk with an adult family member around your neighborhood. Look for evidence of erosion. Try to find areas where there is loose soil, sand, gravel, or rock. (**CAUTION:** *Stay away from any large pile of loose sand or soil—it may slide without warning.*) Which areas have the most erosion? The least erosion? How does the slope of the ground affect the amount of erosion? Sketch or take photographs of the areas showing evidence of erosion.

Developing Hypotheses

Sand Hills

In this lab, you will develop and test a hypothesis about how mass movement affects the size and shape of a sand hill.

Problem

What is the relationship between the height and width of a sand hill?

Materials

Dry sand, 500 mL
Cardboard tube
Tray (about 15 cm × 45 cm × 60 cm)
Wooden barbecue skewer
Masking tape
Spoon
Ruler
Pencil or crayon
Several sheets of white paper

Procedure

1. Begin by observing how gravity causes mass movement in sand. To start, place the cardboard tube vertically in the center of the tray.
2. Using the spoon, fill the cardboard tube with the dry sand. Take care not to spill the sand around the outside of the tube.
3. Carefully lift the sand-filled tube straight up so that all the sand flows out. As you lift the tube, observe the sand's movement.
4. Develop a hypothesis explaining how you think the width of the sand pile is related to its height for different amounts of sand.
5. Empty the sand in the tray back into a container. Then set up your system for measuring the sand hill.
6. Copy the data table into your lab notebook.
7. Following Steps 1 through 3, make a new sand hill.

How to Measure a Sand Hill

1. Cover the bottom of the tray with unlined white paper and tape it firmly in place.
2. Mark off points 0.5 cm apart along one side of the paper in the tray.
3. Carefully draw the sand hill's outline on the paper. The line should go completely around the base of the hill.
4. Now measure the width of the hill against the marks you made along the edge of the paper.
5. Measure the sand hill's height by inserting a barbecue skewer through its center. Make a mark on the skewer at the top of the hill.
6. Remove the skewer and use the ruler to measure how much of the skewer was buried in the hill. Try not to disturb the sand.

DATA TABLE					
Test	1	2	3	4	5
Width					
Height					

8. Measure and record the sand hill's height and width for Test 1. (See the instructions on the bottom of the previous page to help you accurately measure the height and width.)
9. Now test what happens when you add more sand to the sand hill. Place your cardboard tube vertically at the center of the sand hill. Be careful not to push the tube down into the sand hill! Using the spoon, fill the tube with sand as before.
10. Carefully raise the tube and observe the results of the sand's movement.
11. Measure and record the sand hill's height and width for Test 2.
12. Repeat Steps 9 through 11 at least three more times. After each test, record your results. Be sure to number each test.

Analyze and Conclude

1. Make a graph showing how the sand hill's height and width changed with each test. (*Hint:* Use the *x*-axis of the graph for height. Use the *y*-axis of the graph for width.)
2. What does your graph show about the relationship between the sand hill's height and width?
3. Does your graph support your hypothesis about the sand hill's height and width? Why or why not?
4. How would you revise your original hypothesis after examining your data? Give reasons for your answer.
5. **Think About It** Predict what would happen if you continued the experiment for five more tests. Extend your graph with a dashed line to show your prediction. How could you test your prediction?

Design an Experiment

Do you think the use of different materials, such as wet sand or gravel, would produce different results from dry sand? Make a new hypothesis about the relationship between slope and width in hills made of materials other than dry sand. Design an experiment in which you test how these different materials form hills. Obtain your teacher's approval before you try the experiment.

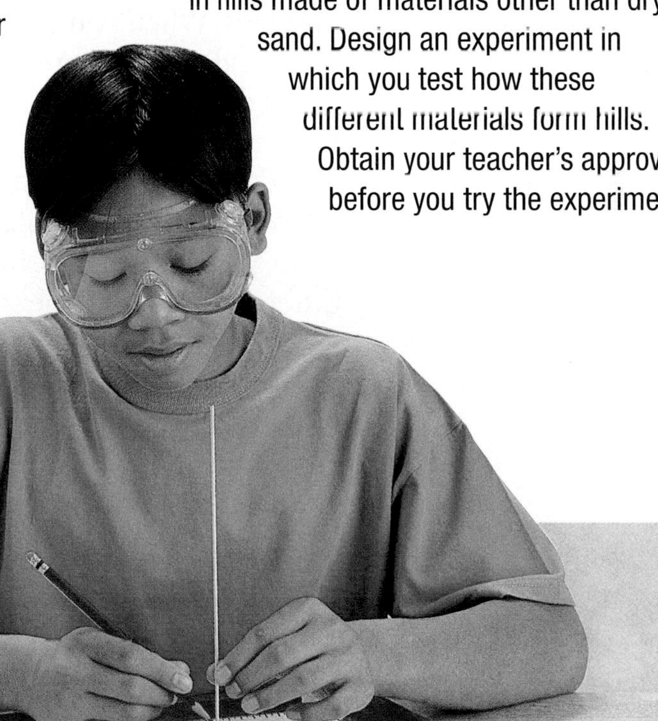

Section 2

Water Erosion

Discover — Activity

How Does Moving Water Wear Away Rocks?

1. Obtain two bars of soap that are the same size and brand.
2. Open a faucet just enough to let the water drip out very slowly. How many drops of water does the faucet release per minute?
3. Place one bar of soap in a dry place. Place the other bar of soap under the faucet. Predict the effect of the dripping water droplets on the soap.

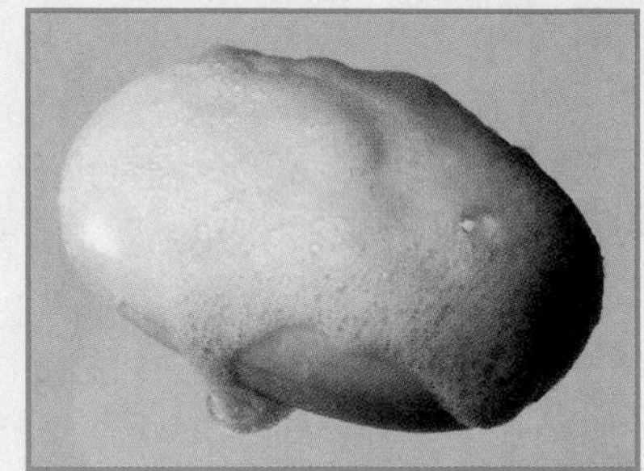

4. Let the faucet drip for 10 minutes.
5. Turn off the faucet and observe both bars of soap. What difference do you observe between them?

Think It Over

Predicting What would the bar of soap under the dripping faucet look like if you left it there for another 10 minutes? For an hour? How could you speed up the process? Slow it down?

Guide for Reading

- **What process is mainly responsible for shaping Earth's land surface?**
- **What features are formed by water erosion?**
- **What features are formed when rivers and streams deposit sediment?**

Reading Tip **Before you read, use the headings to make an outline on water erosion and deposition.**

Walking in the woods in summer, you can hear the racing water of a stream before you see the stream itself. The water roars as it foams over rock ledges and boulders. When you reach the stream, you see water rushing by. Sand and pebbles tumble along the bottom of the stream. As it swirls downstream, it also carries twigs, leaves, and bits of soil. In sheltered pools, insects such as water striders silently skim the water's calm surface. Beneath the surface, you see a rainbow trout hovering in the clear water.

If you visit the stream at other times of year, it will be very different. In winter, the stream freezes. Chunks of ice scrape and grind away at the stream's bed and banks. In spring, the stream floods. Then the flow of water may be strong enough to move large rocks. But throughout the year, the stream continues to erode its small part of Earth's surface.

A woodland stream ▼

Figure 6 A falling raindrop starts the process of erosion. Water flowing across the surface runs together in small rills. Rills combine to form larger gullies. *Predicting What will happen to the land between the gully and the side gully as the two gullies grow wider?*

Runoff and Erosion

Running water creates many landforms. **Moving water is the major agent of the erosion that has shaped Earth's land surface.**

Erosion by water begins with the splash of rain, as you can see in Figure 6. Some rainfall sinks into the ground. Some evaporates or is taken up by plants. The force of a falling raindrop can loosen and pick up soil particles. As water moves over the land, it carries these particles with it. This moving water is called runoff. **Runoff** is all the remaining water that moves over Earth's surface. When runoff flows in a thin layer over the land, it may cause a type of erosion called sheet erosion.

Rills and Gullies Because of gravity, runoff and the material it contains move downhill. As runoff travels, it forms tiny grooves in the soil called **rills.** As the rills flow into one another, they grow larger, forming gullies. A **gully** is a large groove, or channel, in the soil that carries runoff after a rainstorm. As water flows through gullies, it moves soil and rocks with it, thus enlarging the gullies through erosion. Gullies flow only after it rains.

Figure 7 As water erodes gullies, soil can be lost.

Streams and Rivers Gullies join together to form a larger channel called a stream. A **stream** is a channel along which water is continually flowing down a slope. Unlike gullies, streams rarely dry up. Small streams are also called creeks or brooks. As streams flow together, they form larger and larger bodies of flowing water. A large stream is often called a **river.**

Amount of Runoff The amount of runoff in an area depends on five main factors. The first factor is the amount of rain an area receives. A second factor is vegetation. Grasses, shrubs, and trees reduce runoff by absorbing water and holding soil in place. A third factor is the type of soil. Some types of soils absorb more water than others. A fourth factor is the shape of the land. Land that is steeply sloped has more runoff than flatter land. Finally, a fifth factor is how people use the land. For instance, a paved parking lot absorbs no water, so all the rain that falls on it becomes runoff. Runoff also increases when a farmer cuts down crops, since this removes vegetation from the land.

Generally, more runoff means more erosion. In contrast, things that reduce runoff, such as plant leaves and roots, will reduce erosion. Even though deserts have little rainfall, they often have high runoff and erosion. This is because deserts usually have few plants. In wet areas, runoff and erosion may be low because there are more plants to protect the soil.

☑ *Checkpoint* *What factors affect the amount of runoff in a region?*

River Systems

A stream grows into a larger stream or river by receiving water from tributaries. A **tributary** is a stream that flows into a larger stream. A small creek that flows into a large river is a tributary to that river. So too is a large river that adds its water to another large river. For instance, the Missouri River becomes a tributary of the Mississippi River near the city of St. Louis, even though both rivers are about the same size there.

Raindrops Falling

ACTIVITY

Find out how the force of falling raindrops affects soil.

1. Fill a petri dish with fine-textured soil to a depth of about 1 cm. Make sure the soil has a smooth flat surface, but do not pack it firmly in the dish.
2. Place the dish in the center of a newspaper.
3. Fill a dropper with water. Squeeze a large water drop from a height of 1 m onto the surface of the soil. Repeat 4 times.
4. Use a meter stick to measure the distance the soil splashed from the dish. Record your observations.
5. Repeat Steps 1 through 4, this time from a height of 2 m. Which traveled further, the splash from 1 m or the splash from 2 m?

Drawing Conclusions Which test produced the greater amount of erosion? Why?

Look at Figure 8. Notice all the tributaries to the Ohio River. Together, all these streams—from tiny rills to great rivers—form a system that drains a large part of eastern North America. A **drainage basin** is the land area from which a river and its tributaries collect their water.

If you were to follow a river upstream all the way to its source, you would finally reach a divide. A **divide** is the high ground between two drainage basins. The most famous divide within the United States is the Continental Divide, which follows the high ground of the Rocky Mountains. The Continental Divide separates streams that flow into the Gulf of Mexico from streams that flow into the Great Basin or the Pacific Ocean.

Figure 8 The drainage basin of the Ohio River drains much of eastern North America.
Interpreting Maps *What are the tributaries of the Ohio River? Could a tributary come from outside the drainage basin?*

Erosion by Rivers

Scientists classify rivers by identifying certain features that form as a result of erosion. **Through erosion, a river creates valleys, waterfalls, flood plains, meanders, and oxbow lakes.**

Rivers often form on steep mountain slopes. Near its source, a river is often fast-flowing and generally follows a straight, narrow course. The steep slopes along the river erode rapidly. The result is a deep, V-shaped valley.

Waterfalls may occur where a river meets an area of rock that is very hard and erodes slowly. The river flows over this rock and then flows over softer rock downstream. The softer rock wears away faster than the harder rock. Eventually a waterfall develops where the softer rock was removed. This process formed Niagara Falls, shown in Figure 9. Areas of rough water called rapids also occur where a river tumbles over hard rock.

Figure 9 Niagara Falls formed on the Niagara River, which connects Lake Erie and Lake Ontario. A flat layer of tough rock lies over a layer of softer rock that erodes easily. When the softer rock erodes, pieces of the harder rock above break off, creating the waterfall's sharp drop.

Figure 10 The oxbow lake (above) was formerly a part of the channel of the Kasanak River in Alaska. These meanders (right) were formed by a river in Australia.

Lower down on its course, a river usually flows over more gently sloping land. The river spreads out and erodes the land, forming a wide river valley. The flat, wide area of land along a river is a **flood plain.** A river often covers its flood plain when it overflows its banks during floods. On a wide flood plain, the valley walls may be kilometers away from the river itself.

A river often develops meanders where it flows through easily eroded rock or sediment. A **meander** is a looplike bend in the course of a river. As the river widens from side to side, it tends to erode the outer bank and deposit sediment on the inner bank of a bend. Over time, the bend—or meander—becomes more and more curved.

When the gently sloping part of a river flows through an area of sediment or soft rock, it can erode a very wide flood plain. Along this part of a river's course, its channel is deep and wide. Meanders are common along this part of a river. The southern stretch of the Mississippi River is one example of a river that meanders on a wide, gently sloping flood plain.

Sometimes a meandering river forms a feature called an oxbow lake. An **oxbow lake** is a meander that has been cut off from the river. An oxbow lake may form when a river floods. During the flood, high water finds a straighter route downstream. As the flood waters fall, sediments dam up the ends of a meander. The meander has become an oxbow lake.

☑ *Checkpoint* *How does an oxbow lake form?*

Deposits by Rivers

Figure 11 This alluvial fan in Death Valley, California, was formed from deposits by streams from the mountains.

As water moves, it carries sediments with it. Any time moving water slows down, it drops, or deposits, some of the sediment. As the water slows down, fine particles fall to the river's bed. Larger stones quit rolling and sliding. **Deposition creates landforms such as alluvial fans and deltas. It can also add soil to a river's flood plain.** In *Exploring the Course of a River* on pages 622–623, you can see these and other features shaped by rivers and streams.

Alluvial Fans Where a stream flows out of a steep, narrow mountain valley, the stream suddenly becomes wider and shallower. The water slows down. Here sediments are deposited in an alluvial fan. An **alluvial fan** is a wide, sloping deposit of sediment formed where a stream leaves a mountain range. As its name suggests, this deposit is shaped like a fan.

Deltas A river ends its journey when it flows into a still body of water, such as an ocean or a lake. Because the river water is no longer flowing downhill, the water slows down. At this point, the sediment in the water drops to the bottom. Sediment deposited where a river flows into an ocean or lake builds up a landform called a **delta.** Deltas can be a variety of shapes: some are arc-shaped, others are triangle-shaped. The delta of the Mississippi River is an example of a type of delta called a "bird's foot" delta.

Soil on Flood Plains Deposition also occurs during floods. INTEGRATING LIFE SCIENCE Then heavy rains or melting snow cause a river to rise above its banks and spread out over its flood plain. When the flood water finally retreats, it deposits sediment as new soil. Deposition of new soil over a flood plain is what makes a river valley fertile. Dense forests can grow in the rich soil of a flood plain. The soil is also perfect for growing crops.

Figure 12 This satellite image shows part of the Mississippi River delta, which is always growing and changing. ***Observing*** *What happens to the Mississippi River as it flows through its delta? Can you find the river's main channel?*

EXPLORING the Course of a River

The slope and size of a river, as well as the land through which it flows, determine how a river shapes the land.

Waterfalls and rapids Waterfalls and rapids are common where the river passes over harder rock.
V-shaped valley Near its source, a river often flows through a deep, V-shaped valley. As the river flows, it cuts a deeper valley.
Meanders Where a river flows across easily eroded sediment, its channel bends from side to side in a series of meanders.
Oxbow lake
Flood plain A flood plain forms when a river's power of erosion widens its valley rather than deepening it.
Beaches Sand carried downstream by rivers spreads along the coast to form beaches.

Groundwater Erosion and Deposition

When rain falls and snow melts, not all of the water evaporates or becomes runoff. Some water soaks into the ground. There it fills the openings in the soil and trickles into cracks and spaces in layers of rock. **Groundwater** is the term geologists use for this underground water. Like running water on the surface, groundwater affects the shape of the land.

INTEGRATING CHEMISTRY Groundwater can cause erosion through a process of chemical weathering. When water sinks into the ground, it combines with carbon dioxide to form a weak acid, called carbonic acid. Carbonic acid can break down limestone. Groundwater containing carbonic acid flows into cracks in the limestone. Then some of the limestone changes chemically and is carried away in a solution of water. This gradually hollows out pockets in the rock. Over time, these pockets develop into large holes underground, called caves or caverns.

The action of carbonic acid on limestone can also result in deposition. Inside limestone caves, deposits called stalactites and stalagmites often form. Water containing carbonic acid and calcium from limestone drips from a cave's roof. As the water

Figure 13 Over millions of years, chemical weathering of limestone and groundwater erosion created the beautiful shapes in Carlsbad Caverns in New Mexico. ***Interpreting Photos*** *What evidence of deposition do you see in the photo of Carlsbad Caverns?*

Figure 14 A sinkhole, such as this one in Florida, is a characteristic feature of karst topography. Sinkholes can pose a hazard for people who live in a karst region.

evaporates, a deposit of calcite forms. A deposit that hangs like an icicle from the roof of a cave is called a **stalactite** (stuh LAK tyt). Slow dripping builds up a cone-shaped **stalagmite** (stuh LAG myt) from the cave floor.

In rainy regions where there is a layer of limestone near the surface, groundwater erosion can significantly change the shape of the land. Streams are rare, because water sinks easily down into the weathered limestone. Deep valleys and caverns are common. If the roof of a cave collapses because of the erosion of the underlying limestone, the result is a depression called a sinkhole. This type of landscape is called **karst topography** after a region in Eastern Europe. In the United States, there are regions of karst topography in Florida, Kentucky, and Indiana.

Section 2 Review

1. What is the major cause of erosion on Earth's surface?
2. Briefly describe five features formed by rivers and streams as they erode the land.
3. What are the results of deposition along the course of a stream or river?
4. How can groundwater contribute to erosion?
5. **Thinking Critically Comparing and Contrasting** How is an alluvial fan similar to a delta? How is it different?

Science at Home

In a small dish, build a cube out of 27 small sugar cubes. Your cube should be three sugar cubes on a side. Fold a square piece of paper towel to fit the top of the cube. Wet the paper towel, place it on the cube, and let it stand for 15 or 20 minutes. Every few minutes, sprinkle a few drops of water on the paper towel to keep it wet. Then remove the paper towel. What happened to your cube? How is the effect of water on a sugar cube similar to groundwater eroding limestone? How is it different?

Real-World Lab

You and Your Environment

Streams in Action

Erosion can form gullies, wash away topsoil, and pollute rivers with sediment. You can observe the effects of erosion using a stream table.

Problem

How do rivers and streams erode the land?

Skills Focus

making models, observing, predicting

Materials   

plastic tub at least 27 cm × 40 cm × 10 cm
diatomaceous earth
plastic measuring cup
spray bottle
hand lens
watch or clock
water
1 metal spoon
plastic foam cup
blue food coloring
liquid detergent
scissors
2 wood blocks about 2.5 cm thick
bucket to hold 2–3 L of water or a source of tap water
plastic stirrers, 10–12 cm long, with two small holes each
wire 13–15 cm long, 20 gauge

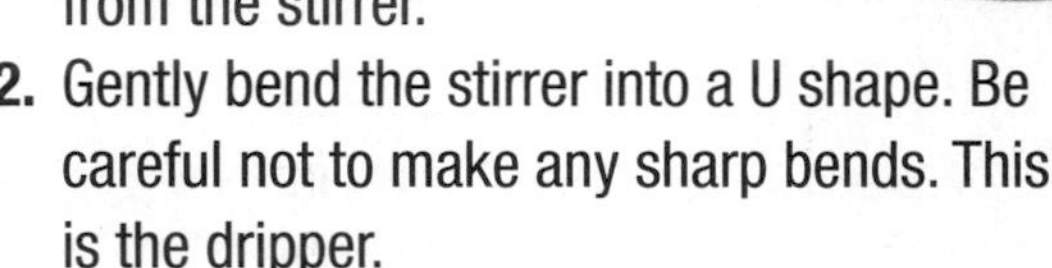

Making the Dripper

1. Insert the wire into one of the two holes in a plastic stirrer. The ends of the wire should protrude from the stirrer.
2. Gently bend the stirrer into a U shape. Be careful not to make any sharp bends. This is the dripper.
3. With scissors, carefully cut two small notches on opposite sides of the top of the foam cup.
4. Fill the cup to just below the notches with water colored with two drops of blue food coloring. Add more food coloring later as you add more water to the cup.
5. Add one drop of detergent to keep air bubbles out of the dripper and increase flow.
6. To start the dripper, fill it with water. Then quickly tip it and place it in one of the notches in the cup, as shown above.
7. Adjust the flow rate of the dripper to about 2 drips per 1 second. (*Hint:* Bend the dripper into more of a U shape to increase flow. Lessen the curve to reduce flow.)

Procedure

Part A Creating Streams Over Time

1. Your teacher will give you a plastic tub containing diatomaceous earth that has been soaked with water. Place the tub on a level surface. **CAUTION:** *Dry diatomaceous earth produces dust that may be irritating if inhaled. To keep the diatomaceous earth from drying out, spray it lightly with water.*
2. One end of the tub will contain more diatomaceous earth. Use the block of wood to raise this end of the tub 2.5 cm.
3. Place the cup at the upper end of the slope with the notches pointing to the left and right.
4. Press the cup firmly down into the earth to secure its position.
5. Start the dripper (see Step 6 in the box above). Allow the water to drip to the right onto the diatomaceous earth.

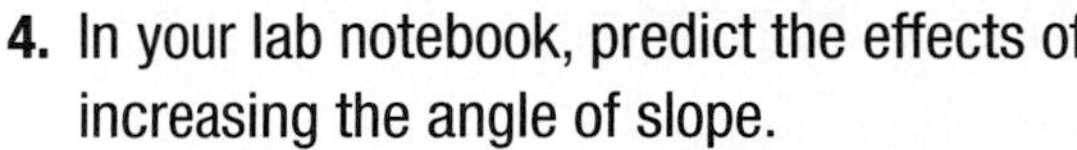

6. Allow the dripper to drip for 5 minutes. (*Hint:* When you need to add more water, be careful not to disturb the dripper.)
7. Observe the flow of water and the changes it makes. Use the hand lens to look closely at the stream bed.
8. After 5 minutes, remove the dripper.
9. In your lab notebook, draw a picture of the resulting stream and label it "5 minutes."
10. Now switch the dripper to the left side of the cup. Restart the dripper and allow it to drip for 10 minutes. Then remove the dripper.
11. Draw a picture and label it "10 minutes."

Part B Changing the Angle of Slope

1. Remove the cup from the stream table.
2. Save the stream bed on the right side of the tub. Using the bowl of the spoon, smooth out the diatomaceous earth on the left side.
3. To increase the angle of slope of your stream table, raise the end of the tub another 2.5 cm.
4. In your lab notebook, predict the effects of increasing the angle of slope.
5. Replace the cup and restart the dripper, placing it in the notch on the left side of the cup. Allow the dripper to drip for 5 minutes. Notice any changes in the new stream bed.
6. At the end of 5 minutes, remove the dripper.
7. Draw a picture of the new stream bed in your lab notebook. Label it "Increased Angle."
8. Follow your teacher's instructions for clean-up after this activity. Wash your hands when you have finished.

Analyze and Conclude

1. Compare the 5-minute stream with the 10-minute stream. How did the length of time that the water flowed affect erosion along the stream bed?
2. Were your predictions about the effects of increasing the angle of slope correct? Explain your answer.
3. What eventually happened to the eroded material that was carried downstream?
4. What other variables besides time and angle of slope might affect the way rivers and streams erode the land?
5. **Apply** Have you ever seen water flowing down a hillside or street after a heavy rain? If so, how much did the land slope in that area? Did you notice anything about the color of the water? Explain.

Design an Experiment

Design a stream table experiment to measure how the amount of sediment carried by a river changes as the volume of flow of the river increases. Obtain your teacher's approval before you try the experiment.

Protecting Homes in Flood Plains

At least ten million American households are located in flood plains. Living near a river is tempting. Riverside land is often flat and easy to build on. Because so many people now live in flood plains, the cost of flood damage has been growing. Communities along rivers want to limit the cost of flooding. They want to know how they can protect the people and buildings already in flood plains. They also want to know how to discourage more people from moving into flood plains.

The Issues

Should the Government Insure People Against Flood Damage? The United States government offers insurance to households in flood plains. The insurance pays part of the cost of repairs after a flood. Insurance helps people, but it is very expensive. Only 17 percent of people who live in flood plains buy the government insurance. Government flood insurance is available only in places that take steps to reduce flood damage. Cities must allow new building only on high ground. The insurance will not pay to rebuild homes that are badly damaged by floodwater. Instead, these people must use the money to find a home somewhere else.

Critics say that insurance just encourages people to move back into areas that flood. Supporters say it rewards towns and cities that make rules to control building on flood plains.

How Much of the Flood Plain Should Be Protected? Government flood insurance is available only in areas where scientists expect flooding about once in 100 years, or once in 500 years. Such figures are just estimates. Three floods occurred in only 12 years in a government flood-insurance area near Sacramento, California.

Should the Government Tell People Where They Can Live? Some programs of flood control forbid all new building. Other programs may also encourage people to move to safer areas. The 1997 flood on the Red River in Grand Forks, North Dakota, is one example. After the flood, the city of Grand Forks offered to buy all the damaged buildings near the river. The city wants to build high walls of earth to protect the rest of the town.

The Grand Forks plan might prevent future damage, but is it fair? Supporters say that since the government has to pay for flood damage, it has the right to make people leave flood plains. Critics of such plans say that people should be free to live where they want, even in risky areas.

Who should decide in which neighborhood no new houses can be built? Who decides which people should be asked to move away from a flood plain? Experts disagree over whether local, state, or United States government officials should decide which areas to include. Some believe scientists should make the decision.

You Decide

1. Identify the Problem
In your own words, describe the controversy surrounding flood plains and housing.

2. Analyze the Options
List several steps that could be taken to reduce the damage done to buildings in flood plains. For each step, include who would benefit from the step, and who would pay the costs.

3. Find a Solution
Your town has to decide what to do about a neighborhood damaged by the worst flood in 50 years. Write a speech that argues for your solution.

SECTION 3 The Force of Moving Water

DISCOVER ACTIVITY

How Are Sediments Deposited?

1. Put on your goggles.
2. Obtain a clear plastic jar or bottle with a top. Fill the jar about two-thirds full with water.
3. Fill a plastic beaker with 200 mL of fine and coarse sand, soil, clay, and small pebbles.
4. Pour the mixture into the jar of water. Screw on the top tightly and shake for two minutes. Be sure to hold onto the jar firmly.
5. Set the jar down and observe it for 10 to 15 minutes.

Think It Over

Inferring In what order are the sediments in the jar deposited? What do you think causes this pattern?

GUIDE FOR READING

- **What enables water to do work?**
- **How does sediment enter rivers and streams?**
- **What factors affect a river's ability to erode and carry sediment?**

Reading Tip **Before you read, rewrite the headings of the section as *how, why,* or *what* questions. As you read, look for answers to these questions.**

The Merrimack River in New Hampshire and Massachusetts is only 180 kilometers long. But the Merrimack does a great deal of work as it runs from the mountains to the sea. The river's waters fall 82 meters through many rapids and waterfalls. During the 1800s, people harnessed this falling water to run machines. These machines could spin thread and weave cloth very quickly and cheaply. Thanks to water power, the towns along the river grew quickly into cities.

Work and Energy

The waters of the Merrimack River could drive machines because a river's water has energy. **Energy** is the ability to do work or cause change. There are two kinds of energy. **Potential energy** is energy that is stored and waiting to be used later. The Merrimack's waters begin with potential energy due to their position above sea level. **Kinetic energy** is the energy an object has due to its motion. **As gravity pulls water down a slope, the water's potential energy changes to kinetic energy that can do work.**

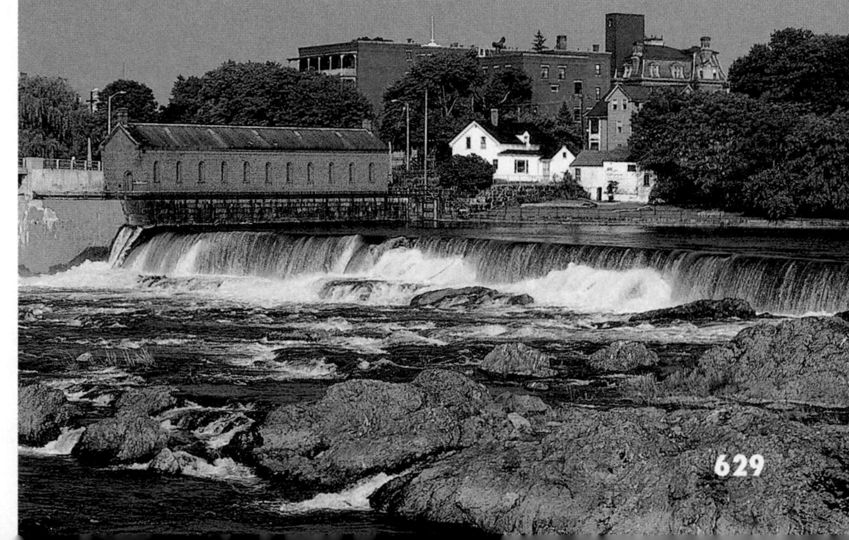

Figure 15 Dams like this one on the Merrimack River in Lowell, Massachusetts, help to harness the power of flowing water.

Social Studies CONNECTION

The cotton mills in Lowell, Massachusetts, were built in the 1820s. The mills employed young women from the farms and small towns of New England. At that time, it was unusual for women to work outside the home. The hours of work at a mill were long and pay was low. But mill work helped these women to earn and save their own money. Most later returned to their hometowns.

In Your Journal

Use library references to find out more about the daily life of the mill workers. Write a diary entry describing a worker's typical day.

When energy does work, the energy is transferred from one object to another. At the textile mills along the Merrimack River, the kinetic energy of the moving water was transferred to the spinning machines. It became mechanical energy harnessed for a human purpose—making cloth. But all along a river, kinetic energy does other work. A river is always moving sediment from the mountains to the sea. At the same time, a river is also eroding its banks and valley.

☑ *Checkpoint* *What are potential energy and kinetic energy?*

How Water Erodes and Carries Sediment

Gravity causes the movement of water across Earth's land surface. But how does water cause erosion? In the process of water erosion, water picks up and moves sediment. Sediment includes soil, rock, clay, and sand. Sediment can enter rivers and streams in a number of ways. **Most sediment washes or falls into the river as a result of mass movement and runoff. Other sediment erodes from the bottom or sides of the river.** Wind may also drop sediment into the water.

Abrasion is another process by which a river obtains sediment. **Abrasion** is the wearing away of rock by a grinding action. Abrasion occurs when particles of sediment in flowing water bump into the streambed again and again. Abrasion grinds down sediment particles. For example, boulders become smaller as they are moved down a streambed. Sediments also grind and chip away at the rock of the streambed, deepening and widening the stream's channel.

The amount of sediment that a river carries is its **load.** Gravity and the force of the moving water cause the sediment load to move downstream. Most large sediment falls to the bottom and moves by rolling and sliding. Fast-moving water actually lifts sand and other, smaller, sediment and carries it downstream. Water dissolves some sediment completely. The river carries these dissolved sediments in solution. If you look at Figure 16, you can observe the different ways in which water can carry sediment. Notice for example, how grains of sand or small stones can move by bouncing.

Figure 16 Rivers and streams carry sediment in several ways. ***Predicting*** *What will eventually happen to a boulder on the bottom of a river?*

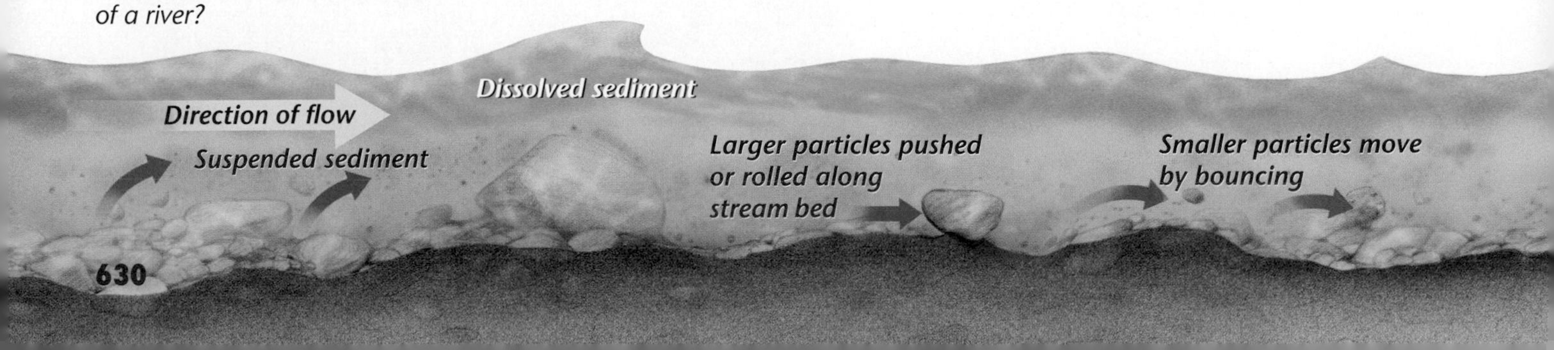

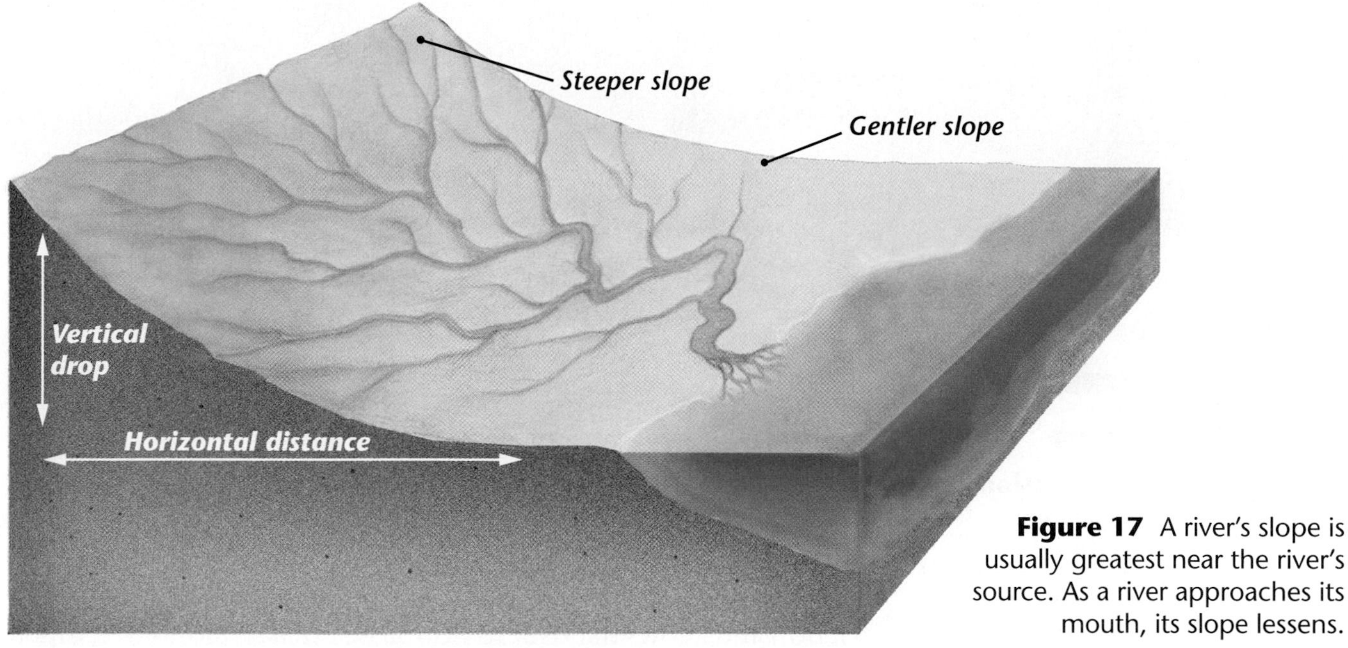

Figure 17 A river's slope is usually greatest near the river's source. As a river approaches its mouth, its slope lessens.

Erosion and Sediment Load

The power of a river to cause erosion and carry sediment depends on several factors. **A river's slope, volume of flow, and the shape of its streambed all affect how fast the river flows and how much sediment it can erode.**

A fast-flowing river carries more and larger particles of sediment. When a river slows down, its sediment load is deposited. The larger particles of sediment are deposited first.

Slope Generally, if a river's slope increases, the water's speed also increases. A river's slope is the amount the river drops toward sea level over a given distance. If a river's speed increases, its sediment load and power to erode may increase. But other factors are also important in determining how much sediment the river erodes and carries.

Volume of Flow A river's flow is the volume of water that moves past a point on the river in a given time. As more water flows through a river, its speed increases. During a flood, the increased volume of water helps the river to cut more deeply into its banks and bed. A flooding river may have hundreds of times more eroding power than the river has at other times. A flooding river can carry huge amounts of sand, soil, and other sediments. It may move giant boulders as if they were pebbles.

Streambed Shape A streambed's shape affects the amount of friction between the water and the streambed. **Friction** is the force that opposes the motion of one surface as it moves across another surface. Friction, in turn, affects a river's speed. Where a river is deep, less water comes in contact with the streambed. This reduces

Developing Hypotheses

ACTIVITY

A geologist is comparing alluvial fans. One alluvial fan is composed of gravel and small boulders. The other fan is composed of sand and silt. Propose a hypothesis to explain the difference in the size of the particles in the two fans. (*Hint*: Think of the characteristics of the streams that formed each alluvial fan.)

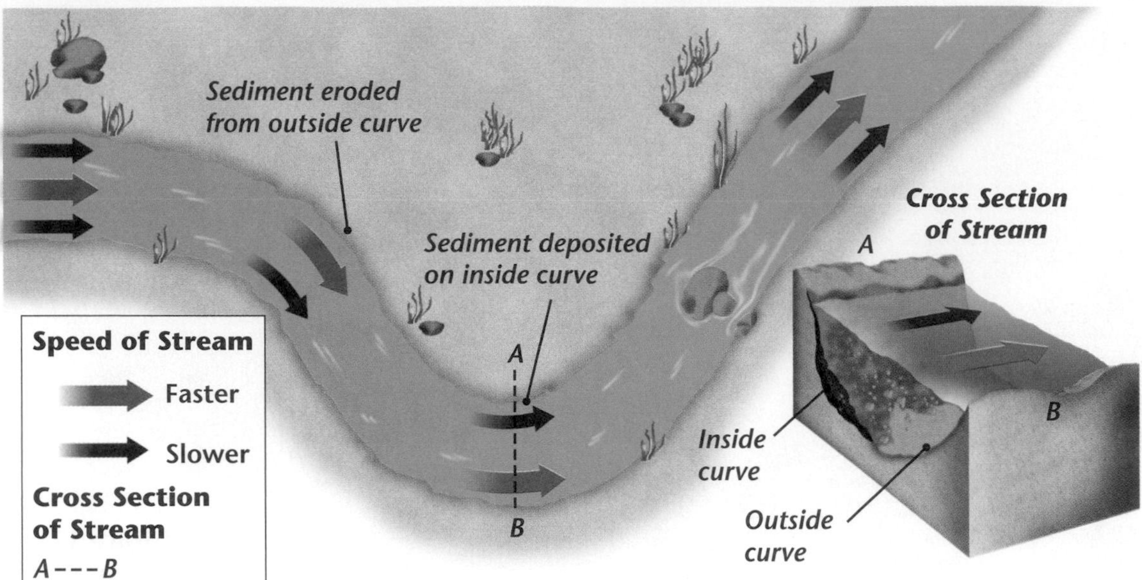

Figure 18 A river erodes sediment from its banks on the outside curve and deposits its sediment on the inside curve.
Relating Cause and Effect *Why does a river deposit sediment on the inside of a curve?*

friction and allows the river to flow faster. In a shallow river, much of the water comes in contact with the streambed. Therefore friction increases, reducing the river's speed.

A streambed is often full of boulders and other obstacles. This roughness prevents the water from flowing smoothly. Roughness thus increases friction and reduces the river's speed. Instead of moving downstream, the water moves every which way in a type of movement called **turbulence.** For example, a stream on a steep slope may flow at a lower speed than a large river on a gentle slope. Friction and turbulence slow the stream's flow. But a turbulent stream or river may have great power to erode.

The shape of a river affects the way it deposits sediment. Where a river flows in a straight line, the water flows faster near the center of the river than along its sides. Deposition occurs along the sides of the river, where the water moves more slowly.

If a river curves, the water moves fastest along the outside of the curve. There, the river tends to cut into its bank. Sediment is deposited on the inside curve, where the water speed is slowest. You can see this process in Figure 18.

Section 3 Review

1. How can moving water on Earth's surface do work?
2. How does a river collect sediment?
3. What are three factors that affect a river's sediment load?
4. Describe three ways that sediment moves in a river.
5. **Thinking Critically Relating Cause and Effect** What effect does increased slope have on a river's speed and sediment load? Explain.

CHAPTER PROJECT 19

Check Your Progress

Make a drawing of the landscape that you plan to model. This landscape will show the land before erosion. What kinds of landforms will you show in the model? Be sure to include a high mountain and a coastline. Make a list of materials that you will use to build your model. Once your teacher has approved your drawing and your list of materials, you may build your first model.

Section 4 Glaciers

Discover Activity

How Do Glaciers Change the Land?

1. Put some sand in a small plastic container.
2. Fill the container with water and place the container in a freezer until the water turns to ice.
3. Remove the block of ice from the container.
4. Holding the ice with paper towels, rub the ice, sand side down, over a bar of soap. Observe what happens to the surface of the soap.

Think It Over

Inferring Based on your observations, how do you think moving ice could change the surface of the land?

Guide for Reading

- **What are the two kinds of glaciers?**
- **How do glaciers cause erosion and deposition?**

Reading Tip **Before you read, preview the headings and key terms in the section. Make a list of predictions about the characteristics of glaciers.**

You are on a boat trip near the coast of Alaska. You sail by vast evergreen forests and snow-capped mountains. Then, as your boat rounds a point of land, you see an amazing sight. A great mass of ice winds like a river between rows of mountains. Suddenly you hear a noise like thunder. Where the ice meets the sea, a giant chunk of ice breaks off and plunges into the water. Carefully, you pilot your boat around the iceberg and toward the mass of ice. It towers over your boat. You see that it is made up of solid ice that is deep blue and green as well as white. What is this river of ice?

Kinds of Glaciers

Geologists define a **glacier** as any large mass of ice that moves slowly over land. **There are two kinds of glaciers—valley glaciers and continental glaciers.**

A **valley glacier** is a long, narrow glacier that forms when snow and ice build up high in a mountain valley. The sides of mountains keep these glaciers from spreading out in all directions. Instead, they usually move down valleys that have already been cut by rivers. Valley glaciers are found on many high mountains.

A **continental glacier** is a glacier that covers much of a continent or large island. Continental glaciers are much larger than

Figure 19 The Mendenhall Glacier in Alaska winds downhill between high mountains.

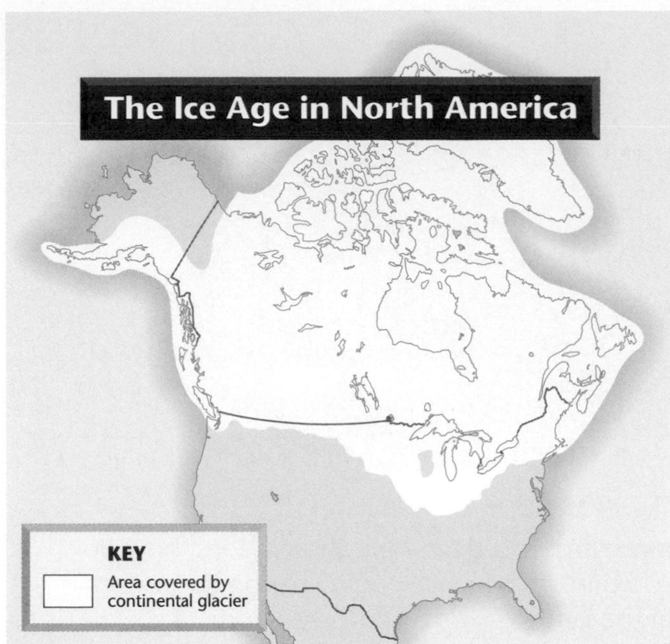

Figure 20 The continental glacier of the last ice age covered most of Canada and Alaska as well as much of the northern United States. The ice age lasted about 70,000 years and ended about 10,000 years ago.

valley glaciers. They spread out over large areas of the land. Today, continental glaciers cover about 10 percent of Earth's land. They cover Antarctica and most of Greenland. The glacier covering Antarctica spreads out over 14 million square kilometers and is over 2 kilometers thick.

Ice Ages

Many times in the past, continental glaciers have covered large parts of Earth's surface. These times are known as **ice ages.** For example, about 9 million years ago, continental glaciers began to form in North America, Europe, and Asia. These glaciers slowly grew and advanced southward. By about 2.5 million years ago, they covered about a third of Earth's land. The glaciers advanced and retreated, or melted back, several times. Figure 20 shows how far south the glaciers came on the North American continent during the most recent ice age. They finally retreated about 10,000 years ago.

How Glaciers Form and Move

Glaciers can form only in an area where more snow falls than melts. High in mountain valleys, temperatures seldom rise above freezing. Snow builds up year after year. The pressure of the weight of more and more snow compacts the snow at the bottom into ice. Once the depth of snow and ice reaches more than 30 to 40 meters, gravity begins to pull the glacier downhill.

Valley glaciers flow at a rate of a few centimeters to a few meters per day. But sometimes a valley glacier slides down more quickly in what is called a surge. A surging glacier can flow as much as 6 kilometers a year. Unlike valley glaciers, continental glaciers can flow in all directions. Continental glaciers spread out much as pancake batter spreads out in a frying pan.

☑ ***Checkpoint*** *How do glaciers form?*

Glacial Erosion

The movement of a glacier changes the land beneath it. Although glaciers work slowly, they are a major force of erosion. **The two processes by which glaciers erode the land are plucking and abrasion.**

As a glacier flows over the land, it picks up rocks in a process called **plucking.** Beneath a glacier, the weight of the ice can break rocks apart. These rock fragments freeze to the bottom of the glacier. When the glacier moves, it carries the rocks with it. Figure 21 shows plucking by a glacier. Plucking can move even huge boulders.

Many rocks remain on the bottom of the glacier, and the glacier drags them across the land. This process, called abrasion, gouges and scratches the bedrock. You can see the results of erosion by glaciers in *Exploring Glacial Landforms* on pages 636–637.

Figure 21 As a glacier moves downhill, the ice plucks pieces of bedrock from the ground. ***Predicting*** *What evidence of plucking might you find after a glacier melts?*

Glacial Deposition

A glacier gathers a huge amount of rock and soil as it erodes the land in its path. **When a glacier melts, it deposits the sediment it eroded from the land, creating various landforms.** These landforms remain for thousands of years after the glacier has melted.

The mixture of sediments that a glacier deposits directly on the surface is called **till.** Till is made up of particles of many different sizes. Clay, silt, sand, gravel, and boulders can all be found in till.

The till deposited at the edges of a glacier forms a ridge called a **moraine.** A terminal moraine is the ridge of till at the farthest point reached by a glacier. Long Island in New York is a terminal moraine from the continental glaciers of the last ice age.

INTEGRATING LIFE SCIENCE Other features left in glacial sediments are prairie potholes. These potholes are shallow depressions in till that were formed by flowing water as the continental glacier melted. Today, prairie potholes contain water for only part of the year. Each prairie pothole is a small oasis for living things. Grasses and moisture-loving plants grow thickly in and around the potholes. In the spring, the potholes brim with water from melting snow or rain. Thousands of migrating ducks and other birds stop off at the potholes to feed and rest on their way north. Some stay to build nests and raise their young.

Figure 22 This prairie pothole in Wisconsin is surrounded by farmland. Prairie potholes were left in till deposited by glaciers.

EXPLORING Glacial Landforms

As glaciers advance and retreat, they sculpt the landscape by erosion and deposition.

Retreating glaciers also create features called kettles. A **kettle** is a small depression that forms when a chunk of ice is left in glacial till. When the ice melts, the kettle remains. The continental glacier of the last ice age left behind many kettles. Kettles often fill with water, forming small ponds or lakes called kettle lakes. Such lakes are common in areas that were covered with ice.

The continental glacier of the last ice age also formed the Great Lakes. Before the ice age, there were large river valleys in the area now occupied by the lakes. As the ice advanced over these valleys, it scooped out loose sediment and soft rock, forming broad, deep basins. The Great Lakes formed over thousands of years as the glaciers melted and these basins filled with water.

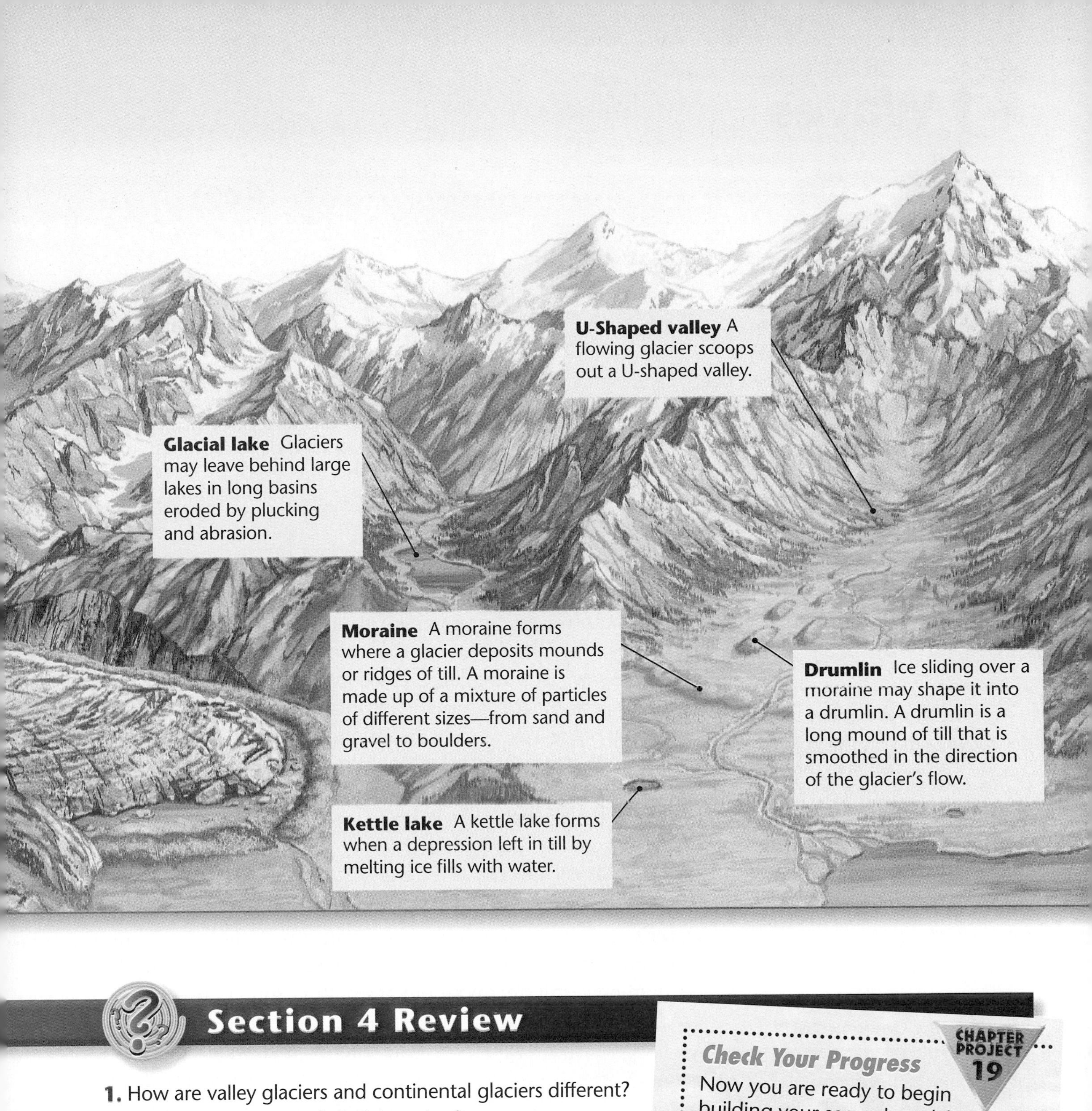

U-Shaped valley A flowing glacier scoops out a U-shaped valley.

Glacial lake Glaciers may leave behind large lakes in long basins eroded by plucking and abrasion.

Moraine A moraine forms where a glacier deposits mounds or ridges of till. A moraine is made up of a mixture of particles of different sizes—from sand and gravel to boulders.

Drumlin Ice sliding over a moraine may shape it into a drumlin. A drumlin is a long mound of till that is smoothed in the direction of the glacier's flow.

Kettle lake A kettle lake forms when a depression left in till by melting ice fills with water.

Section 4 Review

1. How are valley glaciers and continental glaciers different?
2. What are two types of glacial erosion?
3. Describe three features formed by glacial deposition.
4. **Thinking Critically Relating Cause and Effect** Driving through the countryside in Michigan, you and your family come upon a series of small, round lakes. Explain the process that formed these features.

CHAPTER PROJECT 19

Check Your Progress

Now you are ready to begin building your second model. Pattern the model after your drawing that predicts the effects of erosion and deposition. The model will show how gravity, water, and glaciers have changed your model landscape. Where on your model would glaciers be likely to form?

Section 5 Waves

Discover — Activity

What Can Be Learned From Beach Sand?

1. Collect a spoonful of sand from each of two different beaches. The two samples also may come from different parts of the same beach.
2. Examine the first sample of beach sand with a hand lens.
3. Record the properties of the sand grains, for example, color and shape. Are the grains smooth and rounded or angular and rough? Are all the grains in the sample the same shape and color?
4. Examine the second sample and repeat Step 3. How do the two samples compare?

Think It Over

Posing Questions What questions do you need to answer to understand beach sand? Use what you know about erosion and deposition to help you think of questions.

Guide for Reading

- What gives waves their energy?
- How do waves shape a coast?

Reading Tip As you read, make a concept map showing features formed by wave erosion and deposition.

Ocean waves contain energy—sometimes a great deal of energy. The waves that sweep onto the Pacific coast are especially powerful. Created by ocean winds, they carry energy vast distances across the Pacific Ocean. Acting like drills or buzzsaws, the waves erode the solid rock of the coast into cliffs and caves. Waves also carry sediment that forms features such as beaches. But these features do not last long. More waves follow to change the shoreline yet again.

How Waves Form

The energy in waves comes from wind that blows across the water's surface. As the wind makes contact with the water, some of its energy transfers to the water. Large ocean waves are the result of powerful storms far out at sea. But ordinary breezes can produce waves in lakes or small ponds.

The energy that water picks up from the wind causes water particles to move up and down as the wave goes by. But the water particles themselves don't move forward. Only the form of the wave moves. Have you ever watched a wave in a field of tall grass? Each blade of grass moves back and forth but doesn't move from its place. But the energy of the wave moves across the field.

Waves on the Oregon coast ▼

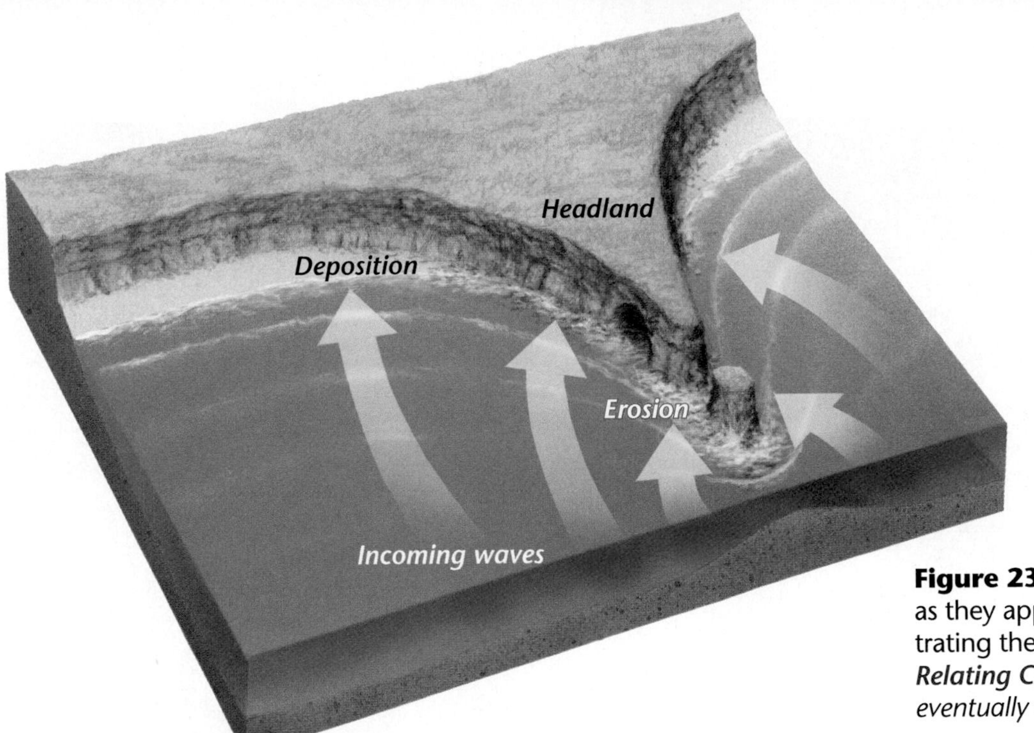

Figure 23 Incoming waves bend as they approach the shore, concentrating their energy on headlands. ***Relating Cause and Effect*** *What will eventually happen to the headlands?*

A wave changes as it approaches land. In deep water, a wave only affects the water near the surface. But as the wave approaches shallow water, the wave begins to drag the bottom. The friction between the wave and the bottom causes the wave to slow down. Now the water actually does move forward with the wave. This forward-moving water provides the force that shapes the land along the shoreline.

Erosion by Waves

Waves are the major force of erosion along coasts. One way waves erode the land is by impact. Large waves can hit rocks along the shore with great force. This energy in waves can break apart rocks. Over time, waves can make small cracks larger. Eventually, the waves cause pieces of rock to break off.

Waves also erode land by abrasion. As a wave approaches shallow water, it picks up sediment, including sand and gravel. This sediment is carried forward by the wave. When the wave hits land, the sediment wears away rock like sandpaper wearing away wood.

Waves coming to shore gradually change direction. The change in direction occurs as different parts of a wave begin to drag on the bottom. Notice how the waves in Figure 23 change direction as they approach the shore. The energy of these waves is concentrated on headlands. A headland is a part of the shore that sticks out into the ocean. Headlands stand out from the coast because they are made of harder rock that resists the waves. But, over time, waves erode the headlands and even out the shoreline.

☑ ***Checkpoint*** *What are two of the processes by which waves can cause erosion?*

Calculating

A sandy coast erodes at a rate of 1.25 meters per year. But a severe storm can erode an additional 3.75 meters from the shore. If 12 severe storms occur during a 50-year period, how much will the coast erode? If you wish, you may use an electronic calculator to find the answer.

ACTIVITY

Figure 24 Waves cut these cliffs on the coast of Australia. The blocks of rock offshore are sea stacks. ***Developing Hypotheses*** *Develop a hypothesis to explain how these sea stacks formed.*

Landforms Created by Wave Erosion

When waves hit a steep, rocky coast, they strike the area again and again. Think of an ax striking the trunk of a tree. The cut gets bigger and deeper with each strike of the blade. Finally the tree falls. In a similar way, ocean waves erode the base of the land along a steep coast. Where the rock is softer, the waves erode the land faster. Over time the waves may erode a hollow area in the rock called a sea cave.

Eventually, waves may erode the base of a cliff so much that the rock above collapses. The result is a wave-cut cliff. You can see an example of such a cliff in Figure 24.

Another feature created by wave erosion is a sea arch. A sea arch forms when waves erode a layer of softer rock that underlies a layer of harder rock. If an arch collapses, the result might be a sea stack, a pillar of rock rising above the water.

☑ *Checkpoint* *How can waves produce a cliff on a rocky coast?*

Deposits by Waves

Waves not only erode the land, they also deposit sediment. **Waves shape the coast through both erosion and deposition.** Deposition occurs when waves slow down and the water drops its sediment. This process is similar to the deposition that occurs on a river delta when the river slows down and drops its sediment load.

Figure 25 This satellite image of Cape Cod in Massachusetts shows how longshore drift can carry sand and deposit it to form a spit. ***Observing*** *How many spits can you find in this image?*

As waves reach the shore, they drop the sediment they carry, forming a beach. A **beach** is an area of wave-washed sediment along a coast. The sediment deposited on beaches is usually sand. Most sand comes from rivers that carry eroded particles of rock into the ocean. But not all beaches are made of sand carried by rivers. Some beaches are made of small fragments of coral or sea shells piled up by wave action. Florida has many such beaches.

The sediment on a beach usually moves down the beach after it has been deposited. Waves usually hit the beach at an angle instead of straight on. These angled waves create a current that runs parallel to the coastline. As repeated waves hit the beach, some of the beach sediment moves down the beach with the current, in a process called **longshore drift.**

One result of longshore drift is the formation of a spit. A **spit** is a beach that projects like a finger out into the water. Spits form as a result of deposition by longshore drift. Spits occur where a headland or other obstacle interrupts longshore drift, or where the coast turns abruptly. Incoming waves carrying sand may build up sandbars, long ridges of sand parallel to the shore.

INTEGRATING ENVIRONMENTAL SCIENCE A barrier beach is similar to a sandbar, but a barrier beach forms when storm waves pile up sand above sea level. Barrier beaches are found in many places along the Atlantic coast of the United States, such as the Outer Banks of North Carolina. People have built homes on many of these barrier beaches. But the storm waves that build up the beaches can also wash them away. Barrier beach communities must be prepared for the damage that hurricanes and other storms can bring.

Section 5 Review

1. How do ocean waves form?
2. Describe two landforms created by wave erosion and two landforms created by wave deposition.
3. Why are headlands eroded faster than the land at the ends of inlets and bays?
4. **Thinking Critically Predicting** You visit a rocky headland by the ocean that has a sea arch and several sea stacks. How might this area change in the next 500 years?

Check Your Progress

CHAPTER PROJECT 19

Now you are ready to add the effects of wave erosion to your model. What landforms will wave erosion produce along the coastline on your model? What materials will you use to model these landforms? When you have finished your second model, make labels for the landforms on your models.

Section 6 Wind

Discover Activity

How Does Moving Air Affect Sediment?

1. Cover the bottom of a pan with a flat layer of cornmeal 1–2 centimeters deep.
2. Gently blow over the layer of cornmeal using a straw to direct your breath. Observe what happens.

CAUTION: *Do not blow the cornmeal in the direction of another student.*

Think It Over

Observing What changes did the wind you created make in the flat layer of cornmeal?

Guide for Reading

- **How does wind cause erosion?**
- **What features result from deposition by wind?**

Reading Tip **Before you read, preview Figure 27. In your notebook, write some predictions about the characteristics of wind erosion.**

Imagine a landscape made almost entirely of sand. One such place is the Namib Desert. The desert stretches for about 1,900 kilometers along the coast of Namibia in Africa. In the southern half of the Namib are long rows of giant sand dunes. A **sand dune** is a deposit of wind-blown sand. Some sand dunes in the Namib are more than 200 meters high and 15 kilometers long. Much of the sand in the dunes originally came from the nearby Orange River. Over thousands of years, wind has swept the sand across the desert, piling up huge, ever-changing dunes.

How Wind Causes Erosion

Wind by itself is the weakest agent of erosion. Water, waves, moving ice, and even mass movement have more effect on the land. Yet wind can be a powerful force in shaping the land in areas where there are few plants to hold the soil in place. As you might guess, wind is very effective in causing erosion in deserts. There few plants can grow, and wind can easily move the grains of dry, light sand.

Figure 26 Wind erosion continues to shape the giant sand dunes in the Namib Desert along Africa's southwestern coast.

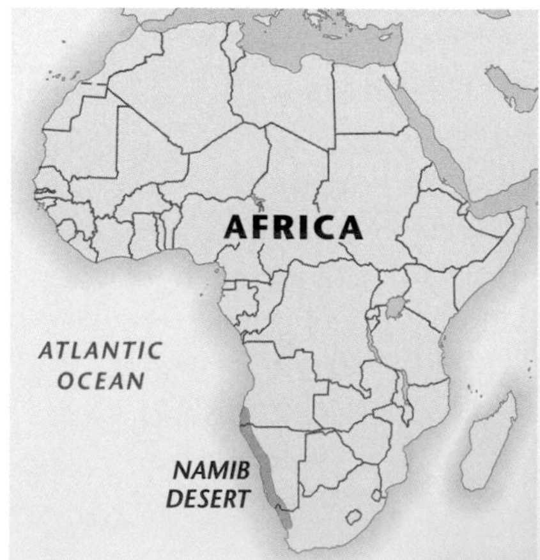

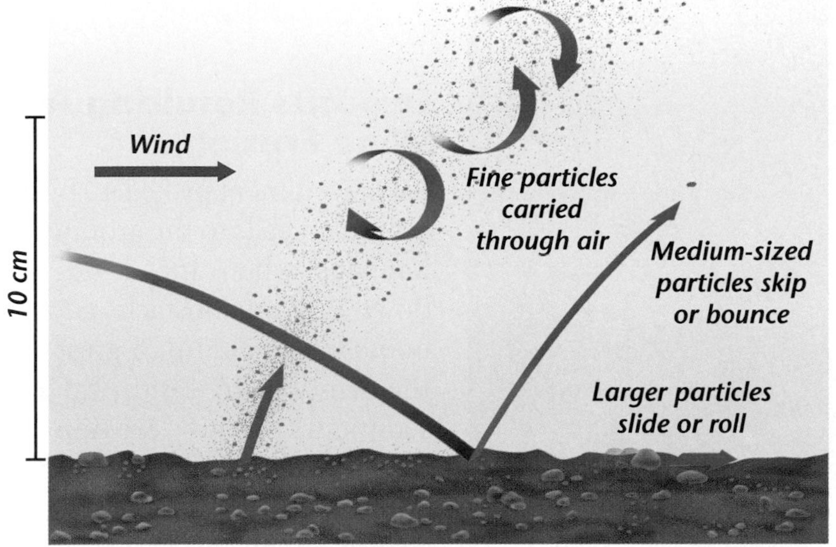

Figure 27 Wind erosion moves sediment particles of different sizes in the three ways shown above. ***Comparing and Contrasting*** *Compare the movement of sediment by wind with the movement of sediment by water in Figure 16 on page 630. How are the processes similar? How are they different?*

The main way that wind causes erosion is by deflation. Geologists define **deflation** as the process by which wind removes surface materials. When wind blows over the land, it picks up the smallest particles of sediment. This sediment is made of bits of clay and silt. The stronger the wind, the larger the particles that it can pick up and move through the air. Slightly heavier particles, such as sand, might skip or bounce for a short distance. But sand soon falls back to the ground. Strong winds can even roll heavier sediment particles over the ground. Figure 27 shows how wind erodes by deflation.

Deflation does not usually have a great effect on the land. However, in parts of the Great Plains in the 1930s, deflation caused the loss of about 1 meter of topsoil in just a few years. In deserts, deflation can sometimes create an area of rock fragments called desert pavement. You can see an area of desert pavement in Figure 28. There, wind has blown away the smaller sediment. All that remains are rocky materials that are too large and heavy to be moved. Where there is already a slight depression in the ground, deflation can produce a bowl-shaped hollow called a blowout.

Figure 28 Wind erosion formed this desert pavement in the Arizona desert. Wind-driven sand may polish and shape individual stones.

Abrasion by wind-carried sand can polish rock, but it causes little erosion. At one time, geologists thought that the sediment carried by wind cut the stone shapes seen in deserts. But now evidence shows that most desert landforms are the result of weathering and water erosion.

☑ ***Checkpoint*** *Where would you be most likely to see evidence of wind erosion?*

Figure 29 Wind carrying fine particles of silt built up this loess deposit near Natchez, Mississippi.

Deposits Resulting From Wind Erosion

All the sediment picked up by wind eventually falls to the ground. This happens when the wind slows down or some obstacle, such as a boulder or a clump of grass, traps the windblown sand and other sediment. **Wind erosion and deposition may form sand dunes and loess deposits.** When the wind strikes an obstacle, the result is usually a sand dune. Sand dunes can be seen on beaches and in deserts where wind-blown sediment has built up.

Sand dunes come in many shapes and sizes. Some are long, with parallel ridges, while others are U-shaped. They can also be very small or very large—some sand dunes in China have grown to heights of 500 meters. Sand dunes move over time. Little by little, the sand shifts with the wind from one side of the dune to the other. Sometimes plants begin growing on a dune. Plant roots can help to anchor the dune in one place.

Sand dunes are most often made of the coarser sediments carried by wind. The finer sediments, including particles of clay and silt, are sometimes deposited in layers far from their source. This fine, wind-deposited sediment is **loess** (LES). Large loess deposits are found in central China and in such states as Nebraska, South Dakota, Iowa, Missouri, and Illinois. Loess helps to form fertile soil. Many areas with thick loess deposits are valuable farmlands.

Section 6 Review

1. Describe how wind erodes the land.
2. How do sand dunes and loess deposits form?
3. What is a blowout and what is the process that produces one?
4. **Thinking Critically Predicting** You visit a beach that has sand dunes covered with dune grass. But where people take a shortcut over one dune, the grass has been worn away. What may eventually happen to the dune if people keep taking this path?

Science at Home

Here's how to make a model of desert pavement. Put a few coins in a shallow pan about 1 centimeter deep. Sprinkle enough flour over the coins to bury them beneath a thin layer of flour. Then blow air gently through a straw across the surface of the flour. Be careful not to draw in any flour through the straw. Be certain the blown flour will not get in your or anyone else's eyes. Ask your family to predict what the surface of the pan would look like if the "wind" continued to blow for a long time.

CHAPTER 19 STUDY GUIDE

Changing Earth's Surface

Key Ideas

- Weathering, erosion, and deposition act to wear down and build up Earth's surface.
- Gravity pulls sediment downhill in the process of mass movement. There are four main types of mass movement: landslides, mudslides, slump, and creep.

Key Terms

erosion	deposition
sediment	mass movement

Water Erosion

Key Ideas

- Moving water is the major force of erosion that has shaped Earth's land surface.
- A river may form V-shaped valleys, waterfalls, meanders, oxbow lakes, and flood plains.
- When a river slows down, it deposits some of the sediment load it carries, forming features such as alluvial fans and deltas.

Key Terms

runoff	drainage basin	delta
rill	divide	groundwater
gully	flood plain	stalactite
stream	meander	stalagmite
river	oxbow lake	karst topography
tributary	alluvial fan	

The Force of Moving Water

INTEGRATING PHYSICS

Key Ideas

- When gravity pulls water down a slope, water's potential energy changes to kinetic energy, and it does work.
- Most sediment washes or falls into streams, or is eroded from the streambed by abrasion.
- The greater a river's slope or volume of flow, the more sediment it can erode.

Key Terms

energy	abrasion	friction
potential energy	load	turbulence
kinetic energy		

Glaciers

Key Ideas

- The two kinds of glaciers are valley glaciers and continental glaciers.
- Glaciers erode the land through plucking and abrasion. Melting glaciers deposit sediment.

Key Terms

glacier	ice age	moraine
valley glacier	plucking	kettle
continental glacier	till	

Waves

Key Ideas

- The energy of ocean waves comes from wind blowing across the water's surface and transferring energy to the water.
- Ocean waves hitting land cause erosion through impact and abrasion. Waves also move and deposit sediment along the shore.

Key Terms

beach	longshore drift	spit

Wind Erosion

Key Ideas

- Wind causes erosion mainly through deflation, the blowing of surface materials.
- Landforms created by wind deposition include sand dunes and loess deposits.

Key Terms

sand dune	deflation	loess

Organizing Information

Flowchart Make a flowchart showing how a stream forms. Your flowchart should include the following terms in the correct order: rills, runoff, gullies, stream, raindrops. Give your flowchart a title. (For tips on making a flowchart, see the Skills Handbook.)

Reviewing Content

Multiple Choice

Choose the answer that best completes the sentence.

1. The eroded materials carried by water or wind are called
   a. stalactites.
   b. desert pavement.
   c. sediment.
   d. moraines.
2. The downhill movement of eroded materials is known as
   a. mass movement.
   b. abrasion.
   c. deposition.
   d. deflation.
3. A mass of rock and soil deposited directly by a glacier is called
   a. load. b. till.
   c. loess. d. erosion.
4. When waves strike a shoreline, they concentrate their energy on
   a. beaches.
   b. cirques.
   c. sand dunes.
   d. headlands.
5. The erosion of sediment by wind is
   a. deposition. b. deflation.
   c. plucking. d. glaciation.

True or False

If the statement is true, write true. If it is false, change the underlined word or words to make the statement true.

6. The process by which sediment in water settles in new locations is mass movement.
7. An area of alluvial fans may be found where groundwater erodes limestone to form valleys, sinkholes, and caverns.
8. Because it is moving, flowing water has a type of energy called kinetic energy.
9. A looplike bend in the course of a river is a meander.
10. The sediment deposited at the edge of a glacier forms a ridge called a kettle.

Checking Concepts

11. What agents of erosion are in part caused by the force of gravity?
12. How do a river's slope and volume of flow affect the river's sediment load?
13. Describe how the speed of flowing water changes where a river bends. How does this affect a river's deposition of sediment?
14. Why does a delta develop when a river flows into a larger body of water?
15. Describe the process by which groundwater can cause erosion and deposition in limestone beneath Earth's surface.
16. What are ice ages?
17. **Writing to Learn** You go on a rafting journey that takes you down a river from the mountains to the sea. Write a letter to a friend describing the features created by erosion and deposition that you see as you travel down the river. Include features near the river's source, along the middle of its course, and where it reaches the ocean.

Thinking Critically

18. **Applying Concepts** Under what conditions would you expect abrasion to cause the most erosion of a riverbed?
19. **Relating Cause and Effect** In a desert, you see an area that looks as if it were paved with rock fragments. Explain how this situation occurred naturally.
20. **Problem Solving** Suppose you are a geologist studying a valley glacier. What method could you use to tell if it is advancing or retreating?
21. **Making Judgments** A salesperson offers to sell your family a new house right on a riverbank for very little money. Why might your family hesitate to buy this house?
22. **Inferring** You see a sandy beach along a coastline. What can you infer about where the sand came from?
23. **Comparing and Contrasting** How are landslides similar to mudflows? How are they different?

Applying Skills

The table below shows how a river's volume of flow and sediment load change over six months. Use the table to answer Questions 24–26.

Month	Volume of Flow (cubic meters/second)	Sediment Load (metric tons/day)
January	1.5	200
February	1.7	320
March	2.6	725
April	4.0	1600
May	3.2	1100
June	2.8	900

24. Graphing Make one graph with the month on the *x*-axis and the volume of flow on the *y*-axis. Make a second graph with the sediment load on the *y*-axis. Compare your two graphs. When were the river's volume of flow and load the greatest? The lowest?

25. Developing Hypotheses Use your graphs to develop a hypothesis about the relationship between volume of flow and sediment load.

26. Relating Cause and Effect What may have occurred in the river's drainage basin in April to cause the changes in volume of flow and sediment load? Explain.

Performance CHAPTER PROJECT 19 Assessment

Project Wrap Up Now you are ready to explain your models of erosion to your class. Label your models to indicate the features that changed during erosion.

Reflect and Record In your journal, write about the easiest and hardest parts of this project. How would you do each model differently if you did the project again?

Test Preparation

Use these questions to prepare for standardized tests.

Read the passage. Then answer Questions 27–30.

This is the story of a great river. The Missouri River is America's second longest river after the Mississippi River. Its vast drainage basin covers parts of 10 states and 2 Canadian provinces. Early settlers called the Missouri the "Big Muddy" because its waters carry a heavy sediment load.

The Missouri River begins in the Rocky Mountains near Three Forks, Montana, where three small streams join. The upper Missouri flows through a deep valley called the Gates of the Mountains. Then at Great Falls, Montana, it plunges down a series of waterfalls and rapids.

Leaving the mountains, the middle Missouri flows across the Great Plains. Major tributaries, such as the Yellowstone and Platte rivers, flow into it. The Missouri has eroded a wide valley as it winds through the plains. Steep ridges called bluffs sometimes form the edges of the valley.

The Missouri ends just north of St. Louis, Missouri, where it flows into the Mississippi.

27. A good title for this passage is
a. The Rivers of America.
b. Following the Missouri River.
c. Tributaries of the Missouri River.
d. Sedimental Journey.

28. A deep valley, waterfalls, and rapids can be found
a. where the Missouri crosses the Plains.
b. nowhere along the Missouri.
c. on the upper Missouri.
d. on the lower Missouri.

29. Along the middle Missouri's valley are features called
a. gullies. **b.** drainage basins.
c. gates. **d.** bluffs.

30. The nickname "Big Muddy" refers to the Missouri's
a. sediment load.
b. source.
c. meanders.
d. tributaries.

INTERDISCIPLINARY EXPLORATION

The Gift of the Nile

What water—

Lush, fertile lands along the Nile contrast with the scorching desert beyond.

- *flows from south to north?*
- *travels through a scorching desert for much of its length?*
- *nourished a remarkable ancient culture that lasted for 3,000 years?*
- *is the longest river in the world?*

It's the Nile River, which gives life to the Egyptian desert.

More than 5,000 years ago, people first began planting seeds and harvesting crops in the valley of the Nile. The great civilization of Egypt rose in these fertile lands. The Nile supplied water for drinking, growing crops, raising animals, and fishing. When the river flooded every year, it brought a new layer of rich soil to the flood plain.

This productive strip of land was the envy of many nations. Fortunately, the deserts west and east of the Nile River helped protect ancient Egypt from invaders. The river provided a route for trade from central Africa downstream to the Mediterranean Sea. Around 600 B.C., Egypt expanded its trade by digging a canal to the Red Sea.

During the months when the Nile flooded, peasants worked as builders for the Pharaoh, or king. They constructed magnificent pyramids and temples, some of which still stand in the desert today.

Blue water lilies grow in the Nile.

Lifeline of Egypt

The wealth of ancient Egypt and the lives of its people depended on the fertile flood plains that bordered the Nile River. Egyptian society was organized in classes to support agriculture. The Pharaoh was the supreme ruler to whom all Egyptians paid taxes. Below the Pharaoh was a small upper class of priests, scribes, and nobles. Traders and skilled workers, who made tools, pottery, and clothing, formed a small middle class. But the largest group in Egyptian society was the peasants. Peasants used the Nile waters to raise crops that fed all of Egypt.

Priests and nobles recorded the history and literature of ancient Egypt on the walls of monuments and temples. They also wrote on papyrus, a paper made from reeds that grew in marshes along the Nile. Many writings were about the Nile.

When scholars finally found the key to hieroglyphics (hy ur oh GLIF iks), Egyptian writing, they discovered hymns, poems, legends, adventure stories, and lessons for young people. The poem at the right is from a hymn to Hapy, the god of the Nile. "Darkness by day" is the Nile filled with silt.

Egyptian writing, called hieroglyphics, decorates the borders of this poem. ▶

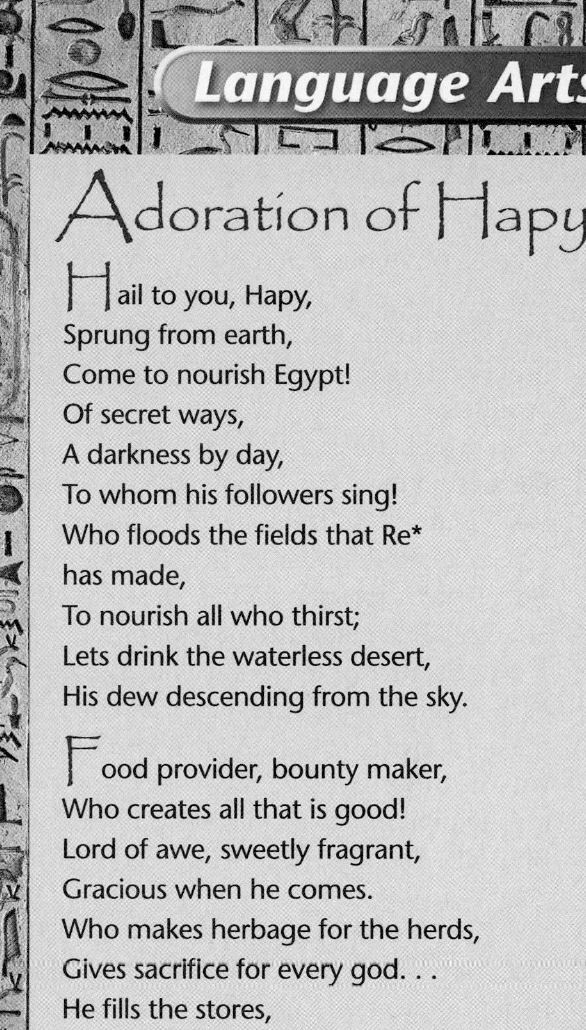

Adoration of Hapy

Hail to you, Hapy,
Sprung from earth,
Come to nourish Egypt!
Of secret ways,
A darkness by day,
To whom his followers sing!
Who floods the fields that Re*
has made,
To nourish all who thirst;
Lets drink the waterless desert,
His dew descending from the sky.

Food provider, bounty maker,
Who creates all that is good!
Lord of awe, sweetly fragrant,
Gracious when he comes.
Who makes herbage for the herds,
Gives sacrifice for every god. . .
He fills the stores,
Makes bulge the barns,
Gives bounty to the poor.

Oh joy when you come!
O joy when you come, O Hapy,
Oh joy when you come!

**Amon-Re, god of the sun*

Language Arts Activity

In this poem, Hapy is a personification of the Nile River. When writers and poets use personification, they give an object or animal human qualities. Write your own story or poem using personification. Choose a subject found in nature, such as a mountain, stream, river, or glacier. Jot down human behaviors and actions for your subject—"the stream gurgles, murmurs, and sighs." Before writing, think about the time, place, characters, and sequence of events in your story.

Science

Fertilizing the Fields

In some parts of Egypt, it hasn't rained in years. Only about 3 percent of Egypt can be farmed. The rest is sun-baked desert. But hot weather and the silt and water brought by the Nile River make the Nile Valley highly productive.

The Nile River is the longest river on Earth, stretching 6,650 kilometers. Its drainage basin is about 3.3 million square kilometers. This is larger than that of the Mississippi River. Three major rivers form the Nile—the White Nile, the Blue Nile, and the Atbara.

The source of the White Nile is just south of the equator near Lake Victoria (about 1,135 meters above sea level). A fairly constant volume of water flows north over rapids and through swamp lands to Khartoum. Here the Blue Nile and the White Nile meet to form the great Nile River.

The Blue Nile starts in the eastern plateau of Ethiopia near Lake Tana (about 1,800 meters above sea level). The Atbara River, the last major tributary of the Nile, also flows in from Ethiopia. Between Khartoum and Aswan, the Nile flows north over six cataracts—huge waterfalls. From Aswan to Cairo, the flood plain stretches out on both sides of the river. It gradually widens to about 19 kilometers. Then in Lower Egypt the river branches out to form the Nile Delta.

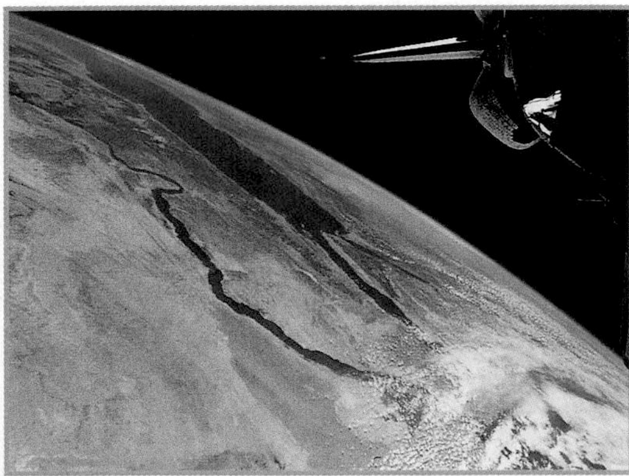

A view from space shows the Nile River winding through the Sahara Desert. A space probe is at the upper right.

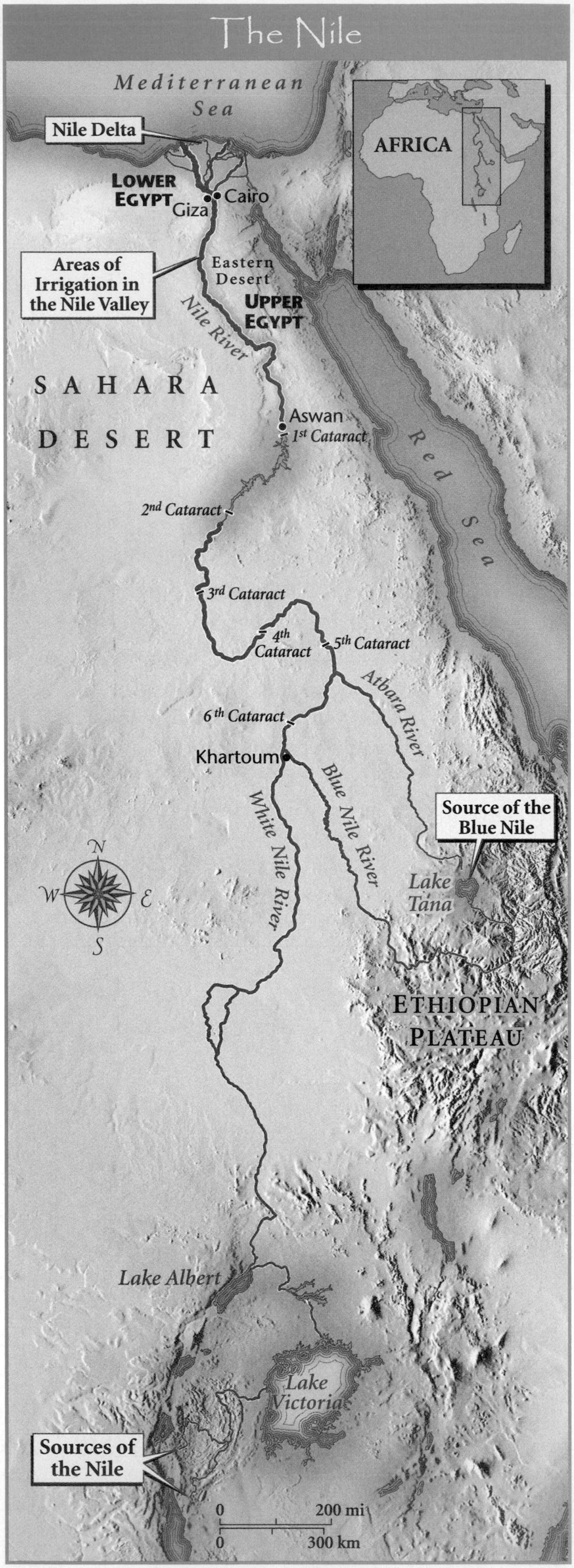

The Nile

Mediterranean Sea
Nile Delta
LOWER EGYPT
Giza
Cairo
AFRICA
Areas of Irrigation in the Nile Valley
Eastern Desert
UPPER EGYPT
Nile River
SAHARA DESERT
Aswan
1st Cataract
Red Sea
2nd Cataract
3rd Cataract
4th Cataract
5th Cataract
Atbara River
6th Cataract
Khartoum
Blue Nile River
White Nile River
Source of the Blue Nile
Lake Tana
N
W
E
S
ETHIOPIAN PLATEAU
Lake Albert
Lake Victoria
Sources of the Nile
0 200 mi
0 300 km

The rushing waters of the Blue Nile carry silt and other sediment from the Ethiopian highlands to the Nile.

Between May and August, heavy rains soak the eastern plateau of Ethiopia and wash rock and silt from the highlands into the Blue Nile. The dark water rushes over rapids and through deep gorges into the Nile River. For thousands of years this rush of water from the Blue Nile and the Atbara caused the seasonal flooding on the Nile. In mid-July, the Nile would begin to rise north of Aswan. When the flood waters went down, the silt remained on the land.

Then in the 1800s and 1900s, Egypt built dams on the Nile to try to control the floodwaters. The Aswan High Dam, the largest of these dams, was completed in 1970. With this dam, the Egyptians finally gained control over annual flooding. The Aswan High Dam holds back water for dry periods and manages surplus water.

In recent years, the population of Egypt and other nations in the Nile basin has grown rapidly. Feeding more people means increasing the area of irrigated cropland. To avoid conflicts, nations must agree to share water. Most of the water in the Blue Nile, for example, comes from Ethiopia. Yet Egypt and Sudan, the nations farther downstream, use about 90 percent of that water. Today, Ethiopia's growing population needs more Nile water. Using water efficiently and sharing it fairly are essential in the Nile basin.

Science Activities

Use the stream table (pages 626–627) to observe how the Nile builds its delta and how the Aswan Dam affects the river. Pour water into the lower end of the stream table to model the sea.

- Make a dam. Cut off the top 2 centimeters from a plastic foam cup. Cut a semicircle for your dam. Cut a small notch in the top of the dam for a spillway.
- Start the dripper to create the Nile. Allow it to flow for 5 minutes. What do you observe where the river flows into the sea?
- Now place the dam halfway down the river. Scoop out a small, shallow reservoir behind the dam. Observe for 5 minutes.

What effect would you say that the Aswan Dam has on the movement of sediment down the Nile?

Basin Irrigation

The ancient Egyptians may have been the first to irrigate their lands. The slope of the flood plain in Egypt is good for irrigation. From south to north, the land slopes down slightly. The land also slopes slightly down to the desert from the river banks on either side of the Nile.

Egyptians used basin irrigation. They divided the flood plain into a series of basins by building low banks of dirt. When the Nile flooded from July to October, it filled the basins. Then, the water level in the Nile and in the basins gradually dropped. This left a rich sediment layer ready for planting.

In November, peasants plowed the fields and scattered seeds. To push the seeds into the ground, they drove sheep over the fields. Egyptians grew crops of wheat, barley, lentils, onions, beans, garlic, vegetables, and fruits in the Nile Valley. The crops usually could feed all of Egypt. The Egyptians traded any surplus crops for lumber, copper, and beautiful minerals that they used for decorations.

When the fields became dry, peasants brought water from irrigation channels, or deep ditches. They also used a tool called a shaduf to take water directly from the Nile. After the harvest in April, farm animals grazed on the lands until the Nile rose again in mid-July. Then a new cycle began.

The flooding of the Nile determined the lives of early Egyptians. Their year began on the day the Nile began to rise, about July 19 on our calendar. The Egyptians were the first people to have a calendar of 365 days. Their year was divided into 3 seasons based on the Nile's flood cycle. Each season had 4 months of 30 days. At the end of the twelve months, the Egyptians had 5 festival days to complete the year.

The shaduf, still used today, dates back to about 2200 B.C. A wooden beam balances on a pivot, like a plank on a see-saw. Hanging from one end of the beam is a bucket. Balancing at the other end is a large stone. A farmer rocks the beam to scoop water from the Nile. Then the farmer swivels the bucket and empties it into an irrigation channel.

This painting from around 1200 B.C. was found on the wall of the Tomb of Sennedjem in Thebes. The panels show Sennedjem and his wife farming in the afterworld. Sennedjem's wife plants grain. Sennedjem harvests wheat with a sickle (top panel) and plows (middle panel). Egyptians cultivated fruit-bearing trees, such as the date palm (bottom panel).

Social Studies Activities

Divide into groups of three to make a time line of an Egyptian calendar year. Each member of the group should choose a four-month season—flooding, planting, or harvesting—to label and illustrate.

- Draw the time line to begin on July 19 and end on July 18.
- Divide the time line into 12 months and 5 days.
- Label the months and seasons.
- Illustrate the seasonal work of the farmers.

The flooded fields of the Nile Delta are separated into lots by irrigation channels.

Mathematics

Measuring the Land

Have you ever measured the length of a room using your feet as the unit of measurement? Around 3000 B.C., ancient Egyptians developed the cubit system of measurement. It was based on the lengths of parts of the arm and hand, rather than the foot. The Egyptian cubit was the length of a forearm from the tip of the elbow to the end of the middle finger. The cubit was subdivided into smaller units of spans, palms, digits, and parts of digits.

Of course, the length of a cubit varied from person to person. So Egypt established a standard cubit, called the Royal Cubit. It was based on the length of the Pharaoh's forearm. The Royal Cubit was a piece of black granite about 52.3 centimeters long. Although the royal architect kept the Royal Cubit, wooden copies were distributed through the land.

Measurement was important to Egyptian life. Every year when the Nile flooded, it wiped out the boundaries for the fields. So after the annual floods, farmers had to measure off new areas. Drawings on the walls of early tombs show that the Egyptians probably had a system for measuring distances and angles on land.

Standard measurement was also necessary for building the massive temples and pyramids that lined the Nile Valley. The cubit stick must have been very accurate, because the lengths of the sides of the Great Pyramid at Giza vary by only a few centimeters.

Egyptians used geometry to measure triangles, squares, and circles to build pyramids. These pyramids at Giza were built around 2500 B.C.

Mathematics Activities

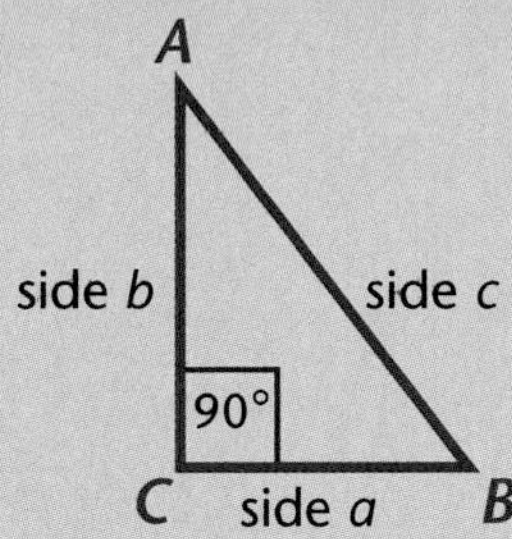

To measure fields and build pyramids, the Egyptians needed to understand geometry. They laid out their fields in squares by first making a right triangle. Look at the diagram. The two shorter sides are the legs. The side opposite the right angle is the hypotenuse. The Egyptians might have known that the sum of the squares of the lengths of the legs is equal to the square of the hypotenuse. The equation is $a^2 + b^2 = c^2$. So if side *a* is 3, and side *b* is 4, and side *c* is 5, then $3^2 + 4^2 = 5^2$, or $9 + 16 = 25$.

Now work in groups of 3 to make your own right triangle.

- Measure one student's arm to make a cubit stick.
- Use the cubit stick to cut one rope 12 cubits long; mark off each of the 12 cubits.
- Have 3 students hold the rope at points *A, B,* and *C* so that side *a* is 3 cubits, side *b* is 4 cubits, and *c* is 5 cubits.

Have you made a right triangle? How do you know? How could you make a square?

Tie It Together

Egyptian Exhibition

Plan a brochure to promote a special exhibition on Egypt at a museum. Half the class can focus on ancient Egypt. The other half can find out about the changes that have occurred on the Nile in the last 100 years. Work in small groups to research and assemble the information and illustrations. You might want to include the following:

- the Rosetta Stone and hieroglyphics
- directions for making a mummy
- the Great Pyramid at Giza
- history and treasures of King Tutankhamen
- religion in ancient Egypt
- model of an irrigation system for fields on the Nile
- maps of ancient and modern Egypt
- construction of the Aswan Dam, 1959–1970
- water control on the Nile in Egypt today
- Nile Delta today

CHAPTER 20

Earth, Moon, and Sun

www.phschool.com

Section 1 Earth in Space

Discover Why Does Earth Have Day and Night?
Sharpen Your Skills Calculating
Skills Lab Reasons for the Seasons

Section 2 Phases, Eclipses, and Tides

Discover How Does the Moon Move?
Sharpen Your Skills Making Models
Skills Lab A "Moonth" of Phases

Integrating Technology 

Section 3 Rockets and Satellites

Discover How Do Rockets Work?
Try This Be a Rocket Scientist

Where's the Moon?

What a view! Though you would have to be in orbit around the moon to see this kind of Earthrise, you don't have to travel at all to see the moonrise from Earth. All you have to do is look in the right direction at the right time and you will see the moon rise in front of you!

In this chapter, you will explore relationships among Earth, the moon, and the sun. In your project, you will observe the position of the moon in the sky every day. These observations will show you the changing positions of Earth and the moon with respect to each other and to the sun.

Your Goal To observe the shape of the moon and its position in the sky every day for one month.

To complete the project you will

- observe and record every day the compass direction in which you see the moon and its height above the horizon
- use your observations to explain the phases of the moon
- develop rules you can use to predict where and when you might see the moon each day throughout a month

Get Started Begin by preparing an observation log. You will want to record the date and time of each observation, the direction and height of the moon, a sketch of its shape, and notes about the cloud cover or other conditions. You can also keep track of the time of moonrise each day.

Check Your Progress You'll be working on this project as you study this chapter. To keep your project on track, look for Check Your Progress boxes at the following points.

Section 1 Review, page 665: Make a map to help you determine the direction of the moon.

Section 2 Review, page 678: Observe the moon every day.

Section 4 Review, page 688: Look for patterns in your observations.

Wrap Up At the end of the chapter (page 691), you will present your observations of the moon using words, drawings, and graphs.

This amazing Earthrise above the moon's horizon was seen by astronaut Michael Collins in the *Apollo 11* moon orbiter *Columbia*.

Earth's Moon

Discover **Why Do Craters Look Different From Each Other?**

Sharpen Your Skills **Calculating**

SECTION 1

Earth in Space

DISCOVER ACTIVITY

Why Does Earth Have Day and Night?

1. Place a lamp with a bare bulb in the middle of a table to represent the sun. Put a globe at the end of the table about 1 meter away to represent Earth.
2. Turn the lamp on and darken the room. Which parts of the globe have light shining on them? Which parts are in shadow?
3. Find your location on the globe. Take about 5 seconds to turn the globe once. Notice when it is lit—day—at your location and when it is dark—night.

Think It Over

Making Models How does one complete turn of the globe represent one day? In this model, how many seconds represent one day? How could you use the model to represent a year?

GUIDE FOR READING

- What causes day and night?
- What causes the cycle of seasons on Earth?

Reading Tip **Before you read, preview the figures and captions in the section. List any terms that are not familiar to you. Then write their definitions as you read about them.**

Ancient Egyptian farmers eagerly awaited the annual spring flood of the Nile River. For thousands of years, their planting was ruled by it. As soon as the Nile's floodwaters withdrew, the farmers had to be ready to plow and plant their fields along the banks of the river. Because of this, the Egyptians wanted to predict when the flood would occur. Around 3000 B.C., people noticed that the bright star Sirius first became visible in the early morning sky every year shortly before the flood began. The Egyptians used this knowledge to predict each year's flood.

Egyptian farmers ▶

Rotation

N

Axis

S

Earth

Revolution

Sun

Earth

Figure 1 Earth rotates on its axis and revolves around the sun.
Applying Concepts What is one full rotation called? What is one complete revolution called?

Days and Years

The ancient Egyptians were among the first people to study the stars. The study of the moon, stars and other objects in space is called **astronomy.**

Ancient astronomers also studied the movements of the sun and the moon as they appeared to travel across the sky. It seemed to them as though Earth were standing still and the sun and moon were moving. Actually, the sun and moon seem to move across the sky each day mainly because Earth is rotating on its axis.

Rotation The imaginary line that passes through Earth's center and the North and South poles is called Earth's **axis.** The north end of the axis currently points toward a point in space near Polaris, the North Star. Earth's spinning on its axis is called its **rotation.** A point on the equator rotates at about 1,600 kilometers per hour. Even most commercial jet planes can't fly this fast!

Earth's rotation on its axis causes day and night. As Earth rotates eastward, the sun appears to move westward across the sky. It is day on the side of Earth facing the sun. As Earth continues to turn to the east, the sun appears to set in the west. Sunlight can't reach the side of Earth facing away from the sun, so it is night there. It takes Earth about 24 hours to rotate once on its axis. As you know, each 24-hour cycle of day and night is called a day.

Revolution In addition to rotating on its axis, Earth travels around the sun. The movement of one object around another object is called **revolution.** One complete revolution around the sun is called a year. Earth's path as it revolves around the sun is called its **orbit.** As it travels around the sun, Earth's orbit is not quite a circle. It is a slightly flattened circle, or oval shape.

☑ *Checkpoint Why do the sun and moon seem to move each day?*

Calculating

ACTIVITY

Earth moves at a speed of about 30 km/sec as it travels around the sun. What distance, in kilometers, does Earth travel in a minute? An hour? A day? A year?

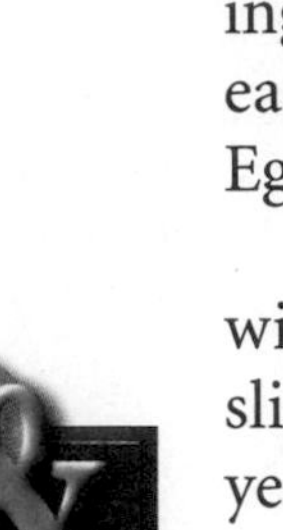

Calendars The Egyptian astronomers counted the number of days between each first appearance of the star Sirius in the morning sky. In this way, they found that there were about 365 days in each year. By dividing the year into 365 days, the ancient Egyptians had created one of the first calendars.

People of many different cultures have struggled to come up with workable calendars. Earth's orbit around the sun takes slightly more than 365 days—actually about $365\frac{1}{4}$ days. Four years of about $365\frac{1}{4}$ days each can be approximated by taking 3 years of 365 days and a fourth year of 366 days. You know this fourth year as a "leap year." During a leap year, an extra day is

Tracking the Cycle of the Year

For thousands of years, people have used observations of the sky to keep track of the time of year.

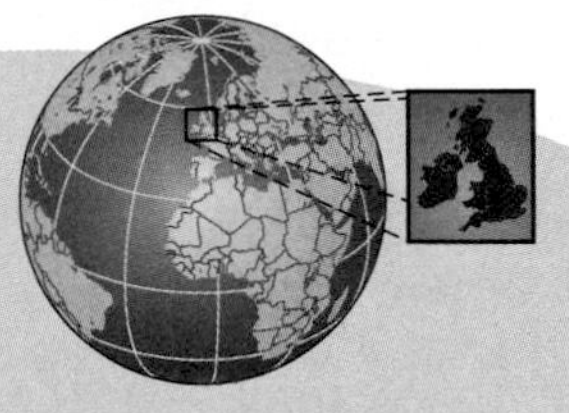

1500 B.C.

British Isles

Ancient peoples complete Stonehenge, a monument with giant stones that mark the directions in which the sun rises and sets on the longest day of the year.

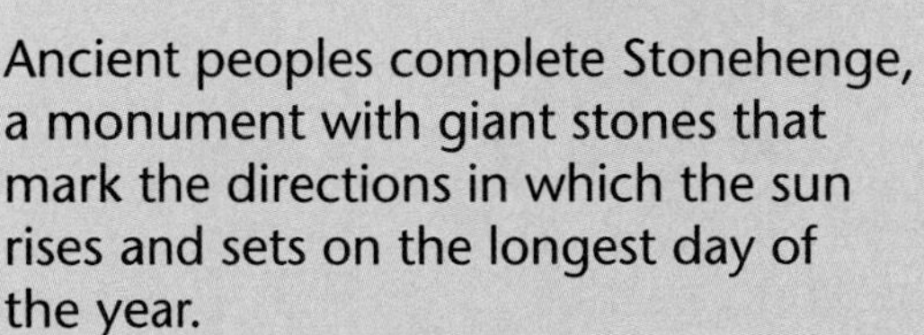

1500 B.C. — **900 B.C.** — **300 B.C.**

1300 B.C.

China

During the Shang dynasty, Chinese astronomers made detailed observations of the sun, planets, and other objects they saw in the night sky. Chinese astronomers calculated that the length of a year is 365.25 days.

300 B.C.

Egypt

Astronomers in Alexandria, Egypt, learned to use an instrument called an astrolabe. Astrolabes were used to find the positions of stars and planets.

added to February, giving it 29 days instead of its usual 28.

Dividing the year into smaller parts was difficult also. Early people used moon cycles as a sort of calendar. The time between one full moon and the next one is about $29\frac{1}{2}$ days. A year of 12 of these "moonths" only adds up to 354 days. The ancient Egyptians worked out a calendar that had 12 months of 30 days each, with an extra 5 days that were not part of any month. The Romans borrowed this calendar and made changes to it. With more changes, it eventually became the calendar we know: 11 months having 30 or 31 days each, plus one month (February) having 28 or 29 days.

In Your Journal

Research one of the accomplishments discussed in the time line. Write a dialogue in which two people from the culture that made the discovery or observation discuss its importance in their lives.

A.D. 1450

Wyoming

Wyoming

The Big Horn Medicine Wheel was built by Native Americans. Individual stones are aligned with the rising and setting sun and several bright stars. The rising of these specific stars may have indicated to people when it was time to move south for the winter.

A.D. 300 **A.D. 900** **A.D. 1500**

A.D. 900

Mexico

The Mayas studied the movement of the sun, the moon, and the planet Venus. They had two different calendars, one with 365 days for everyday use and the other with 260 days for religious uses. These calendars combined to make a 52-year cycle. The Mayas were able to predict astronomical events 3,000 years into the future.

Figure 2 It is warm near the equator because sunlight hits Earth's surface directly and is less spread out. ***Interpreting Diagrams*** *Why is it colder near the poles?*

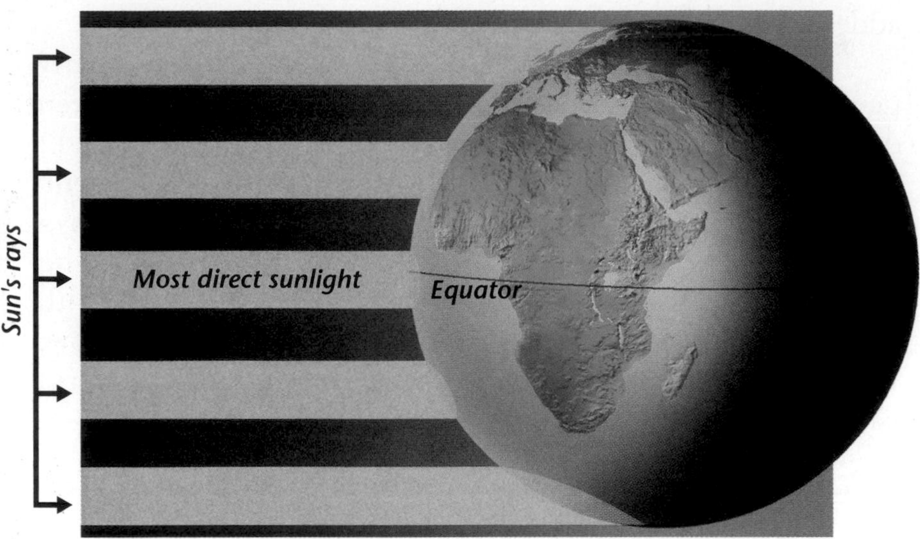

Seasons on Earth

Most places outside the tropics have four distinct seasons: winter, spring, summer, and autumn. But there are great differences in temperature from place to place. For instance, it is warmer near the equator than near the poles. Why is this so?

How Sunlight Hits Earth Figure 2 shows how sunlight hits Earth's surface. Notice that at the equator, sunlight hits Earth's surface directly. Closer to the poles, sunlight hits Earth's surface at an angle. Near the poles, energy from the sun is spread out over a greater area. That is why it is warmer near the equator than near the poles.

Earth's Tilted Axis If Earth's axis were straight up and down relative to the sun, as it appears in Figure 2, temperatures would remain fairly constant year-round. There would be no seasons. **Earth has seasons because its axis is tilted as it moves around the sun.**

Look at Earth's position in space in *Exploring the Seasons* on the next page. Notice that Earth's axis is tilted at an angle of 23.5° from the vertical. As Earth revolves around the sun, its axis is tilted away from the sun for part of the year and toward the sun for part of the year.

When the north end of Earth's axis is tilted toward the sun, the Northern Hemisphere has summer. At the same time, the south end of Earth's axis is tilted away from the sun. As a result, the Southern Hemisphere has winter.

Summer and winter are not affected by changes in Earth's distance from the sun. In fact, when the Northern Hemisphere is having summer, Earth is actually at its greatest distance from the sun.

Math TOOLBOX

Angles

An angle is formed when two lines meet at a point. Angles are measured in degrees (symbol °). A full circle has 360 degrees.

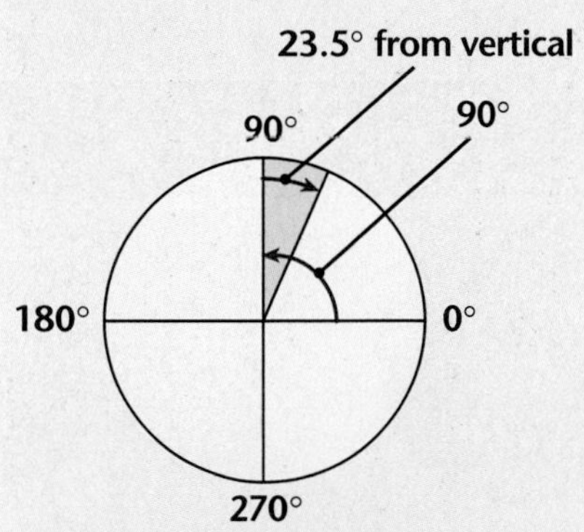

Earth's axis is tilted at an angle of 23.5° from the vertical. When the sun is directly overhead at noon near the equator, its angle from the horizon is 90°. What fraction of a circle is this?

EXPLORING the Seasons

The yearly cycle of the seasons is caused by the tilt of Earth's axis as it revolves around the sun.

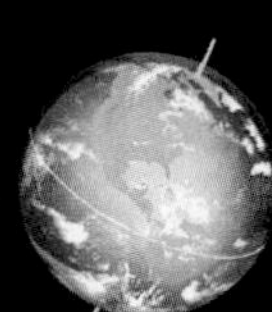
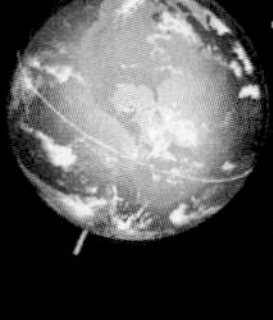

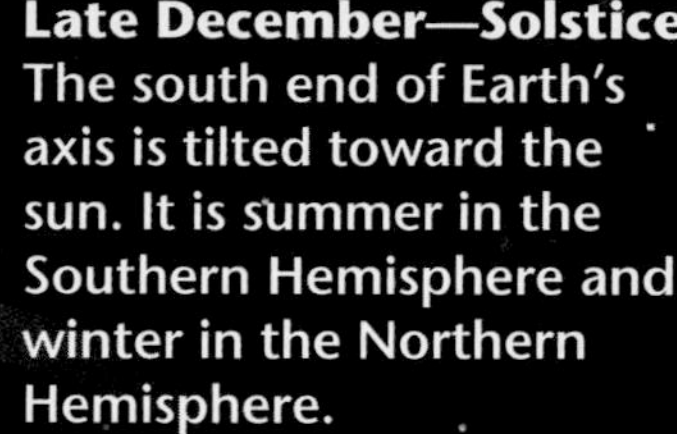

Late December—Solstice
The south end of Earth's axis is tilted toward the sun. It is summer in the Southern Hemisphere and winter in the Northern Hemisphere.

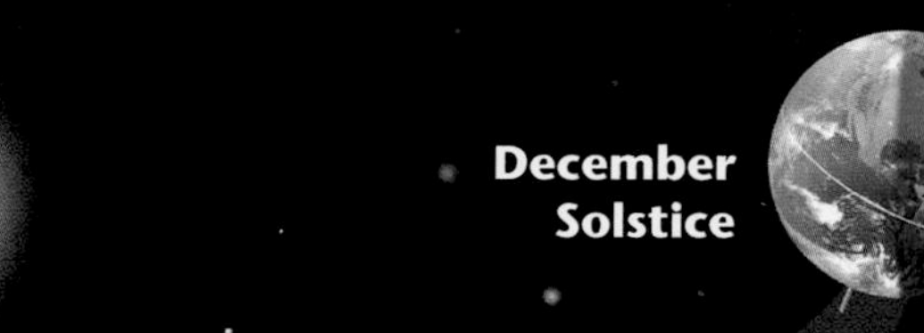

Late June—Solstice
The north end of Earth's axis is tilted toward the sun. It is summer in the Northern Hemisphere and winter in the Southern Hemisphere.

Late March and Late September—Equinoxes
Neither end of Earth's axis is tilted toward the sun. Both hemispheres receive the same amount of energy.

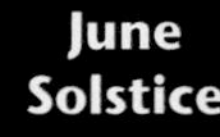

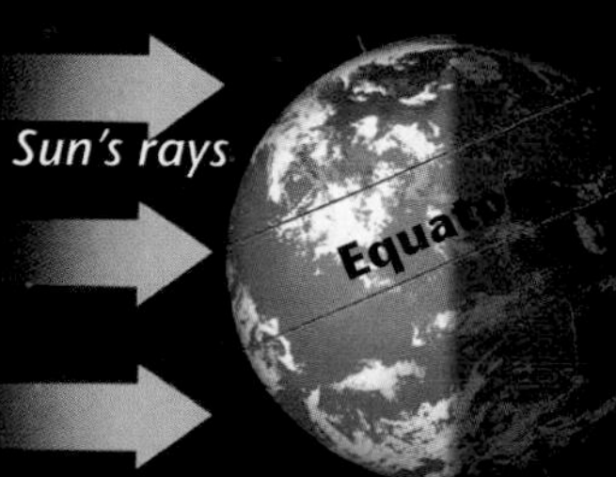

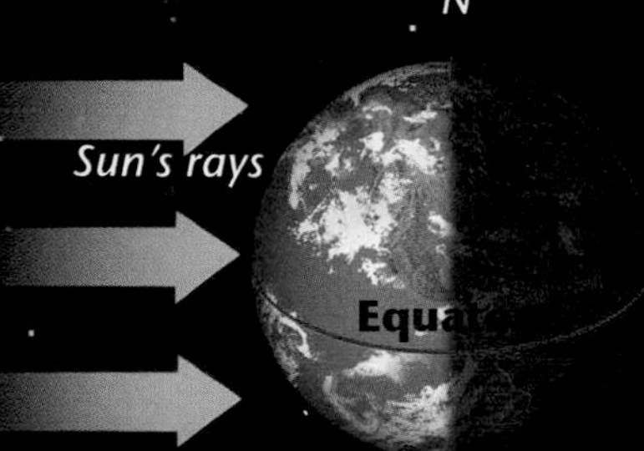

Earth in June In June, the north end of Earth's axis is tilted toward the sun. The noon sun is directly overhead at 23.5° north latitude. **Latitude** is a measurement of distance from the equator, expressed in degrees north or south. (The equator has latitude 0° and the North Pole has latitude 90° north.)

The hemisphere that is tilted toward the sun also has more hours of daylight than the hemisphere that is tilted away from the sun. The combination of direct rays and more hours of sunlight heats the surface more than at any other time of the year. It is summer in the Northern Hemisphere.

At the same time, for any place on Earth south of the equator, the sun's energy is spread over a large area. There are also fewer hours of daylight. The combination of indirect rays and fewer hours of sunlight heats Earth's surface less than at any other time of the year. It is winter in the Southern Hemisphere.

Earth in December Look again at *Exploring the Seasons.* Around December 21, the noon sun is overhead at 23.5° south latitude. People in the Southern Hemisphere receive the most direct sunlight, so it is summer there. At the same time, the sun's rays in the Northern Hemisphere are indirect and there are fewer hours of daylight. So it is winter in the Northern Hemisphere.

Both June and December On two days each year, the noon sun is overhead at either 23.5° south or 23.5° north. Each of these days is known as a **solstice** (SAHL stis). The day when the noon sun is overhead at 23.5° south is the winter solstice in the Northern Hemisphere. It is the summer solstice in the Southern Hemisphere. This solstice occurs around December 21 each year, and is the shortest day of the year in the Northern Hemisphere. At

Figure 3 Spring is the season between the vernal equinox and the summer solstice. The warming temperatures of spring make it the best time to plant flowers like these pansies.

the same time, it is close to the longest day of the year in the Southern Hemisphere.

Similarly, around June 21, the noon sun is overhead at 23.5° north. This is the summer solstice in the Northern Hemisphere and the winter solstice in the Southern Hemisphere.

Earth in March and September Halfway between the solstices, neither hemisphere is tilted toward or away from the sun. This situation only occurs on two days of the year. On these days, the noon sun is directly overhead at the equator.

Each of these days is known as an **equinox,** which means "equal night." During an equinox, the lengths of nighttime and daytime are about the same. The **vernal equinox,** or spring equinox, occurs around March 21, and marks the beginning of spring in the Northern Hemisphere. The **autumnal equinox** occurs around September 23. It marks the beginning of fall in the Northern Hemisphere.

Figure 4 This hungry bear has spent the long winter in a dormant state in a cave in Alaska. ***Applying Concepts*** *Why didn't this bear remain active all winter?*

INTEGRATING LIFE SCIENCE In much of the United States, seasonal changes affect living things. In spring and summer, the sun shines for more hours each day and is higher in the sky. The warmer days allow many plants to begin growing leaves and flowers. Because plants grow more, animals that feed on the plants, from tiny insects to large deer, get more food.

In the fall, the nights get longer, signaling the plants to stop growing and some plants to lose their leaves. With less food available, black bears and some other animals go into a dormant state in which they use very little energy. Others, like many songbirds and waterfowl, travel to warmer climates where food is still available.

Section 1 Review

1. Explain the process that causes day and night.
2. What two factors cause the cycle of the seasons?
3. Compare rotation and revolution.
4. What do the words *solstice* and *equinox* mean? How are they related to the position of Earth's axis?
5. **Thinking Critically Relating Cause and Effect** Are changes in the distance between Earth and the sun important in causing the cycle of the seasons? Explain.

Check Your Progress

CHAPTER PROJECT 20

Begin recording your daily observations of the moon. Sketch a map of the site from which you will be making observations. Which way is north? East? South? West? Each night, observe and record the moon's direction. You should also estimate the moon's altitude, or height in degrees from the horizon. You can do this by making a fist and holding it at arm's length. One fist above the horizon is 10°, two fists are 20°, and so on.

Skills Lab

Observing

REASONS FOR THE SEASONS

In this lab, you will use an Earth-sun model to make observations about factors that contribute to the seasons.

Problem

What effect does the tilt of Earth's axis have on the heat and light received by Earth as it revolves around the sun?

Materials (per pair of students)

books, flashlight, paper, pencil, protractor, toothpick

acetate sheet with thick grid lines drawn on it

plastic foam ball marked with poles and equator

Procedure

1. Make a pile of books about 15 cm high.
2. Tape the acetate sheet to the head of the flashlight. Place the flashlight on the pile of books.
3. Carefully push a pencil into the South Pole of the plastic foam ball, which represents Earth.
4. Use the protractor to measure a 23.5° tilt of the axis of your Earth away from your "flashlight sun," as shown in the first diagram. This represents winter.
5. Hold the pencil so that Earth is steady at this 23.5° angle and about 15 cm from the flashlight head. Turn the flashlight on. Dim the room lights.
6. The squares on the acetate should show up on your model Earth. Move the ball closer if necessary or dim the room lights more. Observe and record the shape of the squares at the equator and at the poles.
7. Carefully stick the toothpick straight into your model Earth about halfway between the equator and the North Pole. Observe and record the length of the shadow.
8. Without changing the tilt, turn the pencil to rotate the model Earth once on its axis. Observe and record how the shadow of the toothpick changes.
9. Tilt your model Earth 23.5° toward the flashlight, as shown in the second diagram. This is summer. Observe and record the shape of the squares at the equator and at the poles. Observe how the toothpick's shadow changes.
10. Rotate the model Earth and note the shadow pattern.

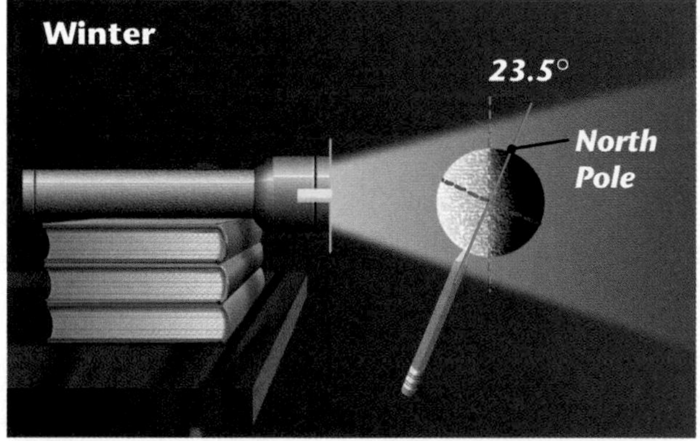

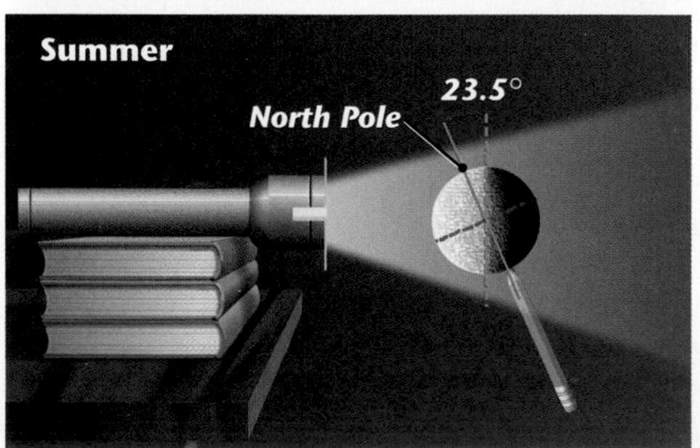

Analyze and Conclude

1. When it is winter in the Northern Hemisphere, which areas on Earth get the most concentrated amount of light? Which areas get the most concentrated light when it is summer in the Northern Hemisphere?
2. Compare your observations of how the light hits the area halfway between the equator and the North Pole during winter (Step 6) and during summer (Step 9).
3. If the squares projected on the ball from the acetate become larger, what can you conclude about the amount of heat distributed in each square?
4. According to your observations, which areas on Earth are consistently coolest? Which areas are consistently warmest? Why?
5. What time of year will the toothpick's shadow be longest? When will the shadow be shortest?
6. How are the amounts of heat and light received in a square related to the angle of the sun's rays?
7. **Think About It** How can you use your observations of an Earth-sun model to explain what causes the seasons?

More to Explore

You can measure how directly light from the sun hits Earth's surface by making a shadow stick. You need a stick or pole about 1 m long. With the help of your teacher, push the stick partway into the ground where it will not be disturbed. Make sure the stick stays vertical. At noon on the first day of every month, measure the length of the stick's shadow. The shorter the shadow, the more directly the sun's rays are hitting Earth. At what time of the year are the shadows longest? Shortest? How do your observations help explain the seasons?

SECTION 2 Phases, Eclipses, and Tides

DISCOVER

How Does the Moon Move?

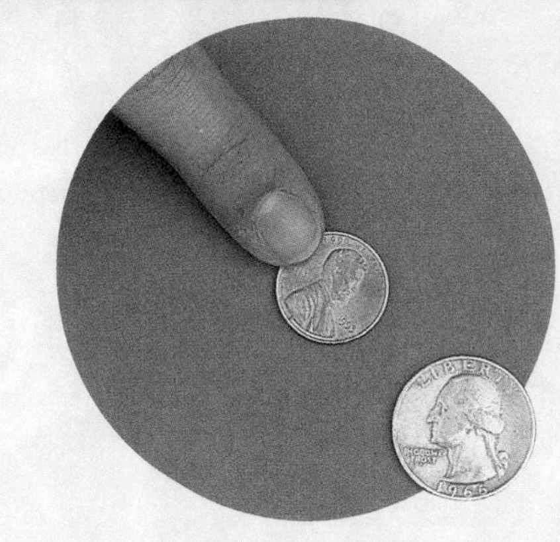

1. Put a quarter flat on your desk to represent Earth. Use a penny flat on your desk to represent the moon.
2. One side of the moon always faces Earth. Move the moon through one revolution around Earth, keeping Lincoln's face always looking at Earth. How many times did the penny make one complete rotation?

Think It Over

Inferring From the point of view of someone on Earth, does the moon seem to rotate? Explain your answer.

GUIDE FOR READING

- What causes the phases of the moon?
- What causes solar and lunar eclipses?
- What causes the tides?

Reading Tip As you read, write a sentence to describe what causes each of the following: phases, solar eclipses, lunar eclipses, tides.

The moon is Earth's closest neighbor in space—much closer than any planet. In fact, the average distance from Earth to the moon is only about 30 times Earth's diameter. Even so, the moon is quite far away. On average, the moon is 384,400 kilometers from Earth. If there were a highway to the moon and you could travel at 100 kilometers per hour, it would take you more than five months to get there.

The moon moves in space just as Earth does. As the moon revolves around Earth and Earth revolves around the sun, the relative positions of the moon, Earth, and sun change. **The positions of the moon, Earth, and the sun cause the phases of the moon, eclipses, and tides.**

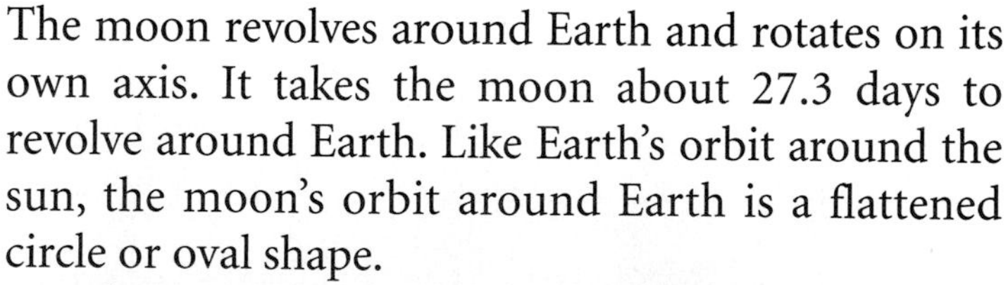

Motions of the Moon

The moon revolves around Earth and rotates on its own axis. It takes the moon about 27.3 days to revolve around Earth. Like Earth's orbit around the sun, the moon's orbit around Earth is a flattened circle or oval shape.

The moon rotates slowly on its own axis once every 27.3 days. Because the moon also revolves around Earth every 27.3 days, a "day" and a "year" on the moon are the same length. As you saw if you

◀ Crescent moon over Fire Island, New York

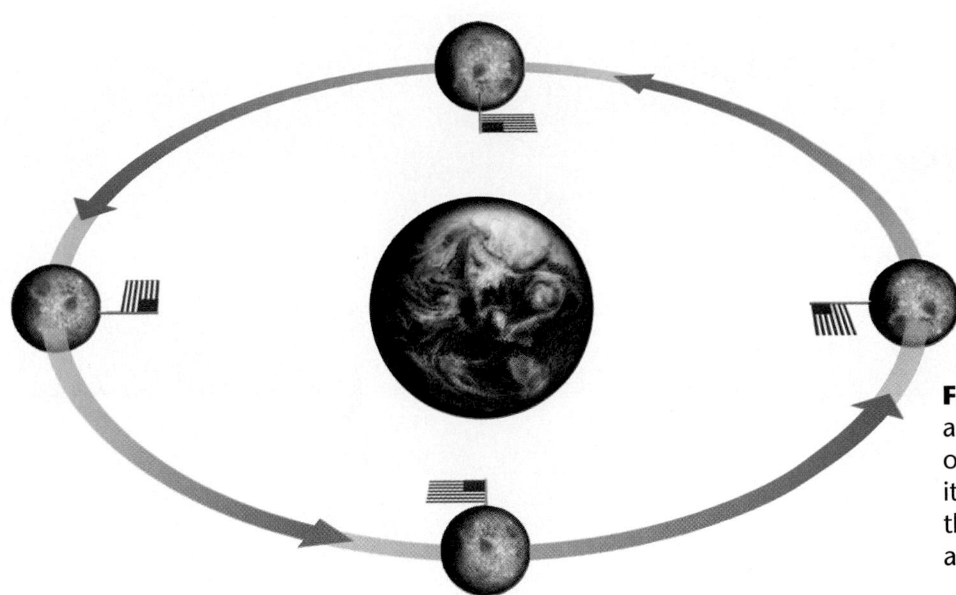

Figure 5 The moon revolves around Earth in the same amount of time the moon takes to rotate on its axis. As a result, the near side of the moon (shown with a flag) always faces Earth.

tried the Discover activity, the same side of the moon, the "near side," always faces Earth. The "far side" of the moon always faces away from Earth, so you never see it from Earth.

***Checkpoint** How many days does it take the moon to revolve once around Earth?*

Phases of the Moon

On a clear night when the moon is full, the bright moonlight can keep you awake. But the moon does not produce the light you see. Instead, it reflects light from the sun. Imagine taking a flashlight into a dark room. If you were to shine the flashlight on a chair, you would see the chair because the light from your flashlight would bounce, or reflect, off the chair. In the same way that the chair wouldn't shine by itself, the moon doesn't give off light by itself. You see the moon because sunlight reflects off it.

When you see the moon in the sky, sometimes it appears round. Other times you see only a thin sliver, or crescent. The different shapes of the moon you see from Earth are called **phases.** The moon goes through its whole set of phases each time it revolves around Earth, that is, about once a month.

What Causes Phases? Phases are caused by changes in the relative positions of the moon, Earth, and the sun. Because the sun lights the moon, half the moon is almost always in sunlight. However, since the moon revolves around Earth, you see the moon from different angles. The half of the moon that faces Earth is not always the half that is sunlit. **The phase of the moon you see depends on how much of the sunlit side of the moon faces Earth.** To understand the changing phases, refer to *Exploring Phases of the Moon* on the next page.

Social Studies CONNECTION

Before there was artificial lighting, the phases of the moon were important in planning activities. For example, the full moon nearest the autumnal equinox is called the harvest moon, and the following full moon is called the hunter's moon.

In Your Journal

Find out about an event that is determined by the phases of the moon, such as the Jewish Passover, the Christian Easter, or the Islamic fast of Ramadan. How is the date of the event calculated?

EXPLORING *Phases of the Moon*

The diagram in the center shows a view of Earth and the moon phases from above. The sun is shining from the right. The outer ring of photos shows the different amounts of the sunlit side of the moon that an observer on Earth sees as the moon revolves around Earth.

First Quarter
You see half of the lighted side of the moon.

Waxing Crescent
You see more and more of the lighted side of the moon. This is called a waxing crescent moon.

Waxing Gibbous
The moon continues to wax. The moon is called gibbous.

Full Moon
You see the whole lighted side of the moon.

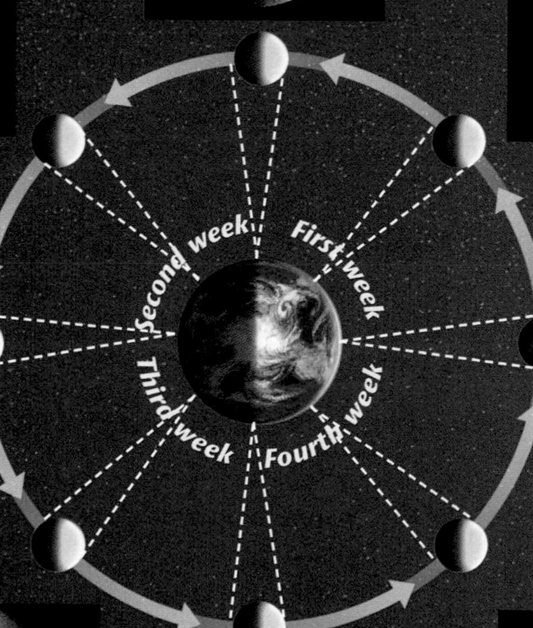

New Moon
The sun lights the side of the moon facing away from Earth. The side of the moon that faces Earth is dark.

Waning Gibbous
The fraction of the lighted side of the moon that you see gets smaller each day.

Third Quarter
You can see half of the moon's lighted side.

Waning Crescent
You see a crescent again.

The Cycle of the Phases During the new moon, the side of the moon facing Earth is not lit. As the moon revolves around Earth, you see more and more of the lighted side of the moon every day, until the side of the moon you see is fully lit. As the moon continues in its orbit, you see less and less of the lighted side of the moon. About 29.5 days after the last new moon, the cycle is complete, and you see a new moon again.

☑ ***Checkpoint*** *Since the moon does not produce light, how can you see it?*

Eclipses

What would you think if you were walking home from school on a sunny afternoon and the sun began to disappear? Would you be frightened? On rare occasions, the moon completely blocks the sun. The sky grows as dark as night even in the middle of a clear day. The air gets cool and the sky becomes an eerie color. If you don't know what is happening, you can become very frightened.

The moon doesn't usually go directly between Earth and the sun or directly behind Earth. As Figure 6 shows, the moon's orbit around Earth is slightly tilted with respect to Earth's orbit around the sun. As a result, in most months the moon revolves completely around Earth without the moon moving into Earth's shadow or the moon's shadow hitting Earth.

When the moon's shadow hits Earth or Earth's shadow hits the moon, an eclipse occurs. An **eclipse** (ih KLIPS) occurs when an object in space comes between the sun and a third object, and casts a shadow on that object. There are two types of eclipses: solar eclipses and lunar eclipses. (The words *solar* and *lunar* come from the Latin words for "sun" and "moon.")

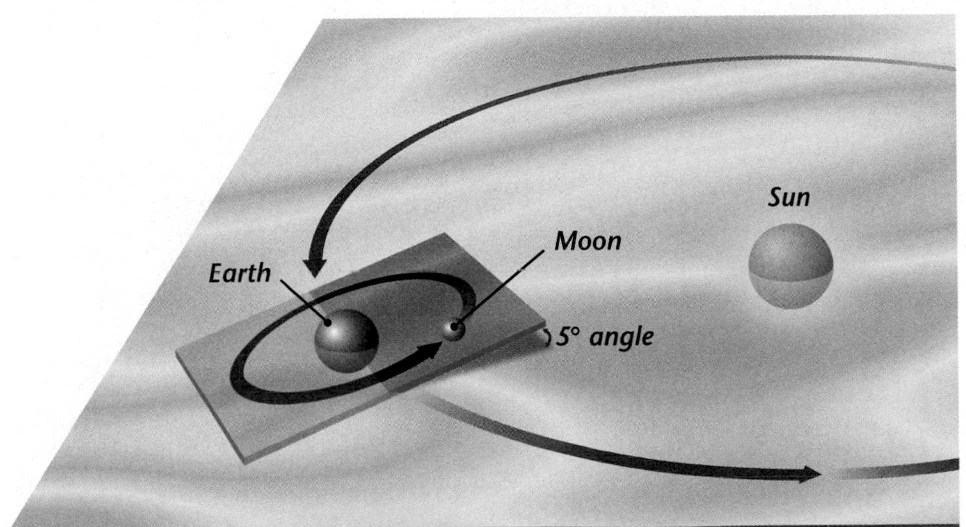

Figure 6 The moon's orbit is tilted with respect to Earth's orbit. So the moon rarely goes directly between Earth and the sun. ***Interpreting Diagrams*** *How large is the angle between Earth's orbit and the moon's orbit?*

Sharpen your Skills

Making Models

ACTIVITY

Here is how you can draw a scale model of a solar eclipse. The moon's diameter is about one fourth Earth's diameter. The distance from Earth to the moon is about 30 times Earth's diameter. Make a scale drawing of the moon, Earth, and the distance between them. (*Hint:* Draw Earth 1 cm in diameter in one corner of the paper.) From the edges of the moon, draw and shade in a triangle just touching Earth to show the moon's umbra during a solar eclipse.

Solar Eclipses

During a new moon, the moon is almost exactly between Earth and the sun. But most months, as you have seen, the moon travels a little above or below the sun in the sky. A **solar eclipse** occurs when the moon passes between Earth and the sun, blocking the sunlight from reaching Earth. The moon's shadow then hits Earth, as shown in Figure 7. So a solar eclipse is really just a new moon in which the moon blocks your view of the sun.

Total Solar Eclipses The darkest part of the moon's shadow, the **umbra** (UM bruh), is cone-shaped. From any point in the umbra, light from the sun is completely blocked by the moon. The moon's umbra happens to be long enough so that the point of the cone can just reach a small part of Earth's surface. Only the people within the umbra experience a total solar eclipse. During a total solar eclipse, the sky is dark. You can see the stars and the solar corona, which is the faint outer atmosphere of the sun.

Partial Solar Eclipses In Figure 7, you can see that the moon casts another shadow that is less dark than the umbra. In this larger part of the shadow, called the **penumbra** (pih NUM bruh), part of the sun is visible from Earth. During a solar eclipse, people in the penumbra see only a partial eclipse. Since part of the sun remains visible, it is not safe to look directly at the sun during a partial solar eclipse (just as you wouldn't look directly at the sun at any other time).

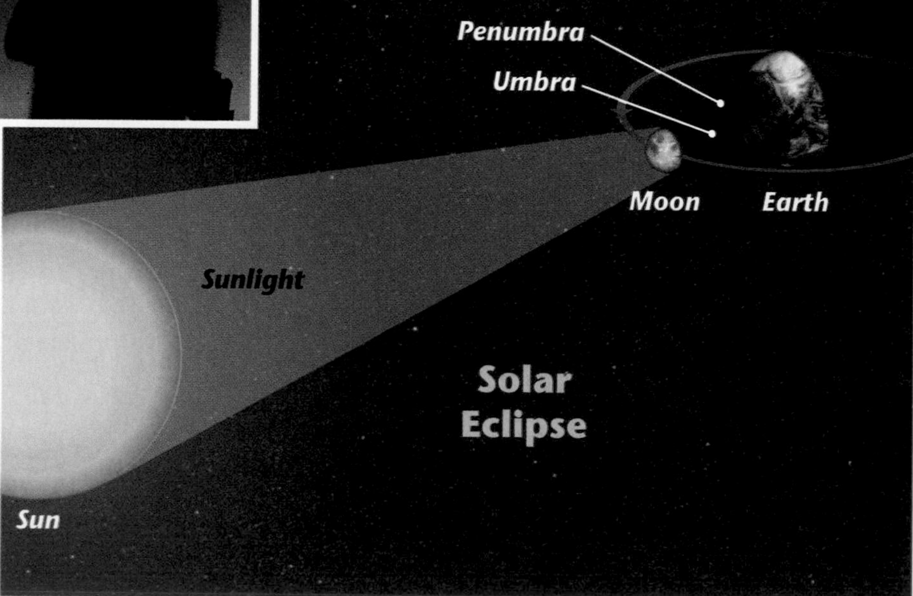

Figure 7 During a solar eclipse, right, the moon blocks light from the sun, preventing the light from reaching Earth's surface. The solar corona surrounding the dark disk of the moon, above, is visible during a solar eclipse.

Figure 8 **A.** During a lunar eclipse, Earth blocks sunlight from reaching the moon's surface. **B.** This photo of the moon was taken during a total lunar eclipse. **C.** This photo was taken during a partial lunar eclipse. ***Interpreting Diagrams*** *What is the difference between Earth's umbra and penumbra?*

Lunar Eclipses

During most months, the moon goes near Earth's shadow but not quite into it. A **lunar eclipse** occurs at a full moon when Earth is directly between the moon and the sun. You can see a lunar eclipse in Figure 8. During a lunar eclipse, Earth blocks sunlight from reaching the moon. The moon is then in Earth's shadow and looks dark from Earth. Because the moon is closest to Earth's shadow during the full moon, lunar eclipses occur only at full moon.

Total Lunar Eclipses Like the moon's shadow, Earth's shadow has an umbra and a penumbra. When the moon is in Earth's umbra, you see a total lunar eclipse. You can see Earth's shadow on the moon before and after the total part of a lunar eclipse.

Unlike a solar eclipse, a lunar eclipse can be seen anywhere on Earth that the moon is visible. So you are more likely to see a total lunar eclipse than a total solar eclipse.

Partial Lunar Eclipses For most lunar eclipses, Earth, the moon, and the sun are not quite in line, and a partial lunar eclipse results. A partial lunar eclipse occurs when the moon passes partly into the umbra of Earth's shadow. The edge of the umbra appears blurry, and you can watch it pass across the moon for two or three hours.

☑ ***Checkpoint*** *Why do lunar eclipses occur only at full moon?*

Making Models

A "Moonth" of Phases

In this lab, you will use a model of the Earth-moon-sun system to explore how the phases of the moon occur.

Problem

What causes the phases of the moon?

Materials

floor lamp with 150-watt bulb
pencils
plastic foam balls

Procedure

1. Place a lamp in the center of the room. Remove the lampshade.
2. Close the doors and shades to darken the room, and switch on the lamp.
3. Carefully stick the point of a pencil into the plastic foam ball so that the pencil can be used as a "handle."
4. Draw 8 circles on a sheet of paper. Number them 1–8.
5. Have your partner hold the plastic foam ball at arm's length in front and slightly above his or her head so that the ball is between him or her and the lamp. **CAUTION:** *Do not look directly at the bulb.*
6. The ball should be about 1 to 1.5 m away from the lamp. Adjust the distance between the ball and the lamp so that the light shines brightly on the ball.
7. Stand directly behind your partner and observe what part of the ball facing you is lit by the lamp. If light is visible on the ball, draw the shape of the lighted part of the ball in the first circle.
8. Have your partner turn 45° to the left while keeping the ball in front and at arm's length.
9. Repeat Step 7. Be sure you are standing directly behind your partner.
10. Repeat Steps 8 and 9 six more times until your partner is facing the lamp again. See the photograph for the 8 positions.
11. Change places and repeat Steps 4–10.

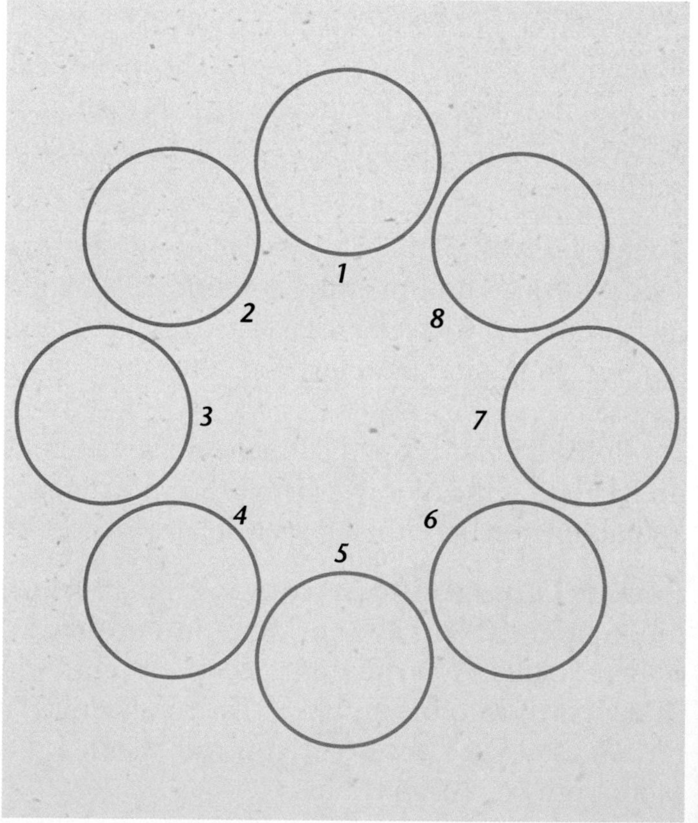

Analyze and Conclude

1. In your model, what represents Earth? The sun? The moon?
2. Refer back to your 8 circles. How much of the lighted part of the ball did you see when facing the lamp?
3. Label your drawings with the names of the phases of the moon. Which drawing represents a full moon? A new moon? Which represents a waxing crescent? A waning crescent?
4. How much of the lighted part of the ball did you see after each turn?
5. Whether you could see it or not, how much of the ball's surface was always lit by the lamp? Was the darkness of the new moon caused by an eclipse? Explain your answer.
6. **Think It Over** How did making a model help you understand the phases of the moon? What are some disadvantages of using models? What is another way to make a model to represent the moon's phases?

More to Explore

Design a model to show a lunar eclipse and a solar eclipse. What objects would you use for Earth, the sun, and the moon? Use the model to demonstrate why there isn't an eclipse every full moon and new moon.

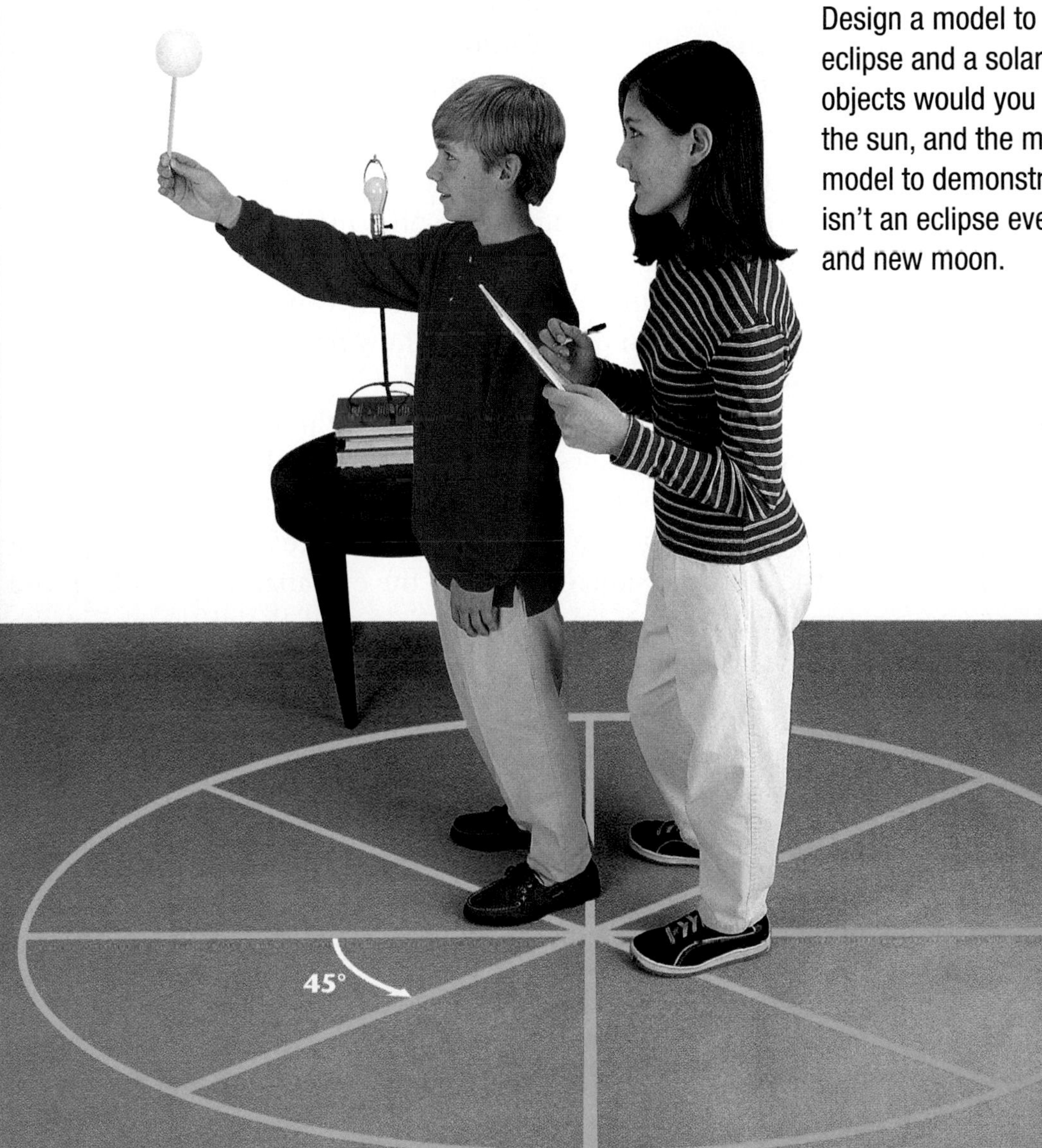

Figure 9 The Hopewell Rocks in New Brunswick, Canada, are partly covered at high tide. At low tide, people can walk along the beach between the rocks. ***Predicting*** *What would happen if these people stayed on the beach too long?*

Tides

Have you ever built a sand castle at an ocean beach? Was it washed away by the rising water? People who spend time near the ocean see the effects of **tides,** the rise and fall of water, every 12.5 hours or so. The water rises for about six hours, then falls for about six hours, in a regular cycle.

What Causes Tides? The force of **gravity** pulls the moon and Earth (including the water on Earth's surface) toward each other. The force of gravity between two objects depends on the masses of the objects and the distance between them. **Tides occur mainly because of differences in how much the moon pulls on different parts of Earth.**

As Earth rotates, the moon's gravity pulls water toward the point on Earth's surface closest to the moon. If that were the only cause, there would be only one high tide at a time, at the point on Earth closest to the moon. Actually, there is a second high tide on the opposite side of Earth, so the explanation must be more complex. The two tides occur because of the difference in the force of gravity from one place to another.

High Tides Look at Figure 10. The force of the moon's gravity at point A, which is closer to the moon, is stronger than the force of the moon's gravity on Earth as a whole. The water near point A is pulled toward the moon more strongly than is Earth as a whole. The water flows toward point A, and a high tide forms.

The force of the moon's gravity at point B, which is farther from the moon, is weaker than the force of the moon's gravity on Earth as a whole. Earth as a whole is pulled toward the moon more strongly than the water at point B, so the water is "left behind." Water flows toward point B, and a high tide occurs there too.

☑ ***Checkpoint*** *Why are there high tides on opposite sides of Earth at the same time?*

High and Low Tides

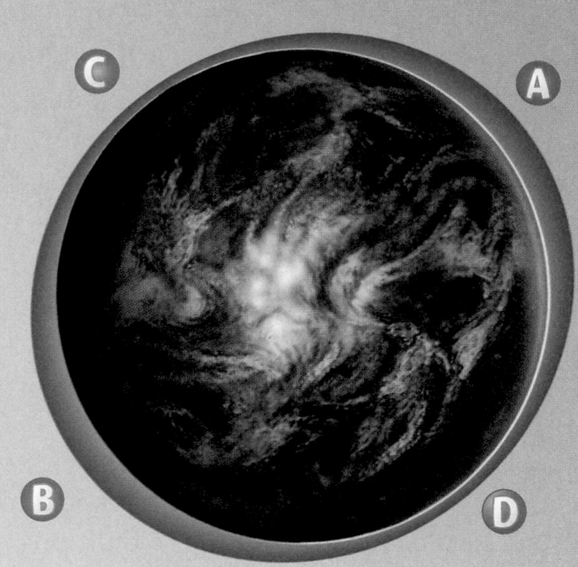

Point A
Closest to the moon, the moon pulls on water at Earth's surface more strongly than on Earth as a whole. Water flows toward Point A, creating a high tide.

Point B
Farthest away from the moon, the moon pulls less strongly on the water at Earth's surface than on Earth as a whole. Earth is pulled away from this point, leaving the water behind. The water that is left behind creates another high tide.

Points C and D
Low tides occur between the two high tides.

Figure 10 Tides occur mainly because of differences in the force of gravity between the moon and different parts of Earth.

The Tide Cycle Between points A and B, water flows away from points C and D, causing low tides to occur. Figure 10 shows that at any one time there are two places with high tides and two places with low tides on Earth. As Earth rotates, one high tide stays on the side of Earth facing the moon. The second high tide stays on the opposite side of Earth. Every location on Earth sweeps through those two high tides and two low tides in a 25-hour cycle.

Spring and Neap Tides The sun's gravity also pulls on Earth's waters. Once a month, at new moon, the sun, Earth, and moon are nearly in a line. The gravity of the sun and the moon pull in the same direction. The combined forces produce a tide with the greatest difference between low and high tide, called a **spring tide.**

What do you think happens at full moon? The moon and the sun are on opposite sides of Earth. However, since there are tides on both sides of Earth, a spring tide is also produced. It doesn't matter in which order the sun, Earth, and moon line up. So spring tides occur twice a month, at the new moon and at the full moon.

Also twice a month, during the moon's first quarter and last quarter phases, the line between Earth and the sun is at right angles to the line between Earth and the moon. The sun's pull is at right angles to the moon's. This arrangement produces a tide with the least difference between low and high tide, called a **neap tide.**

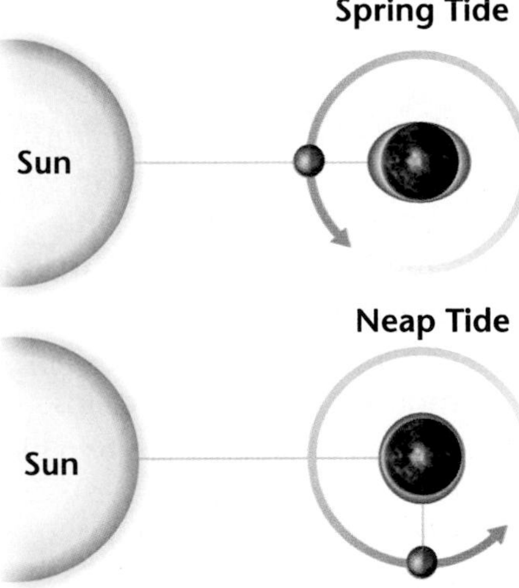

Figure 11 When Earth, the sun, and the moon are in a straight line (top), a spring tide occurs. When the moon is at a right angle to the sun (bottom), a neap tide occurs.

Figure 12 Purple sea stars feed on barnacles at low tide in an intertidal zone in Olympic National Park in Washington State. Both animals have adaptations for keeping moist and holding on that allow them to survive the ever-changing conditions of an intertidal zone.

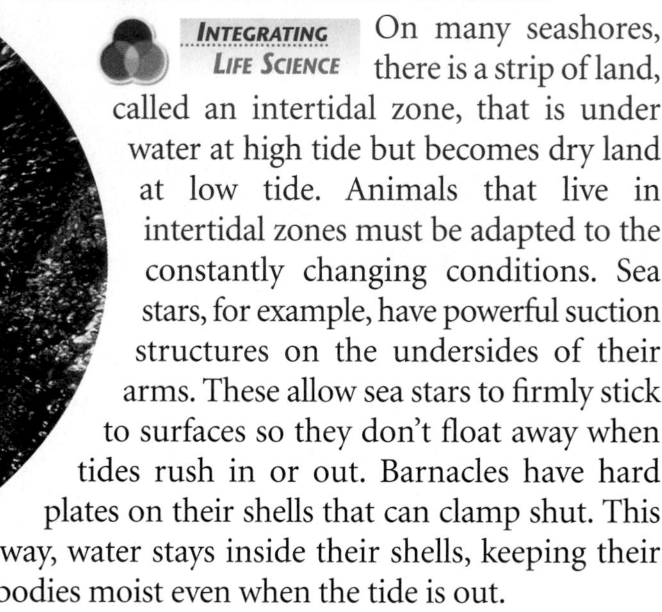

Local Tide Effects Not every place on Earth has two regular tides every day. The shapes of bays, inlets, and the ocean floor can affect the flow of water, so that the height and timing of the tides can vary even in places that are close to each other. Because low tides can expose rocks and make waters too shallow to navigate, it is very important for sailors to keep track of the tides. Even today, you sometimes read in the newspaper that a ship that had run aground at low tide was floated off on the next high tide.

Sometimes, the effects of ocean tides extend far up rivers. Water at the river's mouth flows upstream as the tide comes in. As the tide changes and goes out, the water flows downstream back into the ocean.

INTEGRATING LIFE SCIENCE On many seashores, there is a strip of land, called an intertidal zone, that is under water at high tide but becomes dry land at low tide. Animals that live in intertidal zones must be adapted to the constantly changing conditions. Sea stars, for example, have powerful suction structures on the undersides of their arms. These allow sea stars to firmly stick to surfaces so they don't float away when tides rush in or out. Barnacles have hard plates on their shells that can clamp shut. This way, water stays inside their shells, keeping their soft bodies moist even when the tide is out.

Section 2 Review

1. Why does the moon change its phases as the month progresses?
2. Describe the relative positions of Earth, the sun, and the moon during a solar eclipse and during a lunar eclipse.
3. Explain why there are two high tides and two low tides each day.
4. Why are a "day" and a "year" on the moon the same length?
5. **Thinking Critically Interpreting Diagrams** Make a diagram to show what phase the moon is in during a lunar eclipse.

CHAPTER PROJECT 20

Check Your Progress

Bring your log sheet to class so you can share your observations with classmates. Check the newspaper every day to find the times of moonrise and moonset and record this information. If you can, look for the moon at moonrise or moonset, even during daylight hours. Use your map to keep track of the direction in which you can see the moon.

 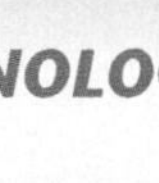

SECTION 3 Rockets and Satellites

DISCOVER ACTIVITY

How Do Rockets Work?

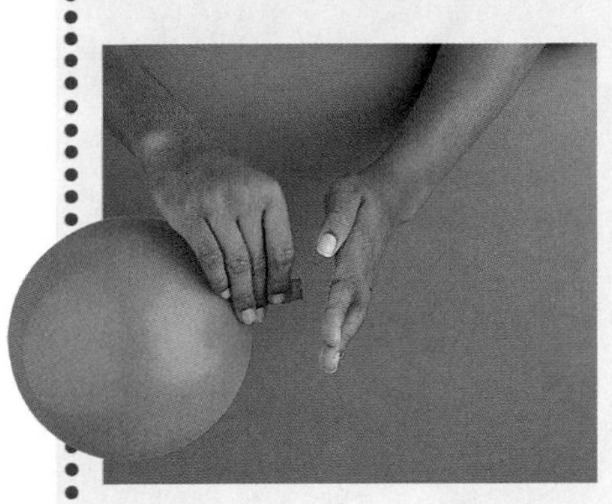

1. Put on your goggles. Blow up a balloon and hold its neck closed with your fingers.
2. Point the balloon toward an area where there are no people. Put your free hand behind the neck of the balloon, so the air will push against your hand. Let go of the balloon.
3. Repeat Steps 1 and 2 without your free hand behind the balloon.

Think It Over

Observing In which direction does the air rush out? In which direction does the balloon go? Does the balloon need to push against something in order to move? Explain your answer.

GUIDE FOR READING

- How do rockets travel in space?
- What are satellites and space stations used for?

Reading Tip Before you read, rewrite the headings in the section as *how, why,* or *what* questions. As you read, look for answers to those questions.

Curiosity about Earth's "neighborhood" in space has led to moon missions, space shuttle missions, space stations, and Mars missions. But without rockets, none of these accomplishments would have been possible.

How Rockets Work

A rocket works in much the way that a balloon is propelled through the air by releasing gas. **A rocket moves forward when gases expelled from the rear of the rocket push it in the opposite direction.** It's a basic law of physics that for every force, or action, there is an equal and opposite force, or reaction. For example, the force of the air going out the back of a balloon is an action force. An equal force, the reaction, pushes the balloon forward.

In a rocket, fuel is burned to make a hot gas. This hot gas is forced out of narrow nozzles in the back of the rocket, propelling the rocket forward.

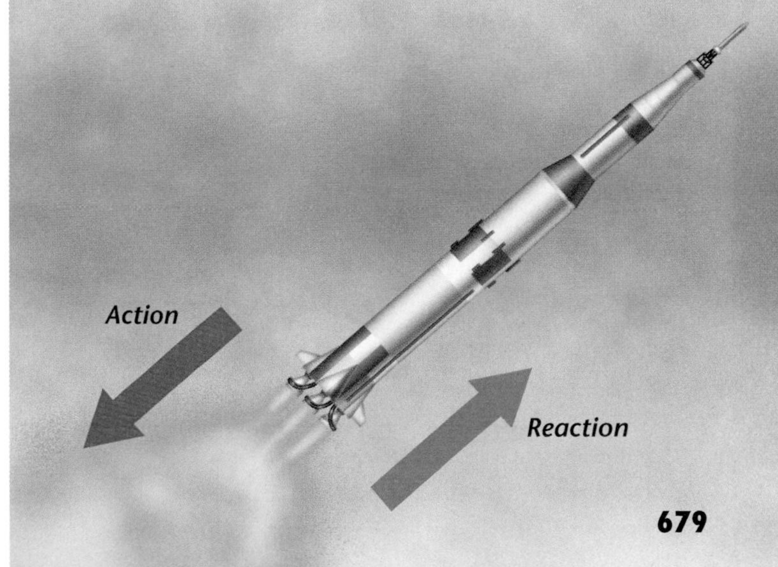

Figure 13 Hot gas is propelled out of the back of a rocket engine. The force of the gas in one direction (action) produces an opposing force (reaction) that propels the rocket forward.

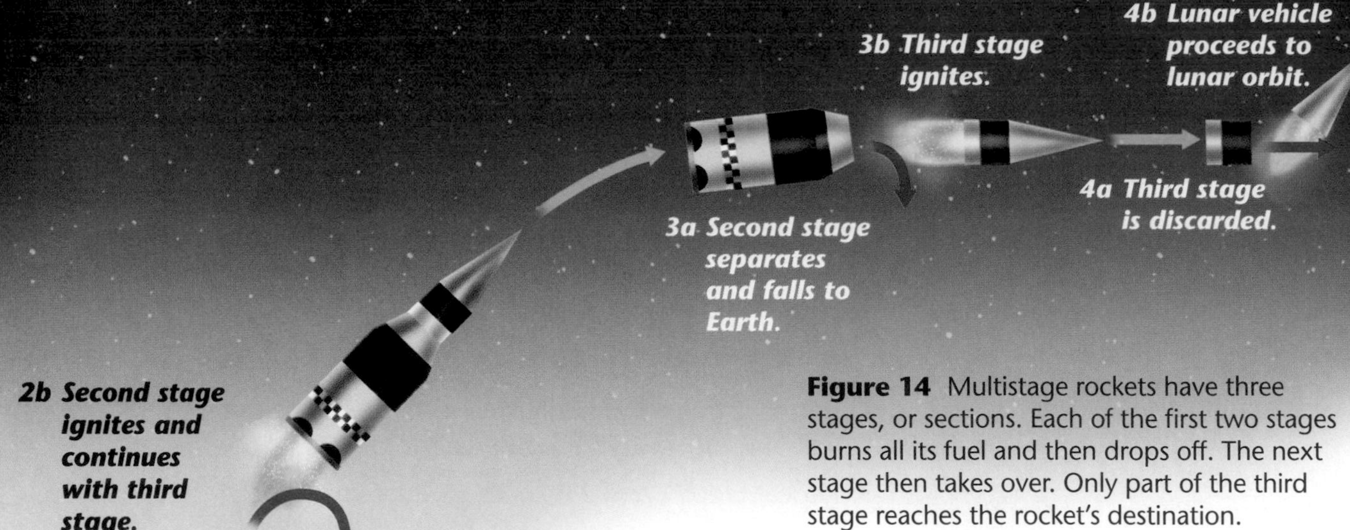

Figure 14 Multistage rockets have three stages, or sections. Each of the first two stages burns all its fuel and then drops off. The next stage then takes over. Only part of the third stage reaches the rocket's destination.

Multistage Rockets

Early rockets, built by the Chinese around the year 1000, used gunpowder as fuel. But gunpowder burns quickly and explosively. A rocket designed to travel out of Earth's atmosphere needs a different sort of fuel that burns slowly and continuously. The American scientist Robert H. Goddard experimented with liquid fuels in the 1920s. He showed that a liquid fuel can provide continuous power. Some solid fuels also burn slowly and continuously.

Another problem remained, however. A rocket can carry only so much fuel. Once the fuel is used up, the rocket falls back to Earth. In 1903, a Russian named Konstantin Tsiolkovsky came up with the idea of multistage rockets. As each stage, or section, of a rocket uses up its fuel, the empty fuel container drops off. Then the next stage ignites and continues up toward the rocket's destination.

The development of powerful multistage rockets in the 1950s and 1960s made it possible to send rockets to the moon and farther into space. Figure 14 shows a rocket similar to the Saturn V that carried the astronauts to the moon. You will learn more about the moon landings in Section 4.

Artificial Satellites

The world was astounded on October 4, 1957, when the Soviet Union launched the first artificial satellite into orbit around Earth. A **satellite** is any natural or artificial object that revolves around an object in space, just as the moon revolves around Earth. This satellite, *Sputnik 1,* revolved around Earth every 96 minutes. Three months later, the United States launched *Explorer 1* into orbit. On April 12, 1961, Yuri Gagarin, a Soviet cosmonaut, orbited Earth, becoming the first person in space.

Since 1957, thousands of artificial satellites, including space stations, have been launched into orbit. **Satellites and space stations are used for communications, navigation, collecting weather data, and research.**

Satellites Artificial satellites are used to relay telephone calls, to measure Earth's atmosphere, and to photograph weather systems, crops, troops, and ships. In addition, two dozen Global Positioning Satellites give off signals that can be picked up by small receivers on Earth. The receiver can then tell you where you are on Earth's surface.

Some satellites are in **geosynchronous orbits,** which means they revolve around Earth at the same rate that Earth rotates. Geosynchronous satellites above the equator seem to hover over a given point on Earth. Geosynchronous satellites are used to relay television signals and to map weather patterns.

Space Stations A space station is a large satellite in which people can live for long periods. The first space station, the Soviet Union's *Salyut,* was launched in 1971. In 1973, the United States launched *Skylab,* which carried a series of telescopes and scientific experiments. The former Soviet Union, of which Russia was part, launched the *Mir* space station in 1986. Astronauts from many countries, including Americans, visited *Mir*. Sixteen countries, including the United States and Russia, are cooperating on the International Space Station, which is now being built in orbit and will eventually provide living quarters and labs for up to seven astronauts.

☑ ***Checkpoint*** *What is a geosynchronous orbit?*

Be a Rocket Scientist

You can build a rocket.

1. Use a plastic or paper cup as the rocket body. Cut out a paper nose cone and tape it to the closed end of the cup.
2. Obtain an empty film canister with a lid that snaps on inside the canister. Go outside to do Steps 3–5.
3. Fill the canister about one-quarter full with water.
4. Put on your goggles. Now add half of a fizzing antacid tablet to the film canister and quickly snap on the lid.
5. Place the canister on the ground with the lid down. Place your rocket over the canister and stand back.

Observing What action happened inside the film canister? What was the reaction of the rocket?

Figure 15 The International Space Station is a cooperative project involving 16 countries, including the United States, Russia, Japan, and Canada. This is an artist's conception of the station in orbit.

Figure 16 The Space Shuttle *Discovery* is launched into space by its own rockets as well as by rockets attached to it. ***Inferring*** *What is one advantage of a reusable space vehicle?*

Space Shuttles

The Saturn V rockets that carried astronauts to the moon in the 1960s and 1970s were very expensive. In addition, they could not be reused because each stage burned up as it fell back through Earth's atmosphere. In the late 1970s, the National Aeronautics and Space Administration (NASA) developed the reusable space shuttles. They are called shuttles because they can go back and forth, or shuttle, between Earth and space. Since the first shuttle was launched in 1981, space shuttles have been the main way that the United States launches astronauts and equipment into space.

NASA is studying several ideas for building better and less expensive ways of launching people and cargo into space. The ideal vehicle would be an aerospace plane that could take off from a runway, travel into space, and land again on a runway.

Section 3 Review

1. How does a rocket work?
2. Describe three uses of satellites and space stations.
3. Which stage of a multistage rocket reaches the final destination?
4. **Thinking Critically Comparing and Contrasting** What is one way that Saturn V rockets and space shuttles are different?

Science at Home

Interview someone who remembers the space programs of the 1950s and 1960s. Prepare your questions in advance, such as: How did you feel when you heard that *Sputnik* was in orbit? How did you feel when the first Americans went into space? Did you watch any of the space flights on television? You may want to record your interview, then write it out in a question-and-answer format.

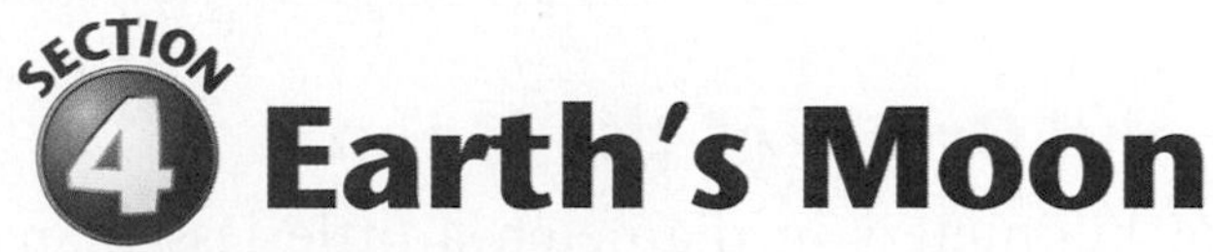

Section 4 Earth's Moon

Discover Activity

Why Do Craters Look Different From Each Other?

The moon's surface has pits in it, called craters.

1. Put on your goggles. Fill a large plastic basin with 2 cm of sand.
2. Drop marbles of different masses from about 20 cm high. Take the marbles out and view the craters they left.
3. Predict what will happen if you drop marbles from a higher point. Smooth out the sand. Now drop marbles of different masses from about 50 cm high.
4. Take the marbles out and view the craters they left.

Think It Over

Developing Hypotheses In which step do you think the marbles were moving faster when they hit the sand? If objects hitting the moon caused craters, how did the speeds of the objects affect the sizes of the craters? How did the masses of the objects affect the sizes of the craters?

Guide for Reading

- **What features of the moon can be seen with a telescope?**
- **How did the Apollo landings help scientists learn about the moon?**

Reading Tip **As you read, write down ways in which the moon's surface is similar to Earth's surface.**

Would you want to take a vacation on the moon? Before you answer, think about these facts. There is no air or liquid water on the moon. Temperatures on the moon's surface range from 100°C, the boiling point of water, to –170°C, well below freezing.

To stay at a comfortable temperature and carry an air supply, the astronauts who landed on the moon had to wear bulky spacesuits. Each spacesuit had a mass of 90 kilograms, about as much as the astronaut himself! Because the moon's gravity is only about one-sixth as strong as Earth's, however, the astronauts were able to leap about like basketball stars despite their heavy spacesuits. What do you think now? Do you still want to go?

Figure 17 Astronaut John W. Young jumps up from the moon's surface as he salutes the flag on April 21, 1972. The machine on the left is the *Apollo 16* lunar lander.

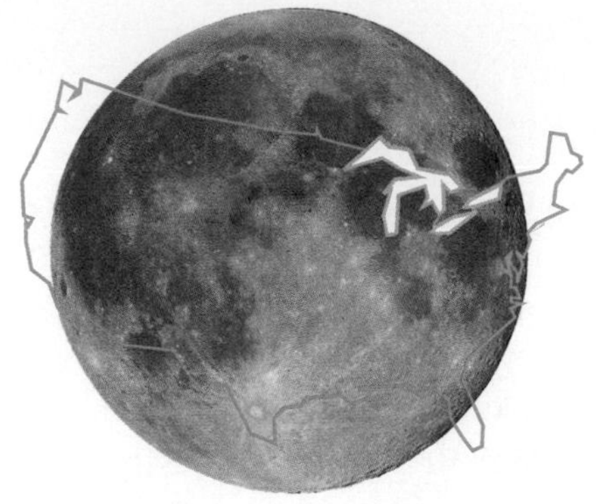

Figure 18 The diameter of the moon is a little less than the distance across the United States.

The Structure and Origin of the Moon

The moon is 3,476 kilometers in diameter, a little less than the distance across the United States. This diameter is only one fourth Earth's diameter. However, the moon contains only one-eightieth as much mass as Earth. Though Earth has a very dense core, the outer layers are less dense. The moon's average density is about the same as the density of Earth's outer layers.

People have long wondered how the moon formed. Scientists have suggested many possible hypotheses. For example, did Earth at one time spin so fast that the material the moon is made of was thrown off? Was the moon formed elsewhere in the solar system and captured by Earth's gravitational pull as it came near? Was the moon formed near Earth at the same time that Earth formed? Scientists have found reasons to reject all of these ideas.

The theory of the moon's origin that best fits the evidence is called the collision theory. It is illustrated in Figure 19. About 4.5 billion years ago, when Earth was very young, an object at least as large as Mars collided with Earth. Material from the object and Earth's outer layers was thrown into orbit around Earth. Eventually, this material combined to form the moon.

Looking at the Moon From Earth

For thousands of years, people could see shapes on the surface of the moon, but didn't know what caused them. The ancient Greeks thought that the moon was perfectly smooth. It was not until about 400 years ago that scientists could study the moon more closely.

Figure 19 This computer simulation shows the collision theory of the moon's origin. In this theory, a large object struck Earth. The resulting debris formed the moon.

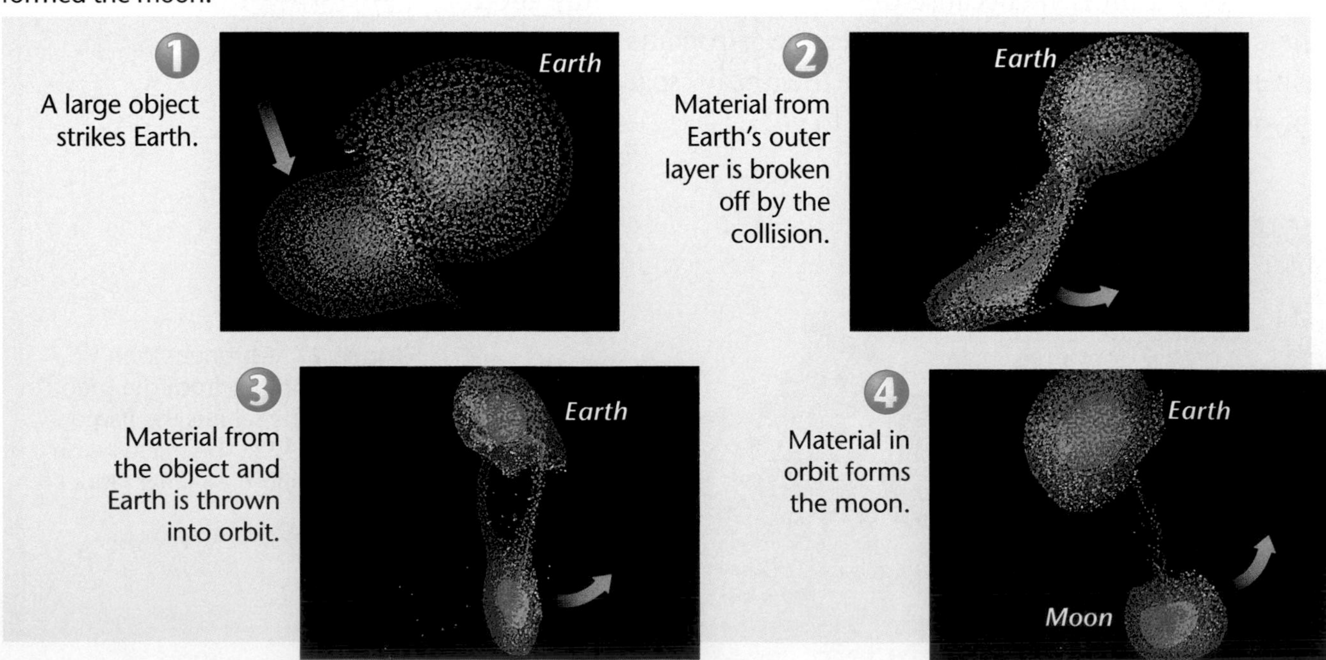

Figure 20 Astronomers have given names to many of the moon's craters and maria. Copernicus is one of the largest craters.

In 1609, the Italian astronomer Galileo Galilei heard about a device that made distant objects appear closer. Galileo soon made his own **telescope** by putting two lenses in a wooden tube. The lenses focused the light coming through the tube, making distant objects seem closer. When Galileo pointed his telescope at the moon, he was able to see much more detail than anyone had ever seen before. **Features on the moon's surface include craters, highlands, and maria.**

Galileo saw that much of the moon's surface is covered with round pits called **craters.** Some craters are hundreds of kilometers across. For 300 years, scientists thought that the craters on the moon had been made by volcanoes. But about 50 years ago, scientists concluded that the craters on the moon were caused by the impacts of meteoroids, rocks from space.

Galileo inferred that some of the other features he saw were highlands, or mountains. The peaks of the highlands and the rims of the craters cast dark shadows, which Galileo could see.

The moon's surface also has dark, flat areas, which Galileo called **maria** (MAH ree uh), the Latin word for "seas." Each one is a "mare" (MAH ray). Galileo thought that the maria might be oceans. Scientists now know that there are no oceans on the moon. The maria are low, dry areas that were flooded with molten material billions of years ago. Since you always see the same maria from Earth, you can tell that the moon always shows the same face to Earth.

☑ ***Checkpoint*** *What are maria?*

Visual Arts CONNECTION

When Galileo observed the moon, he drew pictures like the one below. Galileo had been trained as an artist, so he interpreted his observations as an artist would. Light and shadow are used in art to create the appearance of three-dimensional forms.

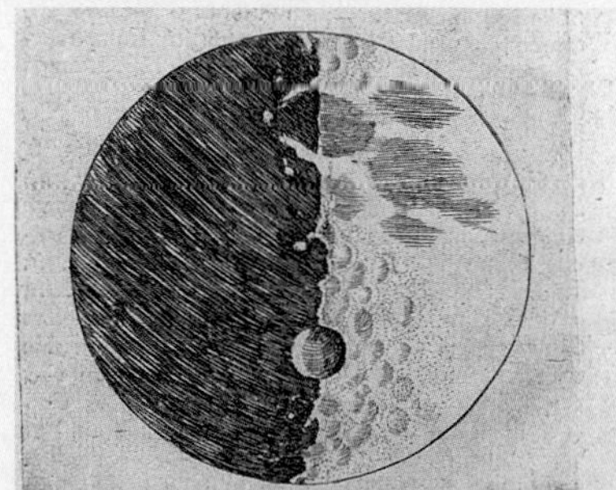

Galileo saw the areas of light and shadow on the moon and concluded that the surface of the moon was not smooth.

In Your Journal

Under a bright light, set up an arrangement of objects. Sketch the outline of the objects. Then observe where the shadows fall. Shade in those areas. Notice how adding shading makes your drawing look more real.

Missions to the Moon

"I believe that this nation should commit itself to achieving the goal, before this decade is out, of landing a man on the moon and returning him safely to Earth." With these words from a May 1961 speech, President John F. Kennedy launched an enormous program of space exploration and scientific research.

Exploring the Moon Between 1964 and 1972, the United States and the Soviet Union sent dozens of rockets to explore the moon. Until spacecraft went to the moon, no one knew what its surface was like. Would spacecraft landing on the moon sink deep into thick dust and be lost? When *Surveyor* spacecraft landed on the moon, they didn't sink in, thus showing that the surface was solid. Lunar orbiters then photographed the moon's surface, so scientists could find a flat, safe spot for a rocket to land.

The Moon Landings In July 1969 three astronauts circled the moon in *Apollo 11.* Once in orbit around the moon, Neil Armstrong and Buzz Aldrin got into a tiny Lunar Module called *Eagle*, leaving Michael Collins in orbit in the Command Module. On July 20, 1969, the *Eagle* descended toward a flat area on the moon's surface called the Sea of Tranquillity. Armstrong and Aldrin were running out of fuel, so they had to find a safe landing spot fast. Billions of people held their breaths as they waited to learn if the astronauts had landed safely on the moon. Finally, a red light flashed on the control panel. "Contact light! Houston, Tranquillity Base here. The *Eagle* has landed," Armstrong radioed to Earth.

After the landing, Armstrong and Aldrin left the *Eagle* to explore the moon. When Armstrong first set foot on the moon, he said, "That's one small step for man, one giant leap for mankind." Armstrong meant to say "That's one small step for *a* man," meaning himself, but in his excitement he never said the "a."

Figure 21 On July 20, 1969, *Apollo 11* astronaut Neil Armstrong became the first person to walk on the moon. He took this photograph of Buzz Aldrin, the second person to walk on the moon. ***Inferring*** *Why was it important for the lunar module to land on a flat spot?*

Figure 22 Astronauts on later missions had a lunar buggy to help them explore the moon's surface.

On the Surface of the Moon Everything the *Apollo 11* astronauts found was new and exciting. Even looking at their footprints taught the astronauts lessons about the moon's soil. The astronauts bounded around the surface, picking up samples of rocks to bring back to Earth for scientists to study.

In later missions, the astronauts were able to stay on the moon for days instead of hours. They even had a lunar buggy to ride around in. The astronauts were also able to land near the highlands, which were more interesting to study than the flat mare where *Apollo 11* landed.

Moon Rocks and Moonquakes The astronauts brought back to Earth 382 kilograms of moon rocks, about half the mass of a small car. **Much of what scientists have learned about the moon came from detailed study of the moon rocks gathered by astronauts.** Almost all of the rocks were formed from the cooling of molten material, so the moon's surface must once have been very hot. Some of the rocks showed that they had been broken apart by impacts and then reformed. So scientists concluded that meteoroids had bombarded the moon's surface.

The astronauts brought measuring instruments to the moon to record some of the meteoroid impacts. One type of device, known as a seismometer, is used to detect earthquakes on Earth. The seismometers on the moon detected extremely weak moonquakes, the result of changes deep under the moon's surface.

Until the *Apollo* astronauts landed, scientists knew very little about the moon's interior. Another kind of instrument the astronauts left behind measured the amount of heat flowing out from the moon's interior, in order to study what the inside of the moon is like. This instrument showed that the moon has cooled almost completely since it was formed.

☑ ***Checkpoint*** *What did scientists discover about the interior of the moon as a result of the moon landings?*

Calculating ACTIVITY

If you went to the moon for a vacation, your weight would only be about one sixth of your weight on Earth. To find your weight on the moon, divide your weight by 6.

If you had to wear a spacesuit that weighed as much as you do, what would be your total weight on the moon?

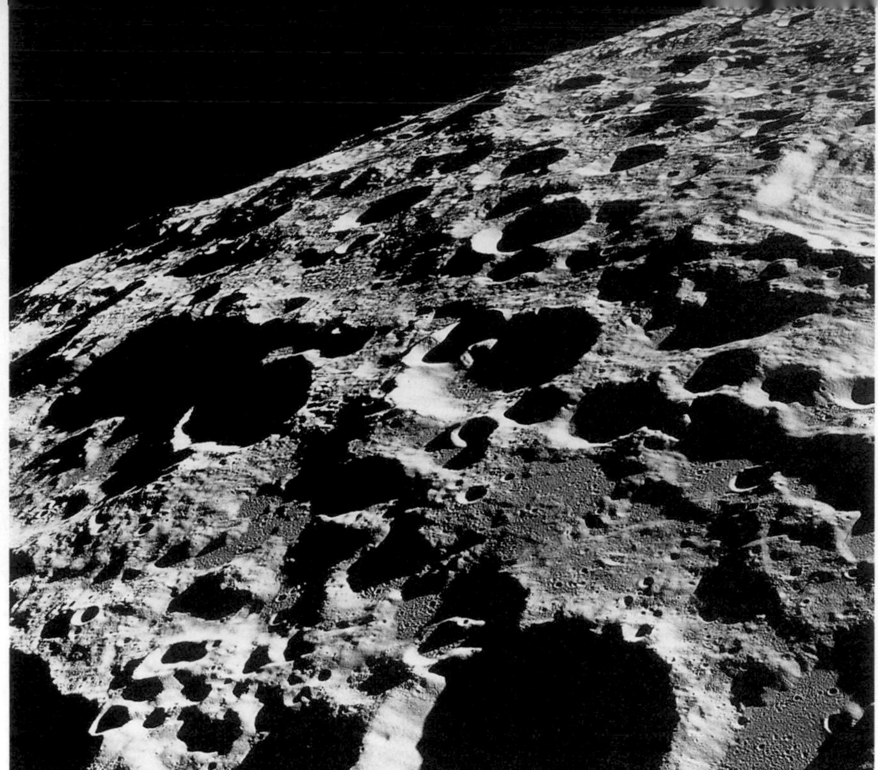

Figure 23 The far side of the moon is much rougher than the side that faces Earth.
Observing *What are the round features in this photograph called?*

Photographs of the Moon The *Apollo* astronauts circled the moon by rocket and photographed all parts of its surface. The pictures show that the far side of the moon is rougher than the near side and has very few maria.

The American *Clementine* spacecraft went to the moon in 1994. It took photographs of the moon through different filters chosen to show what types of minerals are on the moon. The name *Clementine* was chosen because it is the name of the prospector's daughter in the old song "My Darlin' Clementine."

In 1998, the American *Lunar Prospector* spacecraft went to the moon. *Lunar Prospector* mapped the entire moon from an altitude of only 100 kilometers. *Lunar Prospector* found evidence that there is ice frozen into the lunar soil near the moon's poles.

Section 4 Review

1. Name the three kinds of features that Galileo saw on the moon's surface.
2. What did the *Apollo* astronauts do on the moon?
3. How did the craters form on the moon?
4. **Thinking Critically Inferring** Why did scientists once think there were volcanoes on the moon? What evidence from the *Apollo* landings makes this unlikely?

Check Your Progress

CHAPTER PROJECT 20

Compare your observations of the moon early in the day with observations later that day. How does the moon appear to move in the sky during the course of the day? What happens to the appearance of the moon between earlier and later observations? Is there a pattern for each day? (*Hint:* See whether the same pattern holds true for observations later in the month.)

Earth in Space

Key Ideas

- Astronomy is the study of the moon, stars, and other objects in space.
- Earth's rotation on its axis causes day and night.
- One complete revolution of Earth around the sun is called a year.
- Earth has seasons because its axis is tilted as it revolves around the sun.

Key Terms

astronomy	latitude
axis	solstice
rotation	equinox
revolution	vernal equinox
orbit	autumnal equinox

Phases, Eclipses, and Tides

Key Ideas

- The moon revolves around Earth and rotates on its own axis.
- The phase of the moon you see depends on how much of the sunlit side of the moon faces Earth.
- A solar eclipse occurs when the moon passes between Earth and the sun, blocking the sunlight from reaching Earth.
- A lunar eclipse occurs when Earth is directly between the moon and the sun, blocking the sunlight from reaching the moon.
- Tides occur mainly because of differences in how much the moon pulls on different parts of Earth.

Key Terms

phase	lunar eclipse
eclipse	tide
solar eclipse	gravity
umbra	spring tide
penumbra	neap tide

Rockets and Satellites

INTEGRATING TECHNOLOGY

Key Ideas

- A rocket moves in one direction when gases are expelled from it in the opposite direction.
- Satellites and space stations are used for communications, navigation, collecting weather data, and research.

Key Terms

satellite geosynchronous orbit

Earth's Moon

Key Ideas

- Features on the moon's surface include craters, highlands, and maria.
- Much of what scientists have learned about the moon came from detailed study of the moon rocks.

Key Terms

telescope crater maria

Organizing Information

Concept Map Copy the concept map about how Earth moves in space onto a sheet of paper. Then complete it and add a title. (For more on concept maps, see the Skills Handbook.)

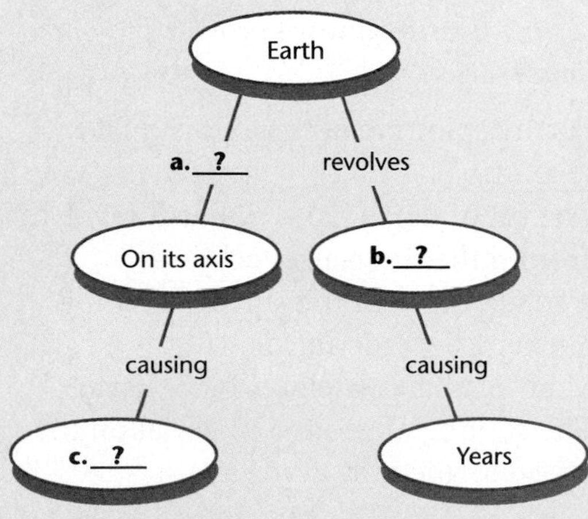

CHAPTER 20 ASSESSMENT

Reviewing Content

Multiple Choice

Choose the letter of the answer that best completes each statement.

1. The movement of Earth around the sun once a year is Earth's
a. orbit.
b. rotation.
c. revolution.
d. axis.

2. The darkest part of a shadow is the
a. umbra.
b. penumbra.
c. eclipse.
d. phase.

3. When Earth's shadow falls on the moon, the shadow causes a
a. new moon.
b. solar eclipse.
c. full moon.
d. lunar eclipse.

4. A satellite in geosynchronous orbit revolves around Earth once each
a. hour.
b. week.
c. month.
d. day.

5. The craters on the moon were caused by
a. highlands. **b.** volcanoes.
c. meteoroid impacts. **d.** maria.

True or False

If the statement is true, write true. If it is false, change the underlined word or words to make the statement true.

6. Earth's spinning on its axis is called revolution.

7. The tilt of Earth's axis as Earth revolves around the sun causes eclipses.

8. A total eclipse of the sun occurs only during a new moon.

9. Many artificial satellites orbit Earth.

10. The cooling of molten material on the moon formed the craters.

Checking Concepts

11. Describe the shape of Earth's orbit.

12. Mars's axis is tilted at about the same angle as Earth's axis. Do you think Mars has seasons? Explain your answer.

13. How does the time it takes the moon to rotate on its axis compare with the time it takes the moon to revolve around Earth?

14. Why isn't there a lunar eclipse every month?

15. Why do more people see a total lunar eclipse than a total solar eclipse?

16. Why is there a high tide on the side of Earth closest to the moon? On the side of Earth furthest from the moon?

17. What basic law of physics explains how a rocket moves forward?

18. Describe the events that formed the moon, according to the collision theory.

19. What did scientists learn by studying the rocks astronauts brought back from the moon?

20. Writing to Learn Imagine that trips to the moon are resuming. You are an astronaut going to the moon. Write a paragraph describing what you see as you arrive. What does the sky look like? What could the rocks you find help scientists learn?

Thinking Critically

21. Relating Cause and Effect How do the changing positions of the moon, Earth, and sun cause spring tides or neap tides on Earth?

22. Applying Concepts At what time does the full moon rise? Is it visible in the eastern sky or the western sky?

23. Posing Questions Suppose you were assigned to design a spacesuit for astronauts to wear on the moon. What questions about the moon would you need to have answered in order to design the spacesuit?

Applying Skills

Use the illustration below to answer Questions 24–26. (*Hint:* The tilt of the Earth's axis is 23.5°.)

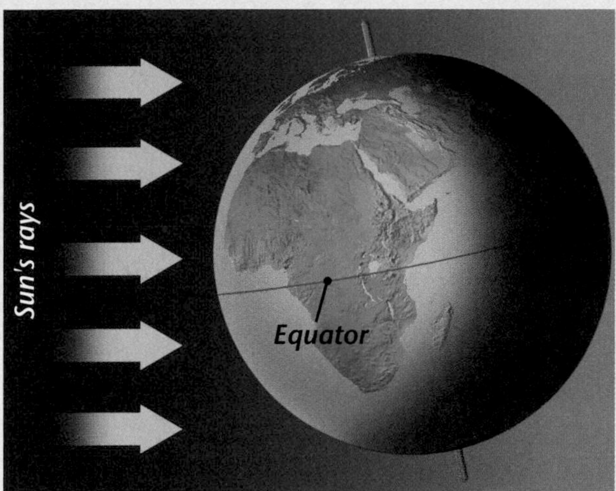

24. **Interpreting Diagrams** On which hemisphere are the sun's rays falling most directly?
25. **Inferring** In the Northern Hemisphere, is it the summer solstice, winter solstice, or one of the equinoxes? How do you know?
26. **Predicting** Six months after this illustration, Earth will have revolved halfway around the sun. Show in a sketch which end of Earth's axis will be tilted toward the sun.

Performance Assessment — Chapter Project 20

Project Wrap Up Now you are ready to present your log, map, and drawings. Here are some ways you can graph your data: time of moonrise for each date; how often you saw the moon at each compass direction; how often you saw the moon at a specific time. Display your graphs. Discuss any patterns you discovered with your classmates. With your classmates, predict when and where you can see the moon.

Reflect and Record In your journal, write about the easiest and hardest parts of this project. What would you do differently if you observed the moon for another month? What observation(s) surprised you? Why?

Test Preparation

Use these questions to prepare for standardized tests.

Study the diagram. Then answer Questions 27–30. Numbers 1, 2, 3, and 4 on the diagram indicate locations of the moon in its orbit around Earth.

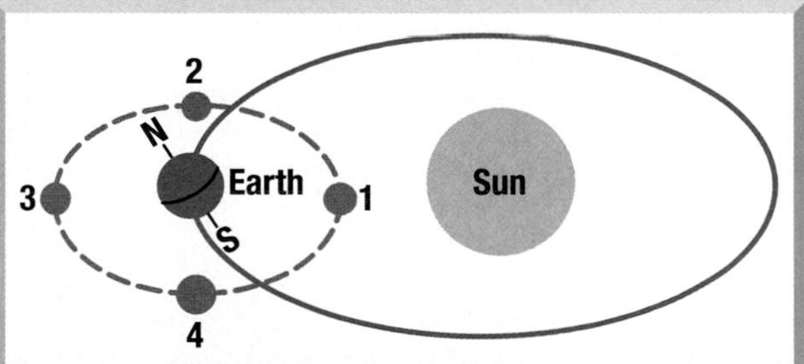

27. About how much time does it take the moon to revolve once around Earth?
    a. one day
    b. 7 days
    c. 27 days
    d. one year
28. Which of the following phases is the moon in at location 1?
    a. new
    b. crescent
    c. half
    d. full
29. At which location(s) could a lunar eclipse occur?
    a. 1 only
    b. 3 only
    c. 1 and 3
    d. 2 and 4
30. Only one side of the moon is visible from earth because
    a. the moon does not rotate on its axis.
    b. the moon does not revolve around Earth.
    c. the moon is in a geosynchronous orbit around Earth.
    d. the moon revolves once and rotates once in the same period of time.

CHAPTER

21 The Solar System

This artist's conception shows the *Cassini* space probe arriving near Saturn's rings in 2004.

www.phschool.com

Observing the Solar System

Discover How Do Mass and Speed Affect an Object's Motion?
Try This A Loopy Ellipse

The Sun

Discover How Can You Safely Observe the Sun?
Try This Viewing Sunspots
Real-World Lab Stormy Sunspots

The Inner Planets

Discover How Does Mars Look From Earth?
Sharpen Your Skills Graphing
Try This Remote Control

PROJECT 21

Model of the Solar System

If you could drive from Earth to the sun at 100 kilometers per hour, your trip would take 170 years. And most distances in the solar system are even greater! The *Cassini* space probe left Earth for Saturn in 1997 traveling much faster than highway speed, but will not arrive at Saturn's rings until 2004. Sizes in the solar system can be huge, too. Compared with some of the other planets in the solar system, Earth is very small. Saturn, for example, is about 10 times Earth's diameter.

In this chapter, you will get to know many of the objects in the solar system. To help you understand the huge distances and sizes, you will design three different scale models of the solar system.

Your Goal To design scale models of the solar system.

To complete this project, you will

- design a model to show the planets' distances from the sun
- design a model to show the planets' sizes relative to the sun
- test different scales to see if you can use the same scale for both size and distance in one model

Get Started Begin by previewing the tables with distances and diameters on pages 707 and 715. Brainstorm with a group of classmates how you will build your models. Prepare a data sheet to record your calculations of scaled-down distances and diameters.

Check Your Progress You will be working on this project as you study this chapter. To keep your project on track, look for Check Your Progress boxes at the following points.

Section 1 Review, page 699: Design a model to show distances.
Section 3 Review, page 713: Design a model to show diameters.
Section 4 Review, page 721: Design one scale model that shows both sizes and distances.

Wrap Up At the end of the chapter (page 735), you will present your design to the class.

The Outer Planets

Discover **How Large Are the Outer Planets?**
Try This **Model Saturn**
Skills Lab **Speeding Around the Sun**

Comets, Asteroids, and Meteors

Discover **Which Way Do Comet Tails Point?**

Integrating Life Science

Is There Life Beyond Earth?

Discover **Is Yeast Alive or Not?**
Sharpen Your Skills **Communicating**

Observing the Solar System

DISCOVER — ACTIVITY

How Do Mass and Speed Affect an Object's Motion?

1. Have your partner push a toy truck across the table toward you. Stop the truck with your hands.
2. Repeat Step 1, but have your partner push the truck a little faster. Was it easier or harder to stop the truck than in Step 1?
3. Now add some rocks or other heavy objects to the truck and repeat Step 1. Your partner should push the truck at the same speed as in Step 1. How hard was it to stop the truck this time compared to Step 1?
4. Repeat Step 2 with the rocks still in the truck. How hard was it to stop the truck this time?

Think It Over

Predicting How hard would it be to stop the truck if your partner pushed it more slowly? If you added more mass to the truck?

GUIDE FOR READING

- **How do the heliocentric and geocentric descriptions of the solar system differ?**
- **What did Kepler discover about the orbits of the planets?**
- **What two factors keep the planets in their orbits?**

Reading Tip **As you read, make a list of the evidence that supports the heliocentric system.**

Have you ever lain outdoors on a starry night, gazing up at the stars? As you watch, the stars seem to move across the sky. The sky seems to be rotating right over your head. In fact, from the Northern Hemisphere, the sky appears to rotate completely around Polaris, the North Star, once every 24 hours.

Now think about what you see every day. During the day, the sun appears to move across the sky. From here on Earth, it seems as if Earth is stationary and that the sun, moon, and stars are all moving around Earth. But is the sky really moving above you? Centuries ago, before there were space shuttles or even telescopes, there was no easy way to find out.

Figure 1 This photo was made by exposing the camera film for several hours. Each star appears as part of a circle, and all the stars seem to revolve around a single point.

Wandering Stars

When the ancient Greeks watched the stars move across the sky, they noticed that the patterns of most of the stars didn't change. Although the stars seemed to move, they stayed in the same position relative to each other. For example, the constellations kept the same shapes from night to night and from year to year.

As they observed the sky more carefully, the Greeks noticed something surprising. Five points of light seemed to wander among the stars. The Greeks called these objects *planets*, from the Greek word meaning "wandering star." The Greeks made very careful observations of the motions of the five planets they could see. You know these planets by the names the ancient Romans later gave them: Mercury, Venus, Mars, Jupiter, and Saturn.

Greek Ideas: Earth at the Center

When you look up at the sky, you can almost imagine that you are under a rotating dome with the stars pasted on it. The Greeks thought that they were inside a rotating dome they called the celestial sphere. Most Greek astronomers believed that the universe is perfect and unchangeable and that Earth is stationary in the center of the celestial sphere. Since *geo* is the Greek word for Earth, an Earth-centered explanation is known as a **geocentric** (jee oh SEN trik) system. **In a geocentric system, Earth is at the center of the revolving planets.**

In A.D. 140, the Greek astronomer Ptolemy (TAHL uh mee) explained the motion of the planets in another way. Like the earlier Greeks, Ptolemy thought that Earth is at the center of the system of planets. Ptolemy also thought that the moon, Mercury, Venus, the sun, Mars, Jupiter, and Saturn revolve around Earth.

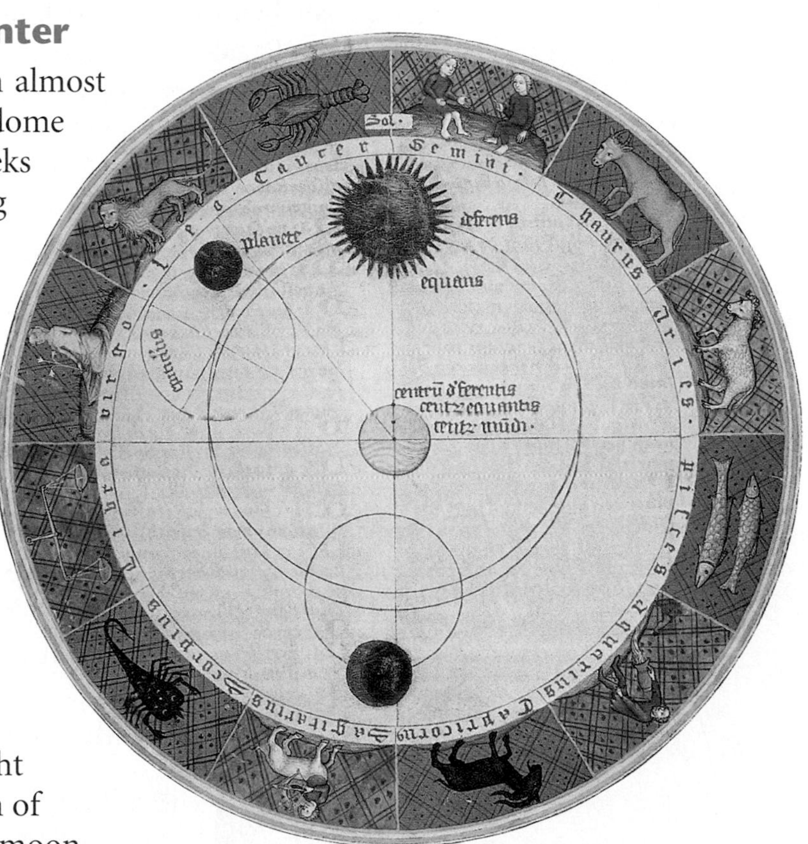

Figure 2 In the 1500s, an astronomy book published this illustration of Ptolemy's system. ***Interpreting Diagrams*** *Where is Earth located in this illustration?*

In Ptolemy's explanation, however, the planets move on little circles that move on bigger circles. Ptolemy thought that this explained why the planets seem to move at different speeds, and even backwards, among the stars. For the next 1,400 years, people believed that Ptolemy's ideas were correct.

☑ ***Checkpoint*** *What is a geocentric system?*

Copernicus's Idea: Sun at the Center

In the early 1500s, the Polish astronomer Nicolaus Copernicus developed another explanation for the motions of the planets. Copernicus thought that the sun is at the center of the system of planets. His sun-centered system is called a **heliocentric** (hee lee oh SEN trik) system. *Helios* is Greek for "sun." **In a heliocentric system, Earth and the other planets revolve around the sun.** Copernicus's explanation included the six planets he knew about: Mercury, Venus, Earth, Mars, Jupiter, and Saturn.

Galileo's Observations

In the 1500s and 1600s, most people still believed Ptolemy's geocentric explanation. However, the Italian astronomer Galileo Galilei, who lived nearly 100 years after Copernicus, thought that the heliocentric explanation was correct.

Recall from Chapter 1 that Galileo was the first scientist to use a telescope to look at objects in the sky. With his telescope, Galileo made two discoveries that supported the heliocentric model. First, Galileo saw four moons revolving around Jupiter. Galileo's observations of Jupiter's moons showed that not everything in the sky revolves around Earth.

Figure 3 From this observatory, Tycho Brahe made accurate observations of the planets for nearly 20 years. His data became the basis for many important discoveries.

Galileo's observations of Venus also supported Copernicus's heliocentric system. Galileo discovered that Venus goes through phases similar to those of Earth's moon. Galileo reasoned that the phases of Venus could not be explained if Earth were at the center of the system of planets. So Ptolemy's geocentric system could not be correct.

Galileo's evidence gradually convinced others that Copernicus's explanation was correct. Today, people talk about the "solar system" rather than the "Earth system." This shows that people accept Copernicus's idea that the sun is at the center.

☑ ***Checkpoint** What two discoveries made by Galileo supported the heliocentric description of the solar system?*

Brahe and Kepler

Copernicus and Galileo had correctly identified the sun as the center of the system of planets. But Copernicus, like Ptolemy, assumed that the orbits of the planets are circles.

Copernicus's ideas were based on observations made by the ancient Greeks. In the late 1500s, Tycho Brahe (TEE koh BRAH uh), a Danish astronomer, made much more accurate observations. Brahe carefully observed the positions of the planets for almost 20 years.

In 1600, a German mathematician, Johannes Kepler, went to work analyzing Brahe's data. Kepler tried to figure out the shape of the planets' orbits. At first, he assumed that the orbits are circles. When Kepler tried to figure out the exact orbit of Mars, however, no circle fit the observations.

Kepler had discovered that the orbit of each planet is an ellipse. An **ellipse** is an elongated circle, or oval shape. Kepler found that if he assumed that Mars's orbit is an ellipse, his calculations fit Brahe's observations better.

Inertia and Gravity

Kepler had discovered the correct shape of the planets' orbits. But he could not explain why the planets stay in orbit. The work of the English scientist Isaac Newton provided the answer to that puzzle. **Newton concluded that two factors—inertia and gravity—combine to keep the planets in orbit.**

Galileo had discovered that a moving object will continue to move until some force acts to stop its motion. This tendency of a moving object to continue in a straight line or a stationary object to remain in place is the object's **inertia.** The more mass an object has, the more inertia it has. As you found if you did the Discover activity, an object with greater inertia is more difficult to start or stop.

Isaac Newton picked up where Galileo had left off. Late in his life, Newton told the story of how watching an apple fall from a tree in 1665 had made him think about motion. He hypothesized that the same force that pulls the apple to the ground also pulls the moon toward Earth. This force, called gravity, attracts all

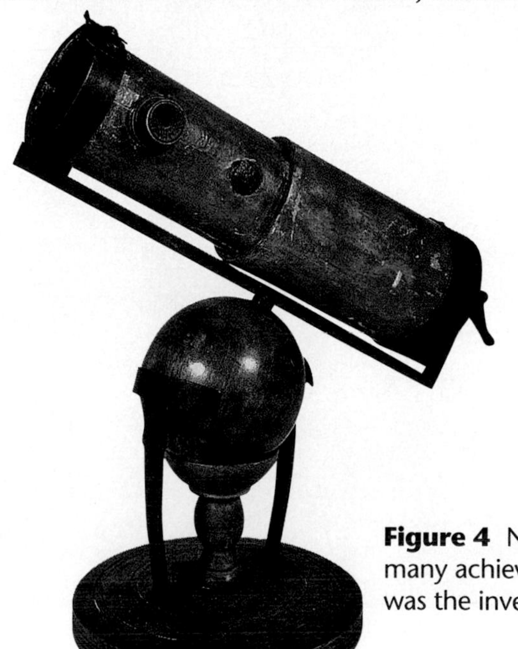

Figure 4 Newton was a man of many achievements. Among them was the invention of this telescope.

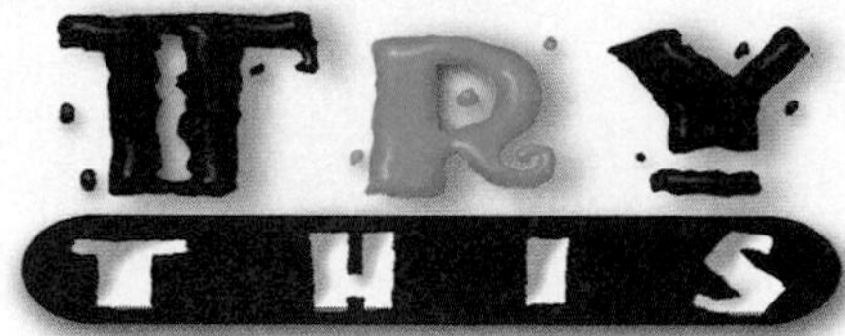

A Loopy Ellipse

You can draw an ellipse.

1. Carefully stick two pushpins about 10 cm apart through a sheet of white paper on top of corrugated cardboard.

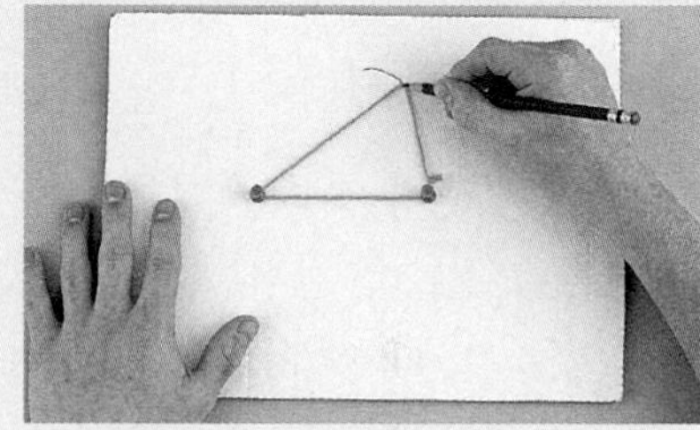

2. Tie the ends of a 30-cm piece of string together. Place the string around the pushpins.
3. Keeping the string tight, move a pencil around inside the string.
4. Now place the pushpins 5 cm apart. Repeat Step 3.

Predicting How does changing the distance between the pushpins affect the ellipse's shape? What shape would you draw if you used only one pushpin?

objects toward each other. The strength of gravity depends on the masses of the objects and the distance between them.

Newton figured out that Earth keeps pulling the moon toward it with gravity. At the same time, the moon keeps moving ahead because of its inertia. Earth curves away as the moon falls toward it, so the moon winds up in orbit around Earth.

In the same way, the planets are in orbit around the sun because the sun's gravity pulls on them while their inertia keeps them moving ahead. Therefore, the planets keep moving around the sun and end up in orbit.

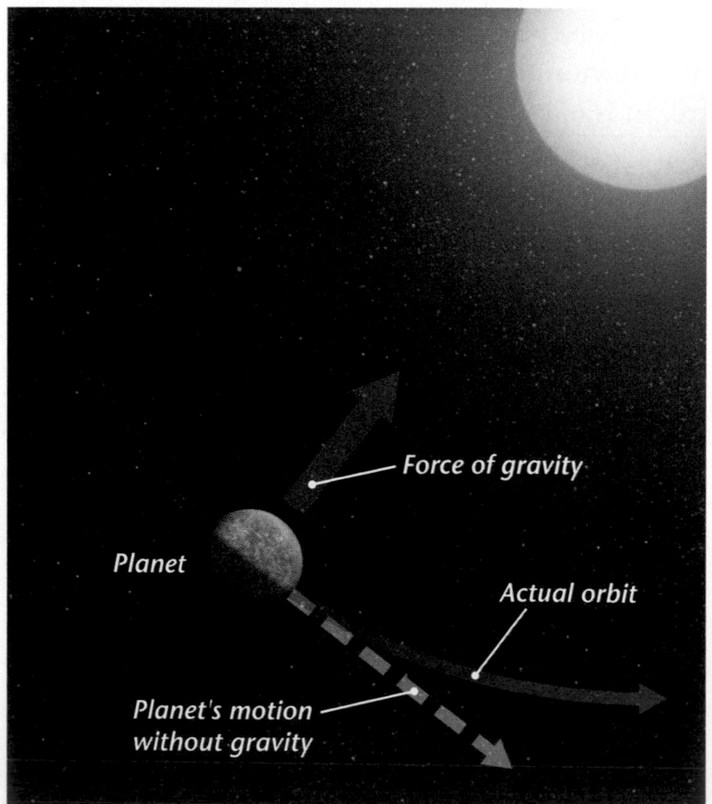

Figure 5 If there were no force of gravity, inertia would make a planet travel in a straight line. But because gravity pulls the planet toward the sun, the planet actually travels in an elliptical orbit around the sun. ***Interpreting Diagrams*** *What would happen if a planet had no inertia?*

Uranus
2,871,000,000 km

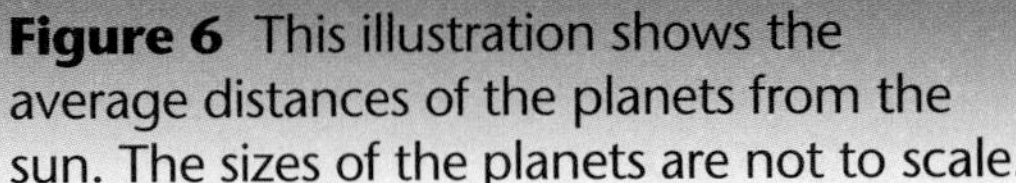

Figure 6 This illustration shows the average distances of the planets from the sun. The sizes of the planets are not to scale.

More to Discover

Since Newton's time, our knowledge about the solar system has increased dramatically. Newton knew of the same six planets the ancient Greeks had known—Mercury, Venus, Earth, Mars, Jupiter, and Saturn. Now astronomers know three more planets—Uranus, Neptune, and Pluto. Astronomers have also identified many other objects in the solar system, such as comets and asteroids, that you will learn about later in this chapter.

Galileo and later astronomers used telescopes on Earth to observe the solar system. Astronomers still use telescopes on Earth, but they have also made close-up observations of the planets from space probes sent far into the solar system. Our understanding of the solar system continues to change every day. Who knows what new discoveries will be made in your lifetime!

Section 1 Review

1. How is Copernicus's description of the system of planets different from Ptolemy's description?
2. How did Galileo's observations of Jupiter's moons help to show that the geocentric explanation is incorrect?
3. What shape are the orbits of the planets? How was the discovery of this orbit shape made?
4. What two factors act together to keep the planets in orbit around the sun?
5. **Thinking Critically Applying Concepts** People usually say that the sun rises in the east, moves across the sky, and sets in the west. Is this description literally correct? Explain.

Check Your Progress

CHAPTER PROJECT 21

Begin by making a table that shows the distances of the planets from the sun. To help visualize the solar system, you can reduce all the distances by the same amount: for example, divide all distances by 100,000 or 1,000,000. You can use the resulting smaller numbers to design a scale model of the solar system. Record your calculations on your data sheet. Now choose a different scale and repeat your calculations. Which scale makes it easier to see the relative distances between the planets and the sun?

SECTION 2

The Sun

DISCOVER — ACTIVITY

How Can You Safely Observe the Sun?

1. Clamp a pair of binoculars to a ring stand.
2. Cut a hole in a 20-cm by 28-cm sheet of thin cardboard so that it will fit over the binoculars, as shown in the photo. The cardboard should cover one lens, but allow light through the other lens. Tape the cardboard on securely. **CAUTION:** *Never look directly at the sun. You will hurt your eyes if you do.*
3. Use the binoculars to project an image of the sun onto a sheet of white paper. The cardboard will shade the white paper. Change the focus and move the paper back and forth until you get a sharp image.

Think It Over

Observing Draw what you see on the paper. What do you see on the surface of the sun?

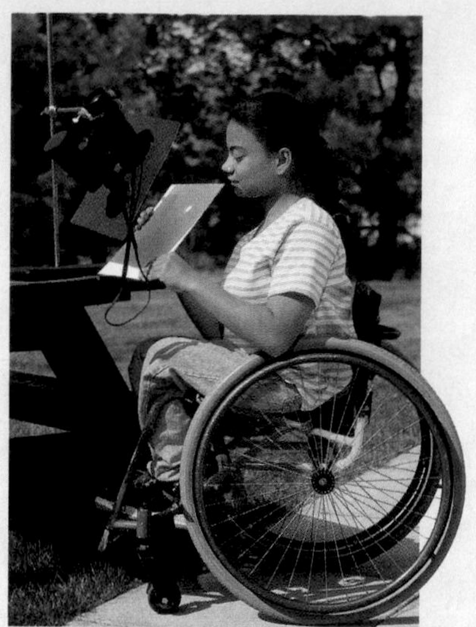

GUIDE FOR READING

- **How does the sun get its energy?**
- **What are the layers of the sun's atmosphere?**
- **What are some features of the sun's surface?**

Reading Tip **As you read, write a sentence defining each boldfaced term in your own words.**

The sun's gravity is by far the most powerful force in the solar system—strong enough to hold all of the planets and comets in orbit! The sun's gravity is so strong because the sun's mass is very large. In fact, 99.8 percent of the mass of the solar system is in the sun.

Like Earth, the sun has an interior and an atmosphere. Unlike Earth, however, the sun does not have a solid surface. The sun is a ball of glowing gas. About three fourths of the sun's mass is hydrogen, one fourth is helium, and very small amounts are other chemical elements.

The Sun's Interior

The interior of the sun is like a giant furnace. Like furnaces in houses, the sun produces energy. But the sun does not get its energy from burning fuels such as oil. **Instead, the sun's energy comes from nuclear fusion.** In the process of **nuclear fusion,** hydrogen atoms join together to form helium. Nuclear fusion occurs only under conditions of extremely high temperature and pressure. The temperature inside the sun's **core,** or center, reaches about 15 million degrees Celsius, high enough for nuclear fusion to occur.

The total mass of the helium produced by nuclear fusion is slightly less than the total mass of the hydrogen that goes into it. The change in mass occurs because some of the matter is converted into energy, including light and heat. The light and heat gradually move from the core of the sun to its atmosphere and escape into space. Some of this light and heat reach Earth, becoming Earth's main source of energy.

There is enough hydrogen fuel in the core of the sun to last for a total of 10 billion years. The sun is now only about 5 billion years old, so you don't have to worry about the sun "burning out" any time soon!

☑ *Checkpoint* *Where in the sun does nuclear fusion occur?*

The Sun's Atmosphere

The sun's atmosphere has three layers: the photosphere, the chromosphere, and the corona. There are no boundaries between the layers of the sun.

The Photosphere The inner layer of the sun's atmosphere is called the **photosphere** (FOH tuh sfeer). The Greek word *photo* means "light," so *photosphere* means the sphere that makes light. When you look at an image or photograph of the sun, you are looking at the photosphere.

The Chromosphere During a total solar eclipse, the moon blocks light from the photosphere. The photosphere no longer provides the glare that keeps you from seeing the sun's faint, outer layers. At the beginning and end of a total eclipse, you can see a reddish glow just around the photosphere. This glow comes from the middle layer of the sun's atmosphere, the **chromosphere.** The Greek word *chromo* means "color," so the chromosphere is the "color sphere."

The Corona In the middle of a total solar eclipse, the moon also blocks light from the chromosphere. At these times an even fainter layer of the sun becomes visible, as you can see in Figure 7. This outer layer, which looks like a white halo around the sun, is called the **corona,** which means "crown" in Latin. From Earth's surface, the corona is only visible during eclipses or from special telescopes. But astronomers can use telescopes in space to observe the corona all the time and to study how it changes.

Figure 7 During a total solar eclipse, you can see light from the corona, the outer layer of the sun's atmosphere. ***Inferring*** *Why is it easiest to photograph the sun's outer layers during a solar eclipse?*

Viewing Sunspots

You can observe changes in the number of sunspots.

1. Make a data table to record the average number of sunspots you see each day.
2. Decide on a time to look for sunspots each day.
3. View the sun in the way described in the Discover activity. **CAUTION:** *Never look directly at the sun. You will hurt your eyes if you do.*
4. Make and record your observations.

Interpreting Data How much did the average number of sunspots change from day to day?

The corona sends out a stream of electrically charged particles called **solar wind.** Normally Earth's atmosphere and magnetic field block these particles. However, near the North and South poles, the particles can enter Earth's atmosphere, where they hit gas molecules and cause them to glow. The result is rippling sheets of light in the sky called auroras.

☑ *Checkpoint* *During what event could you see the sun's corona?*

Features on the Sun

For hundreds of years, scientists have used telescopes to look at the sun. (To protect their eyes, they used a filter or projected the sun onto a white surface, as in the Discover activity.) The dark spots that they saw on the sun's surface became known as sunspots. The spots seemed to move across the sun's surface, which showed that the sun rotates on its axis, just as Earth does. **Features on or above the sun's surface include sunspots, prominences, and solar flares.**

Sunspots As you can see in Figure 8, sunspots look like small, dark areas on the sun's surface. But in fact, they can be as large as Earth. **Sunspots** are areas of gas on the sun that are cooler than the gases around them. Cooler gases don't give off as much light as hotter gases, which is why sunspots look darker than the rest of the photosphere.

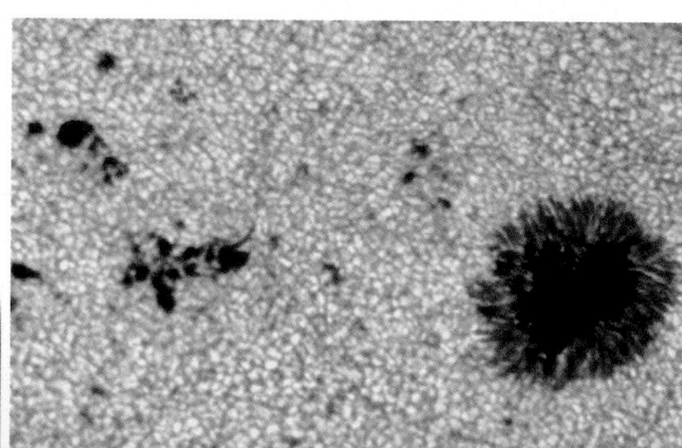

Figure 8 Sunspots are areas of gas on the sun that are cooler than the gas around them. Many of the sunspots in these photos are about as large as Earth.

The number of sunspots on the sun varies over a period of 10 or 11 years. Some scientists have hypothesized that short-term changes in climate on Earth may be related to sunspot cycles. Satellites have recently collected data that show that the amount of energy the sun produces changes slightly from year to year. Some scientists think that these increases and decreases, which may be linked to the number of sunspots, may cause changes in Earth's temperature. Scientists need to make more observations in order to test this hypothesis.

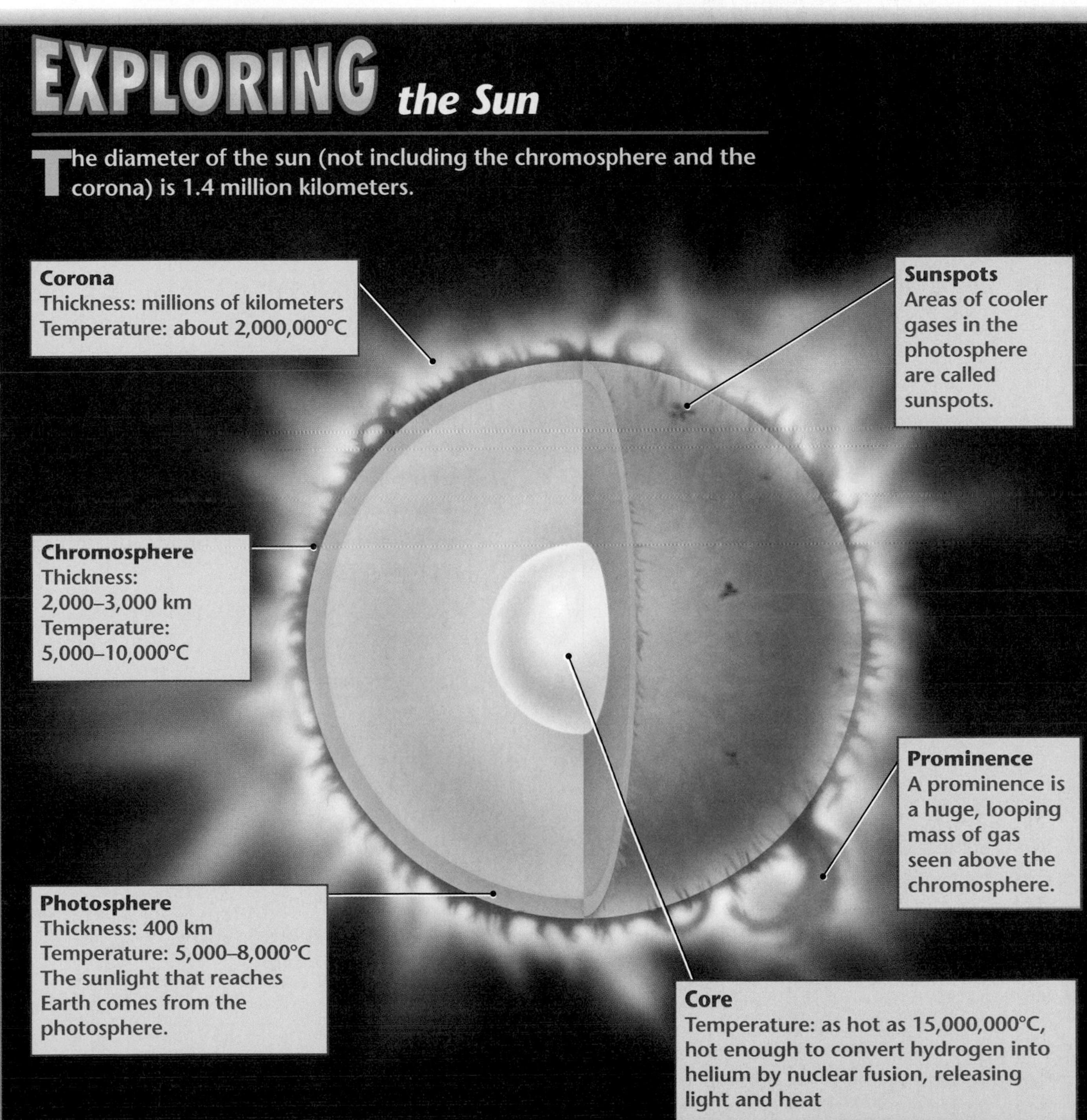

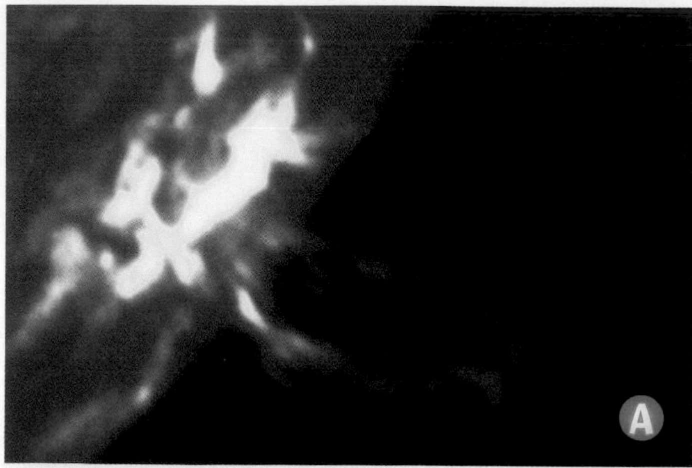

Figure 9 A. Prominences are huge loops of gas that connect different parts of sunspot regions. **B.** Solar flares on the sun release large amounts of energy. ***Relating Cause and Effect*** *How can solar flares affect communications on Earth?*

Prominences Sunspots usually occur in pairs or groups. Reddish loops of gas called **prominences** link different parts of sunspot regions. When a group of sunspots is near the edge of the sun as seen from Earth, these loops can stick out over the edge of the sun. If an eclipse hides the sun's photosphere, astronomers are able to see these loops. Prominences are about the same temperature as the sun's chromosphere, about 10,000 degrees Celsius.

Solar Flares Sometimes the loops in sunspot regions suddenly connect, releasing large amounts of energy. The energy heats gas on the sun to millions of degrees Celsius, causing the hydrogen gas to explode out into space. These explosions are known as **solar flares.**

Solar flares can greatly increase the solar wind from the corona, resulting in an increase in the number of particles reaching Earth's atmosphere. These solar wind particles can affect Earth's upper atmosphere, causing magnetic storms. Magnetic storms sometimes disrupt radio, telephone, and television signals. Magnetic storms can also cause electrical power problems for homes and businesses.

Section 2 Review

1. How is energy produced in the sun's core?
2. Name the layers of the sun's atmosphere.
3. What is the solar wind?
4. Describe three features found on or above the surface of the sun.
5. Why do sunspots look darker than the rest of the sun's photosphere?
6. How does the number of sunspots change over time?
7. **Thinking Critically Comparing and Contrasting** What is the difference between a prominence and a solar flare?

Science at Home

As the source of heat and light, the sun is an important symbol in many cultures. With family members, look around your home and neighborhood for illustrations of the sun on signs, flags, clothing, and in artwork. Which parts of the sun's atmosphere do the illustrations show? Describe the layers of the sun's atmosphere to your family.

Real-World Lab

You and Your Environment

STORMY SUNSPOTS

Problem

How are magnetic storms on Earth related to sunspot activity?

Skills Focus

graphing, interpreting data

Materials

graph paper, pencil, straightedge

Procedure

1. Use the data in the table to make a line graph of sunspot activity between 1967 and 1997.
2. On the graph, label the *x*-axis "Year." Use a scale with 2-year intervals, from 1967 to 1997.
3. Label the *y*-axis "Sunspot Number." Use a scale of 0 through 160 in intervals of 10.
4. Graph a point for the Sunspot Number for each year.
5. Complete your graph by drawing lines to connect the points.

Sunspots

Year	Sunspot Number	Year	Sunspot Number
1967	93.8	1983	66.6
1969	105.0	1985	17.9
1971	66.6	1987	29.4
1973	38.0	1989	157.6
1975	15.5	1991	145.7
1977	27.5	1993	54.6
1979	155.4	1995	17.5
1981	140.4	1997	23.4

Analyze and Conclude

1. Based on your graph, which years had the highest Sunspot Number? The lowest Sunspot Number?
2. How often does the cycle of maximum and minimum activity repeat?
3. When was the most recent maximum sunspot activity? The most recent minimum sunspot activity?
4. Compare your sunspot graph with the magnetic storms graph. What relationship can you infer between periods of high sunspot activity and magnetic storms? Explain.
5. **Apply** During which years do you think electrical disturbances on Earth were most common?

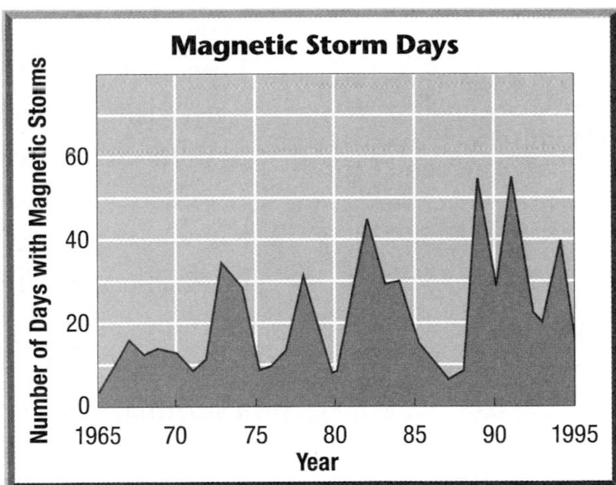

More to Explore

Using the pattern of sunspot activity you found, predict the number of peaks you would expect in the next 30 years. Around which years would you expect the peaks to occur?

SECTION 3 The Inner Planets

DISCOVER ACTIVITY

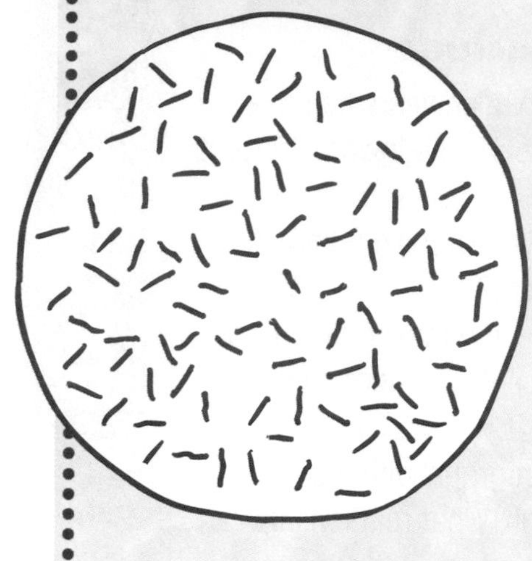

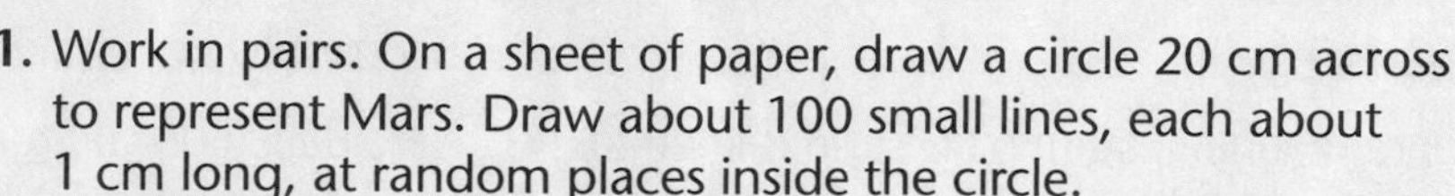

How Does Mars Look From Earth?

1. Work in pairs. On a sheet of paper, draw a circle 20 cm across to represent Mars. Draw about 100 small lines, each about 1 cm long, at random places inside the circle.
2. Have your partner look at your drawing of Mars from the other side of the room. Your partner should draw what he or she sees.
3. Compare your original drawing with what your partner drew. Then look at your own drawing from across the room.

Think It Over

Observing Did your partner draw any connecting lines that were not actually on your drawing? What can you conclude about the accuracy of descriptions of other planets as observed from Earth?

GUIDE FOR READING

- **What are the main characteristics of the inner planets?**

Reading Tip **As you read about each planet, write down the similarities and differences between that planet and Earth.**

Where could you find a planet whose surface is hot enough to melt lead? How about a planet whose atmosphere has almost entirely leaked away? And how about a planet with volcanoes higher than any on Earth? Finally, what about a planet with oceans of water brimming with fish and other life? These are descriptions of the four planets closest to the sun, known as the inner planets

Earth and the other three inner planets—Mercury, Venus, and Mars—are more similar to each other than they are to the five outer planets. **The four inner planets are small and have rocky surfaces.** These planets are often called the **terrestrial planets,** from the Latin word *terra*, which means "Earth." Figure 10 gives a summary of information about the inner planets.

Earth

Our planet's atmosphere extends more than 100 kilometers above Earth's surface. The oxygen you need to live makes up about 20 percent of the gases in Earth's atmosphere. Almost all the rest is nitrogen gas, with small amounts of argon and other gases. Earth's atmosphere also contains water vapor and clouds of water droplets. From space, astronauts can usually see past the clouds to Earth's surface.

Most of Earth, about 70 percent, is covered with water. Perhaps the planet should be named "Water" instead of "Earth"! No other planet in our solar system has oceans like Earth's.

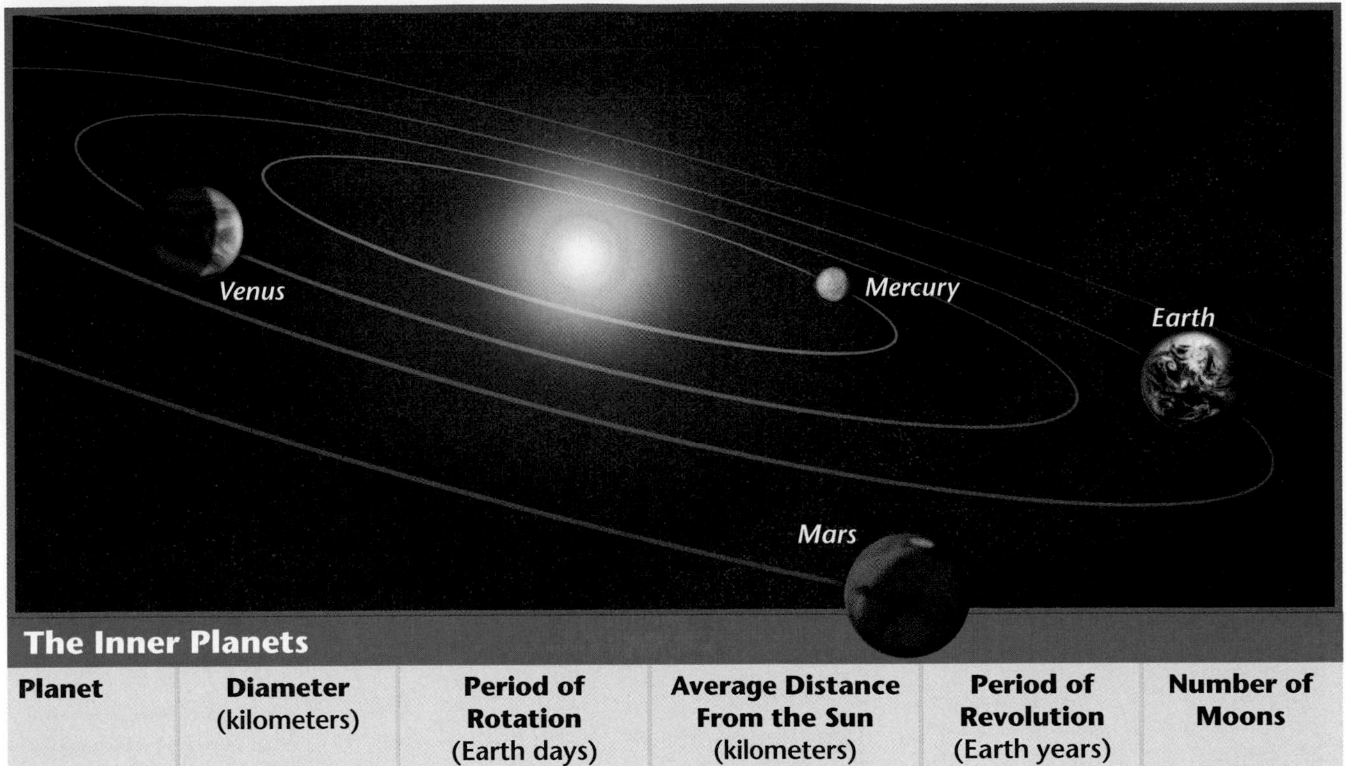

The Inner Planets

Planet	Diameter (kilometers)	Period of Rotation (Earth days)	Average Distance From the Sun (kilometers)	Period of Revolution (Earth years)	Number of Moons
Mercury	4,878	59	58,000,000	0.24	0
Venus	12,104	243	108,000,000	0.62	0
Earth	12,756	1	150,000,000	1	1
Mars	6,794	1.03	228,000,000	1.9	2

Figure 10 The inner planets take up only a small part of the solar system. The diameter of the entire solar system is more than 25 times the diameter of Mars's orbit.

INTEGRATING EARTH SCIENCE As you can see in Figure 11, Earth has three main layers—a crust, a mantle, and a core. The crust includes the solid rocky surface. Under the crust is the mantle, a layer of hot molten rock. When volcanoes erupt, this hot material rises to the surface. Earth has a dense inner core made up mainly of iron and nickel. The outer core is liquid, but the inner core is probably solid.

Scientists have been studying Earth for many years. They use what they know about Earth to make inferences about the other planets. For example, when astronomers find volcanoes on other planets, they infer that these planets have or once had hot material inside them. As we continue to learn more about our own planet, scientists will be able to apply that new knowledge to the study of the other planets.

Figure 11 Earth has a solid, rocky surface. ***Interpreting Diagrams*** *What are Earth's three main layers?*

Figure 12 This photo of Mercury and the closeup view of some of its craters (inset) were taken by the *Mariner 10* space probe.

Mercury

The planet closest to the sun is Mercury. Mercury is not much larger than Earth's moon and has no moons of its own. Astronomers have been able to infer that the interior of Mercury is made up mainly of the dense metals iron and nickel.

Exploring Mercury Because Mercury is so close to the sun, people on Earth never get a good view of Mercury. Much of the knowledge that astronomers have about Mercury's surface came from a single probe, *Mariner 10.* It flew by three times in 1974 and 1975. *Mariner 10* photographed only half of Mercury's surface, so astronomers still don't know much about what the rest of Mercury is like.

Mariner 10's photographs show that, like the moon, Mercury has many flat plains and many craters on its surface. The craters on Mercury have been named for artists, writers, and musicians, including the composers Bach and Mozart.

Mercury's Atmosphere Mercury has an extremely thin atmosphere. Apparently the gases Mercury once had were heated so much that the gas particles moved very fast. Since they were moving so fast, the gas particles escaped from Mercury's weak gravity into space. However, astronomers have detected small amounts of sodium and other gases in Mercury's atmosphere.

Mercury is a planet of extremes. It is so close to the sun that during the day, the side facing the sun reaches temperatures of 430°C. Because Mercury has almost no atmosphere, at night all the heat escapes into space. The temperature drops to –170°C. Mercury thus has a greater range of temperatures than any other planet in the solar system.

☑ ***Checkpoint*** *Why is it difficult for astronomers to learn about Mercury?*

Venus

Whenever you see a bright object in the west after sunset, it is probably Venus. When Venus shines brightly like that, it is known as the "evening star," though of course it really isn't a star. Stars shine with their own light, while Venus shines because it is reflecting light from the sun, just as the other planets and moons do. At other times, you see Venus rise before the sun in the morning. It is then known as the "morning star." At still other times, Venus is too close to the sun in the sky for you to see it from Earth.

Venus is so similar in size to Earth that it is sometimes called Earth's twin. Astronomers also think that the density and internal structure of Venus are similar to Earth's. However, in many other ways, Venus is very different from Earth.

Venus's Rotation Venus takes about 7.5 Earth months to revolve around the sun. It takes about 8 months for Venus to rotate on its axis. Venus rotates so slowly that its "day" is longer than its "year." Oddly, Venus rotates from east to west, the opposite direction from most other planets and moons. This type of rotation is called **retrograde rotation,** from the Latin words for "moving backward." One hypothesis proposed by astronomers to explain this unusual rotation is that Venus was struck by a very large object billions of years ago. Such a collision could have caused the direction of its rotation to change.

Sharpen your Skills

Graphing ACTIVITY

Using data in Figure 10 on page 707, make a line graph of the average distance from the sun and period of revolution of Mercury, Venus, Earth, and Mars. Describe how the two variables are related. If you wish, add data on Jupiter, Saturn, Uranus, Neptune, and Pluto from Figure 19 on page 715.

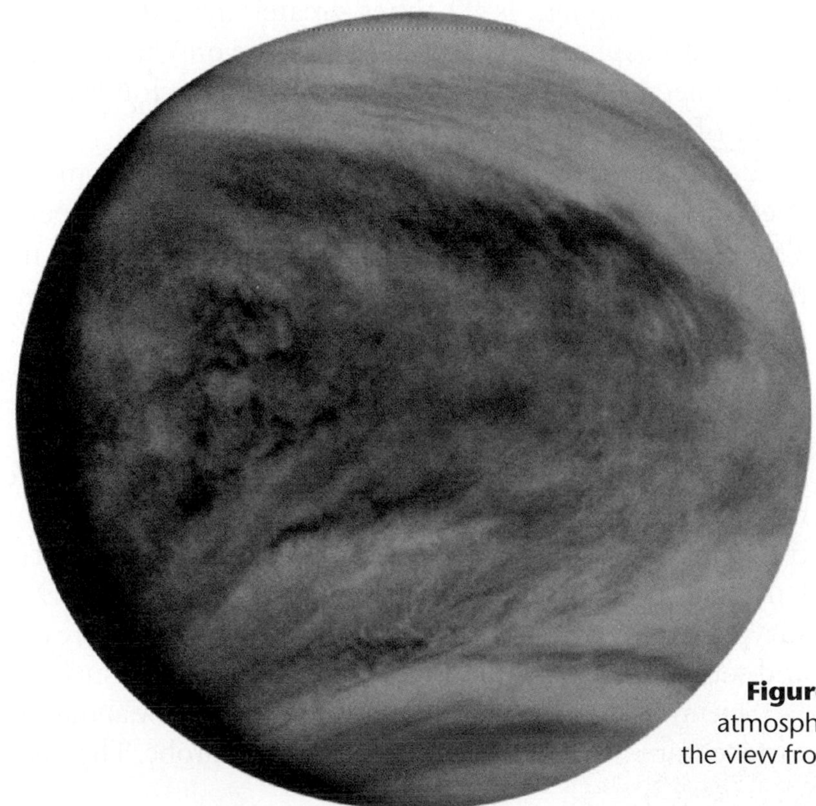

Figure 13 The thick atmosphere of Venus makes the view from space a cloudy one.

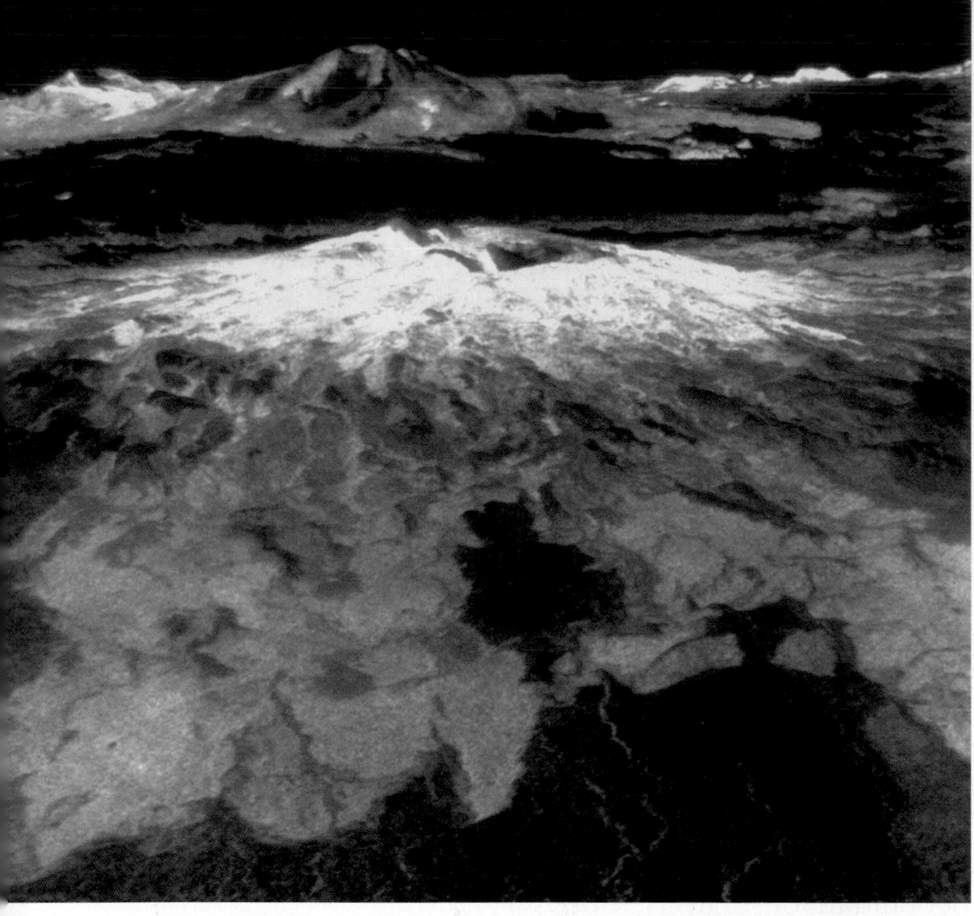

Figure 14 The *Magellan* spacecraft used radar to penetrate Venus's clouds. This three-dimensional image of a volcano on Venus was created by a computer using radar data. The height of the mountains is exaggerated to make them stand out.

Venus's Atmosphere The atmosphere of Venus is so thick that every day is a cloudy one. Venus never has a sunny day. From Earth, astronomers see only a smooth cloud cover over Venus all the time.

If you could stand on the surface of Venus, you would quickly be crushed by the weight of its atmosphere. The pressure of Venus's atmosphere is 90 times greater than the pressure of Earth's atmosphere. You could not breathe on Venus because its atmosphere is mostly carbon dioxide. Also, its clouds are partly made of sulfuric acid.

Because Venus is closer to the sun than Earth, it gets more solar energy than Earth does. Ordinary light from the sun can penetrate Venus's atmosphere and hit its surface. The surface heats up and then gives off heat. Carbon dioxide traps this heat in the atmosphere. So Venus's surface becomes hotter and hotter, until it is about 460°C—hot enough to melt lead. This trapping of heat by the atmosphere is called the **greenhouse effect.**

Music CONNECTION

The English composer Gustav Holst, who lived from 1874 to 1934, composed a group of pieces for orchestra entitled *The Planets.* The seven pieces describe musically the planets Mars, Venus, Mercury, Jupiter, Saturn, Uranus, and Neptune.

In Your Journal

Listen to a recording of one of the pieces from *The Planets.* How did Holst use music to represent the planet? What words would you use to describe what you heard?

Exploring Venus A total of 19 spacecraft have visited Venus, more than have visited any other planet. Some have even penetrated its clouds and landed on its surface. The first spacecraft to land and send back information, *Venera 7,* landed in 1970 but survived for only 23 minutes. Later spacecraft were more durable and sent back pictures and other data from Venus's surface.

Scientists have learned most of what they know about Venus's surface from data collected by the *Magellan* probe. The *Magellan* probe reached Venus in 1990, carrying radar instruments. Radar works through clouds, so *Magellan* was able to map Venus's entire surface.

The *Magellan* views are so detailed that computers can be used to figure out what Venus would look like if you could fly just above its surface. Figure 14 shows one of these radar images. Venus is covered with rock, similar to many rocky areas on Earth. Venus has volcanoes with lava flows, many craters, and strange domes not found on other planets.

☑ *Checkpoint* *Why is the surface of Venus so hot?*

Mars

Mars is called the "red planet" because it has a slightly reddish tinge when you see it in the sky. The atmosphere of Mars is mostly carbon dioxide and has only 1 percent the pressure of Earth's atmosphere. You could walk around on Mars, but you would have to wear an airtight suit and carry your own air, like a scuba diver. Mars has clouds but they are very thin compared to the clouds on Earth.

Canals on Mars? In 1877, an Italian astronomer, Giovanni Schiaparelli (sky ah puh REL ee), announced that he had seen long, straight lines on Mars. He called them *canale,* or channels. In the 1890s and early 1900s, Percival Lowell, an American astronomer, convinced many people that these lines were canals that had been built by intelligent Martians to carry water. Astronomers now know that Lowell was mistaken. There are no canals on Mars.

Astronomers have found that some water remains on Mars in the form of ice at its north pole, as shown in Figure 15. During the winter, this polar ice cap is covered by a layer of frozen carbon dioxide. Mars' south pole has an ice cap made mostly of frozen carbon dioxide.

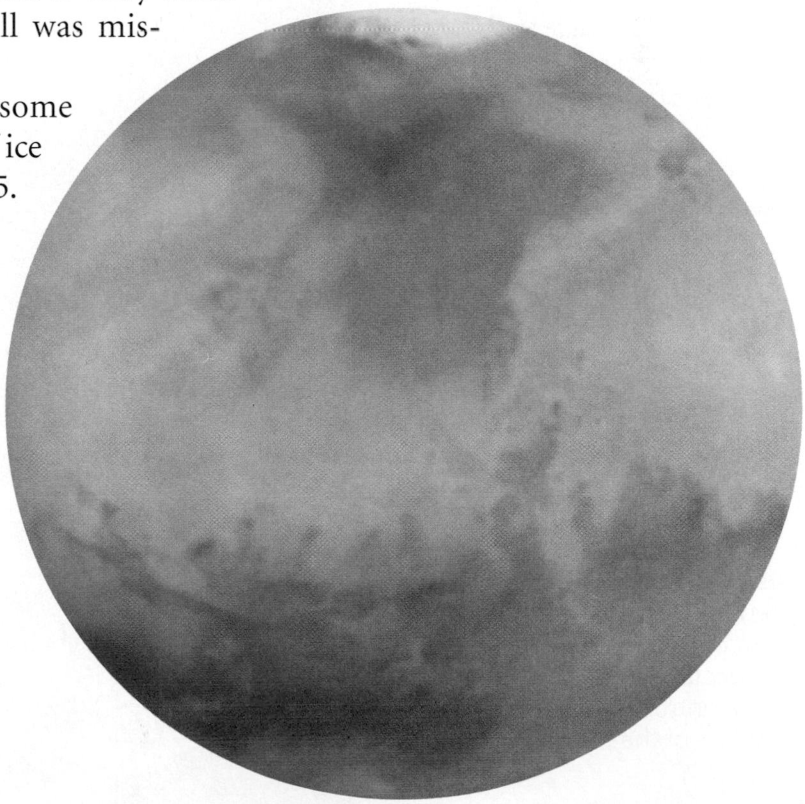

Figure 15 Because of its thin atmosphere and its distance from the sun, Mars is quite cold. Mars has ice caps at both poles.

Remote Control

How hard is it to explore another planet by remote control?

ACTIVITY

1. Tape a piece of paper over the front of a pair of goggles. Have your partner put them on.
2. Walk behind your partner and give him or her directions to move to another part of the room. **CAUTION:** *Do not give directions that would cause your partner to walk into a wall or corner, trip on an obstacle, or hit anything.*
3. Trade places and repeat Steps 1 and 2.

Inferring Which verbal directions worked best? How quickly could you move? How is this activity similar to the way NASA engineers moved *Sojourner* on Mars in 1997? How fast do you think the rover could move?

Seasons on Mars Because the axis of Mars is tilted, Mars has seasons just as Earth does. As the seasons change on the dusty surface of Mars, wind storms arise and blow the dust around. Since the dust is blown off some regions, these regions look darker. A hundred years ago, some people thought these regions looked darker because plants were growing there. Astronomers now realize that it is just that wind storms blow dust off the surface.

Exploring Mars The United States has sent many spacecraft to Mars. The first ones, in the 1960s, seemed to show that Mars is barren and covered with craters like the moon. Later spacecraft showed that regions of Mars have giant volcanoes. Astronomers see signs that hot material flowed down the volcanoes in the past, but they don't think the volcanoes are active now.

In 1976, two NASA spacecraft, *Viking 1* and *Viking 2,* landed on Mars. They sent back close-up pictures from Mars's surface. The pictures showed that the rocks look red because they are covered with a rusty dust. Other parts of the *Viking* spacecraft went into orbit around Mars, sending back detailed pictures.

In 1997, *Mars Pathfinder* landed on Mars. As Figure 16 shows, close-up photographs from *Mars Pathfinder* show no oceans or even puddles of water. Photographs taken from space do show evidence that water flowed on Mars millions of years ago.

Figure 16 The surface of Mars is rugged and rocky. The object at the bottom of the photo is the *Mars Pathfinder* lander. You can see the remote-control rover *Sojourner* in the middle of the photo.

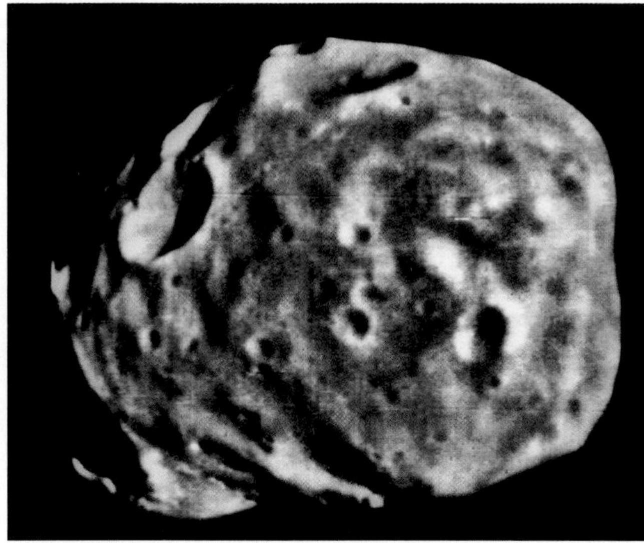

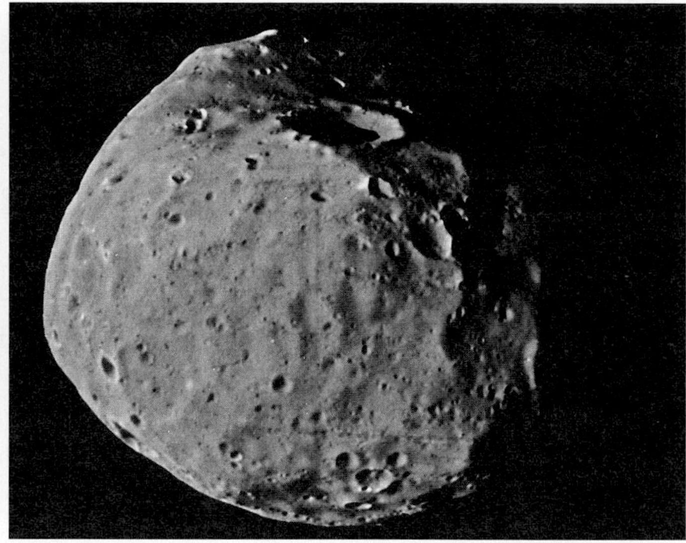

Figure 17 Phobos (left) and Deimos (right) are Mars's two small, crater-covered moons.

Mars Pathfinder carried a microwave-sized remote-control rover, called *Sojourner,* that investigated rocks on Mars. Also in 1997, another probe, *Mars Global Surveyor,* arrived in orbit around Mars, where it began mapping and photographing all of the planet's surface in detail.

Mars's Moons Mars has two very small moons. Phobos, the larger moon, is only 27 kilometers in diameter, about the distance a car can travel on the highway in 15 minutes. Deimos is even smaller, only 15 kilometers in diameter. Close-up views from space show that, like Earth's moon, Phobos and Deimos are covered with craters.

Section 3 Review

1. What features do all of the inner planets have in common?
2. What is Mercury's atmosphere like? Explain.
3. Why can astronomers see the surface of Mars clearly, but not the surface of Venus?
4. How have astronomers been able to study the surface of Venus?
5. What evidence do astronomers have that water once flowed on Mars?
6. **Thinking Critically Relating Cause and Effect** Venus is much farther from the sun than is Mercury. Yet temperatures on Venus are as high as those on the sunny side of Mercury. Explain why.

Check Your Progress

CHAPTER PROJECT 21

Now you will design a model that shows the relative diameters of the planets. Try several different scales to find one for which the smallest planet is clearly visible but the sun would still fit into your classroom. Convert the sun's and planets' diameters to scaled-down diameters and record your results on your data sheet. Compare your scaled-down diameters to objects you are familiar with, such as coins. Include your comparisons in your data sheet.

The Outer Planets

DISCOVER — ACTIVITY

How Large Are the Outer Planets?

Planet Diameters	
Planet	**Diameter**
Earth	1
Jupiter	11
Saturn	9.4
Uranus	4.0
Neptune	3.9
Pluto	0.17

The table shows the diameters of the outer planets compared to Earth. For example, Jupiter's diameter is 11 times Earth's diameter.

1. Measure the diameter of a quarter in millimeters. This represents Earth's diameter. Trace the quarter to represent Earth.
2. If Earth were the size of a quarter, calculate how large Jupiter would be. Now draw a circle to represent Jupiter.
3. Repeat Step 2 for each of the other outer planets.

Think It Over

Classifying List the planets in order from largest to smallest. What is the largest outer planet? Which outer planet is much smaller than Earth?

GUIDE FOR READING

- What are the main characteristics of the gas giant planets?
- How is Pluto different from the other outer planets?

Reading Tip Before you read, preview the photos and captions in this section. Then write down any questions you have. Look for answers as you read.

Most of what astronomers know about the outer planets has come from visits by NASA space probes. *Voyager 1* and *Voyager 2* reached Jupiter in 1979 and sent back close-up views of the planet. *Voyager 1* went on to visit Saturn in 1980. *Voyager 2* also visited Saturn, but then moved on to explore Uranus and Neptune. In 1995, the spacecraft *Galileo* reached Jupiter and dropped a probe into Jupiter's atmosphere.

Structure of the Gas Giants

Compared to Earth, some planets are huge. The largest planet, Jupiter, has a diameter that is 11 times Earth's diameter. Jupiter's mass is more than 300 times Earth's mass. If you could put Earth next to Jupiter, Earth would look like a tiny Chihuahua next to an enormous Great Dane. If Earth were the height of an average student, Jupiter would be as tall as a six-story building.

Jupiter and the other planets farthest from the sun, as seen in Figure 19, are called the outer planets. **The first four outer planets—Jupiter, Saturn, Uranus, and Neptune—are much larger than Earth, and do not have solid surfaces.** Because these four planets are all so large, they are also called the **gas giants.** The fifth outer planet, Pluto, is small and rocky like the terrestrial planets.

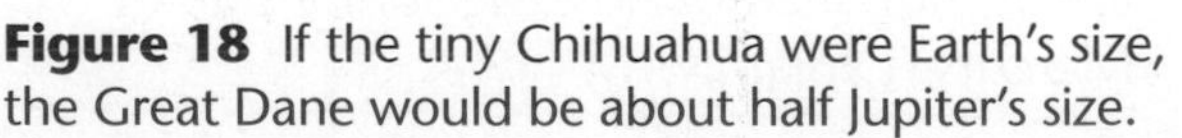

Figure 18 If the tiny Chihuahua were Earth's size, the Great Dane would be about half Jupiter's size.

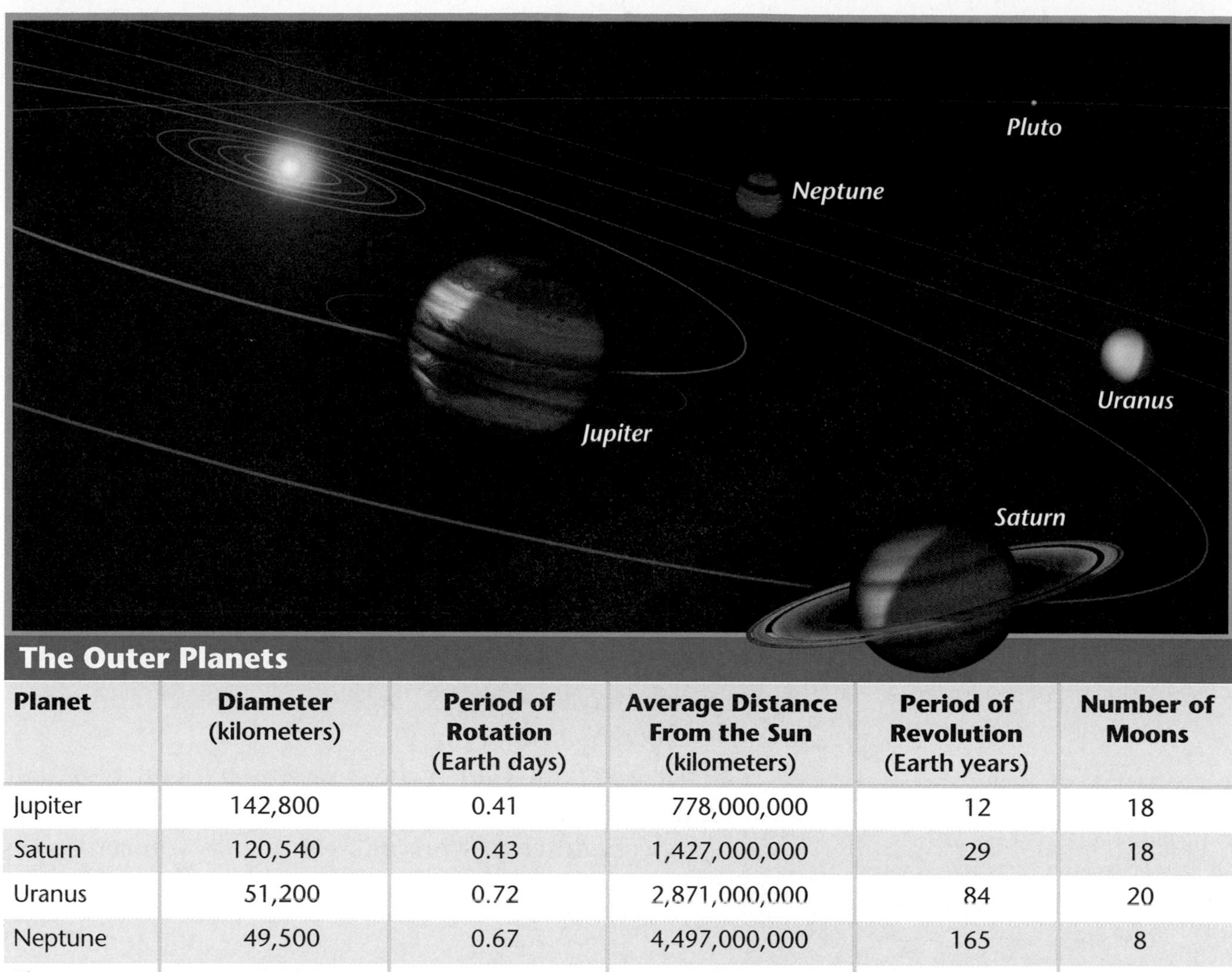

The Outer Planets

Planet	Diameter (kilometers)	Period of Rotation (Earth days)	Average Distance From the Sun (kilometers)	Period of Revolution (Earth years)	Number of Moons
Jupiter	142,800	0.41	778,000,000	12	18
Saturn	120,540	0.43	1,427,000,000	29	18
Uranus	51,200	0.72	2,871,000,000	84	20
Neptune	49,500	0.67	4,497,000,000	165	8
Pluto	2,200	6.4	5,913,000,000	248	1

Figure 19 The outer planets are much farther apart than the inner planets. At this scale, the inner planets are so small and close to the sun that they cannot be shown. ***Observing*** *Which outer planet is closest to the sun?*

Atmospheres Because the gas giants have so much mass, they exert a much stronger gravitational force than the terrestrial planets. The strong gravity keeps the giant planets' gases from escaping, so they have deep atmospheres. The composition of their atmospheres is similar to the gases in the sun. They are, on average, about 75 percent hydrogen, 24 percent helium, and 1 percent other elements.

None of the giant planets has a solid surface. If you could parachute into Jupiter's atmosphere, you would sink into denser and denser gas. You would be crushed by the enormous pressure long before you got to the center, or core, of the planet.

Solid Cores Astronomers think that each of the giant planets has a partly solid core made of rock, ice, frozen carbon dioxide, and other compounds. Each of these cores may have several times as much mass as Earth. But they are buried so deep inside the planets that it has been hard to find out much about them.

☑ ***Checkpoint*** *Why do the gas giants have large atmospheres?*

Jupiter

Jupiter is the most massive planet. In fact, Jupiter is more than 300 times as massive as Earth.

Jupiter's Atmosphere Like all of the gas giant planets, Jupiter has a thick atmosphere made up mainly of hydrogen and helium. Jupiter's atmosphere contains many colorful bands and swirls of thick clouds. An especially interesting feature in Jupiter's atmosphere is its Great Red Spot, a giant area of swirling clouds many times bigger than Earth. The Great Red Spot, shown in Figure 20, appears to be an ongoing storm similar to a hurricane on Earth.

Jupiter's Moons Recall that the astronomer Galileo discovered four of Jupiter's moons. These moons are named Io (EYE oh), Europa, Ganymede, and Callisto. These four moons are Jupiter's largest moons. Io, Ganymede, and Callisto are all larger than Earth's own moon. Since Galileo's time, astronomers have discovered more than a dozen additional moons revolving around Jupiter.

The *Voyager* and *Galileo* probes sent back images that showed detailed views of many of Jupiter's moons. Jupiter's moons are very different from one another, as you can see in Figure 21.

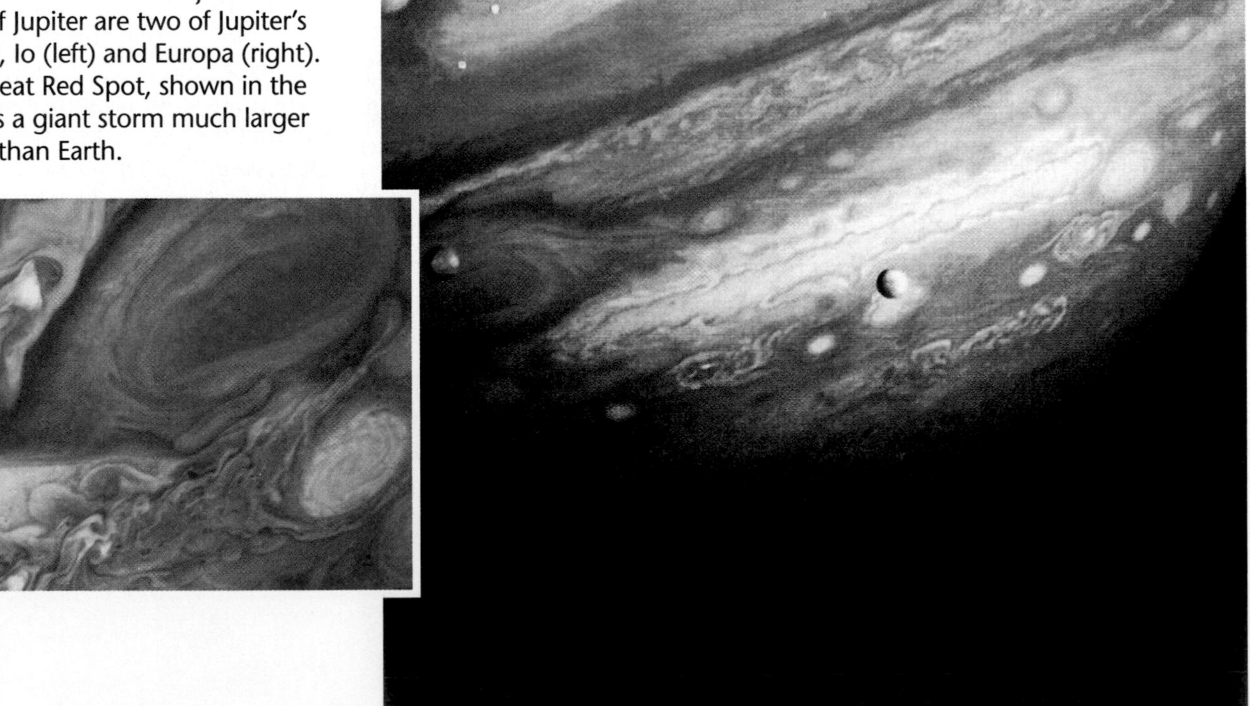

Figure 20 The larger photo of Jupiter was taken by the *Voyager 1* spacecraft. The small objects in front of Jupiter are two of Jupiter's moons, Io (left) and Europa (right). The Great Red Spot, shown in the inset, is a giant storm much larger in size than Earth.

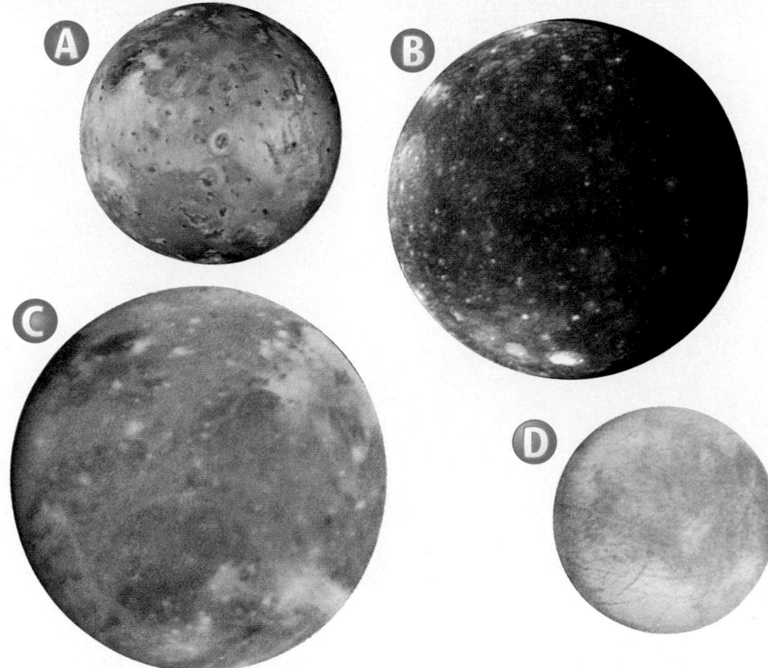

Figure 21 The astronomer Galileo discovered Jupiter's four largest moons. **A.** Io's surface is covered with large, active volcanoes. **B.** Callisto's surface is icy and covered with craters. **C.** Ganymede is the largest of Jupiter's moons. **D.** Europa's icy crust may have liquid water underneath.
Inferring *Why was Galileo able to see only Jupiter's largest moons?*

Io is covered with volcanoes. Over a dozen huge volcanoes are erupting all the time, so Io's surface changes from year to year because of the flows of hot material. The sulfur in the flows gives a variety of colors to Io's surface. From space, Io looks like a giant pizza. Europa has an icy crust that may have liquid water underneath. You will learn more about Europa in Section 6.

Ganymede is the largest of Jupiter's moons and has about twice the mass of Earth's moon. Ganymede's surface is icy and partly covered with craters. Other parts of the surface show giant grooves in the ice. Callisto also has an icy surface. It is so heavily cratered that no part of its surface is free of craters.

☑ ***Checkpoint*** *What are Jupiter's four largest moons?*

Saturn

The second-largest planet in the solar system is Saturn. Saturn is slightly smaller than Jupiter, but including its beautiful rings it has a greater overall diameter. The *Voyager* probes showed that Saturn, like Jupiter, has a thick atmosphere made up mainly of hydrogen and helium. Saturn's atmosphere also contains clouds and storms, but they are less dramatic than those on Jupiter. Saturn is the only planet that is less dense than water.

Saturn's Rings When Galileo first looked at Saturn with a telescope, he could see that something was sticking out on the sides, but he didn't know what it was. A few decades later, another astronomer using a better telescope discovered that Saturn had rings around it. Astronomers later found that these rings are made of chunks of ice and rock, each traveling in its own orbit around Saturn.

Model Saturn

ACTIVITY

Here's how you can build a scale model of Saturn.

1. Use a plastic foam sphere 8 cm in diameter to represent Saturn.
2. Use an overhead transparency to represent Saturn's rings. Cut a circle 18 cm in diameter out of the transparency. Cut a hole 9 cm in diameter out of the center of the circle.
3. Stick five toothpicks into Saturn, spaced equally around its equator. Put the transparency on the toothpicks and tape it to them. Sprinkle baking soda on the transparency.
4. Use a peppercorn to represent Titan. Place the peppercorn 72 cm away from Saturn on the same plane as the rings.

Making Models What do the particles of baking soda represent?

Figure 22 Saturn's rings are made up of ice chunks and rocks of many different sizes. The smaller photo shows that there are actually many small rings. The colors in this photo have been added by a computer. ***Observing*** *Why might it be hard to see Saturn's rings when their edges are facing Earth?*

From Earth, it looks as though Saturn has only a few rings, and that they are divided from each other by narrow, dark regions. The *Voyager* spacecraft discovered that each of these obvious rings is divided into dozens of smaller rings. In all, Saturn has hundreds of rings.

Saturn's rings are broad and thin, like a compact disc. Sometimes the rings are tipped so that observers see them at an angle. Occasionally, they are on edge, and then, because they are so thin, astronomers can't see them at all.

In the last few decades, rings have been discovered around the other three gas giants as well. But the rings around Jupiter, Uranus, and Neptune are not as spectacular as Saturn's.

Saturn's Moons Saturn's largest moon, Titan, is larger than Earth's own moon. Titan was discovered in 1665 but was known only as a point of light until the *Voyagers* went by. The probes showed that Titan has an atmosphere so thick that little light can get through it. Astronomers studying Hubble Space Telescope images can barely see Titan's surface.

Four other moons of Saturn are each over 1,000 kilometers in diameter. They are named Tethys (TEE this), Iapetus (eye AP uh tus), Dione, and Rhea. *Voyager* images show craters and canyons on these moons.

Checkpoint *What are Saturn's rings made of?*

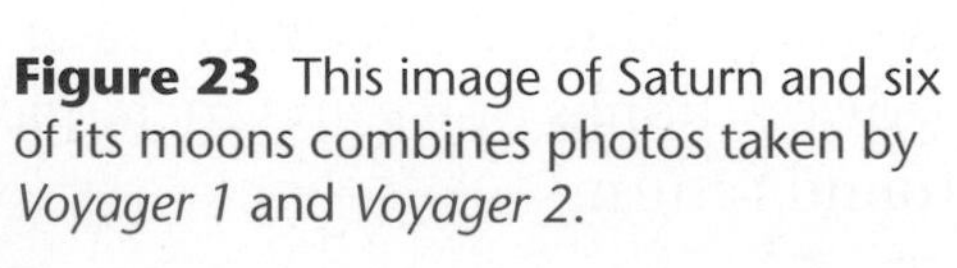

Figure 23 This image of Saturn and six of its moons combines photos taken by *Voyager 1* and *Voyager 2*.

Uranus

Although the gas giant Uranus (YOOR uh nus) is about four times the diameter of Earth, it is still much smaller than Jupiter and Saturn. Uranus is twice as far from the sun as Saturn, so it is much colder. Uranus looks bluish because of traces of methane in its atmosphere.

Discovery of Uranus In 1781, Uranus became the first new planet discovered since ancient times. Astronomer William Herschel, in England, found an object in the sky that did not look like a star. At first he thought it might be a comet. But other astronomers soon calculated its orbit and realized that it was a planet beyond Saturn. The discovery made Herschel famous and started an era of solar system exploration.

Exploring Uranus In 1986, about 200 years after Herschel's discovery, *Voyager 2* arrived at Uranus and sent back our only close-up views of that giant planet. Images from *Voyager 2* show only a few clouds on Uranus's surface, but even these few allowed astronomers to calculate that Uranus rotates in about 17 hours.

Strangely, Uranus's axis is tilted at an angle of about 90° from the vertical, as shown in Figure 24. Viewed from Earth, Uranus is rotating from top to bottom instead of from side to side, the way most of the other planets do. Astronomers think that billions of years ago Uranus was hit by an object that knocked it on its side.

Uranus's Moons Photographs from *Voyager 2* showed that Uranus's five largest moons have icy, cratered surfaces. The craters show that the moons have been hit by rocks from space. Uranus's moons also have lava flows on their surfaces, suggesting that material has erupted from inside each moon. *Voyager 2* images revealed ten moons that had never been seen before. In 1999, astronomers discovered three more moons, for a total of 20.

Language Arts CONNECTION

The ancient Romans named the planets after the gods they worshipped. Mercury was the fast, winged messenger of the gods. Venus was the goddess of beauty and Mars was the god of war. Jupiter was the king of the Roman gods. Saturn was the Roman god of agriculture.

The planets discovered in the last 200 years have also been named after ancient gods. Uranus was the Greek god who was the husband of Gaea, Earth. Neptune was the Roman god of the sea. Pluto was the Roman god of the underworld.

In Your Journal

Look in a reference book to find out more about one of the gods for which a planet has been named. Make a poster showing that god and describing his or her character.

Figure 24 **A.** This composite image of *Voyager 2* photos includes Uranus and five of its 20 moons. **B.** Unlike most other planets, Uranus rotates on its side.

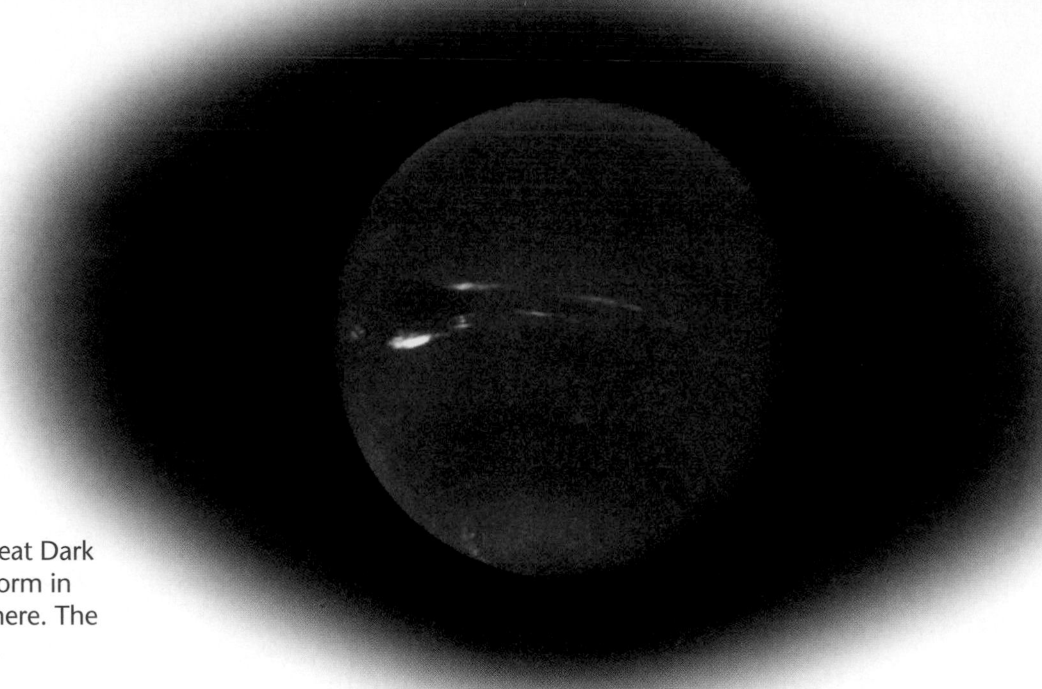

Figure 25 The Great Dark Spot was a giant storm in Neptune's atmosphere. The storm is now gone.

Neptune

Neptune is even farther from the sun than Uranus—in fact, it is 30 times Earth's distance from the sun. Unlike Uranus's nearly featureless blue atmosphere, Neptune's atmosphere contains visible clouds.

Discovery of Neptune The planet Neptune was discovered as a result of a mathematical prediction. Uranus was not quite following the orbit astronomers predicted for it. Astronomers hypothesized that there must be another, unseen planet whose gravity was affecting Uranus's orbit. By 1846, mathematicians in both England and France had calculated the orbit of this new planet. A few months later, an observer in Germany saw an unknown object in the sky. It was the new planet, now called Neptune.

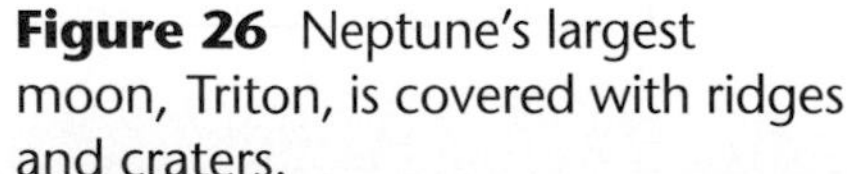

Figure 26 Neptune's largest moon, Triton, is covered with ridges and craters.

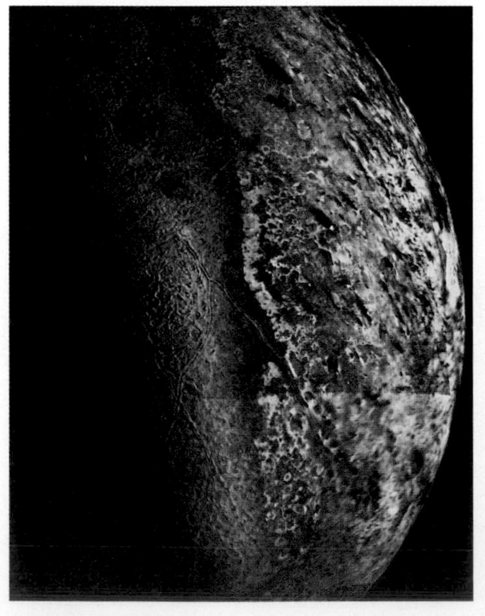

Exploring Neptune In 1989 *Voyager 2* flew by Neptune, where it photographed a Great Dark Spot, as shown in Figure 25, about the size of Earth. Like the Great Red Spot on Jupiter, the Great Dark Spot probably was a giant storm. But the storm didn't last long. Images from the Hubble Space Telescope taken five years later showed that the Great Dark Spot was gone. Other, smaller spots and regions of clouds on Neptune seem to come and go.

Neptune's Moons Astronomers have discovered eight moons revolving around Neptune. Neptune's largest moon is Triton. The *Voyager* photos show that the region near Triton's south pole is covered with a cap of ice, and that dark material erupts from underneath.

☑ ***Checkpoint*** *Before they could see Neptune, what evidence led scientists to conclude that it existed?*

Pluto and Charon

Pluto and its single moon Charon are very different from the gas giants. **Pluto and Charon have solid surfaces and masses much less than that of Earth.** In fact, Pluto is less than two thirds the size of Earth's moon. Since Charon is more than half the size of Pluto, astronomers often consider them to be a double planet instead of a planet and a moon.

Pluto and Charon are so far from the sun that they revolve around the sun only once every 248 Earth years. Because Pluto and Charon are so small and far away, astronomers have been unable to learn much about them.

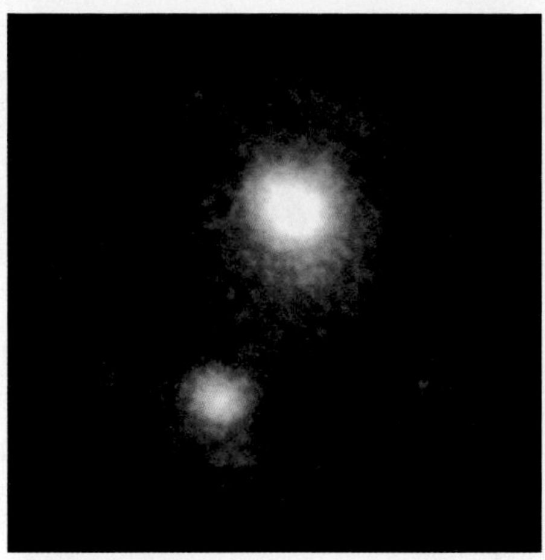

Figure 27 The space between Pluto and Charon couldn't be clearly seen from Earth until 1999, when Pluto and Charon were observed with new telescopes. This photo, taken with the Hubble Space Telescope, clearly shows them as two objects. ***Inferring*** *Why do astronomers often call Pluto and Charon a double planet?*

Discovery of Pluto and Charon The American astronomer Clyde Tombaugh discovered Pluto in 1930. He had been searching for a large object he thought might be affecting Neptune's orbit. Tombaugh spent 10 months looking at hundreds of thousands of images before he found Pluto. Charon was not discovered until 1978, by the astronomer James Christy. Christy was studying photographs of Pluto when he noticed that Pluto seemed to have a "bump." The bump turned out to be Charon.

Is Pluto Really a Planet? Pluto is so small that many astronomers do not think it should be called a planet at all. Pluto may be merely the largest of thousands of objects revolving around the sun out beyond Neptune. If astronomers had found these other objects before they found Pluto, they might not have called Pluto a planet.

Section 4 Review

1. How are the gas giants similar to each other? How are they different?
2. How is Pluto different from the gas giants?
3. What is the most prominent feature of Jupiter's surface? What causes this feature?
4. Why do astronomers think Uranus may have been hit by another object billions of years ago?
5. **Thinking Critically Predicting** Do you think astronomers have found all of the moons of the outer planets? Explain.

Check Your Progress

CHAPTER PROJECT 21

Once you have models that show size and distance separately, design another scale model of the solar system. This time, use the same scale for both size and distance. If your chalkboard is the sun, which planets would be in your classroom? Where would the other planets be with respect to your classroom, school grounds, and town?

Discuss with classmates any problems that would come up in building a model using the same scale for both size and distance. Revise your model as needed.

Skills Lab

Developing Hypotheses

Speeding Around the Sun

In this lab, you will make and test a hypothesis about how a planet's distance from the sun is related to its period of revolution.

Problem

How does a planet's distance from the sun affect its period of revolution?

Materials

string, 1.5 m
plastic tube, 6 cm
meter stick
weight or several washers
one-hole rubber stopper
stopwatch

Procedure 

1. What do you think is the relationship between a planet's distance from the sun and its period of revolution? Write your hypothesis in the form of an "If . . . then . . ." statement.

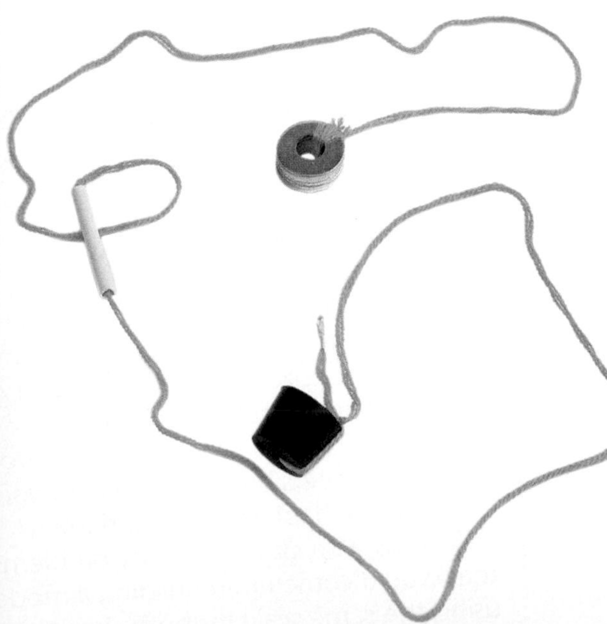

2. To test your hypothesis, you need to make a model planet.
   a. Thread the string through the rubber stopper hole. Tie the end of the string to the main part of the string. Pull tightly to make sure that the knot will not become untied.
   b. Thread the other end of the string through the plastic tube and tie a weight to that end. Have your teacher check both knots.
   c. Hold the plastic tube in your hand above your head. Swing the stopper around above your head. Practice keeping the stopper moving at a constant speed. The circle represents the planet's orbit. **CAUTION:** *Stand away from other students. Make sure the swinging stopper will not hit students or objects. Do not let go of the string.*
3. Before you try different distances for your model planet, copy the data table into your notebook.

DATA TABLE

Distance (cm)	Period of Revolution			
	Trial 1	Trial 2	Trial 3	Average
20				
40				
60				

4. Pull the string so the stopper is 20 cm away from the plastic tube. Swing the stopper just fast enough to keep the stopper moving.

5. Have your partner time how long it takes for the stopper to make 10 revolutions. Divide by 10 to find the period of revolution. Record this number as Trial 1.
6. Repeat Steps 4–5 two more times. Record your results as Trials 2 and 3. Add the results of the three trials together and divide by three to find the average period of revolution.
7. If you pull the stopper out to 40 cm, do you think the period of revolution will increase or decrease? To find out, pull the stopper out to 40 cm and repeat Steps 4–6.
8. Based on your results in Step 7, do you want to revise your hypothesis? Make any needed changes. Then pull the stopper out to 60 cm and repeat Steps 4–6.

Analyze and Conclude

1. Which object in your model represented the sun? Which represented the planet?
2. What force did the pull on the string represent?
3. When you pulled the stopper out to make the orbit larger, did the string then represent a stronger or weaker force of gravity? Why?
4. What happened to the period of revolution when you made the orbit larger in Steps 7 and 8?
5. Did your observations support your hypothesis? Summarize your conclusions based on your observations.
6. Which planets take less time to revolve around the sun—those closer to the sun or those farther away? Use the model to support your answer.
7. **Think About It** What information did you consider when you made your hypothesis? How did having some experimental data help you modify your hypothesis?

Design an Experiment

Write a hypothesis relating the mass of a planet to its period of revolution. Then, using a stopper with a different mass, modify the activity to test your hypothesis. Before you swing the stopper, have your teacher check your knots.

Comets, Asteroids, and Meteors

Discover

Which Way Do Comet Tails Point?

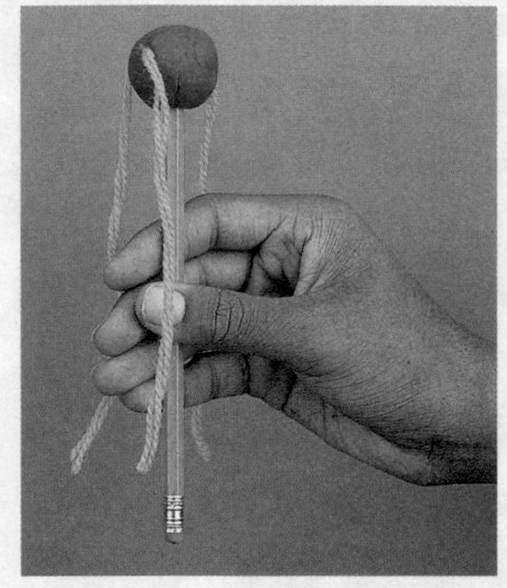

1. Form a small ball out of modeling clay to represent a comet.
2. Using a pencil point, push three 10-cm lengths of string into the ball. The strings represent the comet's tail. Stick the ball onto the pencil point, as shown in the photo.
3. Hold the ball about 1 m in front of a fan. The air from the fan represents the solar wind. Move the ball toward the fan, away from the fan, and from side to side. **CAUTION:** *Keep your fingers away from the fan blades.*

Think It Over

Inferring How does moving the ball affect the direction in which the strings point? What determines which way the tail of a comet points?

Guide for Reading

- **What are the characteristics of comets and asteroids?**
- **Where do meteoroids come from?**

Reading Tip **As you read, make an outline of this section using the headings as the main topics.**

Imagine watching a cosmic collision! That's exactly what happened in July 1994. Eugene and Carolyn Shoemaker and David Levy discovered a new comet in 1993 that had previously broken into pieces near Jupiter. In 1994, the fragments returned and crashed into Jupiter. On Earth, astronomers were fascinated to see the huge explosions—some were as large as Earth!

As this story shows, the sun, planets, and moons aren't the only objects in the solar system. There are also millions of smaller objects, most of which are classified as comets and asteroids.

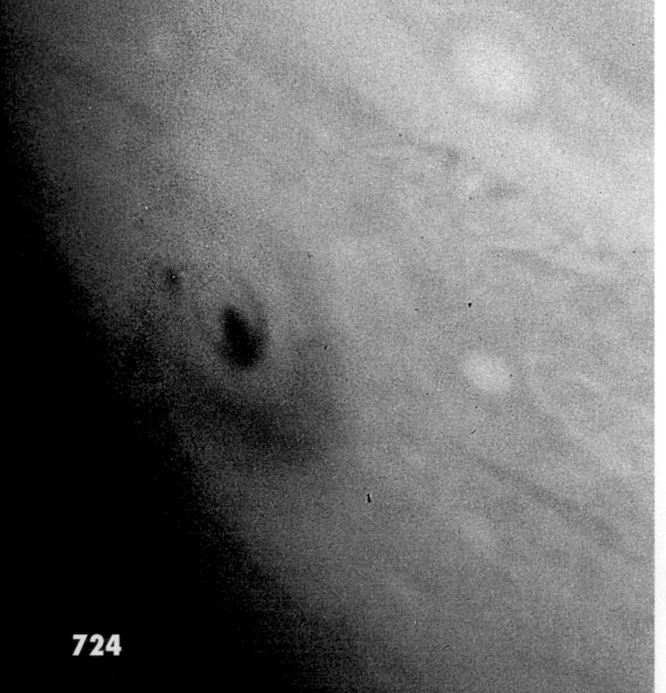

◄ **A dark ring on Jupiter caused by comet Shoemaker-Levy 9**

Comets

One of the most glorious things you can see in the night sky is a comet. A bright comet may be visible only for days or weeks or months, but is well worth seeing. In April 1997, for example, Comet Hale-Bopp and its bright dust tail were clearly visible even without a telescope.

You can think of a **comet** as a "dirty snowball" about the size of an Earth mountain. **Comets are chunks of ice and dust whose orbits are usually very long, narrow ellipses.** Because their orbits are so

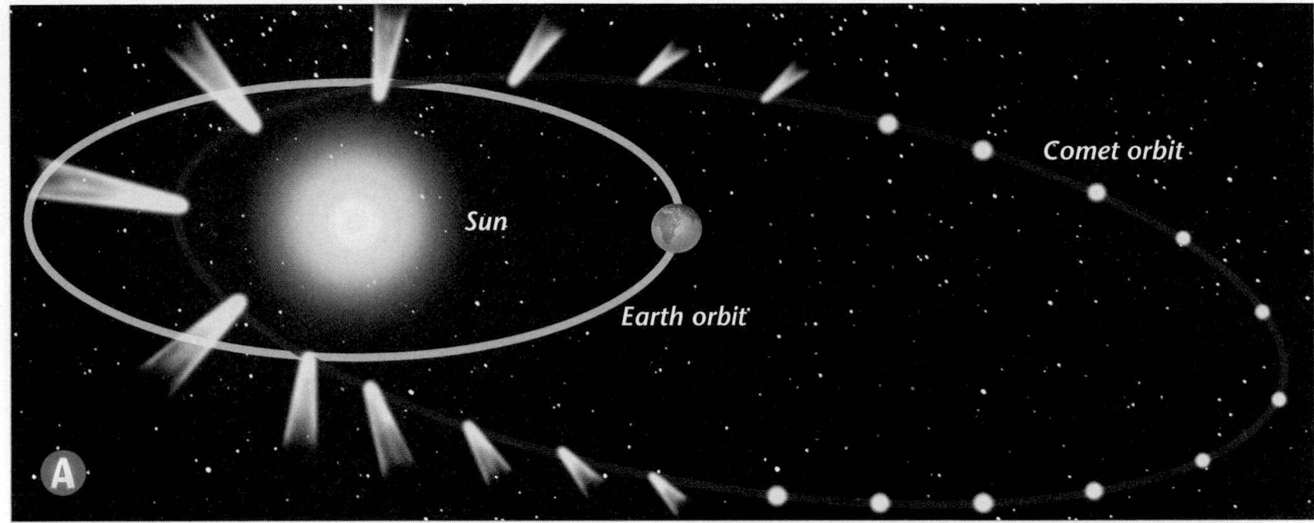

elliptical, few of them pass near Earth. They can usually then be seen only briefly. When a comet gets close enough to the sun, the energy in the sunlight turns the ice into gas, releasing dust. The gas and dust form an outer layer called the coma. Figure 28 shows the inner layer of the comet, which is then called the nucleus. The brightest part of a comet, the comet's head, is made up of the nucleus and coma.

Figure 28 **A.** Most comets revolve around the sun in very long, narrow orbits. **B.** The main parts of a comet are the nucleus, the coma, and the tail. ***Observing*** *What shape is a comet's orbit?*

Remember that the sun's corona produces a stream of particles called the solar wind. Solar wind pushes the gas from a comet away from the sun. Gas and dust form the comet's tail. The tail looks like hair; in fact, the name *comet* means "long-haired star" in Greek.

A comet's tail can be hundreds of millions of kilometers long and stretch across most of the sky. The material is stretched out very thinly, however, so there isn't much mass in a comet tail.

In 1705, Edmond Halley, an English astronomer, calculated the orbits of 24 comets that people had observed over hundreds of years. Halley realized that several of the comets seemed to have the same orbit and suggested that they were actually the same comet. Halley calculated that this comet appeared about every 76 years, and predicted that it would reappear in 1758. When this prediction came true, the comet was named Halley's Comet. In 1986, the last time Halley's Comet appeared, the European Space Agency's *Giotto* spacecraft flew within a few hundred kilometers of it.

☑ ***Checkpoint*** *How did Halley's Comet get its name?*

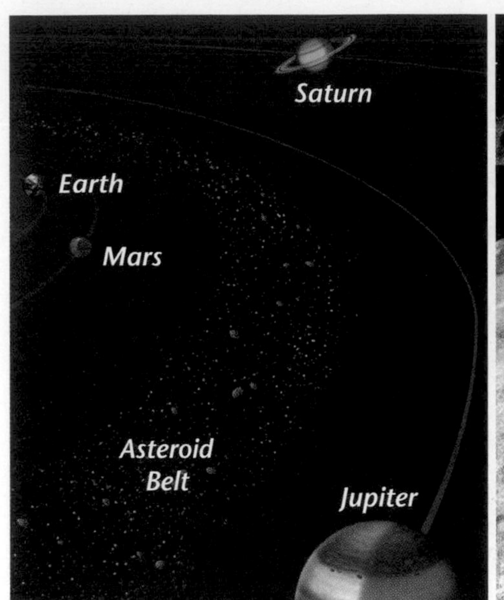

Figure 29 The asteroid belt (left) lies between Mars and Jupiter. Asteroids come in many sizes and shapes, as shown in this artist's depiction (center). NASA's *Galileo* mission photographed the asteroid Gaspra (right) .

Asteroids

Between 1801 and 1807, astronomers discovered four small objects between the orbits of Mars and Jupiter. They named the objects Ceres, Pallas, Juno, and Vesta. Over the next 80 years, astronomers found 300 more. These objects, called **asteroids,** are too small and too numerous to be considered full-fledged planets. **Most asteroids revolve around the sun between the orbits of Mars and Jupiter.** This region of the solar system, shown in Figure 29, is known as the **asteroid belt.**

Astronomers have discovered more than 10,000 asteroids, and more are found every month. Ceres, Pallas, Juno, and Vesta are among the dozen that are over 250 kilometers across.

INTEGRATING EARTH SCIENCE Some asteroids come near the orbit of Earth. Someday, one of these near-Earth asteroids could hit Earth. When a large asteroid hit Earth 65 million years ago, it exploded, making a crater 200 kilometers in diameter near the Yucatán Peninsula of Mexico. The explosion almost certainly raised trillions of tons of dust into the atmosphere, blocking the light from the sun for months. Debris from the explosion probably started huge fires that destroyed much of Earth's forests and grass. Scientists hypothesize that as a result many species of organisms, including the dinosaurs, became extinct.

Meteors

Imagine being outside in the country on a clear night, looking up at the sky. Suddenly, you see a streak of light flashing across the sky. Within seconds, you see another streak. For an hour or so, you see a streak at least once a minute. You are watching a meteor shower. Meteor showers happen regularly, several times a year.

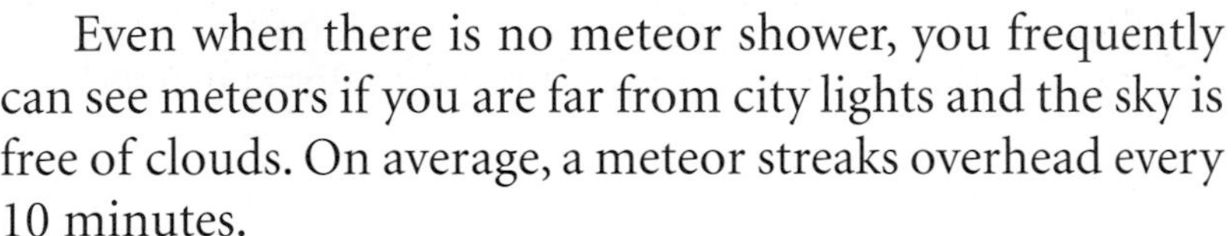

Figure 30 A. Meteor Crater in Arizona is the best-known meteorite crater on Earth. It was formed when a meteorite hit Earth about 40,000 years ago. **B.** Meteoroids make streaks of light, like the one above, as they burn up in the atmosphere.

Even when there is no meteor shower, you frequently can see meteors if you are far from city lights and the sky is free of clouds. On average, a meteor streaks overhead every 10 minutes.

A **meteoroid** is a chunk of rock or dust in space. **Meteoroids usually come from comets or asteroids.** When a comet breaks up, it forms a cloud of dust that continues to move through the solar system. When Earth passes through one of these dust clouds, bits of dust enter Earth's atmosphere.

When a meteoroid enters Earth's atmosphere, friction makes it burn up and produce the streak of light you see in the sky—a **meteor.** If the meteoroid is large enough, it may not burn up completely. Meteoroids that pass through the atmosphere and hit Earth's surface are called **meteorites.** The craters on the moon and on other objects in the solar system were caused by meteoroids.

Meteorites fall all over Earth. Most of them look just like stones, so nobody notices them. A few meteorites are made almost entirely of iron and nickel, and so are unusually heavy for their size. This makes them more likely to be identified as meteorites than as Earth rocks.

Section 5 Review

1. What is a comet made of?
2. Where are most asteroids found?
3. What are the main sources of meteoroids?
4. What is the difference between a meteor and a meteorite?
5. **Thinking Critically Predicting** Describe what might happen if an asteroid the size of the one that hit Earth 65 million years ago hit Earth today.

Science at Home

Meteor showers occur regularly on specific dates. (The Perseids meteor shower, for example, occurs every August 12.) Look in the newspaper or almanac for information about the next meteor shower. With adult family members, go outside on that night and look for meteors. Explain to your family what causes the glow.

SECTION 6 Is There Life Beyond Earth?

DISCOVER ACTIVITY

Is Yeast Alive or Not?

1. Open a package of yeast and pour it into a bowl.
2. Look at the yeast carefully. Make a list of your observations.
3. Fill the bowl about halfway with warm water (about 20°C). Add a spoonful of sugar. Stir the mixture with the spoon. Wait five minutes.
4. Now look at the yeast again and make a list of your observations.

Think It Over

Forming Operational Definitions Which of your observations seem to suggest that yeast is not alive? Which observations suggest that yeast is alive? How can you tell if something is alive?

GUIDE FOR READING

- **What conditions do living things need to exist on Earth?**
- **Why do scientists think Mars and Europa are good places to look for signs of life?**

Reading Tip **As you read, write down evidence to support this statement: Life may exist in other parts of the solar system.**

Most of Antarctica is covered with snow and ice. You would not expect to see rocks lying on top of the whiteness. But surprisingly, in some places people have found rocks lying on the surface. When scientists examined the rocks, they found that the rocks are meteorites. A few of the meteorites came from Mars. Astronomers think that meteoroids hitting the surface of Mars must have blasted chunks of rock into space. The rocks eventually entered Earth's atmosphere and landed in Antarctica.

Recently a team of scientists announced that a meteorite from Mars found in Antarctica shows tiny shapes that look like fossils—the remains of ancient life preserved in rock. Many scientists doubt that the shapes really are fossils. But if they are, it would be a sign that life forms similar to bacteria once existed on Mars. Life other than that on Earth would be called **extraterrestrial life.**

Figure 31 Dr. Ursula Marvin (lying down) studies meteorites such as this one in Antarctica.

The "Goldilocks Conditions"

If you did the Discover activity, you saw that it can be hard to tell whether something is alive or not. But all living things on Earth have several characteristics in common. Living things are made up of one or more cells. Living things take in energy and use it to grow and develop. They reproduce, producing new living things of the same type. Living things also give off waste.

A yeast cell, for example, is a living thing. Each yeast organism has one cell. Yeast cells take in sugar for energy. They reproduce and make new yeast cells. And yeast cells produce carbon dioxide as waste. A yeast cell, then, fulfills all the requirements for a living thing.

Nobody knows whether life exists anywhere other than Earth. Scientists often talk about the conditions needed by "life as we know it." **Earth has liquid water and a suitable temperature range and atmosphere for living things to survive.** Other planets do not have such favorable conditions, which scientists sometimes call the "Goldilocks conditions." That is, the temperature is not too hot and not too cold. It is just right. If Earth were hotter, water would always be a gas—water vapor. If Earth were colder, water would always be solid ice. On Earth, water exists as a liquid as well as a solid and a gas.

Are these the conditions necessary for life? Or are they just the conditions that Earth's living things happen to need? Scientists have only one example of life to study: life on Earth. Unless scientists find life somewhere else, there will be no way to answer these questions.

Communicating

You are writing ACTIVITY a letter to a friend who lives on another planet. Your friend has never been to Earth and has no idea what the planet is like. Explain in your letter why the conditions on Earth make it the ideal place for living things.

☑ *Checkpoint What are some characteristics of all living things?*

Life on Earth

In recent years, astounding discoveries have been made deep under the ocean. Sunlight never penetrates there. But deep-diving submarines have discovered giant tube worms and other animals that live at very high pressure in the dark. Single-celled forms of life have been discovered that are different from plants, animals, or bacteria. These newly discovered life forms get their energy not from sunlight, but from chemicals. Other scientists have found tiny life forms in caves and deep inside solid rocks. Still other scientists have found life surviving in hot springs that had been thought to be too hot to support life.

The range of conditions in which life can exist is much greater than scientists once thought. Perhaps life forms exist that do not even need the "Goldilocks conditions"!

Figure 32 These colonies of microorganisms were discovered deep in a cave in Mexico. ***Inferring*** *How does studying unusual organisms like these help scientists predict what extraterrestrial life might be like?*

Life on Mars?

Recall that Mars is the planet most similar to Earth. That makes Mars the most obvious place to look for living things similar to those on Earth.

The *Viking* Missions In 1970, a spacecraft found regions on the surface of Mars that look like stream beds with criss-crossing paths of water. These shapes, shown in Figure 33, were almost certainly formed by flowing water. **Since life as we know it requires water, scientists hypothesize that Mars may have once had the conditions needed for life to exist.**

Twin *Viking* spacecraft reached Mars in 1976. Each had one part that landed on Mars's surface and another part that stayed in orbit, taking pictures of most of the surface. Each of the *Viking* landers carried a compact biology laboratory meant to search for life forms.

The biology laboratories on the landers tested the Martian air and soil for signs of life. Each laboratory was designed to see if there were life forms that used oxygen and gave off carbon dioxide, as many living things on Earth do. A robot scoop brought some soil from Mars's surface into the lab and added water to see if the sample gave off oxygen. None of these tests showed any evidence of life.

☑ ***Checkpoint*** *What evidence shows that there may once have been running water on Mars?*

Meteorites From Mars Interest in life on Mars was increased by the report in 1996 about the meteorite from Mars that may contain fossils. The scientists' report started a huge debate. What were the tubelike things in the meteorite? Many scientists have suggested that the tiny shapes found in the meteorite do not prove that life forms once existed on Mars. Perhaps the shapes came from natural processes on Mars and are just lumps of hard-ened clay. Perhaps the shapes came from snow that got into cracks in the meteorite after it landed on Earth. Were the shapes

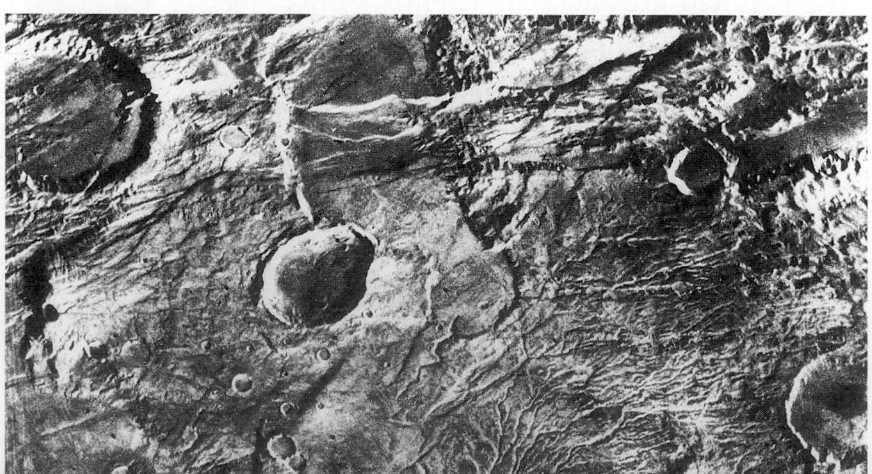

Figure 33 These patterns on the surface of Mars are probably evidence that liquid water once flowed on Mars. ***Applying Concepts*** *Why does this evidence make it more likely that there may once have been life on Mars?*

too deep inside the rocks to be from Earth? Perhaps the shapes are too small to be the remains of life forms. They are only one-hundredth the size of any other known life forms.

The most effective way to answer these questions is to send more probes to Mars. Future Mars missions should be able to bring samples of rocks and soil back to Earth for detailed analysis. Scientists may not yet have evidence of life on Mars, but hope is growing that we can soon solve the mystery.

Life on Europa?

Many scientists think that Europa, one of Jupiter's moons, may have the conditions necessary for life to develop. Photos from *Voyager* and *Galileo* showed that Europa has a very smooth, icy crust with giant cracks in it.

Close-up views from *Galileo* show that Europa's ice has broken up and re-formed, resulting in twisted, house-sized blocks of ice. Similar patterns occur in the ice crust over Earth's Arctic Ocean. Could this mean that there is a liquid ocean under Europa's ice? The water in the ocean could possibly be kept liquid by heat coming from inside Europa. **If there is liquid water on Europa, there might also be life.**

How can scientists study conditions under Europa's ice sheet? Such studies are many years off. People will have to wait for the next generation of space probes to search for liquid water on Europa.

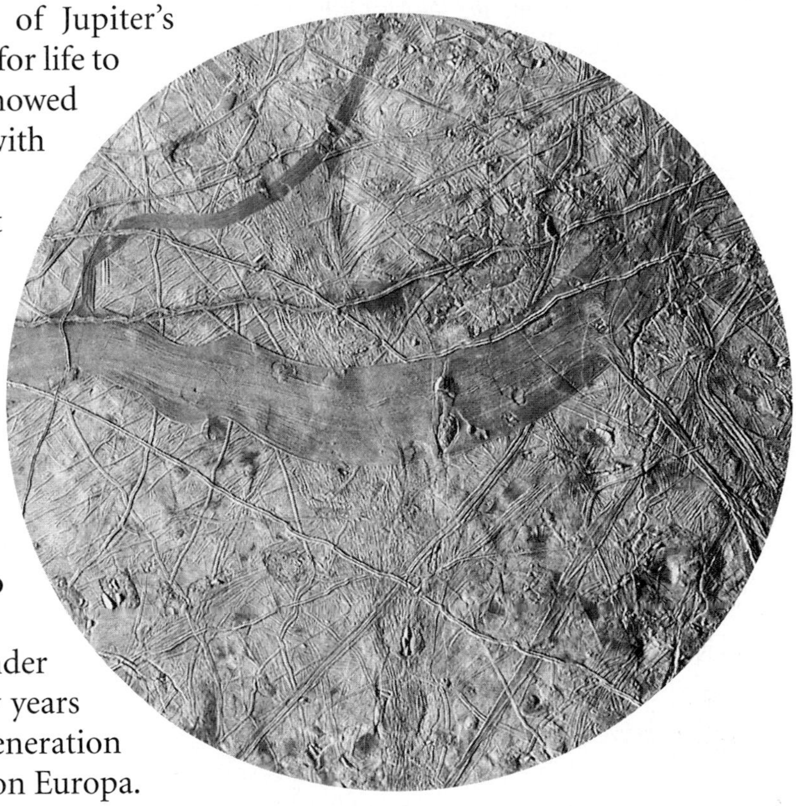

Figure 34 Europa is covered with a layer of ice similar to the ice covering Earth's Arctic Ocean. There may be liquid water under the ice.

Section 6 Review

1. What conditions does life on Earth need to survive?
2. Why do astronomers think there could be life on Europa?
3. How did the *Viking* missions search for life on Mars?
4. **Thinking Critically Applying Concepts** Do you think there could be life as we know it on Venus? Explain. (*Hint:* Review page 66.)

Science at Home

Imagine that scientists have found intelligent extraterrestrial life. With family members, make up a message to send to the extraterrestrials. Remember that they will not understand English, so you should use only symbols and drawings in your message.

Science and Society

Space Exploration—Is It Worth the Cost?

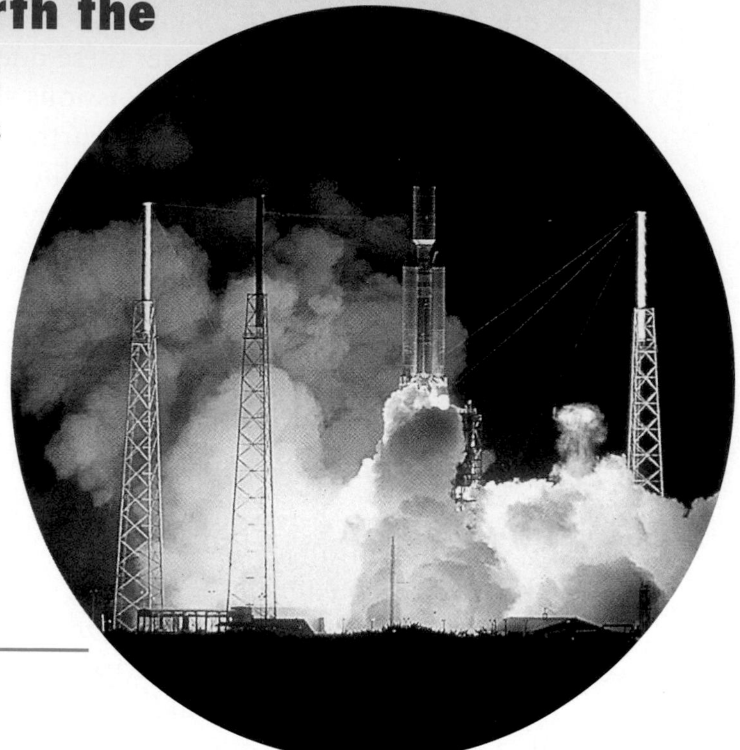

Imagine that your spacecraft has just landed on Mars after a two-month journey from Earth. You've spent years planning for this moment. Canyons, craters, and distant plains stretch out before you. You check your spacesuit and prepare to step out onto the rocky red surface of Mars.

Is such a trip likely? Would it be worthwhile? How much is space flight really worth to human society? Scientists and politicians have already started to debate such questions. Space exploration can help us learn more about the universe. But exploration is risky and expensive. Sending people into space costs billions of dollars and risks human lives. How can we balance the costs and benefits of space exploration?

The Issues

Should Humans Travel Into Space? Many Americans think that Neil Armstrong's walk on the moon in 1969 was one of the great moments in history. Also, learning how to keep people alive in space has led to improvements in everyday life. Safer equipment for firefighters, easier ways to package frozen food, and effective heart monitors have all come out of space program research.

What Are the Alternatives? Space exploration can involve a project to put a person on Mars. It also can involve a more limited use of scientific instruments near Earth, such as the Hubble Space Telescope. Instead of sending people, we could send space probes like *Mars Pathfinder* to other planets.

Is Human Space Exploration Worth the Cost? Scientists who favor human travel into space say that only people can collect certain kinds of information. And using simpler space vehicles that are cheaper to build can also save money. But no one knows if research in space really provides information quicker than research that can be done on Earth. Many critics of space research think that other needs are more important. One United States senator said, "Every time you put money into the space station, there is a dime that won't be available for our children's education or for medical research."

You Decide

1. **Identify the Problem**
   In your own words, list the costs and benefits of space exploration.

2. **Analyze the Options**
   Make a chart of three different approaches to space exploration: sending humans to another planet, doing only Earth-based research, and one other option. What are the benefits and drawbacks of each approach?

3. **Find a Solution**
   Imagine that you are a member of Congress who has to vote on a new budget. There is a fixed amount of money to spend, so you have to decide which needs are most important. Make a list of your top ten priorities. Explain your decisions.

CHAPTER 21 STUDY GUIDE

Observing the Solar System

Key Ideas

- ◆ Ptolemy thought that Earth is at the center of the system of planets.
- ◆ Copernicus thought that the sun is at the center of the planets. Galileo's observations supported Copernicus's theory.
- ◆ Kepler discovered that the orbits of the planets are ellipses.
- ◆ Newton concluded that two factors—inertia and gravity—combine to keep the planets in orbit.

Key Terms

geocentric
heliocentric
ellipse
inertia

The Sun

Key Ideas

- ◆ The sun's energy comes from nuclear fusion.
- ◆ The sun's atmosphere has three layers: the photosphere, the chromosphere, and the corona.
- ◆ Features on or above the sun's surface include sunspots, prominences, and solar flares.

Key Terms

nuclear fusion
core
photosphere
chromosphere
corona
solar wind
sunspot
prominence
solar flare

The Inner Planets

Key Idea

- ◆ The four inner planets—Mercury, Venus, Earth, and Mars—are small and have rocky surfaces. They are often called the terrestrial planets.

Key Terms

terrestrial planets
retrograde rotation
greenhouse effect

The Outer Planets

Key Ideas

- ◆ Four outer planets—Jupiter, Saturn, Uranus, and Neptune—are much larger than Earth.
- ◆ Pluto and Charon have solid surfaces and masses much less than that of Earth.

Key Term

gas giant

Comets, Asteroids, and Meteors

Key Ideas

- ◆ Comets are chunks of ice and dust that usually have long, elliptical orbits.
- ◆ Most asteroids revolve around the sun between the orbits of Mars and Jupiter.

Key Terms

comet
asteroid
asteroid belt
meteoroid
meteor
meteorite

Is There Life Beyond Earth?

INTEGRATING LIFE SCIENCE

Key Ideas

- ◆ Earth has liquid water and a suitable temperature range and atmosphere for living things to survive.
- ◆ Since life as we know it requires water, scientists hypothesize that Mars may have once had the conditions for life to exist.

Key Term

extraterrestrial life

Organizing Information

Compare/Contrast Table On a separate piece of paper, make a table comparing and contrasting the geocentric and heliocentric systems. Include information on the following: object at the center of the system; objects that move around the center; who the system was first proposed by; and who supported the system. (For more on compare/contrast tables, see the Skills Handbook.)

Reviewing Content

Multiple Choice

Choose the letter of the answer that best completes each statement.

1. Copernicus thought that the solar system was
a. celestial.
b. elliptical.
c. geocentric.
d. heliocentric.

2. The part of the sun where nuclear fusion occurs is the
a. photosphere. **b.** chromosphere.
c. corona. **d.** core.

3. Planets with atmospheres composed mostly of carbon dioxide include
a. Earth and Mercury.
b. Venus and Mercury.
c. Venus and Mars.
d. Mercury and Mars.

4. The Great Red Spot is a huge storm on
a. Jupiter. **b.** Neptune.
c. Saturn. **d.** Pluto.

5. Most asteroids orbit the sun
a. between the sun and Mercury.
b. between Earth and Mars.
c. between Mars and Jupiter.
d. between Neptune and Pluto.

True or False

If the statement is true, write true. If it is false, change the underlined word or words to make the statement true.

6. The shape of the orbit of each planet is a <u>circle</u>.

7. Sunspots are regions of <u>cooler</u> gases on the sun.

8. The atmosphere of Venus has <u>higher</u> pressure than the atmosphere of Earth.

9. Aside from the sun, <u>Saturn</u> is the largest source of gravity in the solar system.

10. Conditions favorable to life as we know it are sometimes called the <u>Goldilocks conditions</u>.

Checking Concepts

11. How did Galileo's observations support the heliocentric system?

12. How did Newton's work on orbits add to the work Kepler had done?

13. Why is it usually impossible to see the sun's corona?

14. What are sunspots?

15. Why does Mercury have only a thin atmosphere?

16. How do astronomers explain that Venus rotates in the opposite direction from most planets and moons?

17. What are the major characteristics of the terrestrial planets? How do they differ from the gas giants?

18. Why do some astronomers think that Pluto should not be called a planet?

19. Why does a comet's tail always stream away from the sun?

20. Do living things have to live on the surface of a planet or moon? Where else on a planet or moon could scientists look for evidence of life?

21. Writing to Learn Imagine you are an astronaut on a mission to explore the solar system. Write a trip journal telling the story of your trip from Earth to another terrestrial planet and to a gas giant. Include a description of each planet.

Thinking Critically

22. Relating Cause and Effect How would Earth move if the sun (including its gravity) suddenly disappeared? Explain your answer.

23. Applying Concepts Explain why Venus is hotter than it would be without its atmosphere.

24. Comparing and Contrasting Compare and contrast meteoroids, meteors, and meteorites.

25. Making Generalizations Why would the discovery of liquid water on another planet be important?

Applying Skills

Use the diagram of an imaginary, newly discovered planetary system around Star X to answer Questions 26–28. The periods of revolution of planets A, B, and C are 75 Earth days, 200 Earth days, and 300 Earth days.

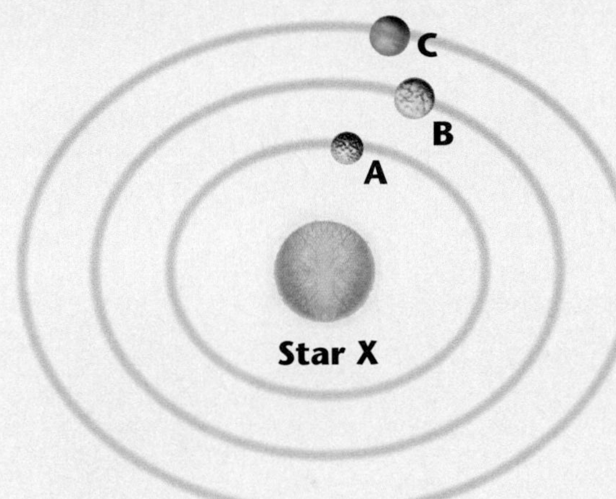

26. **Interpreting Data** Which planet in this new planetary system revolves around Star X in the shortest amount of time?

27. **Making Models** In 150 days, how far will each planet have revolved around Star X? Copy the diagram and sketch the positions of the three planets to find out. How far will each planet have revolved around Star X in 400 days? Sketch their positions.

28. **Drawing Conclusions** Can planet C ever be closer to planet A than to planet B? Study your drawings to figure this out.

Performance — Chapter Project 21 — Assessment

Project Wrap Up Now you are ready to present your solar system. Explain how you were able to work with large distances. Display your data tables showing how you did the calculations and how you checked them for accuracy. Compare the distances in your models to distances inside and outside your classroom.

Reflect and Record In your journal, explain what you would change in your model of the solar system. What would you do to improve the model? How effectively did you use computers or calculators to get the data?

Test Preparation

Use these questions to prepare for standardized tests.

Study the table. Then answer Questions 29–32.

Planet	Period of Rotation (Earth days)	Period of Revolution (Earth years)	Average Distance From the Sun (million kilometers)
Mars	1.03	1.9	228
Jupiter	0.41	12	778
Saturn	0.43	29	1,427
Uranus	0.72	84	2,871
Neptune	0.67	165	4,497

29. Which of these planet's orbits is farthest from Earth's orbit?
    a. Mars **b.** Jupiter
    c. Uranus **d.** Neptune

30. Which planet has a "day" that is most similar in length to a day on Earth?
    a. Mars **b.** Jupiter
    c. Uranus **d.** Neptune

31. Light takes about 8 minutes and 20 seconds to travel from the sun to the Earth, 150 million kilometers away. About how long does it take light to travel from the sun to Jupiter?
    a. 10 minutes **b.** 25 minutes
    c. 43 minutes **d.** 112 minutes

32. Which one of the following conclusions about planets is supported by the information in the table?
    a. As distance from the sun increases, period of rotation increases.
    b. As distance from the sun increases, period of revolution increases.
    c. As distance from the sun increases, period of revolution decreases.
    d. There is no relationship between distance from the sun and period of revolution.

CHAPTER 22

Stars, Galaxies, and the Universe

www.phschool.com

Integrating Physics

Tools of Modern Astronomy

Discover **Are Those Stars Really a Group?**
Try This **Locating Radio Waves**
Sharpen Your Skills **Inferring**
Real-World Lab **Make Your Own Telescope**

Characteristics of Stars

Discover **How Does Your Thumb Move?**
Try This **Star Bright**
Skills Lab **How Far Is That Star?**

Lives of Stars

Discover **What Determines How Long Stars Live?**
Sharpen Your Skills **Predicting**

PROJECT 22

Star Stories

In the spring of 1997, you could easily see comet Hale-Bopp, shown here, without any special equipment. But many of the objects astronomers study just look to you like tiny pinpoints of light—that is, if you can see them at all. However, astronomers have found many ways to learn about these "pinpoints."

In this chapter, you will discover how astronomers study the universe and what they have learned about the stars. In your project, you will find out how people in the past created stories to explain the patterns they saw in the sky. You'll learn how the names of constellations reflect the cultures of the people who named them.

Your Goal To recognize major constellations, learn the stories behind their names, and create your own star myth.

To complete the project you will

- learn the star patterns of at least three major constellations
- research the myths that gave one constellation its name
- write a new star myth

Get Started Begin your project by previewing page 94 to learn what a constellation is. With a group of your classmates, make a list of constellations you have heard about. Then look at the star charts in Appendix B. From the chart for the current season, choose three or four constellations to explore further.

Check Your Progress You'll be working on this project as you study this chapter. To keep your project on track, look for Check Your Progress boxes at the following points.

Section 1 Review, page 744: Locate constellations and research one.

Section 3 Review, page 760: Draw a new picture for the star pattern in your constellation and give it a name.

Section 5 Review, page 768: Write a story about your constellation.

Wrap Up At the end of the chapter (page 771), you will present your constellation along with a story that explains its name.

These telescopes on top of Mauna Kea, a mountain in Hawaii, are used to study distant stars and galaxies.

SECTION 1 Tools of Modern Astronomy

DISCOVER ACTIVITY

Are Those Stars Really a Group?

1. Cut ten pieces of thread to different lengths between 5 cm and 25 cm. Tape a 1-cm plastic foam ball to the end of each piece of thread.
2. Obtain a piece of cardboard about 50 cm by 50 cm. Tape the free ends of the thread pieces to various points on the cardboard.
3. Turn the cardboard over so the balls hang down. While your partner holds the cardboard horizontally, look at the balls from the side.

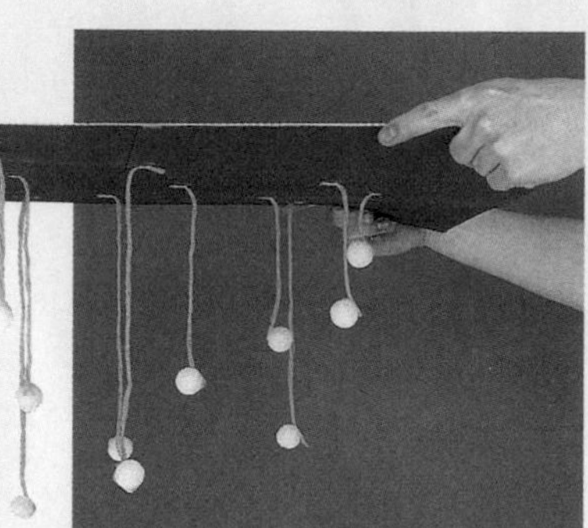

4. Imagine that the balls are stars in a constellation. With one eye closed, sketch the pattern the balls make.

Think It Over

Observing Can you tell which balls are farther away and which are closer? Do you think you can tell how close to each other the stars in a constellation are?

GUIDE FOR READING

- What is the electromagnetic spectrum?
- What is the main purpose of a telescope?
- Why do astronomers use spectrographs?

Reading Tip **Before you read, rewrite the main headings of the section as *how, why,* or *what* questions.**

Before the Civil War, thousands of enslaved African Americans fled north to freedom. Traveling in secret by night, they looked to the stars for direction. They told each other to "follow the drinking gourd"—the star pattern that points to the North Star. Most Americans today call this pattern the Big Dipper.

Patterns of stars in the sky are called **constellations.** Stars in a constellation can look as if they are close together, even though they are at very different distances from Earth. For example, the star at the end of the handle in the Big Dipper is about twice as far from Earth as most of the other stars in the Big Dipper. So the stars in a constellation are not, in fact, all close together. Constellations are just patterns formed by stars that happen to be in the same direction in the sky.

Big Dipper ▶

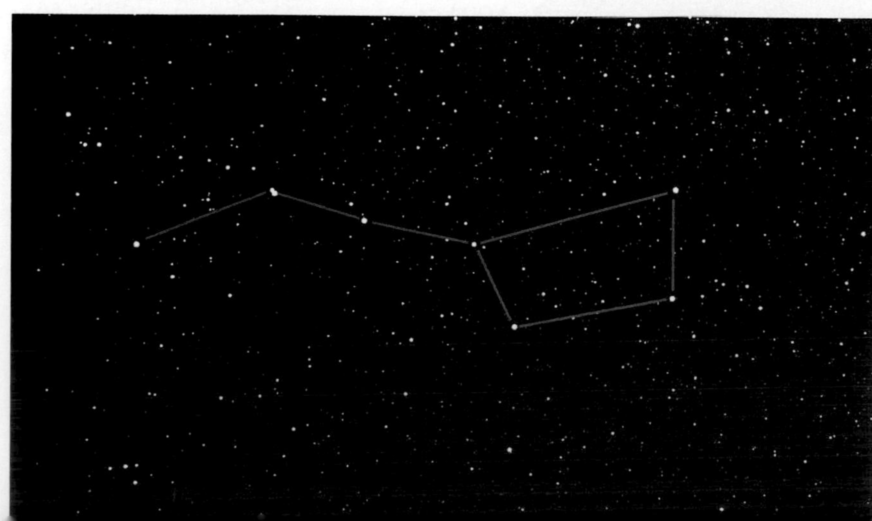

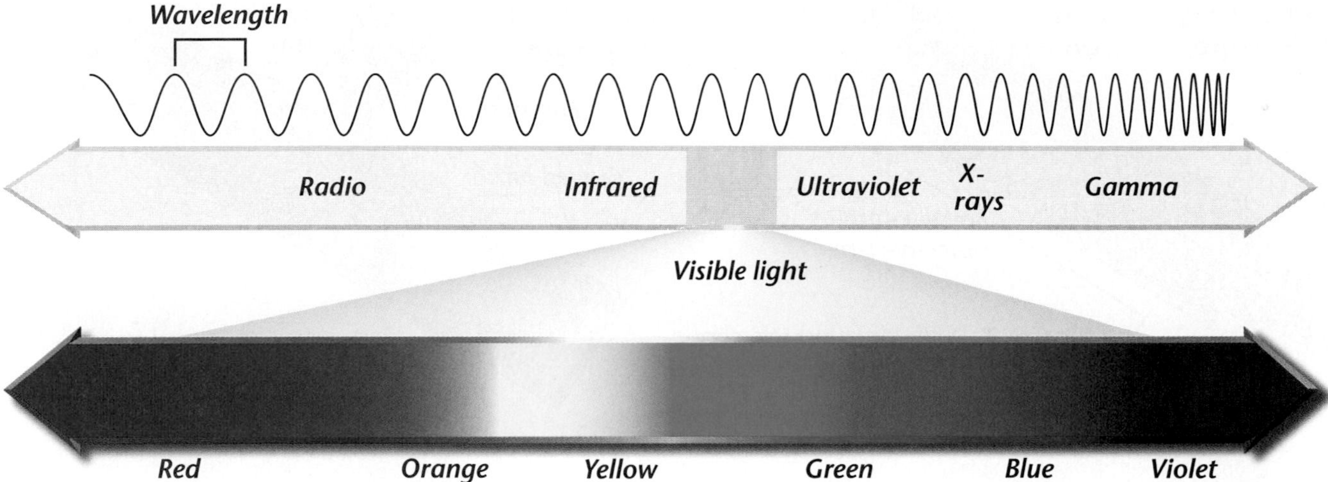

Figure 1 The electromagnetic spectrum ranges from long-wavelength radio waves through short-wavelength gamma rays. ***Interpreting Diagrams*** *Are infrared waves longer or shorter than ultraviolet waves?*

Electromagnetic Radiation

The stars in constellations appear as tiny points of light. In fact, stars are huge spheres of hot glowing gas, like the sun. By using telescopes to study the light from stars, astronomers have learned a great deal about stars and other objects in the sky.

Types of Electromagnetic Radiation Scientists call the light you see with your eyes **visible light.** Light is a form of **electromagnetic radiation** (ih lek troh mag NET ik), or energy that can travel directly through space in the form of waves.

Visible light is only one type of electromagnetic radiation. Many objects give off radiation that you can't see. For example, the glowing coils of an electric heater give off infrared radiation, which you feel as heat. Radio waves carry signals to radios and televisions.

The Electromagnetic Spectrum As you can see in Figure 1, the distance between the crest of one wave and the crest of the next wave is called the **wavelength.** Visible light has very short wavelengths, less than one millionth of a meter. Some electromagnetic waves have even shorter wavelengths. Other waves are much longer, even several meters long.

If you shine white light through a prism, the light spreads out to make a range of different colors with different wavelengths, called a **spectrum.** The spectrum of visible light is composed of the colors red, orange, yellow, green, blue, and violet. **The electromagnetic spectrum includes radio waves, infrared radiation, visible light, ultraviolet radiation, X-rays, and gamma rays.** All these different kinds of electromagnetic waves make up the electromagnetic spectrum, shown in Figure 1.

☑ ***Checkpoint*** *Give two examples of electromagnetic waves that you might use or experience every day.*

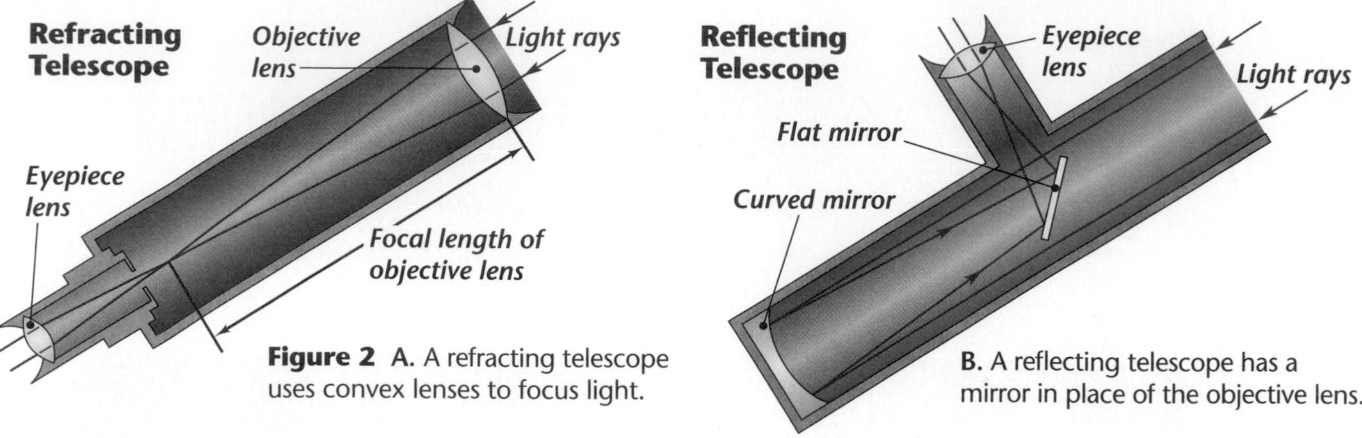

Figure 2 A. A refracting telescope uses convex lenses to focus light.

B. A reflecting telescope has a mirror in place of the objective lens.

Locating Radio Waves

ACTIVITY

You can use an umbrella to focus radio waves.

1. Line the inside of an umbrella with aluminum foil.
2. Turn on a small radio and tune it to a station.
3. Move the radio up and down along the umbrella handle. Find the position where the station is clearest. Radio waves reflecting off the foil focus at this point. Tape the radio to the handle.

4. Hold the umbrella at different angles. At which angle is the station the clearest?

Inferring In which direction do you think the radio station is located? Explain.

Telescopes

Objects in space give off all types of electromagnetic radiation. Many telescopes produce images using visible light. But much of modern astronomy is based on detection of other types of electromagnetic radiation. **Most telescopes collect and focus different types of electromagnetic radiation, including visible light.**

Visible Light Telescopes In 1609, Galileo used a refracting telescope to look at objects in the sky. A **refracting telescope** uses convex lenses to gather a large amount of light and focus it onto a small area. A **convex lens** is a piece of transparent glass, curved so that the middle is thicker than the edges.

Galileo's telescope, like the refracting telescope in Figure 2, used two lenses—an eyepiece lens and an objective lens. When light passes through the objective lens, the lens focuses the light at a certain distance away from the lens. This distance is called the focal length of the lens. Different lenses have different focal lengths. The larger the objective lens, the more light it can collect, making it easier for astronomers to see faint objects.

Isaac Newton built the first **reflecting telescope** in 1668. It used a mirror instead of an objective lens. Like the lenses in a refracting telescope, the mirror in a reflecting telescope focuses a large amount of light onto a small area. The larger the mirror, the more light the telescope can collect. The largest visible light telescopes are now all reflecting telescopes.

Radio Telescopes Devices used to detect radio waves from objects in space are called **radio telescopes.** Most radio telescopes have curved, reflecting surfaces—up to 305 meters in diameter. These surfaces focus radio waves the way the mirror in a reflecting telescope focuses light waves. The surfaces of radio telescopes concentrate the faint radio waves from outer space onto small antennas like those on radios. As with visible light telescopes, the larger a radio telescope is, the more radio waves it can collect.

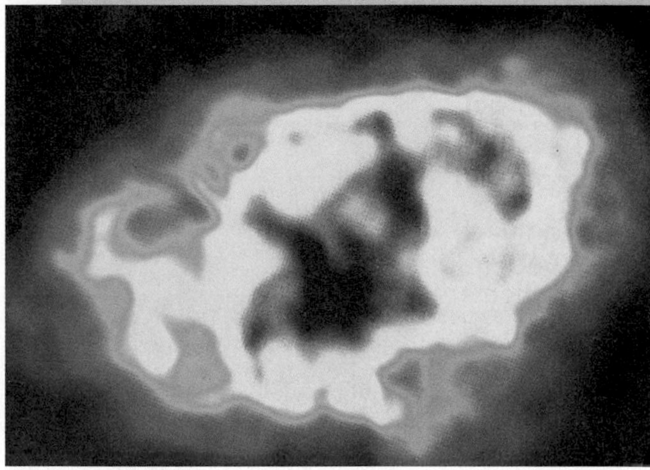

Figure 3 The Crab Nebula is the remains of a star that exploded about 1,000 years ago. The top image was photographed using visible light. The lower image was made using radio waves.

Other Telescopes Some telescopes detect infrared radiation, which has longer wavelengths than visible light. There are also telescopes that detect the shortest wavelengths—ultraviolet radiation, X-rays, and gamma rays.

☑ ***Checkpoint*** *What are two types of visible light telescopes?*

Observatories

A building that contains one or more telescopes is called an **observatory.** Most large observatories are located on mountaintops. Why have astronomers built the largest visible light telescopes on the tops of mountains? Earth's atmosphere makes objects in space look blurry. The sky on some mountaintops is clearer and is not brightened much by city lights.

The best observatory site on Earth is probably the top of Mauna Kea, an ancient volcano on the island of Hawaii. Mauna Kea is so tall—4,200 meters above sea level—that it is above 40 percent of Earth's atmosphere. The sky there is very dark at night, and many nights are free of clouds.

To collect data from visible light telescopes on Earth, astronomers must stay awake all night. Radio telescopes, however, can be used 24 hours a day and do not have to be on mountaintops.

Satellites

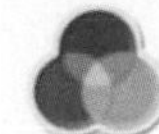

Integrating Technology Most ultraviolet radiation, X-rays, and gamma rays are blocked by Earth's atmosphere. To detect these wavelengths, astronomers have placed telescopes on satellites.

The Hubble Space Telescope is a reflecting telescope with a mirror 2.4 meters in diameter. Because it is above the atmosphere, it makes images in visible light that are about seven times more detailed than the best images from telescopes on Earth. The Hubble Space Telescope can also collect ultraviolet and infrared radiation. The Chandra X-ray Observatory, similar in size to Hubble, makes images in the X-ray portion of the spectrum.

Development of Modern Telescopes

During the last century, astronomers have built larger telescopes, which can collect more light and other types of radiation. Today's astronomers use tools that could not have been imagined 100 years ago.

1897

Yerkes Telescope

The 1-meter-diameter telescope at Yerkes Observatory in Wisconsin is the largest refracting telescope ever built. Because its main lens is so large, the Yerkes telescope can collect more light than any other refracting telescope.

1900 **1920** **1940**

1931

Beginning of Radio Astronomy

Karl Jansky, an American engineer, was trying to find the source of static that was interfering with radio communications. Using a large antenna, he discovered that the static was coming from objects in space giving off radio waves. Jansky's accidental discovery led to the beginning of radio astronomy.

Spectrographs

Most large telescopes today have spectrographs. A **spectrograph** (SPEK truh graf) breaks the light from an object into colors and photographs the resulting spectrum. **Astronomers use spectrographs to get information about stars, including their chemical compositions and temperatures.**

Chemical Compositions Chemical elements in a star's atmosphere absorb light from the star. Each element absorbs light at different wavelengths, and each absorbed wavelength is shown as a dark line on a spectrum. Just as each person has a unique set of fingerprints, each element has a unique set of lines. By comparing

In Your Journal

Research one of these telescopes or another large telescope. Create a publicity brochure in which you describe the telescope's features, when and where it was built, and what types of research it is used for.

1963

Arecibo Radio Telescope

This radio telescope in Puerto Rico was built in a natural bowl in the ground. It is 305 meters in diameter, more than three times the size of the next-largest radio telescope.

1990

Hubble Space Telescope

The Hubble Space Telescope can see objects in space more clearly than any other telescope. Astronauts have visited the telescope several times to repair or replace equipment.

1960 | 1980 | 2000

1980

Very Large Array

The Very Large Array is a set of 27 radio telescopes in New Mexico. The telescopes can be moved close together or far apart. The telescopes are linked, so they can be used as if they were one giant telescope 25 kilometers in diameter.

1999

Chandra X-ray Observatory

The hottest objects in space give off X-rays. NASA launched the Chandra X-ray Observatory into orbit to make detailed images in that part of the spectrum. Chandra X-ray images match Hubble visible-light images in detail.

Figure 4 Astronomers can use line spectrums to find the temperatures of stars.

Inferring ACTIVITY

The lines on the spectrums below are from three different stars. Each of these star spectrums is made up of an overlap of spectrums from the individual elements shown in Figure 4. In star A, which elements have the strongest lines? Which are the strongest in star B? In star C?

a star's spectrum with the known spectrums of different elements, such as those shown in Figure 4, astronomers can infer which elements are found in a star.

Temperatures Most stars have a chemical composition similar to the sun, about 73% hydrogen, 25% helium, and 2% other elements. The amount of energy each of these elements absorbs depends on the temperature of the star. Because of this, stars at different temperatures produce different line spectrums. By comparing a star's spectrum with the known spectrums of elements at different temperatures, astronomers can infer how hot the star is. Hydrogen, for example, produces very strong spectral lines when it is at about 10,000 degrees Celsius. If astronomers do not see a strong hydrogen line on a spectrum, this does not mean there is no hydrogen in the star. It just means that the star is much cooler or hotter than 10,000 degrees Celsius.

Section 1 Review

1. What are the main types of electromagnetic waves, from longest wavelength to shortest?
2. For what purpose are most telescopes designed?
3. What can astronomers tell from looking at a star's spectrum?
4. How are the stars in a constellation related to each other in space?
5. **Thinking Critically Applying Concepts** Why are images from the Hubble Space Telescope clearer than images from telescopes on Earth?

Check Your Progress

CHAPTER PROJECT 22

Using the star charts in Appendix B, try to locate constellations in the night sky. (*Hint:* Remember that you may be looking at a constellation upside down. Also, light conditions may affect how many stars you can see.) Sketch the constellations you can locate and compare them with the ones your classmates saw. Now choose one constellation and research the myths or legends that gave it its name. Find as many stories as you can about your constellation and make notes about them.

Make Your Own Telescope

In this lab you will learn how to construct and use a simple refracting telescope. You can then try out your telescope.

Problem

How can you build a telescope?

Skill Focus

making models, observing, drawing conclusions

Materials

2 paper towel tubes of slightly different diameters
plastic objective lens
plastic eyepiece lens
foam holder for eyepiece (optional)
transparent tape
meter stick

Procedure

1. Fit one of the paper towel tubes inside the other. Make sure you can move the tubes but that they will not slide on their own.

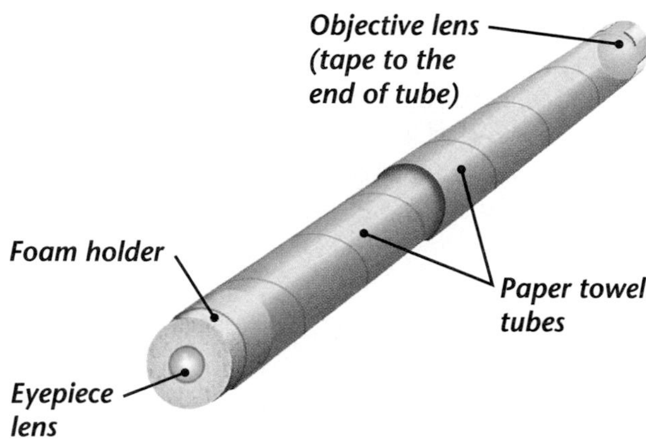

2. Place the large objective lens flat against the end of the outer tube. Tape the lens in place.
3. Insert the small eyepiece lens into the opening in the foam holder.
4. Place the foam eyepiece lens holder into the inner tube at the end of the telescope opposite to the objective lens.
5. Tape a meter stick to the wall. Look through the eyepiece at the meter stick from 5 m away. Slide the tubes in and out to focus your telescope so that you can clearly read the numbers on the meter stick. Draw your telescope. On the drawing, mark the tube position that allows you to read the numbers most clearly.
6. Use your telescope to look at other objects at different distances, both in your classroom and through the window. For each object you view, draw your telescope, marking the tube position at which you see the object most clearly. **CAUTION:** *Do not look at the sun. You will damage your eyes.*

Analyze and Conclude

1. Why do you need two tubes?
2. If you focus on a nearby object and then focus on something farther away, do you have to move the tubes together or apart?
3. How does this telescope compare to the telescopes astronomers use?
4. **Apply** How could you improve on the design of your telescope? What effects would different lenses or tubes have?

More to Explore

With an adult, go outside in the evening a few days after the first-quarter phase and observe the moon. Draw a circle with all the features you see. Label the maria (lowlands) and highlands.

SCIENCE AND SOCIETY

Light Pollution

Imagine you are in a dark theater watching a movie when the lights come on. You can still see the movie, but it seems dull and faded. For the same reason, you may not see very many stars if you live in or near a city. Light from street lights and advertising signs masks much of the starlight. Artificial light that makes it difficult to see the night sky clearly is known as light pollution.

Astronomers build modern observatories far from cities and outdoor lights. But light pollution is still a problem for older observatories and for amateur astronomers like the one in this photo. If light pollution increases, how will you see glittering stars in the night sky, the broad Milky Way, meteor showers, or an occasional passing comet?

The Issues

How Important Are Outdoor Lights?

Artificial lighting is one of the great advantages of the modern age. Street lights make it easier to drive safely, reducing accidents. Night lighting allows businesses to stay open later. In addition, lighting helps people feel safer in their homes and on the streets.

What Can Be Done? Street lights are the biggest cause of light pollution. However, some types of street lights cause more light pollution than others.The three types of street light bulbs are mercury vapor bulbs, high-pressure sodium bulbs, and low-pressure sodium bulbs. Low-pressure sodium lights cause the least problem for astronomers because they shine in only a very narrow range of wavelengths. A simple filter on a telescope can eliminate this light from the telescope's view. In addition, street lights of all types can be shielded so they don't shine upward. They can also be pointed only where the light is needed.

Would Reducing Light Pollution Save Money? Mercury vapor lights are the most common type of street light. High-pressure sodium and low-pressure sodium lights use less electricity, however.

Modifying street lights to reduce light pollution would initially cost a lot of money. However, reducing unneeded light and using light bulbs that require less electricity would also reduce energy usage, which could save money.

You Decide

1. **Identify the Problem**
   In your own words, explain the problem of light pollution.
2. **Analyze the Options**
   List possible solutions. What procedures are involved in each solution? List the advantages and disadvantages of each solution.
3. **Find a Solution**
   Find out what types of street lights your town or city has. Are the lights shielded? Write a letter to your city council proposing a solution to light pollution in your city or town.

Characteristics of Stars

Discover — Activity

How Does Your Thumb Move?

1. Stand facing a wall, at least an arm's length away. Stretch your arm out with your thumb up and your fingers curled.
2. Close your right eye and look at your thumb with your left eye. Line your thumb up with something on the wall.
3. Now close your left eye and open your right eye. How does your thumb appear to move along the wall?
4. Bring your thumb closer to your eye, about half the distance as before. Repeat Steps 2 and 3.

Think It Over

Observing How does your thumb appear to move in Step 4 compared to Step 3? How are these observations related to how far away your thumb is at each step? How could you use this method to estimate distances?

GUIDE FOR READING

- How do astronomers measure distances to nearby stars?
- How are stars classified?

Reading Tip As you read, make a list of the characteristics of stars. Write a sentence describing each characteristic.

Imagine you could travel to the stars at the speed of light. To travel from Earth to the sun would take about 8 minutes, not very long for such a long trip! Yet the next nearest star, Proxima Centauri, is much farther away—a trip to Proxima Centauri would take 4.2 years!

Most stars are much farther away than Proxima Centauri. Our sun and Proxima Centauri are only two of the stars that make up the Milky Way. The Milky Way is a giant flat structure, called a **galaxy,** that contains hundreds of billions of stars. At the speed of light, it would take you 25,000 years to travel the 250 million billion kilometers to the center of our galaxy. If you left our galaxy and traveled at the speed of light for about 2 million years, you would eventually reach another galaxy, the Andromeda Galaxy.

There are billions of galaxies in the **universe,** which astronomers define as all of space and everything in it. Since galaxies are so far apart, most of the universe is empty space. If our galaxy were the size of a dime, the Andromeda Galaxy would be about half a meter away. The rest of the universe, as far as astronomers can see, would extend for about 2 kilometers in all directions.

Distances to Stars

Distances on Earth are often measured in kilometers. However, as you have seen, distances to stars are so large that the kilometer is not a very practical unit. Instead of kilometers, astronomers use a unit called the light-year. In space, light travels at a speed of 300,000 kilometers per second. A **light-year** is the distance that light travels in one year, or about 9.5 million million kilometers. Note that the light-year is a unit of distance, not time.

To help you understand what a light-year is, consider an everyday example. If you bicycle at 10 kilometers per hour, it would take you 1 hour to go to a mall 10 kilometers away. You could say that the mall is "1 bicycle-hour" away.

It takes light about 4.2 years to reach Earth from Proxima Centauri, so Proxima Centauri is 4.2 light-years, or 40 million million kilometers, away.

Figure 5 You and your friend are sitting behind a woman with a large hat. ***Applying Concepts*** *Why is your view of the screen different from your friend's view?*

☑ ***Checkpoint*** *How many kilometers are in three light-years?*

Measuring Distances to Stars

Standing on Earth looking up at the sky, it seems as if there is no way to tell how far away the stars are. However, astronomers have found a way to measure those distances. **Astronomers often use parallax to measure distances to nearby stars.**

Parallax is the apparent change in position of an object when you look at it from different places. For example, imagine that you and a friend have gone to a movie. After you sit down, a woman with a large hat sits down in front of you. Because you and your friend are sitting in different positions, the woman's hat blocks different parts of the screen. If you are sitting on her left, the woman's hat appears to be in front of the dinosaur. But to your friend, who is sitting on her right, she appears to be in front of the bird.

Have the woman and her hat moved? No. But because of your relative positions, she appears to have moved. This apparent movement is parallax.

Astronomers use parallax to measure the distances to nearby stars. They look at a star when Earth is on one side of the sun. Then they

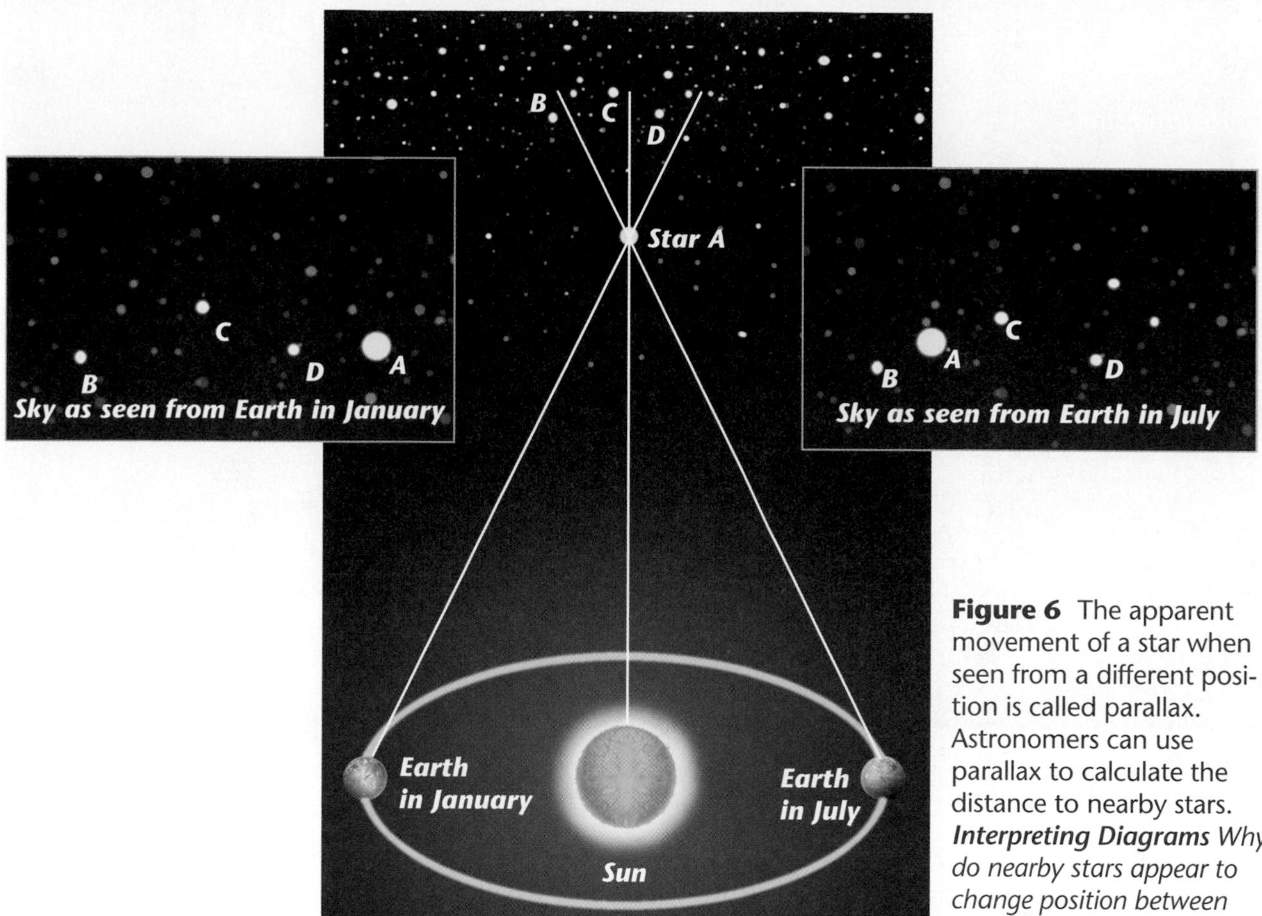

Figure 6 The apparent movement of a star when seen from a different position is called parallax. Astronomers can use parallax to calculate the distance to nearby stars. ***Interpreting Diagrams*** *Why do nearby stars appear to change position between January and July?*

look at the same star again six months later, when Earth is on the other side of the sun. Astronomers measure how much the star appears to move against a background of stars that are much farther away. They can then use this measurement, called the parallax shift, to calculate how far away the star is. The less the star appears to move, the farther away it is.

Parallax cannot be used to measure distances any greater than 1,000 light-years using existing technology. The distance that a star that far away would appear to move when seen from opposite sides of Earth's orbit is too small to measure accurately.

Classifying Stars

Like the sun, all stars are huge spheres of glowing gas. They are made up mostly of hydrogen, and they make energy by nuclear fusion. This energy makes stars shine brightly. The sun is only an average-brightness star. However, the sun is much closer to Earth than any other star. Because it is so close, the sun appears much brighter and much larger then any other star. But the sun is neither the brightest nor the largest star in the galaxy.

Astronomers classify stars according to their physical characteristics. **The main characteristics used to classify stars are size, temperature, and brightness.**

Figure 7 **A.** Stars range in size from tiny neutron stars to enormous supergiants. **B.** The brighter star is Sirius A. The fainter star circled in yellow, Sirius B, is a white dwarf. ***Observing*** *What size star is the sun?*

Sizes of Stars

When you look at stars in the sky, they all appear to be the same size. Many stars are actually about the size of the sun, which is a medium-sized star. However, some stars are much larger than the sun. Very large stars are called **giant stars** or supergiant stars. If the supergiant star Betelgeuse (BAY tul jooz) were located where our sun is, it would be large enough to fill the solar system as far out as Jupiter.

Some stars are much smaller than the sun. White dwarf stars are about the size of Earth. Neutron stars are even smaller, only about 20 kilometers in diameter.

☑ ***Checkpoint*** ***Name five sizes of stars, in order from largest to smallest.***

Color and Temperature of Stars

If you look around the sky at night, you can see slight differences in the colors of the stars. Figure 8 shows the constellation known as Orion the Hunter. The red star in Orion's shoulder is Betelgeuse. The blue-white star in Orion's heel is called Rigel.

A star's color reveals its temperature. Hot objects on Earth display the same range of colors as stars. If you watch a toaster heat up, you can see the wires glow red-hot. The wires inside a light bulb are even hotter and glow white. Similarly, the coolest stars—about 3,200 degrees Celsius—appear reddish in the sky. Reddish Betelgeuse is a cool star. With a surface temperature of about 5,500 degrees Celsius, the sun glows white. The hottest stars in the sky—over 10,000 degrees Celsius—appear slightly bluer than the sun. Blue-white Rigel is a very hot star, more than 15,000 degrees Celsius.

Brightness of Stars

Stars also differ in brightness, the amount of light they give off. The brightness of a star depends upon its size and temperature. Recall from Chapter 21 that the photosphere is the layer of a star that gives off light. Betelgeuse is fairly cool, so each square meter of its photosphere doesn't give off much light. But Betelgeuse is very large, so it shines brightly. Rigel, on the other hand, is very hot, so each square meter of Rigel's photosphere gives off a lot of light. Even though it is much smaller than Betelgeuse, Rigel also shines brightly.

How bright a star looks from Earth depends on both how far the star is from Earth and how bright the star actually is. Because of these two factors, the brightness of a star can be described in two different ways: apparent magnitude and absolute magnitude.

Apparent Magnitude A star's **apparent magnitude** is its brightness as seen from Earth. Astronomers can measure apparent magnitude fairly easily using electronic devices.

Astronomers cannot tell how much light a star gives off just from the star's apparent magnitude. Just as a flashlight looks brighter the closer it is to you, a star looks brighter the closer it is to Earth. For example, the sun looks very bright. This does not mean that the sun gives off more light than all other stars. The sun looks so bright simply because it is so close to Earth.

Social Studies CONNECTION

During the Middle Ages Arab astronomers in Southwest Asia and North Africa named many stars. For example, the star name Algol comes from the Arabic words *Ras al Ghul,* which mean "the demon's head." Other Arabic star names include Aldebaran ("the follower of the Pleiades"), Vega ("swooping eagle"), and Rigel ("the left leg of the giant").

In Your Journal

Many other words used in astronomy and mathematics come from Arabic. Find *zenith, nadir, algorithm,* and *algebra* in a dictionary. Write their definitions in your own words.

Figure 8 The constellation Orion includes the red supergiant star Betelgeuse and the blue supergiant star Rigel.

Figure 9 The stars in a globular cluster are all about the same distance from Earth.

Star Bright ACTIVITY

Here's how you can compare absolute and apparent magnitudes.

1. Dim the lights. Put two equally bright flashlights next to each other on a table. Turn them on.
2. Look at the flashlights from the other side of the room. Think of the flashlights as two stars. Then compare them in terms of absolute and apparent magnitudes.
3. Move one of the flashlights closer to you and repeat Step 2.
4. Replace one of the flashlights with a brighter one. Repeat Step 1 with the unequally bright flashlights. Then repeat Step 2.

Making Models How could you place the flashlights in Step 4 so that they have the same apparent magnitude? Try it.

Absolute Magnitude A star's **absolute magnitude** is the brightness the star would have if it were at a standard distance from Earth. Finding a star's absolute magnitude is more complicated than finding its apparent magnitude. An astronomer must first find out the star's apparent magnitude and its distance from Earth. The astronomer can then calculate the star's brightness if it were at a standard distance from Earth.

Figure 9 shows a globular cluster, a group of 10,000 to 1,000,000 stars that are close together. The stars in a globular cluster are all at about the same distance from Earth. So astronomers study globular clusters to compare the brightnesses of stars. If one star in a globular cluster appears brighter than another star, it really is brighter than that other star.

The Hertzsprung-Russell Diagram

Two of the most important characteristics of stars are temperature and absolute magnitude. About 100 years ago, Ejnar Hertzsprung (EYE nahr HURT sprung) in Denmark and Henry Norris Russell in the United States each made graphs to find out if temperature and brightness are related. They plotted the temperatures of stars on the *x*-axis and their brightness on the *y*-axis. The points formed a pattern.

The graph they made is still used by astronomers. It is called the **Hertzsprung-Russell diagram,** or H-R diagram. As you can see in Figure 10, most of the stars in the H-R diagram form a diagonal line called the **main sequence.** In the main sequence, surface temperature increases as brightness increases. More than 90% of all stars are main-sequence stars. The sun is among the stars on the main sequence. Giant and supergiant stars are higher and farther to the right on the H-R diagram. White dwarfs are hot, but not very bright, so they appear at the bottom center of the diagram.

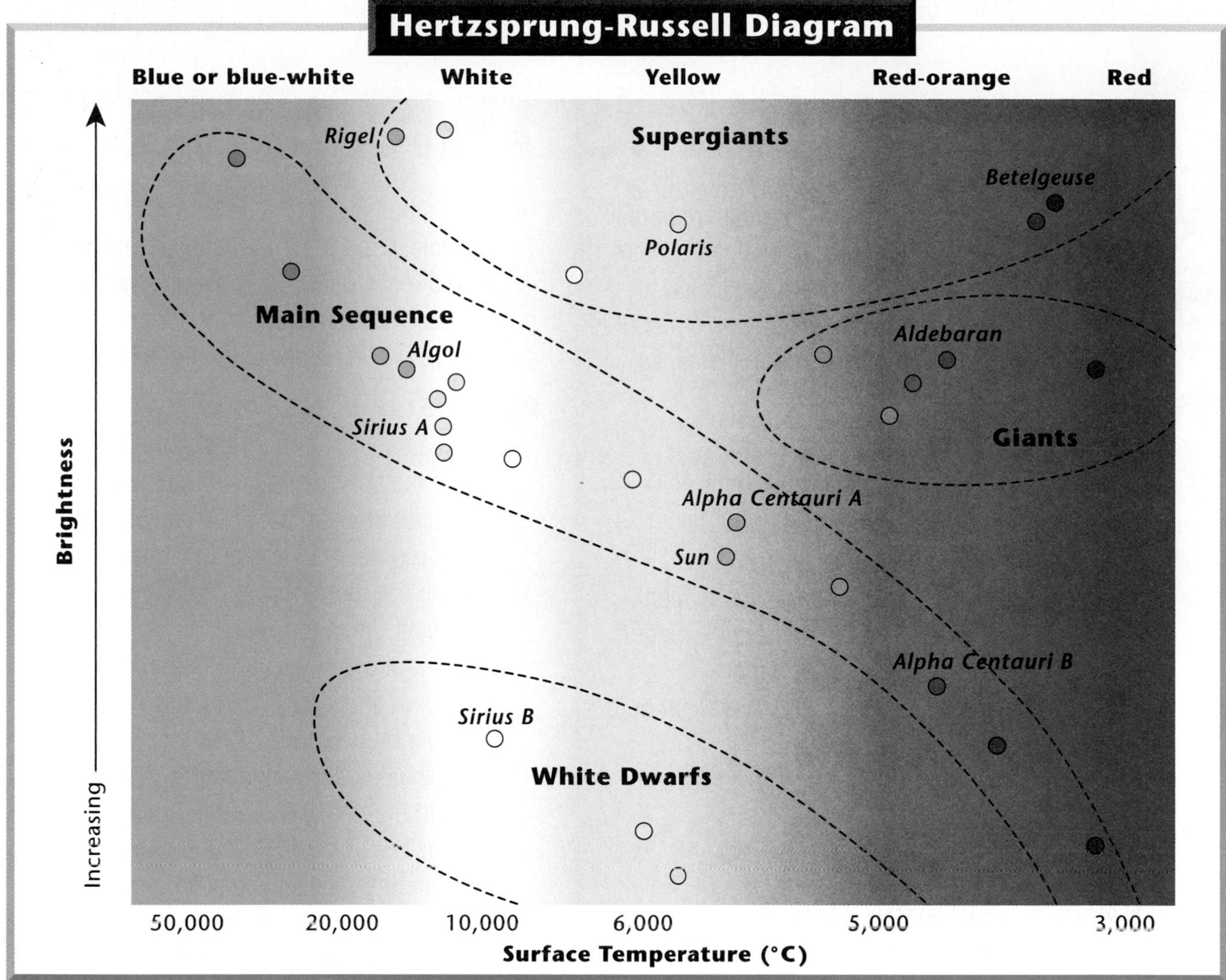

Figure 10 The Hertzsprung-Russell diagram shows the relationship between surface temperature and brightness. ***Interpreting Diagrams*** *Which star is hotter: Rigel or Aldebaran?*

Section 2 Review

1. What is parallax? How is it useful in astronomy?
2. List three characteristics used to classify stars.
3. Which is hotter—a red star or a blue star? Why?
4. **Thinking Critically Applying Concepts** Stars A and B have about the same apparent magnitude, but Star A is about twice as far from Earth as Star B. Which star has the greater absolute magnitude? Explain your answer.

Science at Home

With adult family members, go outside on a clear, dark night. Determine which way is north, south, east, and west. Using the star chart for the correct season in Appendix B, look for the constellation Orion. Find the stars Betelgeuse and Rigel in Orion and explain to your family why they are different colors.

Skills Lab

Measuring

HOW FAR IS THAT STAR?

When astronomers measure parallax, they record the positions of stars on film in cameras attached to telescopes. In this lab, you will set up a model of a telescope and use it to estimate distances.

Problem

How can parallax be used to determine distances?

Materials

masking tape
paper clips
pen
black and red pencils
metric ruler
paper
meter stick
calculator
lamp without a shade, with 100-watt light bulb
copier paper box (without the lid)
flat rectangular table, about 1 m wide

Procedure

Part 1 Telescope Model

1. Place the lamp on a table in the middle of the classroom.
2. Carefully use the tip of the pen to make a small hole in the middle of one end of the box. The box represents a telescope.
3. At the front of the classroom, place the box on a flat table so the hole points toward the lamp. Line the left side of the box up with the left edge of the table.
4. Put a small piece of tape on the table below the hole. Use the pen to make a mark on the tape directly below the hole. The mark represents the position of the telescope when Earth is on one side of its orbit.

Part 2 Star 1

5. Label a sheet of paper Star 1 and place it inside the box as shown in the drawing. Hold the paper in place with two paper clips. The paper represents the film in a telescope.
6. Darken the room. Turn on the light to represent the star.
7. With the red pencil, mark the paper where you see a dot of light. Label this dot A. Dot A represents the image of the star on the film.
8. Move the box so the right edge of the box lines up with the right edge of the table. Repeat Step 4. The mark on the tape represents the position of the telescope six months later, when Earth is on the other side of its orbit.
9. Repeat Step 7, and use a black pencil to mark the second dot B. Dot B represents the image of the star as seen 6 months later from the other side of Earth's orbit.
10. Remove the paper. Before you continue, copy the data table into your notebook.
11. Measure and record the distance in millimeters between dots A and B. This distance represents the parallax shift for Star 1.

DATA TABLE

Star	Parallax Shift (mm)	Focal Length (mm)	Diameter of Orbit (mm)	Calculated Distance to Star (mm)	Calculated Distance to Star (m)	Actual Distance to Star (m)

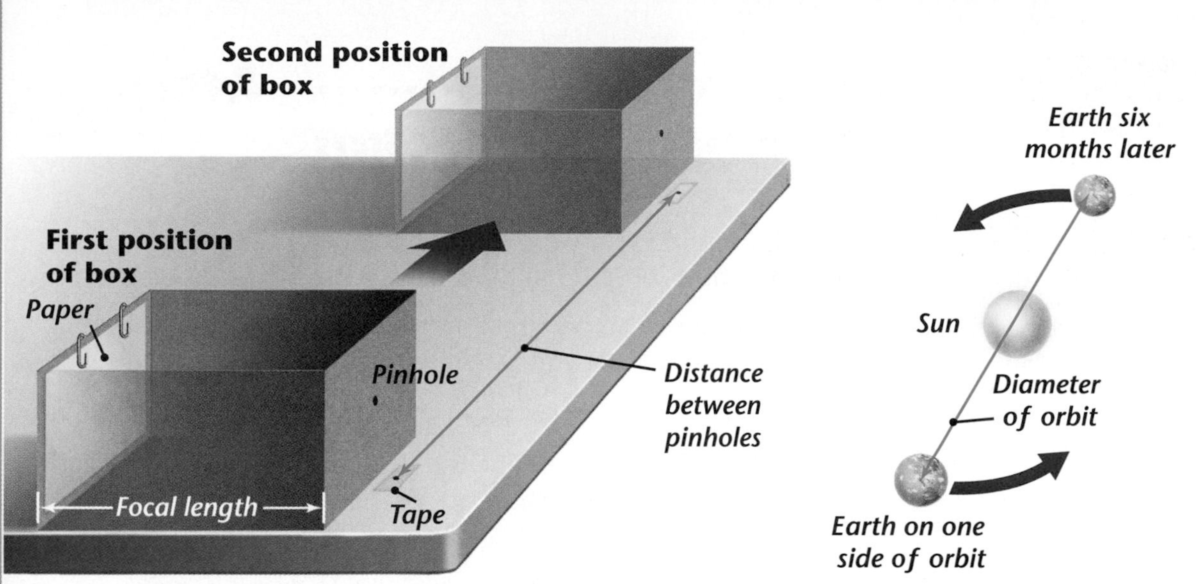

12. Measure and record the distance from the hole in the box to the lamp. This distance represents the actual distance to the star.
13. Measure and record the distance from the hole (lens) to the back of the box in millimeters. This distance represents the focal length of your telescope.
14. Measure and record the distance in millimeters between the marks on the two pieces of masking tape. This distance represents the diameter of Earth's orbit.

Part 3 Stars 2 and 3

15. Move the lamp away from the table—about half the distance to the back of the room. The bulb now represents Star 2. Predict what you think will happen to the light images on your paper.
16. Repeat Steps 6–12 with a new sheet of paper to find the parallax shift for Star 2.
17. Move the lamp to the back of the classroom. The bulb now represents Star 3. Repeat Steps 6–12 with a new sheet of paper to find the parallax shift for Star 3.

Analyze and Conclude

1. What caused the apparent change in position of the dots of light for each star? Explain.
2. Use the following formula to calculate the distance from the telescope to Star 1.

$$\text{Distance} = \frac{\text{Diameter} \times \text{Focal length}}{\text{Parallax shift}}$$

3. Divide your result from Question 3 by 1,000 to get the distance to the light bulb in meters.
4. Repeat Questions 3 and 4 for Stars 2 and 3.
5. Was your prediction in Step 15 correct? Why or why not?
6. Is the parallax shift greater or smaller the farther away the star is? Relate each star's parallax shift to its distance from Earth.
7. **Think About It** How did your calculation for Star 3 compare with the actual distance? What could you do to improve your results?

Design an Experiment

What would happen if you kept moving the lamp away from the box? Is there a distance at which you can no longer find the distance to the star? Design an experiment to find out.

SECTION 3 Lives of Stars

DISCOVER ACTIVITY

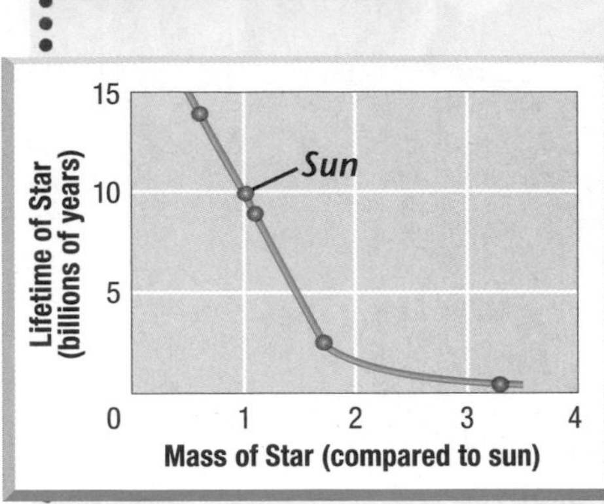

What Determines How Long Stars Live?

1. This graph shows how the mass of a star is related to its lifetime—how long the star lives before it runs out of fuel.
2. How long does a star with 0.8 times the mass of the sun live? How long does a star with 1.7 times the mass of the sun live?

Think It Over

Drawing Conclusions Describe the general relationship between a star's mass and its lifetime.

GUIDE FOR READING

- How does the life of a star begin?
- What determines how long a star will live?
- What happens to a star when it runs out of fuel?

Reading Tip **As you read, make a flowchart showing the stages in the life of a medium-sized star.**

Jocelyn Bell today ▼

In 1967, Jocelyn Bell, a British astronomy student, detected an object in space that appeared to give off regular pulses of radio waves. Some astronomers hypothesized that the pulses might be a signal from an extraterrestrial civilization. At first, astronomers even named the source LGM, for the "Little Green Men" in early science-fiction stories. Eventually, astronomers concluded that the source of the radio waves was a neutron star. A neutron star is a tiny star left over when a giant star explodes. Neutron stars like the one Bell discovered are called **pulsars**, short for pulsating radio sources.

Studying the Lives of Stars

Stars do not last forever. Each star is born, goes through its life cycle, and eventually dies. (Of course, stars are not really alive. The words *born, live,* and *die* are just helpful comparisons.) How did astronomers figure out that the neutron star Bell discovered had been a larger star earlier in its life?

Imagine that you want to study how people age. You wish you could watch a few people for 50 years, but your assignment is due next week! You have to study a lot of people for a short time, and classify the people into different age groups. You may come up with groups like *babies, children, teenagers, young adults, middle-aged people,* and *elderly people.* You don't have time to see a single person go through all these stages, but you know the stages exist.

Astronomers have a similar problem with stars. They can't watch a single star for billions of years, so they study many stars and see how they differ from one another.

A Star Is Born

A star is made up of a large amount of gas in a relatively small volume. A **nebula,** on the other hand, is a large amount of gas and dust spread out in an immense volume. All stars begin their lives as parts of nebulas.

Gravity can pull some of the gas and dust in a nebula together. The contracting cloud is then called a protostar. *Proto* means "earliest" in Greek, so a **protostar** is the earliest stage of a star's life. **A star is born when the contracting gas and dust become so hot that nuclear fusion starts.** Recall from Chapter 21 that nuclear fusion is the process by which atoms of hydrogen are combined to form helium. During fusion, enormous amounts of energy are released.

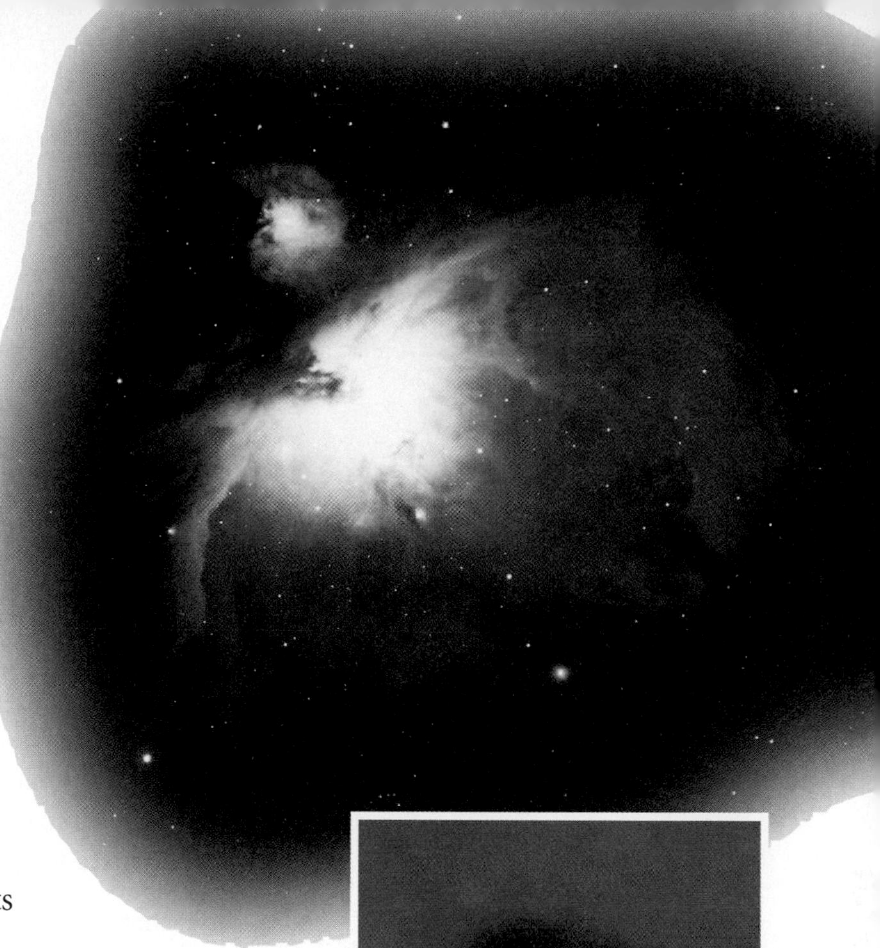

Figure 11 The Orion Nebula, top, is a giant cloud of gas and dust. The Hubble Space Telescope took this photo of a protostar, bottom, in the Orion Nebula. A protostar is a star in the earliest stage of its life. ***Applying Concepts*** *How do some of the gas and dust in a nebula become a protostar?*

Lifetimes of Stars

Before they can tell how old a star is, astronomers must determine its mass. **How long a star lives depends on how much mass it has.**

You might think that stars with more mass would last longer than stars with less mass. However, the reverse is true. You can think of stars as being like cars. A small car has a small gas tank, but it also has a small engine that burns gas slowly. A large car, on the other hand, has a larger gas tank, but it also has a larger engine that burns gas rapidly. So the small car might be able to travel farther on one small tank of gas than the larger car can on one large tank of gas. Small-mass stars use up their fuel more slowly than large-mass stars, so they have much longer lives.

Generally, stars that have less mass than the sun use their fuel slowly, and can live for up to 200 billion years. Medium-mass stars like the sun live for about 10 billion years. Astronomers think the sun is about 4.6 billion years old, so it is almost halfway through its lifetime.

Stars that have more mass than the sun have shorter lifetimes. A star that is 15 times as massive as the sun may live only about ten million years. That may seem like a long time, but it is only one tenth of one percent of the lifetime of the sun.

☑ ***Checkpoint*** *If a star is twice as massive as the sun, will it have a longer or shorter life than the sun?*

Figure 12 Supernova 1987A was the brightest supernova seen in hundreds of years. The arrow in the photo at the left points to the original star, before it exploded. ***Making Generalizations*** *Why were ancient astronomers able to see supernovas?*

Deaths of Stars

When a star begins to run out of fuel, the center of the star shrinks and the outer part of the star expands. The star becomes a red giant or supergiant.

All main sequence stars eventually become red giants or supergiants. However, what happens next depends on the mass of the star, as *Exploring the Lives of Stars* shows. **When a star runs out of fuel, it becomes a white dwarf, a neutron star, or a black hole.**

White Dwarfs Small- and medium-mass stars take 10 billion or more years to use up their nuclear fuel. Then their outer layers expand, and they become red giants. Eventually, the outer parts grow bigger still and drift out into space. The blue-white hot core of the star that is left behind is a **white dwarf.**

White dwarfs are only about the size of Earth, but they have about as much mass as the sun. Since a white dwarf has the same mass as the sun but only one millionth the volume, it is one million times as dense as the sun. A spoonful of material from a white dwarf has as much mass as a large truck. White dwarfs have no fuel, but they glow faintly from leftover energy. When a white dwarf stops glowing, it is dead. Then it is called a black dwarf.

Neutron Stars A dying giant or supergiant star can suddenly explode. Within hours, the star blazes millions of times brighter. The explosion is called a **supernova.** You can see a supernova in Figure 12. After a supernova, some of the material from the star expands into space. This material may become part of a nebula. The nebula can then contract to form a new, "recycled" star. Astronomers think the sun began as a nebula that contained material from a supernova explosion.

After the star explodes, some of the material from the star is left behind. This material forms a neutron star. **Neutron stars** are even smaller and denser than white dwarfs. A neutron star may contain as much as three times the mass of the sun but be only about 20 kilometers in diameter, the size of a large asteroid or a town on Earth.

Predicting ACTIVITY

Find Algol, Polaris, and Sirius B in the H-R diagram on page 109. For each star, write a sentence predicting what the next stages in its life will be.

Black Holes The most massive stars—those having more than 40 times the mass of the sun—become **black holes** when they die. After this kind of star becomes a supernova, more than five times the mass of the sun may be left. The gravity of this mass is so strong that the gas is pulled inward, packing the gas into a smaller and smaller space. Eventually five times as much mass as the sun becomes packed within a sphere 30 kilometers in diameter. At that point, the gravity is so strong that nothing can escape, not even light. The remains of the star become a black hole.

EXPLORING *the Lives of Stars*

A star's life history depends on its mass. The sun is a medium-mass star that will become a white dwarf, then a black dwarf.

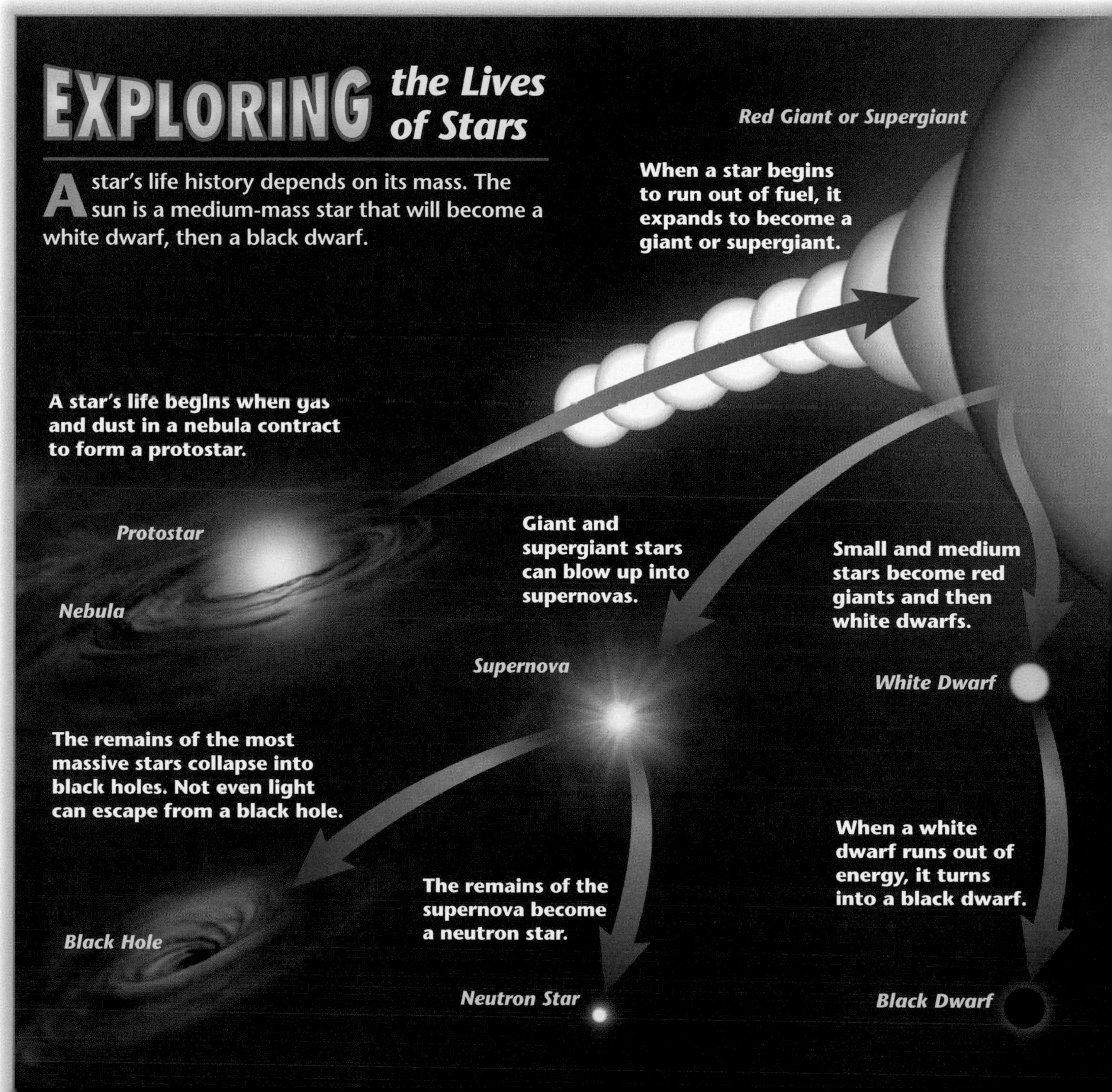

A star's life begins when gas and dust in a nebula contract to form a protostar.

Protostar

Nebula

Red Giant or Supergiant

When a star begins to run out of fuel, it expands to become a giant or supergiant.

Giant and supergiant stars can blow up into supernovas.

Small and medium stars become red giants and then white dwarfs.

Supernova

White Dwarf

The remains of the most massive stars collapse into black holes. Not even light can escape from a black hole.

When a white dwarf runs out of energy, it turns into a black dwarf.

The remains of the supernova become a neutron star.

Black Hole

Neutron Star

Black Dwarf

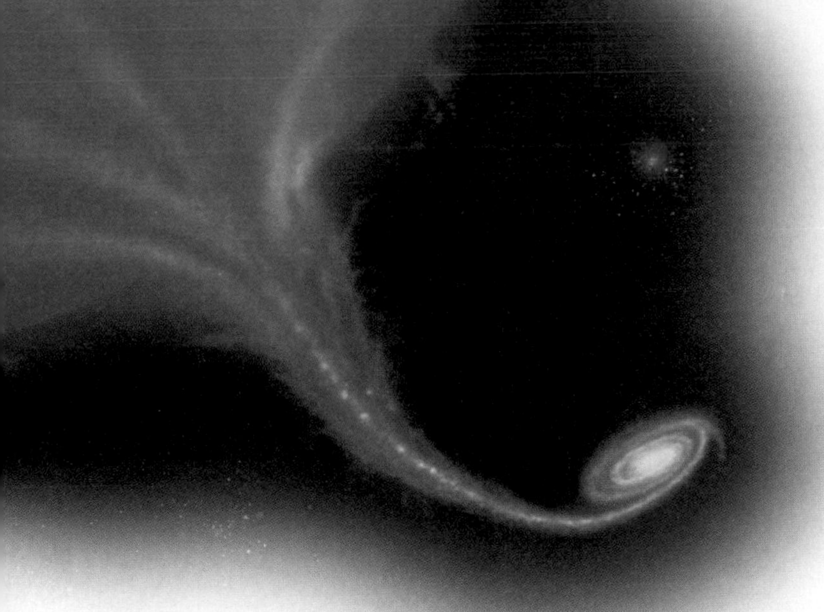

Figure 13 This artist's impression shows a black hole pulling matter from a companion star. The material glows as it is pulled into the black hole. *Applying Concepts If it is impossible to detect a black hole directly, how do astronomers find them?*

No light, radio waves, or any other form of radiation can ever get out of a black hole, so it is not possible to detect a black hole directly. But astronomers can detect black holes indirectly.

For example, gas near a black hole is pulled so strongly that it rotates faster and faster around the black hole. Friction heats the gas up. Astronomers can detect X-rays coming from the hot gas and infer that a black hole is present. Similarly, if another star is near a black hole, astronomers can calculate the mass of the black hole from the effect of its gravity on the star. Scientists are using the Chandra X-ray Observatory to look for black holes by studying sources of X-rays.

Quasars In the 1960s, astronomers discovered objects that are unusual because they are very bright, but also very far away. Many of these objects are about 12 billion light-years away, making them among the most distant objects in the universe. These distant bright objects looked almost like stars. Since *quasi* means "something like" in Latin, these objects were given the name quasi-stellar objects, or **quasars.**

What could be so bright even though it is so far away? Astronomers have concluded that quasars are actually distant galaxies with giant black holes at their centers. Each black hole has a mass a billion times or more as great as that of the sun. As enormous amounts of gas revolve around such a black hole, the gas heats up and shines brightly.

Section 3 Review

1. What is the earliest stage in the life of a star?
2. Why do small-mass stars have longer lifetimes than large-mass stars?
3. What is the difference between stars that become white dwarfs and stars that become neutron stars?
4. What evidence do astronomers use to detect black holes?
5. **Thinking Critically Inferring** What will happen to the sun when it dies? Explain your answer.

Check Your Progress

CHAPTER PROJECT 22

Draw and label the stars in your constellation *without* the connecting lines that form the usual image. What different patterns can you see? (*Hint:* Use a pencil to "doodle" different connections among the stars.) What does each pattern look like? Choose one pattern, and use it to name your constellation. Then write an outline of a brief story that explains why this constellation is in the sky.

Star Systems and Galaxies

DISCOVER

Why Does the Milky Way Look Hazy?

1. Using a pencil, carefully poke at least 20 holes close together in a sheet of white paper.
2. Tape the paper to a chalkboard or dark-colored wall.
3. Go to the other side of the room and look at the paper. From the far side of the room, what do the dots look like? Can you see individual dots?

Think It Over

Making Models How is looking at the paper from the far side of the room like trying to see many very distant stars that are close together? How does your model compare to the photograph of the Milky Way below?

On a clear, dark summer night in the country, you can see a hazy band of light stretched across the sky. This band of stars is called the Milky Way. It looks as if the Milky Way is very far away from Earth. Actually, though, Earth is inside the Milky Way! How is this possible? Before you can understand the answer to this question, you need to know more about how stars are grouped together.

GUIDE FOR READING

- **What is a star system?**
- **What are the three types of galaxies?**

Reading Tip **Before you read, preview the boldfaced terms. As you read, look for a photograph or diagram that illustrates each term.**

Star Systems and Planets

Our solar system has only one star, the sun. **But more than half of all stars are members of groups of two or more stars, called star systems.** If you were on a planet in one of these star systems, you would probably see two or more suns in the sky.

Double and Triple Stars Star systems with two stars are called double stars or **binary stars.** (The prefix *bi* means "two.") Those with three stars are called triple stars. Proxima Centauri is probably part of a triple star system close to our sun. The other two stars in the system, Alpha Centauri A and Alpha Centauri B, form a double star. Scientists are not sure whether Proxima Centauri is really part of the system or is just passing close to the other two stars temporarily.

Astronomers can sometimes detect a binary star even if only one of the stars in the pair can be seen from Earth. For example, the darker star in the pair may pass in front of the other star and eclipse the other star. A system in which one star blocks the light from another is

The Milky Way ▶

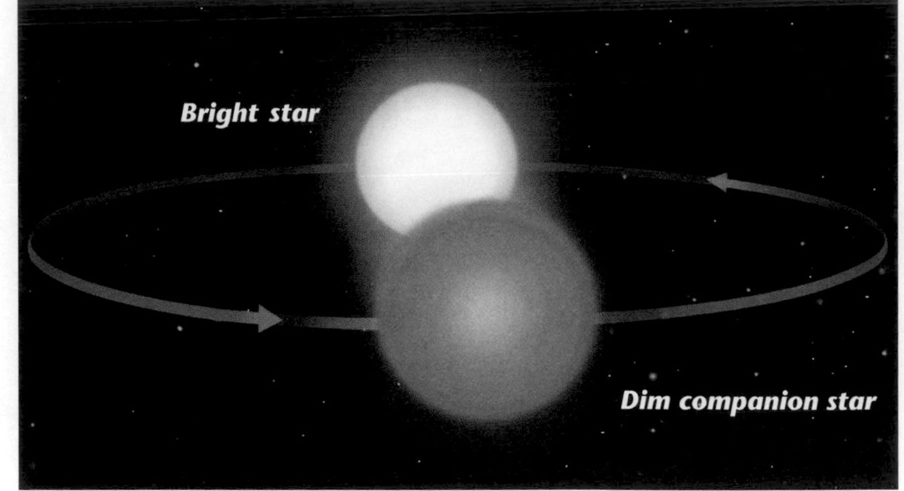

Figure 14 Algol is an eclipsing binary star system consisting of a bright star and a dim companion. Each time the dimmer star passes in front of the brighter one, Algol appears less bright.
Interpreting Diagrams *When does Algol appear brighter?*

called an **eclipsing binary.** As Figure 14 shows, the star Algol is actually an eclipsing binary.

Often astronomers can tell that there is a second star in a system only by observing the effects of its gravity. As the second star revolves around the first star, the second star's gravity makes the first star move back and forth. Imagine you are watching a pair of dancers twirling each other around. Even if one dancer were invisible, you could tell that the invisible dancer was there from watching the motion of the visible dancer.

Figure 15 If you saw someone dancing but couldn't see a partner, you could infer that the partner was there by watching the dancer you could see. Astronomers use a similar method to detect faint stars in star systems.

Planets Around Other Stars In 1995, astronomers discovered a planet revolving around a star using a method similar to the one they use to detect binary stars. The star the astronomers were observing, 51 Pegasi, moved back and forth only very slightly. Therefore, they knew the invisible object could not have enough mass to be a star. They deduced that it must be a planet.

Before this discovery, there was no way to know whether stars other than the sun had planets revolving around them. Now astronomers know that our solar system is not the only one. Most of the planets found beyond our solar system so far are very large, at least half Jupiter's mass. A small planet would be difficult to detect because it would have little gravitational effect on the star it revolved around.

Astronomers are trying to find new ways to use telescopes to see planets directly. Seeing a planet around another star is like trying to see a firefly near a street light. The glare of the light makes it hard to see anything near the light. To see a planet directly, astronomers will have to shield their view from the glare of the star that the planet revolves around. In 2000, astronomers were excited by the discovery of a planet orbiting a star similar to our sun and only 10.5 light-years away.

INTEGRATING LIFE SCIENCE Some scientists hypothesize that life may exist on planets revolving around other stars. A few astronomers are using radio telescopes to search for signals that could not have come from natural sources. Such a signal might be evidence that an extraterrestrial civilization existed and was sending out radio waves.

☑ ***Checkpoint*** *What evidence have astronomers used to conclude that there are planets around other stars?*

Galaxies

Now you are ready to learn about the Milky Way. The Milky Way is the galaxy in which our solar system is located. Like other galaxies, it contains single stars, double stars, star systems, and lots of gas and dust between the stars. The Milky Way Galaxy, often just called "our galaxy," looks milky or hazy because the stars are too close together for your eyes to see them individually. The dark blotches in the Milky Way are clouds of dust that block light coming from stars behind them.

There are billions of galaxies in the universe. **Astronomers have classified most galaxies into three main categories: spiral galaxies, elliptical galaxies, and irregular galaxies.**

A Spiral Galaxy

You can make a model of our galaxy.

1. Using pipe cleaners, make a pinwheel with two spirals.

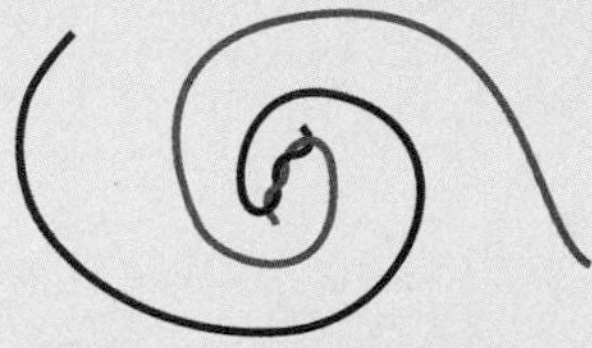

2. View the spirals along the surface of the table. Sketch what you see. Can you see the spiral shape?
3. Next, view the spirals from above the table and sketch them.

Observing The sun is inside a flat spiral galaxy. From Earth's position on the flat surface, is it possible to get a good view of stars in the spiral arms? Why or why not?

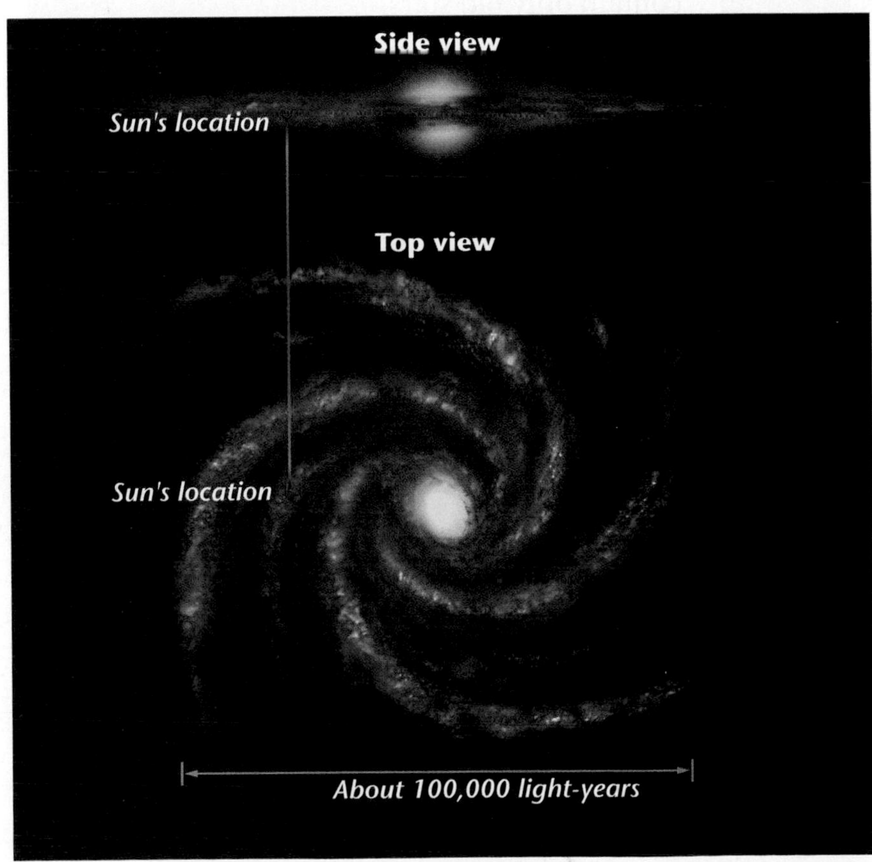

Figure 16 From the side, the Milky Way Galaxy appears to be a narrow disk. The spiral structure would be visible only from above the galaxy.

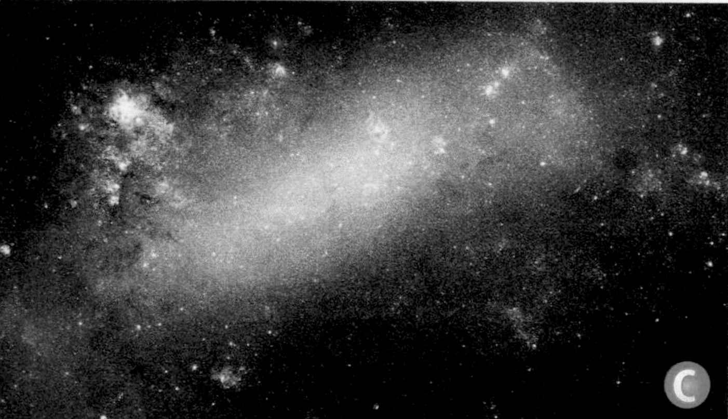

Figure 17 **A.** This spiral galaxy is similar to our galaxy. **B.** An elliptical galaxy looks like a flattened ball. **C.** The Large Magellanic Cloud is an irregular galaxy.

Spiral Galaxies Figure 17A shows a galaxy that has the shape of twin spirals, called a **spiral galaxy.** Astronomers can see other spiral galaxies from different angles. These views show that spiral galaxies have arms that spiral outward, like pinwheels.

Our galaxy has the same spiral, pinwheel shape. It is hard for us to see the spiral shape of our galaxy because our solar system is inside the galaxy, about two thirds of the way out in one of the spiral arms. The Milky Way you see in the sky is the view people on Earth get when they look toward the main part of the rest of our galaxy. The center of our galaxy is about 25,000 light-years from the sun. However, we cannot see the center of our galaxy. The center is hidden from our view by the dust associated with the massive clouds of gas between the sun and the center.

Elliptical Galaxies Not all galaxies have spiral arms. **Elliptical galaxies** look like flattened balls. These galaxies contain billions of stars but have little gas and dust between the stars. Because of the lack of gas and dust, new stars cannot form in most elliptical galaxies. Most elliptical galaxies contain only old stars.

Irregular Galaxies Some galaxies do not have regular shapes. Because of this, they are known as **irregular galaxies.** The Large Magellanic Cloud is an irregular galaxy about 160,000 light-years away from our galaxy. At this distance it is one of the closest neighboring galaxies in the universe.

Section 4 Review

1. What is a star system?
2. Describe the three main types of galaxies.
3. Where is the sun in our galaxy?
4. **Thinking Critically Applying Concepts** Some binary stars are called eclipsing binaries. Explain why this term is appropriate. (*Hint:* Think about Algol as you come up with an answer.)

Science at Home

Plan an evening of stargazing with adult family members. Choose a dark, clear night. Use binoculars if available and the star charts in Appendix B to locate the Milky Way and some interesting stars you have learned about. Explain to your family what you know about the Milky Way and each star you observe.

SECTION 5

History of the Universe

DISCOVER — ACTIVITY

How Does the Universe Expand?

1. Use a marker to put 10 dots on an empty balloon. The dots represent galaxies.
2. Blow up the balloon. What happens to the distances between galaxies that are close together? Galaxies that are far apart?

Think It Over

Inferring If the universe is expanding, do galaxies that are close together move apart faster or slower than galaxies that are far apart?

GUIDE FOR READING

- How did the universe form?
- How did the solar system form?

Reading Tip **Before you read, write down what you have already heard about the big bang theory. Then read how the theory explains the history of the universe.**

The Andromeda Galaxy is the most distant object you can see with your unaided eyes. Light from this galaxy has traveled for 2 million years before reaching your eyes. When that light finally reaches your eye, you are seeing what the galaxy looked like 2 million years ago. It is as though you are looking back in time.

Astronomers have photographed galaxies that are billions of light-years away. Light from these galaxies traveled for billions of years before it reached telescopes on Earth. From these observations, astronomers have inferred that the universe is incredibly old—billions of years old.

Moving Galaxies

To study how and when the universe formed, astronomers use information about how galaxies are moving. Astronomers can measure how far away different galaxies are. By examining the spectrum of a galaxy, astronomers can tell how fast the galaxy is moving and whether it is moving toward our galaxy or away from it. Only a few nearby galaxies are moving toward our galaxy. All of the other galaxies are moving away from our galaxy.

In the 1920s, Edwin Hubble, an American astronomer, discovered that the farther away a galaxy is from us, the faster it is moving away from us. The Hubble Space Telescope was named after Hubble in honor of this and other important discoveries.

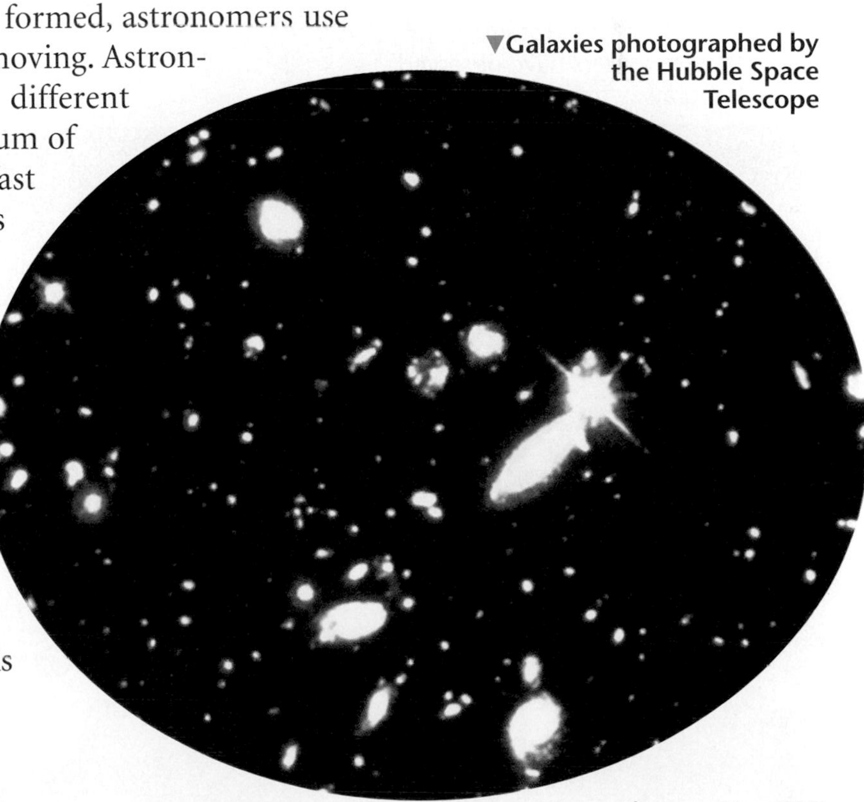

▼Galaxies photographed by the Hubble Space Telescope

Figure 18 The galaxies in the expanding universe are like the raisins in rising bread dough. *Making Models How does rising raisin bread dough model the expanding universe?*

To understand how the galaxies are moving, think of raisin bread dough that is rising. If you could shrink yourself to sit on a raisin, you would see all the other raisins moving away from you as the bread dough rose. The farther away a raisin was from you, the faster it would move away, because there would be more bread dough to expand between you and the raisin. No matter which raisin you sat on, all the other raisins would seem to be moving away from you. You could tell that the bread dough was expanding by watching the other raisins.

The universe is like the raisin bread dough. The galaxies in the universe, like the raisins in the dough, are moving away from each other. In the universe it is space that is expanding, like the dough between the raisins.

The Big Bang Theory

To understand how the galaxies moved in the past, imagine you could run time backward. All of the galaxies would then be moving together instead of apart. All of the matter in the universe would eventually come together at a single point. At that time, billions of years ago, the universe was small, hot, and dense. The universe then exploded in what astronomers call the **big bang.**

According to the big bang theory, the universe formed in an enormous explosion about 10 to 15 billion years ago. Since the big bang, the universe has been expanding rapidly. Because of the big bang, the universe is billions of times larger than it was billions of years ago. To understand this change in size, picture a

Figure 19 All of the distant galaxies astronomers have observed are moving away from our galaxy.

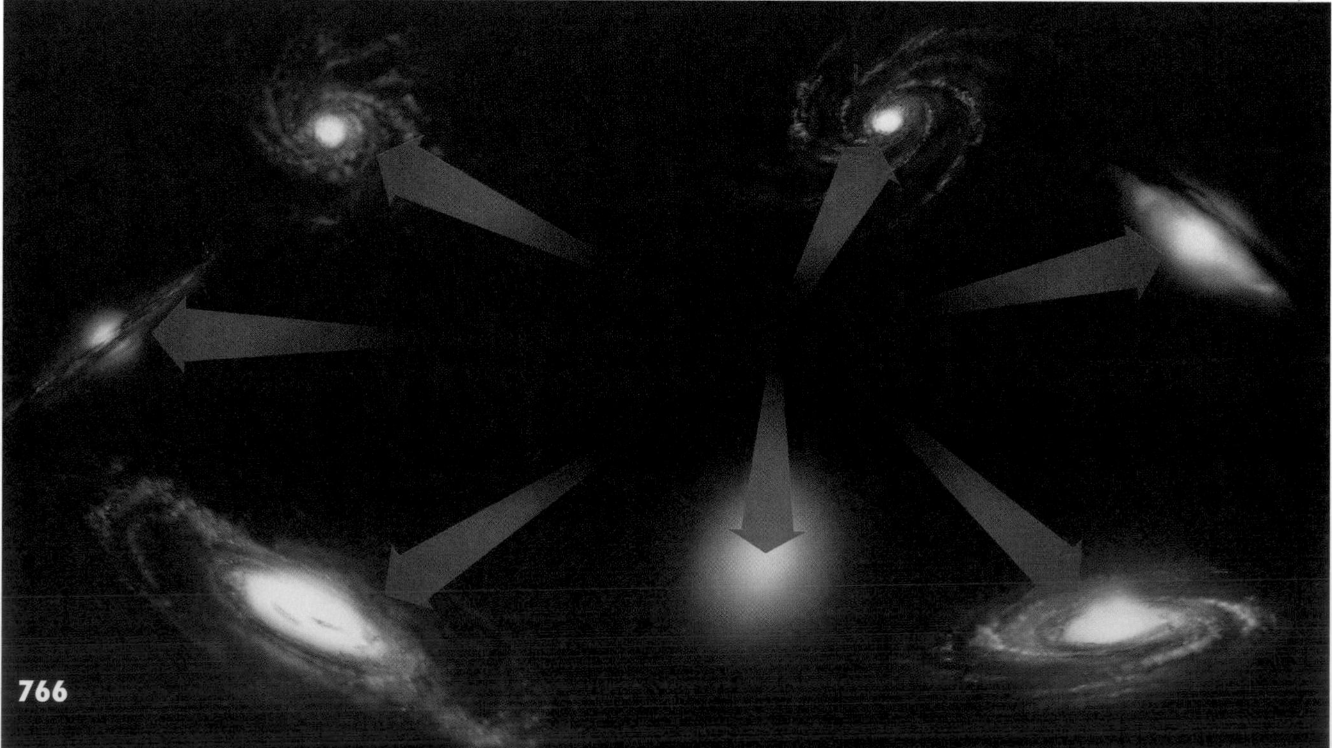

Figure 20 The solar system formed from a collapsing cloud of gas and dust.

tiny pea. Pretend you can blow it up to be as big as Earth. You would be inflating the pea by about a billion times. Like the pea, the universe in which you live was once very small. The universe has been growing rapidly ever since the big bang. Astronomers have concluded that the galaxies are moving away from each other as a result of the big bang.

Since astronomers know approximately how fast the universe is expanding now, they can infer how long it has been expanding. Astronomers estimate that the universe has been expanding for 10 billion to 15 billion years.

☑ *Checkpoint* *Which way are most galaxies moving relative to each other?*

Formation of the Solar System

After the big bang, matter in the universe separated into galaxies. Gas and dust spread throughout space in our galaxy. Where the solar system is now, there was only cold, dark gas and dust.

About five billion years ago, a giant cloud of gas and dust, or nebula, collapsed to form the solar system. Slowly the nebula shrank to form a spinning disk. As gravity pulled some of the gas into the center of the disk, the gas became hot and dense enough for nuclear fusion to begin. The sun was born.

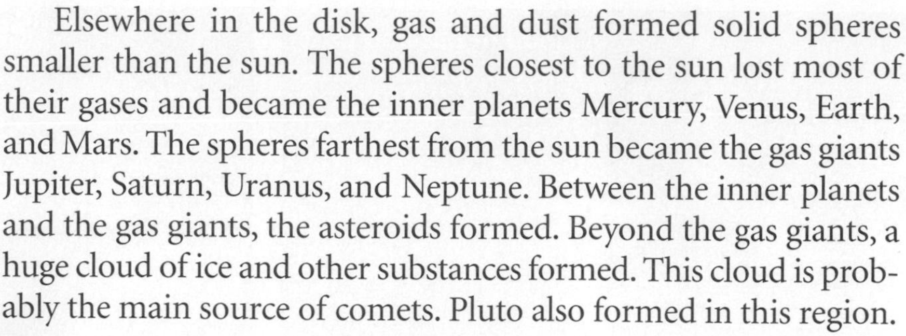

Elsewhere in the disk, gas and dust formed solid spheres smaller than the sun. The spheres closest to the sun lost most of their gases and became the inner planets Mercury, Venus, Earth, and Mars. The spheres farthest from the sun became the gas giants Jupiter, Saturn, Uranus, and Neptune. Between the inner planets and the gas giants, the asteroids formed. Beyond the gas giants, a huge cloud of ice and other substances formed. This cloud is probably the main source of comets. Pluto also formed in this region.

Figure 21 This engineer is checking data from the Hubble Space Telescope. The telescope can be controlled from this room.

The Future of the Universe

What will happen to the universe in the future? One possibility is that the universe will continue to expand, as it is doing now. All of the stars will eventually run out of fuel and burn out, and the universe will be cold and dark. Another possibility is that the force of gravity will begin to pull the galaxies back together. The result will be a reverse big bang, or "big crunch." All of the matter in the universe will be crushed into an enormous black hole.

Which of these possibilities is more likely? The answer depends on how strong the total force of gravity pulling the galaxies together is. This force depends on the total mass of the universe. It is very difficult for astronomers to estimate this mass because much of it is in the form of particles that do not give off electromagnetic radiation. The evidence so far suggests that the total mass of the universe is not great enough to pull the galaxies back together again. However, more research needs to be done to solve this problem.

Astronomy is one of the oldest sciences, but there are still many discoveries to be made and puzzles to be solved about this universe of ours!

Section 5 Review

1. What was the big bang?
2. Describe how the solar system formed.
3. What observations show that the universe is expanding?
4. **Thinking Critically Inferring** What can astronomers infer from the fact that other galaxies are moving away from ours?

Check Your Progress

CHAPTER PROJECT 22

Now you are ready to write the first draft of a story that explains your constellation's name. After you have written a first draft, read it over carefully and look for ways to improve it. Here are things to look for as you edit your first draft. Does the beginning grab the reader's interest? Does your story make sense? Should you add more details? Should you rethink your choice of words? Rewrite and revise as much as necessary.

CHAPTER 22 STUDY GUIDE

Tools of Modern Astronomy

Integrating Physics

Key Ideas

- The electromagnetic spectrum includes radio waves, infrared radiation, visible light, ultraviolet radiation, X-rays, and gamma rays.
- Telescopes collect and focus different types of electromagnetic radiation.
- Astronomers use spectrographs to get information about stars.

Key Terms

constellation
visible light
electromagnetic radiation
wavelength
spectrum
refracting telescope
convex lens
reflecting telescope
radio telescope
observatory
spectrograph

Characteristics of Stars

Key Ideas

- Astronomers use parallax to measure distances to nearby stars.
- The main characteristics used to classify stars are size, temperature, and brightness.

Key Terms

galaxy
universe
light-year
parallax
giant star
apparent magnitude
absolute magnitude
Hertzsprung-Russell diagram
main sequence

Lives of Stars

Key Ideas

- A star is born when nuclear fusion starts.
- The length of a star's life depends on its mass.
- When a star runs out of fuel, it becomes a white dwarf, a neutron star, or a black hole.

Key Terms

pulsar
nebula
protostar
white dwarf
supernova
neutron star
black hole
quasar

Star Systems and Galaxies

Key Ideas

- More than half of all stars are members of groups of two or more stars, called star systems.
- There are three types of galaxies: spiral galaxies, elliptical galaxies, and irregular galaxies.

Key Terms

binary star
eclipsing binary
spiral galaxy
elliptical galaxy
irregular galaxy

History of the Universe

Key Ideas

- According to the big bang theory, the universe formed in an enormous explosion about 10 to 15 billion years ago.
- About five billion years ago, a cloud of gas and dust collapsed to form the solar system.

Key Term

big bang

Organizing Information

Concept Map Copy the concept map about telescopes onto a separate sheet of paper. Then complete it and add a title. (For more on concept maps, see the Skills Handbook.)

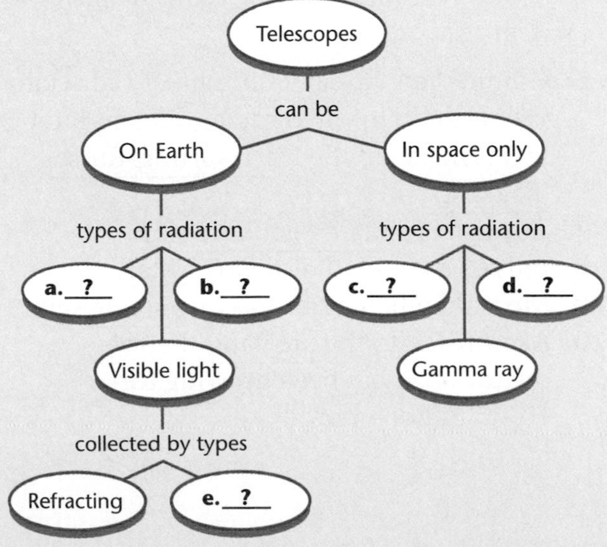

Reviewing Content

Multiple Choice

Choose the letter of the answer that best completes each statement.

1. The Hubble Space Telescope is a
   a. gamma ray telescope.
   b. reflecting telescope.
   c. refracting telescope.
   d. radio telescope.
2. The most common chemical element in a star is
   a. hydrogen.
   b. helium.
   c. carbon.
   d. sodium.
3. To measure the distance to a nearby star, an astronomer would use
   a. apparent magnitude.
   b. quasars.
   c. parallax.
   d. a spectrograph.
4. Stars more massive than the sun
   a. live longer than the sun.
   b. are redder than the sun.
   c. have shorter lives than the sun.
   d. live as long as the sun.
5. The sun formed out of a
   a. pulsar. b. supergiant star.
   c. black hole. d. nebula.

True or False

If the statement is true, write true. If it is false, change the underlined word or words to make the statement true.

6. Gamma rays, X-rays, ultraviolet radiation, visible light, infrared radiation, and radio waves make up the Hertzsprung-Russell diagram.
7. The sun is a main-sequence star.
8. Pulsars are a kind of neutron star.
9. More than half of all stars are single stars.
10. Acccording to the big bang theory, the universe has been growing for 10–15 billion years.

Checking Concepts

11. What types of radiation are included in the electromagnetic spectrum?
12. What kinds of information can astronomers obtain by studying the spectrum of a star?
13. Describe what will happen to the sun when it runs out of fuel.
14. Why can astronomers see the spiral arms of the Andromeda Galaxy more clearly than the spiral arms of the Milky Way Galaxy?
15. Describe the process by which the sun was formed.
16. **Writing to Learn** Imagine you have a spaceship that can travel much faster than the speed of light. Write a letter describing your three-part trip from Earth: to the nearest star other than the sun, to the center of our galaxy, and to the next nearest spiral galaxy.

Thinking Critically

17. **Relating Cause and Effect** Once every three days a small, bright star becomes much dimmer, only to return to its original brightness within six hours. Based on this information, what is causing the small star to become dimmer?
18. **Applying Concepts** Describe a real-world situation involving absolute and apparent magnitudes. (*Hint:* Think about riding in a car at night.)
19. **Comparing and Contrasting** Compare the life histories of a medium-mass star and a high-mass star. How are they similar? How are they different?
20. **Making Generalizations** What does knowing the rate at which the universe is expanding tell astronomers about the big bang?
21. **Applying Concepts** Is a light-year a unit of distance or a unit of time? Explain.

Applying Skills

Use the data about moving galaxies in the table below to answer Questions 22–24.

Cluster of Galaxies	Distance (millions of light-years)	Speed (kilometers per second)
Virgo	80	1,200
Ursa Major	980	15,000
Bootes	2,540	39,000
Hydra	3,980	61,000

22. Graphing Make a line graph showing how each cluster's distance from our galaxy is related to its speed. Put distance on the x-axis and speed on the y-axis.

23. Interpreting Data How are the distance and speed of a galaxy related?

24. Drawing Conclusions Does your graph indicate that the universe is expanding, contracting, or staying the same size? Explain.

Performance Assessment — Chapter Project 22

Project Wrap Up Check the final draft of your story for correct spelling, grammar, punctuation, and usage. Make any necessary changes. Then decide how you will present your new constellation story. For example, you can make a poster showing the constellation, its star pattern, and your story. You can read your story aloud or perform it as a skit or play.

Reflect and Record This project has given you a chance to research information and then present it in writing. In your journal, write what you found easiest and hardest about researching and writing.

Test Preparation

Use these questions to prepare for standardized tests.

Study the diagram. Then answer Questions 25–29.

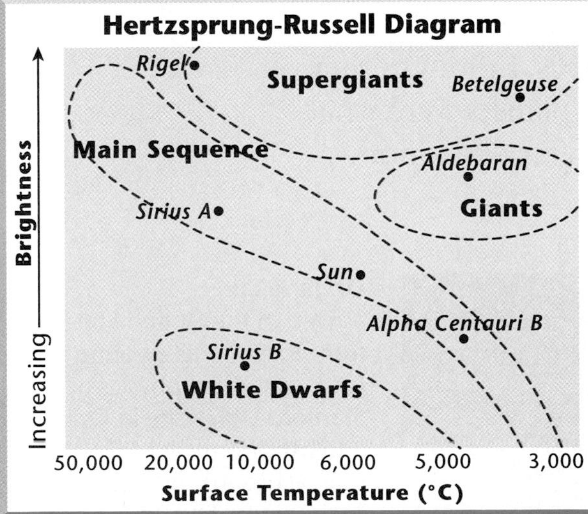

25. To which group do most stars belong?
a. supergiants **b.** giants
c. main sequence **d.** white dwarfs

26. Which star is hotter than the sun?
a. Betelgeuse
b. Aldebaran
c. Alpha Centauri B
d. Sirius B

27. Which star is most likely to be red?
a. Rigel
b. Sirius A
c. Sirius B
d. Betelgeuse

28. Compared to Rigel, Alpha Centauri B is
a. cooler and brighter.
b. cooler and dimmer.
c. hotter and brighter.
d. hotter and dimmer.

29. Which star has a greater absolute magnitude?
a. Rigel
b. Betelgeuse
c. Sirius B
d. Aldebaran

Searching for the home of COMETS

It's a long way from astronomer Jane Luu's office in the Netherlands to the mountaintop in Hawaii where she searches the night sky. But astronomers need dark skies, far from city lights. They also need clean, clear air to see deep into the solar system. That's why Jane Luu travels all the way to the high mountain observatory in Hawaii. Jane Luu has traveled long distances before. Born in Vietnam, she came to the United States at the age of 12.

"As a kid in Vietnam," she says, "I didn't have a single class in science. But after studying physics in college, I got a job at the Jet Propulsion Laboratory, the place where they track all the unmanned space missions. It was a summer job, pretty unimportant stuff. But when I saw the pictures taken by *Voyager I* and *Voyager II* in the mid-1980s, I thought they were spectacular. Those pictures of the planets were what made me go to graduate school in planetary astronomy."

Dr. Jane Luu arrived in the United States from Vietnam as a young girl. Dr. Luu studied physics at Stanford University in California and astronomy at the Massachusetts Institute of Technology. She now works at Leiden University in the Netherlands.

TALKING WITH DR. JANE LUU

What Jane Luu looks at now lies just beyond the farthest planets in our solar system. It's a ring made of millions of ice-rock pieces that circle the sun. Luu and her co-worker David Jewitt first discovered these objects in 1992. The rocky planet Pluto is the biggest object in this ring—called the Kuiper (KY pur) Belt. Pluto travels through space along with an estimated 30,000 other objects that Luu and Jewitt have named "Plutinos" (little Plutos). Objects in the Kuiper Belt sometimes escape from the belt and approach the sun. The sun's heat then makes them light up and become comets.

These color-enhanced images of Jupiter (above), Saturn (right), and Neptune (below) were taken from a *Voyager* spacecraft.

Q ***Why did you start searching for the Kuiper Belt?***

A There were two reasons. We wanted to know if there was anything beyond Neptune besides Pluto. Why should that space be empty when there were so many planets and smaller objects nearer the sun? Scientists had predicted there would be a group of comets not too far beyond Neptune, but no one had seen these objects. There were other people trying to find the same thing, so it was a bit of a race. We're glad we won it.

Q ***Where did you start looking?***

A Most things in the solar system are in a plane, a basically flat disk where the planets and the sun are. So you start looking there. Then, you want to look opposite the sun. Also, you look at a time of the year when the Milky Way, our home galaxy, isn't in the part of the sky you're searching. That's so the light of all those stars doesn't make it hard to see.

Q ***Once you knew where to look, what did you do?***

A We took pictures. We started in 1987 and saw the first object in 1992, five years later. In the beginning we didn't have a computer at the telescope that was fast enough to analyze the pictures. So we'd make three pictures and then take them home to analyze. We'd take images, say a half-hour apart, of the same piece of sky. Then we'd look to see if any point of light had moved

These observatories are located on top of Mauna Kea, an inactive volcano in Hawaii.

between the three pictures. If it moves, we know it's near us in the solar system, and not a distant star. Since our first discovery in 1992, scientists have found about 60 objects in the Kuiper Belt. David and I have found about two thirds of those.

The Kuiper Belt lies beyond the part of the solar system where the planets revolve around the sun. Objects in the Kuiper Belt revolve far from Earth and the sun. Pluto's orbit is on a different plane from the other planets.

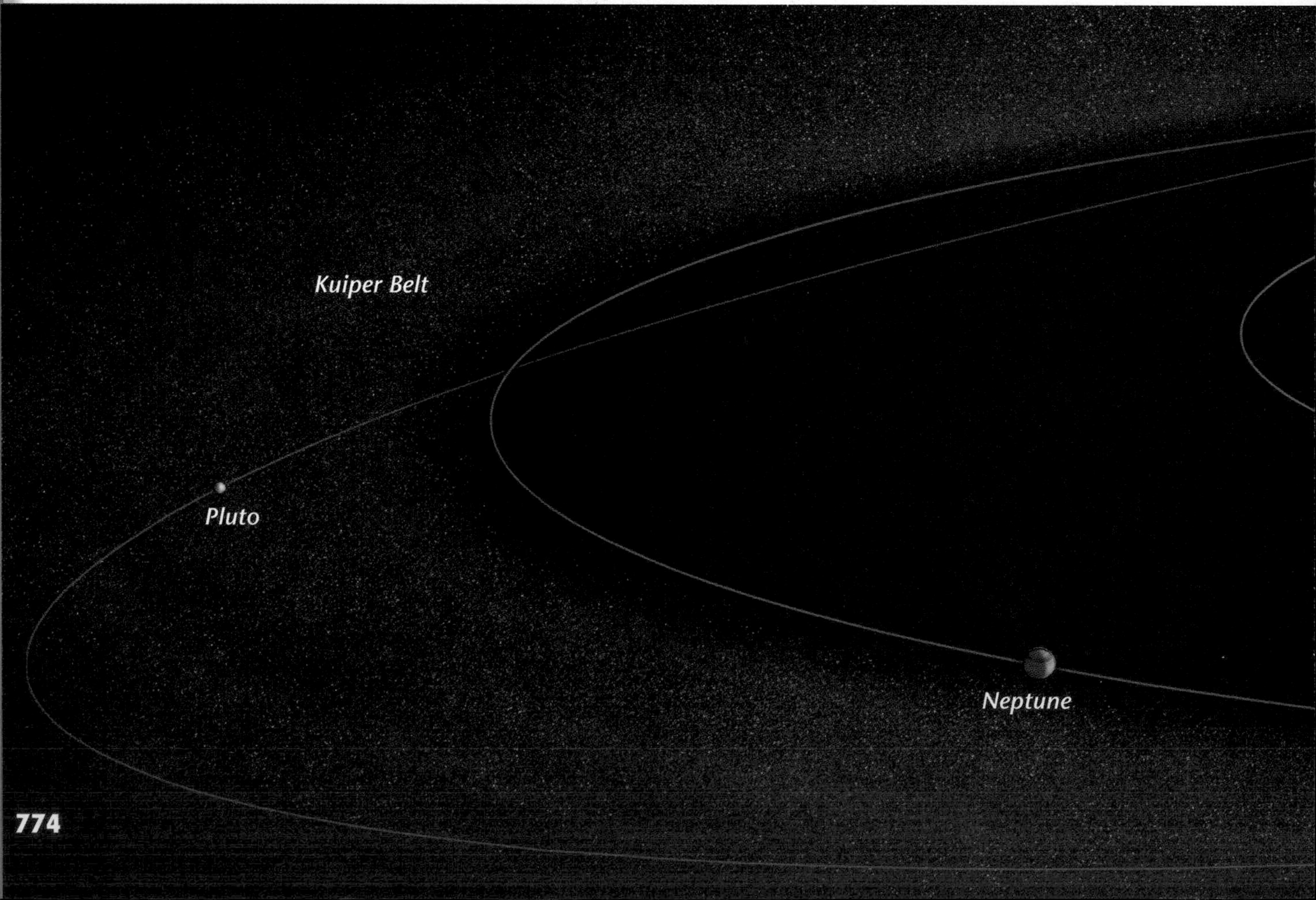

Q ***Do you stay up all night?***

A Yes, we have to. Telescope time is valuable so you don't want to waste a single minute. We observe for a week or so, staying up for 5 or 6 nights in a row. It's hard work, switching from a daytime to a nighttime schedule. In Hawaii, we observe on top of Mauna Kea volcano at 14,000 feet. So we have to add an extra night at the beginning to get used to the altitude and thin air.

Kuiper Belt

Pluto

Neptune

Q ***Five years is a long time to wait for a discovery. Didn't you get discouraged?***

A We told ourselves that after we'd covered a certain part of the sky without finding anything, we would stop. We were pretty near that limit. But the newer cameras could take bigger pictures of the sky. They helped us do in a month what at first had taken two years. We could see something and know right away where to look the next night.

Because I've been lucky, I've participated in discoveries. There's such a satisfaction you get when you solve a puzzle, when you find out something that nobody has known before. And it's really fun after a lot of hard work, when you've finally found what you wanted to find.

In Your Journal

Jane Luu describes working night after night for five years, observing and recording data for one part of the night sky. "It was so time-consuming, and we didn't know if anything was going to come from it." Fortunately, in the end, she was rewarded. How did Jane Luu's persistence, as well as her skill, energy, and step-by-step reasoning, lead to her success?

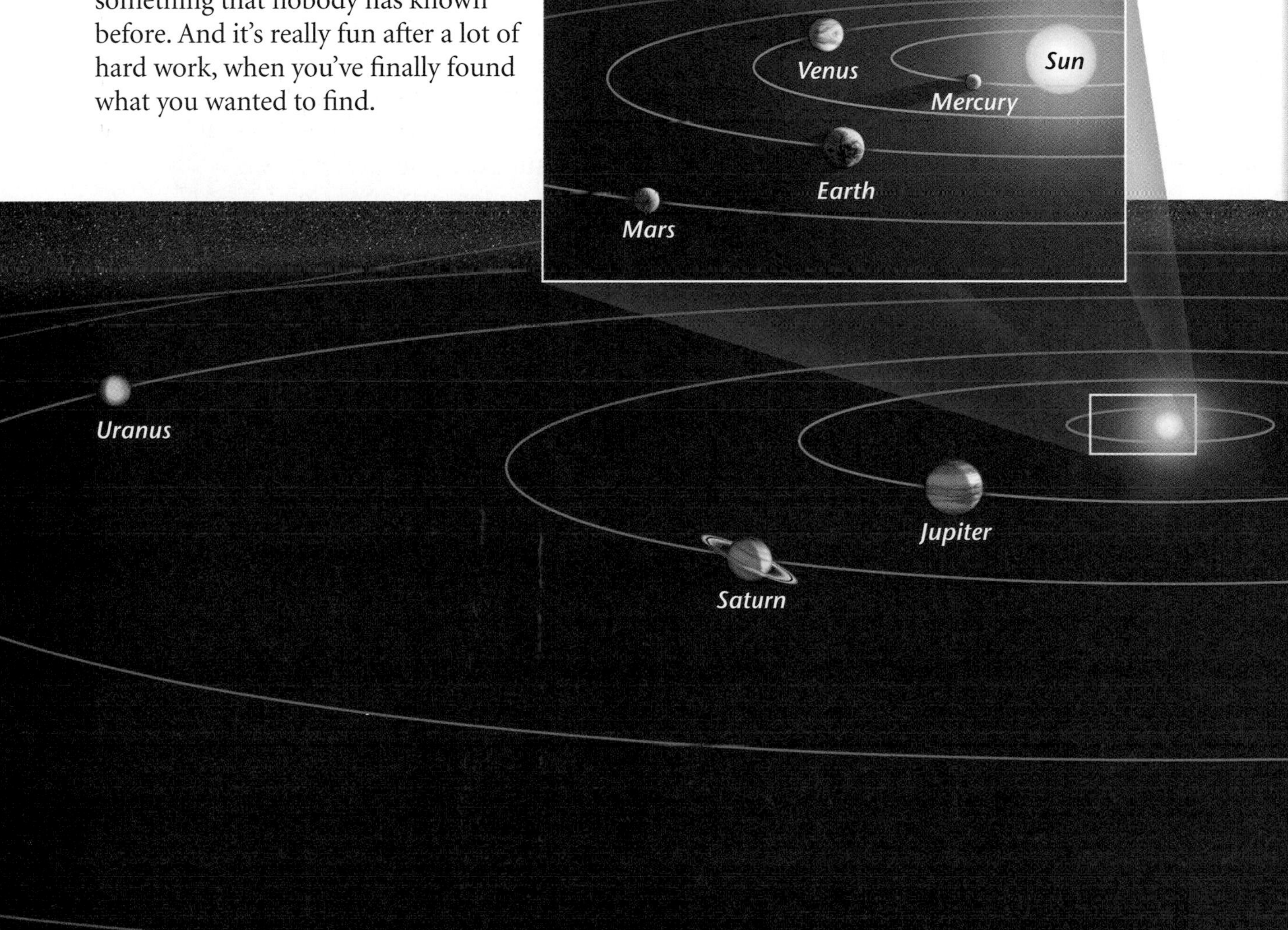

Think Like a Scientist

Although you may not know it, you think like a scientist every day. Whenever you ask a question and explore possible answers, you use many of the same skills that scientists do. Some of these skills are described on this page.

Observing

When you use one or more of your five senses to gather information about the world, you are **observing.** Hearing a dog bark, counting twelve green seeds, and smelling smoke are all observations. To increase the power of their senses, scientists sometimes use microscopes, telescopes, or other instruments that help them make more detailed observations.

An observation must be an accurate report of what your senses detect. It is important to keep careful records of your observations in science class by writing or drawing in a notebook. The information collected through observations is called evidence, or data.

Inferring

When you interpret an observation, you are **inferring,** or making an inference. For example, if you hear your dog barking, you may infer that someone is at your front door. To make this inference, you combine the evidence—the barking dog—and your experience or knowledge—you know that your dog barks when strangers approach—to reach a logical conclusion.

Notice that an inference is not a fact; it is only one of many possible interpretations for an observation. For example, your dog may be barking because it wants to go for a walk. An inference may turn out to be incorrect even if it is based on accurate observations and logical reasoning. The only way to find out if an inference is correct is to investigate further.

Predicting

When you listen to the weather forecast, you hear many predictions about the next day's weather—what the temperature will be, whether it will rain, and how windy it will be. Weather forecasters use observations and knowledge of weather patterns to predict the weather. The skill of **predicting** involves making an inference about a future event based on current evidence or past experience.

Because a prediction is an inference, it may prove to be false. In science class, you can test some of your predictions by doing experiments. For example, suppose you predict that larger paper airplanes can fly farther than smaller airplanes. How could you test your prediction?

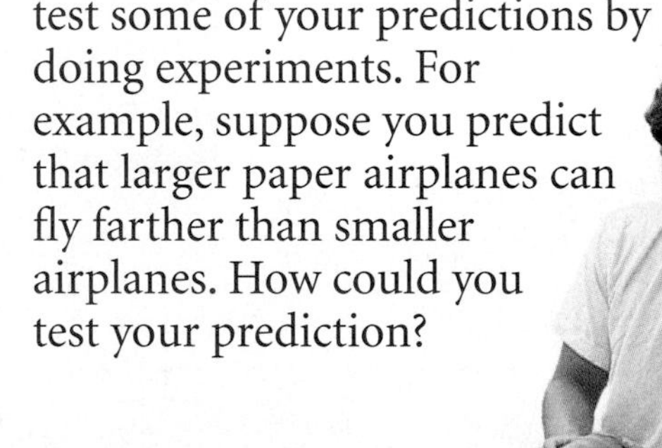

ACTIVITY Use the photograph to answer the questions below.

Observing Look closely at the photograph. List at least three observations.

Inferring Use your observations to make an inference about what has happened. What experience or knowledge did you use to make the inference?

Predicting Predict what will happen next. On what evidence or experience do you base your prediction?

Classifying

Could you imagine searching for a book in the library if the books were shelved in no particular order? Your trip to the library would be an all-day event! Luckily, librarians group together books on similar topics or by the same author. Grouping together items that are alike in some way is called **classifying.** You can classify items in many ways: by size, by shape, by use, and by other important characteristics.

Like librarians, scientists use the skill of classifying to organize information and objects. When things are sorted into groups, the relationships among them become easier to understand.

ACTIVITY Classify the objects in the photograph into two groups based on any characteristic you choose. Then use another characteristic to classify the objects into three groups.

Making Models

Have you ever drawn a picture to help someone understand what you were saying? Such a drawing is one type of model. A model is a picture, diagram, computer image, or other representation of a complex object or process. **Making models** helps people understand things that they cannot observe directly.

Scientists often use models to represent things that are either very large or very small, such as the planets in the solar system, or the parts of a cell. Such models are physical models—drawings or three-dimensional structures that look like the real thing. Other models are mental models—mathematical equations or words that describe how something works.

ACTIVITY This student is using a model to demonstrate what causes day and night on Earth. What do the flashlight and the tennis ball in the model represent?

Communicating

Whenever you talk on the phone, write a letter, or listen to your teacher at school, you are communicating. **Communicating** is the process of sharing ideas and information with other people. Communicating effectively requires many skills, including writing, reading, speaking, listening, and making models.

Scientists communicate to share results, information, and opinions. Scientists often communicate about their work in journals, over the telephone, in letters, and on the Internet. They also attend scientific meetings where they share their ideas with one another in person.

ACTIVITY On a sheet of paper, write out clear, detailed directions for tying your shoe. Then exchange directions with a partner. Follow your partner's directions exactly. How successful were you at tying your shoe? How could your partner have communicated more clearly?

Making Measurements

When scientists make observations, it is not sufficient to say that something is "big" or "heavy." Instead, scientists use instruments to measure just how big or heavy an object is. By measuring, scientists can express their observations more precisely and communicate more information about what they observe.

Measuring in SI

The standard system of measurement used by scientists around the world is known as the International System of Units, which is abbreviated as SI (in French, *Système International d'Unités*). SI units are easy to use because they are based on multiples of 10. Each unit is ten times larger than the next smallest unit and one tenth the size of the next largest unit. The table lists the prefixes used to name the most common SI units.

Common SI Prefixes

Prefix	Symbol	Meaning
kilo-	k	1,000
hecto-	h	100
deka-	da	10
deci-	d	0.1 (one tenth)
centi-	c	0.01 (one hundredth)
milli-	m	0.001 (one thousandth)

Length To measure length, or the distance between two points, the unit of measure is the **meter (m).** The distance from the floor to a doorknob is approximately one meter. Long distances, such as the distance between two cities, are measured in kilometers (km). Small lengths are measured in centimeters (cm) or millimeters (mm). Scientists use metric rulers and meter sticks to measure length.

Common Conversions

1 km = 1,000 m
1 m = 100 cm
1 m = 1,000 mm
1 cm = 10 mm

ACTIVITY The larger lines on the metric ruler in the picture show centimeter divisions, while the smaller, unnumbered lines show millimeter divisions. How many centimeters long is the shell? How many millimeters long is it?

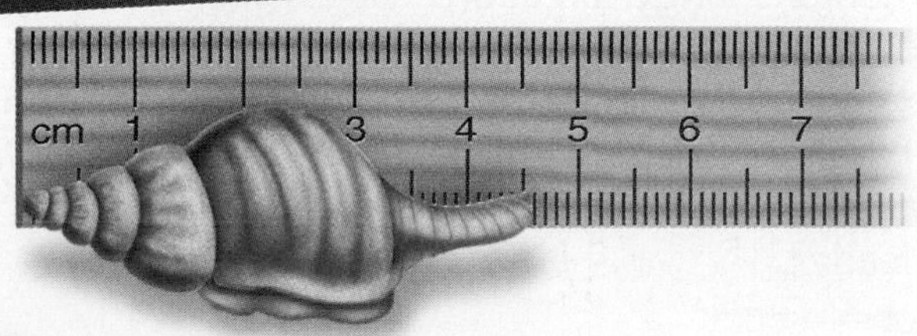

Liquid Volume To measure the volume of a liquid, or the amount of space it takes up, you will use a unit of measure known as the **liter (L).** One liter is the approximate volume of a medium-size carton of milk. Smaller volumes are measured in milliliters (mL). Scientists use graduated cylinders to measure liquid volume.

Common Conversion

1 L = 1,000 mL

ACTIVITY The graduated cylinder in the picture is marked in milliliter divisions. Notice that the water in the cylinder has a curved surface. This curved surface is called the *meniscus*. To measure the volume, you must read the level at the lowest point of the meniscus. What is the volume of water in this graduated cylinder?

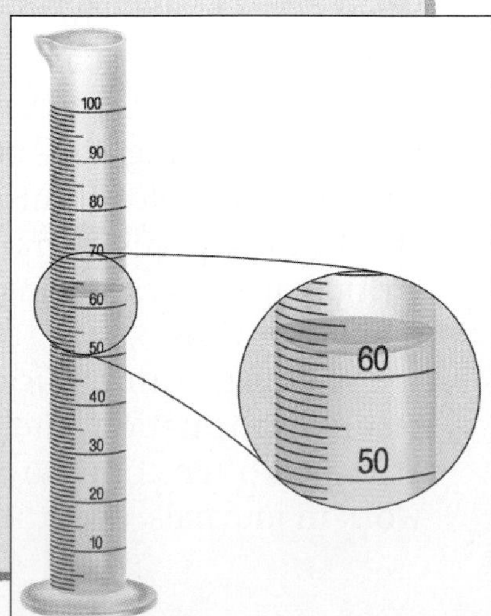

Mass To measure mass, or the amount of matter in an object, you will use a unit of measure known as the **gram (g)**. One gram is approximately the mass of a paper clip. Larger masses are measured in kilograms (kg). Scientists use a balance to find the mass of an object.

Common Conversion

1 kg = 1,000 g

ACTIVITY

The mass of the apple in the picture is measured in kilograms. What is the mass of the apple? Suppose a recipe for applesauce called for one kilogram of apples. About how many apples would you need?

Temperature To measure the temperature of a substance, you will use the **Celsius scale**. Temperature is measured in degrees Celsius (°C) using a Celsius thermometer. Water freezes at 0°C and boils at 100°C.

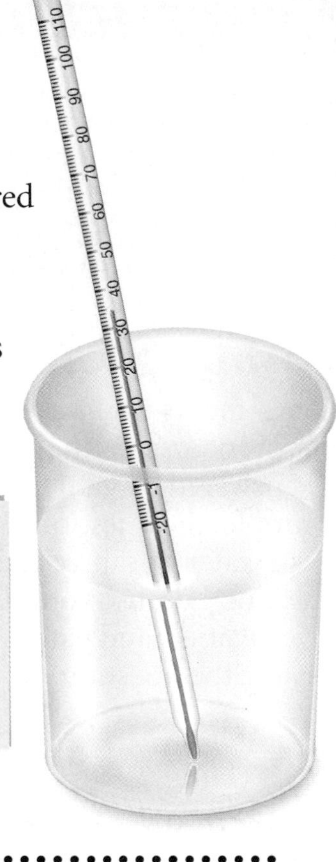

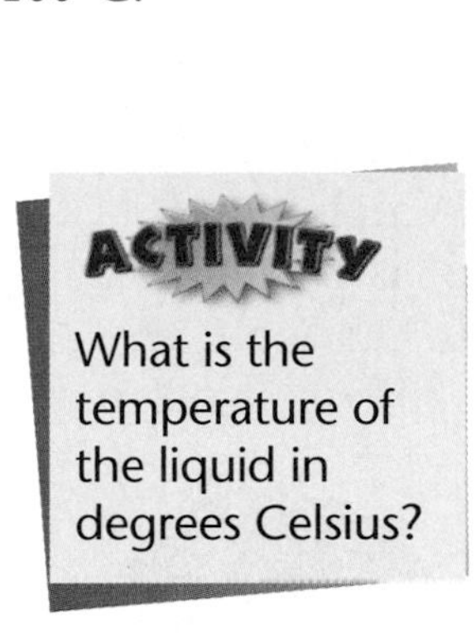

ACTIVITY

What is the temperature of the liquid in degrees Celsius?

Converting SI Units

To use the SI system, you must know how to convert between units. Converting from one unit to another involves the skill of **calculating**, or using mathematical operations. Converting between SI units is similar to converting between dollars and dimes because both systems are based on multiples of ten.

Suppose you want to convert a length of 80 centimeters to meters. Follow these steps to convert between units.

1. Begin by writing down the measurement you want to convert—in this example, 80 centimeters.
2. Write a conversion factor that represents the relationship between the two units you are converting. In this example, the relationship is *1 meter = 100 centimeters.* Write this conversion factor as a fraction, making sure to place the units you are converting from (centimeters, in this example) in the denominator.
3. Multiply the measurement you want to convert by the fraction. When you do this, the units in the first measurement will cancel out with the units in the denominator. Your answer will be in the units you are converting to (meters, in this example).

Example

80 centimeters = __?__ meters

$$80 \text{ centimeters} \times \frac{1 \text{ meter}}{100 \text{ centimeters}} = \frac{80 \text{ meters}}{100}$$

$$= 0.8 \text{ meters}$$

Convert between the following units.

1. 600 millimeters = _?_ meters
2. 0.35 liters = _?_ milliliters
3. 1,050 grams = _?_ kilograms

Conducting a Scientific Investigation

In some ways, scientists are like detectives, piecing together clues to learn about a process or event. One way that scientists gather clues is by carrying out experiments. An experiment tests an idea in a careful, orderly manner. Although experiments do not all follow the same steps in the same order, many follow a pattern similar to the one described here.

Posing Questions

Experiments begin by asking a scientific question. A scientific question is one that can be answered by gathering evidence. For example, the question "Which freezes faster—fresh water or salt water?" is a scientific question because you can carry out an investigation and gather information to answer the question.

Developing a Hypothesis

The next step is to form a hypothesis. A **hypothesis** is a possible explanation for a set of observations or answer to a scientific question. In science, a hypothesis must be something that can be tested. A hypothesis can be worded as an *If*... *then*... statement. For example, a hypothesis might be *"If I add salt to fresh water, then the water will take longer to freeze."* A hypothesis worded this way serves as a rough outline of the experiment you should perform.

Designing an Experiment

Next you need to plan a way to test your hypothesis. Your plan should be written out as a step-by-step procedure and should describe the observations or measurements you will make.

Two important steps involved in designing an experiment are controlling variables and forming operational definitions.

Controlling Variables In a well-designed experiment, you need to keep all variables the same except for one. A **variable** is any factor that can change in an experiment. The factor that you change is called the **manipulated variable.** In this experiment, the manipulated variable is the amount of salt added to the water. Other factors, such as the amount of water or the starting temperature, are kept constant.

The factor that changes as a result of the manipulated variable is called the responding variable. The **responding variable** is what you measure or observe to obtain your results. In this experiment, the responding variable is how long the water takes to freeze.

An experiment in which all factors except one are kept constant is a **controlled experiment.** Most controlled experiments include a test called the control. In this experiment, Container 3 is the control. Because no salt is added to Container 3, you can compare the results from the other containers to it. Any difference in results must be due to the addition of salt alone.

Forming Operational Definitions
Another important aspect of a well-designed experiment is having clear operational definitions. An **operational definition** is a statement that describes how a particular variable is to be measured or how a term is to be defined. For example, in this experiment, how will you determine if the water has frozen? You might decide to insert a stick in each container at the start of the experiment. Your operational definition of "frozen" would be the time at which the stick can no longer move.

EXPERIMENTAL PROCEDURE

1. *Fill 3 containers with 300 milliliters of cold tap water.*
2. *Add 10 grams of salt to Container 1; stir. Add 20 grams of salt to Container 2; stir. Add no salt to Container 3.*
3. *Place the 3 containers in a freezer.*
4. *Check the containers every 15 minutes. Record your observations.*

Interpreting Data

The observations and measurements you make in an experiment are called data. At the end of an experiment, you need to analyze the data to look for any patterns or trends. Patterns often become clear if you organize your data in a data table or graph. Then think through what the data reveal. Do they support your hypothesis? Do they point out a flaw in your experiment? Do you need to collect more data?

Drawing Conclusions

A conclusion is a statement that sums up what you have learned from an experiment. When you draw a conclusion, you need to decide whether the data you collected support your hypothesis or not. You may need to repeat an experiment several times before you can draw any conclusions from it. Conclusions often lead you to pose new questions and plan new experiments to answer them.

ACTIVITY Is a ball's bounce affected by the height from which it is dropped? Using the steps just described, plan a controlled experiment to investigate this problem.

Thinking Critically

Has a friend ever asked for your advice about a problem? If so, you may have helped your friend think through the problem in a logical way. Without knowing it, you used critical-thinking skills to help your friend. Critical thinking involves the use of reasoning and logic to solve problems or make decisions. Some critical-thinking skills are described below.

Comparing and Contrasting

When you examine two objects for similarities and differences, you are using the skill of **comparing and contrasting.** Comparing involves identifying similarities, or common characteristics. Contrasting involves identifying differences. Analyzing objects in this way can help you discover details that you might otherwise overlook.

ACTIVITY

Compare and contrast the two animals in the photo. First list all the similarities that you see. Then list all the differences.

Applying Concepts

When you use your knowledge about one situation to make sense of a similar situation, you are using the skill of **applying concepts.** Being able to transfer your knowledge from one situation to another shows that you truly understand a concept. You may use this skill in answering test questions that present different problems from the ones you've reviewed in class.

ACTIVITY

You have just learned that water takes longer to freeze when other substances are mixed into it. Use this knowledge to explain why people need a substance called antifreeze in their car's radiator in the winter.

Interpreting Illustrations

Diagrams, photographs, and maps are included in textbooks to help clarify what you read. These illustrations show processes, places, and ideas in a visual manner. The skill called **interpreting illustrations** can help you learn from these visual elements. To understand an illustration, take the time to study the illustration along with all the written information that accompanies it. Captions identify the key concepts shown in the illustration. Labels point out the important parts of a diagram or map, while keys identify the symbols used in a map.

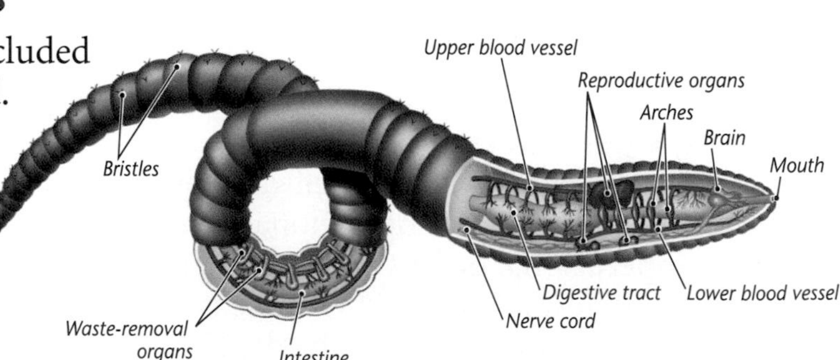

▲ **Internal anatomy of an earthworm**

Study the diagram above. Then write a short paragraph explaining what you have learned.

Relating Cause and Effect

If one event causes another event to occur, the two events are said to have a cause-and-effect relationship. When you determine that such a relationship exists between two events, you use a skill called **relating cause and effect.** For example, if you notice an itchy, red bump on your skin, you might infer that a mosquito bit you. The mosquito bite is the cause, and the bump is the effect.

It is important to note that two events do not necessarily have a cause-and-effect relationship just because they occur together. Scientists carry out experiments or use past experience to determine whether a cause-and-effect relationship exists.

ACTIVITY

You are on a camping trip and your flashlight has stopped working. List some possible causes for the flashlight malfunction. How could you determine which cause-and-effect relationship has left you in the dark?

Making Generalizations

When you draw a conclusion about an entire group based on information about only some of the group's members, you are using a skill called **making generalizations.** For a generalization to be valid, the sample you choose must be large enough and representative of the entire group. You might, for example, put this skill to work at a farm stand if you see a sign that says, "Sample some grapes before you buy." If you sample a few sweet grapes, you may conclude that all the grapes are sweet—and purchase a large bunch.

ACTIVITY

A team of scientists needs to determine whether the water in a large reservoir is safe to drink. How could they use the skill of making generalizations to help them? What should they do?

Making Judgments

When you evaluate something to decide whether it is good or bad, or right or wrong, you are using a skill called **making judgments.** For example, you make judgments when you decide to eat healthful foods or to pick up litter in a park. Before you make a judgment, you need to think through the pros and cons of a situation, and identify the values or standards that you hold.

ACTIVITY

Should children and teens be required to wear helmets when bicycling? Explain why you feel the way you do.

Problem Solving

When you use critical-thinking skills to resolve an issue or decide on a course of action, you are using a skill called **problem solving.** Some problems, such as how to convert a fraction into a decimal, are straightforward. Other problems, such as figuring out why your computer has stopped working, are complex. Some complex problems can be solved using the trial and error method—try out one solution first, and if that doesn't work, try another. Other useful problem-solving strategies include making models and brainstorming possible solutions with a partner.

Organizing Information

As you read this textbook, how can you make sense of all the information it contains? Some useful tools to help you organize information are shown on this page. These tools are called *graphic organizers* because they give you a visual picture of a topic, showing at a glance how key concepts are related.

Concept Maps

Concept maps are useful tools for organizing information on broad topics. A concept map begins with a general concept and shows how it can be broken down into more specific concepts. In that way, relationships between concepts become easier to understand.

A concept map is constructed by placing concept words (usually nouns) in ovals and connecting them with linking words. Often, the most general concept word is placed at the top, and the words become more specific as you move downward. Often the linking words, which are written on a line extending between two ovals, describe the relationship between the two concepts they connect. If you follow any string of concepts and linking words down the map, it should read like a sentence.

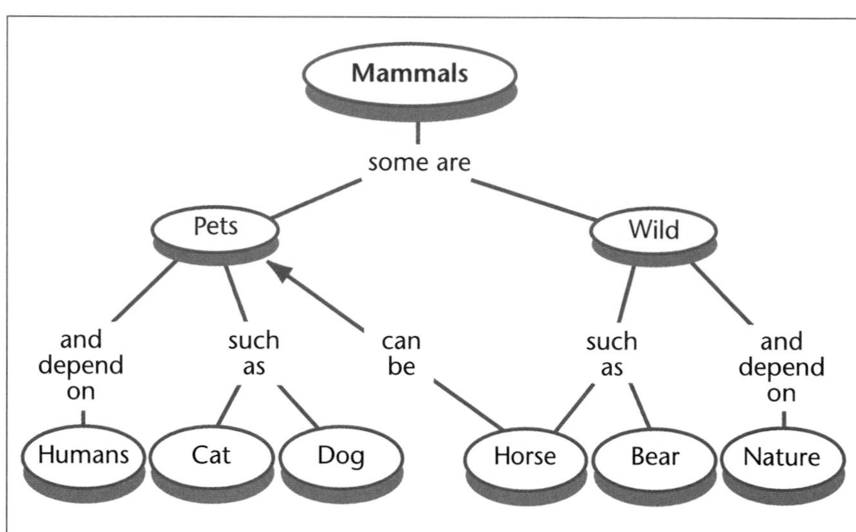

Some concept maps include linking words that connect a concept on one branch of the map to a concept on another branch. These linking words, called cross-linkages, show more complex interrelationships among concepts.

Compare/Contrast Tables

Compare/contrast tables are useful tools for sorting out the similarities and differences between two or more items. A table provides an organized framework in which to compare items based on specific characteristics that you identify.

To create a compare/contrast table, list the items to be compared across the top of a table. Then list the characteristics that will form the basis of your comparison in the left-hand column. Complete the table by filling in information about each characteristic, first for one item and then for the other.

Characteristic	Baseball	Basketball
Number of Players	9	5
Playing Field	Baseball diamond	Basketball court
Equipment	Bat, baseball, mitts	Basket, basketball

Venn Diagrams

Another way to show similarities and differences between items is with a Venn diagram. A Venn diagram consists of two or more circles that partially overlap. Each circle represents a particular concept or idea. Common characteristics, or similarities, are written within the area of overlap between the two circles. Unique characteristics, or differences, are written in the parts of the circles outside the area of overlap.

To create a Venn diagram, draw two overlapping circles. Label the circles with the names of the items being compared. Write the unique characteristics in each circle outside the area of overlap. Then write the shared characteristics within the area of overlap.

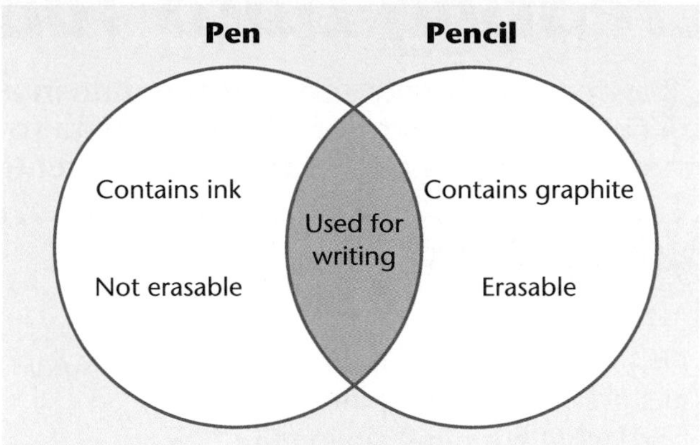

Flowcharts

A flowchart can help you understand the order in which certain events have occurred or should occur. Flowcharts are useful for outlining the stages in a process or the steps in a procedure.

To make a flowchart, write a brief description of each event in a box. Place the first event at the top of the page, followed by the second event, the third event, and so on. Then draw an arrow to connect each event to the one that occurs next.

Preparing Pasta

Boil water

Cook pasta

Drain water

Add sauce

Cycle Diagrams

A cycle diagram can be used to show a sequence of events that is continuous, or cyclical. A continuous sequence does not have an end because, when the final event is over, the first event begins again. Like a flowchart, a cycle diagram can help you understand the order of events.

To create a cycle diagram, write a brief description of each event in a box. Place one event at the top of the page in the center. Then, moving in a clockwise direction around an imaginary circle, write each event in its proper sequence. Draw arrows that connect each event to the one that occurs next, forming a continuous circle.

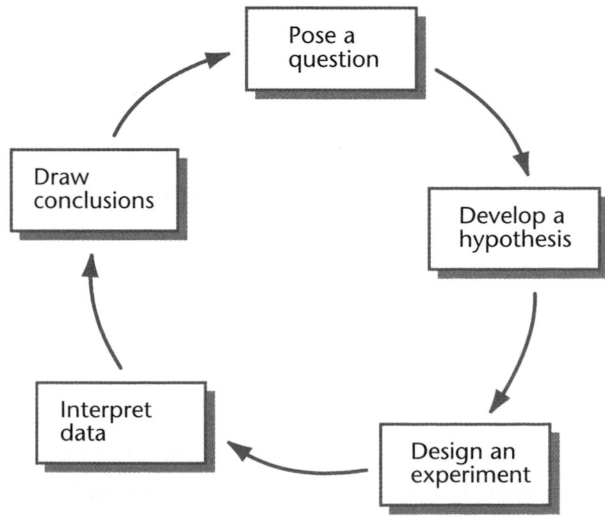

Creating Data Tables and Graphs

How can you make sense of the data in a science experiment? The first step is to organize the data to help you understand them. Data tables and graphs are helpful tools for organizing data.

Data Tables

You have gathered your materials and set up your experiment. But before you start, you need to plan a way to record what happens during the experiment. By creating a data table, you can record your observations and measurements in an orderly way.

Suppose, for example, that a scientist conducted an experiment to find out how many Calories people of different body masses burn while doing various activities. The data table shows the results.

CALORIES BURNED IN 30 MINUTES OF ACTIVITY

Body Mass	Experiment 1 Bicycling	Experiment 2 Playing Basketball	Experiment 3 Watching Television
30 kg	60 Calories	120 Calories	21 Calories
40 kg	77 Calories	164 Calories	27 Calories
50 kg	95 Calories	206 Calories	33 Calories
60 kg	114 Calories	248 Calories	38 Calories

Notice in this data table that the manipulated variable (body mass) is the heading of one column. The responding variable (for Experiment 1, the number of Calories burned while bicycling) is the heading of the next column. Additional columns were added for related experiments.

Bar Graphs

To compare how many Calories a person burns doing various activities, you could create a bar graph. A bar graph is used to display data in a number of separate, or distinct, categories. In this example, bicycling, playing basketball, and watching television are three separate categories.

To create a bar graph, follow these steps.

1. On graph paper, draw a horizontal, or x-, axis and a vertical, or y-, axis.
2. Write the names of the categories to be graphed along the horizontal axis. Include an overall label for the axis as well.
3. Label the vertical axis with the name of the responding variable. Include units of measurement. Then create a scale along the axis by marking off equally spaced numbers that cover the range of the data collected.
4. For each category, draw a solid bar using the scale on the vertical axis to determine the appropriate height. For example, for bicycling, draw the bar as high as the 60 mark on the vertical axis. Make all the bars the same width and leave equal spaces between them.
5. Add a title that describes the graph.

Calories Burned by a 30-kilogram Person in Various Activities

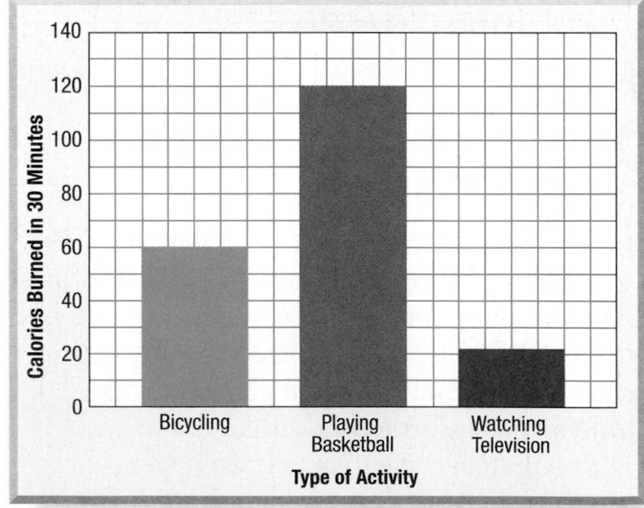

Line Graphs

To see whether a relationship exists between body mass and the number of Calories burned while bicycling, you could create a line graph. A line graph is used to display data that show how one variable (the responding variable) changes in response to another variable (the manipulated variable). You can use a line graph when your manipulated variable is *continuous*, that is, when there are other points between the ones that you tested. In this example, body mass is a continuous variable because there are other body masses between 30 and 40 kilograms (for example, 31 kilograms). Time is another example of a continuous variable.

Effect of Body Mass on Calories Burned While Bicycling

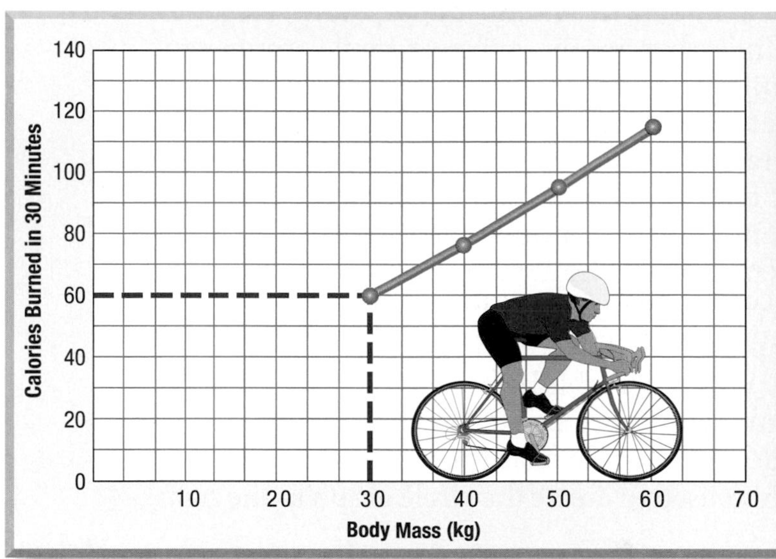

Line graphs are powerful tools because they allow you to estimate values for conditions that you did not test in the experiment. For example, you can use the line graph to estimate that a 35-kilogram person would burn 68 Calories while bicycling.

To create a line graph, follow these steps.

1. On graph paper, draw a horizontal, or *x*-, axis and a vertical, or *y*-, axis.
2. Label the horizontal axis with the name of the manipulated variable. Label the vertical axis with the name of the responding variable. Include units of measurement.
3. Create a scale on each axis by marking off equally spaced numbers that cover the range of the data collected.
4. Plot a point on the graph for each piece of data. In the line graph above, the dotted lines show how to plot the first data point (30 kilograms and 60 Calories). Draw an imaginary vertical line extending up from the horizontal axis at the 30-kilogram mark. Then draw an imaginary horizontal line extending across from the vertical axis at the 60-Calorie mark. Plot the point where the two lines intersect.
5. Connect the plotted points with a solid line. (In some cases, it may be more appropriate to draw a line that shows the general trend of the plotted points. In those cases, some of the points may fall above or below the line. Also, not all graphs are linear. It may be more appropriate to draw a curve to connect the points.)
6. Add a title that identifies the variables or relationship in the graph.

ACTIVITY

Create line graphs to display the data from Experiment 2 and Experiment 3 in the data table.

ACTIVITY

You read in the newspaper that a total of 4 centimeters of rain fell in your area in June, 2.5 centimeters fell in July, and 1.5 centimeters fell in August. What type of graph would you use to display these data? Use graph paper to create the graph.

Circle Graphs

Like bar graphs, circle graphs can be used to display data in a number of separate categories. Unlike bar graphs, however, circle graphs can only be used when you have data for *all* the categories that make up a given topic. A circle graph is sometimes called a pie chart because it resembles a pie cut into slices. The pie represents the entire topic, while the slices represent the individual categories. The size of a slice indicates what percentage of the whole a particular category makes up.

The data table below shows the results of a survey in which 24 teenagers were asked to identify their favorite sport. The data were then used to create the circle graph at the right.

Sports That Teens Prefer

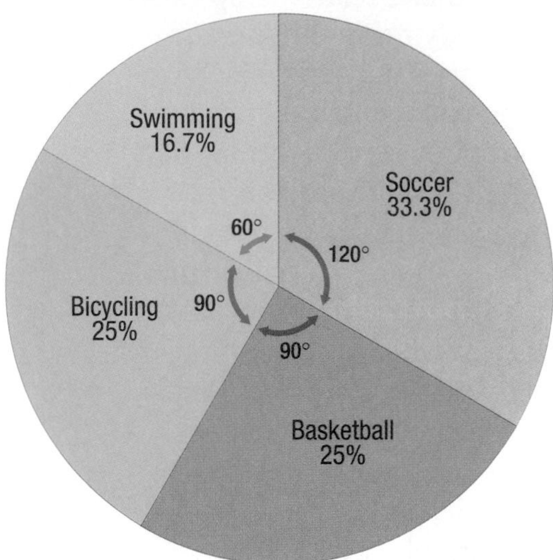

FAVORITE SPORTS

Sport	Number of Students
Soccer	8
Basketball	6
Bicycling	6
Swimming	4

To create a circle graph, follow these steps.

1. Use a compass to draw a circle. Mark the center of the circle with a point. Then draw a line from the center point to the top of the circle.
2. Determine the size of each "slice" by setting up a proportion where x equals the number of degrees in a slice. (NOTE: A circle contains 360 degrees.) For example, to find the number of degrees in the "soccer" slice, set up the following proportion:

$$\frac{\text{students who prefer soccer}}{\text{total number of students}} = \frac{x}{\text{total number of degrees in a circle}}$$

$$\frac{8}{24} = \frac{x}{360}$$

Cross-multiply and solve for x.

$$24x = 8 \times 360$$
$$x = 120$$

The "soccer" slice should contain 120 degrees.

3. Use a protractor to measure the angle of the first slice, using the line you drew to the top of the circle as the 0° line. Draw a line from the center of the circle to the edge for the angle you measured.
4. Continue around the circle by measuring the size of each slice with the protractor. Start measuring from the edge of the previous slice so the wedges do not overlap. When you are done, the entire circle should be filled in.
5. Determine the percentage of the whole circle that each slice represents. To do this, divide the number of degrees in a slice by the total number of degrees in a circle (360), and multiply by 100%. For the "soccer" slice, you can find the percentage as follows:

$$\frac{120}{360} \times 100\% = 33.3\%$$

6. Use a different color to shade in each slice. Label each slice with the name of the category and with the percentage of the whole it represents.
7. Add a title to the circle graph.

ACTIVITY

In a class of 28 students, 12 students take the bus to school, 10 students walk, and 6 students ride their bicycles. Create a circle graph to display these data.

Laboratory Safety

Safety Symbols

These symbols alert you to possible dangers in the laboratory and remind you to work carefully.

Safety Goggles Always wear safety goggles to protect your eyes in any activity involving chemicals, flames or heating, or the possibility of broken glassware.

Lab Apron Wear a laboratory apron to protect your skin and clothing from damage.

Breakage You are working with materials that may be breakable, such as glass containers, glass tubing, thermometers, or funnels. Handle breakable materials with care. Do not touch broken glassware.

Heat-resistant Gloves Use an oven mitt or other hand protection when handling hot materials. Hot plates, hot glassware, or hot water can cause burns. Do not touch hot objects with your bare hands.

Heating Use a clamp or tongs to pick up hot glassware. Do not touch hot objects with your bare hands.

Sharp Object Pointed-tip scissors, scalpels, knives, needles, pins, or tacks are sharp. They can cut or puncture your skin. Always direct a sharp edge or point away from yourself and others. Use sharp instruments only as instructed.

Electric Shock Avoid the possibility of electric shock. Never use electrical equipment around water, or when the equipment is wet or your hands are wet. Be sure cords are untangled and cannot trip anyone. Disconnect the equipment when it is not in use.

Corrosive Chemical You are working with an acid or another corrosive chemical. Avoid getting it on your skin or clothing, or in your eyes. Do not inhale the vapors. Wash your hands when you are finished with the activity.

Poison Do not let any poisonous chemical come in contact with your skin, and do not inhale its vapors. Wash your hands when you are finished with the activity.

Physical Safety When an experiment involves physical activity, take precautions to avoid injuring yourself or others. Follow instructions from your teacher. Alert your teacher if there is any reason you should not participate in the activity.

Animal Safety Treat live animals with care to avoid harming the animals or yourself. Working with animal parts or preserved animals also may require caution. Wash your hands when you are finished with the activity.

Plant Safety Handle plants in the laboratory or during field work only as directed by your teacher. If you are allergic to certain plants, tell your teacher before doing an activity in which those plants are used. Avoid touching harmful plants such as poison ivy, poison oak, or poison sumac, or plants with thorns. Wash your hands when you are finished with the activity.

Flames You may be working with flames from a lab burner, candle, or matches. Tie back loose hair and clothing. Follow instructions from your teacher about lighting and extinguishing flames.

No Flames Flammable materials may be present. Make sure there are no flames, sparks, or other exposed heat sources present.

Fumes When poisonous or unpleasant vapors may be involved, work in a ventilated area. Avoid inhaling vapors directly. Only test an odor when directed to do so by your teacher, and use a wafting motion to direct the vapor toward your nose.

Disposal Chemicals and other laboratory materials used in the activity must be disposed of safely. Follow the instructions from your teacher.

Hand Washing Wash your hands thoroughly when finished with the activity. Use antibacterial soap and warm water. Lather both sides of your hands and between your fingers. Rinse well.

General Safety Awareness You may see this symbol when none of the symbols described earlier appears. In this case, follow the specific instructions provided. You may also see this symbol when you are asked to develop your own procedure in a lab. Have your teacher approve your plan before you go further.

Science Safety Rules

To prepare yourself to work safely in the laboratory, read over the following safety rules. Then read them a second time. Make sure you understand and follow each rule. Ask your teacher to explain any rules you do not understand.

Dress Code

1. To protect yourself from injuring your eyes, wear safety goggles whenever you work with chemicals, burners, glassware, or any substance that might get into your eyes. If you wear contact lenses, notify your teacher.
2. Wear a lab apron or coat whenever you work with corrosive chemicals or substances that can stain.
3. Tie back long hair to keep it away from any chemicals, flames, or equipment.
4. Remove or tie back any article of clothing or jewelry that can hang down and touch chemicals, flames, or equipment. Roll up or secure long sleeves.
5. Never wear open shoes or sandals.

General Precautions

6. Read all directions for an experiment several times before beginning the activity. Carefully follow all written and oral instructions. If you are in doubt about any part of the experiment, ask your teacher for assistance.
7. Never perform activities that are not assigned or authorized by your teacher. Obtain permission before "experimenting" on your own. Never handle any equipment unless you have specific permission.
8. Never perform lab activities without direct supervision.
9. Never eat or drink in the laboratory.
10. Keep work areas clean and tidy at all times. Bring only notebooks and lab manuals or written lab procedures to the work area. All other items, such as purses and backpacks, should be left in a designated area.
11. Do not engage in horseplay.

First Aid

12. Always report all accidents or injuries to your teacher, no matter how minor. Notify your teacher immediately about any fires.
13. Learn what to do in case of specific accidents, such as getting acid in your eyes or on your skin. (Rinse acids from your body with lots of water.)
14. Be aware of the location of the first-aid kit, but do not use it unless instructed by your teacher. In case of injury, your teacher should administer first aid. Your teacher may also send you to the school nurse or call a physician.
15. Know the location of emergency equipment, such as the fire extinguisher and fire blanket, and know how to use it.
16. Know the location of the nearest telephone and whom to contact in an emergency.

Heating and Fire Safety

17. Never use a heat source, such as a candle, burner, or hot plate, without wearing safety goggles.
18. Never heat anything unless instructed to do so. A chemical that is harmless when cool may be dangerous when heated.
19. Keep all combustible materials away from flames. Never use a flame or spark near a combustible chemical.
20. Never reach across a flame.
21. Before using a laboratory burner, make sure you know proper procedures for lighting and adjusting the burner, as demonstrated by your teacher. Do not touch the burner. It may be hot. And never leave a lighted burner unattended!
22. Chemicals can splash or boil out of a heated test tube. When heating a substance in a test tube, make sure that the mouth of the tube is not pointed at you or anyone else.
23. Never heat a liquid in a closed container. The expanding gases produced may blow the container apart.
24. Before picking up a container that has been heated, hold the back of your hand near it. If you can feel heat on the back of your hand, the container is too hot to handle. Use an oven mitt to pick up a container that has been heated.

Using Chemicals Safely

25. Never mix chemicals "for the fun of it." You might produce a dangerous, possibly explosive substance.
26. Never put your face near the mouth of a container that holds chemicals. Many chemicals are poisonous. Never touch, taste, or smell a chemical unless you are instructed by your teacher to do so.
27. Use only those chemicals needed in the activity. Read and double-check labels on supply bottles before removing any chemicals. Take only as much as you need. Keep all containers closed when chemicals are not being used.
28. Dispose of all chemicals as instructed by your teacher. To avoid contamination, never return chemicals to their original containers. Never simply pour chemicals or other substances into the sink or trash containers.
29. Be extra careful when working with acids or bases. Pour all chemicals over the sink or a container, not over your work surface.
30. If you are instructed to test for odors, use a wafting motion to direct the odors to your nose. Do not inhale the fumes directly from the container.
31. When mixing an acid and water, always pour the water into the container first and then add the acid to the water. Never pour water into an acid.
32. Take extreme care not to spill any material in the laboratory. Wash chemical spills and splashes immediately with plenty of water. Immediately begin rinsing with water any acids that get on your skin or clothing, and notify your teacher of any acid spill at the same time.

Using Glassware Safely

33. Never force glass tubing or thermometers into a rubber stopper or rubber tubing. Have your teacher insert the glass tubing or thermometer if required for an activity.
34. If you are using a laboratory burner, use a wire screen to protect glassware from any flame. Never heat glassware that is not thoroughly dry on the outside.
35. Keep in mind that hot glassware looks cool. Never pick up glassware without first checking to see if it is hot. Use an oven mitt. See rule 24.
36. Never use broken or chipped glassware. If glassware breaks, notify your teacher and dispose of the glassware in the proper broken-glassware container. Never handle broken glass with your bare hands.
37. Never eat or drink from lab glassware.
38. Thoroughly clean glassware before putting it away.

Using Sharp Instruments

39. Handle scalpels or other sharp instruments with extreme care. Never cut material toward you; cut away from you.
40. Immediately notify your teacher if you cut your skin when working in the laboratory.

Animal and Plant Safety

41. Never perform experiments that cause pain, discomfort, or harm to animals. This rule applies at home as well as in the classroom.
42. Animals should be handled only if absolutely necessary. Your teacher will instruct you as to how to handle each animal species brought into the classroom.
43. If you know that you are allergic to certain plants, molds, or animals, tell your teacher before doing an activity in which these are used.
44. During field work, protect your skin by wearing long pants, long sleeves, socks, and closed shoes. Know how to recognize the poisonous plants and fungi in your area, as well as plants with thorns, and avoid contact with them. Never eat any part of a plant or fungus.
45. Wash your hands thoroughly after handling animals or a cage containing animals. Wash your hands when you are finished with any activity involving animal parts, plants, or soil.

End-of-Experiment Rules

46. After an experiment has been completed, turn off all burners or hot plates. If you used a gas burner, check that the gas-line valve to the burner is off. Unplug hot plates.
47. Turn off and unplug any other electrical equipment that you used.
48. Clean up your work area and return all equipment to its proper place.
49. Dispose of waste materials as instructed by your teacher.
50. Wash your hands after every experiment.

Appendix B
Using a Laboratory Balance

The laboratory balance is an important tool in scientific investigations. You can use a balance to determine the masses of materials that you study or experiment with in the laboratory.

Different kinds of balances are used in the laboratory. One kind of balance is the triple-beam balance. The balance that you may use in your science class is probably similar to the balance illustrated in this Appendix. To use the balance properly, you should learn the name, location, and function of each part of the balance you are using. What kind of balance do you have in your science class?

The Triple-Beam Balance

The triple-beam balance is a single-pan balance with three beams calibrated in grams. The back, or 100-gram, beam is divided into ten units of 10 grams each. The middle, or 500-gram, beam is divided into five units of 100 grams each. The front, or 10-gram, beam is divided into ten major units of 1 gram each. Each of these units is further divided into units of 0.1 gram. What is the largest mass you could find with a triple-beam balance?

The following procedure can be used to find the mass of an object with a triple-beam balance:

1. Place the object on the pan.
2. Move the rider on the middle beam notch by notch until the horizontal pointer drops below zero. Move the rider back one notch.
3. Move the rider on the back beam notch by notch until the pointer again drops below zero. Move the rider back one notch.
4. Slowly slide the rider along the front beam until the pointer stops at the zero point.
5. The mass of the object is equal to the sum of the readings on the three beams.

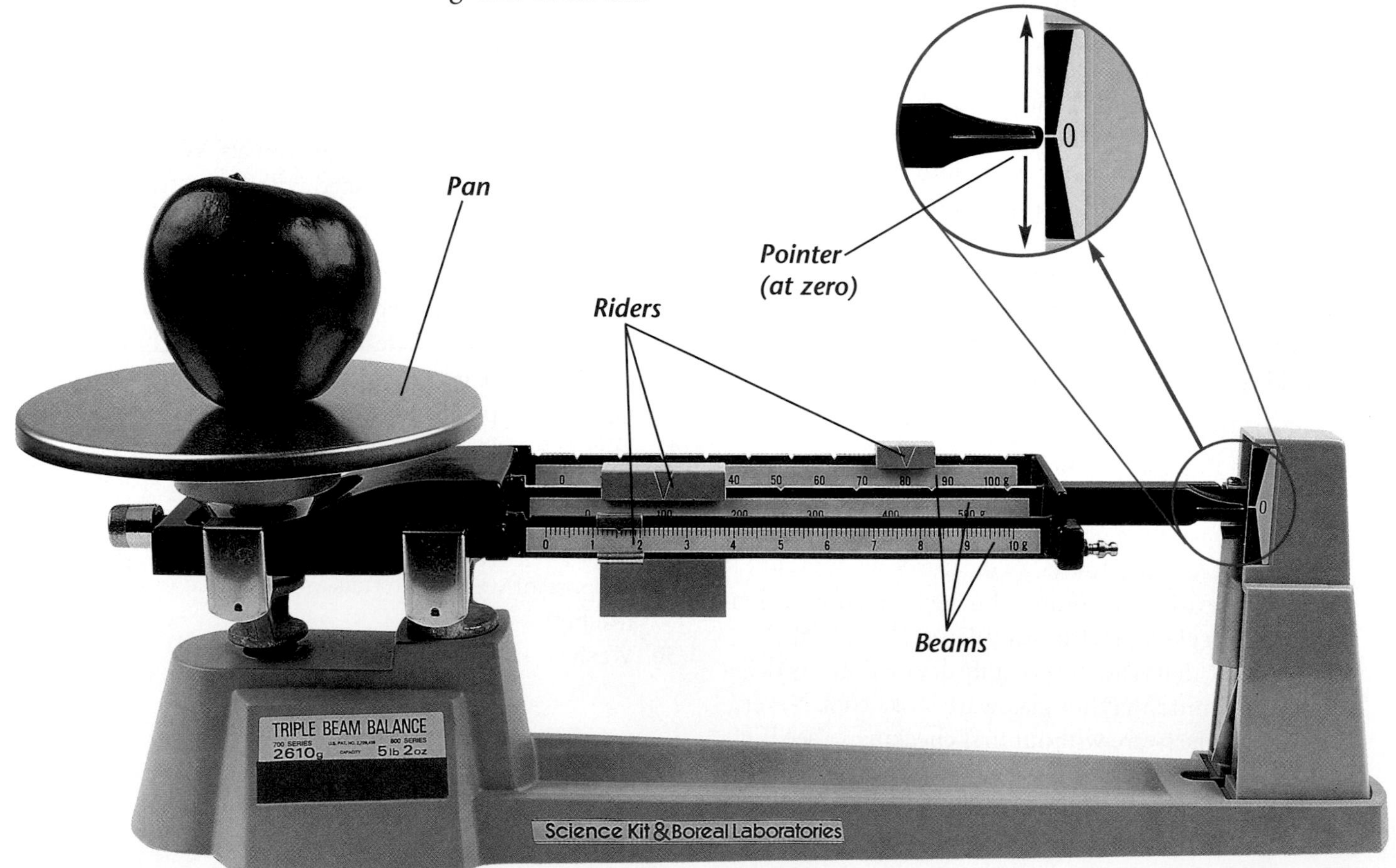

Triple-Beam Balance

List of Chemical Elements

Name	Symbol	Atomic Number	Atomic Mass†
Actinium	Ac	89	(227)
Aluminum	Al	13	26.982
Americium	Am	95	(243)
Antimony	Sb	51	121.75
Argon	Ar	18	39.948
Arsenic	As	33	74.922
Astatine	At	85	(210)
Barium	Ba	56	137.327
Berkelium	Bk	97	(247)
Beryllium	Be	4	9.012
Bismuth	Bi	83	208.980
Bohrium	Bh	107	(264)
Boron	B	5	10.811
Bromine	Br	35	79.904
Cadmium	Cd	48	112.411
Calcium	Ca	20	40.078
Californium	Cf	98	(251)
Carbon	C	6	12.011
Cerium	Ce	58	140.115
Cesium	Cs	55	132.905
Chlorine	Cl	17	35.453
Chromium	Cr	24	51.996
Cobalt	Co	27	58.933
Copper	Cu	29	63.546
Curium	Cm	96	(247)
Dubnium	Db	105	(262)
Dysprosium	Dy	66	162.50
Einsteinium	Es	99	(252)
Erbium	Er	68	167.26
Europium	Eu	63	151.965
Fermium	Fm	100	(257)
Fluorine	F	9	18.998
Francium	Fr	87	(223)
Gadolinium	Gd	64	157.25
Gallium	Ga	31	69.723
Germanium	Ge	32	72.61
Gold	Au	79	196.967
Hafnium	Hf	72	178.49
Hassium	Hs	108	(265)
Helium	He	2	4.003
Holmium	Ho	67	164.930
Hydrogen	H	1	1.008
Indium	In	49	114.818
Iodine	I	53	126.904
Iridium	Ir	77	192.22
Iron	Fe	26	55.847
Krypton	Kr	36	83.80
Lanthanum	La	57	138.906
Lawrencium	Lr	103	(262)
Lead	Pb	82	207.2
Lithium	Li	3	6.941
Lutetium	Lu	71	174.967
Magnesium	Mg	12	24.305
Manganese	Mn	25	54.938
Meitnerium	Mt	109	(268)
Mendelevium	Md	101	(258)
Mercury	Hg	80	200.659
Molybdenum	Mo	42	95.94

Name	Symbol	Atomic Number	Atomic Mass†
Neodymium	Nd	60	144.2
Neon	Ne	10	20.180
Neptunium	Np	93	(237)
Nickel	Ni	28	58.69
Niobium	Nb	41	92.906
Nitrogen	N	7	14.007
Nobelium	No	102	(259)
Osmium	Os	76	190.23
Oxygen	O	8	15.999
Palladium	Pd	46	106.42
Phosphorus	P	15	30.974
Platinum	Pt	78	195.08
Plutonium	Pu	94	(244)
Polonium	Po	84	(209)
Potassium	K	19	39.098
Praseodymium	Pr	59	140.908
Promethium	Pm	61	(145)
Protactinium	Pa	91	231.036
Radium	Ra	88	(226)
Radon	Rn	86	(222)
Rhenium	Re	75	186.207
Rhodium	Rh	45	102.906
Rubidium	Rb	37	85.468
Ruthenium	Ru	44	101.07
Rutherfordium	Rf	104	(261)
Samarium	Sm	62	150.36
Scandium	Sc	21	44.956
Seaborgium	Sg	106	(263)
Selenium	Se	34	78.96
Silicon	Si	14	28.086
Silver	Ag	47	107.868
Sodium	Na	11	22.990
Strontium	Sr	38	87.62
Sulfur	S	16	32.066
Tantalum	Ta	73	180.948
Technetium	Tc	43	(98)
Tellurium	Te	52	127.60
Terbium	Tb	65	158.925
Thallium	Tl	81	204.383
Thorium	Th	90	232.038
Thulium	Tm	69	168.934
Tin	Sn	50	118.710
Titanium	Ti	22	47.88
Tungsten	W	74	183.85
Ununbium	Uub	112	(277)
Ununhexium	Uuh	116	*
Ununnilium	Uun	110	(269)
Ununoctium	Uuo	118	*
Ununquadium	Uuq	114	*
Unununium	Uuu	111	(272)
Uranium	U	92	238.029
Vanadium	V	23	50.942
Xenon	Xe	54	131.29
Ytterbium	Yb	70	173.04
Yttrium	Y	39	88.906
Zinc	Zn	30	65.39
Zirconium	Zr	40	91.224

†Numbers in parentheses give the mass number of the most stable isotope.

*Newly discovered

Periodic Table of the Elements

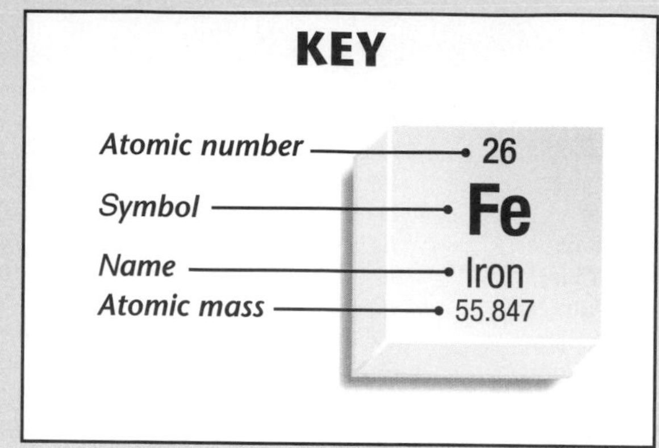

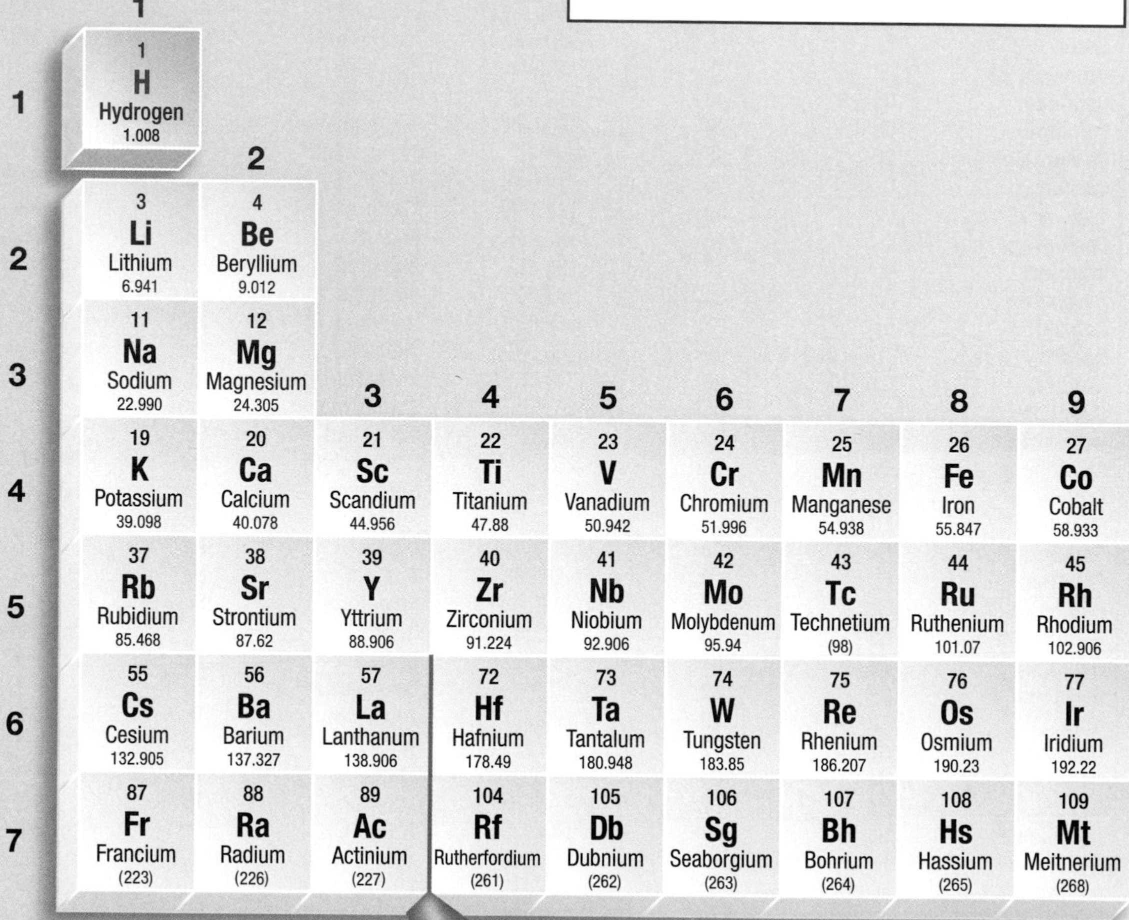

	1	2	3	4	5	6	7	8	9
1	1 H Hydrogen 1.008								
2	3 Li Lithium 6.941	4 Be Beryllium 9.012							
3	11 Na Sodium 22.990	12 Mg Magnesium 24.305							
4	19 K Potassium 39.098	20 Ca Calcium 40.078	21 Sc Scandium 44.956	22 Ti Titanium 47.88	23 V Vanadium 50.942	24 Cr Chromium 51.996	25 Mn Manganese 54.938	26 Fe Iron 55.847	27 Co Cobalt 58.933
5	37 Rb Rubidium 85.468	38 Sr Strontium 87.62	39 Y Yttrium 88.906	40 Zr Zirconium 91.224	41 Nb Niobium 92.906	42 Mo Molybdenum 95.94	43 Tc Technetium (98)	44 Ru Ruthenium 101.07	45 Rh Rhodium 102.906
6	55 Cs Cesium 132.905	56 Ba Barium 137.327	57 La Lanthanum 138.906	72 Hf Hafnium 178.49	73 Ta Tantalum 180.948	74 W Tungsten 183.85	75 Re Rhenium 186.207	76 Os Osmium 190.23	77 Ir Iridium 192.22
7	87 Fr Francium (223)	88 Ra Radium (226)	89 Ac Actinium (227)	104 Rf Rutherfordium (261)	105 Db Dubnium (262)	106 Sg Seaborgium (263)	107 Bh Bohrium (264)	108 Hs Hassium (265)	109 Mt Meitnerium (268)

Lanthanide Series	58 Ce Cerium 140.115	59 Pr Praseodymium 140.908	60 Nd Neodymium 144.24	61 Pm Promethium (145)	62 Sm Samarium 150.36
Actinide Series	90 Th Thorium 232.038	91 Pa Protactinium 231.036	92 U Uranium 238.029	93 Np Neptunium (237)	94 Pu Plutonium (244)

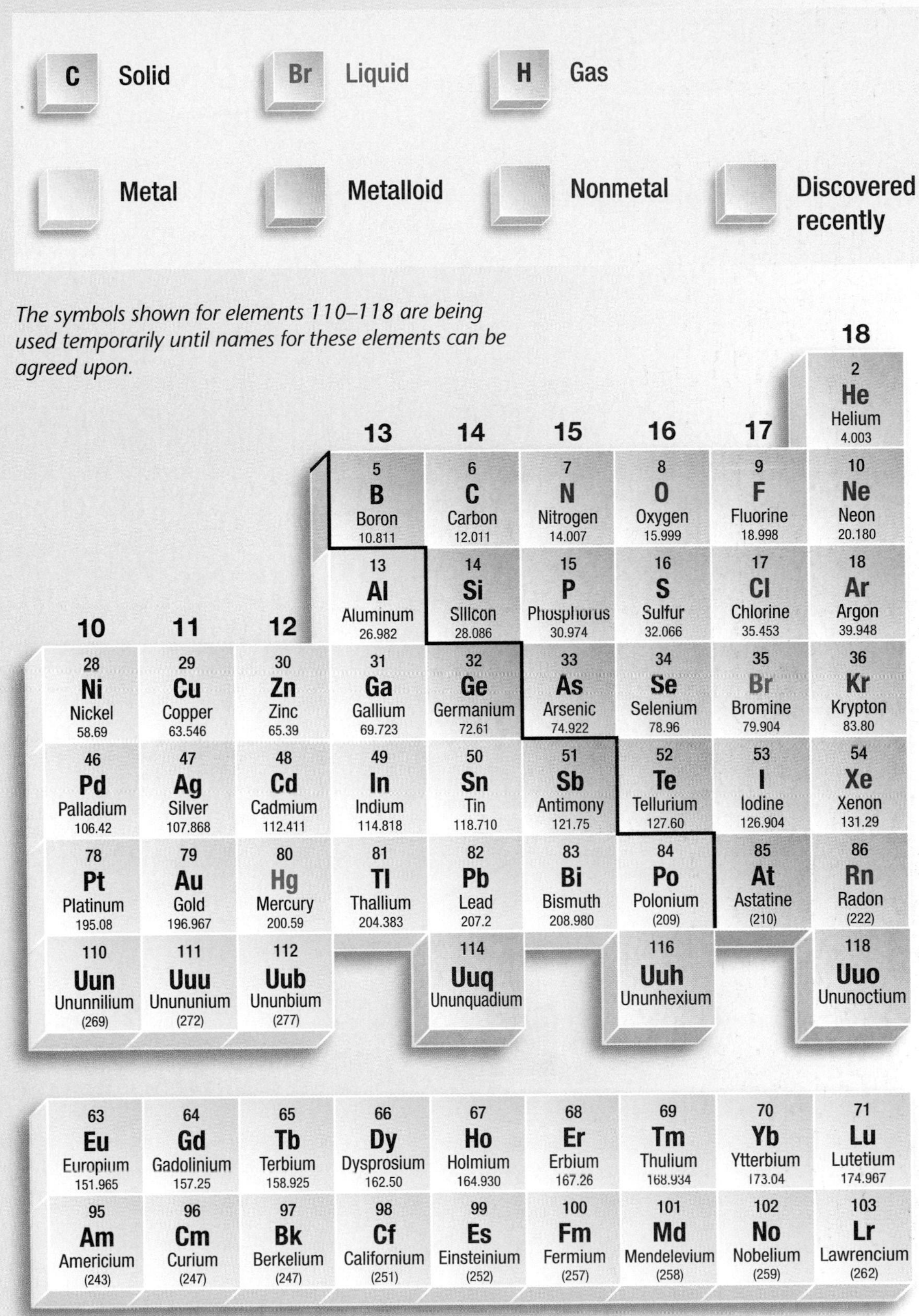

The symbols shown for elements 110–118 are being used temporarily until names for these elements can be agreed upon.

Mass numbers in parentheses are those of the most stable or common isotope.

Physical Map: United States

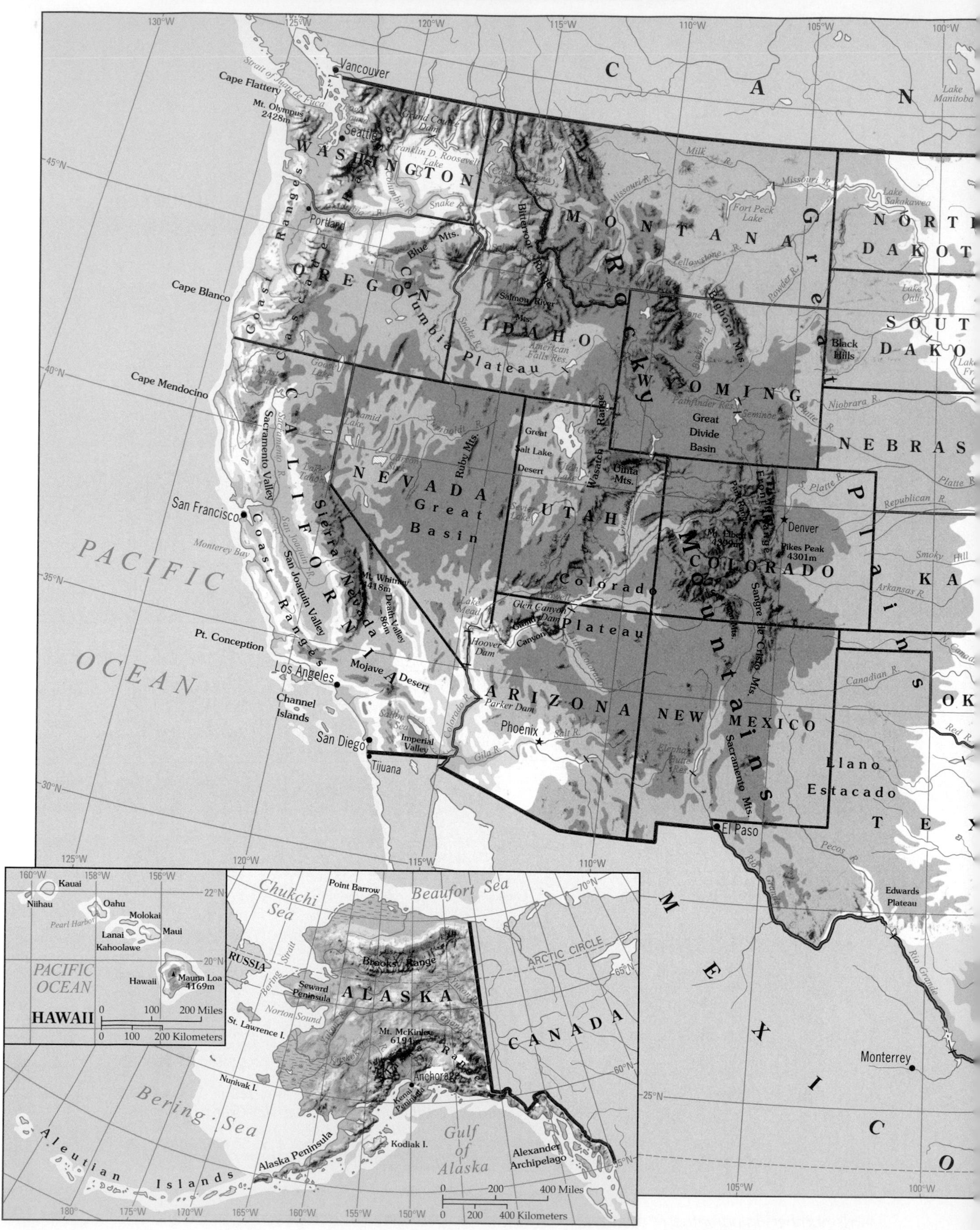

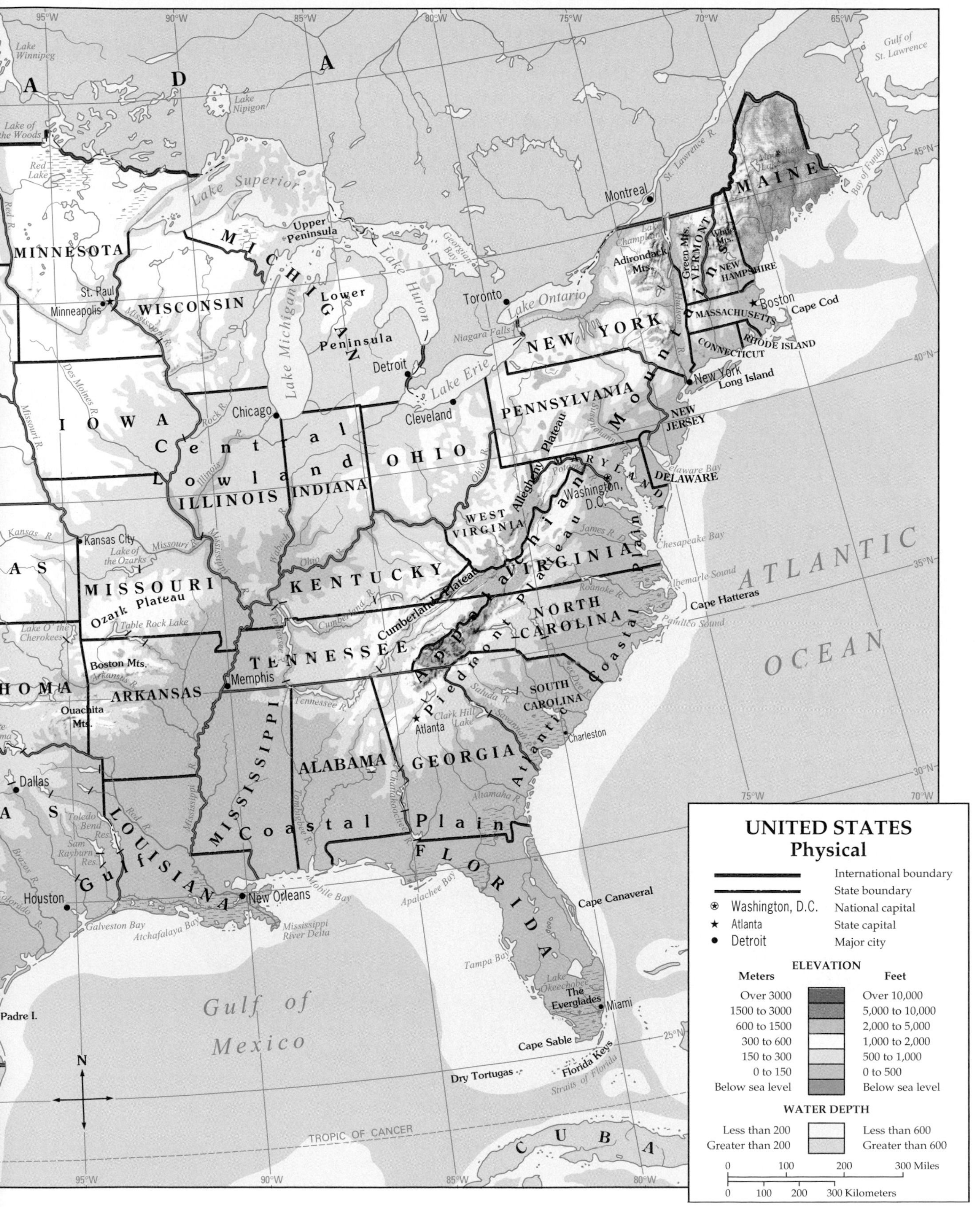
UNITED STATES
Physical
International boundary
State boundary
Washington, D.C. National capital
Atlanta State capital
Detroit Major city
ELEVATION
Meters
Feet
Over 3000
1500 to 3000
600 to 1500
300 to 600
150 to 300
0 to 150
Below sea level
Over 10,000
5,000 to 10,000
2,000 to 5,000
1,000 to 2,000
500 to 1,000
0 to 500
Below sea level
WATER DEPTH
Less than 200
Greater than 200
Less than 600
Greater than 600
0 100 200 300 Miles
0 100 200 300 Kilometers
MINNESOTA
WISCONSIN
MICHIGAN
IOWA
ILLINOIS
INDIANA
OHIO
MISSOURI
KENTUCKY
TENNESSEE
ARKANSAS
MISSISSIPPI
ALABAMA
GEORGIA
FLORIDA
LOUISIANA
SOUTH CAROLINA
NORTH CAROLINA
VIRGINIA
WEST VIRGINIA
PENNSYLVANIA
NEW YORK
NEW JERSEY
DELAWARE
MARYLAND
CONNECTICUT
RHODE ISLAND
MASSACHUSETTS
VERMONT
NEW HAMPSHIRE
MAINE
Central Lowland
Appalachian Mountains
Allegheny Plateau
Cumberland Plateau
Piedmont Plateau
Atlantic Coastal Plain
Gulf Coastal Plain
Ozark Plateau
Boston Mts.
Ouachita Mts.
Adirondack Mts.
Green Mts.
White Mts.
Upper Peninsula
Lower Peninsula
Lake Superior
Lake Michigan
Lake Huron
Lake Erie
Lake Ontario
Lake Winnipeg
Lake of the Woods
Lake Nipigon
Red Lake
Georgian Bay
Lake Champlain
Lake of the Ozarks
Table Rock Lake
Lake O' the Cherokees
Toledo Bend Res.
Sam Rayburn Res.
Clark Hill Lake
Lake Okeechobee
The Everglades
Niagara Falls
St. Lawrence R.
Mississippi R.
Missouri R.
Ohio R.
Red R.
Des Moines R.
Rock R.
Illinois R.
Wabash R.
Tennessee R.
Cumberland R.
Kansas R.
Arkansas R.
Brazos R.
Colorado R.
Tombigbee R.
Chattahoochee R.
Savannah R.
Saluda R.
Altamaha R.
Roanoke R.
James R.
Potomac R.
Susquehanna R.
Hudson R.
Delaware Bay
Chesapeake Bay
Albemarle Sound
Pamlico Sound
Cape Hatteras
Cape Cod
Long Island
Bay of Fundy
Gulf of St. Lawrence
Cape Canaveral
Cape Sable
Florida Keys
Dry Tortugas
Straits of Florida
Tampa Bay
Apalachee Bay
Mobile Bay
Mississippi River Delta
Atchafalaya Bay
Galveston Bay
Padre I.
Gulf of Mexico
ATLANTIC OCEAN
CANADA
CUBA
TROPIC OF CANCER
Minneapolis
St. Paul
Chicago
Detroit
Cleveland
Toronto
Montreal
Boston
New York
Washington, D.C.
Kansas City
Memphis
Atlanta
Charleston
Dallas
Houston
New Orleans
Miami
N
95°W
90°W
85°W
80°W
75°W
70°W
65°W
45°N
40°N
35°N
30°N
25°N

Star Charts

Autumn Sky

To use this chart, hold it up in front of you and turn it so that the direction you are facing is at the bottom of the chart. This chart works best at 34° north latitude, but can be used at other times and latitudes within the continental United States. It works best at the following times: 10:00 P.M. on September 1; 9:00 P.M. on September 15; 8:00 P.M. on September 30.

NORTHERN HORIZON

EASTERN HORIZON

WESTERN HORIZON

SOUTHERN HORIZON

Winter Sky

To use this chart, hold it up in front of you and turn it so that the direction you are facing is at the bottom of the chart. This chart works best at 34° north latitude, but can be used at other times and latitudes within the continental United States. It works best at the following times: 10:00 P.M. on December 1; 9:00 P.M. on December 15; 8:00 P.M. on December 30.

NORTHERN HORIZON

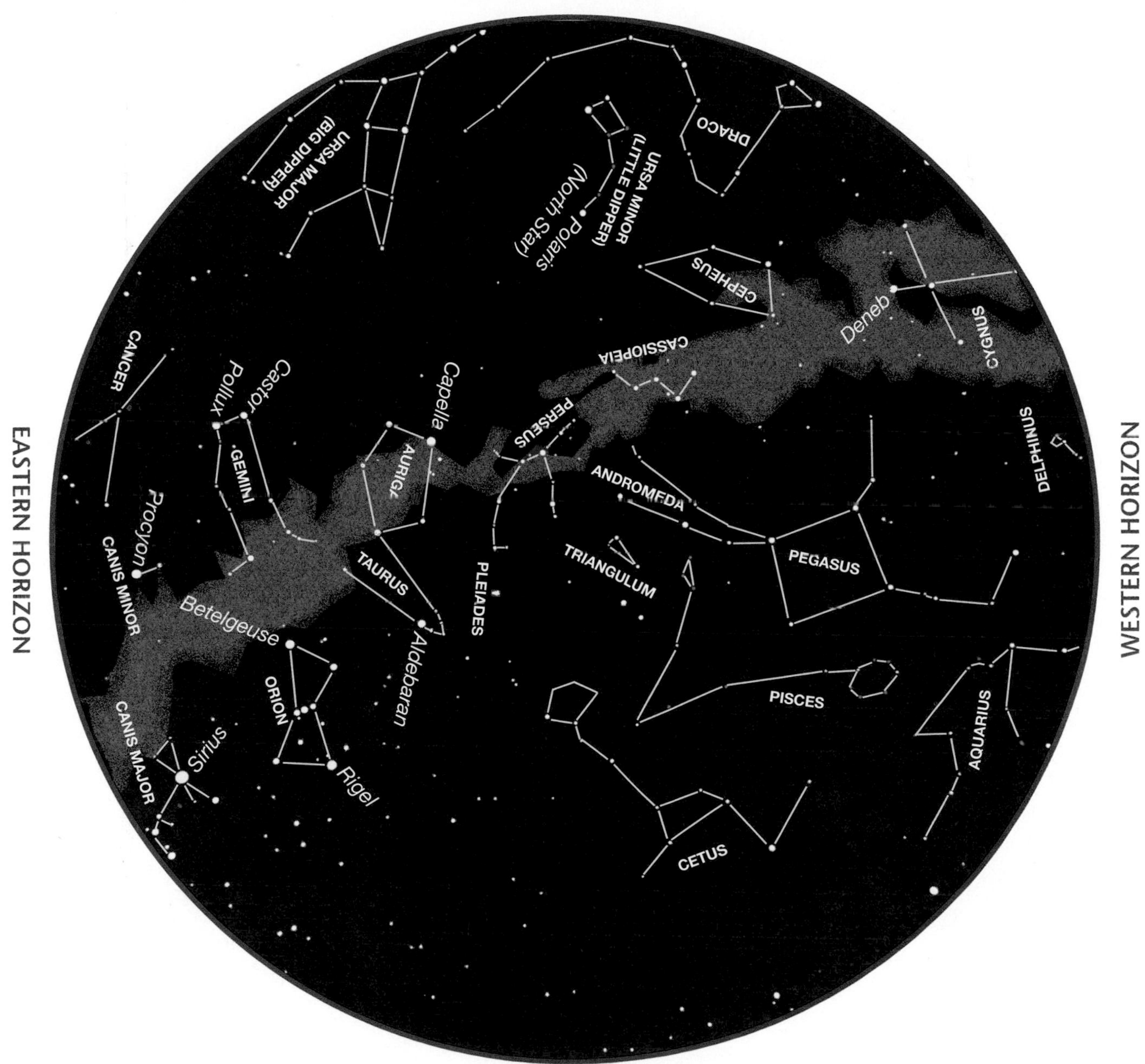

SOUTHERN HORIZON

Spring Sky

To use this chart, hold it up in front of you and turn it so that the direction you are facing is at the bottom of the chart. This chart works best at 34° north latitude, but can be used at other times and latitudes within the continental United States. It works best at the following times: 10:00 P.M. on March 1; 9:00 P.M. on March 15; 8:00 P.M. on March 30.

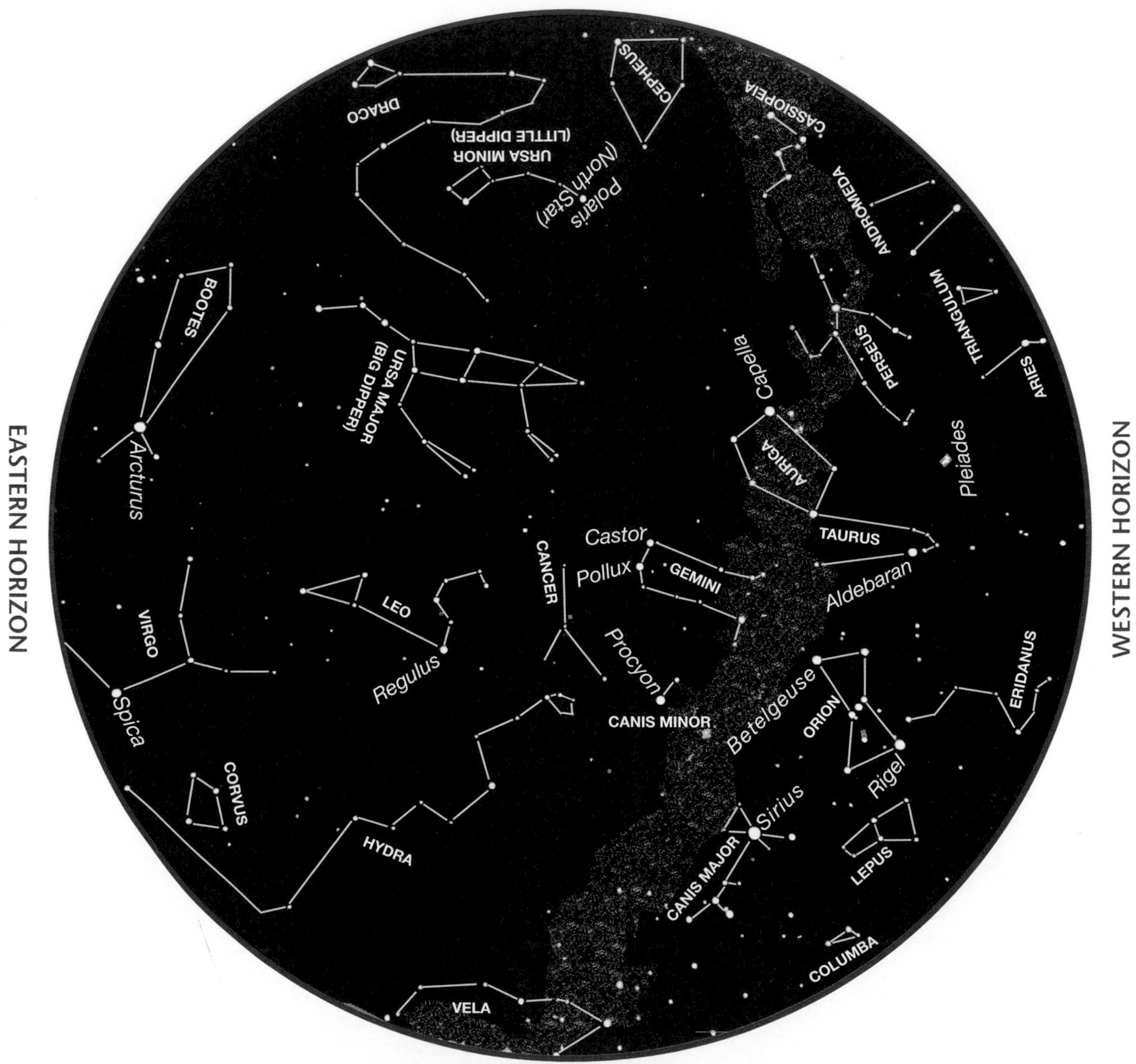

Summer Sky

To use this chart, hold it up in front of you and turn it so that the direction you are facing is at the bottom of the chart. This chart works best at 34° north latitude, but can be used at other times and latitudes within the continental United States. It works best at the following times: 10:00 P.M. on June 1; 9:00 P.M. on June 15; 8:00 P.M. on June 30.

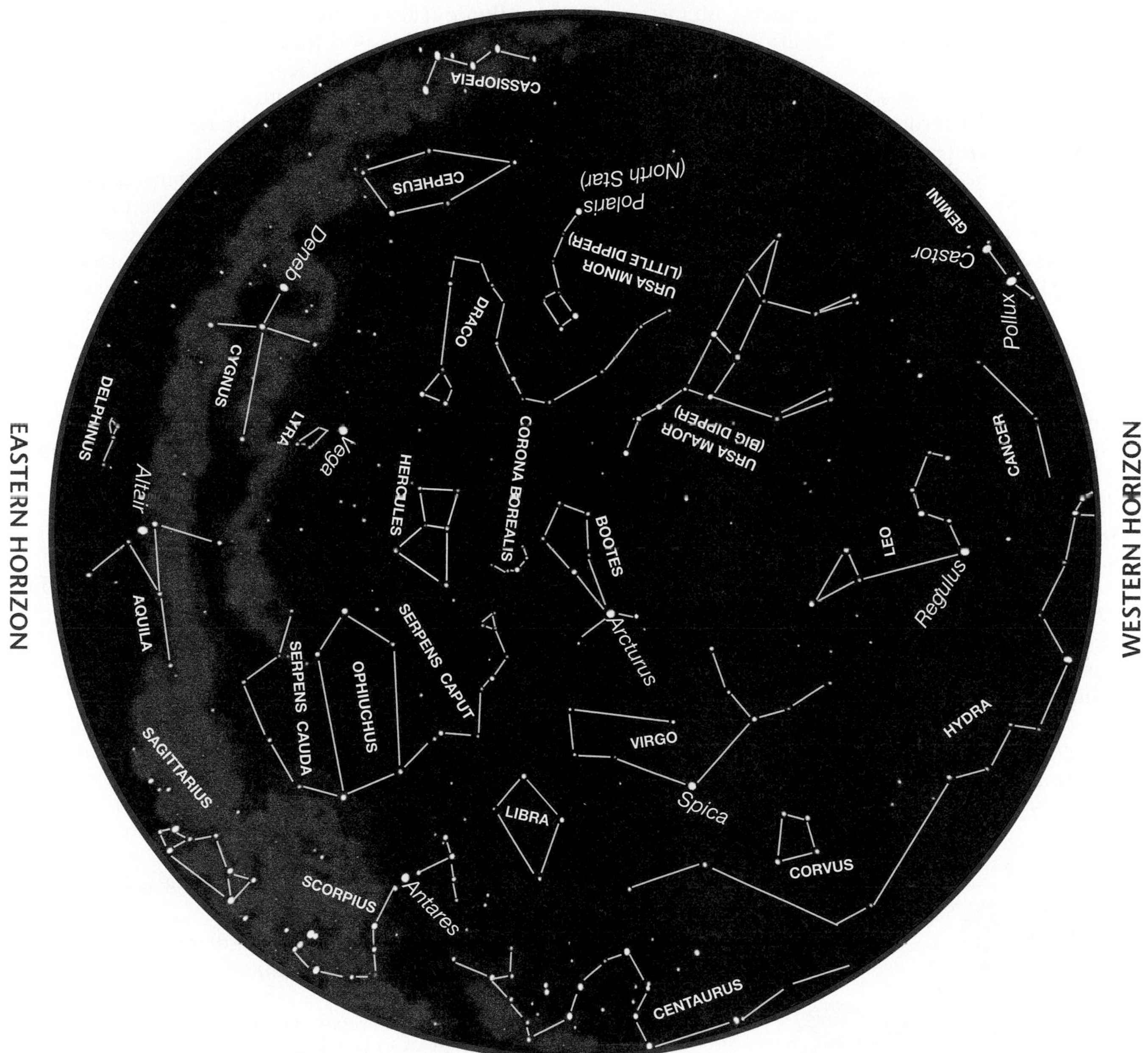

Glossary

abiotic factor A nonliving part of an ecosystem. (p. 20)

abrasion The grinding away of rock by other rock particles carried in water, ice, or wind. (pp. 585, 630)

absolute magnitude The brightness of a star if it were a standard distance from Earth. (p. 752)

absorption The process by which nutrient molecules pass through the wall of the digestive system into the blood. (p. 141)

acid A substance that tastes sour, reacts with metals and carbonates, and turns blue litmus paper red. (p. 394)

acid rain rainwater that is more acid than normal due to the presence of carbonic acid. (p. 404)

acne A bacterial infection of the skin in which the oil glands become blocked and swollen. (p. 120)

acoustics The study of how well sounds can be heard in a particular room or hall. (p. 464)

activation energy The minimum amount of energy needed to get a chemical reaction started. (p. 337)

active immunity Immunity that occurs when a person's own immune system produces antibodies in response to the presence of a pathogen. (p. 228)

adaptation The behaviors and physical characteristics of species that allow them to live successfully in their environments. (p. 34)

addiction A physical dependence on a substance; an intense need by the body for a substance. (p. 199)

adolescence The stage of development between childhood and adulthood when children become adults physically and mentally. (p. 302)

AIDS (acquired immunodeficiency syndrome) A disease caused by a virus that attacks the immune system. (p. 224)

alcoholism A disease in which a person is both physically addicted to and emotionally dependent on alcohol. (p. 277)

allergen A substance that causes an allergy. (p. 234)

allergy A disorder in which the immune system is overly sensitive to a foreign substance. (p. 233)

alluvial fan A wide, sloping deposit of sediment formed where a stream leaves a mountain range. (p. 621)

alveoli Tiny sacs of lung tissue specialized for the movement of gases between the air and the blood. (p. 192)

amino acids Small units that are linked together chemically to form large protein molecules. (p. 130)

amniotic sac A fluid-filled sac that cushions and protects a developing fetus in the uterus. (p. 296)

amplitude The maximum distance the particles of a medium move away from their rest positions as a wave passes through the medium. (p. 425)

amplitude modulation Method of transmitting radio signals by changing the amplitude of the waves. (p. 503)

anabolic steroids Synthetic chemicals that are similar to hormones produced in the body and that may increase muscle size and cause mood swings. (p. 274)

angle of incidence The angle between an incoming wave and an imaginary line drawn perpendicular to the surface of the barrier or new medium. (p. 430)

angle of reflection The angle between a reflected wave and an imaginary line drawn perpendicular to the surface of the barrier. (p. 430)

antibiotic A chemical that kills bacteria or slows their growth without harming the body cells of humans. (p. 232)

antibody A chemical produced by a B cell of the immune system that destroys a specific kind of pathogen. (223)

antigen A molecule on a cell that the immune system can recognize either as part of the body or as coming from outside the body. (p. 222)

antinode A point of maximum amplitude on a standing wave. (p. 434)

anus A muscular opening at the end of the rectum through which digestive waste material is eliminated from the body. (p. 151)

aorta The largest artery in the body. (p. 164)

apparent magnitude The brightness of a star as seen from Earth. (p. 751)

artery A blood vessel that carries blood away from the heart. (p. 162)

asteroid belt The region of the solar system between the orbits of Mars and Jupiter, where many asteroids are found. (p. 726)

asteroids Objects revolving around the sun that are too small and too numerous to be considered planets. (p. 726)

asthma A disorder in which the respiratory passages narrow significantly. (p. 234)

astronomy The study of the moon, stars, and other objects in space. (p. 659)
atherosclerosis A condition in which an artery wall thickens as a result of the buildup of fatty materials. (p. 179)
atmosphere The mixture of gases that surrounds Earth. The outermost of the four spheres into which scientists divide Earth. (p. 558)
atom The smallest particle of an element. (p. 324)
atomic number The number of protons in the nucleus of an atom. (p. 359)
atrium Each of the two upper chambers of the heart that receives blood that comes into the heart. (p. 160)
autonomic nervous system The group of nerves that controls involuntary actions. (p. 258)
autumnal equinox The day of the year that marks the beginning of fall in the Northern Hemisphere. (p. 665)
axis An imaginary line that passes through Earth's center and the North and South poles, about which Earth rotates. (p. 659)
axon A threadlike extension of a neuron that carries nerve impulses away from the cell body. (p. 250)

base A substance that tastes bitter, feels slippery, and turns red litmus paper blue. (p. 399)

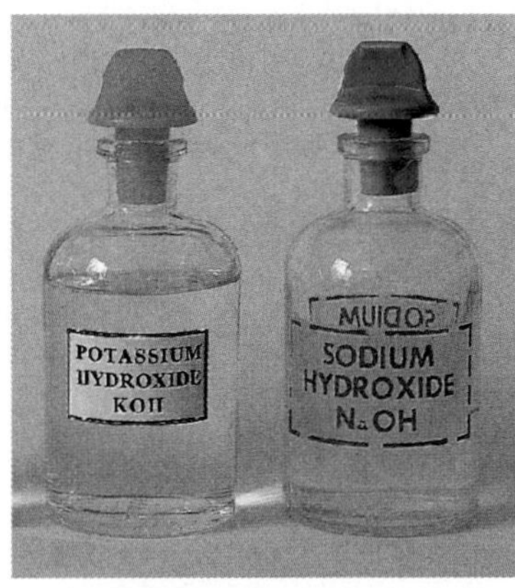

B cell A lymphocyte that produces chemicals that help destroy a specific kind of pathogen. (p. 223)
beach Wave-washed sediment along a coast. (p. 641)
beats The regular changes in loudness of a sound when two sounds of different frequencies are played together. (p. 465)
bedrock The solid layer of rock beneath the soil. (p. 593)
big bang The initial explosion that resulted in the formation and expansion of the universe. (p. 766)
bile A substance produced by the liver that breaks up fat particles. (p. 149)
binary star A star system that contains two stars. (p. 761)
biogeography The study of where organisms live. (p. 58)
bioluminescence Light produced by organisms as a result of a chemical reaction. (p. 499)

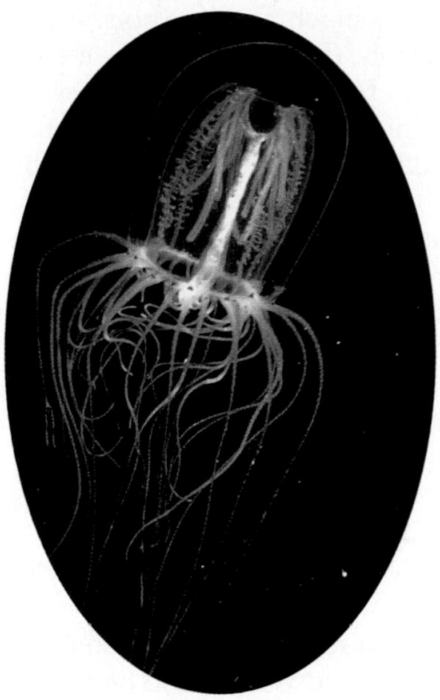

biome A group of ecosystems with similar climates and organisms. (p. 64)
biosphere All living things. One of the four spheres into which scientists divide Earth. (p. 558)
biotic factor A living part of an ecosystem. (p. 19)
birth rate The number of births in a population in a certain amount of time. (p. 27)
black hole The remains of an extremely massive star pulled into a small volume by the force of gravity. (p. 759)
blood pressure The pressure that is exerted by the blood against the walls of blood vessels. (p. 169)
blood transfusion The transference of blood from one person to another. (p. 174)
brain The part of the central nervous system that is located in the skull and controls most functions in the body. (p. 255)
brainstem The part of the brain that controls many body functions that occur automatically. (p. 257)
bronchi The passages that branch from the trachea and direct air into the lungs. (p. 192)
bronchitis An irritation of the breathing passages in which the small passages become narrower than normal and may be clogged with mucus. (p. 200)

C

calorie The amount of energy needed to raise the temperature of one gram of water by one Celsius degree. (p. 127)

camera Optical instrument that uses lenses to focus light and record an image of an object. (p. 541)

cancer A disease in which some body cells divide uncontrollably. (p. 119, 235)

canopy A leafy roof formed by tall trees. (p. 65)

capillary A tiny blood vessel where substances are exchanged between the blood and the body cells. (p. 162)

carbohydrates Nutrients composed of carbon, oxygen, and hydrogen that are a major source of energy and provide the raw materials to make parts of cells. (p. 127)

carbon monoxide A colorless, odorless gas produced when substances—including tobacco—are burned. (p. 199)

carcinogen A substance or a factor in the environment that can cause cancer. (p. 236)

cardiac muscle Muscle tissue found only in the heart. (p. 111)

cardiovascular system The body system that consists of the heart, blood vessels, and blood, and that carries needed substances to cells and carries waste products away from cells. (p. 158)

carnivore Consumer that eats only animals. (p. 48)

carrying capacity The largest population that an area can support. (p. 29)

cartilage A connective tissue that is more flexible than bone and that gives support to some parts of the body. (p. 104)

catalyst A material that increases the rate of a chemical reaction by lowering the activation energy. (p. 340)

cell The basic unit of structure and function in a living thing. (p. 93)

cell membrane The outside boundary of a cell. (p. 93)

central nervous system The brain and spinal cord; the control center of the body. (p. 254)

cerebellum The part of the brain that coordinates the actions of the muscles and helps maintain balance. (p. 257)

cerebrum The part of the brain that interprets input from the senses, controls the movement of skeletal muscles, and carries out complex mental processes. (p. 256)

chemical bond The force that holds atoms together. (p. 325)

chemical change A change in matter that produces a new substance. (p. 321)

chemical digestion The process that breaks large food molecules into smaller molecules. (p. 408)

chemical equation A short, easy way to show a chemical reaction, using symbols instead of words. (p. 328)

chemical formula A combination of symbols that represent the elements in a compound. (p. 329)

chemical reaction The process in which substances undergo chemical changes that results in the formation of new substances. (p. 321)

chemical weathering The process that breaks down rock through chemical changes. (p. 587)

chemistry The study of the properties of matter and how matter changes. (p. 318)

cholesterol A waxy, fatlike substance, found only in animal products, that is an important part of your body's cells; can build up on artery walls. (p. 129)

chromosomes Rod-shaped structures in cells that carry the information that controls inherited characteristics such as eye color and blood type. (p. 290)

chromosphere The middle layer of the sun's atmosphere. (p. 701)

cilia Tiny hairlike extensions of cells that can move together like whips. (p. 190)

climate The typical weather pattern in an area over a long period of time. (p. 61)

cochlea A snail-shaped tube in the inner ear lined with sound receptors; nerve impulses are sent from the cochlea to the brain. (pp. 267, 469)

coefficient A number in front of a chemical formula in an equation that indicates how many molecules or atoms of each reactant and product are involved in a reaction. (p. 332)

combustion A rapid reaction between oxygen and fuel that results in fire. (p. 344)

comet A ball of ice and dust whose orbit is usually a long, narrow ellipse. (p. 724)

commensalism A relationship between two species in which one species benefits and the other is neither helped nor harmed. (p. 39)

community All the different populations that live together in an area. (p. 22)

competition The struggle between organisms for the limited resources in a habitat. (p. 35)

complementary colors Any two colors that combine to form white light or black pigment. (p. 532)

compound A substance made of two or more elements chemically combined in a specific ratio, or proportion. (p. 320)

compression The part of a longitudinal wave where the particles of the medium are close together. (p. 423)

concave lens A lens that is thinner in the center than at the edges. (p. 526)
concave mirror A mirror with a surface that curves inward. (p. 521)
concentrated solution A mixture that has a lot of solute dissolved in it. (p. 387)
concentration The amount of one material in a certain volume of another material. (p. 339)
concussion A bruiselike injury of the brain that occurs when the soft tissue of the cerebrum bumps against the skull. (p. 260)
condensation The process by which a gas changes to a liquid. (p. 55)
cones Cells on the retina that detect color. (p. 537)
coniferous trees Trees that produce their seeds in cones and have needle-shaped leaves. (p. 69)
connective tissue A body tissue that provides support for the body and connects all of its parts. (p. 95)
conservation of mass The principle stating that matter is not created or destroyed during a chemical reaction. (p. 331)
conservation plowing Soil conservation method in which the dead stalks from the previous year's crop are left in the ground to hold the soil in place. (p. 604)
constellation A pattern of stars in the sky. (p. 738)
constructive interference The interference that occurs when two waves combine to make a wave with a larger amplitude. (p. 432)
consumer An organism that obtains energy by feeding on other organisms. (p. 48)
continental drift The very slow motion of the continents. (p. 58)
continental glacier A glacier that covers much of a continent or large island. (p. 633)
contour interval The difference in elevation from one contour line to the next. (p. 575)
contour line A line on a topographic map that connects points of equal elevation. (p. 575)
contour plowing Plowing fields along the curves of a slope to prevent soil loss. (p. 604)
controlled experiment An experiment in which all factors except one are kept constant. (pp. 7, 139, 781)
convex lens A lens that is thicker in the middle than at the edges. (pp. 526, 740)
convex mirror A mirror with a surface that curves outward. (p. 522)
core The central part of the sun, where nuclear fusion occurs. (p. 700)
cornea The clear tissue that covers the front of the eye; the transparent front surface of the eye. (pp. 263, 536)
corona The outer layer of the sun's atmosphere. (p. 701)
coronary artery An artery that supplies blood to the heart itself. (p. 165)
corrosive The way in which acids react with some metals so as to eat away the metal. (p. 395)
covalent bond A chemical bond formed when two atoms share electrons. (p. 369)
crater A round pit on the moon's surface. (p. 685)
crest The highest part of a transverse wave. (p. 422)
crystal An orderly, three-dimensional pattern of ions or atoms in a solid. (p. 367)

cytoplasm The area in a cell between the cell membrane and the nucleus; contains a clear, jellylike substance in which cell structures are found. (p. 93)

D

data The facts, figures, and other evidence collected in an experiment. (pp. 7, 776)
death rate The number of deaths in a population in a certain amount of time. (p. 27)
decibel (dB) A unit of measurement of loudness. (p. 453)
deciduous trees Trees that shed their leaves and grow new ones each year. (p. 68)
decomposer Soil organism that breaks down wastes and the remains of dead organisms and digests them. (pp. 49, 597)
decomposition A chemical reaction that breaks down compounds into simpler products. (p. 334)
deflation Wind erosion that removes surface materials. (p. 643)
degree A unit used to measure distances around a circle. One degree equals $\frac{1}{360}$ of a full circle. (p. 566)
delta A landform made of sediment that is deposited where a river flows into an ocean or lake. (p. 621)
dendrite A threadlike extension of a neuron that carries nerve impulses toward the cell body. (p. 250)
density Ratio of the mass of a substance to its volume. (p. 449)
deposition Process in which sediment is laid down in new locations. (p. 611)
depressant A drug that slows down the activity of the central nervous system. (p. 272)
dermis The lower layer of the skin. (p. 117)

desert An area that receives less than 25 cm of precipitation a year. (p. 66)

destructive interference The interference that occurs when two waves combine to make a wave with a smaller amplitude. (p. 433)

diabetes A condition in which either the pancreas fails to produce enough insulin, or the body's cells can't use it properly. (p. 235)

diaphragm A large, dome-shaped muscle that plays an important role in breathing. (p. 194)

diffraction The bending of waves around a barrier. (p. 432)

diffuse reflection Reflection that occurs when parallel rays of light hit a rough surface and all reflect at different angles. (p. 519)

diffusion The process by which molecules move from an area in which they are highly concentrated to an area in which they are less concentrated. (p. 167)

digestion The process by which the body breaks down food into small nutrient molecules. (pp. 140, 408)

digitizing Converting information to numbers for use by a computer. (p. 572)

dilute solution A mixture that has little solute dissolved in it. (p. 387)

dispersal The movement of organisms from one place to another. (p. 59)

dissonance The sound produced when notes that have no musical relationship are played together. (p. 461)

divide The ridge of land that separates one drainage basin from another. (p. 619)

Doppler effect The apparent change in frequency of a sound as the source moves in relation to the listener. (p. 456)

double bond A chemical bond formed when atoms share two pairs of electrons. (p. 370)

drainage basin The land area from which a river and its tributaries collect their water. (p. 619)

drug Any chemical that causes changes in a person's body or behavior. (p. 270)

drug abuse The deliberate misuse of drugs for purposes other than appropriate medical ones. (p. 271)

Dust Bowl The area of the Great Plains where wind erosion caused soil loss during the 1930s. (p. 603)

ear canal A narrow region leading from the outside of the human ear to the eardrum. (p. 468)

eardrum The membrane that separates the outer ear from the middle ear, and that vibrates when sound waves strike it; a small, tightly stretched, drumlike membrane in the ear. (pp. 267, 469)

echolocation The use of reflection of sound waves to navigate and to locate prey. (p. 474)

eclipse The partial or total blocking of one object by another. (p. 671)

eclipsing binary A star system in which one star periodically blocks the light from another. (p. 762)

ecology The study of how living things interact with each other and their environment. (p. 22)

ecosystem All the living and nonliving things that interact in an area. (p. 18)

egg A female sex cell. (p. 289)

elasticity The ability of a material to bounce back after being disturbed. (p. 449)

electromagnetic radiation Energy that travels through space in the form of electromagnetic waves. (pp. 483, 739)

electromagnetic spectrum The range of electromagnetic waves placed in a certain order. (p. 487)

electromagnetic waves Transverse waves that transfer electric and magnetic energy. (p. 483)

electron dot diagram A representation of the number of valence electrons in an atom, using dots placed around the symbol of an element. (p. 358)

electrons Tiny, negatively charged, high-energy particles that move around outside the nucleus of an atom. (p. 355)

element A substance that cannot be broken down into any other substances by chemical or physical means. (p. 319)

elevation Height above sea level. (p. 559)

ellipse An elongated circle, or oval shape; the shape of the planets' orbits. (p. 697)

elliptical galaxy A galaxy shaped like a flattened ball, containing only old stars. (p. 764)

embryo A developing human during the first eight weeks after fertilization has occurred. (p. 295)

emigration Leaving a population. (p. 28)

emphysema A serious disease that destroys lung tissue and causes difficulty in breathing. (p. 200)

endocrine gland An organ of the endocrine system which produces and releases its chemical products directly into the bloodstream. (p. 284)

endothermic reaction A reaction that absorbs energy in the form of heat. (p. 337)

energy The ability to do work or cause change. (pp. 420, 629)

energy pyramid A diagram that shows the amount of energy that moves from one feeding level to another in a food web. (p. 51)

enzyme A protein that speeds up chemical reactions in the body; a biological catalyst that lowers the activation energy of reactions in cells. (pp. 142, 341)

epidermis The outermost layer of the skin. (p. 116)
epiglottis A flap of tissue that seals off the windpipe and prevents food from entering. (p. 143)
epithelial tissue A body tissue that covers the surfaces of the body, inside and out. (p. 95)
equator An imaginary line that circles Earth halfway between the North and South poles. (p. 565)
equinox The two days of the year on which neither hemisphere is tilted toward or away from the sun. (p. 665)
erosion The process by which water, ice, wind, or gravity moves weathered rock and soil. (pp. 585, 611)
esophagus A muscular tube that connects the mouth to the stomach. (p. 143)
estimate An approximation of a number based on reasonable assumptions. (p. 26)
estrogen A hormone produced by the ovaries that controls the development of adult female characteristics. (p. 292)
estuary A habitat in which the fresh water of a river meets the salt water of the ocean. (p. 73)
evaporation The process by which molecules of a liquid absorb energy and change to the gas state. (p. 54)
excretion The process by which wastes are removed from the body. (p. 203)
exothermic reaction A reaction that releases energy in the form of heat. (p. 337)
exotic species Species that are carried to a new location by people. (p. 60)
extraterrestrial life Life that arises outside of Earth. (p. 728)
eyepiece A lens that magnifies the image formed by the objective. (p. 540)

family Elements in the same vertical column of the periodic table. Also called group. (p. 360)
farsightedness The condition in which distant objects are seen clearly but nearby objects look blurry. (pp. 265, 538)
fats High-energy nutrients that are composed of carbon, oxygen, and hydrogen and contain more than twice as much energy as an equal amount of carbohydrates. (p. 129)
fertilization The joining of a sperm and an egg. (p. 289)
fetus A developing human from the ninth week of development until birth. (p. 297)
fiber A complex carbohydrate, found in plant foods, that cannot be broken down into sugar molecules by the body. (p. 128)
fibrin A chemical that is important in blood clotting because it forms a fiber net that traps red blood cells. (p. 174)
flood plain Wide valley through which a river flows. (p. 620)
fluorescent lights Lights that glow when an electric current causes ultraviolet waves to strike a coating inside a tube. (p. 497)
focal point The point at which rays of light meet, or appear to meet, after being reflected (or refracted) by a mirror (or a lens). (p. 521)
follicle Structure in the dermis of the skin from which a strand of hair grows. (p. 117)
food chain A series of events in which one organism eats another. (p. 49)
Food Guide Pyramid A chart that classifies foods into six groups to help people plan a healthy diet. (p. 136)
food web The pattern of overlapping food chains in an ecosystem. (p. 49)
force A push or a pull. (p. 164)
frequency The number of complete waves that pass a given point in a certain amount of time. (p. 428)
frequency modulation Method of transmitting radio signals by changing the frequency of the waves. (p. 504)
friction The force that opposes the motion of one surface as it moves across another surface. (p. 631)
fuel A material that releases energy when it burns. (p. 344)

galaxy A giant structure that contains hundreds of billions of stars. (p. 747)
gallbladder The organ that stores bile after it is produced by the liver. (p. 149)
gamma rays Electromagnetic waves with the shortest wavelengths and highest frequencies. (p. 494)
gas giants The name given to the first four outer planets: Jupiter, Saturn, Uranus, and Neptune. (p. 714)
geocentric A description of the solar system in which all of the planets revolve around Earth. (p. 695)
geosynchronous orbit The orbit of a satellite that revolves around Earth at the same rate that Earth rotates. (p. 681)
giant star A very large star, much larger than the sun. (p. 750)
glacier A large mass of moving ice and snow on land. (p. 633)
Global Positioning System A method of finding latitude and longitude using satellites. (p. 577)
globe A sphere that represents Earth's surface. (p. 559)
glucose A sugar that is the major source of energy for the body's cells. (p. 128)
grassland An area populated by grasses that gets 25 to 75 centimeters of rain each year. (p. 67)

gravity The attractive force between two objects; its magnitude depends on their masses and the distance between them. (p. 676)
greenhouse effect The trapping of heat by a planet's atmosphere. (p. 710)
groundwater Water that fills the cracks and spaces in underground soil and rock layers. (p. 624)
group Elements in the same vertical column of the periodic table. Also called family. (p. 360)
gully A large channel in soil formed by erosion. (p. 617)

H

habitat The place where an organism lives and that provides the things it needs. (p. 19)
half-life The time it takes for half of the atoms of a radioactive element to decay. (p. 664)
halogen An element belonging to Group 17 of the periodic table. (p. 361)
heart A hollow, muscular organ that pumps blood throughout the body. (p. 160)
heart attack A condition in which blood flow to a part of the heart muscle is blocked, which causes heart cells to die. (p. 179)
heliocentric A description of the solar system in which all of the planets revolve around the sun. (p. 696)
hemisphere One half of the sphere that makes up Earth's surface. (p. 565)
hemoglobin An iron-containing protein that binds chemically to oxygen molecules and makes up most of red blood cells. (p. 172)
herbivore Consumer that eats only plants. (p. 48)
hertz (Hz) Unit of measurement for frequency. (p. 428)
Hertzsprung-Russell diagram A graph relating the temperature and brightness of stars. (p. 752)
hibernation A low-energy state similar to sleep that some mammals enter in the winter. (p. 69)
histamine A chemical that is responsible for the symptoms of an allergy. (p. 234)
hologram A three-dimensional photograph formed by the interference between two laser beams. (p. 546)
homeostasis The process by which an organism's internal environment is kept stable in spite of changes in the external environment. (p. 96)
hormone The chemical product of an endocrine gland that speeds up or slows down the activities of an organ or tissue. (p. 285)
host The organism that a parasite lives in or on. (p. 40)
humus Dark-colored organic material in soil. (p. 594)
hydrogen ion A positively charged ion (H^+) formed of a hydrogen atom that has lost its electron. (p. 400)
hydrosphere Earth's water and ice. One of the four spheres into which scientists divide Earth. (p. 558)
hydroxide ion A negatively charged ion made of oxygen and hydrogen, OH^-. (p. 401)
hypertension A disorder in which a person's blood pressure is consistently higher than normal. (p. 179)
hypothalamus A tiny part of the brain that links the nervous system and the endocrine system. (p. 286)
hypothesis A possible explanation for a set of observations or answer to a scientific question; must be testable. (pp. 6, 780)

I

ice age One time in the past when continental glaciers covered large parts of Earth's surface. (p. 634)
ice wedging Process that splits rock when water seeps into cracks, then freezes and expands. (p. 586)
illuminated Words used to describe an object that can be seen because it reflects light. (p. 496)
image A copy of an object formed by reflected or refracted rays of light. (p. 520)
immigration Moving into a population. (p. 28)
immune response Part of the body's defense against pathogens in which cells of the immune system react to each kind of pathogen with a defense targeted specifically at that pathogen. (p. 222)
immunity The ability of the immune system to destroy pathogens before they can cause disease. (p. 228)
incandescent lights Lights that glow when something inside them gets hot. (p. 496)
index of refraction The amount a ray of light bends when it passes from one medium to another. (p. 524)
indicator A compound that changes color in the presence of an acid or a base. (p. 396)
inertia The tendency of a moving object to continue in a straight line or a stationary object to remain in place. (p. 697)
infectious disease A disease that can pass from one organism to another. (p. 215)
inference An interpretation based on observations and prior knowledge. (p. 5)
inflammatory response Part of the body's defense against pathogens, in which fluid and white blood cells leak from blood vessels into tissues; the white blood cells destroy pathogens by breaking them down. (p. 220)
infrared rays Electromagnetic waves with higher frequencies and shorter wavelengths than radio waves. (p. 490)
infrasound Sound waves with frequencies below 20 Hz. (p. 454)
inhibitor A material that decreases the rate of a reaction. (p. 341)
insulin A chemical produced in the pancreas that enables the body's cells to take in glucose from the blood and use it for energy. (p. 235)

intensity The amount of energy per second carried through a unit area by a wave. (p. 452)

interference The interaction between waves that meet. (p. 432)

interneuron A neuron that carries nerve impulses from one neuron to another. (p. 250)

intertidal zone The area between the highest high-tide line and lowest low-tide line. (p. 74)

involuntary muscle A muscle that is not under conscious control. (p. 108)

ion An atom or group of atoms that has become electrically charged. (p. 364)

ionic bond The attraction between oppositely charged ions. (p. 364)

iris The circular structure that surrounds the pupil and regulates the amount of light entering the eye; the ring of colored muscle around the pupil of the eye. (pp. 263, 536)

irregular galaxy A galaxy that does not have a regular shape. (p. 764)

joint A place where two bones come together. (p. 104)

karst topography A type of landscape in rainy regions where there is limestone near the surface, characterized by caverns, sinkholes, and valleys. (p. 625)

kettle A small depression that forms when a chunk of ice is left in glacial till. (p. 636)

key A list of the symbols used on a map. (p. 564)

kidney A major organ of the excretory system; eliminates urea, excess water, and other waste materials from the body. (p. 203)

kinetic energy The energy an object has due to its motion. (p. 629)

large intestine The last section of the digestive system, where water is absorbed from food and the remaining material is eliminated from the body. (p. 151)

larynx The voice box, located in the top part of the trachea, underneath the epiglottis. (pp. 195, 447)

laser A device that produces coherent light. (p. 543)

latitude A measurement of distance from the equator, expressed in degrees north or south. (pp. 566, 664)

lens The flexible structure that focuses light that has entered the eye (p. 263); also, a curved piece of glass or other transparent material that is used to refract light. (p. 526)

ligament Strong connective tissue that holds together the bones in a movable joint. (106)

light-year The distance that light travels in one year. (p. 748)

limiting factor An environmental factor that prevents a population from increasing. (p. 29)

lithosphere Earth's solid rock outer layer. One of four spheres into which scientists divide Earth. (p. 558)

litter The loose layer of dead plant leaves and stems on the surface of the soil. (p. 596)

liver The largest and heaviest organ inside the body; it breaks down substances and eliminates nitrogen from the body. (p. 149)

load The amount of sediment that a river or stream carries. (p. 630)

loam Rich, fertile soil that is made up of about equal parts of clay, sand, and silt. (p. 594)

loess A wind-formed deposit made of fine particles of clay and silt. (644)

longitude The distance in degrees east or west of the prime meridian. (p. 567)

longitudinal wave A wave that moves the medium parallel to the direction in which the wave travels. (p. 422)

longshore drift The movement of water and sediment down a beach caused by waves coming in to shore at an angle. (p. 641)

loudness Perception of the intensity of a sound. (p. 453)

luminous Word used to describe an object that can be seen because it emits light. (p. 496)

lunar eclipse The blocking of sunlight to the moon that occurs when Earth is directly between the sun and moon. (p. 673)

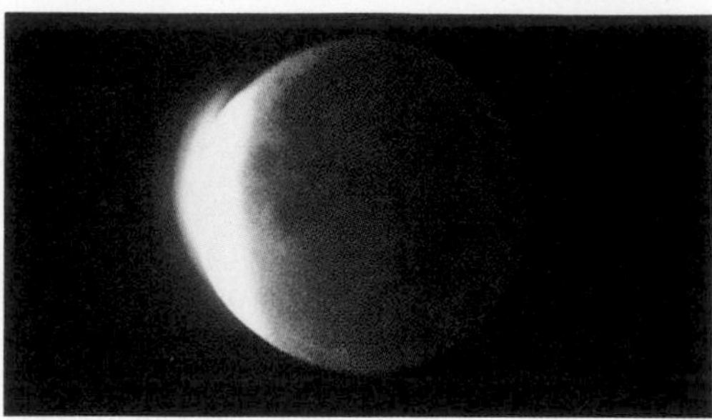

lungs The main organs of the respiratory system. (p. 192)

lymph The fluid that the lymphatic system collects and returns to the bloodstream. (p. 176)

lymph node A small knob of tissue in the lymphatic system that filters lymph. (p. 176)

lymphatic system A network of veinlike vessels that returns the fluid that leaks out of blood vessels to the bloodstream. (p. 176)

lymphocyte White blood cell that reacts to each kind of pathogen with a defense targeted specifically at that pathogen. (p. 222)

magnetic resonance imaging (MRI) A process that uses radio waves to form pictures of the inside of the human body. (p. 489)

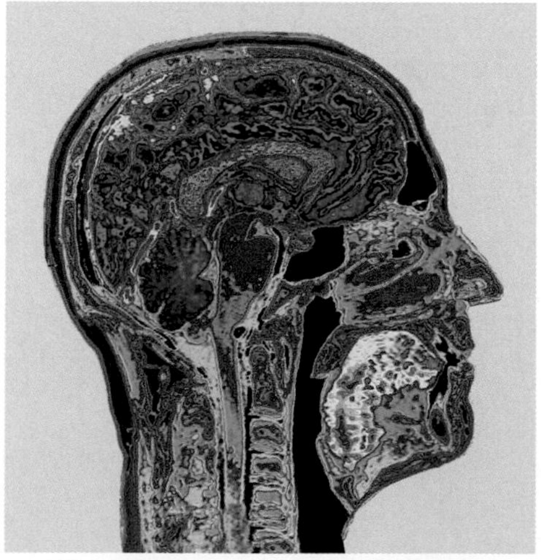

main sequence An area on the Hertzsprung-Russell diagram that runs from the upper left to the lower right and includes more than 90 percent of all stars. (p. 752)

manipulated variable The one factor that a scientist changes during an experiment. (pp. 6, 781)

map A model of all or part of Earth's surface as seen from above. (p. 559)

map projection A framework of lines that helps to show landmasses on a flat surface. (p. 568)

maria Dark, flat regions on the moon's surface. (p. 685)

marrow The soft tissue that fills the internal spaces in bone. (p. 104)

mass movement Any one of several processes by which gravity moves sediment downhill. (p. 611)

matter Anything that has mass and occupies space. (p. 318)

meander A looplike bend in the course of a river. (p. 620)

mechanical digestion The physical process that tears, grinds, and mashes large food particles into smaller ones. (p. 408)

mechanical wave A wave that requires a medium through which to travel. (p. 421)

mechanical weathering The type of weathering in which rock is physically broken into smaller pieces. (p. 585)

medium Material through which a wave travels. (p. 421)

melanin A pigment that gives the skin its color (p. 117)

menstrual cycle The monthly cycle of changes that occurs in the female reproductive system, during which an egg develops and the uterus prepares for the arrival of a fertilized egg. (p. 293)

menstruation The process that occurs if fertilization does not take place, in which the thickened lining of the uterus breaks down and blood and tissue then pass out of the female body through the vagina. (p. 294)

meteor A streak of light in the sky produced by the burning of a meteoroid in Earth's atmosphere. (p. 727)

meteorite A meteoroid that has hit Earth's surface. (p. 727)

meteoroid A chunk of rock or dust in space. (p. 727)

microscope Optical instrument that forms enlarged images of tiny objects. (p. 541)

microwaves Radio waves with the shortest wavelengths and the highest frequencies. (p. 487)

middle ear The space behind the eardrum. (p. 469)

mineral A nutrient that is needed by the body in small amounts and is not made by living things (p. 132); also, a naturally occurring solid that has a crystal structure and a definite chemical composition. (p. 376)

mirage An image of a distant object caused by refraction of light as it travels through air of varying temperature. (p. 525)

mixture Two or more substances that are mixed together but not chemically combined. (p. 320)
molecular compound A compound consisting of molecules of covalently bonded atoms. (p. 370)
molecule A particle made of two or more atoms bonded together. (p. 324)
moraine A ridge formed by the till deposited at the edge of a glacier. (p. 635)
motor neuron A neuron that sends an impulse to a muscle, causing the muscle to contract. (p. 250)
mountain A landform with high elevation and high relief. (p. 556)
mountain range A series of mountains that have the same general shape and structure. (p. 556)
mucus A thick, slippery substance produced by the body. (p. 143)
muscle tissue A body tissue that contracts or shortens, making body parts move. (p. 94)
music A set of tones and overtones combined in ways that are pleasing to the ear. (p. 460)
mutualism A relationship between two species in which both species benefit. (p. 39)

native species Species that have naturally evolved in an area. (p. 60)
natural selection Process by which individuals that are better adapted to the environment are more likely to survive and reproduce than others. (p. 34)
neap tide A tide with the least difference between low and high tides. (p. 677)
nearsightedness The condition in which nearby objects can be seen clearly but distant objects look blurry. (pp. 265, 538)
nebula A large amount of gas and dust in space, spread out in an immense volume. (p. 757)

negative feedback A process in which a system is turned off by the condition it produces; examples of negative feedback systems include regulation of temperature by a thermostat and the regulation of the levels of many hormones in the blood. (p. 288)
neon lights Glass tubes filled with neon that produce light. (p. 498)
nephron One of a million tiny, filtering structures found in the kidneys that removes wastes from blood and produces urine. (p. 204)
neritic zone The region of shallow ocean water over the continental shelf. (p. 74)
nerve A bundle of nerve fibers. (p. 250)
nerve impulse The message carried by a neuron. (p. 249)
nerve tissue A body tissue that carries messages back and forth between the brain and every other part of the body. (p. 94)
neuron A cell that carries messages through the nervous system. (p. 249)
neutralization A reaction of an acid with a base, yielding a solution that is not as acidic or basic as the starting solutions were. (p. 404)
neutron star A tiny star that remains after a supernova explosion. (p. 758)
neutrons Small uncharged particles that are found in the nucleus of an atom. (p. 355)
niche An organism's particular role in an ecosystem, or how it makes its living. (p. 34)
nicotine A drug in tobacco that speeds up the activities of the nervous system, heart, and other organs. (p. 199)
nitrogen fixation The process of changing free nitrogen gas into a usable form. (p. 57)
node A point of zero amplitude on a standing wave. (p. 434)
nodules Bumps on the roots of certain plants that house nitrogen-fixing bacteria. (p. 57)
noise A mixture of sound waves with no pleasing timbre and no identifiable pitch. (p. 461)
noninfectious disease A disease that is not spread from person to person. (p. 233)
nonpolar The description of a covalent bond in which electrons are shared equally, or of a molecule containing nonpolar bonds, or polar bonds that cancel out. (p. 372)
nuclear fusion The process by which hydrogen atoms join together to form helium, releasing energy. (p. 700)
nucleus The control center of a cell that directs the cell's activities and contains information that determines the cell's characteristics (p. 93); also, the central core of the atom, containing protons and usually neutrons. (p. 355)

nutrients Substances in food that provide the raw materials and energy the body needs to carry out all the essential life processes. (p. 126)

O

objective Lens that gathers light from an object and forms a real image. (p. 540)

observatory A building that contains one or more telescopes. (p. 741)

omnivore A consumer that eats both plants and animals. (p. 48)

opaque A material that reflects or absorbs all light that strikes it. (p. 518)

optical fiber Long, thin strand of glass or plastic that can carry light for long distances without allowing the light to fade out. (p. 546)

optic nerve Short, thick nerve that carries signals from the eye to the brain. (p. 537)

orbit The path of an object as it revolves around another object in space. (p. 659)

organ A structure in the body that is composed of different kinds of tissue. (p. 95)

organ system A group of organs that work together to perform a major function in the body. (p. 95)

osteoporosis A condition in which the body's bones become weak and break easily. (p. 107)

ovary Organ of the female reproductive system in which eggs and estrogen are produced. (p. 292)

oviduct A passageway for eggs from an ovary to the uterus; the place where fertilization usually occurs. (p. 292)

ovulation The process in which a mature egg is released from the ovary into an oviduct; occurs about halfway through a typical menstrual cycle. (p. 293)

oxbow lake A meander cut off from a river. (p. 620)

P

pacemaker A group of cells located in the right atrium that sends out signals that make the heart muscle contract and that regulates heartbeat rate. (p. 162)

pancreas A triangular organ that produces enzymes that flow into the small intestine. (p. 150)

parallax The apparent change in position of an object when seen from different places. (p. 748)

parasite The organism that benefits by living on or in its host. (p. 40)

parasitism A relationship in which one organism lives on or inside another and harms it. (p. 40)

passive immunity Immunity in which the antibodies that fight a pathogen come from another organism rather than from the person's own body. (p. 230)

passive smoking The involuntary inhalation of smoke from other people's cigarettes, cigars, or pipes. (p. 201)

pathogen An organism that causes disease. (p. 215)

penis The organ through which both semen and urine leave the male body. (p. 291)

penumbra The part of a shadow surrounding the darkest part. (p. 672)

Percent Daily Value An indication of how the nutritional content of a food fits into the diet of a person who consumes a total of 2,000 Calories a day. (p. 138)

period Elements in the same horizontal row of the periodic table. (p. 360)

peripheral nervous system All the nerves located outside the central nervous system; connects the central nervous system to all parts of the body. (p. 254)

peristalsis Involuntary waves of muscle contraction that keep food moving along in one direction through the digestive system. (p. 143)

permeable Characteristic of a material that is full of tiny, connected air spaces that water can seep through. (p. 589)

phagocyte A white blood cell that destroys pathogens by engulfing them and breaking them down. (p. 221)

pharynx The throat; part of both the respiratory and digestive systems. (p. 190)

phase One of the different shapes of the moon as seen from Earth. (p. 669)

photoelectric effect The movement of electrons in a substance when light is shined on it. (p. 485)

photon A tiny particle or packet of light energy. (p. 485)

photosphere The inner layer of the sun's atmosphere. (p. 701)

photosynthesis The process in which organisms use water along with sunlight and carbon dioxide to make food. (p. 20)

pH scale A range of numbers used to express the concentration of hydrogen ions in a solution. (p. 402)

physical change A change that alters the form or appearance of a material but does not make the material into another substance. (p. 321)

pigment An opaque substance used to color other materials. (p. 532)

pioneer species The first species to populate an area. (p. 79)

pitch Perception of the frequency of a sound. (p. 454)

pituitary gland An endocrine gland just below the hypothalamus that communicates with the hypothalamus to control many body activities. (p. 287)

pixels The tiny dots in a satellite image. (p. 571)

placenta A membrane that becomes the link between the developing embryo or fetus and the mother. (p. 296)

plain A landform made up of flat or gently rolling land with low relief. (p. 556)

plane mirror A flat mirror that produces an upright, virtual image the same size as the object. (p. 520)

plasma The liquid part of blood. (p. 171)
plateau A landform that has high elevation and a more or less level surface. (p. 557)
platelet A cell fragment that plays an important part in forming blood clots. (p. 174)
plucking The process by which a glacier picks up rocks as it flows over the land. (p. 634)
polar The description of a covalent bond in which electrons are shared unequally, or of a molecule containing polar bonds that do not cancel out. (p. 371)
polarized light Light that vibrates in only one direction. (p. 484)
polyatomic ion An ion that is made of more than one atom. (p. 366)
population All the members of one species in a particular area. (p. 21)
population density The number of individuals in a specific area. (p. 25)
pore An opening through which sweat reaches the surface of the skin. (p. 117)
potential energy Energy that is stored and available to be used later. (p. 629)
precipitate A solid that forms from a solution during a chemical reaction. (p. 322)

precipitation Rain, snow, sleet, or hail. (p. 55)
predation An interaction in which one organism kills and eats another. (p. 36)
predator The organism that does the killing in predation. (p. 36)
pressure The force that something exerts over a given area. (p. 168)
prey An organism that is killed in predation. (p. 36)
primary colors Three colors that can be used to make any other color. (p. 531)
primary succession The changes that occur in an area where no ecosystem had existed. (p. 79)
primary wave A longitudinal seismic wave. (p. 439)
prime meridian The line that makes a half circle from the North Pole to the South Pole and that passes through Greenwich, England. (p. 566)
producer An organism that can make its own food. (p. 47)
product A substance formed as a result of a chemical reaction. (p. 330)
prominence A loop of gas that protrudes from the sun's surface, linking parts of sunspot regions. (p. 704)
proteins Nutrients that contain nitrogen as well as carbon, hydrogen, and oxygen; they are needed for tissue growth and repair and play a part in chemical reactions within cells. (p. 130)
protons Small positively charged particles that are found in the nucleus of an atom. (p. 355)
protostar A contracting cloud of gas and dust; the earliest stage of a star's life. (p. 757)
puberty The period of sexual development during the teenage years in which the body becomes able to reproduce. (p. 303)
pulsar A neutron star that produces radio waves. (p. 756)
pupil The opening through which light enters the eye. (pp. 263, 536)

Q

quasar A distant galaxy with a black hole at its center. (p. 760)

R

radar A system of detecting reflected radio waves. (p. 488)
radio telescope A device used to detect radio waves from objects in space. (p. 740)
radio waves Electromagnetic waves with the longest wavelengths and lowest frequencies. (p. 487)
rarefaction The part of a longitudinal wave where the particles of the medium are far apart. (p. 423)

ray Straight line used to represent a light wave. (p. 519)
reactant A substance that enters into a chemical reaction. (p. 330)
real image An inverted image formed where rays of light meet. (p. 521)
rectum A short tube at the end of the large intestine where waste material is compressed into a solid form before being eliminated. (p. 151)
red blood cell A cell in the blood that takes up oxygen in the lungs and delivers it to cells elsewhere in the body. (p. 172)
reflecting telescope Telescope that uses a concave mirror to gather light from distant objects. (pp. 540, 740)
reflection The bouncing back of a wave when it hits a surface through which it cannot pass. (p. 430)
reflex An automatic response that occurs very rapidly and without conscious control. (p. 259)
refracting telescope Telescope that uses two convex lenses to form images. (pp. 540, 740)
refraction The bending of waves as they enter a different medium. (p. 431)
regular reflection Reflection that occurs when parallel rays of light hit a smooth surface and all reflect at the same angle. (p. 519)
relief The difference in elevation between the highest and lowest parts of an area. (p. 559)
replacement A reaction in which one element replaces another in a compound; or when two elements in different compounds trade places. (p. 335)
reproduction The process by which living things produce new individuals of the same type. (p. 289)
resonance The increase in the amplitude of vibration that occurs when external vibrations match the object's natural frequency. (p. 434)
respiration The process in which oxygen and glucose undergo a complex series of chemical reactions inside cells. (p. 189)
responding variable The factor that changes as a result of changes to the manipulated variable in an experiment. (pp. 6, 781)
response What the body does in reaction to a stimulus. (p. 249)
retina The layer of receptor cells at the back of the eye on which an image is focused; nerve impulses are sent from the retina to the brain. (p. 264)
retrograde rotation The spinning motion of a planet from east to west, opposite to the direction of rotation of most planets and moons. (p. 709)
revolution The movement of an object around another object. (p. 659)
rill A tiny groove in soil made by flowing water. (p. 617)
river A large stream. (p. 618)
rods Cells on the retina that detect dim light. (p. 537)
rotation The spinning motion of a planet about its axis. (p. 659)
runoff Water that flows over the ground surface rather than soaking into the ground. (p. 617)

saliva The fluid released when the mouth waters that plays an important role in both mechanical and chemical digestion. (p. 142)
salt An ionic compound made from the neutralization of an acid with a base. (p. 405)

sand dune A deposit of wind-blown sand. (p. 642)
satellite Any object that revolves around another object in space. (p. 680)
satellite images Pictures of the land surface based on computer data collected from satellites. (p. 570)
saturated fats Fats, such as butter, that are usually solid at room temperature. (p. 129)
saturated solution A mixture that has so much solute in it that no more will dissolve. (p. 388)
savanna A grassland close to the equator. (p. 67)
scale Used to compare distance on a map or globe to distance on Earth's surface. (p. 559)
scavenger A carnivore that feeds on the bodies of dead organisms. (p. 48)
science A way of looking at the natural world and the knowledge gained in that process. (p. 4)
scientific inquiry The ways in which scientists study the world around them. (p. 4)
scientific law A statement that describes what scientists expect to happen every time under a particular set of conditions. (p. 10)
scientific theory A well-tested concept that explains a wide range of observations. (p. 10)
scrotum An external pouch of skin in which the testes are located. (p. 290)
secondary color Any color produced by combining equal amounts of any two primary colors. (p. 531)
secondary succession The changes that occur after a disturbance in an ecosystem. (p. 80)

secondary wave A transverse seismic wave. (p. 439)
sediment Earth materials deposited by erosion. (p. 611)
seismic wave A wave produced by an earthquake. (p. 439)
seismograph Instrument used to detect and measure earthquakes. (p. 440)
semen A mixture of sperm cells and fluids. (p. 291)
semicircular canals Structures in the inner ear that are responsible for the sense of balance. (p. 267)
sensory neuron A neuron that picks up stimuli from the internal or external environment and converts each stimulus into a nerve impulse. (p. 250)
skeletal muscle A muscle that is attached to the bones of the skeleton. (p. 109)
small intestine The part of the digestive system in which most chemical digestion takes place. (p. 148)
smooth muscle Involuntary muscle found inside many internal organs of the body. (p. 110)
sod A thick mass of grass roots and soil. (p. 601)
sodium vapor lights Bulbs containing solid sodium plus neon and argon gas that produce light. (p. 498)
soil The loose, weathered material on Earth's surface in which plants can grow. (p. 593)
soil conservation The management of soil to prevent its destruction. (p. 604)
soil horizon A layer of soil that differs in color and texture from the layers above or below it. (p. 595)
solar eclipse The blocking of sunlight to Earth that occurs when the moon is between the sun and Earth. (p. 672)
solar flare An explosion of hydrogen gas from the sun's surface that occurs when loops in sunspot regions suddenly connect. (p. 704)

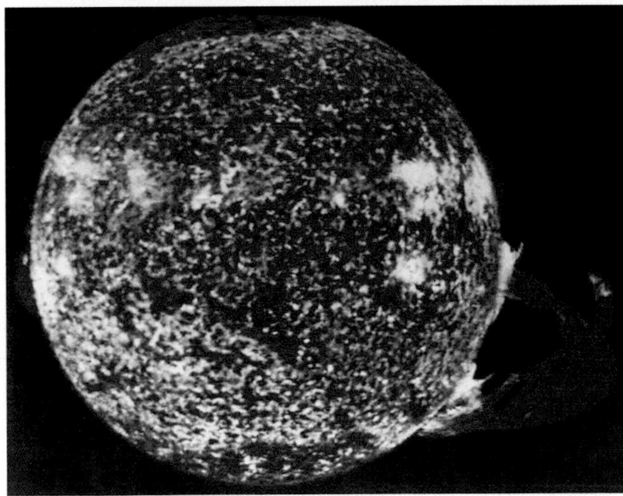

solar wind A stream of electrically charged particles produced by the sun's corona. (p. 702)
solstice The two days of the year on which the noon sun is directly overhead at either 23.5° South or 23.5° North. (p. 664)
solubility A measure of how well a solute can dissolve in a solvent at a given temperature. (p. 388)
solute The part of a solution present in a lesser amount and that is dissolved by the solvent. (p. 385)
solution A well-mixed mixture. (p. 320, 385)
solvent The part of a solution present in the largest amount and that dissolves other substances. (p. 385)
somatic nervous system The group of nerves that controls voluntary actions. (p. 258)
sonar A system of detecting reflected sound waves. (p. 473)
sonogram An image formed by an ultrasound machine. (p. 475)
sound A disturbance that travels through a medium as a longitudinal wave. (p. 446)
species A group of organisms that are similar and can reproduce to produce fertile offspring. (p. 21)
spectrograph An instrument that separates light into colors and photographs the resulting spectrum. (p. 743)
spectroscope An instrument used to view the different colors of light produced by different sources. (p. 496)
spectrum The range of wavelengths of electromagnetic waves. (p. 739)
sperm A male sex cell. (p. 289)
sphygmomanometer An instrument that measures blood pressure. (p. 169)
spinal cord The thick column of nerve tissue that is enclosed by the vertebrae and that links the brain to most of the nerves in the peripheral nervous system. (p. 255)
spiral galaxy A galaxy whose arms curve outward in a pinwheel pattern. (p. 754)
spit A beach formed by longshore drift that projects like a finger out into the water. (p. 641)
spring tide A tide with the greatest difference between low and high tides. (p. 677)
stalactite A calcite deposit that hangs from the roof of a cave. (p. 625)
stalagmite A cone-shaped calcite deposit that builds up from the floor of a cave. (p. 625)
standing wave A wave that appears to stand in one place, even though it is really two waves interfering as they pass through each other. (p. 433)
stimulant A drug that speeds up body processes. (p. 272)
stimulus Any change or signal in the environment that can make an organism react in some way. (p. 249)
stomach A J-shaped, muscular pouch located in the abdomen that expands to hold all of the food that is swallowed. (p. 144)

stream A channel through which water is continually flowing downhill. (p. 618)
stress The reaction of a person's body and mind to threatening, challenging, or disturbing events. (p. 97)
subscript A number in a chemical formula that tells the number of atoms in a molecule or the ratio of elements in a compound. (p. 329)
subsoil The layer of soil beneath the topsoil that contains mostly clay and other minerals. (p. 595)
succession The series of predictable changes that occur in a community over time. (p. 78)
sunspot A dark area of gas on the sun that is cooler than surrounding gases. (p. 702)
supernova The explosion of a dying giant or supergiant star. (p. 748)
surface wave A wave that occurs at the surface between two mediums. (p. 423)
suspension A mixture in which particles can be seen and easily separated by settling or filtration. (p. 384)
symbiosis A close relationship between species that benefits at least one of the species. (p. 39)
symbol A one- or two-letter set of characters that is used to identify an element (p. 329); also, on a map, pictures used by mapmakers to stand for a feature on Earth's surface. (p. 560)
synapse The tiny space between the tip of an axon and the next structure (p. 252)
synthesis A chemical reaction in which two or more simple substances combine to form a new, more complex substance. (p. 333)

T cell A lymphocyte that identifies pathogens and distinguishes one pathogen from the other. (p. 222)
tar A dark, sticky substance produced when tobacco burns. (p. 198)
target cell A cell in the body that recognizes a hormone's chemical structure; a cell to which a hormone binds chemically. (p. 285)
telescope Optical instrument that forms enlarged images of distant objects. (pp. 540, 685)
tendon Strong connective tissue that attaches a muscle to a bone. (p. 110)
terrestrial planets The name given to the four inner planets: Mercury, Venus, Earth, and Mars. (p. 706)
testis Organ of the male reproductive system in which sperm and testosterone are produced. (p. 290)
testosterone A hormone produced by the testes that controls the development of physical characteristics in men. (p. 290)
thermogram An image that shows regions of different temperatures in different colors. (p. 491)
tide The rise and fall of the level of water in the ocean. (p. 676)
till The sediments deposited directly by a glacier. (p. 635)
timbre The overall quality of a sound. (p. 459)
tissue A group of similar cells that perform the same function. (p. 94)
total internal reflection Complete reflection of light by the inside surface of a medium. (p. 548)
tolerance A state in which a drug user, after repeatedly taking a drug, needs larger and larger doses of the drug to produce the same effect. (p. 271)
topographic map A map that shows the surface features of an area. (p. 573)
topography The shape of the land determined by elevation, relief, and landforms. (p. 558)
topsoil Mixture of humus, clay, and other minerals that forms the crumbly, topmost layer of soil. (p. 595)
toxin A poison that is produced by bacterial pathogens and that damages cells. (p. 216)
trachea The windpipe; a passage through which air moves in the respiratory system. (p. 191)
translucent A material that scatters light as it passes through. (p. 518)

transparent A material that transmits light. (p. 518)
transverse wave A wave that moves the medium in a direction perpendicular to the direction in which the wave travels. (p. 422)
tributary A stream that flows into a larger stream. (p. 618)
trough The lowest part of a transverse wave. (p. 422)
tsunami Surface wave on the ocean caused by an underwater earthquake. (p. 439)
tumor An abnormal tissue mass that results from the rapid division of cancerous cells. (p. 236)
tundra An extremely cold, dry biome. (p. 70)

tungsten-halogen lights Bulbs containing a tungsten filament and a halogen gas that produce light. (p. 499)

turbulence A type of movement of water in which, rather than moving downstream, the water moves every which way. (p. 632)

ultrasound Sound waves with frequencies above 20,000 Hz. (p. 454)

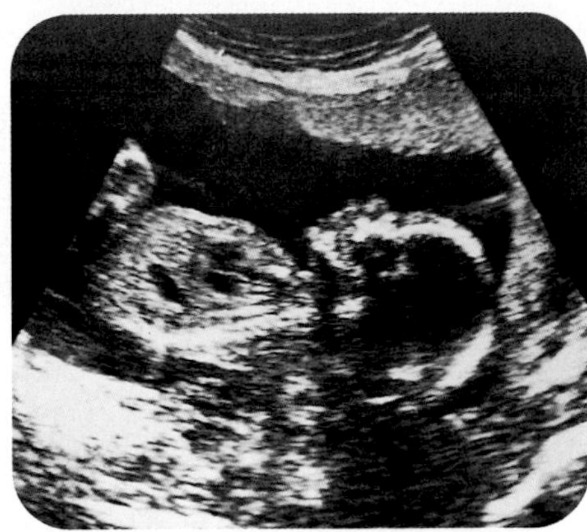

ultraviolet rays Electromagnetic waves with frequencies higher than visible light, but lower than X-rays. (p. 492)

umbilical cord A ropelike structure that forms in the uterus between the embryo and the placenta. (p. 296)

umbra The darkest part of a shadow. (p. 672)

understory A layer of shorter plants that grow in the shade of a forest canopy. (p. 65)

universe All of space and everything in it. (p. 747)

unsaturated fats Fats, such as olive oil and canola oil, that are usually liquid at room temperature. (p. 129)

unsaturated solution A mixture in which more solute can be dissolved. (p. 388)

urea A chemical that comes from the breakdown of proteins and that is removed from the body by the kidneys. (p. 203)

ureter A narrow tube that carries urine from one of the kidneys to the urinary bladder. (p. 203)

urethra A small tube through which urine flows from the body. (p. 204)

urinary bladder A sacklike muscular organ that stores urine until it is eliminated from the body. (p. 204)

urine A watery fluid produced by the kidneys that contains urea and other waste materials. (p. 203)

uterus The hollow muscular organ of the female reproductive system in which a baby develops. (p. 292)

vaccination The process by which harmless antigens are deliberately introduced into a person's body to produce active immunity. (p. 229)

vaccine A substance used in a vaccination that consists of pathogens that have been weakened or killed but can still trigger the immune system into action. (p. 229)

vagina A muscular passageway through which a baby leaves the mother's body. (p. 293)

valence electrons The electrons that are farthest away from the nucleus of an atom and are involved in chemical reactions. (p. 357)

valley glacier A long, narrow glacier that forms when snow and ice build up in a mountain valley. (p. 633)

valve A flap of tissue in the heart or a vein that prevents blood from flowing backward. (p. 160)

variable Any factor that can change in an experiment. (pp. 6, 781)

vein A blood vessel that carries blood back to the heart. (p. 162)

ventricle Each of the two lower chambers of the heart that pumps blood out of the heart. (p. 160)

vernal equinox The day of the year that marks the beginning of spring in the Northern Hemisphere. (p. 665)

vertebrae The 26 small bones that make up the backbone. (p. 101)

vibration A repeated back-and-forth or up-and-down motion. (p. 421)

villi Tiny finger-shaped structures that cover the inner surface of the small intestine and provide a large surface area through which digested food is absorbed. (p. 150)

virtual image An upright image formed where rays of light appear to meet or come from. (p. 520)

visible light Electromagnetic radiation that can be seen with the unaided human eye. (pp. 492, 739)

vitamins Molecules that act as helpers in a variety of chemical reactions within the body. (p. 131)

vocal cords Folds of connective tissue that stretch across the opening of the larynx and produce a person's voice. (p. 195)

voluntary muscle A muscle that is under conscious control. (p. 108)

water cycle The continuous process by which water moves from Earth's surface to the atmosphere and back. (p. 54)

wave A disturbance that transfers energy from place to place. (p. 420)

wavelength The distance between two corresponding parts of a wave. (pp. 427, 739)

weathering The chemical and physical processes that break down rock at Earth's surface. (p. 584)

white blood cell A blood cell that fights disease. (p. 173)

white dwarf The remaining hot core of a star after its outer layers have expanded and drifted out into space. (p. 758)

withdrawal A period of adjustment that occurs when a drug-dependent person stops taking the drug. (p. 272)

X-rays Electromagnetic waves with higher frequencies than ultraviolet rays, but shorter than gamma rays. (p. 493)

zygote A fertilized egg, produced by the joining of a sperm and an egg. (p. 289)

Index

Index

Index

Index

Index

Acknowledgments

Staff Credits

The people who made up the Prentice Hall **Integrated Science** team—representing design, editorial, editorial services, electronic publishing technology, manufacturing & inventory planning, marketing, marketing services, market research, online services & multimedia development, production services, product planning, project office, publishing processes—are listed below. Bold type denotes core team members.

Carolyn Belanger, Suzanne Biron, Peggy Bliss, Patricia Cully, Bob Craton, **Patricia Fromkin,** Jennifer Muncherian, **Phyllis Hawkes,** Roberto Portocarrero, **Richard Stakun-Pickering,** Jennifer Teece, Char Lyn Yeakley.

Illustration

Carmella Clifford: 149, 263, 267, 469(tl)
Bruce Day: 98
Kathleen Dempsey: 426(ctr), 436, 451, 466, 500, 528, 534, 561, 569, 578, 590, 600, 626
John Edwards & Associates: 52, 61, 74–75, 85, 103, 356(bl), 403, 421, 422, 423, 431, 432, 443, 447(t), 456, 457, 510, 511, 512, 566, 567(t), 575, 588, 630, 631, 635, 639, 663, 669, 670, 672, 673, 677, 698–699, 707(t), 715, 726, 750, 759, 762, 763, 766(b), 767
John Edwards & Associates (Dave Fischer): 275
John Edwards & Associates (Henry Hill): 251
David Fuller: 506(br)
Function thru Form: 137
GeoSystems Global Corporation: 65, 66, 68, 70, 84, 559, 567(b), 568, 599, 602, 603, 619(t), 621, 634, 642
Andrea Golden: 76(t), 366(b), 555
Biruta Hansen: 22–23, 34,
Floyd E. Hosmer: 250
Keith Kasnot: 143, 145, 204–205, 286, 287, 296
Jared Lee: 338, 364, 391, 448, 468, 482, 748
Martucci Design: 33, 71, 83, 123, 138, 185, 204, 217, 236, 351, 358, 361, 365, 369, 370, 372, 381, 487, 574, 594, 705, 739(b), 744, 756, 786, 787, 788
Matt Mayerchak: 42, 121, 153, 209, 243, 279, 309, 349, 379, 411(t), 413, 441, 477, 513, 579, 605, 689, 769, 785
William McAllister: 502
Fran Milner: 141, 150, 166–167, 172–173, 192–193, 291, 292, 409(br), 536, 537(t), 551
Morgan Cain & Associates: 47, 93, 116, 144, 160, 165, 171, 175, 196, 211, 219, 223, 252, 258, 288, 325, 328, 332, 337, 340, 341, 345, 347, 355, 356(t), 356(br), 357, 360, 367, 373(t), 377, 386, 390, 402, 413, 415, 425, 426, 427, 430, 433, 434(b), 439, 447(ctr), 453, 454, 459, 465, 473, 490–491, 509, 577, 594, 596–597, 610, 612, 613, 619(b), 632, 643, 659, 662, 666, 671, 679, 680, 681, 691, 703, 707, 719, 725, 735, 745, 749, 753, 755, 766(t), 771, 778(bl, br), 779(tl, br)
Ortelius Design Inc.: 59, 506(tl, bl), 507(bl, br), 544, 545, 564 565, 660, 661
Stephanie Pershing: 443
Judith Pinkham: 113, 118
Matthew Pippin: 54, 416, 434–435, 595, 622–623, 636–637
Pond and Giles: 79, 80
Precision Graphics: 483, 496, 503, 504, 507(t), 519, 520, 521, 522, 524, 525, 526, 527, 533, 538, 540, 541, 542, 543, 546, 549
Pat Rossi: 105(bl, br, tl, tr)
Sandra Sevigny: 95, 101, 159, 176, 255
Nancy Smith: 326, 342, 362, 374, 392, 406
Tim Spransy: 472
Walter Stuart: 50, 161, 191
Robert Warshaw: 515
Alan Witschonke: 88–89
J/B Woolsey Associates: 24, 28, 35, 38, 49, 55,56, 76, 142, 163, 189, 195, 245, 259, 265, 277, 294, 311, 413, 469(tr), 484, 485, 488, 508, 581, 586, 607, 617, 739(t), 740, 782

Photography

Cover Design Studio Montage
Photo Credits bridge: Cosmo Condina/Tony Stone WorldWide
parrot: Corel Stock Photo Library
planets: NASA

Nature of Science
Page xxii b, Courtesy of Elroy Masters; **1b,** Pat O'Hara/DRK Photo; **1 t,** Courtesy of Elroy Masters; **2 bl,** Jeff Foott/Tom Stack & Associates; **2 m,** M. Collier/DRK Photo; **2 t,** Jeff Foott/Tom Stack & Associates; **2 tl,** Vireo; **3 t,** Gilbert Grant/Photo Researchers

What is Science?
Page 4, John Sanford/Science Photo Library/Photo Researchers; **5 bl,** Bruce Henderson/Stock Boston; **5 br,** Index Stock Imagery; **5 t,** John Brooks/Liaison Agency; **6,** David Howell/The Image Works; **7,** Russ Lappa; **8,** D'Andrea/Index Stock Imagery; **9,** James Holmes/Photo Researchers, Inc.; **10,** Richard Haynes; **11,** Russ Lappa; **12 l,** Ben Osborne/Tony Stone Images; **12 r,** Nieto/Jerrican/Photo Researchers; **13 l,** Robin L. Sachs/PhotoEdit; **13 r,** Index Stock Imagery; **14 t,** John Brooks/Liaison Agency.

Chapter 1
Pages 16–17, Tony Craddock/TSI; **18,** Richard Haynes; **18–19,** Shin Yoshino/Minden Pictures; **19,** Carr Clifton/Minden Pictures; **19 inset top,** Corel Corp.; **19 inset,** S. Nielsen/DRK Photo; **20,** John Cancalosi/Tom Stack & Associates; **21,** Patti Murray/Animals Animals; **25 t,** Richard Haynes; **25 b,** Michlo Hoshino/Minden Pictures; **26,** C. Allan Morgan/DRK Photo; **27 t,** Rob Simpson/Visuals Unlimited; **27 b,** Bas van Beek/Leo de Wys; **29,** Mitsuaki Iwago/Minden Pictures; **30 t,** Dan Budnick/Woodfin Camp & Associates; **30 b,** Russ Lappa; **32,** Gary Griffen/Animals Animals; **33,**J. Alcock/Visuals Unlimited; **35 l,** Patti Murray/Animals Animals; **35 tr,** Wayne Lankinen/DRK Photo; **35 br,** Ron Willocks/Animals Animals; **36 l,** Michael Fogden/DRK Photo; **36 r,** D. Holden Bailey/Tom Stack & Associates; **37 l,** Stephen J. Krasemann/ DRK Photo; **37 r,** Donald Specker/Animals Animals; **37 b,** Jeanne White/ Photo Researchers; **39,** Daryl Balfour/TSI; **40,** John Gerlach/DRK Photo;**41,** Tony Craddock/TSI.

Chapter 2
Pages 44–45, Tom McHugh/Steinhart Aquarium/Photo Researchers; **46 t,** Richard Haynes; **46 b,** Byron Jorjorian/TSI; **47,** Breck P. Kent/Animals Animals/Earth Scenes; **48 l,** Stephen J. Krasemann/DRK Photo; **48 tr,** John Cancalosi/DRK Photo; **48 br,** John Netherton/Animals Animals; **49,** S. Nielsen/DRK Photo; **51,** Stephen J. Krasemann/DRK Photo; **53 t,** Richard Haynes; **53 b,** R.J. Erwin/DRK Photo; **57,** Dr. Jeremy Burgess/Science Photo Library/Photo Researchers; **58 t,** Richard Haynes; **58 b,** J. Cancalosi/DRK Photo; **59,** D. Cavagnaro/DRK Photo; **60,** Stephen G. Maka/DRK Photo; **61 t,** John Canalosi/DRK Photo; **61 b,** Russ Lappa; **63,** Richard Haynes; **64,** Russ Lappa; **65 t,** Renee Lynn/TSI; **65 m,** Frans Lanting/Minden Pictures; **65 b,** Mark Hones/Minden Pictures; **66 l,** Joe McDonald/DRK Photo; **66 inset,** Michael Fogden/DRK Photo; **67,** Art Wolfe/TSI; **68 l,** Carr Clifton/Minden Pictures; **68 inset, 69 r,** Stephen J. Krasemann/DRK Photo; **69 inset,** Michael Quinton/Minden Pictures; **70, 71,** Michio Hoshino/Minden Pictures; **72 l,** David Boyle/Animals Animals; **72 r,** Kim Heacox/DRK Photo; **73 l,** Stephen G. Maka/DRK Photo; **73 r,** Steven David Miller/Animals Animals; **74 l,** Anne Wertheim/Animals Animals; **74 r,** Gregory Ochocki/Photo Researchers; **75 l,** Michael Nolan/Tom Stack & Associates; **75 r,** Norbert Wu; **77 l,r,** Russ Lappa; **78 t,78 b,** Tom & Pat Leeson/Photo Researchers; **81,** John Cancalosi/DRK Photo.

Interdisciplinary Exploration
Page 84 tm, Frans Lanting/Minden Pictures; **84 tr,** Alan Carey/Photo Researchers; **84 bl,** Frans Lanting/Minden Pictures; **84 br,** Roy Toft/Tom Stack & Associates; **85 t,** Starin/Ardea London Ltd.; **85 m,** Peter Steyn/Ardea London Ltd.; **85 b,** Tom Brakefield/DRK Photo; **86 t,** Dr. Migel Smith/ Earth Scenes; **86 b,** Werner Forman Archive/Art Resource; **87 l,** Christie's Images; **87 r,** Jose Anzel/Aurora; **89,** Corbis-Bettmann

Chapter 3
Pages **90–91,** Globus, Holway & Lobel/The Stock Market: **92 t,** Richard Haynes; **92 tl,** Russ Lappa; **94 tl,** Robert Becker/Custom Medical Stock; **94 bl,** Fred Hossler/Visuals Unlimited; **94 m,** Clive Brunckill/Allsport; **94 tr,** Biophoto Associates/Science Source/Photo Researchers; **94,** John D. Cunningham/Visuals Unlimited; **96 br,** Lori Adamski Peek/Tony Stone Images; **97,** Paul J. Sutton/Duomo; **99,** Michael P. Manheim/Midwest Stock; **100 t,** Russ Lappa; **100 b,** Cathy Cheney/Stock Boston; **101,** Richard Haynes; **103,** Andrew Syred/Science Photo Library/Photo Researchers; **104,** Salisbury District Hospital/Science Photo Library/Photo Researchers; **105,** William R. Sallaz/Duomo; **106,** The Granger Collection, NY; **107 both,** Superstock; **108 t,** Richard Haynes; **108 bl,** Superstock; **109 tl,** Astrid & Hanns-Frieder Michler/Science Photo Library/ Photo Researchers; **109 bl,** Eric Grave/Photo Researchers; **109 m,** Richard Haynes; **109 r,** Ed Reschke/Peter Arnold; **110 l,** Richard Haynes; **110 r,** Jim Cummins/FPG International; **112,** Superstock; **113, 114 t,** Richard Haynes; **114 b,** Jed Jacobsen/Allsport; **115 l,** David Young Wolff/Tony Stone Images; **115 r,** Lennart Nilsson/ Behold Man; **117 l,** Prof. P. Motta/Dept. of Anatomy/University "La Sapienza," Rome/Science Photo Library/Photo Researchers; **117 r,** Russ Lappa; **118, 119,** Richard Haynes; **120,** Bob Daemmrich/Stock Boston.

Chapter 4

Pages 124–125, Superstock; **126,** Bob Daemmrich/Stock Boston; **127 l,** Richard Haynes; **127 r, 128, 129, 130–131, 131 all, 132 all,** Russ Lappa; **133,** Joan Baron/The Stock Market; **134,** Russ Lappa; **135 t,** Richard Haynes; **135 b,** David Young-Wolff/PhotoEdit; **136,** David Young Wolff/TSI; **139,** David Young-Wolff/ PhotoEdit; **140,** The Granger Collection, NY; **141, 142,** Richard Haynes; **145,** CNRI/Science Photo Library/Photo Researchers; **147, 148 t,** Richard Haynes; **148 b,** Llewellyn/Uniphoto; **150,** Prof. P. Motta/Dept. of Anatomy/University "La Sapienza", Rome/Science Photo Library/Photo Researchers; **151,** CNRI/Science Photo Library/ Photo Researchers; **152,** Donna Day/TSI.

Chapter 5

Pages 156–157, National Cancer Institute/Science Photo Library/Photo Researchers; **158, 159,** Richard Haynes; **160 t,** Erich Lessing/Art Resource; **160 b** Science Photo Library/Photo Researchers; **162–163,** Pete Saloutos/The Stock Market; **164,** Scott Weersing/Allsport; **165,** Richard Haynes; **167,** Prof. P. Motta/Dept. of Anatomy/University "La Sapienza", Rome/Science Photo Library/Photo Researchers; **168,** Cabisco/Visuals Unlimited; **169,** Matt Meadows/Peter Arnold; **170,** Richard Haynes; **171,** Andrew Syred/Science Photo Library/Photo Researchers; **172,** Bill Longcore/Science Source/Photo Researchers; **173 t,** Andrew Syred/Science Photo Library/Photo Researchers; **173 b,** National Cancer Institute/Science Photo Library/Photo Researchers; **174,** Oliver Meckes/Photo Researchers; **176,** Richard Haynes; **178 t,** Daemmrich/Stock Boston; **178 b,** Thom Duncan/Adventure Photo; **179 both,** Custom Medical Stock; **180 t** AP/Wide World Photos; **180 b,** The Granger Collection, NY; **181 t,** Liaison International; **181 b,** Brad Nelson/Custom Medical Stock; **182,** Nicole Katodo/TSI; **183,** both, CustomMedical Stock.

Chapter 6

Pages 186–187, Mark Gibson/The Stock Market; **188 t,** Richard Haynes; **188 b,** Dick Dickinson/Photo Network; **190 l,** Richard Haynes; **190 inset,** Eddy Gray/Science Photo Library/Photo Researchers; **191,** Richard Haynes; **194,** Paul Harris/TSI; **196,** J. Sohm/The Image Works; **197,** Russ Lappa; **198,** Spencer Jones/FPG International; **199,** Ken Karp; **200,** Al Bello/TSI; **201 l,** Clark Overton/Phototake; **201 m,** SIV/Photo Researchers; **201 r,** Martin Rotker/Phototake; **202,** Smoke Free Educational Services; **203, 206,** Richard Haynes; **208,** Ken Karp.

Chapter 7

Pages 212–213, Microworks/Phototake; **214 t,** Richard Haynes; **214 b,** The Granger Collection, NY; **215,** Pete Saloutos/The Stock Market; **216 t,** CNRI/Science Photo Library/Photo Researchers; **216 m,** Biozentrum/Science Photo Library/Photo Researchers; **216 b,** Gucho/CNRI/Science Photo Library/Photo Researchers; **218 t,** Mike Peres/Custom Medical Stock Photo; **218 b,** Scott Camazine/Photo Researchers; **219,** Russ Lappa; **220,** Science Pictures Ltd./Science Photo Library/Photo Researchers; **221,** Lennart Nilsson/Boehringer Ingelheim International GmbH; **222,** Lori Adamski Peek/TSI; **224,** NIBSC/Science Photo Library/Photo Researchers; **225,** Jon Riley/TSI; **226, 227,** Richard Haynes; **228 t,** Russ Lappa; **228 b,** CNRI/Science Photo Library/Photo Researchers; **229,** Aaron Haupt/Photo Researchers; **230 t,** Historical Picture Service/Custom Medical Stock; **230 b,** The Granger Collection, NY; **231 t,** Granger Collection, NY; **231 b,** Giraudon/Art Resource; **233 t,** Richard Haynes; **233 b,** Richard Haynes; **234 l,** Ron Kimball; **234 r,** Andrew Syred/Science Photo Library/Photo Researchers; **235,** Therisa Stack/Tom Stack & Associates; **236,** Dept. of Clinical Radiology, Salisbury District Hospital/Science Photo Library/Photo Researchers; **237,** Yoav Levy/Phototake; **238,** Stevie Grand/Science Photo Library/Photo Researchers; **240 t,** Richard Haynes; **240 bl, 240–241,** The Granger Collection, NY; **242,** Phil Savoie/The Picture Cube.

Chapter 8

Pages 246–247, 1998 Magic Eye Inc.; **248 t,** Richard Haynes; **248 b,** Lee Snider/The Image Works; **249,** Gordon R. Gainer/The Stock Market; **250,** Biophoto Associates/Photo Researchers; **253, 254 t,** Richard Haynes; **254 b,** Milton Feinberg/The Picture Cube; **255,** Richard Haynes; **257,** Art Resouce; **258,** Tom Stewart/The Stock Market; **260,** William Sallaz/Duomo; **261,** Robert E. Daemmrich/ TSI; **262,** Superstock; **264 t,** Prof. P. Motta/Dept. of Anatomy/U. "La Sapienza," Rome/Science Photo Library/Photo Researchers; **264 b,** Lennart Nilsson; **266,** Renee Lynn/TSI; **268 l,** Spencer Grant/The Picture Cube; **268 r,** Lennart Nilsson; **269,** Mugshots/The Stock Market; **270 t,** Russ Lappa; **270 b,** Uniphoto; **271,** Tom Croke/Liaison International; **272,** David Young-Wolff/PhotoEdit; **276,** Index Stock; **278,** Bob Daemmrich/Stock Boston.

Chapter 9

Pages 282–283, Uniphoto; **284,** Keith Kent/Photo Researchers; **285 l,** Chad Slattery/TSI; **285 r,** Nancy Sheehan/The Picture Cube; **289,** Mitsuaki Iwago/Minden Pictures; **290 both,** Dr. Dennis Kunkel/Phototake; **293,** Prof. P.M. Motta & J. Van Blerkom/Science Photo Library/ Photo Researchers; **295 tl,** Stephen R. Swinburne/Stock Boston; **295 tm,** Stephen R. Swinburne/Stock Boston; **295 b,** David Phillips/Science Photo Library/ Photo Researchers; **297,** Lennart Nilsson; **298,** Index Stock; **299 l,** Roy Morsch/The Stock Market; **299 r,** Frauke/Mauritius/H. Armstrong Roberts; **300 l,** Penny Gentieu; **300 r,** Elizabeth Hathol/The Stock Market; **301,** Don Semtzer/TSI; **302 t,** Ken Karp; **302 b,** Roy Morso/The Stock Market; **303 l,** James D. Wilson/Liaison International; **303 r,** Robert E. Daemmrich/TSI; **304,** Mark Burnett/Photo Researchers; **305,** Bruce Dale/National Geographic Society; **306,** David Young-Wolff/Photo Edit; **307,** David Young Wolff/TSI.

Nature of Science Page 312, Courtesy of Alex Martinez; **313 t,** Lawrence Migdale/Stock Boston; **313 b,** Josh Mitchell/TSI; **314 t,mt,b,** PhotoDisc; **314 m,** Russ Lappa; **314 mb,** Steven Maus; **316,** Steven Mays.

Chapter 10

Pages 316–317, Kunio Owaki/The Stock Market; **318,** Reinstein, The Image Works; **319 l,** Cathlyn Melloan/TSI; **319 m,** Bernard Roussel/The Image Bank; **319 r,** Bob Firth/International Stock; **320,** Russ Lappa; **321,** Bob Firth/International Stock; **322,** Steve Elmore/The Stock Market; **323 t,** Charles D. Winters/Photo Researchers; **323 bl,** Russ Lappa; **323 ml,** Wood Sabold/International Stock; **323 mr,** Ken O'Donaghue; **323 br,** Steven Needham/Envision; **324 l,** Russ Lappa; **324 r,** J. Sulley/The Image Works; **325,** Ken Eward/Science Source/Photo Researchers; **327,** Richard Haynes; **328, 330 all,** Russ Lappa; **331,** John D. Cummingham/Visuals Unlimited; **333,** Koitsu Hirota/The Image Bank; **334,** Paul Sisul/TSI; **335 t,** Russ Lappa; **335 b,** Charles D. Winters/Photo Researchers; **336 t,** Richard Haynes; **336 b,** Simon Norfolk/TSI; **337,** Michael Newman/PhotoEdit; **339 tl & tr,** Richard Megna/Fundamental Photographs; **339 b,** AP/Wide World Photos; **340, 342,** Russ Lappa; **343, 344 t,** Richard Haynes; **344 b,** Patrick Donehue/Photo Researchers; **345,** Dorothy Littell/Stock Boston; **346 all,** Russ Lappa; **348,** Dede Gilman/Photo Network; **349 l,** Steven Needham/Envision; **349 r,** Richard Megna/Fundamental Photographs.

Chapter 11

Pages 352–353, Ken Eward/Science Source/Photo Researchers; **354, 355 both, 356 tl,tr, 357 t,** Russ Lappa; **357 b,** Frank Cezus/FPG International; **359,** Richard Megna/Fundamental Photographs; **363 t,** Russ Lappa; **363 b,** Arthur Gurmankin & Mary Morina/Visuals Unlimited; **365 tl,** Lawrence Migdale/Photo Researchers; **365 tr,** Richard Megna/Fundamental Photographs; **365 b, 366,** Russ Lappa; **367,** M. Claye/Jacana/Photo Researchers; **368,** Richard Megna/ Fundamental Photograhs; **369,** Russ Lappa; **371,** George Disario/The Stock Market; **374, 375,** Richard Haynes; **376 l,** Gary Retherford/Photo Researchers; **376 r, 377 l, m,** Paul Silverman/ Fundamental Photographs; **377 r,** Ken Lucas/Visuals Unlimited; **378 t,** Breck P. Kent/Earth Scenes; **378 b,** Russ Lappa.

Chapter 12

Pages 382–383, Minolta Corp.; **384,** Michael Newman/PhotoEdit; **385 t, m,** Russ Lappa; **385 b,** Leonard Lessin/Peter Arnold; **387,** Russ Lappa; **388,** Tony Freeman/PhotoEdit; **389, 392,** Russ Lappa; **393,** Richard Haynes; **394 t,** Russ Lappa; **394 b,** Lawrence Migdale/Photo Researchers; **395 both,** Russ Lappa; **396,** Bob Krist/The Stock Market; **397 tl,** Russ Lappa; **397 tr,** David Young-Wolfe/ PhotoEdit; **397 bl,** Mark C. Burnett/Stock Boston; **397 m, br,** Russ Lappa; **398 b r,** B. Daemmrich/The Image Works; **398 all others,** Russ Lappa; **399,** P. Aprahamian/ Science Photo Library/Photo Researchers; **400,** Russ Lappa; **401 t,** L.S. Stepanowicz/Visuals Unlimited; **401 b,** Tom Pantages; **403,** Richard Haynes; **404 t,** Jenny Hager/The Image Works; **404 b,** Russ Lappa; **405,** George Ranalli/Photo Researchers; **406,** Russ Lappa; **407,** Richard Haynes; **408,** Cleo Photography/Photo Researchers; **410,** Russ Lappa; **411,** Lawrence Migdale/Photo Researchers.

Nature of Science

Page 414 t, Joe Towers/The Stock Market; **414 b,** Bourg/Liaison International; **415,** Leonard Lessin/Peter Arnold; **416–417 both,** NASA.

Chapter 13

Pages 418–419, Jim Pickerell/Folio, Inc.; **420 t,** Richard Haynes; **420 b,** Rob Gilley/Adventure Photo & Film; **422,** Richard Megna/Fundamental Photographs; **424 t,** Richard Haynes; **424 b,** Chris Cole/Duomo; **427, 430, 436, 437,** Richard Haynes; **438 b,** Lynette Cook/Science Photo Library/Photo Researchers; **440 t,** Andrew Ratkino/TSI; **440 inset,** Russell D. Curtis/Photo Researchers.

Chapter 14
Pages 444–445, Bob Kramer /The Picture Cube; **446,** Richard Haynes; **447,** Russell D. Curtis/Photo Researchers; **449,** Russ Lappa; **450 t,** The Granger Collection, NY; **450 b,** Eric Risberg/AP Wide World Photos; **451, 452,** Richard Haynes; **454,** Matt Bostick; **455 t,** Mark C. Burnett/Stock Boston; **455 b,** Martin Bough/Fundamental Photographs; **458 t,** Richard Haynes; **458 b,** Cosmo Condina/TSI; **460,** Michael Newman/PhotoEdit; **461,** Stanley Rowin/The Picture Cube; **462 l,** Spencer Grant/The Picture Cube; **462 r,** Nancy Brown/The Stock Market; **462–463,** Peter Saloutos/The Stock Market; **462–463 t,** Doug Martin/Photo Researchers; **463 r,** PhotoDisc Inc.; **463 b,** Index Stock; **464,** David Ball/The Stock Market; **465,** Neil Nissing/ FPG International; **466–467, 468,** Richard Haynes; **470,** Stephen Frisch/Stock Boston; **471,** Michael Newman/PhotoEdit; **473,** Corbis; **474 t,** Mitch Reardon/Photo Researchers; **474 b,** Francois Gohier/Photo Researchers; **475 t,** Merlin D. Tuttle, Bat Conservation International/Photo Researchers; **475 b,** Charles Gupton/The Stock Market, **475 inset,** Telegraph Color Library/FPG International; **476 all,** Richard Megna/Fundamental Photographs.

Chapter 15
Pages 480–481, Alex Bartel/Science Photo Library/Photo Researchers; **482, 485 t,** Richard Haynes; **485 b,** Russ Lappa; **486,** Richard Haynes; **488,** Matthew McVay/TSI; **489 l,** Jim Roshan; **489 r,** Eric Miller/Liaison International; **489 b,** Vecto Verso/Leo de Wys, Inc.; **491,** Alfred Pasieka/Science Photo Library/Photo Researchers; **492 t,** Fundamental Photographs; **492 b,** Ron Sutherland/Science Photo Library/Photo Researchers; **493,** RNHRD NHS Trust/TSI; **494,** Alfred Pasieka/Science Photo Library/Photo Researchers; **495,** Nordion/Visuals Unlimited; **497,** Bill Horsman/Stock Boston; **498 t,** 98 Kunio Owaki/The Stock Market; **498 b,** Phil Degginger; **499 t,** Aneal E. Vohra/Unicorn Stock Photos; **499 b,** Charles Seaborn/TSI; **501,** Richard Haynes; **503,** Russ Lappa; **505,** Bruce Forster/TSI; **507,** AP/Wide World Photos; **508,** David Ducros/Science Photo Library/Photo Researchers; **512,** Richard Haynes.

Chapter 16
Pages 516–517, Arthur Gurmankin/Mary Morina/Visuals Unlimited; **518 t,** Russ Lappa; **518 b,** Andy Levin/Photo Researchers; **519 l,** Coco McCoy/Rainbow; **519 m,** Michael A. Keller Studios LTD./The Stock Market; **519 r,** Skip Moody/Rainbow; **520 both,** Corel Corp.; **521, 522,** PhotoDisc Inc.; **521 t,** Richard Haynes; **522 b,** Russ Lappa; **522,** Peter A. Simon/The Stock Market; **523 t,** John Kieffer/Peter Arnold; **524 b,** John M. Dunay IV/Fundamental Photographs; **524 both,** David Parker/Photo Researchers; **525,** Richard Megna/Fundamental Photographs; **526,** Russ Lappa; **527 t,** Richard Haynes; **529 b,** David Young-Wolff/PhotoEdit; **530 tl,** Breck P. Kent; **530 b,** Grant Heilman Photography; **531 both,** Michael Dalton/Fundamental Photographs; **532 l** Ralph C. Eagle/Photo Researchers; **532 inset,** Jerome Wexler/Photo Researchers; **532 r, 533 both,** Russ Lappa; **534,** Richard Haynes; **535,** John Coletti/Stock Boston; **536 both,** L.V. Bergman & Associates; **538,** PhotoDisc Inc.; **539 t,** Richard Haynes; **539 b,** Camerique, Inc./The Picture Cube; **541 t,** Richard T. Nowitz/Photo Researchers; **541 b,** Jan Hinsch/Science Photo Library/Photo Researchers; **544 t,** Corbis; **544 b,** Scala/Art Resource, NY; **545 t** Grant Heilman Photography; **545 m,** Corbis; **546,** Blair Seitz/Photo Researchers; **547 tl,** Jon Goell/The Picture Cube; **547 tr,** Bob Daemmrich/Stock Boston; **547 ml,** E.R. Degginger; **547 m,** Grant Heilman Photography; **547 mr,** Spencer Grant/Photo Researchers; **547 bl,** E.R. Degginger; **547 br,** Will & Deni Mcintyre/Photo Researchers.

Nature of Science
Page 552 t, Rob Trubia/Westlight; **552 b,** Courtesy of Christine Darden; **553,** HO/AP/Wide World Photos; **555 l,** AP/Wide World Photos; **555 r,** Courtesy of Christine Darden.

Chapter 17
Pages 556–557, Tom Bean; **558,** The Granger Collection, NY; **560 t,** Tom Bean; **560 b,** David Muench Photography; **562,** ESA/PLI/The Stock Market; **563 both,** Russ Lappa; **564 t,** Bodleian Library, Oxford, U.K.; **564 b,** The Granger Collection, NY; **565 t, br,** The Granger Collection, NY; **565 bl,** British Library, London/Bridgeman Art Library, London/Superstock; **570 t,** Russ Lappa; **570 b, 571 both,** Earth Satellite Corporation/Science Photo Library/Photo Researchers; **572 tl,** Geographix; **572 tr,** Bob Daemmrich/Stock Boston; **573 t,** Richard Haynes; **573 b,** Robert Rathe/Stock Boston; **575,** Paul Rezendes; **576,** U.S. Geological Survey; **577 t,** Ken M. Johns/Photo Researchers; **578,** Richard Haynes; **581,** U.S. Geological Survey.

Chapter 18
Pages 582–583, Mike Mazzaschi/Stock Boston; **584,** Russ Lappa; **585 l,** Ron Watts/Westlight; **585 r,** Jerry D. Greer; **586 l,** Breck P. Kent/Animals Animals/Earth Scenes; **586 r,** Susan Rayfield/Photo Researchers; **587 l,** John Sohlden/Visuals Unlimited; **587 m,** E.R. Degginger/Photo Researchers; **587 r,** Gerald & Buff Corsi/Visuals Unlimited; **589 t,** Chromosohm/Sohm/Photo Researchers; **589 b,** Breck P. Kent/Animals Animals/Earth Scenes; **591,** Richard Haynes; **592,** John G. Ross/Photo Researchers; **593 t,** Richard Haynes; **593 b,** Rod Planck/TSI; **598,** J. M. Labat/Jacana/Photo Researchers; **600,** Richard T. Nowitz/Photo Researchers; **601 t,** Richard Haynes; **601 b,** Jim Brandenburg/Minden Pictures; **602,** Corbis; **603,** AP/Wide World Photos; **604 t,** Larry Lefever/Grant Heilman Photography; **604 b,** Jim Strawser/Grant Heilman Photography; **605,** John G. Ross/Photo Researchers.

Chapter 19
Pages 608–609 & 610, Jim Steinberg/Photo Researchers; **610, 611,** Paul Sequeira/Photo Researchers; **612 t,** Eric Vandeville/Gamma-Liaison Network; **612 b,** Thomas G. Rampton/Grant Heilman Photography; **613,** Steven Holt; **614–615,** Richard Haynes; **616,** Photo Disc; **616–617,** Walter Bibikow/The Viesti Collection; **617 t,** Runk Schoenberger/Grant Heilman Photography; **618,** Inga Spence/Tom Stack & Associates; **619,** David Ball/The Stock Market; **620 l,** Glenn M. Oliver/Visuals Unlimited; **620 r,** Index Stock Photography, Inc.; **621 t,** E.R. Degginger; **621 b,** NASA/SADO/Tom Stack & Associates; **624,** Chuck O'Rear/Westlight; **625,** *St. Petersburg Times*/Gamma-Liaison; **626,** Russ Lappa; **627,** Richard Haynes; **628,** Doug McKay/TSI; **629 t,** Richard Haynes; **629 b,** Eliot Cohen; **633 t,** Richard Haynes; **633 b,** Mark Kelley/Stock Boston; **635,** Grant Heilman Photography; **638,** Craig Tuttle/The Stock Market; **640,** Randy Wells/TSI; **641,** E.R.I.M./TSI; **642 t,** Richard Haynes; **642 b,** Jess Stock/TSI; **643,** Breck P. Kent; **644,** Connie Toops; **645,** Craig Tuttle/The Stock Market.

Interdisciplinary Exploration
Page 648 t, Robert Caputo/Stock Boston; **648–649 b,** David Sanger Photography; **649 l,** Brian Braker/Photo Researchers; **650,** NASA; **651,** Groenendyk/Photo Researchers; **652–653 b,** Thomas J. Abercrombie/National Geographic Society; **652 inset,** Robert Caputo/Stock Boston; **653 t,** Robert Caputo/Stock Boston; **654,** David Ball/The Picture Cube; **655,** Richard Haynes.

Chapter 20
Pages 656–657, NASA; **658 t,** Russ Lappa; **658 b,** Eric Lessing; **660 t,** Corel Corp.; **660 b,** Archive Photos; **661 t,** Courtney Milne/Masterfile; **661 b,** Hazel Hankin/Stock Boston; **664,** Palmer/Kane/TSI; **665,** Art Wolfe/TSI; **667,** Richard Haynes, **668 t,** Richard Haynes; **668 b,** Larry Landolfi/Photo Researchers; **670 mr,** Jerry Lodriguss/Photo Researchers; **670 tl, ml, bl, tm, bm, tr, br,** John Bova/Photo Researchers; **672, 673 tr, 673 br,** Jay M. Pasachoff; **675,** Richard Haynes; **both,** Nancy Dudley/Stock Boston; **678,** Jim Zipp/Photo Researchers; **679 t,** Richard Haynes; **680–682,** NASA; **683 t,** Richard Haynes; **683 b,** NASA; **684 t,** John Bova/Photo Researchers; **684 b all,** Alastair G.W. Cameron/Harvard-Smithsonian Center for Astrophysics; **685 tl,** NASA; **685 br,** Jay M. Pasachoff; **686,** N. Armstrong/The Stock Market; **687,** TSI; **688,** NASA.

Chapter 21
Pages 692–693, NASA; **694 t,** Russ Lappa; **694 b,** Anglo-Australian Observatory, photograph by David Malin; **695–697 b,** The Granger Collection, NY; **697 t,** Richard Haynes; **701,** Digital Vision; **702,** National Solar Observatory; **702 inset, 704 t,** Space Telescope Science Institute; **704 b,** National Solar Observatory; **708 r,** NASA; **708 inset,** A.S.P./Science Source/Photo Researchers; **709–710,** Digital Vision; **711,** NASA; **712,** Jet Propulsion Laboratory; **713 both,** NASA; **714,** TSI; **716 both,** NASA; **717, 718 tr,** Jet Propulsion Laboratory; **718 inset,** Digital Vision; **718 b, 719, 720 both, 721,** NASA; **722–724 t,** Richard Haynes; **724 b,** Space Telescope Science Institute; **726 tr,** Jet Propulsion Laboratory; **727 tl,** U. S. Geological Survey; **727 tr,** Jerry Schad/Photo Researchers; **728,** Ghislaine Grozaz; **729,** James Pisarowicz; **730,** U. S. Geological Survey; **731,** NASA; **732–733,** Jet Propulsion Laboratory.

Chapter 22

Pages 736–737, David Nunuk/Science Photo Library/Photo Researchers; **738 t,** Richard Haynes; **738 b,** John Sanford/Science Photo Library/Photo Researchers; **740,** Russ Lappa; **741 t,** Malin/Pasachoff/Caltech 1992; **741 b,** NRAO/Science Photo Library/Photo Researchers; **742 tl,** Yerkes Observatory; **742–743 tr,** National Astronomy and Ionosphere Center; **742–743 br,** John Sanford/Astrostock; **743 tr,** NASA; **746,** Silver, Burdett & Ginn Publishing; **747 t,** Richard Haynes; **747 b,** Roger Harris/Science Photo Library/Photo Researchers; **750 inset,** UCO/Lick Observatory photo/image; **751,** Luke Dodd/Science Photo library/Photo Researchers; **752** Anglo-Australian Observatory, photograph by David Malin; **756 b,** Open University, UK; **757 tr,** National Optical Astronomy Observatories; **757 br,** Space Telescope Science Institute; **758, 760,** Photo Researchers; **761,** Dennis Di Cicco/Peter Arnold; **762 both,** Richard Haynes; **764 t, 764 m,** Anglo-Australian Observatory, photograph by David Malin; **764 b,** Royal Observatory, Edinburgh/AATB/Science Photo Library/Photo Researchers; **765,** NASA; **768,** David Parker/Science Photo Library/Photo Researchers.

Nature of Science

Page 772 t, Digital Vision; **772 b,** Jane Luu; **772 b background,** David Jewitt and Jane Luu; **773 tr,br,** Jet Propulsion Laboratory; **774 mr,** Digital Vision; **774,** John Sanford/Astrostock Art Resource.

Skills Handbook

Page 776, Mike Moreland/Photo Network; **777 t,** Foodpix; **777 m,** Richard Haynes; **777 b,** Russ Lappa; **780,** Richard Haynes; **782,** Ron Kimball; **783,** Renee Lynn/Photo Researchers.

Appendix

Pages 798–801, Griffith Observer, Griffith Observatory, Los Angeles.